Lecture Notes in Computer Science 5885

Commenced Publication in 1973
Founding and Former Series Editors:
Gerhard Goos, Juris Hartmanis, and Jan van Leeuwen

T0180725

Karin Breitman   Ana Cavalcanti (Eds.)

Formal Methods and Software Engineering

11th International Conference
on Formal Engineering Methods, ICFEM 2009
Rio de Janeiro, Brazil, December 9-12, 2009
Proceedings

 Springer

Volume Editors

Karin Koogan Breitman
Department of Informatics
Pontifícia Universidade Católica do Rio de Janeiro
R. Marques de Sao Vicente 225
Rio de Janeiro, RJ, Brasil 22451-900
E-mail: karin@inf.puc-rio.br

Ana Cavalcanti
University of York
Department of alcc Computer Science
Heslington, York YO10 5DD, UK
E-mail: Ana.Cavalcanti@cs.york.ac.uk

Library of Congress Control Number: 2009938641

CR Subject Classification (1998): D.2.4, D.2, D.3, F.3

LNCS Sublibrary: SL 2 – Programming and Software Engineering

ISSN 0302-9743

ISBN 978-3-642-10372-8 Springer Berlin Heidelberg New York

Typesetting: Camera-ready by author, data conversion by Scientific Publishing Services, Chennai, India
Printed on acid-free paper   SPIN: 12796106   06/3180   5 4 3 2 1 0

Preface

Formal methods for development of computer systems have been extensively studied over the years. A range of semantic theories, specification languages, design techniques, and verification methods and tools have been developed and applied to the construction of programs used in critical applications. The challenge now is to scale up formal methods and integrate them into engineering development processes for the correct and efficient construction and maintenance of computer systems in general. This requires us to improve the state of the art on approaches and techniques for integration of formal methods into industrial engineering practice, including new and emerging practice.

The now long-established series of International Conferences on Formal Engineering Methods brings together those interested in the application of formal engineering methods to computer systems. Researchers and practitioners, from industry, academia, and government, are encouraged to attend and to help advance the state of the art. This volume contains the papers presented at ICFEM 2009, the 11th International Conference on Formal Engineering Methods, held during December 9–11, in Rio de Janeiro, Brazil.

There was a record 121 submissions by authors from 36 countries all around the world. Each submission was reviewed by at least three, and on the average four, Programme Committee members. After extensive discussions, they decided to accept 36 papers. The programme also included two invited talks by Manfred Broy, from the Technische Universität München, Germany, and Augusto Sampaio, from the Universidade Federal de Pernambuco, Brazil. Their invited papers are also included here. This year, authors of a selection of the accepted papers were invited to submit an extended version of their work to a special issue of the *Science of Computer Programming* journal.

ICFEM 2009 was organized jointly by the Pontifícia Universidade Católica do Rio de Janeiro, the University of York, and the Instituto Militar de Engenharia. EasyChair was used to manage the submissions, the reviewing, and the proceedings production. We thank the EasyChair team for a very good tool.

We are grateful to all members of the Programme and Organizing Committees, and to all referees for their hard work. The support and encouragement of the Steering Committee were invaluable assets.

Finally, we would like to thank all the authors of the invited and submitted papers, and all the participants of the conference. They are the main focus of the whole event. We hope they enjoyed it.

December 2009

Karin Breitman
Ana Cavalcanti

Organization

Steering Committee

Keijiro Araki
Jin Song Dong
Chris George
He Jifeng (Chair)
Mike Hinchey
Shaoying Liu
John McDermid
Tetsuo Tamai
Jim Woodcock

Conference Chair

Jim Woodcock

Programme Chairs

Karin Breitman
Ana Cavalcanti

Programme Committee

Luca Aceto
Nazareno Aguirre
Bernhard Aichernig
Keijiro Araki
Michael Butler
Andrew Butterfield
Rance Cleaveland
Jim Davies
Jin Song Dong
Neil Evans
Colin Fidge
John Fitzgerald
Joaquim Gabarro
Alex Garcia
Stefania Gnesi
Hermann Haeusler
James Harland

Mike Hinchey
Thierry Jeron
Steve King
Kim Larsen
Rustan Leino
Michael Leuschel
Zhiming Liu
Shaoying Liu
Patricia Machado
Tom Maibaum
Tiziana Margaria
Ana Melo
Dominique Mery
David Naumann
Marcel Oliveira
Ken Robinson
Markus Roggenbach

Helen Treharne
T. H. Tse
Mark Utting
Marcel Verhoef

Farn Wang
Heike Wehrheim
Wang Yi
Fatiha Zaidi

Local Organization

Karin Breitman
Paulo Rosa
Vera Werneck

External Reviewers

Azma Abdullah
Mohammed Aboulsamh
Wilkerson Andrade
Zoe Andrews
Jens Bendisposto
Peter Bertok
Nathalie Bertrand
Frédéric Besson
Anirban Bhattacharyya
Jean-Paul Bodeveix
Artur Boronat
Dragan Bosnacki
Pontus Bostram
Harald Brandl
Franck van Breugel
Roberto Bruni
Jeremy Bryans
Antonio Bucchiarone
Lin-Zan Cai
Josep Carmona
Emanuela Cartaxo
Chunqing Chen
Jia-Fu Chen
Sylvain Conchon
Morten Dahl
Fredrik Degerlund
Zinovy Diskin
Lydie Du Bousquet
David Déharbe
Andrew Edmunds
Christian Estler
Marc Fontaine

David Friggens
Marie-Claude Gaudel
Thierry Gauthier
Ricard Gavalda
Andreas Griesmayer
Lindsay Groves
Stefan Gruner
Nan Guan
Dominik Haneberg
Arild Haugstad
Magne Haveraaen
Sarah Hickmott
Chung-Hao Huang
Yoshinao Isobe
Mohammad-Javad Izadi
Mahdi Jaghoori
Phil James
Michael Jastram
Kenneth Jogensen
Temesghen Kahsai
Savas Konur
Derrick Kourie
Willibald Krenn
Shigeru Kusakabe
Marcel Kyas
Mounir Lallali
Diego Latella
Axel Legay
Shuhao Li
Yang Liu
Yanhong Liu
Delphine Longuet

Anh Luu
Wissam Mallouli
Hervé Marchand
Nicolas Markey
Will Marrero
Tiago Massoni
Abdul Mat
Ilaria Matteucci
Franco Mazzanti
Stephan Merz
Björn Metzler
Weikai Miao
Hiroshi Mochio
Carroll Morgan
Charles Morisset
Christophe Morvan
Martin Musicante
Nikos Mylonakis
Brian Nielsen
Ulrik Nyman
Liam O'Reilly
Joseph Okika
Francisco Oliveira Neto
Yoichi Omori
Fernando Orejas
Jonathan Ostroff
Johan Oudinet
Jun Pang
Lucian Patcas
Ian Peake
Jordi Petit
Sophie Pinchinat
Pascal Poizat
Fiona Polack
Geguang Pu
Kairong Qian
Shengchao Qin
Alexandre Rademaker
Willard Rafnsson
Silvio Ranise
Germán Regis

Stephan Reiff-Marganiec
Abdolbaghi Rezazadeh
Thomas Ruhroth
Vlad Rusu
Mar Said
Mireille Samia
Osmar Santos
Rudolf Schlatte
Anton Setzer
James Sharp
Leila Silva
Renato Silva
Jennifer Sorge
Martin Stigge
Volker Stolz
David Streader
Jun Sun
Meng Sun
Andrzej Tarlecki
Maurice ter Beek
John Thangarajah
Francesco Tiezzi
Nils Timm
Edward Turner
Saleem Vighio
Frederic Voisin
Chen-Wei Wang
Shuling Wang
Xi Wang
Xu Wang
Stephan Weissleder
James Welch
Burkhart Wolff
Rong-Hsuan Wu
Hsun-Chin Yang
Li-Wei Yao
Naijun Zhan
Shaojie Zhang
Yu Zhang
Liang Zhao

Table of Contents

Invited Papers

Seamless Model Driven Systems Engineering Based on Formal
Models 1
    Manfred Broy

Compositional Verification of Input-Output Conformance via CSP
Refinement Checking 20
    Augusto Sampaio, Sidney Nogueira, and Alexandre Mota

Testing I

Symbolic Query Exploration 49
    Margus Veanes, Pavel Grigorenko, Peli de Halleux, and
    Nikolai Tillmann

Event Listener Analysis and Symbolic Execution for Testing GUI
Applications 69
    Svetoslav Ganov, Chip Killmar, Sarfraz Khurshid, and
    Dewayne E. Perry

An Empirical Study of Structural Constraint Solving Techniques 88
    Junaid Haroon Siddiqui and Sarfraz Khurshid

Protocols

Improving Automatic Verification of Security Protocols with XOR 107
    Xihui Chen, Ton van Deursen, and Jun Pang

Modeling and Verification of Privacy Enhancing Protocols 127
    Suriadi Suriadi, Chun Ouyang, Jason Smith, and Ernest Foo

Role-Based Symmetry Reduction of Fault-Tolerant Distributed
Protocols with Language Support 147
    Péter Bokor, Marco Serafini, Neeraj Suri, and Helmut Veith

Testing II

Implementing and Applying the Stocks-Carrington Framework for
Model-Based Testing 167
    Maximiliano Cristiá and Pablo Rodríguez Monetti

A Statistical Approach to Test Stochastic and Probabilistic Systems 186
  Mercedes G. Merayo, Iksoon Hwang, Manuel Núñez, and Ana Cavalli

Qualitative Action Systems 206
  Bernhard K. Aichernig, Harald Brandl, and Willibald Krenn

Verification

RAFFS: Model Checking a Robust Abstract Flash File Store 226
  Paul Taverne and C. (Kees) Pronk

European Train Control System: A Case Study in Formal
Verification 246
  André Platzer and Jan-David Quesel

Development of Security Software: A High Assurance Methodology 266
  David Hardin, T. Douglas Hiratzka, D. Randolph Johnson,
  Lucas Wagner, and Michael Whalen

Model Checking I

Bounded Semantics of CTL and SAT-Based Verification 286
  Wenhui Zhang

Graded-CTL: Satisfiability and Symbolic Model Checking 306
  Alessandro Ferrante, Margherita Napoli, and Mimmo Parente

Approximate Model Checking of PCTL Involving Unbounded Path
Properties... 326
  Samik Basu, Arka P. Ghosh, and Ru He

Object-Orientation

A Graph-Based Operational Semantics of OO Programs 347
  Wei Ke, Zhiming Liu, Shuling Wang, and Liang Zhao

Modeling and Analysis of Thread-Pools in an Industrial Communication
Platform 367
  Frank S. de Boer, Immo Grabe, Mohammad Mahdi Jaghoori,
  Andries Stam, and Wang Yi

A Verification System for Distributed Objects with Asynchronous
Method Calls 387
  Wolfgang Ahrendt and Maximilian Dylla

Model checking II

A Time-Optimal On-the-Fly Parallel Algorithm for Model Checking of
Weak LTL Properties 407
  Jiří Barnat, Luboš Brim, and Petr Ročkai

Scalable Multi-core Model Checking Fairness Enhanced Systems 426
  Yang Liu, Jun Sun, and Jin Song Dong

Combining Static Model Checking with Dynamic Enforcement Using
the Statecall Policy Language 446
  Anil Madhavapeddy

Event-B

Supporting Reuse of Event-B Developments through Generic
Instantiation 466
  Renato Silva and Michael Butler

A Lazy Unbounded Model Checker for EVENT-B 485
  Paulo J. Matos, Bernd Fischer, and João Marques-Silva

Proof Assisted Model Checking for B 504
  Jens Bendisposto and Michael Leuschel

Compilation

Machine-Checked Sequencer for Critical Embedded Code Generator 521
  Nassima Izerrouken, Marc Pantel, and Xavier Thirioux

Implementing a Direct Method for Certificate Translation 541
  Gilles Barthe, Benjamin Grégoire, Sylvain Heraud,
  César Kunz, and Anne Pacalet

Process Algebra

Algorithmic Verification with Multiple and Nested Parameters 561
  Antti Siirtola and Juha Kortelainen

Verifying Stateful Timed CSP Using Implicit Clocks and Zone
Abstraction 581
  Jun Sun, Yang Liu, Jin Song Dong, and Xian Zhang

Refinement

Modal Systems: Specification, Refinement and Realisation 601
  Fernando L. Dotti, Alexei Iliasov, Leila Ribeiro, and
  Alexander Romanovsky

Refinement-Preserving Co-evolution 620
  Thomas Ruhroth and Heike Wehrheim

Algebraic Specifications

Circular Coinduction with Special Contexts 639
  Dorel Lucanu and Grigore Roşu

The VSE Refinement Method in HETS.............................. 660
  Mihai Codescu, Bruno Langenstein, Christian Maeder, and
  Till Mossakowski

Real-Time Systems

A Compositional Approach on Modal Specifications for Timed
Systems 679
  Nathalie Bertrand, Axel Legay, Sophie Pinchinat, and
  Jean-Baptiste Raclet

An Efficient Translation of Timed-Arc Petri Nets to Networks of Timed
Automata.. 698
  Joakim Byg, Kenneth Yrke Jørgensen, and Jiří Srba

Verifying Ptolemy II Discrete-Event Models Using Real-Time
Maude... 717
  Kyungmin Bae, Peter Csaba Ölveczky, Thomas Huining Feng, and
  Stavros Tripakis

Specifying and Verifying Business Processes Using PPML 737
  Germán Regis, Nazareno Aguirre, and Tom Maibaum

Author Index 757

Seamless Model Driven Systems Engineering Based on Formal Models

Manfred Broy

Institut für Informatik, Technische Universität München
D-80290 München Germany
broy@in.tum.de
http://wwwbroy.informatik.tu-muenchen.de

Abstract. So-called formal methods have been advocated as techniques in software and systems engineering to improve the correctness and reliability of system and software development – in practice with limited success. In contrast, modeling concepts have found high interest in the development of software intensive systems in recent years in industry. Models are not necessary formal and formal methods do not necessarily provide useful models. We discuss the role of models and the advantages, in particular, of formal models in system development with emphasis on their seamless use.

Keywords: Formal methods, models based development.

1 Motivation

Since more than four decades, extensive research in so-called "formal methods" accomplished remarkable results and a rich body of knowledge. Nevertheless the transfer to practice is slow – lagging behind the state of science and sometimes even not making much progress.

Certainly, there are many reasons why it is difficult to bring formal methods closer to practice. Actually, to begin with, there are some misconceptions about the term "*formal methods*". Already, the understanding of the concept of a "method" is not so trivial. The answer to the question what it means that a method is formal is even less obvious. A lot of the work done under the heading "formal methods" is actually not on methods at all, but rather contributes to a formalization and foundation of structures and concepts useful in software and systems engineering.

It is quite clear that people in practice are not prepared to apply formal methods without a clear idea what their advantages are, actually. It is obvious, however, that the state of practise in systems and software engineering is not satisfactory. In fact, there are a lot of projects in systems and software engineering getting into troubles. Typical troubles are that projects run out of budget or they do not deliver in time. Moreover, the quality of software products is often not sufficient. It is noteworthy, however, that functional correctness is only one concern among the many problems software projects have to solve. Therefore, it is not surprising that as long as formal methods, advocated as a silver bullet, however, only addressing correctness, they will not be accepted.

K. Breitman and A. Cavalcanti (Eds.): ICFEM 2009, LNCS 5885, pp. 1–19, 2009.
© Springer-Verlag Berlin Heidelberg 2009

We suggest a more holistic view onto software and systems engineering. *Holistic* means to keep all the different factors in mind that may influence the project results developing engineering techniques that definitely improve the processes and the resulting products.

In the following we restrict our considerations to technical aspects of development in contrast to management issues. Of course, a lot of the problems in software and systems engineering do not come from the software engineering techniques but rather from problems in project management as pointed out by Fred Brooks (see [2]). His book, "The Mythical Man-Month", reflects experience in managing the development of OS/360 in 1964-65. Its central arguments are that large projects suffer from management problems different in kind than small ones, due to division in labor and their critical need is the preservation of the conceptual integrity of the product itself. His central conclusions are that the conceptual integrity can be achieved throughout by chief architects and implementation is achieved through well-managed effort. Brooks's famous law says that adding personnel to a late project makes it later. We do not discuss problems in project management in the following text. However, we want to keep in mind that development techniques cannot be separated completely from project management issues. Therefore, when aiming at integrating formal methods and modelling approaches into processes of software development, the outcome has to improve and to fit to software management issues as well.

A topic closely related to that is the question what the decisive success factors for software and systems engineering technologies are. What we observe today is the enormous size and increase in complexity of systems we have to deal with. So, one major goal in development is a reduction of complexity and a scaling up of methods to the size of the software today. Moreover, we have to accept that technologies have to be cost effective. Techniques that contribute to the quality of the product but do not prove to be affordable are not helpful in practise.

2   Engineering Software Intensive Systems

Engineering is ... the systematic application of scientific principles and methods to the efficient and effective construction of useful structures and machines. Engineering of software intensive systems is still a challenge – but what are the reasons? In spite of the many and famous stories about software bugs, it is not just the problem to get software bug-free.

Applying modeling techniques and formal methods are not primary goals in engineering. The main goal is to improve our abilities to manage the development of software intensive systems. Primary goals of engineering software intensive systems are suitable quality, low evolution costs and timely delivery.

Formal methods basically claim that they can improve the correctness of software. Formal methods provide support in following areas of development:

- formal specification
- formal development rules and
- verification of software.

Sometimes an argument against formal method is that they are not powerful enough to deal with real life systems. This is actually not true! Within the project Verisoft (see [1]) we have demonstrated that software of the size and of complexity as we find it in modern cars today can be formally specified and verified by applying computer-based tools for modelling and interactive theorem proving. This constitutes a proof of concept, that formal methods are powerful enough for today's real life systems. However, we cannot say much about their cost effectiveness.

A second issue is that – at least for safety critical systems – the state of the art in correctness is not so bad, in practise. The reliability of safety critical systems that we are using today is surprisingly good. For instance, reliability of avionic software is not worse than that achieved in the other involved engineering disciplines such as mechanical engineering and electrical engineering. Therefore, a real need to improve our technologies with respect to improving correctness and verification is perhaps not the most pressing goal. However, the reliability of the systems we develop today is achieved by enormous costs. Some expenses go into the redundancy of the systems, while others go into expensive certification processes.

A third issue is that the key problem in software and systems engineering is not just correctness and verification, it is even more the validity of the requirements as they were captured and formulated. This is underlined in the new ISO 26262 (see [6]), on functional safety for software in vehicles, which rightly points out that safety does not just address correctness but has to tackle validity of requirements and their correctness as well.

2.1 Engineering and Modeling Based on First Principles

To make sure that methods are helpful in engineering and really do address key issues, it is advisable to base methods on principles and strategic goals. These principles are a condensed form of the experiences gained in engineering software intensive systems over the years. In the following we list a number of principles and then discuss to what extent these principles can be backed up by formal methods.

One of the simple insights in software and systems engineering is, of course, that not only the way artefacts are described and also not just the methods that are applied are most significant for the quality of the development outcome. What is needed is a deep understanding of the engineering issues taking into account all kinds of not explicitly stated quality requirements. Here formal methods, at least at the state they are today, cannot help a lot. As engineers, we are interested to be sure that our systems are safe with a high probability and address the user needs in a valid way and that during their lifecycle they can be adapted to the requirements to come in the future. In particular, legacy software is one of the nightmares of software engineering and it is completely unclear to what extend formal methods can help here.

The discipline of systems and software engineering has gathered a large amount of development principles and rules of best practice. Examples are principles like:

- Separation of Concerns
- Stepwise refinement
- Modularity and Compositionality
- Decomposition
- Abstraction

- Rigor and formality
- Generality
- Mitigation of risk
- Anticipation of Change
- Incremental Development
- Standardized Patterns
- Scalability

Which of these principles can be supported by formal methods? Certainly, formal methods could contribute to the first five principles – but they have to be explicitly taken care off when designing formal methods. Formal methods certainly can address the principle of "rigor and formality". The last five principles, however, are not addressed by formal methods, per se. They can support these principles, however.

Software Engineering "Maxims" say:

- Adding developers to a project will likely result in further delays and accumulated costs.

- Basic tension of software engineering is in trade-offs like:

    – Better, cheaper, faster — pick any two!

    – Functionality, scalability, performance — pick any two!

- The longer a fault exists in software

    – the more costly it is to detect and correct,

    – the less likely it is to be properly corrected.

- Up to 70% of all faults detected in large-scale software projects are introduced in requirements and design.

- Insufficient communication and transparency in the development team will lead to project failure.

- Detecting the causes of those faults early may reduce their resulting costs by a factor of 100 or more.

How can formal methods support these principles? Some do only address management tasks. However, early fault prevention can definitely be supported by formal methods.

2.2 From Principles to Methods, from Methods to Processes

Given principles, we may ask how to derive from principles methods and from methods development processes. First lets look at principles for which formal techniques provide good support.

2.2.1 Key Steps in Software and Systems Engineering

In fact, looking at projects in practise we may identify the key activities in software and systems engineering. When studying projects and their success factors on the technical side, the latter prove to be always the same, namely, valid requirements, well worked out architectures addressing the needs of the application domain and an appropriate mapping onto technical solutions. Quality assurance is essential, but only a part of it is verification not to forget validation of the requirements.

Therefore, formal methods have to address directly the demands of requirements engineering and of architectural design. If this can be achieved then we actually arrive at formal methods that are useful and can help a lot.

An important issue that is not addressed enough in formal techniques is comprehensibility and understandability. Formal description techniques are precise, of course. But the significant goal is reduction of complexity and ease of understanding – this is why graphical description techniques are so popular! Engineers, users, stakeholders have to understand the artefacts worked out during the development process. Often understanding is even more important then formality. If a formal method precisely captures important properties, but if no engineer is able to understand it properly the way it is formulated then it is not useful in practice.

2.2.2 Requirements Engineering

Gathering requirements based on collecting, structuring, formalizing, specifying, modeling are key activities. One of the big issues is, first of all, capturing and structuring valid requirements. IEEE 830 1998 mentions following quality attributes of requirements documentation:

- correct
- unambiguous
- complete
- consistent
- ranked for importance/stability
- verifiable
- modifiable
- traceable

For a good requirements engineering we do not necessarily need formality of methods to begin with, since from the attributes listed above mainly consistency, unambiguity, and verifiability are supported directly by formal methods.

2.2.3 Architecture Design

For the design of architecture at a logical level we use hierarchies of logical components, on which a detailed design can be based. The difference between architecture and detailed design [7] is expressed as follows:

- Architecture is concerned with the selection of architectural elements, their interactions, and the constraints on those elements and their interactions necessary to provide a framework in which to satisfy the requirements and serve as a basis for the design.
- Design is concerned with the modularization and detailed interfaces of the design elements, their algorithms and procedures, and the data types needed to support the architecture and to satisfy the requirements.

A detailed design is mandatory for systematic module implementation and verification and later system integration, which is the key step in system development, including integration verification.

2.3 Functional Safety: The Example ISO DIS 26262

ISO 26262 is the adaptation of IEC 61508 to comply with needs in functional safety specific to the application sector of E/E systems within road vehicles. It explicitly addresses notions such as:

- functional safety: absence of unreasonable risk due to hazards caused by malfunctioning behaviour of E/E systems
- functional safety concept: specification of the functional safety requirements, with associated information, their assignment to architectural elements, and their interaction necessary to achieve the safety goals
- functional safety requirement: specification of implementation-independent safety behaviour, or implementation-independent safety measure, including its safety-related attributes

ISO 26262 emphasises in a note that there is a difference between

- to perform a function as required (stronger definition, use-oriented) and
- to perform a function as specified, so a failure can result from an incorrect specification.

This addresses the significance of valid specification and validation ("Get the requirements right") as a precondition for useful verification ("Show that the implementation fulfils the requirements").

3   On Formal Engineering Methods

First of all, formalization is a general method in science. It has been created as a technique in mathematics and also in philosophical and mathematical logic with the general aim to express propositions and to argue about them in a fully objective way. In some sense it is the ultimate goal of science to deal with its themes in an absolutely objective way.

Only in the last century, formal logic has entered into engineering. First of all, logic has been turned into an engineering tool by the logic of switching circuits and also by the logic of software systems. Secondly, the logical approaches help in developing software and digital hardware – after all code is a formal artefact.

3.1 Formalization as Scientific Method

Formalization is a general scientific method. It is, in particular, a helpful concept in informatics. Informatics deals with very abstract concepts and notions, which are captured by formalization. So, informatics has worked out a lot of formal notions including concepts like, for instance, computability, computational complexity and so on. These are basic notions and should not be called formal methods. Formalization is an indispensable scientific method for our discipline.

But what does it mean that something is formal? One difficulty is that the term "formal" is used with different meanings. Generally, a formality is *an established procedure or set of specific behaviors*. But this is not what we mean in software and systems engineering if we call something formal.

The following concepts in informatics can be given the attribute formal

- languages (for specification, design, implementation)
- development steps and processes
- rules (calculi)

Predicate logic may provide the best basis to explain the term formal. Assuming that a method requires a language that has a meaning and rules, we can classify the formality of a method as follows

- formal syntax,
- formal semantics (also called the modeling theory),
- formal transformation and deduction rules.

It is important not to confuse scientific work for the formalization of scientific concepts with formal methods in systems and software engineering. Clear concepts that are theoretically justified and produce a proper terminology are of high scientific interest. In engineering, formality is not a goal per se, but rather a powerful mean to achieve other goals.

3.2 About the Concept of a Method

A method defines "how to do or make something".

A method is a very general term and has a flavour that it is a way to reach a particular goal, where the steps to reach that goal are very well defined such that skilled people can perform them. Engineers therefore heavily use methods as ways to reach their sub-goals in the development process.

3.2.1 What Is a Formal Method?

In informatics, formal methods are understood as mathematically-based techniques for the functional specification, development and verification in the engineering of software and hardware systems. The use of formal methods for software and hardware design is motivated by the expectation that, as in other engineering disciplines, applying mathematical techniques can contribute to the correctness, reliability and robustness of a design. However, the high cost of using formal methods means that they are usually used only in the development of high-integrity systems, where safety or security is important.

Some people say that *"formal methods are best described as the application of a fairly broad variety of theoretical computer science fundamentals, in particular logic calculi, formal languages, automata theory, and program semantics, but also type systems and algebraic data types to problems in software and hardware specification and verification."* Formal engineering methods can be used at a number of levels:

1. Formal specification may be the result of requirements engineering and then a program developed from this informally.
2. Formal development and formal verification may be used to produce a program in a more formal manner.
3. Theorem provers help to produce fully formal machine-checked proofs. This can be very expensive and is only practically worthwhile if the cost of mistakes is extremely high (such as in critical parts of microprocessor design).

Further information on this is expanded below.

3.2.2 Why Formal Specification and Verification Is Not Enough

Formal development methods that just aim at formal specification and verification are not sufficient for the real challenge to make software systems reliable and functionally safe such that they fulfil valid requirements of their costumers with expected quality and are constructed in cost effective ways. Pure formalization and verification can only prove a correct relationship between formal specifications and implementations but cannot prove that the systems meet valid requirements.

Therefore the project on the verifying compiler (see [5]) has an essential weakness since it only addresses partial aspects of correctness but not validity.

3.2.3 The Importance of the Formalization of Engineering Concepts

Engineering concepts in systems and software development are complex and abstract. Therefore they are difficult to define and to understand. We see a great potential for formalization in the precise definition of terms and notions in engineering and in the formal analysis of engineering techniques. We see a significant discrepancy between a formal method and the scientific method of formalization.

3.2.4 The Role of Automation and Tools

Any methods used in the engineering of software systems are only helpful if they scale up and are cost effective. This means they have to be supported to a great deal by automation and by tools.

Here formal methods actually can offer something because any tool support requires a sufficient amount of formalization. The better a method can be formalized the better it can be supported by tools.

4 Seamless Model Based Development

Our goal should not be making sure that formal methods are applied – our goal should be to make engineering more effective, more reliable and more efficient.

Model Based Engineering (MBE) is a software development methodology which focuses on creating models, or abstractions, more close to some particular domain concepts rather than programming, computing and algorithmic concepts. It is meant to increase productivity by maximizing compatibility between systems, simplifying the process of design, increasing automation, and promoting communication between individuals and teams working on the system.

4.1 What Is a Model?

A model is simply an *appropriate abstraction for a particular purpose*. This is of course, a very general connotation of model. Having a closer look, models have to be represented and communicated in order to be useful in software engineering. We should keep in mind, however, that an appropriate "Gedankenmodell", which provides a particular way and abstraction of how to think about a problem is useful for the engineer even without an explicit representation for communication. Using Gedankenmodells means to think and argue about a system in a specific way.

We are interested not only in individual models but also in *modelling concepts*. These are hopefully proven techniques to derive certain abstractions for specific purposes. Here is an important point in modelling that goes beyond formal methods, namely, that good modelling concepts provide useful patterns of engineering.

4.1.1 Modeling Requirements

Capturing and documenting requirements is one of the big challenges in the evolution of software intensive systems. As well-known, we have to distinguish between functional requirements and quality requirements. We concentrate in the following mainly on functional requirements. Here modelling techniques help since we can describe the functionality by using formal specification techniques.

A well worked out requirements techniques end up with a complete formal specification of the interface behaviour of the system under construction. Since for many systems the functionality is much too large to be captured in one monolithic specification, specifications have to be structured. For instance, techniques are needed to structure the functionality of large multifunctional systems by hierarchies of sub-functions. The system model, briefly introduced in the appendix, allows specifying the interface behaviour of the sub-functions and at the same moment using modes to specify how they are dependent and to capture the feature interactions. Done in full detail state-machines with input and output capture the behaviour of the sub-services describing the interactions and dependencies between the different sub-functionalities with the help of modes. Such descriptions are worked-out starting from use-cases.

In the end we obtain a fully formalized high level functional specification of a system structured into a number of sub-functions.

4.1.2 Architecture Modeling

A key task is the modelling of architectures. Having modelled the function hierarchy as described above a next step is to design a logical component architecture capturing the decomposition of the system into logical components, again in a hierarchical style. However, logical component architectures provide completely different views in contrast to function hierarchies derived in requirements engineering.

How are the two views related? The overall functionality described by the function hierarchy has to be refined by the interface behaviour of the logical architecture.

4.1.3 From Requirements and Architecture to Implementation, Integration and Verification

Having worked out a complete description of the requirements and the architecture the further development steps are very much guided by the architecture. First of all, the architecture model provides specifications of the components and modules. On this basis, we can do a completely independent implementation of components (following the principle of separation of concerns and modularity), say, in terms of state machine models. From these state machine models we can generate code. Moreover, we can even formally verify architectures before having worked out their implementation. Architectures with components described by state machines can be tested even before implementation and from them we can generate test cases for integration tests. Provided, the architecture is described and specified in detail, we can derive and verify from the architectural specification also properties of the overall functionality as specified by the function hierarchy specification of the system.

Architecture design can be carried out rigorously formally. This is, of course, not so easy for large systems. It is a notable property of formal methods whether they scale and may be applied lightweight.

If early architecture verification is done accurately and if modules are verified properly then during system integration we have not to be afraid of finding many new bugs. Only if architecture verification and component verification are not done properly, significant bugs are discovered much too late during system integration, as it is the case in practice today, if architectures are not verified and modules are not properly specified. Then module verification cannot be done properly; all problems of systems show up only much too late up during system integration and verification.

4.2 Modeling Systems

Based on a comprehensive set of concepts for modeling systems – as shortly outlined in the appendix – an integrated system description approach can be obtained.

4.2.1 The Significance of Terminology and Concepts

One of the big advantages of formal and mathematical techniques in software and systems engineering is not just the possibility to increase automatic tool support, to formalize and to write formal specifications and to do formal verifications. Perhaps, equally important is to have clear notions and clear terminology. In many areas of software and systems engineering terms are not properly chosen. Simple examples are terms like "function" or "feature" or "service", which are frequently used in software and systems engineering without a proper definition. As a result the understanding between the engineers is limited and a lot of time is wasted in confusing discussions.

4.2.2 An Integrated Model for System Specification and Implementation

A specified and implemented system is described by (for the used formal concepts see appendix):

- an identifier k, the system name,
- an interface specification consisting of
  - a syntactic interface description $synif(k) = (I \triangleright O)$
  - an interface behavior specification $specif(k) \in IF[I \triangleright O]$
- an implementation design $dsgn(k)$ for the interface syntactic interface $(I \triangleright O)$, being either
  - an interpreted architecture $dsgn(k) = A = (K, \psi)$,
  - a state machine $dsgn(k) = B = (\Delta, \Lambda)$.

We end up with a hierarchical system model that way, where systems are decomposed into architectures with subsystems called their *components* that again can be decomposed via architectures into subsystems until these are finally realized by state machines. We assume that all identifiers in the hierarchy are unique. Then hierarchical system with name k defines a set of subsystems subs(k).

Each subsystem as part of a specified and implemented system has its own specification and implementation. A system has an implemented behavior by considering only the implementation designs in the hierarchy and a specified behavior considering only the interface specifications in the hierarchy.

A system k is called *correct*, if the interface abstraction of its implementation A = dsgn(k) has an interface abstraction F_A is a refinement of its interface specification specif(k) = F:

$$F \approx>_{ref} F_A$$

On the basis of this formal system model we can classify faults. A system is called *fully correct*, if all its sub-systems are correct. A system is called *faulty*, if some of its subsystems are not correct. A system fault of a system implemented by some architecture is called *architecture fault*, if the interface behavior of the specified architecture is not a refinement of the interface specification of the system. A fault is called *component fault*, if the implemented behavior of a subsystem is not a refinement of the specified behavior. The distinction between architecture faults and component faults is not possible in practice today due to insufficient architecture specification (see [9]).

4.2.3 Modular System Design, Specification, and Implementation

It is essential to distinguish between

- the architectural design of a system and
- the implementation of the components of an architectural design.

An architectural design consists in the identification of components, their specification and the way they interact and form the architecture.

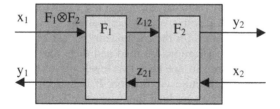

Fig. 1. Composed System

The property of modularity of specification may be characterized as follows. Given two system specifications, where T is a type (for simplicity, here all channels are of the same type) and the $P_i(\dots)$ are the specifying assertions for systems F_i, i = 1, 2:

F_1	
in x_1, z_{21}: T	
out y_1, z_{12}: T	
$P_1(x_1, z_{21}, z_{12}, y_1)$	

F_2	
in x_2, z_{12}: T	
out y_2, z_{21}: T	
$P_2(x_2, z_{12}, z_{21}, y_2)$	

We get the specification of the composed system $F_1 \otimes F_2$ as illustrated in Fig. 1:

$F_1 \otimes F_2$
in x_1, x_2: T
out y_1, y_2: T
$\exists\, z_{12}, z_{21} \in$ Stream T: $P_1(x_1, z_{21}, z_{12}, y_1) \wedge P_2(x_2, z_{12}, z_{21}, y_2)$

The specifying assertion of $F_1 \otimes F_2$ is constructed in a modular way from the specifying assertions of its components by logical "and" and existential quantification for streams denoted by the internal channels.

If the architectural design and the specification of the components is precise enough then we are able to determine the result of the cooperation of the components of the architectures, according to their specification, even without providing an implementation. If the specifications are addressing behaviour of the components and the design is modular, then the behaviour of the architecture can be derived from the behaviour of its components and the way they are connected. In other words, in this case an architecture has given a specification and a specified behaviour. This specified behaviour has to be put into relation with the requirements specification for the system.

Having this in mind, we obtain two possibilities in making use of architecture descriptions. First of all, architecture verification can be done, based on the architecture specification without having to give implementations for the components. How verification is done depends on how the components are described. If component specifications are given by abstract state machines, then the architecture can be simulated and model-checked. If component specifications are given by descriptive specifications in predicate logic, then verification is possible by logical deduction. If the components are described informally only, then we can design test cases for the architecture to see whether architectures conform with system specifications.

Given interface specifications for the components we can first of all implement the components, having the specifications in mind and then verify the components with respect to their specifications. So, we have two levels of verifications, namely, component verification and architecture verification. If both verifications are done carefully enough and if the theory is modular then correctness of the system follows from both verification steps as a corollary.

Finally, for an implemented system for a specified system and we distinguish faults in the architectural design, then the architecture verification would fail, and faults in the component implementation. Note that only if we are careful enough with our specification techniques to be able to specify architectures independent from component implementations then the separation of component test, architecture and integration tests and system tests are meaningful.

Furthermore, for hierarchical systems the scheme of specification, design, and implementation can be iterated for each sub-hierarchy. In any case, we may go on in an idealised top-down development as follows: We give a requirement specification for the system, we do an architectural design and architectural specification for the system, this delivers specifications for components and we can go on with component specification as requirements specification for the step of designing and implementing the components.

4.2.4 Formal Foundation of Methods and Models

As defined, a formal method (or better a formal engineering) method applies formal techniques in engineering. Another way to make use of formalization is the justification of methods by formal theories. Examples are proofs that specification concepts modular or that concepts of refinement are transitive or that transformation rules are correct.

Formal justification of methods or modeling techniques is important. This allows justifying methods or development rules to be used by engineers without further explicit formal reasoning.

5 Seamless Modeling

Being formal is only one attribute of a modeling technique or a development method. There are others – not less important.

5.1 Integration of Modeling Techniques

Modelling techniques and formal techniques have one thing in common. If they are applied only in isolated steps of the development process they will not show their full benefits well enough and, as a result, they often will not be cost effective. If just one step in the development process is formalized and formally verified and if for instance a formal verified program is then given to a compiler, which is not verified, it is unclear whether the effect of the formal verification brings enough benefit.

The same applies to modelling. When high level models of systems are constructed and a number of results have been achieved based on these models, it is not cost effective if then in the next step the model is not used anymore and instead the work is continued by working out different models.

Tab. 1 shows a collection of modelling and development methods as well as their integration into a workflow aiming at a seamless development process by formal models and formal methods. In the requirements engineering the first result should be the function hierarchy as described above. Then the logical component architectures are designed and verified by test cases generated from the functional hierarchies. For the components, test cases can be generated from the component specifications being part of the architecture. Logical test cases can be translated into test cases at the technical level. If the logical architecture is flexible enough, it is a good starting point for working out units of deployment, which then can be deployed and scheduled as part of the technical architecture in terms of distributed hardware structure and its operating systems.

Table 1. Formal Artefacts, Models and Methods in Seamless Model Based Development

Artifact	Based on	Formal Description	Formal method to Work Out	Validation & Verification	Generated artifacts
Business Goals		Goal trees	Logical deduction	Logical analysis	-
Requirements	System and quality model	Tables with attributes and predicate logic Taxonomies	*Use cases* Formalization in predicate logics	Consistency proof Derivation of safety assertions	System assertions System test cases
Data models	*Informal models*	Algebraic data types E/R diagrams Class diagrams	Axiomatization	Proof of consistency and relative completeness	-
System specification	Interface model	Syntactic interface and interface assertions Abstract state machines Interaction diagrams	Stepwise refinement	Proof of safety assertions and requirements Derivation of interaction diagrams	Interaction diagrams System test cases
Architecture	Component and composition	Hierarchy of Data flow diagrams	Decomposition	Architecture verification Architecture simulation	Interaction diagrams Integration tests
Components	Component model	Syntactic interface and interface assertions Abstract state machines	Decomposition of system specification assertions	Consistency analysis	Component tests
Implementation	State machines	State transition diagrams State transition tables	Stepwise derivation of state space and state transition rules	See component verification	
Component verification	State machine runs	Proofs in predicate logics Tests	Proof of interface assertions Test case generation	-	Test runs
Integration	Interactions	Interaction diagrams	Incremental composition	-	Test runs Interaction diagrams
System verification	Interface interaction	System interface assertions System test cases	Proof of interface assertions Test case generation	-	Test runs

From the models of the architecture and its interface descriptions test cases for module tests as well as extensive integration test cases can be generated and executed. The same applies for system test.

5.2   Reducing Costs – Increasing Quality

One of the large potentials of formal models and techniques in development process is their effects to reduce costs. There are mainly four possibilities for cost reduction as numerated below.

1. Avoiding and finding faults early in the process,
2. Applying proven methods and techniques that are standardized and ready for use,
3. Automation of the development task and steps wherever possible,
4. Reuse of implementations, architectures requirements and development patterns wherever possible.

The last step goes into the direction of a product line engineering, which needs a highly worked out modelling and formalization approach to be able to gain all the benefits of such an approach.

6   Concluding Remarks: Towards a Synergy between Formal Methods and Model Based Development

Not surprisingly the synergy between formal methods and model-based development is very deep and not exploited in enough details so far. It is certainly not enough for a formal development method just to provide a formalization of informal approaches like the unified modelling language UML or to develop techniques of model checking certain models that have been worked out in the development process. A much deeper synergy is needed where appropriate formal models directly address the structure of functionality and architecture. This concept requires targeted structure of the models and their relation by refinement. Furthermore, tracing between the models must be a built-in property supporting change requests. Then the whole model structure is always updated and modified in a way such that consistent system models are guaranteed.

Now what is a bottom line? By a first look one might come to the conclusion that formal methods and modelling techniques are not so much different and that, if we add the requirement of formality to a model-based approach, we end up with a formal method. A deeper look, however, shows that there are significant differences.

A formal method emphasizes formality. So obviously being formal is one of the major goals when designing formal methods. Being a method of course is another goal but method is a rather broad term.

The notation of a model, however, addresses an *abstraction for a particular purpose*. Hence a model is much more purpose oriented than a formal method, in general. Actually, many formal methods are not designed for a particular application area or a particular step in the development process. They rather provide possibilities to formalize properties or to prove propositions.

Putting formal methods and modelling together we end up with a more powerful concept, developing formal methods and modelling for a particular purpose, addressing particular issues in the evolution of software intensive systems with the rigour of formality and its possibilities for automation and reuse. This brings in a new quality. Achieving this, however, needs a lot of research starting from useful theories, based on valid principles, finding a good syntax, addressing the application domain and finally integrate in that in the process and supporting it with appropriate tool.

Appendix: Modeling Systems Formally

We are dealing with models of *discrete systems*. A discrete system is a technical or organizational unit with a clear boundary. A discrete system interacts with its environment over this boundary by exchanging messages representing discrete events. In the case of Focus (see [3]) messages are exchanged via channels. Each instance of sending or receiving of a message is a discrete event.

Systems have *syntactic interfaces* that are described by their sets of input and output channels. Channels are used for communication by transmitting messages and to connect systems. Channels have a data type indicating which messages are communicated over the channels. Hence, the syntactic interfaces describe the set of actions for a system that are possible at its interface. Each action consists in the sending or receiving of an instance of a message on a particular channel. A type is a name for a data set, a channel is a name for a communication line, and a stream is a finite or an infinite sequence of data messages.

A discrete system has a semantic interface represented by its interactive behavior. The behavior is modeled by a function mapping the streams of messages given on its input channels to streams of messages provided on its output channels. We call this the *black box behavior* or the *interface behavior* of discrete systems. Let I be a set of typed input channels and O be the set of typed output channels. By (I▶O) this *syntactic interface* is denoted.

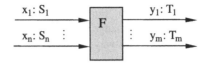

Fig. 2. Graphical Representation of a System F as a Data Flow Node with its Syntactic Interface

Fig. 2 shows the system F with its syntactic interface in a graphical representation by a data flow node.

In FOCUS, a system encapsulates a state and is connected to its environment exclusively by its input and output channels. On channels, streams of messages of the specified type are transmitted. Given a message set M of data elements of type T we represent a *timed stream* s of messages of set M by a function

$$s: \mathbb{N}\backslash\{0\} \to M^*$$

where M^* is the set of finite sequences over the set M. By $(M^*)^\infty$ we denote the set of timed streams. For a timed stream $s \in (M^*)^\infty$ in each time interval $t \in \mathbb{N}\backslash\{0\}$ the sequence $s(t)$ of messages denotes the sequence of messages communicated within time interval t as part of the stream s. Let C be a set of typed channels. A (total) *channel history* is a mapping

$$x : C \to (M^*)^\infty$$

such that x.c is a stream of type Type(c) for each channel $c \in C$. We denote the set of all channel histories for the channel set C both by $\vec{C}$. A function

$$F : \vec{I} \to \wp(\vec{O})$$

represents an *I/O-behavior*. By $\mathbb{F}[I \blacktriangleright O]$ we denote the set of all (total and partial) I/O-behaviors with syntactic interface $(I \blacktriangleright O)$ and by $\mathbb{F}$ the set of all I/O-behaviors. The black box behavior, also called *interface behavior* of a system with syntactic interface $(I \blacktriangleright O)$ is given by an I/O-behavior.

A I/O-behavior $F \in \mathbb{F}[I \blacktriangleright O]$ can be specified by a formula in predicate logic, called *interface assertion*, with the channels as logical identifiers for streams.

Every behavior $F' \in \mathbb{F}[I \blacktriangleright O]$ with

$$F'(x) \subseteq F(x)$$

is called a *refinement* of $F \in \mathbb{F}[I \blacktriangleright O]$; then we write $F \approx_{ref} F'$. A system implementation is *correct* for the specified behavior F if its interface behavior is a refinement of F.

Given a state space Σ a *state machine* (Δ, Λ) with input and output according to the syntactic interface $(I \blacktriangleright O)$ consists of a set $\Lambda \subseteq \Sigma$ of *initial states* as well as of a *state transition function*

$$\Delta: (\Sigma \times (I \to M^*)) \to \wp(\Sigma \times (O \to M^*))$$

For each state $\sigma \in \Sigma$ and each valuation a: $I \to M^*$ of the input channels in I by sequences we obtain by every pair $(\sigma', b) \in \Delta(\sigma, a)$ a successor state σ' and a valuation b: $O \to M^*$ of the output channels consisting of the sequences produced by the state transition. (Δ, Λ) is a Mealy machine with possibly infinite state space.

Given a state machine $A = (\Delta, \Lambda)$ we define a behavior F_A as follows (let Σ be the state space for A)

$$F_A(x) = \{y: \exists \ \sigma: \ \mathbb{N} \to \Sigma: \sigma(0) \in \Lambda$$

$$\wedge \ \forall \ t \in \mathbb{N}: (\sigma(t+1), y(t+1)) \in \Delta(\sigma(t), x(t+1)) \}$$

Here for $t \in \mathbb{N}$ we write x.t for the mapping in $I \to M^*$ where for $c \in I$:

$$(x.t).c = (x.c).t$$

Architectures are concepts to compose systems from subsystems or to decompose systems into subsystems. Architectures describe how the composition of their subsystems takes place. In the following we assume that each system used in architectures as component has a unique name $k \in K$.

A set of component names K with a finite set of interfaces $(I_k \blacktriangleright O_k)$ for each $k \in K$ is called *composable*, if

- the sets of input channels I_k, $k \in K$, are pairwise disjoint,
- the sets of output channels O_k, $k \in K$, are pairwise disjoint,
- the channels in $\{c \in I_k: k \in K\} \cap \{c \in O_k: k \in K\}$ have the same channel types in $\{c \in I_k: k \in K\}$ and $\{c \in O_k: k \in K\}$.

If channel names are not consistent for a set of systems to be used as components we simply rename the channels to make them consistent.

A syntactic architecture $A = (K, \xi)$ with interface $(I_A \blacktriangleright O_A)$ is given by a set K of component names with composable syntactic interfaces $\xi(k) = (I_k \blacktriangleright O_k)$ for $k \in K$.

- $I_A = \{c \in I_k: k \in K\} \setminus \{c \in O_k: k \in K\}$ denotes the set of *input* channels of the architecture,
- $D_A = \{c \in O_k: k \in K\}$ denotes the set of *generated* channels of the architecture,
- $O_A = D_A \setminus \{c \in I_k: k \in K\}$ denotes the set of *output* channels of the architecture,
- $D_A \setminus O_A$ denotes the set of *internal* channels of the architecture,
- $C_A = \{c \in I_k: k \in K\} \cup \{c \in O_k: k \in K\}$ the set of all channels.

By $(I_A \blacktriangleright D_A)$ we denote the *syntactic internal interface* and by $(I_A \blacktriangleright O_A)$ we denote the *syntactic external inte*rface of the architecture.

A syntactic architecture forms a directed graph with its components as its nodes and its channels as directed arcs. The input channels in I_A are ingoing arcs and the output channels in O_A are outgoing arcs.

An interpreted architecture $A' = (K, \psi)$ for a syntactic architecture $A = (K, \xi)$ gives an interface behavior $\psi(k) \in \mathbb{F}[I_k \blacktriangleright O_k]$ for every $k \in K$, where $\xi(k) = (I_k \blacktriangleright O_k)$.

For an interpreted architecture with syntactic internal interface $(I_A \blacktriangleright D_A)$ we define the glass box interface behavior $[\times] A \in \mathbb{F}[I_A \blacktriangleright D_A]$ by the equation (let $\psi(k) = F_k$):

$$([\times] A')(x) = \{ z|D_A: z \in \vec{C}_A \wedge x = z|I \wedge \forall \ k \in K: z|O_k \in F_k(z|I_k) \}$$

For two composable systems $F_k \in \mathbb{F}[I_k \blacktriangleright O_k]$, $k = 1, 2$, we write

$$F_1 \times F_2$$

for $[\times] \{ F_k: k = 1, 2 \}$. Composition of composable systems is associative

$$(F_1 \times F_2) \times F_3 = F_1 \times (F_2 \times F_3)$$

We also write with $K = \{1, 2, 3, \dots \}$

$$[\times] \{F_k \in \mathbb{F}[I_k \blacktriangleright O_k]: k \in K \} = F_1 \times F_2 \times F_3 \times \dots$$

The *black box view* of the interface behavior of an architecture is an abstraction of the glass box view. Given an interpreted architecture with syntactic external interface $(I_A \blacktriangleright O_A)$ and glass box interface behavior $[\times] A' \in \mathbb{F}[I_A \blacktriangleright D_A]$ we define the black box interface behavior $F_{A'} \in \mathbb{F}[I_A \blacktriangleright O_A]$ by

$$F_{A'}(x) = (F(x))|O_A$$

Internal channels are hidden by this composition and in contrast to the glass box view not part of the output.

We get for an interpreted architecture with syntactic external interface $(I_A \blacktriangleright O_A)$ the black box interface behavior $F_A \in \mathbb{F}[I_A \blacktriangleright O_A]$ specified by

$$F_A(x) = \{y \in \vec{O}_A: \exists\, z \in \vec{C}_A : y = z|O_A \wedge x = z|I_A \wedge \forall\, k \in K: z|O_k \in F_k(z|I_k)\}$$

and write

$$F_A = \otimes \{F_k \in \mathbb{F}[I_k \blacktriangleright O_k]: k \in K \}$$

For two composable systems $F_k \in \mathbb{F}[I_k \blacktriangleright O_k]$, $k = 1, 2$, we write

$$F_1 \otimes F_2$$

for $\otimes\{F_1, F_2 \}$. Composition of composable systems is associative:

$$(F_1 \otimes F_2) \otimes F_3 = F_1 \otimes (F_2 \otimes F_3)$$

We also write therefore with $K = \{1, 2, 3, \dots \}$

$$\otimes \{F_k \in \mathbb{F}[I_k \blacktriangleright O_k]: k \in K \} = F_1 \otimes F_2 \otimes F_3 \otimes \dots$$

The idea of the composition of two systems as defined above is shown in Fig. 3 with $C_1 = I_2 \cap D$ and $C_2 = I_1 \cap D$.

In a composed system, the internal channels are used for internal communication.

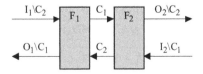

Fig. 3. Composition $F_1 \otimes F_2$

References

1. Botaschanjan, J., Broy, M., Gruler, A., Harhurin, A., Knapp, S., Kof, L., Paul, W.J., Spichkova, M.: On the correctness of upper layers of automotive systems. Formal Asp. Comput. 20(6), 637–662 (2008)
2. Brooks Jr., F.P.: The Mythical Man-Month: Essays on Software Engineering. Addison-Wesley, Reading (1975)
3. Broy, M., Stølen, K.: Specification and Development of Interactive Systems: Focus on Streams, Interfaces, and Refinement. Springer, Heidelberg (2001)
4. Broy, M.: A Theory of System Interaction: Components, Interfaces, and Services. In: Goldin, D., Smolka, S., Wegner, P. (eds.) The New Paradigm, pp. 41–96. Springer, Heidelberg (2006)
5. Hoare, T.: The verifying compiler: A grand challenge for computing research. J. ACM 50(1), 63–69 (2003)
6. ISO DIS 26262
7. Perry, D.E., Wolf, A.L.: Foundations for the Study of Software Architecture. ACM SIGSOFT Software Engineering Notes 17(4) (October 1992)
8. Parnas, D.L.: Some Software Engineering Principles. In: Parnas, D.L. (ed.) Software fundamentals: collected papers, pp. 257–266. Addison-Wesley Longman Publishing Co., Inc., Boston (2001)
9. Reiter, H.: Reduktion von Integrationsproblemen für Software im Automobil durch frühzeitige Erkennung und Vermeidung von Architekturfehlern. Ph. D. Thesis, Technische Universität München, Fakultät für Informatik, forthcoming

Compositional Verification of Input-Output Conformance via CSP Refinement Checking

Augusto Sampaio, Sidney Nogueira, and Alexandre Mota

Centro de Informática
Universidade Federal de Pernambuco
P.O. Box 7851 50740-540 Recife PE, Brazil
{acas,scn,acm}@cin.ufpe.br

Abstract. This paper contributes to a testing theory, based on the CSP process algebra, whose conformance relation (**cspio**) distinguishes input and output events. Although **cspio** has been defined in terms of the standard CSP traces model, we show that our theory can be immediately extended to address deadlock, outputlock and livelock situations if a special output event is used to represent quiescence. This is formally established by showing that this broader view of **cspio** is equivalent to Tretmans' **ioco** relation. Furthermore, we address compositional conformance verification, establishing compositionality properties for **cspio** with respect to process composition operators. Our testing theory has been adopted in an industrial context involving a collaboration with Motorola, whose focus is on the testing of mobile applications. Some examples are presented to illustrate the overall approach.

1 Introduction

Aligned to seminal works that have proposed the use of formal methods as a basis for testing, notably the general testing framework proposed in [9], several approaches have emerged, evolved and consolidated. As a particular benefit of such efforts, the formal characterisation of a conformance notion allows defining test observations, which are the basis for stating and proving properties of the testing artifacts. A conformance relation allows to determine whether an implementation under test (or a model of such an implementation) is valid with respect to a specification. Several conformance relations have been proposed to capture different notions of conformance [26]. For example, **ioco** [24] is a relation that distinguishes input and output events.

Soundness or exhaustiveness of a test suite can only be properly addressed based on some precisely defined conformance relation. Nevertheless, for the purpose of test case generation and execution, a conformance notion plays its role as a formal reference to prove the relevant properties as, for instance, ensuring that an algorithm always generates sound test cases. Once proved, the test case generation algorithm becomes the interface for the practical testing activity, rather than the conformance relation itself.

K. Breitman and A. Cavalcanti (Eds.): ICFEM 2009, LNCS 5885, pp. 20–48, 2009.
© Springer-Verlag Berlin Heidelberg 2009

Therefore, conformance notions end up not being directly used in the process of verifying that an implementation conforms to a specification, as this might be extremely hard (and often impossible) in practice. One reason might be that, in black box testing, the source code is usually unavailable. Even when the source code is available, conformance notions relate specifications with abstract models of implementations, and such models are hardly available. As a consequence, several formal testing theories do not address mechanised strategies to verify conformance.

On the other hand, in more systematic development environments, it might be feasible to assume the existence of design and implementation models; in such contexts, it might be desirable to perform conformance verification in an automated way, as an alternative to constructive refinement proofs. In the ideal scenario in which the model precisely captures the implementation behaviour, conformance verification would replace the testing activity entirely, being equivalent to exhaustive testing. However, in the more realistic situation where the model represents only the more critical aspects of an implementation, a combination of conformance verification and testing would possibly be a promising direction to explore. In such contexts, mechanised conformance verification would play a similar role to classical model checking [8] or, alternatively, refinement checking [17]. For example, in [4] it is shown that although a user can provide an appropriate abstraction when extracting a model from a software implementation, a promising approach is to use a mechanised strategy to search for an abstraction, based on the program and the property under consideration. Using the techniques of predicate abstraction and analysis of spurious error paths, the author shows how to find such abstractions and embeds the solution in the SLAM analysis engine, which forms the core of a recently released Microsoft tool for checking Windows device drivers, called Static Driver Verifier.

Another interesting application of mechanised conformance verification is reported in [2,3], where an approach is presented to generate fault-based testing. In [2], the strategy is to apply a mutation to the original specification and then carry out a mechanical comparison between the two specifications, based on some equivalence relation (in the particular context, strong bisimulation has been adopted). A discriminating sequence resulted as counterexample of the analysis is taken as a test purpose from which test cases are generated. In subsequent work [3], **ioco** is used to compare the two specifications, since **ioco** is also the conformance relation, adopted in [3], to assert the correctness of an implementation.

As with model checking, the mechanical analysis of conformance may easily give rise to state explosion. Therefore, to make the approach more potentially applicable in practice, compositional verification seems essential. Consider a conformance relation, say **rel**, implementation models IUT_1 and IUT_2, and specifications S_1 and S_2. If IUT_1 **rel** S_1 and IUT_2 **rel** S_2, then compositionality implies that, for some operator **op**, $(IUT_1$ **op** $IUT_2)$ **rel** $(S_1$ **op** $S_2)$. For refinement relations used in program development, monotonicity of the language operators is a demand, and, therefore, compositionality is an immediate consequence. However, this is not the case for some conformance relations. Some approaches to compositional verification can be found in [10,11]. For **ioco**, it has been proved [27] that it is not compositional with respect to usual operators like parallelism or hiding, unless the specification is always ready to input (input completeness).

In previous work [18], we introduced a testing theory based on the process algebra CSP [12,20,22]. We defined a conformance relation, **cspio**, that distinguishes input and output, based on the traces model of CSP. Intuitively, this relation captures the **ioco** notion of input-output conformance. However, unlike **ioco** that relates labelled transition systems (LTS), **cspio** relates I/O processes, formed of ordinary CSP processes together with explicit input and output alphabets. Also, **ioco** takes quiescence (deadlock and livelock, for instance) into account and is defined in terms of suspension traces (traces with events representing quiescence), whereas **cspio** ignores quiescence and is defined in terms of ordinary traces. In this paper we show that, when the specification and the model of the implementation are annotated with output events that represent quiescence, **cspio** is equivalent to **ioco**, with respect to a mapping between LTS and CSP processes. We contrast our conformance verification strategy for **cspio**, based on refinement checking, with an on-the-fly verification algorithm for **ioco**. Also, we address compositional conformance verification, by uncovering the conditions necessary to ensure that operators on I/O processes be monotonic with respect to **cspio**. One of the advantages of our formalisation in terms of a process algebra, and of CSP in particular, is that we can benefit from the semantic models and laws of CSP to carry out the proofs. Such proofs can even be mechanised using tools such as the CSP-Prover [14].

As regards practical applications, our work is in the context of a cooperation with Motorola, whose aim is to develop strategies to support the testing of mobile device applications. Figure 1 presents an overview of the overall approach. Application requirements are detailed in use cases; each use case is presented in the form of a tabular template, where each line is split into user action, system state (condition) and system response. The (English) text in each field is written in a controlled natural language (CNL) [23], so that the entire table can be automatically translated into a CSP test model [6].

From the CSP test model, our strategy reported in [18] automatically generates test suites for both individual features and feature interactions, where each feature represents a mobile device functionality. The test case generation can be guided by test purposes, which allow selection based on particular traces of interest. As already mentioned, more generally, we characterise a testing theory in terms of CSP. We have also developed a tool that mechanises the entire generation process. The figure also shows that a complementary activity to testing is automated conformance verification, which is the major contribution of the current paper.

In the next section we discuss input-output conformance in some detail. First we introduce the **ioco** relation and then we give an overview of our approach based on CSP, focusing on the **cspio** relation. Section 3 formally establishes a notion of equivalence between **cspio** and **ioco**. Section 4 addresses compositional

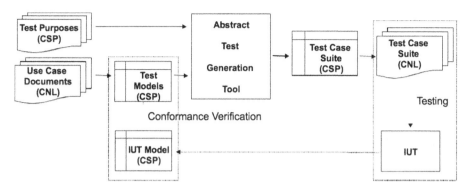

Fig. 1. Overview of the testing strategy

conformance verification, stating and proving compositionality properties for **cspio** with respect to I/O process operators. A summary of our contributions, related and future work are discussed in the final section. Most of the proofs and some auxiliary lemmas are included in the appendix.

2 Conformance Relations

In order to have a precise criteria to compare specifications and implementations, conformance testing [25] requires the definition of an implementation relation between the domain of specifications and that of implementations. In the following subsections we summarise two conformance notions: **ioco** and **cspio**.

2.1 Input-Output Conformance

The relation **ioco** is formally defined in terms of labelled transition systems. We start with some background, necessary both to introduce the relation and later on to establish a connection between **ioco** and **cspio**.

Definition 1 (LTS). *A labelled transition system is a 4-tuple* $\langle Q, L, T, q_0 \rangle$, *where Q is a finite non-empty set of states; L is a finite non-empty set of labels; T is the transition relation, which satisfies $T \subseteq Q \times (L \cup \{\tau\}) \times Q$, with $\tau \notin L$; and $q_0 \in Q$ is the initial state.*

The labels in L represent the observable interactions between the system and its environment; the special label τ represents internal (unobservable) actions. The observable behaviour of a system is captured by its ability to perform sequences of observable actions; each sequence is called a *trace*. The set of all traces over L is denoted by L^*, with ϵ denoting the empty trace. Let $\sigma_1, \sigma_2 \in L^*$ be two traces, then $\sigma_1 \cdot \sigma_2$ is the concatenation of σ_1 and σ_2. As usual, we adopt the convention that μ denotes an action from $L \cup \{\tau\}$ (visible or not), and a denotes a visible action from L. In addition, the operator $\cdot$ is overloaded to combine events to form a sequence, as in $a_1 \cdot a_2$ and to form a sequence from an element and an existing sequence, as in $a \cdot \sigma$.

Definition 2 introduces standard notation for LTS. In the sequel, the intuition of each one is explained, in the same order they are presented. The notation $q \xrightarrow{\mu} q'$ expresses that the system, when in state q, may perform action μ, and move to state q'. We write $q \xrightarrow{\mu_1 \cdot \ldots \cdot \mu_n} q'$ to mean that: starting from state q, and performing a sequence of actions $\mu_1 \cdot \ldots \cdot \mu_n$, each action leading to an adjacent state, the system may reach a state q'. When in state q, if no visible action is performed, which is represented by the empty trace ϵ, $q \xRightarrow{\epsilon} q'$ states that the system may move to a state q', which is reachable by a sequence of internal actions. Similarly, $q \xRightarrow{a} q'$ is used to denote that the system may move from state q to q' by performing a visible action a, which can be preceded or followed by a sequence of internal actions. More generally, $q \xRightarrow{a_1 \cdot \ldots \cdot a_n} q'$ means that: starting from state q, and performing a sequence of visible actions $\sigma = a_1 \cdot \ldots \cdot a_n$, which can be preceded or followed by a sequence of internal actions, the system may reach state q'. Finally, we write $q \xRightarrow{\sigma}$ to denote that from state q, after performing trace σ, the system may reach state q'.

Definition 2 (Notation for transitions). *Let $\langle Q, L, T, q_0 \rangle$ be a labelled transition system with $q, q' \in Q$, $\mu, \mu_i \in L \cup \{\tau\}$, $a, a_i \in L$, and $\sigma = a_1 \cdot \ldots \cdot a_n \in L^*$.*

$q \xrightarrow{\mu} q'$	$=$	$(q, \mu, q') \in T$
$q \xrightarrow{\mu_1 \cdot \ldots \cdot \mu_n} q'$	$=$	$\exists\, q_1, \ldots, q_n : q = q_1 \xrightarrow{\mu_1} q_2 \ldots \xrightarrow{\mu_n} q_n = q'$
$q \xRightarrow{\epsilon} q'$	$=$	$q = q' \;\vee\; q \xrightarrow{\tau \cdot \ldots \cdot \tau} q'$
$q \xRightarrow{a} q'$	$=$	$\exists\, q1, q2 : q \xRightarrow{\epsilon} q1 \xrightarrow{a} q2 \xRightarrow{\epsilon} q'$
$q \xRightarrow{a_1 \cdot \ldots \cdot a_n} q'$	$=$	$\exists\, q_1, \ldots, q_n : q = q_1 \xRightarrow{a_1} q2 \xRightarrow{a_2} \ldots \xRightarrow{a_n} q_n = q'$
$q \xRightarrow{\sigma}$	$=$	$\exists\, q' : q \xRightarrow{\sigma} q'$

As usual, whenever convenient, we do not distinguish between the system, represented as an LTS, and its initial state. Thus, for an LTS p with initial state q_0, we use p and q_0 interchangeably. The following definition makes this explicit for the set of traces of an LTS.

Definition 3 (Traces of an LTS). *Let $p = \langle Q, L, T, q_0 \rangle$ be a labelled transition system, $q \in Q$ a state of p, and $traces(q) = \{\sigma \in L^* \mid q \xRightarrow{\sigma}\}$ the set of traces of p starting from state q. Then, the set of traces of p, denoted $traces(p)$, is defined as $traces(q_0)$.*

Since the **ioco** theory distinguishes between input and output behaviour, the theory models are a kind of LTS that makes this distintion, as defined below.

Definition 4 (IOLTS). *An input-output LTS $p = \langle Q, L, T, q_0 \rangle$ is a labelled transition system in which the set of actions L is partitioned into input actions L_I and output actions L_O: $L_I \cup L_O = L$ and $L_I \cap L_O = \emptyset$. An alternative characterisation splits the alphabet in the tuple $p = \langle Q, L_I, L_O, T, q_0 \rangle$.*

While a specification in the **ioco** theory can be an arbitrary IOLTS, an implementation is characterised as a particular subclass of IOLTS, as defined below.

Definition 5 (Input complete IOLTS). *An IOLTS $p = \langle Q, L_I, L_O, T, q_0 \rangle$ is input complete iff $\forall q : Q, a \in L_I : q \overset{a}{\Longrightarrow}$.*

A state of an input-output transition system where no outputs are enabled, and consequently the system is forced to wait until its environment provides an input, is called suspended, or quiescent. An observer looking at a quiescent state does not see any outputs. This particular observation of seeing nothing can intself be considered an event, which is denoted by δ ($\delta \notin L \cup \{\tau\}$); $q \overset{\delta}{\longrightarrow} q'$ expresses that q allows the observation of quiescence. We use L_δ for $L \cup \{\delta\}$.

Let $available(q) = \{\mu \mid q \overset{\mu}{\longrightarrow} q'\}$ be the set of actions (visible or not) that may be performed from state q.

Definition 6 (Quiescence). *Let $p = \langle Q, L_I, L_O, T, q_0 \rangle$ be an IOLTS.*

1. *A state q of p is quiescent, denoted $\delta(q)$, iff it does not perform an output, neither an internal transition. Formally, $\delta(q) \equiv available(q) \cap (L_O \cup \{\tau\}) = \emptyset$*
2. *The suspension IOLTS, denoted by $\Delta(p)$, is the IOLTS with self transitions in the quiescent states. Formally, $\Delta(p) = \langle Q, L_I, L_O \cup \{\delta\}, T \cup T_\delta, q_0 \rangle$, for $T_\delta = \{q \overset{\delta}{\longrightarrow} q \mid q \in Q \wedge \delta(q)\}$.*
3. *The traces of $\Delta(p)$ are called suspension traces, denoted $Straces(p)$.*

Now we are ready to introduce the conformance notion captured by **ioco**. Informally, an implementation conforms to a specification, according to the **ioco** relation, if and only if, after performing a trace of the specification, the set of output events produced by the implementation (including quiescence) is a subset of that produced by the specification, for the same trace. This is a flexible notion in that it allows partial specifications; an implementation might produce new traces, bacause it is always free to engage on new input events. The traces of an implementation after new inputs can be totally arbitrary, since they are not considered for establishing conformance.

This is similar to refinement notions in languages like B [1], VDM [16] or Z [30], where an operation is refined by weakening the precondition (making it more applicable) or strengthening the postcondition (reducing nondeterminism). On the other hand, it is weaker than refinement relations adopted in process algebras, such as trace inclusion, which does not allow an implementation to engage on new traces.

The formal definition of **ioco** uses some auxiliary notation. The function q **after** $\sigma = \{q' \mid q \overset{\sigma}{\Longrightarrow} q'\}$ yields the set of states reachable from q after a trace σ; $initials(q) = \{a \in L \mid q \overset{a}{\Longrightarrow}\}$ gives the set of visible events that can be triggered from q; and $out(q) = initials(q) \cap (L_O \cup \{\delta\})$ yields the set of outputs (including quiescence) that may be performed in q.

Definition 7 (Input-output conformance). *Let s be an IOLTS and i an input complete IOLTS, both with the same alphabets. Then*

$$i \textbf{ ioco } s \equiv \forall \sigma \in Straces(s) : out(\Delta(i) \textbf{ after } \sigma) \subseteq out(\Delta(s) \textbf{ after } \sigma)$$

As an example, consider the LTS in Figure 2a, which shows the control flow of the Important Messages Feature, a simplified mobile phone functionality. This flow specifies the sequence of actions that the user must perform, and the corresponding system responses, to move a message from the Inbox to the Important Messages folder. The first user action is to scroll to a message, whose effect is to highlight this message. The user then selects the option to move this message to the Important Messages folder. The system reaction is to request storage information from a data base component (omitted here, but considered in Section 2.2). This component then replies indicating whether the message storage is full or not. If it is full, the user action is to clean up some of the old messages (this selection is abstracted here); this triggers another request to the database component, which replies confirming that the clean up has been performed. In any case (whether the storage was originally full or not) the system final response is an indication that the message was moved to the Important Messages folder. Figure 2b shows a conforming implementation. This implementation is valid because it has all the traces of the specification but, in addition, it allows the user to perform the cleanup option at the very beginning (root state); such traces respect conformance as they start with an input event not offered by the specification at its initial state. For simplicity, we omit some transitions necessary for this implementation to be input complete, since they are not relevant for our illustration.

On the other hand, the LTS in Figure 2c is not a valid implementation of the specification. The reason is that, on the left path, this candidate implementation produces the output *msgInfoDisp*, which is not produced by the specification after the corresponding trace. Again, we omit some transitions for this LTS to be input complete.

There are well-established theories, algorithms and tools to generate test cases from LTS specifications, based on the **ioco** relation, notably TGV [15] and TorX [5]. They include soundness and completeness results for test suites, and offer selection strategies based on the idea of test purposes.

2.2 CSP Input-Output Conformance

In this section we introduce a conformance relation, **cspio**, inspired by **ioco**, but formalised in the setting of the CSP process algebra, rather than in terms of LTS. Before defining the relation and presenting some of its properties, we give a brief overview of CSP.

A process is the central element of a CSP specification. Processes can offer events from Σ (the set of all possible events) to establish communication with the environment or with other processes. The alphabet of a CSP process P, denoted by αP, with $\alpha P \subseteq \Sigma$, is the set of events it can communicate.

The CSP primitive process *Stop* specifies a broken process (deadlock), and the primitive *Skip* a process that communicates an event $\checkmark$ and terminates successfully. CSP also provides a rich set of operators to describe the behaviour of concurrent and distributed systems. We introduce some of the operators of CSP using

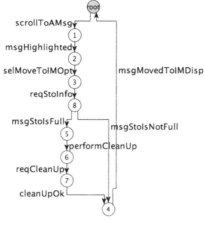

(a) Specification

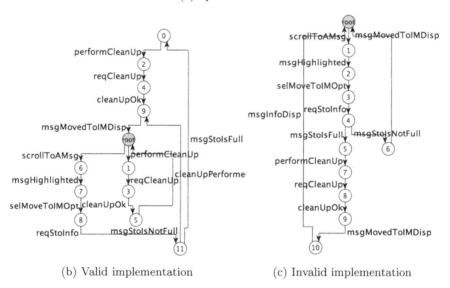

(b) Valid implementation   (c) Invalid implementation

Fig. 2. Important messages mobile feature

the Important Messages feature already considered in the previous section. For instance, the LTS in Figure 2a can be modelled as the process $IM1$ below.

$IM1 = START1;\ IM1$

$START1 = scrollToAMsg \rightarrow msgHighlighted \rightarrow selMoveToIMOpt \rightarrow$
$\qquad\qquad\qquad reqStoInfo \rightarrow (ALT1 \ \Box \ ALT2)$

$ALT1 = msgStoIsNotFull \rightarrow msgMovedToIMDisp \rightarrow Skip$

$ALT2 = msgStoIsFull \rightarrow performCleanUp \rightarrow reqCleanUp \rightarrow cleanUpOk \rightarrow$
$\qquad\qquad\qquad msgMovedToIMDisp \rightarrow Skip$

The process $IM1$ is defined as the sequential composition $START1; \ IM1$, which behaves initially as the process $START1$, and when this process terminates successfully, $IM1$ recurses. The behaviour of $START1$ is given by a sequence of events captured using the prefix operator; a process of the form $a \rightarrow P$ communicates the event a and then behaves like P. After communicating the event $reqStoInfo$, $START1$ behaves as the deterministic choice ($\Box$) between the processes $ALT1$ and $ALT2$; the decision is taken by the environment (for instance, a process that operates in parallel with $IM1$). The process $ALT1$ represents the path that indicates that the storage is not full and, therefore, the message can be moved to the Important Messages folder. The process $ALT2$ captures the situation when the storage is full; some cleaning up is performed so that the message can be moved to the same folder. Both processes terminate successfully (*Skip*).

In addition to these operators, CSP offers several other constructs for combining processes. For example, the nondeterministic choice of processes P and Q is denoted $P \sqcap Q$; the choice is totally arbitrary, with no interference from the environment. The notation P/s denotes the behavior of the process P after the trace s, provided $s \in \mathcal{T}(P)$. The process $P \, [\![\, X \,]\!] \, Q$ stands for the generalised parallel composition of the processes P and Q with synchronisation set X. This expression states that, concerning events in X, the processes P and Q can only communicate when both are ready to engage in the same events. On the other hand, for events not in X, each process can evolve independently. The parallel composition $P \, ||| \, Q$ represents the interleaving between the processes P and Q, and is a special case of parallel composition with an empty synchronisation set, in order to avoid external interference. In this case, both processes communicate any event freely. The process $P \setminus X$ behaves like P, but hides (internalises) all events in X. When composing processes in parallel, it is common to hide the synchronisation set. CSP also includes operators for interruption and piping, among others, but we do not make use of such operators in this work; see [20] for further details.

Although CSP is a very expressive process algebra, and, therefore, convenient to express our theory, there is no semantic distinction between input and output events in CSP. A model in our theory is a tuple $M = (P, A_I, A_O)$, where P is an ordinary CSP process representing the model behaviour, A_I the set of input events, and A_O the set of output events, with $A_I \cap A_O = \emptyset$ and $\alpha P \subseteq A_I \cup A_O$; this model is called an I/O process.

In previous work [18] we have also considered a separate set of events to abstractly represent state conditions, but in our current approach conditions are more concretely modeled as expressions on state variables. In any case, this issue is not relevant for this work, which explores a connection between **cspio** and **ioco**, as well as compositional properties for **cspio**.

As an example, the process $IM1$ introduced above is an ordinary CSP process. The relevant model in our theory is the I/O process $(IM1, A_{I_{IM1}}, A_{O_{IM1}})$, where the alphabet sets $A_{I_{IM1}}$ and $A_{O_{IM1}}$ contain the input and output events, respectively, and are defined as follows.

$$A_{I_{IM1}} = \{scrollToAMsg, selMoveToIMOpt, msgStoIsNotFull, msgStoIsFull,$$
$$\qquad performCleanUp, cleanUpOk\}$$
$$A_{O_{IM1}} = \{msgHighlighted, reqStoInfo, msgMovedToIMDisp, reqCleanUp\}$$

As another example, the database component, responsible for managing the message storage, is specified as the process $DB1$ below, together with its input and output alphabets.

$$A_{I_{DB1}} = \{reqStoInfo, reqCleanUp\}$$
$$A_{O_{DB1}} = \{msgStoIsNotFull, msgStoIsFull, cleanUpOk\}$$

$$DB1 = reqStoInfo \rightarrow (msgStoIsNotFull \rightarrow DB1 \sqcap msgStoIsFull \rightarrow DB1)$$
$$\qquad \square\ reqCleanUp \rightarrow cleanUpOk \rightarrow DB1$$

This process accepts requests concerning storage information or cleaning up (removing) some messages from the storage that represents the Important Messages folder. As a response to the request for storing information, it indicates whether the storage is full or not, abstractly represented as an internal (non-deterministic) choice ($\sqcap$). With respect to the request for cleaning up, the response is an event indicating that it has been performed; for simplicity, the behaviour abstracts the number and the actual messages that are removed. After reacting to any of the two requests the process recurses.

Concerning operators for combining I/O processes, strictly, we define a new algebra, based on CSP, but considering the input and output events. For instance, to combine two I/O processes in parallel requires imposing restrictions on their alphabets, as well as defining the alphabet of the resulting I/O process. The following definition introduces the parallel operator for composing I/O processes.

Definition 8 (I/O parallel composition). *Consider the two I/O processes* $M_1 = (P_1, A_{I_1}, A_{O_1})$ *and* $M_2 = (P_2, A_{I_2}, A_{O_2})$ *so that* $A_{I_1} \cap A_{I_2} = A_{O_1} \cap A_{O_2} = \emptyset$. *Then, the parallel composition of* M_1 *and* M_2, *denoted* $M_1 \|_{io} M_2$, *is defined as*

$$M_1 \|_{io} M_2 = (P_1 \|[X]\| P_2, A_{I_{12}}, A_{O_{12}})$$

where

- $X = (A_{I_1} \cap A_{O_2}) \cup (A_{I_2} \cap A_{O_1})$
- $A_{I_{12}} = (A_{I_1} - A_{O_2}) \cup (A_{I_2} - A_{O_1})$
- $A_{O_{12}} = A_{O_1} \cup A_{O_2}$

To illustrate the combination of I/O processes to form more elaborate I/O processes, consider the process $IM1DB1$, which is the (I/O) parallel composition of $IM1$ and $DB1$: $IM1DB1 = IM1 \|_{io} DB1$. The relevant synchronisation set is

$$Sync = \{cleanUpOk, reqStoInfo, reqCleanUp, msgStoIsFull, msgStoIsNotFull\}$$

and the input and output alphabets of the resulting process are given by:

$$A_{I_{IM1DB1}} = \{selMoveToIMOpt, scrollToAMsg, performCleanUp\}$$

$$A_{O_{IM1DB1}} = \{reqStoInfo, cleanUpOk, reqCleanUp, msgMovedToIMDisp,$$
$$\qquad msgStoIsFull, msgStoIsNotFull, msgHighlighted\}$$

Similarly, we compose the processes $IM2$ and $DB2$ to form a more elaborate component; the resulting process is $IM2DB2 = IM2 \,\|_{io}\, DB2$. The synchronisation set is also given by $Sync$ of the previous example, and the input and output events are as follows.

$$A_{I_{IM2DB2}} = A_{I_{IM1DB1}}$$

$$A_{O_{IM2DB2}} = A_{O_{IM1DB1}} \cup \{cleanUpPerformed\}$$

The hiding operator for I/O processes is defined as follows.

Definition 9 (I/O hiding). *Let $M = (P, A_I, A_O)$ be an I/O process and $X \subseteq A_I \cup A_O$. Then hiding the events of X in M, denoted $M \setminus_{io} X$, is $(P \setminus X, A_I - X, A_O - X)$.*

We illustrate the use of hiding by internalising the synchronisation alphabet of the previous I/O parallel processes: $IM1DB1 \setminus_{io} Sync$ and $IM2DB2 \setminus_{io} Sync$.

As another example of I/O process operator, we introduce external choice.

Definition 10 (I/O external choice). *Consider the following I/O processes $M_1 = (P_1, A_{I_1}, A_{O_1})$ and $M_2 = (P_2, A_{I_2}, A_{O_2})$ so that $A_{I_1} \cap A_{O_2} = A_{I_2} \cap A_{O_1} = \emptyset$. Then the external (deterministic) choice between M_1 and M_2, denoted $M_1 \,\square_{io}\, M_2$, is $(P_1 \,\square\, P_2, A_{I_1} \cup A_{I_2}, A_{O_1} \cup A_{O_2})$.*

Trace semantics is the simplest model for a CSP process. The traces of a process P, given by $\mathcal{T}(P)$, correspond to the set of all possible sequences of events P can communicate. Definition 11 presents the trace semantics of some of the CSP operators. A complete definition for all CSP operators can be found in [20].

Definition 11 (Trace semantics of processes). *Let P and Q be CSP processes and Σ the set of all specified events.*

$$
\begin{aligned}
\mathcal{T}(Skip) &= \{\langle\rangle, \langle\checkmark\rangle\} \\
\mathcal{T}(STOP) &= \{\langle\rangle\} \\
\mathcal{T}(a \to P) &= \{\langle\rangle\} \cup \{\langle a\rangle \frown s \mid s \in \mathcal{T}(P)\} \\
\mathcal{T}(P \,\square\, Q) &= \mathcal{T}(P) \cup \mathcal{T}(Q) \\
\mathcal{T}(P \sqcap Q) &= \mathcal{T}(P \,\square\, Q) \\
\mathcal{T}(P;\, Q) &= (\mathcal{T}(P) \cap \Sigma^*) \cup \{s \frown t \mid s \frown \langle\checkmark\rangle \in \mathcal{T}(P) \wedge t \in \mathcal{T}(Q)\rangle \\
\mathcal{T}(P \setminus X) &= \{s \upharpoonright \Sigma - X \mid s \in \mathcal{T}(P)\} \\
\mathcal{T}(P/s) &= \{t \mid s \frown t \in \mathcal{T}(P)\} \\
\mathcal{T}(P \,\|[\,X\,]\|\, Q) &= \bigcup\{s \,\|[\,X\,]\|\, t \mid s \in \mathcal{T}(P) \wedge t \in \mathcal{T}(Q)\}
\end{aligned}
$$

All processes include the empty trace ($\langle\rangle$). The *Skip* process produces the event $\checkmark$ to indicate successful termination, and *STOP* communicates no visible events. All non-empty traces of $a \to P$ are prefixed by a. Internal and external choices are not distinguished in the traces model. Both result in the union of the traces of the two operands. The traces of sequential composition are the ones of the first process, but removing $\checkmark$ ($\mathcal{T}(P) \cap \Sigma^*$), and those formed of the concatenation of these traces with the ones produced by the second process. The traces resulting from hiding a set of events is given by preserving only those events that are not in X ($s \upharpoonright \Sigma - X$). If $s \frown t$ is a trace of P, then t is a trace of P/s. The semantics of parallel composition uses an operator on traces ($s \,\|[\,X\,]\|\, t$) which takes into account the synchronisation and all possible forms of interleavings between the traces of the two processes operating in parallel.

It is possible to compare the trace semantics of two processes by set inclusion: process Q refines process P, in the traces model, denoted $P \sqsubseteq_\tau Q$, if and only if $\mathcal{T}(Q) \subseteq \mathcal{T}(P)$. This can be mechanically checked using the FDR tool [17]. In case the refinement does not hold, FDR yields a trace (the shortest counter-example), say ce, such that $ce \in \mathcal{T}(Q)$ but $ce \notin \mathcal{T}(P)$.

Other more elaborate semantic models of CSP are the failures and the failures-divergences models. The former captures deadlock situations, whereas the latter captures livelocks as well. See [20] for further details.

As far as we know, CSP Input-Output Conformance (**cspio**) is the only implementation relation that distinguishes input from output events, where specifications and implementations are expressed using CSP processes. This relation assumes as *test hypothesis* [7] that there is a CSP process which specifies an implementation under test (IUT), say IUT. The alphabet of IUT is also assumed to be known, and split into two disjoint sets: inputs and outputs.

The relation is formalised by the following definition, which uses some auxiliary functions: $initials(P) = \{a \mid \langle a \rangle \in \mathcal{T}(P)\}$ yields the set events offered by the process P; and the function $out(M, s)$ gives the set of output events of the process component of the I/O process M, say P_M, after the trace s. Formally, $out(M, s) = $ if $s \in \mathcal{T}(P_M)$ then $initials(P_M/s) \cap A_{O_M}$ else $\emptyset$. The relation **cspio** establishes that any output event observed in an implementation model IUT is also observed in the specification S, after any trace of S. In this case, IUT **cspio** S.

Definition 12 (CSP input-output conformance). *Consider an implementation model* $IUT = (P_{IUT}, A_{I_{IUT}}, A_{O_{IUT}})$ *and a specification* $S = (P_S, A_{I_S}, A_{O_S})$, *such that* $A_{I_S} \subseteq A_{I_{IUT}}$ *and* $A_{O_S} \subseteq A_{O_{IUT}}$. *Then*

$$IUT \ \textbf{cspio} \ S \equiv \forall s : \mathcal{T}(P_S) \bullet out(IUT, s) \subseteq out(S, s)$$

Theorem 1 below captures **cspio** using process refinement. This characterisation uses the process RUN, defined as $RUN(A) = \square\, e : A \bullet e \to RUN(A)$. It offers all the events in A (through an indexed choice operator) and then recurses. The proof of the following theorem can be found in Appendix A.1.

Theorem 1 (Verification of cspio). *Let* $IUT = (P_{IUT}, A_{I_{IUT}}, A_{O_{IUT}})$ *be an implementation model, and* $S = (P_S, A_{I_S}, A_{O_S})$ *a specification, with* $A_{I_S} \subseteq A_{I_{IUT}}$ *and* $A_{O_S} \subseteq A_{O_{IUT}}$. *Then* IUT **cspio** S *holds iff the following refinement holds.*

$$P_S \sqsubseteq_\tau (P_S \ ||| \ RUN(A_{O_{IUT}})) \ |[\, A_{I_{IUT}} \cup A_{O_{IUT}} \,]| \ P_{IUT} \tag{1}$$

As a consequence of Theorem 1, if we know the IUT we can mechanically verify IUT **cspio** S by checking (using FDR) the expression (1).

As an example, consider the process $IM2$ below, which corresponds to the LTS in Figure 2b.

$A_{I_{IM2}} = A_{I_{IM1}}$
$A_{O_{IM2}} = A_{O_{IM1}} \cup \{cleanUpPerformed\}$

$IM2 = START2; IM2$

$START2 = scrollToAMsg \rightarrow msgHighlighted \rightarrow selMoveToIMOpt \rightarrow$
$\qquad\qquad\qquad reqStoInfo \rightarrow (ALT1 \ \square \ ALT2)$
$\qquad \square \ performCleanUp \rightarrow reqCleanUp \rightarrow cleanUpOk \rightarrow$
$\qquad\qquad\qquad cleanUpPerformed \rightarrow Skip$

FDR successfully checks that the following refinement holds, confirming that $IM2$ is a valid implementation of $IM1$.

$$IM1 \sqsubseteq_\tau (IM1 \ ||| \ RUN(A_{O_{IM2}})) \ [\![A_{I_{IM2}} \cup A_{O_{IM2}}]\!] \ IM2$$

As another example, we use FDR to show that the following process is a valid implementation of $DB1$, defined earlier in this section.

$A_{I_{DB2}} = A_{I_{DB1}}$
$A_{O_{DB2}} = A_{O_{DB1}}$

$DB2 = reqStoInfo \rightarrow (msgStoIsNotFull \rightarrow DB2 \ \sqcap \ msgStoIsFull \rightarrow DB2$
$\qquad\qquad\qquad \sqcap \ reqStoInfo \rightarrow DB2)$
$\qquad \square \ reqCleanUp \rightarrow cleanUpOk \rightarrow DB2$

The process $DB2$ allows all the traces of $DB1$, but in addition accepts consecutive input requests for storing information.

The mechanical verification of conformance is an important advantage of our formalisation using CSP. Unlike an explicit algorithm for checking conformance, as presented in [29] for **ioco**, we benefit from the expressive power of the refinement notions and the model checker for CSP to verify conformance in a simple way. Furthermore, we have a formal proof that the refinement expression does capture input-output conformance, whereas the algorithm presented in [29] is not, to our knowledge, proved sound. On the other hand, **cspio** is defined in terms of ordinary traces, whereas **ioco** considers quiescence as well. In the next section we establish a connection between these relations.

3 Relating ioco and cspio

Since **ioco** and **cspio** are defined on different formalisms, a comparison between them requires relating LTS and CSP. As a concrete formalism, LTS is used as an operational model of several process algebras, including CSP. So operational semantics and tools for these languages map the corresponding notations into LTS. We follow the reverse direction. Our approach is to map each LTS transition into a CSP process prefixed with the corresponding event, and whose behaviour is given by recursively mapping the transitions of the target state; transitions with events representing quiescence are mapped likewise. Based on this mapping we then establish that verifying i **ioco** s is the same as checking whether **cspio** holds for the processes resulting from the mapping of i and s. As Theorem 1 gives us a mechanical way of checking **cspio**, we obtain a strategy to verify **ioco** as a byproduct of the results of this section.

The mapping of an LTS into a CSP process is very simple, and uses some auxiliary definitions. Let q be a state and T a transition relation, then we define: $available(q, T) = \{e \mid (q, e, q') \in T\}$ yields the set of available events (visible or not) in state q; $next(q, e, T) = \{q' \mid (q, e, q') \in T\}$ gives the adjacent states of q after the event e; and $m(e) = if\ e \neq \tau\ then\ e\ else\ tau$ is an identity on event names, except in the case of τ that is mapped into tau.

As our testing theory is based on the traces model of CSP, we can simplify the mapping by disregarding nondeterminism, since internal and external choices are not distinguished in the traces model. Internal transitions (with τ events) are mapped as ordinary ones, but replacing τ with tau, a special event such that $tau \notin L$; the fact that τ events must be translated into internal events in the resulting CSP process is captured later one, by internalising such events using the CSP hiding operator, which effectively replaces tau back into τ, at the semantic level.

Definition 13 (LTS to CSP mapping). *Let $p = \langle Q, L \cup \{\tau\}, T, q_0 \rangle$ be an LTS. The following function yields a CSP process whose structure is based on the transitions of p starting from state q.*

$$M(q, T) = \Box\ e : available(q, T) \bullet m(e) \to \Box\ q' : next(q, e, T) \bullet M(q', T)$$

The resulting process is defined as an indexed external choice of processes, each one prefixed by an event of a transition that can be triggered from state q in the LTS. The behaviour after engaging in an event, say e, is given by the recursive call of the mapping function from the target states of the transition triggered by event e.

Although the definition above does not mention quiescence, it actually maps quiescent states, provided the relevant transitions are included in the transition relation. Therefore, $M(q, T \cup T_\delta)$ generates a CSP process annotated with a special event representing quiescence situations. Recall that T_δ has been introduced in Definition 6.

A mapping is usually taken as a definition of an embedded semantics. However, since both the LTS and the resulting CSP processes have a common trace semantics, we can prove that the proposed mapping does preserve traces. Actually, it preserves suspension traces as well, since quiescence is mapped into a special event, as previously explained. This proof is simple but lengthy, and is omitted here.

Lemma 1 (Mapping preserves (suspension) traces). *Let Q be a finite non-empty set of states; L a finite non-empty set of labels; $T \subseteq Q \times (L \cup \{\tau\}) \times Q$ the transition relation over Q and L, with $tau \notin L$. Then,*

$$traces(q) = \mathcal{T}(M(q, T) \setminus \{tau\})$$

This lemma allows us to relate the traces of an LTS, from an arbitrary state q, with the process that results from the mapping. Particularly, for an LTS $p = \langle Q, L_I, L_O, T, q_0 \rangle$, we have that $traces(p) = traces(q_0)$, which, from Lemma 1, is the same as $traces(M(q_0, T) \setminus \{tau\})$.

From the fact that our mapping preserves (suspension) traces, and that both **ioco** and **cspio** are based on trace semantics, it is now possible to formally relate **cspio** and **ioco**.

Theorem 2 (Conformance equivalence). *Let $i = \langle Q_i, L_I, L_O, T_i, q_{0_i} \rangle$ be an input complete IOLTS representing an implementation, $s = \langle Q_s, L_I, L_O, T_s, q_{0_s} \rangle$ an IOLTS representing a specification, $IUT = (M(q_{0_i}, T_i \cup T_{\delta_i}) \setminus \{tau\}, L_I, L_O)$ the I/O process resulting from mapping the suspension IOLTS of i, $\Delta(i)$; and $S = (M(q_{0_s}, T_s \cup T_{\delta_s}) \setminus \{tau\}, L_I, L_O)$ the I/O process obtained from mapping the suspension IOLTS of s, $\Delta(s)$. Then*

$$i \ \textbf{ioco} \ s \equiv IUT \ \textbf{cspio} \ S$$

The above theorem, proved in Appendix A.2, formalises an important contribution of this paper: i **ioco** s can be mechanically verified using FDR to check the expression IUT **cspio** S, provided IUT and S correspond to the mappings of i and s, respectively.

4 Compositional Verification

It has been shown in [27] that, in general, **ioco** is not a compositional relation with respect to parallel composition and hiding. However, compositionality does hold under the assumption that specifications are input complete in the same alphabet of the corresponding implementations. Therefore, given the results of the previous section, it is expected that this holds for **cspio** as well. Nevertheless, our aim is to prove compositionality for all I/O process operators, and not only for parallel composition and hiding; it is also our objective to study weaker assumptions for establishing compositionality for **cspio**.

We assume, however, that the implementation models to be composed are non-observationally terminating; this means that they cannot eventually behave like the *Skip* process. The lemmas and theorems in this section implicitly assume that the implementation models obey this condition. The reason for this restriction is that *Skip* produces the event ✓ in the traces, and this demands a special treatment in our compositional strategy, which is a topic for further investigation. In any case, this is a weaker assumption than input completeness, which clearly implies in non-termination.

Theorem 3, presented in the sequel, states that **cspio** reduces to standard CSP traces refinement, if we assume that the specification is input complete, and that some additional constraints hold concerning the specification and implementation alphabets. First we formalise the notion of input completeness for an I/O process.

Definition 14 (Input complete I/O process). *Let $M = (P, A_I, A_O)$ be an I/O process. Then, M is input complete if, and only if,*

$$\forall t : \mathcal{T}(P) \bullet A_I \subseteq initials(P/t)$$

Input completeness can be mechanically verified by checking a simple refinement expression. The following four lemmas are proved in Appendix A.

Lemma 2 (Input complete I/O process). *Let $M = (P, A_I, A_O)$ be an I/O process. Then, M is input complete if, and only if, $P \sqsubseteq_\tau RUN(A_I)$*

The following two lemmas introduce simple properties of the process RUN. The first one allows to combine two interleaving processes into a single one.

Lemma 3 (RUN composition). *Let X and Y be sets of events, such that $X \cap Y = \emptyset$. Then*

$$RUN(X \cup Y) = RUN(X) \,|||\, RUN(Y)$$

The next property shows that RUN is the unit of parallel composition.

Lemma 4 (RUN unity). *Let P be a non-observationally terminating process, and A a set of events. Then*

$$P \,|[\, A \,]|\, RUN(A) = P$$

This lemma is a simple variation of a law presented in [22] with an explicit condition requiring that P does not terminate with *Skip*.

Another relevant property is that composing a process in parallel in the context of a synchronisation set that includes the process alphabet leads to refinement.

Lemma 5 (Parallel refinement). *Let P and Q be two processes and X a set of events, such that $\alpha_P \subseteq X$ and $\alpha_Q \subseteq X$. Then*

$$P \sqsubseteq_\tau Q \,|[\, X \,]|\, P$$

Based on the previous lemma, we establish that **cspio** is, in general, a weaker relation then traces refinement.

Lemma 6 (cspio weaker than $\sqsubseteq_\tau$). *Let $S = (P_S, A_{I_S}, A_{O_S})$ be a specification and $IUT = (P_{IUT}, A_{I_{IUT}}, A_{O_{IUT}})$ an implementation model, such that $A_{I_S} \subseteq A_{I_{IUT}}$ and $A_{O_S} \subseteq A_{O_{IUT}}$. Then*

$$P_S \sqsubseteq_\tau P_{IUT} \Rightarrow IUT \textbf{ cspio } S$$

Proof

$$\begin{aligned}
& P_S \sqsubseteq_\tau P_{IUT} \\
\Rightarrow\ & \textit{[transitivity of } \sqsubseteq_\tau \textit{ and Lemma 5]} \\
& P_S \sqsubseteq_\tau (P_S \,|||\, RUN(A_O)) \,|[\, A_I \cup A_O \,]|\, P_{IUT} \\
\equiv\ & \textit{[Definition 12]} \\
& IUT \textbf{ cspio } S
\end{aligned}$$

Finally we present our first result concerning the equivalence between **cspio** and traces refinement.

Theorem 3 (cspio equivalent to $\sqsubseteq_\tau$). *Consider an input complete specification denoted by the I/O process $S = (P_S, A_I, A_O)$, and an implementation model $IUT = (P_{IUT}, A_I, A_O)$. Then*

$$IUT \textbf{ cspio } S \equiv P_S \sqsubseteq_\tau P_{IUT}$$

Proof

(IUT **cspio** *$S \Rightarrow P_S \sqsubseteq_\tau P_{IUT}$)*

$\qquad$ *IUT* **cspio** *S*
$\equiv$ *[Theorem 1]*
$\qquad P_S \sqsubseteq_\tau (P_S \;|||\; RUN(A_O)) \,|[\, A_I \cup A_O \,]|\, P_{IUT}$
$\Rightarrow$ *[Lemma 2 and transitivity/monotonicity of $\sqsubseteq_\tau$]*
$\qquad P_S \sqsubseteq_\tau (RUN(A_I) \;|||\; RUN(A_O)) \,|[\, A_I \cup A_O \,]|\, P_{IUT}$
$\equiv$ *[Lemma 3]*
$\qquad P_S \sqsubseteq_\tau RUN(A_I \cup A_O) \,|[\, A_I \cup A_O \,]|\, P_{IUT}$
$\equiv$ *[Lemma 4]*
$\qquad P_S \sqsubseteq_\tau P_{IUT}$

*($P_S \sqsubseteq_\tau P_{IUT} \Rightarrow IUT$ **cspio** *S) follows directly from Lemma 6.*

The fact that each I/O process operator is monotonic with respect to the **cspio** relation is a simple consequence of the above theorem. As an illustration we show the case for parallel composition.

Corollary 1. *Consider the input complete specifications $S_1 = (P_{S_1}, A_{I_1}, A_{O_1})$ and $S_2 = (P_{S_2}, A_{I_2}, A_{O_2})$, and the implementations $IUT_1 = (P_{IUT_1}, A_{I_1}, A_{O_1})$ and $IUT_2 = (P_{IUT_2}, A_{I_2}, A_{O_2})$. Then*

$$(IUT_1 \textbf{ cspio } S_1) \wedge (IUT_2 \textbf{ cspio } S_2) \Rightarrow (IUT_1 \;||_{io}\; IUT_2) \textbf{ cspio } (S_1 \;||_{io}\; S_2)$$

Proof

$\qquad (IUT_1$ **cspio** *S_1) $\wedge$ (IUT_2* **cspio** *S_2)*
$\equiv$ *[Theorem 3]*
$\qquad (P_{S_1} \sqsubseteq_\tau P_{IUT_1}) \wedge (P_{S_2} \sqsubseteq_\tau P_{IUT_2})$
$\Rightarrow$ *[transitivity/monotonicity of $\sqsubseteq_\tau$, and $X = (A_{I_1} \cap A_{O_2}) \cup (A_{I_2} \cap A_{O_1})$]*
$\qquad (P_{S_1} \,|[\, X \,]|\, P_{S_2}) \sqsubseteq_\tau (P_{IUT_1} \,|[\, X \,]|\, P_{IUT_2})$
$\equiv$ *[Definition 8 and Theorem 3]*
$\qquad (IUT_1 \;||_{io}\; IUT_2)$ **cspio** *($S_1 \;||_{io}\; S_2$)*

Therefore, as all CSP operators are monotonic with respect to all CSP refinement relations, including traces refinement, compositionality holds for the operators on I/O processes, since these are defined in terms of the standard CSP operators.

It is worthy contrasting this result with the one obtained in [27]. Apart from proving a property similar to Theorem 3, laborious proofs were necessary to establish monotonicity of each of the two operators considered (parallel composition and hiding). This seems to give some evidence that a formalisation in the setting of a process algebra is a more promising direction to follow in the context of compositional conformance verification.

We have also explored whether compositionality would hold under weaker assumptions. The next theorem shows that **cspio** also reduces to traces refinement when the input events offered by the implementation, after each trace, is a subset of those offered by the specification, for the same trace. Input completeness of the specification (in the same alphabet of the implementation) clearly implies this weaker condition. We define an auxiliary function:

$$in(M, s) \ = \ if \ s \in \mathcal{T}(P_M) \ then \ initials(P_M / s) \ \cap \ A_{I_M} \ else \ \emptyset$$

to capture the set of input events of the I/O process M after the trace s. This can be easily checked using FDR by verifying an expression similar to (1) in Theorem 1, except that $RUN(A_{O_{IUT}})$ is replaced with $RUN(A_{I_{IUT}})$.

Theorem 4 (cspio equivalent to $\sqsubseteq_\tau$). *Let the I/O process $S = (P_S, A_I, A_O)$ represent a specification, and $IUT = (P_{IUT}, A_I, A_O)$ an implementation, and $\forall \, s \bullet in(IUT, s) \subseteq in(S, s)$. Then*

$$IUT \ \textbf{cspio} \ S \equiv P_S \sqsubseteq_\tau P_{IUT}$$

Based on this theorem, whose proof is in Appendix A.6, and on the fact that traces refinement is compositional, we can show that compositionality holds for I/O process operators, similarly to Theorem 3. The case for parallel composition is again used as illustration.

Corollary 2. *Let $S_1 = (P_{S_1}, A_{I_1}, A_{O_1})$ and $S_2 = (P_{S_2}, A_{I_2}, A_{O_2})$ represent specifications, and $IUT_1 = (P_{IUT_1}, A_{I_1}, A_{O_1})$ and $IUT_2 = (P_{IUT_2}, A_{I_2}, A_{O_2})$ stand for implementations. Then*

$$(IUT_1 \ \textbf{cspio} \ S_1) \wedge (IUT_2 \ \textbf{cspio} \ S_2) \Rightarrow (IUT_1 \, ||_{io} \, IUT_2) \ \textbf{cspio} \ (S_1 \, ||_{io} \, S_2)$$

As an example of compositional conformance verification, consider the processes $IM1$, $DB1$, $IM2$ and $DB2$ presented in Section 2.2, where we have also shown that $IM2$ **cspio** $IM1$ and that $DB2$ **cspio** $DB1$. In the same section we have also defined the processes $IM1DB1$ and $IM2DB2$ that capture the parallel compositions of $IM1$ with $DB1$, and of $IM2$ with $DB2$, respectively. The question is whether $IM2DB2$ **cspio** $IM1DB1$?

Our first attempt to justify this conformance is to check whether the conditions of Theorem 3 hold for the parallel compositions of $IM1$ with $DB1$, and of $IM2$ with $DB2$. They trivially fail to hold since neither $IM1$ nor $DB1$ are input complete. Nevertheless, the conditions of Theorem 4 are satisfied, and then we can conclude that $IM2DB2$ conforms to $IM1DB1$; this can be easily confirmed using FDR.

5 Conclusions

We hope to have given some evidence that a characterization of a testing theory in the setting of a process algebra is a promising direction to follow, especially concerning compositional conformance verification, where compositionality of the conformance relation is an essential property. Particularly, we have explored this issue in the context of CSP, through an input-output conformance relation denoted **cspio**. We have analysed in some detail under which conditions compositionality holds for **cspio**. Assuming input completeness of the specification in the same alphabet of the implementation, we have proved that conformance verification reduces to standard traces refinement in CSP and, therefore, compositionality holds since all CSP operators are monotonic with respect to traces refinement, and so are the I/O process operators. We have also shown that compositionality holds under a weaker condition: when the input events offered by the implementation, after each trace, is a subset of those offered by the specification, for the same trace. In such cases, conformance checking also reduces to traces refinement, and, therefore, we obtain an analogous result to the one that assumes input completeness of the specification.

Another contribution of our work is the connection between **cspio** and the well-established **ioco** conformance notion. We have formally shown that these two relations are equivalent if quiescence in an LTS is annotated using a special event in the CSP model. Therefore, it is natural that the closest related works for us to consider are those on **ioco**. Concerning conformance verification, in [29] the authors present an on-the-fly algorithm for mechanically verifying whether **ioco** holds between a specification and a candidate implementation. In contrast, we mechanise such a verification through a simple refinement expression using the CSP model checker FDR. Although **cspio** is defined in terms of standard traces, by using special events to represent quiescence, and based on the established connection with **ioco**, the results hold for suspension traces as well. As regards soundness, the fact that the proposed refinement expression does capture the conformance notion has been proved as a theorem. On the other hand, a proof of soundness of the algorithm presented in [29] has not been reported, to our knowledge.

In [28] the authors present a denotational formalisation of **ioco** in the framework of the Unifying Theories of Programming [13]. Implementations and specifications are represented as reactive process. It is shown that, provided an implementation refines a specification in the reactive processes theory of the UTP, such an implementation is **ioco** conformant to the specification. This result is analogous to our Lemma 6 for traces refinement and **cspio**.

Compositionality for **ioco** has been addressed in [27]. Parallel composition and hiding are defined for LTS, and it is proved that these operators preserve conformance under the assumption that the specification is input complete in the same alphabet of the implementation. Apart from proving a result similar to Theorem 3, laborious proofs were necessary to establish monotonicity of each of the two operators considered. As previously discussed, we have proved that compositionality holds for the I/O process operators, as an immediate consequence of monotonicity of these operators with respect to trace inclusion. Furthermore, we have obtained similar results for weaker conditions, not explored in [27].

There are other approaches to testing that are formalised using CSP. In [19], some implementation relations are defined based on the semantic models of CSP; practical test sets are proposed inspired by these relations. The approach is not, however, completely formal. In [21], two conformance relations are defined, based on the traces and on the failures-divergences models of CSP, and refinement is used to check whether conformance holds, in a similar way as we do here. An instantiation of a well-established theory of formal testing [9] to CSP, using traces and failures refinement as the notion of correctness, is reported in [7]. Compositionality is not explicitly addressed in any of these works. Nevertheless, in [7], compositionality is a direct consequence of adopting one of the CSP semantic models as the conformance relation. None of these works, however, distinguishes input from output.

As a relevant topic for further research, we intend to explore additional compositionality theorems with the weakest possible conditions, for each I/O process operator. As another future direction, we plan to mechanise our proofs using the CSP-Prover [14]; some initial experiments have shown that this is feasible. It is also our aim to consider realistic case studies. Although our testing strategy has been adopted in practice in the Motorola's Brazil Test Center initiative, the focus so far has been on test case generation from use cases, and their execution; we have not yet applied our compositionality results in practice.

Acknowledgements

We thank Thierry Jéron and his group for the constructive discussions related to **ioco** and (compositional) conformance verification. Although mechanical proofs is not in the scope of this paper, we are extremely grateful to Yoshinao Isobe for showing us that the CSP reasoning we conduct in this paper can be fully automated using the CSP-Prover.

References

1. Abrial, J.-R.: The B-book: assigning programs to meanings. Cambridge University Press, New York (1996)
2. Aichernig, B.K., Delgado, C.C.: From faults via test purposes to test cases: On the fault-based testing of concurrent systems. In: Baresi, L., Heckel, R. (eds.) FASE 2006. LNCS, vol. 3922, pp. 324–338. Springer, Heidelberg (2006)
3. Aichernig, B.K., Weiglhofer, M., Wotawa, F.: Improving fault-based conformance testing. ENTCS 220(1), 63–77 (2008)
4. Ball, T.: Automated abstraction of software. In: Automated Technology for Verification and Analysis, Springer, Heidelberg (2006)
5. Belinfante, A., Feenstra, J., de Vries, R.G., Tretmans, J., Goga, N., Feijs, L.M.G., Mauw, S., Heerink, L.: Formal test automation: A simple experiment. In: Proceedings of the IFIP TC6 12th International Workshop on Testing Communicating Systems, pp. 179–196. Kluwer, B.V (1999)
6. Cabral, G., Sampaio, A.: Formal Specification Generation from Requirement Documents. ENTCS 195, 171–188 (2008)

7. Cavalcanti, A., Gaudel, M.-C.: Testing for Refinement in CSP. In: Butler, M., Hinchey, M.G., Larrondo-Petrie, M.M. (eds.) ICFEM 2007. LNCS, vol. 4789, pp. 151–170. Springer, Heidelberg (2007)
8. Clarke, E.M., Emerson, E.A., Sistla, A.P.: Automatic verification of finite-state concurrent systems using temporal logic specifications. ACM Transactions Programming Languages Systems 8(2), 244–263 (1986)
9. Gaudel, M.-C.: Testing Can Be Formal, Too. In: Mosses, P.D., Schwartzbach, M.I., Nielsen, M. (eds.) CAAP 1995, FASE 1995, and TAPSOFT 1995. LNCS, vol. 915, pp. 82–96. Springer, Heidelberg (1995)
10. Godefroid, P.: Compositional dynamic test generation. SIGPLAN Notices 42(1), 47–54 (2007)
11. Gotzhein, R., Khendek, F.: Compositional testing of communication systems. In: Uyar, M.Ü., Duale, A.Y., Fecko, M.A. (eds.) TestCom 2006. LNCS, vol. 3964, pp. 227–244. Springer, Heidelberg (2006)
12. Hoare, C.A.R.: Communicating Sequential Processes. Prentice-Hall, Englewood Cliffs (1985)
13. Hoare, C.A.R., He, J.: Unifying Theories of Programming. Prentice-Hall, Englewood Cliffs (1998)
14. Isobe, Y., Roggenbach, M.: A Generic Theorem Prover of CSP Refinement. In: Halbwachs, N., Zuck, L.D. (eds.) TACAS 2005. LNCS, vol. 3440, pp. 108–123. Springer, Heidelberg (2005)
15. Jard, C., Jéron, T.: TGV: theory, principles and algorithms: A tool for the automatic synthesis of conformance test cases for non-deterministic reactive systems. International Journal on Software Tools for Technology Transfer 7(4), 297–315 (2005)
16. Jones, C.B.: Systematic software development using VDM, 2nd edn. Prentice-Hall, Inc., Upper Saddle River (1990)
17. Formal Systems. Failures-Divergence Refinement - FDR2 User Manual. Formal Systems (Europe) Ltd (June 2005)
18. Nogueira, S., Sampaio, A., Mota, A.: Guided Test Generation from CSP Models. In: Fitzgerald, J.S., Haxthausen, A.E., Yenigun, H. (eds.) ICTAC 2008. LNCS, vol. 5160, pp. 258–273. Springer, Heidelberg (2008)
19. Peleska, J., Siegel, M.: Test automation of safety-critical reactive systems. South African Computer Journal 19, 53–77 (1997)
20. Roscoe, A.W.: The Theory and Practice of Concurrency. Prentice Hall PTR, Englewood Cliffs (1997)
21. Schneider, S.: Abstraction and testing. In: Wing, J.M., Woodcock, J.C.P., Davies, J. (eds.) FM 1999. LNCS, vol. 1708, pp. 738–757. Springer, Heidelberg (1999)
22. Schneider, S.: Concurrent and Real Time Systems: The CSP Approach (Worldwide Series in Computer Science). John Wiley & Sons, Chichester (1999)
23. Torres, D., Leitão, D., Barros, F.A.: Motorola SpecNL: A Hybrid System to Generate NL Descriptions from Test Case Specifications. HIS, 45 (2006)
24. Tretmans, J.: Test Generation with Inputs, Outputs and Repetitive Quiescence. Software—Concepts and Tools 17(3), 103–120 (1996)
25. Tretmans, J.: Testing concurrent systems: A formal approach. In: Baeten, J.C.M., Mauw, S. (eds.) CONCUR 1999. LNCS, vol. 1664, pp. 46–65. Springer, Heidelberg (1999)
26. van der Bijl, M., Peureux, F.: 7 I/O-automata Based Testing. In: Broy, M., Jonsson, B., Katoen, J.-P., Leucker, M., Pretschner, A. (eds.) Model-Based Testing of Reactive Systems. LNCS, vol. 3472, pp. 173–200. Springer, Heidelberg (2005)

27. van der Bijl, M., Rensink, A., Tretmans, J.: Compositional testing with ioco. In: Petrenko, A., Ulrich, A. (eds.) FATES 2003. LNCS, vol. 2931, pp. 86–100. Springer, Heidelberg (2004)
28. Weiglhofer, M., Aichernig, B.: Unifying input output conformance. In: Proceedings of the 2nd International Symposium on Unifying Theories of Programming. LNCS, vol. 5713. Springer, Heidelberg (2008)
29. Weiglhofer, M., Wotawa, F.: On the fly input output conformance verification. In: Proceedings of the IASTED International Conference on Software Engineering, Innsbruck, Austria, pp. 286–291. ACTA Press (2008)
30. Woodcock, J., Davies, J.: Using Z: Specification, Refinement, and Proof. Prentice Hall International, Englewood Cliffs (1996)

A   Proofs

A.1   Theorem 1

The following Lemma is auxiliary to the proof of Theorem 1.

Lemma A1 (Initials of P interleaved). *Let P be a CSP process, and A a set of events. Then*

$$initials((P \;|||\; RUN(A))/s) = initials(P/s) \cup initials(RUN(A)/s)$$

Proof

$$initials((P \;|||\; RUN(A))/s)$$
$= [traces(P/s) \text{ and } initials(P) \Rightarrow initials(P/s) = \{a \mid s \,^\frown \langle a \rangle \in \mathcal{T}(P)\}]$
$$\{e \mid s \,^\frown \langle e \rangle \in \mathcal{T}(P \;|||\; RUN(A))\}$$
$= [def. \; \mathcal{T}(P \;|||\; Q)]$
$$\{e \mid s \,^\frown \langle e \rangle \in \bigcup\{t \;|||\; u \mid t \in \mathcal{T}(P) \wedge u \in \mathcal{T}(RUN(A))\}\}$$
$= [def. \; s \;|||\; t]$
$$\{e \mid s \,^\frown \langle e \rangle \in ($$
$$\qquad \{\langle v \rangle \,^\frown z \mid \langle v \rangle \in \mathcal{T}(P) \wedge z \in (t \;|||\; u) \wedge t \in \mathcal{T}(P/\langle v \rangle) \wedge$$
$$\qquad\qquad u \in \mathcal{T}(RUN(A))\}$$
$$\qquad \cup$$
$$\qquad \{\langle v \rangle \,^\frown z \mid \langle v \rangle \in \mathcal{T}(RUN(A)) \wedge z \in (t \;|||\; u) \wedge t \in \mathcal{T}(P) \wedge$$
$$\qquad\qquad u \in \mathcal{T}(RUN(A)/\langle v \rangle)\}$$
$$\qquad)$$
$$\}$$
$= [set \; comphreension]$
$$\{e \mid s \,^\frown \langle e \rangle \in \{\langle v \rangle \,^\frown z \mid \langle v \rangle \in \mathcal{T}(P) \wedge z \in (t \;|||\; u) \wedge t \in \mathcal{T}(P/\langle v \rangle) \wedge$$
$$\qquad u \in \mathcal{T}(RUN(A))\}\}$$
$$\cup$$
$$\{e \mid s \,^\frown \langle e \rangle \in \{\langle v \rangle \,^\frown z \mid \langle v \rangle \in \mathcal{T}(RUN(A)) \wedge z \in (t \;|||\; u) \wedge t \in \mathcal{T}(P) \wedge$$
$$\qquad u \in \mathcal{T}(RUN(A)/\langle v \rangle)\}\}$$
$= [def. \; initials(P/s)]$
$$initials(P/s) \cup initials(RUN(A)/s)$$

The proof of Theorem 1.

Let the I/O process $IUT = (P_{IUT}, A_{I_{IUT}}, A_{O_{IUT}})$ be an implementation model, and $S = (P_S, A_{I_S}, A_{O_S})$ a specification, with $A_{I_S} \subseteq A_{I_{IUT}}$ and $A_{O_S} \subseteq A_{O_{IUT}}$. Then IUT **cspio** S holds iff the following refinement holds.

$$P_S \sqsubseteq_\tau (P_S \;|||\; RUN(A_{O_{IUT}})) \,|[\, A_{I_{IUT}} \cup A_{O_{IUT}} \,]|\, P_{IUT}$$

Proof

$\qquad P_S \sqsubseteq_\tau (P_S \;|||\; RUN(A_{O_{IUT}})) \,|[\, A_{I_{IUT}} \cup A_{O_{IUT}} \,]|\, P_{IUT}$

$=$ [definition $\sqsubseteq_\tau$]

$\qquad \mathcal{T}((P_S \;|||\; RUN(A_{O_{IUT}})) \,|[\, A_{I_{IUT}} \cup A_{O_{IUT}} \,]|\, P_{IUT}) \subseteq \mathcal{T}(P_S)$

$=$ [$\alpha_P \subseteq \alpha_Q \Rightarrow \mathcal{T}(P \,|[\, \alpha_P \cup \alpha_Q \,]|\, Q) = \mathcal{T}(P \parallel Q)$]

$\qquad \mathcal{T}(P_S \;|||\; RUN(A_{O_{IUT}})) \cap \mathcal{T}(P_{IUT}) \subseteq \mathcal{T}(P_S)$

$=$ [definition $\subseteq$]

$\qquad \forall\, s \bullet s \in (\mathcal{T}(P_S \;|||\; RUN(A_{O_{IUT}})) \cap \mathcal{T}(P_{IUT})) \Rightarrow s \in \mathcal{T}(P_S)$

$=$ [holds when sequence is empty or neither]

$\qquad \langle\rangle \in (\mathcal{T}(P_S \;|||\; RUN(A_{O_{IUT}})) \cap \mathcal{T}(P_{IUT})) \Rightarrow \langle\rangle \in \mathcal{T}(P_S) \wedge$

$\qquad \forall\, s, x \bullet s \,\widehat{}\, \langle x \rangle \in (\mathcal{T}(P_S \;|||\; RUN(A_{O_{IUT}})) \cap \mathcal{T}(P_{IUT})) \Rightarrow$

$\qquad\qquad s \,\widehat{}\, \langle x \rangle \in \mathcal{T}(P_S)$

$=$ [traces property $\forall\, P_S \bullet \langle\rangle \in \mathcal{T}(P_S)$]

$\qquad true \Rightarrow true \wedge$

$\qquad \forall\, s, x \bullet s \,\widehat{}\, \langle x \rangle \in (\mathcal{T}(P_S \;|||\; RUN(A_{O_{IUT}})) \cap \mathcal{T}(P_{IUT})) \Rightarrow$

$\qquad\qquad s \,\widehat{}\, \langle x \rangle \in \mathcal{T}(P_S)$

$=$ [$\wedge$ elimination]

$\qquad \forall\, s, x \bullet s \,\widehat{}\, \langle x \rangle \in (\mathcal{T}(P_S \;|||\; RUN(A_{O_{IUT}})) \cap \mathcal{T}(P_{IUT})) \Rightarrow$

$\qquad\qquad s \,\widehat{}\, \langle x \rangle \in \mathcal{T}(P_S)$

$=$ [def. $\cap$]

$\qquad \forall\, s, x \bullet s \,\widehat{}\, \langle x \rangle \in (\mathcal{T}(P_S \;|||\; RUN(A_{O_{IUT}})) \wedge s \,\widehat{}\, \langle x \rangle \in \mathcal{T}(P_{IUT})) \Rightarrow$

$\qquad\qquad s \,\widehat{}\, \langle x \rangle \in \mathcal{T}(P_S)$

$=$ [set comphreension]

$\qquad \forall\, s, x \bullet x \in \{a \mid s \,\widehat{}\, \langle a \rangle \in \mathcal{T}(P_S \;|||\; RUN(A_{O_{IUT}}))\} \wedge$

$\qquad\qquad x \in \{a \mid s \,\widehat{}\, \langle a \rangle \in \mathcal{T}(P_{IUT})\} \Rightarrow x \in \{a \mid s \,\widehat{}\, \langle a \rangle \in \mathcal{T}(P_S)\}$

$=$ [from $\mathcal{T}(P/s)$ and $initials(P)$ we have

$\quad initials(P/s) = \{a \mid s \,\widehat{}\, \langle a \rangle \in \mathcal{T}(P)\}$]

$\qquad \forall\, s, x \bullet x \in initials((P_S \;|||\; RUN(A_{O_{IUT}}))/s) \wedge x \in initials(P_{IUT}/s) \Rightarrow$

$\qquad\qquad x \in initials(P_S/s)$

$=$ [$\checkmark \notin A_{O_{IUT}}$, $SKIP \;|||\; RUN(A_{O_{IUT}})) \neq SKIP$ and

$\quad initials(P_S) \subseteq (A_{I_{IUT}} \cup A_{O_{IUT}})$]

$\qquad \forall\, s, x \bullet x \in initials((P_S \;|||\; RUN(A_{O_{IUT}}))/s) \cap (A_{I_{IUT}} \cup A_{O_{IUT}}) \wedge$

$\qquad\qquad x \in initials(P_{IUT}/s) \cap (A_{I_{IUT}} \cup A_{O_{IUT}}) \Rightarrow$

$\qquad\qquad x \in initials(P_S/s) \cap (A_{I_{IUT}} \cup A_{O_{IUT}})$

$=$ [$\cap$-dist-$\cup$]

$\qquad \forall\, s, x \bullet x \in (initials((P_S \;|||\; RUN(A_{O_{IUT}}))/s) \cap A_{I_{IUT}}) \cup$

$\qquad\qquad (initials((P_S \;|||\; RUN(A_{O_{IUT}}))/s) \cap A_{O_{IUT}}) \wedge$

$\quad x \in (initials(P_{IUT}/s) \cap A_{I_{IUT}}) \cup (initials(P_{IUT}/s) \cap A_{O_{IUT}}) \Rightarrow$
$\quad x \in (initials(P_S/s) \cap A_{I_{IUT}}) \cup (initials(P_S/s) \cap A_{O_{IUT}})$
$= [\text{Lemma A1}]$
$\quad \forall s, x \bullet x \in ((initials(P_S/s) \cup initials(RUN(I_{O_{IUT}})/s)) \cap A_{I_{IUT}}) \cup$
$\quad\quad (initials(P_S/s) \cup initials(RUN(I_{O_{IUT}})/s)) \cap A_{O_{IUT}}) \wedge$
$\quad\quad x \in (initials(P_{IUT}/s) \cap A_{I_{IUT}}) \cup (initials(P_{IUT}/s) \cap A_{O_{IUT}}) \Rightarrow$
$\quad\quad x \in (initials(P_S/s) \cap A_{I_{IUT}}) \cup (initials(P_S/s) \cap A_{O_{IUT}})$
$= [\text{since } (X \cup initials(RUN(I_{O_{IUT}})/s)) \cap A_{I_{IUT}} = X \cap A_{I_{IUT}} \text{ and }$
$\quad (X \cup initials(RUN(I_{O_{IUT}})/s)) \cap A_{O_{IUT}} = A_{O_{IUT}}]$
$\quad \forall s, x \bullet x \in (initials(P_S/s) \cap A_{I_{IUT}}) \cup A_{O_{IUT}} \wedge$
$\quad\quad x \in (initials(P_{IUT}/s) \cap A_{I_{IUT}}) \cup (initials(P_{IUT}/s) \cap A_{O_{IUT}}) \Rightarrow$
$\quad\quad x \in (initials(P_S/s) \cap A_{I_{IUT}}) \cup (initials(P_S/s) \cap A_{O_{IUT}})$
$= [A_{I_S} \subseteq A_{I_{IUT}}, A_{O_S} \subseteq A_{O_{IUT}}] \text{ and def. } out(M_P, s)]$
$\quad \forall s, x \bullet x \in (initials(P_S/s) \cap A_{I_{IUT}}) \cup A_{O_{IUT}} \wedge$
$\quad\quad x \in (initials(P_{IUT}/s) \cap A_{I_{IUT}}) \cup out(IUT, s) \Rightarrow$
$\quad\quad x \in (initials(P_S/s) \cap A_{I_{IUT}}) \cup out(S, s)$
$= [\text{definition } \cap]$
$\quad \forall s, x \bullet x \in (initials(P_S/s) \cap A_{I_{IUT}}) \cup A_{O_{IUT}} \cap$
$\quad\quad (initials(P_{IUT}/s) \cap A_{I_{IUT}}) \cup out(IUT, s)) \Rightarrow$
$\quad\quad x \in (initials(P_S/s) \cap A_{I_{IUT}}) \cup out(S, s)$
$= [\cap\text{-dist-}\cup]$
$\quad \forall s, x \bullet x \in (initials(P_S/s) \cap A_{I_{IUT}}) \cap (initials(P_{IUT}/s) \cap A_{I_{IUT}} \cup$
$\quad out(IUT, s)) \cup (A_{O_{IUT}} \cap (initials(P_{IUT}/s) \cap A_{I_{IUT}} \cup out(IUT, s)) \Rightarrow$
$\quad\quad x \in (initials(P_S/s) \cap A_{I_{IUT}}) \cup out(S, s)$
$= [\text{set theory, } A \cap A = A]$
$\quad \forall s, x \bullet x \in (initials(P_S/s) \cap initials(P_{IUT}/s) \cap A_{I_{IUT}}) \cup out(IUT, s) \cup$
$\quad\quad (A_{O_{IUT}} \cap (initials(P_{IUT}/s) \cap A_{I_{IUT}} \cup out(IUT, s)) \Rightarrow$
$\quad\quad x \in (initials(P_S/s) \cap A_{I_{IUT}}) \cup out(S, s)$
$= [\text{since } A_{I_{IUT}} \cap A_{O_{IUT}} = \emptyset]$
$\quad \forall s, x \bullet x \in (initials(P_S/s) \cap initials(P_{IUT}/s) \cap A_{I_{IUT}}) \cup out(IUT, s) \Rightarrow$
$\quad\quad x \in (initials(P_S/s) \cap A_{I_{IUT}}) \cup out(S, s)$
$= [\text{definition } \subseteq]$
$\quad \forall s \bullet (initials(P_S/s) \cap initials(P_{IUT}/s) \cap A_{I_{IUT}}) \cup out(IUT, s) \subseteq$
$\quad\quad (initials(P_S/s) \cap A_{I_{IUT}}) \cup out(S, s)$
$= [\text{since } A \cup B \subseteq C \cup D \equiv A \subseteq C \wedge B \subseteq D, \text{ provided } A \cap B = A \cap D =$
$\quad B \cap C = C \cap D = \emptyset; \text{ and, } out(P_M, s) \cap A_{I_{IUT}} = \emptyset]$
$\quad \forall s \bullet (initials(P_S/s) \cap initials(P_{IUT}/s) \cap A_{I_{IUT}}) \subseteq$
$\quad\quad (initials(P_S/s) \cap A_{I_{IUT}}) \wedge$
$\quad\quad out(IUT, s) \subseteq out(S, s)$
$= [\text{since } A \cap B \subseteq A]$
$\quad \forall s \bullet out(IUT, s) \subseteq out(S, s)$
$= [\text{since } \forall s \notin \mathcal{T}(P_{IUT}) \bullet out(IUT, s) = \emptyset \subseteq out(S, s)]$
$\quad \forall s : \mathcal{T}(P_S) \bullet out(IUT, s) \subseteq out(S, s)$
$= [\text{Definition 12}]$
$\quad IUT \textbf{ cspio } S$

A.2   Theorem 2

The following lemma establishes a connection between the output events produced both by the LTS and the corresponding mapped process, after a given trace.

Lemma A2 (Output equivalence). *Let $p = \langle Q, L_I, L_O, T, q_0 \rangle$ be an IOLTS, and $M_p = (M(q_0, T \cup T_\delta) \setminus \{tau\}, L_I, L_O \cup \{\delta\})$ be the I/O process mapped from $\Delta(p)$ be. Then*

$$out(\Delta(p) \text{ after } \sigma) = out(M_p, \sigma)$$

Proof

$$out(\Delta(p) \text{ after } \sigma)$$
$= [def.\ out(q)]$
$$initials(\Delta(p) \text{ after } \sigma) \cap (L_O \cup \{\delta\})$$
$= [def.\ initials(q)]$
$$\{a \in L \mid \Delta(p) \text{ after } \sigma \xrightarrow{a} \} \cap (L_O \cup \{\delta\})$$
$= [def.\ traces(q)]$
$$\{a \mid \langle a \rangle \in traces(\Delta(p) \text{ after } \sigma)\} \cap (L_O \cup \{\delta\})$$
$= [Lemma\ 1\ and\ def.\ P/s]$
$$\sigma \in T(M(q_0, T \cup T_\delta) \setminus \{tau\}) \wedge$$
$$\{a \mid \langle a \rangle \in T((M(q_0, T \cup T_\delta) \setminus \{tau\})/\sigma)\} \cap (L_O \cup \{\delta\})$$
$= [set\ comphreension]$
$$\{a \mid \sigma \in T(M(q_0, T \cup T_\delta) \setminus \{tau\}) \wedge$$
$$\langle a \rangle \in T((M(q_0, T \cup T_\delta) \setminus \{tau\})/\sigma)\} \cap (L_O \cup \{\delta\})$$
$= [set\ comphreension]$
$$if(\sigma \in T(M(q_0, T \cup T_\delta) \setminus \{tau\}))\ then$$
$$\{a \mid \langle a \rangle \in T((M(q_0, T \cup T_\delta) \setminus \{tau\})/\sigma)\} \cap (L_O \cup \{\delta\})$$
$$else\ \emptyset$$
$= [def.\ initials(P)]$
$$if(\sigma \in T(M(q_0, T \cup T_\delta) \setminus \{tau\}))\ then$$
$$initials((M(q_0, T \cup T_\delta) \setminus \{tau\})/\sigma) \cap (L_O \cup \{\delta\})$$
$$else\ \emptyset$$
$= [def.\ out(M, s)]$
$$out(M_p, \sigma)$$

Here the proof of Theorem 2.

Let $i = \langle Q_i, L_I, L_O, T_i, q_{0_i} \rangle$ be an input complete IOLTS representing an implementation, $s = \langle Q_s, L_I, L_O, T_s, q_{0_s} \rangle$ an IOLTS representing a specification, $IUT = (M(q_{0_i}, T_i \cup T_{\delta_i}) \setminus \{tau\}, L_I, L_O)$ the I/O process resulting from mapping the suspension IOLTS of i, $\Delta(i)$; and $S = (M(q_{0_s}, T_s \cup T_{\delta_s}) \setminus \{tau\}, L_I, L_O)$ the I/O process obtained from mapping the suspension IOLTS of s, $\Delta(s)$. Then

$$i \text{ ioco } s \equiv IUT \text{ cspio } S$$

Proof

$$IUT \ \mathbf{cspio} \ S$$
$$\equiv [\text{def. } \mathbf{cspio}]$$
$$\forall \sigma : \mathcal{T}(M(q_{0_s}, T_s \cup T_{\delta_s}) \setminus \{tau\}) \bullet out(IUT, \sigma) \subseteq out(S, \sigma)$$
$$\equiv [\text{Lemma 1 and def. } \Delta(p)]$$
$$\forall \sigma : traces(\Delta(s)) \bullet out(IUT, \sigma) \subseteq out(S, \sigma)$$
$$\equiv [\text{def. } Straces(p)]$$
$$\forall \sigma : Straces(s) \bullet out(IUT, \sigma) \subseteq out(S, \sigma)$$
$$\equiv [\text{Lemma A2}]$$
$$\forall \sigma : Straces(s) \bullet out(\Delta(i) \ \mathbf{after} \ \sigma) \subseteq out(\Delta(s) \ \mathbf{after} \ \sigma)$$
$$\equiv [\text{def. } \mathbf{ioco}]$$
$$i \ \mathbf{ioco} \ s$$

A.3   Lemma 2

The following Lemma is auxiliary. It captures a simple property of traces refinement.

Lemma A3 (Initials and $\sqsubseteq_\tau$). *Let P and Q be CSP processes. Then*

$$P \sqsubseteq_\tau Q \equiv \forall s \bullet initials(Q/s) \subseteq initials(P/s)$$

Proof

$$P \sqsubseteq_\tau Q$$
$$\equiv [traces \ refinement]$$
$$\mathcal{T}(Q) \subseteq \mathcal{T}(P)$$
$$\equiv [def. \subseteq]$$
$$\forall t \bullet t \in \mathcal{T}(Q) \Rightarrow t \in \mathcal{T}(P)$$
$$\equiv [t = s \frown \langle x \rangle \ or \ t = \langle \rangle]$$
$$\forall s, x \bullet s \frown \langle x \rangle \in \mathcal{T}(Q) \Rightarrow s \frown \langle x \rangle \in \mathcal{T}(P)$$
$$\wedge$$
$$\langle \rangle \in \mathcal{T}(Q) \Rightarrow \langle \rangle \in \mathcal{T}(P)$$
$$\equiv [traces \ axiom, \ \langle \rangle \in traces(R)]$$
$$\forall s, x \bullet s \frown \langle x \rangle \in \mathcal{T}(Q) \Rightarrow s \frown \langle x \rangle \in \mathcal{T}(P)$$
$$\equiv [set \ comphreension]$$
$$\forall s, x \bullet x \in \{a \mid s \frown \langle a \rangle \in \mathcal{T}(Q)\} \Rightarrow x \in \{a \mid s \frown \langle a \rangle \in \mathcal{T}(P)\}$$
$$\equiv [\mathcal{T}(P/s) \ and \ initials(P) \Rightarrow initials(P/s) = \{a \mid s \frown \langle a \rangle \in \mathcal{T}(P)\}]$$
$$\forall s, x \bullet x \in initials(Q/s) \Rightarrow x \in initials(P/s)$$
$$\equiv [def. \subseteq]$$
$$\forall s \bullet initials(Q/s) \subseteq initials(P/s)$$

Here follows the proof of Lemma 2.

Let $M = (P, A_I, A_O)$ be an I/O process. Then, M is input complete if, and only if, $P \sqsubseteq_\tau RUN(A_I)$

Proof

$$P \sqsubseteq_\tau RUN(A_I)$$
$\equiv$ [Lemma A3]
$$\forall t \bullet initials(RUN(A_I)/t) \subseteq initials(P/t)$$
$\equiv$ [$\mathcal{T}(RUN(A)) = A^*$ and
$$\forall t \notin A^* \bullet initials(RUN(A)/s) = \emptyset \subseteq initials(P/t)]$$
$$\forall t : \mathcal{T}(P) \bullet A_I \subseteq initials(P/t)$$

A.4   Lemma 3

The findings of this paper are based on trace semantics, then it is enough to proof the equality of Lemma 3 on traces model.

Let X and Y be sets of events, such that $X \cap Y = \emptyset$. Then

$$RUN(X \cup Y) = RUN(X) \, ||| \, RUN(Y)$$

Proof

$$RUN(X) \, ||| \, RUN(Y)$$
$=$ [By $|||$-step, $X \cap Y = \emptyset$ and $RUN(X) =?x : X \to RUN(X)$]
$$?x : X \cup Y \to if \, (x \in X) \, then \, RUN(X) \, ||| \, RUN(Y)$$
$$else \, RUN(X) \, ||| \, RUN(Y)$$
$=$ [By predicate calculus]
$$?x : X \cup Y \to RUN(X) \, ||| \, RUN(Y)$$

Using induction we show:

$$\forall s \bullet s \in \mathcal{T}(RUN(X) \, ||| \, RUN(Y)) \Leftrightarrow s \in \mathcal{T}(RUN(X \cup Y))$$

Base case : $s = \langle \rangle$

Trivially holds.

Inductive case : $s = s' \frown \langle x \rangle$, such that $x \in X \cup Y$

$$s' \frown \langle x \rangle \in \mathcal{T}(?x : X \cup Y \to RUN(X) \, ||| \, RUN(Y))$$
$\equiv$ [applying $|||$-step $\#s$ times]
$$s' \in (X \cup Y)^* \wedge \langle x \rangle \in \mathcal{T}(?x : X \cup Y \to RUN(X) \, ||| \, RUN(Y))$$
$\equiv$ [by induction hypothesis]
$$s' \in (X \cup Y)^* \wedge \langle x \rangle \in \mathcal{T}(?x : X \cup Y \to RUN(X \cup Y))$$
$\equiv$ [by $\to$-step]
$$s' \frown \langle x \rangle \in \mathcal{T}(?x : X \cup Y \to RUN(X \cup Y))$$

The proof above enable us to establish the following equality (in traces) for $RUN(X) \, ||| \, RUN(Y)$.

$= [\text{By traces}]$
$\quad ?x : X \cup Y \to RUN(X \cup Y)$
$= [\text{By }|||\text{-step}]$
$\quad RUN(X \cup Y)$

A.5 Lemma 5

Let P and Q be two processes and X a set of events, such that $\alpha P \subseteq X$ and $\alpha Q \subseteq X$. Then

$$P \sqsubseteq_\tau P\,||[\,X\,]||\,Q$$

Proof

$\qquad P \sqsubseteq_\tau P\,||[\,X\,]||\,Q$
$\equiv [\text{def. } \sqsubseteq_\tau]$
$\qquad \mathcal{T}(P\,||[\,X\,]||\,Q) \subseteq \mathcal{T}(P)$
$\equiv [\text{def } \mathcal{T}(P\,||[\,X\,]||)Q]$
$\qquad \bigcup\{s\,||[\,X\,]||\,t \mid s \in \mathcal{T}(P) \wedge t \in \mathcal{T}(Q)\} \subseteq \mathcal{T}(P)$

We demonstrate it for each production of $s\,||[\,X\,]||\,t$. In the proof consider that $x, x' \in X$ and $y, y' \notin X$.

1. For $s = \langle\rangle$ and $t = \langle\rangle$

   $\qquad \langle\rangle\,||[\,X\,]||\,\langle\rangle = \{\langle\rangle\}$
   $\quad \Rightarrow [\text{traces semantics}]$
   $\qquad (\langle\rangle\,||[\,X\,]||\,\langle\rangle) \subseteq \mathcal{T}(P)$

2. For $s = \langle\rangle$ and $t = \langle x\rangle$

   $\qquad \langle\rangle\,||[\,X\,]||\,\langle x\rangle = \emptyset$
   $\quad \Rightarrow [\text{set theory}]$
   $\qquad (\langle\rangle\,||[\,X\,]||\,\langle x\rangle) \subseteq \mathcal{T}(P)$

3. For $s = \langle x\rangle \frown s'$ and $t = \langle x\rangle \frown t'$

   $\qquad \langle x\rangle \frown s'\,||[\,X\,]||\,\langle x\rangle \frown t' = \{\langle x\rangle \frown z \mid z \in s'\,||[\,X\,]||\,t'\}$
   $\quad \Rightarrow [\text{since } \langle x\rangle \in \mathcal{T}(P) \cap \mathcal{T}(Q) \text{ and assuming inductively } z \in \mathcal{T}(P)]$
   $\qquad (\langle x\rangle \frown s'\,||[\,X\,]||\,\langle x\rangle \frown t') \subseteq \mathcal{T}(P)$

4. For $s = \langle x\rangle \frown s'$ and $t = \langle x'\rangle \frown t'$

   $\qquad \langle x\rangle \frown s'\,||[\,X\,]||\,\langle x'\rangle \frown t' = \emptyset$
   $\quad \Rightarrow [\text{set theory}]$
   $\qquad (\langle x\rangle \frown s'\,||[\,X\,]||\,\langle x\rangle \frown t') \subseteq \mathcal{T}(P)$

5. The assumptions $\alpha Q \subseteq X$ and $\alpha P \subseteq X$ avoid the productions of $s\,||[\,X\,]||\,t$ that follow.

   - $s = \langle\rangle$ and $t = \langle y\rangle$
   - $s = \langle x\rangle \frown s'$ and $t = \langle y\rangle \frown t'$
   - $s = \langle y\rangle \frown s'$ and $t = \langle y'\rangle \frown t'$

A.6   Theorem 4

Let the I/O process $S = (P_S, A_I, A_O)$ be a specification, and consider an implementation $IUT = (P_{IUT}, A_I, A_O)$, and $\forall\, s \bullet in(IUT, s) \subseteq in(S, s)$. Then

$$IUT \textbf{ cspio } S \equiv P_S \sqsubseteq_\tau P_{IUT}$$

Proof

$\qquad P_S \sqsubseteq_\tau P_{IUT}$
$\equiv$ [Lemma A3]
$\qquad \forall\, t \bullet initials(P_{IUT}/t) \subseteq initials(P_S/t)$
$\equiv$ [set theory]
$\qquad \forall\, t \bullet initials(P_{IUT}/t) \cap (A_I \cup A_O) \subseteq initials(P_S/t) \cap (A_I \cup A_O)$
$\equiv$ [∩-∪-dist]
$\qquad \forall\, t \bullet initials(P_{IUT}/t) \cap A_I \cup initials(P_{IUT}/t) \cap A_O \subseteq$
$\qquad\qquad initials(P_S/t) \cap A_I \cup initials(P_S/t) \cap A_O$
$\equiv$ [defs. $in(M_P, s)$ and $out(M_P, s)$]
$\qquad \forall\, t \bullet in(IUT, t) \cup out(IUT, t) \subseteq in(S, t) \cup out(S, t)$
$\equiv$ [$A \cup B \subseteq C \cup D \equiv A \subseteq C \wedge B \subseteq D$, provided
$\qquad A \cap B = A \cap D = C \cap D = B \cap C = \emptyset$]
$\qquad \forall\, t \bullet in(IUT, t) \subseteq in(S, t) \wedge out(IUT, t) \subseteq out(S, t)$
$\equiv$ [def. **cspio**]
$\qquad IUT \textbf{ cspio } S \wedge \forall\, s \bullet in(IUT, s) \subseteq in(S, s)$
$\equiv$ [hypothesis and ∧-elimination]
$\qquad IUT \textbf{ cspio } S$

Symbolic Query Exploration

Margus Veanes[1], Pavel Grigorenko[2,*], Peli de Halleux[1], and Nikolai Tillmann[1]

[1] Microsoft Research, Redmond, WA, USA
{margus,jhalleux,nikolait}@microsoft.com
[2] Institute of Cybernetics, Tallinn University of Technology, Tallinn, Estonia
pavelg@cs.ioc.ee

Abstract. We study the problem of generating a database and parameters for a given parameterized SQL query satisfying a given test condition. We introduce a formal background theory that includes arithmetic,
tuples, and sets, and translate the generation problem into a satisfiability or model generation problem modulo the background theory. We
use the satisfiability modulo theories (SMT) solver Z3 in the concrete
implementation. We describe an application of model generation in the
context of the database unit testing framework of Visual Studio.

1   Introduction

The original motivation behind this work comes from *unit testing* of relational
databases. A typical unit test, first populates the database with concrete *test
tables*, then evaluates a given *test query* with respect to the tables, and finally
checks if the result of the evaluation satisfies a given *test condition*. Typical test
conditions are, checking if the result is empty, nonempty, has a certain number
of rows, or contains a specific value.

In general, a test query may also be *parameterized*, i.e., involve variables in
place of some concrete values, in which case the parameter variables first need
to be instantiated with concrete values in a separate step prior to evaluating the
query. A test query uses domain specific knowledge about the particular database
schema and acts like a usage scenario, much like code in a traditional unit test.
A test condition validates the result. The task of coming up with concrete test
tables and parameters for the test query satisfying the test condition is, on the
other hand, a combinatorial problem that is both error-prone and tedious.

We propose a technique that can be used to automate the above data generation problem for a class of SQL queries. The idea is illustrated in Figure 1 where
Qex is the underlying analysis engine. The expected usage scenario is that the
user supplies the query q as well as the test condition φ, Qex then generates
the sample input tables and the expected output. The generated input tables
are used to populate the database and the query q is executed against the actual database. The actual output is validated against the test condition φ or
compared against the expected output that was generated by Qex.

---

* This work was done during an internship at Microsoft Research, Redmond.

K. Breitman and A. Cavalcanti (Eds.): ICFEM 2009, LNCS 5885, pp. 49–68, 2009.

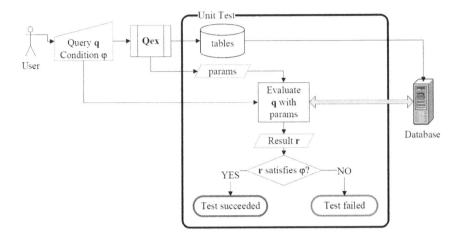

Fig. 1. Using Qex for data generation

We introduce a formal background theory T^Σ that is rich enough to capture the semantics for the class of queries under consideration, and is tailored for automatic analysis with state of the art SMT solvers. A given query q and a test condition φ are translated into a formula ψ in T^Σ. The translation is such that, if the formula ψ is satisfiable modulo T^Σ, i.e., ψ has a model S in T^Σ, then the values of the variables in S, are mapped back to concrete test tables and input parameters for q.

Satisfiability checking combined with finding a concrete model as a witness is usually called *model generation*. We illustrate the use of model generation in the context of the Visual Studio database unit testing framework. In this application, model generation is seen as a black box from the user's perspective. There are other well-known applications of model generation in the context of databases, such as integrity and security constraint checking, where this technique could be useful.

In Section 2 we introduce the background theory T^Σ. In Section 3 we define a formal translation from a class of SQL queries into T^Σ. In Section 4 we introduce an analysis approach of formulas in T^Σ by using satisfiability modulo theories (SMT). In Section 5 we discuss a concrete application for generating database unit tests in Visual Studio, we look at some concrete examples and provide some benchmarks. In Section 6 we discuss future work. Section 7 is about related work.

2   Background T^Σ

We use a fixed state background T^Σ that includes arithmetic, Booleans, tuples, and *finite* sets. The universe is multi-sorted, with all values having a fixed *sort*. The sorts $\mathbb{Z}$, $\mathbb{R}$, and $\mathbb{B}$ are used for integers, reals, and Booleans, respectively; $\mathbb{Z}$ and $\mathbb{R}$ are called *numeric* sorts. The sorts $\mathbb{Z}$, $\mathbb{R}$ and $\mathbb{B}$ are *basic*, so is the *tuple*

$$T^\sigma \qquad ::= x^\sigma \mid \mathit{Default}^\sigma \mid \mathit{Ite}(T^{\mathbb{B}}, T^\sigma, T^\sigma) \mid \mathit{TheElementOf}(T^{\mathbb{S}(\sigma)}) \mid$$
$$\pi_i(T^{\mathbb{T}(\sigma_0,\ldots,\sigma_i=\sigma,\ldots)})$$

$$T^{\mathbb{T}(\sigma_0,\ldots,\sigma_k)} ::= \langle T^{\sigma_0}, \ldots, T^{\sigma_k} \rangle$$

$$T^{\mathbb{Z}} \qquad ::= k \mid T^{\mathbb{Z}} + T^{\mathbb{Z}} \mid k * T^{\mathbb{Z}} \mid \Sigma_i(T^{\mathbb{S}(\mathbb{T}(\sigma_0,\ldots,\sigma_i=\mathbb{Z},\ldots))})$$

$$T^{\mathbb{R}} \qquad ::= r \mid T^{\mathbb{R}} + T^{\mathbb{R}} \mid k * T^{\mathbb{R}} \mid \Sigma_i(T^{\mathbb{S}(\mathbb{T}(\sigma_0,\ldots,\sigma_i=\mathbb{R},\ldots))}) \mid \mathit{AsReal}(T^{\mathbb{Z}})$$

$$T^{\mathbb{B}} \qquad ::= \mathit{true} \mid \mathit{false} \mid \neg T^{\mathbb{B}} \mid T^{\mathbb{B}} \wedge T^{\mathbb{B}} \mid T^{\mathbb{B}} \vee T^{\mathbb{B}}$$
$$T^\sigma = T^\sigma \mid T^{\mathbb{S}(\sigma)} \subseteq T^{\mathbb{S}(\sigma)} \mid T^\sigma \in T^{\mathbb{S}(\sigma)} \mid T^{\mathbb{Z}} \leq T^{\mathbb{Z}} \mid T^{\mathbb{R}} \leq T^{\mathbb{R}}$$

$$T^{\mathbb{S}(\sigma)} \qquad ::= X^{\mathbb{S}(\sigma)} \mid \{T^\sigma \mid_{\bar{x}} T^{\mathbb{B}}\} \mid T^{\mathbb{S}(\sigma)} \cup T^{\mathbb{S}(\sigma)} \mid T^{\mathbb{S}(\sigma)} \cap T^{\mathbb{S}(\sigma)} \mid T^{\mathbb{S}(\sigma)} \setminus T^{\mathbb{S}(\sigma)}$$

$$F \qquad ::= T^{\mathbb{B}} \mid \exists x\, F \mid \exists X\, F$$

Fig. 2. Well-formed expressions in $\mathcal{T}^\Sigma$

sort $\mathbb{T}(\sigma_0,\ldots,\sigma_k)$, provided that each σ_i is basic. The *set sort* $\mathbb{S}(\sigma)$ is not basic and requires σ to be basic.

The universe of values of sort σ is denoted by $\mathcal{U}^\sigma$. Universes of distinct sorts are disjoint.[1] For each sort σ, there is a specific *Default*$^\sigma$ in $\mathcal{U}^\sigma$. In particular, *Default*$^{\mathbb{B}} = \mathit{false}$, *Default*$^{\mathbb{Z}} = 0$, *Default*$^{\mathbb{R}} = 0$, *Default*$^{\mathbb{S}(\sigma)} = \emptyset$, and for a tuple sort the *Default* tuple is the tuple of *Default*'s of the respective element sorts. There is a function $\mathit{AsReal} : \mathcal{U}^{\mathbb{Z}} \to \mathcal{U}^{\mathbb{R}}$ that maps integers to corresponding reals.

We refer to a sort σ together with a semantic constraint on $\mathcal{U}^\sigma$ as a *type*. In particular, the type $\mathbb{Z}^+$ refers to the positive integers, i.e., the constraint is $\forall x^{\mathbb{Z}^+}(x > 0)$. An *enum* or *k-enum* type refers to integers 0 through $k - 1$ for some $k > 0$.

2.1 Expressions

We use an expression language that we also refer to as $\mathcal{T}^\Sigma$. Well-formed expressions or terms of $\mathcal{T}^\Sigma$ are shown in Figure 2. A term t of sort σ is written t^σ; x^σ is a variable of basic sort σ; X^σ is a variable where σ is a set sort. We adopt the convention that upper case letters are used for set variables. Boolean terms are also called *formulas*. We always assume that terms are well-sorted but omit the sorts when they are clear from the context. The set of *free variables* of a term t is denoted by $FV(t)$, these are all the variables that have an occurrence in t that is not in the scope of a quantifier. In particular, $FV(\{t \mid_x \varphi\}) = (FV(t) \cup FV(\varphi)) \setminus \{x\}$, where $\mid_x$ is the comprehension quantifier. A term without free variables is a *closed* term. We write $t[x_0, \ldots, x_{n-1}]$ for a term t where each x_i may occur free in t.

---

[1] We could assume that for distinct set sorts σ_1 and σ_2 the empty set is shared, but we may also assume, as we do here, that there is distinct empty set for each set sort. Either assumption is fine, because all expressions in $\mathcal{T}^\Sigma$ are well-sorted.

Let θ be the substitution $\{x_i \mapsto t_i\}_{i<n}$ (where x_i and t_i have the same sort)[2]; $t\theta$ denotes the application of θ on t. We write also $t[t_0, \ldots, t_{n-1}]$ for $t\theta$. For example, if $t[x]$ is the term $Ite(\{x \mid_x \varphi\} = \emptyset, x + x, x)$ and $\theta = \{x \mapsto x + y\}$ then $t\theta$ or $t[x + y]$ is the term $Ite(\{x \mid_x \varphi\} = \emptyset, (x + y) + (x + y), x + y)$.

We often omit the variables $\bar{x}$ from the comprehension quantifier $\mid_{\bar{x}}$ when they are clear from the context. We also use additional definitions in terms of $\mathcal{T}^\Sigma$ when they are needed. When a definition is obvious (such as $x < y$), we use it without further notice. *We often use the abbreviation $x.i$ for $\pi_i(x)$.*

A term in $\mathcal{T}^\Sigma$ of the form $\{x \mid x = t_1 \vee \cdots \vee x = t_n\}$ (where x is not free in any t_i), is abbreviated by $\{t_1, \ldots, t_n\}$ and is not considered as a comprehension term, but as an *explicit set* term.

2.2   Semantics

A *state* S is a mapping of variables to values. Since $\mathcal{T}^\Sigma$ is assumed to be the background we omit it from S, and assume that S has an implicit part that includes the interpretation for the function symbols of $\mathcal{T}^\Sigma$, for example that $+$ means addition and $\cup$ means set union. By slight abuse of notation, we reuse the function symbols in Figure 2 also to denote their interpretations, e.g., we write π_i also for $\pi_i^{\mathcal{T}^\Sigma}$, and let the context determine whether we refer to the symbol or its interpretation in $\mathcal{T}^\Sigma$. We write $Dom(S)$ for the domain of S. Given two states S_1 and S_2 we write $S_1 \uplus S_2$ for the union of S_1 and S_2 but where the variables in $Dom(S_1) \cap Dom(S_2)$ have the value in S_2.

A *state for* a term t is a state S such that $FV(t) \subseteq Dom(S)$. Given a term t and a state S for t, t^S is the *interpretation* or *evaluation of t in S*, defined by induction over the structure of t. Given a formula φ and a state S for φ, $S \models \varphi$ means that φ^S is *true*. Besides the standard logical connectives, arithmetical operations and set operations, equations (1–4) below show the semantics for the nonstandard constructions of t in Figure 2.

$$Ite(\varphi, t_1, t_2)^S = \begin{cases} t_1^S, \text{ if } S \models \varphi; \\ t_2^S, \text{ otherwise.} \end{cases} \tag{1}$$

$$TheElementOf(t_1^{\mathbb{S}(\sigma)})^S = \begin{cases} a, & \text{if } t_1^S = \{a\}; \\ Default^\sigma, & \text{otherwise.} \end{cases} \tag{2}$$

$$\{t_0 \mid_{x^\sigma} \varphi\}^S = \{t_0^{S \uplus \{x \mapsto a\}} : a \in \mathcal{U}^\sigma, S \uplus \{x \mapsto a\} \models \varphi\} \tag{3}$$

$$\Sigma_i(t_1)^S = \sum_{a \in t_1^S} \pi_i(a) \tag{4}$$

The interpretation of a comprehension with several variables is a straightforward generalization of (3). In (3) it is assumed that there are only *finitely* many a such that $S \uplus \{x \mapsto a\} \models \varphi$, otherwise we may assume that $\{t_0 \mid_{x^\sigma} \varphi\}^S$ is $\emptyset$.[3]

---

[2] We always make the assumption that substitutions are well-sorted in this sense, without further notice.

[3] In our translation from SQL to $\mathcal{T}^\Sigma$, finiteness is guaranteed by construction.

The use of comprehensions as terms is well-defined since sets are *extensional*:
$\forall X\, Y\, (\forall z(z \in X \Leftrightarrow z \in Y) \Leftrightarrow X = Y).$[4]

A state S for a formula φ such that $S \models \varphi$ is a *model* of φ. A formula φ is *satisfiable* if there exists a model of φ, and φ is *valid* if all states for φ are models of φ.

For a closed term t we talk about *evaluation of t*, without reference to any particular state.

Multiplication. We define $n * m$ with Σ_0, where $n > 0$ is an integer.

$$n * m \stackrel{\text{def}}{=} \Sigma_0(\{\langle m, x\rangle \mid 0 \le x < n\}) = \sum_{x=0}^{n-1} \pi_0(\langle m, x\rangle) = \sum_{x=0}^{n-1} m \qquad (5)$$

Note that m may be an integer or a real and the sort of m determines the sort of $n * m$.

Bags. Bags or *multisets* are represented as graphs of maps with positive integer ranges, i.e., a bag b with elements $\{a_i\}_{i<n}$ each having *multiplicity* $m_i > 0$ in b for $i < n$, is represented as a set of pairs $\{\langle a_i, m_i\rangle\}_{i<n}$, thus having the sort $\mathbb{S}(\mathbb{T}(\sigma, \mathbb{Z}))$ for some basic sort σ called the *domain sort* of b. We let $\mathbb{M}(\sigma)$ be the type $\mathbb{S}(\mathbb{T}(\sigma, \mathbb{Z}^+))$ with the additional *map constraint*:

$$\forall X^{\mathbb{M}(\sigma)}\, \forall x^\sigma\, y^\sigma\, ((x \in X \wedge y \in X \wedge x.0 = y.0) \Rightarrow x.1 = y.1).$$

We use the following definitions for dealing with bags.

$$AsBag(Y^{\mathbb{S}(\sigma)}) \stackrel{\text{def}}{=} \{\langle y, 1\rangle \mid y \in Y\}$$
$$AsSet(X^{\mathbb{M}(\sigma)}) \stackrel{\text{def}}{=} \{y.0 \mid y \in X\}$$
$$\Sigma_i^{\text{b}}(X^{\mathbb{M}(\mathbb{T}(\sigma_0,\dots,\sigma_i,\dots))}) \stackrel{\text{def}}{=} \Sigma_0(\{\langle x.1 * x.0.i, x.0\rangle \mid x \in X\}) \quad (\sigma_i \text{ is numeric})$$

Intuitively $AsSet(X)$ eliminates the duplicates from X. Σ_i^{b} is a generalization of the projected sum over sets to bags. Note that $x.1$ above is always positive (thus, the use of $*$ is well-defined). Note that an expression like $X^{\mathbb{M}(\sigma)} \cup Y^{\mathbb{M}(\sigma)}$ is a well-formed expression in $\mathcal{T}^\Sigma$, but it does not preserve the type $\mathbb{M}(\sigma)$.

Example 1. Let $q[X^{\mathbb{M}(\mathbb{T}(\mathbb{Z},\mathbb{Z},\mathbb{Z}))}]$ be the following expression where $\varphi[x]$ is the formula $x < 4$. Intuitively, the query selects the first column and sums up the elements in the second column and groups all entries by the first column (see also Example 2).

$$q[X] = \{\langle x.0.0, \Sigma_1^{\text{b}}(\{y \mid y \in X \wedge x.0.0 = y.0.0 \wedge \varphi[y.0.2]\})\rangle \mid x \in X \wedge \varphi[x.0.2]\}$$

Let $t = \{\langle\langle 0, 2, 1\rangle, 2\rangle, \langle\langle 1, 2, 3\rangle, 1\rangle, \langle\langle 1, 2, 4\rangle, 1\rangle\}$. Consider the evaluation of $q[t]$.

$$q[t] = \{\langle x.0.0, \Sigma_1^{\text{b}}(\{y \mid y \in t \wedge x.0.0 = y.0.0 \wedge \varphi[y.0.2]\})\rangle \mid x \in t \wedge \varphi[x.0.2]\}$$

---

[4] Extensionality of sets is a meta-level property that is not expressible in $\mathcal{T}^\Sigma$.

$$= \{\langle 0, \Sigma_1^{\mathrm{b}}(\{y \mid y \in t \wedge 0 = y.0.0 \wedge \varphi[y.0.2]\})\rangle,$$
$$\langle 1, \Sigma_1^{\mathrm{b}}(\{y \mid y \in t \wedge 1 = y.0.0 \wedge \varphi[y.0.2]\})\rangle\}$$
$$= \{\langle 0, \sum_{a \in \{\langle\langle 0,2,1\rangle,2\rangle\}} \pi_1(a) * \pi_1(\pi_0(a))\rangle,$$
$$\langle 1, \sum_{a \in \{\langle\langle 1,2,3\rangle,1\rangle\}} \pi_1(a) * \pi_1(\pi_0(a))\rangle\}$$
$$= \{\langle 0, 4\rangle, \langle 1, 2\rangle\}$$

3   From SQL to $\mathcal{T}^{\Sigma}$

In this section we show how we translate a class of SQL queries into $\mathcal{T}^{\Sigma}$. We name the translation $\mathbf{Q} : \mathrm{SQL} \rightarrow \mathcal{T}^{\Sigma}$. This section is less formal than Section 2. We omit full details of $\mathbf{Q}$ and illustrate it through examples and templates, which should be adequate for understanding how the general case works. We restrict our focus to queries without side-effects and consider a subset of SELECT statements. We illustrate parts of the concrete grammar with simplified grammar fragments extracted from [1]. Queries that may cause deletion or addition of rows in the database are outside the scope of this paper. Also, queries that use ORDER BY are not handled here. In Section 6 we briefly discuss an extension of our approach for analyzing queries with side-effects, as ongoing and future work. In most cases input tables have primary keys that disallow duplicates. However, in the general case, tables and results of queries are represented as bags whose domain sort is a tuple.

3.1   Data Types

Typical databases use additional data types besides numbers and Booleans. In particular, *strings* are used in virtually every database. So how do we support them? There are two approaches to deal with this. One is to encode the data types in $\mathcal{T}^{\Sigma}$. The other one is to extend $\mathcal{T}^{\Sigma}$ with the corresponding sorts and background theories. In this paper we take the first approach. The main advantage is that we have a smaller core that we need to deal with in the context of analysis, that is discussed in Section 4. The main disadvantage is that the overhead of the encoding may be more expensive than using a built-in theory.

Strings. There are several ways how strings can be encoded in $\mathcal{T}^{\Sigma}$. Suppose that in a given column, all strings have a maximum length k; a possible encoding of a k-string is as a k-tuple of integers, where each character a is encoded as an integer $c(a)$ in the range $[1, 255]$. A further constraint associated with this encoding is that it has the form $\langle c(a_0), \ldots, c(a_l), 0, \ldots, 0\rangle$ for a string $a_0 \cdots a_l$ for $l < k$, and the empty string is the *Default* of the tuple sort. Operations over k-strings, such as extracting a substring, can then be defined in terms of tuple operations.

Commonly, a collection of strings D are used as enums in a given column (for example names of persons), and the only string operations that are relevant are equality and lexicographic ordering $\leq_{\mathrm{lex}}$ over strings in D. In this case one can define a bijection $f_D : D \rightarrow [0, |D| - 1]$ such that, for all $a, b \in D$, $a \leq_{\mathrm{lex}} b$ iff $f_D(a) \leq f_D(b)$, and encode strings in D as $|D|$-enums.

3.2   Nullable Values

We encode nullable values with tuples. Given a basic sort σ, let $?\sigma$ be the sort $\mathbb{T}(\sigma, \mathbb{B})$ with the constraint $\forall x^{?\sigma} (x.1 = false \Rightarrow x.0 = Default^{\sigma})$ and $null^{?\sigma} \overset{\text{def}}{=} Default^{\mathbb{T}(\sigma, \mathbb{B})}$. Operations that are defined for σ are lifted to $?\sigma$. For example, for a numeric sort σ,

$$x^{?\sigma} + y^{?\sigma} \overset{\text{def}}{=} Ite(x.1 \wedge y.1, \langle x.0 + y.0, true \rangle, null^{?\sigma}).$$

The projected sum operation is lifted analogously. The sorts $\mathbb{T}(\sigma, \mathbb{B})$ are not used to represent any other data types besides $?\sigma$. This encoding introduces an overhead for the symbolic analysis and is avoided unless the corresponding value type is declared nullable.

3.3   Query Expressions

We consider top level query expressions that have the form *query_expr* according to the (simplified) grammar:

query_expr ::= *select* | (*query_expr* *set_operation* *query_expr*)
set_operation ::= UNION | EXCEPT | INTERSECT
select ::= SELECT [DISTINCT] *select_list*
              FROM *table_src* [WHERE *condition*] [*group_by_having*]

Set operations such as UNION remove duplicate rows from the arguments and the resulting query. In particular, the translation for UNION is:

$$\mathbf{Q}(\texttt{q1 UNION q2}) \overset{\text{def}}{=} AsBag(AsSet(\mathbf{Q}(\texttt{q1})) \cup AsSet(\mathbf{Q}(\texttt{q2}))).$$

The other set operations have a similar translation.

3.4   Select Clauses

A select clause refers to a particular selection of the columns from a given table by using a *select_list*. In the following translation we translate a *select_list* $\mathbf{l}$ into a sequence of projection indices $(l_0, \ldots, l_n)$ on the table on which the selection is applied.

$$\mathbf{Q}(\texttt{SELECT l FROM t}) \overset{\text{def}}{=} \{\langle \langle x.0.l_0, \ldots, x.0.l_n \rangle, M(x) \rangle \mid x \in \mathbf{Q}(\texttt{t})\} \quad (6)$$

$$\text{where } M(x) = \Sigma_0(\{\langle y.1, y \rangle \mid y \in \mathbf{Q}(\texttt{t}) \wedge \bigwedge_{i=0}^{n} y.0.l_i = x.0.l_i\})$$

Note that multiplicities of the resulting tuples are computed separately, which is needed to preserve the type of the result as a bag. For example, the following is *not* a valid translation, unless $\mathbf{l}$ is *, because the multiplicities are not computed correctly:

$$\{\langle \langle x.0.l_0, \ldots, x.0.l_n \rangle, x.1 \rangle \mid x \in \mathbf{Q}(\texttt{t})\}$$

If the DISTINCT keyword is used then duplicate rows are removed.

$$\mathbf{Q}(\text{SELECT DISTINCT 1 FROM t}) \stackrel{\text{def}}{=} AsBag(AsSet(\mathbf{Q}(\text{SELECT 1 FROM t})))$$

The following property is used in the set conversion:

$$AsSet(\mathbf{Q}(\text{SELECT 1 FROM t})) = \{\langle y.l_0, \ldots, y.l_n \rangle \mid y \in AsSet(\mathbf{Q}(\text{t}))\} \quad (7)$$

An optional WHERE condition is translated into a formula in $\mathcal{T}^{\Sigma}$ and appears as an additional condition in the above comprehensions.

3.5   Join Operations

Join operations are used in FROM statements. In general, a FROM statement takes an argument *table_src*, that, in simplified form, has the grammar:

table_src ::= *table_name* [AS *alias*] | *joined_table*
joined_table ::= *table_src* join *table_src* ON *condition*
join ::= [{INNER | {{LEFT | RIGHT | FULL} [OUTER]}}] JOIN

The condition may use column names of the (aliased) tables and operations on the corresponding data types. We only consider the case of INNER JOIN:

$$\mathbf{Q}(\text{t1 INNER JOIN t2 ON c}) \stackrel{\text{def}}{=} \quad (8)$$
$$\{\langle x_1.0 \times x_2.0, x_1.1 * x_2.1 \rangle \mid x_1 \in \mathbf{Q}(\text{t1}) \wedge x_2 \in \mathbf{Q}(\text{t2}) \wedge \mathbf{Q}(\text{c})[x_1.0, x_2.0]\}$$

where $\mathbf{Q}(\text{c})[y_1, y_2]$ denotes the translation of the condition c to the corresponding formula in $\mathcal{T}^{\Sigma}$, where the column names referring to the tables t1 and t2 occur as corresponding tuple projection operations on y_1 and y_2, respectively. The operation $\times$ is defined as follows, where x is an m-tuple and y is an n-tuple:

$$x \times y \stackrel{\text{def}}{=} \langle \pi_0(x), \ldots, \pi_{m-1}(x), \pi_0(y), \ldots, \pi_{n-1}(y) \rangle$$

The following property holds for the translation:

$$AsSet(\mathbf{Q}(\text{t1 INNER JOIN t2 ON c})) = \quad (9)$$
$$\{y_1 \times y_2 \mid y_1 \in AsSet(\mathbf{Q}(\text{t1})) \wedge y_2 \in AsSet(\mathbf{Q}(\text{t2})) \wedge \mathbf{Q}(\text{c})[y_1, y_2]\}$$

3.6   Grouping and Aggregates

A very common construct is the combined use of GROUP BY with *aggregate* operations. A *group_by_having* expression has the following (simplified) grammar, where a *group_by_item* for us is a column name.

group_by_having ::= *group_by* [HAVING *condition*]
group_by ::= GROUP BY *group_by_list*
group_by_list ::= *group_by_item* [,...n]

This expression appears in a *select* expression, the grammar of which is shown above, and there is a context condition that the columns in *select_list* that are not included in *group_by_list* must be applied to aggregate operations. The context condition is needed to eliminate duplicate rows produced by the select clause by combining the values in the columns not in the *group_by_list* into a single value for the given column. Here we only consider aggregates in combination with grouping.[5] The aggregate operations we consider are SUM, COUNT, MAX, MIN.

Example 2. Assume that X is a table with the columns (A,B,C) where each column has integer type. Consider the following query q.

```
SELECT A, SUM(B) AS D
FROM X
WHERE C < 4
GROUP BY A
```

$\mathbf{Q}(\mathsf{q})$ is $AsBag(q[X])$ with $q[X]$ as in Example 1, where it is shown how

$$q[\begin{array}{|c|c|c|}\hline A & B & C \\\hline 0 & 2 & 1 \\\hline 0 & 2 & 1 \\\hline 1 & 2 & 3 \\\hline 1 & 2 & 4 \\\hline\end{array}]\quad\text{evaluates to}\quad\begin{array}{|c|c|}\hline A & D \\\hline 0 & 4 \\\hline 1 & 2 \\\hline\end{array}.$$

In order to simplify the presentation assume that *select_list* and *group_by_list* are like in Example 2. (Generalization is straightforward, but tedious.) The translation is as follows, where t is SELECT a SUM(b) AS d FROM t1 WHERE c1,

$$\mathbf{Q}(\mathsf{t}\ \text{GROUP BY}\ \mathsf{a}\ \text{HAVING}\ \mathsf{c2})\ \overset{\text{def}}{=}\ AsBag(\{z \mid z \in G \wedge \mathbf{Q}(\mathsf{c2})[z]\})$$
$$\text{where}\ G = \{\langle x.0.0, \Sigma_1^b(\{y \mid y \in \mathbf{Q}(\mathsf{t}) \wedge y.0.0 = x.0.0\})\rangle \mid x \in \mathbf{Q}(\mathsf{t})\}$$

Note that the condition $y.0.0 = x.0.0$ corresponds to *group_list*. Note also that c2 is applied to the result G of the grouping and in the formula $\mathbf{Q}(\mathsf{c2})[z]$, $z.0$ corresponds to a and $z.1$ corresponds to d. The other aggregates are translated similarly. For example, if SUM(b) is replaced by COUNT(b) then in the above translation Σ_1^b is replaced by $Count \overset{\text{def}}{=} \Sigma_1$. For MIN and MAX the projected sum operation is not needed, for example:

$$Min(X^{\mathbb{S}(\sigma)}) \overset{\text{def}}{=} TheElementOf(\{y \mid y \in X \wedge \{z \mid z \in X \wedge z < y\} = \emptyset\}) \quad (10)$$

Although we do not consider the aggregate AVG here, it can be translated as $\Sigma_i^b(X) \div Count(X)$, where $\div$ is division by positive integer in $\mathbb{R}$ and can be defined as follows:

$$r \div k \overset{\text{def}}{=} TheElementOf(\{x^{\mathbb{R}} \mid k * x = r\}). \quad (11)$$

---

[5] In general, aggregates may also be used in a select expression without using grouping.

3.7   Simplifications

Many operations convert bags into sets. There are certain further simplification
rules, besides (7) and (9), that are based on the following properties between
bag an set operations and are used in the translation to reduce operations over
bags to operations over sets, whenever possible.

$$AsSet(AsBag(X^{\mathbb{S}(\sigma)})) = X$$
$$\Sigma_i^{\mathrm{b}}(AsBag(X^{\mathbb{S}(\sigma)})) = \Sigma_i(X)$$
$$AsSet(\{t \mid \varphi\}^{\mathbb{M}(\sigma)}) = \{t.0 \mid \varphi\}$$

Moreover, further simplifications are done at the level of basic sorts, such as
$\pi_i(\langle t_0, \ldots, t_i, \ldots \rangle) = t_i$, that are also used as part of the simplification process.
More accurately, the simplifications are part of an equivalence preserving post
processing phase of $\mathbf{Q}(\mathsf{q})$ for a given query q.

4   Model Generation with SMT

Translation $\mathbf{Q}$ leads to a subclass of expressions in $\mathcal{T}^{\Sigma}$, denoted by $\mathcal{T}_{\mathbf{Q}}^{\Sigma}$. The core
problem we are interested in is *model generation* in $\mathcal{T}_{\mathbf{Q}}^{\Sigma}$.

Definition 1 (Model Generation in $\mathcal{T}_{\mathbf{Q}}^{\Sigma}$). Given a quantifier free formula
$\varphi[X]$ in $\mathcal{T}^{\Sigma}$, and a query q, decide if $\psi = \varphi[\mathbf{Q}(q)]$ is satisfiable, and if ψ is
satisfiable generate a model of ψ.

Our main application is to generate a database for a given query such that the
query satisfies a certain property. In general a query may also include *parameters*,
other than the input tables, e.g., in Example 2, the constant 4 can be replaced
by a parameter variable @x.[6] Thus, one can use model generation for parameter
generation as well as database generation, given a (partially) fixed database and
a parameterized query q, generate a model of $\varphi[\mathbf{Q}(\mathsf{q})]$, where φ represents a test
condition (such as the result being nonempty). Once a model is generated, it is
used to generate a concrete unit test, see Section 5.

For model generation we use the state of the art SMT solver Z3 [25,10]. For
bags and sets we use the built-in theory of extensional arrays in Z3, similarly for
tuples, Booleans, integers and reals. In some cases the formula $\varphi[\mathbf{Q}(\mathsf{q})]$ can be
first simplified, e.g., so that all bags are reduced to sets. Below we describe the
general mechanism without emphasis on such simplifications.

4.1   Eager Expansion

Consider a formula $\psi[\overline{X}]$ as an instance of the model generation problem, where
every X in $\overline{X}$ is a bag variable. The formula ψ may include other free variables
that correspond to parameter variables in the original query. For the analysis,
we introduce a special inductively defined term called a *set describer*, with the
sort $\mathbb{S}(\sigma)$.

---

[6] Parameters are prefixed with the @ sign in the concrete query language we are using.

- The constant $Empty^{\mathbb{S}(\sigma)}$ is a set describer.
- If $t^{\mathbb{S}(\sigma)}$ is a set describer then so is the term $Set(\varphi^{\mathbb{B}}, u^{\sigma}, t)$.

Given a state S for $Set(\varphi, u, t)$, the interpretation in S is,

$$Set(\varphi, u, t)^S = Ite(\varphi, \{u\}, \emptyset)^S \cup t^S, \quad Empty^S = \emptyset.$$

Consider a fixed X in $\overline{X}$ and let t_X be the set describer

$$Set(true, \langle x_1, m_1 \rangle, \ldots Set(true, \langle x_k, m_k \rangle, Empty) \ldots)$$

where k and all the m_j's are some positive integer constants and each x_i is a variable. Thus, t_X describes the set $\{\langle x_1, m_1 \rangle, \ldots, \langle x_k, m_k \rangle\}$. It is also assumed that there is an associated constraint $distinct(x_1, \ldots, x_k)$ stating that all the x_i's are pairwise distinct. Thus t_X is a valid bag term, in any context where the constraint holds.

The *expansion* of $\psi[t_X]$, $\mathbf{Exp}(\psi[t_X])$, eliminates comprehensions and projected sums from $\psi[t_X]$. The definition of $\mathbf{Exp}$ is by induction over the structure of terms. The case of comprehensions is as follows. Here we assume that the comprehension has a single bound variable, the definition is straightforward to generalize to any number bound variables. It is also assumed here that the comprehension has a special form where the bound variable x has a *range expression* $x \in r$ where x is not free in r.

$$\mathbf{Exp}(\{t \mid_x x \in r \wedge \varphi\}) \stackrel{\mathrm{def}}{=} \mathbf{ExpC}(t, x, \mathbf{Exp}(r), \varphi)$$

$$\mathbf{ExpC}(t, x, Empty, \varphi) \stackrel{\mathrm{def}}{=} Empty$$

$$\mathbf{ExpC}(t[x], x, Set(\gamma, u, rest), \varphi[x]) \stackrel{\mathrm{def}}{=} Set(\gamma \wedge \mathbf{Exp}(\varphi[u]), \mathbf{Exp}(t[u]),$$
$$\mathbf{ExpC}(t, x, rest, \varphi))$$

Not all comprehensions are expanded this way, some expressions use specialized expansion rules. For example, for (10), $\mathbf{Exp}(Min(t))$ is replaced by a fresh variable x and the formula

$$Ite\left(\mathbf{Exp}(t) \neq \emptyset, (\mathbf{IsLeq}(x, \mathbf{Exp}(t)) \wedge x \in \mathbf{Exp}(t)), x = 0\right),$$

which is equivalent to $x = Min(t)$, that is included as a top-level conjunct (in $\mathbf{Exp}(\psi[t_X]))$,[7] where

$$\mathbf{IsLeq}(x, Empty) \stackrel{\mathrm{def}}{=} true$$

$$\mathbf{IsLeq}(x, Set(\varphi, u, r)) \stackrel{\mathrm{def}}{=} (\varphi \Rightarrow x \leq u) \wedge \mathbf{IsLeq}(x, r)$$

For Σ_i the expansion is as follows.

$$\mathbf{Exp}(\Sigma_i(t)) \stackrel{\mathrm{def}}{=} \mathbf{Sum}_i(\mathbf{Exp}(t), Empty)$$

$$\mathbf{Sum}_i(Empty, s) \stackrel{\mathrm{def}}{=} 0$$

$$\mathbf{Sum}_i(Set(\gamma, u, rest), s) \stackrel{\mathrm{def}}{=} Ite(\gamma \wedge u \notin s, \pi_i(u), 0) + \mathbf{Sum}_i(rest, Set(\gamma, u, s))$$

---

[7] Note that a formula $\varphi[t]$ is equivalent to the formula $\exists x(\varphi[x] \wedge x = t)$, where x is a fresh variable.

Note that the role of s is to accumulate elements that have already been included in the sum, so that the same element is not added twice.

Regarding multiplication, the general form of (5), that involves a comprehension without a range expression, is not needed. Since all multiplicities in the initial tables t_X are fixed constants, it follows that multiplications are either of the form $k_1 * k_2$, where k_1 and k_2 are constants (in formulas created in (8)), which preserves the constant multiplicities in the resulting table), or multiplicities are finite sums of constants (as in (6)), which provides constant upper and lower bounds for the multiplicities. Multiplication under these constraints is supported in Z3.

It is also possible to expand $t \div u$ as defined in (11), by replacing $\mathbf{Exp}(t \div u)$ with a fresh variable $x^{\mathbb{R}}$ and adding the top-level conjunct $\mathbf{Exp}(u) * x = \mathbf{Exp}(t)$. Here $\mathbf{Exp}(u)$ is also a sum of terms that have constant upper and lower bounds.

The overall approach amounts to systematically enumerating the sizes of the tables and the multiplicities, and searching for a model of the resulting expanded formula.

4.2 Lazy Expansion

The main disadvantage of the eager approach is that it expands all terms upfront, without taking into account if a certain expansion is actually needed in a particular context. An alternative (or complementary) approach is to delay the expansion of (some) terms by delegating the expansion to the proof search engine of the underlying solver. We explain here a high-level view of how to accomplish such delayed or *lazy* expansion in the context of SMT.

In addition to a quantifier free formula ψ that is provided to the SMT solver and for which proof of satisfiability is sought, one can also provide additional universally quantified *axioms*. During proof search, axioms are triggered by matching subexpressions in ψ. An axiom has the form

$$(\forall \bar{x}(\alpha),\ pat_\alpha)$$

where α is a quantifier free formula, pat_α is a quantifier free term, and $FV(\alpha) = FV(pat_\alpha) = \bar{x}$. The axioms typically define properties of uninterpreted function symbols in an extended signature. The high-level view behind the use of the axioms is as follows. If ψ contains a subterm t and there exists a substitution θ such that $t = pat_\alpha\theta$, i.e., t *matches the pattern* pat_α, then ψ is replaced during proof search by (a reduction of) $\psi \wedge \alpha\theta$.[8] Note that, if a pattern is never matched in this way, the use of the corresponding axiom is not triggered. Thus, the use of axioms is inherently incomplete, and it is not guaranteed that the axioms hold in a model of ψ, if one is found, or even if the axioms are consistent.

We illustrate the use of axioms with the projected sum operator. Assume that *Empty*, *Set*, and $\mathbf{Sum}_i$ are new function symbols and assume that we have the following axioms:

---

[8] In general, one can associate several patterns with an axiom, one of which is used for triggering, and one can also use multi-patterns in Z3. A multi-pattern is a collection of patterns all of which must be matched for the axiom to be triggered.

$$\alpha_1 = \forall s (\mathbf{Sum}_i(Empty, s) = 0)$$
$$pat_{\alpha_1} = \mathbf{Sum}_i(Empty, s)$$
$$\alpha_2 = \forall b\, u\, r\, s\, (\mathbf{Sum}_i(Set(b, u, r), s) =$$
$$Ite(b \wedge u \notin s, \pi_i(u), 0) + \mathbf{Sum}_i(r, Ite(b, \{u\}, \emptyset) \cup s))$$
$$pat_{\alpha_2} = \mathbf{Sum}_i(Set(b, u, r), s)$$

Note that, unlike we defined $\mathbf{Sum}_i$ in Section 4.1, the argument s here is not a set describer, but a set valued term that has built-in interpretation in the SMT solver.[9] Let us consider an example reduction, let ψ_0 be the formula:

$$x \leq \mathbf{Sum}_1(Set(true, \langle 1, y \rangle, Set(true, \langle 1, z \rangle, Empty)), \emptyset)$$

The right hand side of ψ_0 matches pat_{α_2}, so ψ_0 reduces to ψ_1:[10]

$$x \leq y + \mathbf{Sum}_1(Set(true, \langle 1, z \rangle, Empty), \{\langle 1, y \rangle\})$$

The same axiom is applied again, and ψ_1 is reduced to ψ_2:

$$x \leq y + Ite(z \neq y, z, 0) + \mathbf{Sum}_1(Empty, \{\langle 1, y \rangle, \langle 1, z \rangle\})$$

Finally, α_1 is used to reduce ψ_2 to $x \leq y + Ite(z \neq y, z, 0)$. Some concrete examples, using the smt-lib format, are given in the technical report [24].

In general, such axioms can be defined for expanding other constructs. The main tradeoff is whether the additional overhead of the axiomatization of the expansion rules and the loss of completeness pays off. One also has to take into account that in the intended application, discussed in Section 5, we are mostly interested in generating small databases.

5   Application to Unit Testing

Returning to the main motivation behind this work, we are primarily interested in the problem of generating a database (a collection of tables) and concrete parameters for a given parameterized query that, when evaluated with respect to the database, satisfies a certain test condition. Examples of standard test conditions are: the answer is empty, the answer is nonempty, and the answer contains a given number of (distinct) rows.

We are abstracting here from the problem of determining what exactly are the intended domains of the values in a column, e.g., a certain column may be declared to have the string type, but effectively the strings are used as enums. In fact, the particular encoding of the domain values depends of the query. We suppose that we have domain specific functions, that enable us to map models generated by the analysis engine, to corresponding concrete tables and parameter values for the query, e.g., that the value 12 in a certain column corresponds to the string "Bob". See also Section 3.1.

---

[9] It is not possible to pattern-match against built-in operations in Z3.
[10] To be precise the reduction takes several steps that are skipped here.

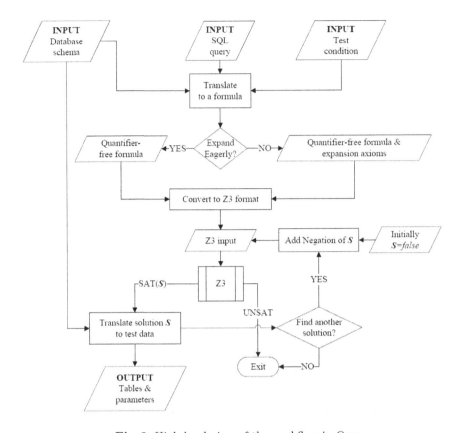

Fig. 3. High-level view of the workflow in Qex

With this encoding in mind, we view the analysis engine here as a black box, called *Qex*, which given a parameterized query, produces a set of tables and parameters to that query. A high-level workflow diagram of Qex is illustrated in Figure 3. One can also see a short video that introduces Qex [18]. In the following we look at some examples and illustrate a concrete application of Qex in the context of generating database unit tests in Visual Studio.

Experiments. We consider here a sample database for an online store that contains tables for products, orders and customers; products have a product id, a name and a price; customers have a customer id and a name; orders have an order id and a customer id. Figure 4 illustrates some sample queries over the database. Query q1 selects customers and related orders based on a constraint on the ids. Query q2 selects those customers and corresponding number of orders, who have more than one order. Query q3 selects "good" customers and has a parameter named @value. Table 1 shows some performance measures of model generation for different input table sizes and test conditions for the queries in Figure 4 using the eager expansion. The total

```
q1: SELECT C.CustomerID, O.OrderID   q2: SELECT C.CustomerID,
    FROM Orders AS O                          Count(O.OrderID)
    JOIN Customers AS C ON               FROM Orders AS O
         O.CustomerID = C.CustomerID     JOIN Customers AS C ON
    WHERE O.CustomerID > 2 AND                O.CustomerID = C.CustomerID
         O.OrderID < 15                  GROUP BY C.CustomerID HAVING
                                                  Count(O.OrderID) > 1
```

```
q3: DECLARE @value AS INT;
    SELECT C.CustomerID, SUM(OP.OrderProductQuantity * P.ProductPrice)
    FROM OrderProducts AS OP
    JOIN Orders AS O ON OP.OrderID = O.OrderID
    JOIN Products AS P ON OP.ProductID = P.ProductID
    JOIN Customers AS C ON O.CustomerID = C.CustomerID
    WHERE @value > 1
    GROUP BY C.CustomerID
    HAVING SUM(OP.OrderProductQuantity * P.ProductPrice) > 100 + @value
```

Fig. 4. Sample queries

evaluation time is divided into *expansion time* t_{exp} and *proof search time* t_{z3} with Z3. The current prototype implementation of the eager expansion algorithm is unoptimized and uses a naive representation of terms in $\mathcal{T}^\Sigma$ without structure sharing, e.g., the size of the expanded term $\mathbf{Q}(q2)$ for $k = 3$ is over 5 million symbols. This is reflected by the fact that in most cases $t_{exp} \gg t_{z3}$, although the actual parameter and table generation takes place during proof search. Note that t_{exp} is independent of the test condition, whereas t_{z3} clearly depends on it. In general, exhaustive search for models, in the case when the formula is unsatisfiable, is more time consuming than when a model exists. Note also that query q2 is unsatisfiable with 1 row in each input table due to the

Table 1. Model generation for sample queries. Evaluation times t_{exp} and t_{z3} are given in seconds; k is the expected number of rows in each of the generated input tables; all multiplicities of rows in input tables are 1.

query	condition	k	check	t_{exp}	t_{z3}
q1	$res \neq \emptyset$	1	sat	.03	.001
		2	sat	.05	.005
		3	sat	.3	.02
		4	sat	1.4	.13
	$res = \emptyset$	1	sat	.03	.001
		2	sat	.05	.006
		3	sat	.3	.12
		4	sat	1.4	2

query	condition	k	check	t_{exp}	t_{z3}
q1	$|res| = 5$	1	unsat	.03	.001
		2	unsat	.05	.01
		3	unsat	.3	.16
		4	unsat	1.4	10
		5	sat	8.4	1.6
q2	$res \neq \emptyset$	1	unsat	.03	.001
		2	sat	.7	.006
		3	sat	26	.03
q3	$res \neq \emptyset$	1	sat	.34	.001
		2	sat	30	.03

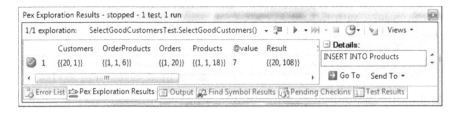

Fig. 5. Screenshot of model generation through Pex integration of Qex in Visual Studio

condition `Count(O.OrderID) > 1`. The actual tables and parameters generated for `q3` using Pex [17] integration in Visual Studio Database edition are illustrated by a screenshot in Figure 5. The integration also generates automatically a unit test. A partial screenshot of the generated unit test is illustrated in Figure 6. The test contains two SQL scripts. The first script prepares the database by deleting old data from the tables and by inserting newly generated rows into the database. The second script declares the given query together with the generated parameter values. The unit test is executed against the actual database, which in this case is provided through MS SQL Server 2005.

```
[TestMethod]
[PexGeneratedBy(typeof(SelectGoodCustomersTest))]
public void SelectGoodCustomers01()
{
    SelectGoodCustomersTest.SelectGoodCustomers();
    DatabaseTestAction preTestAction = new DatabaseTestAction();
    preTestAction.SqlScript =
       "DELETE FROM OrderProducts;\r\nDELETE FROM Orders;\r\nDELETE FROM Products;\r
    DatabaseTestAction testAction = new DatabaseTestAction();
    testAction.SqlScript =
       "DECLARE @value AS INT;\r\n\r\nSET @value = 7;\r\n\r\nSELECT    C.CustomerID,\
    testAction.Conditions
       .Add((TestCondition)(new NotEmptyResultSetCondition()));
    using (ConnectionContext executionContext = DatabaseTestClass.TestService
       .OpenExecutionContext())
    {
        using (ConnectionContext priviledgedContext = DatabaseTestClass.TestService
           .OpenPrivilegedContext())
        {
            ExecutionResult[] preTestResult = DatabaseTestClass.TestService
                .Execute(priviledgedContext, priviledgedContext, preTestAction);
            QexAssert.WriteResults("preTest", preTestResult);
            ExecutionResult[] TestResult = DatabaseTestClass.TestService
                .Execute(executionContext, priviledgedContext, testAction);
                            ⋮
```

Fig. 6. Automatically generated database unit test in Visual Studio

6   Extensions

The Qex project is a new project that has some flavor of model-based testing as well as parameterized unit testing. The current implementation is a prototype that needs further evaluation and case studies. The approach can also be extended in several ways. The choice of the background theory $\mathcal{T}^\Sigma$ was partly motivated with some of those extensions in mind. Here we discuss a few of the extensions that are ongoing and future work.

Side-effects. The background theory $\mathcal{T}^\Sigma$ is an extension of the background theory $\mathcal{T}$ with the projected sum operator and restricted to finite sets; $\mathcal{T}$ is used for symbolic *model program* analysis [23,22] by reduction to SMT solving. The projected sum operation has not been considered in that context; one reason is that it causes undecidability of some fragments that are otherwise decidable. In principle though, model programs can also be based on the background $\mathcal{T}^\Sigma$. A model program can be used to describe an evaluation of a query together with side-effects, where the side-effects are computed as update sets to respective tables that are applied at the end of the evaluation in a single transaction. In this setting one can also symbolically analyze the resulting model program for potential *update inconsistency* [23].

Data types. Another extension is better support for data types that are in the current approach encoded with tuples. This encoding is not fully adequate for supporting commonly used algebraic data types such as trees and lists, or terms in the sense of a free-algebra with a separate sort. The encoding of such data types in $\mathcal{T}^\Sigma$ is both expensive and incomplete (from the analysis point of view). Also, one can adopt existing techniques to represent strings, and solve constraints involving common operations over strings, in the context of an SMT solver [3].

Integration with parameterized unit testing of code. From the practical perspective, more complex unit tests, used for testing store procedures, may use a combination of queries and code. It is possible to combine parameterized unit testing of managed code [20] with query evaluation discussed in this paper.

7   Related Work

Deciding satisfiability of SQL queries requires a formal semantics. While we give meaning to SQL queries by an embedding into our formal background theory $\mathcal{T}^\Sigma$, which is in turn mapped to a logic of an SMT solver, there are other approaches, e.g., defining the semantics in the Extended Three Valued Predicate Calculus [16], or using bags as a foundation [7]. Satisfiability of queries is also related to logic-based approaches to semantic query optimization [5]. The general problem of satisfiability of SQL queries is undecidable and computationally hard for very restricted fragments, e.g., deciding if a query has a nonempty answer is NEXP-hard for nonrecursive range-restricted queries [9].

Several research efforts have considered formal analysis and verification of aspects of database systems, usually employing a possibly interactive theorem prover. For example, one system [19] checks whether a transaction is guaranteed to maintain integrity constraints in a relational database; the system is based on Boyer and Moore-style theorem proving [4].

There are many existing approaches to generate databases as test inputs. Most approaches create data in an ad-hoc fashion. Only few consider a target query. Tsai et.al. present an approach for test input generation for relational algebra queries [21]. They do not consider comprehensions or bags. They propose a translation of queries to a set of systems of linear inequalities, for which they implemented an ad-hoc solving framework which compares favorably to random guessing of solutions. A practical system for testing database transactions is AGENDA [11]. It generates test inputs satisfying a database schema by combining user-provided data, and it supports checking of complex integrity constraints by breaking them into simpler constraints that can be enforced by the database. While this system does not employ a constraint solver, it has been recently refined with the TGQG [6] algorithm: Based on given SQL statements, it generates test generation queries; execution of these queries against a user-provided set of data groups yields test inputs which cover desired properties of the given SQL statements.

Some recent approaches to test input generation for databases employ automated reasoning. The relational logic solver Alloy [13,14] has been used by Khalek et.al. [15] to generate input data for database queries. Their implementation supports a subset of SQL with a simplified syntax. In queries, they can reason about relational operations on integers, equality operations on strings, and logical operations, but not about nullable values, or grouping with aggregates such as SUM; they also do not reason about duplicates in the query results. QAGen [2] is another approach to query-solving. It first processes a query in an adhoc-way, which requires numerous user-provided "knob" settings as additional inputs. From the query, a propositional logic formula is generated, which is then decided by the Cogent [8] solver to generate the test inputs. Recently, test input generation of queries has been combined with test input generation of programs that contain embedded queries in the program text [12], using ad-hoc heuristic solvers for some of the arising constraints from the program and the queries.

8   Conclusion

The current prototype of Qex is a proof-of-concept. Qex can be used in the context of the Unit Testing Framework of Visual Studio Database Edition; a short video is available on the Qex project page [18] that illustrates the integration. For practical usage in an industrial context, we are working on an integration of Qex inside Pex [17]. In the context of Pex, embedded SQL queries in C# code can be translated into formulas that can be conjuncted with path-conditions that are generated by Pex. It is also possible to apply a similar translation to LINQ queries, although, unlike in SQL, the semantics of LINQ queries depends on the order of the rows in the tables. This combination with Pex is possible because the underlying theorem prover Z3 [25] is used in a similar way in both tools and the API of Z3 enables incremental evaluation and backtracking over the search space. In this setting, Qex may be viewed as a database extension of Pex that supports analysis of constraints involving high-level data types, such as sets and maps and aggregate operations. Path conditions generated by Pex establish different contexts where evaluating the same query may yield different tables depending on the parameter values that have been established in the path conditions for covering different code branches.

A practical limitation of the approach is if queries use multiple joins and aggregates and the input tables need to contain a high number of rows in order to satisfy the test condition. Another limitation is the use nonlinear constraints, in particular multiplication, that has currently only limited support in Z3. However, for generating tables we start with singleton tables and increment the number of rows only when a model is not found. We believe that this heuristic should be adequate for most practical applications, although further evaluation is needed. In general, checking for nonsatisfiability (or searching for a model of an unsatisfiable formula) is less efficient than generating a model of a satisfiable formula, this is also reflected in Table 1.

References

1. SELECT (T-SQL), http://msdn.microsoft.com/en-us/library/ms189499.aspx
2. Binnig, C., Kossmann, D., Lo, E., Özsu, M.T.: Qagen: generating query-aware test databases. In: SIGMOD 2007: Proceedings of the 2007 ACM SIGMOD international conference on Management of data, pp. 341–352. ACM, New York (2007)
3. Bjørner, N., Tillmann, N., Voronkov, A.: Path feasibility analysis for string-manipulating programs. In: Kowalewski, S., Philippou, A. (eds.) TACAS 2009. LNCS, vol. 5505, pp. 307–321. Springer, Heidelberg (2009)
4. Boyer, R.S., Moore, J.S.: A computational logic handbook. Academic Press Professional, Inc., San Diego (1988)
5. Chakravarthy, U.S., Grant, J., Minker, J.: Logic-based approach to semantic query optimization. ACM Trans. Database Syst. 15(2), 162–207 (1990)
6. Chays, D., Shahid, J., Frankl, P.G.: Query-based test generation for database applications. In: Proceedings of the 1st International Workshop on Testing Database Systems (DBTest 2008), pp. 1–6. ACM, New York (2008)
7. Chinaei, H.R.: An ordered bag semantics of SQL. Master's thesis, University of Waterloo, Waterloo, Ontario, Canada (2007)
8. Cook, B., Kröning, D., Sharygina, N.: Cogent: Accurate theorem proving for program verification. In: Etessami, K., Rajamani, S.K. (eds.) CAV 2005. LNCS, vol. 3576, pp. 296–300. Springer, Heidelberg (2005)
9. Dantsin, E., Voronkov, A.: Complexity of query answering in logic databases with complex values. In: Adian, S., Nerode, A. (eds.) LFCS 1997. LNCS, vol. 1234, pp. 56–66. Springer, Heidelberg (1997)
10. de Moura, L., Bjørner, N.: Z3: An efficient SMT solver. In: Ramakrishnan, C.R., Rehof, J. (eds.) TACAS 2008. LNCS, vol. 4963, pp. 337–340. Springer, Heidelberg (2008)

11. Deng, Y., Frankl, P., Chays, D.: Testing database transactions with AGENDA. In: ICSE 2005: Proceedings of the 27th international conference on Software engineering, pp. 78–87. ACM, New York (2005)
12. Emmi, M., Majumdar, R., Sen, K.: Dynamic test input generation for database applications. In: Proceedings of the 2007 International Symposium on Software Testing and Analysis (ISSTA 2007), pp. 151–162. ACM, New York (2007)
13. Jackson, D.: Automating first-order relational logic. SIGSOFT Softw. Eng. Notes 25(6), 130–139 (2000)
14. Jackson, D.: Software Abstractions. MIT Press, Cambridge (2006)
15. Khalek, S.A., Elkarablieh, B., Laleye, Y.O., Khurshid, S.: Query-aware test generation using a relational constraint solver. In: ASE, pp. 238–247 (2008)
16. Negri, M., Pelagatti, G., Sbattella, L.: Formal semantics of SQL queries. ACM Transactions on Database Systems 17(3), 513–534 (1991)
17. Pex, http://research.microsoft.com/projects/pex
18. Qex, http://research.microsoft.com/projects/qex
19. Sheard, T., Stemple, D.: Automatic verification of database transaction safety. ACM Trans. Database Syst. 14(3), 322–368 (1989)
20. Tillmann, N., de Halleux, J.: Pex - white box test generation for .NET. In: Beckert, B., Hähnle, R. (eds.) TAP 2008. LNCS, vol. 4966, pp. 134–153. Springer, Heidelberg (2008)
21. Tsai, W.T., Volovik, D., Keefe, T.F.: Automated test case generation for programs specified by relational algebra queries. IEEE Trans. Softw. Eng. 16(3), 316–324 (1990)
22. Veanes, M., Bjørner, N.: Symbolic bounded conformance checking of model programs. In: Pnueli, A., Virbitskaite, I., Voronkov, A. (eds.) Perspectives of System Informatics (PSI 2009). LNCS. Springer, Heidelberg (2009)
23. Veanes, M., Bjørner, N., Gurevich, Y., Schulte, W.: Symbolic bounded model checking of abstract state machines. Int. J. Software Informatics 3(2-3), 149–170 (2009)
24. Veanes, M., Grigorenko, P., de Halleux, P., Tillmann, N.: Symbolic query exploration. Technical Report MSR-TR-2009-65, Microsoft Research (May 2009)
25. Z3, http://research.microsoft.com/projects/z3

Event Listener Analysis and Symbolic Execution for Testing GUI Applications

Svetoslav Ganov, Chip Killmar, Sarfraz Khurshid, and Dewayne E. Perry

The University of Texas at Austin
Austin TX, USA
svetoslavganov@mail.utexas.edu, {khurshid,perry}@ece.utexas.edu

Abstract. Graphical User Interfaces (GUIs) are composed of virtual objects, widgets, which respond to events triggered by user actions. Therefore, test inputs for GUIs are event sequences that mimic user interaction. The nature of these sequences and the values for certain widgets, such as textboxes, causes a two-dimensional combinatorial explosion. In this paper we present Barad, a GUI testing framework that uniformly addresses event-flow and data-flow in GUI applications generating tests in the form of event sequences and data inputs. Barad tackles the two-dimensional combinatorial explosion by pruning regions of the event and data input space. For event sequence generation we consider only events with registered event listeners, thus pruning regions of the event input space. We introduce symbolic widgets which allow us to obtain an executable symbolic version of the GUI. By symbolically executing the chain of listeners registered for the events in a generated event sequence we obtain data inputs, thus pruning regions in the data input space. Barad generates fewer tests and improves branch and statement coverage compared to traditional GUI testing techniques.

Keywords: GUI testing, symbolic execution, test input generation.

1 Introduction

A Graphical User Interface (GUI) provides a convenient way to interact with the computer. GUIs consist of virtual objects (widgets) that are intuitive to use, for example, buttons, edit boxes, etc. In contrast to console applications where there is only one point of interaction (the command line), GUIs provide multiple points (the GUI widgets) each of which can have different states.

A classic challenge in GUI testing is how to select a feasible number of event sequences, given the combinatorial explosion due to arbitrary event interleavings. Consider testing a GUI with five buttons, where any sequence of button clicks is a valid input. Exhaustive testing without repetition requires trying all 120 combinations since triggering one event before another may cause execution of different code paths.

An orthogonal challenge is how to select values for *data widgets*, i.e., GUI widgets that accept user input, such as textboxes, edit-boxes and combo-boxes, and can have an extremely large space of possible inputs. Consider testing a GUI with one text-box

K. Breitman and A. Cavalcanti (Eds.): ICFEM 2009, LNCS 5885, pp. 69–87, 2009.
© Springer-Verlag Berlin Heidelberg 2009

that takes a ten character string as an input. Exhaustive testing requires 10^{26} possible input strings (we limit each character to be alphabetical in lower-case).

Automation of GUI testing has traditionally focused on minimizing event sequences [9] [10] [12] [18] [21]. Data widgets have either been abstracted away by not considering GUI behaviors dependent on data values, generated at random, or selected from a small manually constructed set of values. As a consequence, data dependent behaviors are inadequately tested. Consider generating a string value that is necessary for satisfying an *if*-condition. Random selection is unlikely to generate the desired value. Manual selection requires tedious code inspection. A specification-based (black-box) approach may find this "special" value, however it would require detailed specifications, which often are not provided.

In this paper we present Barad, a novel GUI testing framework for checking GUI applications written in Java with the Standard Widget Toolkit (SWT) [20]. Barad generates event sequences and data inputs providing a systematic approach that uniformly addresses event-flow and data-flow for white-box testing of GUI applications. We detect *event listeners* – instances that register for and respond to events in the GUI. This allows us to consider only events with registered listeners during event sequence generation, thus pruning regions of the event input space. We symbolically execute the chain of listeners registered for the events in a generated event sequence. This allows us to obtain data inputs for the fields of GUI widgets, thus pruning regions in the data input space. Barad is fully automatic, performing bytecode instrumentation, test generation, symbolic execution, and test execution. While our current implementation handles only GUIs written with the SWT library, our approach is generic and can be successfully applied to other Java GUI libraries.

To scale symbolic execution [7] [8] [15] [16] [17] for GUI applications, we introduce symbolic widgets which allow us to perform symbolic manipulation of standard GUI widgets and obtain an executable symbolic version of the GUI. Widget implementations have three concerns: (1) functionality; (2) visualization; and (3) performance. Symbolic widgets focus on functionality, abstracting away the other two concerns. The benefit of this approach is that it enables (1) efficient and systematic dynamic analysis of GUI applications, and (2) generation of inputs for data widgets.

In our previous publication [5] we introduced symbolic analysis of GUI event listeners in isolation for obtaining data inputs without considering event sequence generation and analysis of event listeners in the context of the GUI application (i.e. interactions between event listeners). In this paper we present a novel approach for event sequence generation and symbolic analysis of the GUI application.

We make the following contributions:

- **Symbolic analysis of GUI applications.** We introduce the abstraction of symbolic widgets that enables efficient and systematic dynamic analysis of GUI applications.
- **Event sequence generation.** We present a novel test generation approach and consider only events with registered event listeners, thus pruning regions of the event input space.
- **Data input generation.** By symbolically executing the chain of listeners registered for the events in a generated event sequence we obtain data inputs, thus pruning regions in the data input space.

- • **Implementation.** Barad is fully automatic, performing Java bytecode instrumentation, test generation, symbolic execution, and test execution.
- • **Evaluation.** We evaluate our approach on non-trivial GUI subjects and compare it to traditional GUI testing techniques. Barad generates fewer tests and achieves higher statement and branch coverage.

2 Example

In this section we provide an example how our approach uniformly handles event-flow and data-flow in GUI applications and compare it to conventional GUI testing techniques.

2.1 Fare Calculator

The GUI presented in Figure 1 is an application (313 lines of code) that we developed. It calculates the amount due for a train ticket. A user must provide a passenger class, name, ID, passenger group, and begin and end points. Passenger groups are *Senior*, *Adult*, *Student*, and *Child*.

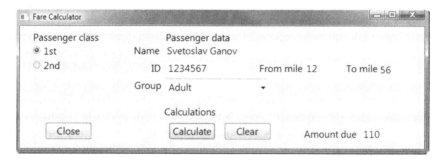

Fig. 1. Screenshot of the Fare Calculator

Each passenger class has its own coefficient that is used during the calculation. Each group has a different base price depending on the distance to be traveled, which is the difference between *From mile* and *To mile*. This application has three event listeners registered for the click events in buttons *Close*, *Calculate*, and *Clear*, respectively. The calculation logic has 22 branches with conditional statements nested three levels deep. The execution of a particular branch depends on the user input both in the form of data and event sequence.

2.2 Input Space

The Fare Calculator consists of two radio buttons, five textboxes, three buttons, and one combo–a total of eleven GUI widgets. Therefore, the number of event sequences with only one event per widget and one value per data widget is slightly less than 4,000,000 (11!). Furthermore, just the input for the ID field of the Fare Calculator, a sequence of ten numeric characters, causes a factor of 10,000,000,000 (10^{10}) increase in the test suite size. Hence, due to the two-dimensional combinatorial explosion in GUI inputs, exhaustive testing of even as simple GUI as the Fare Calculator is unrealistic. Clearly, a systematic approach that prunes regions of the event and data input space is required.

2.3 Test Results

We tested the Fare Calculator with Barad. The process was completed fully automatically. Our results are shown in Table 1.

Table 1. Test results with enabled symbolic analysis

Tests	Branch coverage, %	Statement coverage, %	Time, sec
69	100	100	13.02

The first column presents the total number of tests. The second and the third columns present the branch and statement coverage, respectively. Column four contains the execution time which includes instrumentation, test generation, symbolic execution, and test execution. Barad uses Emma [4] to determine code coverage. Branch coverage was obtained by manual inspection of the code coverage report.

We interpret our results as follows. The application has three event listeners registered for the events of clicking each of the buttons. Hence, during event sequence generation we consider only these three events resulting in six tests with length three without repetition. Each test case was executed on the symbolic version of the GUI and for some tests sets of input values were obtained. Test cases, symbolic execution of which generated sets of input values, were prefixed with events to populate each set of values, thus producing a new test case for each input set. The full branch and statement coverage is due to data values obtained by systematic exploration of all feasible paths during symbolic execution.

Conventional GUI testing techniques [9] [10] [12] [18] [22] exhaustively generate event sequences up to a given bound and adopt a specification based approach to populate inputs—selecting from a predefined set of values. We disabled the symbolic and event listener analysis in Barad to simulate conventional GUI testing. We limited the length of event sequences to be equal to the length of sequences generated by our approach before prefixing with events for data input population. The input values for data widgets were chosen in a widget specific manner as follows: for the textboxes a choice from the set {-1, 0, 1, *Test*, *ThisIsAVeryLongStringValue*, the empty string} was made; for the combo a choice from the set of possible values,

Table 2. Test results with disabled symbolic analysis

Tests	Branch coverage, %	Statement coverage, %	Time, sec
1152	23	87	142.45

namely {*Senior, Adult, Student, Child*} was made. Results of this analysis are presented in Table 2. The first column presents the total number of tests. The second and the third columns present the branch and statement coverage, respectively. Column four contains the execution time which includes test generation and test execution.

2.4 Comparison

Results show that for the Fare Calculator our approach generated more than an order of magnitude fewer tests compared to a traditional approach, while achieving significantly higher branch coverage. The longest event sequence generated by our technique has length eight and consists of the following events: (1) selecting a *Passenger class*; (2) populating the *Name* field; (3) populating the *ID* field; (4) populating the *From mile* field; (5) populating the *To mile* field; (6) selecting the *Calculate* button; (7) selecting the *Clear* button; (8) selecting the *Close* button; Note that our approach generated the minimal set of event sequences with length eight to achieve full path coverage. In contrast, to generate a test case with this length and achieve the same coverage results the traditional approach requires generation of all event sequences with length eight without repetition. Considering the very limited input specifications, this results in 7.6×10^{13} test cases.

3 Background

This section provides the reader with some background about the technique of symbolic execution. It also presents the traditional GUI testing approaches and the GUI model we adopt.

3.1 Symbolic Execution

The main idea behind symbolic execution is to use *symbolic values*, instead of actual data, as input values, and to represent the values of program variables as symbolic expressions. As a result, the output values computed by a program are expressed as a function of the input symbolic values.

The *state* of a symbolically executed program includes the (symbolic) values of program variables, a *path condition* (PC), and a program counter. The path condition is a (quantifier-free) Boolean formula over the symbolic inputs; it accumulates constraints which the inputs must satisfy in order for an execution to follow the particular associated path. The program counter defines the next statement to be executed. A *symbolic execution tree* characterizes the execution paths followed during the symbolic execution of a program. The nodes represent program states and the arcs represent transitions between states.

Consider the code fragment in Figure 2, which swaps the values of integer variables x and y, when x is greater than y. The figure also shows the corresponding symbolic execution tree. Initially, PC is *true* and x and y have symbolic values X and Y, respectively. At each branch point, PC is updated with assumptions about the inputs, in order to choose between alternative paths. For example, after the execution of the first statement, both then and else alternatives of the *if*-statement are possible, and PC is updated accordingly.

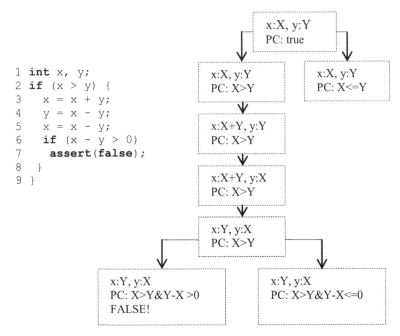

```
1  int x, y;
2  if (x > y) {
3     x = x + y;
4     y = x - y;
5     x = x - y;
6     if (x - y > 0)
7        assert(false);
8  }
9  }
```

Fig. 2. Code that swaps two integers and its symbolic execution tree where transitions are labeled with program control points

If the path condition becomes *false*, i.e., there is no set of inputs that satisfy it, this means that the symbolic state is not reachable, and symbolic execution does not continue for that path. For example, statement (7) is unreachable.

3.2 GUI Testing Approaches

Since contemporary software extensively uses GUIs to interact with users, verifying GUI's reliability becomes important. There are two approaches to building GUIs and these two approaches affect how testing can be performed.

The first approach is to keep the GUI light weight and move computation into the background. In such cases the GUI could be considered as a "skin" for the software. Since the main portion of the application code is not in the GUI, it may be tested using conventional software testing techniques. However, such an approach places architectural limitations on system designers.

The second approach is to merge the GUI and its computations. The most common way of testing such GUIs is by using tools that record and replay event sequences. This is laborious and time consuming. Another technique for checking GUI's correctness is by using tools for automatic test generation, execution, and assessment as the one presented in this paper or the ones described in [9] [12] .

3.3 GUI Model

We take a standard view of a GUI. Let $W = \{w_1, w_2, ... w_n\}$ be the set of GUI widgets. Examples of widgets are *Button, Combo, Label,* etc. Each widget has a set of properties.

Let $P = \{p_1, p_2, ... p_m\}$ be the set of widget properties. Examples of properties are *enabled*, *text*, *visible*, *selection*, etc. Each property has a set of values. Let $V = \{v_1, v_2, ... v_p\}$ be the set of property values. Examples of values are *true*, *false*, etc. A GUI is a triple (W, ρ, v) that consists of a set of widgets, a mapping $\rho : W \rightarrow 2^P$ from widgets to properties, and a mapping $v : P \rightarrow 2^V$ from properties to values.

Let E be the set of all events accepted by the GUI. Each GUI widget w accepts as input a set of user events E_w triggered by user actions which is a subset of E. Examples of events are *clicks*, *mouse moves*, etc.

$$\forall w \in W \mid \exists E_w \subseteq E : accept(w, E_w) \tag{1}$$

Let L be the set of all event listeners in the GUI. Each GUI widget w has zero or more event listeners L_w registered for events performed on the widget which is a subset of L. Each listener l is registered for a set of events E_l which is a subset of all events E_w accepted by the widget. Examples of listeners are *selection listener*, *modification listener*, etc.

$$\forall w \in W \mid \exists L_w \subseteq L \wedge \forall l \in L_w \mid \exists E_l \subseteq E_w \wedge \forall e \in E_l \mid registered(l, e) \tag{2}$$

Since a user interacts with the GUI through events, a GUI test case t from the set T of GUI test cases is an event sequence.

$$\forall t \in T : t = < e_1, e_2, ..., e_p > \tag{3}$$

4 Barad

This section presents Barad, our GUI testing framework. We present the techniques for addressing event-flow and data-flow in GUI applications and our approaches for pruning regions in the event and data input space. We also provide details about the adopted abstractions.

The process of GUI testing performed by Barad is shown on Figure 3. To enable symbolic execution, Barad instruments the bytecode of the tested GUI application replacing concrete entities (widgets, strings, primitives, library classes) with their corresponding symbolic equivalents (symbolic widgets, symbolic strings, symbolic integers etc.) provided by Barad's symbolic library. The bytecode instrumentation is implemented with the ASM library [1]. As a result of the instrumentation phase an executable symbolic version of the GUI is generated. Next, a symbolic analysis of the instrumented version is performed.

During this process event listeners are detected, tests in the form of sequences of events with registered listeners are generated, and then symbolically executed—all paths are systematically explored and their feasibility evaluated by constraint solving.

As a result of this process a log file and a test suite are generated. The test suite consists of event sequences and concrete inputs. Finally, the test suite is executed on the concrete version of the application and a coverage report is generated.

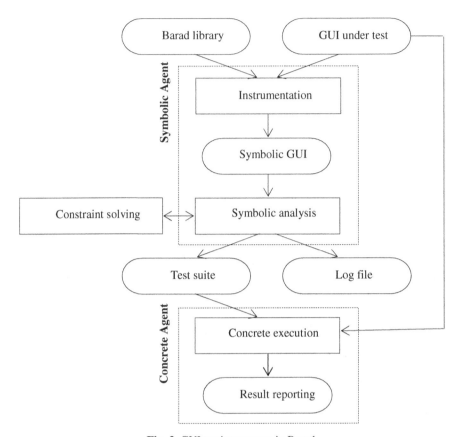

Fig. 3. GUI testing process in Barad

4.1 Event-Flow

To address event-flow in GUI applications we adopt a strategy of pruning regions in the event input space by not considering events for which there is no registered event listener. Since an event listener contains computational logic performed upon a certain event, the lack of a listener for an event renders the event to have no effect on the GUI.

However, such an approach might prevent the execution of a given program path. Consider a simple GUI with one textbox, one button, and a single event listener for the event of pressing the button. Now assume the event listener code has a conditional statement which depends on the value of the textbox.

Since there is no listener for the event of populating the text box and we consider only events with registered listeners, an event for populating the textbox will not be included in any test case. This leads to inadequate testing because of a failure to cover all program paths in the listener. Hence, adopting a strategy for considering only events with registered listeners requires a mechanism for detecting if the code in the event listener in our example depends on the value of the textbox. To determine such a dependency we perform symbolic analysis of the event listener code and generate values for the textbox that would ideally achieve full path coverage of the event listener. Let us assume that we have identified two values "A" and "B" for the textbox which would force the execution to follow different paths at the conditional statement in the listener. In such a case if we generate two tests one including the event for populating "A" in the textbox followed by pressing the button and the other including the event for populating "B" in the textbox followed by pressing the button we will achieve full path coverage of the event listener. Therefore, employing symbolic execution for identifying such dependencies allows us to safely consider only events with registered event listeners. We generate events that populate data widgets, for which no listener exists only in case we have identified values that would force visiting unexplored program paths. More details about our test generation approach are presented in Section 4.4.

To illustrate the reduction in the event input space by considering only events with registered event listeners consider the Fare Calculator from Section 2. The GUI consists of eleven widgets and three event listeners. Considering only one event per widget (some widgets accept more than one event) results in 165 event sequences with length three while considering only events with registered listeners results in only six events sequences with length three.

4.2 Data-Flow

To address data-flow in GUI applications we utilize symbolic execution to obtain inputs for data widgets. We execute symbolically the chain of event listeners registered for the events in a test case. This is achieved by executing each test case on a symbolic version of the application.

In order to obtain a symbolic version of the application, thus enabling symbolic execution of GUIs, we introduce the abstraction of symbolic widgets. Each GUI widget has a symbolic counterpart that has the same fields and provides the same methods, which however represent and operate on symbolic data, respectively. For example, *org.eclipse.swt.widgets.Text* is mapped to a *barad.symboliclibrary.ui.widgets.SymbolicText* and the string field *text* of the former is implemented as a symbolic string in the latter. The corresponding *getter* and *setter* methods, for the *text* field of the *SymbolicText* widget, return as a result and receive as a parameter symbolic strings. To enable the integration of symbolic widgets in our framework, we introduce *symbolic events* and *symbolic event listeners*. Similarly to symbolic widgets, these entities are structurally equivalent to their concrete counterparts and operate with symbolic data.

Symbolic widgets could be envisioned as wrappers that relate sets of variables, representing symbolic primitives and strings, to particular instances in the GUI widget hierarchy. Therefore, constraints and operations on symbolic widgets are constraints and operations on symbolic primitives and strings.

However, symbolic widgets have richer semantics than the set of variables they encapsulate, performing specific to the symbolic and event listener analysis functions: (1) Symbolic widgets wrap the variables related to concrete GUI widgets, allowing us to maintain a mapping from symbolic variables to concrete GUI widgets. This mapping identifies which concrete widgets to be populated with values obtained after concretization of symbolic variables; (2) Symbolic widgets are mapped one-to-one with concrete widgets. This guarantees that the symbolic widget hierarchy is isomorphic to the concrete widget hierarchy and tests generated for the symbolic version of the GUI are applicable to its concrete version; (3) Symbolic widgets detect event listeners at run time. Detecting of event listeners is required by our test generation algorithm; (4) Symbolic widgets implement methods which execute registered event listeners, passing as a parameter a symbolic event. These methods are used for execution of the generated tests; (5) Symbolic widgets, similarly to their concrete counterparts, are referenced by the events passed as parameters to the event listeners. This provides a mechanism of accessing properties of symbolic widgets through events instances.

Symbolic widgets abstract away the visualization layer of their concrete replicas. Such an approach has several advantages. (1) We avoid symbolic execution of the GUI library implementation and focus our analysis on the application logic. Our objective is verifying application correctness, rather than proper behavior of the GUI library. (2) We avoid the native calls made by a GUI widget to the operating system to generate a visual representation of the widget. Our focus, during symbolic execution, is on data-flows in GUI applications and the visual representation of these GUIs is irrelevant to our analysis. Hence, we abstract away unnecessary computations.

Currently Barad supports the symbolic widgets, events, and event listeners required for testing the GUI applications presented in this paper. Our framework is an experimental prototype used to evaluate the applicability of our approach. We did not encounter any widget specific issues, which make defining a symbolic widget challenging. We believe that full support for the SWT library as well as other Java GUI libraries is feasible.

4.3 Symbolic GUI Model

Our view of the symbolic version of a GUI follows the GUI model we have presented in Section 3.3.

Let $W_s = \{w_{s1}, w_{s2}, ...w_{sn}\}$ be the set of symbolic widgets. Each symbolic widget has a set of properties which are symbolic variables $P_s = \{p_{s1}, p_{s2}, ...p_{sm}\}$. Each symbolic property has a set of values it can take during its concretization $V_s = \{v_{s1}, v_{s2}, ...v_{ps}\}$. A symbolic GUI is a triple (W_s, ρ, v) that consists of a set of symbolic widgets, a mapping $\rho: W_s \rightarrow 2^{P_s}$ from symbolic widgets to symbolic properties, and a mapping $v: P_s \rightarrow 2^{V_s}$ from symbolic properties to concrete values.

Let E_s be the set of symbolic events. Each symbolic widget w_s accepts as input a set of symbolic events E_{ws}.

$$\forall w_s \in W_s \mid \exists E_{ws} \subseteq E_s : accept(w_s, E_{ws}) \tag{1}$$

Let L_s be the set of event listeners. Each symbolic widget w_s has zero or more event listeners L_{ws}. Each listener l_s is registered for a set of symbolic events E_{ls}.

$$\forall w_s \in W_s \mid \exists L_{ws} \subseteq L_s \land \forall l_s \in L_{ws} \mid \exists E_{ls} \subseteq E_{ws} \land \forall e_s \in E_{ls} \mid registered(l_s, e_s) \tag{2}$$

4.4 Test Generation Algorithm

Taking advantage of the symbolic widgets we developed our test generation algorithm shown in Figure 4.

```
1. SymbolicModel.executeEventsWithListeners();
2. eventSequences = TestGenerator.generateTests();
3. for (EventSequence s: eventSequences){
4.    in = SymbolicModel.excecuteListenerSequence(s.listeners());
5.    test.addAll(TestGenerator.appendInputs(in, s);
6. }
```

Fig. 4. Test generation algorithm

We represent the GUI events with registered event listeners as an *Events with Listeners Graph* (ELG)—a directed graph with nodes representing events with registered listeners and edges. The existence of an edge from event *e1* to event *e2* means an execution of event *e2* can be performed immediately after the execution of event *e1*. For example, if event *e1* opens a new *form* (GUI window) every event in that form strictly succeeds *e1*. Every time a new event with registered listener is identified a new node is added to the graph.

Since events with registered listeners are detected at runtime by symbolic widgets (intercepting event listener registration calls) and these events can open other forms, all events with registered listeners should be executed at least once (line 1) to build a complete ELG. Such an approach enables handling of multiple GUI windows. Once an ELG has been created we generate test cases performing graph traversals. Our test generation algorithm generates exhaustively test cases in the form of event sequences up to a given bound without repetition (line 2).

We obtain data inputs by symbolically executing the sequence of listeners registered for the events in a test case (line 3-6). Doing so, we capture data dependencies between the event listeners and potentially identify sets of input values for the data widgets in the GUI (line 4). For each such set (if such sets exist) a test case is created by concatenating events for populating data widgets with the values from the set and the events of the test case (line 5).

To illustrate our test generation algorithm, recall the Fare Calculator from Section 2. The algorithm proceeds as follows. Once the symbolic version of the GUI is launched the ELG is constructed by executing every event with registered listener in the GUI (line 1). As a result from this step all three events with registered listeners (for clicking the three buttons) $e1$, $e2$, and $e3$ are identified and used for construction of six event sequences (line 2). The listeners corresponding to these events are symbolically executed (line 4). Without loss of generality, consider the event sequence $(e1, e2, e3)$ symbolically executing the listeners of which generated twenty two sets S of five inputs values $v1 - v5$ each:

$$(e_1, e_2, e_3) \rightarrow \{S_1\{v_1,..., v_5\}, S_2\{v_1,..., v_5\},....., S_{22}\{v_1,..., v_5\}\} \qquad (1)$$

Each input set transitions the GUI to such a state that executing the sequence ($e1$, $e2$, and $e3$) will force visiting of a different program path. Our algorithm constructs a separate test case for each set of values by concatenating the event sequence required to populate these values with the test event sequence (line 5). The generated test cases, where $e(x, y)$ is the event required for populating the value x from value set y, look as follows:

$$e(v_1, S_1), e(v_2, S_1), ..., e(v_5, S_1), e_1, e_2, e_3; \qquad (2)$$

$$...$$

$$e(v_1, S_{22}), e(v_2, S_{22}), ..., e(v_5, S_{22}), e_1, e_2, e_3; \qquad (3)$$

4.5 Symbolic Widget Example

To provide the reader with a better intuition about symbolic widgets we present as an example a partial implementation of the symbolic combo widget. Figure 5 shows the source code. Symbolic combo extends the symbolic widget (line 1) and defines a concrete SWT class it represents (line 2).

```
1. public class SymbCombo extends SymbWidget {
2.    String SWT_CLASS_NAME = "org.eclipse.swt.widgets.Combo";
3.    private List<SymbSelectionListener> mSelectionListeners;
4.    private SymbString mText;
5.    . . .
6.    public SymbCombo(SymbComposite parent, SymbInteger style) {
7.      super(parent, style, "SymbCombo");
8.      . . .
9.      mText = new SymbString(20, this, "text");
10.   }
11.   public String getSWTClassName() {return SWT_CLASS_NAME;}
12.   public void fireSelectionEvent() {
13.     SymbSelectionEvent event = new SymbSelectionEvent(this);
14.     for (SymbSelectionListener l: mSelectionListeners) {
15.       l.widgetSelected(event);
16.     }
17.   }
18.   public void addSelectionListener(SymbSelectionListener l) {
19.     TestGenerator.addELGVertex(this, EventType.SELECTION);
20.     mSelectionListeners.add(l);
21.   }
22.   public StringInterface getText() {
23.     Path.addInputVariable(text);
24.     return text;
25.   }
```

Fig. 5. Symbolic combo snippet

The widget has a list of symbolic listeners (line 3) and a set of symbolic members representing its properties (line 4). In the constructor (lines 6-10) symbolic variables are assigned to the combo's properties (line 9). The symbolic variable receives the combo and the property it represents as parameters to associates itself with that property. The combo exposes the SWT class it represents (line 11) and defines a method for firing a selection event (lines 12-17). Client code can register event listeners (lines 18-21). Upon detection of an event listener a vertex is added to the ELG (line 19). Properties of the symbolic combo are exposed via getter/setter (setter not shown) pairs (lines 22-25). Each symbolic variable representing a widget property is added to the path (multiple additions has no effect) as an input variable (line 23), informing the constraint solver to generate an input value for this variable during the concretization phase.

5   Implementation

This section presents the components of Barad. We discuss the symbolic and concrete agents and provide an overview of the GUI testing mechanism.

5.1 Symbolic Primitives, Strings, and Constraint Solving

Barad supports symbolic operations on all primitive types (*integer, float, Boolean,* and *character*). Supported symbolic operations on integers and floats are: *and, or, addition, difference, multiplication, division, less than, greater than, greater than or equal,* and *less than or equal.* (*Booleans* are represented as integers). For solving numeric constraints Barad has a custom solver implemented via the Choco [2] library.

Supported operations on symbolic strings are: *substring, concat, charAt,* and *trim.* For symbolic string representation and constraint solving we use the work presented in [19], where finite state automata are employed to model the set of possible values for a string variable.

5.2 Barad Agents

Barad consists of two collaborating agents operating on a symbolic and a concrete version of the application, respectively. They perform separate steps in the GUI testing process and can operate as stand-alone testing tools. The *Symbolic Agent* performs our algorithm for symbolic analysis and generates a test suite. The *Concrete Agent* generates and executes tests on the concrete version of the application as well as provides reports for code coverage and detected errors. While these agents operate in a collaborative fashion, test cases are generated by the *Symbolic Agent* and executed by the *Concrete Agent*. The agents run in the same Java Virtual Machine (JVM) and communicate asynchronously via publish-subscribe paradigm.

5.2.1 Symbolic Agent

The Symbolic Agent instruments the GUI bytecode, performs symbolic execution of the instrumented version, and generates test cases as event sequences and data inputs. It is a Java agent that registers in the JVM for class loading events. It intercepts the loading of the main class of the AUT, instruments it, and executes it symbolically in a separate thread. Subsequently loaded classes are also instrumented at loading time.

5.2.2 Concrete Agent

The Concrete Agent generates tests adopting a traditional test generation approach and executes tests on the application. In contrast with conventional GUI testing frameworks, which restart the GUI after executing a test case, the agent performs reinitialization. The agent is a JVM Tool Interface and can detect defects via uncaught exceptions thrown by the GUI at runtime.

6 Evaluation

This section presents two case studies and evaluates the applicability of our GUI testing approach. The first case study is a notepad application which does not exploit data dependent behaviors. The second case study is a workout generator program the behavior of which depends on data inputs. We compare our approach to traditional GUI testing strategies.

6.1 JNotepad

JNotepad is a Java implementation of the popular Notepad text editor. JNotepad provides basic functionalities such as creating, editing, and saving text files; cut, copy,

Table 3. JNotepad application

Windows	Widgets	LOC	Classes	Methods	Branches
8	30	849	9	51	90

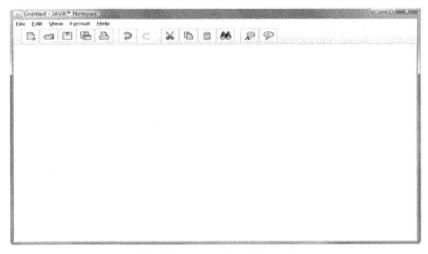

Fig. 6. Screenshot from JNotepad

paste, undo, redo operations etc. We analyze version 2.0 of the application. Table 3 presents a summary of JNotepad and Figure 6 shows a screenshot of the GUI.

For testing JNotepad we configured Barad to ignore all widgets in the *Open*, *Save*, and *SaveAs* dialogs except the text field for specifying a file name and the *OK* and *Cancel* buttons. The file chooser class, used for implementing these dialogs, is provided by the GUI library, testing of which we want to avoid.

First, we tested JNotepad adopting our approach with enabled symbolic and event listener analysis. To limit the number of generated test cases, we configured the maximal length of event sequences before appending data populating events to three. Obtained results are presented in Table 4.

Table 4. Test results with enabled symbolic analysis

Tests	Branch coverage, %	Statement coverage, %	Time, sec
24 058	92	97	1 495

The first column presents the total number of executed tests. The second and third columns present the branch and statement coverage, respectively. The fourth column presents the test generation and execution time (including symbolic analysis). Code coverage was reported by Barad and branch coverage was obtained by manual inspection of the code coverage report.

We next disabled the symbolic and event listener analysis simulating a traditional GUI testing approach. Values for the text boxes were selected from the set {-1, 0, 1, *Test, ThisIsAVeryLongStringValue*, and the empty string}. Table 5 shows the results.

Table 5. Test results with disabled symbolic analysis

Tests	Branch coverage, %	Statement coverage, %	Time, sec
51 694	84	91	2 946

Experimental results show that our approach generated approximately half the number of test as opposed to the traditional technique. The reason for the moderate decrease in the number of test cases generated by Barad is twofold: (1) JNotepad has few data widgets (one textbox in the main, find, and save/open windows, respectively) and does not have much data dependent behavior; (2) JNotepad contains primarily buttons, which accept a single event for which corresponding event listeners exist. Hence, for most of the events accepted by the GUI corresponding listeners exist. Despite the structure of JNotepad, which is not ideal for our technique, we still achieve significant reduction in the number of tests.

6.2 Workout Generator

The Workout Generator is a program the first author developed in his previous experience. The GUI takes as input user's biometric characteristics and generates a weekly workout program. Table 6 summarizes the characteristics of the Workout Generator and Figure 7 shows a screenshot of the GUI.

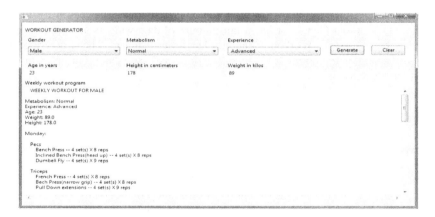

Fig. 7. Screenshot of the Workout Generator

Table 6. Workout Generator application

Windows	Widgets	LOC	Classes	Methods	Branches
1	9	651	3	15	121

The combo boxes could take one of the following values: for Gender - *Male, Female*; for Metabolism - *Slow, Normal*, and *Fast*; and for Experience - *Beginner, Intermediate*, and *Advanced*.

First, we tested the Workout Generator adopting our approach with enabled symbolic and listener analysis. We configured an upper bound of three for the length of event sequences. The results are presented in Table 7.

Table 7. Test results with enabled symbolic analysis

Tests	Branch coverage, %	Statement coverage, %	Time, sec
48	100	100	4.3

We next disabled the symbolic and event listener analysis simulating a traditional GUI testing approach. The values for data widgets were chosen as follows: for text-boxes a value from the set {-1, 0, 1, *Test, ThisIsAVeryLongStringValue*, and the empty string}; for combo-boxes, a value from the set of possible values. We set the maximal length of generated event sequences to three. The results are presented in Table 8.

Table 8. Test results with disabled symbolic analysis

Tests	Branch coverage, %	Statement coverage, %	Time, sec
5 984	76	97	285

Experimental results show that for the Workout Generator our approach generates significantly fewer test compared to the traditional technique. The reason for that is twofold: (1) Workout Generator has a fair amount of data widgets and exploits data dependent behaviors; (2) Workout Generator has fewer listeners. The structure of the Workout Generator is opportune for our technique and we achieve in order of two magnitudes decrease in the number of test.

7 Discussion

The experimental results show that our approach generates fewer tests and achieves higher branch and statement coverage compared to traditional GUI testing techniques. Further, our approach addressed data-flows in GUI applications by generating inputs for data widgets, which force the execution of different program paths. Our technique is especially effective for testing data intensive GUI applications, with data dependent behavior.

Since we perform symbolic analysis, our technique inherits the limitations of symbolic execution with regard to native calls. While our implementation does not handle native calls we can adopt the approach for approximation symbolic execution presented in [16]. Another issue that arises during symbolic execution is handling of loops. We take a standard approach and perform loop unwinding up to a given bound.

Such an approximation inevitably introduces errors. Further, symbolic execution requires solving of path constraints, which in the general case, are undecidable.

The current implementation of Barad supports a subset of the SWT GUI library which prevents us to apply our approach to the written with Swing TerpOffice, an application suite used by Memon et al. in his extensive work in GUI testing.

We currently detect bugs as runtime exceptions. However, specification based oracles that check richer properties would enable more thorough testing of GUIs. We do not report detected bugs since we adopt the same fault detection strategy as the conventional GUI testing performed by Memon et al. Our focus is on reducing test suite size and improving statement and branch coverage.

8   Related Work

To the best of our knowledge, in his Ph.D. dissertation [9] Memon presents the first framework for GUI testing that generates, runs, and assesses GUI tests. The framework focuses on the event-flow of GUI applications. For emulating user input a specification based approach is adopted—using values from a prefilled database. The components of the framework and its extensions are presented in several papers [9], [11], [13], [14], [22]. This framework considers all events accepted by the GUI while we focus on events with event listeners. The framework does not provide a mechanism for obtaining inputs for data widgets. By providing such a mechanism our work is complementary in this respect.

Memon, Banarjee and Nagarajan present a framework for regression testing of nightly/daily builds of GUI applications [12]. This tool addresses rapidly evolving GUI applications executing a small enough test suite that the test process could be accomplished in less than a day/night. This framework is based on the one presented in Memon's PhD dissertation [9] and uses the same test generation algorithm and specification based approach to simulate user inputs. We employ a different test generation algorithm and present a technique for obtaining data inputs.

Another approach is representing the GUI as a Variable Finite State Machine from which after a transformation to an FSM, tests are obtained [18]. This black-box testing technique does not consider user input while focusing on the event-flow. Our approach is white-box with dynamic analysis focusing on event listeners and generates data inputs.

A technique for testing a GUI is transforming the GUI into a FSM and using different techniques to reduce the states of that FSM to avoid state space explosion [21]. In approach the focus is on collaborating selections and user sequences over different objects in the GUI. This is a white-box event centric approach that abstracts away user inputs. We adopt an event listener centric technique and generate data values.

Verification of GUI specifications has been performed via model checking [3]. The authors introduce domain specific abstractions to reduce the state space to be explored. The GUI and its behavior are represented as a Computation Tree Logic in the input language of the SMV model checker via a manual process. In contrast, our approach is fully automatic and aims at test generation rather than at model checking. We see this work as complementary to our approach.

A technique for updating test scripts for evolving GUI applications has been proposed [6]. This enables reuse of existing scripts via detecting script errors due to changes in the GUI. Our work focuses on test generation and is complementary.

A system that automatically extracts a program interface, generates a test driver and a random test suite after completion of which symbolic execution is used to guide the generation of additional tests has been presented [15]. Similarly, we employ symbolic execution to generate tests which maximize coverage by exploring different program paths. We introduce the abstraction of symbolic widgets which allows scaling symbolic execution for GUIs.

Symbolic execution and concrete execution have been combined for test generation [16]. This approach uses approximate symbolic execution for testing code with dynamic data structures. In contrast, we generate inputs in the form of string and numeric data and do not perform concrete execution. We take advantage of the systematic approach for path exploration and scale symbolic execution for GUIs.

Symbolic execution has been used for test data generation [23]. The program is represented as a deterministic FSM and using symbolic execution generates test data. This work deals exclusively with numeric constraints. Barad performs symbolic execution over GUI components (widgets) and strings (in addition to primitives).

9   Conclusion

We presented Barad, a novel GUI testing framework that addresses event-flow as well as data-flow for white-box testing of GUI applications. Barad is fully automatic, performing instrumentation, symbolic execution, test generation, and test execution.

We introduce the abstraction of symbolic widgets. This abstraction enables symbolic analysis to reason about the control flow in GUI applications without analyzing the GUI library implementation. We generate test cases as sequences of events with registered listeners, pruning significant regions of the event input space. We execute symbolically the sequence of listeners registered for the events in a test case enabling a systematic approach to obtain inputs for data widgets.

We evaluate our framework on non trivial GUI subjects. Compared to traditional GUI testing techniques Barad achieves higher statement and branch coverage while generating significantly fewer tests.

Acknowledgements. This material is based upon work partially supported by the NSF under Grant Nos. IIS-0438967, CCF-0702680, and CCF-0845628, and AFOSR grant FA9550-09-1-0351.

References

1. ASM: Java bytecode manipulation and analysis framework,
   http://asm.objectweb.org/
2. Choco: Java library for constraint solving,
   http://sourceforge.net/projects/choco/
3. Dweyer, M., Carr, V., Hines, L.: Model Checking Graphical User Interfaces Using Abstractions. In: Jazayeri, M. (ed.) ESEC 1997 and ESEC-FSE 1997. LNCS, vol. 1301, pp. 244–261. Springer, Heidelberg (1997)

4. Emma: Java code coverage tool, http://emma.sourceforge.net/
5. Ganov, S., Killmar, C., Khurshid, S., Perry, D.: Test Generation for Graphical User Interfaces Based on Symbolic Execution. In AST, 2008.
6. Grechanik, M., Xie, Q., Fu, C.: Maintaining and Evolving GUI-Directed Test Scripts. In: ICSE (2009)
7. King, J.: Symbolic Execution and Program Testing. Communications of the ACM (1976)
8. Lori, C.: A System to Generate Test Data and Symbolically Execute Programs. IEEE Transactions on Software Engineering (1976)
9. Memon, A.: A Comprehensive Framework For Testing Graphical User Interfaces. Ph.D. Thesis, University of Pittsburgh (2001)
10. Memon, A.: Using Tasks to Automate Regression Testing of GUIs. In: AIA (2004)
11. Memon, A., Banarjee, I., Nagarajan, A.: GUI Ripping: Reverse Engineering of Graphical User Interfaces for Testing. In: WRCE (2003)
12. Memon, A., Banarjee, I., Nagarajan, A.: DART: A Framework for Regression Testing Nightly/Daily Builds of GUI Applications. In: ICSM (2003)
13. Memon, A., Banarjee, I., Nagarajan, A.: What Test Oracle Should I use for Effective GUI Testing? In: ASE (2003)
14. Memon, A., McMaster, S.: Call Stack Coverage for GUI Test-Suite Reduction. In: ISSRE (2006)
15. Godefroid, P., Klarlund, N., Sen, K.: DART: Directed Automated Random Testing. In: PLDI (2005)
16. Sen, K., Marinov, D., Agha, G.: CUTE: A Concolic Unit Testing Engine for C. In: ESEC/FSE 2005 (2005)
17. Ramamoorthy, V., Siu-Bun, H., Chen, W.: On the Automated Generation of Program Test Data. In: IEEE TSE (1976)
18. Shehady, R., Siewiorek, D.: A Method to Automate User Interface Testing Using Variable Finite State Machines. In: FTCS, 1997.
19. Shannon, D., Hajra, S., Lee, A., Zhan, D., Khurshid, S.: Abstracting Symbolic Execution with String Analysis. In: TAICPART-MUTATION (2007)
20. SWT: The Standard Widget Toolkit, http://www.eclipse.org/SWT
21. White, L., Almezen, H.: Generating Test Cases for GUI Responsibilities Using Complete Interaction Sequences. In: ISSRE (2000)
22. Xie, Q., Atif, M.: Using a Pilot Study to Derive a GUI Model for Automated Testing. In: TOSEM (2008)
23. Zhang, J., Xu, C., Wang, X.: Path-Oriented Test Data Generation Using Symbolic Execution and Constraint Solving Techniques. In: SEFM (2004)

An Empirical Study of
Structural Constraint Solving Techniques

Junaid Haroon Siddiqui and Sarfraz Khurshid

The University of Texas at Austin
Austin, TX 78712
{jsiddiqui,khurshid}@ece.utexas.edu

Abstract. Structural constraint solving allows finding object graphs that satisfy given constraints, thereby enabling software reliability tasks, such as systematic testing and error recovery. Since enumerating all possible object graphs is prohibitively expensive, researchers have proposed a number of techniques for reducing the number of potential object graphs to consider as candidate solutions. These techniques analyze the structural constraints to prune from search object graphs that cannot satisfy the constraints. Although, analytical and empirical evaluations of individual techniques have been done, comparative studies of different kinds of techniques are rare in the literature. We performed an experiment to evaluate the relative strengths and weaknesses of some key structural constraint solving techniques. The experiment considered four techniques using: a model checker, a SAT solver, a symbolic execution engine, and a specialized solver. It focussed on their relative abilities in expressing the constraints and formatting the output object graphs, and most importantly on their performance. Our results highlight the tradeoffs of different techniques and help choose a technique for practical use.

Keywords: Empirical comparison, software testing tools, model checking, symbolic execution, SAT, state space exploration, systematic testing.

1 Introduction

Generating test inputs for programs that manipulate structurally complex inputs like XML documents or red black trees is a complex operation. Manual generation of these tests is time consuming, error prone, and has fairly limited ability to find bugs whereas systematic testing, which is effective at finding bugs, is not straightforward as there are no simple enumerators for structurally complex inputs.

Automated generation of structurally complex test inputs can be done in two basic ways: using generator functions [52,51] and by solving constraints [5,38]. Generator functions are functions that perform basic operations to construct and build structures (e.g., constructors or mutator methods in Java). Automated testing using generator functions typically uses different orderings of generator functions to produce test inputs. This can however result in the same structures repeated, i.e., redundant tests, and some kinds of structures may never be

K. Breitman and A. Cavalcanti (Eds.): ICFEM 2009, LNCS 5885, pp. 88–106, 2009.

produced. Generator functions are mostly applied for generating larger inputs effectively.

Automated testing by solving structural constraints [5, 38] enables *systematic testing* where the program is tested against all test inputs within given bounds. Even though doing so is feasible only for small bounds, it has been shown to give high code coverage and find faults in programs with structurally complex inputs [32, 38, 49]. Also, by writing constraints we can conveniently describe a whole class of structurally complex test inputs. In this paper, we discuss the techniques that can be used for systematic testing based on structural constraint solving.

The structural constraints used by systematic testing techniques are usually written either as declarative constraints or as imperative constraints. Alloy [30] (one of the techniques discussed here) uses declarative constraints written in relational logic using quantified formulas. The other three techniques that we evaluate use imperative constraints. We call them *imperative* in contrast to *declarative* as they use constraints written in an imperative language (C or Java in our case). We note that these imperative constraints are required to be free of side-effects and hence are declarative in nature (even though they are written in an imperative language).

The contribution of this paper is a controlled experiment for performance analysis of different constraint solving techniques. It also performs an analysis to quantify the tradeoffs of these techniques in writing constraints and in processing outputs. Our results show that even though generic techniques like model checkers and symbolic execution can be used to solve structural constraints, specialized solvers are faster in solving and need the least tweaking of code to work.

The rest of the paper is organized as follows. We provide an overview of the problem of constraint solving in the following subsection, give a background on different techniques and how they solve structural constraints in Section 2. Section 3 describes our experiment; the subjects, analysis strategy, and threats to validity. We discuss experimental results and our analysis in Section 4 and summarize and conclude in Section 5.

1.1 Related Work

The idea of using constraints for representing test inputs has been used for at least three decades [11, 28, 35, 43] and implemented in EFFIGY [35], TEST-GEN [36], and INKA [24] among other tools. However most of this work was to solve constraints on primitive data like integers and not structural constraints.

Goodenough and Gerhart [23] discuss the importance of specification based testing. Test case generation has been automated from specifications by many tools. Some examples are from Z specifications [15], UML statecharts [41], ADL specifications [9], and AsmL specifications [25]. However these specifications are also targeted to primitive types and not structurally complex inputs.

Constraints on complex structures require very different constraint solving techniques, which have only been explored more recently. Directions of research include using model checkers [20, 50], SAT solvers [47], symbolic execution [21, 44], and specialized solvers [5]. Section 2 discusses each of these techniques, their background and recent advancements.

One common problem faced while generating complex structures is isomorphism [45]. Two structures are defined to be isomorphic if they only differ in object identities. For example, if all elements in two nodes of a tree are swapped and all references to these nodes are swapped too, the resulting structure is identical to the original except that pointer values in some nodes would be different. Since, most programs are not concerned with the actual pointer *values* and only with *where* they are pointing, generating isomorphic structures is considered redundant and the algorithms attempt isomorph breaking procedures to reduce generated structures.

For the purpose of comparison and explaining how constraints are written in different approaches, we will take red-black tress [3, 26] as our running example. We pick this representative example as it is one of the more complex structures, one of the structures commonly used for evaluation in previous work, and one that is likely to be familiar.

2   Background of Subject Tools

2.1   JPF — Model Checker

Model checking [10] has traditionally been applied to software [2, 13, 50, 27] for checking event sequences, specified in temporal logic or as a finite state machine of API usage rules. If a program is checked successfully, no input and execution can lead it to an error. Thus model checking provides a strong guarantee. However these techniques did not consider checking properties and validity of complex structures. The model checkers BLAST and SLAM are also used for white-box test input generation [4] targeting to cover specific predicates. The two are also not applied to solving complex structural constraints.

Generalized Symbolic Execution [34] introduced the idea of using a model checker for solving structural constraints. As an enabling technology, the JPF (Java Path Finder) model checker [50] was used. JPF is an explicit-state model checker for Java programs that has been used to find errors in a number of complex systems [42, 6, 1]. It is built on top of a custom Java Virtual Machine (JVM). Therefore it handles all standard Java features and in addition allows nondeterministic choices written as annotations. These annotations are added by method calls to class `Verify`. The following methods in this class are important:

- `randomBool()` returns a nondeterministic boolean value
- `random(n)` returns a nondeterministic integer in [0,n]
- `ignoreIf(cond)` makes JPF backtrack if `cond` is true

Generalized symbolic execution provides a source-to-source translation of a Java program such that it can be symbolically executed by any standard model checker that supports non-deterministic choice. The technique of generalized

```
class RedBlackTree {
    ...
    static Node[] nodes;
    static int maxNode = 0;
    boolean header_accessed = false;
    Node header;
    Node header() {
        if (!header_accessed) {
            header_accessed = true;
            if (maxNode < nodes.length - 1) {
                maxNode++;
                int r = Verify.random(maxNode);
                if( r != maxNode )
                    maxNode--;
                header = nodes[r];
            } else header = nodes[ Verify.random( maxNode ) ];
        }
        return header;
    }
    boolean repOk() {
        if (header() == null)
            return false;
        Set<Node> visited = new java.util.HashSet<Node>();
        visited.add(header());
        LinkedList<Node> workList = new LinkedList<Node>();
        workList.add(header());
        while (!workList.isEmpty()) {
            Node current = workList.removeFirst();
            if (current.left() != null) {
                if (!visited.add(current.left()))
                    return false;
                workList.add(current.left());
            }
            if (current.right() != null) {
                if (!visited.add(current.right()))
                    return false;
                workList.add(current.right());
            }
        }
        if (visited.size() != size() || size() < LOWER_BOUND )
          return false;
        return repOkColors() && repOkKeys();
    }
}
```

Fig. 1. Parts of Red Black Tree predicate written for JPF

symbolic execution is based on *lazy initialization*, i.e. it initializes fields when they are first accessed during symbolic execution of a method. Due to this lazy initialization, the algorithm only executes program paths on non-isomorphic inputs. This can be used for systematic generation of structurally complex inputs by symbolically executing a predicate checking structural constraints.

Figure 1 shows parts of Red Black Tree predicate written for JPF. Note that all accesses to structure variables are through accessors functions. One accessor function for **header** is also shown. It non-deterministically picks one of the nodes that have already been used or one of the new nodes.

Recently, this technique has been optimized by making modifications to Java Path Finder [19]. However these optimizations are specific to one model checker, whereas the original technique can be used on any model checker.

2.2   Alloy — Using a SAT Solver

SAT solvers solve boolean formulas. To use SAT solvers for solving structural constraints, we thus need a language for writing structural constraints, a compiler to translate that language into a boolean formula, and a mapping from the solution of the boolean formula into a solution to the structural constraint.

Alloy [29] provides a declarative language for writing these constraints. It is based on parts of the Z specification [48]. The Alloy Analyzer [31] provides a fully automated tool to solve these constraints using a SAT solver. The latest version of Alloy Analyzer (4.1.10) works with many state-of-the-art solvers like BerkMin [22], MiniSat [47], SAT4J (Java implementation of MiniSat), and ZChaff [40]. Alloy analyzer provides a translation from the declarative language of Alloy with quantifiers to a boolean formula when given bounds. It then translates the solution back to the declarative language.

TestEra [33] builds on Alloy to translate the solutions further back into actual Java structures. TestEra also adds a layer on top of Alloy language to facilitate writing preconditions and postconditions, and allows test case generation based on preconditions and function validation using its postconditions as an oracle. However for the purpose of constraint solving alone, Alloy is sufficient. The Alloy to Java translator component of TestEra can be used to translate Alloy solutions into Java structures. The translation time is insignificant in comparison to the constraint solving time.

We show class invariant for red-black trees modeled in Alloy in Figure 2. Note that this completely models red black trees. Addition of a few more syntactic sugar like definition of Node etc is all that is needed to generate all possible red black trees within given bounds. This concise representation is one of the key benefits of using a declarative language. However the learning curve of declarative

```
all e: rbt.root.*(left+right) |
    // BT: distinct children
    ( no e.(left+right) || e.left != e.right ) &&
    // BT: acyclic
    ( e ! in e.^(left+right) ) &&
    // BT: distinct parent
    lone e.~(left + right) &&
    // BST: ordered
    lt[ e.left.*(right+left).key, e.key ] &&
    gt[ e.right.*(right+left).key, e.key ] &&
    // RBT: red node has black children
    ( e.color in Red && some e.(left + right)
      => e.(left + right).color in Black )

all e, f: rbt.root.*(left+right) |
    // RBT: all paths from root to NIL have same # of black nodes
    (no e.left || no e.right) && (no f.left || no f.right) =>
      #{ p: rbt.root.*(left+right) |
        e in p.*(left+right) && p.color in Black } =
      #{ p: rbt.root.*(left+right) |
        f in p.*(left+right) && p.color in Black }
```

Fig. 2. Red Black Tree constraint written for Alloy

programming for programmers used to program in imperative languages often offsets this benefit. The bounds for Alloy are written as below:

```
run test for 1 rbt, exactly 3 Node
```

The class invariant requires the tree to satisfy binary search tree properties and the additional properties of red-black trees mentioned in comments in Figure 2. The reader is referred to Jackson [29] for detailed discussion of Alloy operators and syntax and to Guibas [26] for red-black tree properties.

2.3   CUTE — Symbolic Execution

The idea of symbolic execution dates back at least three decades [35]. Traditional symbolic execution is a combination of static analysis and theorem proving. In symbolic execution, operations are performed on symbolic variables instead of actual data. On branches, symbolic execution is forked with opposite constraints on symbolic variables in each forked branch. At times, the constraints on symbolic variables can become unsatisfiable signaling unreachable code. Otherwise, end of the function is reached and a formula on symbolic variables is formed. A solution to this formula will give a set of values that will direct an actual execution along the same path.

Renewed interest in symbolic execution is seen in the last decade [7, 12, 18]. Generalized Symbolic Execution [34] extended the concept to concurrent programs and complex structures.

The main problem with symbolic execution is that for large or complex units, it is computationally infeasible to maintain and solve the constraints required for test generation. Larson and Austin [37] combined symbolic execution with concrete execution to overcome this limitation. Their approach was primitive as they used symbolic execution to make the path constraint of a concrete execution and find other input values that can lead to errors along the same path.

DART (Directed Automated Random Testing) [21] is one of the first tools to systematically combine symbolic execution and concrete execution. Similar to previous approach, they formed a path constraint during concrete execution. However after the execution, they backtrack on the path constraint by negating clauses, solve the new constraints, and re-run concrete execution expecting it to follow a new path. When it is not feasible to solve the modified constraints, they substitute random concrete values. Another simultaneous effort was EGT (Execution Guided Test Cases) [8] using a similar approach. Lastly, CUTE (Concolic Unit Testing Engine for C) [44], another tool using similar approach, is the tool that we will be using here. It is the only tool that can handle pointers and complex structures.

The idea of using CUTE to generate test cases has been briefly discussed but not evaluated [44]. There, the authors considered prev pointers in a doubly linked list and discussed the order (big O) of candidates CUTE and Korat (discussed below) explore to find answers. In our evaluations we thoroughly cover this example among others. In particular, we discuss the constants involved (time of

```
int repOk( struct bintree* b ) {
  struct listnode* visited=0, *worklist=0;
  int NODES = 0;
  if( b->root == 0 )
      return 0;
  visited = newnode( b->root, visited );
  ++NODES;
  worklist = newnode( b->root, worklist );
  while( worklist ) {
    struct node* current = worklist->data;
    worklist = worklist->next;
    if( current->left ) {
      if( !addunique( visited, current->left ))
        return 0;
      ++NODES;
      worklist = newnode( current->left, worklist );
    }
    if( current->right ) {
      if( !addunique( visited, current->right ))
        return 0;
      ++NODES;
      worklist = newnode( current->right, worklist );
    }
    if( NODES > UPPER_BOUND )
      return 0;
  }
  if( b->size != vcount || NODES < LOWER_BOUND)
    return 0;
  return repOkColors(b) && repOkKeys(b);
}
```

Fig. 3. Parts of Red Black Tree predicate written for CUTE

exploring one candidate) and constraint rewriting requirements to understand which approach is likely better in practical usage.

We show parts of the red-black tree constraint written in C for use in CUTE in Figure 3. The NODES variable is introduced to keep a count of nodes used. We break the loop when more than UPPER_BOUND nodes have been touched and return false if less than LOWER_BOUND nodes were touched during the execution. This is how we control the desired number of objects when generating structures in CUTE. Rest of the constraint is similar to what was shown in Figure 1.

2.4   Korat — A Specialized Solver

Korat [5] is a framework for automated generation of structurally complex test inputs. It performs *specification based testing*. By using a Java predicate that represents properties of desired inputs, Korat uses backtracking search and explores the input space of the predicate and enumerates inputs for which the predicate returns true. Each enumerated inputs is a desired structurally complex test input. Korat performs *bounded exhaustive testing*: it generates all non-isomorphic test cases within given bounds. Bounded exhaustive testing has been used to successfully find bugs in a fault-tree analyzer [49], a resource discovery architecture, and an XPath compiler.

Korat performs a dynamic analysis of the predicate. It prunes huge portions of the input space by monitoring field accesses during predicate execution. It

```
public boolean repOK() {
    if (root == null)
        return false;
    Set<Node> visited = new HashSet<Node>();
    visited.add(root);
    LinkedList<Node> workList = new LinkedList<Node>();
    workList.add(root);
    while (!workList.isEmpty()) {
        Node current = workList.removeFirst();
        if (current.left != null) {
            if (!visited.add(current.left))
                return false;
            workList.add(current.left);
        }
        if (current.right != null) {
            if (!visited.add(current.right))
                return false;
            workList.add(current.right);
        }
    }
    if (visited.size() != size)
        return false;
    return repOkColors() && repOkKeys();
}
```

Fig. 4. Parts of Red Black Tree predicate written for Korat

```
IFinitization f = FinitizationFactory.create(RedBlackTree.class);

IClassDomain entryDomain = f.createClassDomain(Node.class, numEntries);
IObjSet entries = f.createObjSet(Node.class, true);
entries.addClassDomain(entryDomain);

IIntSet sizes = f.createIntSet(minSize, maxSize);
IIntSet keys = f.createIntSet(-1, numKeys - 1);
IIntSet colors = f.createIntSet(0, 1);

f.set("root", entries);
f.set("size", sizes);
f.set("Node.left", entries);
f.set("Node.right", entries);
f.set("Node.color", colors);
f.set("Node.key", keys);
```

Fig. 5. Korat's specification of bounds for Red Black Tree

backtracks on the last field accessed and makes a non-deterministic assignment to that field. It then uses the new candidate to re-execute the predicate.

Korat, being a specialized solver, produces correct output for every predicate (**repOk**), however it is written. Although, some predicates would cause a faster execution (return after touching as few fields as possible) and some would be slower (return once after checking all checks that can be checked), none would result in an incorrect result. We here show a portion of red-black tree constraint written for Korat in Java in Figure 4. We also show how bounds are given for Red Black Tree in Korat's finitization in Figure 5.

The principle idea of Korat has been used in other applications. In particular, STARC [16] uses the Korat algorithm to repair huge complex structures by running the algorithm in neighborhood of the defective structure. Glass box testing [14] uses the method to be tested to prune Korat's generation. Thus it moves away from the pure black-box approach of Korat.

Korat has been optimized in a number of ways. Instead of running `repOk` from the start for every candidate, efficient backtracking optimization [17] can undo operations done in last execution and proceed from that point for the next candidate. This has shown improvements for STARC and also for Korat. Lastly, Korat has been parallelized for clusters of largely independent machines by random division of work [39] and for high bandwidth clusters by systematic division of work [46].

2.5 Research Questions

The effectiveness of bounded exhaustive testing (generating all test cases satisfying the constraints) has been previously shown in application to many real applications. Here we are concerned with different tools to generate these tests. Thus we are not concerned with the fault detecting capability of these tools, as this capability would be equal (given sufficient time) for all tools in our scenario. We are rather concerned with how to write the tests and interpret the output and most importantly how much time it takes to generate the tests.

We pose the following research questions for our experiment and analysis:

- What are the pros and cons of different tools in writing constraints and defining bounds?
- How is the output of a tool represented and how it can be converted into actual test inputs?
- What are the fastest tools for practical sizes of subject structures?
- How well do the tools perform with more and more complex constraints?
- What are the best tools in terms of time complexity?

Next we describe our experiment and its analysis.

3   The Experiment

3.1 Experimental Subjects

To evaluate the selected tools, we consider six complex structures: three list structures, and three tree structures. Note that these complex structures are the foundation of several data structures used in applications. For example, an XML document, a file system hierarchy, Java or C class hierarchies, expression trees, abstract syntax trees for compiler can all be viewed as trees and are likely to give similar performance to one of the tree structures we consider here. We evaluate the following six structures:

1. Binary Tree
2. Binary Search Tree
3. Red Black Tree
4. Singly Linked List
5. Doubly Linked List
6. Sorted Linked List

Note that a red-black-tree is a binary search tree which is in turn a binary tree. From this, we intend to learn the effect of increasing constraint complexity on tool performance.

To avoid any bias, we took constraints for the above subjects from previous work [5], where available. In some cases, we needed to change the constraints so that the tool under evaluation performs bounded exhaustive testing (as discussed in the previous section).

3.2 Experimental Design

The experiment focused on:

1. Structurally complex constraints (6 constraints of subjects given in previous section)
2. Bounds (we considered 4 bounds for each subject structure)
3. The constraint solver (one of the four constraint solvers discussed in this paper)

On each run, we measured:

1. Time taken to generate all tests
2. Candidates generated to see isomorphism pruning

We also measure qualitative results for:

1. How constraints needed to be converted to run the tool
2. How bounds needed to be converted to run the tool
3. How results from the tool needed to be converted to test cases

Results reported for the experiment were averages of 10 repeated measurements. Thus, for each subject structure and each constraint solver and each given bounds, we ran the tool 10 times and computed the average. The experiments were performed on a Linux machine with Intel Pentium 4 2.8Ghz processor and 4GB RAM.

3.3 Threats to Internal Validity

Threats to internal validity are influences that can affect dependent variables without researcher's knowledge. In this respect, our concerns include the way constraints are written and language differences. Constraints can be written to suit one tool and not the other. We have done our best effort is writing the constraints so that every tool can perform at its best. Language differences matter because one of the tools works in C while the rest work in Java. C implementations are inherently faster so the results of this tool would have a slight edge because of language. However this concern would have been more significant if this tool turned out to be the fastest which is not the case as we see below.

3.4   Threats to External Validity

Threats to external validity are conditions that limit us in generalizing the results of our experiment. Our biggest concerns in this area is that the subject programs might not be representative of complex constraints. To control this threat, we have studied literature regarding the tools and summarized the complex constraints previously studied, we have also studied structures discussed in algorithm books, and have found that the most commonly used complex structures are actually the basis of a large class of data structures. For example, B-trees, AVL trees, Sparse matrices, hash tables are all basically trees or a combination of trees and lists. We considered complex inputs of real programs like compilers (abstract syntax tree), XML parsers (XML Tree), web browser (HTML Tree), File system tree, Java class hierarchies, and expression trees. All of these share constraints with the basic structures we test here. Therefore we believe that our subjects are representative of complex constraints and can be used to evaluate constraint solvers.

3.5   Threats to Construct Validity

Threats to construct validity are situations where measurement instruments do not adequately capture concepts that they are supposed to capture. In this experiment, we measure performance and ease of writing constraints and using results. Measuring performance is always risky on todays multitasking machines. We controlled this threat with repeated measurements and with no sharing of resources. The quantitative analysis about constraint writing is more prone to this threat. We control this threat by providing raw data (how constraints are written, bounds given, results converted) and add our analysis on top of it.

3.6   Analysis Strategy

We summarize all the data first. We then make observations on this data and our observations on the three quantitative criteria of constraint writing, giving bounds, and using results. Finally, we show several comparisons between performance of different techniques in graphical form.

4   Data and Analysis

We provide performance comparison and its analysis followed by quantitative analysis.

4.1   Performance Comparison

Table 1 shows the results of our experiments. The first column lists the complex structures we chose. The next column specifies the size we are using. For Binary Tree, Singly Linked List, and Doubly Linked List, we generate structures up to

Table 1. Results of generating bounded exhaustive test cases for six subject structures by CUTE, Korat, Alloy, and JPF. Time out or tool limitations are represented by a hyphen (-).

Subject	Size	CUTE	Korat	Alloy	JPF
	3	1.761	0.507	0.880	16.349
	4	4.774	0.533	1.085	16.158
Binary Tree	5	15.104	0.567	1.779	16.678
	6	47.427	0.620	5.882	19.405
	7	156.368	0.720	41.866	24.197
	8	527.292	1.048	520.868	48.389
	3	2.580	0.579	1.159	16.415
	4	8.240	0.495	1.423	16.478
Search Tree	5	28.015	0.547	2.529	21.498
	6	95.764	0.746	3.032	43.905
	7	341.444	2.363	6.437	222.893
	8	-	17.515	26.456	1409.366
	3	43.769	0.841	1.571	15.775
	4	82.905	0.875	1.450	17.139
Red Black Tree	5	720.625	0.829	5.293	18.948
	6	-	1.018	4.132	28.186
	7	-	1.687	18.036	57.800
	8	-	5.250	85.277	170.962
	10	0.855	0.389	8.452	16.661
	13	1.073	0.399	602.250	16.414
	50	4.136	0.481	-	18.015
Singly Linked List	100	8.383	0.688	-	23.433
	200	17.273	2.110	-	48.625
	300	27.082	6.138	-	104.517
	400	36.811	13.939	-	200.062
	500	48.849	27.982	-	344.724
	10	1.167	0.408	7.408	16.221
	13	1.523	0.411	130.423	15.242
	50	5.657	0.537	-	18.511
Doubly Linked List	100	11.900	1.047	-	24.547
	200	25.538	4.987	-	63.614
	300	44.332	16.354	-	146.015
	400	67.828	36.503	-	285.589
	500	100.057	72.686	-	501.617
	9	1.292	0.395	2.602	21.333
	11	1.557	0.457	7.409	36.900
	13	1.839	1.026	10.420	108.670
Sorted List	15	2.110	2.286	21.874	439.063
	18	2.821	21.646	-	-
	20	2.797	102.609	-	-
	22	3.036	499.276	-	-

given size while we generate structures of exactly that size for the other three structures. The reason for this is that when generating structures with valid integer ranges of some data variables (e.g. Sorted List), then all tools except CUTE will produce all valid assignments while CUTE will provide a single valid assignment. This makes comparison difficult. We thus chose a fixed size and fixed range of integers such that only one valid assignment exists. The next four columns in the table list the times taken by each tool.

Alloy ran into solver limitations for sizes greater than about 15 nodes for all list structures. Similarly CUTE faced symbolic execution limitations for red black trees. Other numbers not available are time outs for the allocated 15 minutes.

Table 2. Isomorphic Candidates Produced

Subject	CUTE	Korat	Alloy	JPF
Binary Tree	NO	NO	**YES**	NO
Binary Search Tree	NO	NO	NO	NO
Red Black Tree	**YES**	NO	NO	NO
Singly Linked List	NO	NO	**YES**	NO
Doubly Linked List	NO	NO	**YES**	NO
Sorted List	NO	NO	NO	NO

Table 2 shows how well the candidate tools performed in terms of pruning isomorphic candidates. Korat and JPF never produced an isomorphic result. Also from their algorithm, they would never produce a normal isomorphic result according to the definition given previously. Note that their can be domain specific isomorphic results (e.g. isomorphic graphs) which no tool identifies as isomorphic. CUTE produced isomorphic candidates only when it ran into symbolic execution limitations. This happened in our case for red-black trees. Alloy produced isomorphic candidates most often. Its isomorphism pruning is most limited. For example, for a singly linked list, other than the root node and the tail node, it produces more than one isomorphic orderings of the middle nodes.

Lastly, Figure 6 shows six graphs, one for each subject structure and plots the performance of all four tools. The time axis is logarithmic since bounded exhaustive testing is an exponentially growing problem and a logarithmic scale better shows how the tools are performing.

We observe that other than sorted lists, Korat is the fastest tool within 1000s time. For binary tree and Red Black Trees, it also seems to grow the slowest. For Binary Trees and Binary Search Trees, CUTE is growing linear on a logarithmic scale which means it is slightly better in terms of time complexity but the actual problem size where it would take over Korat would be huge.

CUTE is the only tool that handles Sorted Lists successfully, It touches our 1000s limit for generating about 500 element lists. This huge difference is because the other tools internally generate all possible combinations (n!) whereas symbolic execution does not. This is also the motivation around some recent work on Korat and JPF to use symbolic execution for primitives and use the native algorithm for non-primitive fields [51].

Note also in all graphs that CUTE has the best time complexity. It grows exponentially (trees) and sub-exponentially (lists) except for red black trees where symbolic execution faced limitations. Thus when symbolic execution faces limitations and CUTE reverts to take help from concrete execution, we may not get results comparable to other tools. This is one of the key weak points of CUTE for bounded exhaustive generation.

Alloy shows an interesting behavior. It performs better for Binary Search Trees (more complex constraint) than Binary Trees. We believe that this is because SAT solvers solve the easiest clauses first and the former gives it a better chance at doing that. Red black tree performance is in the middle and is better for 4

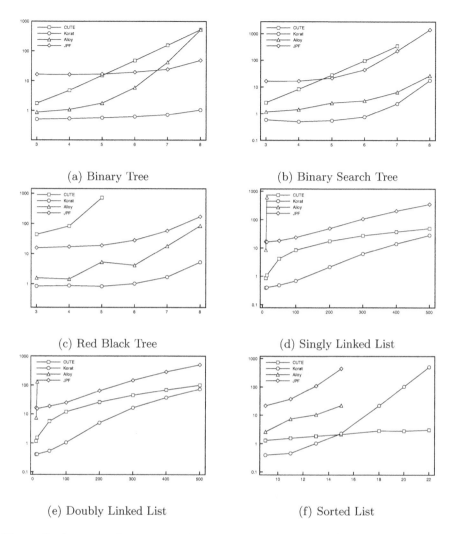

Fig. 6. Performance Comparison of techniques for all six subject structures. Y-axis shows time in seconds on a logarithmic scale. X-axis shows size of structure.

nodes than for 3 (and 6 nodes than for 5). We again believe this has to do with the formation of clauses.

If we carefully note, the graph of JPF is almost at a constant distance above Korat. Indeed, JPF structural constraint solving algorithm and the Korat algorithm principally make the same decisions. JPF is only burdened with running a model checking virtual machine and keeping a lot of additional state which Korat can do without. That is why they have similar time complexity but a different multiplier. Thus we can say that Korat is a much faster specialized implementation of what the JPF structural constraint solving algorithm does without the added overheads of model checking.

Table 3. Comparison of structural constraint solving techniques on non-performance metrics

	Constraints	Bounds	Output
CUTE	Imperative function: Some special care at branches to enable symbolic execution to visit both branches	For linear structures, giving a depth bound in invoking CUTE is enough; for others, special checks needed to be inserted inside the predicate	Each complex structure is available at end of testing function in a separate process
Korat	Imperative function: No special restrictions	An imperative function listing bounds for each object and predicate involved (*finitization*)	Each structure is available in a special function in the same single process
Alloy	Declarative predicate: In relational quantified logic	List of bounds for each object involved	Result is a list of solutions that can be translated into actual heap structures using Alloy to Java translator in TestEra [33]
JPF	Imperative function: Need to use special accessor functions (can be added automatically) that use model checker's non-determinism	Ranges can be specified in special accessor functions	Each complex structure is available at end of testing function in a separate process

4.2   Qualitative Comparison

One of the research goals of our experiment was to discuss some qualitative differences between subject tools. We give summarized results in Table 3 and give a more detailed discussion of each difference below.

Constraint Writing: All tools except Alloy required constraints written in an imperative language. Constraints are required to be free of side-effects. CUTE constraints needed some tweaking to allow symbolic execution to explore all paths. For example, a `return size == 0` statement has to be changed to a branch statement with separate returns. JPF and Korat can use an arbitrary imperative function that is free of side-effects. Alloy required declarative predicates. Declarative specifications are concise and can be significantly smaller than an equivalent imperative specification. The tradeoff is the learning curve of declarative language for programmers used to writing code in imperative languages.

Giving Bounds: Korat and Alloy were the easiest to provide bounds, which is not surprising since they are designed for specification-based, bounded exhaustive checking. They differed in that Alloy required bounds for each *type* whereas Korat was more explicit in requiring bounds for each *field* of each type. Also for primitives, Korat can use lower bounds and upper bounds whereas Alloy would need those bounds as part of specification and not as part of bounds. To limit structures generated by CUTE within bounds, we needed to tweak its imperative predicate. Providing bounds using the JPF approach was simple. In this approach the required arrays (universe of values) were constructed during the testing `Main` method. Values of these arrays are non-deterministically used by accessor functions (possibly automatically added).

Using Results: The JPF approach and CUTE approach produce each result, i.e. structure that represents a test input, in a separate execution (process). This result can directly be used for testing or saved for later use. Korat approach produces each result in the same execution (process). The result can be saved. Direct testing has to be careful about using a new process to avoid crashing of Korat due to faulty code. In previous work, these results have been distributed for parallel test execution [39]. Alloy produces solutions to declarative specifications. These need to be converted to the corresponding imperative language for actual test use. One tool in this area is Alloy to Java converter used in TestEra [33]. This tool can generate actual Java structures corresponding to Alloy output.

Treatment of primitive fields: While the key benefit of structural constraint solving is non-primitive fields (pointers to objects), primitive fields also pose a limitation. All the surveyed tools except CUTE try all possible values for a given primitive field. This often results in exponential or factorial amount of time. CUTE excels in this area by providing a single valid solution for such fields.

5   Summary and Conclusions

In this paper, we performed an empirical study of using four different techniques for constraint solving to perform bounded exhaustive testing. Bounded exhaustive testing has been previously shown effective at finding faults in real programs. Here, our goal is to compare the performance of these tools. We considered the CUTE tool based on symbolic execution, the JPF model checker, the Alloy tool based on SAT, and the specialized solver Korat . Our key results are:

- The fastest tool for most of the subjects of small size is Korat. However it degrades in performance when several constraints are on primitive fields.
- The JPF constraint solving approach using lazy initialization is effectively a slower Korat.
- Alloy provides the most concise way of writing predicates. For programmers knowledgeable in declarative languages, it can significantly reduce time to write or maintain specifications.
- CUTE provides better time complexity than most tools however the slope constant is fairly high. This is because of the symbolic execution overhead.
- CUTE requires some tweaking of class invariants to enable bounded exhaustive generation.
- No tool gives better non-isomorphic generation for exhaustive enumeration than the Korat algorithm (and likewise lazy initialization using JPF).
- All tools except CUTE provide bounded exhaustive checking by design and CUTE focuses on generating one input per path.

Our results also provide directions for future work. We see two main directions of research:

- Using symbolic execution to improve the specialized solver Korat.
- While Alloy provides an intuitive way to write specifications (after the learning curve), its solving capability is limited to smaller sizes (see list data structure) and can often produce isomorphic candidates. We believe using a combination of solvers, such as SAT, SMT, string constraint solvers, and set constraint solvers, is likely to provide significantly more efficient solving.
- Similar to parallelization for Korat [39, 46], we are working on parallel symbolic execution. Other tools, such as Alloy, can also gain from parallel execution, both on commodity parallel machines and bigger clusters.

Acknowledgements

We thank Darko Marinov for insightful and detailed discussions and comments. This material is based upon work partially supported by the NSF under Grant Nos. IIS-0438967, CCF-0702680, and CCF-0845628, and AFOSR grant FA9550-09-1-0351.

References

1. Artho, C., Drusinksy, D., Goldberg, A., Havelund, K., Lowry, M., Păsăreanu, C.S., Roşu, G., Visser, W.: Experiments with Test Case Generation and Runtime Analysis. In: Börger, E., Gargantini, A., Riccobene, E. (eds.) ASM 2003. LNCS, vol. 2589, pp. 87–107. Springer, Heidelberg (2003)
2. Ball, T., Rajamani, S.K.: Automatically Validating Temporal Safety Properties of Interfaces. In: Dwyer, M.B. (ed.) SPIN 2001. LNCS, vol. 2057, pp. 103–122. Springer, Heidelberg (2001)
3. Bayer, R.: Symmetric Binary B-trees: Data Structure and Maintenance Algorithms. Acta informatica 1(4), 290–306 (1972)
4. Beyer, D., Chlipala, A.J., Majumdar, R.: Generating Tests from Counterexamples. In: Proc. 2004 Int. Conf. Softw. Eng (ICSE), pp. 326–335 (2004)
5. Boyapati, C., Khurshid, S., Marinov, D.: Korat: Automated Testing based on Java Predicates. In: Proc. 2002 Int. Symp. Softw. Testing and Analysis (ISSTA), pp. 123–133 (2002)
6. Brat, G., et al.: Experimental Evaluation of Verification and Validation Tools on Martian Rover Software. Form. Methods Syst. Des. 25(2-3), 167–198 (2004)
7. Bush, W.R., Pincus, J.D., Sielaff, D.J.: A Static Analyzer for Finding Dynamic Programming Errors. Softw. Pract. Exper. 30(7), 775–802 (2000)
8. Cadar, C., et al.: EXE: Automatically Generating Inputs of Death. In: Proc. 13th Conf. Comput. and Commun. Security (CCS), pp. 322–335 (2006)
9. Chang, J., Richardson, D.: Structural Specification-Based Testing: Automated Support and Experimental Evaluation. In: Nierstrasz, O., Lemoine, M. (eds.) ESEC 1999 and ESEC-FSE 1999. LNCS, vol. 1687, pp. 285–302. Springer, Heidelberg (1999)

10. Clarke, E.M.: The Birth of Model Checking. 25 Years of Model Checking: History, Achievements, Perspectives, 1–26 (2008)
11. Clarke, L.A.: A System to Generate Test Data and Symbolically Execute Programs. IEEE Trans. Softw. Eng. 2(3), 215–222 (1976)
12. Coen-Porisini, A., et al.: Using Symbolic Execution for Verifying Safety-critical Systems. In: Proc. 3rd joint meeting of the Euro. Softw. Eng. Conf. (ESEC) and Symp. Foundations of Softw. Eng. (FSE), pp. 142–151 (2001)
13. Corbett, J., et al.: Bandera: Extracting Finite-state Models from Java Source Code. In: Proc. 2000 Int. Conf. Softw. Eng. (ICSE), pp. 439–448 (2000)
14. Darga, P.T., Boyapati, C.: Efficient Software Model Checking of Data Structure Properties. In: Proc. 21st Annual Conf. Object Oriented Prog. Syst., Lang., and Applications (OOPSLA), pp. 363–382 (2006)
15. Donat, M.R.: Automating Formal Specification-Based Testing. In: Bidoit, M., Dauchet, M. (eds.) CAAP 1997, FASE 1997, and TAPSOFT 1997. LNCS, vol. 1214, pp. 833–847. Springer, Heidelberg (1997)
16. Elkarablieh, B., et al.: STARC: Static Analysis for Efficient Repair of Complex Data. In: Proc. 22nd Annual Conf. Object Oriented Prog. Syst., Lang., and Applications (OOPSLA), pp. 387–404 (2007)
17. Elkarablieh, B., Marinov, D., Khurshid, S.: Efficient Solving of Structural Constraints. In: Proc. 2008 Int. Symp. Softw. Testing and Analysis (ISSTA), pp. 39–50 (2008)
18. Flanagan, C., et al.: Extended Static Checking for Java. In: Proc. 2002 Conf. Prog. Lang. Design and Implementation (PLDI), pp. 234–245 (2002)
19. Gligoric, M., et al.: Optimizing Generation of Object Graphs in Java PathFinder. In: Proc. 2nd Int. Conf. Softw. Testing Verification and Validation (ICST), pp. 51–60 (2009)
20. Godefroid, P.: Model Checking for Programming Languages using VeriSoft. In: Proc. 24th Symp. Principles of Prog. Lang. (POPL), pp. 174–186 (1997)
21. Godefroid, P., Klarlund, N., Sen, K.: DART: Directed Automated Random Testing. In: Proc. 2005 Conf. Prog. Lang. Design and Implementation (PLDI), pp. 213–223 (2005)
22. Goldberg, E., Novikov, Y.: BerkMin: A Fast and Robust SAT-solver. Discrete Appl. Math. 155(12), 1549–1561 (2007)
23. Goodenough, J.B., Gerhart, S.L.: Toward a Theory of Test Data Selection. In: Proc. Int. Conf. Reliable Softw. Technol., pp. 493–510 (1975)
24. Gotlieb, A., Botella, B., Rueher, M.: Automatic Test Data Generation using Constraint Solving Techniques. In: Proc. 1998 Int. Symp. Softw. Testing and Analysis (ISSTA), pp. 53–62 (1998)
25. Grieskamp, W., et al.: Generating Finite State Machines from Abstract State Machines. In: Proc. 2002 Int. Symp. Softw. Testing and Analysis (ISSTA), pp. 112–122 (2002)
26. Guibas, L.J., Sedgewick, R.: A Dichromatic Framework for Balanced Trees. In: Proc. 19th Annual Symp. Foundations of Comput. Sci. (FOCS), pp. 8–21 (1978)
27. Henzinger, T., et al.: Software Verification with BLAST. In: Proc. 10th Int. SPIN Workshop on Model Checking of Softw., pp. 235–239 (2003)
28. Huang, J.C.: An Approach to Program Testing. ACM Comput. Surv. 7(3), 113–128 (1975)
29. Jackson, D.: Alloy: A Lightweight Object Modelling Notation. ACM Trans. Softw. Eng. and Methodology 11(2), 256–290 (2002)
30. Jackson, D.: Software Abstractions: Logic, Language, and Analysis. The MIT Press, Cambridge (2006)

31. Jackson, D., Schechter, I., Shlyakhter, I.: ALCOA: The Alloy Constraint Analyzer. In: Proc. 2000 Int. Conf. Softw. Eng. (ICSE), pp. 730–733 (2000)
32. Khurshid, S., Marinov, D.: Checking Java Implementation of a Naming Architecture Using TestEra. Electr. Notes Theor. Comput. Sci. 55(3) (2001)
33. Khurshid, S., Marinov, D.: TestEra: Specification-Based Testing of Java Programs using SAT. Automated Softw. Eng. J. 11(4), 403–434 (2004)
34. Khurshid, S., Păsăreanu, C.S., Visser, W.: Generalized symbolic execution for model checking and testing. In: Garavel, H., Hatcliff, J. (eds.) TACAS 2003. LNCS, vol. 2619, pp. 553–568. Springer, Heidelberg (2003)
35. King, J.C.: Symbolic Execution and Program Testing. Commun. ACM 19(7), 385–394 (1976)
36. Korel, B.: Automated Test Data Generation for Programs with Procedures. In: Proc. 1996 Int. Symp. Softw. Testing and Analysis (ISSTA), pp. 209–215 (1996)
37. Larson, E., Austin, T.: High Coverage Detection of Input-related Security Faults. In: Proc. 12th USENIX Security Symp., p. 9 (2003)
38. Marinov, D., Khurshid, S.: TestEra: A Novel Framework for Automated Testing of Java Programs. In: Proc. 16th Int. Conf. Automated Softw. Eng. (ASE), p. 22 (2001)
39. Misailovic, S., et al.: Parallel Test Generation and Execution with Korat. In: Proc. 6th joint meeting of the Euro. Softw. Eng. Conf. (ESEC) and Symp. Foundations of Softw. Eng. (FSE), pp. 135–144 (2007)
40. Moskewicz, M.W., et al.: Chaff: Engineering an Efficient SAT Solver. In: Proc. 38th Design Automation Conf. (DAC), pp. 530–535 (2001)
41. Offutt, J., Abdurazik, A.: Generating Tests from UML Specifications. In: Proc. 2nd Int. Conf. Unified Modeling Language, pp. 416–429 (1999)
42. Penix, J., et al.: Verification of Time Partitioning in the DEOS Scheduler Kernel. In: Proc. 2000 Int. Conf. Softw. Eng. (ICSE), pp. 488–497 (2000)
43. Ramamoorthy, C.V., Ho, S.B.F., Chen, W.T.: On the Automated Generation of Program Test Data. IEEE Trans. Softw. Eng. 2(4), 293–300 (1976)
44. Sen, K., Marinov, D., Agha, G.: CUTE: A Concolic Unit Testing Engine for C. In: Proc. 5th joint meeting of the Euro. Softw. Eng. Conf. (ESEC) and Symp. Foundations of Softw. Eng. (FSE), pp. 263–272 (2005)
45. Shlyakhter, I.: Generating Effective Symmetry-breaking Predicates for Search Problems. Discrete Appl. Math. 155(12), 1539–1548 (2007)
46. Siddiqui, J.H., Khurshid, S.: PKorat: Parallel Generation of Structurally Complex Test Inputs. In: Proc. 2nd Int. Conf. Softw. Testing Verification and Validation (ICST), pp. 250–259 (2009)
47. Sorensson, N., Een, N.: An Extensible SAT-solver. In: Proc. 6th Int. Conf. Theor. and Applications of Satisfiability Testing (SAT), pp. 502–518 (2003)
48. Spivey, J.M.: The Z Notation: A Reference Manual. Prentice-Hall, Inc., Englewood Cliffs (1989)
49. Sullivan, K., et al.: Software Assurance by Bounded Exhaustive Testing. In: Proc. 2004 Int. Symp. Softw. Testing and Analysis (ISSTA), pp. 133–142 (2004)
50. Visser, W., et al.: Model Checking Programs. In: Proc. 15th Int. Conf. Automated Softw. Eng. (ASE), p. 3 (2000)
51. Visser, W., Păsăreanu, C.S., Khurshid, S.: Test Input Generation with Java PathFinder. In: Proc. 2004 Int. Symp. Softw. Testing and Analysis (ISSTA), pp. 97–107 (2004)
52. Xie, T., Marinov, D., Notkin, D.: Rostra: A Framework for Detecting Redundant Object-Oriented Unit Tests. In: Proc. 29th Int. Conf. Automated Softw. Eng. (ASE), pp. 196–205 (2004)

Improving Automatic Verification of Security Protocols with XOR

Xihui Chen[1,2], Ton van Deursen[1,*], and Jun Pang[1]

[1] Faculty of Sciences, Technology and Communication
University of Luxembourg, 6, rue Richard Coudenhove-Kalergi, L-1359 Luxembourg
[2] School of Computer Science and Technology
Shandong University, Jinan, 250101 China

Abstract. Küsters and Truderung recently proposed an automatic verification method for security protocols with exclusive or (XOR). Their method reduces protocols with XOR to their XOR-free equivalents, enabling efficient verification by tools such as ProVerif. Although the proposed method works efficiently for verifying secrecy, verification of authentication properties is inefficient and sometimes impossible.

In this paper, we improve the work by Küsters and Truderung in two ways. First, we extend their method for authentication verification to a richer class of XOR-protocols by automatically introducing bounded verification. Second, we improve the efficiency of their approach by developing a number of dedicated optimizations. We show the applicability of our work by implementing a prototype and applying it to both existing benchmarks and RFID protocols. The experiments show promising results and uncover a flaw in a recently proposed RFID protocol.

1 Introduction

Cryptographic security protocols typically consists of a series of message exchanges among two or more agents over a hostile network. They aim to achieve various security goals such as authentication, secrecy, key agreement, privacy, and anonymity. However, designing secure protocols is an error-prone task and incorrect protocols may become ideal entry points for various attacks. Starting from the seminal work by Lowe [1], automated symbolic verification methods for security protocols have shown their strength in finding attacks and proving correctness of security protocols.

As attacks that rely on cryptographic primitives are hard to prove and difficult to be automatically checked, cryptographic primitives are usually treated as functions without any algebraic properties in symbolic methods. This is called the perfect cryptography assumption [2], namely no cryptographic message can be opened without the correct key. Based on this assumption, many automatic tools have been designed and implemented, among which ProVerif [3] is considered as the state of the art [4]. However, ProVerif cannot uncover attacks that

---

* Ton van Deursen was supported by a grant from the Fonds National de la Recherche (Luxembourg).

K. Breitman and A. Cavalcanti (Eds.): ICFEM 2009, LNCS 5885, pp. 107–126, 2009.
© Springer-Verlag Berlin Heidelberg 2009

make use of certain algebraic properties of cryptographic primitives. Cortier, Delaune and Lafourcade give a survey on algebraic properties of common cryptographic primitives and attacks making use of them [5]. Therefore, some relaxation of the perfect assumption needs to be investigated. Exclusive or (XOR) is one binary operator with typical algebraic properties that has drawn a lot of interest. For example, XOR is often used in radio frequency identification (RFID) systems, which have become popular in recent years.

We call security protocols employing the exclusive or operator ($\oplus$) XOR-protocols. The $\oplus$-operator has the following four properties.

$$x \oplus (y \oplus z) = (x \oplus y) \oplus z \qquad \text{(associativity)} \qquad (1)$$
$$x \oplus y = y \oplus x \qquad \text{(commutativity)} \qquad (2)$$
$$x \oplus 0 = x \qquad \text{(neutral element)} \qquad (3)$$
$$x \oplus x = 0 \qquad \text{(nilpotence)} \qquad (4)$$

In order to detect attacks on XOR-protocols, we need to model intruders with the ability of exploring the above algebraic properties, in addition to the perfect cryptography assumption.

Related work. In the literature, several approaches have been proposed to deal with the verification of XOR-protocols [6,7,8], but few of them are practical to implement. A few tools can cope with a certain class of XOR-protocols [8,9], all of them have strict restrictions on the range of protocols they can be applied to. For example, the tool of Cortier, Keighren, and Steel can only handle protocols with the $\oplus$-operator and symmetric encryption. More recently, Küsters and Truderung proposed a more general approach [10] to automatic verification of cryptographic XOR-protocols based on ProVerif. Their main idea is to reduce protocol analysis with XOR to the XOR-free case. The XOR-reduction step transforms Horn theories modeling XOR-protocols to the ones free from algebraic properties of the $\oplus$-operator, by computing a family of legal substitutions for terms containing $\oplus$. Thus, verification is reduced to a syntactic derivation problem. They implement their transformation step in a tool called XorProverif [10]. The use of ProVerif allows the modeling of essential cryptographic primitives and the verification of security protocols with an unbounded number of sessions. However, there are still a few limitations of this XOR-reduction approach – only $\oplus$-linear protocols can be handled (see Sect. 2 for the definition of $\oplus$-linearity) and it is likely to suffer from exponential blow up of the number of substitutions (Lem. 12, [10]). In this paper, we develop several methods to tackle these restrictions of the XOR-reduction approach, and implement a prototype to evaluate and illustrate our methods by experiments on existing benchmarks and recent RFID protocols.

Our main contribution. One goal of this research is to develop a systematic method to improve efficiency of the XOR-reduction approach. Our first idea is to reduce the number of substitutions during the transformation, by exploring the freshness of nonces generated during the executions of the XOR-protocols. By this further reduction, the time taken by ProVerif for verification is decreased and some false attacks can be removed as well.

We also propose a new approach to use *bounded verification* to make the XOR-reduction approach available to verify authentication of more protocols which violate ⊕-linearity. In this approach, session identifiers are considered as constants instead of variables [10] and we can verify protocols using models with a certain bounded number of sessions. Our bounded verification can be further optimized by restricting the order between sessions and by checking the secrecy property first. RFID protocols are a special class of protocols that require authentication. They often use the ⊕-operator to build protocol messages. In terms of the characteristics of RFID protocols, more optimizations can be introduced and their protocol models could be much more simplified.

We implement a prototype to evaluate and illustrate our methods: it first automatically transforms the original Horn theory of an XOR-protocol to a multi-session model, then it reduces the model XOR-free and performs the introduced optimizations when necessary. In the end, ProVerif is applied to the final result of the transformations. A number of XOR-protocols including RFID protocols have been analyzed and experimental results show that our approach is effective and improves the verification of XOR-protocols based on the XOR-reduction approach. In one case, a new attack is detected on a RFID protocol in its multi-session model.

Structure of this paper. In Sect. 2, we present the main idea of the XOR-reduction approach with a running example. The concepts of bounded verification are introduced in Sect. 3. Several different ways to do optimizations are presented in Sect. 4. We discuss our implementation and experimental results in Sect. 5. We conclude the paper in Sect. 6.

2 Preliminaries

In this section, we illustrate how security protocols with ⊕ can be modeled by Horn theories and explain the main ideas behind the reduction process proposed by Küsters and Truderung. More details can be found in the original paper [10].

2.1 Basic Concepts

We use Σ to denote a finite signature containing the binary function symbol ⊕ and V to denote a set of variables. The set of terms is defined as usual over Σ and V. We use $s \sqsubseteq t$ to denote that s is a subterm of t. Terms containing no variables are *ground* and are also called *messages*. For a unary predicate q and a (ground) term t, we call $q(t)$ a (ground) *atom*. A *substitution* σ is a set of pairs $\{t_1/x_1, \ldots, t_n/x_n\}$, where $t_1, \ldots, t_n$ are terms and $x_1, \ldots, x_n$ are variables. We use $dom(\sigma)$ to denote the domain of σ, which contains the variables $x_1 \ldots x_n$. A term is *standard* if its top symbol is not ⊕, otherwise it is called *non-standard*. Equations (1)-(4) define a congruence relation $\sim$ on terms. A term is in *reduced form* if equations (1)-(2) and equations (3)-(4), when interpreted as reductions from left to right, can no longer be applied.

A Horn clause is of the form of $a_1, \ldots, a_n \rightarrow a_0$ where $a_0, \ldots, a_n$ are atoms. A set of Horn clauses constitutes a Horn theory. Given a ground atom a, we use $T \vdash a$ to denote that there is a derivation π for a from the Horn theory T. A derivation π is a sequence of ground atoms $b_1, \ldots, b_\ell$ with $b_\ell = a$. For each b_i there exists a substitution σ of a Horn clause $a_1, \ldots, a_n \to a_0$ in T, we have $a_1\sigma, \ldots, a_n\sigma \to a_0\sigma$ where $a_0\sigma = b_i$ and for every $j \in \{1, \ldots, n\}$ there exists $k \in \{1, \ldots, i-1\}$ with $a_j\sigma = b_k$. Similarly, if the congruence relation $\sim$ is used instead of syntactic equality $=$, we can say a can be derived from T modulo $\oplus$, denoted by $T \vdash_\oplus a$.

One crucial notion in [10] is $\oplus$-*linearity*. A term is $\oplus$-linear if for each of its subterms of the form $t \oplus s$, t or s is ground. For example, $a \oplus x$ is $\oplus$-linear while $a \oplus x \oplus y$ is not, where x, y are variables and a is a constant. The concept of $\oplus$-linearity extends to Horn theories and derivations in a straightforward way. Küsters and Truderung also define the notion of C-*domination* [10]. Let C denote a finite set of standard reduced ground terms such that C does not contain two terms m and m' such that $m \neq m'$ and $m \sim m'$. We use $C^\oplus$ to denote the $\oplus$-closure of C, that is,

$$C^\oplus = \{t \mid \text{there exist } c_1, \ldots, c_n \in C \text{ s.t. } t \sim c_1 \oplus \cdots \oplus c_n\}.$$

A term is C-*dominated* if for each of its subterms of the form $t \oplus s$, it is true that either t or s is in $C^\oplus$. The concept of C-domination extends to Horn clauses and derivations. A Horn theory is called C-dominated if each clause in T is C-dominated, except for the rule $I(x), I(y) \to I(x \oplus y)$ which models the intruder's ability to perform XOR operations. The set C is always finite and must be chosen as small as possible in order to make the XOR-reduction efficient (see Lem. 2 and Lem. 12 in [10]).

2.2   Modeling Protocols by Horn Theories

A Horn theory modeling security protocols contains three parts: *initial intruder facts*, *intruder rules*, and *protocol rules*. It uses the predicate I. A fact $I(t)$ means that the intruder can obtain the term t. The initial intruder facts represent the initial intruder knowledge, typically names of principals and public keys, for instance, $I(a)$ denotes that the intruder knows the name a and $I(pub(sk_a))$ denotes that the intruder knows the public key of a where sk_a represents its private key. The set of Dolev-Yao intruder [2] rules representing the ability to derive new messages can be found in [10], where a special clause $I(x), I(y) \to I(x \oplus y)$, called the $\oplus$-*rule*, is used to allow the intruder to perform the XOR operation on arbitrary messages. The protocol rules represent the actions performed in a protocol. Each rule i is of the form $I(t_1), \ldots, I(t_i) \to I(s_i)$ where $t_1, \ldots, t_i$ describe messages the principal has received up to step i and $I(s_i)$ describes the message the principal will send out at step i.

The secrecy property of a term t can be formulated as the fact that $I(t)$ cannot be derived from the set of clauses, while authentication properties are often expressed as correspondence assertions of the form $end(x) \to begin(x)$, where x describes the value on which both agents agree [11]. Due to the difference, we give the Horn theories for secrecy and authentication verification of our running

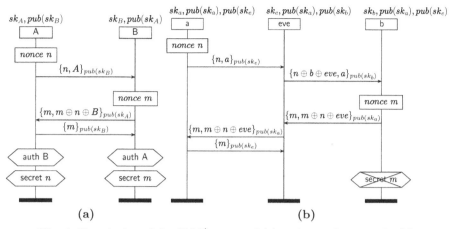

Fig. 1. Description of the $NSL'_\oplus$ protocol (a) and one of its attacks (b)

example $NSL'_\oplus$ separately. Fig. 1(a) depicts the $NSL'_\oplus$ protocol, which is a variation of the protocol by Lowe [1] that fixes a vulnerability in the Needham-Schroeder protocol [12].

In this paper, we use *role* to refer to the protocol steps an agent expects to carry out, for instance A and B in Fig. 1(a)[1]. For example, agent a playing role A has two steps. To start, a generates a nonce and sends the first message to the agent playing role B. Then upon receiving the second message and checking its correctness, a sends back the last message. A *run* is the execution of a role by an agent. Several runs can be executed at the same time. By *session*, we mean a (prefix of a) complete run of an agent. Let P denote the sets of participants and H be the set of honest agents. The notations sk_a and $pub(sk_a)$ represent the private and the corresponding public key of $a \in P$. Comon-Lundh and Cortier prove that for secrecy (authentication properties), only two (three) participants [13] need to be considered. Therefore, we have $P = \{a, b\}$, $H = \{a\}$ for $NSL'_\oplus$-sec and $P = \{a, b, c\}$, $H = \{a, b\}$ for $NSL'_\oplus$-auth. We use $n(a, b)$ to denote the nonce in the first message in which $a \in P$ is the generator and $b \in P$ is the receiver, and $m(b, a)$ in the second message to denote the nonce sent from b to a. Encryption of a term t under a key k is denoted by $\{t\}_k$.

Model for secrecy verification $NSL'_\oplus$-sec. We model the protocol using the following clauses:

$$I(\{n(a, b), a\}_{pub(sk_b)}) \text{ for } a \in H, b \in P \quad (5)$$

$$I(\{x, a\}_{pub(sk_b)}) \rightarrow I(\{m(b, a), m(b, a) \oplus x \oplus b\}_{pub(sk_a)}) \text{ for } b \in H, a \in P \quad (6)$$

$$I(\{y, y \oplus n(a, b) \oplus b\}_{pub(sk_a)}) \rightarrow I(\{y\}_{pub(sk_b)}) \text{ for } a \in H, b \in P \quad (7)$$

---

[1] We use message sequence charts for the descriptions of protocols and/or their possible attacks, where capital letters represent roles and small letters are used to represent agents.

We denote the set of clauses above by $NSL'_\oplus$-sec. One attack breaking the secrecy claim of $m(b, a)$ is described in Fig. 1(b) where the adversary impersonates a to b. After receiving the message $\{n(a, eve), a\}_{pub(sk_e)}$, it makes use of the algebraic properties of XOR and its knowledge of the protocol to send out a message $\{n(a, eve) \oplus b \oplus eve, a\}_{pub(sk_b)}$ to b. It replays the response from b, $\{m(b, a), m(b, a) \oplus n(a, eve) \oplus eve\}_{pub(sk_a)}$, to a. In the end, the adversary can obtain $m(b, a)$ by decrypting the last message from a.

Model for authentication $NSL'_\oplus$-auth. For authentication verification, nonces generated in a session are typically chosen as the parameter x in the events $begin(x)$ and $end(x)$. To guarantee their freshness and prevent replay attacks, session identifiers need to be added to nonces to make expressing correspondence of sessions possible. The following Horn theory models the protocol rules to verify if role A can be authenticated by B.

$$I(\{n(a, b, sid), a\}_{pub(sk_b)}) \text{ for } a \in H, b \in P \quad (8)$$

$$I(\{x, a\}_{pub(sk_b)}) \rightarrow I(\{m(b, a, sid), m(b, a, sid) \oplus x \oplus b\}_{pub(sk_a)}) \text{ for } b \in H, a \in P \quad (9)$$

$$begin(a, b, y), I(\{y, y \oplus n(a, b, sid) \oplus b\}_{pub(sk_a)}) \rightarrow I(\{y\}_{pub(sk_b)}) \text{ for } a \in H, b \in P \quad (10)$$

$$I(\{m(b, a, sid)\}_{pub(sk_b)}) \rightarrow end(a, b, m(b, a, sid)) \text{ for } b \in H, a \in P \quad (11)$$

The set of clauses we defined above is denoted by $NSL'_\oplus$-auth.

2.3   The XOR-Reduction Process

We refer to the process of reducing the deduction problem modulo XOR to the one without XOR for C-dominated theories as XOR-reduction. XOR-reduction aims to construct a Horn theory that can be analyzed by ProVerif and makes sure that any derivation obtained from the theory modulo XOR can also be derived from the constructed one.

Each C-dominated term can be turned into normal form after fixing a linear ordering on C. The operator $\ulcorner \cdot \urcorner$ denotes this operation. Any two C-dominated terms t and t' such that $t \sim t'$ have the same normal form, that is $\ulcorner t \urcorner = \ulcorner t' \urcorner$. If all terms in $C^\oplus$ are in normal form, we have the set $C^\oplus_{norm}$. A *fragile subterm* t' of a C-dominated term t is a non-ground, standard term occurring in a subterm of t of the form $t' \oplus s$ or $s \oplus t'$. We use $\mathcal{F}(t)$ to represent the set of all fragile subterms of t. The concept of fragile subterms extends to Horn clauses.

For example, the dominating set for $NSL'_\oplus$-sec is

$$\{m(a, b), m(a, a), n(a, b), n(a, a), a, b\}.$$

Considering the term $m(b, a) \oplus x \oplus b$ in rule (6), its fragile subterm is x.

Definition 1 (Def. 4 in [10]). *Let t be a C-dominated term. The family of substitutions $\sum(t)$ for t with respect to $\mathcal{F}(t)$ is defined as follows. The domain of every substitution in $\sum(t)$ is the set of all variables which occur in some $s \in \mathcal{F}(t)$. Consider a substitution $\sigma \in \sum(t)$. For each $x \in dom(\sigma)$ one of the following three cases holds: (i) $\sigma(x) = x$; (ii) $x \in \mathcal{F}(t)$ and $\sigma(x) = c \oplus x$ for some $c \in C^\oplus_{norm}$, $c \neq 0$; (iii) x occurs in a fragile subterm s and there exists a substitution σ' in normal form satisfying $s\sigma' \in C^\oplus$ then $\sigma(x) = \sigma'(x)$.*

Now given a Horn theory modulo XOR, T, we can reduce it to an XOR-free one T^+ as follows

$$\ulcorner r_1 \sigma \urcorner, \cdots, \ulcorner r_n \sigma \urcorner \to \ulcorner r_0 \sigma \urcorner \qquad \text{for each } \sigma \in \sum(\langle r_0, \ldots, r_n \rangle) \qquad (12)$$

$$I(c), I(c') \to I(\ulcorner c \oplus c'\urcorner) \qquad \text{for each } c, c' \in C_{norm}^\oplus \qquad (13)$$

$$I(c), I(x) \to I(c \oplus x) \qquad \text{for each } c \in C_{norm}^\oplus \qquad (14)$$

$$I(c), I(c' \oplus x) \to I(\ulcorner c \oplus c'\urcorner \oplus x) \text{ for each } c, c' \in C_{norm}^\oplus \qquad (15)$$

$$I(c \oplus x), I(c' \oplus x) \to I(\ulcorner c \oplus c'\urcorner) \qquad \text{for each } c, c' \in C_{norm}^\oplus \qquad (16)$$

where rule (12) is applied to each rule $r_1, \ldots, r_n \to r_0$ of T. The Horn clauses except for the $\oplus$-rule can be simulated by the rules in (12). The rules (13)-(16) are used to simulate the $\oplus$-rule. Küsters and Truderung prove that a message can be derived from T modulo XOR if and only if it can be derived from T^+ only with a syntactic derivation, that is, no algebraic properties of XOR need to be considered.

We take $NSL'_\oplus$-sec as an example to show how the reduction works. It is $\oplus$-linear with dominating set $C = \{m(a,b), m(a,a), n(a,b), n(a,a), a, b\}$. We suppose the order on C is how they are listed. The set $C_{norm}^\oplus$ can also be computed. Since only the Horn clauses in (6) and (7) have a fragile subterm x, we need to compute its set of substitutions whose domain is $\{x\}$. Other clauses should be included in the new theory unchanged.

Consider an instantiated clause of rule (6)

$$I(\{x, a\}_{pub(sk_a)}) \to I(\{m(a,a), m(a,a) \oplus x \oplus a\}_{pub(sk_a)}) \qquad (17)$$

According to Def. 1, case (i) always holds so it gives $\sigma_1(x) = x$. Case (ii) gives 63 substitutions such as $\sigma_i(x) = m(a,a) \oplus n(a,a) \oplus x$. For case (iii), we have another 64 substitutions. For instance, $\sigma_j(x) = m(a,b) \oplus n(a,a)$ will be included. In the end, we have 128 substitutions in total. For each of them, we obtain an instance of rule (6). For example, after applying σ_i we have:

$$I(\{m(a,a) \oplus n(a,a) \oplus x, a\}_{pub(sk_a)}) \to I(\{m(a,a), n(a,a) \oplus a \oplus x\}_{pub(sk_a)})$$

We can obtain the reduced Horn clauses for other instantiated clauses in a similar way. The clauses (13)-(16) model the $\oplus$-rule. In our running example, for instance, $I(m(a,a) \oplus a), I(a \oplus x) \to I(m(a,a) \oplus x)$ will be an instance of clause (15).

3   Bounded Verification of Authentication Protocols

In the Horn theory based approach new protocol runs do not necessarily use fresh nonces [10]. Therefore, nonces from different runs need to be disambiguated. The standard solution is to add a special *session identifier variable* (*sid*) to terms representing nonces. During verification, *sid* is automatically instantiated by a fresh random value. Freshness of nonces is only required when verifying security properties that need correspondence at run level. Note the difference between $m(a, b, sid)$ and $m(a, b)$ in $NSL'_\oplus$-auth and $NSL'_\oplus$-sec, respectively.

As a consequence, Horn theories that are $\oplus$-linear when verifying secrecy can become non-$\oplus$-linear when verifying authentication properties. For instance, $NSL'_\oplus$-auth is not $\oplus$-linear since it contains a term $m(b, a, sid) \oplus x \oplus b$, where both $m(b, a, sid)$ and x are non-ground. As observed by Küsters and Truderung [10], sid is a special variable, because it cannot be substituted by C-dominated terms. In the sequel, we call variables that can be substituted by C-dominated terms C-*variables*. Protocol models that are not $\oplus$-linear solely because of the introduction of session identifiers form a special class of XOR-protocols, which we call *nonce-$\oplus$-linear*.

Definition 2 (Nonce-$\oplus$-linear). *A term is* nonce-$\oplus$-linear *if for each of its subterms of the form* $s \oplus t$, *s or t contains no C-variables.*

For example, the term $h(n(a, b, sid)) \oplus x$ is nonce-$\oplus$-linear while $h(n(a, b, sid) \oplus x) \oplus y$ is not, where $n(a, b, sid)$ is a nonce and x, y are variables. The concept of nonce-$\oplus$-linearity extends to Horn clauses and theories in a similar fashion to $\oplus$-linearity.

By instantiating the variable sid with a fixed finite set $S = \{s_1, \ldots, s_n\}$ of session identifiers, nonce-$\oplus$-linear protocols can be transformed into $\oplus$-linear protocols. Note that S must not intersect with T. We then obtain the multi-session Horn theory T_n by replacing sid with each $s_i \in S$.

Definition 3 (Multi-session Horn Theory). *Let T be a Horn theory, and let σ_i ($1 \leq i \leq n$) be the substitutions mapping sid to s_i and the identity map for other terms. Then multi-session Horn theory of T is defined by*

$$T_n = \bigcup_{1 \leq i \leq n} \sigma_i(T)$$

Clearly, transforming a nonce-$\oplus$-linear Horn theory into a multi-session Horn theory as in Def. 3 makes it $\oplus$-linear.

We now give a theorem about the correctness of our multi-session transformation. Suppose there is a C-dominated message using at most n sessions of any agent to derive. We can derive it from T if and only if it can also be derived from $T_n^\oplus$ through syntactic derivations. Since $T_n^\oplus$ is XOR-free, ProVerif can be used to analyze it.

Theorem 1. *Given a nonce-$\oplus$-linear Horn theory T, the corresponding multi-session XOR-free Horn theory $T_n^\oplus$ and a C-dominated message f which can be derived using at most n sessions of participating agents, $T \vdash_\oplus f$ iff $T_n^\oplus \vdash f$.*

In the sequel, let T_n be the n-session model transformed from T. We prove the theorem by proving the following two lemmas.

Lemma 1. *If π is a syntactic derivation for f from $T_n^\oplus$, then π is a derivation for f from T modulo XOR.*

Proof. From Lem. 13 in [10], if there is a derivation π for f from $T_n^\oplus$, then π is also a derivation for f from T_n modulo XOR. Therefore, to prove this lemma it suffices to prove that if π is a derivation for f from T_n modulo XOR, then it is also a derivation for f from T. Thus, we need to prove each $\pi(i)$ can be obtained by a derivation modulo XOR from T and $\pi_{<i}$. (We use $\pi(i)$ to denote the i-th atom in π, and $\pi_{<i}$ to denote those atoms $\pi(j)$ with $j < i$.)

Suppose $\pi(i)$ is obtained using a protocol rule $r_1, \ldots, r_m \rightarrow r_0$ in T_n. There exists a substitution θ with $r_0\theta \sim \pi(i)$ and for each $k \in \{1, \ldots, m\}$, we have $j < i$ such that $r_k\theta \sim \pi(j)$. By Def. 3, there must be a rule $r'_1, \ldots, r'_m \rightarrow r'_0$ in T and a substitution σ such that for each $\ell \in \{0, \ldots, m\}$, $r_\ell = r'_\ell\sigma$. Thus for each $k \in \{1, \ldots, m\}$, we have $j < i$ such that $r'_k(\sigma\theta) = (r'_k\sigma)\theta = r_k\theta \sim \pi(j)$. Thus we obtain $r'_0(\sigma\theta) = r_0\theta \sim \pi(i)$ using the rule $r'_1, \ldots, r'_m \rightarrow r'_0$.

Lemma 2. *If π is a derivation for f from T modulo XOR, then $\ulcorner\pi\urcorner$ is a derivation for f from $T_n^\oplus$.*

Proof. Let S be the set of session identifiers occurring in π and suppose its size is n. By Def. 3, we obtain a multi-session theory T_n using S. From Lem. 15 in [10], we know if π' is a derivation for f from T_n modulo XOR, then $\ulcorner\pi'\urcorner$ is a syntactic derivation for f from $T_n^\oplus$. Thus, to prove this lemma, it suffices to prove π is also a derivation from T_n. Now, we have to prove each $\pi(i)$ is obtained by a derivation modulo XOR from T_n and $\pi_{<i}$.

Suppose $\pi(i)$ is obtained from a rule $r_1, \ldots, r_m \rightarrow r_0$ in T. Then there exists a substitution θ with $r_0\theta = \pi(i)$ such that for each $k \in \{1, \ldots, m\}$, we have $j < i$ and $r_k\sigma = \pi(j)$. The domain of θ can be divided into two parts; session identifiers V_1 and C-variables V_2. It is clear that there exist two substitutions σ and θ' such that $r_j\theta = r_j\sigma\theta'$ where $dom(\sigma) = V_1$ and $dom(\theta') = V_2$. From Def. 3, there exists a rule $r'_1, \ldots, r'_m \rightarrow r'_0$ in T_n such that for each $\ell \in \{0, \ldots, m\}$ $r'_\ell = r_\ell\sigma$. Thus we obtain $\pi(i) = (r_0\sigma)\theta' = r'_0\theta'$ from $r'_1, \ldots, r'_m \rightarrow r'_0$.

From the above two lemmas, we immediately obtain that $T \vdash_\oplus f$ iff $T_n^\oplus \vdash f$.

4   Optimizations of XOR-Reduction

4.1   Optimization Based on Nonce Freshness

Recall that a protocol model in a Horn theory T consists of a set of rules r_i ($i \in \{1, \ldots n\}$) of the form $I(t_1), \ldots, I(t_i) \rightarrow I(s_i)$. Such rules should be read as "after receiving the messages $t_1, \ldots, t_i$ the agent sends s_i". The terms on both sides may contain C-variables to which substitutions are applied in the XOR-reduction process. Consider a rule r_i in which some t_j ($1 < j \leq i$) and s_i contain a variable x. If r_i generates a nonce m, substituting m for x may lead to false attacks. For example, applying substitution $\sigma(x) = m(b, a) \oplus x$ to rule (6) gives

$$\{m(b, a) \oplus x, a\}_{pub(sk_b)} \rightarrow \{m(b, a), b \oplus x\}_{pub(sk_a)},$$

indicating a pre-play of the nonce $m(b, a)$ by the adversary, contradicting freshness of nonces. We call rules that are vulnerable to this type of illegal substitutions *challenging rules*. To identify challenging rules we assume a strict total order $\prec$ on protocol rules of a role according to the execution order of the protocol steps, and use $t \sqsubseteq r$ to denote that a term t appears in the Horn clause r (formally t is a subterm of the left-hand side or right-hand side of the rule r).

Definition 4 (Challenging Rule). *Let M be the set of nonces occurring in a Horn theory and $R = \{r_1, \cdots, r_n\}$ the corresponding set of protocol rules. We say r_i is a challenging rule if there exists $m \in M$ such that $m \sqsubseteq r_i$ and for each $r_j \in R$ such that $r_j \prec r_i$, $m \not\sqsubseteq r_j$.*

We now define which terms in a clause can be cancelled by applying a substitution to them.

Definition 5 (Cancelling Term Set). *Let t be a C-dominated term and $s \sqsubseteq t$ be a fragile term. We define the set of cancelling terms $\mathcal{N}(s, t)$ to be a set of terms such that there exists a substitution for s resulting in cancellation of another subterm of t:*

$$\mathcal{N}(s, t) = \{s' | \exists u \text{ s.t. } s \oplus u \oplus s' \sqsubseteq t \vee s' \oplus u \oplus s \sqsubseteq t\}.$$

For example, the cancelling term set $\mathcal{N}(x, t)$ for $t = m(a, b) \oplus x \oplus a$ is $\{m(a, b), a\}$.

Now, let M be a set of nonces that are freshly generated in rule r. We can restrict the set of C-dominated substitutions for r to substitutions that do not cancel any term with $m \in M$.

Definition 6 (Legal Substitution). *Let t be a C-dominated term and M be the set of nonces that are freshly generated. Then σ is a legal substitution for t if it contains all variables x that occur in t and for each x one of the following three cases holds:*

  i. *$\sigma(x) = x$,*
 ii. *$x \in \mathcal{F}(t), \sigma(x) = c \oplus x$ for some $c \in C_{norm}^{\oplus}, c \neq 0$ and for each $m \in M$, there does not exist $n \in \mathcal{N}(x, t)$ such that $m \sqsubseteq n \wedge n \sqsubseteq c$.*
iii. *if x occurs in a fragile subterm s and there exists a substitution σ' in normal form satisfying $s\sigma' \in C^{\oplus}$ and for each $m \in M$, there does not exist $n \in \mathcal{N}(s, t)$ such that $m \sqsubseteq n \wedge n \sqsubseteq s\sigma'$, then $\sigma(x) = \sigma'(x)$.*

Recall that there are 128 substitutions for clause (17). Clearly, $\mathcal{N}(x, t)$ is $\{m(a, a), a\}$ where $t = m(a, a) \oplus x \oplus a$. Since $m(a, a)$ is fresh in this challenging rule, $M = \{m(a, a)\}$. According to Def. 6, any substitution in cases (ii) and (iii) having $m(a, a)$ as a subterm is not legal. For instance, the substitutions such as $\sigma(x) = m(a, a) \oplus x$ and $\sigma(x) = m(a, a) \oplus n(a, a)$ are removed. Applying this optimization removes 64 rules.

4.2   Optimization Based on Session Ordering

The bounded verification that we have introduced in Sect. 3 extends the class of XOR-protocols that can be automatically verified. However, their verification is often inefficient. Recall that the number of rules of an XOR-reduced protocol grows exponentially in the size of the dominating set. Therefore, in particular the verification of protocols that are nonce-$\oplus$-linear but not $\oplus$-linear becomes less efficient if the number of sessions grows. In this section, we aim to reduce the number of rules obtained from the XOR-reduction process by computing a dominating set for each rule with fragile subterms.

We first observe that the session identifiers we introduced in Sect. 3 are only needed to disambiguate nonces from different sessions. They carry no other information and do not appear anywhere else in the protocol specification. We can therefore enforce an order on the challenging rules that create these nonces. In the following we assume that each role of a protocol contains at most one challenging rule, but we note that our theory can be extended to roles with more than one challenging rule.

Let $Cr(s_i)$ be the challenging rule of an agent in session $s_i \in \{s_1, \ldots, s_n\}$. In these sessions, the agent plays the same role and communicates with the same partner as well. We now extend the order $\prec$ introduced in Sect. 4.1 by defining the order between these challenging rules such that $Cr(s_i) \prec Cr(s_j)$ if and only if $i < j$. The main observation for this optimization is that by fixing an order on the execution of the challenging rules, we can eliminate illegal substitutions. In order to do so, we compute a dominating set for each rule having fragile subterms separately. This dominating set only contains nonces that have been generated in previous sessions (based on $\prec$).

As a starting point we take a dominating set C (see Sect. 2.1). We then eliminate terms that contain subterms that are generated in later challenging rules. Let $Nt(Cr)$ denote the set of nonces generated in challenging rule Cr. Then the dominating set C' for rule r is defined by the set C from which any term that depends on a nonce that is generated after or in r is eliminated:

$$C'(r) = \{s \in C | \text{there does not exist } n \in \bigcup_{r \prec r'} Nt(r') \cup Nt(r) \text{ s.t. } n \sqsubseteq s\}.$$

With the size of the dominating set decreasing, the number of substitutions decreases as well. Consider an instance of rule (9) in $NSL'_\oplus$-auth. Suppose two sessions s_1 and s_2 in which agent b plays role B and talks to a. Let r_1 and r_2 represent the rules in session s_1 and s_2 respectively:

$$I(\{x, a\}_{pub(sk_b)}) \rightarrow I(\{m(b, a, s_1), m(b, a, s_1) \oplus x \oplus b\}_{pub(sk_a)})$$
$$I(\{x, a\}_{pub(sk_b)}) \rightarrow I(\{m(b, a, s_2), m(b, a, s_2) \oplus x \oplus b\}_{pub(sk_a)})$$

Since they are both challenging rules with $Nt(r_1) = \{m(b, a, s_1)\}$ and $Nt(r_2) = \{m(b, a, s_2)\}$, and we also have $r_1 \prec r_2$, the dominating set $C'(r_1)$ cannot contain terms with $m(b, a, s_1)$ and $m(b, a, s_2)$ as subterms.

4.3   Secrecy-Based Authentication Verification

By the result of Comon-Lundh and Cortier [13], we need one more participant to verify authentication than secrecy (see Sect. 2.2). Therefore, Horn theories for verifying authentication are generally bigger than models of the same protocols for verifying secrecy. The situation becomes worse when bounded verification is applied. We propose to optimize verification of authentication properties by first verifying secrecy for certain terms in the Horn theory.

Consider two nonce-$\oplus$-linear Horn theories T_{sec} and T_{auth}. Let F be the set of facts that ProVerif will check for their secrecy when deriving the goals in T_{auth}. With the results from the secrecy verification for F using T_{sec}, we can prevent ProVerif from deriving these facts during authentication verification.

For the sake of efficiency, F should be carefully chosen. Typically, F contains shared keys and C-dominated terms. The observation is that by this choice we can eliminate the rules violating secrecy after reduction. For example, for $NSL'_{\oplus}$ after reduction of its two-session model, we have a rule:

$$I(\{n(a,b,s_1),c\}_{pub(sk_b)}) \rightarrow I(\{m(b,c,s_1),m(b,c,s_1)\oplus n(a,b,s_1)\oplus b\}_{pub(sk_c)}).$$

If we know that $n(a,b,s_1)$ is secret, according to this rule and the $\oplus$-rule the intruder can obtain it after decrypting the message and computing the XOR of $m(b,c,s_1)\oplus n(a,b,s_1)\oplus b$ with $m(b,c,s_1)$ and b. This contradicts the secrecy of $n(a,b,s_1)$. To identify these rules, we define *secrecy-violating rules*:

Definition 7 (Secrecy-violating Rule). *Let S be a set of verified secrets and r be a reduced rule. We say r is a secrecy-violating rule if after repeatedly using the intruder rules, the intruder can obtain a secret $t \in S$.*

This optimization concentrates on finding secrecy-violating rules in order to reduce the size of the resulting Horn theory. Therefore, we can improve the efficiency of verification using ProVerif. We only implemented a light-weight process to remove some of the rules automatically. How to remove all such rules is an interesting research topic.

4.4   RFID-Based Optimizations

Radio frequency identification (RFID) systems are used to identify tagged objects through wireless channels. Since tags must be manufactured at a very low cost, only simple operations can be performed by the tag. Therefore, XOR is an operator that is often used in RFID protocols. Compared to general security protocols, RFID protocols have their own characteristics that allow optimization of the verification process. In this section, we discuss three characteristics and present their corresponding optimizations.

During communications, readers are initiators and they aim to authenticate tags. Tags receive challenges and run the steps described by the protocol. For this reason, an agent can only play one role: an agent is either *reader* or *tag*. This allows us to simplify the Horn theories for verification of authentication. For instance, assume $NSL'_{\oplus}$ is used as an RFID protocol and let the set of protocol participants be $\{tag, reader, intruder\}$. In rule (8) of $NSL'_{\oplus}$-auth, a can only be substituted by *reader* while b can be substituted by either *tag* or *intruder*.

Since information such as keys is embedded in tags, only the readers of the same system can talk to tags. Moreover, tags always belong to one RFID system. There never exist secrets shared between the intruder and tags. We therefore do not model the intruder as an insider, preventing the derivation of insider-attacks.

In particular, we propose to remove the rules in which *tag* believes to be talking to *intruder*. For example, with the assumption that $NSL'_\oplus$ is an RFID protocol, in rule (9), we have $a \in \{tag\}, b \in \{reader\}$. In this way, we decrease the number of Horn clauses in the model. In particular, the size of dominating set will be smaller as a number of nonces is removed.

We observe that tags are manufactured in such a way that they can only have one active protocol execution at a time. Therefore, we do not have to model attacks that rely on a parallel execution of two or more runs of one tag. Hence, a tag's runs are completely sequential. For bounded verification, the order $\prec$ introduced in Sect. 4.1 can be extended to all rules of the tag. Suppose there are ℓ rules in a session and n sessions are modeled in total. Let $r(i, s_k)$ be the rule that represents the ith step of the tag in session $s_k \in \{s_1, \ldots, s_n\}$. Given $i, j \le \ell, k_1, k_2 \le n$, we have $r(i, s_{k_1}) \prec r(j, s_{k_2})$ if $(i < j \wedge k_1 = k_2) \vee (k_1 < k_2)$. Now, the optimization in Sect. 4.2 can be applied to the simplified models with the strict order on the tag's rules.

4.5   Optimization Based on $\oplus$-Rule Reduction

In the implementation of XorProverif, Küsters and Truderung introduce a compact way to represent clauses (13)-(16). They do not keep all the copies for every pair $c, c' \in C_{norm}^\oplus$, but rather introduce a function $xtab(c, c', \ulcorner c \oplus c' \urcorner)$ to denote clauses of the form of (13). The Horn clauses (14)-(16) are represented below:

$$xarg(x), I(x), I(y) \rightarrow I(x \oplus y)) \tag{18}$$

$$xarg(x), I(x \oplus y), I(x) \rightarrow I(y) \tag{19}$$

$$xtab(x, y, z), I(x \oplus t), I(y) \rightarrow I(z \oplus t) \tag{20}$$

$$xtab(x, y, z), I(x \oplus t), I(y \oplus t) \rightarrow I(z) \tag{21}$$

where $xarg(x)$ denotes $x \in C_{norm}^\oplus$ in the first two clauses and x, y, z are variables in the last two. When instantiating rule (20) with the substitution $\{a/x, b/y, \ulcorner a \oplus b \urcorner / z\}$, we have $xtab(a, b, \ulcorner a \oplus b \urcorner), I(a \oplus t), I(b) \rightarrow I(\ulcorner a \oplus b \urcorner \oplus t)$. Similarly, for substitution $\{b/x, a/y, \ulcorner a \oplus b \urcorner / z\}$ we have $xtab(b, a, \ulcorner a \oplus b \urcorner), I(b \oplus t), I(a) \rightarrow I(\ulcorner a \oplus b \urcorner \oplus t)$. As shown by this example, rule (20) requires both $xtab(a, b, \ulcorner a \oplus b \urcorner)$ and $xtab(b, a, \ulcorner a \oplus b \urcorner)$ existing in the Horn theory to capture both scenarios. By introducing the following symmetric clause to rule (20)

$$xtab(x, y, z), I(y \oplus t), I(x) \rightarrow I(z \oplus t)$$

we can remove $xtab(b, a, \ulcorner a \oplus b \urcorner)$ as long as $xtab(a, b, \ulcorner a \oplus b \urcorner)$ remains in the Horn theory in the previous example, since the second substitution is captured by the newly introduced clause. In this way, we can remove rules of the form $xtab(a, b, \ulcorner a \oplus b \urcorner)$. With the size of the dominating set $C_{norm}^\oplus$ becoming larger, the number of reduced rules also becomes larger.

5   Implementation and Experiments

In order to validate our ideas, we have built an implementation [14] of the bounded verification (as descried in Sect. 3) and the optimizations (as described in Sect. 4). In order to check the effects of our improvements, we have compared our implementation with that of XorProverif.

5.1   Implementation

We use SWI prolog for our implementation. The input Horn theory consists of three parts: (1) declaration of function symbols that are used in the theory, (2) necessary initial intruder facts, intruder rules, and protocol rules, (3) verification goals, either secrecy or authentication. We introduce a function *nonce* to declare nonces, and an auxiliary function to provide necessary information about a protocol rule including its position and session. The latter is needed in order to implement optimizations in Sect. 4.

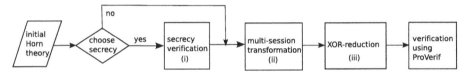

Fig. 2. Structure of the implementation

As shown in Fig. 2, our implementation mainly performs three steps. Each step takes the output of its previous step as the input Horn theory and outputs a new Horn theory after. The input Horn theory at the very beginning must be nonce-$\oplus$-linear. Step (i) is optional. It can choose a set of terms to check if they are secret, and the results of the secrecy verification are added to the output. Step (ii) transforms its input into a multi-session $\oplus$-linear model, which is necessary for bounded verification (see Sect. 3). Step (iii) checks $\oplus$-linearity and computes C-dominating sets as done by XorProverif. It also applies optimizations as described in Sect. 4 whenever possible and reduces the Horn theory to the XOR-free one. In the end, ProVerif performs the last part of the verification.

5.2   Experiments

We first present experimental results for secrecy verification with optimizations applied to the XOR-reduction step and compare them with XorProverif (see Tab. 1). Then we apply bounded verification to a number of nonce-$\oplus$-linear protocols including some RFID protocols to check authentication (see Tab. 2). All experiments are performed on a Dell Latitude E5500 laptop with a 2.26GHz Intel Core™ 2 Duo P8400 processor and 2GB RAM.

Secrecy verification. We first describe the protocols in that we use for our experiments.

The first protocol we consider is our running example $NSL'_\oplus$-sec. We propose two fixes to the protocol that counter the attack depicted in Sect. 2.2. In $NSL'_\oplus$-fix-0, we replace the message $\{m, m \oplus n \oplus b\}_{pub(sk_a)}$ with $\{m \oplus n, b\}_{pub(sk_a)}$ and in $NSL'_\oplus$-fix-1 with $\{m, h(m \oplus n) \oplus b\}_{pub(sk_a)}$, where h denotes a hash function. Note that these protocols are only meant to fix the secrecy flaw.

The protocol $NSL_\oplus$ is the example used by Küsters and Truderung [10] where the second message is of the form $\{m, n \oplus b\}_{pub(sk_a)}$. CCA is short for Common Cryptographic Architecture (CCA) API [15], designed by IBM. This series of CCA protocols are also checked by Küsters and Truderung [10].

Inspired by Millen's ffgg protocol [16], we design a family of protocols which we call *fgms*. The family contains protocols that can be attacked in n sessions, but not in $n - 1$ sessions, for any n. In order to attack the secrecy claim, the algebraic properties of $\oplus$ need to be used.

The specification of fgms-2, the protocol that can be attacked in two sessions but not in one, is as follows. Role A and B initially share a secret k. An agent in role A initiates the protocol by sending $\{n_a, k\}_k$ to B. The agent playing role B does not verify the values of n_a and k inside the encryption, but only the encryption key k. He then generates a nonce n_b and replies with $\langle x, n_b, \{n_b \oplus y, x\}_k \rangle$. The protocol is shown in Fig. 3.

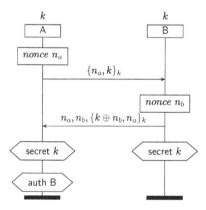

Fig. 3. Description of the fgms-2 protocol

We can obtain the protocol fgms-3 by adding an extra nonce to both messages. The first message is replaced by $\{n_a, n'_a, k\}_k$ and the second message by $n_a, n_b, \{n'_a \oplus n_b, k, n_a\}_k$. In a similar way fgms-n for any $n > 2$ can be designed.

Tab. 1 gives the reduction time required by XorProverif (referred to as 'XPv') and our implementation (referred to as 'optimized'), and the ProVerif verification time with and without our optimizations. From the results, we observe a big improvement for $NSL'_\oplus$ and its fixes, if our optimization for secrecy is applied. For the CCA protocols, due to the optimization in Sect. 4.5, the analysis also becomes more efficient. For the fgms family of protocols, without our optimization ProVerif cannot terminate.

Table 1. Results for secrecy verification (n.t. for non-terminating)

XOR-protocols	correct	reduction		ProVerif time		saved
		XPv	optimized	- opt.	+ opt.	
$NSL'_\oplus$-sec	no	0.67s	0.52s	16.12s	7.16s	55.6%
$NSL'_\oplus$-fix-0	yes	0.13s	0.12s	0.14s	0.08s	42.9%
$NSL'_\oplus$-fix-1	yes	0.71s	0.53s	14.95s	6.60s	55.9%
$NSL_\oplus$	no	0.07s	0.07s	0.02s	0.01s	50%
CCA-0	no	0.24s	0.22s	129s	117s	9.3%
CCA-1A	yes	0.09s	0.09s	0.69s	0.64s	7.2%
CCA-1B	yes	0.12s	0.11s	1.17s	1.11s	5.1%
CCA-2B	yes	0.20s	0.18s	12.7s	10.4s	18.1%
CCA-2C	yes	0.25s	0.22s	69.60s	64.34s	7.6%
CCA-2E	yes	0.09s	0.09s	1.48s	1.34s	9.5%
fgms-2	no	0.06s	0.06s	n.t.	0.21s	-
fgms-3	no	0.07s	0.07s	n.t.	0.37s	-
fgms-4	no	0.07s	0.07s	n.t.	0.40s	-
fgms-5	no	0.08s	0.08s	n.t.	0.51s	-

Bounded verification of authentication properties. For the analysis of our verification method for authentication we use the following protocols.

The protocols containing $NSL'_\oplus$ in their names include our running example and one of its fixes. Lee et al. [17] and Song and Mitchell [18] proposed RFID protocols, which we call LAK06 and SM08 after the last names of the

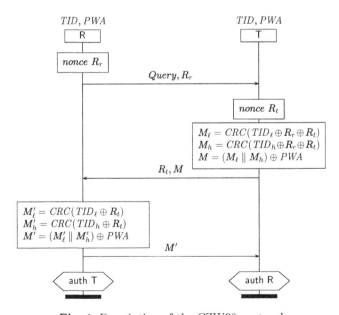

Fig. 4. Description of the CZW08 protocol

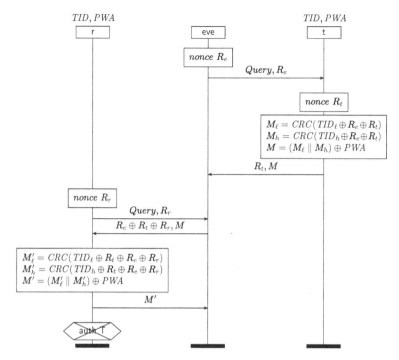

Fig. 5. An attack on the CZW08 protocol

authors. Attacks on both protocols have been reported by Van Deursen and Radomirović [19]. We also analyze a variant of the protocol by Choi et al. [20] (CLL09).

Our final example is the mutual RFID authentication protocol proposed by Cai et al. [21], which is depicted in Fig. 4. In order to comply with the EPCglobal C1G2 specification, the protocol only uses a 16-bit Pseudo-Random Number Generator (PRNG) and a 16-bit Cyclic Redundancy Check (CRC). The reader R and tag T share secrets TID (*Tag Identifier*) and PWA (*Access Password*). The reader starts by sending a query and a nonce R_r. The tag generates a nonce R_t and computes the XOR of PWA and the concatenation of M_ℓ and M_h, as given in Fig. 4.

The reader checks the the correctness of the received message before sending the response. Burmester et al. give two attacks on the protocol [22], which both rely on the homomorphic properties of CRC functions.

Using our prototype, we find a new attack on tag authentication using bounded verification. To impersonate a tag the intruder proceeds as follows. He challenges the tag with any nonce R_e and obtains the reply $\langle R_t, (CRC(TID_l \oplus R_e \oplus R_t) \parallel CRC(TID_h \oplus R_e \oplus R_t)) \oplus PWA \rangle$. This message suffices for the intruder to respond to any reader challenge R_r by replacing R_t in the message with $R_e \oplus R_r \oplus R_t$. The attack is depicted in Fig. 5.

Tab. 2 gives the number of sessions (#sid) used for multi-session transformation, the time used for our optimized XOR-reduction, the verification time taken

Table 2. Results of bounded verification of authentication

XOR-protocols	correct	#sid	reduction	ProVerif time		saved	#derivations	
				- opt.	+ opt.		- opt.	+ opt.
$NSL'_\oplus$-authA	no	1	4.47s	17.67s	7.39s	58.2%	2	1
$NSL'_\oplus$-authA-fix-0	yes	1	6.50s	0.132	0.072s	45.5%	1	1
$NSL'_\oplus$-authA-fix-0	yes	2	97.2s	6916s	2907s	58.0%	2	2
$NSL'_\oplus$-authB-fix-0	no	1	3.01s	0.32s	0.08s	75.0%	1	1
LAK06	no	1	0.152s	0.012s	0.004s	66.7%	8	4
SM08	no	1	0.128s	0.036s	0.016s	55.6%	8	4
CLL09	yes	1	0.068s	0.124s	0.064s	48.4%	13	5
CLL09	no	2	0.62s	244.4s	139.4s	42.9%	156	14
CZW08	no	1	0.17s	0.064s	0.028s	56.2%	8	4

by ProVerif after the multi-session transformation (without the optimizations) and our bounded verification with optimizations, and the number of generated derivations (#derivations). For general protocols, we apply the optimization in Sect. 4.2. For RFID protocols, the optimization in Sect. 4.4 is also applied. The table clearly shows that our optimizations can reduce both the verification time by ProVerif, and the number of derivations.

6   Conclusion and Future Work

In this paper, we have focused on the verification of security protocols with XOR. We improve the XOR-reduction approach of Küsters and Truderung [10] for the verification of XOR-protocols modeled by Horn theories.

First, we extend their approach for authentication verification to a richer class of XOR protocols using the idea of bounded verification. We consider session identifiers as constants instead of variables [10] and verify protocols using models with a bounded number of sessions. The corresponding transformation process is performed automatically.

Second, we make their approach more efficient by developing a number of dedicated optimizations including the usage of freshness of generated nonces and secrecy of certain terms to reduce the number of substitutions, restricting session order in our bounded verification, and exploring the specific characteristics of RFID protocols. All these ideas have been implemented in a prototype. The experimental results show the feasibility of our methods and the reduction in verification time by ProVerif looks in all respects promising. We also found a new attack on a recently proposed RFID protocol.

We conjecture that our optimizations presented in the current paper do not sacrifice the soundness of Küsters and Truderung's approach. However, their formal correctness proofs are left for the future. There are several ways to proceed. Our implementation is still preliminary, we want to improve it and test it with more experiments. Especially we are interested in bigger examples. We want to extend our work by identifying more optimizations. Küsters and Truderung have extended their reduction approach to protocols with Diffie-Hellman exponentiation [23]. It will be interesting to see to what extent our optimizations can be applied to those protocols as well.

Acknowledgement. We thank the anonymous referees for their valuable comments.

References

1. Lowe, G.: Breaking and fixing the Needham-Schroeder public-key protocol using FDR. In: Margaria, T., Steffen, B. (eds.) TACAS 1996. LNCS, vol. 1055, Springer, Heidelberg (1996)
2. Dolev, D., Yao, A.C.C.: On the security of public key protocols. IEEE Transactions on Information Theory 29(2), 198–207 (1983)
3. Blanchet, B.: An efficient cryptographic protocol verifier based on prolog rules. In: Proc. 14th IEEE Computer Security Foundations Workshop, pp. 82–96. IEEE Computer Society, Los Alamitos (2001)
4. Cremers, C., Lafourcade, P., Nadeau, P.: Comparing state spaces in automatic protocol analysis. In: Formal to Practical Security. LNCS, vol. 5458, pp. 70–94. Springer, Heidelberg (2009)
5. Cortier, V., Delaune, S., Lafourcade, P.: A survey of algebraic properties used in cryptographic protocols. Journal of Computer Security 14(1), 1–43 (2006)
6. Comon-Lundh, H., Shmatikov, V.: Intruder deductions, constraint solving and insecurity decision in presence of exclusive or. In: Proc. 8th Annual IEEE Symposium on Logic in Computer Science, pp. 271–280. IEEE Computer Society Press, Los Alamitos (2003)
7. Comon-Lundh, H., Delaune, S.: The finite variant property: How to get rid of some algebraic properties. In: Giesl, J. (ed.) RTA 2005. LNCS, vol. 3467, pp. 294–307. Springer, Heidelberg (2005)
8. Cortier, V., Keighren, G., Steel, G.: Automatic analysis of the security of XOR-based key management schemes. In: Grumberg, O., Huth, M. (eds.) TACAS 2007. LNCS, vol. 4424, pp. 538–552. Springer, Heidelberg (2007)
9. Lowe, G.: Casper: A compiler for the analysis of security protocols. In: Proc. 10th Computer Security Foundations Workshop, pp. 18–30. IEEE Computer Society Press, Los Alamitos (1997)
10. Küsters, R., Truderung, T.: Reducing protocol analysis with XOR to the XOR-free case in the horn theory based approach. In: Proc. 15th ACM Conference on Computer and Communications Security, pp. 129–138. ACM Press, New York (2008)
11. Blanchet, B.: Automatic verification of correspondences for security protocols. Journal of Computer Security 17(4), 363–434 (2009)
12. Needham, R.M., Schroeder, M.D.: Using encryption for authentication in large networks of computers. Communications of the ACM 21(12), 993–999 (1978)
13. Comon-Lundh, H., Cortier, V.: Security properties: two agents are sufficient. Science of Computer Programming 50(1-3), 51–71 (2004)
14. Chen, X., van Deursen, T., Pang, J.: Improving automatic verification of protocols with XOR (implementation) (2009), http://satoss.uni.lu/software/
15. International Business Machines Corporation: CCA basic services reference and guide (2003), http://www-306.ibm.com/security/cryptocards/pdfs/CCA_Basic_Services_241_Revised_20030918.pdf

16. Millen, J.K.: A necessarily parallel attack. In: Proc. Workshop on Formal Methods and Security Protocols (1999)
17. Lee, S., Asano, T., Kim, K.: RFID mutual authentication scheme based on synchronized secret information. In: Proc. Symposium on Cryptography and Information Security (2006)
18. Song, B., Mitchell, C.J.: RFID authentication protocol for low-cost tags. In: Proc. 2nd ACM Conference on Wireless Network Security, pp. 140–147. ACM Press, New York (2008)
19. van Deursen, T., Radomirović, S.: Algebraic attacks on RFID protocols. In: Jaap-Henk, H. (ed.) WISTP 2009. LNCS, vol. 5746, pp. 38–51. Springer, Heidelberg (2009)
20. Choi, E.Y., Lee, D.H., Lim, J.I.: Anti-cloning protocol suitable to EPCglobal class-1 generation-2 RFID systems. Computer Standards & Interfaces (in press, 2009)
21. Cai, Q., Zhan, Y., Wang, Y.: A minimalist mutual authentication protocol for RFID system and BAN logic analysis. In: Proc. ISECS Colloquium on Computing, Communication, Control and Management, pp. 449–453 (2008)
22. Burmester, M., Medeiros, B., Munilla, J., Peinado, A.: Secure EPC gen2 compliant radio frequency identification (2009), http://eprint.iacr.org/
23. Küsters, R., Truderung, T.: Using ProVerif to analyze protocols with Diffie-Hellman exponentiation. In: Proc. 22th IEEE Computer Security Foundations Symposium, pp. 157–171. IEEE Computer Society, Los Alamitos (2009)

Modeling and Verification of Privacy Enhancing Protocols

Suriadi Suriadi, Chun Ouyang, Jason Smith, and Ernest Foo

Queensland University of Technology, Australia
{s.suriadi,c.ouyang,j4.smith,e.foo}@qut.edu.au

Abstract. Privacy enhancing protocols (PEPs) are a family of protocols that allow secure exchange and management of sensitive user information. They are important in preserving users' privacy in today's open environment. Proof of the correctness of PEPs is necessary before they can be deployed. However, the traditional provable security approach, though well established for verifying cryptographic primitives, is not applicable to PEPs. We apply the formal method of Coloured Petri Nets (CPNs) to construct an executable specification of a representative PEP, namely the Private Information Escrow Bound to Multiple Conditions Protocol (PIEMCP). Formal semantics of the CPN specification allow us to reason about various security properties of PIEMCP using state space analysis techniques. This investigation provides us with preliminary insights for modeling and verification of PEPs in general, demonstrating the benefit of applying the CPN-based formal approach to proving the correctness of PEPs.

1 Introduction

As a response to the increasing number of incidents compromising the privacy of millions of users [1], there has been an increase in the research related to privacy enhancing protocols (PEPs). PEP is a generic term that refers to protocols whose main purpose is to preserve users privacy in an open communication environment (e.g. over the Internet). For example, emulating the off-line anonymity afforded by cash transactions, a PEP ensures that when a user purchases goods on-line, the on-line seller does not learn the identity of the user. A PEP normally *applies* complex cryptographic primitives (such as custodian-hiding group encryption and verifiable encryption) to achieve the privacy-enhancing features. Recently, the Trusted Platform Module (TPM) technology - which provides secure hardware storage of cryptographic keys and implementation of common cryptographic primitives - has also been used in PEPs [2].

An important issue in the design of applied cryptographic protocols, such as PEPs, is to ensure they work correctly and do not contain errors that may weaken the original security protections provided by the cryptographic primitives employed. Formal methods are necessary for the construction of unambiguous and precise models that can be analysed to identify errors and verify correctness before implementation. The application of formal methods has been demonstrated

K. Breitman and A. Cavalcanti (Eds.): ICFEM 2009, LNCS 5885, pp. 127–146, 2009.
© Springer-Verlag Berlin Heidelberg 2009

to lead to reliable and trustworthy security protocols [3, 4, 5]. However, to the best of our knowledge, no existing work provides a formal verification of PEPs.

In the domain of cryptography, the main method to verify a cryptographic primitive is the provable security approach [6]. This approach aims to prove some standard security properties of cryptographic primitives by reducing the proof of those properties to some hard (normally mathematical) problem within the context of a simplified standard attack model with well-defined boundaries (such as the random oracle model). It is however not suitable for verification of PEPs and the reasons are two-fold. On the one hand, the security properties of a PEP are *behavioral* properties and proof of these properties can hardly be reduced to pure mathematical problems. On the other hand, the simplified assumptions employed in the provable security approach are not applicable to PEPs due to the expanded threat environment in which PEPs operate. In PEPs, one needs to consider attacks introduced by the existence of multi-party entities and attacks targeted at the *design* of a protocol, not directly at the cryptographic primitives employed. The lack of computer-aided tools in the provable security approach also makes such an approach not scalable when modeling and verifying a large system such as PEPs. While provable security has been used to verify certain types of protocols (notably key establishment protocols), we note that it is nevertheless not suitable to verify behavioral properties.

Coloured Petri Nets (CPNs) [7] are a widely-used formal method for system specification, design, simulation and verification. They provide a graphical-oriented modeling language capable of expressing concurrency, synchronisation, non-determinism, and system concepts at different levels of abstraction. CPNs combine Petri nets [8] and the functional programming language Standard ML (SML) [9]. Petri nets are used to model concurrency, synchronisation and resource sharing, and support an abundance of analysis techniques such as the well-known state space techniques. SML is used to capture data manipulation and to create compact and parameterisable models. CPN Tools [10] is a graphical tool supporting the construction, simulation and analysis of CPN models.

In this paper, we propose a CPN-based approach for modeling and verification of PEPs. CPNs are used to construct a formal specification of a representative PEP, namely the Private Information Escrow Bound to Multiple Conditions Protocol (PIEMCP) [11]. PIEMCP involves large multi-party communication and employs complex cryptographic primitives and TPM functionalities. The hierarchical structuring mechanism of CPNs supports a modular and systematic approach in capturing the behavior of PIEMCP at different levels of abstraction. Using SML, a wide variety of cryptographic primitives and the processing of these primitives are captured in meta-models that are embedded in higher levels of the protocol operations. By parameterising the protocol model with different types of attacks, a large number of attack scenarios are captured for analysis. The CPN model of PIEMCP is executable and can be analysed to verify the security behavior of the protocol. The analysis of PIEMCP is performed using the state space generated from the parameterized CPN model and the selective runtime protocol session data stored as external files.

The contributions of this paper are two-fold. First of all, it demonstrates the use of CPN to model and verify the security behavior of PEPs. To the best of our knowledge, this is the first attempt at the formal verification of a PEP. Secondly, the paper proposes several modeling and analysis techniques that have been applied to other PEPs [12, 13]. These techniques may be used as preliminary guidelines for a general CPN-based approach for modeling and verification of PEPs. Also, efficiency is another major concern in PEPs due to the use of resource-intensive cryptographic primitives. The CPN model of PIEMCP developed in this paper can be easily extended in the future to allow a simultaneous analysis of both the protocol performance and security behavior.

The rest of the paper is structured as follows. Sect. 2 provides some background information about PIEMCP. Sect. 3 proposes the modeling approach and describes selected parts of the CPN model of PIEMCP. Based on this CPN model, Sect. 4 details the verification of a set of security behaviors of PIEMCP. Sect. 5 reviews related research efforts. Finally, in Sect. 6 we summarize our contribution and discuss future work.

2   Overview of PIEMCP

The PIEMCP [11] is used in a federated single-sign on (FSSO) environment whereby a user only has to authenticate once to an identity provider (IdP) to access services from multiple service providers (SPs). The entities involved are users, IdPs, SPs, and an anonymity revocation manager (ARM) or some referees. An IdP assures SPs that although users are anonymous, when certain conditions are fulfilled, the users' identities can be revealed. A user's identity refers to a set of personally identifiable information (PII). Although the services that SPs provide can be delivered without the need of PII, they require the PII to be revealed by an ARM *or* some referees when certain conditions are satisfied.

The PIEMCP consists of four stages, namely PII escrow (PE), key escrow (KE), multiple conditions (MC) binding, and revocation. An execution of the protocol involves two distinct sessions: the *escrow session* which consists of a sequential execution of the PE, KE and MC stages, and the *revocation session* which consists of an execution of the revocation stage. A user can run n escrow sessions, during which his/her PII is hidden (anonymous). At least one escrow session has to be completed before a revocation session can start. During the revocation session, the user's PII linked to a specific SP in a specific escrow session is revealed. For n escrow sessions, each with m-number of SPs, up to $n \times m$ revocation sessions can be performed.

The PIEMCP has two variants: the first variant (PIEMCP-T) uses a trusted ARM for anonymity revocation, and the second variant (PIEMCP-NT) uses a group of referees instead of ARM. In both variants, most of the operations, especially those in the PE, KE and MC stages, are performed in a similar way. Therefore, we describe the main operations in one of them, the PIEMCP-NT. Fig. 1 depicts the message exchanges between the different entities within the four stages of this protocol.

The *PE stage* begins when a user requests a service from a service provider SP1. This triggers the agreement of conditions (*Cond*1) whose fulfillment allows the PII to be revealed. SP1 then sends a message NT-PE-1 containing *Cond*1 to an IdP to escrow the user's PII. The IdP contacts the user to obtain his encrypted PII. The user encrypts the PII using a Verifiable Encryption (VE) scheme under a freshly generated key pair (public and private keys). The user sends to the IdP NT-PE-2 comprising the VE ciphertext and the public key used for the encryption. The user keeps the private key, which is needed to decrypt the ciphertext. Next, the user and the IdP engage in a cryptographic "proof-of-knowledge" (PK) protocol (NT-PE-3). This is to prove to the IdP that the VE ciphertext given correctly hides some *certified* PII without letting the IdP learn the value of the PII itself. We denote this operation as PKVE. The output of PKVE is an acceptance or rejection of the VE ciphertext.

The *KE stage* is started when the PK-VE outputs an acceptance of the ciphertext. The IdP and the user then engage in another PK protocol - the Direct Anonymous Attestation (DAA) (NT-KE-1). This is to convince the IdP that the user is using a valid TPM device while concealing the identity of the TPM device. A successful DAA prompts the user's TPM to generate (1) a universal custodian-hiding verifiable group encryption (UCHVE) of the VE private key under *Cond*1 and (2) a TPM proof of a correct UCHVE execution. A UCHVE produces n ciphertext pieces for a group of n referees among whom there are t ($t \leq$ n) *designated* referees, and only designated referees can decrypt these ciphertext pieces. At least k ($k \leq t$) decrypted pieces are required to recover the VE private key (i.e. k is the *threshold* value). Both the n ciphertext pieces and the TPM proof are sent to the IdP in NT-KE-2. The IdP then verifies the proof and if correct, prepares a response NT-KE-3 to SP2 which includes the VE of PII (from the PE stage) and the UCHVE of the VE private key. SP1 now has the ciphertext of the PII (from the PE stage) and the ciphertext of the corresponding private key. With the help of referees, SP1 can recover the user's PII when *Cond*1 is fulfilled, but *cannot* decrypt these ciphertexts until that time.

In the *MC stage*, the user goes to another service provider SP2. This time SP2 (instead of SP1 in the PE stage) needs the IdP to escrow the VE private key in NT-MC-1 under different conditions *Cond*2 (*Cond*1 $\neq$ *Cond*2). The IdP requests the user's TPM to produce a new UCHVE ciphertext of the VE private key and the associated TPM proof in NT-MC-2. The user replies with the requested encryption and proof in NT-MC-3. The IdP verifies the proof and if correct, prepares a response NT-MC-4 to SP2 which includes the VE of PII (from the PE stage) and the UCHVE of the VE private key (bound to *Cond*2). SP2 now has the data that, with referees' help, can reveal the PII when *Cond*2 are satisfied, but yet *cannot* decrypt these ciphertexts at this point. Note that the user may go to a third provider SP3, in which case, only the MC stage needs to be executed.

The *revocation stage* is executed when the agreed conditions are satisfied and when a user has completed at least one escrow session. Assuming that *Cond*1 is satisfied, SP1 sends a revocation request NT-REV-1 comprising n ciphertext pieces to the n referees with *Cond*1. Each referee checks if *Cond*1 is fulfilled,

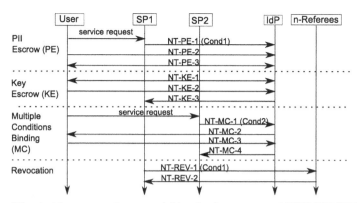

Fig. 1. Message exchanges within the four stages of PIEMCP-NT

and if so, the referee tries to decrypt the given ciphertext piece. Only the designated referees can decrypt the ciphertext pieces. If decryption is successful, each designated referee sends the decrypted data NT-REV-2 to SP1. When k or more decrypted data are received, SP1 can recover the VE private key, and subsequently decrypt the VE ciphertext to recover the PII.

In the above we described the normal execution of PIEMCP-NT (i.e. without attacks). However, each of the parties involved in PIEMCP (both variants) may behave maliciously resulting in different attack scenarios. The design goal of PIEMCP is to achieve the expected security behavior with and without considering the attacks. In the next section, a CPN model of PIEMCP is presented which can be configured to capture possible attack and non-attack senarios. The model is then used as a basis for the verification of PIEMCP in Sect. 4.

3   CPN Model of PIEMCP

CPN Preliminaries. CPNs are a class of high-level nets that enhance Petri nets with data types. A CPN consists of two types of nodes, *places* (drawn as ellipses) and *transitions* (rectangles), and directed edges known as *arcs*. A place is typed by a *color set* and contains collections (*multi-sets*) of data items called *tokens* of the same type as the place. A transition represents an event and may have a *guard* associated with it. The guard is a boolean expression enclosed in square brackets. Arcs connect places to transitions and transitions to places, and are inscribed by expressions comprising variables, constants and functions. Variables are typed and can be assigned values known as *binding*. CPNs use a variant of SML for net inscriptions and declarations of variables and types.

A transition's *input places* have arcs going to the transition, while its *output places* have arcs coming from the transition. A transition is *enabled* if: 1) sufficient tokens exist in each input place to match each respective input arc inscription when evaluated for a particular binding of its variables, and 2) the transition guard evaluates to true for the same binding. If a transition is enabled, it can *occur* (or be *fired*). The occurrence of a transition removes tokens specified by the respective arc inscriptions from input places, and deposits tokens specified by inscriptions on the output arcs into output places. The state of a CPN is called a *marking*. It consists of tokens distributed on each place of the CPN. The occurrence of transitions represent stage changes.

CPNs support hierarchical modeling which facilitates the construction of large models by using a number of CPN modules called *pages*. Each page is linked to a *substitution transition* (sub-transition) at a higher level of the model. By means of the hierarchical structuring mechanism it is possible to capture different abstraction levels of the modeled system in the same CPN model.

3.1   Modeling Approach

The PIEMCP (both variants) is modeled using hierarchical CPNs. There is one top-level (main) page and four sub-pages capturing the four stages of PIEMCP. Each of these sub-pages is named according to the stage it models. The PE page has one further sub-page. The PE page, KE page, and MC page can be executed in a loop to form an escrow session. The number of escrow sessions to be executed is parameterized. The revocation page can be executed after the completion of at least *one* escrow session. Below, we introduce three modeling approaches that are specific to PEPs. These approaches are demonstrated in Sect. 3.2.

Cryptographic primitive abstraction. To capture complex cryptographic behaviors, we firstly model the representation of a ciphertext as a CPN colour set, and then capture its operations by describing them as SML functions. This approach is flexible and inclusive as virtually any type of cryptographic primitives can be captured. The CPN `record` type can encode the necessary information to represent a primitive properly, and the SML can be used to simulate the operations. Expressing cryptographic operations as functions promotes reuse which leads to a cleaner and more concise model. In Sect. 3.2, we demonstrate this approach by modeling a VE ciphertext and a zero-knowledge operation (PK-VE). The complexity of UCHVE ciphertext prevents use from describing it due to the space constraint. However, it is available in the full-version of this paper [14].

We also propose a technique to capture the commonly-used message signing and verification operations. We define a CPN colour set for the message to be signed, followed by a definition of its signature. A signed message is a pair consisting of the message and its signature. The verification of a signed message upon the receipt of the message is *enforced* within a transition guard. If the signature verification fails, the message integrity and/or authenticity are compromised. As a result, the guard returns a false value, thus halting any further processing on the message - an expected fail-stop behavior.

TPM provable execution. We propose an approach to model a TPM's provable execution behavior [15]. Our model depicts how an entity can generate the *expected* TPM proof based on some known information, and compare it with the received TPM-generated output and its corresponding proof. In this way an incorrect TPM-generated output can be detected. The demonstration of this approach is available in the full-version of this paper [14].

parameterized attack. We propose a parameterisation approach to modeling attacks such that one or more attacks can be switched on or off depending on the environmental assumptions. In general, attacks can come from both external intruders (i.e. external entities attempt to access and break the protocol) and malicious insiders (i.e. protocol entities attempt to compromise a users PII to achieve some personal advantage). At this point, we scope our work to only consider malicious insiders - which we think is of a greater concern in PEPs.[1] To this end, the attack models specifying those from external intruders, such as the Dolev-Yao intruder model [16], are not used. There are many attacks that a malicious insider could launch. Creating a new model to capture each type of attack (existing or new) scales poorly as the number of attacks grows. Parameterisation allows the re-use of the existing model while allowing it to behave differently according to the attacks being set - virtually allowing thousands of possible attack scenarios to be captured. We have modeled 17 types of attacks in our model, each with a possible value of 'true' or 'false', thus capturing $2^{17} = 131072$ possible attack scenarios. The attack parameters can be encoded in the arc-inscriptions, transition guards, or transition code-regions (attached to a transition where one can specify side-operations upon execution of the transition, e.g. writing data to an external file). The advantage of this approach is that we do not have to change the structure of the model at all to obtain different behaviors.

In addition, we introduce two general modeling approaches. First, *session-data capture* is applied to capture runtime protocol data generated and received by entities for analysis. We take advantage of the executable CPN model by interfacing it with a set of output text files which store the session data during the execution of the model. Session data are firstly represented as CPN colour sets. Then, functions are written to read session data from text files into the appropriate CPN variables, and to write back the updated variables into text files. This allows easy reading, storing, and updating of session data during the model execution without having to maintain tokens in various places across multiple CPN pages, thus avoiding the application of the 'vacuum cleaner' functionality [17] to remove tokens at the end of each session. Next, we generate *one-time* random data which improves on the simple random (possibly repeated) number generation function supported in the current CPN Tools.

3.2 Model Description

Selected parts of the PIEMCP-NT CPN model (the main page, the PE page, and the revocation page) are described to demonstrate the above modeling approaches. Relevant CPN colour sets definitions are provided in Table 1. The entire model consists of 6 pages, 108 places, 79 transitions, 77 colour sets, 38 functions, 29 code-regions, and 21 parameters.

---

[1] While many types of attacks from external intruders (e.g. eavesdropping, message modification) can be mitigated through the use of secure communication channels (e.g. Secure Sockets Layer (SSL)), attacks from malicious insider could result in a misuse of PII without having to break the security of the communication channel.

Table 1. Colour Sets Definition

```
colset K_PUB_VE = INT;
colset K_PRIV_VE = INT;
colset K_SIGN_GEN = INT;
colset PII = STRING;
colset LABEL = STRING;
colset PROVABILITY = BOOL;
colset SP_REQ = record genCond:STRING * conditions1:STRING * <other fields omitted>
colset SP_REQ_SIG = record message:SP_REQ * key:K_SIGN_GEN;
colset SIGNED_SP_REQ = record message:SP_REQ * signat:SP_REQ_SIG;
colset COMMITMENT_PII = record message:PII * random:RANDOM;
colset SIGNATURE_GEN = record message:MSG * key:K_SIGN_GEN * provable: PROVABILITY;
colset SIGNED_MSG = record message:MSG * signat:SIGNATURE_GEN;
colset CIPHER_VE_PII = record message:PII * key:K_PUB_VE * label:LABEL * provable:PROVABILITY;
colset DEC_REQ = record conditions:LABEL * uchvePiece:CIPHER_UCHVE_KVE_PIECE;
colset DEC_REQ_SIGNATURE = record message:DEC_REQ * key:K_SIGN_GEN * provable:BOOL;
colset SIGNED_DEC_REQ = record message:DEC_REQ * signat:DEC_REQ_SIGNATURE;
```

Main page. Fig. 2 shows the main page of PIEMCP-NT. The protocol starts with a user and a service provide SP1 agreeing on a set of conditions (transition U_SP1_GENERATE_ CONDITIONS) before proceeding to execute the PE stage (sub-transition PII_ Escrow) and then the KE stage (sub-transition Key_Escrow). Upon completion of the KE stage, the user goes to another service provider SP2. Similarly, they need to agree on a set of conditions (transition U_SP2_GENERATE_ CONDITIONS) before starting the MC stage (sub-transition Multiple_Conditions). The completion of the MC stage marks the completion of one session which triggers the storage of the session data accumulated by all entities. The number of sessions executed is parameterized by the value of

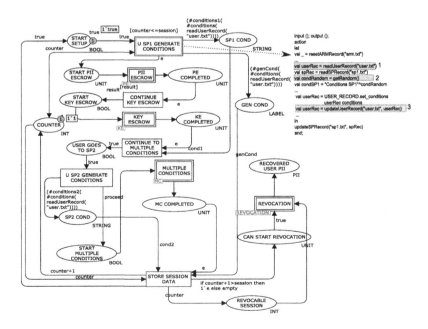

Fig. 2. The PIEMCP-NT CPN – Main page

session. Thus, if value of counter is less than or equal to session (note the guard for the transition U SP1 GENERATE CONDITIONS), the model will execute another session. Otherwise, the guard will disable the transition, and a token will be placed at the place SP1_REVOCATION_CONDITIONS_FULFILLED which triggers the start of a revocation stage which, if successful, results in the revelation of the user's PII represented by a token in the place RECOVERED_USER_PII.

This page also demonstrates the session data capture approach. The shaded text number 1 in Fig. 2 shows a code region which calls the function to read the user session data from a text file to a variable of type USER_RECORD. After performing some update operations on the variable (the one-time random number generator function is called in shaded text number 2), the update function is called to store the updated user session data into the text file again (shaded text number 3).

PE page. This page models the PE stage of PIEMCP-NT (Fig. 3). Here, we demonstrate the message signing and verification approach. The place SP1_PII_REQ_SIGNATURE, of type SIGNED_SP_REQ, represents the NT-PE-1 message. From Table 1, this colour set represents a SP1-signed message whose content is *Cond*1. Other messages are omitted here for simplicity. As the IdP receives this message, the IdP first verifies the signature validity. As explained in Sect. 3.1, such a validation is captured in a transition guard. In this case, the transition guard at the IDP_VERIFIES_SP1_REQ_AND_STARTS_PII_ESCROW transition captures the signature validation process. If it returns true, the signature is valid and the transition is enabled, allowing PE stage to progress normally.

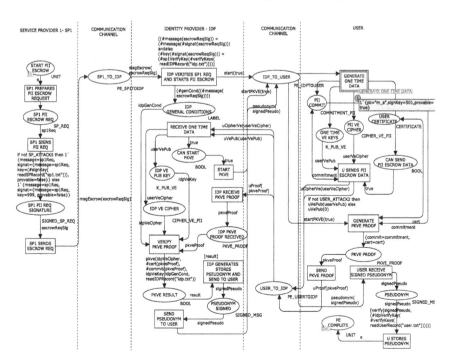

Fig. 3. The PIEMCP-NT CPN – PE page

The user then encrypts the PII. Here, we demonstrate how complex crypto-graphic primitive behaviors can be modeled. The VE ciphertext is defined as a CPN colour set of type `CIPHER_VE_PII` (see Table 1) which is a record consisting of four fields: the message itself, the public encryption key, the label under which the message is encrypted, and the provability property. A provable ciphertext means that the recipient of the ciphertext can be convinced that the received ciphertext correctly encrypts some claimed value (in this case the user's PII) without the recipient learning the value of either the PII itself or the decryption key. We consider the `message` field inside a CPN colour set that represents a ciphertext to be *unreadable*. The VE operations, including the encryption and decryption operations, are captured as functions. The VE ciphertext of PII is represented by a token in the place `PII VE CIPHER`.

Next, the user sends the `NT-PE-2` message (containing the VE ciphertext of PII, and the public VE key) - represented by the transition `U_SENDS_PII_ESCROW_DATA`. Upon receiving `NT-PE-2`, the PK-VE operation is triggered (`NT-PE-3`). Here, we demonstrate how a complex zero-knowledge proof protocol, such as PKVE is modeled in CPN. We break this operation into three transitions: `START_PKVE` (triggered by IdP to signal user the start of such a protocol), the `GENERATE_PKVE_PROOF` transition, executed on the user side to generate the re-quired PKVE proof data, and the `VERIFY_PKVE_PROOF` executed by the IdP to verify the given PKVE proof data. The result of PKVE is represented by the place `PKVE_RESULT`. The essential processing required on the IdP to verify the correctness of the proof is captured by the function `pkve` called as arc inscription from the transition `VERIFY_PKVE_PROOF` to the place `PKVE_RESULT`.

There are two parameterized attacks: `SP_ATTACK5` (arc inscription from transition `SPI_SIGNS_PII_REQ` to place `SPI_PII_REQ_SIGNATURE`), and `USER_ATTACK2` (from transition `U_SENDS_PII_ESCROW_DATA` to place `USER_TO_IDP`). `USER_ATTACK2` depicts the behavior of a malicious user who gives an incorrect VE public key to the IdP in the `NT-PE-2` message. Thus, when `USER_ATTACK2` is set to 'true', the user will send an incorrect VE public key value represented by a value of '0', otherwise, a correct value is sent. `SP_ATTACK5` depicts the behavior of a malicious SP1 who uses an invalid signature key to sign the SP1 request message.

Revocation page. This page captures the UCHVE threshold decryption process (Fig. 4). Due to space limitation, it is impossible to go into the de-tail how we model such a threshold decryption process. Nevertheless, note the place `UCHVE_PIECE_DECRYPT_SUCCESS` and its corresponding output arc. The arc inscription requires t (representing the threshold value) successful decrypted pieces of the UCHVE group encryption by referees before the message (that is, the VE private key) can happen. Also note the parameterized malicious refer-ees' behavior (`REF_ATTACK2`) who attempt to pool all decrypted UCHVE pieces amongst themselves with the hope of being able to recover the VE private key. Since our protocol assume that there is at least one honest designated referee, we assign such role to referee 2 (hence, we do not model referee 2 participating in the attack). This page also demonstrates how CPN can be used to capture concurrent processing required during the threshold decryption process.

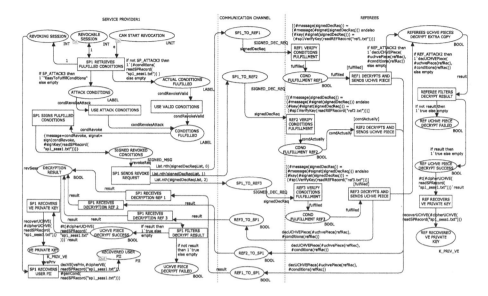

Fig. 4. Revocation page

4   Verification of the PIEMCP

We verify the correctness of PIEMCP using state space analysis. The basic idea behind the state space method of CPNs is to compute all reachable states and state changes of the system based on the CPN model. The verification of PIEMCP is carried out in two stages: the basic behavior verification and security behavior verification. The basic behavior verification is performed through standard state space analysis. It includes the analysis of proper session termination, deadlock freedom, livelock freedom, and absence of unexpected dead transitions. The security behavior verification is the focus of the paper.

Verifying the security behavior of PIEMCP is complicated due to the numerous avenues by which attackers could break the security protection provided by the protocol. We propose to scope the verification of the security behavior of PIEMCP within a set of plausible known attack scenarios. The result of such a verification is the assurance that the desired security behavior is achieved within the set of attack scenarios. As attacks are parameterized in the model, new types of attack scenarios can be added to the existing model without requiring major changes or a new model to be developed. A protocol is proved to be secure if the set of security properties hold in both the presence and absence of attacks. This is especially true in the case of PEPs whose main service (privacy) is in itself already a security behavior. When no attacks are modeled, we expect the security behavior to be fulfilled; when attacks are included, we expect the protocol to either detect it (and therefore stop), or be immune from those attacks.

The verification of the security behavior of the PIEMCP is performed as follows: firstly, the security behaviors of PIEMCP are formalized as Computational

Tree Logic (CTL) and/or standard state space statements; next, the formalized statements are used as queries for model-checking the state space generated from the PIEMCP CPN. Session data analysis is used when appropriate.

CPN Tools support state space analysis and model-checking the state space via ASK-CTL [18]. ASK-CTL is an implementation of a subset of CTL (mainly the "until" operator). It implements two basic operators to capture this logic: EXIST_UNTIL(A_1, A_2) and FORALL_UNTIL(A_1, A_2). The EXIST_UNTIL operator means that there must be at least *one* path, from a given state, whereby A_1 is true for every state in the path until the last state where A_2 is true. The FORALL_UNTIL operator is similar, except that it requires *all* paths to fulfill A_1 until A_2 is true. Based on these two operators, there are also POS and EV operators, where POS(A) = EXIST_UNTIL(TT, A), and EV(A) = FORALL_UNTIL(TT, A) (TT refers to a true value). These operators check the reachability of a state where A is true. POS checks if there is at least one path that leads to A, while EV checks if all paths lead to A. The NF operator contains a state formula function which returns a boolean value. There are many other ASK-CTL operators which we do not use, thus, not elaborated. CPN Tools contain a model checker which takes an ASK-CTL formula as an argument, checks the formula against the current state space of the CPN model, and returns the truth value of the given formula. Both the ASK-CTL logic and model checker are implemented in SML and thereby queries are formulated directly in SML syntax.

For simplicity, we consider a minimum full protocol execution. The PIEMCP CPN model is parameterized to execute two escrow sessions sequentially, followed by one revocation session. Note that it is possible for both the escrow and revocation session to run in parallel, however, modeling such concurrency does not capture any additional behaviors of the protocol as these two sessions are distinct, i.e. they do not interfere with each other. The state space generated from the above in the absence of attack behavior contains 147 nodes and 226 arcs. Next, the CPN model is parameterized to include a number of known attacks, resulting in a set of parameterized CPN models. Each of these models is executed to generate the state space for analysis of certain security properties.

Below, we define four security behaviors for PIEMCP and discuss in detail how we implement the first two properties in ASK-CTL queries in CPN Tools (the details of the queries for the other properties are available in the full version of this paper [14]). Fig 5 includes a set of notations to be used in the definition of these properties.

Let $T = \{t_s | s \in \{1, 2, ..., n\}\}$ be the set of (executed) escrow sessions, $P = \{SP_i | i \in \{1, 2, ..., n\}\}$ be the set of SPs. $\forall t_s \in T$, $\forall SP_i \in P$:

- v_i^s represents a VE ciphertext that SP_i holds for session t_s;
- u_i^s represents a UCHVE ciphertext that SP_i holds for t_s;
- v_{usr}^s represents a user-generated VE ciphertext for t_s;
- $\overline{u}_i^s$ represents the user-generated UCHVE ciphertext for SP_i in t_s;
- C_i^s represents the set of agreed conditions between a user and SP_i in t_s;
- G^s is the set of the general conditions in t_s;
- k^s represents the one-time VE public key that an IDP receives in t_s.

Fig. 5. List of notations to be used in the definition of security properties

4.1 Multiple Conditions

When PIEMCP runs without attacks, it is expected to reach the end of every escrow session, and also each SP should receive an escrowed PII that is cryptographically bound to conditions which are different from one SP to another. However, an attack may occur during an escrow session and as a result it is not possible for the PIEMCP to reach the end of that session. In the PIEMCP CPN, when the protocol reaches the end of an escrow session s, the place MC_COMPLETE on the Main page ($P_{\text{MC\_COMPLETE}}^{\text{Main}}$) is marked by 1'e and the place COUNTER on the same page ($P_{\text{COUNTER}}^{\text{Main}}$) is marked by a token of integer carrying the value of 1's. This can be specified by the following predicate:

$$\text{SessionEnd}^s(M_i) = (\text{Marking}(M_i, P_{\text{MC\_COMPLETE}}^{\text{Main}}) = 1\text{'e}) \text{ AND } (\text{Marking}(M_i, P_{\text{COUNTER}}^{\text{Main}}) = 1\text{'s})$$

where $M_i \in \mathbb{M}$ i.e. the set of reachable markings (states) of the PIEMCP CPN.

*Property 1 (**Multiple Conditions**).* When there is no attack:

- ϕ_1^{mc}: $\forall t_s \in T$, EV(SessionEnd^s);[2] and
- ϕ_2^{mc}: $\forall t_s \in T$, $\forall M$ such that SessionEnd$^s(M)$=true, $\forall SP_i, SP_j \in P$, if $i \neq j$, then Cond(u_i^s) $\neq$ Cond(u_j^s).[3]

When an attack occurs:

- ϕ_3^{mc}: $\exists t_s \in T$, NOT(POS(SessionEnd^s)).[4]

To verify this property, we use both ASK-CTL and session data analysis. In a normal environment (i.e. without an attack), ϕ_1^{mc} states that the end of the session is reachable. It can be directly queried using ASK-CTL formulas (see

Table 2. ASK-CTL and session-data queries for Multiple Conditions property

```
1    fun SessionEnd_1 n = Mark.Main'MC_COMPLETED 1 n = 1'() andalso Mark.Main'COUNTER 1 n = 1'1;
2    fun SessionEnd_2 n = Mark.Main'MC_COMPLETED 1 n = 1'() andalso Mark.Main'COUNTER 1 n = 1'2;
3    val MC_Phi1_1 = EV(NF("", SessionEnd_1));
4    val MC_Phi1_2 = EV(NF("", SessionEnd_2));
5    val sp1Rec1 = readSPRecord("sp1_sess1.txt");
6    val sp1Rec2 = readSPRecord("sp1_sess2.txt");
7    val sp2Rec1 = readSPRecord("sp2_sess1.txt");
8    val sp2Rec2 = readSPRecord("sp2_sess2.txt");
9    val cipherUCHVE11 = #cipherUCHVE(sp1Rec1);
10   val cipherUCHVE21 = #cipherUCHVE(sp2Rec1);
11   val cipherUCHVE12 = #cipherUCHVE(sp1Rec2);
12   val cipherUCHVE22 = #cipherUCHVE(sp2Rec2);
13   val MC_Phi2 = #label(cipherUCHVE11) <> #label(cipherUCHVE21) andalso
14                 #label(cipherUCHVE12) <> #label(cipherUCHVE22);
15   val MC_Phi3_1 = NOT(POS(NF("", SessionEnd_1)));
16   val MC_Phi3_2 = NOT(POS(NF("", SessionEnd_2)));
17   val multipleConditions =
18   if not SP_ATTACK7 then (eval_node MC_Phi1_1 InitNode andalso
19   eval_node MC_Phi1_2 InitNode andalso MC_Phi2) else
20   (eval_node MC_Phi3_1 InitNode andalso eval_node MC_Phi3_2 InitNode);
```

---

[2] SessionEnd^s must eventually become true.

[3] Each SP holds a UCHVE ciphertext bound to a unique set of conditions.

[4] It is not possible to reach the end of an existing session.

line 1-4 in Table 2). By running two sessions, we have $s \in \{1, 2\}$. From the main page of the PIEMCP CPN, it is obvious that the session data is stored when $\texttt{SessionEnd}^s$ becomes true in each session. Therefore, ϕ_2^{mc} (which formalizes the 'different conditions within a session clause') can be directly verified using the saved session data as shown in line 5-14 of Table 2. We have parameterized the model with one attack parameter that may compromise this property: $\texttt{SP\_ATTACK7}$ which depicts the scenario of SPs colluding to use the same condition string with the same user in a session. In such a scenario, we expect the protocol to behave in a fail-stop manner - therefore, ϕ_3^{mc} states that the protocol cannot reach the end of both sessions. ϕ_3^{mc} is directly translated into ASK-CTL queries as shown in line 15-16 of Table 2. Finally, after formulating the queries, we execute the formulas to check if all of the predicates hold (line 17-20).

4.2 Zero-Knowledge

When there are no attacks, before the revocation of a user's PII for an escrow session, IdP, SPs and referees must not learn the value of the user's PII but at the same time be convinced that its encryption is correct. When the attacks occur, it is expected that *at least* one of the encryptions is corrupted. For example, if a user-generated VE ciphertext is correct, the place $\texttt{PKVE\_RESULT}$ on the PE page is marked by $1\texttt{'true}$; otherwise, the place is marked by $1\texttt{'false}$. Fig. 6 lists the predicates specifying the acceptance (i.e. conviction) or rejection of the user's encryption data by IdP and SPs while the user's PII is not revealed. Finally, an escrow session cannot be revoked until the user's encryption data has been all accepted. The place $\texttt{REVOCABLE\_SESSION}$ on the $\texttt{Main}$ page records the revocable sessions in terms of session numbers. Thus, we define the predicate Revocable-$\text{Session}^s(M_i) = 1's \in \text{Marking}(M_i, P_{\texttt{REVOCABLE\_SESSIONs}}^{\texttt{Main}})$ over $\mathbb{M}$ which indicates if a session t_s has been revoked.

$\forall t_s \in T$:

- $\text{TrueUsrVE}^s(M_i) = (\text{Marking}(M_i, P_{\texttt{PKVE\_RESULT}}^{\texttt{PE}})=1\texttt{'true})$ AND $(\text{Marking}(M_i, P_{\texttt{COUNTER}}^{\texttt{Main}})=1's)$
- $\text{FalseUsrVE}^s(M_i) = (\text{Marking}(M_i, P_{\texttt{PKVE\_RESULT}}^{\texttt{PE}})=1\texttt{'false})$ AND $(\text{Marking}(M_i, P_{\texttt{COUNTER}}^{\texttt{Main}})=1's)$
- $\text{TrueUsrTPM}^s(M_i) = (\text{Marking}(M_i, P_{\texttt{PK\_DAA\_RESULT}}^{\texttt{KE}})=1\texttt{'true})$ AND $(\text{Marking}(M_i, P_{\texttt{COUNTER}}^{\texttt{Main}})=1's)$
- $\text{FalseUsrTPM}^s(M_i) = (\text{Marking}(M_i, P_{\texttt{PK\_DAA\_RESULT}}^{\texttt{KE}})=1\texttt{'false})$ AND $(\text{Marking}(M_i, P_{\texttt{COUNTER}}^{\texttt{Main}})=1's)$
- $\text{TrueUCHVEinKE}^s(M_i) = (\text{Marking}(M_i, P_{\texttt{TPM\_PROOF\_RESULT}}^{\texttt{KE}})=1\texttt{'true})$ AND $(\text{Marking}(M_i, P_{\texttt{COUNTER}}^{\texttt{Main}})=1's)$
- $\text{FalseUCHVEinKE}^s(M_i) = (\text{Marking}(M_i, P_{\texttt{TPM\_PROOF\_RESULT}}^{\texttt{KE}})=1\texttt{'false})$ AND $(\text{Marking}(M_i, P_{\texttt{COUNTER}}^{\texttt{Main}})=1's)$
- $\text{TrueUCHVEinMC}^s(M_i) = (\text{Marking}(M_i, P_{\texttt{TPM\_PROOF\_RESULT}}^{\texttt{MC}})=1\texttt{'true})$ AND $(\text{Marking}(M_i, P_{\texttt{COUNTER}}^{\texttt{Main}})=1's)$
- $\text{FalseUCHVEinMC}^s(M_i) = (\text{Marking}(M_i, P_{\texttt{TPM\_PROOF\_RESULT}}^{\texttt{MC}})=1\texttt{'false})$ AND $(\text{Marking}(M_i, P_{\texttt{COUNTER}}^{\texttt{Main}})=1's)$

where $M_i \in \mathbb{M}$ i.e. the set of reachable markings (states) of the PIEMCP CPN.

Fig. 6. List of predicates specifying acceptance or rejection of user's encryption data

*Property 2 (**Zero-knowledge**).* Without attacks:

- ϕ_1^{zk}: $\forall t_s \in T$, $\text{EV}(\text{TrueUsrVE}^s) \wedge \text{EV}(\text{TrueUsrTPM}^s) \wedge \text{EV}(\text{TrueUCHVEinKE}^s)$
  $\wedge\ \text{EV}(\text{TrueUCHVEinMC}^s)$;

- ϕ_2^{zk}: $\forall t_s \in T$, NOT(POS(FalseUsrVE^s)) $\land$ NOT(POS(FalseUsrTPM^s)) $\land$ NOT(POS(FalseUCHVEinKE^s)) $\land$ NOT(POS(FalseUCHVEinMC^s)); and
- ϕ_3^{zk}: $\forall t_s \in T$, FORALL_UNTIL(NOT(RevocableSession^s), ϕ_1^{zk}).

With attacks:

- ϕ_4^{zk}: $\forall t_s \in T$, NOT(POS(TrueUsrVE^s)) $\land$ NOT(POS(TrueUsrTPM^s)) $\land$ NOT(POS(TrueUCHVEinKE^s)) $\land$ NOT(POS(TrueUCHVEinMC^s)); and
- ϕ_5^{zk}: $\forall t_s \in T$, POS(FalseUsrVE^s) $\lor$ POS(FalseUsrTPM^s) $\lor$ POS(FalseUCHVEinKE^s) $\lor$ POS(FalseUCHVEinMC^s);
- ϕ_6^{zk}: $\forall t_s \in T$, NOT(POS(RevocableSession^s)).

For brevity, Table 3 only show queries related to **TrueUsrVE^s**, **FalseUsrVE^s** and RevocableSession^s (queries related to other predicates are performed in the same manner as for the first two predicates). ϕ_1^{zk}, ϕ_2^{zk} and ϕ_3^{zk} can be directly translated into ASK-CTL queries as shown in line 12-17 of Table 3. These three predicates are finally executed at line 18-19, where the zero-knowledge property of no attacks holds if all three predicates return true.

We have modeled six attacks that may compromise this property, which are parameterized as **USER_ATTACK1**, **USER_ATTACK2**, **USER_ATTACK3**, **USER_ATTACK4**, **SP_ATTACK12**, **SP_ATTACK22**. The formulas ϕ_4^{zk}, ϕ_5^{zk} and ϕ_6^{zk} are directly translated into ASK-CTL queries as shown in line 23-28 of Table 3. These predicates are executed at line 29-30 and all must return true if the zero-knowledge property with attacks is to hold.

```
1    fun TrueUsrVE_1 n = Mark.PE'PKVE_RESULT 1 n = 1'true andalso Mark.Main'COUNTER 1 n = 1'1;
2    fun TrueUsrVE_2 n = Mark.PE'PKVE_RESULT 1 n = 1'true andalso Mark.Main'COUNTER 1 n = 1'2;
3    ...
4    fun FalseUsrVE_1' n = Mark.PE'PKVE_RESULT 1 n = 1'false andalso Mark.Main'COUNTER 1 n = 1'1;
5    fun FalseUsrVE_2' n = Mark.PE'PKVE_RESULT 1 n = 1'false andalso Mark.Main'COUNTER 1 n = 1'2;
6    ...
7    fun RevocableSession_1 n = List.exists (fn y => y=1) (Mark.Main'REVOCABLE_SESSION 1 n);
8    fun RevocableSession_2 n = List.exists (fn y => y=2) (Mark.Main'REVOCABLE_SESSION 1 n);
9
10   NO ATTACKS (NA)
11   ==================
12   val ZK_Phi1 = eval_node EV(NF("",TrueUsrVE_1)) InitNode andalso ...
13                 eval_node EV(NF("",TrueUsrVE_2)) InitNode andalso ...;
14   val ZK_Phi2 = eval_node NOT(POS(NF("",FalseUsrVE_1))) InitNode andalso ...
15                 eval_node NOT(POS(NF("",FalseUsrVE_2))) InitNode andalso ...;
16   val ZK_Phi3 = FORALL_UNTIL(NOT(NF("",RevocableSession_1)), ZK_Phi1_1 initNode) andalso
17                 FORALL_UNTIL(NOT(NF("",RevocableSession_2)), ZK_Phi1_2 initNode);
18   val zeroKnowledgeNA = eval_node ZK_Phi1 InitNode andalso eval_node ZK_Phi2 InitNode andalso
19                 eval_node ZK_Phi3 InitNode;
20
21   WITH ATTACKS (WA)
22   ====================
23   val ZK_Phi4 = eval_node NOT(POS(NF("",TrueUsrVE_1))) InitNode andalso ...
24                 eval_node NOT(POS(NF("",TrueUsrVE_2))) InitNode andalso ...;
25   val ZK_Phi5 = eval_node POS(NF("",FalseUsrVE_1)) InitNode orelse ...
26                 eval_node POS(NF("",FalseUsrVE_2)) InitNode orelse ...;
27   val ZK_Phi6 = eval_node NOT(POS(NF("",RevocableSession_1))) InitNode andalso
28                 eval_node NOT(POS(NF("",RevocableSession_2))) InitNode;
29   val zeroKnowledgeWA = eval_node ZK_Phi4 InitNode andalso eval_node ZK_Phi5 InitNode andalso
30                 eval_node ZK_Phi6 InitNode;
```

Table 3. ASK-CTL and session-data queries for Zero-knowledge property

4.3   Enforceable Conditions

When PIEMCP is executed, a user's PII should never be revealed unless all designated referees agree that the cryptographically bound conditions are satisfied. This property should hold regardless of whether there is an attack or not. We define the following: $\forall t_s \in T$, $\forall M_i \in \mathbb{M}$,

- $\mathsf{HasRefPKVE}^s(M_i) = \mathsf{Marking}(M_i, P_{\mathrm{REF\_RECOVERED\_VE\_PRIVATE\_KEY}}^{\mathrm{Revocation}}) \neq$ empty,
- $\mathsf{HasRecUsrPII}^s(M_i) = \mathsf{Marking}(M_i, P_{\mathrm{RECOVERED\_USER\_PII}}^{\mathrm{Revocation}}) \neq$ empty,
- *threshold* $\in \{2..n\}$ specifies the minimum referees needed for a successful PII revocation, and
- *revCondition* denotes the actual status of a revocation condition which is either true or false.

*Property 3 (**Enforceable Conditions:**)*

- ϕ_1^{ec}: $\forall t_s \in T$, NOT(POS($\mathsf{HasRefPKVE}^s$));
- ϕ_2^{ec}: if *revCondition*=true then $\forall t_s \in T$ where t_s is being revoked,
  - ϕ_{2a}^{ec}: $|P_{\mathrm{UCHVE\_PIECE\_DECRYPT\_SUCCESS}}^{\mathrm{Revocation}}| <$ *threshold* and
  - ϕ_{2b}^{ec}: NOT(POS($\mathsf{HasRecUsrPII}^s$));
- ϕ_3^{ec}: if *revCondition*=false then $\forall t_s \in T$ where t_s is being revoked,
  - ϕ_{3a}^{ec}: $|P_{\mathrm{UCHVE\_PIECE\_DECRYPT\_SUCCESS}}^{\mathrm{Revocation}}| \geq$ *threshold* and
  - ϕ_{3b}^{ec}: EV(POS($\mathsf{HasRecUsrPII}^s$)).

While there are attacks that can be launched to compromise this property (parameterized by SP_ATTACK4, REF_ATTACK1, REF_ATTACK2, the above definition remains the same. Standard state space queries, and ASK-CTL queries are used to verify this property. ϕ_1^{ec} states that the marking indicating illegal recovery of private VE key by the referees must not be reached *at any time*. When some conditions for session t_s are not fulfilled, the number of decrypted UCHVE pieces must be fewer than the threshold value required (ϕ_{2a}^{ec}), and that the marking which indicates the revelation of the user PII must not be reached too (ϕ_{2b}^{ec}). When conditions are fulfilled, we expect the number of decrypted UCHVE pieces to be greater or equal to the threshold value (ϕ_{3a}^{ec}), and that the user PII must eventually be revealed (ϕ_{3b}^{ec}).

In summary, the predicates ϕ_1^{ec}, ϕ_{2b}^{ec} and ϕ_{3b}^{ec} can be directly translated into ASK-CTL queries, while ϕ_{2a}^{ec} and ϕ_{3a}^{ec} are verified using the standard state space query UpperIntegerBound (i.e. the maximum number of tokens that can reside in a place). See [14] for details.

4.4   Conditions Abuse Resistant

During the execution of PIEMCP, an SP and an IdP must not be able to make the user encrypt the PII, or the VE private key, under a set of conditions different from those originally agreed. Similarly, an SP or IdP must not be able to successfully revoke the user's PII using conditions different from those originally agreed. In the following definition, we have used the notations shown in Fig. 5.

*Property 4 (**Conditions Abuse Resistant**).* No attack:

- ϕ_{1a}^{car}: $\forall t_s \in T$, $G^s = \text{Cond}(v_{usr}^s)$ and
- ϕ_{1b}^{car}: $\forall t_s \in T$, $\forall SP_i \in P$, $C_i^s = \text{Cond}(\overline{u}_i^s)$

With attacks: $\forall t_s \in T$, $\forall M_i \in \mathbb{M}$, let:

- $\text{PE\_End}^s(M_i) = (\text{Marking}(M_i, P_{\text{PE\_COMPLETE}}^{\text{Main}})=1\text{'e})$ AND $(\text{Marking}(M_i, P_{\text{COUNTER}}^{\text{Main}})=1\text{'s})$
- $\text{KE\_End}^s(M_i) = (\text{Marking}(M_i, P_{\text{KE\_COMPLETE}}^{\text{Main}})=1\text{'e})$ AND $(\text{Marking}(M_i, P_{\text{COUNTER}}^{\text{Main}})=1\text{'s})$

then:

- for attacks that manipulate the general conditions, ϕ_{2a}^{car}: $\text{NOT}(\text{POS}(\text{PE\_End}^s))$;
- for attacks that manipulate conditions with SP_1, ϕ_{2b}^{car}: $\text{NOT}(\text{POS}(\text{KE\_End}^s))$;
- for attacks that manipulate conditions with $SP_{2,3,...,y}$,
  ϕ_{2c}^{car}: $\text{NOT}(\text{POS}(\text{SessionEnd}^s))$;
- for attacks that use wrong conditions for revocation,
  - ϕ_{2d}^{car}: Transition $T_{\text{USE\_ATTACK\_CONDITIONS}}^{\text{Revocation}}$ is not dead $\wedge$
  - ϕ_{2e}^{car}: $\text{NOT}(\text{POS}(\text{HasRecUsrPII}^s)) \wedge \text{NOT}(\text{POS}(\text{HasRefPKVE}^s))$.

In a normal environment (no attacks), ϕ_{1a}^{car} states that the cryptographically bound conditions (or label) used to produce a VE ciphertext must be the same as the one originally agreed. Similar explanation applies to ϕ_{1b}^{car}. When there are attacks targeting the general conditions used in the PE stage (parameterized by USER_ATTACK1, SP_ATTACK1, we expect the PE stage to fail stop (hence ϕ_{2a}). For attacks targeting the conditions used during the KE stage (with SP1 - parameterized by USER_ATTACK4, SP_ATTACK11), we expect the KE stage to fail stop (hence ϕ_{2b}^{car}). For attacks targeting the conditions used during the MC stage (for subsequent SPs - parameterized by SP_ATTACK2), we expect the MC stage to fail stop (hence ϕ_{2c}^{car}). For attacks targeting the use of invalid conditions during the revocation stage (parameterized by SP_ATTACK3, we expect that $T_{\text{USE\_ATTACK\_CONDITIONS}}^{\text{Revocation}}$ is not a dead transition (i.e. a transition that can never fire), and that the marking which indicate the revelation of user PII, or the illegal revelation of VE private key to *not* be reached (hence ϕ_{2d}^{car} and ϕ_{2e}^{car}).

In summary, ϕ_{1a}^{car}, ϕ_{1b}^{car}, and ϕ_{2d}^{car} can be verified using state space queries (notably the search nodes and token value comparisons queries). ϕ_{2a}^{car}, ϕ_{2b}^{car}, ϕ_{2c}^{car}, and ϕ_{2e}^{car} can be directly translated into ASK-CTL queries. See [14] for details.

5   Related Work

We briefly review several formal methods that have been used to verify security protocols. Earlier work, such as Burrows, Abadi, and Needham (BAN) logic [19], use the modal logic approach whereby the security of a protocol is assessed by studying the evolution of beliefs and/or knowledge over the course of the protocol to evaluate their adequacy for some pre-defined protocol objectives. We do not use this method because it is not evident if this approach is able to capture and verify behavioral properties. Besides, the modal logic approach is generally considered a weaker approach in comparison to other formal methods [20].

Formal methods based on process algebra have also been used to model and verify security protocols (such as LySa [5] and CSP [21]). Process algebra allows the modeling of a system's behavior (including concurrency) as a set of algebraic statements. Common verification techniques used with process algebra include equational reasoning and model checking [22]. For example, Pi-Calculus [23] supports *labeled transition* semantics in modeling a system. This allows the verification of protocols through state exploration techniques such as model checking. However, we choose not to use process algebra approach due to its complexity which tends to (unnecessarily) complicate even simple things [17]. In comparison to the graphical-based modeling approach in CPN, this is a less intuitive approach to modeling large distributed systems such as PEPs. Model validation can only be performed by users who are experts in both the protocol itself *and* the process algebra syntax. While one still needs to understand the concept of CPN, the intuitive graphical-based modeling approach is a more human-friendly approach and thus easier to learn. The interactive and simulatable CPN model help modelers in detecting inconsistencies between a model and its original protocol specification, thus facilitating effective model validation.

State exploration techniques (such as state space analysis and model checking) have also been widely used for security protocol analysis. Examples of formal methods belonging to this category are the Automated Validation of Internet Security Protocols and Applications (AVISPA) tool [3], Scyther [24], and ProVerif [25]. These are state-of-the-art tools capable of automatically detecting attacks in many security protocols. Nevertheless, the main reason we do not use these tools is because the types of security properties verifiable by these tools are not relevant to PEPs. Instead, they are mostly relevant to authentication and key agreement protocols, i.e. *secrecy*, *authenticity*, and their variants. When protocols related to privacy are verified using these tools, the privacy property is reduced to confidentiality and authenticity. We argue that this is a simplistic approach to verifying privacy and that privacy does not simply equate to confidentiality and/or authenticity. The *behavior* of a protocol in preserving/violating a user's privacy is just as important. As stated in the introduction, it is the behavior of the protocol that we are interested to verify.

Similar to process algebra, these tools also lack the rich graphical and simulation support of CPN.[5] Finally, it is not evident if concurrent processing (as oppose to concurrent protocol execution supported in Scyther) is supported in these tools. Therefore, we do not find these tools to be suitable for our purpose. Although CPN has been widely used to analyze industrial communication protocols (such as Transmission Control Protocol (TCP)), its use in the area of security protocols is still very new with limited documented cases. For example, Al-Azzoni et al [4] used CPN to model and verify the Tatebayashi, Matsuzaki, and Newman (TMN) key exchange protocol [26]. The main difference between

---

[5] Scyther provides some static graphical support. However, it falls short of interactive protocol simulation and graphically-driven protocol specification.

our work and theirs is that they focus on verifying the *secrecy* property of the TMN protocol, while our work focus on verifying the security behavior of PEPs.

Our work has not reached the maturity of the other methods discussed. However, we see its potential. By exploiting the intuitiveness of CPN's graphical-based modeling approach (which is also based upon a solid underlying mathematical foundation) in combination with its rich modeling capability (hierarchical modeling, concurrent processing, flexible colour sets definition, model parameterization, etc), performance analysis capability, and its powerful verification techniques, CPN has the potential to be an easy-to-use yet powerful formal method for modeling and verifying large multi-party PEPs.

6   Conclusion

We have shown that CPNs can be used to model complex PEPs using CPN and verify its behavioral properties using state space analysis, ASK-CTL (model checking language), and session data analysis. We have also proposed several modeling techniques, notably the cryptographic primitive abstraction (capturing complex primitives and zero-knowledge proof protocol), TPM provable execution, parameterized attacks, and session data capture. We have also shown how a set of behavioral properties can be formalized which can be directly verified using the existing state space, ASK-CTL, and session data queries.

Future work involves using the model to conduct a performance analysis of the protocol and to assess its efficiency in deployment. We will also be looking at refining and generalizing the modeling techniques proposed in this paper such that they can be applied to other PEPs. CPN Tools can be improved by providing a better user front-end to simplify and automate the tasks required in the modeling and verification of PEPs. The function of such a front-end could be as simple as aiding users with the configuration of the model parameters, to a full-blown automation whereby a user without any knowledge of CPN can generate the required back-end CPN model with only a PEP specification. As to the issue of attack behavior, so far we have considered in the protocol verification a set of known attack scenarios, while ultimately the goal is to achieve an automated attack detections for PEPs using the CPN-based approach.

References

1. Holtzman, D.H.: Privacy Lost. Jossey-Bass (2006)
2. WP 14.1: PRIME (Privacy and Identity Management for Europe) - Framework V3 (March 2008)
3. Team, T.A.: AVISPA v1.1 User Manual. Information Society Technologies Programme (June 2006), http://avispa-project.org/
4. Al-Azzoni, I., Down, D.G., Khedri, R.: Modeling and verification of cryptographic protocols using coloured petri nets and design/cpn. Nordic Journal of Computing 12(3), 201–228 (2005)
5. Bodei, C., Buchholtz, M., Degano, P., Nielson, F., Nielson, H.R.: Static validation of security protocols. J. Comput. Secur. 13(3), 347–390 (2005)

6. Koblitz, N., Menezes, A.: Another look at provable security. J. Cryptology 20(1), 3–37 (2007)
7. Jensen, K.: Coloured Petri Nets - Basic Concepts, Analysis Methods and Practical Use, 2nd edn. Monographs in Theoretical Computer Science, vol. 1. Springer, Berlin (1997)
8. Murata, T.: Petri nets: Properties, analysis and applications. Proceedings of the IEEE 77(4), 541–580 (1989)
9. Gilmore, S.: Programming in standard ml 1997: A tutorial introduction. Technical report, The University of Edinburgh (1997)
10. Jensen, K., Kristensen, L.M., Wells, L.: Coloured petri nets and cpn tools for modelling and validation of concurrent systems. STTT 9(3-4), 213–254 (2007)
11. Suriadi, S., Foo, E., Smith, J.: Private information escrow bound to multiple conditions. Technical report, Information Security Institute - Queensland University of Technology (2008), http://eprints.qut.edu.au/17763/1/c17763.pdf
12. Suriadi, S., Foo, E., Josang, A.: A user-centric federated single sign-on system. Journal of Network and Computer Applications 32(2), 388–401 (2009)
13. Suriadi, S., Foo, E., Smith, J.: A user-centric protocol for conditional anonymity revocation. In: Furnell, S.M., Katsikas, S.K., Lioy, A. (eds.) TrustBus 2008. LNCS, vol. 5185, pp. 185–194. Springer, Heidelberg (2008)
14. Suriadi, S., Ouyang, C., Smith, J., Foo, E.: Modeling and verification of privacy enhancing security protocols. Technical report, ISI, Queensland University of Technology (April 2009) http://eprints.qut.edu.au/20088/
15. McCune, J.M., Parno, B., Perrig, A., Reiter, M.K., Isozaki, H.: Flicker: an execution infrastructure for TCB minimization. In: Sventek, J.S., Hand, S. (eds.) EuroSys, pp. 315–328. ACM, New York (2008)
16. Dolev, D., Yao, A.C.C.: On the security of public key protocols. IEEE Transactions on Information Theory 29(2), 198–207 (1983)
17. van der Aalst, W.: Pi calculus versus petri nets: Let us eat humble pie rather than further inflate the pi hype. In: BPTrends, pp. 1–11 (May 2005)
18. Christensen, S., Mortensen, K.H.: Design/CPN ASK-CTL Manual - Version 0.9. University of Aarhus, Aarhus C, Denmark (1996)
19. Burrows, M., Abadi, M., Needham, R.: A logic of authentication. ACM Trans. Comput. Syst. 8(1), 18–36 (1990)
20. Meadows, C.: Open issues in formal methods for cryptographic protocol analysis. In: DISCEX 2000, pp. 237–250. IEEE Computer Society Press, Los Alamitos (2000)
21. Lowe, G.: Breaking and fixing the needham-schroeder public-key protocol using FDR. In: Margaria, T., Steffen, B. (eds.) TACAS 1996. LNCS, vol. 1055, pp. 147–166. Springer, Heidelberg (1996)
22. Baeten, J.C.M.: A brief history of process algebra. Theor. Comput. Sci. 335(2-3), 131–146 (2005)
23. Milner, R.: Communicating and Mobile Systems: the Pi-Calculus. Cambridge University Press, Cambridge (1999)
24. Cremers, C.J.: The scyther tool: Verification, falsification, and analysis of security protocols. In: Gupta, A., Malik, S. (eds.) CAV 2008. LNCS, vol. 5123, pp. 414–418. Springer, Heidelberg (2008)
25. Blanchet, B.: An Efficient Cryptographic Protocol Verifier Based on Prolog Rules, pp. 82–96 (June 2001)
26. Tatebayashi, M., Matsuzaki, N., Newman Jr., D.B.: Key distribution protocol for digital mobile communication systems. In: Brassard, G. (ed.) CRYPTO 1989. LNCS, vol. 435, pp. 324–334. Springer, Heidelberg (1989)

Role-Based Symmetry Reduction of Fault-Tolerant Distributed Protocols with Language Support*

Péter Bokor, Marco Serafini, Neeraj Suri, and Helmut Veith

Technische Universität Darmstadt, Germany
{pbokor,marco,suri,veith}@cs.tu-darmstadt.de

Abstract. Fault-tolerant (FT) distributed protocols (such as group membership, consensus, etc.) represent fundamental building blocks for many practical systems, e.g., the Google File System. Not only does one desire rigor in the protocol design but especially in its verification given the complexity and fallibility of manual proofs. The application of model checking (MC) for protocol verification is attractive with its full automation and rich property language. However, being an exhaustive exploration method, its scalable use is very much constrained by the overall number of different system states. We observe that, although FT distributed protocols usually display a very high degree of symmetry which stems from permuting different processes, MC efforts targeting their automated verification often disregard this symmetry. Therefore, we propose to leverage the framework of symmetry reduction and improve on existing applications of it by specifying so called role-based symmetries. Our secondary contribution is to define a high-level description language called FTDP to ease the symmetry aware specification of FT distributed protocols. FTDP supports synchronous as well as asynchronous protocols, a variety of fault types, and the specification of safety and liveness properties. Specifications written in FTDP can directly be analyzed by tools supporting symmetry reduction. We demonstrate the benefit of our approach using the example of well-known and complex distributed FT protocols, specifically Paxos and the Byzantine Generals.

1 Introduction

Model checking (MC) is a verification approach that exhaustively and automatically simulates the system by starting it from initial states and generating paths to verify that some specified properties hold along every path [7]. For designers of distributed systems, in particular of *fault-tolerant (FT) distributed protocols*, MC represents a useful tool for automatic verification of formal properties which are usually hand-proved. Not only can MC provide supporting evidence of the correctness of the proofs: it can also serve as a powerful tool for fast prototyping and debugging of protocols by showing counterexamples, i.e., runs violating

---

* Research supported in part by Microsoft Research, IBM Faculty Award and CASED.

K. Breitman and A. Cavalcanti (Eds.): ICFEM 2009, LNCS 5885, pp. 147–166, 2009.

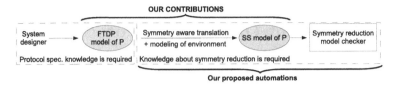

Fig. 1. The proposed approach for verifying a FT distributed protocol P

a certain property. However, the use of MC in the design and verification of distributed systems is still limited. In this paper, we identify (and tackle) two major barriers that prevent a widespread use of MC for distributed protocols.

The first barrier is that the design of a model still requires significant MC specific expertise. Distributed systems designers typically use a pseudocode which primarily represents the process behavior and which abstracts many details required by the model checker. When the properties of an algorithm are hand-proved, only those predicates about the system and fault model which are needed in the proofs are enunciated. With automatic verification, however, the system and fault model need to be explicitly encoded into the model. This, together with the fact that the input languages of MC often require detailed understanding of the internal model representation used by the model checker, makes it difficult and error-prone for distributed systems designers to define models for MCs.

The second major limitation to the adoption of MC for verification of distributed systems is that the number of system states generated by the MC becomes very often unfeasible, i.e., *state space explosion*. Existing approaches to MC of FT distributed protocols disregard the fact that the *symmetric* nature of such systems can lead to significant state space reductions. For example, in many consensus protocols all processes execute the same algorithm and it is irrelevant to model which processes agree on a value as long as this is the same for all processes.

Paper Contributions. This paper introduces the FTDP language which (a) allows writing models of FT distributed protocols using a simple pseudocode-like language and (b) forces the specification of symmetric systems to yield a sound and complete abstraction which effectively limits state space explosion. FTDP addresses both discussed barriers. It allows the system designer to concentrate on writing the pseudocode of the protocol behavior. The system and fault model can be defined by picking the desired properties from a palette of pre-defined templates which represent typical and well-known abstractions expressing the properties of the communication channels (e.g. synchrony, reliability) and of faults (e.g. crashes, Byzantine). FTDP also mitigates the state explosion problem by showing and discussing how *symmetry reduction* [10,8,16] can be integrated into automated model verification transparently to the system designer.

The basic idea of symmetry reduction is to identify groups of symmetric system states such that it is sufficient to explore one representative state in each group. However, the process of identification of symmetric states, commonly called *symmetry detection*, is a complex task. Automatic detection of symmetries in a model in order to produce a smaller, symmetry-reduced model is at least as complex as exploring the original model. It is therefore up to the designer to identify symmetries and express them in a language supporting symmetry reduction like SS [10]. FTDP identifies symmetries from the pseudocode of the system by leveraging *roles*. Roles are independent processes which partition the operations executed by the nodes participating in the protocol. They are explicitly defined, for example, in the Paxos protocol (leaders, acceptors and learners) [11] and in the OM protocol (commander and lieutenants) [15]. Implicit roles can be commonly identified in many distributed protocols (e.g., [1,6,18]). In our experimental evaluations we show that *role-based* symmetry reduction of distributed algorithms is very efficient as it can reach almost optimal state reduction for the detected symmetries. We also show that a role-based approach can be exponentially more efficient in the number of roles than the common, simplistic symmetry detection approach which considers nodes as the symmetric unit in the system [10,8].

Our overall verification approach is depicted in Figure 1. The system designer writes a protocol's pseudocode using the FTDP language. By doing this, it also selects the appropriate system and fault model. FTDP is then automatically translated to the language SS. SS is general and comes with a precise proof of the correctness of symmetry detection. During the translation, FTDP uses roles to specify the symmetries of the system. The SS model of the protocol is then given as an input to a symmetry reduction model checker, which automatically explores the system state and verifies the properties.

In order to show the viability of the approach, we present the FTDP models of the Paxos and Oral Messages (OM) protocols. Both are fundamental consensus protocols which representatively show how FTDP can be used over different system models (asynchronous vs. synchronous) and over different fault models (crash vs. Byzantine). These protocols also demonstrate how roles are commonly used in distributed algorithms. Experimental verification shows that our approach can reduce the size of the state space of multiple orders of magnitude over non-symmetric models as well as over node-based symmetry reductions.

A Motivating Example. We give the intuition of the proposed approach through the example of a simple reliable storage protocol. The protocol operations here, of different phases of information exchange and consequent decision/termination steps, are representative of a broad class of distributed FT protocols. This protocol implements a *regular read/write storage* (RS) assuming that only a strict minority of all processes can crash [17]. Channels are authenticated, i.e., a receiver process can identify the sender of the message. A message can be lost, duplicated or delayed but it cannot be forged. An RS is implemented on top of read/write registers each of them located on a different physical node. RS defines two roles, a single *writer* and n *readers* that can write/read to/from the RS respectively. Being a fault-tolerant solution, processes should be able to access the RS even if some registers are unaccessible. Figure 2(a) sketches how the protocol works if $n = 4$ in a setting where the registers are located on the

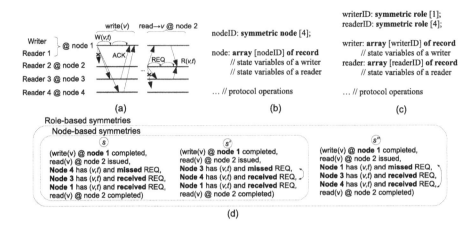

Fig. 2. (a) Example of the regular read/write storage protocol. (b-c) Outline of the pseudocode of the same protocol using the usual node-based and the proposed role-based symmetries resp. (d) The benefit of the role-based approach: the node-based approach cannot detect that global state s'' is symmetric with global states s and s'.

same physical nodes as the readers and where the writer and one reader are located on the same node. The writer can write a value v into RS by invoking write(v). This operation consists of requesting every register to update its value to v together with the writer's latest timestamp (t). The write completes if any majority of the registers have sent an acknowledgement. Even though reader 2 does not have v locally, it can use the RS protocol to obtain the value by invoking a read operation. The reader first requests every register to report the value with the latest timestamp, waits for a reply from a majority of all registers and returns the value with the largest timestamp among the replies. MC must verify that the RS is *regular*, i.e., a read always returns a value v that was actually written and v is not older than the value written by the last preceding write.[1]

Figure 2(b) shows the template of the pseudocode specification of the RS protocol used to detect node-based symmetries by construction. The designer specifies that the system consists of nodes, each of them able to host a writer and a reader. Nodes are declared to be symmetric, i.e., their local states are interchangeable. Symmetry violations are prevented in the specification language by disallowing the definition of symmetry-breaking operations. The global state of the system at each instant of time is given by an array storing the local state of each node of the system.

Figure 2(c), on the other hand, depicts the pseudocode-template of the same protocol with the ability of detecting role-based symmetries (like in FTDP). Every role, writer and reader, is defined to be symmetric. There is one writer process and four reader processes. The assignment of processes to physical nodes needs not be modeled because the properties of RS does not specify nodes. The

---

[1] An operation op_1 precedes op_2 if op_1 completes before op_2 is invoked.

global state of the system is the set of arrays, each of them belonging to a role, storing the local state of each role instance. The benefit of the role-based approach is demonstrated by an example in Figure 2(d). Three global states s, s' and s'' are shown which only differ regarding which node has missed a read request. *All* these global states are symmetric because each of them can be obtained from another by permuting the IDs of the readers. However, the node-based approach cannot detect that s'' is symmetric with s and s' because the model has to remember that reader 1, which is the only one hosted on the same node as the writer, has received the read request. Therefore, the model checker explores two states (s or s' and s'') in the node-based model. In contrast, it suffices to explore a single state (arbitrarily selected among s, s' and s'') in the role-based model.

Related Work. A recent survey of general applications and tools for symmetry reduction is [16]. Our work is related to symmetry detection and to approaches that are specific to automated formal verification of FT distributed protocols. We assume that the model checker can distinguish between symmetric states; related techniques are also surveyed in [16].

The proposed solution assumes that the system consists of a finite number of processes. This strong assumption enables us to provide full automation and an expressive property language. Our recent brief announcement [4] provides a summary level overview of the approach. A powerful tool for the specification and the analysis of distributed systems is provided by the TLA+ language and the TLC model checker [13]. TLC supports symmetry reduction and requires that the user detects symmetries. FTDP models automatically detect symmetry and can be also translated into TLA+. +CAL [14] is a language allowing high-level specification of algorithms which, similarly to FTDP and SS, is automatically translated into TLA+. +CAL does not support the specification of symmetries and is lower-level (and also more general) than FTDP. For example, the modeling of message-based communication and faults must be implemented by the user.

Other work uses model checkers with no symmetry reduction support to verify consensus protocols under the crash fault model and the Heard-Of system model [23,24]. The latter model assumes that a message which is sent in a communication round cannot arrive in later rounds. This additional assumption facilitates verification of consensus protocols, but is only sound for systems implementing it. The symmetry detection approach of FTDP can also be extended to exploit symmetry under the Heard-Of system model. Since FTDP restricts to finite models, the technique of abstracting protocols using infinite time stamps into a finite representation [23] can be combined with our approach.

Another work verifies the optimistic termination of Byzantine consensus protocols [25]. This approach differs from ours in many aspects: it is specific to consensus protocols, it uses a dedicated verification engine, it does not use symmetries, and it does not verify the entire protocol but rather focuses on optimistic cases. Model checking of self-stabilizing algorithms was proposed by using symbolic techniques that are (under favorable conditions) insensitive to the large number of initial states [22]. However, different but symmetric initial states need

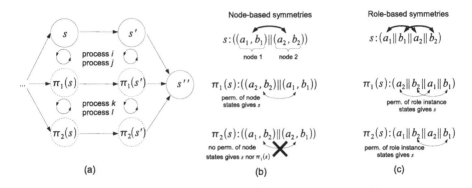

Fig. 3. (a) Example symmetric state space with symmetry reduction. The dashed line states are not explored leading to state space reduction. (b) If the system has two nodes, each running instances of two roles a and b, where instances of a have states a_1 and a_2 and instances of b has states b_1 and b_2, symmetric state $\pi_2(s)$ is not detected in the classic node-based approach but (c) is detected in the role-based approach.

not be explored, which, if combined with explicit state model checking, does not suffer from the drawback of symbolic approaches. Work that uses MC to verify specific FT distributed protocols but that disregards symmetry (e.g., [21]) can naturally leverage our technique.

2   A Role-Based Approach to Tackling Symmetry

Symmetries of Distributed Protocols. A typical example of symmetries in the state space, or *state graph*, of the system is when all nodes in a distributed system execute the same process. The intuition is that a (global) system state s where two processes i and j assume different local states is symmetric with another state $\pi(s)$ where these two local states are swapped. Formally, *symmetry* [8] is a permutation π acting on all reachable system states satisfying that for every state s and its successor s' it holds that $\pi(s')$ is a successor of $\pi(s)$.[2] Figure 3 (a) shows a simple case of a symmetric state graph, where any pair among $s, \pi_1(s)$ and $\pi_2(s)$ is symmetric.

Symmetry reduction [16] exploits such symmetries to ease model checking. The idea is that the system exhibits indistinguishable behavior when started from symmetric states if the property under verification does not distinguish symmetric states. By using this technique a reduced model, or *reduced state graph*, is explored which is defined such that every state s of the reduced model is a representative state among all states of the original model that are symmetric with s, and two states are connected in the reduced model if any two states of the corresponding sets of symmetric states are connected in the original model.

---

[2] More generally, the pairs of symmetric states s and $\pi(s)$ yield a bi-simulation for the state graph.

In Figure 3(a) the reduced state graph contains only the representative states s, s', s'', and their relations.

Detecting Symmetries. The definition of symmetry shows that all relations and states in the non-reduced state space may have to be visited to *automatically detect* symmetries, although this entails the very same complexity we want to eliminate. Therefore, we take the approach of creating symmetric models *by construction*, where the exploration of the state space is not needed because symmetries are indicated by the system designer. In order to indicate symmetries in the model the designer uses a special data type called *scalarsets*. Scalarsets were introduced in the SS language and define subranges with restricted operations, e.g., scalarset values can only be checked for equivalence and arrays with scalarset index type cannot be indexed by constants. The restrictions guarantee that any permutation of scalarset values results in symmetric states.

Efficient Symmetry Detection via Roles. We observe that most FT distributed protocols are expressed, or can be easily expressed, in terms of *roles*. Protocols are executed by computing elements, termed processors or *nodes*. Each node executes one or more state machines, called *processes*, whose state consists of input and output message buffers and a local state. State transitions are atomic and are activated by either reading a message from the input buffer or by responding to an internal event (e.g. timeouts). Possible effects of a state transition are changing the local state of the process and writing new messages in its output buffer.

As protocols normally consist of a single process p_i per node $i \in [1, n]$, it is natural to model the system as the parallel composition $p_1 || \ldots || p_n$ and to represent the current system state as a *configuration*, i.e., a tuple containing for each node i the local state of its process p_i. This is done by existing symmetry reduction approaches for distributed protocols, which use a single scalarset to represent the IDs of nodes in the current configuration (e.g. [10,8]). Each node is thus modeled as an atomic entity and two configurations are symmetric if the states of the nodes can be permuted. We call this approach *node-based*.

The key idea of FTDP is that it lets the designer define a set R of *roles*, which are independent processes having non-intersecting states and whose state transitions are activated by non-intersecting sets of incoming messages and internal events. The behavior of each process p_i is expressed in FTDP as the parallel composition $p_i = r_i^1 || \ldots || r_i^{k_i}$, where each r_i^j is an instance of a role in R and where each role has at most one instance per process. Our *role-based* symmetry detection identifies symmetries by permuting the states of multiple role instances rather than the states of nodes as a whole. FTDP models each role in R with a separated scalarset whose size is determined by the number of the corresponding role instances in the system. In other words, we do not model the local state of a node but the local state of each role instance separately. This is possible because the properties of the protocol specify roles rather than nodes.

We illustrate the difference between role- and node-based approaches using the example state graph of Figure 3 (a). All states $s, \pi_1(s)$ and $\pi_2(s)$ are symmetric but only a role-based approach may be able to detect all existing symmetries. Consider for example that these states model a protocol where each of the two nodes executes instances of two roles $\{a, b\} = R$ as in Figures 3 (b) and (c). A node-based approach can detect the symmetry of s and $\pi_1(s)$ because two node states are permuted, but no symmetry is detected between $\pi_2(s)$ and any of the previous states. This symmetry can be detected by our role-based approach because role instances, rather than nodes, are modeled as basic symmetric entities.

The role-based approach can yield an exponentially larger number of symmetric states compared to classic node-based approaches. In the best-case, the model reduced using the symmetries detected by the role-based approach contains less states than the original model by a factor of at most $\prod_{i=1...|R|} n_i!$, where R is the set of roles and n_i is the number of processes executing role $r_i \in R$. This is because every state in the reduced model corresponds to at most $n_i!$ different states in the original model where n_i instances of r_i are permuted. In our experiments we show that this best-case reduction is almost reached for both Paxos and OM(1), so the identified reductions are very efficient. Furthermore, role-based detection can lead to an exponential best-case gain in terms of state reduction compared to the classic node-based approach in common systems. Assume that all n nodes execute all roles, i.e., $n_i = n$ for all i. In this case, the maximum benefit of symmetry reduction with the node-based symmetry detection approach is $n!$, which is $(n!)^{|R|-1}$ times less than with the role-based approach. Note that there is no guarantee that the reduced state space remains intractably large. In fact, symmetry reduction is able to mitigate state space explosion instead of fully tackling it.

3   The FTDP Language by Example: Modeling Paxos

Our goal is to create a language which, besides detecting symmetries, is able to faithfully model a broad class of FT distributed protocols. Models written in our language resemble the pseudocode of protocols so that system designers can easily use it.

We now present the FTDP language through the example of the Paxos protocol [11]. The complete FTDP model to verify the safety of Paxos is very compact and as depicted in Figures 4 and 5. The syntax of FTDP can be found in the Appendix.

Paxos solves the *consensus* problem, where each process keeps a local value and only one of these values is delivered to all processes. It assumes asynchronous, lossy channels with out-of-order delivery and at most a minority of processes which can crash. In a didactic paper [12] successive to [11], Lamport explicitly mentions three roles for each process, *leaders*, *acceptors* and *learners*. Leaders send a *proposal*, composed of the current local value and a proposal number, to all acceptors. An acceptor accepts a proposal only if it has not yet received any other proposal with a higher proposal number. A proposal is termed as *chosen* if a majority of acceptors accepts it. A chosen proposal can be learnt by the learners by collecting the accepted proposals from the acceptors. Consensus

Table 1. Overview of system models available in the FTDP language

Channel Models		
Synchrony	Asynchronous / Synchronous	(No / Existing) known upper bound on computation and message transmission delays
Reliability	Lossy / Reliable	Sent messages (are not / are) eventually received
Authentication	Authenticated	The receiver can identify the sender of the message
Delivery order	Out-of-order / FIFO	Sent messages (are not / are) received in the same order as they are sent
Duplication	No	Sent messages are not duplicated by the channel
Channel size	B-bounded	At most B messages can be sent but not yet received
Fault Models		
Status	Correct / Crash faulty / Byzantine faulty	Process always follows specification / Process eventually stops / Process does not follow specification

requires that (a) it is impossible that two proposals with different values are ever chosen (*safety*) and (b) a proposal is eventually learnt (*liveness*).[3]

Palette of System Models and API. The FTDP language supports multiple common system models that usually appear in FT distributed protocols. We model systems as parallel compositions of processes, i.e., role instances, communicating via messages sent through point-to-point directed channels. A summary of the different channel and fault models that can be selected by the user in FTDP are depicted in Table 1. A global parameter of every FTDP model determines a specific channel model. A field called `status` denotes for each process whether the process is correct, crash faulty or Byzantine.

Incoming messages activating state transitions are referred by the special variable `msg`, which has a user defined message type. A set of variables of the form `2roleName[k]` is used for sending a message to the kth process executing in the specified role (e.g., `2leader[k]`). These variables are written by the sender process and have a user defined message type.

FTDP Model Structure and Declarations. Every FTDP model defines four blocks for the definitions of roles and message types (`type`), state variables (`var`), initial assignments of the variables (`init`), and rules updating the variables (`rules`). The first three blocks for Paxos are depicted in Figure 4. A role is defined for leaders and acceptors by the role name and the number of the corresponding role instances `m` and `n`, which are constant model parameters (line 1 and 2). In order to verify safety we only need to model that a proposal is chosen so learners are not modeled explicitly. The type of messages is defined between lines 3-7. We define messages using a record where the value of the first field indicates the message type.

In every FTDP model, an array is defined for each role (lines 8-15 and 16-19), which stores the local states of role instances. The local state consists of the values of all state variables of the corresponding process. For example, proposal

---

[3] Note that in MC terms a liveness property differs from a safety property in that it can only be violated through infinite runs.

```
 1 type   leaderID: role[m];                                          // m processes are leaders
 2         acceptorID: role[n];                                        // n processes are acceptors
 3         Msg: record
 4               msgType: enum {READ,READ_REPL,WRITE};                 // message type
 5               propNo: 1..m*L;
 6               currPropNo: 0..m*L;
 7               val: 0..m end;
 8 var     leader: array[leaderID] of record
 9               propVal: 1..m;                                        // proposed value
10               propNoPool: array[1..L] of 1..m*L;                    // proposal no. pool, L: size of the pool
11               propNoID: 0..L;                                       // index of current proposal no.
12               readReplCnt:  0..[(n+1)/2];                           // READ-REPL message counter
13               readReplHighestProp: record                          // highest received prop. and its value
14                     propNo: 0..m*L;
15                     val:0..m end end;
16         acceptor: array[acceptorID] of record
17               currPropNo: 0..m*L;                                   // no. of the last accepted prop. , 0 is def. val.
18               acceptedVal: 0..m;                                    // val. of the last accepted prop. , 0 is def. val.
19               highestPropNo: m*L end;                               // highest observed prop. no, 0 is def. val.
20 init
21  [](i₁:leaderID)[](i₂:leaderID)[](j₁:acceptorID)...[](j_{[(n+1)/2]}:acceptorID)   initRule:       // maj. of acceptors is corr (m=2,L=2)
22      if  i₁≠i₂∧ j₁≠...≠j_{[(n+1)/2]}  then                         // acceptors are distinct
23          undefine leader;    undefine acceptor;                    // set all variables to undefine value
24          leader[i₁].propVal:=1;   leader[i₂].propVal:=2;           // leader i proposes i
25          leader[i₁].propNoPool[1]:=1;   leader[i₁].propNoPool[2]:=3;  // init disjoint prop. no. pools
26          leader[i₂].propNoPool[1]:=2;   leader[i₂].propNoPool[2]:=4;
27          leader[i₁].propNoID:=0;   leader[i₂].propNoID:=0;
28          leader[i₁].status=corr;   leader[i₂].status=corr;         // leaders are correct
29          for  k:acceptorID  do
30                acceptor[k].currPropNo:=0;
31                acceptor[k].highestPropNo:=0;
32                if  k=j₁∨...∨k=j_{[(n+1)/2]}
33                      then  acceptor[k].status:=corr  else  acceptor[k].status:=crash  endif endfor endif;
```

Fig. 4. Paxos modeled in FTDP — Declaration of types and variables, initialization with two leaders

numbers are stored in an array called `propNoPool` (line 10). The FTDP model of Paxos is parametric in the size of this array (L). The Paxos protocol assumes that the sets of proposal numbers are disjoint for different leaders. We implement this by assigning in the `init` block distinct values in $[1..m \cdot L]$ to the elements of the `propNoPool` arrays.

We specify symmetry by declaring that the local states of role instances can be freely permuted. The syntax of the FTDP language guarantees that the permutation yields symmetric states. This results in state space reduction if two processes of the same role have different local states which can be permuted in two different (global) system states in the original model. For example, the local state of two acceptors can differ when only one of them receives a leader's message. On the other hand, role-based symmetry detection cannot achieve the theoretically maximum benefit when the two acceptors can have the same local state, for example because both receive the leader's message.

State Initialization and Transitions. Initialization rules are used to set the initial values of process variables and the fault model of each process. Since asynchronous communication and concurrent operations between leaders are more challenging to handle than leader crashes, the initialization rule of Figure 4 sets all leaders as correct and selects a minority of crash faulty acceptors (lines 21-33). For simplicity of the presentation, we assume that m=2 and L=2. The initialization rule is parametric in the process IDs so that there is a distinct rule for each possible assignment of the parameters i_1, i_2 and $j_1 \ldots j_{\lceil(n+1)/2\rceil}$ to process IDs. For example, in case of $n = 3$, the assignment $i_1 = 1, i_2 = 2, j_1 = 1, j_2 = 3$ determines one instance of the rule.

Each FTDP *rule* corresponds to a state transition which can update the local state and send messages. The rules for Paxos, separated by [], are depicted in Figure 5. Rules are labeled for an easier reference. For example, the rule labeled as **leaderElect** (lines 36-43) handles an internal event triggered by leader election which makes leader i propose its value. Other rules are parameterized by i and j, the receiver and the sender of a message. Rules in FTDP can be guarded by a Boolean condition (lines 37, 46, 54, 68). For example, **leaderElect** is executed only if there is some unused proposal number left in the pool (line 37).

Temporal Properties in FTDP. Safety in Paxos requires that once a proposal with a value *val* is chosen, no other proposal is chosen at some time in the future with a value different from *val*. Such properties can be naturally written

```
35 rules
36 [](i:leaderID) leaderElect:                                          // the protocol is initiated by leader
37      if  leader[i].propNoID < L  then
38          leader[i].propNoID := leader[i].propNoID + 1;               // take next proposal no.
39          leader[i].readReplCnt := 0;                                 // reset reply counter
40          leader[i]readReplHighestProp.propNo := 0;                   // reset the READ_REPL w/ highest prop. no.
41          for  k : acceptorID  do                                     // leader initializes read phase...
42              2acceptor[k].msgType := READ;                           // ...by sending READ mess. to each acceptor
43              2acceptor[k].propNo := leader[i].propNoPool[leader[i].propNoID]  endfor endif;
44 []
45 [](i:acceptorID)[](j:leaderID) onReceiveREAD:                        // upon receipt of READ mess. at acceptor
46      if  msg.msgType = READ  then
47          if  msg.propNo > acceptor[i].highestPropNo  then            // make a promise, otherwise discard mess.
48              acceptor[i].highestPropNo := msg.propNo;
49              2leader[j].msgType := READ_REPL;                        // acceptor i completes read phase...
50              2leader[j].propNo := msg.propNo;                        // ... by sending a READ-REPL message to the leader
51              2leader[j].currPropNo := acceptor[i].currPropNo;
52              if  acceptor[i].currPropNo > 0  then  2leader[j].val := acceptor[i].acceptedVal  endif endif endif;
53 [](i:leaderID)[](j:acceptorID) onReceiveREAD_REPL:                   // upon receipt of READ_REPL mess. at leader
54      if  leader[i].readReplCnt < [(n+1)/2]  then                     // leader waits for majority, else discards mess.
55          if  msg.currPropNo > leader[i].readReplHighestProp.propNo  then   // updates the highest prop. received so far
56              leader[i].readReplCnt := leader[i].readReplCnt + 1;     // increment counter
57          if  msg.currPropNo > leader[i].readReplHighestProp.propNo  then   // updates the highest prop. received so far
58              leader[i].readReplHighestProp.propNo := msg.currPropNo;
59              leader[i].readReplHighestProp.val := msg.val  endif;
60          if  leader[i].content.readReplCnt = [(n+1)/2]  then         // if enough READ-REPL messages received
61              for  k : acceptorID  do                                 // leader initiates the write phase...
62                  2acceptor[k].msgType := WRITE;                      // ...by sending a WRITE mess. to each acc.
63                  2acceptor[k].propNo := leader[i].propNoPool[leader[i].propNoID];
64                  if  leader[i].readReplHighestProp.propNo = 0
65                      then  2acceptor[k].val := leader[i].propVal;
66                      else  2acceptor[k].val := leader[i].readReplHighestProp.val;  endif endfor endif endif endif;
67 [](i:acceptorID)[](j:leaderID) onReceiveWRITE:                       // upon receipt of WRITE mess. at acceptor
68      if  msg.msgType = WRITE  then
69          if  msg.propNo ≥ acceptor[i].highestPropNo  then            // accept if no promise prohibits this, else discard mess.
70              acceptor[i].currPropNo := msg.propNo;     acceptor[i].acceptedVal := msg.val  endif endif;

71 safety:   ∧_{val=1,2}  G( ∃(i_1:acceptorID)...∃(i_{[(n+1)/2]}:acceptorID)
72                          i_1 ≠ ... ≠ i_{[(n+1)/2]} ∧
73                          acceptor[i_1].currPropNo = ... = acceptor[i_{[(n+1)/2]}].currPropNo ∧
74                          acceptor[i_1].acceptedVal = val ⇒
75                              (F  ∃(j_1:acceptorID)...∃(j_{[(n+1)/2]}:acceptorID)
76                                  j_1 ≠ ... ≠ j_{[(n+1)/2]} ∧
77                                  acceptor[j_1].currPropNo = ... = acceptor[j_{[(n+1)/2]}].currPropNo ⇒
78                                      acceptor[j_1].acceptedVal = val  ))
```

Fig. 5. Paxos modeled in FTDP — Rules and safety property

in temporal logics. FTDP supports Computation Tree Logic (CTL*) which is a powerful temporal logic containing other useful logics like CTL or LTL. For example, safety can be defined in FTDP by using the temporal operators **G** ("always") and **F** ("eventually") (Figure 5, lines 71-78).[4] The basic assumption of role-based symmetries is that the property does not specify which role instance is executed by which physical node. In fact, the specification of such properties is impossible in FTDP as the model does not have the notion of nodes.

4   Symmetry Reduction of FTDP Models

The syntax of FTDP hides the modeling of channels and faulty processes from the user. These are modeled in the SS translation of FTDP models. In other words, FTDP defines syntactic sugar for SS. The translation between FTDP and SS guarantees that out-of-order delivery, message losses and process faults are considered in all possible ways. Therefore, no case can be overlooked which is necessary for a sound verification process. The soundness of verification is also affected by the property of the protocol. The property language of FTDP supports a broad class of properties that is provably preserved by symmetry reduction. We now give an overview of the translation between FTDP and SS and our property preservation results. The precise semantics of FTDP can be found in our technical report available online [3].

Faithful Model of Environment. Channels are modeled via message buffers. An input buffer is an array or a multiset depending on whether the channel is FIFO or delivers messages out-of-order. The size of each input buffer is bounded by B. Output buffers correspond to the API variables in the form `2roleName[k]` and can contain a single message. The transmission of a message is modeled by moving it from the output buffer of the sender process into the input buffer of the recipient process. In case this buffer is full the message is discarded (lossy channels) or the sender must wait until all the messages it is sending can be copied into the input buffers of the recipients (reliable channels). We model authenticated channels by defining at each process a buffer for each other process. A process receives and processes a message by removing it from the input buffer. In lossy channels it is decided non-deterministically if a message in the input buffer is lost, in which case it is removed without processing.

A crash faulty process that has not yet crashed is modeled such that it correctly follows the process specification. Upon receiving a message from a crash faulty process, it is decided non-deterministically if the message is actually processed. If not, the sender is considered to be crashed and the message is discarded as it had not been sent. In such a way we also model scenarios where a process crashes after it has sent a message to only a subset of processes.

---

[4] Note that because of the implication in line 77 it is not required that another proposal is ever chosen.

The state of a Byzantine process is not modeled. We model a process receiving a message from a Byzantine sender by non-deterministically selecting an arbitrary message from the domain. Thus, the size of this domain directly affects the size of the state space.

A system is synchronous if there is a known upper bound on message computation and delivery time, and is considered asynchronous otherwise. We model synchronous systems by assuming that a correct process waiting for a message is able to perfectly detect if the sender is faulty and the message will never arrive. Therefore, we introduce a Boolean flag `msg.absent` which is true if and only if the sender is either Byzantine faulty and fails to send a message or is crashed. The message itself (`msg`) contains the necessary information about which message is missing.

Property Preservation. Symmetry reduction is sound to use only if it preserves the properties in FTDP, which is provided by the following theorem:

Theorem 1. *[10,8] Let P be an SS model and AP a set of Boolean expressions defined over the variables in P. Given the state graph representation M of P, let the reduced state graph M_R be obtained from M by the permutation of scalarset values. M_R preserves every CTL* property f over AP, that is, f holds in M iff f holds in M_R.*

The property language of FTDP is essentially CTL* where the quantifiers, for example in the safety property of Paxos of Figure 5, are syntactic sugar for ANDs and ORs. Since the translation from FTDP to SS does not change AP, the above theorem justifies the soundness of our proposed approach as depicted in Figure 1. The details of the proof can be found in [3]. Note that every proposition p in AP is symmetric in that it cannot distinguish between specific role instances. Formally, in FTDP p must be quantified (existentially or universally) over the IDs of role instances. This constraint about AP enables the preservation of a class of properties as general as CTL*. We remark that the same constraint is needed if we restrict to a simpler class of properties such as simple invariants. Techniques where less symmetric properties can be preserved, at a price of less reduction, are surveyed in [16].

5   Experiments

We tested our approach on the representative synchronous and asynchronous Paxos and the OM(1) protocols. These two protocols represent a wide spectrum of different system and fault models. Different from Paxos, OM(1) is a synchronous, Byzantine fault tolerant consensus protocol using reliable channels. It defines two roles, a single commander who proposes its local value and n lieutenants who will agree on the same value if at most one general or lieutenant is Byzantine and $n \geq 3$ (IC1). Moreover, if the commander is correct its local value must be the agreed value (IC2). Conditions IC1-2 are called the interactive consistency (IC) conditions. The full FTDP model of OM(1) can be found in the Appendix (Figure 8).

Protocol	Param.	Property	Symm. red.	States	Gain	Effic.	Time	Result
			No	1,591,897			268 s	Verified
		safety	Node-based	795,945	2x	33%	226 s	Verified
Paxos			**Role-based**	**136,915**	**12x**	**96%**	32 s	Verified
	$m = 2$	Erroneous	No	649,301			61 s	CE found
	$n = 3$	safety (chosen	Node-based	325,074	2x	-	226 s	CE found
	$L = 1$	= accepted)	**Role-based**	**57,677**	**11x**	-	12 s	CE found
Faulty Paxos			No	1,114,891			126 s	CE found
(always accept		safety	Node-based	562,298	2x	-	122 s	CE found
proposals)			**Role-based**	**101,239**	**11x**	-	20 s	CE found
			No	1,797			0.1 s	Verified
	$n = 3$	IC1-2	Node-based	941	2x	31%	3 s	Verified
			Role-based	**345**	**5x**	**85%**	0.1 s	Verified
			No	150,417			9.6 s	Verified
OM(1)	$n = 4$	IC1-2	Node-based	26,401	6x	24%	17 s	Verified
			Role-based	**6,999**	**22x**	**90 %**	7.4 s	Verified
			No	-			-	No mem.
	$n = 5$	IC1-2	Node-based	2,402,167	-	-	4 h	Verified
			Role-based	**490,839**	-	-	2 h	Verified
Faulty OM(1)			No	934			0.1 s	CE found
(two Byzantine	$n = 3$	IC1	Node-based	843	1.1x	-	2.9 s	CE found
faults)			**Role-based**	**200**	**5x**	-	0.1 s	CE found

(a)

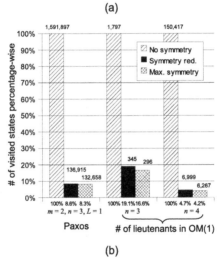

(b)

Fig. 6. (a) Results of model checking Paxos and OM(1) with Murφ using no, node-based and role-based symmetry reduction: "Verified" if the property can be proved, "No mem." if the state space explodes, and "CE found" if a counterexample was identified. (b) Comparison between the maximum and measured benefit of role-based symmetry reduction ($n = 5$, OM(1) see table).

We used the Murφ symmetry reduction model checker [9] as it implements the SS language.[5] Since Murφ only supports invariants, i.e., properties that must hold in all states of the model, we instrumented our SS models by monitors to check properties containing temporal operators. Monitors save system states that

---

[5] Other symmetry reduction model checkers like SymmSpin [5] or SMC [20] can also be used if the SS translation of FTDP models is adapted for the input language of the model checker. The SMC model checker supports liveness properties as well.

are specified by the property (e.g., the first chosen proposal in Paxos) and use it as a reference in other states (e.g., where a new proposal is chosen). Properties that cannot be defined via invariants and monitors, like liveness in Paxos, cannot be verified using Murφ and thus are excluded from the experiments.

Murφ uses different heuristics to minimize the (time and space) overhead of checking whether a state is symmetric with a previously visited one. Therefore, Murφ might also expand states that are symmetric. The results of the experiments are depicted in Figure 6 using Murφ's "heuristic fast canonicalization" algorithm. The results of Figure 6(a) include a comparison of the node-based and role-based approaches, the verification of the properties of both protocols as well as false properties and fault-injected protocols where, for each case, a counterexample was found. Our experiments cover for both protocols those (non-trivial) settings that were feasible to verify with Murφ. All experiments were executed on DETERlab machines [2], equipped with a Xeon processor and 4 GB memory and running a Linux installation with Fedora 6 core. The results show that symmetry reduction was able to achieve a benefit of at least one magnitude in terms of the number of visited states. Furthermore, OM(1) with 5 lieutenants could not be verified without symmetry reduction because the queue of unexplored states ran out of memory.

Figure 6 also compares the size of the reduced model (in terms of the number of visited states) with the lower bound on the number of non-symmetric states, i.e., the theoretical maximum benefit of node-based and role-based symmetries (see Section 2). The proportion of these two numbers is called *efficiency* [10]. It can be seen that both protocols are almost optimally symmetric with respect to their roles (approaching 100% efficiency). This is also highlighted in Figure 6(b) where we compare the size of the reduced model (middle bar) with the lower bound (rightmost bar), and relate them to the size of the original model (leftmost bar). This comparison cannot be done for OM(1) with $n = 5$ because the size of the original model is unknown. We can observe that the difference between the achieved and maximum benefit is within 3% of the size of the original model.

The node-based models assume that the number of nodes equals $max\{n_i\}$, i.e., the maximum number of processes executing the same role. Nodes can be arbitrarily allocated for role instances as long as no node hosts more than one role instance of the same role. Our experiments show that the role-based symmetry detection approach is superior to the node-based one in terms of the number of explored states. Note that even in the case of OM(1), where the theoretical maximum benefit is the same for the node-based and role-based approaches, the measured benefit is considerably higher with role-based symmetry detection. Intuitively, this is because the node-based model has to remember whether a lieutenant is hosted on the same node as the commander.

6   Conclusion

We have created FTDP, a pseudocode-like specification language for FT distributed protocols which can be directly used to model check the target protocol against its properties without specific MC expertise. FTDP flexibly supports the most used system and fault models and is able to specify symmetries of the protocol if it is divided into roles, a term familiar to protocol designers. We have shown that FTDP can naturally and compactly specify complex and widely-used distributed protocols such as Paxos and OM. Our role-based symmetry detection approach can be exponentially more efficient than the node-based approach. Our experiments on the MC of these protocols have shown that they are highly symmetric with respect to their roles as the experienced benefit approaches the theoretical maximum, and that the reduction in terms of the number of visited states is very significant, that is, around one order of magnitude.

References

1. Attiya, H., Bar-Noy, A., Dolev, D.: Sharing memory robustly in message-passing systems. J. ACM 42(1), 124–142 (1995)
2. Benzel, T., et al.: Design, deployment, and use of the deter testbed. In: DETER Community Workshop on Cyber Security Experimentation and Test (2007)
3. Bokor, P., Serafini, M., Suri, N., Veith, H.: Role-based symmetry reduction of fault-tolerant distributed protocols with language support. TR-TUD-DEEDS-04-04-2009 (2009), http://www.deeds.informatik.tu-darmstadt.de/peter/FTDP_SR.pdf
4. Bokor, P., Serafini, M., Suri, N., Veith, H.: Brief announcement: Practical symmetry reduction of fault-tolerant distributed protocols. DISC (to appear, 2009)
5. Bošnacki, D., Dams, D., Holenderski, L.: Symmetric SPIN. Journal on Softw. Tools for Techn. Transfer 4(1), 92–106 (2002)
6. Castro, M., Liskov, B.: Practical Byz. fault tolerance. In: Proc. OSDI, pp. 173–186 (1999)
7. Clarke, E., Grumberg, O., Peled, D.: Model Checking. MIT Press, Cambridge (2000)
8. Clarke, E.M., Enders, R., Filkorn, T., Jha, S.: Exploiting symmetry in temporal logic model checking. Formal Methods Sys. Design 9(1-2), 77–104 (1996)
9. Dill, D.L., Drexler, A.J., Hu, A.J., Yang, C.H.: Protocol verification as a hardware design aid. In: Proc. ICCD: Int. Conf. on Computer Design on VLSI in Computer & Processors, pp. 522–525 (1992)
10. Ip, C.N., Dill, D.L.: Better verification through symmetry. Formal Methods Sys. Design 9(1-2), 41–75 (1996)
11. Lamport, L.: The part-time parliament. ACM Trans. Comp. Sys. 16(2), 133–169 (1998)
12. Lamport, L.: Paxos made simple. ACM SIGACT News 32(4), 18–25 (2001)
13. Lamport, L.: Specifying Systems: The TLA+ Language and Tools for Hardware and Software Engineers. Addison-Wesley Longman Publishing Co., Inc., Amsterdam (2002)
14. Lamport, L.: Checking a multithreaded algorithm with +CAL. In: Dolev, S. (ed.) DISC 2006. LNCS, vol. 4167, pp. 151–163. Springer, Heidelberg (2006)
15. Lamport, L., Shostak, R., Pease, M.: The Byzantine Generals Problem. ACM Trans. Program. Lang. Syst. 4(3), 382–401 (1982)
16. Miller, A., Donaldson, A., Calder, M.: Symmetry in temporal logic model checking. ACM Comput. Surv. 38(3), 8 (2006)
17. Chockler, G., Guerraoui, R., Keidar, I., Vukolic, M.: Reliable distributed storage. Computer 42(4), 60–67 (2009)

18. Serafini, M., Suri, N., et al.: A tunable add-on diagnostic protocol for time-triggered systems. In: Proc. DSN, pp. 164–174 (2007)
19. Sistla, A.P., Godefroid, P.: Symmetry and reduced symmetry in model checking. ACM Trans. Program. Lang. Syst. 26(4), 702–734 (2004)
20. Sistla, A.P., et al.: SMC: A symmetry-based model checker for verification of safety and liveness properties. ACM Trans. Softw. Eng. Methodol. 9(2), 133–166 (2000)
21. Steiner, W., et al.: Model checking a fault-tolerant startup algorithm: from design exploration to exhaustive fault simulation. In: Proc. DSN, pp. 189–198 (2004)
22. Tsuchiya, T., Nagano, S., Paidi, R.B., Kikuno, T.: Symbolic Model Checking for Self-Stabilizing Algorithms. IEEE Trans. Parallel Distrib. Syst. 12(1), 81–95 (2001)
23. Tsuchiya, T., Schiper, A.: Model checking of consensus algorithms. In: Proc. SRDS, pp. 137–148 (2007)
24. Tsuchiya, T., Schiper, A.: Using BMC to verify consensus algorithms. In: Taubenfeld, G. (ed.) DISC 2008. LNCS, vol. 5218, pp. 466–480. Springer, Heidelberg (2008)
25. Zielinski, P.: Automatic verification and discovery of byzantine consensus protocols. In: Proc. DSN, pp. 72–81 (2007)

A   The Syntax of FTDP

Figure 7 depicts the BNF syntax of FTDP. As usual, the operator "[]" is used to select array elements and "." to address fields of a record. The names of non-terminals specific to FT distributed protocols are prefixed by "FTDP". The following types are pre-defined in every model: the roles used by the protocol ($\langle$FTDP-roleDecls$\rangle$) and the type of a message (Msg). The first type defines for each role $\langle$FTDP-roleType$\rangle$ the number of role instances. A message is modeled through a record of fields. For simplicity, the language allows the definition of one type of message only. This is not a limitation because the same type can be used to model various messages. Every FTDP model maintains for each role an array $\langle$FTDP-roleState$\rangle$ to store the local state of each role instance.

Every FTDP model must define at least one initial state. This is done via $\langle$rule$\rangle$. A simple rule is defined by a sequence of statements ($\langle$stmt$\rangle$) and labeled for easier reference. A statement is used to update the values of process variables. Rules are separated by using the [] operator. Parameterized rules can be defined by writing []($\langle$id$\rangle$: $\langle$typeExpr$\rangle$). This means that a rule is defined for every possible value of id. The execution of a rule means that the statements defined by the rule are executed. The state of the protocol is updated through the execution of a rule. If multiple rules are defined any of them can be executed. This is how the FTDP language supports non-determinism.

The statement undefine(v) can be used to assign a special undefined value to all values in variable v. The predicate isundefined(v) is used to check if all values in v assume the undefined value. Otherwise, a variable var can be assigned a value val by writing var:=val. Conditional and iterative statements are defined similar to ordinary programming languages.

Rules that describe how correct processes or processes that have not yet crashed update their variables are defined via $\langle$FTDP-rule$\rangle$. These rules can be combined similarly to $\langle$rule$\rangle$. The rule $\langle$FTDP-onTransition$\rangle$ defines an event

```
<FTDP>                  ::= type <FTDP-roleDecls>
                               Msg: record <decls> end;
                               <decls>
                            var <FTDP-roleState>
                            init <rule>
                            rules <FTDP-rule>
<FTDP-roleDecls>        ::= <FTDP-roleType> : role [<num>]; {<FTDP-roleType> : role [<num>];}
<FTDP-roleType>         ::= <id>
<FTDP-roleState>        ::= <FTDP-roleName>: array[<FTDP-roleType>] of record <decls> end
                          | <FTDP-roleState> ; <FTDP-roleState>
<FTDP-roleName>         ::= <id>
<FTDP-rule>             ::= <FTDP-onReceipt>
                          | <FTDP-onTransition>
                          | ELSE
                          | [] (<id>:<typeExpr>) <FTDP-rule>
                          | <FTDP-rule> [] <FTDP-rule>
<FTDP-label>            ::= string
<FTDP-onReceipt>        ::= [](i:<FTDP-roleId>)[](j:<FTDP-roleId>) <FTDP-label> :
                            if <FTDP-guard> then <stmt> endif
<FTDP-guard>            ::= <boolExpr>
<FTDP-onTransition>     ::= [](i:<FTDP-roleId>) <FTDP-label> : if <FTDP-guard> then <stmt> endif
<decls>                 ::= <id>: <typeExpr> {; <id>: <typeExpr>}
<typeExpr>              ::= <id>
                          | <num> .. <num>
                          | bool
                          | record <decls> end
                          | array [<num> .. <num>] of <typeExpr> | array [<id>] of <typeExpr>
                          | enum {<id>{, <id>}}
<rule>                  ::= <FTDP-label> : <stmt>
                          | [] (<id>:<typeExpr>) <rule>
                          | <rule> [] <rule>
<stmt>                  ::= <var> := <term>
                          | undefine(<var>)
                          | if <boolExpr> then <stmt> {else <stmt>} endif
                          | for <id>:<typeExpr> do <stmt> endfor
                          | <stmt> ; <stmt>
<boolExpr>              ::= <term> = <term>
                          | <term> > <term>
                          | ¬<boolExpr>
                          |  <boolExpr> ∧ <boolExpr>
                          |  ∀ (<id>:<typeExpr>) <boolExpr>
                          |  ∃(<id>:<typeExpr>)<boolExpr>
                          | isundefined(<boolExpr>)
<term>                  ::= <var> | <num>
                          | <term> + <term> | <term> * <term>
<var>                   ::= <id> | <var>.<id> | <var>[<term>]
<id>                    ::= string
<num>                   ::= string
```

Fig. 7. The syntax of the FTDP language

handler of the ith role instance in the specified role (⟨FTDP-roleId⟩) to update its local state in response to an internal event. Another rule ⟨FTDP-onReceipt⟩ defines an event handler for the receipt of a message. The rule is parameterized by a reference to the receiver and sender role instances (i and j). Both rules are guarded by a Boolean condition (⟨FTDP-guard⟩) to govern which handler is

Table 2. List of predefined variables in FTDP modeling a protocol with k roles ($j \in [1..k]$). Variables can be read-only (R), read/write (RW), and write-only (W). Proc. i is defined in the FTDP rule.

Name	Type	Scope	Usage	Description
msg	Msg	rules	R	Latest mess. received by proc. i from j
msg.absent	bool	rules	R	True iff the mess. was not sent
roleName[i].status	{corr,crash,byz}	init	RW	Status of proc. i in role "roleName"
2roleName$j$	array[roleIdj] of Msg	rules	W	Proc. i's mess. to "roleName$j$" inst.

```
type        commanderID: scalarset[1];                                    // one commander
            lieutenantID: scalarset[n]                                    // n lieutenants
            Msg: record comm: Boolean end
var         commander: array[commanderID] of record
                command: Boolean end;                                     // commander's order
                hasProposed: Boolean;                                     // flags that corr. commander has sent order
            lieutenant: array[lieutenantID] of record
                commands: array[lieutenantID] of Boolean;                 // commands received by lieutenant
                decision: Boolean; end                                    // decision: accepted order
init
[](i:lieutenantID)[](comm:Boolean) init1:                                 // corr. commander orders "comm"
            undefine lieutenant;
            for k:commanderID do
              commander[k].command:=comm;
              commander[k].hasProposed:=false;
              commander[k].status:=corr;
            endfor;
            for k:lieutenantID do                                         // i^th lieutenant is Byzantine
                if  k=i  then  lieutenant[k].status:=byz  else  lieutenant[k].status:=corr   endif endfor;
[]
[](i:commanderID) init2:                                                  // Byzantine commander
            undefine commander;
            undefine lieutenant;
            commander[i].status:=byz;
            for k:lieutenantID do  lieutenant[k].status:=corr endfor;     // correct lieutenants
rules
[](i:commanderID) propose:                                                // correct commander sends order
   if  ¬commander[i].hasProposed  then
            for k:lieutenantID do  2lieutenant[k].comm:=command  endfor;
            commander[i].hasProposed:=true
   endif
[]
[](i:lieutenantID)[](j:commanderID) recProp:                              // correct lieut. i receives order from commander
   if  isundefined(lieutenant[i].commands[i])  then                       // if lieutenant has not already received it
     if  msg.absent                                                       // order stored at commands[i] at lieut. i
       then   lieutenant[i].commands[i]:=defVal                           // defVal upon send omission
       else   lieutenant[i].commands[i]:=msg.comm                         // store received order otherwise
     endif;
     for k:lieutenantID do                                               // forward order to other lieutenants
         if  k≠i  then  2lieutenant[k].comm:=lieutenant[i].commands[i]  endif endfor
   endif
[]
[](i:lieutenantID)[](j:lieutenantID) recComm:                             // correct lieut. i receives command from lieut. j
   if  isundefined(lieutenant[i].commands[j])  then                       // if i has not already received it
     if  msg.absent
       then   lieutenant[i].commands[j]:=defVal
       else   lieutenant[i].commands[j]:=msg.comm
     endif;
     if  ∀(k:lieutenantID)¬isundefined(lieutenant[i].commands[k])  then   // majority voting
         if   ∃(i_1:lieutenantID)...∃(i_{(n+1)/2}:lieutenantID)i_1≠...≠i_{(n+1)/2}∧
         lieutenant[i].commands[i_1]=¬defVal∧...∧lieutenant[i].commands[i_{(n+1)/2}]=¬defVal
               then   lieutenant[i].decision:=¬defVal
               else   lieutenant[i].decision:=defVal                      // defVal if no majority exists
     endif
   endif;
[]
ELSE

IC1: F(  ∀(i:lieutenantID)∀(j:lieutenantID)                               // agreement is always achieved
         lieutenant[i].status=corr∧lieutenant[j].status=corr⇒
         ¬isundefined(lieutenant[i].decision)∧¬isundefined(lieutenant[j].decision)∧
         lieutenant[i].decision=lieutenant[j].decision   )
IC2: G(  ∀(i:commanderID)∀(j:lieutenantID)                                // correct comm.'s order is decided
         commander[i].status=corr∧¬isundefined(lieutenant[j].decision)⇒
         commander[i].command=lieutenant[j].decision   )
```

Fig. 8. OM(1) and its properties specified in FTDP

executed. In order to avoid deadlocks in our models the **ELSE** rule can be used which executes the empty statement if no other rule can be executed.

The list of pre-defined variables and their description is depicted in Table 2. The use of these variables is better explained in Section 3 and in [3].

Symmetry by Construction. We define conditions C1-C5 to ensure that the symmetry of an FTDP model is not broken. These conditions can be verified through simple syntactic checking. We assume that they are (automatically) checked by an interpreter.

(C1) An array with role index type can only be indexed by a variable of exactly the same type.
(C2) A term of role type may not appear as an operand to + or any other operator in a term.
(C3) Variables of role type may only be compared using =.
(C4) For all assignments $d := t$, the types of d and t may be (possible different) subranges or exactly matching roles.
(C5) Variables, elements of arrays and fields of records written by any iteration of a "for" statement indexed by a role type must be disjoint from the set of variables, elements of arrays and fields of records referenced (read or written) by other iterations.

The Property Language. We adopt the Computation Tree Logic (CTL*) [7] to define properties of FT distributed protocols. Properties of an FTDP model can be defined via the CTL* temporal operators based on *AP* (atomic properties), where *AP* contains all Boolean expressions in the FTDP language. We refer to our technical report [3] for more details about CTL*.

Implementing and Applying the Stocks-Carrington Framework for Model-Based Testing

Maximiliano Cristiá[1,2,3] and Pablo Rodríguez Monetti[1,2,3]

[1] Flowgate Consulting
[2] CIFASIS-CONICET
[3] FCEIA, Universidad Nacional de Rosario
{mcristia,prodriguez}@flowgate.net

Abstract. In this paper we describe the functional features and the architecture of a tool implementing the Stocks-Carrington framework (TTF) for model based testing (MBT). The resulting prototype, called Fastest, makes it easy to generate test cases from Z specifications. We not only apply the ideas of the referred framework but we also use a technique based on finite models to find test cases, which has proved to increase the level of automation during the whole testing process. The paper also discusses problems and challenges that have appeared during the development of the tool, and introduces real case studies and an analysis of the results obtained so far.

1 Introduction

Current industrial practice in software testing is mostly manual: test template[1] definition, test case derivation and the determination of success or failure are all manual, tedious, resource consuming and error prone activities. These activities make poor use of software engineers' skills, changing analytical tasks for a repetitive manual work. Within this picture many software development companies seldom perform serious testing of their programs. In this paper we introduce a tool, called Fastest [1], which automates test suite definition and test case derivation for unit testing, by applying the Test Template Framework (TTF) proposed by Stocks and Carrington [2,3,4] for model-based testing (MBT).

The main contributions of the paper are: (a) a flexible, efficient and automatic implementation of the TTF which, as far as we have investigated, does not exist yet; (b) the implementation of a technique to automatically derive abstract test cases from test objectives, which was not originally proposed by Stocks and Carrington; and (c) an analysis of the application of Fastest to two industrial-strength case studies and several toy examples.

Since this paper is about MBT we will shortly introduce this technique; for a deeper presentation the reader may consult [5]. In order to test a program

---

[1] Test templates are also called *test classes* or *test objectives*; we will use all of them as synonymous.

K. Breitman and A. Cavalcanti (Eds.): ICFEM 2009, LNCS 5885, pp. 167–185, 2009.

P it is necessary to have a formal specification Op of it and follow the process depicted in Fig. 1. From Op, abstract test cases (t) are derived by executing the conceptual step named *gen*. Abstract test cases are abstract since they are written in the same language than Op. Then each t is refined into a concrete test case (x), i.e. in a test case written in the same language than P. The *exec* step represents the actual execution of P with input x, which produces an output $P(x)$. This output is abstracted to the specification level when the *abs* step is executed. The specification is used again to verify whether the test has uncovered an error or not, during the final step *compr*. The abstract pair (t, y) is conveniently substituted in Op: if it reduces to *true* then no error was discovered, and if it reduces to *false* or $P(x)$ cannot be abstracted into t, an error was found.

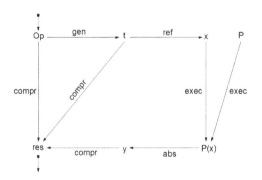

Fig. 1. A general description of the MBT process

All of the steps of Fig. 1 can be mechanized to a great extent. In this article we introduce a specific implementation of the *gen* step based on the TTF. It is worth to mention that, although the Z notation is one of the most used formal notations in industry and that the TTF is a straightforward and powerful MBT technique for Z, there is no implementation of the Stocks and Carrington framework as automatic as ours.

The paper is structured as follows. The next section presents a brief introduction to the TTF. In Sect. 3 we show the functional and architectural features of Fastest, while a representative example is run in Sect. 4. Section 5 presents the results of applying Fastest to some industrial cases studies and to some toy examples, as well. Our work is compared to similar approaches in Sect. 6. Finally, Sect. 7 describes our conclusions and future work.

2   The Test Template Framework

In this section we introduce MBT from the perspective of Stocks and Carrington, without mention any particular implementation or tool. Precisely, in Sect. 3 we introduce our implementation which also refines the framework.

Phil Stocks and David Carrington introduced in [2,3,4] a formal framework to conduct model-based testing of Z specifications [6], including a rigorous and disciplined technique for defining and structuring abstract test templates and test cases. They also proposed new testing tactics[2] specifically suited to the Z notation. According to them, testing tactics are the mechanisms that must be used to partition the input space to build a so called testing tree.

We make use of an example to explain the TTF, but we assume the reader is fluent in the Z notation.

2.1   A Simple Pool of Sensors

The following Z model describes a simple pool of sensors which records the highest reading of each sensor. The KMR operation[3] takes as input a sensor ID, $s?$, and a reading, $r?$, of it. If $s?$ is a valid ID and if $r?$ is greater than the current reading of $s?$, KMR replaces the current reading for $r?$. If some condition does not hold, then the operation fails and nothing is changed.

$$[SENSOR]$$
$$MaxReadings == [smax : SENSOR \nrightarrow \mathbb{Z}]$$

$$
\begin{array}{l}
\hline
\ \_\ KMROk _____ \\
\ \Delta MaxReadings \\
\ s? : SENSOR;\ r? : \mathbb{Z} \\
\hline
\ s? \in \mathrm{dom}\ smax \\
\ smax\ s? < r? \\
\ smax' = smax \oplus \{s? \mapsto r?\} \\
\hline
\end{array}
\qquad
\begin{array}{l}
\hline
\ \_\ KMRE2 _____ \\
\ \Xi MaxReadings \\
\ s? : SENSOR;\ r? : \mathbb{Z} \\
\hline
\ s? \in \mathrm{dom}\ smax \\
\ r? \leq smax\ s? \\
\hline
\end{array}
$$

$$KMRE1 == [\Xi MaxReadings;\ s? : SENSOR \mid s? \notin \mathrm{dom}\ smax]$$
$$KMR == KMROk \vee KMRE1 \vee KMRE2$$

2.2   Testing Tactics, Test Classes and Testing Trees

The TTF starts by defining, for each Z operation, the *input space* (*IS*) and the *valid input space* (*VIS*). The *IS* is the set defined by all of the possible values of the input and state variables of the operation. For instance, the *IS* of *KMR* is:

$$IS == [smax : SENSOR \nrightarrow \mathbb{Z};\ s? : SENSOR;\ r? : \mathbb{Z}]$$

In turn, the *VIS* is the subset of *IS* for which the operation is defined. The *VIS* of *KMR* is equal to its *IS* since the operation is total. More formally, the *VIS* of an operation *Op* can be defined as follows:

---

[2] Here we preferred testing tactic instead of the original term *testing strategy* because we believe the former has a narrow scope than the last.

[3] *KMR* stands for *KeepMaxReadings*.

$$VIS_{Op} == [IS_{Op} \mid \text{pre } Op]$$

Stocks and Carrington suggest to divide the *VIS* into equivalence classes, called *test classes*, by applying one or more *testing tactics*. The test classes obtained in this way can be further subdivided into more test classes by applying other testing tactics. This procedure can continue until either the engineer considers that the test classes are reasonable small, or there is a reasonable number of them, or each of the functional alternatives is covered by only one test class. Within the TTF all these test classes are represented as a *testing tree*, as shown in Fig. 3. The authors indicate that it is convenient for the testing process that tactics produce a mathematical partition of either the *VIS* or a test class. In this way, test classes are indeed equivalence classes in the sense that if the program fails for a particular element it should fail for any other element of the class. Test cases are taken only from the leaves of the testing tree as we will see shortly.

Within the TTF the authors defined a number of testing tactics that together provide a sound method for calculating tests objectives. Furthermore, they propose that new tactics should be added for particular projects, systems, requirements, etc. Then, any tool implementing the TTF should enable the inclusion and parametrization of testing tactics. Two of the testing tactics proposed within the TTF are the following:

- *Disjunctive Normal Form (DNF)*. By applying this tactic the predicate of the operation is written in DNF and the *VIS* or a test class is partitioned in as many test classes as terms has the predicate. The precondition of each term is conjoined to the predicate of the *VIS* or the test class being divided.
- *Standard Partitions (SP)*. This tactic uses the mathematical operators appearing in the predicate to generate more test objectives. A *standard partition* is a partition of the domain of a given mathematical operator in sets called *sub-domains*. In practice, standard partitions are expressed as conditions that must hold of the operator's operands. These conditions are used to divide a test class. Figure 2 shows one possible standard partition for the $<$ operator.

We will apply both tactics to *KMR*. First we apply DNF to the *VIS* and then Standard Partitions is applied to the expression $smax\ s? < r?$ of *KMROk*. The resulting testing tree is shown in Fig. 3. Some of the nodes of the testing tree are shown below as Z schema boxes. It is worth to mention that the predicates of the objectives in a given level contain the predicates of the upper level. This is the reason for which test cases are drawn only from the leaves.

1. $a < 0, b < 0$	4. $a = 0, b < 0$	7. $a > 0, b < 0$
2. $a < 0, b = 0$	5. $a = 0, b = 0$	8. $a > 0, b = 0$
3. $a < 0, b > 0$	6. $a = 0, b > 0$	9. $a > 0, b > 0$

Fig. 2. Possible standard partition for $a < b$

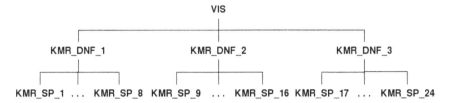

Fig. 3. Testing tree of *KMR*

_____ *KMR_DNF_1* _____
$smax : SENSOR \nrightarrow \mathbb{Z}$
$s? : SENSOR$
$r? : \mathbb{Z}$
_____
$s? \in \text{dom } smax$
$smax \ s? < r?$

_____ *KMR_DNF_2* _____
$smax : SENSOR \nrightarrow \mathbb{Z}$
$s? : SENSOR$
$r? : \mathbb{Z}$
_____
$s? \notin \text{dom } smax$

_____ *KMR_SP_1* _____
$smax : SENSOR \nrightarrow \mathbb{Z}$
$s? : SENSOR$
$r? : \mathbb{Z}$
_____
$s? \in \text{dom } smax$
$smax \ s? < r?$
$smax \ s? < 0$
$r? < 0$

_____ *KMR_SP_9* _____
$smax : SENSOR \nrightarrow \mathbb{Z}$
$s? : SENSOR$
$r? : \mathbb{Z}$
_____
$s? \in \text{dom } smax$
$smax \ s? < r?$
$smax \ s? > 0$
$r? > 0$

_____ *KMR_SP_2* _____
$smax : SENSOR \nrightarrow \mathbb{Z}$
$s? : SENSOR$
$r? : \mathbb{Z}$
_____
$s? \in \text{dom } smax$
$smax \ s? < r?$
$smax \ s? < 0$
$r? = 0$

_____ *KMR_DNF_3* _____
$smax : SENSOR \nrightarrow \mathbb{Z}$
$s? : SENSOR$
$r? : \mathbb{Z}$
_____
$s? \in \text{dom } smax$
$r? \leq smax \ s?$

_____ *KMR_SP_19* _____
$smax : SENSOR \nrightarrow \mathbb{Z}$
$s? : SENSOR$
$r? : \mathbb{Z}$
_____
$s? \in \text{dom } smax$
$r? \leq smax \ s?$
$smax \ s? < 0$
$r? < 0$

_____ *KMR_SP_20* _____
$smax : SENSOR \nrightarrow \mathbb{Z}$
$s? : SENSOR$
$r? : \mathbb{Z}$
_____
$s? \in \text{dom } smax$
$r? \leq smax \ s?$
$smax \ s? < 0$
$r? = 0$

For instance, *KMR_DNF_3* is defined by the same variables declared in *VIS*, and its predicate is one of the terms of the predicate of *KMR* after writing it in *DNF*. In turn, the predicate of *KMR_SP_20* is the conjunction between the predicate of *KMR_DNF_3* and the instantiation of the second predicate of the standard partition shown in Fig. 2.

The second step of the TTF methodology suggests to prune the testing tree. In effect, some test objectives are empty because they are contradictions. In these cases it is impossible to find abstract test cases. For instance, class *KMR_SP_20* must be pruned, among others. Stocks and Carrington do not give a recipe on how this can be automated. In Sect. 3.6 we give a very short description of a technique that we are currently implementing in Fastest.

Finally, the engineer has to choose at least one element for each of the remaining leaves of the testing tree. These are the abstract test cases. Here, we can see one of the main benefits of the TTF: the model, the test classes and the test cases are all expressed in the same notation. For example, the following schema boxes represent abstract test cases of the corresponding test objectives. Note that the method naturally provides traceability between objectives and abstract test cases by using schema inclusion. Within the TTF a test case is a sort of assignment of constant values to state and input variables, rather than a sequence of operations leading to the desired state, as is suggested by other approaches [7,8,9].

$$
\begin{array}{|l}
\underline{\quad KMR\_SP\_1\_TCASE \quad} \\
KMR\_SP\_1 \\
\hline
r? = -1 \\
smax = \{(sensor0, -2)\} \\
s? = sensor0 \\
\end{array}
$$

$$
\begin{array}{|l}
\underline{\quad KMR\_SP\_6\_TCASE \quad} \\
KMR\_SP\_6 \\
\hline
r? = 1 \\
smax = \{(sensor0, 0)\} \\
s? = sensor0 \\
\end{array}
$$

$$
\begin{array}{|l}
\underline{\quad KMR\_SP\_2\_TCASE \quad} \\
KMR\_SP\_2 \\
\hline
r? = 0 \\
smax = \{(sensor0, -1)\} \\
s? = sensor0 \\
\end{array}
$$

$$
\begin{array}{|l}
\underline{\quad KMR\_SP\_9\_TCASE \quad} \\
KMR\_SP\_9 \\
\hline
r? = 2 \\
smax = \{(sensor0, 1)\} \\
s? = sensor0 \\
\end{array}
$$

We want to remark that there is a clear distinction between test objectives and test cases: the formers are predicates, and the latter are constants. In other papers test cases are the same than test objectives [10,11,12]. We think that this difference is essential to the MBT process because the selection of constants satisfying test objectives is a very time consuming task if it is not done automatically. Although the TTF suggests that the selection of abstract test cases from test classes is a rather easy task, the authors do not give any clue on how to automate this step. In Sect. 3.7 we show the method we have developed.

3   Fastest: An Implementation of the TTF

The goal of this section is to describe both the functional and architectural features of Fastest. Also we show some design and implementation details that we believe contribute to the development of MBT tools. Since the Community Z Tools framework [13,14] is a key component of Fastest we comment on how it was integrated into our tool.

Fastest is an open-source software available in the section Tools at http://www.flowgate.net (which includes a rather complete user manual).

3.1   Conceptual Description

As shown in Fig. 4, Fastest receives a Z specification in LATEX format using the CZT package. The Z specification must verify the ISO standard [15]. The specification is transformed into an internal representation more amenable to parsing and static analysis. Then, the user has to enter a list of the operations to test as well as the tactics to apply to each of them. In a third step Fastest generates the testing tree of each operation. After the trees are generated, the user can browse them and their test classes, and he can prune any node. Once the user is done with pruning, he can instruct Fastest to find one abstract test case for each leaf in all the test trees. Although the method to find abstract test cases has proved to be quite automatic, it is worth to say that it does not guarantee to find abstract test cases for all test objectives, as we will see in a following subsection. The user can export all the results –test classes and abstract test cases– in LATEX format.

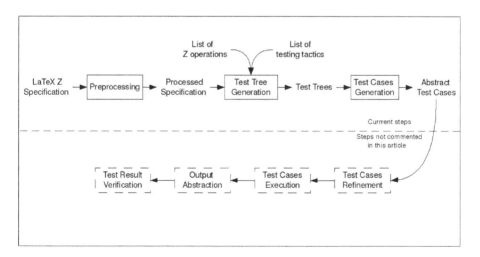

Fig. 4. Fastest's testing process. The dotted line divides the steps reported in this paper from those not included here.

3.2   The Architecture of Fastest

Fastest was envisioned as a client-server application [16]. The main reason for thinking of a distributed system came from the realization that calculating abstract test cases from test objectives in large projects could be a hard computing problem, but highly parallelizable as well –we will come back to this point in Sect. 3.7. Then, we thought of an scalable application using the idle computer power present in a corporate network. On the other side, since testing a large application is usually carried on by a group of testers, a client-server architecture allows the team to work concurrently from different workstations by running a client process per tester. However, in such a large project there is shared information –such as the definition or parametrization of some testing tactics, test cases already calculated, theorems that help to prune testing trees, etc.– that all the clients and servers should be able to access. Hence, a typical Fastest installation has a data server that is known to all other processes, some client processes and a number of testing servers.

The client is organized following the Implicit Invocation architectural style [17]. The main architectural invariant of this style is that the components that announce events do not know which other components will react to them. A consequence of this property is the possibility to add, remove and change components without affecting the others [18]. For instance, it would be quite easy to add a component that is called whenever a new test case is calculated, that stores it on disc or that refines it to a given programming language.

The client has a simple text-based user interface from which the user can issue commands and read their output. All the components of this architecture were implemented as Java programs.

3.3   The CZT Framework

The Community Z Tools (CZT) project [13,14] is an open source Java framework created in 2003 with the goal of building a toolkit for the Z notation or its dialects. These tools include editors, parsers, type-checkers and so on, to work with Z specifications written in LaTeX, Unicode or XML. The following CZT services have been used in Fastest:

- CZT Parser and the Annotated Syntax Trees (AST)
- CZT Type-checker
- CZT ZLive specification animator

Although we were benefited greatly from all these services, perhaps the most important was ZLive. The ZLive project provides an evaluator of Z expressions and predicates. In other words, ZLive takes a Z model and values for the input and state variables and calculates the values of the output and next state variables –it is worth to mention that ZLive does not cover the whole Z notation yet.

We used this facility to calculate test cases from test templates as is described in Sect. 3.7.

·3.4   Testing Tactics in Fastest

As we have said earlier, the first step of the TTF is to apply some testing tactics to each operation of the Z model. Fastest features a user command (`addtactic`) that allows the user to build the list of tactics to be applied to each operation, by entering the name of an operation, the testing tactic name and a few more parameters depending on the tactic –for more details on the syntax of user commands go to Sect. 4. The current version implements DNF, Standard Partitions and two new tactics proposed by us: Free Types (FT) and In Set Extension (ISE). FT works on the variables of a free (enumerated) type, partitioning the *VIS* or the test class in as many classes as elements has the type. More formally, if the *VIS* of a given operation declares $v : T$, where $T ::= V_1 \mid \ldots \mid V_n$, then the class is partitioned in n templates where each of them has a predicate of the form $v = V_i$. This tactic is useful since enumerated types usually codify specific states, operational modes, etc. Hence, by applying it there will be at least one test case for each of those situations. ISE consist in partitioning an objective which contains a precondition of the form $v \in \{e_1, \ldots, e_n\}$, where v is a variable and $e_1, \ldots, e_n$ are expressions, in n new objectives each of which contains, also, a predicate of the form $v = e_i$.

Since Standard Partitions is a general tactic that can be applied to a number of mathematical operators, Fastest has a configuration file where the user can define, modify or read partitions for all the operators he or she needs. Figure 5 shows a typical standard partition for the $\cap$ operator. As the reader may note, the user writes the standard partitions in a simple and intuitive LATEX-based language. In this way Fastest implements one important feature of the TTF.

Another important aspect of Fastest is a key design decision that allows users to add new tactics. The only thing a user has to do is to program a class implementing the `Tactic` interface. This class has methods to configure and apply testing tactics.

```
\cap : operator(S,T);
S = \{\}, T = \{\};
S = \{\}, T \neq \{\};
S \neq \{\}, T = \{\};
S \neq \{\}, T \neq \{\}, S \cap T = \{\};
S \neq \{\}, T \neq \{\}, S \subset T;
S \neq \{\}, T \neq \{\}, T \subset S;
S \neq \{\}, T \neq \{\}, T = S;
S \neq \{\}, T \neq \{\}, (S \cap T) \neq \{\},
\lnot(S \subseteq T), \lnot (T \subseteq S), T \neq S;
end operator;
```

Fig. 5. Fastest's standard partition for $S \cap T$

3.5   Fastest's Automatic Generation of Testing Trees

Once the engineer has entered the list of testing tactics for each operation, the only thing he or she has to do to build the testing trees is to run command `genalltt`. In other words, the sole manual work for the engineer, up to this point, is to enter the names of the tactics and other simple parameters: Fastest reads the definition of each testing tactic and builds automatically each node of each testing tree by manipulating the Z text.

3.6   Pruning Testing Trees in Fastest

Applying one tactic after another usually yields many empty test classes that is advisable to prune from the tree. Besides, the engineer might want to prune some nodes to reduce the number of tests to run for various reasons. Then, a tool implementing the TTF should feature a way to automatically prune testing trees as well as some manual way. Fastest current version implements only manual pruning.

Automatic pruning involves some automatic way of finding contradictions, which is in general an unsolvable problem. After trying to use the automated theorem prover Z/EVES [19], which solves some cases but not all of them, we have envisioned a light-weight method. This technique is being implemented and rests on the peculiarities of the problem within the TTF. We think that a full description of the method deserves its own paper, so here we just give some tips. First, we assume that test class predicates are conjunctions of atomic predicates. Second, Fastest would be delivered with a list of so called *elimination theorems*, which are parametrized conjunctions of atomic predicates that yield a contradiction –for instance $f = \varnothing \wedge \operatorname{dom} f \neq \varnothing$, where the name and type of f are parameters. Third, we let the user to extend the list with his own theorems. Fourth, some simplification or rewrite rules are applied to each test class. Finally, Fastest applies all the elimination theorems to each test class, which means to seek the contradictory predicates inside the test class' predicate. Hence, if some class is a contradiction but Fastest fails to prune it, the user can add an elimination theorem that will prune similar test classes in future projects. However, we still think of combining our method with Z/EVES.

For manual pruning, Fastest provides three commands (`prunebelow`, `prune-from` and `unprune`) that allow the engineer to prune subtrees and restore them in case of mistake. See Sect. 4 for more details.

3.7   Finding Abstract Test Cases with Finite Models

We have based our method for calculating abstract test cases from test objectives on the following:

> **Conjecture.** For most of the predicates appearing in real specifications, a small finite model will suffice to find an element verifying that predicate; and if there is no element verifying the predicate, it is because the predicate is a contradiction.

Then, the method consists of building a finite model for each test class by calculating the Cartesian product between a very small finite set of values for each variable in the *VIS*. Later, Fastest evaluates –using ZLive– the class' predicate on each element of the model. Although this technique might appear inefficient and is certainly inelegant, it has proved to be quite accurate, as we show in Sect. 5. In part the efficiency has been achieved by exploiting the highly parallelizable nature of the problem. In effect, Fastest asks each testing server to calculate a test case of a particular test class. Then, the time to find abstract test cases decrease proportionally with the number of available testing servers. This parallelization is so efficient because each calculation is completely independent from each other; synchronization is only needed when testing servers communicate a result to a client.

Then, every time Fastest asks a testing server to find an abstract test case from a given test class, it can happen one and only one of the following:

- Some element in the finite model satisfies the class' predicate, then we have the desired test case.
- There is no element in the finite model satisfying the predicate because it is a contradiction –and was not pruned in the previous step.
- There is no element in the finite model satisfying the predicate, but the predicate is not a contradiction. In this case Fastest lets the user to suggest a new finite model or part of it for the conflicting class (see command `setfinitemodel` in Sect. 4).

The key point here is what finite sets Fastest considers for each variable in the test class. By applying the first versions of the tool to some real case studies we were able to define a set of heuristics that make it possible to find a very high number of test cases, while minimizing the number of evaluations. These heuristics are the following:

- The finite sets for types $\mathbb{N}$ or $\mathbb{Z}$ are built from the numerical constants appearing in the predicate –if there are no such constants then we take $\{0, 1, 2\}$ and $\{-1, 0, 1\}$, respectively.
- The finite sets for enumerated types are the types themselves.
- The finite sets for basic types are built by generating three constant names of each type. For example, if *CHAR* is a basic type, we assume the existence of $char1, char2, char3 : CHAR$, and then we take $\{char1, char2, char3\}$ as the finite set for any variable of type *CHAR*. We think of them as being three different constant elements.
- If a variable declared in the *VIS* does not appear in the predicate of a test class, then the finite set for that variable is any singleton –since the value of such a variable has no influence whatsoever on the evaluation of the predicate.
- If the predicate of a test class contains an atomic predicate of the form $var = VAL$, where *var* is a variable declared in the *VIS* and *VAL* is a constant value, then the finite set for *var* is just $\{VAL\}$ –since it will be impossible to satisfy the predicate with any other value.
- The finite sets for types such as $\text{seq } X$, $X \nrightarrow Y$, and so on, are built recursively from the finite sets considered for the more basic types.

The current version of Fastest does not cover the whole Z notation yet –in part because ZLive does not either. Hence, the Z models can only have variables of the following types: basic types, enumerated types, $\mathbb{N}$, $\mathbb{Z}$, set extensions, ranges, power sets, Cartesian products, binary relations, total functions, partial functions, sequences or any valid combination of them. For instance, Fastest does not yet support variables of schema types, $A \twoheadrightarrow B$, $A \rightarrowtail B$, $A \rightarrowtail\!\!\!\!\to B$, $\mathbb{P}_1 A$ and $\mathbb{N}_1$. Axiomatic definitions are not supported neither. Although these are obvious limitations they do not impeded us to apply Fastest to real world examples, as shown in Sect. 5.

4   Running an Example

In this section we use Fastest to run the example shown in Sect. 2. We will refer to some Z schema defined in that section.

Fastest is run from a command window with the following command:

```
java -jar fastest.jar
```

Assuming the specification is stored in a file called **sensors.tex** it is loaded with:

```
loadspec sensors.tex
```

Before generating a testing tree the user needs to select one or more operations to test. In our example we select *KMR*.

```
selop KMR
```

Now it is time to apply the testing tactics. Fastest applies DNF by default. Standard Partitions is applied to the expression *smax s? < r?* present in schema *KMROk* with:

```
addtactic KMR SP < smax~s? < r?
```

Test trees are generated with the command **genalltt**, which needs no parameters. Now the engineer can either prune the tree or calculate abstract test cases. Assume he or she wants to prune the tree. In order to perform manual pruning the user first needs to see the contents of each node in the testing tree. Fastest provides command **showsch** to print the LATEX text of any node. Since all the descendants of *KMR_DNF_2* contain an undefined expression *–smax s?* because *s? ∉ dom smax–* they can be pruned manually by issuing:

```
prunebelow KMR_DNF_2
```

while individual empty test classes can be pruned with **prunefrom**, as follows:

```
prunefrom KMR_SP_4
```

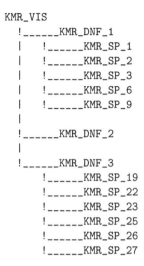

```
KMR_VIS
  !_____KMR_DNF_1
  |    !_____KMR_SP_1
  |    !_____KMR_SP_2
  |    !_____KMR_SP_3
  |    !_____KMR_SP_6
  |    !_____KMR_SP_9
  |
  !_____KMR_DNF_2
  |
  !_____KMR_DNF_3
       !_____KMR_SP_19
       !_____KMR_SP_22
       !_____KMR_SP_23
       !_____KMR_SP_25
       !_____KMR_SP_26
       !_____KMR_SP_27
```

Fig. 6. Testing tree for *KMR* after pruning all the empty nodes

The testing tree resulting after pruning all the empty test classes is shown in Fig. 6, which was generated with command **showtt**.

Abstract test case generation is initiated by **genalltca**, without any parameters. After some time, the engineer can see that Fastest found an abstract test case for all test objectives except for *KMR_SP_1* and *KMR_SP_9*. The reason is that while Fastest will choose, in this case, the set $\{-1, 0, 1\}$ as the finite set for $\mathbb{Z}$, their predicates can only be satisfied by considering either two strictly positive or negative numbers. Hence, the user must help Fastest to find the right finite models. The commands are as follows:

```
setfinitemodel KMR_SP_1 -fm "\num == \{-1, -2\}"
setfinitemodel KMR_SP_9 -fm "\num == 1 \upto 2"
```

By running **genalltca** again Fastest will find abstract test cases for those two leaves.

As the reader can see, Fastest features an interesting level of automation. To date, the most human-time consuming task is pruning testing trees, but automatic pruning will be included in the next version as we explained in Sect. 3.6.

5   Empirical Assessment

We do not assess MBT against other forms of testing, nor the relative suitability of the TTF because it has been done elsewhere [5,20]. However, we think it is worth to mention that Fastest is the only tool providing an implementation of the TTF where most of its steps are automatic, and that it is one of the few tools for MBT for the Z notation [5] –see Sect. 6. Rather, what we want is to assess Fastest with respect to its ability to find abstract test cases from tests objectives.

Table 1. Summary of the case studies (part one)

N°	Case study	Real/Toy	LOZC	State	Operations	Tactics
1	SWPDC	Real	1,238	18	17	DNF, SP, ISE, FT
2	Plavis	Real	608	13	13	DNF, SP, FT
3	Scheduler	Toy	240	3	10	DNF, SP
4	Security class	Toy	172	4	7	DNF, SP
5	Savings accounts	Toy	171	1	5	DNF, SP
6	Lift	Toy	152	6	3	DNF
7	Symbol table	Toy	78	1	3	DNF, SP

In particular we are interested in two measurements: (a) the percentage of non-empty test classes for which Fastest automatically finds an abstract test case; and (b) the computing time necessary to calculate (a). Since testing trees are built almost instantaneously, we did not pay attention to this step.

Here we report the results of applying Fastest to two real-world, industrial-strength systems from the aerospace sector, and to five toy examples borrowed from the Z and MBT literature, and proposed by us as well. Tables 1 and 2 summarize the results of these experiments; note that both tables are related by column **N°**. In Sect. 5.1 we briefly describe each case study.

Table 1 gives an idea of the complexity of the models being "tested". **LOZC** stands for lines of Z code (in LaTeX format); **State** indicates the number of state variables in each model; and **Operations** gives the number of Z operations in each model. The last column shows the testing tactics that we have applied in the experiments. We applied at most two tactics to every operation in all experiments, except in one operation of the Scheduler case study, where three tactics were applied.

Table 2 gives an idea of the complexity of testing. **Classes** is the total number of test objectives right after applying the tactics, some of which were manually pruned, as is indicated in the third column, either because they are empty test classes or because they will not contribute significantly to test the target application. After pruning remains the **Possible** test objectives. Columns **Auto**, **Manual**, **Time** and **Ratio** are the most important for us. The first two of these indicate the number of test cases derived automatically and manually, respectively –by manually we mean that the engineer had to issue a `setfinitemodel` command to help Fastest to find a test case in a given test class. Percentages are with respect to column **Possible** because we want to assess the effectiveness of our method for finding abstract test cases from non empty test classes. As the reader can observe, our conjecture (Sect. 3.7) was true even in the real-world experiments. In our opinion this implies some uniformity in specifications: although Z is a general purpose notation, users tend to specify using the same kind of predicates. Otherwise, so simple a heuristic could not have yield so high percentages. It was quite surprising for us that this simple heuristic have been useful for specifications of systems of such diverse domains (see Sect. 5.1).

Before analyzing the last two columns of Table 2, it is necessary to give some details about the platform used for performing the experiments. All the

Table 2. Summary of the case studies (part two)

N°	Classes	Pruned	Possible	Auto (%)	Manual (%)	Time	Ratio
1	225	123	112	91 (81.25%)	21 (18.75%)	124:00'	1:06'
2	232	128	117	104 (88.88%)	13 (11.11%)	158:00'	1:21'
3	213	174	29	28 (96.55%)	1 (3.44%)	3:00'	0:06'
4	36	16	20	20 (100%)	0 (0%)	0:20'	0:01'
5	97	74	23	23 (100%)	0 (0%)	4:50'	0:12'
6	17	1	16	16 (100%)	0 (0%)	7:30'	0:28'
7	18	10	10	10 (100%)	0 (0%)	0:10'	0:01'
Averages				**95.24%**	**4.76%**		**0:27'**

experiments were conducted over the same hardware and software: an Intel Centrino Duo of 1.66 GHz with 1 Gb of main memory, running Linux Ubuntu 8.04 with kernel 2.6.24-24-generic and Java SE Runtime Environment (build 1.6.0_14-b08). Fastest was run in application mode –i.e. not in client-server mode–, what did not make use of parallelization, except for the concurrency that the Intel chip and the Linux kernel can provide. The last two columns show the total computing time (in minutes) necessary to find one test case for all **Possible** test objectives, and the computing time per test case, respectively.

In spite of the good results we got so far, there is a key issue that we need to solve –in fact we are doing it as we write this article. The problem is how and how efficient can empty test classes be automatically pruned from testing trees. This point is important because, as the reader can see, there is a large number of empty test classes in all the experiments. To perform the experiments we analyzed one by one all the classes for which Fastest failed to find an abstract test case, just to find that close to 100% were actually empty –by the way, this fact supports the second part of our conjecture (Sect. 3.7). If most of the empty test classes cannot be pruned automatically, then Fastest either will require a non trivial amount of human effort, or the engineer could skip some test cases.

5.1 Description of the Case Studies

In this section we give a brief informal description of each case study.

SWPDC. Simplified version of the communication protocol between two computers of a Brazilian satellite. The protocol roughly follows the directives of the ESA standard ECSS-E-70-41A. This model has operations to load a program in the memory of one of the computers, to transmit a data between the computers, to interact with some hardware devices, to dump the memory, and so on.

Plavis. Simpler version of SWPDC.

Scheduler. This model was borrowed from [5]. Basically, we translated the B model described in that book into Z.

Security class. A security class is a computer security concept belonging to mandatory access control [21]. A security class is composed of an element –called security level– that belongs to a totally ordered set and a set of elements –called categories– of other type. Then, there are operations to consult the security level or the set of categories, to change either one, etc.

Savings accounts. This is a typical example of a Z model. A bank has many savings accounts where money can be deposited and withdrawn, the balance can be checked, a new account can be created and an existing account can be closed.

Lift. This model was borrowed from [22].

Symbol table. This model was borrowed from [2].

6   Related Work

In this section we compare Fastest with other similar tools. Clearly, TinMan [23,24] is an obligatory reference since it is the implementation of the TTF by its own authors. However, TinMan is not as automatic as Fastest because the engineer has to enter by hand: (a) the predicates of the derived test classes, and (b) the values of the constants for the abstract test cases. In other words, as far as we understood, all the calculation is the engineer's responsibility while TinMan assist him or her in managing the specification, test objectives and abstract test cases. Although management of hundreds of test cases is a real problem, the automatic features of Fastest (a) avoid human error, and (b) save human effort for the analytical work.

Confimiq launched in 2002 a tool called Conformiq Test Generator (CTQ) [25] which calculates and executes test cases from UML Statechars models. CQT was surpassed by another tool by Conformiq named Qtronic. While CQT needed both a model of the environment of the system and a model of the system itself, Qtronic only needs a model of the system. Besides, Qtronic supports concurrent, multi-thread or non-deterministic models and time restrictions. Smartesting's Test Designer [26] is another tool that works with UML models. Test Designer also provides facilities for simulation. Two tools from IBM's Telelogic, Telelogic Statemate & Telelogic Rhapsody [27], also work from UML and Statechart models. All these tools have many advantages with respect to Fastest, basically because they are the result of many years of development, but they have a nontrivial disadvantage for data-intensive systems. Statecharts are not particularly well suited to modeling that kind of system and, strictly speaking, UML models are not formal, while Z has proved to be a very good formal notation for this kind of specification. In fact, every Statecharts model can be translated into a Z specification.

UniTESK Lab. is part of the Institute for System Programming of the Russian Academy of Sciences. This laboratory has developed a couple of similar MBT tools named CTESK and JavaTESK. These tools use models written in extensions of the C and Java programming languages developed also at UniTESK. As far as we understand both tools are aimed at system testing and not particularly for unit testing. ModelJUnit is an extension of JUnit that supports MBT based on FSM written in Java [28]. An obvious limitation of these tools is their dependency on programming languages, but it also can be their strength since programmers might find it easier to write models in languages similar to the ones they routinely work with.

Rave [29] uses tabular models derived from the work done by David L. Parnas at the U.S Naval Research Laboratory. T-VEC, the company which developed Rave, also advertises T-VEC Tester [30] which uses Simulink and Stateflow models. Reactis [31], from Reactive Systems, also uses Simulink and Stateflow models from which it generates test cases.

In the open source community we found a Java implementation of MBT called org.tigrismbt. This tool generates sequences of tests from FSM written as graphs in graphml format.

LTG/B from LEIRIOS (now Smartesting) [5] shares some similarities with Fastest. This tool uses B models [32] –which are similar to Z models– and is based on the symbolic animation of formal specifications and two test generation strategies: analysis of cause-effect and analysis of boundaries. One difference with Fastest is that LTG/B generates sequences of operations that put the system in the desired state, rather than giving the values of state variables to put the system in that state, as the TTF suggests.

Helke and others in [10] use Isabelle/HOL to calculate test classes, although the title of the paper indicates that test cases are generated. However, in this work an automatic pruning technique is well described and empirically assessed. There are numerous papers proposing algorithms or techniques for automatically generating test cases from Z specifications, like [11,12], but none of them shows the implementation of the proposed tool, or they are not based on the TTF, or they actually does not generate test cases but just test templates.

For an up-to-date list of MBT tools consult [33].

As this survey shows there are no implementations of MBT tools for the Z formal notation as automatic as Fastest. This situation combined with the relative widespread use of the Z formal notation in industry and the advantages of the TTF, led us to implement the framework in order to provide such a tool to the Z community.

7   Conclusions and Future Work

We presented a tool, called Fastest, that automates the generation of unit tests from Z models based on the Stocks-Carrington framework for model-based testing. A simple method is proposed to find abstract test cases from test objectives and an empirical analysis based on seven models from different domains is also shown. The architecture of the tool was briefly introduced and a toy example was executed. We think that the architecture presents some interesting features such as the possibility of distributing the calculation of test cases, the way by means of which new testing tactics can be added and the existing ones can be configured, the integration with the CZT project, etc. It is worth to mention that Fastest is still a prototype that needs to be extended in many ways.

As the empirical study shows, we can conclude that, an apparently rough method to calculate abstract test cases, based on a practical conjecture about the form of real-world specifications, proved to be very accurate and reasonable efficient and, combined with the architecture, scalable as well. On the other side, the direct implementation of the TTF framework made it possible to take advantage of all its interesting properties.

However, among others, we need to improve on automatic pruning of test trees to dramatically reduce the amount of human effort during the testing process. We also sketched our ideas on this regard. Also, more testing tactics proposed within the TTF, such as specification mutation and sub-domain propagation, have to be implemented. In turn, these tactics can be assembly in higher-level test design strategies. The user interface prays for an improvement. Finally, it will be necessary to support the whole Z notation, but this is tied, to some extent, to the improvement of CZT's ZLive animator.

Acknowledgments. We would like to thank Flowgate Consulting and CIFASIS for their support in writing this paper. The reviewers gave us an excellent feedback. Particularly, we want to thank reviewer number two who made a number of suggestions to improve this paper.

References

1. Fastest, `http://www.flowgate.net/?lang=en&seccion=herramientas`
2. Stocks, P., Carrington, D.: A Framework for Specification-Based Testing. IEEE Transactions on Software Engineering 22(11), 777–793 (1996)
3. Stocks, P.: Applying Formal Methods to Software Testing. PhD thesis, Department of Computer Science, University of Queensland (1993)
4. Maccoll, I., Carrington, D.: Extending the Test Template Framework. In: Proceedings of the Third Northern Formal Methods Workshop (1998)
5. Utting, M., Legeard, B.: Practical Model-Based Testing: A Tools Approach. Morgan Kaufmann Publishers Inc., San Francisco (2006)
6. Spivey, J.M.: The Z Notation: A Reference Manual. Prentice-Hall, Inc., Upper Saddle River (1989)
7. Souza, S., Maldonado, J., Fabbri, S. Masiero, P.: Statecharts Specifications: A Family of Coverage Testing Criteria. In: CLEI 2000 - XXVI Latin-American Conference of Informatics, CLEI (2000)
8. Bernard, E., Legeard, B., Luck, X., Peureux, F.: Generation of Test Sequences from Formal Specifications: GSM 11-11 Standard Case Study. International Journal of Software Practice and Experience 34(10), 915–948 (2004)
9. Dick, J., Faivre, A.: Automating the Generation and Sequencing of Test Cases from Model-Based Specifications. In: Larsen, P.G., Woodcock, J.C.P. (eds.) FME 1993. LNCS, vol. 670, pp. 268–284. Springer, Heidelberg (1993)
10. Helke, S., Neustupny, T., Santen, T.: Automating Test Case Generation from Z Specifications with Isabelle. In: Till, D., Bowen, J.P., Hinchey, M.G. (eds.) ZUM 1997. LNCS, vol. 1212, pp. 52–71. Springer, Heidelberg (1997)
11. Hierons, R.M.: Testing from a Z Specification. Softw. Test., Verif. Reliab. 7(1), 19–33 (1997)

12. Burton, S., York, H.: Automated Testing from Z Specifications. Technical report, Department of Computer Science – University of York (2000)
13. Malik, P., Utting, M.: CZT: A framework for Z tools. In: Treharne, H., King, S., Henson, M.C., Schneider, S. (eds.) ZB 2005. LNCS, vol. 3455, pp. 65–84. Springer, Heidelberg (2005)
14. Community Z Tools, http://czt.sourceforge.net
15. ISO: Information Tchnology – Z Formal Specification Notation – Syntax, Type System and Semantics. Technical Report ISO/IEC 13568, International Organization for Standardization (2002)
16. Clements, P., Garlan, D., Bass, L., Stafford, J., Nord, R., Ivers, J., Little, R.: Documenting Software Architectures: Views and Beyond. Pearson Education, London (2002)
17. Shaw, M., Garlan, D.: Software architecture: perspectives on an emerging discipline. Prentice-Hall, Upper Saddle River (1996)
18. Garlan, D., Kaiser, G.E., Notkin, D.: Using Tool Abstraction to Compose Systems. Computer 25(6), 30–38 (1992)
19. Saaltink, M.: The Z/EVES System. In: Till, D., Bowen, J., Hinchey, M.G. (eds.) ZUM 1997. LNCS, vol. 1212, pp. 72–85. Springer, Heidelberg (1997)
20. Legeard, B., Peureux, F., Utting, M.: A comparison of the BTT and TTF test-generation methods. In: Bert, D., Bowen, J., Henson, M.C., Robinson, K. (eds.) B 2002 and ZB 2002. LNCS, vol. 2272, pp. 309–329. Springer, Heidelberg (2002)
21. Bishop, M.: Computer Security. Art and Science. Addison-Wesley, Reading (2003)
22. Hörcher, H.M., Peleska, J.: Using Formal Specifications to Support Software Testing. Software Quality Journal 4, 309–327 (1995)
23. Murray, L., Carrington, D., Maccoll, I., Strooper, P.: TinMan - A Test Derivation and Management Tool for Specification-Based Class Testing. In: Technology of ObjectOriented Languages and Systems (TOOLS), pp. 222–233 (1999)
24. Murray, L.: Software Requirements Specification for TinMan - Version 1.0. Technical Report 99-02, The Univesity of Qeensland (1999)
25. Conformiq, http://www.conformiq.org
26. Smartesting, http://www.smartesting.com
27. Telelogic: Telelogic Statemate & Telelogic Rhapsody, http://modeling.telelogic.com/products/
28. Utting, M.: Model JUnit, http://www.cs.waikato.ac.nz/~marku/mbt/modeljunit/
29. T-VEC: Requirements-Based Automated Verification, http://www.t-vec.com/solutions/rave.php
30. T-VEC: T-vec Tester for Simulink and Stateflow, http://www.t-vec.com/solutions/simulink.php
31. Reactis, http://www.reactive-systems.com
32. Abrial, J.R.: The B-book: Assigning Programs to Meanings. Cambridge University Press, New York (1996)
33. Utting, M.: Commercial MBT Tools, http://www.cs.waikato.ac.nz/~marku/mbt/CommercialMbtTools.pdf

A Statistical Approach to Test Stochastic and Probabilistic Systems[*]

Mercedes G. Merayo[1], Iksoon Hwang[2], Manuel Núñez[1], and Ana Cavalli[2]

[1] Departamento de Sistemas Informáticos y Computación
Universidad Complutense de Madrid, 28040 Madrid, Spain
`mgmerayo@fdi.ucm.es, mn@sip.ucm.es`
[2] Software-Networks Department, Telecom & Management SudParis
9, rue Charles Fourier, 91011, Evry Cedex, France
`Iksoon.Hwang@it-sudparis.eu, Ana.Cavalli@it-sudparis.eu`

Abstract. In this paper we introduce a formal framework to test systems where non-deterministic decisions are probabilistically quantified and temporal information is defined by using random variables. We define an appropriate extension of the classical finite state machines formalism, widely used in formal testing approaches, to define the systems that we are interested in. First, we define a conformance relation to establish, with respect to a given specification, what a *good* implementation is. In order to decide whether a system is conforming, we apply different statistic techniques to determine whether the (unknown) probabilities and random variables governing the behaviour of the implementation match the (known) ones of the specification. Next, we introduce a notion of test case. Finally, we give an alternative characterization of the previous conformance relation based on how a set of test is passed by the implementation.

1 Introduction

Formal testing techniques [20,28,5,31] allow to test the correctness of a system with respect to a specification. Formal testing originally targeted the functional behavior of systems, such as determining whether the tested system can perform certain actions and it does not perform some non-expected ones. However, many systems require to deal with non-functional properties such as probabilities or time. On the one hand, the number of systems that incorporate non-determinism and probabilistic behavior in order to ensure fairness and robustness in communication protocols is increasing. Some of them such as Ethernet and IEEE 802.11 have long been deployed in real networks where the exponential back-off algorithm works in a nondeterministic way. Some security protocols such as non-repudiation protocols have been proposed where the key for decrypting a message already sent is delivered with a given probability to ensure the fairness

---

[*] Research supported by the Spanish MEC project WEST/FAST (TIN2006-15578-C02-01), the MATES project (CCG08-UCM/TIC-4124) and by the UCM-BSCH programme to fund research groups (GR58/08 - group number 910606).

K. Breitman and A. Cavalcanti (Eds.): ICFEM 2009, LNCS 5885, pp. 186–205, 2009.

of the protocol [24]. Regarding the temporal behavior it is a critical aspect for developing useful models of real-time systems. In fact, there are several proposals that allow to explicitly represent the probability of performing a certain task [19,10,9,7,27] as well as the time consumed by the system while performing tasks, being it either given by fix amounts of time [30,26] or defined in probabilistic/stochastic terms [15,3,21,4].

In this paper we use a suitable extension of the well known finite state machine formalism (FSM), *Probabilistic-Stochastic Finite State Machine (PSFSM)* introduced in [13], that allows to express in a natural way both probabilistic and temporal aspects. The *probabilities* allow to quantify the non-deterministic choices that a system may undertake. We consider a variant of the *reactive* interpretation of probabilities (see for example [19]). Intuitively, a reactive interpretation imposes a probabilistic relation among transitions labelled by the same action but choices between different actions are not quantified. In our setting we are able to express probabilistic relations between transitions outgoing from a state and having the same input action (the output may vary). The *stochastic information* represents the time consumed between the input is applied and the output is received and it will be given by *random variables*. The main idea is that time information is incremented with some kind of probabilistic information. That is, instead of having expressions such as "the message a will be received in t units of time" we will have expressions such as "the message a is expected to be received with probability $\frac{1}{2}$ in the interval $(0, 1]$, with probability $\frac{1}{4}$ in $(1, 2]$, and so on".

There has been a lot of work to test the functional correctness of non-deterministic FSMs with respect to input/output sequences [11,23,29,17]. More recently models with probabilities have been studied [2,12,19,33,8,22] while some of them also include time information [18,34,25]. Nevertheless, there have been relatively few studies on testing whether the probabilities and stochastic information of a system is correctly implemented with respect to its specification. Implementation relations to assess conformance based on the observed executions of the implementation have been proposed in [22,25,14].

In this paper, we propose a methodology to test whether the probabilities and random variables of the transitions are correctly implemented. We might require that any transition of the implementation must have the same associated probability and delay, that is, an identically distributed random variable. Even though this is a very reasonable notion to define correctness, if we assume a black-box testing framework then we do not know the internal details of the implementations. So, we cannot check whether the corresponding random variables are identically distributed or the probabilities are equal to the ones established in the specification. In fact, we would need an infinite number of observations to assure it. Thus, we give a more *realistic* method based on a finite set of observations. The idea will be to check that the observed outputs and execution times in the implementation, *fit* the probabilities and random variables, respectively, established in the specification. This notion of *fitting* will be given by means of interval estimation (probabilities) and hypothesis contrasts (stochastic time).

We also introduce a notion of test and how to test implementations that can be represented by using our notion of finite state machine. In addition, we provide an algorithm that derives test suites from specifications. The main result of our paper indicates that these test suites have the same distinguishing power as the two conformance relations presented, in the sense that an implementation successfully passes a test suite iff it is conforming to the specification. Since the testing methodology is based on a finite set of observations, a test verdict is assigned with a given confidence level. When we test probabilities using interval estimation, different confidence levels and confidence interval length provide different quality of testing.

The rest of the paper is structured as follows. In Section 2, we define a PSFSM and notations related to testing. In Section 3, we give our conformance relations. In Section 4, we formally define a notion of test, as well as the application of tests to implementations and two notions of successfully passing a test suite. A test generation method for testing from PSFSMs is presented in Section 5. In Section 6, the basic ideas behind testing of probabilities using interval estimation and checking random variables by means of hypothesis contrast are introduced. Finally, in Section 7 we present our conclusions.

2   Preliminaries

In this section we extend the finite state machine formalism in order to deal with probabilities and stochastic time. On the one hand, probabilities attached to the transitions allow us to quantify the non-determinism of the system. On the other hand, stochastic time, represented by means of random variables, let us model the time that outputs take to be executed. We will consider that the domain of random variables is a set of numeric time values Time. Since this is a *generic* time domain, the specifier can choose whether the system will use a discrete/continuous time domain. We simply assume that $0 \in$ Time.

In addition, we denote by C^* the set of all finite sequences with elements in C, $\bar{c}$ denotes a sequence with length greater than 0 while ε denotes the empty sequence. Following, we introduce some basic concepts that will be used along the paper.

Definition 1. *We denote by $\mathcal{V}$ the set of random variables ($\xi, \psi, \ldots$ range over $\mathcal{V}$). Let ξ be a random variable. We define its probability distribution function as the function $F_\xi :$ Time $\longrightarrow [0,1]$ such that $F_\xi(x) = P(\xi \leq x)$, where $P(\xi \leq x)$ is the probability that ξ assumes values less than or equal to x. Let $\xi, \xi' \in \mathcal{V}$ be random variables. We write $\xi = \xi'$ if for any $x \in$ Time we have $F_\xi(x) = F_{\xi'}(x)$. We will denote by θ the random variable which probability distribution function is defined by $F(x) = 1$ for all $x \in$ Time.*

Given two random variables ξ and ψ we consider that $\xi + \psi$ denotes a random variable distributed as the addition of the two random variables ξ and ψ.

We will use the delimiters $\{$ and $\}$ to denote multisets. Given a set E, we denote by $\wp(E)$ the multisets of elements belonging to E.

A Probabilistic-Stochastic Finite State Machine is a non-deterministic finite state machine in which every transition has associated both a probability and a random variable. As we said before, the latter represents the expected distribution of times to execute the transition.

Definition 2. *A Probabilistic Stochastic Finite State Machine, in short PSFSM, is a tuple $M = (S, s_0, Li, Lo, P_T, P_\mathcal{V})$ where S is a finite set of states, with $s_0 \in S$ being the initial state, Li and Lo denote the finite input and output alphabets, respectively, $P_T : S \times Li \times Lo \times S \to [0, 1]$ is the probability-transition function and $P_\mathcal{V} : S \times Li \times Lo, S \to \mathcal{V}$ the time function. For all $s \in S$ and $a \in Li$, $\sum_{p \in P_T(s,a,x,s')} p = 1$. For all $(s, a, x, s') \in S \times Li \times Lo \times S$ if $P_T(s, a, x, s') = p > 0$ and $P_\mathcal{V}(s, a, x, s') = \xi$ then (s, a, x, p, ξ, s') is a transition of M.*

M is observable if for every state s, input a and output x there is at most one transition leaving s with input a and output x. PSFSM M is completely specified if for every state s and input a there exists at least one transition outgoing from s and labelled with input a. M is said to be initially connected if every state is reachable from the initial state.

Intuitively, a transition (s, a, x, p, ξ, s') indicates that if the machine is in state s and receives the input a then with probability p the machine emits the output x and it moves to state s' before time t with probability $F_\xi(t)$.

We do not allow that a PSFSM has two transitions with the same initial and final states s, s' and the same input/output a/x. Let us note that this condition does not really limit the behaviors that we can define. If we consider two different transitions, $(s, a, x, p_1, \xi_1, s')$ and $(s, a, x, p_2, \xi_2, s')$, they have the same meaning that the one provided by a unique transition (s, x, y, p, ξ, s') where $p = p_1 + p_2$ and $\xi = \frac{p_1}{p} \cdot \xi_1 + \frac{p_2}{p} \cdot \xi_2$.

Let us remark that non-deterministic choices will be resolved before the timers indicated by random variables start counting, that is, we follow a *pre-selection* policy. Thus, if we have several transitions, outgoing from a state s, associated with the same input a, and the system receives this input, then the system *at time* 0 will choose which one of them to perform according to the probabilities. So, we do not have a *race* between the different timers to decide which one is faster. In order to avoid side-effects, we will assume that all the random variables appearing in the definition of a PSFSM are independent. Let us note that this condition does not restrict the distributions to be used. In particular, there can be random variables identically distributed even though they are independent.

In this paper, we assume that both implementation and specification can be modeled by observable PSFSMs with the same input alphabet, completely specified and initially connected. If a PSFSM is not completely specified, it is possible to transform it to a completely specified PSFSM by adding a self-loop transitions for each missing input with an empty output. If the specification is not initially connected, we can consider only a sub-machine which consists of states and transitions reachable from the initial state of the system. It is also assumed that there is an upper bound on the number of states of the implementation.

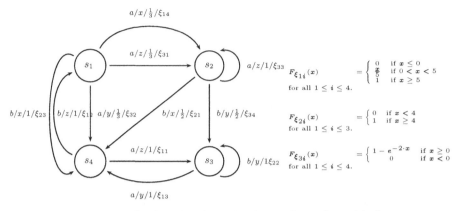

Fig. 1. Example of Probabilistic Stochastic Finite State Machine

Example 1. Let us consider the machine depicted in Figure 1. Each transition has associated a probability and a random variable. In the following we explain how these random variables are distributed. Let us consider that the random variables ξ_{1i} are *uniformly distributed* in the interval $[0, 5]$. Uniform distributions assign equal probability to all the times in the interval. The random variable ξ_{2i} follow a Dirac distribution in 4. The idea is that the corresponding delay will be equal to 4 time units. Finally, ξ_{3i} are *exponentially* distributed with parameter 2.

Let us consider the transition $(s_1, a, x, \frac{1}{3}, \xi_{14}, s_2)$. Intuitively, if the machine is in state s_1 and receives the input a then it will produce the output x with probability $\frac{1}{3}$ after a time given by ξ_{14}. For example, we know that this time will be less than 1 time unit with probability $\frac{1}{5}$, it will be less than 3 time units with probability $\frac{3}{5}$, and so on. Finally, once 5 time units have passed we know that the output x has been performed, that is, we have probability 1.

The functions P_T and P_V can be extended to P_T^* and P_V^* respectively to be applied to input and output sequences.

Definition 3. *Let $M = (S, s_0, Li, Lo, P_T, P_V)$ be a PSFSM. Let $\bar{a}/\bar{x}$ be an input/output sequence and $s \in S$. We define the probability of reaching state s' from s with $\bar{a}/\bar{x}$ as:*

$$P_T^*(s, \varepsilon, x, s') = \begin{cases} 1 \text{ if } x = \varepsilon \wedge s' = s \\ 0 \text{ otherwise} \end{cases}$$

$$P_T^*(s, \bar{a}a, \bar{x}x, s') = \begin{cases} P_T^*(s, \bar{a}, \bar{x}, s'') \cdot P_T(s'', a, x, s') \text{ if } \exists\, s'' \in S : P_T(s'', a, x, s') > 0 \\ \qquad\qquad\qquad\qquad\qquad\qquad\qquad\qquad \wedge \\ \qquad\qquad\qquad\qquad\qquad\qquad\qquad\qquad P_T(s, \bar{a}, \bar{x}, s'') > 0 \\ 0 \qquad\qquad\qquad\qquad\qquad\qquad \text{otherwise} \end{cases}$$

The random variable that defines the time that the system takes to reach the state s' from s performing the output sequence $\bar{x}$ if it receives the input sequence $\bar{a}$ is given by:

$$P_{\mathcal{V}}^*(s, \varepsilon, x, s') = \theta$$

$$P_{\mathcal{V}}^*(s, \bar{a}a, \bar{x}x, s') = \begin{cases} P_{\mathcal{V}}^*(s, \bar{a}, \bar{x}, s'') + P_{\mathcal{V}}(s'', a, x, s') \text{ if } \exists\, s'' \in S: P_T(s'', a, x, s') > 0 \\ \qquad\qquad\qquad\qquad\qquad\qquad\qquad\qquad \wedge \\ \qquad\qquad\qquad\qquad\qquad\qquad\qquad P_T(s, \bar{a}, \bar{x}, s'') > 0 \\ \theta \qquad\qquad\qquad\qquad\qquad\qquad\qquad \text{otherwise} \end{cases}$$

In a slight abuse of notation $P_T^*(s, \bar{a}, \bar{x})$ denotes the probability that M produces output sequence $\bar{x}$ when it receives input sequence $\bar{a}$ when in state s. In the same way, $P_{\mathcal{V}}^*(s, \bar{a}, \bar{x})$ denotes the random variable that defines the time that M takes to produce the output sequence $\bar{x}$ when it receives input sequence $\bar{a}$ when in state s.

Next, we introduce the notion of *trace*. As usual, a trace is a sequence of input/output pairs. In addition, we have to record the time that the trace needs to be performed. An *evolution* is a trace starting at the initial state of the machine.

Definition 4. Let $M = (S, s_0, Li, Lo, P_T, P_{\mathcal{V}})$ be a PSFSM. We say that a tuple $(s, s', (i_1/o_1, \ldots, i_r/o_r), \xi)$ is a *timed trace*, or simply *trace*, of M if there exist $(s, s_1, i_1, o_1, \xi_1), (s_1, s_2, i_2, o_2, \xi_2), \ldots, (s_{r-1}, s', i_r, o_r, \xi_r)$ transitions of M such that $\xi = \sum \xi_i$.

We say that $(i_1/o_1, \ldots, i_r/o_r)$ is a *non-timed evolution*, or simply *evolution*, of M if we have that $(s_0, s', (i_1/o_1, \ldots, i_r/o_r), \xi)$ is a trace of M. We denote by NTEvol(M) the set of non-timed evolutions of M.

We say that the pair $((i_1/o_1, \ldots, i_r/o_r), \xi)$ is a *timed evolution* of M if we have that $(s_0, s', (i_1/o_1, \ldots, i_r/o_r), \xi)$ is a trace of M. We denote by TEvol(M) the set of timed evolutions of M. □

Traces are defined as sequences of transitions. The random variable associated with the trace is computed from the ones corresponding to each transition belonging to the sequence. In fact, this random variable is obtained by adding the time values associated with each of the transitions conforming the trace.

3 Conformance Relations for PSFSMs

In order to test against a specification it is necessary to say what it means for the implementation to conform to the specification. In our framework we need to consider two different levels of conformance: *functional* and *temporal*. The former only takes into account functional aspects of the system while the performance of the system, that is, the time that the system takes to perform the actions is ignored. The fact that we consider a black box framework avoid us to *see* the probabilities and the random variables assigned to the transitions in the implementation under test. In order to *estimate* the probabilities associated with each choice of the implementation we will consider a set of observations. By collecting the observations of the implementation the probabilities will be estimated by an interval with a certain level of confidence, which is called *confidence interval*, and compared with the corresponding probabilities of the specification. We define a notion of functional conformance by following the ideas underlying our methodology. Intuitively, we do not request that the probabilities of the implementation be equal to the corresponding in the specification but that this fact happens up to a certain probability.

In addition to requiring this notion of *functional* conformance, we have to ask for some conditions on delays. As we have indicated, we are not able to check whether the random variables are indeed identically distributed. Thus, we give a notion of temporal conformance based on finite sets of observations. This relation takes into account the observations that we may get from the implementation. We will collect a sample of time values and we will *compare* this sample with the random variables appearing in the specification. By comparison we mean that we will apply a hypothesis contrast to decide, with a certain confidence, whether the sample could be generated by the corresponding random variable.

Definition 5. *Let M be a PSFSM. We say that $(\bar{\sigma}, t)$, with $\bar{\sigma} = a_1/x_1, \ldots, a_n/x_n$, is an observed timed execution of M, or simply timed execution, if the observation of M shows that the time elapsed between the acceptance of the input a_1 and the observation of the output x_n is t units of time.*

Let $\Phi = \{\bar{\sigma}_1, \ldots, \bar{\sigma}_m\}$ and let $H = \{(\bar{\sigma}'_1, t_1), \ldots, (\bar{\sigma}'_n, t_n)\}$ be a multiset of timed executions. We say that $Sampling_{(H,\Phi)} : \Phi \longrightarrow \wp(\mathtt{Time})$ is a sampling application of H for Φ if $Sampling_{(H,\Phi)}(\bar{\sigma}) = \{t \mid (\bar{\sigma}, t) \in H\}$, for all $\bar{\sigma} \in \Phi$.

We say that $SeqSampling_{(H,\Phi)} : \Phi \longrightarrow \wp(\Phi)$ is a sequence sampling application of H for Φ if $SeqSampling_{(H,\Phi)}(\bar{a}/\bar{x}) = \{\bar{\sigma} \mid (\bar{\sigma}, t) \in H \wedge \bar{\sigma} = \bar{a}/\bar{x}'\}$, for all $\bar{a}/\bar{x} \in \Phi$.

Let ξ be a random variable and H be a a multiset of timed executions. We denote by $\gamma(\xi, H)$ the confidence of ξ on H. Let $0 < \alpha < 1$ and $\Phi = \{\bar{\sigma}_1, \ldots, \bar{\sigma}_m\}$. We denote by $CI_\alpha(\Phi)$ the confidence interval from Φ with confidence level α.

In the previous definition, an observed timed execution simply contains the observation of a sequence of input/output actions associated with the amount of time that the implementations take to perform it. Regarding the definition of sampling applications, on the one hand, we assign to each sequence the set of total observed times corresponding to its execution by the implementation; on the other hand, the sequence sampling application assign to each input sequence the set of output sequences observed. Let us note that $\gamma(\xi, H)$ takes values in the interval $[0, 1]$. Intuitively, bigger values of $\gamma(\xi, H)$ indicate that the observed sample H is more likely to be produced by the random variable ξ. That is, this function decides how *similar* the probability distribution function generated by H and the one corresponding to the random variable ξ are. Finally, let us note that the confidence interval length depends on the sample size and α. Larger sample size results in shorter confidence interval, which means that we can estimate the probability from the sample H more precisely. Higher values of α result in larger confidence interval and we can have higher possibility that the actual probability lies within the obtained confidence interval.

Definition 6. *Let M and M' be PSFSMs, H be a multiset of timed executions of M', $0 < \alpha < 1$, $\Phi = \{\bar{\sigma} \mid \exists\, t : (\bar{\sigma}, t) \in H\}$, and let us consider $SeqSampling_{(H,\Phi)}$. We say that M' (α, H)-probabilistically conforms to M, denoted by $M' \sqsubseteq_{p,(\alpha,H)} M$ if for all $\bar{\sigma} = \bar{a}/\bar{x} \in \Phi$ such that $P_T^*(s_0, \bar{a}, \bar{x}) > 0$ we have*

$$P_T^*(s_0, \bar{a}, \bar{x}) \in CI_\alpha(SeqSampling_{(H,\Phi)}(\bar{\sigma}))$$

Intuitively the idea is that the probabilities associated to the sequences in the M' are similar enough to the corresponding ones in M. In addition, we require conditions over the execution times.

Definition 7. *Let M and M' be PSFSMs, H be a multiset of timed executions of M', $0 \leq \alpha \leq 1$, $\Phi = \{\bar{\sigma} \mid \exists\, t : (\bar{\sigma}, t) \in H\}$, and let us consider $Sampling_{(H,\Phi)}$. We say that M' is (α, H)-stochastically conformance to M, denoted by $M' \sqsubseteq_{s,(\alpha,H)} M$ if for all $\bar{\sigma} = \bar{a}/\bar{x} \in \Phi$ we have*

$$\gamma\left(P_{\mathcal{V}}^*(s_0, \bar{a}, \bar{x}), Sampling_{(H,\Phi)}(\bar{\sigma})\right) > \alpha$$

The implementation M' must probabilistically conform to the specification M. Besides, for all observation, the execution time values *fit* the random variable indicated by M. This notion of *fitting* is given by the function γ that it is formally defined in the next Section.

4 Definition and Application of Tests

We consider that tests represent sequences of inputs applied to an implementation. Once an output is received, the tester checks whether it belongs to the set of expected ones or not. In the latter case, a fail signal is produced. In the former case, either a pass signal is emitted (indicating successful termination) or the testing process continues by applying another input. If we are testing an implementation with input and output sets L_I and L_O, respectively, tests are deterministic acyclic L_I/L_O labelled transition systems (i.e. trees) with a strict alternation between an input action and the set of output actions. After an output action we may find either a leaf or another input action. Leaves can be labelled either by *pass* or by *fail*. In addition, we have to check if the implementation behaves according to probabilities established in the specification. We have also to detect whether wrong timed behaviors appear. Thus, tests have to include capabilities to deal with probabilities and time. On the one hand, tests will include *probabilities*. In our proposal, we will *estimate* the probabilities by applying a test several times and we will use *statistical results* to establish the number of times we need to apply the test to obtaining a required confidence level. On the other hand, we will include *random variables*. The idea is that we will record the time that it takes for the implementation to arrive to that point. We will collect a sample of times (one for each test execution) and we will *compare* this sample with the random variable. By comparison we mean that we will apply a contrast to decide, with a certain confidence, whether the sample could be generated by the corresponding random variable.

Definition 8. A *test case* is a tuple $T = (S, L_I, L_O, \lambda, s_0, S_I, S_O, S_F, S_P, \zeta, \eta)$ where S is the set of states, L_I and L_O, with $L_I \cap L_O = \emptyset$ are the sets of input and output actions, respectively, $\lambda \subseteq S \times L_I \cup L_O \times S$ is the transition relation, $s_0 \in S$ is the initial state, and the sets $S_I, S_O, S_F, S_P \subseteq S$ are a partition of S. The transition relation and the sets of states fulfill the following conditions:

- S_I is the set of *input* states. We have that $s_0 \in S_I$. For all input state $s \in S_I$ there exists a unique outgoing transition $(s, a, s') \in \lambda$. For this transition we have that $a \in L_I$ and $s' \in S_O$.
- S_O is the set of *output* states. For all output state $s \in S_O$ we have that for all $o \in L_O$ there exists a unique state s' such that $(s, o, s') \in \lambda$. In this case, $s' \notin S_O$. Moreover, there do not exist $i \in L_I, s' \in S$ such that $(s, i, s') \in \lambda$.
- S_F and S_P are the sets of *fail* and *pass* states, respectively. We say that these states are *terminal*. Thus, for all state $s \in S_F \cup S_P$ we have that there do not exist $a \in L_I \cup L_O$ and $s' \in S$ such that $(s, a, s') \in \lambda$.

Finally, we have two timed functions. $\zeta : S_P \longrightarrow \mathcal{V}$ is a function associating random variables, to compare with the time that took the implementation to perform the outputs, with passing states. $\eta : S_P \longrightarrow (0, 1]$ is a function associating probabilities with passing states.

We say that a test case T is *valid* if the graph induced by T is a tree with root at the initial state s_0. We say that a set of tests $\mathcal{T}_{st} = \{T_1, \ldots, T_n\}$ is a *test suite*.

Let $\bar{\sigma} = i_1/o_1, \ldots, i_r/o_r$. We write $T \overset{\bar{\sigma}}{\Longrightarrow} s^T$ if $s^T \in S_F \cup S_P$ and there exist states $s_{12}, s_{21}, s_{22}, \ldots s_{r1}, s_{r2} \in S$ such that $\{(s_0, i_1, s_{12}), (s_{r2}, o_r, s^T)\} \subseteq \lambda$, for all $2 \le j \le r$ we have $(s_{j1}, i_j, s_{j2}) \in \lambda$, and for all $1 \le j \le r - 1$ we have $(s_{j2}, o_j, s_{(j+1)1}) \in \lambda$. □

Let us remark that $T \overset{\bar{\sigma}}{\Longrightarrow} s^T$ implies that s^T is a terminal state. Next we define the application of a test suite to an implementation. We say that the test suite $\mathcal{T}_{st}$ is *passed* if for all test the terminal states reached by the composition of implementation and test are *pass* states.

Definition 9. Let I be PSFSM and $T = (S_t, L_I, L_O, \lambda_T, s_0, S_I, S_O, S_F, S_P, \zeta, \eta)$ be a valid test, $\bar{\sigma} = i_1/o_1, \ldots, i_r/o_r$, s^T be a state of T, and $\bar{t} = (t_1, \ldots, t_r)$. We write $I \parallel T \overset{\bar{\sigma}}{\Longrightarrow} s^T$ if $T \overset{\bar{\sigma}}{\Longrightarrow} s^T$ and $\bar{\sigma} \in \text{NTEvol}(I)$.

We write $I \parallel T \overset{\bar{\sigma}}{\Longrightarrow}_{\bar{t}} s^T$ if $I \parallel T \overset{\bar{\sigma}}{\Longrightarrow} s^T$ and $(\bar{\sigma}, \bar{t})$ is a observed timed execution of I. In this case we say that $(\bar{\sigma}, \bar{t})$ is a *test execution* of I and T.

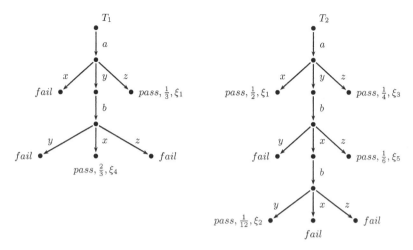

Fig. 2. Examples of Test Cases: $L_I = \{a, b\}$ and $L_O = \{x, y, z\}$

We say that I *passes* the test suite $\mathcal{T}_{st}$, denoted by $\text{pass}(I, \mathcal{T}_{st})$, if for all test $T \in \mathcal{T}_{st}$ there do not exist $\bar{\sigma} \in \text{NTEvol}(I)$, $s^T \in S$ such that $I \parallel T \overset{\bar{\sigma}}{\Longrightarrow} s^T$ and $s^T \in S_F$. □

Let us remark that since we are assuming that implementations are completely specified and initially connected, the testing process will conclude only when the test reaches either a fail or a success state.

In addition to this notion of passing tests, we will have probabilistic and time conditions. We apply these conditions to the set of *observed timed executions*, not to evolutions of the implementations. In fact, we need a set of test executions associated to each evolution to evaluate if they match these conditions. In order to increase the degree of reliability, we will not take the classical approach where passing a test suite is defined according only to the results for each test. In our approach, we will put together all the observations, for each test, so that we have more samples for each evolution. In particular, some observations will be used several times. In other words, an observation from a given test may be used to check the validity of another test sharing the same observed sequence.

Definition 10. *Let I be a PSFSM and $\mathcal{T}_{st} = \{T_1, \ldots, T_n\}$ be a test suite. Let $H_1, \ldots, H_n$ be test execution samples of I and $T_1, \ldots, T_n$, respectively. Let $H = \bigcup_{i=1}^{n} H_i$, $\Phi = \{\bar{\sigma} \mid \exists\, \bar{t} : (\bar{\sigma}, \bar{t}) \in H\}$, and $\bar{\sigma} \in \Phi$. We define the set $\text{Test}(\bar{\sigma}, \mathcal{T}_{st}) = \{T \mid T \in \mathcal{T}_{st} \wedge I \parallel T \overset{\bar{\sigma}}{\Longrightarrow} s^T\}$.*

Let us consider $0 < \alpha < 1$, $\text{Sampling}_{(H, \Phi)}$ and $\text{SeqSampling}_{(H, \Phi)}$. We say that the implementation I probabilistically $(\alpha, H)-$passes the test suite $\mathcal{T}_{st}$ if $\text{pass}(I, \mathcal{T}_{st})$ and for all $\bar{\sigma} = \bar{a}/\bar{x} \in \Phi$ we have that for all $T \in \text{Test}(\bar{\sigma}, \mathcal{T}_{st})$ it holds $\eta(s^T) \in CI_\alpha(\text{SeqSampling}_{(H, \Phi)}(\bar{\sigma}))$.

We say that the implementation I stochastically $(\alpha, H)-$passes the test suite $\mathcal{T}_{st}$ if $\text{pass}(I, \mathcal{T}_{st})$ and for all $\bar{\sigma} \in \Phi$ we have that for all $T \in \text{Test}(\bar{\sigma}, \mathcal{T}_{st})$ it holds $\gamma(\zeta(s^T), \text{Sampling}_{(H, \Phi)}(\bar{\sigma})) > \alpha$.

Intuitively, an implementation passes a test if there does not exist an evolution leading to a fail state. Once we know that the functional behavior of the implementation is correct with respect to the test, we need to check probabilistic and time conditions. The set H corresponds to the observations of the (several) applications of the tests belonging to the test suite $\mathcal{T}_{st}$ to I. Thus, we have to decide whether, for each evolution $\bar{\sigma}$, the frequency (that is, $\mathtt{SeqSampling}_{(H,\Phi)}(\bar{\sigma})$) and the observed time values (that is, $\mathtt{Sampling}_{(H,\Phi)}(\bar{\sigma})$) *match* the probabilities and the definition of the random variables appearing in the successful state of the tests corresponding to the execution of that evolution (that is, $\eta(s^T)$ and $\zeta(s^T)$).

5   Derivation of Test Suites

In this section we present an algorithm to derive tests from specifications. We will derive test suites that are sound and complete with respect to the implementation relations introduced in Section 3. The basic idea underlying test derivation consists in traversing the specification in order to get all the possible evolutions in an appropriate way. First, we introduce some additional notation.

Definition 11. Let $M = (S, s_0, Li, Lo, P_T, P_\mathcal{V})$ be a PSFSM. We define the function $\mathtt{out} : S \times Li \longrightarrow \wp(Lo)$ such that for all $s \in S$ and $i \in I$ it returns the set of outputs

$$\mathtt{out}(s, a) = \{x \mid \exists s', p, \xi : P_T(s, a, x, s') = p > 0 \land P_\mathcal{V}(s, a, x, s') = \xi\}$$

We define the function $\mathtt{after} : S \times Li \times Lo \times \mathcal{V} \times [0, 1] \longrightarrow ((S \times \mathcal{V} \times [0, 1]) \cup \{\mathtt{error}\})$ such that for all $s \in S, a \in Li, x \in Lo, p \in [0, 1]$ and $\xi \in \mathcal{V}$ we have

$$\mathtt{after}(s, a, x, \xi, p) = \begin{cases} (s', \xi + \xi', p \cdot p') & \text{if } \exists s', p', \xi' : P_T(s, a, x, s') = p' > 0 \land \\ & \qquad\qquad P_\mathcal{V}(s, a, x, s') = \xi' \\ \mathtt{error} & \text{otherwise} \end{cases}$$

$\square$

The function $\mathtt{out}(s, a)$ computes the set of output actions associated with those transitions that can be executed from s after receiving the input a. The function $\mathtt{after}(s, a, x, \xi, p)$ computes the *situation* that is reached from a state s after receiving the input a, producing the output x, when the duration of the previous testing process is given by ξ with probability p. Let us also remark that due to the assumption that PSFSMs are observable we have that $\mathtt{after}(s, a, x, \xi, p)$ is uniquely determined. Finally, we will apply this function only when the side condition holds, that is, we will never receive $\mathtt{error}$ as result of applying $\mathtt{after}$.

The algorithm to derive tests from a specification is given in Figure 3. By considering the possible available choices we get a test suite extracted from the specification M. We denote this test suite by $\mathtt{tests}(M)$.

Input: A specification $M = (S, s_{in}, Li, Lo, P_T, P_V)$.
Output: A test case $T = (S, Li, Lo, \lambda, s_0, S_I, S_O, S_F, S_P, \zeta, \eta)$.

Initialization: $S' := \{s_0\};\ Tran', S_I, S_O, S_F, S_P := \emptyset;\ S_{aux} := \{(s_{in}, \theta, 0, s_0)\}$.
Inductive Cases: Choose one of the following two options until $S_{aux} = \emptyset$.

1. If $(s^M, \xi, p, s^T) \in S_{aux}$ then perform the following steps:
   (a) $S_{aux} := S_{aux} - \{(s^M, \xi, p, s^T)\};\ S_P := S_P \cup \{s^T\};\ \zeta(s^T) := \xi;\ \eta(s^T) := p$.
2. If $S_{aux} = \{(s^M, \xi, p, s^T)\}$ and $\exists\, a \in Li : \mathbf{out}(s^M, a) \neq \emptyset$ then perform the following steps:
   (a) $S_{aux} := \emptyset$; Choose a such that $\mathbf{out}(s^M, a) \neq \emptyset$.
   (b) Consider a fresh state $s' \notin S'$ and let $S' := S' \cup \{s'\}$.
   (c) $S_I := S_I \cup \{s^T\};\ S_O := S_O \cup \{s'\};\ Tran' := Tran' \cup \{(s^T, a, s')\}$.
       {Add an input transition labelled by a and consider all outputs}
   (d) For all $x \notin \mathbf{out}(s^M, a)$ do {These outputs lead to a fail state}
       – Consider a fresh state $s'' \notin S'$ and let $S' := S' \cup \{s''\}$.
       – $S_F := S_F \cup \{s''\};\ Tran' := Tran' \cup \{(s', x, s'')\}$.
   (e) For all $x \in \mathbf{out}(s^M, a)$ do
       {These outputs are *expected*. At most one of them will lead to an
       input state where the test continues; the rest will lead to pass
       states}
       – Consider a fresh state $s'' \notin S'$ and let $S' := S' \cup \{s''\}$.
       – $Tran' := Tran' \cup \{(s', x, s'')\}$.
       – $(s_1^M, \xi', p') := \mathbf{after}(s^M, a, x, \xi, p);\ S_{aux} := S_{aux} \cup \{(s_1^M, \xi', p', s'')\}$.

Fig. 3. Derivation of tests from an observable specification

Next we explain how our algorithm works. A set of *pending situations* S_{aux} keeps those tuples denoting the possible states, random variables and probabilities that could appear in a state of the test whose outgoing transitions have not been completed yet. More precisely, a tuple $(s^M, \xi, p, s^T) \in S_{aux}$ indicates that we did not complete the state s^T of the test, the current state in the traversal of the specification is s^M, and the accounting for the elapsed duration in the specification from the initial state is given by ξ. In addition, p reflects the probability associated to the transitions traversed in the specification for reaching the current state.

Following with the explanation of the algorithm, the set S_{aux} initially contains a tuple with the initial states (of both specification and test) and the initial situation of the process, that is, duration θ and probability 0. For each tuple belonging to S_{aux} we may choose one possibility. It is important to remark that the second step can be applied only when the set S_{aux} becomes singleton. So, our derived tests correspond to valid tests as introduced in Definition 8. The first possibility simply indicates that the state of the test becomes a passing state. The second possibility takes an input and generates a transition in the test labelled by this input. Then, the whole sets of outputs is considered. If the output is not expected by the specification (step 2.(d) of the algorithm) then a transition leading to a failing state is created. This could be simulated by a single branch in the test, labelled by `else`, leading to a failing state (in the algorithm we suppose that *all* the possible outputs appear in the test). For the expected outputs (step 2.(e) of the algorithm) we create a transition with the corresponding output and include the appropriate tuple into the set S_{aux}.

Let us note that finite tests are constructed simply by considering a step where the second inductive case is not applied. The algorithm provide us with a test suite extracted from the specification S that we denote by `tests`(S).

Let us comment on the *finiteness* of our algorithm. If we do not impose any restriction on the implementation (e.g. a bound on the number of states) we cannot determine some important information such as the maximal length of the traces that the implementation can perform. In other words we would need a *fault coverage criterion* to generate a finite test suite. Obviously, one can impose restrictions such as "generate n tests" or "generate all the tests with m inputs" and *completeness* will be obtained up to that coverage criterion. Since we do not assume, by default, any criteria, all we can do is to say that this is the, in general, test suite that allows to prove completeness, that is, we obtain full fault coverage but taking into account that the derived test suite will be, in general, infinite.

Next, we present the results that relate implementation relations and application of test suites derived from a specification. The result holds because the temporal and probabilistic conditions required to conform to the specification and to pass the test suite are in fact the same. Due to space limitations, we cannot include in this paper the proof of the theorem. In spite of the differences, the proof is an adaptation of that in [25].

Theorem 1. (Soundness and Completeness) Let I and S be PSFSMs, H be a multiset of timed executions of I, $0 < \alpha < 1$. We have that:

- $I \sqsubseteq_{p,(\alpha,H)} S$ iff I *probabilistically* (α, H)−*passes* `tests`(S).
- $I \sqsubseteq_{s,(\alpha,H)} S$ iff I *stochastically* (α, H)−*passes* `tests`(S).

□

The derived test suite is *sound* and *complete*, up to a given confidence level α and for a sample H, with respect to the conformance relations $\sqsubseteq_{s,(\alpha,H)}$ and $\sqsubseteq_{p,(\alpha,H)}$. Specifically, for a given specification S, the test suite `tests`(S) can be used to distinguish those (and only those) implementations that conform with respect to $\sqsubseteq_{s,(\alpha,H)}$ and $\sqsubseteq_{p,(\alpha,H)}$. However, we cannot say that the test suite is complete since both the notion of passing tests and the considered implementation relations have a probabilistic component. So, we can talk of *completeness* up to a certain confidence level.

6   Estimation of Probabilities and Random Variables

When testing from a non-deterministic FSMs, it is necessary to make an assumption: *implementations have a fairness property such that if an input sequence is applied to the implementation a finite number of times, all possible execution paths in the implementation that can be followed using the input sequence are traversed.* This is the so-called *complete-testing assumption.* Under this assumption, we need to apply the test sequences a minimum number of times to the implementation in order to observe all output sequences that can be produced. In addition, in our approach, we need to estimate the probabilities associated to each input/output sequence in order to determine if they fulfill the requirements specified. Moreover, we need to check if the random variables are correctly implemented. In order to do it we collect a set of timed executions corresponding to the observations of the several applications of the tests belonging to a test suite to the implementation. Nevertheless, this technique does not allow us to determine the probabilities and the random variables of the implementation. We only can *estimate* the probabilities and decide with a certain confidence, whether the sample could be generated by the corresponding random variable in the specification. We use *statistical results* to establish the number of times we need to apply the test to obtaining a required confidence level.

6.1   Checking Correctness of Probabilities

In general, test sequence repetition numbers are neither large enough to satisfy the complete-testing assumption nor large enough to estimate exact probabilities. In such a case, the testing process is a hypothesis test [32]. When we check the probability of a given input/output sequence the following two hypotheses are considered in this paper.

H_0 : *the probability of the implementation is correct*
H_1 : *the probability of the implementation is not correct.*

Let us denote by P_{EP} and P_{NEF} test-pass probability of equivalent machines and test-fail probability of faulty machines respectively. The probability $(1 - P_{EP})$ corresponds to type I error of hypothesis H_0 which is the probability that the hypothesis H_0 is rejected when it is true. The probability $(1 - P_{NEF})$ corresponds to type II error of hypothesis H_0 which is the probability that the hypothesis H_0 is accepted when it is false. When we test probabilities using interval estimation, the numbers of test application will be determined such that P_{EP} and P_{NEF} are not less than a given value where the types of faulty machines can be described further in hypothesis H_1.

   If there are two executable transitions t_1 and t_2 from a state s when an input is applied where the transition probabilities are p and $1 - p$ respectively, a random variable X defined as follows is a Bernoulli random variable:

$$\begin{cases} X = 0 \text{ if transition } t_1 \text{ is selected for execution from state } s. \\ X = 1 \text{ if transition } t_2 \text{ is selected for execution from state } s. \end{cases}$$

Selecting a transition between t_1 and t_2 for execution can be considered as an *experiment* (or a *trial*). If Y represents the number of times t_1 was selected after n independent experiments, Y is said to be a *binomial* random variable with parameters (n, p). The observed data after n independent experiments is called a *sample* where n is the *sample size*. The probability p can be estimated by an interval with a certain degree of confidence, which is called the *confidence interval*, after n independent experiments. The Agresti-Coull interval [1] which is one of the recommended intervals by Brown *et al.* [6] for p with $100(1 - \alpha)\%$ confidence is given by

$$\tilde{p} - \kappa\sqrt{\frac{\tilde{p}(1 - \tilde{p})}{\tilde{n}}} \leq p \leq \tilde{p} + \kappa\sqrt{\frac{\tilde{p}(1 - \tilde{p})}{\tilde{n}}}$$

where $\tilde{Y} = Y + \kappa^2/2$, $\tilde{n} = n + \kappa^2$, $\tilde{p} = \tilde{Y}/\tilde{n}$, and κ is such that $P\{|Z| \leq \kappa\} = 1 - \alpha$ where Z is a standard normal variable. For the case when $\alpha = 0.05$, the value 2 is used instead of 1.96 for κ in the Agresti-Coull interval. If $n \geq 40$, the Agresti-Coull interval provides good coverage even for p very close to 0 or 1 [6].

Suppose that an implementation PSFSM M_I has a transition with probability p' while the probability in the specification PSFSM M is p. The following criteria can be used for testing:

$$\begin{cases} Pass \text{ if } p \text{ is included in the obtained confidence interval for } p'; \\ Fail \text{ otherwise.} \end{cases}$$

Let d denote half of the obtained confidence interval length. According to the value of p' we will have the following results. If $p' = p$, $100(1 - \alpha)\%$ of the time the implementation will have a pass verdict. When we test probabilities using interval estimation, therefore, we can ensure that P_{EP} is never less than a given value, $(1 - \alpha)$. If $|p' - p| > 2d$, $100(1 - \alpha/2)\%$ of the time, the implementation will have a fail verdict and P_{NEF} is ensured to be not less than a given value, $(1 - \alpha/2)$. If $0 < |p' - p| \leq 2d$, we cannot provide any meaningful upper or lower bound of P_{NEF} as the range is too wide, from α to $(1 - \alpha/2)$ according to the difference between p and p'.

We now explain how to determine test sequence repetition numbers for testing probabilities. Test sequence repetition numbers will be determined so that P_{EP} and P_{NEF} are ensured to be not less than $(1 - \alpha)$ and $(1 - \alpha/2)$ respectively where faulty implementations are such that the difference of the probability is more than $2d$. For correct implementations, ideally, $100(1 - \alpha)\%$ of the time, p will be contained in any size of confidence interval. Therefore, P_{EP} is independent of d and we can always ensure P_{EP} as far as we have a reliable confidence interval. In order to have $P_{NEF} \geq 1 - \alpha/2$, the test sequence repetition number n should satisfy the following condition.

$$n > \left(\frac{\kappa}{d}\right)^2 \hat{p}(1 - \hat{p}) - \kappa^2$$

where

$$\hat{p} = \begin{cases} p + d \text{ if } p \leq 0.5 \\ p - d \text{ otherwise} \end{cases}$$

If there are j probabilities to test in a test sequence ts and there are k test sequences in a test suite which have at least two probabilities to test, κ should satisfy the following condition when we test the probabilities of the test sequence.

$$P\{|Z| < \kappa\} = \begin{cases} (1-\alpha)^{1/k} & \text{if } j = 2 \\ (1-\alpha)^{1/(j+k-1)} & \text{if } j > 2 \end{cases}$$

For further details about the determination of test sequence repetition numbers for testing probabilities can be found at [16].

6.2 Checking Correctness of Random Variables

Goodness-of-fit tests indicate whether or not it is sensible to assume that a random sample comes from a specific distribution. Hypothesis Test model for Goodness-of-fit tests are a form of hypothesis testing where the null and alternative hypotheses are

- H_0: Sample data come from the stated distribution.
- H_A: Sample data do not come from the stated distribution.

The underlying idea is that a sample will be *rejected* if the probability of observing that sample from a given random variable is low. In practice, we will check whether the probability to observe a *discrepancy* lower than or equal to the one we have observed is low enough.

Three goodness-of-fit tests are the most frequently used. Chi-square test can be applied for both continuous and discrete distributions. Kolmogorov-Smirnov and Anderson-Darling test only can be used for continuous distributions. Due to the fact that our models may present random variables associated to discrete and continuous distributions functions, we will present a methodology based on Chi-square test to measure the confidence degree that a random variable has on a sample.

The mechanism is the following. Once we have collected a sample of size n we perform the following steps:

- We split the sample into k classes which cover all the possible range of values. We denote by O_i the *observed frequency* at class i (i.e. the number of elements belonging to the class i).
- We calculate the probability p_i of each class, according to the proposed random variable. We denote by E_i the *expected frequency*, which is given by $E_i = np_i$.
- We calculate the *discrepancy* between observed frequencies and expected frequencies as $X^2 = \sum_{i=1}^{k} \frac{(O_i - E_i)^2}{E_i}$. When the model is correct, this discrepancy is approximately distributed as a random variable χ^2 .
- We estimate the number of freedom degrees of χ^2 as $k - r - 1$. In this case, r is the number of parameters of the model which have been estimated by maximal likelihood over the sample to estimate the values of p_i (i.e. $r = 0$ if the model completely specifies the values of p_i before the samples are observed).

– We will *accept* that the sample follows the proposed random variable if the
probability of obtaining a discrepancy greater or equal to the discrepancy
observed is high enough, that is, if $X^2 < \chi_\alpha^2(k-r-1)$ for some α high enough.
Actually, as the margin to accept the sample decreases as α increases, we can
obtain a measure of the validity of the sample as $\mathtt{max}\{\alpha\,|\,X^2 < \chi_\alpha^2(k-r-1)\}$.

According to the previous steps, we can now present an operative definition
of the function γ which is used in this paper to compute the confidence of a
random variable on a sample.

Definition 12. *Let ξ be a random variable and J be a multiset of real numbers
representing a sample. Let X^2 be the discrepancy level of J on ξ calculated as
explained above by splitting the sampling space into k classes*

$$C = \{[0, a_1), [a_1, a_2), \ldots, [a_{k-2}, a_{k-1}), [a_{k-1}, \infty)\}$$

*where k is a given constant and for all $1 \leq i \leq k - 1$ we have $P(\xi \leq a_i) = \frac{i}{k}$. We define the confidence of ξ on J with classes C, denoted by $\gamma(\xi, J)$, as
$\mathtt{max}\{\alpha\,|\,X^2 < \chi_\alpha^2(k - 1)\}$.*

The previous definition indicates that in order to perform a contrast hypothesis, we split the collected values in several intervals having the same expected
probability. We compute the value for X^2 as previously described and check this
figure with the tabulated tables corresponding to χ^2 with $k - 1$ freedom degrees
(see, for example, www.statsoft.com/textbook/sttable.html).

Let us comment on some important details. First, given the fact that the random variables that we use in our framework denote the passing of time, we do not
need classes to cover negative values. Thus, we will suppose that the class containing 0 will also contain all the negative values. Second, the number of classes
and how many data contain each class will affect the power of the test, that is,
how sensitive it is to detecting departures from the null hypothesis. Power will
not only be affected by the number of classes and how they are defined, but by
the sample size and shape of the null and underlying distributions. Some useful
rules can be given in order to determine it. When data are discrete, tabulation
can be used to categorize the data. Continuous data present a more difficult
challenge. One defines classes by segmenting the range of possible values into
non-overlapping intervals. Elements can then be defined by the endpoints of the
intervals. In general, power is maximized by choosing endpoints such that each
element is equiprobable, that is, the probabilities associated with an observation
falling into a given class are divided as evenly as possible across the intervals. A
good starting point for choosing the number of classes is to use the value $2 \cdot n^2/5$,
each of them containing at least 5 elements.

Example 2. Let us consider a device that produces real numbers belonging to the
interval $[0, 1]$. We would like to test whether the device produces these numbers
randomly, that is, it does not have a number or sets of numbers that have a
higher probability of being produced than others. Thus, we obtain a sample

from the machine and we apply the contrast hypothesis to determine whether the machine follows a uniform distribution in the interval $[0, 1]$. First, we have to decide how many classes we will use. Let us suppose that we take $k = 10$ classes. Thus, for all $1 \leq i \leq 9$ we have $a_i = 0.i$ and $P(\xi \leq a_i) = \frac{i}{10}$. So, $C = \{[0, 0.1), [0.1, 0.2) \dots [0.8, 0.9), [0.9, \infty)\}$.

Let us suppose that the multiset of observed values, after we sort them, is:

$$J = \left\{ \begin{array}{l} 0.00001, 0.002, 0.0876, 0.8, \\ 0.1, 0.11, 0.123, \\ 0.21, 0.22, 0.22, 0.2228, 0.23, 0.24, 0.28, \\ 0.32, 0.388, 0.389, 0.391 \\ 0.4, 0.41, 0.42, 0.4333 \\ 0.543, 0.55, 0.57, \\ 0.62, 0.643, 0.65, 0.67, 0.68, 0.689, 0.694 \\ 0.71, 0.711, 0.743, 0.756, 0.78, 0.788, \\ 0.81, 0.811, 0.82, 0.845, 0.8999992, \\ 0.91, 0.93, 0.94, 0.945, 0.9998 \end{array} \right\}$$

Since the sample has 48 elements we have that the expected frequency in each class, E_i, is equal to 4.8. In contrast, the observed frequencies, O_i, are $4, 3, 7, 4, 4, 3, 7, 6, 5, 5$. Next, we have to compute

$$X^2 = \sum_{i=1}^{10} \frac{(O_i - E_i)^2}{E_i} = 4.08333$$

Finally, we have to consider the table corresponding to χ^2 with 9 degrees of freedom and find the maximum α such that $4.08333 < \chi_\alpha^2(9)$. Since $\chi_{0.9}^2(9) = 4.16816$ and $\chi_{0.95}^2(9) = 3.32511$ we conclude that, with probability at least 0.9, the machine produces indeed random values.

7   Conclusions

In this paper we have presented a notion of finite state machine to specify, in an easy way, both probabilities that quantified the non-deterministic choices and the passing of time due to the performance of actions. In addition, we have presented two implementation relations based on the notion of conformance. First, the implementation must conform to the specification regarding functional aspects. It requires to take into account the probabilities associated to the transitions in the specification. Second, we require that the implementation complies with the temporal requirements specified by means of random variables. In order to check that the implementation fulfills the probabilities and random variables established in the specification, we apply statistical results. Additionally, we introduce a notion of test, how to apply a test suite to an implementation, and what is the meaning of successfully passing a test suite. Even though implementation relations and passing of test suites are, apparently, unrelated concepts, we provide a link between them: We give an algorithm to derive test suites from specifications in such a way that a test suite is successfully passed iff the implementation conforms to the specification. This result, usually known as *soundness* and *completeness*, allows a user to check the correctness of an implementation, applying a derived test suite.

References

1. Agresti, A., Coull, B.A.: Approximate is better than exact for interval estimation of binomial proportions. The American Statistician 52(2), 119–126 (1998)
2. Alur, R., Courcoubetis, C., Yannakakis, M.: Distinguishing tests for nondeterministic and probabilistic machines. In: 27th ACM Symp. on Theory of Computing, STOC 1995, pp. 363–372. ACM Press, New York (1995)
3. Bernardo, M., Gorrieri, R.: A tutorial on EMPA: A theory of concurrent processes with nondeterminism, priorities, probabilities and time. Theoretical Computer Science 202(1-2), 1–54 (1998)
4. Bravetti, M., Gorrieri, R.: The theory of interactive generalized semi-Markov processes. Theoretical Computer Science 282(1), 5–32 (2002)
5. Brinksma, E., Tretmans, J.: Testing transition systems: An annotated bibliography. In: Cassez, F., Jard, C., Rozoy, B., Dermot, M. (eds.) MOVEP 2000. LNCS, vol. 2067, pp. 187–195. Springer, Heidelberg (2001)
6. Brown, L.D., Cai, T.T., Dasgupta, A.: Interval estimation for a binomial proportion. Statistical Science 16, 101–133 (2001)
7. Cazorla, D., Cuartero, F., Valero, V., Pelayo, F.L., Pardo, J.J.: Algebraic theory of probabilistic and non-deterministic processes. Journal of Logic and Algebraic Programming 55(1–2), 57–103 (2003)
8. Cheung, L., Stoelinga, M., Vaandrager, F.: A testing scenario for probabilistic processes. Journal of the ACM 54(6), Article 29 (2007)
9. Cleaveland, R., Dayar, Z., Smolka, S.A., Yuen, S.: Testing preorders for probabilistic processes. Information and Computation 154(2), 93–148 (1999)
10. van Glabbeek, R., Smolka, S.A., Steffen, B.: Reactive, generative and stratified models of probabilistic processes. Information and Computation 121(1), 59–80 (1995)
11. Hierons, R.M.: Testing from a non-deterministic finite state machine using adaptive state counting. IEEE Transactions on Computers 53(10), 1330–1342 (2004)
12. Hierons, R.M., Merayo, M.G.: Mutation testing from probabilistic finite state machines. In: 3rd Workshop on Mutation Analysis, Mutation 2007, pp. 141–150. IEEE Computer Society Press, Los Alamitos (2007)
13. Hierons, R.M., Merayo, M.G.: Mutation testing from probabilistic and stochastic finite state machines. Journal of Systems and Software (in press, 2009)
14. Hierons, R.M., Merayo, M.G., Núñez, M.: Testing from a stochastic timed system with a fault model. Journal of Logic and Algebraic Programming 78(2), 98–115 (2009)
15. Hillston, J.: A Compositional Approach to Performance Modelling. Cambridge University Press, Cambridge (1996)
16. Hwang, I., Cavalli, A.: Testing from a probabilistic FSM using interval estimation. Technical Report 09004LOR, TELECOM & Management SudParis (2009)
17. Hwang, I., Kim, T., Hong, S., Lee, J.: Test selection for a nondeterministic FSM. Computer Communications 24(12), 1213–1223 (2001)

18. Kwiatkowska, M., Norman, G., Segala, R., Sproston, J.: Automatic verification of real-time systems with discrete probability distributions. Theoretical Computer Science 282(1), 101–150 (2002)
19. Larsen, K., Skou, A.: Bisimulation through probabilistic testing. Information and Computation 94(1), 1–28 (1991)
20. Lee, D., Yannakakis, M.: Principles and methods of testing finite state machines: A survey. Proceedings of the IEEE 84(8), 1090–1123 (1996)
21. López, N., Núñez, M.: A testing theory for generally distributed stochastic processes. In: Larsen, K.G., Nielsen, M. (eds.) CONCUR 2001. LNCS, vol. 2154, pp. 321–335. Springer, Heidelberg (2001)
22. López, N., Núñez, M., Rodríguez, I.: Specification, testing and implementation relations for symbolic-probabilistic systems. Theoretical Computer Science 353(1-3), 228–248 (2006)
23. Luo, G.L., von Bochmann, G., Petrenko, A.: Test selection based on communicating nondeterministic finite-state machines using a generalized Wp-method. IEEE Transactions on Software Engineering 20(2), 149–161 (1994)
24. Markowitch, O., Roggeman, Y.: Probabilistic non-repudiation without trusted third party. In: 2nd Conf. on Security in Communication Network (1999)
25. Merayo, M.G., Núñez, M., Rodríguez, I.: Formal testing from timed finite state machines. Computer Networks 52(2), 432–460 (2008)
26. Nicollin, X., Sifakis, J.: An overview and synthesis on timed process algebras. In: Larsen, K.G., Skou, A. (eds.) CAV 1991. LNCS, vol. 575, pp. 376–398. Springer, Heidelberg (1992)
27. Núñez, M.: Algebraic theory of probabilistic processes. Journal of Logic and Algebraic Programming 56(1-2), 117–177 (2003)
28. Petrenko, A.: Fault model-driven test derivation from finite state models: Annotated bibliography. In: Cassez, F., Jard, C., Rozoy, B., Dermot, M. (eds.) MOVEP 2000. LNCS, vol. 2067, pp. 196–205. Springer, Heidelberg (2001)
29. Petrenko, A., Yevtushenko, N., von Bochmann, G.: Testing deterministic implementations from their nondeterministic FSM specifications. In: 9th IFIP Workshop on Testing of Communicating Systems, IWTCS 1996, pp. 125–140. Chapman & Hall, Boca Raton (1996)
30. Reed, G.M., Roscoe, A.W.: A timed model for communicating sequential processes. Theoretical Computer Science 58, 249–261 (1988)
31. Rodríguez, I., Merayo, M.G., Núñez, M.: $\mathcal{HOTL}$: Hypotheses and observations testing logic. Journal of Logic and Algebraic Programming 74(2), 57–93 (2008)
32. Ross, S.M.: Introduction to Probability and Statistics for Engineers and Scientists. John Wiley & Sons, Chichester (1987)
33. Segala, R., Lynch, N.: Probabilistic simulations for probabilistic processes. Nordic Journal of Computing 2(2), 250–273 (1995)
34. Uyar, M.Ü., Batth, S.S., Wang, Y., Fecko, M.A.: Algorithms for modeling a class of single timing faults in communication protocols. IEEE Transactions on Computers 57(2), 274–288 (2008)

Qualitative Action Systems*

Bernhard K. Aichernig, Harald Brandl, and Willibald Krenn

Institute for Software Technology, Graz University of Technology, Austria
{aichernig,hbrandl,wkrenn}@ist.tugraz.at

Abstract. An extension to *action systems* is presented facilitating the modeling of continuous behavior in the discrete domain. The original action system formalism has been developed by Back et al. in order to describe parallel and distributed computations of discrete systems, i.e. systems with discrete state space and discrete control. In order to cope with hybrid systems, i.e. systems with continuous evolution and discrete control, two extensions have been proposed: *hybrid action systems* and *continuous action systems*. Both use differential equations (relations) to describe continuous evolution. Our version of action systems takes an alternative approach by adding a level of abstraction: continuous behavior is modeled by Qualitative Differential Equations that are the preferred choice when it comes to specifying abstract and possibly non-deterministic requirements of continuous behavior. Because their solutions are transition systems, all evolutions in our *qualitative action systems* are discrete.

Based on hybrid action systems, we develop a new theory of qualitative action systems and discuss how we have applied such models in the context of automated test-case generation for hybrid systems.

1 Introduction

The most important aspect of any technical system is to meet the expectations set. More precisely, any technical system has to fulfill the requirements that lead to the design of the system. To improve our confidence in a given system, a variety of quality assurance techniques have been developed, including formal (verification) methods. In the case where the system's internals are not accessible, we have to rely on testing techniques that exercise the system with predefined inputs and – hopefully – demonstrate compliance with the expected behavior. One testing methodology that particularly addresses the problem of comparing the expected behavior defined by the requirements with the observed behavior of the implemented system is called black-box testing. Black-box means that details of the implementation are of no concern during testing. Only the input/output behavior is being looked at. Because testing should yield verdicts, any black-box testing approach needs information about the expected (correct) system behavior. One particular testing approach that

---

* Research herein was funded by the EU project ICT-216679, Model-based Generation of Tests for Dependable Embedded Systems (MOGENTES).

K. Breitman and A. Cavalcanti (Eds.): ICFEM 2009, LNCS 5885, pp. 206–225, 2009.

automates test-case generation, execution, and verdict generation is model-based testing.

This paper presents a new approach to model-based test case generation for hybrid systems. Commonly, hybrid automata are used to model hybrid systems, i.e. systems with continuous evolution and discrete control. Overly simplified one might say that hybrid automata are normal automata but with differential equations attached to each discrete state: the differential equations describe the continuous evolution of the system in the particular state. Hence, switching between discrete states in the automaton means changing the continuous evolution. While differential equations are a very precise tool to describe the continuous behavior of a system, they are not necessarily the best choice for model-based testing.

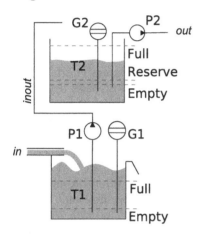

Fig. 1. Two-Tank Pump System

Consider the example hybrid system of Figure 1 and the task to automatically derive tests. The first step toward a system model is to know the (informal) *system requirements*: in the two-tank system in Figure 1 tank $T1$ is on a lower level than the tank $T2$. $T1$ is being filled with water having some inflow rate *in*. Both tanks $(T1, T2)$ are connected by the pump $P1$ that is controlled such that: if the water level in $T2$ decreases below a certain *Reserve* mark and $T1$ is full, pump $P1$ starts pumping water until $T2$ is full or $T1$ gets empty. In addition, the controller needs to control the pump $P2$ that is pumping water out of $T2$: $P2$ shall be turned on as long as a button *WaterRequest* is pressed and there is enough water in $T2$ ($T2$ not *Empty*). Note that the signal *WaterRequest* and the inflow rate *in* are not controllable, hence *T1* may overflow.

Given these requirements, one is able to derive a formal model. As an example, the continuous dynamics of the system may be expressed by two coupled differential equations: $\dot{x}_1 = (in - inout)/A_1$ and $\dot{x}_2 = (inout - out)/A_2$. Here, A_1 and A_2 are the base areas of the two tanks and x_1 and x_2 denote the current level in the tanks. The variables *in*, *inout*, and *out* denote the flow rates into $T1$, between $T1$ and $T2$, and out of $T2$ respectively.

Observe that for testing whether some given implementation of this two-tank system conforms to the stated requirements we do not need to know the exact numerical value of the water level at all times, nor do we care about the exact time information! Also, we would need to incorporate additional knowledge, such as the exact base areas of the tanks, in order to solve these equations numerically: in reality we might not have all information that is required for such a detailed model. Informal requirements, as in our example, mostly describe evolutions of hybrid systems in a qualitative manner like "when something increases to a certain value another thing will start descreasing. Finally, in order to transform the informal requirements to the differential equation model, one needs experience in physics, and applied mathematics. To put a long story short: for our purposes of conformance testing, the full differential model – most of the time – requires (and carries) too much detail.

In such cases, where accurate numerical information about the system is not available, or no precise numerical value about the evolution of the system is needed, a technique called *Qualitative Reasoning* (QR) can be applied [1]. Instead of describing the evolutions of a system in terms of differential equations, QR uses qualitative constraints, so called *Qualitative Differential Equations*. In QR, simulation algorithms like QSIM solve the underlying constraint problem in order to predict future system behavior. Most importantly, QR abstracts away from time and exact numerical values and works on value-intervals, separated by so called landmarks.

Given Qualitative Reasoning to describe the continuous evolutions of a system, we rely on action systems for the discrete part. Action systems have been extensively studied [2,3,4]. Most notably, a solid theoretical basis defines the notion of refinement between different action systems. Also, object-oriented and hybrid extensions have been proposed that make action systems a natural contender for modeling discrete and hybrid systems. By combining these two formalisms, we obtain the notion of *Qualitative Action Systems* that inherit the strengths of both, action systems and qualitative reasoning. In particular we gain the formal foundation for model-based test case generation through action refinement and the ability for high-level hybrid systems specification.

The reminder of this paper is organized as follows. First, Section 2 discusses the modeling of hybrid systems in the continuous domain by means of hybrid action systems. Next, in Section 3 we present our extension to hybrid action systems and discuss qualitative abstraction of continuous models. Then, Section 4 discusses the refinement from qualitative to hybrid models. In Section 5 we explain how our qualitative action systems serve as models for conformance testing. Finally, we discuss related work (Section 6) before drawing our conclusions in Section 7.

2   Hybrid Modeling

In the preceding section we have argued for qualitative action systems, an action-systems-based hybrid system model that does not depend on differential equations to describe continuous behavior. In this section we present the theoretical foundations of our qualitative action system, namely *hybrid action systems* of Rönkkö and Sere [5].

Per definition, a hybrid system comprises discrete and continuous parts. In our two-tank example, the discrete part is formed by the controller that needs to start and stop different pumps. The environment, i.e. the tanks and the water, form the continuous part. In the remainder of this paper, we will take advantage of the compositionality of action systems to express this separation of concerns. More precisely, our hybrid model is formed as parallel composition of the controller and the environment: *system* ≡ *controller*||*environment*. This approach yields important consequences: we are working with a *closed system* and all test cases we derive are tests for the whole system.

2.1 Discrete Part: Controller

For a detailed controller design the requirements given in the introduction are too imprecise. We therefore need to give a more precise picture of the discrete part of our hybrid system:

1. If a button *WaterRequest* is pressed (on) and provided $T2$ is not empty (water level above *Reserve*), start pump P2 and pump water out of tank $T2$.
2. If P2 is running and *WaterRequest* is not pressed then stop P2.
3. If P2 is running and the water level of $T2$ drops to *Empty* stop P2.
4. If tank $T2$ gets empty (water level below *Reserve* mark), and $T1$ is full then pump water out of tank $T1$ into tank $T2$ by starting pump P1.
5. If pump P1 is running and the water level in tank $T1$ drops to *Empty* then stop P1.
6. If pump P1 is running and the water level in tank $T2$ reaches *Full* then stop P1.

Because the given requirements can be mapped to discrete system properties, we are free to use the conventional action-system methodology [3,6] without any hybrid additions to model the controller of our system. Syntactically, an action system AS can be represented as

$$AS =_{df} |[\mathbf{var}\ Y : T \bullet S_0; \mathbf{do}\ A_1 \square \ldots \square A_n \mathbf{od}\ ]| : I$$

where Y denotes the list of S_0-initialized discrete model variables. Similarly, T is the list of types $\langle T_1, \ldots, T_{|Y|} \rangle$ for Y. Variables may be decorated with $*$ to denote read/write-export. The body of an action system is formed by a set of guarded commands $A_1 \ldots A_n$ that are separated by non-deterministic choice operators $\square$ and embedded in a loop-forever statement **do** ... **od**. Each guarded command A_i is of the form *guard* → *action*, meaning that if the *guard*-predicate is satisfied then the *action*-statement can be executed. Finally, I denotes a set of imported variables.

Informally, executing an action system means to initialize all variables with their corresponding initial values before steadily choosing one enabled guarded command and executing the associated *action*-statement. If no guarded command is enabled, or an action aborts, the action system halts execution. Termination of an action system means the termination of the control over the system [6].

Coming back to our running example, we need to create at least four guarded commands in order to model the given requirements: we need to turn on/off both pumps P1 and P2. By setting a state variable $PX\_running$ to true/false we are modeling switching on/off the pump PX. In addition, we set the flow rate produced by the pump PX. Hence, a guarded command for turning on P2 might look like

$$g_3 \rightarrow P2\_running := true; out := (0, Max]$$

with g_3 standing for some guard and $out := (0, Max]$ for a non-deterministic assignment of some flow-rate from the interval $(0, Max]$ to the out-pipe. Based on this knowledge, the action system of the controller can be given as follows.

$$
\begin{aligned}
Controller =_{df} |[\ \textbf{var} \quad & P1\_running, P2\_running : Bool, \\
& out^*, inout^* : Real \\
\bullet \ & P1\_running := false; P2\_running := false; \\
& out := 0; inout := 0; \\
\textbf{do} \quad & g_1 \rightarrow P1\_running := true; inout := (0, Max] \\
\square \ & g_2 \rightarrow P1\_running := false; inout := 0 \\
\square \ & g_3 \rightarrow P2\_running := true; out := (0, Max] \\
\square \ & g_4 \rightarrow P2\_running := false; out := 0 \\
\textbf{od} \quad & \\
]| : \quad & WaterRequest, x_1, x_2
\end{aligned}
$$

The two sensors for the water level and the external button for pumping water out of the tank system are modeled as imported variables x_1, x_2, and $WaterRequest$. The given action system still has general guards g_1 to g_4 instead of concrete ones. Hence, we need to find the correct guards so that our controller behavior matches the requirements. Starting with the first requirement that specifies when P2 should be enabled we can replace g_3 by

$$g_3 =_{df} WaterRequest \wedge \neg P2\_running \wedge x_2 > Reserve$$

Requirements 2 and 3, dealing with cases when to stop P2, can be translated into guard g_4:

$$g_4 =_{df} P2\_running \wedge (\neg WaterRequest \vee x_2 = Empty)$$

Similarly, g_1 and g_2 can be given as follows.

$$g_1 =_{df} x_2 \leq Reserve \wedge x_1 = Full \wedge \neg P1\_running$$
$$g_2 =_{df} P1\_running \wedge (x_1 \leq Empty \vee x_2 = Full)$$

2.2 Continuous Part: Environment

While the controller can be modeled as a discrete system, the environment model depends on continuous evolutions. So we have to use an extended version of conventional action systems, namely hybrid action systems, to model the environment. Hybrid action systems add the notion of a *differential action* that describes a continuous evolution of the system. Differential actions are similar to guarded commands in that both are atomic and both have a guard that needs to be fulfilled so that the action is a candidate for execution. However, differential actions, denoted by *guard* :→ *action*, extend the notion of a discrete guarded command: first, the action-part is formed by a first-order autonomous differential equation that describes the continuous evolution. Second, the guard is checked during the evolution whether it still holds. If the guard is found to not hold anymore, the continuous evolution is aborted. Therefore, the guard of a differential action is also called *evolution guard*. Combining discrete and differential actions yields a hybrid action system.

Definition 1 (Hybrid Action System).

$$HS =_{df} |[\textbf{var } X : T \bullet X := E; \textbf{alt } H \textbf{ with } DH]| : I$$

*where **H** are discrete actions (guarded commands) and **DH** differential actions.*

In the introduction we have already shown that the continuous dynamics of our example system can be modeled by two coupled differential equations: $\dot{x}_1 = (in - inout)/A_1$ and $\dot{x}_2 = (inout - out)/A_2$. Here, A_1 and A_2 are the base areas of the two tanks and x_1 and x_2 denote the current level in the tanks. The variables *in*, *inout*, and *out* denote the flow rates into $T1$, between $T1$ and $T2$, and out of $T2$ respectively. The hybrid action system of the environment contains the differential equations describing the water flows as differential action in the **with** clause:

$$
\begin{aligned}
&Environment =_{df} |[\textbf{ var} \quad && x_1\,{}^*, x_2\,{}^* : Real, \\
& && \bullet\ x_1 := 0; x_2 := 0; \\
& \quad\quad\quad \textbf{alt} && \\
& \quad\quad\quad \textbf{with} && true :\to \\
& && \dot{x}_1 = (in - inout)/A_1 \wedge \dot{x}_2 = (inout - out)/A_2 \\
& \quad\quad]| : && inout, out
\end{aligned}
$$

Notice that in our case the evolution guard is true, hence the system will never leave the continuous evolution. This might be a problem since we also have discrete actions in our system which would never be eligible candidates for execution. As already said, when a differential action is being carried out, it may only be aborted if the evolution guard becomes false. Hence, for a reactive system, it must be ensured that the evolution guard becomes false eventually. This happens when the environment changes its behavior (mode switch to another continuous action) or the controller interacts with the environment. In order to constrain interleavings between discrete and differential actions, so called *prioritized alternation* is applied: as long as discrete actions are ready to run, the system will choose them instead of differential actions that might also be enabled at the same time. Only if no discrete action is enabled, the system tries to run a differential action. This execution model underlies the assumption that the controller is fast enough to reach a stable state before the next environmental interaction takes place. Notice that by including all negated guards of discrete actions within the evolution guards of differential actions, the behavior can be changed to give discrete actions ultimate priority. This is known as *interrupted prioritized alternation*. For details, see [5].

In the remainder of this subsection we give a more formal definition of differential actions. We use this theoretical framework later on to lift differential actions to qualitative ones.

Differential actions in hybrid action systems express initial value problems of ordinary differential equations (ODEs). Given a set of continuous variables related by a set of ODEs and an initialization vector, there exists a unique function vector as solution to the initial value problem. The ODEs in differential actions are autonomous: this property means that the variable used for differentiation does not occur otherwise in the ODE. Because we are differentiating with respect to time-variable t, differential actions must not contain t. As an example, $\dot{y} + y = 0$ is an autonomous first order ODE but $\dot{y} + y + t = 0$ is not.

A differential action $e :\rightarrow d$ consists of an evolution guard $e : PRED(X, Y)$ and a differential relation $d : PRED(X, \dot{X}, Y)$. Both, the evolution guard and the differential relation, are predicates over sets of discrete model variables Y and continuous model variables X. Relations over higher order derivatives can be modeled via additional variables. The following definition characterizes the evolutions of a differential action: ϕ.

Definition 2 (Evolutions).

$$\phi \text{ is an evolution of } \quad e :\rightarrow d \quad \text{iff} \quad SF_c(\phi, e, d) \wedge \Delta_c(\phi, e) > 0 \qquad (1)$$

$$\text{an evolution } \phi \text{ is terminating} \quad \text{iff} \quad \Delta_c(\phi, e) < \infty \qquad (2)$$

$$SF_c(\phi, e, d) =_{df} \phi.0 = X \wedge \dot{\phi}.0 = \dot{X} \wedge$$
$$\forall \tau : \mathbb{R}_0^+ \cdot (e \implies d)[X := \phi.\tau, \dot{X} := \dot{\phi}.\tau] \qquad (3)$$

$$\Delta_c(\phi, e) =_{df} inf\{\tau : \mathbb{R}_0^+ \cdot \neg e[X := \phi.\tau]\} \qquad (4)$$

A function ϕ is a solution to the differential action if it satisfies the predicate SF_c as shown in Formula 3. The predicate demands that the function has to start at the current system state and fulfills the differential relation d as long as the evolution guard is true. The termination time Δ_c (see Equation 4) states the boundary time when the evolution guard is not satisfied by ϕ. Notice that Δ_c is defined as $\Delta_c(\phi, e) =_{df} \infty$ when ϕ satisfies e forever. Function ϕ is called an evolution if it satisfies Proposition 1 and it is said to be terminating if it lasts for a finite period of time, cf. Proposition 2.

The semantics of a differential action is expressed by its weakest precondition:

Definition 3 (WP of Differential Actions).

$$wp(e :\rightarrow d, post) =_{df}$$
$$\forall \phi \cdot SF_c(\phi, e, d) \wedge \Delta_c(\phi, e) > 0 \implies$$
$$\Delta_c(\phi, e) < \infty \wedge post[X := \phi.(\Delta_c(\phi, e)), \dot{X} := \dot{\phi}.(\Delta_c(\phi, e))]$$

The weakest precondition says that of all continuously differentiable functions, those that are evolutions for the given differential action must be terminating and end in a state fulfilling the post-condition. Because in qualitative reasoning the first derivation is part of the state space, Definition 3 extends the definition in [5] with $\dot{X}$ as additional state variable. The same adaptation applies to the initial value condition in (3), Definition 2.

2.3 Putting It All together

In order to get our complete system model, we need to parallel compose the controller and the environment models. Unfortunately, parallel composition of hybrid action systems is more complicated than that of ordinary action systems because linear superposition of differential actions is necessary. The intuitive reason for this is the fact that only one differential action can be executed at a time, so the parallel composition of two systems executing two differential actions at the same time can only be modeled by superposition of the two actions.

In our two-tank example, however, we only have one differential action, so we do not need to apply any superposition calculation. Hence the parallel composition of *Controller* and *Environment* becomes trivial as we only need to combine the elements of both action systems, and correct the import statement. Before doing so, however, we need to fix one issue: because we want our controller (= discrete actions) to interrupt the continuous flow, we need to change the evolution guard of our differential action. Instead of making it trivially true, we need to insert the conjunction of all negated guards of the discrete actions. In effect, we are using *interrupted prioritized alternation* instead of prioritized alternation.

Merging controller and environment under interrupted prioritized alternation yields the following result. Notice that the guards g_1 to g_4 do not change.

$$
\begin{aligned}
System =_{df} \,\|[\ \textbf{var} \quad & x_1\,^*, x_2\,^* : Real, \\
& P1\_running, P2\_running : Bool, out^*, inout^* : Real \\
\bullet \ & x_1 := 0; x_2 := 0; out := 0; inout := 0; \\
& P1\_running := false; P2\_running := false; \\
\textbf{alt} \quad & g_1 \rightarrow P1\_running := true; inout := (0, Max] \\
\square \ & g_2 \rightarrow P1\_running := false; inout := 0 \\
\square \ & g_3 \rightarrow P2\_running := true; out := (0, Max] \\
\square \ & g_4 \rightarrow P2\_running := false; out := 0 \\
\textbf{with} \quad & \neg(g_1 \vee g_2 \vee g_3 \vee g_4) :\rightarrow \\
& \dot{x}_1 = (in - inout)/A_1 \wedge \dot{x}_2 = (inout - out)/A_2 \\
\,]| : \quad & Water Request, in
\end{aligned}
$$

The hybrid model adequately represents our controlled system. The only external signals left are *WaterRequest* and *in*. However, for testing our requirements we are only interested in the qualitative aspects of the environment. The next section presents this abstraction step.

3   Qualitative Modeling

We now lift the continuous model developed within the last section to a discrete one by applying qualitative abstraction. As the name suggests, qualitative modeling abstracts away from quantitative values: in case of qualitative reasoning we are giving up exact numerical values for value intervals, separated by so called landmarks. We also lose exact time information. To support the intuitive understanding of qualitative functions and the difference to continuous ones, we sketch the process of qualitative abstraction in the following. (Further details can be found in Section 3.2.)

Given are the continuous (time dependent) function f and the landmarks $\langle zero, med, high, max \rangle$. After assigning exact numerical values to these landmarks, we can draw a diagram like the one in the upper right corner of Figure 2: the abscissa reflects passing time, while the ordinate measures the output of the continuous function. Value abstraction (v-abs), which is one of two parts of qualitative abstraction, lifts the exact numerical value to a qualitative one. Qualitative values are pairs of an interval or landmark and an abstract value $(-, 0, +)$ for the slope of the continuous function. For example, at time point zero the output of the continuous function is below the landmark *med* but above the landmark *zero*, hence in the interval *zero..med*, and the slope of the function is zero. Value abstraction will therefore return the pair $(zero..med, 0)$ as qualitative value. The second abstraction we need to employ in order to map a continuous

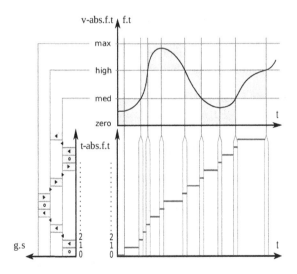

Fig. 2. (*Diagram bottom, right.*) Function *t-abs* partitions time into equivalence classes. (*Diagram on top.*) Function *v-abs* partitions the range of f into equivalence classes. Equivalence classes are denoted by shaded areas, slope omitted. (*Diagram to the left.*) The resulting qualitative function g is depicted on the left. The qualitative slope is represented by circle, triangle up, and triangle down symbols. Thereby the circle stands for "0", triangle up denotes "+", and triangle down represents "-".

function to a qualitative one is time-abstraction (t-abs). Starting again at the upper right diagram in Figure 2 we can see the workings of time-abstraction in the diagram below (bottom right). Informally stated, as long as value abstraction returns the same qualitative value over passing time on a continuous function, the "qualitative time" is the same, i.e. there is no need to create a new qualitative state within the qualitative function that is being constructed. Taking value abstraction and time abstraction together, we get the resulting qualitative function g depicted in the diagram on the bottom to the left.

Commonly, ordinary differential equations are used to specify continuous behavior instead of continuous functions: similar to ordinary differential equations in the continuous domain, qualitative reasoning (QR) knows about qualitative differential equations (QDEs) to describe qualitative functions. Notice that QDEs can be thought of as a constraint system. As is the case with ordinary differential equations, QDEs describe the relations between model variables. Within the domain of QR, these model-variables are also called *quantities.*

Note that QDEs can be derived from ordinary differential equations (ODEs). As an example, the first order ODE $\dot{x} = -3x$ yields the following QDEs: $d/dt(q, \hat{q})$ and $M^-(q, \hat{q})$. Here, the first QDE states that $\hat{q}$ is the qualitative derivation of q. In the second QDE M^- expresses a negative monotonic function relation with $\hat{q} = f.q$ and $\dot{f}.q < 0$.

Given a set of QDEs, an initial state, and a qualitative simulation engine, e.g., QSIM [1], the solution to the QDEs is a transition system[1] (TS) containing all possible behaviors that may evolve over time, i.e. all traces starting from the initial state. Due to incomplete system knowledge, leading to under-constraint specifications, and because of abstraction the solution sets to QDEs usually are large. In addition spurious behavior may occur, i.e. behavior that is not possible in any "real" system. However, the solution-TS is deterministic and each state binds all quantities $q \in Q$ to a certain *qualitative value.* Each qualitative value is of type $QS_q \times \delta$: the *quantity space* QS_q forms a strict total order and is populated with *landmarks* and open intervals in-between. Landmarks distinguish important states of a system, e.g., water freezes below 0°C and starts boiling around 100°C. When we refer to either landmarks or intervals, we speak about *quantity values* (not to be confused with qualitative values!) or "values in the quantity space". Notice that the landmark zero is always included and infinity may be expressed by landmarks, e.g., $+/-\infty$. Also, the open intervals separating landmarks do not have explicit names and we skip mentioning them when specifying a quantity space. Besides values in the quantity space, a qualitative value also consists of a *qualitative derivation* (abstracted gradient $\frac{\partial}{\partial t}$) of ordered type $\delta =_{df} \langle -, 0, + \rangle$.

To make the terminology clearer, we consider our example system comprising the *quantities* $\{x_1, x_2, in, inout, out\}$. In our example, the quantity x_2 has the *quantity space* $\langle 0, Empty, Reserve, Full \rangle$ and may take a *qualitative value* of ($Reserve..Full, +$) with $Reserve..Full$ representing an interval between landmarks and + as abstract derivation. This means that the real value of x_2 is increasing somewhere between $Reserve$ and $Full$.

---

[1] Certain QDEs may also be solved analytically, see [7].

3.1 Qualitative Action Systems

After laying out the terminology of QR and discussing the basic ideas, we come back to our running example and lift the hybrid action system to a qualitative one. We do this by replacing differential actions by *qualitative actions*.

Definition 4 (Qualitative Action). *A qualitative action* $e_q :\rightarrow d_q$ *comprises an abstract, qualitative evolution guard* $e_q : PRED(Y, Q)$ *and a set of qualitative differential equations* $d_q : PRED(Q)$.

Note that in contrast to differential actions, we can not use discrete state variables Y within d_q because of incompatible types. Whenever the guard of the qualitative action becomes true the action is a candidate for execution by simulating (solving) the according QDEs with the current initial values, i.e. the system state. As in differential actions, the execution of the qualitative action halts when the evolution guard does not hold anymore. However, in contrast to differential actions based on differential equations[2], there might exist several different evolutions, all starting from the same initial value. Hence, there can be several different final states.

In order to lift our continuous system to a qualitative one, we need to transform the differential actions to qualitative ones. In particular we need to lift the differential equations to QDEs. However, before we can do this in our example, we need to think about the landmarks the system knows about. Fortunately, most of the landmarks were already given within Figure 1: the model *quantities* x_1 and x_2 (x_1, x_2 are now *qualitative* variables!) have the quantity spaces $T1 = \langle 0, Empty, Full \rangle$ and $T2 = \langle 0, Empty, Reserve, Full \rangle$ respectively. For simplicity we omit an additional landmark *Overflow* for tank $T1$ and assume that when the water climbs above *Full* it will overflow. The flow rates have the quantity space $FR = \langle 0, Max \rangle$. We also need to introduce auxiliary quantities in order to be able to set up the QDEs. The auxiliary quantities only have to link different QDEs, so they only need a coarse quantity space, $NZP = \langle -\infty, 0, \infty \rangle$. The resolution of the quantity spaces depends on the guards of actions in the system and on the relations (QDEs) between quantities. It is in the response of the designer to find the right level of abstraction to express the system requirements appropriately.

The following qualitative actions are written in the *QSIM* [1] notation. Here, $add(x_1, x_2, y)$ means the addition of the quantities $x_1 + x_2 = y$ and the predicate $d/dt(x_1, diff_1)$ means that $diff_1$ is the qualitative derivative of x_1. Note that during qualitative abstraction constant factors, in this example the base areas of the tanks $A1$ and $A2$, are neglected. Hence, given the ordinary differential equation describing the water level of the first tank in our example, $\dot{x}_1 = (in - inout)/A_1$ (all variables are $\in \mathbb{R}$), we can deduce following qualitative differential equations (all variables are $\in QS \times \delta$):

$$d/dt(x_1, diff_1) \wedge add(diff_1, inout, in)$$

---

[2] Note that differential actions based on differential *relations* may also yield several different evolutions.

In our example, the abstraction for the second ordinary differential equation is equally straight forward. By taking everything together, we get the resulting *qualitative action system.*

$$QSystem =_{df} \lVert \textbf{var} \quad x_1 *: T1, x_2 *: T2, out^*, inout^*: FR$$
$$diff_1, diff_2 :: NZP$$
$$P1\_running, P2\_running : Bool$$
$$\bullet \; x_1 := (0,0); x_2 := (0,0);$$
$$out := (0,0); inout := (0,0);$$
$$P1\_running := false; P2\_running := false;$$
$$\textbf{alt} \quad g_1 \rightarrow P1\_running := true; inout := (0..Max, 0)$$
$$\square \; g_2 \rightarrow P1\_running := false; inout := (0,0)$$
$$\square \; g_3 \rightarrow P2\_running := true; out := (0..Max, 0)$$
$$\square \; g_4 \rightarrow P2\_running := false; out := (0,0)$$
$$\textbf{with} \quad \neg(g_1 \vee g_2 \vee g_3 \vee g_4) :\rightarrow$$
$$add(diff_2, out, inout) \wedge add(diff_1, inout, in) \wedge$$
$$d/dt(x_1, diff_1) \wedge d/dt(x_2, diff_2)$$
$$\rVert : \qquad Water Request, in$$

Note that x_1, x_2, *inout*, *out* are now quantities, i.e. qualitative model variables, and that the continuous (but qualitative) evolution of the system is interrupted every time one of the guards g_1 to g_4 becomes true.

After presenting the fundamental idea behind qualitative action systems, we discuss the exact semantics in the remainder of this subsection. We start by giving an characterization of the solution to a QDE: the solution to a QDE d_q with a given initial value assignment is a transition system $\psi : TS =_{df} (S, s_0, T, v)$. The transition system consists of a set of states $S \subset \mathbb{N}_0$, an initial state $s_0 =_{df} 0$, a transition relation $T : S \times S$, and a valuation function $v : S \mapsto (Q \mapsto QS \times \delta)$ binding states to value assignments for all quantities $q \in Q$. The transition system is defined via trace semantics as follows:

$$Traces(\psi) =_{df} \{\langle v.s_0, v.s_1, \ldots \rangle \mid i \in \mathbb{N}_0 \wedge s_i \in S \wedge s_0 = 0 \wedge T(s_i, s_{i+1})\}$$

Notice that each trace is a qualitative function (cf. *g.s* in the bottom left diagram in Figure 2). Similar to differential actions, solutions to qualitative actions have the following properties:

Definition 5.

$$g \text{ is an evolution of } e_q :\rightarrow d_q \quad iff \quad SF_q(g, e_q, d_q) \wedge \Delta_q(g, e_q) > 0 \qquad (5)$$
$$an\ evolution\ g\ is\ terminating \quad iff \quad \Delta_q(g, e_q) < \infty \qquad (6)$$
$$SF_q(g, e_q, d_q) =_{df} g.0 = Q \wedge \forall s : dom(g) \cdot (e_q \implies d_q)[Q := g.s] \qquad (7)$$
$$\Delta_q(g, e_q) = \begin{cases} min(x = \{i \mid i \in \mathbb{N}_0 \wedge \neg e_q[Q := g.i]\}) & if\ x \neq \{\} \\ 0 & else \end{cases} \qquad (8)$$

Predicate SF_q (7) states that a qualitative function, i.e. a trace g, is a valid solution to the qualitative action if it is contained in the solution of the qualitative differential equation whenever the evolution guard is satisfied. Furthermore the initial value must match the current system state. Formula (8) takes a qualitative function and returns the "time", i.e. the state number, when it first violates the evolution guard. Propositions (5) and (6) define when a qualitative function is an evolution and terminating respectively.

Similar to differential actions, we define the weakest precondition of a qualitative action as follows:

Definition 6 (WP of Qualitative Actions).

$$wp(e_q :\longrightarrow d_q,\ post) =_{df}$$
$$\forall \psi : TS \cdot \forall g \in Traces.\psi \cdot SF_q(g, e_q, d_q) \wedge \Delta_q(g, e_q) > 0 \implies$$
$$\Delta_q(g, e_q) < \infty \wedge post[Q := g.\Delta_q(g, e_q)]$$

3.2   Qualitative Abstraction

As we want to have a formal link between quantitative functions and their qualitative counterparts, we look at the abstraction of time-dependent functions. In the following we will develop this abstraction function

$$\alpha_q : C^1 \mapsto (\mathbb{N}_0 \overset{\sim}{\mapsto} QS_q \times \delta)$$

mapping a continuous function f to a qualitative function g, hence $\alpha_q.f = g$.

The abstraction process is two-fold: (1) concrete real values are mapped to qualitative values and (2) continuous time is mapped to a sequence (of states). Given a time-dependent function $f : C^1$, iterated application with progressing time values will give a trajectory, i.e. a trace through the range of this function. Given such a trajectory, we use a value abstraction function $v\text{-}abs_q : C^1 \mapsto (\mathbb{R}_0^+ \overset{\sim}{\mapsto} QS_q \times \delta)$ that maps quantitative values into the qualitative domain and a time abstraction function $t\text{-}abs_q : C^1 \mapsto (\mathbb{R}_0^+ \mapsto \mathbb{N}_0)$ that maps continuous time to a discrete state to derive the qualitative function $g : \mathbb{N}_0 \overset{\sim}{\mapsto} QS_q \times \delta$. The class of functions g is denoted by QF.

Hence, we define the abstraction from continuous values to qualitative values as follows:

Definition 7 (Value Abstraction). *Given a continuous function $f : C^1$, its corresponding quantity q, and a value abstraction function*

$$v\text{-}abs_q : C^1 \mapsto (\mathbb{R}_0^+ \overset{\sim}{\mapsto} QS_q \times \delta).$$

For each concrete value $f(t)$ in the range of the continuous function f the corresponding abstract quantity value is calculated by the function application $v\text{-}abs_q.f.t$.

Note, that our $v\text{-}abs_q$ results in a partial mapping modeling the case where the abstract quantity space (landmarks, intervals) does not cover the full range of f. For example given a quantity space $\langle 0, max = 10 \rangle$ and the function f exceeding this maximum $f.t > 10$, then the abstraction is undefined. Therefore in QR special landmarks covering the border intervals up to infinity are usually added. Hence in the following, we assume $v\text{-}abs_q$ being total.

Value abstraction is necessary but not sufficient: abstracting from time is also needed for our qualitative abstraction mapping α.

Definition 8 (Qualitative Abstraction). *The abstraction α is a mapping of continuous time-dependent functions $f : \mathbb{R}_0^+ \mapsto \mathbb{R}$ to qualitative state-dependent functions $g : \mathbb{N}_0 \rightsquigarrow QS_q \times \delta$ such that:*

$$\forall f : C^1 \cdot \forall t : \mathbb{R}_0^+ \cdot \exists s : \mathbb{N}_0 \cdot \alpha.f.s = g.s = v\text{-}abs_q.f.t \tag{9}$$

Furthermore, a state and its successor must not have equal values:

$$\forall s_1, s_2 \in \textbf{dom}(g) \cdot s_2 = s_1 + 1 \implies g.s_1 \neq g.s_2 \tag{10}$$

*with **dom** giving the domain of a function.*

See Figure 2 for a sketch of the abstraction of a given function.

Corollary 1 (Time Scale Abstraction). *By skolemization of the existential quantifier in (9), we introduce a function $t\text{-}abs_q : C^1 \mapsto (\mathbb{R}_0^+ \mapsto \mathbb{N}_0)$ partitioning the domain of $f : \mathbb{R}_0^+ \mapsto \mathbb{R}$ into qualitative equivalence classes:*

$$\forall f : C^1 \cdot \forall t : \mathbb{R}_0^+ \cdot \alpha.f.(t\text{-}abs_q.f.t) = g.(t\text{-}abs_q.f.t) = v\text{-}abs_q.f.t$$

$$= \forall f : C^1 \cdot \alpha.f \circ t\text{-}abs_q.f = g \circ t\text{-}abs_q.f = v\text{-}abs_q.f$$

This mapping $t\text{-}abs_q$ represents our time scale abstraction.

Furthermore, function $t\text{-}abs$ has the following properties:

Definition 9.

$$\forall f : C^1 \cdot \forall t_1, t_2 : \mathbb{R}_0^+ \cdot t_1 < t_2 \implies t\text{-}abs.f.t_1 \leq t\text{-}abs.f.t_2 \tag{11}$$

$$\forall f : C^1 \cdot \forall t : \mathbb{R}^+ \cdot \exists \epsilon > 0 : \mathbb{R} \cdot t\text{-}abs.f.t - t\text{-}abs.f.(t - \epsilon) \leq 1 \tag{12}$$

$$t\text{-}abs.f.0 = 0 \tag{13}$$

The definition basically says that $t\text{-}abs$ has to be increasing over time and that it must not step-over a state, in other words, it has to sequentially visit all numbers $\in \mathbb{N}_0$ up to the current value. A property of time scale abstraction is the fact, that finite trajectories result in finite qualitative traces but the reverse may not be true. For instance the trace $\langle (0..\boldsymbol{max}, +), (\boldsymbol{max}, 0) \rangle$ may be refined into an exponential function which has the landmark $\boldsymbol{max}$ as limit value:

$$\lim_{t \to \infty} \boldsymbol{max} \cdot (1 - e^{-t}) = \boldsymbol{max}.$$

In practice we may not have access to the function definition of f but we may have access to samples of f. The well known sampling theorem describes conditions under which f can be reconstructed from samples. Similarly, given a sampling interval $T_s > 0 : \mathbb{R}$, a sample number $t_\sqcap$, and a trace of abstracted samples $\langle v\text{-}abs.f.(0 \cdot T_s), \dots, v\text{-}abs.f.(t_\sqcap \cdot T_s), \dots \rangle$, it is not always possible to re-construct an abstract qualitative function g from these qualitative values: Within a qualitative function g, the values may either change to the next value of the quantity space or the next value of the qualitative derivation in one discrete time-step. The following definition, in which q^1 and q^2 denote qualitative values, states this property formally. Because quantity spaces form a strict total order, we can define an indexing function ind that returns the index $i \in \mathbb{N}_0$ of a given value from the quantity space of a quantity q: $ind_q : QS_q \mapsto \{0 \le i < |QS_q|\}$. Furthermore, $ind_\delta(-) = 0, ind_\delta(0) = 1, ind_\delta(+) = 2$.

Definition 10 (Continuity of Qualitative Samples).

$\exists T_s > 0 : \mathbb{R} \cdot \forall 0 \le \epsilon < T_s : \mathbb{R} \cdot \forall t_\sqcap : \mathbb{N}_0 \cdot$

$v\text{-}abs_q.f.(t_\sqcap \cdot T_s + \epsilon) = q^1 \wedge v\text{-}abs_q.f.((t_\sqcap + 1) \cdot T_s + \epsilon) = q^2 \wedge Cont(q^1, q^2)$

where

$Cont(q^1, q^2) =_{df} v_1, v_2 : QS_q \cdot \delta_1, \delta_2 : \delta \cdot$

$q^1 = (v_1, \delta_1) \wedge q^2 = (v_2, \delta_2) \wedge$

$|ind_q.v_1 - ind_q.v_2| \le 1 \wedge |ind_\delta.\delta_1 - ind_\delta.\delta_2| \le 1$

Whenever a system conforms to the given definition (and adheres to the sampling theorem to prevent aliasing), we are able to compute a qualitative function g that represents the continuous function f out of the observed sample values.

4   Refinement of Qualitative Actions

For blackbox testing the behavior of a system might be specified on different abstraction levels. This abstraction level determines the data refinement relation which is usually implemented in the test adapter. This means that observed events from the implementation are translated to events in the specification language and vice versa. In the following we describe the refinement between qualitative and differential actions in more detail.

Data refinement is shown by using the following data refinement relation r:

Definition 11 (Refinement Relation).

$$r =_{df} Q = \beta.(X, \dot{X}) \quad where \quad \beta.(\phi.t, \dot{\phi}.t) = (v\text{-}abs.\phi).t$$

As described in [8] the weakest precondition semantics of differential actions covers not only the relation between pre- and post-states but also the flow between these states. This provides an ordering on the pre-states with respect to time. However, since the points of observation are only at pre/post states on the action level the intermediate flow states are hidden.

In order to characterize refinement between qualitative and hybrid action systems it is worthwhile to note that both can be rewritten into a pre/post condition normal form:

Lemma 1 (Conjunctive Normal Form). *Since both, differential actions C and qualitative actions A are conjunctive predicate transformers they can be rewritten into a normal form [9]: $\{p\}; [R]$. Here, the predicate p is an assert statement establishing the precondition. If the precondition holds the demonic update statement $[R]$ is executed and the statement aborts otherwise.*

$$C = \{p_C\}; [Q_C] =$$
$$\{\forall \phi : C^1 \cdot SF_c(\phi, e, d) \wedge \Delta_c(\phi, e) > 0 \Rightarrow \Delta_c(\phi, e) < \infty\};$$
$$\exists \phi : C^1 \cdot SF_c(\phi, e, d) \wedge \Delta_c(\phi, e) > 0 \wedge X := \phi.(\Delta_c(\phi, e)) \wedge \dot{X} := \dot{\phi}.(\Delta_c(\phi, e))$$

and

$$A = \{p_A\}; [Q_A] =$$
$$\{\forall \psi : TS \cdot \forall g \in Traces.\psi \cdot SF_q(g, e_q, d_q) \wedge \Delta_q(g, e_q) > 0 \Rightarrow \Delta_q(g, e_q) < \infty\};$$
$$\exists \psi : TS, g \in Traces.\psi \cdot SF_q(g, e_q, d_q) \wedge \Delta_q(g, e_q) > 0 \wedge Q' = g.\Delta_q(g, e_q)$$

The rewriting of $\mathbf{wp}$ semantics into normal form is straightforward and can be found in [5].

Given this normal form, the following refinement law expresses the well-known fact that under refinement preconditions are weakened and postconditions are strengthened.

Theorem 1 (Refinement Law). *A qualitative action is refined by a continuous action if*

$$[\ \neg\infty_q(Q, e_q, d_q) \wedge r \implies \neg\infty_c(X, e_c, d_c)) \ ] \quad and$$
$$[\ (\neg\infty_q(Q, e_q, d_q) \wedge r \wedge (\exists\phi : C^1 \cdot SF_c(\phi, e_c, d_c) \wedge \Delta_c(\phi, e_c) > 0$$
$$\wedge X' = \phi.\Delta_c(\phi, e_c) \wedge \dot{X}' = \dot{\phi}.\Delta_c(\phi, e_c)))$$
$$\implies$$
$$\exists Q', \psi : TS, g \in Traces.\psi \cdot (SF_q(g, e_q, d_q) \wedge Q' = g.\Delta_q(g, e_q) \wedge r) \ ]$$

with $[\ ]$ denoting universal quantification over the observations before $(X, \dot{X}, Q)$ and after execution $(X', \dot{X}', Q')$. The termination predicates are defined as:

$$\neg\infty_q(Q, e_q, d_q) =_{df} \forall\psi : TS, g \in Traces.\psi \cdot SF_q(g, e_q, d_q) \wedge$$
$$\Delta_q(g, e_q) > 0 \implies \Delta_q(g, e_q) < \infty$$
$$\neg\infty_c(X, e_c, d_c) =_{df} \forall\phi : C^1 \cdot SF_c(\phi, e_c, d_c) \wedge \Delta_c(\phi, e_c) > 0 \implies \Delta_c(\phi, e_c) < \infty$$

Proof.

$A \sqsubseteq_r C$
$\equiv \quad \{L \text{ simulation, Lemma 1}\}$
$\{p_A\}; [Q_A]; [r] \supseteq [r]; \{p_C\}; [Q_C]$
$\equiv \quad \{wp \text{ of sequential composition}\}$

$$wp(\{p_A\}, wp([Q_A], wp([r], post))) \implies wp([r], wp(\{p_C\}, wp([Q_C], post)))$$

$$\equiv$$

$$\forall \sigma, \gamma \cdot wp(\{p_A\}, \forall \sigma' \cdot Q_A.\sigma.\sigma' \wedge r.\sigma' \subseteq \gamma) \implies wp([r], \forall \sigma' \cdot p_C.\sigma' \wedge Q_C.\sigma' \subseteq \gamma)$$

$$\equiv$$

$$\forall \sigma, \gamma \cdot p_A.\sigma \wedge \forall \sigma' \cdot Q_A.\sigma.\sigma' \wedge r.\sigma' \subseteq \gamma \implies (\forall \sigma' \cdot r.\sigma.\sigma' \implies p_C.\sigma' \wedge Q_C.\sigma' \subseteq \gamma)$$

$$\equiv \quad \{\implies \text{ by specialization } (\gamma := Q_A; r), \Leftarrow \text{ by transitivity of} \subseteq\}$$

$$\forall \sigma, \sigma' \cdot p_A.\sigma \wedge r.\sigma.\sigma' \implies p_C.\sigma' \wedge Q_C.\sigma' \subseteq Q_A; r$$

$$\equiv$$

$$(\forall \sigma, \sigma' \cdot p_A.\sigma \wedge r.\sigma.\sigma' \implies p_C.\sigma') \wedge$$

$$(\forall \sigma, \sigma', \gamma \cdot p_A.\sigma \wedge r.\sigma.\sigma' \wedge Q_C.\sigma'.\gamma \implies \exists \sigma'' \cdot Q_A.\sigma.\sigma'' \wedge r.\sigma''.\gamma)$$

$$\equiv \quad \{\text{definitions}\}$$

$$[\ \neg\infty_q(Q, e_q, d_q) \wedge r \implies \neg\infty_c(X, e_c, d_c))\ ] \quad and$$

$$[\ (\neg\infty_q(Q, e_q, d_q) \wedge r \wedge (\exists \phi : C^1 \cdot SF_c(\phi, e_c, d_c) \wedge \Delta_c(\phi, e_c) > 0 \wedge$$

$$X' = \phi.\Delta_c(\phi, e_c) \wedge \dot{X}' = \dot{\phi}.\Delta_c(\phi, e_c)))$$

$$\implies$$

$$\exists Q', \psi : TS, g \in Traces.\psi \cdot (SF_q(g, e_q, d_q) \wedge Q' = g.\Delta_q(g, e_q) \wedge r)\ ] \qquad \square$$

5   Testing

Testing of hybrid systems is an extension to testing of continuous systems as, e.g., presented in [10]: in hybrid systems, the state space of discrete actions has to be explored in addition to the continuous behavior. As a qualitative action may describe several different evolutions due to the inherent non-determinism, simulating the continuous behavior yields a set of post-states, hence a set of qualitative action systems with different internal state. Further simulation of the qualitative action system then has to take all these possible outcomes into consideration, which most likely yields a state-space explosion problem. In order to prevent full state exploration, online testing is an interesting alternative because the system is able to cut down on possible evolutions due to observations of the real system.

In contrast to our previous work, where whole trajectories are tested against specified traces, this work builds on the weakest precondition semantics of differential/qualitative actions. This has as consequence, that only the pre/post states of actions are observable but not the trajectories/traces in between. For our running example we apply *traces refinement* [11] as conformance relation. For visualization we also show the behavior in between the pre/post states of evolutions.

The system may be initialized with both tanks being empty and both pumps turned off. Figure 3 shows a concrete trajectory and the according abstract trace through the system consisting of four evolutions. (1) In the first evolution both pumps are turned off and the inflow *in* fills tank $T1$ up to the *Full* level. (2)

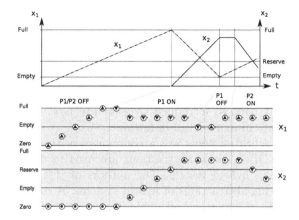

Fig. 3. Example Test Case consisting of four Evolutions

When $T1$ is full pump $P1$ is activated and delivers water to $T2$, so the water level x_2 is increasing. (3) When the water level x_1 drops to *Empty* the pump $P1$ is turned off. Since $P2$ still is turned off, x_2 remains constant. Due to the in-flow, the water level in tank $T1$ increases. (4) In the last evolution pump $P2$ is started which empties tank $T2$ below the *Reserve* water level.

In our case observable behaviors are traces consisting of the valuation of model variables during action execution. We denote one valuation in such a trace as event. In order to decide implementation conformance the observed behavior is simulated on the qualitative action system. It can be seen that there exists a qualitative function (trace) that corresponds to the observed concrete behavior. Based on the test case generation approach in [11] test cases are traces in the specification where one unspecified event has been appended. Such a trace has to be refused by the implementation by showing deadlock behavior. Otherwise the traces refinement does not hold leading to a *fail* verdict. For our example this means that the trace in Figure 3 extended with a state, e.g., $\langle x_1 = (Empty..Full, +), x_2 = (Empty..Reserve, +)\rangle$, must result in a deadlock. This is true since the implementation cannot follow the specified trajectory of the last state where x_2 changes its direction from decreasing to increasing.

6   Related Research

Most relevant to our research are different extensions to action systems that allow modeling of hybrid systems. The work in [6] presents *continuous action systems*. They are similar to conventional action systems except for the fact that continuous functions are used as values for variables (attributes). There also is an implicit attribute *now* that shows the present time and starts at zero. In this model, actions are urgent, meaning that if at some particular time a guard of an action is satisfied, the action is executed. An action may assign new functions to attributes in order to change the future behavior. An action is also thought of being atomic and instantaneous. Composition of continuous action systems is analogous to that of action systems, which means that a parallel composition does not incur the superposition-overhead as outlined earlier in the case of hybrid action systems. We could also use continuous actions systems as a basis for our qualitative action system: since continuous action systems speak about traces, it would be a natural fit to our abstraction function α_q. However, time scale abstraction makes it hard to introduce an attribute *now*. That said, we will explore the differences in more detail in future.

Abstractions of hybrid systems are a common way to deal with inherent system complexity. Often, these abstractions are used to decide over properties of the underlying hybrid system. The authors of [12] summarize results for property-preserving abstractions of hybrid systems. A combination of ideas taken from predicate abstraction and qualitative reasoning has been recently proposed in [13]: based on hybrid automata, the author presents a procedure for constructing sound abstractions for hybrid systems and also discusses which abstractions should be chosen. Abstract models of hybrid systems, besides being useful for deciding over properties, are also a common way of specifying systems. This is the intended use of qualitative action systems. Related work in qualitative modeling of hybrid systems can be found, e.g., in [14] where the authors present *Qualitative Charon*, a qualitative modeling language that is based on *Charon* and qualitative reasoning.

The work in [10] presents an approach for testing continuous systems against Qualitative Reasoning models. A tool named *Garp3* serves as modeling and simulation tool. In a subsequent step test purposes or coverage criteria [15,16] are specified to steer the automated test case generation from QR transition systems. For executing generated abstract test cases inputs are refined to the implementation level whereas outputs (a sequence of samples) are abstracted to the specification level. In order to decide implementation conformance the work in [10] introduces the conformance relation *qrioconf* which is an adaptation of the well known *ioco* relation by Jan Tretmans. The testing approach is demonstrated on a small *Matlab Simulink* implementation where two introduced errors were discovered.

7   Conclusions

In this work, we have formalized an abstraction from continuous functions to discrete qualitative traces. This abstraction relation served subsequently for the definition of (data) refinement between hybrid action systems and the newly introduced qualitative action systems. Furthermore the weakest precondition semantics for qualitative actions was introduced and a refinement theorem between qualitative and differential actions was presented. We also showed with an example how qualitative action systems can be used to specify hybrid systems. Finally, model-based testing applications have been discussed. The contributions can be summarized as follows: (1) To our best knowledge this is the first time that qualitative reasoning techniques from AI have been integrated into a classical formal method. (2) This allows us to model hybrid systems in a purely discrete domain providing an abstraction layer suitable for expressing requirements. (3) The presented notion of refinement establishes a notion of correctness, a method for step-wise development. The results form part of our ongoing development of formal testing techniques for hybrid embedded-systems.

References

1. Kuipers, B.: Qualitative Reasoning: Modeling and Simulation with Incomplete Knowledge. MIT Press, Cambridge (1994)
2. Back, R.J., Kurki-Suonio, R.: Decentralization of process nets with centralized control. In: Proceedings of the 2nd ACM SIGACT-SIGOPS Symp. on Principles of Distributed Computing, Montreal, Quebec, Canada, pp. 131–142. ACM, New York (1983)
3. Back, R.J., Sere, K.: Stepwise refinement of action systems. Structured Programming 12, 17–30 (1991)
4. Back, R.J., von Wright, J.: Trace refinement of action systems. In: Jonsson, B., Parrow, J. (eds.) CONCUR 1994. LNCS, vol. 836, pp. 367–384. Springer, Heidelberg (1994)
5. Rönkkö, M., Ravn, A.P., Sere, K.: Hybrid action systems. Theoretical Computer Science 290, 937–973 (2003)
6. Back, R.J., Petre, L., Porres, I.: Continuous action systems as a model for hybrid systems. Nordic Journal of Computing 8(1), 2–21 (2001)
7. Schaefer, P.: Analytic solution of qualitative differential equations. In: Proceedings of the AAAI 1991 (1991)
8. Rönkkö, M., Sere, K.: Refinement and continuous behaviour. In: Vaandrager, F.W., van Schuppen, J.H. (eds.) HSCC 1999. LNCS, vol. 1569, pp. 223–237. Springer, Heidelberg (1999)
9. Back, R.J.J., Akademi, A., Wright, J.V.: Refinement Calculus: A Systematic Introduction. Springer-Verlag New York, Inc., Secaucus (1998)
10. Aichernig, B.K., Brandl, H., Wotawa, F.: Conformance testing of hybrid systems with qualitative reasoning models. In: Finkbeiner, B., Gurevich, Y., Petrenko, A.K. (eds.) Model-Based Testing, MBT 2009, pp. 45–59 (2009)
11. Cavalcanti, A., Gaudel, M.C.: Testing for refinement in CSP. In: Butler, M., Hinchey, M.G., Larrondo-Petrie, M.M. (eds.) ICFEM 2007. LNCS, vol. 4789, pp. 151–170. Springer, Heidelberg (2007)
12. Rajeev, A., Henzinger, T.A., Lafferriere, G., Pappas, G.J.: Discrete abstractions of hybrid systems. Proceedings of the IEEE 88(7), 971–983 (2000)
13. Tiwari, A.: Abstractions for hybrid systems. Formal Methods in Systems Design 32, 57–83 (2008)
14. Oleg, S., Hyoung Seok, H.: Qualitative modeling of hybrid systems. In: Proc. of the Montreal Workshop (2001)
15. Brandl, H., Fraser, G., Wotawa, F.: QR-model based testing. In: AST'08: Proceedings of the 3rd international workshop on automation of software test, pp. 17–20. ACM, New York (2008)
16. Brandl, H., Fraser, G., Wotawa, F.: Coverage-based testing using qualitative reasoning models. In: Proc. of SEKE 2008, Knowledge Systems Institute Graduate School, pp. 393–398 (2008)

RAFFS: Model Checking
a Robust Abstract Flash File Store

Paul Taverne and C. (Kees) Pronk

Delft University of Technology, The Netherlands
paultaverne@gmail.com, c.pronk@tudelft.nl

Abstract. This paper presents a case study in modeling and verifying
a POSIX-like file store for Flash memory. This work fits in the context of
Hoare's verification challenge and, in particular, Joshi and Holzmann's
mini-challenge to build a verifiable file store. We have designed a simple
robust file store and implemented it in the form of a Promela model. A
test harness is used to exercise the file store in a number of ways. Model
checking technology has been extensively used to verify the correctness
of our implementation. A distinguishing feature of our approach is the
(bounded) exhaustive verification of power loss recovery.

1 Introduction

A software product should meet all of its requirements and fully conform to its
specification. Testing and other quality assessment techniques can only help to
approach this goal [9]. Proving that a piece of software will always work correctly
requires the use of formal methods. Two approaches to using formal methods
exist: *Post facto* and *correctness by construction* [29]. The first approach uses
technologies like model checking to determine the correctness of (an abstraction
of) an existing implementation. This is often called *verification*. The second
approach can be used to construct an implementation starting from an abstract
formal specification. This technique is sometimes referred to as *refinement*.

Tony Hoare has proposed a Grand Challenge project [17], whose long-term
vision is to develop methodologies and a set of automated tools that can be used
to verify whether a piece of software meets its requirements [5]. One of the steps
towards the realization of this vision is to build a repository [40] of formalized
software designs and verified implementations, which can be used to test and
develop the before mentioned tools.

The first case study for the Verification Grand Challenge was Mondex [40], a
smartcard functioning as an electronic purse. At the VSTTE conference [41] in
Zürich in 2005, Gerard Holzmann proposed a *mini-challenge*: build a verifiable
file store specifically designed to work with Flash memory [30,23]. The mini-
challenge defines strict robustness requirements. The file store should be able
to cope with unexpected power loss without getting corrupted. It should also
be able to recover from faults specific to Flash memory, such as bad blocks and
bit corruption. The mini-challenge has been embraced by the Formal Methods

K. Breitman and A. Cavalcanti (Eds.): ICFEM 2009, LNCS 5885, pp. 226–245, 2009.

community. It has for example been a case study for the ABZ conference [2,1] and has also been a topic at several VSR-net workshops. Precursors of this paper have been presented at several GC6 workshops [14].

This paper presents our work contributing to the mini-challenge project. This work is experimental in nature. Our approach is unique in that it forms a kind of middle road between abstracting an existing implementation and the correctness by construction approach. We have designed a simple file store called RAFFS, which is short for **R**obust **A**bstract **F**lash **F**ile **S**tore. This file store and its surrounding environment has been implemented in the modeling language Promela [18]. The environment includes a Flash memory and a test harness that interacts with the file store. RAFFS is capable of fixing inconsistencies that may be present in the file store after a power failure. Our model includes the injection of such power failures. For simplicity reasons we have assumed that the Flash memory is fully reliable. Bit flips and bad blocks are thus not included in the model.

A 'proof of correctness' for our file store implementation is obtained by (exhaustive, but bounded) model checking. At the end of the paper we present some measurements relating model checking particulars (such as memory usage and running time) to the 'depth' of testing by the test harness.

In Section 2 we give an overview of related work and in Section 3 we discuss the quirks of Flash memory. Section 4 will discuss abstractions and simplifications that we have applied to our model. Section 5 will give some implementation details, Section 6 will give verification results. Finally, Section 7 will provide conclusions and suggestions for future work.

2   Related Work

File systems are abundant in computer systems, however the correctness of their implementations is seldom proved. We will first discuss several papers based upon the refinement approach.

A number of authors have used refinement approaches [4], [6], [7], [10], [11], [25], [31] and [33]. Of particular note, Morgan and Sufrin [33] give a specification of the Linux file system using the Z-notation [38]. They explicitly abstract from issues such as data representation and the physics of the underlying storage medium. Their specification is one-level only; there are no refinement steps towards an implementation. Arkoudas et al. [4] prove an implementation of a file system correct by establishing a simulation relation between a specification of the file system and an implementation. The specification models the file system as an abstract map from file names to sequences of bytes. In the implementation, fixed sized blocks are used to store the contents of the files. The implementation assumes an ideal storage medium. Their proofs use the Athena system [3] and automatic theorem provers. Kang and Jackson [31] use Alloy [28] to construct a formal model of a Flash file system. Their model includes the underlying hardware and the file system software with basic operations such as read and write. A fault tolerance scheme addresses memory issues such as the management of block erasures, wear leveling and garbage collection.

As examples of the verification approach, we mention two important papers. Galloway et al. [13] use model checking to investigate the correctness of a Linux Virtual File System (VFS). They downscale existing VFS code by slicing away code and abstracting data. They transform C-code by hand into Promela and SMART models. This turns out to be a challenging task, partly because of the shallow VFS documentation. They had to reduce the sizes of their file system data structures (such as inodes) to similar values as we have used during the construction of our RAFFS. However, due to the well known state explosion problem, they seem unable to perform exhaustive model checking, whereas we have been able to apply exhaustive model checking widely. Yang et al. give an important start to the verification of a file system using model checking [42]. Like in our approach, Yang et al. check file systems for storage errors and they use model checking to verify that a file store, upon encountering such errors, will reboot into a known legal state. They operate the OS and several known file stores from within the model checker whereas we have separated out the file store. The article by Mühlberg and Lüttgen [34] is also an example of exhaustive testing of existing code using model checking. They use BLAST [16] to check device drivers for memory safety (illegal pointer de-references) and locking behaviour.

We have created a POSIX-like file store using a Flash memory. Our file system includes files, directories, reads and writes, block erasure and garbage collection. Since we have assumed the Flash memory to be reliable, we did not model wear, bad blocks, and bit corruption. A distinguishing feature of our model is that it includes the simulation of general system failure in the form of power loss. Our file store has been designed to always recover to a consistent state. Where others have mainly focused on the verification of specifications, we have focused on verification of the implementation. Our implementation supports multiple simultaneous users of the file store.

3   Flash in a Nutshell

For compatibility with existing operating systems, it is desirable that a Flash memory acts as a block based device. Most Flash device drivers emulate a block based device. All Flash specific behavior is then handled in a special layer called the Flash Translation Layer (FTL) [27].

Flash memory has a hierarchical structure similar to common block based storage devices, but has some restrictions with regard to its usage. The memory is divided in small chunks called pages. Pages are grouped together into blocks. A page is the smallest access unit for reading and writing. Writing to a Flash page, which is called programming, has an important limitation. It is only possible to change bit values from 1 to 0. In an empty (read: erased) page all bits have value 1. An empty page can be programmed with any desired data. But once a page has been programmed, it can not be overwritten with arbitrary data. It must first be erased, resetting all bits back to value 1. Erasing is a special operation for Flash memory. The smallest unit for erasing is a block, making it impossible to erase individual pages.

Consequences of the above mentioned limitations are that page content can not be overwritten and that pages with obsolete content can not be erased immediately. The first issue is solved by performing *out of place updates*. This means that instead of overwriting data in its existing location, the data is written to a different (free) location. The original data is marked as obsolete. A garbage collection algorithm is responsible for erasing blocks that contain pages with obsolete content. Valid content can be moved elsewhere when needed.

Moving data around puts a new problem on the table. The file store must know where every single piece of data is stored. This information is part of the metadata stored in for example inodes. Updating an inode whenever a data address changes would result in a vicious circle. This problem is solved by adding a level of indirection between the translation of logical addresses to physical addresses. The indirection and the moving of the data is handled by the FTL. From the point of view of the file store data can then be overwritten in its current logical location and addresses stored in inodes do not need to be updated. The FTL maintains a mapping table in RAM to translate logical addresses into physical ones. The logical address that is associated with the contents of a Flash page is stored in a special part of the page called the *spare data region* along with other metadata used by the FTL. The mapping table can be rebuild by reading this metadata from Flash (during mounting).

Flash memory is well known to have some reliability problems. For example bits may randomly flip value due to electrical interference in the memory. Deterioration of the material of which the memory is made can lead to damaged blocks. We have excluded these issues from our model and have assumed a perfectly reliable Flash memory where no data corruption or unexpected data loss may occur. Properly dealing with these reliability issues is a very complex task and depends heavily on statistics. Our Promela model of a downscaled file store is not intended to be used for statistical analysis. Instead we use exhaustive verification to prove complete correctness.

4   Abstractions

4.1   POSIX Compatibility

The mini-challenge project suggests using a subset of the POSIX standard [35,36,12]. Our highly abstracted file store API is not fully POSIX compatible. We will compare our API with the abstract formal specification [33] from Morgan and Sufrin. An overview of the file store API functions in RAFFS is given in Figure 1.

There are some differences between our API and the formal specification. In the formal specification, a directory is encoded and stored as a file, and all API functions operate on files. In our model, a clear distinction is made between files and directories, and there are separate functions for dealing with these objects. This design choice simplifies the implementation and downscaling of the file store. For example, a directory inode can now be stored in a single page, instead of multiple.

Our model does not contain *file descriptors*, or *channels* as they are called in the formal specification. We have abstracted those away to reduce memory usage. Thus the functions *open*, *close*, and *seek* are not present in our model. Instead of a file descriptor, all functions in our API have a parameter *path* which is used to uniquely identify the inode on which the function operates.

In our model, each inode always has a name. There is no separate naming system like in the formal specification. As a consequence, our model lacks the *link* and *unlink* functions. We have added two delete functions for removing files and directories.

The handling of data also differs from the formal specification. Our API functions only have a single unit of data as input or output, instead of a sequence of data units. The reason for this abstraction is to reduce the complexity of the file store implementation. Changing this, possibly as part of future work, will not have an impact on the robustness quality of RAFFS.

The formal specification lacks clear definitions of error conditions. We have clearly defined error conditions for all API functions. Our implementation checks for those conditions and returns appropriate error codes.

```
fs_api_create_file(path);
fs_api_file_exists(path);
fs_api_file_size(path);
fs_api_file_append(path, data);
fs_api_file_modify(path, offset, data);
fs_api_file_read(path, offset);
fs_api_file_truncate(path, size);
fs_api_delete_file(path);
fs_api_create_dir(path);
fs_api_dir_exists(path);
fs_api_dir_size(path);
fs_api_dir_get_child_name(path, index);
fs_api_delete_dir(path);
fs_api_mount();
fs_api_unmount();
```

Fig. 1. File store API function prototypes

4.2   Abstractions Applied

The goal of our project is to perform (exhaustive) verification of our state-based model, which requires that the model must have a low complexity. In the current context, complexity means the size of the state space. The bigger the state space, the more memory and time is needed to perform verification.

Abstracting an existing implementation would be a time consuming task; far more work than we could accomplish in a short period of time. Others abstracted parts of an existing file store [13] which proved to be a difficult task. We have decided to design a basic file store from scratch. So instead of abstracting a complex design, we have directly made an abstracted design. The advantage of this method is that we had complete freedom in the design choices, allowing us to keep things simple, while also making a robust design. We were not forced to think within the paradigm of other designers. We are confident that this choice has resulted in a model with a much lower complexity than could have achieved if we would have attempted to abstract (and modify) an existing implementation. A disadvantage of making a whole new design and implementation is of course that it is difficult to compare our work with other designs and implementations. Making the design more similar to real-life file stores is envisioned as future work. Our current efforts should be seen as a demonstration of the capabilities of model checking and the complexities involved with verifying a file store implementation.

There are many abstractions and simplifications in our model. The simplified API and the assumption that the Flash memory is reliable have already been discussed. Another simplification is related to inodes. In the model there are two distinct types of inodes, namely a file and a directory. A file contains a sequence of data units. A directory contains an unordered list of references to child inodes. Both types of inodes are assumed to be able to always fit into a single page. They will thus never span multiple pages. The data of a directory is not encoded as file data and is not stored as a file. When a page is used to store file data instead of an inode, then we assume that a page can fit exactly X units of data, regardless of how big a page really is. A unit of data in the model is a single bit.

There are different types of data abstractions in the model. The first type of abstraction is the compact representation of data. For example, file names and paths are not represented by character sequences, but by numerical values. These numerical values can easily be stored as short sequences of bits. The values themselves are not really important in an abstract model. We only need a certain number of distinct values.

The second type of abstraction is to limit ranges of values. Everything in the model is scaled down to a small size. Sizes in the model are specified by constant values. This allows us to easily modify those sizes when desired. The values of these constants have been carefully chosen to scale down the file store as far as possible without sacrificing functionality. For example, every single error condition in each API function must be reachable.

The flash memory in the model currently consists of just 4 blocks, each having two pages, giving a total of 8 pages. The maximum number of inodes that can be present in the file store is currently set to 4. The maximum size of a file is 3 data units. The maximum number of children of a directory is 2.

5   Implementation

In the sections below we will discuss the model that we have constructed. This discussion will necessarily be limited. Further details can be obtained from [39]. Our model has a layered design, consisting of five layers as shown in Figure 2. The arrows indicate which layer uses functionality from another layer. The bottom two layers are the Flash memory and its driver, to be discussed in Section 5.1. The next two layers belong to our file store implementation, named RAFFS, which is discussed in Section 5.2. The top layer serves as a test harness for RAFFS. This test harness is discussed in Section 5.3. In Section 5.4

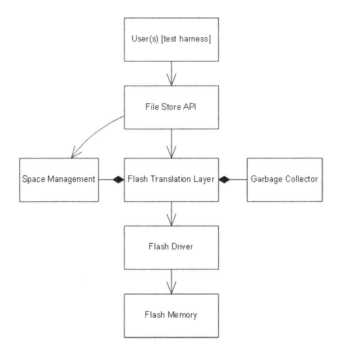

Fig. 2. UML layer diagram

we explain how power loss has been modeled. Section 5.5 discusses how the design of RAFFS has been adapted to meet the robustness requirement. Finally, Section 5.6 explains the issues of verifying a model that contains multiple users.

5.1 Flash Memory and Its Driver

The bottom layer in our implementation is the Flash memory. We have modeled the Flash as a simple data structure, namely an array of pages. Each page consists of two parts, the data region and the spare data region. The data region

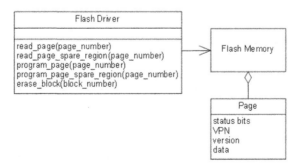

Fig. 3. Flash Memory and Driver

is used for storing inode metadata or file data. Its size is chosen so that it is exactly large enough to fit the largest possible inode in the model. The spare data region is used for storing metadata used by the file store, and the Flash Translation Layer in particular. This metadata includes three page status bits, a version field, and a virtual page number.

The second layer in the model is the Flash driver, which has functions to read or program a page, and to erase a block. Details of both layers are shown in Figure 3.

5.2   RAFFS

The third layer is the Flash Translation Layer (FTL), which implements Flash specific behavior and emulates a generic block based storage device. It exposes functions to the file store API layer for writing, updating, and deleting data in a logical location. The FTL maps logical addresses to physical ones and performs *out of place updates* as explained in Section 3. We use a simple mapping scheme based on virtual page numbers (VPN) [8]. Other schemes exist that are more memory efficient because they use a smaller mapping table [32]. However, due to the extremely small scale of our Flash memory, implementing such a complex scheme would require increasing the number of Flash blocks. Using a different scheme is therefore not worthwhile for us in terms of both complexity and memory efficiency.

The FTL applies a two step programming protocol [26] when writing data to a Flash page. This protocol is a required for robustness reasons.

The FTL contains a simple garbage collection algorithm for recovering space occupied by pages with obsolete content. The FTL in our model is also responsible for the management of free space. To ensure that enough free space is available to successfully complete an operation, each API function must reserve an amount of free locations that equals the number of writes that it is planning to perform.

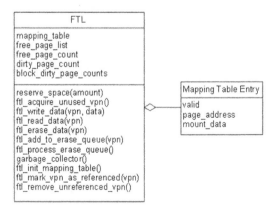

Fig. 4. Flash Translation Layer

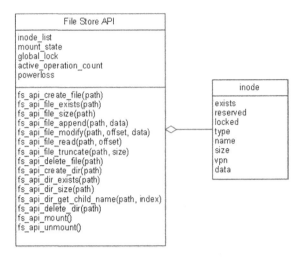

Fig. 5. File Store API

The UML diagram in Figure 4 shows the functions that the FTL exposes to the file store API layer. The fourth layer is the file store API, which was already discussed in Section 4.1. A UML diagram with details of this layer is shown in Figure 5.

5.3 Test Harness

The fifth and topmost layer is the user layer, which functions as a test harness in our model. A user is a Promela process that calls file store API functions. Multiple concurrent user processes are allowed to be present in our model. We use simple techniques to prevent processes from interfering with each others' operations. Shared data structures are either locked for exclusive access or values are read and updated within a single atomic block. Locking is for example applied to inodes.

We have made several variations of our model, each with a different testing purpose, and with a different implementation of the user layer. Four variants will be discussed in this paper; SU (single user), $SUPL$ (single user with power loss), MU (multiple users), and $MUPL$ (multiple users with power loss). The SU variant is discussed below, the SUPL variant is discussed in Section 5.4, and the MU and MUPL variants are discussed in Section 5.6.

To verify the correctness of the file store, we must consider all possible states in which the file store can reside, and all possible transitions between those states. The SU variant of our model contains a single user process that performs a random sequence of file store API calls. In each step of the sequence, the file store API function and its inputs are chosen non-deterministically. Performing full verification on this model will, with an infinite sequence, examine the entire state space.

The behavior of every file store API call should be exactly as described in the specification. We verify this by comparing the result of each API call with the result given by a reference implementation using assertions. The idea is that incorrect behavior will always lead to an unexpected result being returned at some point in the sequence. Because of the state-based nature of our model, the reference implementation has to be fully integrated in the code. If the model would be used for simulation only, then an external reference implementation could be used. Holzmann used an external reference implementation during randomized differential testing of his own Flash file store model [15].

Because the reference implementation needs to be integrated into our model and because our file store API is unique, we were forced to make our own reference implementation. The reference implementation has thus also been written in Promela. This implementation has not been verified to be correct, we can only assume it is correct. Proving its correctness is a task for future work. Suppose that one of the two implementations contains a bug. This bug would only go unnoticed only if both implementations would exhibit the exact same incorrect behavior. However, since the two implementations are considerably different such a situation is unlikely.

The reference implementation in our model is an extremely abstracted implementation of a file store. It maintains a private list of inodes that are expected to exist in the file store. All relevant data is stored in those inodes, including file contents. The file store API functions operate directly on the inode list. The reference implementation is much less complex compared to our RAFFS implementation, as there is no storage medium, and no Flash specific behavior. The code size of the reference implementation is an order of magnitude smaller than the RAFFS implementation.

The sequences of API calls that are performed by the test harness have a configurable length. This allows us to control the 'depth' of our verification. Increasing the sequence length will increase the size of the state space. An unbounded model would be far too complex for performing exhaustive verification. The impact of the bound will be discussed in Section 6.2.

As said before, the input parameters for the chosen API function are generated non-deterministically. The generated values of the input parameters fall in a domain of potentially valid input values. This means values which, in certain situations, could lead to a successful file store operation, while in other situations they will trigger an error condition in the file store API function. Values that always trigger an error fall outside of the inspected domain. We have tested such 'invalid' inputs in a separate deterministic test suite.

Besides comparing results with a reference implementation, we have also implemented a series of consistency checks which are performed after each file store API call. These consistency checks compare metadata stored in RAM by the file store with metadata stored on the Flash memory using assertions. Inodes and the mapping table of the FTL are examples of such metadata.

5.4   Power Loss

One of the goals in our project is to make the file store robust so that it can cope with power failures. If power loss occurs while there are unfinished file store operations, the contents of the Flash memory may be in an inconsistent state. The mount operation is responsible for detecting inconsistencies and recovering the system to a valid consistent state. The robustness requirement specifies that an unfinished operation must either be completed, or that all changes made by such an unfinished operation must be undone.

A second variant of our model, named *SUPL*, is an extension of the SU variant discussed in the previous section. The main difference is the addition of power loss in the model. Promela has a special language construct called *unless* that we have used in this variant. The *unless* construct works similar to an exception handler. It contains a main sequence of statements and an escape sequence. Before a statement from the main sequence is executed, an escape condition is checked. If this condition evaluates to true, execution jumps to the escape sequence. The remaining statements in the main sequence are not executed.

The code that we want to be susceptible to power loss is put inside an *unless* construct. A second Promela process is used to trigger power loss. When power loss occurs, execution of the file store code is aborted. All data that the file store maintains in RAM is cleared and the file store is re-mounted. During mounting the contents of the Flash memory is checked for consistency and corrections are made. After mounting a new sequence of API calls is performed. In our model, multiple subsequent power loss situations take place. They can occur at any time, even during mounting.

Figure 6 shows pseudo code for the model variant SUPL. From the point of view of the user there can be two valid situations when power loss has occurred during an operation. One in which the operation was completed successfully, and one in which the operation was not performed at all. We therefore let the reference implementation maintain two states. Each state consists of an inode list and the amount of available free space. The first state is the 'before' state, where the chosen API function has not been performed. The second state is the 'after' state, where the chosen API function was performed successfully by the reference implementation. If a power loss situation occurs, then after mounting we compare the state of the file store from the RAFFS implementation with the two states from the reference implementation and pick the first one that matches (function *select_expected_state* in the pseudo code). The reference implementation will continue with that state as both the new after and before state. If neither state matches, then the robustness requirement was not met and there is a bug in the model. If the chosen API function completes without the occurrence power loss, then the return values of both implementations are compared (function *compare_results* in the pseudo code). The return value either is an error code (negative value), a data value (positive value), or a void (zero value). The states of the reference implementation are also synchronized, the before state being set equal to the after state.

The results presented in Section 6.2 were obtained using a model that triggers a fixed number of 2 power loss situations during each sequence. Triggering more power losses, for example by using an infinite loop, will increase the complexity of the model.

```
bool  powerloss ;

PROCESS_USER() {
   initialize_system ;
   while(1) {
      {
         mount;
         select_expected_state ;
         perform_consistency_checks ;
         while(1) {
            choose_api_function ;
            generate_inputs ;
            perform_api_call_reference ;
            perform_api_call ;
            compare_results ;
            perform_consistency_checks ;
         }
      } unless {
         powerloss == 1
      }
      reboot ;
   }
}

PROCESS_TRIGGER_POWERLOSS() {
   /* multiple power loss situations */
   powerloss = 1;
   powerloss = 1;
   ...
}
```

Fig. 6. Pseudo code for SUPL test harness

5.5   Mounting and Order of Operations

The mount operation reads inode metadata from Flash and stores it in RAM. It fills the FTL mapping table and is also responsible for correcting inconsistencies in the file store metadata residing on the Flash memory. Our solution for making the file store robust involves making changes to the contents of the Flash memory in a specific order. Given that order, a small set of generic corrective actions will always result in fixing all inconsistencies. The resulting state will be one in which all unfinished operations have either been completed or been undone.

To explain the specific order in which Flash content modifications are made during the various file store operations, we first classify two types of operations. Operations that add inodes or modify data are classified as *constructive*. Operations that remove inodes or data are classified as *destructive*.

We make use of three relations between different pieces of information stored on the Flash memory to decide which corrective actions must be taken by the mount algorithm. Firstly, all inodes (except the root) are referenced by the inode of its parent directory. Secondly, every data page is referenced (through its VPN) by a file inode. Thirdly, when two pages have identical VPN value, the version field can be used to determine which one is the newest copy. If no relation between an inode can be found with another inode, then this inode is called an orphan. Unreferenced data pages are handled in a similar way. Orphaned entities will be removed during mounting. Items that become orphaned during the removal process will be removed as well.

For destructive operations, the idea is to create orphans as quickly as possible. The operation can then always be completed if aborted unexpectedly. For example, when removing a file, the very first step to take is updating the inode of its parent directory. The file inode and any related data, will then become orphaned.

For constructive operations, the idea is to keep all new and modified data orphaned as long as possible. Also, existing data must be kept intact. Then the changes made by the operation can always be undone if aborted. When creating a file, the first step is to create the inode of the file and the last step is to update the inode of its parent directory. The functions in the file store API should thus not overwrite file data. Instead they must write updated data to a new virtual location. The old data locations are deleted at the end of the operation (when they have become orphaned). By preserving the old data, a rollback is possible.

The four corrective actions that our mount algorithm makes are: (1) removing unreferenced inodes, (2) removing unreferenced data pages, (3) removing pages with content of which a newer version was found, (4) removing pages that have state invalid. Removing means marking as obsolete. The actual erasing is done later by the garbage collector. A page can have state invalid if power loss occurred during the first step of the two step programming protocol.

5.6 Multiple Users

The verification method that we have described in the previous sections was performed with a single user process. Even though our implementation supports multiple users, it is not possible to apply the same method to a model with multiple simultaneous users. The reason is that the expected result of each API call is not predictable. We have two variants of our model that contain multiple users; variant *MU* without power loss injection, and variant *MUPL* with power loss injection. In these variants each user again executes a sequence of file store API calls, but this time the results are not compared to a reference implementation. Only general consistency checks are performed. Our main focus with these variants has been on verifying the absence of deadlock. We hope to do more extensive verification in the future. Additional processes cause the state space to explode, making it currently impossible to perform any exhaustive model checking on the multi user variants, even with a bounded model.

6   Verification and Results

The model checking tool SPIN [22] was used for verification of our model. Results of our verification efforts are presented and discussed in Section 6.2. First we will present a method that we developed for compact storage of variables.

6.1   CCVS: Custom Compact Variable Storage

Our model contains many variables with a small size, typically of the special Promela variable type *unsigned*. SPIN maps such variables onto (larger) integer type variables (byte/short/int). As a result, the size of the state vector can be larger than strictly required. Inspired by the work of Ruys [37] we have implemented a generic method for storing the values of multiple variables into a single integer type variable, which then serves as a container. The purpose of this storage method is to reduce memory usage during verification. Bit arithmetic is used for reading and writing the values of individual variables from such a container variable. CCVS makes heavy use of preprocessor macros. We have currently defined variables both as normal individual variables and using our CCVS method. One of these two storage methods is chosen with a preprocessor flag. Disabling CCVS can be useful for debugging purposes, since it obfuscates the variables.

6.2 Results

We will first discuss results obtained for the *SU* variant that was described in Section 5.3. We have been able to perform exhaustive verification for sequences (of file store API calls) up to length 6 with a memory usage less than 1 GB. Using a machine equipped with a 2.3 GHz Intel Xeon CPU and 32 GB of RAM we were able to go up to length 8. Sequences of length 15 and 31 have been extensively tested using the bitstate hashing technique [20].

It is important to note that, thanks to the small scale of the file store, short sequences will already result in many interesting situations being tested. Based on experience gained by making a deterministic test suite, we can say that the majority of error conditions and corner cases in the file store are reachable at length 5 or below. Sequences with a length above 8 mainly involve exploring states that could be considered variations of states reachable at shorter lengths. Complete verification, with an unbounded sequence, is currently infeasible. Nevertheless, the results that we have obtained give us confidence that our implementation functions as intended and expected. In the future we plan to extend the reachable part of the entire state space by starting with different initial states.

Results from our exhaustive verification runs can be found in Table 1, Table 2, and Table 3. Each table shows the number of states, the memory usage, and the execution time for different sequence lengths of file store API calls. The difference between the three tables is the state compression method that was chosen in SPIN. No compression was used for the results listed in Table 1, *state*

Table 1. Results for variant SU. Compression: none.

Sequence length	CCVS	States	Memory (MB)	Time (s)
2	no	129,835	21	0.2
2	yes	137,581	14	0.2
3	no	1,140,027	168	1.7
3	yes	1,217,514	105	1.7
4	no	9,332,851	1,387	14.5
4	yes	10,039,814	876	14.0

Table 2. Results for variant SU. Compression: -DCOLLAPSE.

Sequence length	CCVS	States	Memory (MB)	Time (s)
2	no	129,835	7	0.4
2	yes	137,581	7	0.3
3	no	1,140,027	43	3.6
3	yes	1,217,514	39	3.0
4	no	9,332,851	344	29.0
4	yes	10,039,814	319	24.4

vector collapse [21] was used for Table 2, and *minimized DFA encoding* [24] was used for Table 3.

CCVS proved to be very useful for reducing memory usage during verification of our model. To our surprise it also consistently reduced the time needed to verify the model, despite the additional computations that it makes. The benefit of CCVS is particularly significant when using SPIN's minimized DFA encoding technique (Table 3), where it reduced memory usage by more than half. The results show that minimized DFA encoding gives the lowest memory usage, even without CCVS, at the cost of a significantly longer execution time. We have used this powerful compression technique, in combination with CCVS, during the rest of our verification efforts since memory is the most scarce resource available to us.

Table 3. Results for variant SU. Compression: -DMA.

Sequence length	CCVS	States	Memory (MB)	Time (s)
2	no	129,835	6	3.4
2	yes	137,581	4	2.0
3	no	1,140,027	27	34.2
3	yes	1,217,514	14	19.3
4	no	9,332,851	147	317.0
4	yes	10,039,814	60	164.0
5	yes	67,763,329	249	1,170.0
6	yes	365,532,240	900	6,710.0
7	yes	1,801,435,400	5,989	33,800.0
8	yes	8,010,865,300	18,577	156,000.0

The use of model checking proved particularly useful during the verification of the model variant SUPL that included power loss injection, which was discussed in section 5.4. By analyzing all possible execution interleavings of the processes in the model, we have been able to verify that our implementation is always able to recover to a valid consistent state, regardless of the moments at which power loss situations occur.

We have been able to perform exhaustive verification for a sequence length of 5 on a machine with 32 GB RAM. Results for verification runs on the SUPL variant are listed in Table 6.2. The applied state compression technique was

Table 4. Results for variant SUPL. Compression: -DMA.

Sequence length	CCVS	States	Memory (MB)	Time (s)
2	yes	13,205,390	98	268.0
3	yes	93,392,252	882	2,040.0
4	yes	727,651,040	5,434	16,700.0
5	yes	5,467,663,300	28,584	134,000.0

very efficient with a compression of 95.4% at length 5. This means that without compression the verification run would have required 626 gigabyte of memory. Without CCVS it would have even been double that amount. The execution time of 37 hours is long but in our case more than acceptable. Being able to trade time for reduction in memory usage has allowed us to perform exhaustive verification for sequences longer than would otherwise have been possible.

We already started using the described verification methods during the development of our implementation. This has helped us to find flaws in our implementation quickly and effectively. Like a compiler can point out syntax errors in its input, a verifier can reveal errors in the functioning of its input. By analyzing and fixing our mistakes, we gained a better understanding of the functioning of the model. This knowledge was beneficial for the remainder of the development cycle.

We found a few bugs in our implementation through model checking. In our garbage collection algorithm we found a bug that would probably have never been discovered without the help of model checking techniques. A few free pages are always implicitly reserved for garbage collection so that valid content can be moved from a dirty block to other blocks, before the dirty block is erased. It turned out that the situation in which a power failure occurs right before the erasure of a block was not properly handled. In that case the number of available free pages could decrease below the minimum amount needed to perform garbage collection on an arbitrary dirty block. This flaw was fixed by adjusting the garbage collection algorithm to process the dirtiest blocks first.

We have been unable to perform exhaustive verification on the MU and MUPL variants of our model. The state space explodes when multiple Promela processes are used in a model. Approximative verification has been applied on these variants using SPIN's bitstate hashing technique. Bitstate hashing explores only a subset of the entire state space. Based upon the results obtained and the complexity estimates given by Spin, it is difficult to estimate the full size of the state space. Results of this testing have therefore been omitted from this paper. Our focus up till now has been mainly in the single user variants. We plan to shift our focus to the multi user variants in the near future.

7   Conclusion and Further Work

We have presented the construction of a POSIX-like file store for Flash memory, specially designed for model checking. The system has been constructed using the Promela modeling language. The model abstracts from a real file store by reducing various data structures and by reducing the number of operations supported.

Distinguishing features of our model are the exhaustive verification of the code and the ability to inject multiple power losses in the functioning system. Upon recovery from power loss, the system status is restored into a known correct state. This mechanism has been exhaustively verified. Multiple user processes exercise the model to its full extent under exhaustive verification using a test harness. The paper gives quantitative results of the model checking process such as the compression mechanisms used, number of states investigated, memory usage and running time.

The exhaustive verification makes our approach stand out from other ways of verifying a file system. In [13] the code of a Linux VFS is downscaled and transformed into Spin and SMART models. Although the authors of that paper downscale to similar values as we have used, they seemed unable to use exhaustive verification on their model. Additionally our model verifies Flash particulars such as out of place updates and garbage collection. Our approach differs from [42] in that we test a special purpose file store for Flash memory whereas they concentrate upon existing file systems. Compared to various papers based upon the refinement approach we have constructed real code, resulting in a functioning system.

The middle road between the above approaches we have followed by constructing an abstract model in Promela has proven to be very useful to test a design concept on a reduced scale. Our model proved to be truly effective in verifying the ability of the RAFFS implementation to recover from power loss.

We can't claim full verification of our implementation because of the bounds that we have set in the model to limit the size of the state space, and also because of the assumption that our reference implementation is correct. However, the results that we have obtained give us high confidence in the correctness of our implementation. Our efforts could be considered as an extreme form of testing.

RAFFS has no direct practical application since it is a highly abstracted design and implementation. That was also never our intention. Our work gives a good indication of the complexities involved with model checking a file store implementation. Even an abstracted and downscaled file store is too complex to perform unbounded exhaustive verification with currently available hardware and technologies. The inevitable dependency on data is one of the causes of the enormous size of the state space.

We envisage reducing some of the current severe abstractions in the model. A goal is to make our implementation more realistic and more comparable to existing implementations and specifications. We want to make the file store API more similar to POSIX. A desirable modification is to store directories as files like is done in UNIX. This will also require upscaling the file store. The page based mapping in the FTL can be replaced by a more complex (and more memory efficient) block based mapping.

Since obtaining the results presented in this paper we have continued optimizing our code in an effort to further reduce the size of the state space and the memory usage. Depending on the model variant, we have been able to achieve reductions in memory usage up to 50%.

Our test harness currently always starts with the same initial state of the file store. This is going to be changed so that the initial state can be read from an input file. Files containing valid initial states will be generated through simulation runs.

The capabilities of model checkers have recently been expanded with multithreading [19], opening up the possibility of significant performance gains. The continued growth of memory sizes will allow us to test longer sequences, and/or increase the complexity of the model.

References

1. ABZ conference: case study details, http://www.cs.york.ac.uk/circus/mc/abz/
2. ABZ conference (October 2008), http://www.abz2008.org/
3. Arkoudas, K.: Athena, http://www.cag.csail.mit.edu/~kostas/dpls/athena/
4. Arkoudas, K., Zee, K., Kuncak, V., Rinard, M.: On verifying a file system implementation. In: Davies, J., Schulte, W., Barnett, M. (eds.) ICFEM 2004. LNCS, vol. 3308, pp. 373–390. Springer, Heidelberg (2004)
5. Bicarregui, J.C., Hoare, C.A.R., Woodcock, J.C.P.: The verified software repository: a step towards the verifying compiler. Formal Aspects of Computing 18(2), 143–151 (2006)
6. Butler, M.: Some filestore developments with Event-B and RODIN. In: Workshop at ICFEM (2007)
7. Butterfield, A., Woodcock, J.: Formalising flash memory: First steps. In: ICECCS, pp. 251–260 (2007)
8. Chang, Y.-H., Hsieh, J.-W., Kuo, T.-W.: Endurance enhancement of flash-memory storage systems: an efficient static wear leveling design. In: DAC 2007: Proceedings of the 44th annual conference on Design automation, pp. 212–217. ACM, New York (2007)
9. Dijkstra, E.W.: Notes on structured programming. In: Dahl, O.J., Dijkstra, E.W., Hoare, C.A.R. (eds.) structured programming, Ch. 1, pp. 1–82. Academic Press, London (1972)
10. Ferreira, M.A., Silva, S.S., Oliveira, J.N.: Verifying Intel Flash file system core specification. In: Modelling and Analysis in VDM: Proceedings of the Fourth VDM/Overture Workshop. Newcastle University, CS-TR-1099 (May 2008)
11. Freitas, L., Fu, Z., Woodcock, J.: Posix file store in Z/Eves: an experiment in the verified software repository. In: ICECCS, pp. 3–14 (2007)
12. Freitas, L., Woodcock, J., Butterfield, A.: POSIX and the verification grand challenge: a roadmap. In: 13th Int'l Conference on Engineering Complex Computer Systems (ICECCS 2008). IEEE, Los Alamitos (2008)
13. Galloway, A., Lüttgen, G., Mühlberg, J.T., Siminiceanu, R.I.: Model-checking the Linux virtual file system. In: Jones, N.D., Müller-Olm, M. (eds.) VMCAI 2009. LNCS, vol. 5403, pp. 74–88. Springer, Heidelberg (2009)
14. Grand Challenge 6, http://vsr.sourceforge.net/gc6index.htm

15. Groce, A., Holzmann, G., Joshi, R.: Randomized differential testing as a prelude to formal verification. In: ICSE 2007: Proceedings of the 29th Int'l conference on Software Engineering, pp. 621–631. IEEE Computer Society, Los Alamitos (2007)
16. Henzinger, T.A., et al.: Temporal safety-proofs for systems code. In: Brinksma, E., Larsen, K.G. (eds.) CAV 2002. LNCS, vol. 2404, pp. 526–538. Springer, Heidelberg (2002)
17. Hoare, T., Misra, J.: Verified software: theories, tools, experiments (July 2005), http://vstte.ethz.ch
18. Holzmann, G.J.: Promela language reference, http://www.spinroot.com/spin/Man/promela.html
19. Holzmann, G.J., Bošnački, D.: The design of a multi-core extension of the Spin model checker. IEEE Transactions on Software Engineering 33(10) (October 2007)
20. Holzmann, G.J.: An improved reachability analysis technique. Software Practice and Experience 18, 137–161 (1988)
21. Holzmann, G.J.: State compression in SPIN. In: Proc. Third SPIN Workshop, Twente University, The Netherlands (1997)
22. Holzmann, G.J.: The SPIN Model Checker: Primer and Reference Manual. Addison-Wesley Professional, Reading (2003)
23. Holzmann, G.J., Joshi, R., Groce, A.: New challenges in model checking. In: Grumberg, O., Veith, H. (eds.) 25 Years of Model Checking. LNCS, vol. 5000, pp. 65–76. Springer, Heidelberg (2006)
24. Holzmann, G.J., Puri, A.: A minimized automaton representation of reachable states. Software Tools for Technology Transfer 2(3), 270–278 (1999)
25. Houston, I., King, S.: CICS project report: Experiences and results from the use of Z. In: Prehn, S., Toetenel, H. (eds.) VDM 1991. LNCS, vol. 551, pp. 588–596. Springer, Heidelberg (1991)
26. ICFEM Flash File System Workshop. Modelling Flash Memory (November 2007)
27. Intel Corporation. Intel Flash File System Core Reference Guide, version 1 edition (October 2004)
28. Jackson, D.: Software Abstractions. The MIT-Press, Cambridge (2006)
29. Jones, C., O'Hearn, P., Woodcock, J.: Verified software: A grand challenge. IEEE Computer: Software Technologies 39(4), 93–95 (2006)
30. Joshi, R., Holzmann, G.J.: A mini challenge: build a verifiable filesystem. Formal Aspects of Computing 19(2), 269–272 (2007)
31. Kang, E., Jackson, D.: Formal modeling and analysis of a flash filesystem in Alloy. In: Börger, E., Butler, M., Bowen, J.P., Boca, P. (eds.) ABZ 2008. LNCS, vol. 5238, pp. 294–308. Springer, Heidelberg (2008)
32. Liu, Z., Yue, L., Wei, P., Jin, P., Xiang, X.: An adaptive block-set based management for large-scale flash memory. In: SAC 2009: Proceedings of the, ACM symposium on Applied Computing, pp. 1621–1625. ACM, New York (2009)
33. Morgan, C., Sufrin, B.: Specification of the UNIX filing system. IEEE Trans. Software Eng. 10(2), 128–142 (1984)
34. Mühlberg, J.T., Lüttgen, G.: Blasting Linux code. In: Brim, L., Haverkort, B.R., Leucker, M., van de Pol, J. (eds.) FMICS 2006 and PDMC 2006. LNCS, vol. 4346, pp. 211–226. Springer, Heidelberg (2007)
35. Part 1: Base definitions POSIX. ISO/IEC 9945-1:2003
36. Part 2: System Interfaces POSIX. ISO/IEC 9945-2:2003
37. Ruys, T.C.: Towards Effective Model Checking. PhD thesis, University of Twente, Enschede (March 2001)
38. Spivey, J.M.: The Z notation: a reference manual. Prentice-Hall, Inc., Upper Saddle River (1989)

39. Taverne, P.: Raffs: Model checking a robust abstract flash file store. Master's thesis, Delft University of Technology (2009), `http://repository.tudelft.nl/view/ir/uuid%3A2b4a1434-8169-481d-9824-fe79e9c4874c/`
40. Verified software repository, `http://vsr.sourceforge.net`
41. Verified software: Theories, tools, experiments (October 2005), `http://vstte.inf.ethz.ch/`
42. Yang, J., Twohey, P., Engler, D., Musuvathi, M.: Using model checking to find serious file system errors. ACM Trans. Comput. Syst. 24(4), 393–423 (2006)

European Train Control System: A Case Study in Formal Verification[*]

André Platzer[1] and Jan-David Quesel[2]

[1] Computer Science Department, Carnegie Mellon University, Pittsburgh, PA
[2] University of Oldenburg, Department of Computing Science, Germany

Abstract. Complex physical systems have several degrees of freedom. They only work correctly when their control parameters obey corresponding constraints. Based on the informal specification of the *European Train Control System* (ETCS), we design a controller for its cooperation protocol. For its free parameters, we successively identify constraints that are required to ensure collision freedom. We formally prove the parameter constraints to be sharp by characterizing them equivalently in terms of reachability properties of the hybrid system dynamics. Using our deductive verification tool KeYmaera, we formally verify controllability, safety, liveness, and reactivity properties of the ETCS protocol that entail collision freedom. We prove that the ETCS protocol remains correct even in the presence of perturbation by disturbances in the dynamics. We verify that safety is preserved when a PI controlled speed supervision is used.

Keywords: formal verification of hybrid systems, train control, theorem proving, parameter constraint identification, disturbances.

1 Introduction

Complex physical control systems often contain many degrees of freedom including how specific parameters are instantiated or adjusted [1,2,3]. Yet, virtually all of these systems are hybrid systems [4] and only work correctly under certain constraints on these parameters. The *European Train Control System* (ETCS) [5] has a wide range of different possible configurations of trains, track layouts, and different driving circumstances. It is only safe for certain conditions on external parameters, e.g., as long as each train is able to avoid collisions by braking with its specific braking power on the remaining distance to the rear end of the next train. Similarly, internal control design parameters for supervisory speed control and automatic braking triggers need to be adjusted in accordance with the underlying train dynamics. Moreover, parameters must be constrained such that the system remains correct when passing from continuous models with instant reactions to sampled data discrete time controllers of hardware implementations. Finally, parameter choices must preserve correctness robustly in the presence of

---

[*] *All propositions have been verified in KeYmaera!* This research was supported by DFG SFB/TR14 AVACS, and by NSF under grants no. CNS-0931985, CCF-0926181.

K. Breitman and A. Cavalcanti (Eds.): ICFEM 2009, LNCS 5885, pp. 246–265, 2009.

disturbances caused by unforeseen external forces (wind, friction, . . .) or internal modelling inaccuracies of ideal-world dynamics, e.g., when passing from ideal-world dynamics to *proportional-integral* (PI) controller implementations.[1] Yet, determining the range of external parameters and the choice of internal design parameters for which complex control systems like ETCS are safe, is not possible just by looking at the model, even less so in the presence of disturbance.

Likewise, it is difficult to read off the parameter constraints that are required for correctness from a failed verification attempt of model checkers [6,7,8], since concrete numeric values of a counterexample trace cannot simply be translated into a generic constraint on the free parameters of the system which would have prevented this kind of error. While approaches like counterexample-guided abstraction refinement [9,8] are highly efficient in undoing automatic abstractions of an abstract hybrid system from spurious counterexamples, they stop when true counterexamples remain in the concrete system. For discovering constraints on free parameters, though, even concrete models will have counterexamples until all required parameter constraints have been identified.

Instead, we use our techniques based on symbolic decompositions [10] for systematically exploring the design space of a hybrid system and for discovering correctness constraints on free parameters. For a complex physical system, we show step by step how a control system can be developed that meets its control design goals and desired correctness properties. Starting from a coarse skeleton of the ETCS cooperation protocol obtained from its official specification [5], we systematically develop a safe controller and identify the parameter constraints that are required for collision freedom. Although these parameter constraints are safety-critical, they are not stated in the official specification [5]. Rather, they result from the system dynamics and objectives and need to be made explicit to find safe choices. The constraints are nontrivial especially those needed to ensure a safe interplay of physics and sampled control implementations. Using the parametric constraints so discovered, we verify correctness properties of the ETCS cooperation protocol that entail collision freedom. We verify rich properties, including safety, controllability, reactivity, and liveness, which are not uniformly expressible and verifiable in most other approaches. Moreover, we verify those correctness properties of the parametric ETCS case study almost fully automatically in our verification tool KeYmaera [11]. Compared to our preliminary short report [12] we prove 12 additional properties including PI control and disturbance extensions.

Contributions. We show how realistic fully parametric hybrid systems for traffic protocols can be designed and verified using a logic-based approach. For ETCS, we identify all relevant safety constraints on free parameters, including external system parameters and internal design parameters of controllers. Safe control choices will be important for more than two million passengers in Europe per day. Our first contribution is that we characterize safe parameter choices equivalently in terms of properties of the train dynamics and that we verify controllability, reactivity, safety, and liveness properties of ETCS. Our second contribution is that we show

---

[1] PI is a standard control technique and also used for controlling trains [2].

how to verify ETCS with a proportional-integral (PI) controller. In contrast to their routine use in control, giving formal proofs for the correct functioning of PIs has been an essentially unsolved problem. Other issues often arise from verification results for ideal-world dynamics that cease to hold for real-world dynamics. Our third contribution is to show how to extend ETCS verification to the presence of disturbances in the dynamics, which account for friction etc. Most notably, the ETCS model with its rich set of properties is out of scope for other approaches. ETCS further illustrates a more general phenomenon in hybrid systems: safely combining dynamics with control requires parameter constraints that are much more complicated than the original dynamics.

Related Work. Model checkers for hybrid systems, for example HYTECH [4] and PHAVer [8], verify by exploring the state space of the system as exhaustively as possible. In contrast to our approach they need concrete numbers for most parameters and cannot verify liveness or existential properties, e.g., whether and how a control parameter can be instantiated so that the system is always safe.

Batt et al. [3] give heuristics for splitting regions by linear constraints that can be used to determine parameter constraints. Frehse et al. [13] synthesize parameters for linear hybrid automata. However, realistic systems like ETCS require non-linear parameter constraints and are out of scope for these approaches.

Tomlin et al. [14] show a game-theoretic semi-decision algorithm for hybrid controller synthesis. For systems like ETCS, which are more general than linear or o-minimal hybrid automata, they suggest numerical approximations. We give exact results for fully parametric ETCS using symbolic techniques.

Peleska et al. [15] and Meyer et al. [1] verify properties of trains. They do not verify hybrid dynamics or the actual movement of trains. The physical dynamics is crucial for faithful train models and for showing actual collision freedom, because, after all, collision freedom is a property of controlled movement.

Cimatti et al. [16] analyze consistency of informal requirements on ETCS expressed as temporal properties. Our work is complementary, as we focus on developing and verifying an actual hybrid systems controller that can be implemented later on, not the consistency of the requirement specification properties.

Structure of this Paper. In Sect. 2 we summarize differential dynamic logic [10] which we use for modelling ETCS. We introduce a formal model for parametric ETCS in Sect. 3. We refine and verify it using symbolic decompositions [10] in Sect. 4. More complex control models, namely PI controllers are the topic of Sect. 5. In Sect. 6, we generalize the physical transmission model to the presence of disturbances and verify ETCS with disturbances. Section 7 gives experimental results in our verification tool KeYmaera. Proofs are given in [17].

2   Preliminaries: Differential Dynamic Logic

In this section, we survey *differential dynamic logic* d$\mathcal{L}$ [10] which is tailored for specifying and verifying rich correctness properties of parametric hybrid systems.

Both its ability to express rich properties and the structural decomposition techniques for d$\mathcal{L}$ are highly beneficial for expressing and discovering the required parameter constraints for ETCS. We only develop the theory as far as necessary and refer to [10] for more background on d$\mathcal{L}$ and the sequent proof calculus for d$\mathcal{L}$ which is implemented in KeYmaera [11].

The logic d$\mathcal{L}$ is a first-order logic with built-in correctness statements about hybrid systems. It is designed such that parametric verification analysis can be carried out directly in d$\mathcal{L}$. Generalizing the principle of dynamic logic to the hybrid case, d$\mathcal{L}$ combines hybrid system operations and correctness statements about system states within a single specification and verification language. d$\mathcal{L}$ uses *hybrid programs* (HP) [10] as a program notation for hybrid systems that is amenable to deductive structural decomposition in d$\mathcal{L}$. In addition to standard operations of discrete programs, HPs have continuous evolution along differential equations as a basic operation. For example, the movement of a train braking with force b can be expressed by placing the differential equation $\tau.p'' = -b$ (where $\tau.p''$ is the second time-derivative of $\tau.p$) at the appropriate point inside a HP. Together with the change of variable domain from $\mathbb{N}$ to $\mathbb{R}$, differential equations constitute a crucial generalization from discrete dynamic logic to d$\mathcal{L}$.

The syntax of hybrid programs is shown together with an informal semantics in Tab. 1. The basic terms (called θ in the table) are either real numbers, real-valued variables or arithmetic expressions built from those.

The effect of $x := \theta$ is an instantaneous discrete jump assigning θ to x. That of $x' = \theta \wedge \chi$ is an ongoing continuous evolution controlled by the differential equation $x' = \theta$ while remaining within the evolution domain χ. The evolution is allowed to stop at any point in χ but it must not leave χ. For unrestricted evolution, we write $x' = \theta$ for $x' = \theta \wedge true$. Systems of differential equations and higher-order derivatives are defined accordingly: $\tau.p' = v \wedge \tau.v' = -b \wedge \tau.v \geq 0$, for instance, characterizes the braking mode of a train with braking force b that holds within $\tau.v \geq 0$ and stops at speed $\tau.v \leq 0$ at the latest.

The test action $?\chi$ is used to define conditions. It completes without changing the state if χ is true in the current state, and it aborts all further evolution, otherwise. The nondeterministic choice $\alpha \cup \beta$ expresses alternatives in

Table 1. Statements of hybrid programs (F is a first-order formula, α, β are HPs)

Statement	Effect
$\alpha;\ \beta$	sequential composition, first performs α and then β afterwards
$\alpha \cup \beta$	nondeterministic choice, following either α or β
α^*	nondeterministic repetition, repeating α some $n \geq 0$ times
$x := \theta$	discrete assignment of the value of term θ to variable x (jump)
$x := *$	nondeterministic assignment of an arbitrary real number to x
$(x_1' \sim_1 \theta_1 \wedge \cdots \wedge$ $x_n' \sim_n \theta_n \wedge F)$	continuous evolution of x_i along differential (in)equation system $x_i' \sim_i \theta_i$, with $\sim_i \in \{\leq, =\}$, restricted to evolution domain F
$?F$	check if formula F holds at current state, abort otherwise
if(F) then α	perform α if F is true, do nothing otherwise
if(F) then α else β	perform α if F is true, perform β otherwise

the behavior of the hybrid system. The if-statement can be expressed using the test action and the choice operator. Its semantics is that if the condition is true, the then-part is executed, otherwise the else-part is performed, if there is one, otherwise the statement is just skipped. The sequential composition $\alpha; \beta$ expresses that β starts after α finishes. Nondeterministic repetition α^* says that the hybrid program α repeats an arbitrary number of times. These operations can be combined to form any other control structure. For instance, $(?\tau.v \geq m.r; \tau.a := A) \cup (?\tau.v \leq m.r; \tau.a := -b)$ says that, depending on the relation of the current speed $\tau.v$ of some train and its recommended speed $m.r$, $\tau.a$ is chosen to be the maximum acceleration A if $m.e - \tau.p \geq 0$ or maximum deceleration $-b$ if $m.e - \tau.p \leq 0$. If both conditions are true (hence, $m.e - \tau.p = 0$) the system chooses either way. The random assignment $x := *$ nondeterministically assigns any value to x, thereby expressing unbounded nondeterminism, e.g., in choices for controller reactions. For instance, the idiom $\tau.a := *; ?\tau.a > 0$ randomly assigns any positive value to the acceleration $\tau.a$.

The d$\mathcal{L}$-*formulas* are defined by the following grammar (θ_i are terms, x is a real-valued variable, $\sim \in \{<, \leq, =, \geq, >\}$, ϕ and ψ are formulas, α is a HP):

$$\theta_1 \sim \theta_2 \mid \neg\phi \mid \phi \wedge \psi \mid \phi \vee \psi \mid \phi \rightarrow \psi \mid \phi \leftrightarrow \psi \mid \forall x\, \phi \mid \exists x\, \phi \mid [\alpha]\phi \mid \langle\alpha\rangle\phi$$

The formulas are designed as an extension of first-order logic over the reals with built-in correctness statements about HPs. They can contain propositional connectives $\wedge, \vee, \rightarrow, \leftrightarrow, \neg$ and real-valued quantifiers $\forall, \exists$ for quantifying over parameters and evolution times. For HP α, d$\mathcal{L}$ provides correctness statements like $[\alpha]\phi$ and $\langle\alpha\rangle\phi$, where $[\alpha]\phi$ expresses that all traces of system α lead to states in which ϕ holds. Likewise, $\langle\alpha\rangle\phi$ expresses that there is at least one trace of α to a state satisfying ϕ. As d$\mathcal{L}$ is closed under logical connectives, it provides conditional correctness statements like $\phi \rightarrow [\alpha]\psi$, saying that α satisfies ψ if ϕ holds at the initial state, or even nested statements like the reactivity statement $[\alpha]\langle\beta\rangle\phi$, saying that whatever HP α is doing, HP β can react in some way to ensure ϕ. As a closed logic, d$\mathcal{L}$ can also express mixed quantified statements like $\exists m\, [\alpha]\phi$ saying that there is a choice of parameter m such that system α always satisfies ϕ, which is useful for determining parameter constraints.

3   Parametric European Train Control System

The European Train Control System (ETCS) [5,1] is a standard to ensure safe and collision-free operation as well as high throughput of trains. Correct functioning of ETCS is highly safety-critical, because the upcoming installation of ETCS level 3 will replace all previous track-side safety measures in order to achieve its high throughput objectives. In this section, we present a system skeleton, which corresponds to a simple representation of the train dynamics and controller reflecting the informal ETCS cooperation protocol [5]. This system is actually unsafe. In Sect. 4, we will systematically augment this skeleton with the parameter constraints that are required for safety but not stated in [5].

3.1 Overview of the ETCS Cooperation Protocol

ETCS level 3 follows the *moving block principle*, i.e., movement permissions are neither known beforehand nor fixed statically. They are determined based on the current track situation by a *Radio Block Controller* (RBC). Trains are only allowed to move within their current *movement authority* (MA), which can be updated by the RBC using wireless communication. Hence the train controller needs to regulate the movement of a train locally such that it always remains within its MA. After MA, there could be open gates, other trains, or speed restrictions due to tunnels. The automatic train protection unit (*atp*) dynamically determines a safety envelope around a train τ, within which it considers driving safe, and adjusts the train acceleration $\tau.a$ accordingly. Fig. 1a illustrates the dynamic assignment of MA. The ETCS controller switches according to the protocol pattern in Fig. 1b which corresponds to a simplified version of Damm et al. [2]. When approaching the end of its MA the train switches from *far* mode (where speed can be regulated freely) to negotiation (*neg*), which, at the latest, happens at the point indicated by *ST* (for *start talking*). During negotiation the RBC grants or denies MA-extensions. If the extension is not granted in time, the train starts braking in the correcting mode (*cor*) returning to *far* afterwards. Emergency messages announced by the RBC can also put the controller into *cor* mode. If so, the train switches to a failsafe state (*fsa*) after the train has come to a full stop and awaits manual clearance by the train operator.

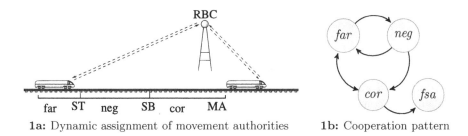

1a: Dynamic assignment of movement authorities   **1b:** Cooperation pattern

Fig. 1. ETCS train cooperation protocol

Lemma 1 (Principle of separation by movement authorities). *If each train stays within its MA and, at any time, MAs issued by the RBC form a disjoint partitioning of the track, then trains can never collide (proof see [17]).*

Lemma 1 effectively reduces the verification of an unbounded number of traffic agents to a finite number. We exploit MAs to decouple reasoning about global collision freedom to local cooperation of every traffic agent with its RBC. In particular, we verify correct coordination for a train without having to consider gates or railway switches, because these only communicate via RBC mediation and can be considered as special reasons for denial of MA-extensions. We only need to prove that the RBC handles all interaction between the trains by assigning or revoking MA correctly and that the trains respect their MA. However, to enable the RBC to guarantee disjoint partitioning of the track it has to rely on properties like appropriate safe rear end computation of the train. Additionally, safe operation of the train plant in conjunction with its environment depends on proper functioning of the gates. As these properties have a more static nature, they are much easier to show once the actual hybrid train dynamics and movements have been proven to be controlled correctly.

As trains are not allowed to drive backwards without clearance by track supervision personnel, the relevant part of the safety envelope is the closest distance to the end of its current MA. The point SB, for *start braking*, is the latest point where the train needs to start correcting its acceleration (in mode *cor*) to make sure it always stays within the bounds of its MA. In Sect. 4, we derive a necessary and sufficient constraint on SB that guarantees safe driving.

We generalize the concept of MA to a vector $m = (d, e, r)$ meaning that beyond point $m.e$ the train must not have a velocity greater than $m.d$. Additionally, the train should try not to outspeed the *recommended speed* $m.r$ for the current track segment. Short periods of slightly higher

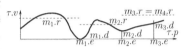

Fig. 2. ETCS track profile

speed are not considered safety-critical. Fig. 2 shows an example of possible train behavior in conjunction with the current value of m that changes over time due to RBC communication.

For a train $\tau = (p, v, a)$ at position $\tau.p$ with current velocity $\tau.v$ and acceleration $\tau.a$, we want to determine sufficient conditions ensuring safety and formally verify that $\tau.v$ is always safe with respect to its current MA, thus satisfying:

$$\tau.p \geq m.e \;\rightarrow\; \tau.v \leq m.d \qquad (\mathcal{S})$$

Formula $(\mathcal{S})$ expresses that the train's velocity $\tau.v$ does not exceed the strict speed limit $m.d$ after passing the point $m.e$ (i.e., $\tau.p \geq m.e$). Generalized MA are a uniform composition of two safety-critical features. They are crucial aspects for ensuring collision free operation in ETCS (Lemma 1) and can take into account safety-critical velocity limits due to bridges, tunnels, or passing trains. For example high speed trains need to reduce their velocity while passing non-airtight or freight trains with a pressure-sensitive load within a tunnel. Our model captures this by reducing the speed component $m.d$ of m.

3.2   Formal Model of Fully Parametric ETCS

For analyzing the proper functioning of ETCS, we have developed a formal model of ETCS as a hybrid program (see Fig. 3) that is based on the informal specification [5]. RBC and train are independent distributed components running in parallel. They interoperate by message passing over wireless communication. As the RBC is a purely digital track-side controller and has no dependent continuous dynamics, we can express parallelism equivalently by interleaving using nondeterministic choice ($\cup$) and repetition (*): the decisions of the train controller only depend on the point in time where RBC messages arrive at the train, not the communication latency. Thus, the nondeterministic interleaving in ETCS

$ETCS_{\text{skel}}$: $(train \cup rbc)^*$
$train$: $spd; atp; drive$
spd : $(?\tau.v \leq m.r; \tau.a := *; ? - b \leq \tau.a \leq A)$
             $\cup(?\tau.v \geq m.r; \tau.a := *; ? - b \leq \tau.a \leq 0)$
atp : if $(m.e - \tau.p \leq SB \vee rbc.message = emergency)$ then $\tau.a := -b$ fi
$drive$: $t := 0; (\tau.p' = \tau.v \wedge \tau.v' = \tau.a \wedge t' = 1 \wedge \tau.v \geq 0 \wedge t \leq \varepsilon)$
rbc : $(rbc.message := emergency) \cup (m := *; ?m.r > 0)$

Fig. 3. Formal model of parametric ETCS cooperation protocol (skeleton)

where either the train or $(\cup)$ the RBC chooses to take action faithfully models every possible arrival time without the need for an explicit channel model. The $*$ at the end of $ETCS_{\text{skel}}$ indicates that the interleaving of train and RBC repeats arbitrarily often. Successive actions in each component are modelled using sequential composition $(;)$. The train checks for its offset to the recommended speed (in spd) before checking if emergency breaking is necessary (in atp).

Train Controller. As it is difficult to use highly detailed models for the train and its mechanical transmission like in [2] directly in the verification and parameter discovery process, we first approximate it by a controller with a ranged choice for the effective acceleration $\tau.a$ between its lower bound $(-b)$ and upper bound (A). (We will refine the dynamics in Sect. 5 and 6.) This controller provides a model that we can use both to derive parameter constraints, and to overapproximate the choices made by the physical train controller [2]. For Sect. 3–4, we model the continuous train dynamics by the differential equation system

$$\tau.p' = \tau.v \wedge \tau.v' = \tau.a \wedge t' = 1 \wedge \tau.v \geq 0 \wedge t \leq \varepsilon \ . \tag{$\mathcal{I}$}$$

It formalizes the ideal-world physical laws for movement, restricted to the evolution domain $\tau.v \geq 0 \wedge t \leq \varepsilon$ in $drive$. The primed variables stand for the first time-derivative of the respective unprimed variable. Therefore, $\tau.p'$ gives the rate with which the position of the train changes, i.e., the velocity $(\tau.p' = \tau.v)$. The velocity itself changes continuously according to the acceleration $\tau.a$, i.e., $\tau.v' = \tau.a$. The train speeds up when $\tau.a > 0$ and brakes when $\tau.a < 0$. In particular, for $\tau.a < 0$, the velocity would eventually become negative, which would mean the train is driving backwards. But that is prohibited without manual clearance, so we restrict the evolution domain to non-negative speed $(\tau.v \geq 0)$. Time can be measured by clocks, i.e. variables changing with constant slope 1 $(t' = 1)$. To further account conservatively for delayed effects of actuators like brakes or for delays caused by cycle times of periodic sensor polling and sampled data discrete time controllers, we permit the continuous movement of the train to continue for up to $\varepsilon > 0$ time units until control decisions finally take effect. This is expressed using the invariant region $t \leq \varepsilon$ on the clock t that is reset using the discrete assignment $t := 0$ before the continuous evolution starts. When the system executes the system of differential equations in $drive$, it can follow a continuous evolution respecting the constraints of $(\mathcal{I})$.

The speed supervision *spd* has two choices ($\cup$). The first option in Fig. 3 can be taken if the test $?\tau.v \leq m.r$ succeeds, the second one if the check $?\tau.v \geq m.r$ is successful. If both succeed, either choice is possible. The *spd* chooses the acceleration $\tau.a$ to keep the recommended speed $m.r$ by a random assignment $\tau.a := *$, which assigns an arbitrary value to $\tau.a$. By the subsequent test $? - b \leq \tau.a \leq 0$ an acceleration is chosen from the interval $[-b, 0]$ if the current speed $\tau.v$ exceeds $m.r$ (otherwise the full range $[-b, A]$ is available). Our controller includes controllers optimizing speed and energy consumption as secondary objectives.

As a supervisory controller, the automatic train protection (*atp* in Fig. 3) checks whether the point SB has been passed ($m.e - \tau.p \leq SB$) or a message from the RBC was received notifying of a track-side emergency situation. Both events cause immediate braking with full deceleration $-b$. Thus, *atp* decisions take precedence over *spd* speed advisory. In the case where $m.e - \tau.p > SB$ but no emergency message arrived the decisions made by *spd* take effect.

Radio Block Controller. We model the RBC as a controller with two possible choices ($\cup$). It may choose to demand immediate correction by sending emergency messages (*rbc.message* := *emergency*) or update the MA by assigning arbitrary new values to its three components ($m := *$). These nondeterministic changes to m reflect different real-world effects like extending $m.e$ and $m.d$ if the heading train has advanced significantly or, instead, notify of a new recommended speed $m.r$ for a track segment. We will identify safety-critical constraints on MA updates in Sect. 4.2.

4   Parametric Verification of Train Control

The model in Fig. 3 from the informal specification is unsafe, i.e., it does not always prevent collisions. To correct this we identify free parameter constraints by analyzing increasingly more complex correctness properties of ETCS. Using these constraints we refine the train control model iteratively into a safe model with constraints on design parameter choices and physical prerequisites on external parameters resulting from the safety requirements on the train dynamics.

Iterative Refinement Process. For discovering parametric constraints required for system correctness, we follow an *iterative refinement process* using structural symbolic decomposition in d$\mathcal{L}$: first, we decompose the uncontrolled system dynamics to a first-order formula characterizing the controllable state region, which specifies for which parameter combinations the system dynamics can actually be controlled safely by any control law. Next, we successively add partial control laws to the system while leaving its decision parameters (like SB or m) free and use structural symbolic decomposition again to discover parametric constraints that preserve controllability under these control laws. This step we repeat until the resulting system is proven safe. Finally, we prove that the discovered parametric constraints do not over-constrain the system inconsistently by showing that it remains live.

In practice, variants of the controllable domain constitute good candidates for inductive invariants, and the parameter constraints discovered ensure that the control choices taken by the controller never leave the controllable domain.

4.1 Controllability Discovery in Parametric ETCS

By analyzing the uncontrolled train dynamics, we obtain a controllability constraint on the external train parameters, i.e., a formula characterizing the parameter combinations for which the train dynamics can be controlled safely by any control law at all. For our analysis we choose the following assumptions

$$\tau.v \geq 0 \wedge m.d \geq 0 \wedge b > 0 \qquad (\mathcal{A})$$

stating that the velocity is non-negative, the movement authority issued by the RBC does not force the train to drive backwards, and the train has some positive braking power b. The controllability constraint is now obtained by applying the d$\mathcal{L}$ proof calculus [10] to the following d$\mathcal{L}$ formula:

$$(\mathcal{A} \wedge \tau.p \leq m.e) \rightarrow [\tau.p' = \tau.v \wedge \tau.v' = -b \wedge \tau.v \geq 0]\mathcal{S} .$$

This means that starting in some state where $(\mathcal{A})$ holds and the train has not yet passed $m.e$ ($\tau.p \leq m.e$) every possible evolution of the train system that applies full brakes ($\tau.v' = -b$) is safe, i.e. does not violate $(\mathcal{S})$. This d$\mathcal{L}$ formula only holds if $\tau.v^2 - m.d^2 \leq 2b(m.e - \tau.p)$. We prove that the so discovered constraint, illustrated in Fig. 4, characterizes the set of states where the train dynamics can still respect MA by appropriate control choices (expressed by the left-hand side d$\mathcal{L}$ formula):

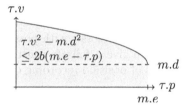

Fig. 4. Controllable region

Proposition 1 (Controllability). *The constraint* $\tau.v^2 - m.d^2 \leq 2b(m.e - \tau.p)$ *is a controllability constraint for the train* τ *with respect to property* $(\mathcal{S})$ *on page 252, i.e., the constraint retains the ability of the train dynamics to respect the safety property. Formally, with* $\mathcal{A} \wedge \tau.p \leq m.e$ *as regularity assumptions, the following equivalence is a valid d$\mathcal{L}$ formula:*

$$[\tau.p' = \tau.v \wedge \tau.v' = -b \wedge \tau.v \geq 0](\tau.p \geq m.e \rightarrow \tau.v \leq m.d)$$
$$\equiv \tau.v^2 - m.d^2 \leq 2b(m.e - \tau.p)$$

This formula expresses that *every run* of a train in braking mode satisfies $(\mathcal{S})$ if and only if condition $\tau.v^2 - m.d^2 \leq 2b(m.e - \tau.p)$ holds initially. Observe how the above equivalence reduces a d$\mathcal{L}$ formula about future controllable train dynamics to a single constraint on the current state. We use this key reduction step from safe train dynamics to controllably safe state-constraints by analyzing whether each part of the ETCS controller preserves train controllability.

Definition 1 (Controllable state). *A train τ is in a controllable state, if the train is always able to stay within its movement authority m by appropriate control actions, which, by Proposition 1, is equivalent to*

$$\tau.v^2 - m.d^2 \leq 2b(m.e - \tau.p) \wedge \mathcal{A} \ . \tag{$\mathcal{C}$}$$

ETCS cannot be safe unless trains start and stay in controllable states. Hence we pick $(\mathcal{C})$ as a minimal candidate for an inductive invariant. This invariant will be used to prove safety of the system by induction even automatically using the technique in [18].

4.2   Iterative Control Refinement of ETCS Parameters

Starting from the constraints for controllable trains, we identify constraints for their various control decisions and refine the ETCS model correspondingly.

RBC Control Constraints. For a safe functioning of ETCS it is important that trains always respect their current MA. Consequently, RBCs are not allowed to issue MAs that are physically impossible for the train like instantaneous full stops. Instead RBCs are only allowed to send new MAs that remain within the controllable range of the train dynamics. For technical reasons the RBC does not reliably know the train positions and velocities in its domain of responsibility to a sufficient precision, because the communication with the trains has to be performed wirelessly with possibly high communication delay and message loss. Thus, we give a failsafe constraint for MA updates which is reliably safe even for loss of position recording communication.

Proposition 2 (RBC preserves train controllability). *The constraint*

$$m_0.d^2 - m.d^2 \leq 2b(m.e - m_0.e) \wedge m_0.d \geq 0 \wedge m.d \geq 0 \tag{$\mathcal{M}$}$$

ensures that the RBC preserves train controllability $(\mathcal{C})$ when changing MA from m_0 to m, i.e., the following formula is valid:

$$\forall \tau \Big(\mathcal{C} \rightarrow [m_0 := m; \ rbc] \ (\mathcal{M} \rightarrow \mathcal{C}) \Big) \ . \tag{1}$$

This RBC controllability is characterized by the following valid formula:

$$m.d \geq 0 \wedge b > 0 \rightarrow [m_0 := m; \ rbc] \ \Big(\mathcal{M} \leftrightarrow \forall \tau \left(((\langle m := m_0 \rangle \mathcal{C}) \rightarrow \mathcal{C}) \right) \Big) \ . \tag{2}$$

Constraint $(\mathcal{M})$ characterizes that an extension is safe if it is possible to reduce the speed by braking with deceleration b from the old target speed $m_0.d$ to the new target speed $m.d$ within the extension range $m.e - m_0.e$, regardless of the current speed of train τ. It imposes constraints on feasible track profiles. Property (1) expresses that, for all trains in a controllable state $(\mathcal{C})$, every RBC change of MA m_0 to m that complies with $(\mathcal{M})$ enforces that the train is still in a controllable state $(\mathcal{C})$. Constraint $(\mathcal{M})$ is characterized by the equivalence (2), expressing that for every decision of rbc, $(\mathcal{M})$ holds for the RBC change from m_0 to m if and only if *all* trains $(\forall \tau)$ that were controllable $(\mathcal{C})$ for the previous MA (set using $\langle m := m_0 \rangle$) remain controllable for the new MA m.

Train Control Constraints. Now that we found constraints characterizing when the cooperation of train and RBC is controllable, we need to find out under which circumstances the actual control choices by *spd* and *atp* retain controllability. In particular, the design parameter SB (start braking point relative to the end of the movement authority) needs to be chosen appropriately to preserve ($\mathcal{C}$). First we show that *there is* a choice of SB:

Proposition 3. *For all feasible RBC choices and all choices of speed control, there is a choice for SB that makes the train always stay within its MA, i.e., for controllable states, we can prove:*

$$\mathcal{C} \rightarrow [m_0 := m;\ rbc](\mathcal{M} \rightarrow [spd]\langle SB := *\rangle[atp;\ drive]\mathcal{S})\ .$$

The formula expresses that, starting in a controllable region $\mathcal{C}$, if the RBC updates the MA from m_0 to m respecting ($\mathcal{M}$), then after arbitrary *spd* choices, the train controller is still able to find some choice for SB ($\langle SB := *\rangle$) such that it always respect the fresh MA when following *atp* and *drive*. Since Proposition 3 is provable in KeYmaera we know that there is a safe solution for ETCS. On the formula level the assumptions are expressed using implications such that the formula does not make any proposition if either ($\mathcal{C}$) is not initially satisfied or the RBC does not respect ($\mathcal{M}$). The train controller is split up into the proposition that for all executions of the speed supervision ([*spd*]) there is a choice for SB ($\langle SB := *\rangle$) such that the automatic train protection unit (*atp*) always preserves safety during the execution of the trains movement in the *drive* phase. For *atp* and *drive* we again make a statement over all possible executions of the components. Only the choice of SB is existentially quantified.

To find a particular constraint on the choice of SB, we need to take the maximum reaction latency ε of the train controllers into account. With $\varepsilon > 0$, the point where the train needs to apply brakes to comply with m is not determined by ($\mathcal{C}$) alone, but needs additional safety margins to compensate for reaction delays. Therefore, we search for a constraint that characterizes that for every possible end of the movement authority ($\forall m.e$) and train position ($\forall \tau.v$), train movement with an acceleration of A preserves ($\mathcal{C}$) if it started in a state where ($\mathcal{C}$) holds and the point SB has not been passed yet ($m.e - \tau.p \geq SB \wedge \mathcal{C}$).

Proposition 4 (Reactivity constraint). *If the train is in a controllable state, the supervisory ETCS controller reacts appropriately in order to maintain controllability iff SB is chosen according to the following equivalence*

$$\left(\forall m.e\, \forall \tau.p\, (m.e - \tau.p \geq SB \wedge \mathcal{C} \rightarrow [\tau.a := A;\ drive]\,\mathcal{C})\right)$$
$$\equiv SB \geq \frac{\tau.v^2 - m.d^2}{2b} + \left(\frac{A}{b} + 1\right)\left(\frac{A}{2}\varepsilon^2 + \varepsilon\, \tau.v\right)\ . \tag{$\mathcal{B}$}$$

Constraint ($\mathcal{B}$) on SB is derived using a projection of the train behavior to the worst-case acceleration A in a state where SB has not been passed yet. We choose this projection because the train controller needs to ensure that it can

$ETCS_r$: $(train_r \cup rbc_r)^*$
$train_r$: $spd;\ atp_r;\ drive$
atp_r : $SB := \frac{\tau.v^2 - m.d^2}{2b} + \left(\frac{A}{b} + 1\right)\left(\frac{A}{2}\varepsilon^2 + \varepsilon\ \tau.v\right);\ atp$
rbc_r : $(rbc.message := emergency)$
$\cup_{-}\left(m_0 := m; m := *; ?m.r \geq 0 \wedge m.d \geq 0 \wedge m_0.d^2 - m.d^2 \leq 2b(m.e - m_0.e)\right)$

Fig. 5. Refined parametric ETCS cooperation protocol with bug-fixes to Fig. 3

drive safely with maximum acceleration A for ε time units even right before passing SB in order for an acceleration choice of A to be safe constraint $(\mathcal{B})$ is not obvious from the system model. After discovering constraint $(\mathcal{B})$, it can be explained in retrospect: It characterizes the relative braking distance required to reduce speed from $\tau.v$ to target speed $m.d$ with braking deceleration b, which corresponds to controllability and is expressed by the term $\frac{\tau.v^2 - m.d^2}{2b}$. In addition, it involves the distance travelled during one maximum reaction cycle of ε time units with acceleration A, including the additional distance needed to reduce the speed down to $\tau.v$ after accelerating with A for ε time units (expressed by $\left(\frac{A}{b} + 1\right)\left(\frac{A}{2}\varepsilon^2 + \varepsilon\ \tau.v\right)$). This extra distance results from speed changes and depends on the relation $\frac{A}{b}$ of maximum acceleration A and braking power b.

Propositions 1–4 prove equivalences. Hence, counterexamples exist for the ETCS skeleton in Fig. 3 whenever the parameter constraints are not met. Consequently, these constraints must be respected for correctness of *any* model of ETCS controllers, including implementation refinements. It is, thus, important to identify these safety constraints early in the overall design and verification process.

4.3   Safety Verification of Refined ETCS

By augmenting the system from Fig. 3 with the parametric constraints obtained from Propositions 1–4, we synthesize a safe system model completing the ETCS protocol skeleton. The refined model is presented in Fig. 5 which bug-fixes the model in Fig. 3 taken from the informal specification (*spd, atp, drive* as in Fig. 3).

Proposition 5 (Safety). *Starting in a controllable state, this global and unbounded-horizon safety formula about the refined ETCS system in Fig. 5 is valid:*

$$\mathcal{C} \to [ETCS_r](\tau.p \geq m.e \to \tau.v \leq m.d)\ .$$

This provable formula states that, starting in a controllable region $(\mathcal{C})$, the augmented ETCS model is safe, i.e., trains always respect their movement authority.

As an example to illustrate the proof structure for the verification of Proposition 5, consider the sketch in Fig. 6. By convention, such proofs start with the conjecture at the bottom and proceed by decomposition to the leaves. We need to prove that universal controllability $(\mathcal{C})$ implies safety $(\mathcal{S})$ at all times. As the system consists of a global loop, we prove that $(\mathcal{C})$ is an invariant of this loop and strong enough to imply ($\mathcal{S}$). It can be shown easily that the invariant ($\mathcal{C}$) is initially valid (left branch) and implies the postcondition ($\mathcal{S}$) (right branch). As usual, proving that invariant ($\mathcal{C}$) is preserved by the loop body is the most challenging part of the proof in KeYmaera (middle branch), which splits into two cases. For the left case, we have to show that the RBC preserves the invariant, which can be proven like Proposition 2. For the right case, we show that the train controller preserves the invariant. The proof splits due to the choice in the spd

$$m.e - \tau.p \geq SB \qquad m.e - \tau.p \geq SB$$
$$\left(\begin{array}{c} m.e - \tau.p \leq SB \\ \diagdown \qquad \diagup \end{array} \right)$$
$$\tau.v \geq m.r \qquad \tau.v \leq m.r$$
$$m := * \quad rec \qquad \diagdown \qquad \diagup$$
$$\mathcal{C} \rightarrow [r\dot{b}c_r]\mathcal{C} \quad \mathcal{C} \rightarrow [train_r]\mathcal{C}$$
$$\diagdown \qquad \qquad |$$
$$\mathcal{C} \rightarrow [train_r \cup rbc_r]\mathcal{C}$$
$$\mathcal{C} \rightarrow \mathcal{C} \qquad | \qquad \mathcal{C} \rightarrow \mathcal{S}$$
$$\diagdown \qquad \diagup$$
$$\mathcal{C} \rightarrow [ETCS_r]\mathcal{S}$$

Fig. 6. Proof sketch for Proposition 5

component depending on the relation of the current speed to the recommended speed ($\tau.v$ vs. $m.r$). The next split on both of these branches depends on the relation of ($m.e - \tau.p$) and SB. If the train has passed point SB (middle case) the system is safe (Proposition 1), because the invariant describes a controllable state and the atp applies brakes. The outer branches, where the train has not yet passed SB, can be proven using Proposition 4.

4.4 Liveness Verification of Refined ETCS

In order to show that the discovered parameter constraints do not over-constrain the system inconsistently, we show liveness, i.e., that an ETCS train is able to reach every track position with appropriate RBC permissions.

Proposition 6 (Liveness). *The refined ETCS system is live, i.e., assuming the RBC can safely grant the required MAs because preceding trains are moving on, trains are able to reach any track position P by appropriate RBC choices:*

$$\tau.v \geq 0 \wedge \varepsilon > 0 \ \rightarrow \ \forall P \langle ETCS_r \rangle \tau.p \geq P$$

The formula expresses that, starting in a state where the velocity is non-negative and the maximum evolution time is positive, every point P ($\forall P$) can be reached ($\tau.p \geq P$) by some execution of the ETCS model ($\langle ETCS_r \rangle$). Here the diamond modality is used to say that not all, but *some* appropriate execution reaches a state where the postcondition ($\tau.p \geq P$) holds. For showing that the system is live, a more liberal initial state is possible with regard to the controllability of the train. It is easy to see from the domain restrictions ($\tau.v \geq 0 \wedge t \leq \varepsilon$) in drive that the assumptions ($\tau.v \geq 0$) and $\varepsilon > 0$ are necessary.

4.5 Full Correctness of ETCS

By collecting Propositions 1–6, we obtain the following main result of this paper, which demonstrates the feasibility of d$\mathcal{L}$-based parametric discovery and verification supported by our theorem prover KeYmaera. It gives important insights in the fully parametric ETCS case study and yields conclusive and fully verified choices for the free parameters in ETCS. By virtue of the parametric formulation, this result applies to all concrete instantiations of the ETCS cooperation protocol from Sect. 3, including controllers that further optimize speed or model refinements in hardware implementations.

Theorem 1 (Correctness of ETCS cooperation protocol). *The ETCS system augmented with constraints* $(\mathcal{B})$ *and* $(\mathcal{M})$ *is correct as given in Fig. 5. Starting in any controllable state respecting* $(\mathcal{C})$, *trains remain in the controllable region at any time. They safely respect movement authorities issued by the RBC so that ETCS is collision-free. Further, trains can always react safely to all RBC decisions respecting* $(\mathcal{M})$. *ETCS is live: When tracks become free, trains are able to reach any track position by appropriate RBC actions. Furthermore, the augmented constraints* $(\mathcal{C})$ *and* $(\mathcal{B})$ *are necessary and sharp: Every configuration violating* $(\mathcal{C})$ *or* $(\mathcal{B})$, *respectively, gives rise to a concrete counterexample violating safety property* $(\mathcal{S})$. *Finally, every RBC choice violating* $(\mathcal{M})$ *gives rise to a counterexample in the presence of lossy wireless communication channels.*

5 Inclusion and Safety of PI Controllers

Trains use *proportional-integral* (PI) controllers for speed supervision [2] like most physical control systems do. A PI uses a linear combination of the proportional and integral values of the difference between the current $(\tau.v)$ and the target system state $(m.r)$ to determine control actions. The proportional part uses the current error $\tau.v - m.r$ of the system state compared to the target state with some factor l, whereas the integral part sums up previous errors $\int (\tau.v - m.r)dt$ with some factor i. Damm et al. have identified a detailed train model with a PI controller [2]. The resulting PI corresponds to the differential equation system

$$\tau.p' = \tau.v \wedge \tau.v' = \min\Big(A, \max\big(-b, \, l(\tau.v - m.r) - i\,s - c\,m.r\big)\Big)$$
$$\wedge s' = \tau.v - m.r \wedge t' = 1 \wedge \tau.v \geq 0 \wedge t \leq \varepsilon \ . \quad (\mathcal{P})$$

The position of the train $\tau.p$ changes according to its velocity $\tau.v$ $(\tau.p' = \tau.v)$ and $\tau.v$ changes according to the acceleration determined by PI equations. Variable s tracks the integral part of the controller: differential equation $s' = \tau.v - m.r$ corresponds to integral equation $s = \int (\tau.v - m.r)dt$. Thus $i\,s$ represents the integral share of the error scaled by i in the PI. Since trains do not drive backwards by braking, the system contains an evolution domain stating that the speed remains non-negative $(\tau.v \geq 0)$. PI $\mathcal{P}$ influences the velocity by changing the acceleration of the train according to proportional and integral changes compared to recommended speed $m.r$. The parameters l, i and c are derived from the train physics and chosen in a way such that the controller does not oscillate. Note that classical PIs use $c = 0$. We also allow $c \neq 0$, which is used in the refined PI controller identified in [2] for additional attenuation. Following [2], the controller further obeys physical bounds for the acceleration and is restricted to values between $-b < 0$ and $A > 0$ using min, max functions.

In this section we relate this model for the train control with the approximation $(\mathcal{I})$ used in Sect. 3–4. First, we prove that our abstraction is a valid overapproximation by showing that whatever the PI controller $(\mathcal{P})$ does, the ideal-world physical controller for $(\mathcal{I})$ can reach the same point within the same time. Unlike $(\mathcal{I})$, we cannot simply solve PI $(\mathcal{P})$ in polynomial arithmetic to prove properties. We use differential invariants [19,18] instead for proofs.

Proposition 7 (PI inclusion). *Starting from 0, every possible execution of the PI controller $(\mathcal{P})$ can be imitated by the ranged controller*

$$spd_s := (\tau.a := *; \ ?\tau.a \geq -b \wedge \tau.a \leq A)$$

for the dynamics $(\mathcal{I})$ such that they are in the same place at the same time:

$$[\mathcal{P} \wedge t'_\pi = 1] \langle (spd_s; \ t := 0; \ \mathcal{I} \wedge t'_\tau = 1)^* \rangle \ (\pi.p = \tau.p \wedge t_\pi = t_\tau)$$

That is, for every evolution of $(\mathcal{P})$, spd_s can choose its options such that $(\mathcal{I})$ reaches the same point $\pi.p$ at the same time t_π. Here t_π is a clock $(t'_\pi = 1)$ measuring the time the first controller $(\mathcal{P})$ consumes and t_τ measures the time needed by the second controller to reach the same position at the same time.

The ranged controller spd_s is less restrictive than spd, because it allows more liberal acceleration choices. As the previous propositions do not depend on the value of $m.r$ showing the inclusion property for spd_s is sufficient.

With the constraints in $ETCS_r$, we verify that the fully parametric PI controller combined with the automatic train protection atp_r preserves safety:

Proposition 8 (Safety of the PI-controlled system). *For trains in controllable state, the $ETCS_r$ system with a PI controller for speed regulation is safe, i.e., when replacing drive by $(\mathcal{P}_e \wedge t' = 1 \wedge t \leq \varepsilon)$ for (continuous) speed supervision and with emergency braking according to Fig. 5. This corresponds to the physical train model identified in [2].*

6 Disturbance and the European Train Control System

In Sect. 3–4, we assumed direct control of acceleration. In reality, acceleration results from physical transmission of corresponding forces that depend on the electrical current in the engine [2]. As a conservative overapproximation of these effects, we generalize the ETCS model to a model with *differential inequalities* [19], where we also take into account disturbances in the physical transmission of forces (including wind, friction etc.):

$$\tau.p' = \tau.v \wedge \tau.a - l \leq \tau.v' \leq \tau.a + u \wedge t' = 1 \wedge \tau.v \geq 0 \wedge t \leq \varepsilon \qquad (\mathcal{I}_d)$$

with a disturbance within the interval $[-l, u]$. That is, the acceleration $\tau.a$ chosen by the train controller can take effect with an error bounded by $-l$ and u, because the derivative $\tau.v'$ of the velocity will not need to be $\tau.a$ exactly in $(\mathcal{I}_d)$, but $\tau.v'$ can vary arbitrarily between $\tau.a - l$ and $\tau.a + u$ over time. We generalize the differential equation $(\mathcal{I})$ in component *train* from Fig. 3 and Fig. 5 by replacing it with the differential inequality $(\mathcal{I}_d)$ and denote the result by *train*$_d$.

Notice that, unlike $(\mathcal{I})$, we cannot simply solve differential inequality $(\mathcal{I}_d)$, because its actual solution depends on the precise value of the disturbance, which is a quantity that changes over time. Thus, solutions would only be relative to this disturbance function and a reachability analysis would have to consider all choices of this function, which would require higher-order logic. Instead, we verify using differential invariants [19,18] as a sound first-order characterization.

6.1   Controllability in ETCS with Disturbances

The controllability characterization from Proposition 1 carries over to train control with disturbance when taking into account the maximum disturbance u on the braking power b that limit the effective braking power to $(b - u)$:

Proposition 9 (Controllability despite disturbance). *The constraint*

$$\tau.v^2 - m.d^2 \leq 2(b - u)(m.e - \tau.p) \wedge m.d \geq 0 \wedge b > u \geq 0 \wedge l \geq 0 \qquad (\mathcal{C}_d)$$

is a controllability constraint *with respect to property* $(\mathcal{S})$ *for the train* τ *with disturbance* $(\mathcal{I}_d)$, *i.e., it retains the ability of the train dynamics to respect the safety property despite disturbance. Formally, with* $\mathcal{A} \wedge \tau.p \leq m.e \wedge b > u \geq 0 \wedge l \geq 0$ *as regularity assumptions, the following equivalence holds:*

$$[\tau.p' = \tau.v \wedge \tau.a - l \leq \tau.v' \leq \tau.a + u \wedge t' = 1 \wedge \tau.v \geq 0 \wedge t \leq \varepsilon]\mathcal{S}$$
$$\equiv \tau.v^2 - m.d^2 \leq 2(b - u)(m.e - \tau.p)$$

Here $(\mathcal{C}_d)$ results from $(\mathcal{C})$ by replacing b with $(b - u)$. In worst case disturbance, the train cannot brake with deceleration $-b$ but instead might be off by u. To guarantee that the train is able to stay within its MA the controller has to assume maximum guaranteed deceleration $-(b - u)$ when making control decision.

6.2   Iterative Control Refinement of Parameters with Disturbances

When taking into account worst-case effects of disturbance on control, reactivity constraint $(\mathcal{B})$ carries over to the presence of disturbance in the train dynamics:

Proposition 10 (Reactivity constraint despite disturbance). *For trains in controllable state, the supervisory ETCS controller reacts appropriately despite disturbance in order to maintain controllability iff SB is chosen according to the following provable equivalence:*

$$\left(\forall m.e \, \forall \tau.p \left((m.e - \tau.p \geq SB \wedge \tau.v^2 - m.d^2 \leq 2(b - u)(m.e - \tau.p)) \rightarrow \right. \right.$$

$$\left. \left. [\tau.a := A; \ drive_d](\tau.v^2 - m.d^2 \leq 2(b - u)(m.e - \tau.p)) \right) \right)$$

$$\equiv SB \geq \frac{\tau.v^2 - m.d^2}{2(b - u)} + \left(\frac{A + u}{b - u} + 1 \right) \left(\frac{A + u}{2} \varepsilon^2 + \varepsilon \tau.v \right) \qquad (\mathcal{B}_d)$$

$$ETCS_d : (train_d \cup rbc_d)^*$$
$$train_d : spd;\ atp_d;\ drive_d$$
$$atp_d : SB := \frac{\tau.v^2 - m.d^2}{2(b-u)} + \left(\frac{A+u}{b-u} + 1\right)\left(\frac{A+u}{2}\varepsilon^2 + \varepsilon\tau.v\right);$$
$$\text{if } (m.e - \tau.p \le SB \vee rbc.message = emergency) \text{ then } \tau.a := -b \text{ fi}$$
$$drive_d : t := 0;\ (\tau.p' = \tau.v \wedge \tau.a - l \le \tau.v' \le \tau.a + u \wedge t' = 1 \wedge \tau.v \ge 0 \wedge t \le \varepsilon)$$
$$rbc_d : (rbc.message := emergency)$$
$$\cup\ (m_0 := m;\ m := *;$$
$$?m.r \ge 0 \wedge m.d \ge 0 \wedge m_0.d^2 - m.d^2 \le 2(b-u)(m.e - m_0.e))$$

Fig. 7. Parametric ETCS cooperation protocol with disturbances

For reactivity $(\mathcal{B}_d)$ not only the maximum deceleration but also the maximum acceleration matters. Therefore, we need to substitute every b by $(b-u)$ but also every A with $(A+u)$ which is the maximum acceleration under disturbance to get a (provable) reactivity constraint for the disturbed system.

6.3 Safety Verification of ETCS with Disturbances

When we augment the ETCS model by the constraints $(\mathcal{B}_d)$ and $(\mathcal{M}_d)$, where $(\mathcal{M}_d)$ results from $(\mathcal{M})$ by again replacing every b by $(b-u)$, ETCS is safe even in the presence of disturbance when starting in a state respecting $(\mathcal{C}_d)$.

Proposition 11 (Safety despite disturbance). *Assuming the train starts in a controllable state satisfying $(\mathcal{C}_d)$, the following global and unbounded-horizon safety formula about the ETCS system with disturbance from Fig. 7 is valid:*

$$\mathcal{C}_d \to [ETCS_d](\tau.p \ge m.e \to \tau.v \le m.d)\ .$$

This safety proof generalizes to ETCS with disturbance, using differential induction [19,18] with a time-dependent version of $(\mathcal{B}_d)$ as differential invariant:

$$m.e - \tau.p \ge \frac{\tau.v^2 - m.d^2}{2(b-u)} + \left(\frac{A+u}{b-u} + 1\right)\left(\frac{A+u}{2}(\varepsilon - t)^2 + (\varepsilon - t)\tau.v\right)$$

7 Experimental Results

Tab. 2 shows experimental results for verifying ETCS in our d$\mathcal{L}$-based verification tool KeYmaera [11]. The results are from a system with two quad core Intel Xeon E5430 (2.66 GHz per core, using only one core) and 32 gigabyte of RAM. All correctness properties and parameter constraints of ETCS can be verified with 91% to 100% degree automation. More than 91% of the proof steps are fully automatic. The proofs are 100% automatic in 6 properties and require minor guidance in 7 more challenging cases. Tab. 2 gives the number of user interactions necessary in the column Int, for comparison the total number of applied proof rules in column Steps. In most cases proofs can be found automatically [18].

Table 2. Experimental results for the European Train Control System

Case study			Int	Time(s)	Memory(MB)	Steps	Dim
Controllability	Proposition 1		0	1.3	29.6	14	5
Refinement	Proposition 2	eqn. (1)	0	1.7	29.0	42	12
RBC Control	Proposition 2	eqn. (2)	0	2.2	29.0	42	12
Reactivity	Proposition 3		8	133.4	118.7	229	13
Reactivity	Proposition 4		0	86.8	688.2	52	14
Safety	Proposition 5		0	249.9	127.8	153	14
Liveness	Proposition 6		4	27.3	100.7	166	7
Inclusion	Proposition 7	PI	19	766.2	354.4	301	25
Safety	Proposition 8	PI	16	509.0	688.2	183	15
Controllability	Proposition 9	disturbed	0	5.6	30.8	37	7
Reactivity	Proposition 10	disturbed	2	34.6	74.3	78	15
Safety	Proposition 11	disturbed	5	389.9	41.7	88	16

For more complicated properties beyond the capabilities of currently available decision procedures for real arithmetic, KeYmaera needs more user guidance but they can still be verified with KeYmaera! We see that the formula complexity and symbolic state dimension (Dim) has more impact on the computational complexity than the number of proof steps in d$\mathcal{L}$ decompositions, which indicates good scalability in terms of the size of the system model.

8   Summary

As a case study for parametric verification of hybrid systems, we have verified controllability, reactivity, safety, and liveness of the fully parametric cooperation protocol of the European Train Control System. We have demonstrated the feasibility of logic-based verification of parametric hybrid systems and identified parametric constraints that are both sufficient and necessary for a safe collision-free operation of ETCS. We have characterized these constraints on the free parameters of ETCS equivalently in terms of corresponding reachability properties of the underlying train dynamics. We have verified a corresponding fully parametric PI controller and proven that the system remains correct even when the train dynamics is subject to disturbances caused, e.g., by the physical transmission, friction, or wind.

We have shown how the properties of train control can be expressed in d$\mathcal{L}$. Our experimental results with KeYmaera show a scalable approach by combining the power of completely automatic verification procedures with the intuition behind user guidance to tackle even highly parametric hybrid systems and properties with substantial quantifier alternation (reactivity or liveness) or disturbance.

We have verified all propositions formally in the KeYmaera tool. We present proof sketches in [17].

Acknowledgments. We like to thank Johannes Faber and Ernst-Rüdiger Olderog for useful remarks on preliminary versions of this paper. Additionally, we like to thank the anonymous referees for their helpful comments.

References

1. Meyer, R., Faber, J., Hoenicke, J., Rybalchenko, A.: Model checking duration calculus: A practical approach. FACS 20(4–5), 481–505 (2008)
2. Damm, W., Mikschl, A., Oehlerking, J., Olderog, E.R., Pang, J., Platzer, A., Segelken, M., Wirtz, B.: Automating verification of cooperation, control, and design in traffic applications. In: Jones, C.B., Liu, Z., Woodcock, J. (eds.) Formal Methods and Hybrid Real-Time Systems. LNCS, vol. 4700, Springer, Heidelberg (2007)
3. Batt, G., Belta, C., Weiss, R.: Model checking genetic regulatory networks with parameter uncertainty. In: Bemporad, A., Bicchi, A., Buttazzo, G. (eds.) HSCC 2007. LNCS, vol. 4416, Springer, Heidelberg (2007)
4. Alur, R., Henzinger, T.A., Ho, P.H.: Automatic symbolic verification of embedded systems. IEEE Trans. Software Eng. 22(3), 181–201 (1996)
5. ERTMS User Group, UNISIG: ERTMS/ETCS System requirements specification. Version 2.2.2 (2002), http://www.era.europa.eu
6. Henzinger, T.A.: The theory of hybrid automata. In: LICS, IEEE CS Press, Los Alamitos (1996)
7. Mysore, V., Piazza, C., Mishra, B.: Algorithmic algebraic model checking II. In: Peled, D.A., Tsay, Y.-K. (eds.) ATVA 2005. LNCS, vol. 3707, pp. 217–233. Springer, Heidelberg (2005)
8. Frehse, G.: PHAVer: Algorithmic verification of hybrid systems past HyTech. In: Morari, M., Thiele, L. (eds.) HSCC 2005. LNCS, vol. 3414, pp. 258–273. Springer, Heidelberg (2005)
9. Clarke, E., Grumberg, O., Jha, S., Lu, Y., Veith, H.: Counterexample-guided abstraction refinement for symbolic model checking. J. ACM 50(5) (2003)
10. Platzer, A.: Differential dynamic logic for hybrid systems. J. Autom. Reasoning 41(2), 143–189 (2008)
11. Platzer, A., Quesel, J.D.: KeYmaera: A hybrid theorem prover for hybrid systems. In: Armando, A., Baumgartner, P., Dowek, G. (eds.) IJCAR 2008. LNCS (LNAI), vol. 5195, pp. 171–178. Springer, Heidelberg (2008), http://symbolaris.com/info/KeYmaera.html
12. Platzer, A., Quesel, J.D.: Logical verification and systematic parametric analysis in train control. In: Egerstedt, M., Mishra, B. (eds.) HSCC 2008. LNCS, vol. 4981, pp. 646–649. Springer, Heidelberg (2008)
13. Frehse, G., Jha, S.K., Krogh, B.H.: A counterexample-guided approach to parameter synthesis for linear hybrid automata. In: Egerstedt, M., Mishra, B. (eds.) HSCC 2008. LNCS, vol. 4981, pp. 187–200. Springer, Heidelberg (2008)
14. Tomlin, C., Lygeros, J., Sastry, S.: A Game Theoretic Approach to Controller Design for Hybrid Systems. Proceedings of IEEE 88, 949–969 (2000)
15. Peleska, J., Große, D., Haxthausen, A.E., Drechsler, R.: Automated verification for train control systems. In: FORMS/FORMAT (2004)
16. Cimatti, A., Roveri, M., Tonetta, S.: Requirements validation for hybrid systems. In: Bouajjani, A., Maler, O. (eds.) CAV 2009. LNCS, vol. 5643. Springer, Heidelberg (2009)
17. Platzer, A., Quesel, J.D.: European train control system: A case study in formal verification. Report 54, SFB/TR 14 AVACS, ISSN: 1860-9821, avacs.org (2009)
18. Platzer, A., Clarke, E.M.: Computing differential invariants of hybrid systems as fixedpoints. Form. Methods Syst. Des. 35(1), 98–120 (2009) Special CAV 2008 issue
19. Platzer, A.: Differential-algebraic dynamic logic for differential-algebraic programs. J. Log. Comput (2008), doi:10.1093/logcom/exn070

Development of Security Software: A High Assurance Methodology

David Hardin[1], T. Douglas Hiratzka[1], D. Randolph Johnson[2], Lucas Wagner[1], and Michael Whalen[1]

[1] Rockwell Collins, Inc.
[2] National Security Agency

Abstract. This paper reports on a project to exercise, evaluate and enhance a methodology for developing high assurance software for an embedded system controller. In this approach, researchers at the National Security Agency capture system requirements precisely and unambiguously through functional specifications in Z. Rockwell Collins then implements these requirements using an integrated, model-based software development approach. The development effort is supported by a tool chain that provides automated code generation and support for formal verification. The specific system is a prototype high speed encryption system, although the controller could be adapted for use in a variety of critical systems in which very high assurance of correctness, reliability, and security or safety properties is essential.

1 Introduction

In order to study advanced high speed electronics technology, hardware research engineers at the National Security Agency started a project to build a prototype high speed encryption system. The system architecture they arrived at is shown in Fig. 1.

In this design, the Data Accelerators handle input/output functions, data formatting, and enforcement of some security policy rules. The encrypt core and decrypt core perform the actual encryption and decryption. These six subsystem blocks are in the high speed data paths. The control block manages the subsystem blocks but lies outside the high speed data path. An important consequence of this architecture is that the High Speed Crypto Controller (HSCC) does not need to be implemented using any exotic high speed electronics technology. The critical HSCC design goals are high reliability and achieving very high assurance of functional correctness and essential security properties. As a result, project responsibility for implementing the data accelerators and the crypto cores remained with the hardware engineering organization while responsibility for the HSCC was passed to the High Confidence Software and Systems (HCSS) Division.

Because of the general research mission of the HCSS division, the project now had two main goals. The first goal was to deliver a working controller. The second goal was to exercise, evaluate, and try to enhance a strong software development methodology. Since this is a security system, the methodology has to support a full range of development aspects from requirements through very rigorous evaluation by independent evaluators. And, in addition to being rigorous, it should also be cost-effective

K. Breitman and A. Cavalcanti (Eds.): ICFEM 2009, LNCS 5885, pp. 266–285, 2009.

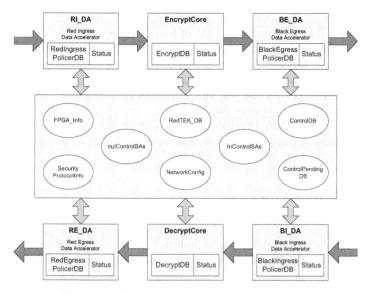

Fig. 1. High-Speed Crypto Functional Block Diagram

in time and money. Given these goals, and the limited resources of a research organization, we in the HCSS division needed an industrial partner. We found the ideal partner in Rockwell Collins.

One reason for teaming with Rockwell Collins was their capability with the AAMP7G microprocessor and high-assurance FPGA development. The AAMP7G supports strict time and space partitioning in hardware, and has received an NSA MILS certificate based in part on a formal proof of correctness of its separation kernel microcode, as specified by the EAL-7 level of the Common Criteria [5]. The formal verification of the AAMP7G partitioning system was conducted using the ACL2 theorem prover, and culminated in the proof of a theorem that the AAMP7G partitioning microcode implements a high-level security policy [4].

Perhaps more important than their hardware capabilities, Rockwell Collins has a very solid approach to software development. It features an integrated, model-based development toolchain with a focus on providing a domain-specific modeling environment that abstracts the implementation details, promotes architectural level design, and provides automated transformations between the problem domain formalisms and the target platform. The tools simplify code development and facilitate the application of automated formal analysis tools. In addition, the toolchain is capable of interfacing directly to a simulation environment, providing another level of assurance of design correctness.

For its part, HCSS researchers have experience in the Z specification language [10]. They have written Z functional specifications and design descriptions for several internal development projects. In the Tokeneer project [1,2], HCSS researchers played the role of customers and read and commented on draft specifications and designs in Z written by Praxis High Integrity Systems. In addition to experience in the requirements stage of development, HCSS people are familiar with the security evaluation work done by other NSA personnel.

The approach we chose for this project was for HCSS to take the lead in writing control software requirements in the form of functional specifications in Z. Rockwell Collins would take these specifications as input into their established development process. They would look for opportunities to strengthen the process, including the support for evaluation, or save time and money by taking advantage of the formal specifications. Everyone would see where the tool support was good or in need of improvement. This is a report on our experience. It is only incidentally about high-speed electronics technology or cryptography. Furthermore, because of limited space, we do not discuss in this paper data separation or any other properties of the hardware, for example, of the sort described by McComb and Wildman [6].

2 Z Specification Work

Over the last ten years, HCSS researchers have worked with other organizations using Z in support of a variety of development projects. We use the Z/EVES [9] support tool and have found it quite suitable for our needs. Based on our experience, we chose to use Z to write functional specifications on this high assurance controller project.

Most of the people involved in using Z over the years had some relevant technical background. An author of this paper is a trained mathematical logician who was involved in writing the ISO standard for Z and participated actively in all the projects. Most others had backgrounds in electrical engineering, mathematics or computer science, but began with no formal methods experience at all. Some had no technical background. Since there was only one occasion in which a number of people wanted to learn Z at about the same time, the usual pattern was individual learning. The newcomer started reading a Z textbook and asked more experienced people questions whenever something was not clear. They joined the small working group (two to four people) and quickly progressed from observers to active participants. When new features of the language came up, they were explained and discussed to make sure that everyone had the correct understanding. This informal on-the-job training approach has worked quite well. We have never had anyone decide that Z or formal methods were too difficult. Quite the opposite, in fact. Those who have expressed an opinion have said that learning the notation was not as hard as they thought it would be.

Our experience is that writing a good functional specification or system design document in Z is hard work. That is because writing a good functional specification or system design document is hard work. The clarity and organization obtained through using an expressive mathematically based notation such as Z makes the work easier, not harder.

On this project we tried to follow good habits acquired over the years. We think carefully about names and try to use clear helpful names and well chosen abbreviations. We have a house style for notational details such as capitalization. The important point is that both writers and readers of Z benefit greatly from a consistent style. The specific details of the style are not nearly as important as the fact that there is a set of standard conventions. In our finished documents, we adhered strictly to the principle that every Z paragraph was immediately preceded by an accurate English translation. No naked Z allowed.

The order in which we specify different aspects of the system matters. We usually start in the middle. That is, think first about the primary activity of the system when everything is working correctly. Define important data structures, introducing given types and other basic data types as needed. Define operations in the normal, successful case. Usually the inputs, outputs, preconditions, postconditions, and invariants are fairly clear. Then consider all the possible error cases. These are usually associated with the ways in which preconditions on the inputs fail or assumed invariants fail. Finally, combine all the possible cases, correct and faulty.

Since this project was to produce the controller for a crypto system, we had to describe, at a suitable level of abstraction, the main work of the system. On the outbound data path, this includes accepting, filtering and formatting data in the Red Ingress data accelerator, encryption in the encrypt core, and formatting and sending data out in the Black Egress data accelerator. The inbound data path is a mirror image with a decrypt core.

From this basic system analysis, we could see what control data structures had to be provided by the controller to properly manage the system. Basically, the system had to match each incoming piece of user data with the right cryptographic algorithm and key material. Secondary functions such as managing and updating key material were handled next. We had to define a system control protocol to convey system management messages back and forth between the controller and the other subsystems. After specifying this basic functionality of the system and the controller, we worked on the functional description of the subsystems.

This was when we realized that the Ingress data accelerators would also receive data such as new key material addressed to the system itself. This should not be encrypted or decrypted but instead passed to the controller. Similarly, the Egress data accelerators would have to send out data from the controller addressed to external recipients. After finishing all six subsystem specifications, we revisited the combined system level-controller specification to incorporate all the added functionality not previously considered. At this point we have complete and final Z specifications for the six subordinate subsystems and are doing the final revised specification for this version of the controller.

There were two aspects of the Z work on this project which were new to us. Because the encrypt and decrypt core subsystems were being developed by one team, the data accelerators by another team, and only the controller by our team with Rockwell Collins, we decided to write the specifications as separate documents. Actually, the top level system specification and the controller specification were so intertwined, they were in one document. The need to integrate a number of separate specifications was one we had not encountered before. The challenge of keeping all seven specification documents consistent was addressed in two ways. On the conceptual level, the fact that the same people (with one change) wrote all the documents and we were all conscious of the need for consistency was sufficient for us to keep each other honest. We could and did refer to previously written documents to check on details.

Where careful thinking was not sufficient was on the level of small details. Our goal was the possibility of merging (the Z content in) all seven documents into a unified system specification which was syntactically correct, type correct, and semantically correct. This goal could be met only if all the tiny details of spelling, capitalization, presence of underscores, etc. were coordinated to make names intended to have the same meaning in the different documents appear exactly the same and names intended to have different meanings differ in some detail. This is a task for which a computer is far more effective than a whole team of human beings. We took advantage of the capability of Z/EVES to export and import Z between its internal representation and LaTeX mark up. We devised an approach and wrote some Python scripts to automate the process and use Z/EVES to help with the required checking. The new tool support did not eliminate the need for careful thinking and attention to detail, but gave us much greater confidence that we have done things right.

The work described in this paper is all part of an ongoing research program. An early version of a system specification was written over a period of about eighteen months. It consisted of 185 pages of Z and English. Using that document, specifications for the six subordinate subsystems and a lower level communication protocol, totaling 290 pages, were written in about eight months. Finally, a revised controller specification estimated to contain 255 pages of Z and English is being written in about four months. In each case two or three people were involved.

3 Model Based Development

Model-based development (MBD) refers to the use of domain-specific, graphical modeling languages that can be executed and analyzed before the actual system is built. The use of such modeling languages allows the developers to create a model of the system, execute it on their desktop, analyze it with automated tools, and use it to automatically generate code and test cases.

The next section discusses the use of MBD in the HSCC software development process.

3.1 HSCC Software Development Using MBD

Software for the HSCC system was developed in two parts. System software (drivers and interrupt/trap handling) and portions of the high-level application code (message formatting and control processing) were implemented in hand-coded SPARK. This code includes information flow annotations to enable use of the Praxis toolchain and provide assurance of correctness.

Database transactions were designed and developed using the Rockwell Collins MBD tool-chain, Gryphon [12]. Simulink/Stateflow models were created for each database transaction. Each model was then tested via simulation in the Reactis tool to discover and correct obvious errors. When complete, the Gryphon framework is used to translate the model into the Prover tool. Gryphon supports several back-end formal analysis tools, including Prover, NuSMV and ACL2; for this project Prover was deemed to have the best combination of performance and automation. Prover is used to exhaustively verify each transaction preserves properties (derived from Z specifications) about the database it is acting upon. The proven correct Simulink model was then used to generate SPARK-compliant Ada95 for use on the target. Fig. 2 below illustrates the process flow.

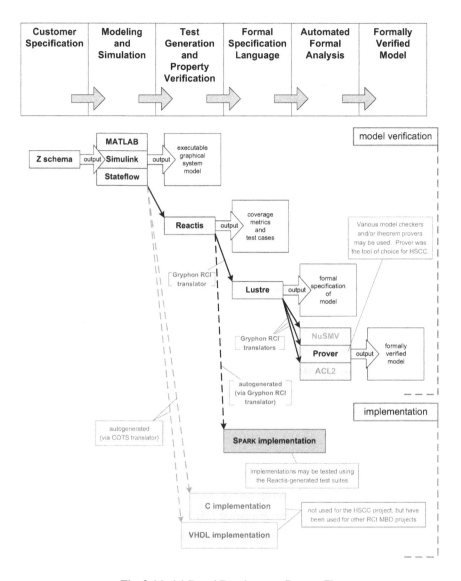

Fig. 2. Model-Based Development Process Flow

The following sections briefly describe each tool involved in the HSCC software development process.

3.1.1 Simulink®, Stateflow®, MATLAB®

Simulink®, Stateflow®, and MATLAB® are products of The MathWorks, Inc. [11] Simulink is an interactive graphical environment for use in the design, simulation, implementation, and testing of dynamic systems. The environment provides a customizable set of block libraries from which the user assembles a system model by selecting and connecting blocks. Blocks may be hierarchically composed from predefined blocks. Simulink was chosen for development because it is the standard model-based development environment at Rockwell Collins and has extensive existing tool support, including support for formal analysis.

3.1.2 Reactis

Reactis® [8], a product of Reactive Systems, Inc., is an automated test generation tool that uses a Simulink/Stateflow model as input and auto-generates test code for the verification of the model. The generated test suites target specific levels of coverage, including state, condition, branch, boundary, and modified condition/decision coverage (MC/DC). Each test case in the generated test suite consists of a sequence of inputs to the model and the generated outputs from the model. Hence, the test suites may be used in testing of the implementation for behavioral conformance to the model, as well as for model testing and debugging.

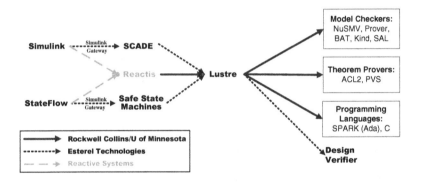

Fig. 3. Rockwell Collins Gryphon Translator Framework

3.1.3 Gryphon

Gryphon [12] refers to the Rockwell Collins tool suite that automatically translates from two popular commercial modeling languages, Simulink/Stateflow® and SCADE™ [3], into several back-end analysis tools, including model-checkers and theorem provers Gryphon also supports code generation into Spark/Ada and C. An overview of the Gryphon framework is shown in Fig. 3. Gryphon uses the Lustre formal specification language (the kernel language of SCADE) as its internal representation. Gryphon has been in development at Rockwell Collins for the last 6 years, and has been used on several significant formal verification efforts involving Simulink models.

3.1.4 Prover

Prover [7] is a best-of-breed commercial model checking tool for analysis of the behavior of software and hardware models. Prover can analyze both finite state models and infinite-state models, that is, models with unbounded integers and real numbers, through the use of integrated decision procedures for real and integer arithmetic.

Prover supports several proof strategies that offer high performance for a number of different analysis tasks including functional verification, test-case generation, and bounded model checking (exhaustive verification to a certain maximum number of execution steps).

3.1.5 Custom Code Generation

By leveraging its existing Gryphon translator framework, Rockwell Collins designed and implemented a tool-chain capable of automatically generating SPARK-compliant Ada95 source code from Simulink/Stateflow models.

3.2 Transaction Development

Simulink/Stateflow models are used as the common starting point for both the implementation and analysis. Each model corresponds to a single database transaction. Model inputs correspond to SPARK procedure "in" parameters and outputs correspond to "out" parameters. Note the database object used by each transaction model may appear as both an input and an output if the database is modified by the transaction. In this case, the database object access appears as an "in out" parameter in the generated code. For each database, one model must be created to initialize the data object, as well as models to perform necessary transactions (add, delete, lookup) on the database. Additional models are required for the formal analysis to model invariants on the database object. This topic will be covered in more detail in subsequent sections.

The screenshot in Fig. 4 below shows a sample Simulink model which contains the "Dest_Encr_Addr_Found" lookup function performed on the Routing Table. This function performs a lookup in the Routing Table to determine if the specified destination encryptor address is found in the table. The inputs (at left) are the routing table ("Rt_Tbl") and the destination encryptor address ("Dest_Encr_Addr") for which to search. The output (at right) is the boolean value ("Found") resulting from the search. The rectangular block in the center is a Simulink subsystem block which implements the database lookup.

Fig. 4. Destination Encryptor Address Found model

Typically, a transaction model will contain a Stateflow chart inside the Simulink model. Stateflow is well-suited to the implementation of the database operations. The screenshot in Fig. 5 below shows the contents of the of the Simulink subsystem block. The heavy vertical bar at the left is a Simulink Bus Selector. Simulink Bus Objects are roughly analogous to a record in Ada or SPARK. (The Reactis tool does not allow Bus Objects as inputs to Stateflow charts, so a Bus Selector is used to separate the

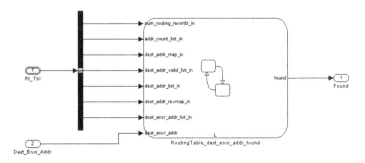

Fig. 5. Sample Simulink Subsystem

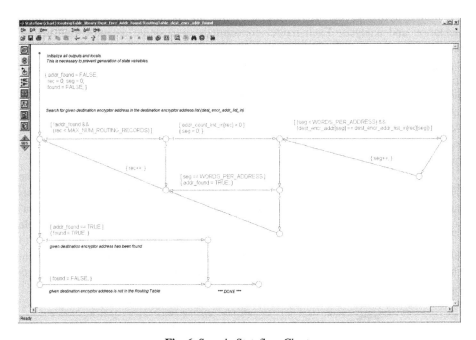

Fig. 6. Sample Stateflow Chart.

component parts of the Bus Object into separate inputs to the Stateflow chart.) The large rounded rectangle block is a Stateflow chart.

Fig. 6 shows the expanded Stateflow chart of the Dest_Encr_Addr_Found model, which implements the database search. Statements are attached to various transitions. Those in curly brackets ("{ }") represent assignment statements. Statements in square brackets ("[ ]") represent conditional expressions. Conditional transitions are executed only if the expression evaluates to "true".

As stated earlier, a model must be built for each transaction in each database. In the case of the Routing Table, these are:

- Init – procedure to initialize the routing table data structure (called upon reset)
- Add – database transaction to add a routing record to the routing table

- Delete – database transaction to remove a routing record from the routing table
- Dest_Encr_Addr_Found – database query to determine existence of destination encryptor address
- Get_Dest_Addr_List – database lookup to return list of addresses mapped to an encryptor address
- Get_Dest_Encr_Addr – database lookup to return encryptor address mapped to a destination address

Fig. 7 below show the interfaces provided by each model, alongside the generated SPARK procedure signature.

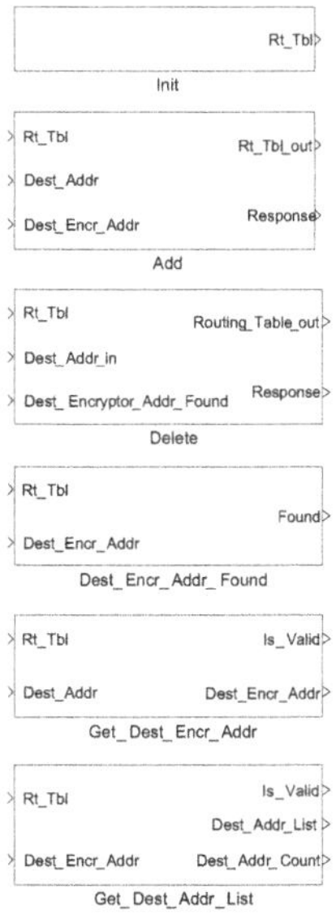


```
procedure Init (
    Rt_Tbl :out    Routing_Table_Types.Routing_Table_Type)
;

procedure Add (
    Rt_Tbl :in out    Routing_Table_Types.Routing_Table_Type ;
    Dest_Addr :in    Routing_Table_Types.Address_Type ;
    Dest_Encryptor_Addr in Rout  ing_Table_Types.Address_Type ;
    Response :out  Unsigned.Word)
;

procedure Delete (
    Rt_Tbl :in out    Routing_Table_Types.Routing_Table_Type ;
    Dest_Addr :in    Routing_Table_Types.Address_Type ;
    Dest_Encryptor_Addr_Found in Boolean ;
    Response :out  Unsigned.Word)
;

procedure Dest_Encr_Addr_Found (
    Rt_Tbl :in    Routing_Table_Types.Routing_Table_Type ;
    Des t_Encr_Addr :in    Routing_Table_Types.Address_Type ;
    Found :out Boolean )
;

procedure Get_Dest_Encr_Addr (
    Rt_Tbl :in    Routing_Table_Types.Routing_Tabe_Type ;
    Dest_Addr :in    Routing_Table_Types.Address_Type ;
    Is_Valid :out  Boolean ;
    Dest_Encr_Addr out    Routing_Table_Types.Address_Type )
;

procedure Get_Dest_Addr_List (
    Rt_Tbl :  in Routing_Table_Types.Routing_Table_Type ;
    Dest_Addr :  in R outing_Table_Types.Address_Type ;
    Is_Valid :  out Boolean ;
    Dest_Addr_List :  out Routing_Table_Types.Dest_Addr_List_Type ;
    Dest_Addr_Count :  out Unsigned.Word)
;
```

Fig. 7. Transaction Models and associated SPARK Signatures

3.3 Invariant Modeling

To perform formal analysis on the transaction models, it is first necessary to model any invariants on the data structures. These invariants are taken directly from the Z specification. As an example, the following invariants appear in the Z specification for the Routing Table:

$$\forall\, kda: knownDestAddresses;\ rr_1, rr_2: routingRecords$$
$$\bullet\ kda \in rr_1.destinationAddresses \wedge kda \in rr_2.destinationAddresses$$
$$\Rightarrow rr_1 = rr_2$$
$$\forall\, rr_1, rr_2: routingRecords$$
$$\bullet\ rr_1.destinationEncryptorAddress = rr_2.destinationEncryptorAddress$$
$$\Rightarrow rr_1 = rr_2$$

Fig. 8. Z Specification Invariant Sample

This specification indicates that no duplicate destination addresses or duplicate encryptor addresses may appear in the Routing Table. These invariants are checked by the "no_dups" model (shown in Fig. 9 below). Given a routing table input ("Rt_Tbl"), the model checks that no duplicate destination encryptor addresses exist in the data structure and sets the output booleans accordingly. Note that the number of boolean outputs in the model is determined by the internal representation of the routing table data structure, and that the condition in which all four boolean outputs are "false" indicates that both invariants hold.

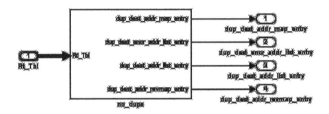

Fig. 9. Sample Invariant Model

3.4 Formal Verification

This section illustrates the approach to performing formal analysis on a database transaction. The necessary models include both the transaction model and any invariant models associated with the relevant database(s). In the formal analysis we are establishing two kinds of properties: 1.) data invariants over the databases (as defined by the Z schemas defining each database) and 2.) transaction requirements that ensure that the operation performed by a model matches the Z schema for that transaction.

3.4.1 Proof Strategy

The proof strategy employed for the data invariants is induction over the sequence of transactions that are performed. We first verify that the Simulink models responsible for initializing each database establish the data invariant for that database. This step provides the basis for our induction. We then prove every transaction that modifies a database maintains the invariant for that database. More concretely, on the "init" models, we use the model checker to determine whether or not the data invariants hold on the model outputs. For the other transactions, the proof strategy is to assume the invariants in the input "pre" database (prior to performing the transaction), and then use the model checker to determine whether the invariants hold in the output "post" database (resulting from performing the transaction).

We prove all the invariants required by the Z specification and also additional invariants involving implementation details related to realizing the Z databases in Simulink/Stateflow. For example, a linked-list representation is used for many of the finite sets described in the Z document. In this case, additional invariants establish that the linked list is a faithful representation of the finite set.

The transaction requirements for each operation are specified as additional properties that must hold on the "post" database. For example, when deleting an element, these properties ensure that the element in question has been removed from the database.

3.4.2 Stateless Transactions

Transactions on HSCC databases (and transactional database systems in general) are designed to perform a complete unit of work, or fail without making any modifications to the database. This indicates that each transaction can be developed without the use of internal state. It is this property of transactional databases that greatly simplifies the model-checking effort, because proofs can be obtained using just bounded model-checking to depth 1, instead of (for example) automated k-inductive reasoning. Taking advantage of this property made the most difficult proof obligations tractable, and reduced the time of simpler proofs from hours to minutes.

3.4.3 Routing Table Example

As an example, we present the proof system for the DeleteRoutingEntry transaction, which deletes an entry from a routing record in the routing table. The Z schema which specifies the RoutingTable is shown below in Fig. 10. The specification describes the contents of the database, the maximum size of the database, and further constraints on the data (no duplicate addresses, as discussed previously).

$$
\begin{array}{l}
\underline{RoutingTable}\\
routingRecords: \mathbb{F}\ RoutingRecord\\
knownDestAddresses: \mathbb{F}\ NETWORK\_ADDRESS\\
maxNumRoutingRecords: \mathbb{N}\\
\hline
\# \ routingRecords \leqslant maxNumRoutingRecords\\
knownDestAddresses = \cup \{\ rt: routingRecords \bullet rt.destinationAddresses\ \}\\
\forall\ kda: knownDestAddresses;\ rr_1,\ rr_2: routingRecords\\
\quad \bullet\ kda \in rr_1.destinationAddresses \wedge kda \in rr_2.destinationAddresses\\
\quad \Rightarrow rr_1 = rr_2\\
\forall\ rr_1,\ rr_2: routingRecords\\
\quad \bullet\ rr_1.destinationEncryptorAddress = rr_2.destinationEncryptorAddress\\
\quad \Rightarrow rr_1 = rr_2
\end{array}
$$

Fig. 10. Z specification of the Routing Table database

For a complete understanding of the proof strategy, it is necessary to present the underlying representation of the Routing Table, shown in Fig. 11.

The number of routing records currently in the database is represented as "num_routing_records". The "addr_count_list" array maintains the number of valid destination addresses, on a "per routing record" basis. The "dest_addr_map" 2-D array holds pointers to the destination addresses. Each row corresponds to a routing record. The "dest_encr_addr_list" contains the destination encryptor addresses (one per routing record). Since an "address" may be a IPv4 or IPv6, this array is sized to contain eight 16-bit values. Taken collectively, a slice across the three arrays (addr_count_list, dest_addr_map, and dest_encr_addr_list), as shown by the dashed arrows, represents a single routing record, which comprises one or more destination addresses mapped to a single destination address. Since 3-D arrays are not supported by the toolchain (specifically, not by Reactis), a mapping array is used. The dest_addr_map array contains

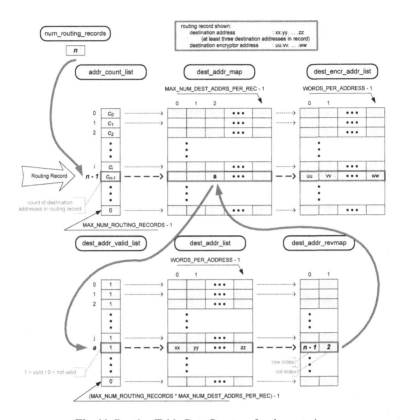

Fig. 11. Routing Table Data Structure Implementation

not the actual destination address, but rather an index into another array which holds all of the known destination addresses. Together, the "dest_addr_valid_list" array and the "dest_addr_list" array form the list of known destination addresses. The dest_addr_ valid_list is an array of booleans, indicating whether the corresponding row of the dest_addr_list array contains a known address. (Note that all-zeros is accommodated as a valid address, so a valid flag must accompany the list of addresses.) As with the dest_encr_addr_list array, the dest_addr_list is sized to hold either an IPv4 or IPv6 address (eight 16-bit values). In order to support reverse lookups (destination encryptor address → destination address), we employ a mapping array which contains the row and column indices (into the dest_addr_map array) for a given destination address. Constant array bounds are indicated in the figure. The maximum number of routing records in the table is defined as MAX_NUM_ROUTING_RECORDS. The maximum number of destination addresses mapped to a destination encryptor address is MAX_NUM_DEST_ADDRS_PER_REC. The number of values required to represent the largest address (IPv6, in the current implementation) is WORDS_PER_ ADDRESS.

The transaction to be model-checked in this example will be the DeleteRoutingEntry transaction. Its Z specification is shown in Fig. 12.

$\underline{\quad DeleteRoutingEntry}$_____
$\Delta RoutingTable$
$ControlDB$
$destinationAddress?: NETWORK\_ADDRESS$
$modRoutingRecord, delRoutingRecord: RoutingRecord$
$response!: Response$
_____

$destinationAddress? \in knownDestAddresses$
$delRoutingRecord$
$\quad = (\mu\ rr: routingRecords \mid destinationAddress? \in rr.destinationAddresses)$
$\# delRoutingRecord.destinationAddresses \geqslant 2$
$\Rightarrow modRoutingRecord.destinationAddresses$
$\quad = delRoutingRecord.destinationAddresses \setminus \{destinationAddress?\}$
$\quad \wedge modRoutingRecord.destinationEncryptorAddress$
$\qquad = delRoutingRecord.destinationEncryptorAddress$
$\quad \wedge routingRecords' = routingRecords \setminus \{delRoutingRecord\} \cup \{modRoutingRecord\}$
$\# delRoutingRecord.destinationAddresses = 1$
$\wedge delRoutingRecord.destinationEncryptorAddress$
$\quad \notin \{\ cr: controlRecords \cdot cr.destinationEncryptorAddress\ \}$
$\Rightarrow routingRecords' = routingRecords \setminus \{delRoutingRecord\}$
$response! = success$

Fig. 12. Z Specification of DeleteRoutingEntry

From the specification of the DeleteRoutingEntry function, the inputs are the routing table object, the destination address (the address to be deleted), and a boolean ("Dest_Encryptor_Addr_Found") which indicates whether the destination encryptor address (mapped to the destination address) exists in the Control database. (This lookup is performed by the caller of the DeleteRoutingEntry function.) Although the Z specification is for only the successful case (error cases are handled in separate schemas), the model must properly trap and handle all error cases. The RoutingTable Delete model is shown in Fig. 13 below. Outputs are the updated routing table object ("Routing_Table_out") and the response code ("Response"). Note that this is the same Simulink model (Delete.mdl) used for code generation. The model for the invariant discussed previously is also shown in Fig. 13. This model checks for any duplicate entries in the routing table.

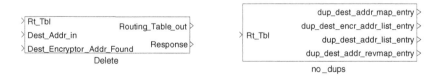

Fig. 13. DeleteRoutingEntry Model and "no_dups" Invariant Model

Given the underlying representation of the routing table, additional invariants must be constructed to complete the infrastructure for model verification. One such model, "is_consistent" determines whether the database is in a valid, consistent state. For example, checks are performed to ensure that each "count" value (e.g. num_routing_records, addr_count_list array elements) is within valid bounds. Mapping array elements are checked to ensure they point to valid entries in their target arrays. Finally, all unused array elements are checked to ensure they have been cleared (set to zero) by any previous Delete operations. (The data structure is initialized to all zeros upon reset by calling an "init" function.) The "is_consistent" model is shown in Fig. 14 below.

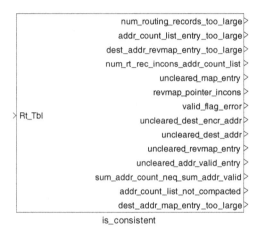

Fig. 14. Routing Table "is_consistent" Invariant Model

Since the Delete operation removes at most one destination address, the resulting routing table must be a subset of the original table. A transaction requirement model has been constructed to check that the "post" routing table object is a subset of the "pre" object. The t2_contains_tl model shown in Fig. 15 checks if Rt_Tbl_2 "contains" Rt_Tbl_1, and sets the output boolean ("t2_contains_t1") accordingly. Additionally, the model returns the difference in counts (of destination addresses) between the two input routing table objects.

Finally, the resulting routing table must not contain the destination address which was to be deleted. The "address_deleted" requirement model in Fig. 15 checks for the existence of the specified address and returns a boolean result.

Fig. 15. Routing Table "t2_contains_t1" and "address_deleted" Invariant models

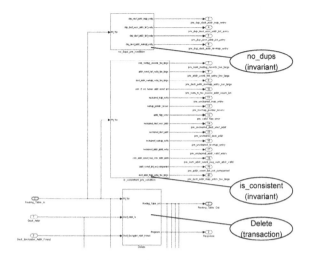

Fig. 16. Sample Formal Analysis Model (part 1)

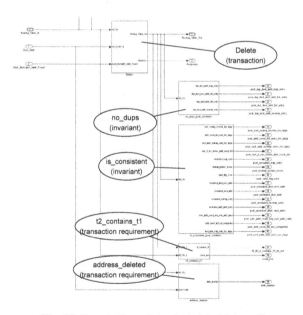

Fig. 17. Sample Formal Analysis Model (part 2)

Given the transaction model, the collection of invariant models, and the transaction requirement models, the approach is to assume the data invariants hold prior to performing the Delete operation, and then verify that the invariants and transaction requirement models hold following the Delete operation. The proof model is shown in Fig. 16 and Fig. 17. Due to the size of the model, the screenshot has been split into two parts for better readability.

Fig. 16 shows the preconditions portion of the proof model. This contains the delete transaction model along with the invariants which are assumed to be true for the "pre" table, namely the "no_dups" (check for duplicated addresses) and "is_consistent" (check for a valid, consistent state).

Fig. 17 shows the postconditions portion of the proof model. This includes the delete model and the invariants which are to be verified against the resulting routing table. The invariants are "no_dups", "is_consistent", "t2_contains_t1", and "address_deleted". If all these invariants are true (i.e. the post-conditions are true), then the correctness of the delete operation is verified.

The model-hierarchy used to perform the proof analysis is translated to the Prover imperative language using the Gryphon translation framework and discharged by the Prover model checker.

3.4.4 Formal Verification Results Summary

The formal verification effort for the project as a whole resulted in the proof of some 840 properties for the HSCC databases, of which 140 were written by the verification team, and the remainder (mainly well-formedness checks) automatically generated by the Gryphon framework. Verification required less than 5% of total project effort over the course of seven calendar months.

3.4.5 Caveat

Due to the demands of a fully-functioning cryptographic system, it will be necessary to populate databases with hundreds, if not thousands of elements. The extreme size of these databases makes model-checking the fully-sized system impossible, due to state-space explosion. Instead, in this effort, a small representative sized database (n=3) was verified in formal analysis. The design of each transaction model allows the user to configure the size of a database to be configured at compile time with a global variable. The claim can be made this is sufficient, due to the design of the database transaction models, however no attempt to prove this claim have been made. Future work at Rockwell Collins will be focused on proving this claim, and it will be discussed further in the Future Work section of this document.

3.5 Code Generation

Code generation is performed after a transaction is proven to satisfy all of its invariant properties. This is accomplished through the use of a proprietary translation tool that leverages the existing Gryphon framework to generate SPARK-compliant Ada95 source code for use on the AAMP7G.

All of the transactions are compiled into single Ada95 package for use by the system programmer. The procedures in the package declaration are shown in Fig. 7.

4 Future Work

Whenever all the subsystems are available, NSA researchers will integrate them into a demonstration system. We also plan to organize the assurance evidence produced in this phase and ask our evaluation organization for their assessment. We won't get a full evaluation of our prototype system, but expect to get expert advice on possible areas for improvement to our assurance case. Depending on available resources, we plan to add functionality missing from the current system. For example, this version can use connections to peer system established and entered by hand. A full system must be capable of automatically establishing and tearing down connections as needed. For another example, this version manages cryptographic key material internally, including limited key update capability. It does not have the capability of requesting and receiving new key material from an external source. This capability would be essential in a real system.

Rockwell Collins will continue this research initiative by investigating two key issues.

The selection of Simulink/Reactis tool-chain caused considerable difficulty due to the lack of an orthogonal type system: Simulink currently does not support arrays of record-types (called *buses* in Simulink). Reactis further restricts the type system by only supporting arrays of one or two dimensions. Consequently, databases could not be designed in an intuitive way, simply to satisfy the Simulink type system. This factor drove up transaction development time, increased the number and complexity of proof obligations, and hampered the development of the proprietary code generator. SCADE, by Esterel Technologies, is a model-development environment similar to Simulink, but features an orthogonal type system, and fits directly into the Gryphon toolchain off the shelf. A comparison of the transaction development process with both Simulink/Reactis and SCADE tool-chains would reveal whether or not the use of SCADE results in significant reductions in development time and cost.

Each transaction was checked to satisfy invariants over a finite-sized database. This partial proof provides a high degree of assurance, however it would be ideal to obtain a proof that each transaction satisfies invariants over databases of arbitrary length. One major obstacle to obtaining this general proof is the use of various FOR loops within each transaction to traverse the elements of a database. Because these loops are typically limited by constants defined at compile time, it would be necessary to prove these loops preserve the transaction invariant over an arbitrary number of iterations. Software model-checkers, such as SLAM by Microsoft, handle this problem with some degree of success. Research would focus on techniques employed by software model-checkers to overcome this problem.

5 Conclusion

Our experiences developing the HSCC system have shown that the methodology described in this paper is a viable process for the development of high-assurance software for use in cryptographic systems.

NSA-provided specifications written in the Z formal notation proved to be superior to those written in English-language in producing a complete and unambiguous set of software requirements. Using these specifications as the main development artifact, Rockwell Collins was able to quickly and accurately determine the necessary pre and post conditions for each database transaction.

The use of a model-based approach to transaction development provides early simulation capabilities, leading to earlier discovery of errors in both the specification and in the implementation. The use of automated code generation removes the possibility of human coding errors. The application of automated model checkers provides a proof of correctness at a level unattainable through traditional software testing methods. With all of these components in our software development approach, we have exercised a viable methodology to deliver high-assurance software with a much greater level of confidence than software developed through traditional approaches.

The use of SPARK information flow annotations for Ada95 code at the system level provides assurance the system code is properly routing information to each of the devices in the HSCC architecture. Hardware enforced (AAMP7G partitioning) red/black separation serves as the final sentinel in preventing unintended red/black communication. In our judgment, the methodology described in this paper is sturdy enough to support full EAL-7 certification of a production encryptor based on this research prototype.

Despite the apparent advantages of the proposed methodology, some aspects of the approach need further development before the methodology can readily be employed.

The most serious limitation is the relatively poor support in portions of the toolchain for composite data structures. For many of the databases in the HSCC system, multi-dimensional arrays would have been the natural representation chosen, had Reactis allowed their use. Instead, multiple two-dimensional arrays were used, leading to a more complex implementation and an increased burden in development of the proof infrastructure models. Arrays of structures would have been a natural choice to represent some of the databases, but Simulink does not support such data structures. The use of the SCADE tool, or improvements to the Mathworks tool-suite may address some or all of these issues.

Another limitation is the relatively small size of databases for which transaction proofs are able to be obtained. Further research will look into identifying methods to leverage existing transaction proofs to obtain general proofs of arbitrarily sized databases.

References

1. AdaCore Inc, Tokeneer product description at AdaCore,
   http://www.adacore.com/home/products/sparkpro/tokeneer/
2. Barnes, J., Chapman, R., Johnson, R., Widmaier, J., Cooper, D., Everett, W.: Engineering the Tokeneer Enclave Protection Software. In: Proceedings of IEEE International Symposium on Secure Software Engineering (ISSSE) (2006)
3. Esterel Technologies, Inc., SCADE Suite product description,
   http://www.esterel-technologies.com/products/scade-suite
4. Greve, D., Richards, R., Wilding, M.: A Summary of Intrinsic Partitioning Verification. In: Proceedings of ACL 2004, Austin, TX (November 2004)
5. Hardin, D.: Invited Tutorial: Considerations in the Design and Verification of Microprocessors for Safety-Critical and Security-Critical Applications. In: Cimatti, A., Jones, R. (eds.) Proceedings of the Eighth International Conference on Formal Methods in Computer-Aided Design (FMCAD 2008), pp. 1–8 (November 2008)
6. McComb, T., Wildman, L.: Verifying Abstract Information Flow Properties in Fault Tolerant Security Devices. In: Liu, Z., He, J. (eds.) ICFEM 2006. LNCS, vol. 4260, pp. 621–638. Springer, Heidelberg (2006)
7. Prover Technologies, Inc. Prover SL/DE plug-in product description,
   http://www.prover.com/products/prover_plugin

8. Reactive Systems, Inc. Reactis product description,
   http://www.reactive-systems.com

9. Saaltink, M.: The Z/EVES System. In: Bowen, J.P., Hinchey, M.G., Till, D. (eds.) ZUM 1997. LNCS, vol. 1212, pp. 72–86. Springer, Heidelberg (1997)

10. Spivey, J.M.: The Z Notation: A Reference Manual, 2nd edn. International Series in Computer Science. Prentice Hall, Englewood Cliffs (1992)

11. The Mathworks, Inc., Simulink product description,
   http://www.mathworks.com/Simulink

12. Whalen, M., Cofer, D., Miller, S., Krogh, B.H., Storm, W.: Integration of formal analysis into a model-based software development process. In: Leue, S., Merino, P. (eds.) FMICS 2007. LNCS, vol. 4916, pp. 68–84. Springer, Heidelberg (2008)

Bounded Semantics of CTL and SAT-Based Verification⋆

Wenhui Zhang

Laboratory of Computer Science
Institute of Software, Chinese Academy of Sciences
P.O.Box 8718, Beijing 100080, China
zwh@ios.ac.cn

Abstract. Bounded model checking has been proposed as a complementary approach to BDD based symbolic model checking for combating the state explosion problem, esp. for efficient error detection. This has led to a lot of successful work with respect to error detection in the checking of LTL, ACTL (the universal fragment of CTL) and ACTL* properties by satisfiability testing. The use of bounded model checking for verification (in contrast to error detection) of LTL and ACTL properties has later also been studied. This paper studies the potentials and limitations of bounded model checking for the verification of CTL and CTL* formulas. On the theoretical side, we first provide a framework for discussion of bounded semantics, which serves as the basis for bounded model checking, then extend the bounded semantics of ACTL to a bounded semantics of CTL, and discuss the limitation of developing such a bounded semantics for CTL*. On the practical side, a deduction of a SAT-based bounded model checking approach for ACTL properties from the bounded semantics of CTL is demonstrated, and a comparison of such an approach with BDD-based model checking is presented based on experimental results.

1 Introduction

Bounded semantics of LTL with existential interpretation and that of ECTL (the existential fragment of CTL), and the characterization of these existentially interpreted properties have been studied and used as the theoretical basis for SAT-based bounded model checking [3,21]. This has led to successful works with respect to error detection in the checking of LTL and ACTL (the universal fragment of CTL) properties by satisfiability testing [2]. It is considered as a complementary technique to BDD-based model checking [5,4,20,7] for combating the state explosion problem [6], esp. for efficient error detection [22]. Bounded semantics of existential LTL and that of ECTL, and the characterization of such properties are consistent with the fact that the witness of the properties can be searched within a fragment of the valid paths. For verification purposes, one need to reach a completeness threshold or some termination

---

⋆ Supported by the National Natural Science Foundation of China under Grant No. 60573012, 60721061 and 60833001.

K. Breitman and A. Cavalcanti (Eds.): ICFEM 2009, LNCS 5885, pp. 286–305, 2009.

criteria [17,9,16,10,1] in order to show the non-existence of a counter-example. This may not be as efficient. On the other hand, the principle of bounded model checking for verification (called bounded verification for short) should be similar to bounded error detection, such that we start with a small bounded model, if this is not sufficient, we increase the bound, until we have a conclusion or we run out of resources. With this principle in mind, bounded verification should check whether every representative part (a k-path or a set of such paths) of the system satisfies some property, and according to this, conclude whether the system satisfies this property. Bounded verification of general LTL formulas has been considered in [27], which can equivalently be formulated as that a model satisfies an LTL formula φ if there is a k-model (a restricted model where all paths are truncated to only have k transitions) such that every k-path starting with some initial state satisfies φ. The paper provides a sufficient condition (not a sufficient and necessary condition) and has discussed that in some special cases such as when dealing with LTL formulas restricted to pUq, the sufficient condition is actually a sufficient and necessary condition (for formulas of the form Fp, a similar characterization is already known [2]). Similar ideas have then been applied to ACTL formulas [28] and a similar result was obtained, and an implementation with experimental results was reported in [26]. These approaches for verification of LTL and ACTL formulas are based on bounded semantics of existential LTL and ECTL with some kinds of weakening, which result in an incomplete bounded characterization (i.e. with only a sufficient condition) of LTL and ACTL formulas. This problem has then been studied in [29] and a bounded semantics for ACTL and a characterization of ACTL properties by propositional formulas were provided. An improvement of the SAT-based encoding of the verification problem was considered in [8].

In this paper, on the theoretical side, we first propose a framework for discussion of bounded semantics, then extend the bounded semantics of ACTL to a sound and complete bounded semantics of CTL, and show that there is no such sound and complete semantics for CTL* in the given framework. On the practical side, we apply the bounded semantics of CTL to derive a SAT-based characterization of ACTL properties, and compare such a characterization with BDD based verification approaches.

2   Bounded Semantics

In this section, we provide a framework for discussion of bounded semantics. The framework defines some properties of bounded semantics.

A Kripke structure is a quadruple $M = \langle S, T, I, L \rangle$ where S is a set of states, $T \subseteq S \times S$ is a transition relation which is total, $I \subseteq S$ is a set of initial states and $L : S \rightarrow 2^{AP}$ is a labeling function that maps each state to a subset of propositions of AP.

An infinite path $\pi = \pi_0 \pi_1 \cdots$ of M is an infinite sequence of states such that $(\pi_i, \pi_{i+1}) \in T$ for all $i \geq 0$. A finite path π of M is a finite prefix of an infinite path of M. Given a path $\pi = \pi_0 \pi_1 \cdots$, we use π^i to denote the subpath of π

starting at π_i, use $\pi(s)$ to denote a path with $\pi_0 = s$. Then $\exists \pi(s).\varphi$ means that there is a path π with $\pi_0 = s$ such that φ holds, and $\forall \pi(s).\varphi$ means that for every path π with $\pi_0 = s$, φ holds.

Semantics of temporal logics is defined with respect to Kripke structures. For brevity, a Kripke structure is called a model. We require a semantic relation to be compositional. We first define what we mean by compositionality with respect to path quantifiers (universal and existential) and with respect to propositional connectives (conjunction and disjunction).

Definition 1 (Compositionality w.r.t. Path Quantifiers). *Let M be a model and s be a state. Let $\models$ be a relation defined for path formulas and state formulas. The relation $\models$ is compositional with respect to path quantifiers, if the following hold:*

- *$M, s \models A\varphi$ iff $M, \pi(s) \models \varphi$ for all $\pi(s)$ of M.*
- *$M, s \models E\varphi$ iff $M, \pi(s) \models \varphi$ for some $\pi(s)$ of M.*

Let a *structure* be either a combination of M and a state or of M and a path (either a finite one or an infinite one).

Definition 2 (Compositionality w.r.t. Prop. Connectives). *Let S be a structure. Let $\models$ be a relation. The relation $\models$ is compositional with respect to propositional connectives, if the following hold:*

- *$S \models \varphi \vee \psi$ iff $S \models \varphi$ or $S \models \psi$*
- *$S \models \varphi \wedge \psi$ iff $S \models \varphi$ and $S \models \psi$*

The compositionality property is a formalization of the standard understanding of the path quantifiers and the propositional connectives. In addition, we formulate a consistency property with respect to the labeling at given positions (in a sequence of states).

Definition 3 (Consistency w.r.t. Labeling). *Let M be a model and s be a state. Let $\models$ be a relation defined for path formulas and state formulas. Let X be the next-time operator. Let p be a proposition. The relation $\models$ satisfies the consistency property, if the following hold:*

- *$M, s \models p$ iff $p \in L(s)$.*
- *$M, \pi \models X^n p$ iff $p \in L(\pi_n)$ when π_n is the $(n+1)$-th state of π.*

A simple compositional semantic relation is a relation which is compositional with respect to both propositional connectives and path quantifiers (whenever applicable) and satisfies the consistency property. For brevity, such a relation is called a *simple relation*. A compositional semantic relation is either a simple compositional semantic relation or a propositional combination of such relations. For brevity, such a relation is called a *semantic relation*.

Without loss of generality, a propositional combination of simple relations may be written as a disjunction of conjunctions of such relations, for instance, a semantic relation $\models$ may be written as $\bigvee_{i=1}^{m} \bigwedge_{j=1}^{n} \models_{i,j}$. Then $S \models \varphi$ iff there is an i such that $S \models_{i,j} \varphi$ holds for all j.

A bounded semantics is then represented by a family of semantic relations each defined on a bounded structure with a parameter indicating the bound. Let us call such a structure a k-structure.

Definition 4 (Soundness and Completeness). *Let $\mathcal{S}_k$ be a k-structure of $\mathcal{S}$. The bounded semantics defined by $\models_k$ is sound and complete with respect to a given relation $\models$, iff the following hold:*

- *(Soundness) If $\mathcal{S}_k \models_k \varphi$ for some $k \geq 0$, then $\mathcal{S} \models \varphi$.*
- *(Completeness) If $\mathcal{S} \models \varphi$, then there is a $k \geq 0$ such that $\mathcal{S}_k \models_k \varphi$.*

Remark. The purpose of this framework is to formalize the usual understanding of good bounded semantics. It excludes some definitions from being considered as semantic definitions, for instance, the following one: $M, s \models A\varphi$ iff $L(\mathcal{A}(M, s)) \subseteq L(\mathcal{A}(\varphi))$ where $L(\mathcal{A}(M, s))$ and $L(\mathcal{A}(\varphi))$ are the languages of the automata constructed from respectively the structure M, s and the LTL formula φ, because it does not comply with compositionality and lacks good characteristics of a semantic definition of temporal logics. For the definition of the semantics of $M, s \models A\varphi$, it is reasonable to look for other kinds of definitions (with good structure and intuition).

3   On CTL

In this section, we provide a bounded semantics for CTL, and formulate a bounded model checking and verification principle for CTL properties.

Computation tree logic (CTL) is a propositional branching-time temporal logic [13] introduced by Emerson and Clarke as a specification language for finite state systems. Let AP be a set of propositional symbols. The set of CTL formulas is defined as follows:

Every member of AP is a CTL formula.
The logical connectives of CTL are: $\neg$, $\wedge$, and $\vee$.
If φ and ψ are CTL formulas, then so are:
$\neg\varphi$, $\varphi \wedge \psi$, and $\varphi \vee \psi$.
The temporal operators are: EX, ER, EU, AX, AR, and AU.
If φ and ψ are CTL formulas, then so are:
$EX\,\varphi$, $EF\,\varphi$, $EG\,\varphi$, $E(\varphi\,R\,\psi)$, $E(\varphi\,U\,\psi)$, $AX\,\varphi$, $AF\,\varphi$, $AG\,\varphi$, $A(\varphi\,R\,\psi)$, and $A(\varphi\,U\,\psi)$.

3.1   Semantics of CTL

Let M be a model, s a state, φ a CTL formula. The relation that φ holds on s in M is denoted $M, s \models \varphi$.

Definition 5 (Semantics of CTL). *Let p be a propositional symbol, φ and ψ CTL formulas. Let $\pi = \pi_0\pi_1\cdots$ denote an infinite path of M. The relation $M, s \models \varphi$ is defined as follows.*

$M, s \models p$	iff $p \in L(s)$
$M, s \models \neg\varphi$	iff $M, s \not\models \varphi$
$M, s \models \varphi \wedge \psi$	iff $(M, s \models \varphi)$ and $(M, s \models \psi)$
$M, s \models \varphi \vee \psi$	iff $(M, s \models \varphi)$ or $(M, s \models \psi)$
$M, s \models AX\varphi$	iff $\forall\pi(s).(M, \pi_1 \models \varphi)$
$M, s \models AF\psi$	iff $\forall\pi(s).(\exists k \geq 0.(M, \pi_k \models \psi)$
$M, s \models AG\psi$	iff $\forall\pi(s).(\forall k \geq 0.(M, \pi_k \models \psi)$
$M, s \models A(\varphi U \psi)$	iff $\forall\pi(s).(\exists k \geq 0.(M, \pi_k \models \psi \wedge \forall j < k.(M, \pi_j \models \varphi)))$
$M, s \models A(\varphi R \psi)$	iff $\forall\pi(s).(\forall k \geq 0.(M, \pi_k \models \psi \vee \exists j < k.(M, \pi_j \models \varphi)))$
$M, s \models EX\varphi$	iff $\exists\pi(s).(M, \pi_1 \models \varphi)$
$M, s \models EF\psi$	iff $\exists\pi(s).(\exists k \geq 0.(M, \pi_k \models \psi)$
$M, s \models EG\psi$	iff $\exists\pi(s).(\forall k \geq 0.(M, \pi_k \models \psi)$
$M, s \models E(\varphi U \psi)$	iff $\exists\pi(s).(\exists k \geq 0.(M, \pi_k \models \psi \wedge \forall j < k.(M, \pi_j \models \varphi)))$
$M, s \models E(\varphi R \psi)$	iff $\exists\pi(s).(\forall k \geq 0.(M, \pi_k \models \psi \vee \exists j < k.(M, \pi_j \models \varphi)))$

A CTL formula is in negation normal form (NNF), if the symbol $\neg$ is applied only to propositional symbols. Every formula can be transformed into an equivalent formula in NNF. The sublogic ACTL is the subset of CTL formulas that can be transformed into NNF formulas such that the temporal operators are restricted to $\{AX, AF, AG, AU, AR\}$. The sublogic ECTL is the subset of CTL formulas that can be transformed into NNF formulas such that the temporal operators are restricted to $\{EX, EF, EG, EU, ER\}$.

Definition 6. *Let φ be an ACTL formula. φ is true in M, denoted $M \models \varphi$, iff φ is true at all initial states of M.*

Definition 7. *Let φ be an ECTL formula. φ is true in M, denoted $M \models \varphi$, iff φ is true at some initial states of M.*

3.2   Bounded Semantics of CTL

Since every CTL formula can be transformed into an equivalent formula in NNF, we only consider formulas in NNF. Therefore, in the following, a formula refers to such a CTL formula unless otherwise stated. For simplicity, we fix the model under consideration to be $M = \langle S, T, I, L \rangle$, and in the sequel, M refers to this model, unless otherwise stated.

k-Path. Let $k \geq 0$. A k-path of M is a finite path of M with length $k + 1$. π is a k-path, if $\pi = \pi_0 \cdots \pi_k$ such that $\pi_i \in S$ for $i = 0, ..., k$ and $(\pi_i, \pi_{i+1}) \in T$ for $i = 0, ..., k - 1$. A k-path may start at anywhere in the model. For the idea of a k-path, the reader is referred to [3].

Bounded Model. The k-model of M is a structure $M_k = \langle S, Ph_k, I, L \rangle$ where Ph_k is the set of all different k-paths of M. M_k can be considered as an approximation of M. For the idea of a bounded model, the reader is referred to [21].

Loop. A loop is a k-path π such that $\pi_i = \pi_j$ for some $0 \leq i < j \leq k$. Let $lp(\pi)$ denote that π is a loop. An important property of a loop is that if π is a prefix of π', then $lp(\pi) \rightarrow lp(\pi')$. Note that this notation of loop is different from the one defined in [3], which is a loop such that the last element has a successor to some element in the loop. Such a loop does not have the property stated above.

Definition 8 (Bounded Semantics of CTL). *Let M_k be the k-model of M, s a state, p a propositional symbol, φ and ψ CTL formulas. The relation that φ holds on s in M_k is denoted $M_k, s \models \varphi$. Let $\pi = \pi_0 \cdots \pi_k$ denote a k-path of Ph_k. The relation $\models$ is defined as follows.*

$M_k, s \models p$ iff
$p \in L(s)$
$M_k, s \models \neg p$ iff
$p \notin L(s)$
$M_k, s \models \varphi \wedge \psi$ iff
$(M_k, s \models \varphi)$ and $(M_k, s \models \psi)$
$M_k, s \models \varphi \vee \psi$ iff
$(M_k, s \models \varphi)$ or $(M_k, s \models \psi)$
$M_k, s \models AX\varphi$ iff
$k \geq 1 \wedge \forall \pi(s).(M_k, \pi_1 \models \varphi)$
$M_k, s \models AF\psi$ iff
$\forall \pi(s).(\exists i \leq k.(M_k, \pi_i \models \psi))$
$M_k, s \models AG\psi$ iff
$\forall \pi(s).(lp(\pi) \wedge (\forall i \leq k.(M_k, \pi_i \models \psi)))$
$M_k, s \models A(\varphi U \psi)$ iff
$\forall \pi(s).(\exists i \leq k.(M_k, \pi_i \models \psi \wedge \forall j < i.(M_k, \pi_j \models \varphi)))$
$M_k, s \models A(\varphi R \psi)$ iff
$\forall \pi(s).(\forall i \leq k.(M_k, \pi_i \models \psi \vee \exists j < i.(M_k, \pi_j \models \varphi)) \wedge$
$(\exists j \leq k.(M_k, \pi_j \models \varphi) \vee lp(\pi)))$
$M_k, s \models EX\varphi$ iff
$k \geq 1 \wedge \exists \pi(s).(M_k, \pi_1 \models \varphi)$
$M_k, s \models EF\psi$ iff
$\exists \pi(s).(\exists i \leq k.(M_k, \pi_i \models \psi))$
$M_k, s \models EG\psi$ iff
$\exists \pi(s).(lp(\pi) \wedge (\forall i \leq k.(M_k, \pi_i \models \psi)))$
$M_k, s \models E(\varphi U \psi)$ iff
$\exists \pi(s).(\exists i \leq k.(M_k, \pi_i \models \psi \wedge \forall j < i.(M_k, \pi_j \models \varphi)))$
$M_k, s \models E(\varphi R \psi)$ iff
$\exists \pi(s).(\forall i \leq k.(M_k, \pi_i \models \psi \vee \exists j < i.(M_k, \pi_j \models \varphi)) \wedge$
$(\exists j \leq k.(M_k, \pi_j \models \varphi) \vee lp(\pi)))$

This semantics of CTL is an extension of the ACTL bounded semantics given in [29]. Note that an extension of the ECTL and ECTL* bounded semantics given in [21] to a bounded semantics of CTL* has been done in [23], however the bounded semantics given in [23] is not regarded as a sound one within our framework[1]. We establish that for CTL, the bounded semantics given above is sound by first presenting some lemmas.

Lemma 1. *If $M_k, s \models \varphi$, then $M_{k+1}, s \models \varphi$.*

A formal proof is to be based on structural induction. The main arguments are explained as follows. For the first, we observe that every k-path in M_k is a prefix of a path in M_{k+1}, and every $(k + 1)$-path in M_{k+1} is an extension of a path in M_k. By looking at the definition, we can be assured that there is no problem in the cases of AX, AF, AU, EX, EF, EU. By recognizing that the semantics of AG and EG can be derived from that of AR and ER (also in this bounded semantics), we only need to look further at the two cases AR and ER. We first consider the case of AR. Suppose that $M_k, s \models A(\varphi R \psi)$ holds and $M_{k+1}, s \models A(\varphi R \psi)$ does not hold. Then there is a $\pi(s)$ such that

$$\forall i \leq k + 1.(M_{k+1}, \pi_i \models \psi \vee \exists j < i.(M_{k+1}, \pi_j \models \varphi))$$
$$\wedge (\exists j \leq k + 1.(M_{k+1}, \pi_j \models \varphi) \vee lp(\pi))$$

(denote hereafter by (*)) does not hold. Let π' be the k-path that is at the same time a prefix of π. If $lp(\pi')$ does not hold, then $\forall i \leq k.(M_k, \pi_i \models \psi \vee \exists j < i.(M_k, \pi_j \models \varphi)) \wedge (\exists j \leq k.(M_k, \pi_j \models \varphi))$ holds. Then by the induction hypothesis, we have $\forall i \leq k.(M_{k+1}, \pi_i \models \psi \vee \exists j < i.(M_{k+1}, \pi_j \models \varphi)) \wedge (\exists j \leq k.(M_{k+1}, \pi_j \models \varphi))$. This contradicts to that (*) does not hold. If $lp(\pi')$ holds, then $\forall i \leq k.(M_k, \pi_i \models \psi \vee \exists j < i.(M_k, \pi_j \models \varphi)) \wedge lp(\pi')$ holds. Similarly, by the induction hypothesis, we have $\forall i \leq k.(M_{k+1}, \pi_i \models \psi \vee \exists j < i.(M_{k+1}, \pi_j \models \varphi))$ and since $lp(\pi')$ implies $lp(\pi)$, the only possible case that may fail (*) is that $(M_{k+1}, \pi_{k+1} \models \psi \vee \exists j < k + 1.(M_{k+1}, \pi_j \models \varphi))$ does not hold. Let $\pi = \pi_0 \cdots \pi_k \pi_{k+1}$. Since $lp(\pi')$ holds, we have that $\pi_i = \pi_j$ for some $0 \leq i < j \leq k$. Let $\pi'' = \pi_0 \cdots \pi_i \pi_{j+1} \cdots \pi_k \pi_{k+1}$. Then π'' is a prefix (not necessarily a proper one) of some k-path starting with s. Since $M_k, s \models A(\varphi R \psi)$, $\forall i \leq k.(M_k, \pi_i'' \models \psi \vee \exists j < i.(M_k, \pi_j'' \models \varphi)) \wedge (\exists j \leq k.(M_k, \pi_j'' \models \varphi) \vee lp(\pi''))$ holds. Let the position of π_{k+1} in π be $l + 1$ (i.e. $\pi_l'' = \pi_{k+1}$). We obtain that $(M_k, \pi_l'' \models \psi \vee \exists j < l.(M_k, \pi_j'' \models \varphi))$ holds. Again, by the induction hypothesis, $(M_{k+1}, \pi_l'' \models \psi \vee \exists j < l.(M_{k+1}, \pi_j'' \models \varphi))$ holds. By comparing π and π'', we obtain that $(M_{k+1}, \pi_{k+1} \models \psi \vee \exists j < k + 1.(M_{k+1}, \pi_j \models \varphi))$ holds. This contradicts to that (*) does not hold. For the case of ER, the reasoning is similar.

Lemma 2. *If $M_n, s \models \varphi$ for some $n \geq 0$, then $M, s \models \varphi$.*

According to Lemma 1, if $M_n, s \models \varphi$ for some n, then $M_k, s \models \varphi$ holds for a large k. Given a model, all properties other than those of the form

$$AG\psi, A(\varphi R \psi), EG\psi, E(\varphi R \psi)$$

can be witnessed by finite paths. Let k be larger than the length of such paths and also larger than the number of reachable states of M. Suppose that a property of

---

[1] The bounded semantics stated that a property is true iff the property is true in a bounded model for a given k (not for some $k \geq 0$ as in our framework), and since the given k is very large, it is not useful as a basis for establishing an efficient bounded model checking approach.

the form $AG\psi, A(\varphi R\psi), EG\psi, E(\varphi R\psi)$ such that φ does not hold in any state of π and ψ must hold in all states of π, and therefore a prefix is not sufficient for showing the truth of such a property. Since AG and EG can be considered as subcases of AR and ER, we only consider $A(\varphi R\psi)$ and $E(\varphi R\psi)$. Assume the aforementioned situation occurs and $A(\varphi R\psi)$ holds in the bounded semantics. We want to show that $\varphi R\psi$ also holds on such a path π. For the first, the situation implies that ψ is true on every state of every k-path of which the set of states is a subset of that of π. For the second, the set of states of all these k-paths with the starting state π_0 covers the set of states of π. These two conditions guarantee that ψ is true on every state of π and therefore $\varphi R\psi$ holds on π. For the case of $E(\varphi R\psi)$, since π satisfies $(\varphi R\psi)$ in the bounded semantics such that ψ holds on all states of π, an infinite path in which all states satisfying ψ can be constructed, therefore $E(\varphi R\psi)$ holds.

Lemma 3. *If* $M, s \models \varphi$, *then* $M_k, s \models \varphi$ *for some* $k \geq 0$.

By looking at the definitions, the bounded semantics is similar to the normal semantics, except that the bounded semantics has a few additional constraints. Let k be sufficiently large. Then the two conditions $k \geq 1$ and $lp(\pi)$ in the bounded semantics hold without any problem. By simplifying the bounded semantics based on this fact, the difference between the bounded semantics and the normal semantics is that the paths in the bounded semantics are restricted to k-paths, while the paths in the normal semantics are infinite paths. Therefore if $M, s \models \varphi$ holds, then $M_k, s \models \varphi$ holds for a sufficiently large k (large enough to make $lp(\pi)$ true for all k-paths). In particular, the number of reachable states of M will be such a k.

Theorem 1 (Soundness and Completeness). $M, s \models \varphi$ *iff* $M_k, s \models \varphi$ *for some* $k \geq 0$.

This theorem is a combination of the above lemmas.

Completeness Threshold. The completeness threshold of the problem $M, s \models \varphi$ is defined as the least k such that if $M_k, s \models \varphi$ does not hold then $M_{k'}, s \models \varphi$ does not hold for all $k' > k$. Theorem 1 guarantees the existence of such a completeness threshold.

Lemma 4. *The completeness threshold of the problem* $M, s \models \varphi$ *exists.*

If the completeness threshold ct of the problem $M, s \models \varphi$ is known, then the problem is almost solved. If $ct = 0$, then we only need to check whether $M_0, s \models \varphi$ holds. If $ct > 0$, then we know that $M_{ct}, s \models \varphi$ holds and therefore $M, s \models \varphi$ also holds. Therefore the complexity of knowing the completeness threshold is the same as solving the problem.

Corollary 1. *Let* ct_0 *be an over-approximation of the completeness threshold of* $M, s \models \varphi$. $M, s \models \varphi$ *iff* $M_k, s \models \varphi$ *for some* $k \leq ct_0$.

Let $|M|$ denote the number of reachable states of M. $|M|$ is an over-approximation of the completeness threshold of $M, s \models \varphi$ for any CTL formula φ.

For a given triple M, s, φ, we may use a more accurate over-approximation. Similar to the definitions in [17,9], let the initial recurrence diameter of a state s of M be the number of states in the longest loop-free path between s and any reachable state, and the recurrence diameter of M be the number of states in the longest loop-free path between any two reachable states. Let $ct(M, s, \varphi)$ denote the completeness threshold of $M, s \models \varphi$. Let p, q be propositional formulas. Then the initial recurrence diameter of s of M is an over-approximation of $ct(M, s, A(pUq))$, while the recurrence diameter of M is an over-approximation of $ct(M, s, A(pUA(qUr)))$.

Bounded Model Checking Principle for CTL. Let M be a model, s a state and φ a CTL formula. The bounded model checking principle[2] may be formulated as follows.

Let ct_0 be an over approx. of $ct(M, s, \varphi)$;
Let $k = 0$;
If $M_k, s \models \varphi$ holds, report that φ holds;
If $k = ct_0$, report that φ does not hold;
Increase k, go to the first "if"-test;

Because CTL is closed under negation, Theorem 1 also provides a basis for bounded model checking and verification (emphasizing the possibility to check whether a formula is true or the negation of the formula is true without using a completeness threshold or other termination criteria)[3] of CTL properties.

Corollary 2. *$M, s \models \varphi$ iff there is a k such that $M_k, s \models \varphi$ and there is no k such that $M_k, s \models \neg\varphi$.*

Note that $\neg\varphi$ represents the NNF formula equivalent to $\neg\varphi$ and $M_k, s \not\models \varphi$ is not equivalent to $M_k, s \models \neg\varphi$.

Bounded Model Checking and Verification. Let M be a model, s a state and φ a CTL formula. The bounded model checking and verification principle may be formulated as follows.

Let $k = 0$;
If $M_k, s \models \varphi$ holds, report that φ holds;
If $M_k, s \models \neg\varphi$ holds, report that φ does not hold;
Increase k, go to the first "if"-test;

---

[2] We call this a principle, not a model checking approach, in the sense that a direct implementation may not be efficient for general CTL properties. Later we shall develop an implementable approach for bounded model checking and verification of ACTL formulas.

[3] This is not possible with the bounded semantics defined in [3,21] for model checking, respectively, LTL and ACTL properties.

This approach is guaranteed to terminate by Corollary 2. One of the features of this bounded model checking and verification principle is that we do not have to worry about the completeness threshold which is important in the previous bounded model checking principle.

4   On CTL*

In this section, we discuss the possibility of extending the bounded semantics of CTL to CTL*, and prove that there are no such extensions in our framework of bounded semantics, in contrast to that there is a natural extension (within this framework) of the bounded semantics of ECTL to that of ECTL* [24].

We first introduce CTL* . The temporal logic CTL* was proposed in [14] as a unifying framework subsuming both CTL and LTL. This extension of CTL waives the restriction of the use of path quantifiers and path operators such that they can be used separately. Then there are two types of formulas in CTL*. One is state formulas and the other is path formulas. Let AP be a set of propositional symbols. The set of CTL* formulas over AP is defined as follows:

If $p \in AP$, then p is a state formula.
If φ_0 and φ_1 are state formulas,
then $\neg\varphi_0$, $\varphi_0 \wedge \varphi_1$ and $\varphi_0 \vee \varphi_1$ are state formulas.
If ψ is a path formula, then $E\psi$ and $A\psi$ are state formulas.
If φ is a state formula, then φ is a path formula.
If ψ_0 and ψ_1 are path formulas,
then $\neg\psi_0$, $\psi_0 \wedge \psi_1$, $\psi_0 \vee \psi_1$, $X\psi_0$, $F\psi_0$, $G\psi_0$, $\psi_0 U \psi_1$ and $\psi_0 R \psi_1$
are path formulas.

4.1   Semantics of CTL*

Let M be a model, s a state of M, π a path of M. The relation ψ holds on π in M for a path formula ψ is denoted by $M, \pi \models \psi$, and the relation φ holds on s in M for a state formula φ is denoted by $M, s \models \varphi$.

Definition 9. *(Semantics of CTL*) Let φ be a state formula and ψ be a path formula. The relation $M, \pi \models \psi$ and $M, s \models \varphi$ are defined as follows.*

$M, s \models p$ *iff* $p \in L(s)$
$M, s \models \neg\varphi_0$ *iff* $M, s \not\models \varphi_0$
$M, s \models \varphi_0 \wedge \varphi_1$ *iff* $M, s \models \varphi_0$ *and* $M, s \models \varphi_1$
$M, s \models \varphi_0 \vee \varphi_1$ *iff* $M, s \models \varphi_0$ *or* $M, s \models \varphi_1$
$M, s \models E\psi_0$ *iff* $\exists\pi(s).(M, \pi \models \psi_0)$
$M, s \models A\psi_0$ *iff* $\forall\pi(s).(M, \pi \models \psi_0)$
$M, \pi \models \varphi$ *iff* $M, \pi_0 \models \varphi$
$M, \pi \models \neg\psi_0$ *iff* $M, \pi \not\models \psi_0$
$M, \pi \models \psi_0 \wedge \psi_1$ *iff* $M, \pi \models \psi_0$ *and* $M, \pi \models \psi_1$
$M, \pi \models \psi_0 \vee \psi_1$ *iff* $M, \pi \models \psi_0$ *or* $M, \pi \models \psi_1$

$M, \pi \models X\psi_0$ iff $M, \pi^1 \models \psi_0$
$M, \pi \models F\psi_0$ iff $\exists k \geq 0.M, \pi^k \models \psi_0$
$M, \pi \models G\psi_0$ iff $\forall k \geq 0.M, \pi^k \models \psi_0$
$M, \pi \models \psi_0 U\psi_1$ iff $\exists k \geq 0.\forall j < k.(M, \pi^k \models \psi_1 \wedge M, \pi^j \models \psi_0)$
$M, \pi \models \psi_0 R\psi_1$ iff $\forall j \geq 0.(M, \pi^j \models \psi_1) \vee \exists k \geq 0.((M, \pi^k \models \psi_0) \wedge (\forall j \leq k.(M, \pi^j \models \psi_1))$

The restriction of CTL* to path formulas such that path quantifers (E,A) do not occur in the formulas is LTL. The restriction of CTL* to state formulas such that temporal path operators (X,F,G,U,R) and path quantifers (E,A) occur in pair and each path operator is immediately preceded by a path quantifer is CTL.

A CTL* formula is in NNF, if the negation $\neg$ is applied only to propositional symbols. Every CTL* formula can be transformed into an equivalent formula in NNF. The restriction of CTL* to NNF formulas not containing the existential path quantifier is called ACTL*. The restriction of CTL* to NNF formulas not containing the universal path quantifier is called ECTL*.

Definition 10. *Let φ be an ACTL* formula. φ is true in M, denoted $M \models \varphi$, iff φ is true at all initial states of M. Let φ be an ECTL* formula. φ is true in M, also denoted $M \models \varphi$, iff φ is true at some initial state of M.*

4.2 Bounded Semantics of CTL*

Let $\models_k$ be a family of bounded relations each defined as a propositional combination of simple relations with respect to $\models$ (for state formulas) as follows.

$$\bigvee_{i=1}^{m} (\bigwedge_{j=1}^{n} \models_k^{i,j})$$

Since $\models_k^{i,j}$ is a simple relation for state formulas, when evaluating formulas of the form $A\varphi$, it must be related to the corresponding path relation. For clarity, we use a different notation for the corresponding path relation. Let $\models_{k,p}^{i,j}$ denote the relation $\models_k^{i,j}$ for path formulas. Then $M_k, s \models_k^{i,j} A\varphi$ iff $M_k, \pi(s) \models_{k,p}^{i,j} \varphi$ for every k-path $\pi(s)$, according to the compositionality of the relation.

Each $\models_{k,p}^{i,j}$ may also be defined by a disjunction of conjunctions of simple relations for path formulas. Let such a definition be as follows.

$$\bigvee_{x=1}^{a_{i,j}} (\bigwedge_{y=1}^{b_{i,j}} \models_{k,p}^{i,j,x,y})$$

Suppose that $M_k, s \models_k A\varphi$ holds. Then there is some i such that for all j and every k-path $\pi(s)$, $M_k, \pi(s) \models_{k,p}^{i,j} \varphi$ holds.

Let $R(i)$ be $\bigwedge_{j=1}^{n} \bigvee_{x=1}^{a_{i,j}} (\bigwedge_{y=1}^{b_{i,j}} \models_{k,p}^{i,j,x,y})$.

Expanding $R(i)$ to a disjunction of conjunctions of simple relations, we may write $R(i)$ as $\bigvee_{x=1}^{r}(\models_{k,p,i,x})$ where $\models_{k,p,i,x}$ is a conjunction of simple relations consistent with the definition of $R(i)$.

Suppose that $M_k, s \models_k A\varphi$ holds. Then there is some i and x such that for every k-path $\pi(s)$, $M_k, \pi(s) \models_{k,p,i,x} \varphi$ holds.

Lemma 5. *Suppose a sound and complete bounded semantics with respect to $\models$ is defined by the family of bounded relations $\models_k$. Then the following hold:*

- *If $M_k, \pi \models_{k,p,i,x} Gp$, then $p \in L(\pi_n)$ for all $n \in \{0, ..., k\}$.*
- *If $M_k, \pi \models_{k,p,i,x} Fp$, then $p \in L(\pi_n)$ for some $n \in \{0, ..., k\}$.*

Proof. Suppose that $\models_k$ is such a family of relations defining the bounded semantics and $M_k, \pi \models_{k,p,i,x} Gp$ without requiring every π_i satisfy p. Then we can construct a model M' such that $\pi \in M'_k$ and a formula φ (a disjunction of conjunctions of formulas of the form $X^n q$ where $0 \le n \le k$ and q is a propositional formula characterizing the $(n+1)$-th state of a path) characterizing the k-paths starting at π_0 that are not identical to π. Then we have $M'_k, \pi' \models_{k,p,i,x} \varphi \vee Gp$ for every k-path π' starting at π_0. Then according to the completeness of $\models_k$, we obtain that $M', \pi_0 \models A(\varphi \vee Gp)$ which is obviously not true, since not every state along the path starting with π_0, not characterized by φ, satisfies p. This is a contradiction. Therefore the first property must hold. Similarly, the second property must hold.

Theorem 2. *There is no sound and complete bounded semantics with respect to the semantics of CTL^*.*

Proof. Suppose that $\models_k$ is such a family of relations defining the bounded semantics. Let M be the model shown in Fig. 1. Let φ be $A(Gp \vee Fr)$.

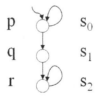

Fig. 1. Model with two loops

Since $M, s_0 \models \varphi$, there is a $k \ge 0$ such that $M_k, s_0 \models_k \varphi$ according to the completeness of $\models_k$. There are following three types of k-paths in M_k that starts with s_0.

- $(s_0)^{k+1}$
- $(s_0)^k s_1$ for $k \ge 1$.
- $(s_0)^i s_1 (s_2)^j$ for $k \ge 1$ and $i + j = k$.

By Lemma 5 and the compositionality of the relation, the only possibility for $M_k, s_0 \models_k \varphi$ to hold is the case when $k = 0$, since $(s_0)^k s_1$ does not satisfy $Gp \vee Fr$ for any relation corresponding to $\models_{k,p,i,x}$. When $k = 0$, there is only one path in M_0, namely s_0. Then $M_0, s_0 \models_k \varphi$.

Let M' be the modification of M such that a self-loop from s_1 to s_1 is added, as shown in Fig. 2.

Fig. 2. Model with three loops

Let M'_0 be the 0-model of M'. Since $M'_0 = M_0$, we have $M'_0, s_0 \models_k \varphi$ for $k = 0$ as well. Then we obtain $M', s_0 \models \varphi$ according to the soundness of $\models_k$. This is not a correct conclusion. Therefore $\models_k$ does not have the properties as claimed. We conclude that the theorem holds.

On ACTL*. The proof above also shows that there are no sound and complete bounded semantics for ACTL*. On the other hand, for ECTL*, a sound and complete bounded semantics is available [24].

5   Applications

The bounded semantics of CTL may serve as a basis for developing a bounded model checking algorithm for checking CTL formulas based on QBF (quantified boolean formulas)-solvers [19]. However, in this section, we will rather concentrate on checking ACTL formulas based on SAT (boolean satisfiability)-solvers, because the universal properties are considered typical in system specifications [11], and of the efficiency of SAT-solvers.

5.1   Further Development for ACTL Properties

For the practical use of the verification principle, the main problem is how to verify $M_k, s \models \varphi$ and $M_k, s \models \neg\varphi$. Since there are many bounded paths in M_k (an over estimation of the number of bounded paths is $|M|^{k+1}$), a brute-force checking of the validity of the two problems is not practical. The development in this section for the verification of ACTL properties is similar to that presented in [21,29], only that this is now developed under the bounded semantics of CTL that admits bounded model checking and verification principle.

Definition 11 (Submodels). *Let $M_k = \langle S, Ph_k, I, L \rangle$ be the k-model of M. $M_k^n = \langle S, Ph_k^n, I, L \rangle$ is a submodel of M_k, if $Ph_k^n \subseteq Ph_k$ where n denotes the size of Ph_k^n. We write $M_k^n \leq M_k$ for this relation and call M_k^n a (k, n)-submodel of M_k.*

Let M_k^b be a (k, b)-submodel of M_k. Let the relation $M_k^b, s \models \varphi$ be defined similar to the relation $M_k, s \models \varphi$, only with paths restricted to that of M_k^b. For a sufficiently large n, an ACTL formula is satisfied in a k-model iff it is satisfied in all submodels of size n, and an ECTL formula is satisfied in a k-model iff it is satisfied in some submodel of size n. Note that since we do not have $M_k, s \models \varphi$ iff $M_k, s \not\models \neg\varphi$, the above two statements are different, and need to be considered separately. Obviously, if we put $n = |M|^{k+1}$, the statements hold. However, we are interested in smaller n.

Let φ be an ACTL formula and ψ be an ECTL formula. Let $n_k^a(\varphi)$ be the least number such that for all s, $M_k, s \models \varphi$ iff $M_k', s \models \varphi$ for all $(k, n_k^a(\varphi))$-submodels M_k'. Let $n_k^e(\psi)$ be the least number such that for all s, $M_k, s \models \psi$ iff $M_k', s \models \psi$ for some $(k, n_k^e(\psi))$-submodel M_k'. We consider over-approximations of $n_k^a(\varphi)$ and $n_k^e(\psi)$.

Definition 12. *Let φ be an ACTL formula. $f_k(\varphi)$ is defined as follows.*

$f_k(p)$	$= 0 \; if \; p \in AP$
$f_k(\neg p)$	$= 0 \; if \; p \in AP$
$f_k(\varphi_0 \wedge \varphi_1)$	$= \max(f_k(\varphi_0), f_k(\varphi_1))$
$f_k(\varphi_0 \vee \varphi_1)$	$= f_k(\varphi_0) + f_k(\varphi_1)$
$f_k(AX\varphi)$	$= f_k(\varphi) + 1$
$f_k(AF\varphi)$	$= (k+1) \cdot f_k(\varphi) + 1$
$f_k(AG\varphi)$	$= f_k(\varphi) + 1$
$f_k(A(\varphi_0 U \varphi_1))$	$= k \cdot \max(f_k(\varphi_0), f_k(\varphi_1)) + f_k(\varphi_0) + f_k(\varphi_1) + 1$
$f_k(A(\varphi_0 R \varphi_1))$	$= k \cdot f_k(\varphi_0) + \max(f_k(\varphi_0), f_k(\varphi_1)) + 1$

Lemma 6. *Let φ be an ACTL formula. $n_k^a(\varphi) \leq f_k(\varphi)$.*

Let φ be an ACTL formula. Then $M_k, s \models \varphi$ iff $M_k', s \models \varphi$ for all $(k, f_k(\varphi))$-submodels M_k'. The reasoning is similar to that presented in [21,29] and is omitted, although the definition of the semantics and the definition of the over-approximation of the necessary number of paths are different[4]. Similarly, we have the following lemma.

Lemma 7. *Let ψ be an ECTL formula. $n_k^e(\psi) \leq f_k(\neg\psi)$.*

By Corollary 2 and the above two lemmas, we have the following theorem.

Theorem 3. *Let φ be an ACTL formula. $M, s \models \varphi$ iff there is a k such that $M_k', s \models \varphi$ for all $(k, f_k(\varphi))$-submodels M_k'' and there is no k such that $M_k'', s \models \neg\varphi$ for some $(k, f_k(\varphi))$-submodel M_k''.*

Definition 13. *Let φ be an ACTL formula. $M_k^b \models \varphi$ iff $M_k^b, s \models \varphi$ for all $s \in I$.*

---

[4] For simplicity, we do not present functions for calculating over-approximations for $n_k^a(\varphi)$ and $n_k^e(\varphi)$ separately, such that the definition of $f_k()$ may in some cases seem to be unnecessarily large.

Definition 14. *Let ψ be an ECTL formula. $M_k^b \models \psi$ iff $M_k^b, s \models \psi$ for some $s \in I$.*

The following statement follows from Theorem 3.

Corollary 3. *Let φ be an ACTL formula. $M \models \varphi$ iff there is a k such that $M_k' \models \varphi$ for all $(k, f_k(\varphi))$-submodels M_k'' and there is no k such that $M_k'' \models \neg\varphi$ for some $(k, f_k(\varphi))$-submodel M_k''.*

Bounded Model Checking and Verification for ACTL. Let M be a model and φ an ACTL formula. The corresponding bounded model checking and verification approach is as follows.

Let $k = 0$;
If $M_k' \models \varphi$ for all $(f_k(\varphi), k)$-models M_k', report that the property holds;
If $M_k' \models \neg\varphi$ for some $(f_k(\varphi), k)$-model M_k', report that the property does not hold;
Increase k, go to the first "if"-test;

5.2   SAT-Based Implementation

A SAT-based characterization of the above approach for ACTL can then be developed[5]. The development follows from the idea of [21,29] and is therefore omitted. It has then been implemented (the tools is called VERBS[6] hereafter) and an experimental study has been carried out with a comparison to SMV (release 2.5.4.3), an implementation of the BDD-based symbolic model checking technique [20]. The experiments are carried out on a Sun Blade 1000 with 750 MHz and 512 MB. In the experiments, VERBS internally calls MiniSat-1.14 [12].

Model. The model consists of global boolean variables $p[0], ..., p[n-1], q[0], ..., q[n-1], r[0], ..., r[n-1]$ and three processes p, q, r, each of which has in addition one local variable and has n transitions. The transitions of p written in the first order transition system are as follows:

$$ss = a_0 \quad \longrightarrow (p[0], ss) := (\neg p[0], a_1);$$
$$ss = a_1 \quad \longrightarrow (p[1], ss) := (\neg p[1], a_2);$$
$$\vdots$$
$$ss = a_{n-2} \longrightarrow (p[n-2], ss) := (\neg p[n-2], a_{n-1});$$
$$ss = a_{n-1} \longrightarrow (p[n-1], ss) := (\neg p[n-1], a_0);$$

Within the process, the variables $p[i]$ are initially set to 0 for all $i \in \{0, ..., n-1\}$, and the variable ss (acting as the program counter, which takes one of the values of $\{a_0, ..., a_{n-1}\}$) is initially a_0 (in practice, a_i is interpreted as number i). The other two processes are similar.

---

[5] For CTL, as mentioned earlier, a QBF-based characterization maybe developed, however, it is unclear whether it is possible to develop a SAT-based characterization.

[6] This is available from the webpage "http://lcs.ios.ac.cn/~zwh/verbs/".

Properties. Let $\varphi(i)$ be $\neg p[i] \wedge \neg q[i] \wedge \neg r[i]$. The following types of properties are considered.

$$PT1 : A(\neg\varphi(i)\,R\,A(\neg\varphi(j)\,R\,\varphi(k)))$$
$$PT2 : A(\neg\varphi(i)\,R\,A(\varphi(j)\,U\,\neg\varphi(k)))$$
$$PT3 : A(\varphi(i)\,U\,A(\neg\varphi(j)\,R\,\varphi(k)))$$
$$PT4 : A(\varphi(i)\,U\,A(\varphi(j)\,U\,\neg\varphi(k)))$$

Experimental Results and Discussion. There are n^3 properties of each type (i, j, k range from 0 to $n - 1$). The experimental data for $n = 9$ (with 729 properties of each type) is summarized in Table 1. The explanation of the symbols in the table is as follows.

A	number of true properties of each of the types in the model
B	number of false properties of each of the types in the model
C	range of time (in seconds) for the true properties by SMV
D	range of time (in seconds) for the false properties by SMV
E	range of time (in seconds) for the true properties by VERBS
F	range of time (in seconds) for the false properties by VERBS
G	percentage of true properties in which VERBS has advantage
H	percentage of false properties in which VERBS has advantage
600+	the time is greater than the given time limit, 600 seconds

The data show that SMV, within each type of properties, is not very sensitive to the concrete properties being verified, with respect to the usage of time, on the other hand, VERBS is sensitive to the concrete properties. As the types of properties are considered, VERBS has an advantage between 18.2 and 67.5 percent (on the other hand, SMV has an advantage between 32.5 and 81.8 percent) for the properties true in the model. In average, for these properties, VERBS has advantage in 41.7 percent of cases, while SMV has advantage in 58.3 percent of the cases. For the properties false in the model, VERBS performs a lot better[7].

In order to have some idea on the asymptotic behavior of the performance, we have also carried out experiments with $n = 13$ with 2197 properties of each type. The experimental data is summarized in Table 2. As the types of properties are considered, the relative advantage and disadvantage are similar (or slightly better in average) when the size of the problem increases.

For the given time limit and the experimental environment, it is expected that, for instance, when n increases to a relatively big number, the verification of the properties using SMV will be ineffective for all of the problem instances, on the other hand, a significant percentage of the problem instances can still be verified or falsified by VERBS within the time limit.

In summary, this example has illustrated that, with respect to ACTL properties, VERBS and SMV have their own advantages both for verification and falsification. The former has advantage when a small k is sufficient for either verification or falsification. The latter has advantage on the opposite situations.

---

[7] Note that VERBS does not have counterexample generation functionality yet, while SMV uses some time on the counterexample generation.

Table 1. Summary of the Experimental Data for $n = 9$

	PT1	PT2	PT3	PT4
A	204	405	324	525
B	525	324	405	204
C	8 - 8	13-16	11-13	13 - 26
D	9 - 12	21-29	13-18	37 - 48
E	0 - 600+	0 - 600+	0- 600+	0-600+
F	0 - 31	0-8	0-41	0 - 28
G	22.5%	18.2%	67.5%	58.8%
H	94.8%	100.0%	66.1%	100.0%

Table 2. Summary of the Experimental Data for $n = 13$

	PT1	PT2	PT3	PT4
A	650	1183	1014	1547
B	1547	1014	1183	650
C	53 - 54	131 - 156	76 - 89	131 - 266
D	59 - 81	232 - 286	89 - 127	419 - 507
E	0 - 600+	0 - 600+	0 - 600+	0 - 600+
F	0 - 340	0 - 600+	0 - 600+	0 - 600+
G	24.3%	18.1%	72.8%	59.5%
H	96.8%	99.6%	72.7%	96.3%

Mutual Exclusion. Experiments have also been carried out with a mutual exclusion algorithm [18], with two processes. Three problem instances are considered, one for verification of mutual exclusion property, one for liveness and one for non-starvation. Let the two processes be identified by $p1$ and $p2$ and let req, cri represent the process states for having just made request for entering the critical region and having just entered the critical region, respectively. The three properties are as follows:

$$AG(\neg(p1.cri \wedge p2.cri))$$
$$AG((p1.req \vee p2.req) \rightarrow AF(p1.cri \vee p2.cri))$$
$$AG((p1.req \rightarrow AF(p1.cri)) \wedge (p2.req \rightarrow AF(p2.cri)))$$

The verification process correctly verified the first two properties and falsified the last one. The bounds for verification and falsification are respectively 35, 35, 4 for the three properties in the experiment.

Coherence. Experiments have also been carried out with an asynchronous communication mechanism (ACM) with rereading and overwriting [15]. The model is specified as a set of conditional rewriting rules. The coherence property specified in [15] is that if some process starts to read and some starts to write, then the read-process will operates on the first element of the ACM and the write-process will operates on the last element of the ACM. The memory of the ACM of the instance of our model has length 6. Let the memory be denoted by

$x[0]x[1]...x[5]$. Let $s \in \{1, .., 6\}$ denote the length of the part of the memory that is in use. Let read-operation on a memory cell containing a be denoted by ra, let the write-operation on a memory cell containing a be denoted by wa. Let $y \in x$ denote $x[0] = y \vee \cdots \vee x[5] = y$. Then one instance of the property is specified as follows.

$$AG(s = 6 \rightarrow$$
$$(ra \in x \rightarrow ra = a[0] \wedge (wa \in x \rightarrow wa = a[5])))$$

The verification process correctly verified this property and falsified incorrect ones, for instance, when we change $wa = a[5]$ to $wa = a[4]$ in the property. The bounds reached are respectively 42, 12 for the two properties, the correct one and the modified one, in the experiment.

6   Concluding Remarks

We have provided a framework for discussion of bounded semantics. This framework has formalized what is the usual understanding of bounded semantics, such that we have a framework to discuss this particular kind of semantics. The traditional bounded semantics presented in [3,21,24] fall into this framework and is sound and complete for their target languages, while the bounded semantics of CTL* presented in [23] are considered unsound. In this framework, we have provided a sound and complete bounded semantics for CTL formulas and identified the limitation of such semantics, namely, there are no such sound and complete bounded semantics for CTL*.

The bounded semantics of CTL differs from the previously developed bounded semantics [3,21,24,29] in that the target language is closed under negation such that it can be used to check both a formula and its negation[8], and used as the basis for bounded model checking and verification in the sense discussed in Section 3. The bounded semantics of CTL is then refined in order to develop a SAT-based algorithm for checking ACTL properties. This algorithm is implemented, and experimental comparison with a BDD-based model checking tool SMV is carried out. The experimental results show that this bounded semantics based approach has advantage when a small k is sufficient for verification or error detection of given ACTL properties, while BDD-based approaches has advantage in the rest of cases. One of the important features of this approach based on CTL bounded semantics is that we do not have to be worried about over-approximations of the completeness threshold and the termination criteria which are one of the difficulties of bounded model checking and have been devoted a lot of research effort [17,9,16,10,1].

Experiments have also been carried out on models for instances of a mutual exclusion algorithm [18] and an asynchronous communication mechanism with rereading and overwriting [15]. For future research, one the theoretical side,

---

[8] The semantics of CTL* presented in [23] can also be used to check a formula and its negation, but it is not a sound semantics in our framework as pointed out in Section 3.2.

we may further investigate bounded semantics of temporal logics, and at the practical side, we may improve the efficiency of the current bounded semantics based approaches in order to extend potential advantages of such an approach.

Acknowledgments. The author thanks anonymous referees for their constructive critics that helped improving this paper.

References

1. Awedh, M., Somenzi, F.: Termination Criteria for Bounded Model Checking: Extensions and Comparison. Electr. Notes Theor. Comput. Sci. 144(1), 51–66 (2006)
2. Biere, A., Cimmatti, A., Clarke, E., Strichman, O., Zhu, Y.: Bounded Model Checking. Advances in Computers, vol. 58. Academic Press, London (2003)
3. Biere, A., Cimmatti, A., Clarke, E., Zhu, Y.: Symbolic Model Checking without BDDs. In: Cleaveland, W.R. (ed.) TACAS 1999. LNCS, vol. 1579, pp. 193–207. Springer, Heidelberg (1999)
4. Burch, J.R., Clarke, E.M., McMillan, K.L., Dill, D.L., Hwang, J.: Symbolic model checking: 10^{20} states and beyond. LICS, pp. 428–439 (1990)
5. Bryant, R.: Graph based algorithms for boolean function manipulation. IEEE Transaction on Computers 35(8), 677–691 (1986)
6. Bryant, R.E.: On the Complexity of VLSI Implementations and Graph Representations of Boolean Functions with Application to Integer Multiplication. IEEE Trans. Computers 40(2), 205–213 (1991)
7. Bryant, R.: Binary decision diagrams and beyond: enabling technologies for formal verification. In: CAD 1995, pp. 236–243 (1995)
8. Chen, W., Zhang, W.: Bounded Model Checking of ACTL formulae. In: TASE 2009, pp. 90–99 (2009)
9. Clarke, E.M., Kroening, D., Ouaknine, J., Strichman, O.: Completeness and Complexity of Bounded Model Checking. In: Steffen, B., Levi, G. (eds.) VMCAI 2004. LNCS, vol. 2937, pp. 85–96. Springer, Heidelberg (2004)
10. Clarke, E.M., Kroening, D., Ouaknine, J., Strichman, O.: Computational challenges in bounded model checking. STTT 7(2), 174–183 (2005)
11. Clarke, E.M., Grumberg, O., Peled, D.: Model Checking. The MIT Press, Cambridge (1999)
12. Een, N., Sorensson, N.: An Extensible SAT-solver. In: Giunchiglia, E., Tacchella, A. (eds.) SAT 2003. LNCS, vol. 2919, pp. 502–518. Springer, Heidelberg (2004)
13. Allen Emerson, E., Clarke, E.M.: Using Branching-time Temporal Logics to Synthesize Synchronization Skeletons. Science of Computer Programming 2(3), 241–266 (1982)
14. Allen Emerson, E., Halpern, J.Y.: Sometimes and Not Never revisited: on branching versus linear time temporal logic. J. ACM 33(1), 151–178 (1986)
15. Gorgonio, K., Xia, F.: Modeling and verifying asynchronous communication mechanisms using coloured Petri nets. In: ACSD 2008, pp. 138–147 (2008)
16. Heljanko, K., Junttila, T.A., Latvala, T.: Incremental and complete bounded model checking for full PLTL. In: Etessami, K., Rajamani, S.K. (eds.) CAV 2005. LNCS, vol. 3576, pp. 98–111. Springer, Heidelberg (2005)
17. Kroening, D., Strichman, O.: Efficient computation of recurrence diameters. In: Zuck, L.D., Attie, P.C., Cortesi, A., Mukhopadhyay, S. (eds.) VMCAI 2003. LNCS, vol. 2575, pp. 298–309. Springer, Heidelberg (2003)

18. Lamport, L.: A fast mutual exclusion algorithm. ACM Transactions on Computer Systems 5(1), 1–11 (1987)
19. Le Berre, D., Simon, L., Tacchella, A.: Challenges in the QBF arena: the SAT 2003 evaluation of QBF solvers. In: Giunchiglia, E., Tacchella, A. (eds.) SAT 2003. LNCS, vol. 2919, pp. 468–485. Springer, Heidelberg (2003)
20. McMillan, K.L.: Symbolic Model Checking. Kluwer Academic Publishers, Dordrecht (1993)
21. Penczek, W., Wozna, B., Zbrzezny, A.: Bounded Model Checking for the Universal Fragment of CTL. Fundamenta Informaticae 51, 135–156 (2002)
22. Prasad, M.R., Biere, A., Gupta, A.: A survey of recent advances in SAT-based formal verification. STTT 7(2), 156–173 (2005)
23. Tao, Z.-H., Zhou, C.-H., Chen, Z., Wang, L.-F.: Bounded Model Checking of CTL. J. Comput. Sci. Technol. 22(1), 39–43 (2007)
24. Wozna, B.: ATCL* properties and Bounded Model Checking. Fundam. Inform. 63(1), 65–87 (2004)
25. Xu, L., Chen, W., Xu, Y., Zhang, W.: Improved Bounded Model Checking for Universal Fragment of CTL. Journal of Computer Science and Technology 24(1), 96–109 (2009)
26. Xu, Y., Chen, W., Xu, L., Zhang, W.: Evaluation of SAT-based Bounded Model Checking of ACTL Properties. In: Proceedings of the 1st Joint IEEE/IFIP Symposium on Theoretical Aspects of Software Engineering (TASE 2007), pp. 339–348. IEEE Computer Society Press, Los Alamitos (2007)
27. Zhang, W.: SAT-based verification of LTL formulas. In: Brim, L., Haverkort, B.R., Leucker, M., van de Pol, J. (eds.) FMICS 2006 and PDMC 2006. LNCS, vol. 4346, pp. 277–292. Springer, Heidelberg (2007)
28. Zhang, W.: Verification of ACTL properties by bounded model checking. In: Moreno Díaz, R., Pichler, F., Quesada Arencibia, A. (eds.) EUROCAST 2007. LNCS, vol. 4739, pp. 556–563. Springer, Heidelberg (2007)
29. Zhang, W.: Model checking with SAT-based characterization of ACTL formulas. In: Butler, M., Hinchey, M.G., Larrondo-Petrie, M.M. (eds.) ICFEM 2007. LNCS, vol. 4789, pp. 191–211. Springer, Heidelberg (2007)

Graded-CTL: Satisfiability and Symbolic Model Checking*

Alessandro Ferrante[1], Margherita Napoli[2], and Mimmo Parente[2]

[1] Embedded Systems Research Unit, Bruno Kessler Foundation, IRST
Via Sommarive, 18, 38123, Povo (TN), Italy
ferrante@fbk.eu
[2] Dip.to di Informatica ed Applicazioni "R.M. Capocelli", Università of Salerno
Via Ponte don Melillo, 84084, Fisciano (SA), Italy
{napoli,parente}@dia.unisa.it

Abstract. In this paper we continue the study of a strict extension of the Computation Tree Logic, called *graded-CTL*, recently introduced by the same authors. This new logic augments the standard quantifiers with graded modalities, being able thus to express "There exist at least k" or "For all but k" futures, for some constant k. One can thus describe properties useful in system design, which cannot be expressed with CTL, like a sort of redundant liveness property asking whether there is more than one path satisfying that "something good eventually happens", making thus the system more tolerant to possible faults. Graded-CTL formulas can also be used to determine whether there are more than a given number of bad behaviors of a system: this, in the model-checking framework, means that one can verify the existence of a user-defined number of counterexamples for a given specification and generate them, in a unique run of the model-checker.

Here we show both theoretical and applicative contributions. On the theoretical side we give a simple algorithm to *decide* this logic, and we prove that the satisfiability problem is EXPTIME-complete when the constants of the quantifiers are represented in unary. On the applicative side we propose *symbolic* algorithms to solve the model checking problem. One of the main characteristics of these algorithms is that, though the computation of "distinct" counterexamples has inherently high complexity when the model is represented symbolically, we have designed them to make the generation of multiple counterexamples as easy and quick as possible. The symbolic algorithms have been implemented using BDD data structures, and have been integrated into the well known NuSMV model checker, that has been modified to accept specifications expressed in graded-CTL. The test results we report are very comfortable in the sense that both the running time and the size of the BDDs produced are comparable to those obtained with specifications expressed in classical CTL.

* Work partially supported by M.I.U.R. grant ex-60%: "Metodi formali per la verifica automatica di sistemi" and by the National Research Project (PRIN'07) "Integrating automated reasoning in model checking: towards push-button formal verification of large-scale and infinite-state systems".

1   Introduction

Recently a new logic strictly more expressive than CTL has been introduced by the same authors in [FNP08, FNP10], called graded-CTL. It augments the existential and universal quantifiers with *graded* modalities that allow to reason about either *at least* or *all but* any number of futures. In literature, graded modalities have been intensively studied in various logic frameworks. In classical logics $\exists^{>k}$ and $\forall^{\leq k}$ are called *counting quantifiers*, see e.g. [GOR97, GMV99, PST00], in modal logics they are called *graded* modalities, see e.g. [Fin72, Tob01], and in description logics one speaks about *number restriction* of properties describing systems, see e.g. [HB91]. A different extension of CTL (RCTL) has been also defined in [EMSS92], where bounds are placed on the temporal modalities, instead of on the path quantifiers, bounding thus the maximum number of permitted transitions along a path.

Simple examples of graded-CTL are the formula $E^{>k}\mathcal{F}(critic1 \wedge critic2)$, which expresses that there exist more than k possibilities to violate the mutual exclusion property to enter the critical section of a system, and the formula $E^{>k}\mathcal{F}good$ which expresses the fact that the system has several ways to reach a good state. Formulas of these types cannot be expressed in CTL and not even in classical μ-calculus. Consider the two Kripke structures in the following figure, they cannot be distinguished by any CTL formula, while on the contrary, only the first is a model for the graded-CTL formula $E^{>1}\mathcal{X}p$, which says that there is more than one next state where p holds.

Another favorable point for studying this new logic is when we want to express that exactly one path satisfies a path formula, say for example $\mathcal{G}\varphi$, which means that φ holds forever in the states along a path: we can use the graded-CTL formula $E^{>0}\mathcal{G}\varphi \wedge \neg E^{>1}\mathcal{G}\varphi$. This latter example also shows that there is a great difference between a graded-CTL formula and the CTL formula obtained simply by ignoring the constant grading the path quantifiers: not only the models of the two formulas are different but even the satisfiability may change since, the deletion of the constants from $E^{>0}\mathcal{G}p \wedge \neg E^{>1}\mathcal{G}p$ produces a CTL formula which is not satisfiable.

Our contribution is on both a theoretical and an applicative side. For the former we give a simple algorithm to decide the satisfiability of a graded-CTL formula φ in time $2^{\mathcal{O}(|\varphi|^4)}$, when the grading constants occurring in the quantifiers of φ are expressed in unary. On the applicative side, we deal with the model-checking framework for the graded-CTL logic. In [FNP10] it has been shown that the graded-CTL model-checking problem can be solved in polynomial time and independently from the constant values grading the path quantifiers of the formula (and thus the representation of the constants does not affect the running time of the model checking algorithm). Here, we propose symbolic algorithms for solving the model checking problem. As widely known, symbolic model checking [BCM+90] is a technique that allows, by representing and manipulating sets of vertices, to manage models with very high number of states. This have also been applied to the model checking of CTL [CE81] by revealing a very high efficiency in practice, especially in hardware verification [McM93].

We have implemented our algorithms with *Binary Decision Diagrams*, BDDs [Bry92], and have integrated them in the NuSMV model-checker [CCG+02] (and actually are collaborating with the development team for the integration of graded-CTL in the next official release of NuSMV). Besides being more expressive than CTL, a motivation for the use of graded-CTL in the model checking framework, is its close relation to the counterexamples generated by the model-checker tools. In fact these tools generate one counterexample for each run and they are used as a step in the *Check/Analyze/Fix* loop: *Check* the model against a specification, *Analyze* the counterexample generated by the tool and re-design the model after having *Fixed* the errors. The Check stage is often expensive, in terms of time resources, so it would be desirable to minimize the number of runs of the model-checkers. The complexity of the Analyze stage depends on the time the designer needs to interpret the counterexamples, and this task can be facilitated by providing more meaningful counterexamples. With respect to this, we think that graded-CTL can be much useful, in fact by using the graded modalities we can get more counterexamples with a unique run of the model checker and, hopefully, one does not have to undergo again through the time-consuming three stage cycle, c.f. [CG07, CIW+01, DRS03].

Clearly, it is possible in principle, to modify a tool checker to let it generate multiple counterexamples without changing the logic. Anyway, this is not likely to be done for essentially two reasons. First suppose that for example a system designer desires two evidences to the CTL formula $E\mathcal{F}E\mathcal{G}p$. He cannot choose the "type" of the evidences unless he uses a graded-CTL formula, either $E^{>0}\mathcal{F}E^{>1}\mathcal{G}p$ or $E^{>1}\mathcal{F}E^{>0}\mathcal{G}p$, which allow to get different evidences according to the needs (and not following a policy hard-coded once and for all into the tool). Second, it is not a trivial task to symbolically implement an algorithm that analyzes the model looking for *distinct* counterexamples (consider, for example, the inherent difficulty in the symbolic implementation of a DFS); our algorithms, instead, have been explicitly designed to make the computation of distinct counterexamples as quick and easy as possible.

We have implemented the symbolic algorithms into the well known NuSMV model checker, version 2.4.3, and have tested it on various examples. We report some results obtained from examples of the official NuSMV web site. Other tests and the package for graded-CTL can be found at `http://gradedctl.dia.unisa.it`. The experimental results indicate that there is no substantial overhead both in time and in size of BDDs needed to process graded-CTL formulas with respect to the classical CTL ones.

Related Works. In [KSV02], complexity issues related to the satisfiability problem for the μ-calculus when the universal and existential quantifiers are augmented with graded modalities, have been investigated. They have shown that this problem is EXPTIME-complete, retaining thus the same complexity as in the case of classical μ-calculus, though strictly extending it. There, the values of the constants grading the quantifiers are represented in binary.

In [BMM09] a logic with the same expressivity of our graded-CTL logic is considered, though their interpretation of the graded quantifiers is different and seems to be less natural than ours. Consider in fact the formula $E^{>k}\mathcal{G}\text{TRUE}$: in our logic it extends the CTL formula $E\mathcal{G}\text{TRUE}$ (having the intuitive meaning that *at least k different paths stem*); in their interpretation it is a contradiction, since it has no models. Also they solve the satisfiability problem, anyway the complexity of the translations between our and their logics prevents the two results to be derived from each other. The main differences between these two results is that theirs is in time $2^{\mathcal{O}(|\varphi|^5)}$.

In the last years, symbolic computations have also been applied to other kinds of problems. In [BGS06] the authors show a symbolic algorithm for the computation of the maximum flow in a 0-1 network, while in [GPP07] graph connectivity related problems are studied from a symbolic point of view. Recently symbolic techniques have also been applied to the satisfiability problem for the modal logic **K** [PSV05] and for CTL [Mar05].

The rest of the paper is organized as follows: in Section 2 we give the definitions of graded-CTL. In Section 3 we solve the satisfiability problem. In Section 4 we give the symbolic algorithms for the graded-CTL model checking problem. In Section 5 we describe the implementation of our algorithm into NuSMV and present the experimental results of the tests. In Section 6 we give our conclusions and outline some future research directions.

2 Graded-CTL Logic

In this section we recall the graded-CTL logic introduced in [FNP10]. The well-known temporal logic CTL [CE82] is a branching-time logic in which temporal operators express properties about a possible future and are preceded by a path quantifier. With this logic one can express properties that have to be true either *immediately after now* ($\mathcal{X}$), or *each time from now* ($\mathcal{G}$), or *from now until something happens* ($\mathcal{U}$), and it is possible to specify, through a path quantifier, that each property must hold either in *some possible futures* (E) or in *each possible future* (A). The graded-CTL logic extends CTL with graded quantifiers allowing to express also that a temporal property must hold either in *more than a given number* or in *all but a given number* of possible futures. The graded-CTL operators consist of the temporal operators $\mathcal{U}$ and $\mathcal{X}$, the boolean connectives $\wedge$ and $\neg$, and the graded path quantifier $E^{>k}$ (*for at least $k+1$ distinct futures*). Given a set of atomic propositions AP, the syntax of the graded-CTL formulas is:

$$\varphi := p \mid \neg\psi_1 \mid \psi_1 \wedge \psi_2 \mid E^{>k}\mathcal{X}\psi_1 \mid E^{>k}\mathcal{G}\psi_1 \mid E^{>k}\psi_1\mathcal{U}\psi_2$$

where $p \in AP$, ψ_1 and ψ_2 are graded-CTL formulas and k is a non-negative integer. The graded-CTL formulas, as in standard CTL, are also called *state-formulas* and $\mathcal{X}\psi_1$, $\mathcal{G}\psi_1$ and $\psi_1\mathcal{U}\psi_2$, are called, as usual, *path-formulas*. The semantics of graded-CTL is defined with respect to a *Kripke Structure*, by means of a satisfiability relation $\models$. A Kripke structure over a set of atomic propositions AP is a tuple $\mathcal{K} = \langle S, s_{in}, R, L \rangle$, where S is a finite set of states, $s_{in} \in S$ is the initial state, $R \subseteq S \times S$ is a transition relation, with the property that for each state s there is a *successor* t such that $(s, t) \in R$, and $L : S \to 2^{AP}$ is a state labeling function. In the rest of the paper, with $\mathcal{K}$ we always denote the Kripke structure $\langle S, s_{in}, R, L \rangle$.

The relation $\models$ is defined as follows:

- $(\mathcal{K}, s) \models p$ iff $p \in L(s)$;
- $(\mathcal{K}, s) \models \psi_1 \wedge \psi_2$ iff $(\mathcal{K}, s) \models \psi_1$ and $(\mathcal{K}, s) \models \psi_2$;
- $(\mathcal{K}, s) \models \neg\psi_1$ iff $\neg((\mathcal{K}, s) \models \psi_1)$
- $(\mathcal{K}, s) \models E^{>k}\mathcal{X}\psi_1$ iff there exist $k+1$ different successors $s_0, \ldots, s_k$ of s such that $(\mathcal{K}, s_i) \models \psi_1$ for all $0 \leq i \leq k$;

To define the semantics for $\mathcal{G}$ and $\mathcal{U}$ operators, let us first introduce the notion of *distinct* paths which plays an important role. The length $|\pi|$ of a path π in $\mathcal{K}$ is the number of its states, and $\pi[i]$ denotes the i-th state in π, $0 \leq i < |\pi|$. Two paths π_1 and π_2 are *distinct* if there exists an index $0 \leq i < \min\{|\pi_1|, |\pi_2|\}$ such that $\pi_1[i] \neq \pi_2[i]$. Observe that from this definition if a path is the prefix of another path, then they are not distinct.

- $(\mathcal{K}, s) \models E^{>k}\mathcal{G}\psi_1$ iff there exist $k+1$ pairwise distinct infinite paths π_j, $0 \leq j \leq k$, starting from s and such that $(\mathcal{K}, \pi_j[h]) \models \psi_1$, for all $h \geq 0$. These paths π_j are said to satisfy the path-formula $\mathcal{G}\psi_1$.
- $(\mathcal{K}, s) \models E^{>k}\psi_1\mathcal{U}\psi_2$ iff there exist $k+1$ pairwise distinct finite paths π_j of length $i_j + 1$, for $0 \leq j \leq k$, and starting from s such that:

  1. $(\mathcal{K}, \pi_j[i_j]) \models \psi_2$, and
  2. for every $0 \leq h < i_j$, $(\mathcal{K}, \pi_j[h]) \models \psi_1$;

  These paths π_j are said to satisfy the path-formula $\psi_1\mathcal{U}\psi_2$.

We say that a state s in $\mathcal{K}$ satisfies a state-formula φ if $(\mathcal{K}, s) \models \varphi$ and $\mathcal{K}$ models (or also is a model of) φ, if $(\mathcal{K}, s_0) \models \varphi$

Observe that we have expressed the syntax of graded-CTL with one of the possible minimal sets of operators. Other temporal operators can be easily derived from those. For example, the temporal operator $\mathcal{F}$ (*eventually*) can be expressed by: $E^{>k}\mathcal{F}\psi_1 \Leftrightarrow E^{>k}\text{TRUE}\mathcal{U}\psi_1$. Moreover, the path quantifier $E^{=k}$ can be expressed, as shown in the introduction, since $E^{=k}\psi$ is equivalent to $E^{>k-1}\psi \wedge \neg E^{>k}\psi$, and also the graded extension of the universal quantifier, $A^{\leq k}$, can be defined, with the meaning that *all the paths starting from a node s, but at most k pairwise distinct paths, satisfy a given path-formula*. The quantifier $A^{\leq k}$ is the dual operator of $E^{>k}$ and can obviously be re-written in terms of $\neg E^{>k}$. The formulas $A^{\leq k}\mathcal{X}\psi_1$ and $A^{\leq k}\mathcal{G}\psi_1$ are equivalent to respectively $\neg E^{>k}\mathcal{X}\neg\psi_1$ and $\neg E^{>k}\mathcal{F}\neg\psi_1$, while the formula $A^{\leq k}\psi_1\mathcal{U}\psi_2$ with $k > 0$ deserves more attention. In fact, we have that $A^{\leq k}\psi_1\mathcal{U}\psi_2$ is equivalent to $\neg E^{>k}\neg(\psi_1\mathcal{U}\psi_2)$, but this formula is not a graded-CTL formula because of the occurrence of the innermost negation. This latter can be expressed in graded-CTL in the following way:

$$A^{\leq k}\psi_1 \mathcal{U}\psi_2 \iff \neg E^{>k}\mathcal{G}(\psi_1 \wedge \neg\psi_2) \ \wedge \neg E^{>k}(\psi_1 \wedge \neg\psi_2)\mathcal{U}(\neg\psi_1 \wedge \neg\psi_2)\wedge \\ \bigwedge_{i=0}^{k-1} \left(\neg E^{>k-1-i}\mathcal{G}(\psi_1 \wedge \neg\psi_2) \ \vee \ \neg E^{>i}(\psi_1 \wedge \neg\psi_2)\mathcal{U}(\neg\psi_1 \wedge \neg\psi_2)\right) \tag{1}$$

Equivalence (1) holds because if a path does not satisfy $\psi_1\mathcal{U}\psi_2$ then it satisfies either $\theta_1 = \mathcal{G}(\psi_1 \wedge \neg\psi_2)$ or $\theta_2 = (\psi_1 \wedge \neg\psi_2)\mathcal{U}(\neg\psi_1 \wedge \neg\psi_2)$ and, moreover, the paths satisfying θ_1 are all distinct from the paths satisfying θ_2.

Let us now recall the definitions of the graded-CTL satisfiability and model-checking problems. The **graded-CTL SAT** is the problem of verifying whether a Kripke structure exists which models a given graded-CTL formula. The **graded-CTL model-checking**, given a Kripke structure $\mathcal{K}$ and a graded-CTL formula φ, is the problem of verifying whether $\mathcal{K}$ models φ.

In spite of the augmented expressiveness, the complexity of the graded-CTL model-checking problem remains the same as that of CTL, since this problem is solved in polynomial time and independently from the constant values grading the path quantifiers of the formula.

Let $|\varphi|$ be the number of the temporal and the boolean operators occurring in a graded-CTL formula φ.

Theorem 1. *[FNP10] The graded-CTL model-checking problem for a Kripke structure $\mathcal{K}$ and a graded-CTL formula φ can be solved in time $\mathcal{O}(|R| \cdot |\varphi|)$.*

Distinct paths. Since graded-CTL requires to count the paths satisfying a formula, we have introduced the notion of *distinct* paths. Now we briefly discuss this definition. For the globally operator we had no choice since we have to distinguish infinite paths. On the contrary the other temporal operators require a deeper reasoning. The most reasonable choice in this case is to count distinct finite evidences of a formula. In fact, the different choice to count infinite distinct paths (as done for the globally operator) may cause loss of information, as illustrated by the fact that the validity of the formula $E^{>k}\mathcal{F}$ *safe* no longer ensures that a system has more ways to reach safe states. In fact also paths that diverge after the last safe state would be counted as distinct.

Another possible choice is to consider as distinct two evidences of $\psi_1\mathcal{U}\psi_2$ also in the case that one is the prefix of the other (this logic, in a certain sense, allows to count the number of states satisfying a formula in a Kripke structure). However, it can be proved quite immediately, that this choice leads to a logic that is no more expressive than ours.

3   The SAT Problem

In this section we show that SAT problem for graded-CTL is ExpTime-complete when the grading constants in the path quantifiers are expressed in unary. The membership proof is based on the reduction of the SAT problem to the emptiness problem for Büchi Automata on Infinite Trees. Since an infinite tree can be seen as a special Kripke structure with an infinite set of states, we can easily extend the semantics of the graded-CTL logic to infinite trees and we say that an infinite tree T is a model (i.e. satisfies) a graded-CTL formula φ iff $(T, root(T)) \models \varphi$.

Given a graded-CTL formula φ, we consider the set E_φ of the subformulas $E^{>k}\theta$ of φ occurring in positive form, that is we do not include in E_φ the subformulas $\neg E^{>k}\theta$. Our algorithm to solve the graded-CTL SAT problem is based on the fact that graded-CTL, as stated in the following lemma, obeys to a *Tree Model Property*.

First, we define for a graded-CTL formula φ the set $ecl(\varphi)$ (that we call *extended closure* of φ) as the minimal set of graded-CTL formulas such that

- TRUE is in $ecl(\varphi)$ and φ is in $ecl(\varphi)$;
- if $\psi_1 \wedge \psi_2$ is in $ecl(\varphi)$, then both ψ_1 and ψ_2 are in $ecl(\varphi)$
- if $E^{>k}\mathcal{X}\psi_1$ ($k \geq 0$) is in $ecl(\varphi)$, then ψ_1 is in $ecl(\varphi)$;
- if $E^{>0}\mathcal{G}\psi_1$ is in $ecl(\varphi)$, then ψ_1 is in $ecl(\varphi)$;
- if $E^{>0}\psi_1\mathcal{U}\psi_2$ is in $ecl(\varphi)$, then both ψ_1 and ψ_2 are in $ecl(\varphi)$;
- if $E^{>k}\theta$ is in $ecl(\varphi)$ with $k > 0$ and either $\theta = \mathcal{G}\psi_1$ or $\theta = \psi_1\mathcal{U}\psi_2$, then $E^{>i}\theta$ is in $ecl(\varphi)$ for all $0 \leq i \leq k - 1$;
- if ψ is in $ecl(\varphi)$ then $\neg\psi$ is in $ecl(\varphi)$;

To get ecl finite, we assume that $\neg\neg\varphi$ is replaced by φ.

Lemma 1. *If a graded-CTL formula φ is satisfiable, then it is satisfiable on a 2^{AP}-labeled infinite tree with branching degree bounded by $b = \hat{k} + l + 1$, where $\hat{k}$ is the sum of the grading constants occurring in the subformulas in E_φ and l is the number of these subformulas.*

Proof. Let $\mathcal{K}$ be a model of φ and let us consider its unwinding T; obviously T satisfies φ. Suppose that the branching degree of T is greater than b; we will show how to modify T to obtain a tree with branching degree at most b and that still satisfies φ. Let $x \in T$ be a node having $n > b$ children. Let us denote by $F(x)$ a minimal subset $ecl(\varphi)$ containing the graded-CTL formulas that have to be satisfied in x in order to have that T is a model of φ. If $F(x)$ contains only boolean combinations of atomic proposition or formulas of the type $\neg E^{>k}\theta$, we choose one child of x and prune all subtrees rooted in the remaining children of x. Each other formula in $F(x)$ not containing path quantifiers still holds true, because it only depends on the labeling of the node x, and each other formula in $F(x)$ of the kind $\neg E^{>k}\theta$ is still satisfied in x because we have only deleted paths starting from x.

Suppose now that $F(x)$ contains also the formulas $E^{>k_1}\theta_1, \ldots, E^{>k_t}\theta_t$. From the minimality of $F(x)$, it follows that $\theta_i \neq \theta_j$, for $i \neq j$, and thus $k_1 + \ldots + k_t \leq \hat{k}$ and $t \leq l$. Consider, for each $1 \leq i \leq t$, a minimal set C_i of children of x that, all together, allow x to satisfy $E^{>k_i}\theta_i$. More precisely, called $m_y = max\{h|(K, y) \models \exists^{>h-1}\theta_i\}$, for a child y of x, $k_i < \sum_{y \in C_i} m_y$, and, for any proper subset C_i' of C_i, $k_i \geq \sum_{y \in C_i'} m_y$. From this definition it follows that $m_y \neq 0$ for every $y \in C_i$ and thus $|C_i| \leq k_i + 1$ for all $1 \leq i \leq t$. Now we prune from T all the subtrees rooted in children of x that are not in $C_1 \cup \ldots \cup C_t$. Since $|C_1 \cup \ldots \cup C_t| \leq k_1 + \ldots + k_t + t \leq b$, now the node x has at most b children. Reasoning as above, formulas in $F(x)$ that either do not contain path quantifiers or are of kind $\neg E^{>k}\theta$ are still satisfied in x. Moreover, the formula $E^{>k_i}\theta_i$ is still satisfied in x because of the x's children that are in C_i.

By iterating this procedure on each node with degree greater than b, we obtain that there exists an infinite tree with branching degree at most b whose root satisfies φ, and this completes the proof. □

Now we show how to solve the SAT problem for a graded-CTL formula in time exponential in the size of the formula. Since $|\varphi|$ is the number of the temporal and the boolean operators occurring in a graded-CTL formula φ, we analyze the complexity of the problem with respect to $|\varphi|_u = |\varphi| + \hat{k}$

Theorem 2. *The satisfiability of a graded-CTL formula φ can be decided in time $2^{\mathcal{O}(|\varphi|_u^4)}$ if the constants appearing in the graded operators of φ are expressed in unary.*

Proof. To prove the theorem, we reduce the satisfiability problem for graded-CTL to the nonemptiness problem of *Nondeterministic Büchi Tree Automata* (NBTA). In particular, we show that for each graded-CTL formula there is an NBTA $\mathcal{A}_\varphi = \langle 2^{AP}, Q, Q_0, \delta, \mathcal{F} \rangle$ that accepts all and only the 2^{AP}-labeled infinite trees satisfying φ, whose branching degree is bounded by b. It is easy to show that $\mathcal{L}(\mathcal{A}_\varphi) \neq \emptyset$ iff φ is satisfiable. From Lemma 1 we have that if $\mathcal{L}(\mathcal{A}_\varphi) = \emptyset$ then φ is not satisfiable. On the other side, if $\mathcal{L}(\mathcal{A}_\varphi) \neq \emptyset$, since an NBTA accepts only regular trees, an infinite regular tree exists satisfying φ; and thus a model for φ exists, since, as it is well known, any regular infinite tree is the unwinding of a Kripke structure.

Let us now describe the automaton $\mathcal{A}_\varphi$. The idea is that each state of the automaton is a set of graded-CTL formulas that have to be satisfied in a node x and the automaton decides, based on the current state and on the label of x, the formulas that have to be satisfied in each child of x. More precisely, the set of the states of the automaton $\mathcal{A}_\varphi$ is the subset $Q \subseteq 2^{ecl(\varphi)}$ such that for all $q \in Q$ the following consistency rules hold:

- if $\psi_1 \wedge \psi_2 \in q$ then $\psi_1 \in q$ and $\psi_2 \in q$,
- if $\neg(\psi_1 \wedge \psi_2) \in q$ then either $\neg\psi_1 \in q$ or $\neg\psi_2 \in q$,
- if $E^{>k}\mathcal{G}\psi_1 \in q$ $(k \geq 0)$ then $\psi_1 \in q$,
- if $E^{>0}\psi_1\mathcal{U}\psi_2 \in q$ then either $\psi_1 \in q$ or $\psi_2 \in q$,
- if $E^{>k}\psi_1\mathcal{U}\psi_2 \in q$ $(k > 0)$ then $\psi_1 \in q$,
- if $\neg E^{>0}\psi_1\mathcal{U}\psi_2 \in q$ then $\neg\psi_2 \in q$,
- for all $\psi \in ecl(\varphi)$, $\psi \in q$ iff $\neg\psi \notin q$.

The set of initial states is the subset $Q_0 \subseteq Q$ containing all the states q such that $\varphi \in q$. A state $q \in Q$ is final iff it satisfies the following properties: *(i)* FALSE $\notin q$, *(ii)* q doesn't contain any formula of kind $E^{>k}\theta$ with $k > 0$ and either $\theta = \mathcal{G}\psi_1$ or $\theta = \psi_1\mathcal{U}\psi_2$, *(iii)* if q contains a formula of kind $E^{>0}\psi_1\mathcal{U}\psi_2$ then it also contains ψ_2 and *(iv)* if q contains a formula of kind $\neg E^{>0}\mathcal{G}\psi_1$ then it also contains $\neg\psi_1$.

Let us now describe the transition function of $\mathcal{A}_\varphi$. Let us suppose that the automaton is in a state $q \in Q$ and is reading the label σ of a node x with $deg(x)$ children. With its transition function, the automaton assigns to each child x a state including a set of formulas chosen as follows, for each $\psi \in q$.

- if $\psi = \text{TRUE}$, then TRUE is added to the set of formulas of each child; analogously for $\psi = \text{FALSE}$;
- if $\psi = p$ ($p \in AP$) and $p \in \sigma$ (resp. $p \notin \sigma$), then TRUE (resp. FALSE) is added to the set of formulas of each child; analogously for $\psi = \neg p$;
- if $\psi = E^{>k}\mathcal{X}\psi_1$ ($k \geq 0$), then $k+1$ children are chosen and ψ_1 is added to the sets of formulas of these children;
- if $\psi = \neg E^{>k}\mathcal{X}\psi_1$ ($k \geq 0$), then at most k children are chosen and ψ_1 is added to the sets of formulas of these children and $\neg\psi_1$ is added to the sets of formulas of the remaining children;
- if $\psi = E^{>k}\mathcal{G}\psi_1$ ($k \geq 0$), then t children $x_1, \ldots, x_t$ and t positive integers $k_1 \ldots, k_t$ are chosen, such that $k_1 + \ldots + k_t + t = k+1$, and $E^{>k_j}\mathcal{G}\psi_1$ is added to the set of formulas of x_j, for all $1 \leq j \leq t$;
- if $\psi = E^{>0}\psi_1\mathcal{U}\psi_2$ and $\neg\psi_2 \in q$, then a child is chosen and $E^{>0}\psi_1\mathcal{U}\psi_2$ is added to the set of formulas of that child;
- if $\psi = E^{>k}\psi_1\mathcal{U}\psi_2$ ($k > 0$), then t children $x_1, \ldots, x_t$ and t positive integers $k_1, \ldots, k_t$ are chosen, such that $k_1 + \ldots + k_t + t = k+1$, and $E^{>k_j}\psi_1\mathcal{U}\psi_2$ is added to the set of formulas x_j, for all $1 \leq j \leq t$;
- if $\psi = \neg E^{>k}\theta$ (with either $\theta = \mathcal{G}\psi_1$ or $\theta = \psi_1\mathcal{U}\psi_2$ and $k \geq 0$) and $\psi_1 \in q$, then $deg(x)$ non negative integers $k_1, \ldots, k_{deg(x)}$ are chosen, such that $k_1 + \ldots + k_{deg(x)} \leq k$, and $\neg E^{>k_j}\theta$ is added to the set of formulas of the j-th child, for all $1 \leq j \leq deg(x)$;
- in the remaining cases, TRUE is added to the set of formulas of each child.

Let us evaluate the size of the automaton and the running time of the algorithm. It is easy to see that $|ecl(\varphi)| = \mathcal{O}(|\varphi|_u)$, therefore the automaton has $2^{\mathcal{O}(|\varphi|_u)}$ states. In the worst case, the function δ contains all the tuples of states with length $b = \mathcal{O}(|\varphi|_u)$, therefore the transition function has total size $|\delta| \leq |Q|^{b+1} = 2^{\mathcal{O}(|\varphi|_u^2)}$ and the size of the automaton is $|\mathcal{A}_\varphi| = 2^{\mathcal{O}(|\varphi|_u^2)}$. Since the nonemptiness problem for an NBTA can be solved in time quadratic in the length of the string representing the automaton [VW86], we obtain that our algorithm works in time $\mathcal{O}(|\mathcal{A}_\varphi|^2) = 2^{\mathcal{O}(|\varphi|_u^4)}$.   □

From the previous theorem and the EXPTIME-completeness of the SAT problem for CTL, the following corollary holds.

Corollary 1. *The SAT problem for graded-CTL is* EXPTIME-*complete.*

4   Symbolic Model Checking Algorithms

In this section we give symbolic algorithms to solve the graded-CTL model checking problem. Let us recall that a *symbolic algorithm* manipulates sets and uses basic set operations, such as union, intersection, and complementation. In symbolic model-checking, states and transitions are represented as boolean functions on the set of the atomic propositions, that in turn, can be represented as the set of variable assignments. In this framework, the fundamental symbolic operation is the computation of the *pre-image* of a set of destination states, (i.e., the states having a successor in the given set). This is performed by using the classical *existential quantification* operation on boolean functions (corresponding to a *projection* on sets). In graded-CTL model-checking, the counterpart of the pre-image is the computation of the *number of successors* that a state has in the destination set, called *image-size*. The image-size function is computed with the existential quantification on multisets (corresponding to a projection on multiset). A Multiset is used to distinguish multiple occurrences of elements and is represented by a pair (M, m) where M is a set of elements and m is a multiplicity function that returns the number of occurrences of the element in input. The projection on multiset is performed with the $\uplus$ operator which sums the multiplicity functions of two multisets. Moreover, our algorithms use also the function $multisetToSet((M, m), i)$ that returns the set of the elements of M having multiplicity greater than i, that is $multisetToSet((M, m), i) = \{s \in M \mid m(s) > i\}$. Some details on the implementation of the above functions can be found in the next section.

It is known that symbolic model-checking algorithms are in the practical cases very efficient, and this depends on the practical efficiency of the data structures used to represent and manipulate sets and multisets. Therefore, as also suggested in [BGS06], we will measure the asymptotic complexity of our algorithms in terms of the *number of pre-image and image-size computations* (we will call **pre** and **imgSize** the functions that compute respectively the pre-image and the image-size).

We denote, for a graded-CTL formula φ, with $[\varphi]$ the set of states of the Kripke structure where φ holds.

Let us now show how to model check formulas of kind $E^{>k}\theta$ $(k \geq 0)$. If $\theta = \mathcal{X}\psi_1$ and $[\psi_1]$ has already been computed, then φ can be easily checked by a function $existNext(\mathcal{K}, k, [\psi_1])$ that first computes the image-size (S, m) of $[\psi_1]$ and then returns the set of states $s \in S$ such that $m(s) > k$ (i.e., $multisetToSet((S, m), k)$).

Therefore we have the following lemma.

Lemma 2. *Given a formula* $\varphi = E^{>k}\mathcal{X}\psi_1$ $(k \geq 0)$, *there is a symbolic algorithm that takes as input* $[\psi_1]$ *and solves the model checking problem for* φ *by using* $\mathcal{O}(1)$ **imgSize** *computations.*

Now let us show how to solve the model checking problem for a formula $\varphi = E^{>k}\theta$ with either $\theta = \psi_1 \mathcal{U}\psi_2$ or $\theta = \mathcal{G}\psi_1$ $(k \geq 0)$.

Lemma 3. *Given a formula* $\varphi = E^{>k}\psi_1 \mathcal{U}\psi_2$ $(k \geq 0)$, *there is a symbolic algorithm that takes in input* $[\psi_1]$ *and* $[\psi_2]$ *and solves the model checking problem for* φ *with* $\mathcal{O}(k \cdot |S|)$ **pre** *and* **imgSize** *computations.*

Proof. We can solve the model checking problem for φ by using the following function *existUntil*.

Function $existUntil(\mathcal{K}, k, [\psi_1], [\psi_2])$

1. $S^0 \leftarrow [\psi_2]; PRED \leftarrow pre(\mathcal{K}, S^0) \cap [\psi_1];$
2. **while** $PRED \nsubseteq S^0$ **do** $S^0 \leftarrow S^0 \cup PRED; PRED \leftarrow pre(\mathcal{K}, S^0) \cap [\psi_1];$
3. $[E^{>0}\psi_1\mathcal{U}\psi_2] \leftarrow S^0;$ Let $(S, sumSucc)$ be such that $sumSucc(s) = 0$ for all $s \in S;$
4. **for** $i \leftarrow 1$ **to** k **do**
5. $(S, succ) \leftarrow imgSize([E^{>i-1}\psi_1\mathcal{U}\psi_2]);$
6. $(S, sumSucc) \leftarrow (S, sumSucc) \uplus (S, succ);$
7. $S^i \leftarrow multisetToSet((S, sumSucc), i) \cap [\psi_1];$
8. $PRED \leftarrow pre(\mathcal{K}, S^i) \cap [\psi_1];$
9.   **while** $PRED \nsubseteq S^i$ **do** $S^i \leftarrow S^i \cup PRED; PRED \leftarrow pre(\mathcal{K}, S^i) \cap [\psi_1];$
10. $[E^{>i}\psi_1\mathcal{U}\psi_2] \leftarrow S^i;$
11. **end**
12. **return** $[E^{>k}\psi_1\mathcal{U}\psi_2];$

For $k = 0$, this function essentially resembles the classical CTL symbolic model checking algorithm [BCM+90]. For $k > 0$ we use, for a state $s \in S$ and $1 \le i \le k$, the functions *succ* and *sumSucc*, defined as follows:

$$succ_s^{i-1} = |\{s' \in [E^{>i-1}\psi_1\mathcal{U}\psi_2] \text{ s.t. } (s, s') \in R\}| \text{ and}$$
$$sumSucc_s^i = \sum_{j=0}^{i-1} succ_s^j.$$

The function $succ_s^{i-1}$ is the number of successors of s satisfying $E^{>i-1}\psi_1\mathcal{U}\psi_2$. Let us observe that if t is a successor of s from which i paths start, each satisfying $\psi_1\mathcal{U}\psi_2$, then t satisfies $E^{>j}\psi_1\mathcal{U}\psi_2$, for $0 \le j < i$, and thus t contributes for i times in the computation of $sumSucc_s^k$. Then $(\mathcal{K}, s) \models \psi$ iff $s \in [\psi_1]$ and one of these two conditions holds:

1. $sumSucc_s^k > k$, that is from the successors of s, $k + 1$ paths stem, each satisfying $\psi_1\mathcal{U}\psi_2$;
2. there is one successor of s satisfying $E^{>k}\psi_1\mathcal{U}\psi_2$.

Based on the above observations, the function *existUntil* satisfies the following invariants, at the end of the i-th iteration:

- the multiset $(S, succ)$ contains the values $succ_s^{i-1}$ for all $s \in S$,
- the multiset $(S, sumSucc)$ contains the values $sumSucc_s^i$ for all $s \in S$ and
- $S^i = [E^{>i}\psi_1\mathcal{U}\psi_2]$.

The proof can be easily obtained by induction on i (it is useful to recall that, given (M, m_1) and (M, m_2), $(M, m_1) \uplus (M, m_2) = (M, m)$ with $m(s) = m_1(s) + m_2(s)$ for all $s \in M$). In particular, to compute S^i, the function computes first the set $\{s \in S \text{ s.t. } sumSucc_s^i > i\}$ (line 6), that is the set of the states satisfying the condition 1 above, and then it applies a least fixpoint algorithm starting from this set (lines 7-8) to compute the set of the states having a successor satisfying $E^{>i}\psi_1\mathcal{U}\psi_2$, according to the condition 2.   □

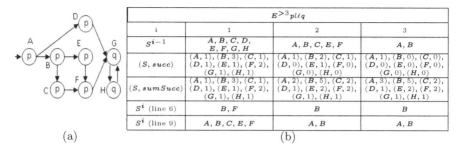

$E^{>3}p\mathcal{U}q$			
i	1	2	3
s^{i-1}	$A,B,C,D,$ E,F,G,H	A,B,C,E,F	A,B
$(S,succ)$	$(A,1),(B,3),(C,1),$ $(D,1),(E,1),(F,2),$ $(G,1),(H,1)$	$(A,1),(B,2),(C,1),$ $(D,0),(E,1),(F,0),$ $(G,0),(H,0)$	$(A,1),(B,0),(C,0),$ $(D,0),(E,0),(F,0),$ $(G,0),(H,0)$
$(S,sumSucc)$	$(A,1),(B,3),(C,1),$ $(D,1),(E,1),(F,2),$ $(G,1),(H,1)$	$(A,2),(B,5),(C,2),$ $(D,1),(E,2),(F,2),$ $(G,1),(H,1)$	$(A,3),(B,5),(C,2),$ $(D,1),(E,2),(F,2),$ $(G,1),(H,1)$
s^i (line 6)	B,F	B	B
s^i (line 9)	A,B,C,E,F	A,B	A,B

(a)   (b)

Fig. 1. An execution of the function $existUntil$

In Figure 1(b) an execution of the function $existUntil$ on the Kripke structure of figure 1(a) and the formula $E^{>3}p\mathcal{U}q$ is reported.

Lemma 4. *Given a formula $\varphi = E^{>k}\mathcal{G}\psi_1$ ($k \geq 0$), there is a symbolic algorithm that takes in input $[\psi_1]$ and solves the model checking problem for φ with $\mathcal{O}(k \cdot |S|)$ pre and imgSize computations.*

Proof. By using a similar reasoning as done in Lemma 3, we can solve the model checking for φ by using the following function $existGlobally$, that is quite similar to the function $existUntil$.

Function $existGlobally(\mathcal{K}, k, [\psi_1])$
---
1. $S^0 \leftarrow [\psi_1]; PRED \leftarrow pre(\mathcal{K}, S^0) \cap [\psi_1];$
2. **while** $PRED \neq S^0$ **do** $S^0 \leftarrow PRED; PRED \leftarrow pre(\mathcal{K}, S^0) \cap [\psi_1];$
3. $[E^{>0}\mathcal{G}\psi_1] \leftarrow S^0;$ Let $(S, sumSucc)$ be such that $sumSucc(s) = 0$ for all $s \in S;$
4. **for** $i \leftarrow 1$ *to* k **do**
5. $\quad (S, succ) \leftarrow imgSize([E^{>i-1}\mathcal{G}\psi_1]);$
5. $\quad (S, sumSucc) \leftarrow (S, sumSucc) \uplus (S, succ);$
6. $\quad S^i \leftarrow multisetToSet((S, sumSucc), i) \cap [\psi_1];$
7. $\quad PRED \leftarrow pre(\mathcal{K}, S^i) \cap [\psi_1];$
8. $\quad$ **while** $PRED \not\subseteq S^i$ **do** $S^i \leftarrow S^i \cup PRED; PRED \leftarrow pre(\mathcal{K}, S^i) \cap [\psi_1];$
9. $\quad [E^{>i}\mathcal{G}\psi_1] \leftarrow S^i;$
10. **end**
11. **return** $[E^{>k}\mathcal{G}\psi_1];$

They essentially differ in the calculus of the base $[E^{>0}\theta]$, for which they resemble the classical CTL symbolic model checking algorithm [BCM$^+$90].   □

Now we are ready to show our symbolic algorithm to solve the graded-CTL model checking problem.

Theorem 3. *The graded-CTL model checking problem can be solved with a symbolic algorithm that performs $\mathcal{O}(\tilde{k} \cdot |S| \cdot |\varphi|)$ calls to the functions pre and imgSize, where $\tilde{k}$ is the maximum grading constant appearing in φ.*

Proof. Algorithm 1 solves the graded-CTL model-checking. It uses the functions $existNext$, $existUntil$ and $existGlobally$ of Lemmas 2, 3 and 4.

Algorithm 1. $gradedCTL(\mathcal{K}, \varphi)$

---

1. **Input:** A Kripke structure and a graded-CTL formula φ.
2. **Output:** The set of states where φ holds.
3. **If** $\varphi = p$ $(p \in AP)$ **then return** $\{s \in S$ s.t. $p \in L(s)\}$;
4. **If** $\varphi = \neg\psi_1$ **then return** $S \setminus GradedCTL(\mathcal{K}, \psi_1)$;
5. **If** $\varphi = \psi_1 \wedge \psi_2$ **then return** $GradedCTL(\mathcal{K}, \psi_1) \cap GradedCTL(\mathcal{K}, \psi_2)$;
6. **If** $\varphi = E^{>k}\mathcal{X}\psi_1$ $(k \geq 0)$ **then return** $existNext(\mathcal{K}, k, GradedCTL(\mathcal{K}, \psi_1))$;
7. **If** $\varphi = E^{>k}\psi_1\mathcal{U}\psi_2$ $(k \geq 0)$ **then return**
   $existUntil(\mathcal{K}, k, GradedCTL(\mathcal{K}, \psi_1), GradedCTL(\mathcal{K}, \psi_2))$;
8. **If** $\varphi = E^{>k}\mathcal{G}\psi_1$ $(k \geq 0)$ **then return** $existGlobally(\mathcal{K}, k, GradedCTL(\mathcal{K}, \psi_1))$;

From previous Lemmas, the number of calls to the functions *pre* and *imgSize* is

$$
T(\mathcal{K}, \varphi) = \begin{cases}
\mathcal{O}(1) & \text{if } \varphi = p \\
\mathcal{O}(1) + T(\mathcal{K}, \psi_1) & \text{if } \varphi = \neg\psi_1 \\
\mathcal{O}(1) + T(\mathcal{K}, \psi_1) + T(\mathcal{K}, \psi_2) & \text{if } \varphi = \psi_1 \wedge \psi_2 \\
\mathcal{O}(1) + T(\mathcal{K}, \psi_1) & \text{if } \varphi = E^{>k}\mathcal{X}\psi_1 \text{ with } k \geq 0 \\
\mathcal{O}(k \cdot |S|) + T(\mathcal{K}, \psi_1) + T(\mathcal{K}, \psi_2) & \text{if } \varphi = E^{>k}\psi_1\mathcal{U}\psi_2 \text{ with } k \geq 0 \\
\mathcal{O}(k \cdot |S|) + T(\mathcal{K}, \psi_1) & \text{if } \varphi = E^{>k}\mathcal{G}\psi_1 \text{ with } k \geq 0
\end{cases}
$$

from which we have that $T(\mathcal{K}, \varphi) = \mathcal{O}(\tilde{k} \cdot |S| \cdot |\varphi|)$. $\qquad\square$

Let us remark that in the syntax of graded-CTL logic we have not included the operator $A^{\leq k}$. In fact, as stated in section 2, this operator can be expressed in terms of $\neg E^{>k}$. Anyway, doing so there is an efficiency problem for the $\mathcal{U}$ operator that causes an efficiency loss for the model checking algorithm. In fact, from equivalence (1) one should evaluate $k + 1$ formulas of kind $E^{>k}\mathcal{G}\theta_1$ and $k + 1$ formulas of kind $E^{>k}\theta_1\mathcal{U}\theta_2$. Anyway, we show here that it is possible to avoid these extra evaluations by using a smarter algorithm.

From the equivalence (1), indeed, it is easy to see that, given a state $s \in S$, if $max_1(s)$ and $max_2(s)$ denote the maximum number of distinct paths, starting from s, satisfying $\mathcal{G}(\psi_1 \wedge \neg\psi_2)$ and $(\psi_1 \wedge \neg\psi_2)\mathcal{U}(\neg\psi_1 \wedge \neg\psi_2)$ respectively, then $(\mathcal{K}, s) \models E^{>k}\neg(\psi_1\mathcal{U}\psi_2)$ iff $max_1(s) + max_2(s) > k$. In fact, there do not exist paths satisfying both the two path-formulas, thus the two sets are disjoint and $max_1(s) + max_2(s)$ is the maximum number of distinct paths violating $\psi_1\mathcal{U}\psi_2$.

Function $forallUntil(\mathcal{K}, k, [\psi_1], [\psi_2])$

---

1. $[\psi_1 \wedge \neg\psi_2] \leftarrow [\psi_1] \cap (S \setminus [\psi_2])$; $[\neg\psi_1 \wedge \neg\psi_2] \leftarrow (S \setminus [\psi_1]) \cap (S \setminus [\psi_2])$;
2. $(S, max_1) \leftarrow maxPathsGlobally(\mathcal{K}, [\psi_1 \wedge \neg\psi_2], k + 1)$;
3. $(S, max_2) \leftarrow maxPathsUntil(\mathcal{K}, [\psi_1 \wedge \neg\psi_2], [\neg\psi_1 \wedge \neg\psi_2], k + 1)$;
4. **return** $multisetToSet((S, max_1) \uplus (S, max_2), k)$;

The function $forallUntil$ uses the functions $maxPathsGlobally(\mathcal{K}, [\theta_1], i)$ and $maxPathsUntil(\mathcal{K}, [\theta_1], [\theta_2], i)$ to compute $max_1(s)$ and $max_2(s)$, respectively, for all $s \in S$. These two functions returns, for each state $s \in S$, the maximum number (bounded by i) of distinct paths starting from s and satisfying $\mathcal{G}\theta_1$ and $\theta_1\mathcal{U}\theta_2$, respectively. The function $maxPathUntil$ can be implemented with a simple modification of the function *existUntil*: execute the *for* loop until $k + 1$, instead of k, and return the multiset $(S, sumSucc)$. Analogously, the function *maxPathGlobally* can be implemented as a simple modification of the function *existGlobally*. In this way, if $[\psi_1]$ and $[\psi_2]$ are known, also the model checking of a formula $A^{\leq k}\psi_1 \mathcal{U} \psi_2$ requires time $\mathcal{O}(k \cdot |S|)$ and we have the following theorem.

Theorem 4. *The model checking problem for a graded-CTL formula φ possibly including* forall *subformulas can be solved with a symbolic algorithm that performs $\mathcal{O}(\tilde{k} \cdot |S| \cdot |\varphi|)$ calls to the functions* pre *and* imgSize, *where $\tilde{k}$ is the maximum grading constant appearing in φ.*

5   Implementation and Experimental Results

In this section we show the experimental results obtained by implementing our symbolic algorithms that we have integrated into the model checker tool NuSMV [CCG⁺02]. NuSMV is based on the CUDD library [Som05], for the treatment of BDDs, that allows also the use of *Algebraic Decision Diagrams*, ADDs in short [BFG⁺97]. These are a generalization of BDDs in which the leaves can be integers and are used to represent multisets. By using ADDs to manipulate multisets one gets several advantages, like natural transformations between sets and multisets (that are frequently used in our algorithms) and very efficient performances in practice. As said in the previous section, the basic operations we use are $\uplus$, *imgSize* and *mutlisetToSet*. Their implementation quite naturally come from simple applications on ADDs of known BDD operations. More precisely, the $\uplus$ operator is obtained by applying to ADDs the classical *apply*: when the computation reaches two leaves x and y of an ADD, the result is a leaf with the sum of x and y. In a similar way, the implementation of the *imgSize* function is an application of the classical *pre* function, with the $\cup$ operator substituted by the $\uplus$ operator. Finally, the *multisetToSet* function is implemented by moving into a 1-node each leaf with value greater than k and into a 0-node the remaining leaves and then by compacting the resulting BDD. The enrichment of NuSMV with the graded-CTL model-checking capability, has implied the modification of the internal parser to allow the use of the syntax for graded-CTL specifications. Let us recall that NuSMV implements direct CTL model-checking procedures only for the operators $E\mathcal{X}$, $E\mathcal{G}$ and $E\mathcal{U}$ and derives from these the procedures for all the other operators (since all the transformations are linear in the size of the formula). In our setting instead, since the transformation of formulas $A^{\leq k}\mathcal{U}$ in terms of $E^{>k}\mathcal{G}$ and $E^{>k}\mathcal{U}$ is inefficient (the size of the resulting formula is $2(k + 1)$ times the size of the original formula), we directly implement all the procedures given in section 4.

We have also implemented the *generation* of the counterexamples, that differently from what happens in CTL, returns trees (constituted by evidences of the negation of the formula) instead of paths. As said into section 1, the implementation of an algorithm for the generation of $k + 1$ distinct evidences of a non trivial path-formula is not easy. More precisely, given a state s, while it is easy to implement an algorithm that returns $k + 1$ distinct evidences of the path-formula $\mathcal{X}\psi_1$ (simply compute the forward-image of s, intersect it with $[\psi_1]$ and pick $k+1$ states from the resulting set), for $\mathcal{G}\psi_1$ and $\psi_1\mathcal{U}\psi_2$ we have to implement a more complex algorithm. We explain here how to use some partial results of our symbolic algorithms (namely, the sets $[E^{>i}\theta]$, $0 \leq i \leq k$, with $\theta = \mathcal{G}\psi_1$ or $\theta = \psi_1\mathcal{U}\psi_2$) to quickly compute a tree of evidences.

When one has to compute a tree of evidences, it is necessary to decide whether it is better to compute a "wide" tree or a "tall" tree, in the sense that one should decide whether, for the case under examination, it is more significant to "distinguish" the evidences as soon as possible or as late as possible. Consider for example the following model and let us look for a counterexample of the formula $\neg E^{>3}\mathcal{G}p$.

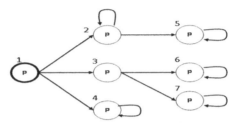

In this case a tall evidence tree will be constituted by all paths which differ only for the number of times that they traverse the self-loop on the state 2, while a large tree includes other more significant evidences.

The technique we have implemented in our tool can be used to find both kinds of tree. The default is to return wide trees (which from our tests seems to be better). Once we have computed the sets $[E^{>i}\theta]$, $0 \leq i \leq k$, by using the functions *existUntil* and *existGlobally*, it is possible to compute a wide evidence tree by executing the following procedure with $s = s_{in}$.

Procedure $evidences(\mathcal{K}, k, s, \theta)$
---
1. **if** $k = 0$ **then**
2. $\quad$ compute an evidence for θ from s as done in NuSMV;
3. **else**;
4. $\quad$ $count \leftarrow 0; i \leftarrow 0$;
5. $\quad$ **while** $count <= k$ **do**
6. $\quad\quad$ **if** $i < k$ **then**
7. $\quad\quad\quad$ $SUCC(s, i) \leftarrow forwardImg(s) \cap ([E^{>i}\theta] \setminus [E^{>i+1}\theta]); k' \leftarrow i$
8. $\quad\quad$ **else**
9. $\quad\quad\quad$ $SUCC(s, i) \leftarrow forwardImg(s) \cap [E^{>i}\theta]; k' \leftarrow \left\lceil \frac{(k-count)}{|SUCC(s,i)|} \right\rceil$
10. $\quad\quad$ **end**
11. $\quad\quad$ **forall** $t \in SUCC(s, i)$ **do**
12. $\quad\quad\quad$ add t to as child of s; $evidences(\mathcal{K}, k', t, \theta); count \leftarrow count + k'$
13. $\quad\quad$ **end**
14. $\quad\quad$ $i \leftarrow i + 1$;
15. $\quad$ **end**
16. **end**

The procedure *evidences* determines $k+1$ evidences starting from a state s in the following way: for each $0 \leq i < k$ it computes the set of successors of s that satisfy $E^{>i}\theta$ and do not satisfy $E^{>i+1}\theta$ (line 7)[1] and from each of these successors it recursively computes a set of $i+1$ distinct evidences. The variable *count* counts the number of evidences that have already been computed. If they are enough (that is, *count* $> k$) then the procedure ends; otherwise it repeats the computation for $i+1$. The *load-balancing* applied to the successors of a node when $i = k$ (lines 9) by giving $k' \leftarrow \left\lceil \frac{(k-count)}{|SUCC(s,i)|} \right\rceil$ is used to avoid to enter in a loop of states all satisfying $E^{>k}\theta$. Note that, the procedure generates the evidences by trying to differentiate them immediately on the successors of each state, thus generating a wide evidence tree.

Our experiments have been executed on a workstation equipped with a CPU Intel Core 2 duo 2.33GHz, with 4GB of RAM and Linux 2.6 operating system. The tool software, other tests and other details (that due to lack of space we have not included in the paper) can be found at http://gradedctl.dia.unisa.it.

As said into the introduction, our motivation to introduce this new graded logic and use it to model check, is mainly to reduce the debugging times: thus to measure the performance of our algorithm/approach one should take into consideration also the *potential* savings obtained in avoiding to go through the cycle Check/Analyze/Fix again. We report now some results measured on CPU time and BDD size on various examples. The examples to test our algorithm have been chosen from the official site of NuSMV. As said before there is no exact method to compare the results of our approach with respect to the classical one. We have chosen to proceed as follows: for each example, we have considered a graded-CTL specification φ and have measured the CPU time and the BDD size to model-check it by varying the values of the constants grading the quantifiers in φ. The first row of each example is the result of running NuSMV on the

Table 1.

k	syncarb5				p-queue				dme1.16	
	$E^{>k}\chi(e2.Token)$		$E^{>k}[!e2.Token\ U\ e2.Token]$		$E^{>k}\mathcal{G}(out\_1[1]=0)$		$A^{\leq k}\mathcal{F}(out\_1[1]=0)$		$E^{>k}\chi e\_1.req$	
	Time	♯BDD	Time	♯BDD	Time	♯BDD	Time	♯BDD	Time	♯BDD
−	0,000	1248	0,000	1255	0,024	33717	0,020	33717	1,320	244734
0	0,000	1248	0,000	1255	0,024	33866	0,020	33866	1,320	244734
1	0,000	1600	0,000	1660	0,056	82361	0,020	41377	1,460	320986
2	0,000	1602	0,000	1694	0,060	92013	0,020	41377	1,664	416145
3	0,000	1603	0,000	1695	0,060	92016	0,024	41377	1,740	443526
5	0,000	1607	0,000	1702	0,060	101671	0,024	41377	2,064	572134
8	0,000	1613	0,000	1714	0,064	102708	0,024	41378	2,736	783876
10	0,000	1614	0,000	1716	0,064	102710	0,024	41380	2,860	830999
15	0,000	1614	0,000	1721	0,068	102715	0,024	41385	3,304	949405
20	0,000	1623	0,000	1738	0,072	104081	0,028	41390	4,248	1168181
50	0,000	1614	0,000	1798	0,104	107395	0,028	41420	9,689	1732683

---

[1] The *forwardImg*, giving the set of successors, can be computed analogously to the computation of the *pre − image*.

given specification with (classical) non-graded quantifiers. The second row is the result of running our tool on the given specification with all the grading values to zero: this to underline that there is no overhead due to the grading, on formulas semantically equivalent. All the remaining rows are the results obtained by using other values of the grading quantifiers, to see how the complexity increases, related to those values.

The Table 1 reports the results for formulas with one graded quantifier. In two cases ($dme1.16$ and p-$queue$ with specification $E^{>k}\mathcal{G}(out\_1[1] = 0)$) one can observe a small increasing in the CPU time, with respect to the time needed for the corresponding CTL formula. In the remaining examples, the CPU time remains almost the same (most are approximatively equal to 0) for all the specifications and for all the values of the constant k. Moreover, also the BDD size increases

Table 2.

k_1	k_2	robot $A^{\leq k_1}\mathcal{G}$ $(pT1.start \to$ $A^{\leq k_2}\mathcal{G}$ $!pT1.finish)$		syncarb5 $A^{\leq k_1}\mathcal{X}A^{\leq k_2}\mathcal{F}$ $(el.ack\_out \wedge$ $el.Persistent)$		k_1	k_2	k_3	abp8 $A^{\leq k_1}\mathcal{G}(A^{\leq k_2}\mathcal{F}$ $(sender.state =$ $get) \wedge A^{\leq k_3}\mathcal{F}$ $(receiver.state =$ $deliver))$		$E^{>k_1}\mathcal{G}(E^{>k_2}\mathcal{F}$ $(sender.state =$ $get) \wedge E^{>k_3}\mathcal{F}$ $(receiver.state =$ $deliver))$	
		Time	#BDD	Time	#BDD				Time	#BDD	Time	#BDD
—	—	0,072	59240	0,000	1321	—	—	—	3,804	1743784	3,052	1616154
0	0	0,072	59449	0,000	1321	0	0	0	3,804	1743794	3,296	1616164
1	0	0,140	96107	0,000	1739	1	0	0	3,832	1750366	5,316	679676
2	0	0,152	97197	0,000	1758	2	0	0	3,832	1750366	6,808	1541032
5	0	0,172	98288	0,000	1791	5	0	0	3,836	1750366	11,765	845117
10	0	0,188	104991	0,000	1829	10	0	0	3,840	1750366	22,321	845117
0	1	0,148	96705	0,000	1739	0	1	1	3,832	1750366	8,237	1345388
1	1	0,160	96705	0,000	1739	1	1	1	3,840	1750366	10,253	679137
2	1	0,224	103426	0,000	1828	5	1	1	3,844	1750366	17,177	845117
5	1	0,236	104517	0,000	1861	10	1	1	3,848	1750366	27,142	845117
10	1	0,264	111220	0,000	1899	0	3	1	3,832	1750366	11,929	1296220
0	2	0,156	97795	0,000	1758	1	3	1	3,840	1750366	13,957	679137
1	2	0,220	103426	0,000	1828	5	3	1	3,860	1750366	20,481	845117
2	2	0,160	97795	0,000	1758	10	3	1	3,872	1750366	31,722	845117
5	2	0,240	104517	0,000	1880	0	5	1	3,864	1750366	15,273	1320804
10	2	0,268	111220	0,000	1918	1	5	1	3,872	1750366	17,385	679137
0	5	0,168	98886	0,000	1792	10	5	1	3,872	1750366	34,058	845117
1	5	0,240	104517	0,000	1862	0	1	3	3,860	1750366	11,725	1345400
2	5	0,244	104517	0,000	1880	1	1	3	3,864	1750366	13,717	679137
5	5	0,188	98886	0,000	1792	10	1	3	3,872	1750366	30,718	845117
10	5	0,276	105589	0,000	1919	0	3	3	3,860	1750366	14,737	1658777
0	10	0,196	105589	0,000	1834	1	3	3	3,868	1750366	16,677	1026555
1	10	0,256	111220	0,000	1904	10	3	3	3,876	1750366	32,950	845117
2	10	0,272	11220	0,000	1922	0	5	3	3,868	1750366	18,141	1316462
5	10	0,284	105589	0,000	1921	1	5	3	3,872	1750366	20,145	679137
10	10	0,220	105589	0,000	1834	10	5	3	3,880	1750366	37,318	845117
50	10	0,528	159213	0,000	1946	10	10	10	3,876	1750366	61,120	845117
50	50	0,564	152510	0,004	1981	50	50	50	3,884	1750366	310,011	845117

very slowly. The Table 2 reports the results for more complex formulas, with two or three graded quantifiers. For some examples, one can observe that the CPU time and the BDD size are not affected by the value of the constant, while in the examples *robot* and *abp8* with the second specification, one can notice an increasing of the CPU time which grows.

Finally, let us note that we have used values for the grading constants in the range $[0, \ldots, 50]$, but we think that in practice a reasonable upper bound should be much smaller, as high values would mean a number of counterexamples too big to deal with.

6   Conclusions and Future Works

In this paper we have considered an expressive extension of classical CTL and have proved that the SAT problem is EXPTIME-complete when the values in the formula are represented in unary. An open problem is hence to establish the complexity of the same problem when the values are in binary (recall that for the case of the model checking problem the complexity for Graded CTL is the same as CTL, even when the constants are expressed in binary). We have also shown symbolic algorithms for model checking against specifications given in this logic and have extended the NuSMV model checker to accept such specifications. The experimental results have indeed shown that the usual performances of NuSMV on classical CTL specifications are still retained.

Besides its augmented expressiveness, with respect to classical CTL specifications, the motivation to study this logic is in the possibility of reducing debugging time. As it is well established, the generation of more than one counterexample is highly desirable, though the size of the counterexamples and their poor human-readability becomes more and more crucial, when more counterexamples are generated. One of the main problems arising is that of determining counterexamples which are as much significant as possible. An approach to this problem is given by a different semantics of graded-CTL which allows to distinguish system behaviors, satisfying a formula, that are completely disjoint. This semantics, called *edge-disjoint* semantics, has been defined in [FNP10] and requires the edge-disjointness of the paths satisfying a path-formula. With this approach one can detect different counterexamples which depend on different and completely independent "errors" in the model. Moreover, this edge-disjointness requirement turns out to be useful also when fault tolerance is required. For this reason, it should be useful to investigate the symbolic model checking problem for edge-disjoint semantics of graded-CTL. Another aspect to consider is the concurrency: partial order techniques have been used to avoid the state explosion, c.f. [God90, GKPP99], also in symbolic model checking, [KGS06]. It would be worthwhile to investigate whether such approach can be usefully applied in our setting to get counterexamples which do not differ only for the interleaving ordering of concurrent actions.

Finally, let us observe that during the model checking process, the system is sometimes abstracted in order to deal with the state explosion problem of the

Kripke structures. But since graded-CTL is a logic based on counting paths satisfying given properties, it is not preserved under most of the usual abstractions (since all of these modify the number of paths in the Kripke structure). Clearly, this situation is inherent to every logic based on counting paths and/or successors such as graded-μ-calculus [KSV02] and graded-HML (Hennessy-Milner Logic) [CDL99]. However in [CDL99] the *resource bisimulation* has been introduced to "discriminate processes according to the number of different computations they can perform to reach specific states". It can be easily shown that graded-CTL logic preserves the resource bisimulation.

Acknowledgments. The authors thank Francesco Sorrentino for his help and his enthusiasm in the early stage of the implementation of our tool.

References

[BCM+90] Burch, J.R., Clarke, E.M., McMillan, K.L., Dill, D.L., Hwang, L.J.: Symbolic model checking: 10^{20} states and beyond. In: Proceedings of the Fifth Annual IEEE Symposium on Logic in Computer Science (LICS 1990), pp. 428–439. IEEE Computer Society Press, Los Alamitos (1990)

[BFG+97] Bahar, R.I., Frohm, E.A., Gaona, C.M., Hachtel, G.D., Macii, E., Pardo, A., Somenzi, F.: Algebraic decision diagrams and their applications. Formal Methods in System Design 10(2/3), 171–206 (1997)

[BGS06] Bloem, R., Gabow, H.N., Somenzi, F.: An algorithm for strongly connected component analysis in $n \log n$ symbolic steps. Formal Methods in System Design 28(1), 37–56 (2006)

[BMM09] Bianco, A., Mogavero, F., Murano, A.: Graded computation tree logic. In: LICS 2009 (2009)

[Bry92] Bryant, R.E.: Symbolic boolean manipulation with ordered binary-decision diagrams. ACM Computing Surveys 24(3), 293–318 (1992)

[CCG+02] Cimatti, A., Clarke, E.M., Giunchiglia, E., Giunchiglia, F., Pistore, M., Roveri, M., Sebastiani, R., Tacchella, A.: NuSMV 2: An openSource tool for symbolic model checking. In: Brinksma, E., Larsen, K.G. (eds.) CAV 2002. LNCS, vol. 2404, pp. 359–364. Springer, Heidelberg (2002)

[CDL99] Corradini, F., De Nicola, R., Labella, A.: Models of nondeterministic regular expressions. J. Comput. Syst. Sci. 59(3), 412–449 (1999)

[CE81] Clarke, E.M., Emerson, E.A.: Design and synthesis of synchronization skeletons using branching-time temporal logic. In: Kozen, D. (ed.) Logic of Programs 1981. LNCS, vol. 131, pp. 52–71. Springer, Heidelberg (1982)

[CE82] Clarke, E.M., Emerson, E.A.: Usig branching time temporal logic to synthesize synchronization skeletons. Science of Computer Programming 2, 241–266 (1982)

[CG07] Chechik, M., Gurfinkel, A.: A framework for counterexample generation and exploration. International Journal on Software Tools for Technololy Transfer 9(5), 429–445 (2007)

[CIW+01] Copty, F., Irron, A., Weissberg, O., Kropp, N.P., Kamhi, G.: Efficient debugging in a formal verification environment. In: Margaria, T., Melham, T.F. (eds.) CHARME 2001. LNCS, vol. 2144, pp. 275–292. Springer, Heidelberg (2001)

[DRS03]   Dong, Y., Ramakrishnan, C.R., Smolka, S.A.: Model checking and evidence exploration. In: Workshop on Model Based Development: Features, Components and Architectures (ECBS 2003), pp. 214–223 (2003)

[EMSS92]   Emerson, E.A., Mok, A.K., Sistla, A.P., Srinivasan, J.: Quantitative temporal reasoning. Real-Time Systems 4(4), 331–352 (1992)

[Fin72]   Fine, K.: In so many possible worlds. Notre Dame Journal of Formal Logic 13(4), 516–520 (1972)

[FNP08]   Ferrante, A., Napoli, M., Parente, M.: CTL model-checking with graded quantifiers. In: Cha, S(S.), Choi, J.-Y., Kim, M., Lee, I., Viswanathan, M. (eds.) ATVA 2008. LNCS, vol. 5311, pp. 18–32. Springer, Heidelberg (2008)

[FNP10]   Ferrante, A., Napoli, M., Parente, M.: Model checking for graded CTL. Fundamenta Informaticae (to appear, 2010); Journal version of [FNP 2008]

[GKPP99]   Gerth, R., Kuiper, R., Peled, D., Penczek, W.: A partial order approach to branching time logic model checking. Information and Computation 150(2), 132–152 (1999)

[GMV99]   Ganzinger, H., Meyer, C., Veanes, M.: The two–variable guarded fragment with transitive relations. In: LICS, pp. 24–34 (1999)

[God90]   Godefroid, P.: Using partial orders to improve automatic verification methods. In: Clarke, E., Kurshan, R.P. (eds.) CAV 1990. LNCS, vol. 531, pp. 176–185. Springer, Heidelberg (1991)

[GOR97]   Grädel, E., Otto, M., Rosen, E.: Two–variable logic with counting is decidable. In: LICS, pp. 306–317 (1997)

[GPP07]   Gentilini, R., Piazza, C., Policriti, A.: Symbolic graphs: Linear solutions to connectivity related problems. Algorithmica 50(1), 120–158 (2007)

[HB91]   Hollunder, B., Baader, F.: Qualifying number restrictions in concept languages. In: KR, pp. 335–346 (1991)

[KGS06]   Kahlon, V., Gupta, A., Sinha, N.: Symbolic model checking of concurrent programs using partial orders and on-the-fly transactions. In: Ball, T., Jones, R.B. (eds.) CAV 2006. LNCS, vol. 4144, pp. 286–299. Springer, Heidelberg (2006)

[KSV02]   Kupferman, O., Sattler, U., Vardi, M.Y.: The complexity of the graded μ–calculus. In: Voronkov, A. (ed.) CADE 2002. LNCS (LNAI), vol. 2392, pp. 423–437. Springer, Heidelberg (2002)

[Mar05]   Marrero, W.: Using bdds to decide ctl. In: Halbwachs, N., Zuck, L.D. (eds.) TACAS 2005. LNCS, vol. 3440, pp. 222–236. Springer, Heidelberg (2005)

[McM93]   McMillan, K.L.: Symbolic Model Checking. Kluwer Academic Publishers, Dordrecht (1993)

[PST00]   Pacholski, L., Szwast, W., Tendera, L.: Complexity results for first–order two–variable logic with counting. SIAM Journal of Computing 29(4), 1083–1117 (2000)

[PSV05]   Pan, G., Sattler, U., Vardi, M.Y.: Bdd-based decision procedures for the modal logic k. Journal of Applied Non-classical Logics 49 (2005)

[Som05]   Somenzi, F.: Cudd: Cu decision diagram package, release 2.4.1 (2005), http://vlsi.colorado.edu/~fabio/CUDD

[Tob01]   Tobies, S.: PSPACE reasoning for graded modal logics. Journal Log. Comput. 11(1), 85–106 (2001)

[VW86]   Vardi, M.Y., Wolper, P.: Automata-theoretic techniques for modal logics of programs. J. of Computer and System Sciences 32(2), 183–221 (1986)

Approximate Model Checking of PCTL Involving Unbounded Path Properties

Samik Basu[1], Arka P. Ghosh[2], and Ru He[1]

[1] Department of Computer Science, Iowa State University
[2] Department of Statistics, Iowa State University
{sbasu,apghosh,rhe}@iastate.edu

Abstract. We study the problem of applying statistical methods for approximate model checking of probabilistic systems against properties encoded as PCTL formulas. Such approximate methods have been proposed primarily to deal with state-space explosion that makes the exact model checking by numerical methods practically infeasible for large systems. However, the existing statistical methods either consider a restricted subset of PCTL, specifically, the subset that can only express bounded until properties; or rely on user-specified finite bound on the sample path length. We propose a new method that does not have such restrictions and can be effectively used to reason about unbounded until properties. We approximate probabilistic characteristics of an unbounded until property by that of a bounded until property for a suitably chosen value of the bound. In essence, our method is a two-phase process: (a) the first phase is concerned with identifying the bound k_0; (b) the second phase computes the probability of satisfying the k_0-bounded until property as an estimate for the probability of satisfying the corresponding unbounded until property. In both phases, it is sufficient to verify bounded until properties which can be effectively done using existing statistical techniques. We prove the correctness of our technique and present its prototype implementations. We empirically show the practical applicability of our method by considering different case studies including a simple infinite-state model, and large finite-state models such as IPv4 zeroconf protocol and dining philosopher protocol modeled as Discrete Time Markov chains.

1 Introduction

A number of techniques has been developed over the past decade for model checking probabilistic systems [16,15,8,13] against probabilistic temporal properties (e.g. PCTL [9], CSL [1]). While [9,3,7,1,2] rely on exploration of entire state-space of the probabilistic systems and applying linear equation solvers to obtain the exact probability with which the system satisfies a property; [22,10,17] sample a finite set of paths in the system and infer the approximate probability of satisfiability of a property by the whole system using probabilistic arguments.

While numerical verification method provides exact solutions, it requires complete knowledge of the system and may fail for systems with large state-space

K. Breitman and A. Cavalcanti (Eds.): ICFEM 2009, LNCS 5885, pp. 326–346, 2009.

(state-space explosion problem). It is in this situation, sampling based statistical verification methods are useful. However, two important issues need to be addressed before any statistical verification approach can be applied effectively. They stem from the fact that samples only explore partial state-space of the system and therefore, the accuracy of the verification results depends on the size N of the sample (i.e., the number of sample paths) and also on the length k of each sample path. The bound k becomes particularly important when the property of interest is *unbounded*, i.e., $\varphi_1 \cup \varphi_2$. The semantics of the property states that a path satisfies the property if and only if there exists a state in the path which satisfies φ_2 and in all states before it φ_1 is satisfied. Note that, φ_1 can be satisfied any number of times in a path before φ_2 is satisfied for the first time. Therefore, in any path of finite length, where every state satisfies $\varphi_1 \wedge \neg\varphi_2$, it is impossible to infer whether the extension of the path will eventually satisfy or not satisfy $\varphi_1 \cup \varphi_2$. However, such problem is not present when the property under consideration has a specific bound (*bounded* path property): $\varphi_1 \cup^{\leq k} \varphi_2$, i.e., φ_2 must be satisfied in k steps from the start state, which, in turn, implies that paths of length k are enough to verify such properties. of the existing sampling based statistical.

We propose to reduce the problem of verifying $(\varphi_1 \cup \varphi_2)$ into that of its bounded counter-part $(\varphi_1 \cup^{\leq k_0} \varphi_2)$. The reduction is possible only when a suitable k_0 can be obtained for which the $\mathsf{P}(s, \varphi_1 \cup^{\leq k_0} \varphi_2)$ (i.e., probability of satisfying of $\varphi_1 \cup^{\leq k_0} \varphi_2$ at state s) is a *good* approximation of $\mathsf{P}(s, \varphi_1 \cup \varphi_2)$. In other words, the bound k_0 is large enough to make the difference between $\mathsf{P}(s, \varphi_1 \cup^{\leq k_0} \varphi_2)$ and $\mathsf{P}(s, \varphi_1 \cup \varphi_2)$ small. Such k_0 provides an approximate upper bound of the sample path lengths needed for our statistical verification technique. We obtain k_0 using the probability of satisfying another bounded until property: $\psi_k := (\varphi_1 \cup^{\leq k} \varphi_2) \vee (\neg\varphi_2 \cup^{\leq k} (\neg\varphi_1 \wedge \neg\varphi_2))$. It states that the property $(\varphi_1 \cup \varphi_2)$ is either satisfied (first disjunct) or unsatisfied (second disjunct) in at most k steps. We prove that the suitable k_0 is one for which $\mathsf{P}(s, \psi_{k_0})$ is close to 1, and the degree of "closeness" is related to ϵ, the overall measure of accuracy of the entire statistical method.

In essence, there are two phases in our method. The first phase estimates $\mathsf{P}(s, \psi_k)$ for $k = 0, 1, 2, \ldots$ and chooses k_0 which satisfies $\mathsf{P}(s, \psi_{k_0}) \geq 1 - \epsilon_0$, where $\epsilon_0 < \epsilon$. In the second phase, $\mathsf{P}(s, (\varphi_1 \cup^{\leq k_0} \varphi_2))$ is estimated which, in turn, serves as an estimate of $\mathsf{P}(s, (\varphi_1 \cup \varphi_2))$. The computations for each phase involves only *bounded-path* properties and can be carried out efficiently using the existing sampling techniques such as [10].

Illustrative Example. To provide an intuitive explanation of why the proposed technique is useful and effective, we present a simple toy example (Figure 1) where the proposed method is applied successfully and where both the numerical method and the existing statistical verification method as

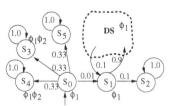

Fig. 1. A simple example

implemented in popular PRISM model checker [11] fail. The example contains a probabilistic transition system containing $6 + n$ states where n is some large integer. The state s_0 is the start state of the system. The dotted segment in the figure represents some "complicated" transition structure on n different states (see [19] for the specification). We will refer to this segment as DS. Let proposition φ_1 hold in all states except s_2 and s_5, and proposition φ_2 hold in states s_3 and s_4. The objective is to find the probability of satisfying the property $(\varphi_1 \ \cup \ \varphi_2)$ at state s_0. From the probabilities specified in the figure, we know that the resultant probability is 0.66 as only two paths $(s_0, s_3, \ldots)$ and $(s_0, s_4, \ldots)$ satisfy the property.

We experimented with the PRISM model checker [11] using the above example. PRISM's numerical method fails as the large state-space (large n) results in state-space explosion. PRISM's statistical method takes as input a parameter ϵ and provides approximate result within ϵ error margin. Our experiments with several $\epsilon > 0$ failed to provide any estimate. This is because, PRISM's statistical method requires that every sample of a pre-specified length can infer with certainty whether the property $(\varphi_1 \ \cup \ \varphi_2)$ is satisfied or not. The failure happens when at least one sample ends in DS where the above requirement does not hold.

In terms of ψ_k introduced earlier, the above requirement in PRISM's statistical method is equivalent to $P(s_0, \psi_k) = 1$, for some pre-specified bound k ($k = 10,000$ by default in PRISM). In general, it is not possible to appropriately find a good value for k such that $P(s_0, \psi_k) = 1$. In contrast, we claim that it is not necessary to verify whether $P(s_0, \psi_k)$ is equal to 1. The necessary precision in sampling based method can be obtained by identifying a k (specifically a k_0) for which $P(s_0, \psi_k)$ is close to 1. In the above example, such a bound can be immediately obtained as the sample paths $(s_0, s_1, \ldots)$ have very low probability (≤ 0.01). Once such a bound is obtained, we compute $P(s_0, \varphi_1 \ \cup^{\leq k_0} \ \varphi_2)$ which approximately coincides with $P(s_0, \varphi_1 \ \cup \ \varphi_2)$. In our experiments, with $n \approx 10^8$, while the PRISM model checker fails to provide any result, our method identifies a bound $k_0 = 190$ and estimates the probability to be equal to 0.6601.

Contributions. The contributions of our approach are summarized as follows:

1. We present a methodology for selecting a suitable bound k_0 using which unbounded until properties for probabilistic systems can be verified using the corresponding k_0-bounded until properties.
2. The reduction allows us to re-use existing results of statistical verification of bounded until properties to identify the bound on sample size N required to infer results within a pre-specified error margin. We present an implementation which directly uses the techniques developed and available in the widely used PRISM model checker.
3. The technique is independent of the system model and property logic. For explanation and experiments, we use probabilistic transition systems modeled as Discrete Time Markov Chains (DTMC) and property logic expressed in PCTL. However, the technique is equally applicable for Continuous Time Markov Chains (CTMC) and until properties expressible in CSL.

4. Our technique can be also effectively applied in setting where the probabilistic system is viewed as a black-box and for probabilistic systems containing infinite number of states; the reason being our technique does not depend on the system state-space and transition structure, our technique only requires the availability of sample simulations of the system under consideration.
5. We theoretically prove the correctness of our technique and present research prototype of our implementation to empirically show the applicability of our technique using several examples: probabilistic dining philosopher, IPv4 zeroconf protocol and a probabilistic model for queue. The prototype and all examples are available at [19].

Organization.   Section 2 discusses related work. Section 3 provides a brief overview of probabilistic transition systems and probabilistic temporal logic PCTL. Section 4 presents our solution methodology and its correctness proof. The implementation and experimental results are discussed in Sections 5. Finally, Section 6 concludes with the summary of our work.

2   Related Work

Statistical method based on Monte Carlo simulation and sequential hypothesis testing [20] for verifying time bounded until CSL properties in CTMC is developed by Younes and Simmons [22]. Similar techniques are proposed and discussed in [21]. Sen et al. [17] introduce a new statistical model checking algorithm for handling unbounded until properties based on Monte Carlo simulation and hypothesis testing. However, the technique suffers from the drawback that it requires some prior knowledge of the actual probability of satisfying unbounded until property for obtaining valid results. Furthermore, the validity of the technique requires that the system being analyzed does not contain self-loops in any state [23]. Zapreev [24] also proposes a statistical technique for verifying unbounded until properties. However, this technique requires knowledge of the model structure and relies on user-specified sample size and sample path lengths.

Closest to our approach is the technique proposed by Herault et al. in [10]. The proposed method based on Monte Carlo simulation uses estimation from Chernoff-Hoeffding inequality [12] to verify a subset of LTL formula, EPF (Essentially Positive Fragment) in DTMC. The algorithm includes the checking of the unbounded until properties. However, it fails to completely control the error in the procedure. The reason is essentially as follows. The sample path length used in the procedure has a pre-specified upper bound. If a simulation reaches that bound and fails to infer a decided result, the technique assumes that the simulation, if allowed to proceed, will eventually have results defending the null hypothesis ([5]) of the testing procedure. This assumption allows the method to control Type I Error (the error that the null hypothesis H_0 is true but the test incorrectly rejects H_0) within a pre-specified limit. However, as the authors state in [10], the proposed technique cannot determine the appropriate upper bound of simulation path length to control the number of the undecided simulations. As such, the method loses the control of Type II Error (the error that the null hypothesis H_0 is false but the test incorrectly accepts H_0).

This technique ([10]) is incorporated in the popular probabilistic model checker PRISM [11]. The distinguishing feature of PRISM's statistical approach is that unlike [10] which allows the undecided simulations, PRISM requires that every simulation terminates with a decided result. This requirement makes it necessary to appropriately identify the bound on sample length for which simulation run of each sample will have a decided result; if such bound is not used, PRISM's simulation based technique fails to compute the result and requests the user to re-run the experiment with a new bound.

Our technique, a natural extension of [10], addresses this problem by using a two phase method where in the first phase an appropriate bound in sample length is obtained and in the second phase the bound obtained in the first phase is used to compute the result for unbounded until properties.

3   Background

The explanation and theoretical results of our technique are presented for probabilistic transition systems modeled as DTMC and until properties expressed in the logic of PCTL. However, the results are extensible to other modeling paradigms (CTMC and semi-Markov chains [6]) and until properties expressed in corresponding property logics (CSL).

3.1   Probabilistic Transition Systems and PCTL

Definition 1. *A probabilistic transition system [10] $PTS = (S, s_I, T, L)$, where S is a finite set of states, $s_I \in S$ is the initial or start state, $T : S \times S \to [0,1]$ is a transition probability function such that $\forall s : \sum_{s' \in S} T(s, s') = 1$, and $L : S \to \mathcal{P}(AP)$ is the labeling function which labels each state with a set of atomic propositions $\subseteq AP$ that holds in that state.*

Paths and Probability Measures. A path in PTS, denoted by π, is a finite or infinite sequence of states $(s_0, s_1, s_2, s_3, \ldots)$ such that for all $i \geq 0 : s_i \in S$ and $T(s_i, s_{i+1}) > 0$. We denote the set of all infinite paths starting from s as $Path(s)$. $\pi[i]$ denotes the i-th state in the path π and $|\pi|$ is the length of π in terms of the number of transitions in π. For example, for an infinite path π, $|\pi| = \infty$, while for a finite path $\pi = (s_0, \ldots, s_n)$, $|\pi| = n, n \geq 0$. The cylinder set, denoted by $C_s(\pi)$, for a state s and π a finite length path starting from s, is defined as $C_s(\pi) = \{\pi' : \pi' \in Path(s) \land \pi \text{ is prefix of } \pi'\}$. Essentially, $C_s(\pi)$ is the set of all infinite paths $\in Path(s)$ with the common finite length prefix π. For any finite path π with $|\pi| = n$ we define

$$P(\pi) = \begin{cases} 1 \text{ if } n = 0 \\ T(\pi[0], \pi[1]) \times \ldots \times T(\pi[n-1], \pi[n]) \text{ otherwise} \end{cases}$$

For a cylinder $C_s(\pi)$, define $Pr(C_s(\pi)) = P(\pi)$. It is well-known that this probability measure $Pr(\cdot)$ extends uniquely over all sets in the relevant σ-algebra.

PCTL Syntax and Semantics. Properties of PTS can be expressed using PCTL, an extension of standard CTL augmented with probabilistic specifications. Let φ represent a state formula and ψ represent a path formula. Then PCTL syntax is defined as follows:

$$\varphi \to tt \mid a \in AP \mid \neg\varphi \mid \varphi \wedge \varphi \mid \mathsf{P}_{\bowtie r}(\psi) \quad \text{and} \quad \psi \to X\varphi \mid \varphi \,\mathsf{U}\, \varphi \mid \varphi \,\mathsf{U}^{\leq k}\, \varphi$$

In the above, $\bowtie \in \{\leq, \geq, <, >\}$, $r \in [0,1]$ and $k \in \{0,1,\ldots\}$. Note that we always use state formulas to specify the properties of a PTS and path formulas only occur inside $\mathsf{P}_{\bowtie r}(.)$. A state s (or a path π) satisfying a state formula φ (or a path formula ψ) is denoted by $s \models \varphi$ (or $\pi \models \psi$), and is inductively defined as follows:

$$s \models tt \text{ for all } s \in S \qquad s \models a \Leftrightarrow a \in L(s) \qquad s \models \neg\varphi \Leftrightarrow s \not\models \varphi$$
$$s \models \varphi_1 \wedge \varphi_2 \Leftrightarrow s \models \varphi_1 \text{ and } s \models \varphi_2 \qquad s \models \mathsf{P}_{\bowtie r}(\psi) \Leftrightarrow \mathsf{P}(s,\psi) \bowtie r$$

In the above, $\mathsf{P}(s,\psi) = Pr(\{\pi \in Path(s) : \pi \models \psi\})$. In other words, $s \models \mathsf{P}_{\bowtie r}(\psi)$ holds if and only if the probability *that ψ is true for an outgoing infinite path from state s* is $\bowtie r$. For any infinite path π:

$$\pi \models X\varphi \Leftrightarrow \pi[1] \models \varphi$$
$$\pi \models \varphi_1 \,\mathsf{U}^{\leq k}\, \varphi_2 \Leftrightarrow \exists 0 \leq i \leq k : \pi[i] \models \varphi_2 \wedge \forall j < i : \pi[j] \models \varphi_1$$
$$\pi \models \varphi_1 \,\mathsf{U}\, \varphi_2 \Leftrightarrow \exists i \geq 0 : \pi[i] \models \varphi_2 \wedge \forall j < i : \pi[j] \models \varphi_1$$

Note that $\varphi_1 \,\mathsf{U}\, \varphi_2 \equiv \exists k : \varphi_1 \,\mathsf{U}^{\leq k}\, \varphi_2$. We refer to properties of the form $\varphi_1 \,\mathsf{U}\, \varphi_2$ as unbounded as the bound k is not known.

4   Verifying Unbounded Until Properties

The objective of our work is to reduce the probabilistic model checking for unbounded until properties to bounded until properties. The main problem that needs to be addressed to realize such a reduction involves identifying (a) a suitable bound k_0 for checking the bounded until property (in each simulation) (done in *Phase I*), and (b) a bound on the number of simulations (each of length k_0) (done in *Phase II*), such that a suitable statistical sampling based verification result of bounded until property approximately coincides with that of the unbounded until property within a pre-specified error limit (See Theorem 1 for a precise statement).

4.1   Rationale

The paths belonging to the semantics of $\varphi_1 \,\mathsf{U}\, \varphi_2$ (Section 3.1) can be partitioned into two groups for each $k \geq 1$: one includes the paths that satisfy the property in $\leq k$ steps; while the other includes the paths that satisfy the property in $> k$ steps. I.e., the semantics of $\varphi_1 \,\mathsf{U}\, \varphi_2$ can be written as

$$\pi \models \varphi_1 \,\mathsf{U}\, \varphi_2$$
$$\Leftrightarrow \forall k : \begin{bmatrix} \exists 0 \leq i < k : \pi[i] \models \varphi_2 \wedge \forall j < i : \pi[j] \models \varphi_1 \\ \vee \\ \exists i > k : \pi[i] \models \varphi_2 \wedge \forall j_1 < i : \pi[j_1] \models \varphi_1 \wedge \forall j_2 \leq k : \pi[j_2] \models \neg\varphi_2 \end{bmatrix}$$
$$\Leftrightarrow \pi \models \forall k : \left[(\varphi_1 \,\mathsf{U}^{\leq k}\, \varphi_2) \vee (\varphi_1 \,\mathsf{U}^{>k}\, \varphi_2) \right]$$

Since, $(\varphi_1 \ U^{\leq k} \ \varphi_2) \wedge (\varphi_1 \ U^{>k} \ \varphi_2) = f\!f$, by law of total probability

$$\mathsf{P}(s, \varphi_1 \ U \ \varphi_2) = \mathsf{P}(s, \varphi_1 \ U^{\leq k} \ \varphi_2) + \mathsf{P}(s, \varphi_1 \ U^{>k} \ \varphi_2) \qquad (1)$$

In other words, from the fact that probabilities $\in [0, 1]$,

$$0 \leq \mathsf{P}(s, \varphi_1 \ U \ \varphi_2) - \mathsf{P}(s, \varphi_1 \ U^{\leq k} \ \varphi_2) = \mathsf{P}(s, \varphi_1 \ U^{>k} \ \varphi_2) \qquad (2)$$

Next consider the property $\varphi_1 \ U^{>k} \ \varphi_2$.

$\pi \models \varphi_1 \ U^{>k} \ \varphi_2$
$\Leftrightarrow \exists i > k : \pi[i] \models \varphi_2 \ \wedge \ \forall j_1 < i : \pi[j_1] \models \varphi_1 \ \wedge \ \forall j_2 \leq k : \pi[j_2] \models \neg\varphi_2$
$\Rightarrow \forall i \leq k : \pi[i] \models \varphi_1 \wedge \neg\varphi_2$
$\Leftrightarrow \varphi_1 \ U \ \varphi_2$ is neither satisfied nor unsatisfied in k steps from $\pi[0]$
$\Leftrightarrow \pi \models \neg(\varphi_1 \ U^{\leq k} \ \varphi_2) \ \wedge \ \neg(\neg\varphi_2 \ U^{\leq k} \ (\neg\varphi_1 \wedge \neg\varphi_2))$

Let $\psi_k = (\varphi_1 \ U^{\leq k} \ \varphi_2) \vee (\neg\varphi_2 \ U^{\leq k} \ (\neg\varphi_1 \wedge \neg\varphi_2))$, i.e., ψ_k is the property that is satisfied by a path π only when the satisfiability of $\varphi_1 \ U \ \varphi_2$ can be proved or disproved in k steps from the start state $(\pi[0])$. Therefore, from the above $(\varphi_1 \ U^{>k} \ \varphi_2) \Rightarrow \neg\psi_k$ and

$$\mathsf{P}(s, \varphi_1 \ U^{>k} \ \varphi_2) \leq \mathsf{P}(s, \neg\psi_k) = 1 - \mathsf{P}(s, \psi_k) \qquad (3)$$

From Equations 2 and 3, for any $k \geq 1$ we obtain

$$0 \leq \mathsf{P}(s, \varphi_1 \ U \ \varphi_2) - \mathsf{P}(s, \varphi_1 \ U^{\leq k} \ \varphi_2) \leq 1 - \mathsf{P}(s, \psi_k) \qquad (4)$$

Our objective is to select a k_0 such that for any given ϵ_0.

$$\mathsf{P}(s, \psi_{k_0}) \geq 1 - \epsilon_0 \qquad (5)$$

In that case,

$$0 \leq \mathsf{P}(s, \varphi_1 \ U \ \varphi_2) - \mathsf{P}(s, \varphi_1 \ U^{\leq k_0} \ \varphi_2) \leq 1 - \mathsf{P}(s, \psi_{k_0}) \leq \epsilon_0 \qquad (6)$$

In other words, by choosing an appropriate k_0, the probability of satisfying unbounded path property $\varphi_1 \ U \ \varphi_2$ can be made close (within an error margin of ϵ_0, for any arbitrarily small choice of ϵ_0) to the probability of satisfying the bounded path property $\varphi_1 \ U^{\leq k_0} \ \varphi_2$.

Remark 1. The above argument assumes that as $k \to \infty$, limit of $\mathsf{P}(s, \psi_k) \geq 1 - \epsilon_0$ (Equation 5). But since, $\mathsf{P}(s, \psi_k) = 1 - \mathsf{P}(s, \neg\psi_k)$, the above requirement is equivalent to stating

$$\lim_{k \to \infty} \mathsf{P}(s, \neg\psi_k) \leq \epsilon_0 \qquad (7)$$

When the above limit is zero, Equation 7 is satisfied for any ϵ_0 and hence our method is also valid for any $\epsilon_0 \geq 0$. When the limit is non-zero, our method works for any ϵ_0 that satisfies the inequality in Equation 7. Note that, the requirement of satisfying this inequality does not restrict the applicability of our technique to any specific class of properties or models; our technique can be applied for any until property and for any model as long as the above requirement is satisfied. Further note that, PRISM's statistical method is equivalent to choosing $\epsilon_0 = 0$ in our method and hence will fail to provide result whenever this limit is non-zero. In other words, whenever PRISM's statistical verification method is successful in computing a result, our method also terminates with a result, and furthermore, our method is able to estimate probabilities for some cases where PRISM's statistical method fails (as discussed in Section 1).

The implication of a non-zero limit is that $\mathsf{P}(s, \neg(tt\ \mathsf{U}\ (\varphi_2 \vee \neg\varphi_1))) > 0$, which happens if and only if there exists an infinite path in the model with positive probability where every state satisfies $(\varphi_1 \wedge \neg\varphi_2)$. In this case, any statistical verification method, which does not analyze model transition structure, may not be able to provide result. However, this feature of not analyzing the model allows application of statistical verification methods (including ours) for the purpose of estimating the probability of properties in black-box systems and in systems with infinite number of states (see Section 5.1), where information regarding transition structure may not be available. The proposed method will work as long as it is possible to obtain sample paths of any finite length from such systems and the property can be verified (to be true, untrue or undecided) for these paths.

4.2   Two-Phase Model Checking

The discussion in previous subsection (specifically, Equations 5 and 6) motivates our two phase method. In the first phase, we determine k_0 suitably and in the second phase we estimate $\mathsf{P}(s, \varphi_1\ \mathsf{U}^{\leq k_0}\ \varphi_2)$.

The main challenge in achieving the first objective is that the function $F(\cdot)$, where $F(k) = \mathsf{P}(s, \psi_k), k \geq 1$, is not known in a typical situation. If this function was known, getting k_0 that satisfies Equation 5 could have been achieved by simply inverting this (non-decreasing) function. We address this issue by considering a natural estimator of this function: for each k, estimate $\mathsf{P}(s, \psi_k)$ by the proportion of N_1 Monte Carlo simulation paths that satisfy ψ_k (similar to the GAA (Generic Approximation Algorithm) algorithm described in [10]). This is done for all $k \geq 1$ until for some k_0, the estimate satisfies Equation 5.

Once k_0 is obtained, in the second phase we estimate $\mathsf{P}(s, \varphi_1\ \mathsf{U}^{\leq k_0}\ \varphi_2)$. This estimate is computed as the proportion of N_2 Monte Carlo simulation paths (each of length at most k_0) that satisfy $\varphi_1\ \mathsf{U}^{\leq k_0}\ \varphi_2$. This also can be thought of as a simple application of the GAA algorithm for bounded until properties described in [10].

Finally, motivated by Equation 6, $\mathsf{P}(s, \varphi_1\ \mathsf{U}\ \varphi_2)$ is estimated from the estimated value of $\mathsf{P}(s, \varphi_1\ \mathsf{U}^{\leq k_0}\ \varphi_2)$. The two phases for computing k_0 and then computing $\mathsf{P}(s, \varphi_1\ \mathsf{U}^{\leq k_0}\ \varphi_2)$ are carried out "independently", i.e., involving separate samples (of sizes N_1 and N_2 respectively), which enables us to combine the errors in two phases to guarantee a certain precision. The number of Monte Carlo simulation paths used in the two phases and the value of k_0 are chosen in such a way that the final estimate is correct within a pre-specified error limit (see Theorem 1). The steps in our method are summarized as follows:

<u>Main Steps.</u> *Algorithm:* U2B$(M, s, \varphi_1 \ \mathsf{U} \ \varphi_2, \epsilon, \delta)$

Input: model M, initial state s, property $\varphi_1 \ \mathsf{U} \ \varphi_2$, precision parameter ϵ, confidence parameter δ

1. *Phase I*: Obtaining k_0
   (a) Choose $N_1 \geq N_1^* = 9 \log(\frac{4}{\delta})/2\epsilon^2$. From M, obtain N_1 Monte Carlo simulation paths of length $k = 1$. Let for $i = 1, \ldots, N_1$, $X_i = 1$ if the i-th simulation satisfies ψ_k; $X_i = 0$ otherwise.
   (b) Estimate $\mathsf{P}(s, \psi_k)$ as the proportion of the simulation paths satisfying ψ_k, i.e
   $$\widehat{\mathsf{P}}(s, \psi_k) = \frac{1}{N_1} \sum_{i=1}^{N_1} X_i. \tag{8}$$
   (c) Verify if Equation 5 is satisfied by the estimate in Equation 8 with the current value of k and $\epsilon_0 = \frac{\epsilon}{3}$. More precisely, if
   $$\widehat{\mathsf{P}}(s, \psi_k) \geq 1 - \epsilon_0 \geq 1 - \frac{\epsilon}{3}, \tag{9}$$
   then $k_0 = k$ and proceed to *Phase II*. Otherwise, increase k by 1 and generate one more transition for each of the existing N_1 simulation paths, creating N_1 paths of increased (by 1) length. Define $X_i, i = 1, \ldots, N_1$ as in Step 2(a) using these extended simulation paths and repeat the Step 2(b)-(c).

2. *Phase II*: Estimating $\mathsf{P}(s, \varphi_1 \ \mathsf{U}^{\leq k_0} \ \varphi_2)$
   (a) Choose $N_2 \geq N_1^* = 36 \log(\frac{4}{\delta})/\epsilon^2$. From M, obtain N_2 Monte Carlo simulation paths (of length at most k_0). Let for $i = 1, \ldots, N_2$, $Y_i = 1$ if the i-th simulation path satisfies $\varphi_1 \ \mathsf{U}^{\leq k_0} \ \varphi_2$; $Y_i = 0$ otherwise.
   (b) Estimate $\mathsf{P}(s, \varphi_1 \ \mathsf{U}^{\leq k_0} \ \varphi_2)$ as the proportion of the simulation paths that satisfy $\varphi_1 \ \mathsf{U}^{\leq k_0} \ \varphi_2$, i.e
   $$\widehat{\mathsf{P}}(s, \varphi_1 \ \mathsf{U}^{\leq k_0} \ \varphi_2) = \frac{1}{N_2} \sum_{i=1}^{N_2} Y_i. \tag{10}$$
   Return $\widehat{\mathsf{P}}(s, \varphi_1 \ \mathsf{U}^{\leq k_0} \ \varphi_2)$, as the estimate for $\mathsf{P}(s, \varphi_1 \ \mathsf{U} \ \varphi_2)$

The proof of the following result provides the proof of correctness of our approach described above.

Theorem 1. *Given any precision parameter $\epsilon > 0$ and confidence parameter $\delta > 0$, the estimator* U2B$(M, s, \varphi_1 \ \mathsf{U} \ \varphi_2, \epsilon, \delta)$ *with the chosen values of k_0, N_1^*, N_2^* satisfies the following:*
$$Pr\left(|\ U2B(M, s, \varphi_1 \ \mathsf{U} \ \varphi_2, \epsilon, \delta) - P(s, \varphi_1 \ \mathsf{U} \ \varphi_2)\ | > \epsilon\right) \leq \delta. \tag{11}$$

4.3 Proof of Correctness

This subsection is devoted to the proof of the Theorem 1. We begin by discussing auxiliary results in theoretical statistics that will be used in the proof. We discuss properties of the estimation procedure separately for the two phases.

Phase I: Estimating k_0

The function $F(\cdot)$ introduced in Subsection 4.2 can be thought of as the cumulative distribution function (c.d.f) of a random variable K = the minimum number of transitions required to verify $\varphi_1 \cup \varphi_2$ along a randomly selected simulation path in the given model. In that case, our estimation process in *Phase I* is equivalent to estimating this c.d.f using N_1 independent samples collected from the distribution of this variable K. In fact, our estimate $\widehat{\mathsf{P}}(s, \psi_k)$ (as a function of k) is the usual empirical c.d.f estimator $\hat{F}_{N_1}(\cdot)$ of the true c.d.f $F(\cdot)$. It is well-known that $k \geq 1$, $\hat{F}_{N_1}(k)$ converges to $F(k)$, as $N_1 \to \infty$ at a suitable rate, for *each* k. For the proof of Theorem 1, we need the rate, *uniform* in k, at which this convergence takes place. This is provided by the celebrated Dvoretzky-Kiefer-Wolfowitz (DKW) inequality (see for example, [14]): For each $\epsilon_1 > 0, N_1 \geq 1$, $Pr\left(\sup_{k \geq 1} |\hat{F}_{N_1}(k) - F(k)| > \epsilon_1\right) \leq 2e^{-2N_1(\epsilon_1)^2}$. This result, restated in terms of $\mathsf{P}(s, \psi_k) = F(k)$ and $\widehat{\mathsf{P}}(s, \psi_k) = \hat{F}_{N_1}(k)$, for each k, yields the following lemma, which will be needed for our proof of Theorem 1.

Lemma 1. *Given any $\epsilon_1 > 0$ and $N_1 \geq 1$,*

$$Pr\left(\sup_{k \geq 1} |\widehat{\mathsf{P}}(s, \psi_k) - \mathsf{P}(s, \psi_k)| > \epsilon_1\right) \leq 2e^{-2N_1(\epsilon_1)^2}.$$

Phase II: Estimating $\mathbf{P}(s, \varphi_1 \cup^{\leq k_0} \varphi_2)$

In this phase, we estimate the probability of the *bounded* until property $\varphi_1 \cup^{\leq k_0} \varphi_2$ in M, with $k_0 \geq 1$ determined in *Phase I*. For any given $k \geq 1$, our algorithm in *Phase II* is simply the GAA algorithm (c.f. [10]) of estimating the probability of a *bounded* until property $\varphi_1 \cup^{\leq k} \varphi_2$ in M. Hence using the same technique (i.e. using Chernoff-Hoeffding bound) we get for each $\epsilon_2 > 0$, $Pr\left(|\widehat{\mathsf{P}}(s, \varphi_1 \cup^{\leq k} \varphi_2) - \mathsf{P}(s, \varphi_1 \cup^{\leq k} \varphi_2)| > \epsilon_2\right) \leq 2e^{-N_2(\epsilon_2)^2/4}$. Now since the above inequality is true for all $k \geq 1$, it is true *conditional* on the simulations of *Phase I*, for $k = k_0$. But the two phases are carried out independently, which means the above statement must be true *unconditionally* as well, for $k = k_0$. Summarizing this discussion, we have

Lemma 2. *Given any $\epsilon_2 > 0$ and $N_2 \geq 1$,*

$$Pr\left(|\widehat{\mathsf{P}}(s, \varphi_1 \cup^{\leq k_0} \varphi_2) - \mathsf{P}(s, \varphi_1 \cup^{\leq k_0} \varphi_2)| > \epsilon_2\right) \leq 2e^{-N_2(\epsilon_2)^2/4}.$$

Now we use the results in Lemmas 1 and 2 to complete the proof of Theorem 1.

Proof (of Theorem 1). Using triangle inequality (after adding and subtracting suitable terms) yields the following

$$|\,\mathsf{U2B}(M, s, \varphi_1 \cup \varphi_2, \epsilon, \delta) - \mathsf{P}(s, \varphi_1 \cup \varphi_2)\,| = |\,\widehat{\mathsf{P}}(s, \varphi_1 \cup^{\leq k_0} \varphi_2) - \mathsf{P}(s, \varphi_1 \cup \varphi_2)\,|$$
$$\leq |\,\widehat{\mathsf{P}}(s, \varphi_1 \cup^{\leq k_0} \varphi_2) - \mathsf{P}(s, \varphi_1 \cup^{\leq k_0} \varphi_2)\,|$$
$$+ \,|\,\mathsf{P}(s, \varphi_1 \cup \varphi_2) - \mathsf{P}(s, \varphi_1 \cup^{\leq k_0} \varphi_2)\,|. \qquad (12)$$

Recall that, from Equation 9, we have $1 - \widehat{\mathsf{P}}(s, \psi_k) \leq \epsilon/3$. Hence, using Equation 4 and triangle inequality, we get the following bound on the last term in Equation 12

$$| P(s, \varphi_1 \cup \varphi_2) - P(s, \varphi_1 \cup^{\leq k_0} \varphi_2) | \leq (1 - P(s, \psi_{k_0}))$$
$$\leq (1 - \widehat{P}(s, \psi_{k_0})) + | \widehat{P}(s, \psi_{k_0}) - P(s, \psi_{k_0}) |$$
$$\leq \frac{\epsilon}{3} + \sup_{k \geq 1} | \widehat{P}(s, \psi_k) - P(s, \psi_k) | . \qquad (13)$$

Combining Equation 12 with Equation 13, we get the following bound

$$| \text{U2B}(M, s, \varphi_1 \cup \varphi_2, \epsilon, \delta) - P(s, \varphi_1 \cup \varphi_2) | \leq$$
$$| \widehat{P}(s, \varphi_1 \cup^{\leq k_0} \varphi_2) - P(s, \varphi_1 \cup^{\leq k_0} \varphi_2) | + \tfrac{\epsilon}{3} + \sup_{k \geq 1} | \widehat{P}(s, \psi_k) - P(s, \psi_k) |$$

Hence, the left side of the above inequality is greater than ϵ (see Equation 11 in Theorem 1) implies that at least one of the terms on the right side is greater than $\epsilon/3$. Therefore, we obtain the following:

$$Pr \left(| \text{U2B}(M, s, \varphi_1 \cup \varphi_2, \epsilon, \delta) - P(s, \varphi_1 \cup \varphi_2) | > \epsilon \right)$$
$$\leq \quad Pr \left(| \widehat{P}(s, \varphi_1 \cup^{\leq k_0} \varphi_2) - P(s, \varphi_1 \cup^{\leq k_0} \varphi_2) | > \frac{\epsilon}{3} \right)$$
$$+ Pr \left(\sup_{k \geq 1} | \widehat{P}(s, \psi_k) - P(s, \psi_k) | > \frac{\epsilon}{3} \right) \quad \leq \quad \delta. \qquad (14)$$

The last inequality follows from the bounds in Lemmas 1 and 2 with $\epsilon_1 = \epsilon/3$ and $\epsilon_2 = \epsilon/3$, since with $N_i \geq N_i^*, i = 1, 2$, we have $2e^{-2N_1(\epsilon_1)^2} \leq \delta/2$ (i.e, $N_1 \geq \frac{1}{2\epsilon_1^2} log(\frac{4}{\delta}) \geq \frac{9}{2\epsilon^2} log(\frac{4}{\delta})$) and $2e^{-N_2(\epsilon_2)^2/4} \leq \delta/2$ (i.e., $N_2 \geq \frac{4}{\epsilon_2^2} log(\frac{4}{\delta}) \geq \frac{36}{\epsilon^2} log(\frac{4}{\delta})$). This completes the proof of Theorem 1.

Remark 2. Observe that there are three error bounds that are derived from ϵ each of which is assigned to $\frac{\epsilon}{3}$: ϵ_0 (From Equation 9), ϵ_1 (From Lemma 1) and ϵ_2 (From Lemma 2). While ϵ_0 is the measure of closeness of $\widehat{P}(s, \psi_k)$ to 1, ϵ_1 and ϵ_2 capture the closeness of the estimated and true probabilities in each phase. In other words, smaller ϵ_0 will lead to larger value for k_0 (sample path length), while smaller ϵ_1 and ϵ_2 values will result in larger values for sample size in each phase, N_1 and N_2. The proof of our theorem holds as long as $\epsilon_0 + \epsilon_1 + \epsilon_2 = \epsilon$. The choice of these values can be fine tuned in the experiments.

5   Prototype Implementation and Experiments

In the following sections we discuss the implementation of our technique. We have developed two variations of implementation; one is based on the PRISM model checker, and the other is a stand-alone implementation using XSB [18] logic programming environment. We will refer to the former as I_{PRISM} and the latter as I_{XSB}. The reason for these two variations is that the PRISM model checker does not allow input models with infinite state-space, while our technique can be applied to such models. As such, to provide proof of concept, I_{XSB} has been developed which can take input models with any state-space. The I_{PRISM} is used to directly compare the precision of our technique against that of PRISM's numerical and statistical methods. The prototype implementations and all examples are available at [19].

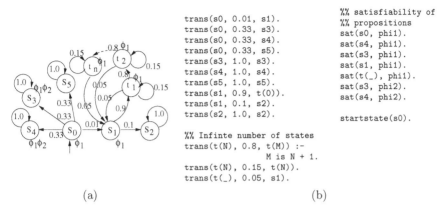

```
trans(s0, 0.01, s1).
trans(s0, 0.33, s3).
trans(s0, 0.33, s4).
trans(s0, 0.33, s5).
trans(s3, 1.0, s3).
trans(s4, 1.0, s4).
trans(s5, 1.0, s5).
trans(s1, 0.9, t(0)).
trans(s1, 0.1, s2).
trans(s2, 1.0, s2).

%% Infinte number of states
trans(t(N), 0.8, t(M)) :-
                M is N + 1.
trans(t(N), 0.15, t(N)).
trans(t(_), 0.05, s1).
```

```
%% satisfiability of
%% propositions
sat(s0, phi1).
sat(s4, phi1).
sat(s3, phi1).
sat(s1, phi1).
sat(t(_), phi1).
sat(s3, phi2).
sat(s4, phi2).

startstate(s0).
```

(a)   (b)

Fig. 2. (a) Model of infinite state system. (b) Logical encoding of the model.

Experimental Setup. For our experiments, we have used $\epsilon = 0.025$ and $\epsilon_0 = \frac{\epsilon}{10}$, $\epsilon_1 = \frac{\epsilon}{2}$, $\epsilon_2 = 2\frac{\epsilon}{5}$ (see Remark 2). For these values, the sample size in phase I is $N_1^* = 19172$ and in phase II is $N_2^* = 239658$ (see Section 4.3, proof of Theorem 1). These values allow for high precision in terms of sample path length without compromising on the time required to obtain the results, where the computation time is directly proportional to the number of the samples being used in each phases. All experiments are conducted on Red Hat Enterprise Linux 5.1 running on Intel Core 2 Duo 3GHz CPU and 2GB memory.

5.1 Logical Encoding of U2B: I_{XSB}

We use XSB tabled logic programming language [18] to encode the algorithm U2B. XSB system is an extension of Prolog-style SLD resolution with tabling. Predicates or relations in XSB are defined as logical rules of the form

$$\text{Goal :- SubGoal\_1, SubGoal\_2, } \ldots \text{, SubGoal\_N}$$

where the predicate Goal evaluates to true if each of the SubGoals in the rhs of :- evaluates to true, i.e., $\text{SubGoal\_1} \wedge \text{SubGoal\_2} \wedge \ldots \wedge \text{SubGoal\_N} \Rightarrow \text{Goal}$. A rule with empty rhs is referred to as a *fact*. We encode the model using such logical rules. Details of our implementation and its usage are available at [19].

Case study: infinite state system. Figure 2(a) presents a variant of the model presented in Figure 1. The segment DS in Figure 1 is replaced by an infinite chain of states: $t_0, t_1, \ldots, t_n$ where $n \geq 0$ is not pre-specified. It is not possible to specify such a system in PRISM as it requires the input model to be of finite state-space.

Figure 2(b) presents our logical encoding of the model in Figure 2(a). Each transition is specified using a **trans** predicate which has three parameters: the source state (first parameter), the destination state (third parameter) and the probability associated with the transition (second parameter). Observe that the transition relation with source state t(N) is defined using three rules. The first rule leads to infinite transition sequence as it specifies that the destination state is t(M) where M is obtained by increasing N by 1. The predicates sat and startstate specifies the propositions/formulas satisfied at each state and the start state of the model respectively. In this case, φ_1 is satisfied in all states except s_2 and s_5, φ_2 is satisfied in s_3 and s_4, and the start state is s_0.

Given that the objective is to compute $P(s_0, \varphi_1 \cup \varphi_2)$, our implementation successfully identifies the bound $k_0 = 248$ (phase I) and estimates the probability to be equal to 0.6598 (phase II). Observe from the transition probabilities, the actual value for $P(s_0, \varphi_1 \cup \varphi_2)$ is 0.66 as there are two paths that satisfies $\varphi_1 \cup \varphi_2$.

Recall that it is not possible to specify the infinite state model (Figure 2(a)) in PRISM. Furthermore, PRISM's numerical method is not applicable due to infinite number of states in the model. However, technique used in PRISM's statistical model checking method can be applied as (similar to ours) it does not depend on the model transition structure. As such, we have also implemented in I_{XSB} a prototype version of PRISM's statistical technique. Our experiments using PRISM's statistical method is not successful in estimating the probability as in every sample there exists at least one sample execution where the given until property is not verifiable (i.e., it cannot be decided whether the path satisfies the until property or not). In Section 1, we have discussed similar results for the example model in Figure 1.

5.2 Implementation Based on PRISM: I_{PRISM}

We re-use sampling based statistical verification method implemented in the PRISM model checker to evaluate the effectiveness of our technique. Given a property $\varphi = \varphi_1 \cup \varphi_2$, our implementation generates $\psi_k^1 = \varphi_1 \cup^{\leq k} \varphi_2$ and $\psi_k^2 = \neg \varphi_2 \cup^{\leq k} (\neg \varphi_1 \wedge \neg \varphi_2)$ for different values of k. The PRISM sampling based technique is then used with sample size N_1^* to estimate the probabilities $p_1(k)$ and $p_2(k)$ of satisfying ψ_k^1 and ψ_k^2 respectively. Observe that $\psi_k = \psi_k^1 \vee \psi_k^2$ and $\psi_k^1 \wedge \psi_k^2 = f\!f$. As such, the probability of satisfying ψ_k is obtained from $p(k) = p_1(k) + p_2(k)$. Once, $p(k) \geq 1 - \epsilon_0$ is obtained for some k, where ϵ_0 is suitably selected from ϵ, the corresponding value of k is recorded as k_0 (Step 1c of Algorithm U2B). In the second phase, the k_0 is used to obtain the probability of satisfying the property $\varphi_1 \cup^{\leq k_0} \varphi_2$ and PRISM's sampling based technique is again invoked with sample size N_2^* (Step 2 of Algorithm U2B). The result is the estimate of probability for satisfying $\varphi_1 \cup \varphi_2$.

5.3 Precision Evaluation Using PRISM

We have described an example (Figure 1) where PRISM's numerical and statistical methods fail to provide result. The exact specification of the model (in PRISM specification language) is provided in [19]. For PRISM's numerical method, we have experimented using both Jacobi and Gauss-Seidel variations. The numerical method fails to compute the result due to state-space explosion. For PRISM's statistical method, we have experimented by varying the error margin from 0.01 (default) to 0.05 and sample path length from 10000 (default) to

Table 1. Experimental results for illustrative example in Figure 1 where exact probability is 0.66

| | PRISM | | | Our Technique | |
| Numerical | Statistical | | | $\epsilon = 0.025, \delta = 0.01$ | |
	ϵ	Sample path-length	k_0	prob	
out-of-memory	0.010	100000 (no-result)			
	0.015	100000 (no-result)			
	0.020	500000 (no-result)	2649	0.6587	
	0.025	500000 (no-result)			
	0.030	1000000 (no-result)			
	0.050	1000000 (no-result)			

1000000; in each experiment, PRISM fails to provide result due to the presence of a sample path where the given until property is not verifiable. On the other hand, our method successfully estimates the probability within the pre-specified error bound (actual probability is 0.66, estimate from our technique is 0.6587 with $\epsilon = 0.025$ and $\delta = 0.01$). Table 1 summarizes the results.

In the following, we will further compare our technique using examples from the existing literature. The objective of the comparison is to show that (a) our technique does not require users to pre-specify the upper-bound of the length of the sample paths; (b) our technique uses smaller sample path lengths than PRISM's statistical method; and (c) our technique provides good probability estimates, i.e., close to the probability results computed by numerical methods.

Zeroconf Protocol. We have experimented using IPv4 zeroconf protocol modeled as PTS [4] (Figure 3(a)); the same model is used in [17]. The model contains $n+3$ states $\{s_0, s_1, \ldots, s_n, s_{ok}, s_{err}\}$. The state s_0 is the start state and the propositions ok and err are satisfied in states s_{ok} and s_{err} respectively. The transition labels denote the probability of the corresponding transitions. Our objective is to compute $P(s_0, \neg ok \, U \, err)$ for the model. The top half of Table 2 presents our experimental results for different values of the n and the transition probabilities q and r. The results show that both PRISM's sampling based method and our method provide good probability estimates (close to PRISM's numerical solutions). In all the experiments, PRISM is able to provide results using the default setting for number of Jacobi iterations (10000 for numerical method) and

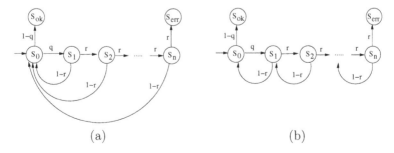

(a)   (b)

Fig. 3. (a) Ipv4 zeroconf protocol and (b) n-buffer Queue

Table 2. Experimental results for (a) Zeroconf and (b) Queue Protocol

(n, q, r)	PRISM		Our Technique	
	Numerical	Statistical (Default settings) $\epsilon = 0.01, \delta = 1.0E\text{-}10$	$\epsilon = 0.025$ $\delta = 0.01$	
	prob (#Jacobi)	prob (max sample path-length)	k_0	prob
$(10, 0.9, 0.9)$	0.8097 (86)	0.8117 (86)	47	0.8095
$(20, 0.9, 0.9)$	0.5975 (308)	0.6020 (398)	183	0.6000
$(40, 0.9, 0.9)$	0.1529 (824)	0.1562 (1173)	555	0.1542
$(60, 0.9, 0.9)$	0.0215 (1009)	0.0223 (1334)	667	0.0213
$(80, 0.9, 0.9)$	0.0026 (1056)	0.0027 (1586)	708	0.0028
$(100, 0.9, 0.9)$	3.24E-4 (1080)	3.42E-4 (1489)	676	3.55E-4
	Results for model in Figure 3(a)			
$(80, 0.9, 0.5)$	0.1022 (12176)	0.1087 (20111)	8768	0.1071
$(100, 0.7, 0.5)$	0.0230 (15728)	0.0237 (23057)	7552	0.0223
$(100, 0.9, 0.5)$	0.0832 (17452)	0.0876 (27727)	12677	0.0875
$(120, 0.9, 0.5)$	0.0702 (23444)	0.0745 (39537)	18057	0.0742
$(140, 0.9, 0.5)$	0.0607 (30102)	0.0639 (56189)	22034	0.0646
$(160, 0.9, 0.5)$	0.0534 (37376)	0.0574 (65429)	26372	0.0553
$(180, 0.9, 0.5)$	0.0477 (45228)	0.0507 (94567)	32565	0.0498
$(200, 0.9, 0.5)$	0.0431 (53662)	fail (100000)	41192	0.0452
	Results for model in Figure 3(b)			

the maximum length of sample path (10000 for statistical method). However, observe that the maximum sample path length (`max sample path-length`) required by PRISM's statistical method is larger than the bound k_0 obtained and used by our method in all experiments.

Queue with parameterized size. We have also experimented using the same property against an n-size queue model (Figure 3(b)) which is similar to Zeroconf protocol model. The bottom half of Table 2 shows the corresponding experimental results. Observe that PRISM's numerical method fails to compute results using default number of Jacobi iterations (10000). We have increased the number of these iterations for obtaining the result and the corresponding maximum iteration required is also shown in the table. PRISM's sampling based technique also fails to provide result using the default sample path length (10000). We have experimented by increasing the sample path lengths and report the corresponding maximum sample path length required for each case. It should be noted that in general, it is not possible to pre-specify these parameters (number of Jacobi iterations or the maximum sample path length). For $(n, q, r) = (200, 0.9, 0.5)$ and for sample path length 100000, PRISM's statistical method is not able to consistently provide results; it fails whenever a sample path is examined where it cannot be decided whether the given until property is satisfied or not. For each experiment, our method consistently uses smaller sample path length (k_0 computed in phase I) compared to PRISM's statistical method, and is successful in providing a good probability estimate.

Dining Philosopher Protocol. We use a DTMC model for dining philosopher protocol. Our objective is to compute for the start state s_0, $P(s_0, \text{allhungry U eat}_1)$, where `allhungry` is true in states where none of the philosophers are eating (do not have one of the forks) and eat_1 is true in states

Table 3. Experimental results for Dining Philosopher Protocol

| # Philos | PRISM | | Our Technique $\epsilon = 0.025$ | |
| | Numerical | Statistical (Default Settings) $\epsilon = 0.01, \delta = 1.0\text{E}{-}10$ | $\delta = 0.01$ | |
	prob	prob (max sample path-length)	k_0	prob
10	0.0999	0.0997 (50)	33	0.0989
20	-	0.0492 (64)	46	0.0495
30	-	0.0333 (80)	58	0.0327
40	-	0.0242 (103)	68	0.0242
50	-	0.0199 (107)	76	0.0196
60	-	0.0164 (114)	83	0.0163
70	-	0.0140 (127)	91	0.0137
100	-	0.0099 (162)	114	0.0096

where philosopher 1 is eating (has both forks). In short, the objective is to compute probability that 1-st philosopher eats before anyone else can eat.

Table 3 presents the experimental results obtained by varying the number of philosophers. PRISM's numerical method fails to compute the probability of satisfying the property due to memory constraints when the number of philosophers is ≥ 20, while both our method and PRISM's sampling based method are successful in estimating the probability.

5.4 Summary of Experimental Results

The experimental results empirically show the advantages of our method. First, our method provides good estimates of the exact result and uses smaller sample path lengths than PRISM's statistical method in all experiments. Whenever PRISM statistical verification provides an estimate, our method also terminates with an estimate using comparatively smaller sample path lengths (Tables 2, 3). Second, our method does not require the user to pre-specify a sample path length which is required in PRISM's statistical method and which may not be possible to correctly specify in general. In fact, as PRISM's statistical method requires the verifiability of the given until property in all samples, its result (i.e., whether it can provide an estimate or fail due to at least one sample where property is unverifiable) may vary from one experiment to another for the same sample path length. In short, our method succeeds in computing results even for some cases when PRISM's statistical method fails (Table 1). Finally, being based on sampling, our method does not require the construction of the entire model and does not suffer from the state-space explosion problem which may render numerical method unusable (Table 3). Our method can be effectively used in the setting where the system is a black-box or has infinite number of states, and only samples in the form of simulation runs of the system are available (Section 5.1).

5.5 Discussion on Optimization

In the above experiments, we are not addressing optimization with respect to execution time directly. This is because, our first objective is to present a provably correct, systematic sampling based method for automatically verifying unbounded until probabilistic properties. Our experiments show that the proposed technique indeed can solve the problem of probabilistic model checking of until properties in an unsupervised fashion (as opposed to trial-and-error method relying on the user to try different sample path length bounds). However, for complete understanding of our current implementation we present here brief discussion on timing results of our technique and provide a roadmap for developing a full-fledged standalone tool based on our technique that is likely to be as fast as existing statistical verification tools like the one implemented in PRISM model checker.

Efficiently Obtaining k_0. We have shown that the upper bound of sample path length required for our technique is considerably smaller than that required by PRISM's statistical method. Naive approach for computing such a bound will involve iteratively computing the $\widehat{P}(s, \psi_k)$ for $k = 1, 2, 3, \ldots$ till a k_0 is obtained for which $\widehat{P}(s, \psi_{k_0}) \geq 1 - \epsilon_0$ (Equation 9).

However, in our experiments we have observed that this approach is be too time consuming when the value of k_0 is large. For instance, the experiments with queue model (Table 2(b)) require a large number of iterations (starting from initial value of k being 1) to obtain the appropriate value of k_0 (≥ 8500). To address this issue (i.e., reduce the number of iterations), we have developed and optimized iterative procedure for computing k_0. The optimization involves increasing the value of k not by pre-specified fixed increments (e.g., by 1), but by Δ_k such that the bound k_0 can be computed in lesser number of iterations in phase I. This strategy involves computing Δ_i (the increment of k after $i - 1$ iterations) from the proportion of the differences between two consecutive estimates ($p(i - 1) = \widehat{P}(s, \psi_{k_{i-1}})$ and $p(i - 2) = \widehat{P}(s, \psi_{k_{i-2}})$) and the target $1 - \epsilon_0$. That is,

$$\forall i \geq 2 : \Delta_i = \begin{cases} \Delta_{i-1} \left[\frac{(1-\epsilon_0)-p(i-1)}{p(i-1)-p(i-2)} \right] & \text{if the denominator is non-zero} \\ \Delta_{i-1} & \text{otherwise} \end{cases}$$

We initialize $k_1 = 1$, $\Delta_1 = 1$ and assume that $p(0) = 0$. Using this strategy, it is likely that the target $(1 - \epsilon_0)$ will be reached with fewer jumps (compared to the strategy which employs pre-specified fixed incremented of k). However, it may happen that k_0, thus obtained, is not be the smallest possible one. Note that the choice of k_0 is not unique, and having a small k_0 actually reduces the computational overhead for the second phase of our method. To remedy this possibility of "overshooting", we use a binary-search strategy to ensure a small value of k_0: If for some $i \geq 2$, for $a = k_{i-1}$, $\widehat{P}(s, \psi_a)$ is below the target $(1 - \epsilon_0)$ and for $b = k_i$, $\widehat{P}(s, \psi_b)$ overshoots the target by certain pre-specified margin (e.g., $\widehat{P}(s, \psi_b) > 1 - \epsilon_0/2$), then we choose next $k_{i+1} = a + \frac{a+b}{2}$; we also reset $a = k_{i+1}$. If for this new k_{i+1}, $\widehat{P}(s, \psi_{k_{i+1}})$ is less than the target, then the next value of $k_{i+2} = b - \frac{b-a}{2}$ and we reset $b = k_{i+2}$; otherwise, $k_{i+2} = a + \frac{b-a}{2}$ as before. The computation terminates either (a) when a value of k_0 is obtained for which $\widehat{P}(s, \psi_{k_0})$ is above the target but within the pre-specified margin; or (b) when $b - a \leq 1$ and k_0 is set to b. Clearly, for different models and choice of the property, the value of k_0 will be different and it will depend on the behavior of the random variable K (with c.d.f $F(\cdot)$). (For more discussion on how different the probability distributions of this random variable can look like, see [19].)

Figures 4(a), (b) and (c) illustrate the increments in k with successive estimates of $\widehat{P}(s, \psi_k)$ (iteration number is shown in parenthesis wherever possible; e.g., in Figure 4(a), at iteration 2, $k = 91$ and $\widehat{P}(s, \psi_k) = F(k) = 0.5989$). The graphs show that the increment in k adapts to the rate at which the corresponding estimated probability increases with k, assuming a local linear approximation of the $F(\cdot)$ function (see Section 4.2). Using this strategy, k increases with smaller "jumps" (smaller Δ−values) when $P(s, \psi_k)$ has a high rate of increase, while the increments in k gets larger when the rate of increase of $P(s, \psi_k)$ is slow. Observe that in Figure 4(b) (queue model with $(n, q, r) = (120, 0.9.0.5)$), the binary search strategy is not deployed as the first k for which $1 - \epsilon_0 \le \widehat{P}(s, \psi_k)$ is such that $\widehat{P}(s, \psi_k) < 1 - \epsilon_0/2$. However, in Figures 4(a) and (c), the binary search strategy is used to obtain a smaller value of k_0. For example (Figure 4(a)), for zeroconf model with $(n, q, r) =$

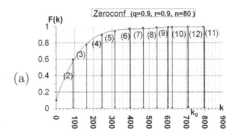

(a)

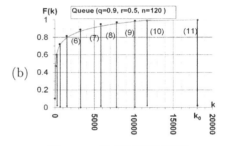

(b)

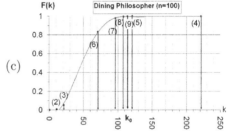

(c)

Fig. 4. $F(k) = \widehat{P}(s, \psi_k)$ against k for (a) Zeroconf, (b) Queue, and (c) Dining philosopher

$(80, 0.9, 0.9)$, at 11-th iteration where $k = 792$, $\widehat{P}(s, \psi_k) > 1 - \epsilon_0/2$, i.e., $\widehat{P}(s, \psi_k)$ overshoots the target value by the pre-specified margin ($\epsilon_0/2$). The binary search strategy is fired, which uses the current value (792 in iteration 11) and previous value (625 in iteration 10) of k and computes the new value of $k = 708$.

The bounds (k_0) and the probability estimates presented in Tables 1, 2 and 3) are obtained by using the above optimized strategy. Table 4 presents some of the experiments already discussed and shows the number of iterations used in Phase I of our technique to obtain the appropriate k_0. The table also compares the timing results of our method as implemented in $\mathtt{I_{PRISM}}$ against PRISM's statistical verification method. Note that the time taken by our technique is of the same order as the time taken by PRISM's statistical method. The main overhead in our implementation is due to the fact that it requires multiple sample

Table 4. Timing results (in seconds)

Model	PRISM Statistical Method Time	Our Technique			
		Phase I			Phase II
		k_0	iterations	Time	Time
Example (Figure. 1)	no-result	2649	8	21	75
Zeroconf ($n : 20, q : 0.9, r : 0.9$)	11	183	10	5	7
Zeroconf ($n : 80, q : 0.9, r : 0.9$)	31	708	12	16	20
Queue ($n : 80, q : 0.9, r : 0.5$)	219	8768	11	77	139
Queue ($n : 180, q : 0.9, r : 0.5$)	532	32565	14	225	331
Dining philosopher (# philos: 20)	61	46	8	23	43
Dining philosopher (# philos: 100)	709	114	9	278	523

analysis for each increments in k in phase I. For example, consider that in the i-th iteration of phase I, our method examines sample of size N_1^*, where each sample path is of length k_i. Further consider that, the estimate of satisfying ψ_{k_i} is not greater than $1 - \epsilon_0$ (Equations 8, 9). In that case, we increase (either by a fixed value or by Δ_i) the sample path length to k_{i+1} and recompute the estimate of satisfying $\psi_{k_{i+1}}$. In other words, in the i-th iteration, if a path $(s_0, s_1, \ldots, s_{k_i})$ does not satisfy ψ_{k_i}, then in the $i + 1$-th iteration, we want to consider the path $(s_0, s_1, \ldots, s_{k_i}, \ldots, s_{k_{i+1}})$ and check whether $\psi_{k_{i+1}}$ is satisfied in this path. However, as our current implementation relies on the PRISM-generated samples and the implementation does not modify the way such samples are generated, instead of extending $(s_0, s_1, \ldots, s_{k_i})$ by $(s_0, s_1, \ldots, s_{k_i}, \ldots, s_{k_{i+1}})$, our implementation obtains a completely new sample path of length k_{i+1}, i.e., $(s'_0, s'_1, \ldots, s'_{k_{i+1}})$ where $s'_0 = s_0$. While this does not invalidate the theoretical basis of our technique, it incurs an additional overhead of obtaining new sample paths (instead of extending the existing ones). The overhead can be completely avoided if the PRISM sample generation method is updated to allow for the extension of sample paths. Incorporating our method inside PRISM by updating the existing sample generation technique is likely to further enhance the efficiency of our optimized two-phase technique and, in turn, will further broaden the scope of application of the PRISM model checker.

6   Conclusion

We presented an approximate statistical method for probabilistic model checking of unbounded until properties. Our technique is based on the reduction of verification of such properties to verification of bounded path properties in two phases. We theoretically proved the correctness of our technique and empirically showed the applicability of our technique. As our technique does not require knowledge of the system transition structure, it can be applied effectively for black-box systems and also for systems containing infinite number of states.

In our experiments, we observed that even if PRISM's statistical method fails with the default value of simulation path length, it can be made to work for some of the experiments if one can choose a sufficiently large path length.

Such a choice can be made by some strategy similar to what we proposed here. However, such a strategy cannot guarantee the correctness of the result within the error bounds. This is because this method would amount to (a) choosing k_0 and (b) estimating the probability using the *same* set of simulation paths, and this will not provide the estimates that are provably correct within the specified error bounds. That is why we recommend a two-phase procedure, where these two objectives ((a) and (b)) are met using two *independent* samples of paths and it also enables us to prove its correctness (Theorem 1).

In addition to incorporating our technique in the PRISM model checker (see discussion in Section 5.5), as part of future work, we are planning to investigate the applicability of our technique for probabilistic LTL properties where properties of the form $\varphi_1 \cup \varphi_2 \cup \varphi_3$ are expressible, unlike PCTL (the logic used in this paper) which cannot express nested path properties.

Acknowledgments. We thank Dr. Andrew S. Miner and anonymous reviewers for providing valuable suggestions and insightful comments. We acknowledge the contributions of Paul Jennings for incorporating initial implementation of our method in PRISM model checker. This work is supported in part by NSF grants CNS0709217, CCF0702758.

References

1. Aziz, A., Sanwal, K., Singhal, V., Brayton, R.: Model checking continuous time markov chains. ACM Transactions on Computational Logic 1(1), 162–170 (2000)
2. Baier, C., Haverkort, B., Hermanns, H., Katoen, J.-P.: Model-Checking Algorithms for Continuous-Time Markov Chains. IEEE Transactions on Software Engineering 29(6), 524–541 (2003)
3. Bianco, A., de Alfaro, L.: Model checking of probabilistic and nondeterministic systems. In: Thiagarajan, P.S. (ed.) FSTTCS 1995. LNCS, vol. 1026, pp. 499–513. Springer, Heidelberg (1995)
4. Bohnenkamp, H., van der Stok, P., Hermanns, H., Vaandrager, F.: Cost-optimization of the ipv4 zeroconf protocol. In: Intl. Conf. on Dependable Systems and Networks (2003)
5. Casella, G., Berger, R.L.: Statistical Inference. Duxbury (2002)
6. Cinlar, E.: Introduction to Stochastic Processes. Prentice-Hall, Englewood Cliffs (1975)
7. Courcoubetis, C., Yannakakis, M.: The complexity of probabilistic verification. Journal of ACM 42(4), 857–907 (1995)
8. Duflot, M., Kwiatkowska, M., Norman, G., Parker, D.: A formal analysis of bluetooth device discovery. Intl. Journal on Software Tools for Technology Transfer 8, 621–632 (2006)
9. Hansson, H., Jonsson, B.: A logic for reasoning about time and reliability. Formal Aspects of Computing 6(5), 512–535 (1994)
10. Herault, T., Lassaigne, R., Magniette, F., Peyronnet, S.: Approximate probabilistic model checking. In: Steffen, B., Levi, G. (eds.) VMCAI 2004. LNCS, vol. 2937, pp. 73–84. Springer, Heidelberg (2004)
11. Hinton, A., Kwiatkowska, M., Norman, G., Parker, D.: Prism: A tool for automatic verification of probabilistic systems. In: Hermanns, H., Palsberg, J. (eds.) TACAS 2006. LNCS, vol. 3920, pp. 441–444. Springer, Heidelberg (2006)

12. Hoeffding, W.: Probability inequalities for sums of bounded random variables. Journal of the American Statistical Association 58 (1963)
13. Kwiatkowska, M., Norman, G., Parker, D.: Using probabilistic model checking in systems biology. ACM SIGMETRICS Perf. Eval. Review 35, 14–21 (2008)
14. Massart, P.: The tight constant in the Dvoretzky-Kiefer-Wolfowitz inequality. Annals of Probability 18, 1269–1283 (1990)
15. Norman, G., Shmatikov, V.: Analysis of probabilistic contract signing. Journal of Computer Security 14, 561–589 (2006)
16. Roy, A., Gopinath, K.: Improved probabilistic models for 802.11 protocol verification. In: Etessami, K., Rajamani, S.K. (eds.) CAV 2005. LNCS, vol. 3576, pp. 239–252. Springer, Heidelberg (2005)
17. Sen, K., Viswanathan, M., Agha, G.: On statistical model checking of stochastic systems. In: Etessami, K., Rajamani, S.K. (eds.) CAV 2005. LNCS, vol. 3576, pp. 266–280. Springer, Heidelberg (2005)
18. The XSB Group. The XSB logic programming system (2009), http://xsb.sourceforge.net
19. Two-phase pmck (2008), http://www.cs.iastate.edu/~sbasu/pmck
20. Wald, A.: Sequential tests of statistical hypotheses. The Annals of Mathematical Statistics 16(2) (1945)
21. Younes, H.L., Kwiatkowska, M., Norman, G., Parker, D.: Numerical vs. statistical probabilistic model checking. Intl. Journal on Software Tools for Technology Transfer 8(3) (2006)
22. Younes, H.L.S., Simmons, R.G.: Probabilistic verification of discrete event systems using acceptance sampling. In: Brinksma, E., Larsen, K.G. (eds.) CAV 2002. LNCS, vol. 2404, p. 223. Springer, Heidelberg (2002)
23. Younes, H.L.S., Simmons, R.G.: Statistical probabilistic model checking with a focus on time-bounded properties. Information and Computation 204(9) (2006)
24. Zapreev, I.S.: Model Checking Markov Chains: Techniques and Tools. PhD thesis, University of Twente, The Netherlands (2008)

A Graph-Based Operational Semantics of OO Programs*

Wei Ke[1,2], Zhiming Liu[3], Shuling Wang[3,**], and Liang Zhao[3]

[1] School of Computer Science and Engineering, Beihang University, Beijing, China
[2] Macao Polytechnic Institute, Macao
[3] United Nations University - International Institute for Software Technology, Macao
`wsl@iist.unu.edu`

Abstract. We present a mathematical model of class graphs, object graphs and state graphs which naturally capture the essential OO features. A small-step operational semantics of OO programs is defined in the style of classical structural operational semantics, in which an execution step of a command is defined as a transition from one state graph to another obtained by simple operations on graphs. To validate this semantics, we give it an implementation in Java. This implementation can also be used for simulation and validation of OO programs, with the visualization of state graph transitions during the execution. A distinct feature of this semantics is location or address independent. Properties of objects and OO programs can be described as properties of graphs in terms of relations of navigation paths (or attribute strings).

Keywords: OO programs, operational semantics, object graphs, state graphs.

1 Introduction

A formal semantic model in general makes (or should make) two major contributions. The first is to provide *conceptual clarification* for better understanding so as to master the complexity better, and the second is to support the development of techniques and tools for reasoning about programs. The work we present in this paper is primarily motivated by the former, but it is promising in help to establish a basis for advancing the state of the art of the techniques and tool support for verification and analysis of OO programs.

1.1 Motivation

The behavior of an OO program is complex and reasoning about it is hard. The main reason is that its execution states contain related objects with complex

---

* Supported by the projects HighQSoftD, HTTS and ARV funded by Macao Science and Technology Development Fund; and grants from STCSM No. 08510700300 and CNSF No. 60970031.
** Corresponding author. UNU-IIST, P.O. Box 3058, Macau.

K. Breitman and A. Cavalcanti (Eds.): ICFEM 2009, LNCS 5885, pp. 347–366, 2009.

structures and properties. These structures are determined by the class structure of the program. Complexity is in general the cause of breakdowns of a system and OO programs are typically prone to errors of null pointers (or references), inaccessible objects and aliases [20].

Because of the complexity and the challenge in understanding OO programs, there are a big number of traditional semantic theories of OO programs (e.g. [25,1,18,8]), operational or denotational, which use the basic theory of sets, functions and relations in defining the states of a program. As pointed out in [23], such an approach "often needs to include in the syntax definition of runtime concepts", such as locations to indicate a value that may change over time. This need and the lack of clarity about the structural properties of the states of OO programs are the main source of the complexity of these traditional theories. The complexity hinders the way of our thinking about the execution of a program and makes it difficult to formulate clear assertions about executions. Formulating clear assertions is the first step for analysis of the correctness of a program [20]. We should admit that the existing operational semantic definitions of OO programs are not as elaborate and comprehensive as the classical structural operational semantics (SOS) for traditional procedural programs and the rewriting systems for functional programming. There are a range of work on defining logics for OO programs [31,30,32]. But those logics are not as easy to understand as the Hoare-logic for the analysis and design of traditional procedural programs.

1.2   Contribution

We define an operational semantics for an OO programming language of the rCOS method of component-based and object-oriented model driven design [26]. This language is originally defined with a denotational semantics and a refinement calculus [18,37]. We define objects of a class and execution states of a program as directed labeled graphs. A node represents an object or a simple datum. However, in the former case, a node is not labeled by an explicit reference value, but by the name of its runtime type, which is a name of a class of the program. An edge is labeled by the name of a field of the source object referring to the target object.

It is well known that an object or a family of related objects can be represented as a graph, in which nodes are objects and edges are their attributes [15,19,37]. Intuitively, a state at anytime of the execution of an OO program consists of the existing objects and their relations at that time, and can thus be represented as a graph. Each step of the execution is to change the graph, and the changes of a graph can be defined by operations on graphs, such as swinging an edge and adding a new subgraph denoting a newly created object.

However, the definitions of the execution states and the operational semantics are more subtle. First, an invocation to a method of an object does not only manipulate the fields of "*this*" object (*self* instead of "*this*" is used in this paper), but also the temporarily declared variables. Moreover, the scope of the execution changes when another method is called inside this method. To address this issue, the edges of the temporary variables are arranged on the top of the state graph in a *stack*, according to their scopes, linked by specially $-labeled edges. Hence, a change of the scope of execution is done by *pushing* in or *popping* out a scope node of the state graph (see Sec. 3). Second, a small step semantics of a method invocation is not straight forward in general. Furthermore, unlike the existing semantic definitions such as that of [25], our definition does not use address variables.

Nevertheless, with the careful combination of the notions of scope stacks and object graphs (representing the object heaps in classical models) in the concept of execution state graphs, the model is indeed simple and defined as a classical SOS transition system, using only the basic notion of graphs and operations on graphs.

A distinct feature of our model is its location or address independency. In other words, it does not explicitly refer to object references or nodes in state graphs. This is important as OO programs only use variables and navigation paths, but do not refer to addresses or references. Variables and navigation paths are "evaluated" as nodes in a state graph. Properties of objects and states, such as conflict-freedom among aliases, accessibility of one object by another and absence of null references, can be described as predicates [9] or relations of such paths. Some concrete examples of properties of OO programs are given in Section 6. This shows that the graphs can be used to interpret a graph-based logic, such as Logics of Aliasing [6], and the operational semantics as the basis to develop a graph-based Hoare-logic for static analysis of OO programs.

While we are lifting objects and states to graphs and treating them as instance values of variables in the manner as we model programs with only pure data, we also lift the class definitions of a program and the declarations as a whole as type graphs, called *class graphs* [37]. This allows us to define a simple type system of the language. Furthermore, with structural refinement relations defined for class graphs in our earlier work [37], the operational semantics will support a rewriting system for proving equivalence upto structural refinement mapping among programs.

We also show in Section 5 that both the type system and the operational semantics are easy to implement. The implementation is written in Java directly according to the semantic rules, and a program produces the visualized graphs step by step during its execution. Therefore, the language can be directly used for simulation and validation.

We introduce in the next section the syntax of our oo language. We define in Section 3 class graphs, object graphs and state graphs, followed by their operations. The operational semantics is defined in Section 4, and its implementation in Section 5. We show in Section 6 examples of properties of oo programs that can be stated and analyzed within this model. Conclusions are drawn in Section 7 with a discussion on related work and future work.

2   An Object-Oriented Language

We assume four disjoint sets: $\mathcal{C}$ of class names, $\mathcal{D}$ of names of primitive data types such as *Int* and *Bool*, $\mathcal{A}$ of names of attributes and variables and $\mathcal{M}$ of names

$$
\begin{array}{llll}
prog & ::= cdecls \bullet Main & cdecls & ::= cdecl \mid cdecl; cdecls \\
adef & ::= visib\ T\ a = l & visib & ::= \mathsf{private} \mid \mathsf{protected} \mid \mathsf{public} \\
mdef & ::= m(\overline{S\ x}; \overline{T\ y})\{c\} & Main & ::= (\overline{ext}; c) \\
e & ::= le \mid self \mid (C)e \mid l \mid f(\overline{e}) & le & ::= x \mid e.a \\
l & ::= d \mid null & ext & ::= T\ x = l \\
\end{array}
$$

$$
\begin{array}{lll}
cdecl & ::= [\mathsf{private}]\ \mathsf{class}\ C\ [\mathsf{extends}\ D]\ \{\overline{adef}; \overline{mdef}\} \\
c & ::= \mathsf{skip} \mid C.new(le) \mid le := e \mid \mathsf{var}\ T\ x\ [= e] \mid \mathsf{end}\ x \mid e.m(\overline{e}; \overline{le}) \mid c; c \mid c \triangleleft b \triangleright c \mid b * c \\
b & ::= true \mid false \mid e = e \mid \neg b \mid b \wedge b \mid b \vee b \\
\end{array}
$$

Fig. 1. Syntax of rCOS

of methods. Let $\mathcal{T}$ be the union of $\mathcal{C}$ and $\mathcal{D}$. The OO programming language we consider is the one of rCOS [18] and its syntax is given in Fig. 1. It supports most of the essential OO features, including inheritance, type casting, dynamic binding and recursive objects.

In Fig. 1, the terminals T and S are type names in $\mathcal{T}$, a an attribute (or field) name, m a method name, d a constant datum of a primitive type, f a built-in operation of a primitive data type, and x and y variables. Any text occurring in a pair of square brackets is optional, while an overlined text $\overline{u}$ denotes a sequence of elements $u_1 \cdot u_2 \cdots u_k$. The concatenation of two sequences is denoted by $\overline{u} \cdot \overline{v}$. We do not distinguish between an element and a singleton sequence.

The language is similar to Java. A program $prog$ is a sequence of class declarations $cdecls$ followed by a main method $Main$. $Main$ also declares $prog$'s external variables $\overline{ext}$. We could follow Java to declare a class with $\overline{ext}$ as its attributes and the method $main()$, but it would cause some hiccups in our discussion. We would like to follow the classical manner in defining the semantics and do not want expressions to have side effects. Therefore, object creation is of the form $C.new(le)$ rather than $le := C.new()$. And method invocations are not allowed to occur in expressions. Instead, a method can have result parameters. Because rCOS is also used as a specification language, it allows a method to return a number of outputs. It also allows direct assignments to a navigation path of the form $x.a_1.\ldots.a_k$, denoted in general by le, according to the accessibility of the attributes. For simplicity, the overriding of attributes is not allowed and the overriding of a method preserves the method signature.

3   Class Graphs, Object Graphs and State Graphs

We define class graphs, object graphs, and state graphs; and discuss their relations. We also define some graph operations that we need.

3.1   Class Graphs

The *class graph* is a *directed and labeled graph* [37]. A node represents a class of objects or a type of data and it is labeled by its type name in $\mathcal{T}$. All nodes are labeled by different names (this is different from object graphs that are defined

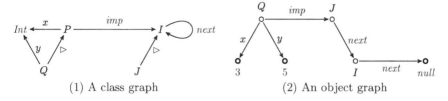

(1) A class graph   (2) An object graph

Fig. 2. Class and object graphs

later). There are two kinds of edges. An edge of the first kind is an *attribute edge* representing that an instance of the source node has a property (attribute) of the type of the target node, and it is labeled by the attribute name. An edge of the other kind represents that the source node is a direct subclass of the target node, and it is labeled by the designated symbol $\triangleright$. The class graph of a program is the one containing all the classes defined in the program.

The class graph of a well-formed program has the following conditions:

1. a node labeled by a primitive data type is a leaf,
2. the labels of the outgoing edges of a node are all different, and this implies that we do not consider multiple inheritance, and
3. there is no $\triangleright$-loop in the graph.

An example of class graph is shown in Fig. 2(1) which contains four classes.

We use $C \triangleright D$ to denote that C is a direct subclass of D, and $\preceq$ the subtype relation, which is the extension of the reflexive and transitive closure of $\triangleright$ on $\mathcal{T}$.

Given a class C in a class graph of a program, $attr(C)$ is the set of labels of the outgoing edges from C and thus the attributes directly defined in C, and $Attr(C)$ defines the set of attributes of C as well as those of all its superclasses. These functions can be calculated from the class graph.

To represent more static features of the program, we extend the class graph. For example, we can annotate an attribute edge a of the source node C with the initial value $init(C, a)$. Let $method(C)$ be the methods defined in C. Then the partial functions $mtype(C, m)$ and $mbody(C, m)$ give the type and body of a method m of class C, respectively.

$$mtype(C, m) \;\hat{=}\; \begin{cases} (S; T) & \text{if } m(S\,x; T\,y)\{c\} \in method(C) \\ mtype(D, m) & \text{otherwise, if } C \triangleright D \end{cases}$$

$$mbody(C, m) \;\hat{=}\; \begin{cases} (x; y; c) & \text{if } m(S\,x; T\,y)\{c\} \in method(C) \\ mbody(D, m) & \text{otherwise, if } C \triangleright D \end{cases}$$

These functions are used for method look-up when defining the semantics of method invocation. The main use of the class graph of a program is first for static type checking of the expressions and commands of the program by traversing the graph and using the information and the associated functions defined on it. It is also used for the dynamic checking of the validity of the execution state, which is defined as an instance graph of a class graph, called a *state graph* (see Section 3.3). For details, we refer to the full version of the paper [24].

3.2   Object Graphs

An object graph describes a family of objects and their relations, with nodes representing objects or values and their outgoing edges labeled by their attributes. The target of an edge is the node representing the object or value that the attribute refers to.

Let $\mathcal{N}$ be an infinite set of node names and $\mathcal{L}$ the set of constant values including the *null* object and values of primitive types.

Definition 1 (Object Graph). *An object graph is a directed and labeled graph* $G = \langle N, E, T, F \rangle$, *where*

- $N \subseteq \mathcal{N}$ *is the set of nodes, denoted by* $G.node$,
- $E \subseteq N \times \mathcal{A} \times N$ *is the set of edges, denoted by* $G.edge$,
- $T : N \rightharpoonup \mathcal{C}$ *is a partial mapping from nodes to types, denoted by* $G.type$,
- $F : N \rightharpoonup \mathcal{L}$ *is a partial mapping from nodes to values, denoted by* $G.value$,

such that

1. *a node is either an object node or a value node:* $\operatorname{dom}(T) \cap \operatorname{dom}(F) = \emptyset$ *and* $\operatorname{dom}(T) \cup \operatorname{dom}(F) = N$,
2. *labels of the outgoing edges from a node are different, and*
3. *all value nodes are leaves, having no outgoing edges.*

An example of object graph is shown in Fig. 2(2) with three objects of class Q, J and I, respectively.

We write $n_1 \xrightarrow{a} n_2$ for the edge $(n_1, a, n_2) \in G.edge$. Given a set $ns \subseteq G.node$ of nodes (or a single node), $in(ns)$ and $out(ns)$ respectively denote the sets of incoming edges to and outgoing from them. For a non-empty path p, i.e. a sequence of consecutive edges, we define $source(p)$ and $target(p)$ to be the starting node and the destination of p, respectively; $first(p)$ and $last(p)$ the first and last edges, respectively.

3.3   State Graphs

A state at a moment of time in the execution of an OO program consists of the existing objects, the attribute links between them, the values of data attributes, which form an object graph at that time; together with the variables and their values.

Roughly speaking, each step of the execution of the program in a state is to change the state by creating a new object, forming a new link, changing a link, or modifying a data attribute. Obviously, all these changes of the state can be considered as simple operations on the initial object graph.

However, we are interested in a small step semantics, and we need to define the semantics of changes of local variables and nested method invocations. We first define the notion of *state graph* which introduces stacks into object graphs.

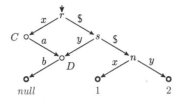

Fig. 3. A state graph

Definition 2 (State Graph). *A state graph is a rooted, directed and labeled graph* $G = \langle N, E, T, F, r \rangle$, *where*

- *N, T and F are defined as in Definition 1 of object graphs,*
- *$E \subseteq N \times (\mathcal{A} \cup \{self, \$\}) \times N$ is the set of edges, denoted by $G.edge$,*
- *$r \in N$ is the root of the graph and it has no incoming edges, denoted by $G.root$,*
- *starting from r, the $\$$-edges, if there are any, form a path such that except r each node on the path has only one incoming edge.*

An example of state graph is shown in Fig. 3.

Informally, a $\$$-edge connects a pair of nodes that correspond to adjacent scopes. We call the $\$$-path of G the *stack* of the state graph and call the nodes on this path, the *scope nodes*. When entering a new scope, a new node together with an edge from it to the current top node are pushed onto the top of the stack, and when exiting a scope, the top node is popped out (together with the outgoing edges from it). The outgoing edges of a scope node, other than the $\$$-edge, represent the variables defined in the scope.

Take the example shown in Fig. 3. When the execution enters var y; var x; $\cdots$; end x; end y, it pushes a new node s onto the top of node n with variable y being attached to it; then when the execution proceeds to var x; $\cdots$; end x; end y, a new scope is entered and thus a new node r is pushed onto the top of node s with the newly declared variable x being attached to it. Note that it is allowed to define variables in different scopes with the same name, for example x in both scopes r and n. In this case, the one defined in the most recent scope, for example x in scope r, will hide the others. At the end, when the execution proceeds to end x; end y, r together with x is popped out, then the node s will be popped out together with y.

A state graph represents a proper execution state of a program only if it satisfies the conditions *2* and *3* of object graphs and the following two well-formedness conditions:

1. the sets of scope nodes, object nodes and value nodes are disjoint, and
2. the source of each edge labeled by *self* is a scope node and its target is an object node.

In the rest of the paper, we always assume a state graph is well-formed. Besides, a state graph is called *stable* if it does not contain $\$$-edges, i.e. the stack is empty.

A node n is *accessible* in G, denoted by $\mathsf{access}(G, n)$, if it is reachable via a path starting from the root node, and G is *connected* if all nodes are accessible. Given a state graph G, we can always get a connected subgraph by removing all the inaccessible nodes together with their associated edges. Such a subgraph of G is unique, called the *connected part* of G, denoted by $G^\bullet$.

The sequence of edge labels $a_1.a_2 \ldots a_k$ uniquely determines the target node of a path from the root node $G.root \xrightarrow{a_1} \cdots \xrightarrow{a_k} n_k$, and it therefore uniquely represents an object or a value, depending on the type of the target node. We call such a sequence of edge labels a *trace* and ignore the difference between a path starting from the root and its trace.

In an abstract model, we do not distinguish graphs with only different node names, and this can be formalized by the notion of graph isomorphism. Two connected state graphs G and G' are *isomorphic* if there is a bijective function g from $G.node$ to $G'.node$ such that

1. $g(G.root) = G'.root$,
2. $n_1 \xrightarrow{a} n_2$ in $G.edge$ iff $g(n_1) \xrightarrow{a} g(n_2)$ in $G'.edge$, and
3. $G.type(n) = G'.type(g(n))$ and $G.value(n) = G'.value(g(n))$.

Two state graphs are isomorphic if their connected parts are isomorphic. Isomorphic state graphs have the same set of traces. For simplicity, we assume the mapping $G.value$ is injective and thus all leaves represent different values. We do not distinguish a value node from its value. We assume a value node is in the state when needed, as otherwise it can always be added.

3.4   Correctly Typed Object Graphs and State Graphs

An object (or state) graph G is *correctly typed* w.r.t. a class graph Γ (called Γ-typed) if

1. the type of each object node of G is a type in Γ, and
2. for the label a of each attribute edge of G, there is an a-edge from some supertype of the source node to some supertype of the target node in Γ,

For example, the object graph in Fig. 2(2) is correctly typed w.r.t. the class graph in Fig. 2(1).

A state graph G is a *valid* state of a program *prog* if G is correctly typed *w.r.t.* the class graph of *prog* and the outgoing edges of the target of the \$-path in G are labeled by the external variables of *prog*.

In the rest of the paper, we are only interested in correctly typed object graphs and valid state graphs, while we do not explicitly mention the program or its class graph when there is no confusion.

3.5   Graph Operations

We define a few basic operations on state graphs, which we will use in the semantic definitions. Assume a state graph $G = \langle N, E, T, F, r \rangle$.

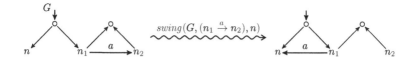

Fig. 4. Edge swing

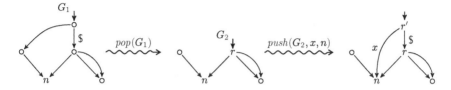

Fig. 5. Stack push and pop

Swing an edge. The most often operation for changing a state G is done by an assignment $e'.a := e$. It causes the swing of the a-edge to point to the object or value of e. For an edge $d = (n_1 \xrightarrow{a} n_2)$ and a node n of G,

$$swing(G, d, n) \mathrel{\hat{=}} G[E[d \to n]/E] \quad \text{where} \quad E[d \to n] \mathrel{\hat{=}} (E \setminus \{d\}) \cup \{n_1 \xrightarrow{a} n\}.$$

The substitution $G[E'/E]$ means that only the component E is substituted by E', without changing anything else. Fig. 4 shows the edge swing. For a path p, we use $swing(G, p, n)$ for $swing(G, last(p), n)$.

Create an object. Adding an object node is slightly tricky and we need to consider the type of the node and its attributes. Creation of a new object of class C and attach it to the trace p in G is defined by

$$new(G, C, p) \mathrel{\hat{=}} swing(G', p, n) \quad \text{where } n \notin N,$$
$$G' = \langle N \cup \{n\}, E \cup \{n \xrightarrow{a} init(C, a) \mid a \in Attr(C)\}, T \cup \{n \mapsto C\}, F, r \rangle.$$

Stack operations. For a sequence of variables $\bar{x} = x_1 \cdots x_k$ and nodes $\bar{n} = n_1 \cdots n_k$, $push(G, \bar{x}, \bar{n})$ adds a new scope with outgoing edges labeled by $\bar{x}$ and pointing to the nodes $\bar{n}$, accordingly:

$$push(G, \bar{x}, \bar{n}) \mathrel{\hat{=}} \langle N \cup \{r'\}, E \cup \{r' \xrightarrow{x_1} n_1, \cdots, r' \xrightarrow{x_k} n_k, r' \xrightarrow{\$} r\}, T, F, r' \rangle$$
$$\text{where } r' \notin N.$$

As shown in Fig. 5, ending a scope pops the root out of the stack by simply removing it, as well as all its outgoing edges, from the graph, but the next node on the stack becomes the root.

$$pop(G) \mathrel{\hat{=}} \langle N \setminus \{r\}, E \setminus out(r), T, F, r_{next} \rangle \qquad \text{if } r \xrightarrow{\$} r_{next} \in E$$

4   Operational Semantics

Using the state graphs, we now simply follow the classical routine to define the evaluation of an expression and then the state transition rules.

4.1   Evaluation of Expressions

In an OO program, an expression is formed from constants and navigation paths. A navigation path represents a node, either a value node or an object node, which is the target node of the path from the root of the current execution state. A composite expression of the form $f(e_1, \ldots, e_n)$ only applies to expressions which are evaluated to data values.

Formally speaking, given a state G, the evaluation of an expression e returns an object node or value. We use $eval(G, e)$ to denote the value of e in state G, and $rtype(G, e)$ to denote the type $G.type(eval(G, e))$ if $eval(G, e)$ is an object node. Type $rtype(G, e)$ is called the *runtime type* or *current type* of e in state G.

For an expression e, the *trace* of e, $trace(G, e)$, is the trace starting from the root and ending at the node which represents the result of the evaluation of e in G. To calculate $trace(G, e)$, we first define a partial function $search(G, n, w)$ which finds the trace of w, which is either a simple variable x or $self$, from the scope node n node-by-node down the stack:

$$search(G, n, w) \;\widehat{=}\; \begin{cases} w & \text{if } \exists n' \bullet n \xrightarrow{w} n' \in G.edge \\ \$.search(G, n_1, w) & \text{otherwise, if } \exists n_1 \bullet n \xrightarrow{\$} n_1 \in G.edge \end{cases}$$

The recursion always terminates as there is only finite number of scope nodes, and there is no $-loop. The function $trace(G, e)$ is defined as

$$trace(G, w) \;\widehat{=}\; search(G, G.root, w)$$
$$trace(G, e.a) \;\widehat{=}\; trace(G, e).a$$
$$trace(G, (C)e) \;\widehat{=}\; trace(G, e)$$

For the example graph G_0 in Fig. 3, $trace(G_0, x) = x$ and $trace(G_0, y) = \$.y$. From now on, when there is only one state graph, we omit the argument G in the graph operations that we have defined.

The evaluation and the runtime type of an expression e in G are determined inductively as follows.

1. If e is a constant value l of type T, then $eval(e) = l$ and $rtype(e) = T$,
2. If e is a variable x or $self$, e can be evaluated in G only when $trace(e)$ exists in G. Let $n = target(trace(e))$. If n is an object node, $eval(e) = n$ and $rtype(e) = G.type(n)$, otherwise $eval(e) = G.value(n)$ and $rtype(e)$ is the type of $eval(e)$.
3. If e is of the form $e'.a$, e can be evaluated in G only when $trace(e)$ exists in G. Let $n = target(trace(e))$. If n is an object node, $eval(e) = n$ and $rtype(e) = G.type(n)$, otherwise $eval(e) = G.value(n)$ and $rtype(e)$ is the type of $eval(e)$.

$$(\text{Assign}) \ \langle le := e, G \rangle \to swing(G, trace(le), eval(e))$$

$$(\text{New}) \ \langle C.new(le), G \rangle \to new(G, C, trace(le)) \qquad (\text{End}) \ \langle \text{end } x, G \rangle \to pop(G)$$

$$(\text{Dcl-I}) \ \langle \text{var } T \ x = e, G \rangle \to push(G, x, eval(e)) \qquad (\text{Dcl}) \ \langle \text{var } T \ x, G \rangle \to add(push(G, x, init(T))$$

$$(\text{Enter})$$
$$\langle \textit{enter } (C, S, T, x, y, e, ve, re), G \rangle \to push(G, self \cdot x \cdot y \cdot y^*, eval(e) \cdot eval(ve) \cdot init(T) \cdot po(G, re))$$

$$(\text{Leave}) \ \langle \textit{leave } (y, re), G \rangle \to pop(swing(G, spo(G, y^*, re), eval(y)))$$

$$(\text{Invk}) \ \frac{rtype(e) = C \qquad mtype(C, m) = (S; T) \qquad mbody(C, m) = (x; y; c)}{\langle e.m(ve; re), G \rangle \to \langle \textit{enter } (C, S, T, x, y, e, ve, re) ; c; \textit{leave } (y, re), G \rangle}$$

Fig. 6. Operational semantics for commands in rCOS

4. If e is a type cast $(C)e'$, then $eval(e) = eval(e')$ and $rtype(e) = rtype(e')$, provided $rtype(e') \preceq C$.
5. If e is of the form $f(e')$, $eval(e) = f(eval(e'))$ and $rtype(e)$ is the type of $eval(e)$.

4.2 Semantic Rules

We define a small step semantics for our language by giving the transition relation between *configurations*. There are two kinds of configurations:

- a *non-terminated configuration* is a pair $\langle c, G \rangle$, where c is a command and G is a state;
- a *terminated configuration* is a state G, representing the completion of the execution of a command.

Fig. 6 gives only the semantic rules that are relevant to the object-oriented features. The rules of sequential composition, conditional choice and iteration are defined in [24] in the standard way in which an operational semantics for an imperative language is defined.

The semantics of assignment, object creation, local scope declaration and un-declaration are defined by simple graph operations. The assignment $le := e$ swings the trace of le to the value of e, and $C.new(le)$ creates a new initial instance of class C and swings the trace of le to the new instance. A local variable declaration var $T \ x \ [= e]$ adds the variable x to a new scope by pushing it onto the stack of the state; while end x pops the root out of the state. We use $init(T)$ to denote the initial value (or "zero" value) of type T. For example, $init(Int) = 0$, $init(Bool) = false$ and $init(C) = null$ for any class type C. An uninitialized variable will be set to the initial value of its declared type.

The semantics of method invocations deserves some more explanation because of the dynamic binding and *early binding* of return parameters. Intuitively, the method invocation $e.m(ve, re)$ first records the value of the actual value parameter ve in the formal value parameter of m, and then executes the body c of

m. At the end it returns the value of the formal return parameter to the actual return parameter re. However, the precise definition is more complex because of the following issues.

Method look-up.   First, dynamic binding of the method to the runtime type of e requires the look-up for the signature $mtype(C, m) = (S; T)$ and the definition $mbody(C, m) = (x; y; c)$ of m. This is handled in Rule (INVK).

Enter to set execution environment.   Then, the parent object of actual result parameter re in the initial state should be recorded before it is possibly changed by the body command of the method. This is the "early result parameter binding" semantics. In addition to have $self$ for recording e, the formal value parameter x for holding the actual value parameter ve and the formal return parameter y being the initial value of T, we need an auxiliary variable y^*, which corresponds to the formal return parameter y and does not occur in the program, to record the parent object of re in the initial state. Therefore, we introduce an *implementation command* $enter\ (C, S, T, x, y, e, ve, re)$ whose semantics is defined by Rule (ENTER), which sets a new scope with variables $self$, x, y and y^* which are respectively initialized properly according to the above discussion. Function $po(G, re)$ returns the parent object of re in G which is going to be recorded by y^*.

$$po(G, re) \ \hat{=} \ \begin{cases} eval(G, e) & \text{if } re = e.a \\ \bot & \text{otherwise} \end{cases}$$

Return result.   When the execution is leaving the body of m, if re is of the form $e.a$, the attribute a of the old parent object of re must be swung to the value of the formal result parameter y. For this, we recover the trace by the function

$$spo(G, y^*, re) \ \hat{=} \ \begin{cases} y^*.a & \text{if } re = e.a \\ \$.trace(pop(G), x) & \text{if } re = x \end{cases}$$

The return of the method invocation is carried out by the implementation command $leave\ (y, re)$ whose semantics is in Rule (LEAVE) defined by the swing and pop operations.

Note that the use of these implementation commands instead of the direct use of commands var $S\ x = ve$; var $T\ y$ and $re := y$; end y; end x is to avoid possible name conflicts between actual parameters ve, re and formal parameters x, y used as local variables in the method body. Instead of implementation commands, literal values of the form Val v are used in [25], which actually model addresses of variables.

For the type safety of the semantics, we expect to prove that a type-correct command can be well executed, but there are the following cases of exceptions.

- **Exception 1 (null reference):** the evaluation of an expression $e.a$ or the execution of a command $e.m(ve, re)$ fails, if e is evaluated to *null*.
- **Exception 2 (illegal downcast):** the evaluation of an expression $(C)e$ fails, if the runtime type of e is not a subtype of C.

These two cases of exceptions cannot be checked and avoided statically. However, if none of them happens, the execution of a type-correct command will not get blocked, i.e. it never enters a configuration which is non-terminated but unable to run according to any semantic rule.

Theorem 1 (Type safety of commands). *For a non-terminated configuration* $\langle c, G \rangle$, *if* c *is type-correct, then*

- *either there exists a state* G' *such that* $\langle c, G \rangle \to G'$,
- *or there exists a configuration* $\langle c', G' \rangle$ *such that* c' *is type-correct and* $\langle c, G \rangle \to \langle c', G' \rangle$,

unless one of the exception cases happens.

The strict definition of type-correctness and the proof of this theorem are given in our technical report [24].

Execution of programs. The semantics of a program is to execute the main command under the initial state graph, whose root records the external variables referring to their initial values. For example, the initial configuration of the program $cdecls \bullet (T_1\ x_1 = l_1, \cdots, T_k\ x_k = l_k; c)$ is $\langle c, G_{init} \rangle$, where

$$G_{init} = \langle \{r, n_1, \cdots, n_k\}, \{r \xrightarrow{x_i} n_i \mid 1 \leq i \leq k\}, \emptyset, \{n_i \mapsto l_i \mid 1 \leq i \leq k\}, r \rangle.$$

As a direct deduction of Theorem 1, the execution of a well-typed program will not get blocked. And if it terminates, the final state is also a stable one.

Theorem 2 (Type safety of programs). *For a well-typed program* $prog = \Gamma \bullet (T_1\ x_1 = l_1, \cdots, T_k\ x_k = l_k; c)$,

- *either there exists a stable state* G_{end} *such that* $\langle c, G_{init} \rangle \to G_{end}$,
- *or there exists a configuration* $\langle c', G' \rangle$ *such that* c' *is type-correct and* $\langle c, G_{init} \rangle \to \langle c', G' \rangle$,

unless one of the exception cases happens.

5   Implementation

We use Java as the implementation language, and ANTLR as the parser generator, because of its Java origin and powerful grammar specification language. The implementation consists of

1. a parser (**pa**), which translates programs into class graphs and commands;
2. a type checker (**tc**), which checks class graphs and commands following the well-typedness rules and definitions;
3. a transformer (**tr**), which transforms state graphs by applying the main command to an initial graph, in small steps, following the semantic rules;
4. an observer (**ob**), which intercepts, layouts and exports intermediate graphs to descriptions in the PGF/T*ik*Z language to be incorporated into TEX documents.

$$\bigcirc \!\!\longrightarrow\! \Gamma, (\overline{ext}, c) := \mathbf{pa} \text{ program} \longrightarrow \mathbf{tc}\ (\Gamma, \overline{ext}) \text{ as } \Delta_{init}, c, \Gamma \longrightarrow \langle c, G \rangle := \langle c, \overline{ext} \text{ as } G_{init} \rangle$$

$$\bullet\!\!\longleftarrow G_{end} := G \longleftarrow \overset{c\, =\, null}{\Diamond} \longrightarrow \langle c, G \rangle := \mathbf{tr}\ \Gamma, \langle c, G \rangle \longrightarrow \mathbf{ob}\ G$$

Fig. 7. Flowchart of program processing

Fig. 7 shows the overall flow of how a program is processed, where Δ, Γ and G stand for type context, class and state graphs, respectively. The Kamada-Kawai algorithm [22] is used in our implementation to auto-layout state graphs, and the results appear to be reasonably pleasing.

Graph representation. Class graphs and state graphs forbid a node having outgoing edges with duplicated labels. This enables us to store the nodes $N \subseteq \mathcal{N}$ and the edges $E \subseteq N \times \mathcal{A} \times N$ of a graph G in a mapping $S : \mathcal{N} \to \mathcal{A} \to \mathcal{N}$. With such a representation, it is efficient to retrieve the target from a source and a label, and all the outgoing edges from a source. Leaf nodes are also stored as sources mapped to nothing in the mapping for membership tests. We have $N = \mathrm{dom}\, S$, $label(out(n)) = \mathrm{dom}\, S(n)$ and $target(n, a) = S(n)(a)$, where n is a node and a is a label.

Nodes are implemented as a Java interface `Node`, and they are identified by instance identities of the objects, such as type names and constant values, implementing the interface. These objects can thus be treated as nodes directly.

The Java API uses two kinds of equality: reference equality (`==`) and content equality (`equals`). According to their natures, nodes are identified by references, while names, values and labels are identified by contents. Since each name or value instance stored in a graph is also a node, we introduce an additional mapping to look up its identity (if exists in the graph) from its content. This resembles the `intern` method of class `String` in the Java API, which ensures that there is only one string object for each string value in use. Ordered contents can be stored as keys in class `TreeMap`, while unordered object identities have to be used as hash values and stored in class `HashMap`.

Graph transformation and optimization. State graphs are immutable in our implementation, which allows intermediate graphs to be retrieved. Every transformation of a graph returns a new graph. Identical nodes and labels in different graphs may refer to the same representation objects, while each graph keeps its own mappings of the elements, reducing the cost of new graph creations.

A garbage collection operation (gc) is performed after each step of execution to get rid of those inaccessible elements, and the operation is effectively done by a depth first search (dfs) on the graph. Primitive graph operations are first performed on a temporary graph, that we call the *increment graph*, and their grand effect is added upon the base graph with only one dfs. The relations in the increment graph override those in the base graph. There is no need for a decrement graph, since the only operation that may remove elements is the gc.

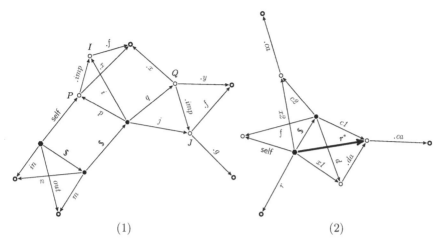

(1)   (2)

Fig. 8. Examples of auto-generated state graphs

A new graph is constructed while performing the *dfs* by adding visited entries to the mappings representing the new graph. We never remove entries from the mappings, allowing us to implement our curried mappings using Maps of Maps, where removals of entries may cause a *domino effect*.

Examples. Two examples in Fig. 8 illustrate the graph system. Fig. 8(1) is an instance of the bridge pattern, and Fig. 8(2) illustrates the capture of parent objects of actual result parameters. They are generated by the auto-layout algorithm.

In Fig. 8(1), there is an explicit pointer in each abstraction object pointing to its implementor object. It is hard to see subclass relations in state graphs, since attribute origins are merged along the inheritance path when objects are instantiated. Q is a subclass of P, and they are abstractions; J is a subclass of I, and they are implementors. We also see the relation between formal and actual parameters, for the graph is obtained within a method invocation.

In Fig. 8(2), the result parameter r will be bound to an attribute $c1.ca$ upon the method return. We record the parent object $c1$ using an edge with auxiliary label r^* to avoid losing it, in the case of $c1$ being pointed to somewhere else during the method invocation.

6   Properties of OO Programs

A main motivation of the semantics is that we wish to help in reasoning about OO programs. It is then crucial that properties can be clearly, easily and precisely thought about, described and understood. The advantage of our model in this aspect comes from intuitiveness and theoretical maturity of graphs. As shown in [20], many important properties of OO programs can easily be interpreted as assertions of state graphs. Simple but useful assertions include *acyclic nodes*, *acyclic graphs*, *sink* (or *leaf*) *nodes*, and *reachability* (*credibility*) of one node from another. In this section we show how within our semantics, properties of programs can be described without explicitly referring to locations.

6.1   Object Aliasing and Confinement

In an OO program, an *accessible object* is referred to by a navigation expression (or path) which is evaluated as a trace in our model. In a state, a navigation path e can represent an object that can further extend to $e.a$ for any attribute a of the object or a sink node (or called leaf). It is a leaf, denoted by $leaf(e)$, when in the state, e is an object whose attributes are not defined (i.e. $e.a$ is evaluated to $\perp$ for all attributes a of the object), an object whose class does not declare any attribute, a *null* object, or a constant value of a data type.

Two paths are *aliasing*, denoted by $e_1 \approx e_2$, if their traces target at the same node. This is obviously an equivalence relation, and thus aliasing expressions share many properties. For example, they can reach the same objects, and they reach any of these objects through the same paths. Formally, let p be a sequence of attribute names, $e_1\langle p \rangle e_2$ means that the object referred to by e_2 can be reached from the object referred to by e_1 via p. We have $e \approx e_1 \wedge e_1\langle p \rangle e_2 \Rightarrow e\langle p \rangle e_2$. We can use $e_1 \xrightarrow{+} e_2$ to denote that e_2 is reachable from e_1 through a non-empty path, and $e_1 \xrightarrow{*} e_2$ is defined as $(e_1 \approx e_2) \vee (e_1 \xrightarrow{+} e_2)$. Notice that aliasing is also a cause of cycles in a state. Formally, e is cyclic, denoted by $cyc(e)$, if it can reach itself via a non-empty path, i.e. $e \xrightarrow{+} e$. We use $acyc(e)$ to denote that e is acyclic.

There are more subtle and interesting graph properties, such as *dominance* of one node by another. Node n_1 *dominates* node n_2, denoted by n_1 dominates n_2, if every trace to n_2 passes through n_1. It holds for G iff

$$n_2 \notin delete(G, \{n_1\})^\bullet.node.$$

where $delete(G, ns)$ removes from G the nodes ns and all their associated edges.

We can use these properties to define language mechanisms for managing aliasing and encapsulation of heap-allocated objects. Ownership [11,10] is one of them, and it provides a notion of object-level encapsulation. Each object has an owner, and it can only be accessed through its owner, i.e. it is dominated by its owner. With predicates of navigation paths, this relation can be represented as e_1 owns e_2, asserting that the object that e_1 refers to owns the object that e_2 refers to, if the node of e_1 dominates the node of e_2.

Similarly, an edge d is the *bridge* for a node n, denoted by d bridges n, if every trace to n goes through d. It holds for G iff

$$n \notin G[(E \setminus \{d\})/E]^\bullet.node$$

Given two navigation paths e_1 and e_2, we can then define the relation bridges, such that e_1 bridges e_2 if the last edge of e_1 is the bridge for the node of e_2. The property of unique or aliasing free references [27,5] can then be specified: a variable or field annotated by the keyword uniq is a *null* object or the only name to refer the object. We define uniq e to denote that e is either *null* or the unique trace to its target object.

$$\text{uniq } e \; \hat{=} \; e = \textit{null} \lor \forall e' \preceq e \bullet e' \text{ bridges } e$$

where $e' \preceq e$ denotes that e' is a (non-empty) prefix of e.

6.2   Separation of Graphs

Given a connected state graph G, let $G.store$ be the subgraph, called the *store* of G, which contains the nodes on the \$-path of G and their outgoing edges. The subgraph obtained from G by removing the edges of the store (and the nodes becoming isolated because of the removal of these edges) is called the *heap* of G, denoted by $G.heap$. Note that $G = G.store \cup G.heap$, and $G.store.edge \cap G.heap.edge = \emptyset$.

The separation logic [32,29] can be interpreted in our model. A state G is a *separating composition* of two graphs G_1 and G_2, denoted by $G = G_1 * G_2$, if $G = G_1 \cup G_2$, $G_1.store = G_2.store$ and $G_1.heap.edge \cap G_2.heap.edge = \emptyset$. The separating conjunction $p * q$, asserting that the heap graph can be split into two object graphs for which p and q hold respectively, is defined as

$$\llbracket p * q \rrbracket\, G \; \hat{=} \; \exists G_1, G_2 \bullet G = G_1 * G_2 \land \llbracket p \rrbracket\, G_1 \land \llbracket q \rrbracket\, G_2.$$

For example, assume that q is an invariant of a class C. To ensure that a method (possibly overriding a method of C) of an object of a subclass D of C preserves this invariant, the assertion $\{q * \mathit{true}\}\, mbody(D, m)\, \{q * \mathit{true}\}$ is checked. Notice that q only mentions fields of C, and the separation is to divide the state of the object into the attributes inherited from C and those newly declared in D.

Chen and Sanders [9] propose a pointer logic based on a mixed model of graphs and functions, which extends separation logic with more flexible relational compositions. Our graphs are simpler, but can also define those compositional relations such as the relation G_1 access G_2, which asserts that there is a node (object) of G_1 that can access a node of G_2.

Hoare and O'Hearn [21] propose a unification of the ideas of separation in CSP and Concurrent Separation Logic [7]. We can also write properties by the idea of trace separation since traces and nodes are unified in our model .

7   Conclusions

Different semantic models provide different ways of thinking about the programs they define. Compared to other semantic models in the large body of literature, the simple graph model of this paper provides, in our opinion, more clarity on the OO features, including inheritance, type casting, dynamic binding, aliasing, local variable (un-)declaration, and early binding of result parameters in method invocations. Furthermore, the discussion on possible applications in Section 6 shows that this model is simple enough and helps in formulating clear assertions about executions of programs. It is also rich enough for defining more sophisticated language mechanisms, such as ownership and confinement, and a powerful logic to describe and prove important properties of programs.

The semantics is location independent and thus more abstract compared to most existing operational semantic definitions. We believe that a trace model similar to the one of Hoare and He [20] can be defined for our language and proved fully abstract w.r.t. the operational semantics given in this paper.

In an UTP approach, Harwood, Cavalcanti, and Woodcock use "path groups" to represent aliasing sets and defined a relation semantics for OO programs without explicit reference to memories [17]. Predicate-transformer models of object orientation have been considered by Naumann [28] and Cavalcanti and Naumann [8] and have been progressively developed by Sampaio and Borba et al. [3,4]. We believe that the structural properties of the state graphs and the simple operations on them would leverage the understanding of these theories too.

Another advantage of our approach, and of graph-based approach in general [23], is that it allows us to use a single mathematical structure, for the static class structure (class graph), the runtime state (state graph), and the flow of control (transition graph), of the program.

There is a large community working on graph-based approaches to software design, known as the area of graph transformations [33,13,14,16,36,2]. However, the major focus in this area is software architecture design and reconfiguration, and thus graphs are required to have hierarchies and hyper-edges. The graph transformation systems there are mostly developed within a heavy use of theories of algebras and categories, which most computer scientists and software engineers find difficult to comprehend. There is, however, some work on defining programming languages, including execution semantics, by graph transformation systems (e.g. [23,12]). However, it heavily uses the Rich Abstract Syntax Graph (R-ASG) to gain the power of unification of context information and formal syntactical transformations from programs to graphs. It leaves the formal semantics of R-ASG undefined. Therefore, while the simulation of a program is nicely supported by a tool, it is not clear how assertions of executions can be formulated and reasoned about. The community of functional programming also applies graph rewriting systems to definitions of functional languages, e.g. [35,34].

Future work. We plan to develop a graph-based assertional logic for static analysis of OO programs, and then investigate its application in automated techniques of verification and analysis. We will define a fully abstract semantics for rCOS, which is now used for component-based model driven development [26]. Further, we plan to extend the work to define an operational semantics of multi-threaded programs for their verification and analysis.

Acknowledgment.   We are grateful to our colleagues Charles Morisset, Volker Stolz and Xu Wang for the discussions and comments. We would also like to thank Yifeng Chen, Zongyan Qiu and Naijun Zhan for their comments and suggestions they gave during a visit to them by two of the authors, Zhiming Liu and Shuling Wang.

References

1. Abadi, M., Cardelli, L.: A Theory of Objects. Springer, Heidelberg (1996)
2. Baresi, L., Heckel, R., Thöne, S., Varró, D.: Style-based refinement of dynamic software architectures. In: 4th Working IEEE/IFIP Conference on Software Architecture, pp. 155–164. IEEE Computer Society, Los Alamitos (2004)
3. Borba, P., Sampaio, A., Cavalcanti, A., Cornélio, M.: Algebraic reasoning for object-oriented programming. Sci. Comput. Program. 52(1-3), 53–100 (2004)
4. Borba, P., Sampaio, A., Cornélio, M.: A refinement algebra for object-oriented programming. In: Cardelli, L. (ed.) ECOOP 2003. LNCS, vol. 2743, pp. 1–37. Springer, Heidelberg (2003)
5. Boyland, J.: Alias burying: Unique variables without destructive reads. Software Practice and Experience 31(6), 533–553 (2001)
6. Bozga, M., Iosif, R., Lakhnech, Y.: On logics of aliasing. In: Giacobazzi, R. (ed.) SAS 2004. LNCS, vol. 3148, pp. 344–360. Springer, Heidelberg (2004)
7. Brookes, S.: A semantics for concurrent separation logic. Theor. Comput. Sci. 375(1-3), 227–270 (2007)
8. Cavalcanti, A., Naumann, D.: A weakest precondition semantics for an object-oriented language of refinement. In: Woodcock, J.C.P., Davies, J., Wing, J.M. (eds.) FM 1999. LNCS, vol. 1709, pp. 1439–1460. Springer, Heidelberg (1999)
9. Chen, Y., Sanders, J.W.: Compositional reasoning for pointer structures. In: Uustalu, T. (ed.) MPC 2006. LNCS, vol. 4014, pp. 115–139. Springer, Heidelberg (2006)
10. Clarke, D., Noble, J., Potter, J.: Simple ownership types for object containment. In: Knudsen, J.L. (ed.) ECOOP 2001. LNCS, vol. 2072, pp. 53–76. Springer, Heidelberg (2001)
11. Clarke, D., Potter, J., Noble, J.: Ownership types for flexible alias protection. SIGPLAN Not. 33(10), 48–64 (1998)
12. Corradini, A., Dotti, F.L., Foss, L., Ribeiro, L.: Translating Java code to graph transformation systems. In: Ehrig, H., Engels, G., Parisi-Presicce, F., Rozenberg, G. (eds.) ICGT 2004. LNCS, vol. 3256, pp. 383–398. Springer, Heidelberg (2004)
13. Corradini, A., Montanari, U., Rossi, F.: Graph processes. Fundamenta Informaticae 26(3,4), 241–265 (1996)
14. Ehrig, H., Ehrig, K., Prange, U., Taentzer, G.: Fundamental theory for typed attributed graphs and graph transformation based on adhesive HLR categories. Fundamenta Informaticae 74(1), 31–61 (2006)
15. Ferreira, A.P.L., Foss, L., Ribeiro, L.: Formal verification of object-oriented graph grammars specifications. ENTCS 175(4), 101–114 (2007)
16. Große-Rhode, M., Parisi-Presicce, F., Simeoni, M.: Spatial and temporal refinement of typed graph transformation systems. In: Brim, L., Gruska, J., Zlatuška, J. (eds.) MFCS 1998. LNCS, vol. 1450, pp. 553–561. Springer, Heidelberg (1998)
17. Harwood, W., Cavalcanti, A., Woodcock, J.: A theory of pointers for the UTP. In: Fitzgerald, J.S., Haxthausen, A.E., Yenigun, H. (eds.) ICTAC 2008. LNCS, vol. 5160, pp. 141–155. Springer, Heidelberg (2008)
18. He, J., Li, X., Liu, Z.: rCOS: A refinement calculus for object systems. Theor. Comput. Sci. 365(1-2), 109–142 (2006)
19. Heckel, R., Küster, J.M., Taentzer, G.: Confluence of typed attributed graph transformation systems. In: Corradini, A., Ehrig, H., Kreowski, H.-J., Rozenberg, G. (eds.) ICGT 2002. LNCS, vol. 2505, pp. 161–176. Springer, Heidelberg (2002)

20. Hoare, C.A.R., He, J.: A trace model for pointers and objects. In: Guerraoui, R. (ed.) ECOOP 1999. LNCS, vol. 1628, pp. 1–17. Springer, Heidelberg (1999)
21. Hoare, T., O'Hearn, P.: Separation logic semantics for communicating processes. ENTCS 212, 3–25 (2008)
22. Kamada, T., Kawai, S.: An algorithm for drawing general undirected graphs. Information processing letters 31(1), 7–15 (1989)
23. Kastenberg, H., Kleppe, A., Rensink, A.: Defining object-oriented execution semantics using graph transformations. In: Gorrieri, R., Wehrheim, H. (eds.) FMOODS 2006. LNCS, vol. 4037, pp. 186–201. Springer, Heidelberg (2006)
24. Ke, W., Liu, Z., Wang, S., Zhao, L.: Graph-based type system, operational semantics and implementation of an object-oriented programming language. Technical Report 410, UNU-IIST, P.O. Box 3058, Macau (2009), http://www.iist.unu.edu/www/docs/techreports/reports/report410.pdf
25. Klein, G., Nipkow, T.: A machine-checked model for a Java-like language, virtual machine, and compiler. ACM TOPLAS 28(4), 619–695 (2006)
26. Liu, Z., Morisset, C., Stolz, V.: rCOS: Theory and tool for component-based model driven development. Technical Report 406, UNU-IIST, P.O. Box 3058, Macau (2009), http://www.iist.unu.edu/www/docs/techreports/reports/report406.pdf (to appear in LNCS)
27. Minsky, N.: Towards alias-free pointers. In: Cointe, P. (ed.) ECOOP 1996. LNCS, vol. 1098, pp. 189–209. Springer, Heidelberg (1996)
28. Naumann, D.A.: Predicate transformer semantics of a higher-order imperative language with record subtyping. Sci. Comput. Program. 41(1), 1–51 (2001)
29. Parkinson, M., Bierman, G.: Separation logic and abstraction. SIGPLAN Not. 40(1), 247–258 (2005)
30. Pierik, C., de Boer, F.: A syntax-directed Hoare logic for object-oriented programming concepts. In: Najm, E., Nestmann, U., Stevens, P. (eds.) FMOODS 2003. LNCS, vol. 2884, pp. 64–78. Springer, Heidelberg (2003)
31. Poetzsch-Heffter, A., Müller, P.: A programming logic for sequential Java. In: Swierstra, S.D. (ed.) ESOP 1999. LNCS, vol. 1576, pp. 162–176. Springer, Heidelberg (1999)
32. Reynolds, J.: Separation logic: A logic for shared mutable data structures. In: Proc. 17th Annual IEEE Symposium on Logic in Computer Science. IEEE Computer Society, Los Alamitos (2002) (invited paper)
33. Rozenberg, G. (ed.): Handbook of Graph Grammars and Computing by Graph Transformation. Foundations, vol. 1. World Scientific, Singapore (1997)
34. van Eekelen, M., de Mol, M.: Mixed lazy/strict graph semantics. In: Proc. 16th International Workshop on Implementation and Application of Functional Languages, pp. 245–260. Christian-Albrechts-Universitaet zu Kiel (2004)
35. van Eekelen, M., Smetsers, S., Plasmeijer, M.: Graph rewriting semantics for functional programming languages. In: Proc. 5th Annual Conference of European Association for Computer Science Logic, pp. 106–128. Springer, Heidelberg (1996)
36. Wermelinger, M., Fiadero, J.L.: A graph transformation approach to software architecture reconfiguration. Sci. Comput. Program. 44(2), 133–155 (2002)
37. Zhao, L., Liu, X., Liu, Z., Qiu, Z.: Graph transformations for object-oriented refinement. Form. Asp. Comput. 21(1-2), 103–131 (2009)

Modeling and Analysis of Thread-Pools in an Industrial Communication Platform*

Frank S. de Boer[1], Immo Grabe[1,2], Mohammad Mahdi Jaghoori[1],
Andries Stam[3], and Wang Yi[4]

[1] CWI, Amsterdam, The Netherlands
[2] Christian-Albrechts-University Kiel, Germany
[3] Almende, The Netherlands
[4] University of Uppsala, Sweden

Abstract. Thread pools are often used as a pattern to increase the throughput and responsiveness of software systems. Implementations of thread pools may differ considerably from each other, which urges the need to analyze these differences in a formal manner. We use an object-oriented paradigm to model different thread pools in the context of the ASK system, an industrial communication platform. We use *behavioral interfaces*, high-level behavioral specifications for the objects, as a starting-point for analysis. Based on these behavioral interfaces, functional aspects are modeled in Creol, a high-level modeling language for concurrent objects. We use UPPAAL to create real-time models and to perform schedulability analysis with respect to the behavioral interfaces. We finally check conformance between the real-time and Creol models using test-cases generated from the behavioral interfaces.

1 Introduction

Thread pools are an important design pattern used frequently in industrial practice to increase the throughput and responsiveness of software systems, as for instance in the ASK system [4]. The ASK system is an industrial communication platform providing mechanisms for matching users requiring information or services with potential suppliers. A thread pool administrates a collection of computation units referred to as threads and assigns tasks to them. This administration includes dynamic creation or removal of such units, as well as scheduling the tasks based on a given strategy like 'first come first served' or priority based scheduling.

In this paper, we propose the use of the *Credo* tool suite in order to capture the various aspects of thread pools and provide a general framework for their analysis. The *Credo* tool suite offers a methodology for the top-down design and compositional analysis of dynamically reconfigurable systems of concurrent objects [11]. We tailor *Credo* methodology to model and analyze the thread

---

* This work has been supported by the EU-project IST-33826 *Credo: Modeling and analysis of evolutionary structures for distributed services*.

K. Breitman and A. Cavalcanti (Eds.): ICFEM 2009, LNCS 5885, pp. 367–386, 2009.

pools in ASK. The core of this methodology consists of two different *executable* modeling languages:

Creol [13] is a high-level object-oriented modeling language for describing the interactions between concurrent objects. Creol focuses on modeling the data and control flow thus reflecting the architectural issues of the implementation at a high level of abstraction. It abstracts from scheduling issues.

Timed Automata [3] are used to model scheduling policies as well as the behavioral interfaces of objects which describe the timings of incoming messages and their deadlines. At this level, we abstract from architectural details of the model and focus on schedulability analysis (no deadline miss).

After modeling in Creol and analyzing schedulability with timed automata, we need to establish the conformance between the two models. This is achieved by testing. Test cases are generated from behavioral interface specifications. As observed, the behavioral interfaces are central to the analyses in *Credo*.

Modeling the Architecture. The ASK system has been developed and evolved over years; different subsystems of ASK use specialized thread pools to address issues like the size of the pool, dynamic creation of threads, load balancing, etc. The implementation of ASK contains thousands of lines of C code, that are difficult to understand and analyze. In this paper, we provide a high-level Creol model that is only tens of lines of Creol code with less distracting implementation details, and is thus more amenable to analysis.

The intended use of the Creol modeling language is to provide a formal object-oriented solution to modeling distributed software systems [13,8]. The Creol modeling language is implemented by means of an interpreter given in Maude [5] and supported by an Eclipse modeling and analysis environment (developed in the *Credo* project [7]) which includes a compiler and type-checker, a simulation platform that allows both closed world and open world simulation as well as guided simulation, and a graphic display of the simulations.

In Creol, objects are concurrent, i.e., conceptually, each object encapsulates its own processor. Therefore, each object has a single thread of execution. Creol objects communicate by asynchronous message passing. The message queue is implicit in the objects. Furthermore, the scheduling policy is underspecified, i.e., messages in the queue are processed in a nondeterministic order. The running method can voluntarily release the processor using special commands allowing another message to be scheduled. For example, a method can test whether an asynchronous call has been completed, and if not, release the processor; thus modeling synchronous calls.

The abstraction from the internal message queue of each object and the related scheduling policies is one of the most important characteristics of Creol which allows for abstractly modeling a variety of thread pools. In this paper, we give an example of an abstract model in Creol of a basic pool where the threads share the task queue. The shared task queue is naturally represented *implicitly* inside a Creol object (called a resource-pool) that basically forwards the queued tasks to its associated threads also represented as Creol objects (called monks).

Analyzing Schedulability. We perform schedulability analysis on the automata models of thread pools; this verifies whether tasks are performed within their deadlines. In the context of the ASK system, schedulability ensures that the response times for service requests are always bounded by the deadlines. We use UPPAAL [16] for this purpose. To analyze the *schedulability* of thread pools, their behavioral interfaces are modeled with timed automata. A behavioral interface describes the (expected) arrival times and the deadlines of the tasks; namely, the workload on the thread pool. A given scheduling policy, e.g., earliest deadline first (EDF), is also specified with timed automata. This determines where to insert a newly generated task in the message queue of the resource-pool object. The tasks correspond to the monks in the Creol model.

We provide two approaches to schedulability analysis of thread pools. Once the threads are assumed to run in parallel. This is in line with the assumption in Creol that monk objects, representing the threads, have dedicated processors. Next, we model a situation in which all threads share the same processor. In this case, we model a time-sharing CPU allocation scheme to the concurrent threads. To this end, we use one extra clock for each thread to compute the idle times when it is preempted.

Finally, we test conformance between the timed automata models and the underlying Creol models by generating test cases from the behavioral interfaces. We use the test cases to drive the execution of the Creol model extended with an abstract implementation of the given scheduling policy on the simulation platform.

Related Work. The schedulability analysis in this paper can be seen as the continuation of our previous work [12] on modular analysis of a single-threaded concurrent object with respect to its behavioral interface. In this paper, we extend the schedulability analysis to the case of a multi-threaded scheduler (representing an object-oriented thread pool).

Schedulability has been studied for actor languages [18] and event driven distributed systems [10]. Unlike these works, we work with non-uniformly recurring tasks as in task automata [9] which fits better to the nature of message passing in object-oriented languages. The main difference is that in our work, multiple objects share the same task queue. These objects are once modeled as using the same processor, therefore scheduled using a time-sharing policy; next we model them as using independent processors, therefore each object runs in parallel to the others.

The work of [6,15] is based on extracting automata from code for schedulability analysis. However, they deal with programming languages and timings are usually obtained by profiling the real system. Our work is applied on high-level model. Therefore, our main focus is on studying different scheduling policies and design decisions. *Credo* offers techniques for testing conformance with the C code [1], which is not covered in this paper.

Outline. In section 2 we give a short introduction to timed automata and the Creol language. The current implementation of the ASK system is explained in section 3. We model the different features and the scheduling of selected thread pools of the ASK system in section 4. Schedulability analysis and testing of conformance between the Creol model of a thread-pool and its behavioral interface is discussed in section 5. We conclude with section 6.

2   Preliminaries

2.1   Timed Automata

In this section, we define timed automata. We use timed automata to specify behavioral interfaces and perform schedulability analysis.

Definition 1 (Timed Automata). *Suppose $\mathcal{B}(C)$ is the set of all clock constraints on the set of clocks C. A timed automaton over actions Σ and clocks C is a tuple $\langle L, l_0, \longrightarrow, I \rangle$ representing*

- *a finite set of locations L (including an initial location l_0);*
- *the set of edges $\longrightarrow \subseteq L \times \mathcal{B}(C) \times \Sigma \times 2^C \times L$; and,*
- *a function $I : L \mapsto \mathcal{B}(C)$ assigning an invariant to each location.*

An edge (l, g, a, r, l') implies that action 'a' may change the location l to l' by resetting the clocks in r, if the clock constraints in g (as well as the invariant of l') hold. Since we use UPPAAL [16], we allow defining variables of type boolean and bounded integers. Variables can appear in guards and updates.

A timed automaton is called *deterministic* if and only if for each $a \in \Sigma$, if there are two edges (l, g, a, r, l') and (l, g', a, r', l'') from l labeled by the same action a then the guards g and g' are disjoint (i.e., $g \wedge g'$ is unsatisfiable).

Networks of timed automata. A system may be described as a collection of timed automata communicating with each other. In these automata, the action set is partitioned into input, output and internal actions. The behavior of the system is defined as the parallel composition of those automata $A_1 \parallel \cdots \parallel A_n$. Semantically, the system can delay if all automata can delay and can perform an action if one of the automata can perform an internal action or if two automata can synchronize on complementary actions (inputs and outputs are complementary). In a network of timed automata, variables can be defined locally for one automaton, globally (shared between all automata), or as parameters to the automata.

A location can be marked *urgent* in an automaton to indicate that the automaton cannot spend any time in that location. This is equivalent to resetting a fresh clock x in all of its incoming edges and adding an invariant $x \leq 0$ to the location. In a network of timed automata, the enabled transitions from an urgent location may be interleaved with the enabled transitions from other automata (while time is frozen). Like urgent locations, *committed* locations freeze time; furthermore, if any process is in a committed location, the next step must involve an edge from one of the committed locations.

IF ::= **interface** $N\{(Par)\}^?\{$**inherits** $Inh\}^?$
      begin $\{$**with** N $Msig^+\}^?$ **end**
Inh ::= $\{N\{(E)\}^?\}^+_,$
Par ::= $\{\{v\}^+_, : N\}^+_,$
$Msig$ ::= **op** $N\{(\{$**in** $Par\}^?$ $\{$**out** $Par\}^?)\}^?$
CL ::= **class** $N\{(Par)\}^?$
      $\{$**contracts** $Inh\}^?$ $\{$**inherits** $Inh\}^?$
      begin $Vdcl^?\{\{$**with** $N\}^?$ $Mtd\}^*$ **end**
$Vdcl$ ::= **var** $\{\{v\}^+_, : N\{= e\}^?\}^+_,$

Mtd ::= $\{Msig == \{Vdcl;\}^?$ $S\}^+$
g ::= $b \mid t? \mid \neg g \mid g \wedge g$
p ::= $x.m \mid m$
S ::= $\epsilon \mid s; S$
s ::= $(S) \mid V := E \mid$ **skip**
    $\mid v :=$ **new** $N(E) \mid !p(E)$
    $\mid t!p(E) \mid t?(V) \mid p(E;V)$
    $\mid$ **if** b **then** S **else** S **end**
    $\mid$ **await** $g \mid$ **await** $t?(V)$
    $\mid$ **await** $p(E;V) \mid$ **release**

Fig. 1. BNF grammar for Creol. Curly brackets are used as meta parenthesis, superscript ? for optional parts, superscript * for repetition zero or more times, whereas $\{...\}^+_,$ denotes repetition one or more times with , as delimiter. Identifiers N denote interface, class, type, or method names. Capitalized terms such as E, V, and S, denote lists of the syntactic categories of the corresponding lower-case terms [13,14].

2.2   Creol

The (simplified) syntax of Creol is given in Fig. 1. Here we introduce the basic concepts of Creol. A comprehensive presentation of the formal semantics of Creol (given in rewrite logic, see [13]) is beyond the scope of this paper.

Creol objects are typed by interfaces, whereas classes can implement (indicated by the keyword **contracts**) as many interfaces as necessary. Co-interfaces are used to restrict possible callers, i.e., if a co-interface is specified only objects implementing the co-interface are allowed to call methods in the scope of the interface. A co-interface is specified by the keyword **with**. The combination of interfaces as types and co-interfaces enforces type-safe communication. Creol provides the keyword **this** to refer to the actual object and the keyword **caller** to refer to a caller of a method. In Creol concurrent objects communicate via asynchronous method calls. After sending an asynchronous method call, e.g. $t!p(E)$ where t denotes a future to retrieve the value later and $p(E)$ the method call, the process continues execution. The return value of a method call is retrieved via a get operation on the future, e.g. $t?(V)$ where t denotes the future and V the variables to store the result in. Note that get is a blocking operation, i.e. the process blocks until the return value of the method call is computed. A process can also test a method call for termination, e.g. **await** $t?(V)$. In case the future has been calculated the statement is equivalent to $t?(V)$. In case the future has not yet been calculated the statement releases control over the processor. We use $p(E;V)$ as a shorthand for $t!p(E); t?(V)$ and **await** $p(E;V)$ as a shorthand for $t!p(E);$ **await** $t?(V)$.

Each object in Creol, upon creation, starts its active behavior by executing its run operation if defined. When receiving a method call a new process is created inside the object to handle the method call. The processes inside an object are interleaved by means of processor release points. A processor release point is reached if a process terminates or reaches a special condition. The **await** keyword opens such a condition. If the condition is false, the processor is released;

```
 1 interface Simple begin
 2     with Simple op callMe
 3     with Any op response
 4 end

 6 class Easy contracts Simple begin
 7     op run == await this.callMe()
 8     with Simple op callMe == ! caller.response()
 9     with Any op response == skip
10 end
```

Fig. 2. A simple Creol model

otherwise, the process continues. The conditions can also query method calls for termination, e.g. **await** $t?(V)$. A process which has not yet started its execution or which is waiting on a condition, that is true, is called enabled. Upon processor release, an enabled process is (nondeterministically) chosen to start or continue its execution.

Creol is backed by its formal operational semantics and its strong typing allows for dynamic class upgrades [19]. Since Creol semantics is given in rewrite logic [17], Creol specifications can be executed and analyzed on the Maude [5] platform. Maude is a rewrite engine that offers analyses like simulation, model checking, etc., on transition systems specified using rewrite logic.

Fig. 2 shows a simple Creol model. The Simple interface defines a callMe operation that can be called only by instances of type Simple, while the response operation does not require any special co-interface. The run method in a class defines its active behavior; thus the class Easy starts with calling its own callMe operation. It waits until the call to callMe has terminated.

3   ASK System

ASK is an industrial software system for connecting people to each other. The system uses intelligent matching functionality in order to find effective connections between requesters and responders in a community. ASK has been developed by Almende [2], a Dutch research company focusing on the application of self-organisation techniques in human organisations and agent-oriented software systems. The system is marketed by ASK Community Systems [4]. ASK provides mechanisms for matching users requiring information or services with potential suppliers. Based on information about earlier established contacts and feedback of users, the system learns to bring people into contact with each other in the most effective way. Typical applications for ASK are workforce planning, customer service, knowledge sharing, social care and emergency response. Customers of ASK include the European mail distribution company TNT Post, the cooperative financial services provider Rabobank and the world's largest pharmaceutical company Pfizer. The amount of people using a single ASK configuration varies from several hundreds to several thousands.

An Overview of the ASK System

The primary goal of the ASK system is to connect people to other people in the most effective way. The system acts as a *mediator* in establishing the contacts: people can contact the system via various media like telephone or email, and the system itself is also able to contact people via those media. In determining the *effectiveness* of contact establishment, multiple aspects play a role. For example, the rating of *human knowledge and skills* is important in cases where people request contact with specialists or service providers. In these cases, the ASK system is able to ask participants for feedback on the quality of service after the contact. This feedback can be used for optimization of subsequent requests of the same kind. A different role is played by *time schedules*, which indicate when certain people can be reached for certain purposes. The ASK system differentiates between regular plannings and ad-hoc schedules caused by sudden events or delays. Different *communication media* play another role. In most ASK configurations, voice communication (phone, VoIP) is the primary communication medium used, but different media like email and SMS are supported by ASK as well. Moreover, people can own various phone numbers and email addresses, for which they can indicate preferences and time or service dependent usage constraints. The ASK system is able to exploit knowledge about the reachability of people via specific media, for example in the context of emergency response systems, where people must be contacted within a certain time window. In general, learning from past experiences of all kinds and forecasting based on these experiences plays a crucial role in ASK.

The software of ASK can be technically divided into three parts: the *web front-end*, the *database* and the *contact engine* (see Figure 3). The *web front-end* acts as a configuration dashboard, via which typical domain data like users, groups, phone numbers, mail addresses, interactive voice response menus, services and scheduled jobs can be created, edited and deleted. This data is stored in a *database*, one for each configuration of ASK. The feedback of users and the knowledge derived from earlier established contacts are also stored in this database. Finally, the *contact engine* consists of a quintuple of components *Reception*, *Matcher*, *Executer*, *Resource Manager* and *Scheduler*, which handle inbound and outbound communication with the system and provide the intelligent matching and scheduling functionality.

The "heartbeat" of the contact engine is the *Request loop*, indicated with thick arrows. Requests loop through the system until they are fully completed. The *Reception* component determines which steps must be taken by ASK in order to fulfil (part of) a request. The *Matcher* component searches for appropriate participants for a request. The *Executer* component determines the best way in which the participants can be connected. ASK clearly separates the medium and resource independent request loop from the level of media-specific resources

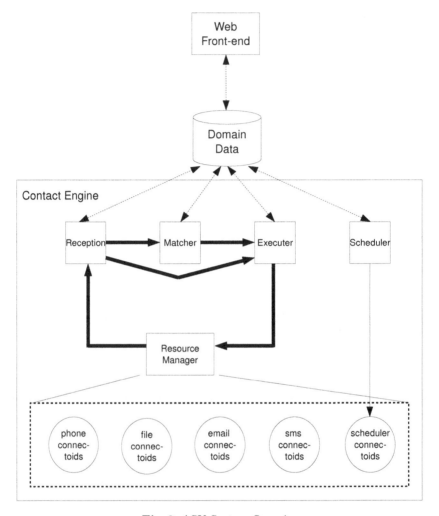

Fig. 3. ASK System Overview

needed for fulfilling the request, called *connectoids* (e.g., a connected phone line, a sound file being played, an email being written, an SMS message to be sent). The *Resource Manager* component acts as a bridge between these two levels. Finally, a separate *Scheduler* component schedules requests based on job descriptions in the database.

Thread-Pools in ASK

Each component in the ASK system is equipped with a thread-pool called an *abbey*. The threads within the pool are called *monks*. Two types of abbeys are currently in use, although many more have been created in the past at Almende:

- The so-called *Determinate Abbey* (Dabbey) uses a fixed amount of monks, which get their tasks from a task array with an amount of "slots" equal to the number of monks. The operation of putting a task in an empty slot of the task array blocks if no empty slot is available.
- Another type of abbey is the *Self-scaling Abbey* (Sabbey). This abbey uses an infinite task queue and a variable amount of monks. Monks are created and "poisoned" at run-time by a special monk called the *shepherd*, which does so by keeping track of the ratio between the amount of tasks to be handled and the amount of available monks.

4   Modeling

4.1   Object-Oriented Modeling

In this section, we introduce the "low-level" Creol model of the Determinate Abbey in order to illustrate the need for abstraction. The low-level model covers all implementation-level details like locks on global variables, explicit tasks and explicit task queues, etc.

In the Determinate Abbey, tasks and monks are kept in lists of fixed size, and tasks are implemented (cf. Appendix A). The Dabbey class contains two class variables *DabbeyTaskList* and *DabbeyMonkList* to store the tasks-to-be-executed and the monks. In the more abstract model, we represent the task queue by the *message queue* of an object and we abstract from the explicit list of monks.

In the low-level model, an array of tasks is represented by a list, called states. An element of the list models a slot for a task resp. the status of the task assigned to the slot:

- "READY" denotes an empty spot for a task.
- "CREATING" denotes a task in creation.
- "OPEN" denotes a task ready for execution.
- "BUSY" denotes a task that is executed.

We use two functions operating on the list:

- index(list ,status) returns the index of an element with the given status.
- replace(list ,status,index) sets the status of the element at the given index.

A pair of counters keeps track of the number of free spots in the array, readyCounter, and the task waiting for execution, openCounter. The methods *testAndSetCreating*, *testAndSetBusy*, *setTaskOpen*, *setTaskReady* and *setTask* use the replace function to model the different phases of the execution of a task. In this manner, we realize an explicit representation of an array in terms of a simple list. For the analysis of the thread-pool, the fact that we use an array is an implementation detail and irrelevant to the analysis. Creol methods are executed mutually exclusive so the methods *testAndSetCreating* and *testAndSetBusy* in fact model "test-and-set" operations. Overall we model a lock on the array providing us with mutually exclusive access and ensuring consistency of the list and the task handling.

```
1  class Monk(myPool: ResourcePool) contracts Monk begin
2    op run == !myPool.request()
3    with ResourcePool op task == skip; run(;)
4  end
5  class ResourcePool(nofMonks: Int) contracts ResourcePool
6  begin
7    var freeMonks: Set[Monk];
8    op init == var monk: Monk; var n: Int := nofMonks;
9      freeMonks := {};
10     while (n>0) do monk:=new Monk(this); n:=n−1 end
11   op chooseMonk(out monk:Monk) == await ˜isempty(freeMonks);
12     monk := choose(freeMonks);
13     freeMonks := remove(freeMonks,monk)
14   op task == var monk: Monk; chooseMonk(;monk); !monk.task()
15   with Monk op request == freeMonks := add(freeMonks,caller)
16   with Outside op addTask == !task()
17 end
```

Fig. 4. The high-level Minimal Abbey

The low-level model of the Self-scaling Abbey is even more complex. Tasks and Monks are kept in queues, while a triplet of counters is used to count the number of tasks, monks and busy monks. Creation and deletion of monks is done by a "shepherd" monk. Monks are killed by letting them execute a "poison" task, which causes the monk to terminate. In Appendix C, the looping shepherd task is shown. Once this task is executed by a monk, that monk acts as the shepherd in the abbey. Note in particular the large amount of class parameters, which are needed inside the task to manage the amount of monks in the monk queue. In fact, the dynamicity of the amount of monks, which is in itself an important property of the Self-scaling Abbey, can be modeled in a more abstract manner. The focus should be on the principle of and constraints on creation and deletion, instead of on the specific solution as implemented in the ASK system.

High-Level Models. As a high-level base model, we created a *Minimal Abbey* (Mabbey), as shown in Figure 4. The Mabbey acts as the "mother" of all abbeys – the Determinate Abbey and the Self-scaling Abbey are derived from it, as well as other types of abbeys. The two most important classes are the *Monk* class and the *ResourcePool* class. Their class specifications and interfaces they contract are shown in Figure 4.

The task list is modeled implicitly, in terms of the message queue of the object. By using the proper way of messaging, i.e. synchronous or asynchronous, blocking and non-blocking behavior for inserts in the queue can be modeled.

The size of the queue can be limited by means of a class variable *nofTasks* which represents the number of tasks currently in the task queue (this construct is used in the Determinate Abbey). A list for the monks is not modeled: it is not needed at this level of abstraction. A variable *freeMonks* is used to hold all monks which are currently not executing a task. Based on simple requests issued by the monks themselves, the monks are added to the list of free monks. Tasks are modeled in terms of simple methods inside the monk class – this is enough, as for our analysis the functional differences between *tasks*, as opposed to the differences between *thread-pools*, is irrelevant.

4.2   Real-Time Modeling in UPPAAL

In this section, we model a thread-pool using timed automata in UPPAAL. We use these UPPAAL models in the next section for schedulability analysis of real-time models of the ASK system. We model a thread-pool as a scheduler automaton taking tasks from a queue and dispatching them among concurrent threads. This model can be seen as an extension of the framework for schedulability analysis of concurrent objects [12] to a situation in which objects share the message/task queue.

We separate the task queue in two parts: an *execution* part and a *buffer*. The execution part includes the tasks that are being executed. This part needs one slot for each thread and is therefore as big as the number of threads; we assume a fixed number of threads given a priori. Before beginning their execution, tasks are queued based on a given scheduling strategies, e.g., EDF, FPS, etc., in the rest of the queue (i.e., the buffer part).

In the rest of this section, we show two approaches in modeling concurrent threads sharing a task queue. At a higher level of abstraction, we can assume that the threads run in parallel as if each has its own processing unit. We can alternatively model a time-sharing scheduling policy where the 'executing' threads share the processor; therefore, each task runs a period of time before it is interrupted by the scheduler to run the next one. In both cases, when a task reaches the execution part, it will not be put back to the buffer part. We call this *weak non-preemption*, i.e., in the special case of one thread, it behaves like a non-preemptive scheduler. The scheduler (responsible for dispatching methods) and the queue (responsible for receiving messages) can be modeled in the same automaton or separately.

Time-Sharing. In this model, execution threads share one CPU. Therefore, the tasks in the execution part of the queue are interleaved. We call a thread active if a task is assigned to it. At its turn, each active thread gets a fixed time slot (called a *quantum*) for execution. If the assigned task does not finish within this quantum, the thread is preempted and the control is given to the next active thread. Recall that we use weak non-preemption, i.e., once a task is in the execution part it cannot be put back into the buffer part.

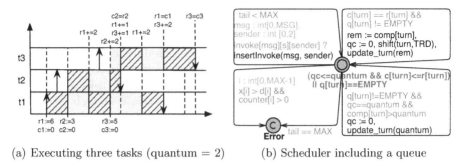

(a) Executing three tasks (quantum = 2)   (b) Scheduler including a queue

Fig. 5. Modeling a time-sharing scheduler for a thread-pool

In this model, each task is modeled only as a computation time. This abstraction is necessary to enable the modeling of preemption of tasks at any arbitrary time (i.e., the selected quantum). Figure 5.(a) shows intuitively how three threads are scheduled. The up-arrows show when a task is released. A down-arrow indicates the completion of the task, after which the thread remains inactive in this scenario. The tasks assigned to t1, t2 and t3 have the computation times of 6, 3 and 5, respectively, and the preemption quantum is 2.

We associate to each thread a clock c and an integer variable r for response time, i.e., the execution plus idle time, which is updated dynamically while an active thread is idle. A task finishes when its clock reaches the expected response time value (c=r shown in green in Figure 5.(a)). When a task is assigned to a thread, only at the next quantum the thread becomes active, i.e., the thread clock is reset to zero and r is given the computation time of the task. In Figure 5.(a), the active period of the threads is shown in gray, during which the hatched pattern denotes when the thread has the CPU. At every context-switch (shown by dashed lines in Figure 5.(a)), the response-time variables of all idle threads are increased to reflect their recent idle time.

Figure 5.(b) shows the formal model of the time-sharing scheduler, which includes the message queue. The clock qc is used to keep track of time slots. The invariant on the initial location of the automaton ensures progress when a context-switch should occur and on the other hand it does not deadlock when the queue is empty (q[turn]==EMPTY). The edges on the right-side of the automaton model context-switch; in update_turn response-time variables are updated:

```
for (i = 0; i < TRD; i++) {
  if (q[i] != EMPTY) {
    if (i != turn) r[i] += quantum;
    else comp[ca[i]] -= quantum;  // remaining computation time
} }
```

The first check q[i] != EMPTY makes sure that the thread i is active, i.e., a task is assigned to it. The variable turn shows the thread that was just running.

For threads i != turn the response time r[i] is increased to cover their idle time, whereas for the thread that is just stopped we update comp, the remaining computation time. The value of comp is used when a task finishes before a quantum is reached, e.g., tasks t2 and t3 in Figure 5.(a). In this case, the response time of idle threads is increased by comp instead of quantum.

Finally the variable turn is updated at every context-switch, such that the next active thread is selected. If it happens that there are no more active threads, i.e., the last task just finished, turn will keep its old value, as modeled in the for loop below:

```
turn = (turn + 1) % TRD;
for (i=0; q[turn]==EMPTY && i<TRD-1; i++) {
  turn = (turn + 1) % TRD;
}
```

The edges on the left model insertion of tasks into the queue using the insertInvoke function, in which the scheduling policy can be modeled. In this model, the deadline or priority values for tasks can be modeled statically. Each queue slot is assigned a clock x which shows how long a task sits in that queue slot. The automaton also takes care that when a task misses its deadline (x[i] > d[i]) or the queue is full (tail == MAX), it goes to the Error state.

Parallel Threads. In this model, every thread is assumed to have a dedicated processing unit, but they share one task queue. This model is more accurate when we can rely on the fact that the real system will run on a multi-core CPU and each thread will in fact run in parallel to the others. In this model, the queue and the scheduling strategy are modeled in separate automata. Figure 6.(a) shows a queue of size MAX which stores the tasks in the order of their arrival. This automaton is parameterized in s which holds the identity of the object. It accepts any message from any sender on the invoke channel, using the UPPAAL 'select' statement on msg and sender. To check for deadlines, a clock x is assigned to each task in the queue, which is reset when the task is added, i.e., in insertInvoke function.

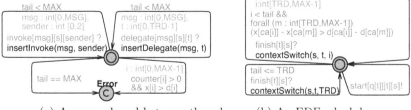

(a) A queue shared between threads   (b) An EDF scheduler

Fig. 6. A scheduler for parallel threads in UPPAAL

This model allows us to specify tasks as timed automata; therefore, tasks can create subtasks with self-calls. As a result, we don't need c and r. The `delegate` channel is dedicated to self calls that create subtasks inheriting the parent's deadline. To identify the parent, it receives the thread identity as t. Inheriting the deadline is modeled by reusing the clock x assigned to the parent task (which is in turn assigned to thread t). The number of tasks (and subtasks) assigned to clock x[i] is stored in `counter[i]`. This is handled in the `insertDelegate` function. The queue goes to `Error` state if a task misses its deadline ($x[i] > d[i]$) or the queue is full.

Figure 6.(b) shows how a scheduling strategy can be implemented. This automaton should be replicated for every thread, thus parameterized in t as well as the object identity s. The different instances of this automaton will be assigned each to one slot in the queue, namely q[t]. This example models an EDF (earliest deadline first) scheduling strategy. The remaining time to the deadline of a task at position i in the queue is obtained by `x[ca[i]]-d[ca[i]]`. When the thread t finishes its current task (`finish[t][s]`), it selects the next task from the buffer part of the queue for execution by putting it in q[t]; next, it is started (`start[q[t]][t][s]`).

5   Analysis

We use timed automata to do schedulability analysis of our program model in UPPAAL. This analysis provides as a result a scheduling for a given strategy like Earliest-Deadline-First. We take the resulting strategy to the Maude level and test the model against it.

5.1   Schedulability Analysis of the Automata Model

Schedulability analysis is checking whether tasks can be accomplished before their deadlines. In this section, we analyze the schedulability of the timed automata models of thread pools given in the previous section. Tasks in this model correspond to the methods of monk objects (cf. the Creol models in Section 4). The model of a thread pool is not enough for schedulability analysis, because we need to know how fast tasks are generated and what their deadlines are. The timed automaton specifying the task generation patterns serves as the behavioral interface of the thread pool. The behavioral interface can be seen as a model of

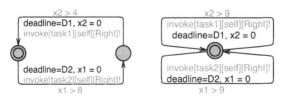

Fig. 7. Generating task instances sequentially (left) or in parallel (right)

the environment and captures the work-load of the ASK system. In this section, we assume two threads and therefore two instances of the monk object.

Figure 7 shows two models of behavioral interfaces for our model of thread pools. In these diagrams, **Right** shows the identity of an object in the environment that sends messages task1 and task2 to the resource pool under analysis; the identity of the thread pool is given as **self**. In one model, the tasks are generated independently with an inter-arrival time of at least 9 time units between every two occurrences of the instances of the same task type. In the other model, tasks are generated one after the other in a sequential manner.

To perform schedulability analysis by model checking, we need to find a reasonable queue length to make the model finite. The execution part of the queue is as big as the number of threads, and the buffer part is at least of size one. As in single-threaded situation of objects [12], a system is schedulable only if it does not put more than $\lceil D_{max}/B_{min} \rceil$ messages in its queue, where D_{max} is the biggest deadline in the system, and B_{min} is the best-case execution time of the shortest task. As a result, schedulability is equivalent to the **Error** state not being reachable with a queue of length $\lceil D_{max}/B_{min} \rceil$. Therefore, schedulability analysis does not depend on whether an upper bound on queue length is assumed (Dabbey) or not (Sabbey). When analyzing the Determinate Abbeys (Dabbeys), one can assume a smaller queue bound if necessary to check for queue overflow situations.

To use the time-sharing model of a thread pool, a task is modeled as a computation time. The two task types are given the computation times of 3 and 6 time units. This model is analyzed with a queue length of three where two concurrent threads are assumed. Given the behavioral interface with parallel task generation, the minimum deadline for which the model is schedulable is 7 and 9 for task1 and task2, respectively. For sequential task generation, the deadlines can be reduced to 5 and 6 for task1 and task2, respectively.

When the thread pool for parallel threads is applied, one can model tasks as timed automata; two simple task models are given in Figure 8.(a). In this model, task1 has a computation time of between 2 to 3 time units, and task2 takes 6 time units to execute. Using either of the two behavioral interfaces above, the model is schedulable with the deadlines 3 and 6 for task1 and task2, respectively. In parallel generation of tasks, parallel threads can handle the tasks faster, and

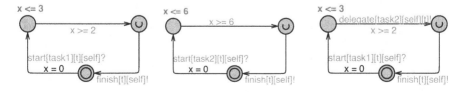

(a) Modeling tasks as computation times   (b) Generating a subtask

Fig. 8. Modeling tasks (corresponding to monks) for parallel threads

therefore, smaller deadlines are needed for schedulability. It turns out that the parallelism of the threads does not affect the schedulability of tasks that are created sequentially.

More complicated models can include sub-task generation. Figure 8.(b) shows a model of task1 which creates an instance of task2. The schedulability analysis of this model with a queue length of three fails due to queue overflow. This implies that a determinate abbey with a too small buffer size can fail. By increasing the size of the queue to four, the model will be schedulable given a deadline of 9 to the task1 (and task2 still needs a deadline of 6). This shows that a determinate abbey can still be useful if a big enough buffer size is used.

5.2   Conformance Testing

From the analysis of the behavioral interfaces we get a sequence of time-stamped tasks with their deadlines of the form

$$(t_1, \text{task}_1(c_1, d_1)), \ldots, (t_n, \text{task}_n(c_n, d_n))$$

where t_i denotes the time at which $task_i$ has been queued, where $task_i$ has the computation time c_i and deadline d_i. For analysis, we assume a scheduling strategy like Earliest Deadline First (EDF).

We use this information to provide a discrete time model for our Creol model. Instead of modeling continuos time, e.g., by means of ticks, we *jump* from a time-stamp to the next time-stamp. This is implemented by a variation of the Creol interpreter. Assuming $(t_i, \text{task}_i(c_i, d_i))$ is the task with the smallest time-stamp at a given point, $(t_i, \text{task}_i(c_i, d_i))$ is removed from the queue and execution of task_i starts. The first thing to check is whether task_i can be computed in time, i.e. whether $t_i + c_i \leq d_i$. If this condition is violated we report a scheduling error indicating a conformance conflict, since the analysis of the timed automata returns a *sound* scheduling. Otherwise, assume that task_i was assigned to monk_j a new time-stamp $t_i + c_i$ is introduced indicating when monk_j is available again. Depending on an assumption on the execution times of the tasks (optimistic or pessimistic) the shortest or longest execution time can be chosen or an arbitrary execution time within the given limits.

As long as there are monks available we jump to the next smallest time-stamp and schedule the associated event. In case we run out of monks we *jump* to the next time-stamp t_f at which point a monk is again available. Now every task_i with time-stamp $t_i \leq t_f$ can be scheduled and the actual task to be scheduled is selected according to the implemented strategy, e.g., in the case of a EDF, the task with the closest deadline among the schedulable tasks is selected.

When all the tasks in the test case have been consumed, we compare the Maude scheduling to the UPPAAL scheduling. The UPPAAL scheduling can be easily obtained by simulating the scheduler automaton (cf. Section 4) put together with a linear timed automaton representing the test-case. If any deviation between the Maude and UPPAAL schedulings is observed, we have found a counter-example to conformance.

6   Conclusion

In this paper, we employed the *Credo* methodology for the design and analysis of thread pools in an industrial communication platform. This methodology is based on a separation of concerns between high-level modeling of architectural features of thread pools (in Creol) and their analysis for schedulability (using timed automata). We use timed automata to specify scheduling policies; whereas the high-level Creol models abstract from scheduling concerns and focus on the architectural modeling using concurrent objects.

Behavioral interfaces are central to the analyses. Thread pools are analyzed for schedulability with respect to the task generation pattern given in the behavioral interfaces modeling the work-load. We also derive test cases from the behavioral interfaces for checking conformance between the timed automata and Creol models, thus bridging the gap between the two levels of abstraction.

Future work consists, first of all, of an implementation of the method for testing conformance between a Creol model of a thread-pool and the timed automata models. Another line of future research consists of real-time extensions of the Creol language itself to support a full development cycle, so that one can generate code for application-specific schedulers from Creol models.

References

1. Aichernig, B., Griesmayer, A., Schlatte, R., Stam, A.: Modeling and testing multi-threaded asynchronous systems with creol. ENTCS 243, 3–14 (2009); Proceedings of the 2nd International Workshop on Harnessing Theories for Tool Support in Software (TTSS 2008)
2. The Almende research company, http://www.almende.com/
3. Alur, R., Dill, D.L.: A theory of timed automata. Theoretical Computer Science 126(2), 183–235 (1994)
4. The ASK community systems, http://www.ask-cs.com/
5. Clavel, M., Durán, F., Eker, S., Lincoln, P., Martí-Oliet, N., Meseguer, J., Quesada, J.F.: Maude: specification and programming in rewriting logic. Theoretical Computer Science 285(2), 187–243 (2002)
6. Closse, E., Poize, M., Pulou, J., Sifakis, J., Venter, P., Weil, D., Yovine, S.: TAXYS: A tool for the development and verification of real-time embedded systems. In: Berry, G., Comon, H., Finkel, A. (eds.) CAV 2001. LNCS, vol. 2102, pp. 391–395. Springer, Heidelberg (2001)
7. Credo - modeling and analysis of evolutionary structures for distributed services, http://credo.cwi.nl/
8. de Boer, F.S., Clarke, D., Johnsen, E.B.: A complete guide to the future. In: De Nicola, R. (ed.) ESOP 2007. LNCS, vol. 4421, pp. 316–330. Springer, Heidelberg (2007)
9. Fersman, E., Krcal, P., Pettersson, P., Yi, W.: Task automata: Schedulability, decidability and undecidability. Information and Computation 205(8), 1149–1172 (2007)
10. Garcia, J.J.G., Gutierrez, J.C.P., Harbour, M.G.: Schedulability analysis of distributed hard real-time systems with multiple-event synchronization. In: Proc. 12th Euromicro Conference on Real-Time Systems, pp. 15–24. IEEE Computer Society Press, Los Alamitos (2000)

11. Grabe, I., Jaghoori, M.M., Aichernig, B., Baier, C., Blechmann, T., de Boer, F., Griesmayer, A., Johnsen, E.B., Klein, J., Klüppelholz, S., Kyas, M., Leister, W., Schlatte, R., Stam, A., Steffen, M., Tschirner, S., Xuedong, L., Yi, W.: Credo methodology. Modeling and analyzing a peer-to-peer system in Credo. In: 3rd International Workshop on Harnessing Theories for Tool Support in Software (TTSS 2009). ENTCS, Elsevier, Amsterdam (to appear, 2009)
12. Jaghoori, M.M., de Boer, F.S., Chothia, T., Sirjani, M.: Schedulability of asynchronous real-time concurrent objects. J. Logic and Alg. Prog. 78(5), 402–416 (2009)
13. Johnsen, E.B., Owe, O.: An asynchronous communication model for distributed concurrent objects. Software and Systems Modeling 6(1), 35–58 (2007)
14. Johnsen, E.B., Owe, O., Yu, I.C.: Creol: A type-safe object-oriented model for distributed concurrent systems. Theoretical Computer Science 365(1-2), 23–66 (2006)
15. Kloukinas, C., Yovine, S.: Synthesis of safe, QoS extendible, application specific schedulers for heterogeneous real-time systems. In: Proc. 15th Euromicro Conference on Real-Time Systems (ECRTS 2003), pp. 287–294. IEEE Computer Society Press, Los Alamitos (2003)
16. Larsen, K.G., Pettersson, P., Yi, W.: UPPAAL in a nutshell. STTT 1(1-2), 134–152 (1997)
17. Meseguer, J.: Conditioned rewriting logic as a united model of concurrency. Theoretical Computer Science 96(1), 73–155 (1992)
18. Nigro, L., Pupo, F.: Schedulability analysis of real time actor systems using coloured petri nets. In: Agha, G.A., De Cindio, F., Rozenberg, G. (eds.) APN 2001. LNCS, vol. 2001, pp. 493–513. Springer, Heidelberg (2001)
19. Yu, I.C., Johnsen, E.B., Owe, O.: Type-safe runtime class upgrades in creol. In: Gorrieri, R., Wehrheim, H. (eds.) FMOODS 2006. LNCS, vol. 4037, pp. 202–217. Springer, Heidelberg (2006)

A   A Class for the Low-Level Determinate Abbey

```
1 interface Dabbey inherits Abbey begin
2 end

4 class Dabbey(size: Int) contracts Dabbey begin
5     var taskList: DabbeyTaskList;
6     var monkList: DabbeyMonkList;
7     op init ==
8         taskList := new DabbeyTaskList(size);
9         monkList := new DabbeyMonkList(size, taskList)
10    with Any op dispatchTask(in task: Task) ==
11        var i: Int;
12        taskList.testAndSetCreating(;i);
13        taskList.setTask(i,task;);
14        taskList.setTaskOpen(i;)
15 end
```

B   The TaskList Class for the Low-Level Determinate Abbey

```
 1 class DabbeyTaskList(size: Int) contracts DabbeyTaskList
 2 begin
 3    ...
 4    with Dabbey op testAndSetCreating(out index: Int) ==
 5       await readyCounter > 0;
 6       index := index(states, "READY");
 7       states := replace(states, "CREATING", index);
 8       readyCounter := readyCounter − 1
 9    with DabbeyMonk op testAndSetBusy(out index: Int) ==
10       await openCounter > 0;
11       index := index(states, "OPEN");
12       states := replace(states, "BUSY", index);
13       openCounter := openCounter − 1
14    with Dabbey op setTaskOpen(in index: Int) ==
15       states := replace(states, "OPEN", index);
16       openCounter := openCounter + 1
17    with DabbeyMonk op setTaskReady(in index: Int) ==
18       states := replace(states, "READY", index);
19       readyCounter := readyCounter + 1
20    ...
21 end
```

C   The Shepherd Task Class of the Self-scaling Abbey

```
 1 class ShepherdTask(
 2    taskId: Int, taskCounter: Counter, monkCounter: Counter,
 3    busyCounter: Counter, mmax: Int, mrate: Int,
 4    taskQueue: SabbeyTaskQueue, monkQueue: SabbeyMonkQueue)
 5    contracts ShepherdTask
 6 begin
 7    op shepherdLoop ==
 8       ...
 9       taskCounter.val(;t); monkCounter.val(;m);
10       busyCounter.val(;mbusy); mfree := m − mbusy;
11       if ((m < mmax) && ((mfree − t) < (m / mrate))) then
12          amountToCreate := t − mfree + (m / mrate);
13          if (amountToCreate > (mmax − m)) then
14             amountToCreate := mmax −m
```

```
15            end;
16            monkQueue.createMonks(amountToCreate;)
17        end;
18        if (mfree > (m / 2)) then
19            task := new PoisonTask(0);
20            taskQueue.enqueueTask(task;)
21        end;
22        release;
23        shepherdLoop(;)
24    ...
25 end
```

D   ResourcePool Class for the High-Level Self-scaling Abbey

```
1 class ResourcePool(nofMonks: Int, maxNofMonks: Int)
2    contracts ResourcePool begin
3  var freeMonks: Set[Monk]; var nofTasks: Int;
4  ...
5  op task ==
6    var monk: Monk; chooseMonk(;monk);
7    !monk.task(); nofTasks := nofTasks - 1
8  op poisonTask ==
9    var monk: Monk;
10   chooseMonk(;monk);
11   !monk.poisonTask()
12 op shepherd == var monk: Monk;
13   await (nofTasks>nofMonks*2) || (#(freeMonks)>nofMonks/2);
14   if (nofTasks > nofMonks*2) then
15     if (nofMonks < maxNofMonks) then
16       monk := new Monk(this);
17       nofMonks := nofMonks + 1
18     end else if (nofMonks > 1) then
19       poisonTask(;);
20       nofMonks := nofMonks - 1
21   end end
22 ...
23 with Outside op addTask ==
24   nofTasks := nofTasks + 1;
25   !task(); !shepherd()
26 end
```

A Verification System for Distributed Objects with Asynchronous Method Calls*

Wolfgang Ahrendt[1] and Maximilian Dylla[1,2]

[1] Chalmers University of Technology, Gothenburg, Sweden
[2] Saarland University, Saarbrücken, Germany

Abstract. We present a verification system for Creol, an object-oriented modeling language for concurrent distributed applications. The system is an instance of KeY, a framework for object-oriented software verification, which has so far been applied foremost to sequential Java. Building on KeY characteristic concepts, like dynamic logic, sequent calculus, explicit substitutions, and the taclet rule language, the system presented in this paper addresses functional correctness of Creol models featuring local cooperative thread parallelism and global communication via asynchronous method calls. The calculus heavily operates on communication histories which describe the interfaces of Creol units. Two example scenarios demonstrate the usage of the system.

1 Introduction

The area of object-oriented program verification made significant progress during the last decade. Systems like Boogie [6], ESC/Java2 [23], KeY [9], and Krakatoa [22] provide a high degree of automation, elaborate user interfaces, extensive tool integration, support for various specification languages, and high coverage of a real world target language (Spec# in case of Boogie, Java in case of the other mentioned tools).

However, this development mostly concerns *sequential, free-standing* applications. When it comes to verifying functional properties of *concurrent* and *distributed* applications, the situation is different. Even if there is a rich literature on the verification of 'distributed formalisms' (based for instance on process calculi [35,27,36]), there are hardly any systems yet matching the aforementioned characteristics. Moreover, many formalisms lack a connection to the dominating paradigm of today's software engineering, *object-orientation*, which is an obstacle for the integration into software development environments and methods.

This work is a contribution towards effective and integrated verification of concurrent, distributed systems. We present a verification system that is built on two foundations: the Creol modeling language for concurrent and distributed object-oriented systems [32], and the KeY approach and system for the verification of object-oriented programs [9]. By combining KeY's proving technology

* This work has partially been supported by the EU-project FP7-ICT-2007-3 *HATS: Highly Adaptable and Trustworthy Software using Formal Methods.* and the EU COST action IC0701: *Formal Verification of Object-Oriented Software.*

with Creol's novel approach to modular modeling of components, we achieve a *system for highly modular verification of concurrent, distributed object-oriented applications.* While being a prototype system yet, past experience with the technological and conceptual basis justifies the perspective of future versions to enjoy similar features as state-of-the-art sequential verification systems already do.

Creol is an executable object-oriented modeling language. It features concurrency in two ways. First of all, different objects execute truly in parallel, as if each object had its own processor. Objects have references to each other, but cannot access each other's internal state. Consequently, there is no remote access to attributes, like 'o.a' in other languages. The only way for objects to exchange information is through methods. Calls to methods are *asynchronous* [31], in the sense that the calling code is able to continue execution even before the callee replies. Mutual information hiding is further strengthened by object variables being typed by interfaces only, not by classes. The loose coupling of objects, their strong information hiding and true parallelism, is what suggest *distributed* scenarios, with each object being identified with a node. The second type of concurrency is object internal. Each call to a method spawns a separate thread of execution. Within one object, these threads execute *interleaved*, with only one thread running at a time. Here, the key to modularity is the cooperative nature of the scheduling: a thread is only ever interrupted when it actively releases control, at 'release points'.

Altogether, Creol allows highly *modular verification.* Within one class, the various methods can be proved correct in isolation, in spite of the shared memory (the attributes), by guaranteeing and assuming a *class invariant* at each release point in the code. At the inter-object level, the vehicle to connect the verification of the various classes is the *'history'* of inter-object communications. Interface specifications are expressed in terms of the history, and class invariants relate the history with the internal state. The fact that each object has only partial knowledge about the global communication history is modeled by *projecting* the global history onto the individual objects [30].

Our system is based on the KeY framework for verifying object-oriented software. The most elaborate instance of KeY is a verification system for sequential Java [9]. Other target languages of KeY are C [39], ASMs [40], and hybrid systems [42]. All these have in common that they use *dynamic logic, explicit substitutions*, and a *sequent calculus* realized by the *'taclet'* language. These concepts, to be introduced in the course of the paper, have proved to be a solid foundation of a long lasting and far reaching research project and system for verifying functional correctness of Java [9]. Dynamic logic features full source code transparency, like Hoare logic, but is more expressive than that. Explicit (simultaneous) substitutions, called *updates*, provide a compact representation of the symbolic state, and allow a natural forward style symbolic execution. Apart from verification, updates are also employed for test case generation and symbolic debugging. Sequent calculi are well-suited for the interleaved automated and interactive usage. And finally, *taclets* provide a high-level rule language capturing both the logical and the operational meaning of rules. They are well suited both for the base logic and for the axiomatization of application specific operations and predicates. KeY has been used in a number of case studies, like the verification of the *Java Card API Reference Implementation* [38], the *Mondex* case study (the most substantial benchmark in the Grand Challenge repository) [44], the *Schoor-Waite algorithm* [12], and the electronic purse application *Demoney* [37]. The system is also used for teaching in various courses at Chalmers University and several other universities.

However, the KeY approach has so far almost only been applied to the sequential setting.[1] It is precisely the described modularity of Creol that allowed us to base our verification system on the same framework. The main challenges for adjusting the KeY approach to Creol were the handling of asynchronous method calls, the handling of release points, and, most of all, the extensive usage of the communication history throughout the calculus.

The structure of the paper is as follows. Sect. 2 introduces Creol, and gives examples of its usage. In Sect. 3, we describe the logic and calculus characteristic for KeY, insofar as they are (largely) independent of the particular target language. Thereafter, Sect. 4 presents a KeY style logic and calculus for Creol specifically. Sect. 5 discusses system oriented aspects of KeY for Creol, including a small account on taclets. Sect. 6 then demonstrates the usage of the systems in examples. In Sect. 7, we discuss related work, and draw conclusions.

2   Overview of Creol

In this section, we introduce our slightly adapted version of Creol, using an automated teller machine scenario adapted from [29]. The example will also be used to discuss Creol verification in later sections.

The scenario we consider has three kinds of actors. There are several teller machines (class ATM), several users (class User), and one server (class Server). In the course of a certain session, a teller machine communicates with one user, and with the server, as depicted in Fig. 1.

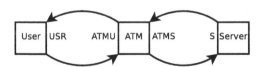

Fig. 1. Communication of the automated teller machine

The picture shows that, while User and Server implement one interface each (USR resp. S), the class ATM implements two interfaces, ATMU and ATMS, dedicated for the communication in either of the directions. The Creol definition of the interfaces is given in Fig. 2. (We omit ATMS, which is empty.)

We can observe that the signature of operations contains (possibly empty) lists for **in**- and **out**-parameters. The operations offered by interfaces appear in the

---

[1] See Sect.7 for an exception.

```
interface USR                          interface ATMU
begin                                  begin
  with ATMU                              with USR
    op giveCode(in; out code:Int)           op insert(in cardId:Int; out)
    op withdraw(in; out amount:Int)      end
    op dispense(in amount:Int; out)
    op returnCard(in; out)
end


interface S
begin
  with ATMS
    op authorize(in cardId:Int, code:Int; out ok:Bool)
    op debit(in cardId:Int, amount:Int; out ok:Bool)
end
```

Fig. 2. The interfaces of the automated teller machine

scope of '**with** *cointerface*', with the meaning that those operations can only be called from instances of classes implementing that *cointerface*. For instance, the server cannot call insert on a teller machine, not even if it was in the possession of an ATMU typed reference. Another consequence of cointerfaces is that the implementations of operations have a well-typed reference to the caller, without that reference being passed explicitly as an input parameter.

The class ATM in Fig. 3 is an example for a class definition. Variables are implicitly initialized with *false* or 0 for primitive types, and null for labels and object references. Some variables are declared of type **Label**[...], like **var** li:**Label**[**Int**].

```
class ATM implements ATMS, ATMU
begin
  var server : S;
  with USR
    op insert(in card:Int; out) ==
        var li:Label[Int]; var lb:Label[Bool]; var l:Label[];
        var l2:Label[]; var code:Int; var ok:Bool; var am:Int;
        li!caller.giveCode(); li?(code);
        lb!server.authorize(card,code); lb?(ok);
        if ok
        then li!caller.withdraw(); li?(am);
          lb!server.debit(card,am); lb?(ok);
          if ok
          then l!caller.dispense(am); l2!caller.returnCard(); l?(); l2?()
          else l!caller.returnCard(); l?() end
        else l!caller.returnCard(); l?() end; return()
end
```

Fig. 3. The class implementing the teller machine

Later, the execution of the call li!caller.giveCode(), for instance, allocates a new label, and assigns it to li. The label is later used in the *reply* statement li?(code), to associate the reply with the respective call. The effect of the reply is that code is assigned the output of the (li-labeled) call to giveCode, *provided that the corresponding reply message has already arrived.* Otherwise, the statement blocks, without the thread releasing control. (This 'busy waiting' can be avoided by the **await** statement, see below.) The effect of li?(x) is similar to treating x as a *future variable* [15,5] or *promise* [34]. In a label type **Label**[T], the T indicates the type of the output of the called operation.

Note that the calls to dispense and returnCard are executed before any of the replies is asked back. This allows the two called methods to execute *interleaved* on the processor of the called object. (Note that the calls went to the same object.) In general, arbitrary code can be executed in between a call and the corresponding reply. We want to highlight that the implementation of insert extensively uses the caller reference, which is known to be of type USR, for callbacks. This style of coupling communicating objects might clarify the distribution of operations over interfaces in the teller machine scenario (cf. Fig. 2).

We discuss further features of Creol not captured by the above example. New objects are created by $x :=$ **new** $C(e^*)$, where C is a class identifier supplied with a list of class parameters. As indicated earlier, $l?(x^*)$ blocks execution, *without releasing control*, until the corresponding reply message has arrived. In contrast, the command **await** $l?$ releases control if the reply for l has not yet arrived, such that the scheduler can pass control to another thread of this object. Other release points are **await** b, releasing control if the Boolean expression b is false, and the unconditioned **release**. The example code above did not contain release points, but see the buffer example in Sect.6.1 (Fig. 7).

In Creol, expressions have no effect on the state. We model errors, like division by zero, by non-terminating (and non-releasing) blocking. The same holds for a call on the null reference and a reply on the null label.

3   The KeY Approach: Logic, Calculus, and System

3.1   Dynamic Logic with Explicit Substitutions

KeY is a deductive verification system for *functional correctness*. Its core is a theorem prover for formulas in *dynamic logic* (DL) [25], which, like Hoare logic [26], is transparent with respect to the programs that are subject to verification. DL is a particular kind of *modal logic*. Different parts of a formula are evaluated in different worlds (states), which vary in the interpretation of functions and predicates. The modalities are 'indexed' with pieces of program code, describing how to reach one world (state) from the other. DL extends full first-order logic with two additional (mix-fix) operators: $\langle . \rangle$. (diamond) and $[.]$. (box). In both cases, the first argument is a *program* (fragment), whereas the second argument is another DL formula. A formula $\langle p \rangle \phi$ is true in a state s if execution of p terminates when started in s and results in a state where ϕ is true. As for the other operator, a formula $[p]\phi$ is true in a state s if execution of p, when started in s, *either* does not terminate *or* results in a state where ϕ is true. In other words, the difference between the operators is the one between total and partial correctness.[2]

DL is closed under all logical connectives. For instance, the following formula states equivalence of p and q w.r.t. the "output", the program variable x.

$$\forall\ v.\ (\ \langle p \rangle\ \mathsf{x} \doteq v\ \leftrightarrow\ \langle q \rangle\ \mathsf{x} \doteq v\ )$$

A frequent pattern of DL formulas is $\phi \rightarrow \langle p \rangle\psi$, stating that the program p, when started from a state satisfying ϕ, terminates with ψ being true afterwards. The formula $\phi \rightarrow [p]\psi$, on the other hand, does not claim termination, and corresponds to the Hoare triple $\{\phi\}\ p\ \{\psi\}$.

The main advantage of DL over Hoare logic is increased expressiveness: pre- or postconditions can contain programs themselves, for instance to express that a linked structure is acyclic. Also, the relation of different programs to each other (like the correctness of transformations) can be expressed elegantly.

All major program logics (Hoare logic, wp calculus, DL) have in common that the resolving of assignments requires substitutions in the formula, in one way or the other. In the KeY approach, the effect of substitutions is delayed, by having *explicit substitutions* in the logic, called *'updates'*. This allows for accumulating and simplifying the effect of a program, in a forward style. Elementary updates have the form $x := e$, where x is a location (in the case of Creol, an attribute or local variable) and e is a (side-effect free) expression. Elementary updates are combined to simultaneous updates, like in $x_1 := e_1 \,|\, x_2 := e_2$, where e_1 and e_2 are evaluated in the same state. For instance, x := y | y := x stands for exchanging the values of x and y. Updates are brought into the logic via the update modality $\{\,.\,\}.$, connecting arbitrary updates with arbitrary formulas, like in x < y $\rightarrow$ {x := y | y := x} y < x. A typical usage of updates during proving is in formulas of the form $\{\mathcal{U}\}\langle p \rangle\phi$, where $\mathcal{U}$ is an update, accumulating the effects of program execution up to a certain point, p is the remaining program yet to be executed, and ϕ a postcondition. A full account of KeY style DL is found in [11].

3.2   Sequent Calculus

The heart of KeY, the prover, uses a sequent calculus for reducing proof obligations to axioms. A sequent is a pair of sets of formulas written as $\phi_1, ..., \phi_m \vdash \psi_1, ..., \psi_n$. The intuitive meaning is that, if all $\phi_1, ..., \phi_m$ hold, at least one of $\psi_1, ..., \psi_n$ must hold. Rules are applied bottom-up, reducing the provability of the conclusion to the provability of the premises. In Fig. 4 we present a selection of the rules dealing with propositional connectives and quantifiers (see [24] for the full set). $\phi[v/e]$ denotes a formula resulting from replacing v with e in ϕ.

---

[2] Just as in standard modal logic, the diamond vs. box operators quantify existentially vs. universally over states (reached by the program). In case deterministic programs, however, the only difference between the two is whether termination is claimed or not.

impRight $\dfrac{\Gamma, \phi \vdash \psi, \Delta}{\Gamma \vdash \phi \to \psi, \Delta}$ andRight $\dfrac{\Gamma \vdash \phi, \Delta \quad \Gamma \vdash \psi, \Delta}{\Gamma \vdash \phi \wedge \psi, \Delta}$ allRight $\dfrac{\Gamma \vdash \phi[v/c], \Delta}{\Gamma \vdash \forall v.\phi, \Delta}$

with c a new constant

Fig. 4. A selection of first-order rules

When it comes to the rules dealing with programs, many of them are not sensitive to the side of the sequent and can even be *applied to subformulas*. For instance, $\langle \mathsf{skip}; \omega \rangle \phi$ can be rewritten to $\langle \omega \rangle \phi$ regardless of where it occurs. For that we introduce the following syntax

$$\dfrac{\lfloor \phi' \rfloor}{\lfloor \phi \rfloor}$$

for a rule stating that the premise sequent $\lfloor \phi' \rfloor$ is constructed by replacing ϕ with ϕ' *anywhere* in the conclusion sequent $\lfloor \phi \rfloor$. In Fig. 5 we present some rules dealing with statements. (assign and if are simplified, see Sect. 4.1.) The schematic modality $\langle\!\langle \cdot \rangle\!\rangle$ can be instantiated with both $[\cdot]$ and $\langle \cdot \rangle$, though consistently within a single rule application. Total correctness formulas of the form $\langle \mathsf{while} \ldots \rangle \phi$ are proved by combining induction with unwind.

assign $\dfrac{\lfloor \{x := e\}\langle\!\langle \omega \rangle\!\rangle \phi \rfloor}{\lfloor \langle\!\langle x := e; \omega \rangle\!\rangle \phi \rfloor}$ if $\dfrac{\lfloor (b \to \langle\!\langle s_1; \omega \rangle\!\rangle \phi) \wedge (\neg b \to \langle\!\langle s_2; \omega \rangle\!\rangle \phi) \rfloor}{\lfloor \langle\!\langle \mathsf{if}\ b\ \mathsf{then}\ s_1\ \mathsf{else}\ s_2\ \mathsf{end}; \omega \rangle\!\rangle \phi \rfloor}$

unwind $\dfrac{\lfloor \langle\!\langle \mathsf{if}\ b\ \mathsf{then}\ s; \mathsf{while}\ b\ \mathsf{do}\ s\ \mathsf{end}\ \mathsf{end}; \omega \rangle\!\rangle \phi \rfloor}{\lfloor \langle\!\langle \mathsf{while}\ b\ \mathsf{do}\ s\ \mathsf{end}; \omega \rangle\!\rangle \phi \rfloor}$

Fig. 5. Dynamic logic rules

Because updates are essentially delayed substitutions, they are eventually resolved by application to the succeeding formula, e.g., $\{u := e\}(u > 0)$ leads to $e > 0$. Update application is only defined on formulas *not* starting with box or diamond. For formulas of the form $\{\mathcal{U}\}\langle s \rangle \phi$ or $\{\mathcal{U}\}[s]\phi$, the calculus first applies rules matching the first statement in s. This leads to nested updates, which are in the next step merged into a single simultaneous update. Once the box or diamond modality is completely resolved, the entire update is applied to the postcondition.

4   A Calculus for Creol Dynamic Logic

Building on the logic and the calculus presented in the previous section, we proceed with the sequent rules handling Creol statements. For the full set of rules, see [20].

4.1 Sequential Constructs

We start with assignments. As soon as the right side is simply a variable or literal (summarized as 'terminal expression', te) the assignment can be transformed to an update, such that the effect will eventually (not immediately) be applied to the postcondition. The same applies for implicit assignments in variable declarations. We give only the rule for integer variable declaration.

$$\text{assign}\ \ \frac{\lfloor \{x := te\}\langle\!\langle\omega\rangle\!\rangle\phi\rfloor}{\lfloor \langle\!\langle x := te;\ \omega\rangle\!\rangle\phi\rfloor} \qquad \text{intDecl}\ \ \frac{\lfloor \{i := 0\}\langle\!\langle\omega\rangle\!\rangle\phi\rfloor}{\lfloor \langle\!\langle \textbf{var}\ i\ :\ \textbf{Int};\ \omega\rangle\!\rangle\phi\rfloor}$$

The same mechanism can be used for operator expressions, as long as all arguments are terminal *and* errors can be excluded. For instance, a division can be shifted to an update iff the divisor is not zero. Otherwise, execution blocks. This semantics is captured by the following rule.

$$\text{DivTerminal}\ \ \frac{\lfloor (\neg te_2 \doteq 0 \to \{x := te_1/te_2\}\langle\!\langle\omega\rangle\!\rangle\phi) \wedge (te_2 \doteq 0 \to \langle\!\langle\textbf{block};\ \omega\rangle\!\rangle\phi)\rfloor}{\lfloor \langle\!\langle x := te_1/te_2;\ \omega\rangle\!\rangle\phi\rfloor}$$

An error could occur arbitrarily deep in an expression. Therefore, expressions are unfolded until they consist only of a top level operator applied to terminal expressions. This is exemplified by the following rules (x' and x'' are new program variables).

$$\frac{\lfloor \langle\!\langle x' := e_1;\ x'' := e_2\ ;\ x := x' + x'';\ \omega\rangle\!\rangle\phi\rfloor}{\lfloor \langle\!\langle x := e_1 + e_2;\ \omega\rangle\!\rangle\phi\rfloor} \qquad \frac{\lfloor \{x := te_1 + te_2\}\langle\!\langle\omega\rangle\!\rangle\phi\rfloor}{\lfloor \langle\!\langle x := te_1 + te_2;\ \omega\rangle\!\rangle\phi\rfloor}$$

In the left rule e_i are non-terminal expressions. As all expressions are unfolded, nested divisions will eventually be analyzed by DivTerminal. Other statements using expressions, like **if**, are unfolded in the same way, until the condition is terminal and the following rule applies:

$$\text{if}\ \ \frac{\lfloor (tb \doteq \textsf{true} \to \langle\!\langle p;\ \omega\rangle\!\rangle\phi) \wedge (tb \doteq \textsf{false} \to \langle\!\langle q;\ \omega\rangle\!\rangle\phi)\rfloor}{\lfloor \langle\!\langle\textbf{if}\ tb\ \textbf{then}\ p\ \textbf{else}\ q\ \textbf{end};\ \omega\rangle\!\rangle\phi\rfloor}$$

Note that application of this rule may lead to proof branching in subsequent steps. As for **while**, the unwind rule was presented in Sect. 3.2. An alternative rule using a loop invariant is discussed in section 4.3. That rule, however, only covers the box operator. Finally, the rules for the **block** statement reflect the fact that a non-terminating program is always partially correct, but never totally correct:

$$\text{blockBox}\ \ \frac{\lfloor true\rfloor}{\lfloor [\textbf{block};\ \omega]\phi\rfloor} \qquad \text{blockDia}\ \ \frac{\lfloor false\rfloor}{\lfloor \langle\textbf{block};\ \omega\rangle\phi\rfloor}$$

4.2 Interface and Class Invariants

The verification process of Creol programs is completely modular. This means we verify only one method (of one class) at the time and do not consider any other code during this process. Instead, we take into account the other threads of the object by guaranteeing the class invariant at release points and assuming it again when execution proceeds. As for the behavior of other objects, that is represented by using specification of their interfaces. An additional construct in the proof is the communication history, which both the specifications as well as the class invariants talk about. These concepts for reasoning about Creol were introduced in [17,19].

The communication history can be viewed as a list of messages of method invocations, method completions, and object creations. For modular reasoning we always consider projections of the system wide history $\mathcal{H}$. Every interface is specified by an interface invariant $inv_I(\mathcal{H}/o/I)$, with o ranging over objects of type I. The system wide history $\mathcal{H}$ is projected $(\mathcal{H}/o/I)$ to messages concerning o and talking about methods declared in I. During verification at method calls and replies, $\mathcal{H}/\text{this}/I$ is checked against the specification. Continuing the previous example of Fig. 2 the interface USR is equipped with the following invariant:

$$\mathcal{H}/o/\mathsf{USR} \le (\rightarrow \mathsf{giveCode}[\cdot \rightarrow \mathsf{withdraw}[\cdot \rightarrow \mathsf{dispense}]]\cdot \rightarrow \mathsf{returnCard})^*$$

where $\cdot$ is appending, $\rightarrow$ are invocation messages, $\leftarrow$ are completion messages, brackets are used for optional occurrence, and $*$ is the Kleene star. The parameters and communication partners are omitted for brevity. The invariant expresses that the history of the interface is always a *prefix* of this regular expression, such that an interaction with the user always begins with requesting PIN code and ends with requesting removal of the card. The interface S is specified by:

$$\mathcal{H}/o/\mathsf{S} \le \left(\rightarrow \mathsf{authorize}(cid, .) \cdot \begin{pmatrix} \leftarrow \mathsf{authorize}(false)| \\ \leftarrow \mathsf{authorize}(true)\cdot \rightarrow \mathsf{debit}(cid, .)\cdot \leftarrow \mathsf{debit}(.) \end{pmatrix}\right)^*$$

Communication partners are omitted. The dot '.' is used as a wildcard for a parameter. Parameters (including the card id cid) and communication partners are quantified universally. The meaning of the invariant is that only after authorization can the debit procedure be attempted.

We turn to the class invariant $inv_C(\mathcal{H}/\text{this}, \overline{\mathcal{W}})$, which forms a contract between all threads of the object. $\overline{\mathcal{W}}$ is the vector of class attributes. Those might get overwritten by other threads during suspension of this thread, but the invariant expresses properties of $\overline{\mathcal{W}}$ every thread is respecting. The class invariant is parametrized by $\mathcal{H}/\text{this}$ which is the projection of the system wide history to the object the invariant belongs to. It contains all messages sent to or by the object this. A class invariant consists of several parts:

$$inv_C(\mathcal{H}/\text{this}, \overline{\mathcal{W}}) \triangleq F(\mathcal{H}/\text{this}, \overline{\mathcal{W}}) \wedge Wf(\mathcal{H}/\text{this}) \wedge \forall obj \bigwedge_I inv_I(\mathcal{H}/\text{this}/obj/I)$$

$F(\mathcal{H}/\text{this}, \overline{\mathcal{W}})$ relates the state of the ordinary class attributes $\overline{\mathcal{W}}$ with the history, reflecting the refinement of the fully abstract interface specification to the local state. $Wf(\mathcal{H}/\text{this})$ is a predicate being interpreted to true for well-formed histories. A well-formed history starts with the creation message of this, contains invocation messages for all completion messages, and does not include any object references being null. Then, all invariants of all interfaces I invoked or implemented by the class of this put in a conjunction to ensure that all methods respect them. *obj* are the objects known by this. Now we can formulate the proof obligation for a method. The precondition is the class invariant, instantiated with a history ending on an invocation of the method. After executing the *body* the invariant holds again for the history ending with its completion message.

$$\vdash inv_C(\mathcal{H}/\text{this}, \overline{\mathcal{W}}) \to [body] inv_C(\mathcal{H}/\text{this}, \overline{\mathcal{W}}) \tag{1}$$

Let us proceed with an example for a class invariant. For class ATM of Fig. 3, the formula F is:

$$F_{ATM}(\mathcal{H}/\text{this}, \overline{\mathcal{W}}) \triangleq \neg\text{server} \doteq \text{null} \wedge \forall cid.sum_{wd}(\mathcal{H}/cid) \doteq sum_{deb}(\mathcal{H}/cid)$$

It states that the reference server is never null and the sum of all withdrawn money for all cards cid equals the sum of the money debited. More detailed, $sum_{wd}(h)$ calculates the sum of the money withdrawn in the history h. (In the equations, msg is used as the 'otherwise case'.)

$$sum_{wd}(\epsilon) = 0$$
$$sum_{wd}(h \cdot \to \text{withdraw}(am)) = sum_{wd}(h) + am$$
$$sum_{wd}(h \cdot msg) = sum_{wd}(h)$$

$sum_{deb}(h)$ is the sum of the money debited from the corresponding bank account. Only successful debit calls are counted.

$$sum_{deb}(\epsilon) = 0$$
$$sum_{deb}(h \cdot \to \text{debit}(am, cid) \cdot \leftarrow \text{debit}(true)) = sum_{deb}(h) + am$$
$$sum_{deb}(h \cdot msg) = sum_{deb}(h)$$

In the system such equations are realized as taclets (see Sect. 5).

4.3   Concurrent Constructs

There are two different levels of communication, namely inter-thread communication within one object via shared memory (the class attributes $\overline{\mathcal{W}}$) and inter-object communication via method calls and replies. We start with the rules concerning the first and focus on the latter further below. In this section we abbreviate $\mathcal{H}/\text{this}$ by $\mathcal{H}$.

The simplest form of a release point is **release**. As mentioned before the class invariant forms a contract between all threads of an object. So the rule for **release** forces us to show that the class invariant is established in the current state, before releasing the processor. When this thread resumes, the invariant can be assumed before the remaining code ω is executed.

$$\text{release} \; \frac{\Gamma \vdash inv_C(\mathcal{H}, \overline{\mathcal{W}}), \Delta \qquad \Gamma \vdash \{U_{\mathcal{H}, \overline{\mathcal{W}}}\}[\omega]\phi, \Delta}{\Gamma \vdash [\textbf{release}; \omega]\phi, \Delta}$$

Here, $U_{\mathcal{H},\overline{W}}$ is the update $\mathcal{H},\overline{W} := \mathsf{some}\ H,\overline{W}.(inv_C(H,\overline{W}) \wedge \mathcal{H} \leq H)$. The update $U_{\mathcal{H},\overline{W}}$ represents an arbitrary but fixed system state satisfying the class invariant in which execution continues. By $\mathcal{H} \leq H$ we denote that the old history $\mathcal{H}$ is a prefix of the new one H. The update is necessary because values of the class attributes could have been overwritten by other threads, and because $\mathcal{H}$ might have grown meanwhile.

Note that this rule, as well as all rules in this section, can also be applied when the modality is preceded by updates, which is the typical scenario. These updates are preserved in the instantiation of the premises (see [11]).

The **await** b statement is handled by a similar rule, with the additional assumption that the guard b holds when execution resumes. A minor complication is that we also must assume that evaluation of b does not block due to an error. The two assumptions together are expressed via $\langle x := b \rangle x \doteq \mathsf{true}$.

$$\mathsf{awaitExp}\ \frac{\Gamma \vdash inv_C(\mathcal{H},\overline{W}), \Delta \quad \Gamma \vdash \{U_{\mathcal{H},\overline{W}}\}(\langle x := b \rangle x \doteq \mathsf{true} \rightarrow [\omega]\phi), \Delta}{\Gamma \vdash [\mathbf{await}\ b;\ \omega]\phi, \Delta}$$

By replacing $\langle x := b \rangle x \doteq \mathsf{true}$ with $Comp(\mathcal{H}, l)$ in the above rule, we get a rule for **await** $l?$. The predicate $Comp(\mathcal{H}, l)$ is valid if a completion message with the label l is contained in the history $\mathcal{H}$. The handling of $Comp(\mathcal{H}, l)$ in the proof is discussed further below.

Partial correctness of a loop can also be shown with help of a loop invariant $inv_{loop}(\mathcal{H}, \overline{mod})$, where $\overline{mod}$ is the modifier set of the loop (all variables assigned in the loop). To be most general, all class attributes could be included in the modifier set. The history could be omitted as a parameter of the loop invariant if there are no method calls, method completions or object creations in the loop body.

$$\mathsf{loopInv}\ \frac{\begin{array}{ll} \Gamma \vdash \langle x:=b \rangle true \rightarrow inv_{loop}(\mathcal{H}, \overline{mod}) \wedge Wf(\mathcal{H}), \Delta & \text{(init. valid)} \\ \Gamma \vdash \{U_{\mathcal{H},\overline{mod}}^{loop}\}(\langle x:=b \rangle x \doteq \mathsf{true} \rightarrow [p]inv_{loop}(\mathcal{H}, \overline{mod})), \Delta & \text{(preserving)} \\ \Gamma \vdash \{U_{\mathcal{H},\overline{mod}}^{loop}\}(\langle x:=b \rangle x \doteq \mathsf{false} \rightarrow [\omega]\phi), \Delta & \text{(use-case)} \end{array}}{\Gamma \vdash [\mathbf{while}\ b\ \mathbf{do}\ p\ \mathbf{end};\ \omega]\phi, \Delta}$$

The update $U_{\mathcal{H},\overline{mod}}^{loop}$ is defined as:

$$\mathcal{H}, \overline{mod} := \mathsf{some}\ H, \overline{m}.(Wf(H) \wedge \mathcal{H} \leq H \wedge inv_{loop}(H, \overline{m}))$$

It creates a new history H and a new modifier set, such that the loop invariant holds. If the condition b of the loop contains an exceptions the implication of all branches are true.

Analogous to $Comp(\mathcal{H}, l)$ there are predicates $Invoc(\mathcal{H}, l)$ and $New(\mathcal{H}, o)$ which guarantee the existence of an invocation message with label l and an object creation message with reference o in the history $\mathcal{H}$, respectively. During a proof, uncertainty is inherent in the projection of the history to this, as there could be incoming method invocations at any time. When dealing with method calls we only state the existence of a corresponding message in the history. We do not append it to the history. In general all rules of Sect. 4.1 would need to cover potential extensions, using the prefix predicate $\leq$. It is however equivalent to extend the history on access (release points, method calls, etc.).

To exemplify some properties of the predicates dealing with the history we give the following formula which is a tautology.

$$Comp(\mathcal{H}_0, l) \wedge \mathcal{H}_0 \leq \mathcal{H}_1 \rightarrow Comp(\mathcal{H}_1, l) \tag{2}$$

Besides $Comp$, New, as well as $Invoc$ are monotonous w.r.t. $\leq$. Additionally, the contra-position is used in our proof system.

We turn attention towards method invocation $l!o.mtd(\overline{p_{in}})$. Its execution assigns a unique reference to l, and extends the history by the corresponding invocation message:

$$\text{invoc} \quad \frac{\begin{array}{c} \Gamma \vdash Wf(\mathcal{H}) \wedge inv_I(\mathcal{H}/o/I), \Delta \\ \Gamma \vdash o \doteq \text{null} \rightarrow \langle\!\langle \textbf{block}; \ \omega \rangle\!\rangle \phi, \Delta \\ \Gamma \vdash \neg o \doteq \text{null} \rightarrow \{l := (\text{this}, o, mtd, \overline{p_{in}}, i)\}\{U_{\mathcal{H}}^{invoc}\}\langle\!\langle \omega \rangle\!\rangle \phi, \Delta \end{array}}{\Gamma \vdash \langle\!\langle l!o.mtd(\overline{p_{in}}); \ \omega \rangle\!\rangle \phi, \Delta}$$

If o is null, execution blocks. In the first branch, the invariant of the remote interface I must be shown (I being the type of o). The index i is new and assures uniqueness of the label l. The abbreviation $U_{\mathcal{H}}^{invoc}$ for the update, is in its full form:

$$\mathcal{H} := \text{some } H.(Wf(H) \wedge \mathcal{H} \leq H \wedge inv_I(H/o/I, \overline{p_{in}}) \wedge Invoc(H, l) \wedge \neg Invoc(\mathcal{H}, l))$$

The new history contains the invocation message $Invoc(H, l)$. As the label l is unique the invocation message must not be included in the previous history ($\neg Invoc(\mathcal{H}, l)$), which prefixes the new one ($\mathcal{H} \leq H$). The new history H is well-formed ($Wf(H)$) and it respects the interface invariant $inv_I(H/o/I, \overline{p_{in}})$ where the in-parameters $\overline{p_{in}}$ are added as they occur in the appended invocation message.

A completion statement $l?(\overline{p_{out}})$ assigns the return parameters of the method call identified by the label l to p_{out}. If the label l is null, execution blocks.

$$\text{comp} \quad \frac{\begin{array}{c} \Gamma \vdash Invoc(\mathcal{H}, l) \wedge Wf(\mathcal{H}) \wedge inv_I(\mathcal{H}/l.callee/I), \Delta \\ \Gamma \vdash l \doteq \text{null} \rightarrow [\textbf{block}; \ \omega] \phi, \Delta \\ \Gamma \vdash \neg l \doteq \text{null} \rightarrow \{U_{\mathcal{H}, \overline{p_{out}}}^{comp}\}[\omega]\phi, \Delta \end{array}}{\Gamma \vdash [l?(\overline{p_{out}}); \ \omega]\phi, \Delta}$$

As we are extending the history with a completion message, we check the existence of the corresponding invocation message by $Invoc(\mathcal{H}, l)$ to ensure well-formedness. The selector $callee$ delivers the reference of the sender of the completion message. $U_{\mathcal{H}, \overline{p_{out}}}^{comp}$ is analogous to $U_{\mathcal{H}}^{invoc}$ where the only difference is that $\overline{p_{out}}$ is overwritten and $Comp$ is used instead of $Invoc$.

$$\mathcal{H}, \overline{p_{out}} := \text{some } H, \bar{p}. \left(\begin{array}{c} Wf(H) \wedge \mathcal{H} \leq H \wedge inv_I(H/l.callee/I, \bar{p}) \\ \wedge Comp(H, l) \wedge \neg Comp(\mathcal{H}, l) \end{array} \right)$$

We omit the rule for object creation, mentioning only that the new reference is constructed by the pair (this, i), here i is an object local, successively incremented index. An alternative, fully abstract modeling of object creation in DL is investigated in [4] and can be adapted also here.

Finally, we consider the **return** statement. It sends the completion message belonging to the method call of the verification process and the thread terminates afterwards. The class invariant is not explicitly mentioned in the following rule as it is contained in ϕ (see previous section).

$$\text{return } \frac{\Gamma \vdash Invoc(\mathcal{H}, l) \wedge Wf(\mathcal{H}) \wedge inv_I(\mathcal{H}/\mathsf{caller}/I), \Delta \qquad \Gamma \vdash \{U_{\mathcal{H}}^{return}\}\phi, \Delta}{\Gamma \vdash \langle\!\langle \mathbf{return}(\overline{p_{out}}) \rangle\!\rangle \phi, \Delta}$$

Here, l is the label of the message which created the thread subject to verification, I the corresponding interface, and caller the corresponding caller. The update $U_{\mathcal{H}}^{return}$ adds the completion message to the history which must not occur in the previous history.

$$\mathcal{H} := \mathsf{some}\ H.(Wf(H) \wedge \mathcal{H} \leq H \wedge inv_I(H/\mathsf{caller}/I) \wedge Comp(H, l) \wedge \neg Comp(\mathcal{H}, l))$$

5   A System for Creol Verification

The verification system for Creol is based on KeY[9]. Written in Java and published under the GNU general public license, it is available from the project's website[3]. The current version is a prototype which provides the functionalities presented in this paper. It has a graphical user interface where the proof tree and open proof goals are displayed. Other features are pretty-printing and syntax-highlighting of the subformula/subterm currently pointed at with the mouse pointer. This enables a context sensitive menu offering only the rules applicable to the highlighted subformula/subterm. Apart from the rule name, tool-tips describe the effect of a rule. Besides interactive application of rules, automatic strategies can be configured. A more detailed description of the KeY interface is available in [3].

Problem files, logical rules, and axiomatizations of data types are written in the *taclet* language [43]. In Fig. 6 the rule impRight from Fig. 4 and the equation Eq. (2) are defined in the taclet language. A `find` describes the formula the rule is applicable to, `replacewith` specifies the replacement for the `find` formula, `assumes` characterizes further assumptions not subject to replacements, and `add` causes its argument to be added. The arrow `==>` indicates on which side of the sequent the formulas are found, replaced or added. Writing a semicolon between two occurrences of `replacewith` or `add` causes a branching. Taclets omitting the sequence arrow `==>` are rewriting rules applicable in all contexts.

The theory explained in the previous section needed some small extensions to be run in the system. First, the `some` quantifier was not implemented, but

---

[3] `www.key-project.org`

```
impRight {\find(==> phi -> psi)        compMon {\find(Comp(H1,L) ==>)
          \replacewith(==> psi)                \assumes(Prefix(H1,H2) ==>)
          \add(phi ==>) }                      \add(Comp(H2,L) ==>) }
```

Fig. 6. Rules in the taclet language

is expressed by another formula. For example, the update formula like $\{\mathcal{H} :=$ some $H.(Wf(H) \wedge \mathcal{H} \leq H)\}\phi$ is rewritten to:

$$\forall H_0.(\mathcal{H} \doteq H_0 \rightarrow \forall H_1.\{\mathcal{H} := H_1\}((Wf(H_1) \wedge H_0 \leq H_1) \rightarrow \phi))$$

The old value of $\mathcal{H}$ is saved in H_0, and the new variable H_1 is assigned to $\mathcal{H}$. The implication assures that H_1 has the desired properties when evaluating ϕ.

Finally, there are different prefix predicates $\leq_I$ where I is an interface. Thereby the interface invariant for I' is monotonous on $\leq_I$ if $I' \neq I$. The rules invoc, comp, and return use $\leq_I$ where I is the interface the message the rule adds corresponds to. Release points and the loop invariant use a prefix predicate $\leq_{all}$ which is not monotonous for interface specifications.

The Creol parser is written in about 3900 lines of code using ANTLR as parser generator. The adaptions in the KeY-system took another 5000 lines. Finally, the rules written in the taclet language are about 1700 lines long.

6   Verification Examples

6.1   Unbounded Buffer

We give an implementation for an unbounded first-in-first-out (FIFO) buffer. This example is adapted from [18]. The interface contains two methods put and get which can be used to put into and to obtain an element from the buffer.

interface FifoBuffer
begin with Any
        op put(**in** x:Any; **out**)
        op get(**in**; **out** x:Any)
end

The interface invariant expresses that the sequence of elements retrieved from the buffer are a prefix of the elements put into the buffer. This ensures the FIFO property. Additionally, no element must equal null. We define $inv_I(\mathcal{H}, callee)$ (slightly simplified) as:

$$out(\mathcal{H}/I, callee) \leq in(\mathcal{H}/I, callee) \wedge \forall x.(x \in in(\mathcal{H}/I, callee) \rightarrow \neg x \doteq \text{null})$$

where I is FifoBuffer and in, out are defined as:

$$
\begin{aligned}
in(\epsilon, o) &= \epsilon & out(\epsilon, o) &= \epsilon \\
in(h \cdot o_2 \leftarrow o.put(x;), o) &= in(h, o) \cdot x & out(h \cdot o_2 \leftarrow o.get(;x), o) &= out(h, o) \cdot x \\
in(h \cdot msg, o) &= in(h, o) & out(h \cdot msg, o) &= out(h, o)
\end{aligned}
$$

Note that we do not guarantee that a caller gets the same objects it has put into the buffer. Such a buffer can be used for fair work balancing where a request is put into the buffer and workers take them out again.

The implementation of the buffer, given in Fig. 7, uses a chain of objects where each of them can store one element. The attribute cell is null if the object does not store an element. In next the reference to the following chain of objects is stored. Requests are forwarded to it if the object cannot serve them alone. The variable cnt holds the number of elements stored in cell and all following objects. Calls of get on an empty buffer are suspended until there are elements in the buffer.

```
class BufferImpl implements FifoBuffer
var cell:Any; var cnt:Int; var next:FifoBuffer;
begin with Any
        op put(in x:Any; out) ==
            if cnt=0 then cell:=x
                    else if next=null then next:=new Buffer end;
                        var l:Label[]; l!next.put(x); l?()
            end;
            cnt:= cnt+1; return()
        op get(in ; out x:Any) ==
            await (cnt>0);
            if cell=null then var l:Label[Any]; l!next.get(); l?(x)
                        else x:=cell; cell:=null
            end;
            cnt:=cnt−1; return(x)
end
```

Fig. 7. The class implementing the buffer

For the class invariant we define another term $buf(o_1, o_2, h)$ which for an object o_1 and its next object o_2 reconstructs from the history h the elements in cell and all following objects.

$$buf(o_1, o_2, h) = \begin{cases} \epsilon & \text{if } h \doteq \epsilon \vee o_1 \doteq \text{null} \vee o_2 \doteq \text{null} \\ buf(o_1, o_2, h') \cdot x & \text{if } h \doteq h' \cdot o_1 \leftarrow o_2.put(x;) \\ rest(buf(o_1, o_2, h')) & \text{if } h \doteq h' \cdot o_1 \leftarrow o_2.get(; x) \\ buf(o_1, o_2, h') & \text{otherwise } h \doteq h' \cdot msg \end{cases}$$

rest removes the first element of a sequence. Let us proceed with the class invariant. The attribute cnt equals the number of elements in cell and all following buffer cells. The interface invariant of FifoBuffer has to hold for both the interface called and implemented by the class. Additionally, we state that the sequence of values put into the current cell equals the sequence of values obtained from the buffer with the cell and the content of the following buffer appended.

$$|\text{cell} \cdot buf(\mathcal{H}/\text{next, this, next})| \doteq \text{cnt}$$
$$\wedge(\neg\text{next} \doteq \text{null} \rightarrow inv_I(\mathcal{H}/\text{next, next})) \wedge inv_I(\mathcal{H}, \text{this})$$
$$\wedge in(\mathcal{H}, \text{this}) \doteq out(\mathcal{H}, \text{this}) \cdot \text{cell} \cdot buf(\mathcal{H}/\text{next, this, next})$$

In the above formula I, is instantiated by FifoBuffer and $\mathcal{H}$ is an abbreviation for $\mathcal{H}/\text{this}$. If cell is null it is omitted. The example with the given specifications was proved interactively by the system. The method put was verified in 1024 proof steps and 80 branches, whereas get needed 587 proof steps and 43 branches. Great parts of the proof were transformations of the sequences the buffer was specified with. However they went rather smoothly as the problem of the equality of two sequences is human-readable even if the automated strategy gets stuck. It seems that a logical toolbox expressing sets, relations and other well-understood mathematical notions would simplify the process of specifying and verifying other case studies.

6.2   Automated Teller Machine

The example of the automated teller machine distributed throughout the paper was successfully verified in 2495 steps (27 branches) by the system. As the implementation of the class makes heavy use of asynchronous method calls and (co)interfaces, it has been shown that our system can deal with them. The amount of method calls produces a chain of prefixed histories where the monotonicity of properties has to be used often. This leads to a number of predicates expressing properties of histories on the left-hand-side of the sequent. Hence, the automated strategy must use the monotonicity with care to improve readability if a branch cannot be closed by it. The experiences with specifications in form of regular expressions were promising. They are easy to write down and a automated strategy can deal with them as the number of successor states is usually limited which narrows the search space of the proof.

7   Discussion and Conclusion

Creol's notion of inter-object communication is inspired by notions from process algebras (CSP [27], CCS [35], π-calculus [36]), which however model synchronous communication mostly. Moreover, Creol differs from those in integrating the notion of processes in the object-oriented setting, using named objects and methods rather than named channels. This also introduces more structure to the message passing (calls, replies, caller references, cointerfaces). The message passing paradigm on the inter-object level is combined with the shared memory paradigm on the local inter-thread level. Early approaches to the verification of shared memory concurrency are interference freedom based on proof outlines [41] and the rely/guarantee method [33]. Other approaches use object invariants as a combined assumption/guarantee, both in the sequential setting to achieve modularity [7,8], and in the concurrent setting [28]. Compared to the last mentioned works, Creol is more restrictive in that it forces shared memory to be entirely object internal. All knowledge of remote data is contained in fully abstract interface specifications talking about the communication history. Communication histories appeared originally both in the CSP as well as the object-oriented setting [14,27], and were used for specification and verification for instance in [45,16].

KeY is among the state-of-the-art approaches to the verification of (at first) sequential object-oriented programs, together with systems like Boogie [6], ESC/Java(2) [23], and Krakatoa [22]. In comparison to those, KeY is unique in that it does not merely generate verification conditions for an external off-the-shelf prover, but employs a calculus where symbolic execution of programs is interleaved with first-order theorem proving strategies. This goes together with the nature of first-order DL, which syntactically interleaves modalities and first-order operators. The cornerstone for KeY style symbolic execution, the updates, have similarities to generalized substitutions in formalisms such as the B method [2]. Updates are, however, tailored to symbolic execution rather than modeling (for instance, conflicts are resolved via right-win). The KeY tool uses these updates not only for verification, but also for test case generation with high code based coverage [21] and for symbolic debugging. The role of updates is largely orthogonal to the target language, allowing us to fully reuse this machinery for Creol.

As for Creol's thread concurrency model, this differs from many other languages in that it is *cooperative*, meaning the programmer actively releases control (conditionally). This simplifies reasoning considerably as compared to reasoning about *preemptive* concurrency, where atomicity has to be enforced by dedicated constructs. There is work on verifying a limited fragment of concurrent Java with KeY [10]. Here, the main idea is to prove the correctness of all permutations of schedulings at once. In [1], concurrent correctness of Java threads is addressed by combining sequential correctness with interference freedom tests and cooperation tests.

Very related to our work is the extension of the Boogie methodology to concurrent programs [28], targeting concurrent Spec#. From the beginning, this work is deeply integrated into an elaborate formal development environment, with all the features mentioned the first paragraph of this paper. The methodology requires users to annotate code with commands in between which an object is allowed to violate its invariant. This is combined with ownership of objects by threads. Just as in our system, invariants have to be established at specific points, and can be assumed at others. Also similar is the erasing of knowledge, there with the havoc statement, here with the *some* operator. Differences (apart from the asynchronous method calls) are the purely cooperative nature of our threads, and that our shared memory is object local, which makes ownership trivial. Connected to this is the inherently fully abstract specification of remote object interfaces, employing histories. The Boogie approach can simulate histories as well (see Fig. 1 in [28]), but it lies in the responsibility of the user whether or not the simulated history reflects the real one.

The system presented in this paper is still a prototype. It supports Creol dynamic logic, but the front-end for loading code and generating proof obligations is yet unfinished. This however will not be a real challenge, given the KeY infrastructure. Also, the automated strategies are very rudimentary yet. We currently achieve an automation of 90% (automatic per total proof steps), which is very low by our standards. As we are only at the beginning of the work on automated strategies tailored to Creol, there is great potential here. The true challenge has been the omnipresence of the history, and it is here that future research on verification in this domain will focus on. This concerns various levels: better support for history based specifications, like a library of frequently used queries on histories, or the usage of specification patterns [13], extended and configurable proof support for history based reasoning, and improved presentation on the syntax level and in the user interface.

We consider Creol's approach to modular object-oriented modeling as a good basis for scaling 'sequential formal methods' to the concurrent distributed setting, in particular when targeting functional correctness. The key is a very strong separation of concerns, which however naturally follows ultimate object-oriented principles. KeY has proved to be a good conceptual and technical basis for such an undertaking, which we argue can lead to an efficient and user-friendly environment for the verification of distributed object applications.

Acknowledgments

The authors would like to thank Frank de Boer, Einar Broch Johnsen, Olaf Owe, and Martin Steffen for fruitful discussions on the subject, Richard Bubel and Markus Drescher for their comments on drafts of this paper, Richard Bubel moreover for his guidance concerning implementation issues, and the anonymous reviewers for detailed comments.

References

1. Ábrahám, E., de Boer, F.S., de Roever, W.-P., Steffen, M.: An assertion-based proof system for multithreaded Java. Theor. Comput. Sci. 331(2-3), 251–290 (2005)
2. Abrial, J.-R.: The B-book: assigning programs to meanings. Cambridge University Press, Cambridge (1996)
3. Ahrendt, W.: Using KeY. In: Beckert, et al. (eds.) [9], pp. 409–451
4. Ahrendt, W., de Boer, F.S., Grabe, I.: Abstract object creation in dynamic logic. In: Cavalcanti, A., Dams, D. (eds.) Proc. 16th International Symposium on Formal Methods (FM 2009). LNCS, Springer, Heidelberg (to appear, 2009)
5. Baker Jr., H.C., Hewitt, C.: The incremental garbage collection of processes. SIGPLAN Not. 12(8), 55–59 (1977)
6. Barnett, M., Chang, B.-Y.E., DeLine, R., Jacobs, B., Leino, K.R.M.: Boogie: A modular reusable verifier for object-oriented programs. In: de Boer, F.S., Bonsangue, M.M., Graf, S., de Roever, W.-P. (eds.) FMCO 2005. LNCS, vol. 4111, pp. 364–387. Springer, Heidelberg (2006)
7. Barnett, M., DeLine, R., Fändrich, M., Leino, K.R.M., Schulte, W.: Verification of object-oriented programs with invariants. Journal of Object Technology 3(6), 27–56 (2004)
8. Barnett, M., Naumann, D.: Friends need a bit more: Maintaining invariants over shared state. In: Kozen, D. (ed.) MPC 2004. LNCS, vol. 3125, pp. 54–84. Springer, Heidelberg (2004)
9. Beckert, B., Hähnle, R., Schmitt, P.H. (eds.): Verification of Object-Oriented Software. LNCS (LNAI), vol. 4334. Springer, Heidelberg (2007)

10. Beckert, B., Klebanov, V.: A dynamic logic for deductive verification of concurrent programs. In: Hinchey, M., Margaria, T. (eds.) Conference on Software Engineering and Formal Methods (SEFM). IEEE Press, Los Alamitos (2007)
11. Beckert, B., Klebanov, V., Schlager, S.: Dynamic logic. In: Beckert, et al. (eds.) [9], pp. 69–177
12. Bubel, R.: The Schorr-Waite-Algorithm. In: Beckert, et al. (eds.) [9], pp. 569–587
13. Bubel, R., Hähnle, R.: Pattern-driven formal specification. In: Beckert, et al. (eds.), [9], pp. 295–315
14. Dahl, O.-J.: Can program proving be made practical? Les Fondements de la Programmaion, 57–114 (December 1977)
15. de Boer, F.S., Clarke, D., Johnsen, E.B.: A complete guide to the future. In: De Nicola, R. (ed.) ESOP 2007. LNCS, vol. 4421, pp. 316–330. Springer, Heidelberg (2007)
16. de Boer, F.S.: A Hoare logic for dynamic networks of asychronously communicating deterministic processes. Theor. Comput. Sci. 274(1-2), 3–41 (2002)
17. Dovland, J., Johnsen, E.B., Owe, O.: A Hoare logic for concurrent objects with asynchronous method calls. Technical Report 315, Department of Informatics, University of Oslo (2006)
18. Dovland, J., Johnsen, E.B., Owe, O.: A compositional proof system for dynamic object systems. Technical Report 351, Department of Informatics, University of Oslo (2008)
19. Dovland, J., Johnsen, E.B., Owe, O.: Observable behavior of dynamic systems: Component reasoning for concurrent objects. Electron. Notes Theor. Comput. Sci. 203(3), 19–34 (2008)
20. Dylla, M.: A verification system for the distributed object-oriented language Creol. Master's thesis, Chalmers University of Technology, Gothenburg, Sweden (June 2009)
21. Engel, C., Hähnle, R.: Generating unit tests from formal proofs. In: Gurevich, Y., Meyer, B. (eds.) TAP 2007. LNCS, vol. 4454, Springer, Heidelberg (2007)
22. Filliâtre, J.-C., Marché, C.: The Why/Krakatoa/Caduceus platform for deductive program verification. In: Damm, W., Hermanns, H. (eds.) CAV 2007. LNCS, vol. 4590, Springer, Heidelberg (2007)
23. Flanagan, C., Leino, K.R.M., Lillibridge, M., Nelson, G., Saxe, J.B., Stata, R.: Extended static checking for Java. In: Conference on Programming Language Design and Implementation, pp. 234–245. ACM Press, New York (2002)
24. Giese, M.: First-order logic. In: Beckert, et al. (eds.) [9], pp. 21–68.
25. Harel, D., Kozen, D., Tiuryn, J.: Dynamic Logic. MIT Press, Cambridge (2000)
26. Hoare, C.A.R.: An axiomatic basis for computer programming. Commun. ACM 12(10), 576–580, 583 (1969)
27. Hoare, C.A.R.: Communicating Sequential Processes. Prentice-Hall, Englewood Cliffs (1985)
28. Jacobs, B., Leino, K.R.M., Piessens, F., Schulte, W.: Safe concurrency for aggregate objects with invariants. In: Conference on Software Engineering and Formal Methods, pp. 137–147. IEEE Computer Society, Los Alamitos (2005)
29. Johnsen, E.B., Owe, O.: A compositional formalism for object viewpoints. In: Jacobs, B., Rensink, A. (eds.) Proceedings of the 5th International Conference on Formal Methods for Open Object-Based Distributed Systems (FMOODS 2002), pp. 45–60. Kluwer Academic Publishers, Dordrecht (2002)

30. Johnsen, E.B., Owe, O.: Object-oriented specification and open distributed systems. In: Owe, O., Krogdahl, S., Lyche, T. (eds.) From Object-Orientation to Formal Methods: Essays in Memory of Ole-Johan Dahl. LNCS, vol. 2635, pp. 137–164. Springer, Heidelberg (2004)

31. Johnsen, E.B., Owe, O.: An asynchronous communication model for distributed concurrent objects. Software and Systems Modeling 6(1), 35–58 (2007)

32. Johnsen, E.B., Owe, O., Yu, I.C.: Creol: A type-safe object-oriented model for distributed concurrent systems. Theoretical Computer Science 365(1-2) (2006)

33. Jones, C.B.: Development Methods for Computer Programs Including a Notion of Interference. PhD thesis, Oxford University, UK (1981)

34. Liskov, B., Shrira, L.: Promises: linguistic support for efficient asynchronous procedure calls in distributed systems. In: Conference on Programming Language design and Implementation, pp. 260–267. ACM, New York (1988)

35. Milner, R.: A Calculus of Communication Systems. LNCS, vol. 92. Springer, Heidelberg (1980)

36. Milner, R.: Communicating and Mobile Systems: the Pi Calculus. Cambridge University Press, Cambridge (1999)

37. Mostowski, W.: The demoney case study. In: Beckert, et al. (eds.) [9], pp. 533–568

38. Mostowski, W.: Fully verified Java Card API reference implementation. In: Beckert, B. (ed.) Verify 2007. CEUR WS, vol. 259 (July 2007)

39. Mürk, O., Larsson, D., Hähnle, R.: KeY-C: A tool for verification of C programs. In: Pfenning, F. (ed.) CADE 2007. LNCS (LNAI), vol. 4603, pp. 385–390. Springer, Heidelberg (2007)

40. Nanchen, S., Schmid, H., Schmitt, P.H., Stärk, R.: The ASMKeY theorem prover. Technical Report 436, ETH Zürich (2004)

41. Owicki, S.S., Gries, D.: An axiomatic proof technique for parallel programs. Acta Informatica 6, 319–340 (1976)

42. Platzer, A., Quesel, J.-D.: KeYmaera: A hybrid theorem prover for hybrid systems. In: Armando, A., Baumgartner, P., Dowek, G. (eds.) IJCAR 2008. LNCS (LNAI), vol. 5195, pp. 171–178. Springer, Heidelberg (2008)

43. Rümmer, P.: Construction of proofs. In: Beckert, et al. (eds.) [9], pp. 179–242

44. Schmitt, P.H., Tonin, I.: Verifying the Mondex case study. In: Hinchey, M., Margaria, T. (eds.) Proc. 5th IEEE Int. Conf. on Software Engineeging and Formal Methods (SEFM), pp. 47–56. IEEE Press, Los Alamitos (2007)

45. Soundararajan, N.: Axiomatic semantics of communicating sequential processes. ACM Trans. Program. Lang. Syst. 6(4), 647–662 (1984)

A Time-Optimal On-the-Fly Parallel Algorithm for Model Checking of Weak LTL Properties⋆

Jiří Barnat, Luboš Brim, and Petr Ročkai⋆⋆

Faculty of Informatics, Masaryk University
Brno, Czech Republic
{barnat,brim,xrockai}@fi.muni.cz

Abstract. One of the most important open problems of parallel LTL model-checking is to design an on-the-fly scalable parallel algorithm with linear time complexity. Such an algorithm would give the optimality we have in sequential LTL model-checking. In this paper we give a partial solution to the problem. We propose an algorithm that has the required properties for a very rich subset of LTL properties, namely those expressible by weak Büchi automata.

1 Introduction

Formal verification is nowadays an established part of the design methodology in many industrial applications. Moreover, it is no more regarded only as a supplementary vehicle to more traditional coverage oriented testing and simulation activities, ruther it takes in many situation the role of the primary validation technique. In [14] the authors report about replacing testing with symbolic verification in the recent Intel Core i7 processor design.

Traditional verification techniques are computationally demanding and memory-intensive in general and their scalability to extremely large and complex systems routinely seen in practice these days is limited. Verifying complex systems with a high degree of fidelity implies exceedingly large state spaces that must be analyzed. These state spaces are typically too large to fit into memory of a single contemporary computer, unless substantial simplification leading to removal of important features from the model are made. One solution to deal with the memory problems is to use more powerfull parallel computers. Enormous recent progress in hardware architectures, which has measured several orders of magnitude with respect to various physical parameters such as computing power, memory size at all hierarchy levels from caches to disks, power consumption, networking, physical size and cost, has made parallel computers easily available. On the other hand, this architectural shift requires introducing algorithmic changes

---

⋆ This work has been partially supported by the Czech Science Foundation grants No. 201/09/1389 and P201/09/P497, and by the Academy of Sciences grants No. 1ET408050503 and 1ET400300504.

⋆⋆ The third author has been partially supported by Red Hat, Inc.

K. Breitman and A. Cavalcanti (Eds.): ICFEM 2009, LNCS 5885, pp. 407–425, 2009.

to our tools. Without them we will not be able to fully utilize the power of parallel computers.

In this paper we consider parallel explicit-state LTL model-checking. Explicit-state model checking is a branch of model checking in which the states and transitions are stored explicitly as the model checking program traverses through the state space. The main practical problem with explicit model checking is the state space explosion. To reduce the state explosion effect, explicit model checking works on-the-fly to gradually generate and check the state space, being thus able to find a counter-example without ever constructing the complete state space.

In the case of automata-based approach to explicit-state LTL model-checking the verification problem is reduced to checking the non-emptiness of a Büchi automaton, hence the detection of a reachable accepting cycle in a rooted directed graph. The best known on-the-fly algorithms use depth-first-search (DFS) strategies.

It is well-known that DFS based algorithms are difficult to parallelize. For this reason parallel explicit-state LTL model-checking algorithms rely on other state exploration strategies than DFS. Typically, they use some variant of breath-first-search (BFS) strategy, which is well suited for parallelization. Several different algorithms have been proposed for parallel explicit-state LTL model-checking. Contrary to the serial case, it is difficult to identify the best algorithm among them. One of the reasons is that some of these algorithms have higher time complexity, but work on-the-fly, while others are on-the-fly with worse time complexity.

One of the main open problems in explicit-state LTL model-checking is to develop a parallel algorithm that works on-the-fly and has linear time complexity. In this paper we propose a parallel on-the-fly linear algorithm for LTL model-checking of weak LTL properties. Weak LTL properties are those that are expressible by weak Büchi automata, i.e. automata in which there is no cycle with both accepting and non-accepting state on its path. The studies of temporal properties [8,5] reveal that verification of up to 90% of LTL properties leads to a weak case. The most common weak LTL properties are the response properties, e.g. properties stating that whenever A happens, B happens eventually. An important aspect of our approach is that there is no difference in handling weak and non-weak LTL formulas. However, if it is required, we can perform test for a weak case within the model checking procedure with no impact on both theoretical complexity and practical performance.

Our algorithm extends the linear parallel OWCTY algorithm [5] by a heuristic for early accepting cycle discovery. The heuristic is based on the MAP algorithm [4], in partiucalr it employs the fact that if an accepting state is its own predecessor, it lies on an accepting cycle. The new algorithm thus combines the basic OWCTY algorithm with a limited propagation of selected accepting states as performed within MAP algorithm.

The new algorithm is able to detect accepting cycle and produce the so called counter-example without constructing the entire state space, hence it can be classified as on-the-fly algorithm. Since it relies on a heuristic method, a natural question is how much on-the-fly the algorithm actually is. Unfortunately, there is no standard way to compare LTL model-checking algorithms regarding this aspect. For DFS-based sequential algorithms the question is easier to answer and has been discussed by several authors. For parallel algorithms the situation is much complicated. Therefore, we identify some simple criteria for the degree of "on-the-flyness" of an algorithm, and subsequently classify our algorithm according these criteria.

Our new algorithm has been implemented in the multi-core version of the parallel LTL model-checker DiVinE [3,2]. The tool is available from its web-page [7] and is also distributed as a part of Fedora 11 release.

We proceed as follows: Section 2 establishes the necessary notions used in the algorithm. Section 3 then presents the algorithm itself. Section 4 discusses the on-the-fly notion in more detail and also contains discussion on related work. Section 5 reports results on experimental evaluation of the algorithm, and Section 6 contains the conclusions and an open questions.

2   Preliminaries

Automata-theoretic approach to explicit-state LTL model-checking [19] exploits the fact that every set of executions expressible by an LTL formula can be described by a *Büchi automaton*. In particular, the approach suggests to express all system executions by a *system automaton* and all executions not satisfying the formula by a *property* or *negative claim automaton*. These automata are combined into their synchronous product in order to check for the presence of system executions that violate the property expressed by the formula. The language recognized by the *product automaton* is empty if and only if no system execution is invalid.

The language emptiness problem for Büchi automata can be expressed as an *accepting cycle detection problem* in a graph. Each Büchi automaton can be naturally identified with an *automaton graph* which is a directed graph $G = (V, E, s, A)$ where V is the set of states ($n = |V|$), E is a set of edges ($m = |E|$), s is an initial state, and $A \subseteq V$ is a set of accepting states. We say that a cycle in G is accepting if it contains an accepting state. Let $\mathcal{A}$ be a Büchi automaton and $G_{\mathcal{A}}$ the corresponding automaton graph. Then $\mathcal{A}$ recognizes a nonempty language iff $G_{\mathcal{A}}$ contains an accepting cycle reachable from s. The LTL model-checking problem is thus reduced to the accepting cycle detection problem in the automaton graph.

The optimal sequential algorithms for accepting cycle detection use depth-first search strategies to detect accepting cycles. The individual algorithms differ in their space requirements, length of the counter-example produced, and other aspects. For a recent survey we refer to [18]. The well-known *Nested DFS* algorithm is used in many model checkers and is considered to be the best suitable algorithm for explicit-state sequential LTL model checking. The algorithm was proposed by Courcoubetis et al. [6] and its main idea is to use two interleaved searches to detect reachable accepting cycles. The first search discovers accepting states while the second one, the nested one, checks for self-reachability. Several modifications of the algorithm have been suggested to remedy some of its disadvantages [12]. Another group of optimal algorithms are *SCC-based algorithms* originating in Tarjan's algorithm for the decomposition of the graph into strongly connected components (SCCs) [17]. While Nested DFS is more space efficient, SCC-based algorithms produce shorter counter-examples in general. For a survey we refer to [16]. The time complexity of all these algorithms is linear in the size of the graph, i.e. $\mathcal{O}(m + n)$, where m is the number of edges and n is the number of states.

The effectiveness of the *Nested DFS* algorithm is achieved due to the particular order in which the graph is explored and which guarantees that states are not re-visited more than twice. In fact, all the best-known algorithms rely on the same exploring principle, namely the *postorder* as computed by the DFS. It is a well-known fact that the postorder problem is P-complete and, consequently a scalable parallel algorithm which would be directly based on DFS postorder is unlikely to exist.

Several solutions to overcome the postorder problem in a parallel environment have been suggested. The parallel algorithms were developed employing additional data structures and/or different search and distribution strategies. In the next section we present two of them. For a survey on other algorithms we refer to [1].

3   Algorithm

The proposed algorithm combines the OWCTY [5] approach with a heuristic for early accepting cycle discovery based on the MAP algorithm [4].

The basic OWCTY algorithm uses topological sort for cycle detection – a linear time algorithm that does not depend on DFS postorder and can thus be parallelized reasonably well. However, topological sort algorithm cannot detect *accepting cycles* as such. Therefore, the OWCTY algorithm uses other provisions to eliminate detection of non-accepting cycles. In particular, the algorithm computes a set of states predecessed by an accepting cycle, the so called approximation set. If the algorithm terminates and the set is empty, there is no accepting cycle in the graph. The set is computed in several phases as follows. First, a phase called INITIALIZE is executed to explore the complete state space of the automaton and to set up internal data for use by subsequent phases. Note that all reachable states are initially part of the approximation set. This phase is the one where we apply our "on-the-fly" heuristics. The latter two phases are called ELIM-NO-ACCEPTING and ELIM-NO-PREDECESSORS. These phases remove states from the approximation set that cannot be part of an accepting cycle. They are executed repeatedly until a fix-point is reached. An important observation is that if the underlying automaton graph is weak (system automaton was produced with weak negative claim Büchi automaton), the phases need to be executed exactly once. Further details of the algorithm and its phases can

---

Algorithm 1. DETECTACCEPTINGCYCLE

Require: Implicit definition of G=(V,E,ACC)
1: INITIALIZE()
2: $oldSize \leftarrow \infty$
3: **while** $(ApproxSet.size \neq oldSize) \wedge (ApproxSet.size > 0)$ **do**
4:     $oldSize \leftarrow ApproxSet.size$
5:     ELIM-NO-ACCEPTING()
6:     ELIM-NO-PREDECESSORS()
7: **return** $ApproxSet.size > 0$

Algorithm 2. INITIALIZE

1: $s \leftarrow$ GETINITIALSTATE()
2: $ApproxSet \leftarrow \{s\}$
3: $ApproxSet.setMap(s, 0)$
4: $Open.pushBack(s)$
5: **while** $Open.isNotEmpty()$ **do**
6:     $s \leftarrow Open.popFront()$
7:     **for all** $t \in$ GETSUCCESSORS(s) **do**
8:         **if** $t \notin ApproxSet$ **then**
9:             $ApproxSet \leftarrow ApproxSet \cup \{t\}$
10:            $Open.pushBack(t)$
11:        **if** ISACCEPTING(t) **then**
12:            **if** $t = s \vee ApproxSet.getMap(s) = t$ **then**
13:                ACCEPTINGCYCLEFOUND()
14:                **return true**
15:            $ApproxSet.setMap(t, \text{MAX}(t, ApproxSet.getMap(s)))$
16:        **else**
17:            $ApproxSet.setMap(t, ApproxSet.getMap(s))$

---

be found in [5]. For clarity, we just list the pseudo-code of the new combined algorithm.

The original MAP algorithm is based on propagation of maximum accepting predecessors and, similarly to OWCTY, its execution is organized into multiple passes. Each pass fully propagates (this includes re-propagation) maximum (according to given order) accepting predecessors of all states. Even a single pass of such algorithm is super-linear, up to n passes may need to be executed. After each pass, states constituting maximum accepting predecessors are marked as non-accepting and next pass is executed. The MAP algorithm finishes when a state is found to be its own maximum accepting predecessor (this means that an accepting cycle has been discovered in the state space), or when there are no reachable accepting states.

The idea of propagating one accepting predecessor along all newly discovered edges is at heart of the proposed heuristic extension of OWCTY. If the propagated accepting state is propagated into itself, an accepting cycle is discovered

Algorithm 3. ELIM-NO-ACCEPTING

```
 1: ApproxSet' ← ∅
 2: for all s ∈ ApproxSet do
 3:     if ISACCEPTING(s) then
 4:         Open.pushBack(s)
 5:         ApproxSet' ← ApproxSet' ∪ {s}
 6:         ApproxSet'.setPredecessorCount(s, 0)
 7: ApproxSet ← ApproxSet'
 8: while Open.isNotEmpty() do
 9:     s ← Open.popFront()
10:     for all t ∈ GETSUCCESSORS(s) do
11:         if t ∈ ApproxSet then
12:             ApproxSet.increasePredecessorCount(t)
13:         else
14:             Open.pushBack(t)
15:             ApproxSet ← ApproxSet ∪ {t}
16:             ApproxSet.setPredecessorCount(t, 0)
```

Algorithm 4. ELIM-NO-PREDECESSORS

```
 1: for all s ∈ ApproxSet do
 2:     if ApproxSet.getPredecessorCount(s) = 0 then
 3:         Open.pushBack(s)
 4: while Open.isNotEmpty() do
 5:     s ← Open.popFront()
 6:     ApproxSet ← ApproxSet ∖ {s}
 7:     for all t ∈ GETSUCCESSORS(s) do
 8:         ApproxSet.decreasePredecessorCount(t)
 9:         if ApproxSet.getPredecessorCount(t) = 0 then
10:             Open.pushBack(t)
```

and the computation is terminated. Likewise the MAP algorithm, an accepting state to be propagated is selected as a maximal accepting state among all accepting states visited by the traversal algorithm on a path from the initial state of the graph to the currently expanded state. Since the INITIALIZE phase of OWCTY needs to explore full state space, we can employ it to perform limited accepting cycle detection using maximal accepting state propagation. Unlike the MAP algorithm, we however avoid any re-propagation to keep the INITIALIZE phase complexity linear in the size of the graph. This means that some accepting cycles that would be actually discovered using re-propagation, may be missed. In particular, there are three general reasons for not discovering an accepting cycle with our heuristics. First, the maximum accepting predecessor of the cycle may not lie on the cycle itself, see Figure 1(a). Second, the maximum accepting predecessor value does not reach the originating state due to the absence of a fresh path (path made of yet unvisited states), see Figure 1(b). And third, the

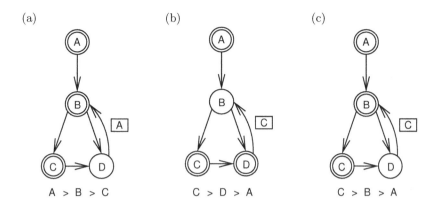

Fig. 1. Three scenarios where no accepting cycle will be discovered using accepting state propagation. a) Maximal accepting predecessor is out of the cycle. b) There is no fresh path back to the maximal accepting state. c) Wrong order of propagation, $C \to D$ is explored before $B \to D$, hence, C is propagated from D.

maximum accepting predecessor value does not reach the originating state due to a wrong propagation order, see Figure 1(c).

When the algorithm encounters an accepting state that is being propagated, it terminates early, producing a counter-example. On the other hand, if the INITIALIZE phase of OWCTY fails to notice an accepting cycle, the rest of the original OWCTY algorithm is executed. Either the algorithm finds an accepting cycle (and again, produce a counter-example) or, it proves that there are no accepting cycles in the underlying graph.

An interesting feature of our algorithm is a possibilty to propagate more values simultaneously. Generally, the more values are propagated the more successful the INITIALIZE phase might be in discovering accepting cycles. Consider for example the case (a) in Figure 1. If two largest accepting states are propagated, A and B in this case, the cycle would be detected. Similarly, if the algorithm considers multiple distinct orderings and propagates maximal accepting states for each of them, the cycle in the case (a) in Figure 1 could be detected. This would, however, require B to be a maximal accepting state for some ordering.

4   On-the-Fly Verification

In automated verification, parallel techniques both for symbolic and explicit state approaches have been considered. While the symbolic set representations, which often employs canonical normal forms for propositional logic like BDDs, have been a breakthrough in the last decade (with the capacity to handle spaces of the size 10^{20} and beyond), they often turned out to not scale well with the problem sizes. Moreover, the success of their application to a given verification problem cannot be estimated in advance, since neither the size of the system in terms of lines of code nor other known metrics for the system size have proved to be useful for such estimates. Moreover, the use of BDDs is often sensible to the used variable ordering, which is sometimes difficult to determine.

For this reason, SAT-based model checking, in particular in the forms of bounded model checking and equivalence checking have recently become very popular. They still benefit from the use of symbolic methods, but tend to be more scalable as they no longer rely on canonical normal forms like BDDs. Many algorithms used in SAT solvers could also benefit from parallel processing capabilities, even though this has not yet been a topic of the mainstream research.

An alternative is the use of explicit state set representations. Clearly, for most real world systems, the state spaces are far too big for a simple explicit representation. However, many techniques like partial order reduction approach have been developed to reduce the state spaces to be examined. In contrast to symbolically represented state sets, explicit state space representations can directly benefit from multiprocessor systems and explicit state based model checking scales very well with the number of available processors.

Let alone partial order reduction techniques, another important method for coping with the state explosion problem in explicit state model checking, is the so called *on-the-fly* verification. The idea of the on-the-fly verification builds upon an observation that in many cases, especially when a system does not satisfy its specification, only a subset of the system states need to be analyzed in order to determine whether the system satisfies a given property or not. On-the-fly approaches to model checking (also reffered to as local algorithmic approaches) attempt to take advantage of this observation and construct new parts of the state space only if these parts are needed to answer the model checking question.

As mentioned in Section 2 explicit-state automata-theoretic LTL model checking relies on three procedures: the construction of an automaton that represents the negation of the LTL property (negative-claim automaton), the construction of the state space, i.e. the product automaton of system and negative-claim automata, and the check for the non-emptiness of the language recognized by the product automaton.

An interesting observation is that only those behaviors of the examined system are present in the product automaton graph that are possible in the negative-claim automaton. In other words, by constructing the product automaton graph the system behaviors that are not relevant to the validity of the verified LTL formula are pruned out. As a result, any LTL model checking algorithm that builds upon exploration of the product automaton graph may be considered as an on-the-fly algorithm. We will denote such an algorithm as Level 0 on-the-fly algorithm in the classification given below.

When the product automaton graph is constructed, an accepting cycle detection algorithm is employed for detection of accepting cycles in the product automaton graph. However, it is not necessary for the algorithm to have the product automaton constructed before it is executed. On the contrary, the run of the algorithm and the construction of the underlying product automaton graph may interleave in such a way that new states of the product automaton are constructed *on-the-fly*, i.e. when they are needed by the algorithm. If this is the case, the algorithm may terminate due to the detection of an accepting cycle before the product automaton graph is fully constructed and all of its states are visited.

Those LTL model checking algorithms that may terminate before the state space is fully constructed are generally denoted as on-the-fly algorithms. If there is an error in the state space (accepting cycle), an on-the-fly algorithm may terminate in two possible phases: either an error is found before the interleaved generation of the product automaton graph is complete (i.e. before the algorithm detects that there are no new states to be explored), or an error is found after all states of the product automaton have been generated and the algorithm is aware of it. The first type of the termination is henceforward referred to as *early termination* (ET). Note that the awareness of completion of the product automaton construction procedure is important. If the algorithm detects the error by exploring the last state of the product automaton graph before it detects that it was actually the last unexplored state of the graph, we consider it to be an early termination.

We classify "on-the-flyness" of accepting cycle detection algorithms according to the capability of early termination as follows. An algorithm is

- *level 0 on-the-fly algorithm*, if there is a product automaton graph containing an error for which the algorithm will never early terminate.
- *level 1 on-the-fly algorithm*, if for all product automaton graphs containing an error the algorithm may terminate early, but it is not guaranteed to do so.
- *level 2 on-the-fly algorithm*, if for all product automaton graphs containing an error the algorithm is guaranteed to early terminate.

Note that level 0 algorithms are sometimes considered as on-the-fly algorithms and sometimes as non-on-the-fly algorithms depending on research community. Since a level 0 algorithm explores full state space of the product automaton graph it may be viewed as if it does not work on-the-fly. However, as explained above, just the fact that the algorithm employs product automaton construction is a good reason for considering the whole procedure of LTL model checking with a level 0 algorithm as an on-the-fly verification process.

To give examples of algorithms with appropriate classification we consider algorithms OWCTY, MAP, and Nested DFS. OWCTY algorithm is level 0 algorithm, MAP algorithm is level 1 algorithm and Nested DFS is level 2 algorithm. From the description in the previous section it is clear, that the algorithm we propose in this paper falls in the category of level 1.

It is not possible to give an analytical estimate of the percentage of the state space an on-the-fly algorithm needs to explore before early termination happens. Therefore, it is always important to accompany the classification of an algorithm by an experimental evaluation. This is in particular the case for level 1, where the experiments may give more accurate measure of the effectiveness of the method involved.

So far we have spoken only about the on-the-flyness status of a state space exploration algorithm. Nevertheless, *on-the-fly* LTL model checking procedure also denotes an approach that avoids explicit a priori construction of the negative claim automaton. We adapt the notation of [13] and denote this type of on-the-flyness as *truly* on-the-fly approach to LTL model checking. Note that truly on-the-flyness and algorithmic on-the-flyness are independent of each other and truly on-the-fly approach may be combined with on-the-fly algorithms of any level.

As for the state space exploration algorithms, the efficiency of the on-the-flyness of the algorithm may also be improved by other techniques. It might be the case that even the level 2 on-the-fly algorithm fails to discover an error, if the examined state space is large enough to exhaust system memory before an error is found. This issue has been addressed by methods of directed model checking [10,11,9], which combines model-checking with heuristic search. The heuristic guides the search process to quickly find a property violation so that the number of explored states is small. It is worthy to note that our approach can be extended with directed search as well.

5   Experiments

To experimentally evaluate efficiency of our approach we conducted numerous experiments employing models from BEEM [15]. All measured values were obtained using the verification tool `DiVinE-MC` version 1.4 [3,7]. The experiments were performed on a workstation equipped with two dual-core Intel Xeon 5130 @ 2.00 GHz processors, 16 GB of RAM, and 64-bit Linux-based operating system. For scalability experiments we also employed 16 way AMD Opteron 885 (8x dual-core) with 64 GB of RAM.

5.1   On-the-Flyness

For validation of the on-the-fly aspect of our new algorithm we originally selected 212 instances of verification problems with invalid LTL specification from BEEM database. However, we discovered that many of the instances resulted in a state space containing a self-loop over an accepting state (trivial accepting cycle). Such an accepting cycle can be easily detected using any graph traversal algorithm using just a simple self-loop test for each accepting state. After pruning out these unwanted cases, our benchmark contained 90 verification problems. An overview of the verification problems used to validate on-the-flyness of our approach is given in Figure 2.

We list experimental results in a few tables that all have a common structure. Each table row represents a single experimental configuration of the algorithm we run. Column *Algorithm* gives the configuration of the experiment. Columns *Visited states*, *Memory (MB)*, and *Time (s)* give the total number of distinct states generated, the total amount of memory consumed, and the total time of verification, respectively, for the whole benchmark set of verification problems. Column *ET ratio* reports on the number of *Early terminations* that happened for the experiment configuration. For example, if the *ET ratio* says 78/90, it means that for 78 verification problems out of 90, an accepting cycle was detected before the full state space was constructed.

Model	LTL Properties	Validity
anderson	G((!cs0) -> F cs0)	No
driving_phils	G(ac0 -> F gr0)	No
	GF ac0	No
elevator2	G(r1->(F(p1 && co)))	No
	G(r1->(!p1U(p1U(p1&& co))))	No
	G(r1->(!p1U(p1U(!p1U(p1U(p1&&co))))))	No
	F(G p1)	No
elevator	G(waiting0 ->(F in_elevator0))	No
iprotocol	F consume	No
	G F consume	No
	((G F dataok) && (G F nakok)) -> (G F consume)	No
lamport	G (wait0 -> F (cs0))	No
	G((!cs0) -> F cs0)	No
lifts	(GF pressedup0) -> (GF moveup)	No
	G (pressedup0 -> F moveup)	No
	((! moveup) U pressedup0) || G (! moveup)	No
mcs	G (wait0 -> F (cs0))	No
	G((!cs0) -> F cs0)	No
peterson	G (wait0 -> F (cs0))	No
	G((!cs0) -> F cs0)	No
	GF someoneincs	No
phils	GF eat0	No
	G (one0 -> F eat0)	No
	GF someoneeats	No
protocols	(pready U prod0) -> ((cready U cons0) || G cready)	No
	F (consume0 || consume1)	No
	G F (consume0 || consume1)	No
rether	G (res0 -> (rt0 R !cend))	No
	GF rt0	No
	G (want0 -> (! ce U (ce U (!ce && (rt0 R !ce)))))	No
szymanski	G (wait0 -> F (cs0))	No
	G((!cs0) -> F cs0)	No
	GF someoneincs	No

Fig. 2. Selected BEEM models with invalid LTL properties

To identify the configuration of the algorithm in the experiment we use the following notation. $W = x$ denotes that the algorithm was performed using x CPU cores (x workers in DiVinE-MC terminology), $V = y$ denotes that the algorithm involved y different value propagations at the same time. Note that for $V = 0$ no values were propagated in order to early detect accepting cycles and the full state space of all verification problems had to be constructed. By *DFS* and *BFS* keys we distinguish whether the underlying search order employed for the initial reachability was a local depth-first or local breadth-first one, respectively. Also, since the behavior of the algorithm is non-deterministic (if more than one CPU cores are used) all values reported are actually average values obtained from ten independent runs of the corresponding experiment.

Before analyzing the experimental results, it is also important to explain the implementation of the technique we use to identify accepting states to be propagated. In particular, the algorithm always propagates the maximal accepting state it has encountered with respect to the given order of accepting states. To be able to efficiently decide about order of two given states, we decided not to compare the contents of the corresponding state vectors, but rather to use the unique pointers to memory addresses where the two state vectors are stored. For a state s, we denote the pointer by `ptr(s)`. Note that the ordering of states depends on properties of the memory managment system of the platform the program is running on. in practice, the ordering of states depends on the order in which the states were allocated, hence, on the order in which the states were examined. Some experiments employed multiple different orderings for identification of states to be propagated. Different orderings were achieved by performing various bit alternations in the bit representation of the pointer. Concrete techniques used in different configurations of our algorithm are listed in the following table.

Algorithm	Propagated values		
Configuration	1st	2nd	3rd
V=0	—	—	—
V=1	`ptr(s)`	—	—
V=2	`ptr(s)`	`ptr(s) xor 0x555`	—
V=3	`ptr(s)`	`ptr(s) xor 0x555`	`ptr(s) xor 0xFFFF`

In Figure 3 we report results for single core experiments. It can be seen that the value propagation is quite successful regarding the early termination. Compared with the algorithm that performs no value propagation the algorithms with value propagations can save non-trivial amount of memory and reduce the runtime needed for verification, which definitely justifies our new algorithm to be considered as an algorithm that *works on-the-fly*. Other interesting aspect that can be read from the table are as follows. The more values are propagated, the larger is the ratio of early terminations, DFS mode seems to be slightly better in states and memory, but the BFS mode is better in detecting the presence of an

Algorithm	Visited states	Memory (MB)	Time (s)	ET ratio
BFS, V=0, W=1	52 047 342	6 712	760	0/90
BFS, V=1, W=1	23 157 474	4 858	295	66/90
BFS, V=2, W=1	23 173 041	4 949	297	67/90
BFS, V=3, W=1	20 175 952	4 796	237	78/90
DFS, V=0, W=1	52 047 342	6 716	760	0/90
DFS, V=1, W=1	19 849 655	4 583	272	56/90
DFS, V=2, W=1	20 971 228	4 753	277	61/90
DFS, V=3, W=1	17 090 024	4 502	240	68/90
Nested DFS	622 984	1 736	7	90/90

Fig. 3. Single core experiments

Algorithm	Visited states	Memory (MB)	Time (s)	ET ratio
BFS, V=1, W=1	6 820 499	2 829	40	66/66
BFS, V=2, W=1	6 854 458	2 893	41	67/67
BFS, V=3, W=1	5 621 320	3 194	36	78/78
DFS, V=1, W=1	3 930 520	2 257	23	56/56
DFS, V=2, W=1	5 173 954	2 546	31	61/61
DFS, V=3, W=1	1 802 949	2 518	12	68/68
Nested DFS	622 984	1 736	7	90/90

Fig. 4. Single core experiments restricted to runs with early termination

Algorithm	Visited states	Memory (MB)	Time (s)	ET ratio
BFS, V=0, W=1	52 047 342	6 712	760	0/90
BFS, V=0, W=2	52 047 342	9 072	503	0/90
BFS, V=0, W=3	52 047 342	10 065	441	0/90
BFS, V=0, W=4	52 047 342	10 874	395	0/90
DFS, V=0, W=1	52 047 342	6 716	760	0/90
DFS, V=0, W=2	52 047 342	9 069	504	0/90
DFS, V=0, W=3	52 047 342	10 036	441	0/90
DFS, V=0, W=4	52 047 342	10 888	396	0/90

Fig. 5. Experiments involving various number of CPU cores but no value propagation

Algorithm	Visited states	Memory (MB)	Time (s)	ET ratio
BFS, V=1, W=1	23 157 474	4 858	295	66/90
BFS, V=1, W=2	17 203 306	5 748	130	74/90
BFS, V=1, W=3	20 244 429	6 955	122	74/90
BFS, V=1, W=4	18 632 114	7 576	102	72/90
DFS, V=1, W=1	19 849 655	4 583	272	56/90
DFS, V=1, W=2	18 996 947	5 890	136	77/90
DFS, V=1, W=3	22 826 318	7 037	138	73/90
DFS, V=1, W=4	18 833 201	7 685	100	72/90

Algorithm	Visited states	Memory (MB)	Time (s)	ET ratio
BFS, V=2, W=1	23 173 041	4 949	297	67/90
BFS, V=2, W=2	17 540 622	5 976	132	75/90
BFS, V=2, W=3	19 199 233	6 956	115	76/90
BFS, V=2, W=4	18 856 858	7 647	102	73/90
DFS, V=2, W=1	20 971 228	4 753	278	61/90
DFS, V=2, W=2	18 557 211	5 909	136	76/90
DFS, V=2, W=3	21 429 842	6 944	125	75/90
DFS, V=2, W=4	18 601 625	7 712	98	72/90

Algorithm	Visited states	Memory (MB)	Time (s)	ET ratio
BFS, V=3, W=1	20 175 952	4 796	237	78/90
BFS, V=3, W=2	16 421 989	6 006	127	78/90
BFS, V=3, W=3	17 335 622	6 765	108	80/90
BFS, V=3, W=4	15 462 219	7 435	89	78/90
DFS, V=3, W=1	17 090 024	4 502	240	68/90
DFS, V=3, W=2	17 932 103	5 882	129	80/90
DFS, V=3, W=3	21 174 728	6 984	126	76/90
DFS, V=3, W=4	18 676 721	7 754	97	75/90

Fig. 6. Experiments involving various configurations of the algorithm and various number of CPU cores

accepting cycle on-the-fly. An interesting observation is the correspondence of the ratio of early terminations and the amount of visited states and time needed. For example, in *DFS, V=3, W=1* case, the ET ratio is 68/90 = 75%, the amount of avoided states is 35 millions which is 67% of the total of state spaces, and the time spared is 520 seconds, i.e. 72%. For comparison we also report the overall

Algorithm	Visited states	Memory (MB)	Time (s)	ET ratio
exp 0, BFS, V=3, W=4	15 271 625	7 408	85	79/90
exp 1, BFS, V=3, W=4	14 831 048	7 388	86	78/90
exp 2, BFS, V=3, W=4	16 324 239	7 541	90	78/90
exp 3, BFS, V=3, W=4	14 979 049	7 400	91	78/90
exp 4, BFS, V=3, W=4	16 064 605	7 453	90	77/90
exp 5, BFS, V=3, W=4	15 950 789	7 445	87	80/90
exp 6, BFS, V=3, W=4	14 726 197	7 401	85	79/90
exp 7, BFS, V=3, W=4	15 601 260	7 441	94	78/90
exp 8, BFS, V=3, W=4	15 308 205	7 413	90	79/90
exp 9, BFS, V=3, W=4	15 565 178	7 462	90	75/90
Maximum	16 324 239	7 541	94	80/90
Minimum	14 726 197	7 388	85	75/90
Average	15 462 220	7 435	88.8	78.1/90

Algorithm	Visited states	Memory (MB)	Time (s)	ET ratio
exp 0, DFS, V=3, W=4	19 126 324	7 802	98	75/90
exp 1, DFS, V=3, W=4	17 513 441	7 622	101	75/90
exp 2, DFS, V=3, W=4	19 289 379	7 814	98	73/90
exp 3, DFS, V=3, W=4	18 234 139	7 734	97	73/90
exp 4, DFS, V=3, W=4	16 135 286	7 504	87	78/90
exp 5, DFS, V=3, W=4	19 586 932	7 833	98	74/90
exp 6, DFS, V=3, W=4	19 237 964	7 803	94	78/90
exp 7, DFS, V=3, W=4	20 121 416	7 885	105	74/90
exp 8, DFS, V=3, W=4	18 956 781	7 784	93	78/90
exp 9, DFS, V=3, W=4	18 565 549	7 767	97	75/90
Maximum	20 121 416	7 885	105	78/90
Minimum	16 135 286	7 504	87	73/90
Average	18 676 721	7 754	96.8	75.3/90

Algorithm	Visited states	Memory (MB)	Time (s)	ET ratio
BFS, V=3, W=4	15 462 220	7 435	88.8	78.1/90
DFS, V=3, W=4	18 676 721	7 754	96.8	75.3/90

Fig. 7. Non-deterministic behavior of the algorithm demonstrated on version V=3 and 4 CPU cores. Comparison of BFS and DFS search order strategies.

Model	LTL Properties	Validity
anderson	GF someoneincs	Yes
elevator2	G(r0->(!p0U(p0U(!p0U(p0U(p0&&co))))))	Yes
lamport	GF someoneincs	Yes
leader_filters	F leader	Yes
rether	GF (nact0)	Yes
szymanski	GF someoneincs	Yes

Fig. 8. Selected BEEM model instances with valid LTL properties

Model	16-way AMD Opteron					4-way Intel Xeon			
	1	2	4	8	16	1	2	3	4
anderson	11:41	6:27	4:46	2:45	1:56	9:39	5:23	4:10	3:56
elevator2	9:27	5:40	3:28	2:07	1:35	8:18	4:51	3:50	3:05
lamport	23:12	13:23	8:10	5:16	3:39	19:41	10:58	8:28	6:49
leader_filters	9:04	5:10	3:08	2:25	1:45	7:34	5:02	3:23	2:53
rether	2:22	1:12	58	38	27	2:06	1:05	58	55
szymanski	1:20	51	39	33	28	1:09	43	39	35

Fig. 9. Scalability experimental results of liveness checking on a selection of models with valid properties

values of visited states and time needed if the serial Nested DFS algorithm is used.

Figure 4 gives the overall values if only the cases, where early termination happened, are considered. The table demonstrates, that if early termination succeeds, the efficiency of our new algorithm is quite close to the optimal but serial Nested DFS algorithm. Note the increase in the number of visited states in case *DFS, V=2, W=1* compared to *DFS, V=1, W=1*. We explain this by the fact, that in the case of *V=2* the memory requirements to store a single state vector differs from the case *V=1*, hence, pointers to addresses of state vectors are reordered due to the underlying memory management.

Before we discuss how the algorithm performs with respect to early termination if multiple CPU cores are used, we first look into how the algorithm behaves if no value propagation is used. As it can be seen from Figure 5, using more CPU cores not only renders shorter running times, but it also increases the overall memory consumption. This can be easily explained by the overhead related to multiple threads. For example, in DiVinE-MC every thread maintains its own hash table. However, there is an interesting phenomenon, also independent of the search order used, that the increase from one core to two cores is approximately twice as big as any further increase from n cores to n+1 cores. Our guess is that for a single core run, the tool consumes less memory as the

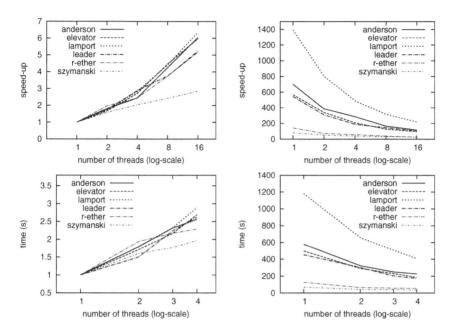

Fig. 10. Runtimes and speedup plots as measured on 16-way AMD Opteron 885 and 4-way Intel Xeon platforms

underlying memory management need not pre-allocate large memory blocks to prevent fragmentation.

In Figure 6 we present an overview of our experimental study. We conclude from the experimental results that our parallel algorithm for accepting cycle detection works in an on-the-fly manner. The experimental data demonstrate that using more accepting states for the propagation increases the successfulness of early termination, though it is disputable whether it actually reduces demands on computing resources. An interesting point is that unlike the single core case, in parallel processing *BFS* variants outperform *DFS* ones. This result is however, bound to the ordering of states in the state space.

Finally, data in Figure 5 demonstrate the non-deterministic behavior of parallel runs. It can be observed that the early termination ratio and the demands on computational resources vary, however, the deviation is relatively small which is very important from the practical point of view.

5.2 Scalability

In order to demonstrate the scalability aspects of the new algorithm we selected various valid instances from the BEEM database. See Figure 8 for details. In Figure 9 we report on run-times needed to complete the corresponding verification tasks. It can be seen that the efficiency of parallel computation is slightly deteriorating as the number of cores involved in the computation reaches the maximum number of available cores. Nevertheless, the run-times consistently decrease as the number of cores involved increases. The speedup and run-times are also given as graphs in Figure 10.

6   Conclusions

In this paper we described a new parallel algorithm for accepting cycle detection problem, i.e. explicit-state LTL model-checking. The algorithm emerged as a combination of two existing parallel algorithms, OWCTY and MAP, keeping the best of both. In particular, the new parallel algorithm is scalable and time-optimal for majority of LTL properties, likewise the OWCTY algorithm, but it is also able to detect some accepting cycles on-the-fly, likewise the MAP algorithm. No such algorithm has been known so far.

We also performed large experimental study. It demonstrated that using our new algorithm significantly reduces computation resources needed to complete the verification task in many cases.

As for the future work, we can see many options. First of all, we have the impression that one could further improve the results by clever selection of ordering function. It is clear that technique to select states to be propagated influences the experimental results a lot. It is still unclear how far one can get with a good ordering function in practice. Another future goal is to incorporate directed search in the INITIALIZE phase of the algorithm. Directed search is known to significantly increase efficiency of early termination in serial case, we expect this to be the case also for parallel algorithms. And finally, we still do not have the answer to the open problem of existence of parallel scalable and optimal level 2 on-the-fly algorithm for weak LTL properties and level 1 or better for full LTL.

References

1. Barnat, J., Brim, L., Černá, I.: I/O Efficient Accepting Cycle Detection. In: Damm, W., Hermanns, H. (eds.) CAV 2007. LNCS, vol. 4590, pp. 281–293. Springer, Heidelberg (2007)
2. Barnat, J., Brim, L., Černá, I., Moravec, P., Ročkai, P., Šimeček, P.: DiVinE – A Tool for Distributed Verification (Tool Paper). In: Ball, T., Jones, R.B. (eds.) CAV 2006. LNCS, vol. 4144, pp. 278–281. Springer, Heidelberg (2006)
3. Barnat, J., Brim, L., Ročkai, P.: DiVinE Multi-Core – A Parallel LTL Model-Checker. In: Cha, S(S.), Choi, J.-Y., Kim, M., Lee, I., Viswanathan, M. (eds.) ATVA 2008. LNCS, vol. 5311, pp. 234–239. Springer, Heidelberg (2008)
4. Brim, L., Černá, I., Moravec, P., Šimša, J.: Accepting Predecessors are Better than Back Edges in Distributed LTL Model-Checking. In: Hu, A.J., Martin, A.K. (eds.) FMCAD 2004. LNCS, vol. 3312, pp. 352–366. Springer, Heidelberg (2004)
5. Černá, I., Pelánek, R.: Distributed Explicit Fair Cycle Detection. In: Ball, T., Rajamani, S.K. (eds.) SPIN 2003. LNCS, vol. 2648, pp. 49–73. Springer, Heidelberg (2003)
6. Courcoubetics, C., Vardi, M., Wolper, P., Yannakakis, M.: Memory efficient algorithms for the verification of temporal properties. In: Clarke, E., Kurshan, R.P. (eds.) CAV 1990. LNCS, vol. 531, pp. 233–242. Springer, Heidelberg (1991)

7. DiVinE – Distributed Verification Environment, Masaryk University Brno, `http://divine.fi.muni.cz`
8. Dwyer, M.B., Avrunin, G.S., Corbett, J.C.: Property Specification Patterns for Finite-State Verification. In: Proc. Workshop on Formal Methods in Software Practice, pp. 7–15. ACM Press, New York (1998)
9. Edelkamp, S., Jabbar, S.: Large-scale directed model checking LTL. In: Valmari, A. (ed.) SPIN 2006. LNCS, vol. 3925, pp. 1–18. Springer, Heidelberg (2006)
10. Edelkamp, S., Leue, S., Lluch-Lafuente, A.: Directed explicit-state model checking in the validation of communication protocols. STTT 5(2-3), 247–267 (2004)
11. Edelkamp, S., Lluch-Lafuente, A., Leue, S.: Directed Explicit Model Checking with HSF-SPIN. In: Dwyer, M.B. (ed.) SPIN 2001. LNCS, vol. 2057, pp. 57–79. Springer, Heidelberg (2001)
12. Geldenhuys, J., Valmari, A.: More efficient on-the-fly LTL verification with Tarjan's algorithm. Theor. Comput. Sci. 345(1), 60–82 (2005)
13. Hammer, M., Knapp, A., Merz, S.: Truly On-the-Fly LTL Model Checking. In: Halbwachs, N., Zuck, L.D. (eds.) TACAS 2005. LNCS, vol. 3440, pp. 191–205. Springer, Heidelberg (2005)
14. Kaivola, R., Ghughal, R., Narasimhan, N., Telfer, A., Whittemore, J., Pandav, S., Slobodová, A., Taylor, C., Frolov, V., Reeber, E., Naik, A.: Replacing Testing with Formal Verification in Intel Core i7 Processor Execution Engine Validation. In: CAV 2009. LNCS, vol. 5643, pp. 414–429. Springer, Heidelberg (2009)
15. Pelánek, R.: BEEM: Benchmarks for Explicit Model Checkers. In: Bošnački, D., Edelkamp, S. (eds.) SPIN 2007. LNCS, vol. 4595, pp. 263–267. Springer, Heidelberg (2007)
16. Schwoon, S., Esparza, J.: A Note on On-The-Fly Verification Algorithms. In: Halbwachs, N., Zuck, L.D. (eds.) TACAS 2005. LNCS, vol. 3440, pp. 174–190. Springer, Heidelberg (2005)
17. Tarjan, R.: Depth First Search and Linear Graph Algorithms. SIAM Journal on Computing, 146–160 (January 1972)
18. Vardi, M.Y.: Automata-Theoretic Model Checking Revisited. In: Cook, B., Podelski, A. (eds.) VMCAI 2007. LNCS, vol. 4349, pp. 137–150. Springer, Heidelberg (2007)
19. Vardi, M.Y., Wolper, P.: An automata-theoretic approach to automatic program verification. In: Proc. IEEE Symposium on Logic in Computer Science, pp. 322–331. Computer Society Press (1986)

Scalable Multi-core Model Checking Fairness Enhanced Systems

Yang Liu, Jun Sun, and Jin Song Dong

School of Computing,
National University of Singapore
{liuyang,sunj,dongjs}@comp.nus.edu.sg

Abstract. Rapid development in hardware industry has brought the prevalence of multi-core systems with shared-memory, which enabled the speedup of various tasks by using parallel algorithms. The Linear Temporal Logic (LTL) model checking problem is one of the difficult problems to be parallelized or scaled up to multi-core. In this work, we propose an on-the-fly parallel model checking algorithm based on the Tarjan's strongly connected components (SCC) detection algorithm. The approach can be applied to general LTL model checking or with different fairness assumptions. Further, it is orthogonal to state space reduction techniques like partial order reduction. We enhance our PAT model checker with the technique and show its usability via the automated verification of several real-life systems. Experimental results show that our approach is scalable, especially when a system search space contains many SCCs.

1 Introduction

In recent years, the growth of computer CPU speed is slowly being replaced by the growth of number of CPUs (or CPU-cores) in the industry. To make full usage of the CPU cores naturally raises interest in applying parallelism in various problems. In this work, we focus on the parallelism of model checking fairness enhanced systems, which emits two challenges stated as follows.

Firstly, efficient parallel solution of many problems may result in dramatically different approaches from those to solve the same problems sequentially. Classical examples are list rankings, connected components, depth-first search in planar graphs etc. In the area of Linear Temporal Logic (LTL) model checking, the two best known enumerative sequential algorithms based on fair-cycle detection are the Nested Depth First Search (NDFS) algorithm [10,18] (e.g., implemented in the model checker SPIN [16]) and SCC-based algorithms [32,31] based on Tarjan's algorithm for strongly connected components (SCCs) detection [33]. However, both algorithms strongly rely on inherently sequential depth-first search of post-ordering of vertices (P-complete computation [28]). Hence it is difficult to adapt them to parallel architectures. Consequently, different techniques and algorithms are needed. Several existing parallel versions of LTL model checking algorithms are ineffective or hard to scale up. For example, SCC based parallel

K. Breitman and A. Cavalcanti (Eds.): ICFEM 2009, LNCS 5885, pp. 426–445, 2009.

algorithms [8,12,9,7,3] gives quadratic or cubic order of the search space. Multi-core SPIN [17] is only applicable to two cores for liveness properties. Note that unlike LTL model checking, deadlock-free or reachability analysis is a verification problem with efficient parallel solution. The reason is that the exploration of the state space can be partitioned using breadth-first search [17]. In this work, we will focus on the liveness properties.

Second, fairness, concerned with a fair resolution of non-determinism, is often important but expensive to be combined with model checking algorithms. Fairness is an abstraction of the fair scheduler in a multi-threaded programming environment or the relative speed of the processors in distributed systems. Without fairness, verification of liveness properties often produces unrealistic loops during which one process or event is infinitely ignored by the scheduler or one processor is infinitely faster than others. It is important to rule out those counterexamples and utilize the computational resource to identify the real bugs. However, systematically ruling out counterexamples due to lack of fairness is highly non-trivial. It requires flexible specification of fairness as well as efficient verification under fairness. Fairness and model checking with fairness have attracted much theoretical interests for decades [14,24,21]. Their practical implications in system/software design and verification have been discussed extensively. In our previous works [32,31], we present a unified on-the-fly model checking algorithm which handles a variety of fairness including process-level weak/strong fairness, event-level weak/strong fairness, strong global fairness, etc. However, none of these works paid attention to parallel verification.

Contributions. In this work, we propose an algorithm with the capacity of parallel verification of systems with various fairness constraints in the multi-core architecture with share-memory.

SCC-based LTL model checking algorithms conduct a depth first search starting from the root node, and check whether the SCC in the subtree is fair whenever a SCC is identified. Previous parallel algorithms focus on partition of the graph based on special properties of the nodes inside the SCCs, which requires multiple traverses of the whole search graph. These approaches are not practical for large systems, especially when there is a counterexample. Based on our previous work, we propose an on-the-fly parallel algorithm based on an improved version of Tarjan's algorithm. In our approach, a main thread performs the DFS searching of Tarjan's algorithm. Whenever a SCC is detected, a new worker thread is forked to process the found SCC. SCC processing contains both fair loop detection and fairness constraints satisfaction checking (if there is fairness assumption in the system), hence a fair amount of workload is divided to the worker threads to achieve load balancing. When a counterexample is identified in any worker thread, it will inform the main thread to stop the DFS and all other live worker threads. This makes our approach on-the-fly, i.e., without generating the entire search space. We have proved the correctness of our approach in the multi-core architecture with shared memory.

Effective reduction techniques are the keys to resolve the infamous "state explosion" problem in model checking, such as partial order reduction (to reduce the search space by exploring independence of system transitions), symmetric reduction (to handle large or even unbounded number of similar processes). We show that all these reductions are compatible with our algorithm, if these reductions are applicable (see Section 4.3 for details).

Our engineering effort realizes this technique in our home-grown PAT model checker (available at http://pat.comp.nus.edu.sg). We show its usability via automated verification of several real-life systems. The experiments show that our technique offers a scalable verification support for multi-core model checking.

Section Organization. The rest of the paper is structured as follows. Section 2 introduces our computational model, together with a family of different fairness notions. Section 3 presents a sequential fairness model checking algorithm based on SCC detection. Section 4 describes our proposed parallel algorithm in the shared-memory platform. Section 5 shows some experimental results to demonstrate the effectiveness of parallel algorithm. Section 6 discusses related work and Section 7 concludes.

2   Background

In this work, system models are described in the setting of Labeled Transition Systems (LTS). All the algorithms proposed in this paper are applicable to the models that can be interpreted as LTSs implicitly by defining a complete set of operational semantics. For example, PAT accepts modeling languages like Communicating Sequential Processes# (CSP#) [29], Web Service modeling language, real-time system modeling language. This section gives the LTS semantics and defines different fairness constraints based on it.

Let e be an event (in process algebra, e.g., CSP), which could be either an abstract event (e.g., a synchronization barrier if shared by multiple processes) or a data operation (e.g., a sequential program). Let Σ be the set of all events in the model.

Definition 1 (LTS). *A Labeled Transition System $\mathcal{L}$ is a 3-tuple $(S, init, \rightarrow)$ where S is a set of system configurations/states, $init \in S$ is the initial system configuration and $\rightarrow \subseteq S \times \Sigma \times S$ is a labeled transition relation.*

In this work, we focus on infinite system executions explained as follows. Finite behaviors are extended to infinite ones by appending infinite idling events at the rear. Given two states s and s' in S, we write $s \xrightarrow{e} s'$ to denote a transition from s to s' with event e. Given a LTS $\mathcal{L} = (S, init, \rightarrow)$, an execution $E = \langle s_0, e_0, s_1, e_1, \cdots \rangle$ is an infinite sequence of alternating states and events, where $s_0 = init$ and for all $i \geq 0$ such that $s_i \xrightarrow{e_i} s_{i+1}$. Given a LTL property ϕ, $\mathcal{L}$ satisfies ϕ if and only if every execution of $\mathcal{L}$ satisfies ϕ.

Without fairness constraints, a system may behave freely as long as it starts with an initial state and conforms to the transition relation. A fairness constraint restricts the set of system behaviors to only those fair ones. Given a LTL property ϕ, verification under fairness means verifying whether all fair executions of the system satisfy ϕ. In the following, we briefly review a variety of different fairness constraints. The following notions are used to define fairness. $enabledEvt(s)$ is the set of enabled events at state s, i.e., e is in $enabledEvt(s)$ if and only if there exist $s' \in S$ such that $s \xrightarrow{e} s'$. If the system is constituted by multiple processes running in parallel, we write $enabledPro(s)$ to be the set of enabled processes, which may make a move given the system state s. Given a transition $s \xrightarrow{e} s'$, we write $engagedPro(s, e, s')$ to be the set of participating processes, which have made some progress during the transition. Notice that if e is synchronized by multiple processes, the set contains all the participating processes. We write $engagedEvt(s, e, s')$ to denote $\{e\}$. In the following, we use $E = \langle s_0, e_0, s_1, e_1, \cdots \rangle$ to denote an execution.

Weak fairness [24,25]. There are two different levels of weak fairness, i.e. event-level weak fairness (EWF) or process-level weak fairness (PWF). E satisfies event-level weak fairness, if and only if for every action e, if e eventually becomes enabled forever in E, then $e_i = e$ for infinitely many i, i.e., $\Diamond\Box$ e is $enabled$ $\Rightarrow$ $\Box\Diamond$ e is $engaged$. Intuitively, event-level weak fairness states that if an event becomes enabled forever after some steps, then it must be engaged infinitely often. E satisfies process-level weak fairness, if and only if for every process p, if p eventually becomes enabled forever in E, then $p \in engagedProc(s_i, e_i, s_{i+1})$ for infinitely many i, which equals to $\Diamond\Box$ p is $enabled$ $\Rightarrow$ $\Box\Diamond$ p is $engaged$ in LTL. Intuitively, process-level weak fairness states that if a process becomes enabled forever after some steps, then it must be engaged infinitely often. From another point of view, process-level weak fairness guarantees that each process is only finitely faster than the others. Weak fairness is equivalent to justice conditions [25]. An alternative formulation of weak fairness is that every computation should contain infinitely many particular states (e.g. states where an event or a process is disabled or has just engaged).

Strong fairness [23,11,27]. Strong fairness is particularly useful in the analysis of systems that use semaphores, synchronous communication, and other special coordination primitives. Likewise, there are two levels of strong fairness. E satisfies event-level strong fairness (ESF) if and only if, for every event e, if e is infinitely often enabled, $e = e_i$ for infinitely many i, which equals to $\Box\Diamond$ e is $enabled$ $\Rightarrow$ $\Box\Diamond$ e is $engaged$ in LTL. It states that if an event is infinitely often enabled, it must be infinitely often engaged. E satisfies process-level strong fairness (PSF) if and only if, for every process p, if p is infinitely often enabled, then $p \in engagedProc(s_i, e_i, s_{i+1})$ for infinitely many i, which equals to $\Box\Diamond$ p is $enabled$ $\Rightarrow$ $\Box\Diamond$ p is $engaged$ in LTL. Process-level strong fairness means that if a process is repeatedly enabled, it must eventually make some progress. Verification under (event-level/ process-level) strong fairness (or compassion condition) has been discussed previously [13,15,20,26,32,31].

Strong global fairness [11]. E satisfies strong global fairness (SGF) if and only if, for every s, e, s' such that $s \xrightarrow{e} s'$, if $s = s_i$ for infinite many i, $s_i = s$ and $e_i = e$ and $s_{i+1} = s'$ for infinitely many i. Intuitively, it states that if a *step* (from s to s' by engaging in event e) can be taken infinitely often, then it must actually be taken infinitely often. Different from the previous notions of fairness, strong global fairness concerns about both events and states, instead of events only. It can be shown by a simple argument that strong global fairness is stronger than event-level strong fairness. Because it concerns about both events and states, it is 'event-level' and 'process-level'. Strong global fairness requires that an infinitely enabled event must be taken infinitely often in *all* contexts, whereas event-level strong fairness only requires the enabled event to be taken in *one* context. Many population protocols reply on strong global fairness, e.g., protocols presented in [1,11].

3   Sequential Model Checking under Fairness

Given a LTS $\mathcal{L}$ and a LTL formula ϕ, model checking is about searching for an execution of $\mathcal{L}$ which fails ϕ. In automata-based model checking, the negation of ϕ is translated to an equivalent Büchi automaton $\mathcal{B}$, which is then composed with the LTS representing the system model. Model checking under fairness is to search for an infinite execution which is accepting to the Büchi automaton and at the same time satisfies the fairness constraints. Equivalently, it is to search a loop or a Strongly Connected Components (SCC) in the state graph such that the infinite execution traversing through every state/edges of the loop or SCC satisfies the fairness constraints.

SCC-based verification algorithms rely on the SCC detection, most of which are based on Tarjan's algorithm for identifying SCCs [33]. Figure 1 presents a sequential unified algorithm for automata-based model checking of LTL under fairness [31]. The algorithm works by searching on-the-fly for fair strongly connected subgraphs, which may constitute counterexamples. The basic idea is to identify one SCC at a time and then check whether it is fair or not. If it is, the search is over. Otherwise, the SCC may be partitioned into several smaller strongly connected subgraphs, which are then checked recursively one by one.

We briefly explain how the algorithm works. Interested readers should refer to [31] for details. Assumes that *States* is the set of states and *Transitions* is the set of transitions[1]. At the top level is a while-loop, which stops only if all states have been visited. At line 2, Tarjan's algorithm is used to identify a SCC [13]. If the found *scc* is fair, a counterexample is generated (at line 5) and the algorithm returns false. Without fairness assumptions, a SCC is fair if and only if it is accepting to the Büchi automaton (i.e. Büchi fair). The complexity of checking whether *scc* is fair or not under fairness assumption is linear in the size of *scc*. For instance, under weak fairness, we must first identify the set of processes/events that are always enabled and compare the set with the set of processes/events that make progress.

If *scc* is not fair, a procedure *prune* is used to prune *bad states* from *scc* (at line 8). Bad states are the reasons why *scc* is not fair. The intuition behind the pruning is that there may be a fair strongly connected subgraph in the remaining

---

[1] Both of which may be constructed on-the-fly instead of known before-hand.

procedure *mc*(*States*, *Transitions*)
1. **while** there are un-visited states
2.   **let** *scc* := *tarjan*(*States*, *Transitions*);
3.   mark states in *scc* as visited;
4.   **if** *isFair*(*scc*) = *true* **then**   – *
5.   generate a counterexample;   – *
6.   **return** *false*;   – *
7.   **else**   – *
8.   *scc* = *prune*(*scc*);   – *
9.   **if** *mc*(*scc*, *Transitions*) = *false* **then**   – *
10.   **return** *false*;   – *
11.   **endif**   – *
12.   **endif**   – *
13. **endwhile**
14. **return** *true*;

Fig. 1. Algorithm for sequential model checking under fairness [31]

states after eliminating the bad states. By simply modifying *isFair* and *prune* method, the algorithm can be used to handle different fairness. For instance, the following defines the functions for event-level strong fairness [31].

$$isFair(scc) = true \text{ if and only if } \forall s : scc \; enabledEvt(s) \subseteq engagedEvt(scc)$$

where $engagedEvt(scc) = \{a \mid \exists s, s' : scc \; s \xrightarrow{a} s'\}$ is the set of events labeling a transition between two states in *scc*, i.e. the set of events that can be engaged if an execution visits only states in *scc*. Intuitively, *scc* satisfies event-level strong fairness if and only if all enabled events are engaged in the SCC.

$$prune(scc) = \{s : scc \mid enabledEvt(s) \subseteq engagedEvt(scc)\}$$

In this setting, a state is bad if it enables an event which is not engaged in the SCC. It is clear that if the SCC contains a fair strongly connected subgraph, no state constituting the subgraph is pruned.

At line 9, a recursive call is made to check whether there is a fair strongly connected subgraph within the remaining states. The call terminates in two ways. One is that a fair subgraph is found (at line 6) and the other is that all states in *scc* are pruned (at line 14).

Example 1. Assume that the automaton shown in Figure 2 is the product of a LTS and a Büchi automaton. Further assume that state 2 is an accepting state, i.e. any traces which visits state 2 infinitely often is accepting the Büchi automaton. There are two SCCs, namely *scc1* which is composed of state 1 only and *scc2* which is composed of state 0, 2 and 3. State 0 is a bad state in *scc2* under event-level strong fairness since $a \in enabledEvt(state\ 0)$ whereas $a \notin engagedEvt(scc2)$. Notice that state 3 is not a bad state. As a result, state

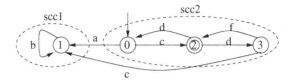

Fig. 2. ESF Model Checking Example

0 is pruned. Next, in the recursive call, the SCC composed of state 2 and 3 are identified. However, state 3 becomes a bad state now because event c is now enabled but not engaged. State 3 is pruned then. Lastly, state 2 is pruned. Because *scc*1 does not contain an accepting state, it fails all *isFair* test. As a result, no counterexample is found.   □

After a SCC has been fully examined (i.e., all pruned) at line 12, the algorithm repeats from line 2 to check the next SCC. We remark that the algorithm is a natural candidate for exploring multi-core parallelism. Firstly, examining weather a SCC is fair or whether it contains fair strongly connected subgraph is time consuming, and hence checking multiple SCCs in parallel is likely to generate significant saving. SCC fairness checking is linear in the number of transitions connecting states of the SCC. Checking whether a SCC contains a fair strongly connected subgraph is expensive. In the worst case, only one state is pruned each time and therefore the complexity is bounded by the number of transitions times the number of states. Secondly, different SCCs naturally exclude each other and therefore checking them in parallel will not cause significant computational or communication overhead.

4   Parallel Model Checking in Shared-Memory Platform

In this section, we present a parallel approach at the challenges of shared-memory architecture and its specific characteristics. We will detail the algorithm design, its complexity and correctness.

4.1   Shared-Memory Platform

We work with a model based on threads that share all memory, although they have separate stacks in their shared address space and a special thread-local storage to store thread-private data. Our working environment is .NET framework (version 2.0) in Microsoft Windows platform, with its implementation of threads as lightweight processes. Switching contexts among different threads is cheaper than switching contexts among full-featured processes with separate address spaces, so using threads in the system incurs only a minor penalty.

Critical Sections, Locking and Lock Contention. In a shared-memory setting, access to memory, that may be used for writing by more than a single thread, has to be controlled through the use of mutual exclusion, otherwise, race conditions will occur. This is generally achieved through use of a "mutual exclusion device", so-called mutex. A thread wishing to enter a critical section has to lock[2] the associated mutex, which may block the calling thread if the mutex is locked already by some other thread. An effect called resource or lock contention is associated with this behavior. This occurs, when two or more threads happen to need to enter the same critical section (and therefore lock the same mutex), at the same time. If critical sections are long or they are entered very often, contention starts to cause observable performance degradation, as more and more time is spent waiting for mutexes.

Memory Management and Thread Communication. Microsoft .NET common language runtime requires that all resources be allocated from the managed heap. Objects are automatically freed when they are no longer needed by the application. The communication between threads can be achieved simply by object reference passing.

4.2 Parallel Fairness Model Checking Algorithm

The SCC-based verification algorithm presented in the previous section is recursive and employs a sequential DFS search, which exhibits some challenges in parallelism.

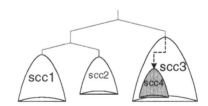

The sequential algorithm in Figure 1 can be illustrated in the figure above. When a SCC is detected, it will be analyzed and pruned until empty or there is a counterexample detected (*scc4* in above graph). Taking a close look at the algorithm, we observe that there are four actions applied in each detected SCC: (1) fairness testing (line 4), (2) bad states pruning (line 8), (3) counterexample generation (line 5), (4) recursive sub-SCC detection (line 9). The first three actions are local to the detected SCC. Although the recursive sub-SCC detection is complicated, we can create a local copy of the Tarjan algorithm to search for "SCC" in the pruned states. In this way, each SCC can be processed independent. Therefore, we can put the workload of SCC analysis into separate threads to achieve concurrency. Inspired by these observations, we present a SCC-based parallel model checking algorithm with four parts: *Tarjan thread, SCC worker thread, SCC worker thread pool* and *parallel model checker*. The detailed algorithms are illustrated as follows.

---

[2] In .NET framework, keyword **lock** is used to achieve this effect.

stopped = *false*;

procedure *run(threadPool, States, Transitions)*

1. *visited* = ∅;
2. **while** there are states in *States* but not in *visited*
3.   **if** *stopped* **then** {**return**; }
4.   **let** *scc* = *tarjan(States, Transitions)*;
5.   *visited* = *visited* ∪ *scc*;
6.   **if** *forking conditions* **then**
7.   *threadPool.forkWorkerThread(scc, Transitions)*;
8.   **else**
9.   process *scc* locally
10.   **endif**
11. **endwhile**
12. **return**;

Fig. 3. Tarjan Thread Implementation

Tarjan thread. Figure 3 presents the implementation of *Tarjan thread*, which identifies all SCCs using Tarjan's algorithm. Tarjan thread has one public variable *stopped* and the thread starting procedure *run*. *stopped* is a control variable to stop this thread (line 3) as soon as a worker thread reports a counterexample. When *Tarjan thread* starts, the *run* procedure will perform a DFS to detect all SCCs in the search space using Tarjan's algorithm. This process is similar to *mc* procedure in Figure 1. When a SCC *scc* is detected at line 4, if the forking conditions at line 6 are satisfied, then a new SCC worker thread will be forked and added in to the worker thread pool (line 7). Otherwise *scc* will processed locally in the *Tarjan thread* (line 9). This local process is the same as the *SCC worker thread* (which will be explained later), which stops this thread if a counterexample is found. Forking conditions can be that the size of *scc* is bigger than some threshold or the thread pool is full. We add this checking to achieve better efficiency and workload balance. If the size of *scc* is small (e.g., only few nodes), the overhead of creating a thread is much bigger than processing it locally. If the thread pool is full, processing the found *scc* locally is probably more efficient than creating a long waiting queue in the thread pool.

SCC worker thread. *SCC worker thread* works on a detected SCC to report whether the SCC contains a counterexample or not within the given SCC states and transitions. It basically resembles the code from line 4 to 12 (highlighted using _*) in Figure 1. If the detected SCC is not fair, it will prune the states according to the given fairness type. Otherwise it will terminate and return false. If the pruned *scc* has fewer states, a local copy of the Tarjan's algorithm will continue the searching. Upon the termination of *SCC worker thread*, a notification will send to the thread pool to notify the result.

threadQueue = empty queue;
jobFinished = false;
procedure *forkWorkerThread(States, Transitions)*
1. **lock**(*threadQueue*);
2.   **if**(*!jobFinished*)
3.   **let** *wt = new workerThread(States, Transitions)*;
4.   register *wt.termination* to *threadTermination* procedure
5.   *threadQueue.enqueue(wt)*;
6.   **endif**
7. **unlock**(*threadQueue*);

procedure *threadTermination(thread)*
8. **lock**(*threadQueue*);
9.   **if** thread produces counterexample ∧ *!jobFinished* **then**
10.   terminate all other threads
11.   terminate tarjan thread
12.   *jobFinished = true*;
13.   **endif**
14.   *threadPool.remove(thread)*
15. **unlock**(*threadQueue*);

procedure *allThreadsJoin()*
16. **while**(has running threads)
17.   busy wait
18. **endwhile**

Fig. 4. Thread Pool Implementation

SCC worker thread pool. The implementation of the *SCC worker thread pool* is presented in Figure 4. The thread pool has a working queue *threadQueue*[3] to store all active worker threads. Private variable *jobFinished* indicates whether a counterexample has been found or not. Procedure *forkWorkerThread* creates a new worker thread (line 3) and puts it into the working queue (line 5), if the counterexample is not found (line 2). A lock is used on *threadQueue* (at line 1 and 7) to prevent *Tarjan thread* working too fast to add two or more threads at same time. This is possible because during the process of forking the first thread, *Tarjan thread* may find another SCC and want to fork a new thread. At line 4, we register the termination event of the *worker thread* to procedure *threadTermination*, which means upon the termination of the worker thread, the thread pool will be notified and procedure *threadTermination* will be triggered. When procedure *threadTermination* is triggered, if the termination thread has located a counterexample and no one does it before (line 9), thread

---

[3] In our implementation, *threadQueue* is realized by System.Threading.ThreadPool object in .NET Framework. The thread scheduling is managed by the thread pool automatically.

procedure *pmc*(*States*, *Transitions*)
1. initialize worker thread pool *threadPool*
2. **let** *tarjan* = *tarjanThread.run*(*threadPool*, *States*, *Transitions*);
3. *tarjan.join*();
4. *threadPool.allThreadsJoin*();
5. **if** counterexample is found **then**
6.   **return** *false*;
7. **return** *true*;

Fig. 5. Parallel Model Checker Implementation

pool will terminate[4] all other active threads (line 10) and *Tarjan thread* (by setting *stopped* flag to true) (line 11). Flag *jobFinished* is set to true at line 12, hence new threads shall not be forked anymore. !*jobFinished* checking in line 9 is necessary to prevent terminating same threads twice. In the end, the termination thread is removed from thread pool in line 12. During this process *threadQueue* is locked to prevent data race. Procedure *allThreadsJoin* does busy-waiting until all threads terminate.

Parallel model checker. Lastly, *parallel model checker* is shown in Figure 5. It conducts the verification by creating the *Tarjan thread* and thread pool. Once *Tarjan thread* starts, it will wait for *Tarjan thread* to join (i.e., successfully terminate) (line 3). The termination can be that all states are explored, or a counterexample is found locally, or *stopped* flag is set to false. Afterwards, it will wait for thread pool to terminate (line 4). The procedure will return false if any counterexample is found in *tarjan thread* or any worker thread.

4.3   Complexity and Soundness

In this section, we discuss the complexity of the parallel model checking algorithm and prove its soundness.

For the sequential version of the algorithm, the time complexity for verification under no fairness, event-level or process-level weak fairness or strong global fairness are similar, i.e., all linear in the number of system transitions. All states in one SCC are discarded at once in all cases and, therefore, no recursive call is necessary. Furthermore, the *prune* function is linear in the number of transitions of a SCC. In comparison, SPIN's model checking algorithm under process-level weak fairness increases the run-time expense of a verification run by a factor that is linear in the number of running processes. Verification under event-level or process-level strong fairness is in general expensive. In the worst case (i.e., the whole system is strongly connected and only one state is pruned every time), the *prune* method may be invoked at most $\#S$ times, where $\#S$ is the number

---

[4] Thread termination can be achieved by thread killing or asking the thread to voluntarily give up. The second way is safer and adopted in our approach. One example is the stopped flag in *Tarjan thread*.

of system states. Thus, the time complexity is bounded by $\#S \times \#T$ where $\#T$ is the number of transitions. In practice, however, if the property is false, a counterexample is usually identified quickly, because our algorithm constructs and checks SCCs on-the-fly. Even if the property is true, our experience suggests that the worst case scenario is rare in practice.

For the parallel version of the algorithm, the time and space complexity is exactly same as the sequential version. This is not surprising because the parallel algorithm simply splits SCC analysis into worker threads. The parallel algorithm is designed for a shared memory framework, the SCCs and their transitions are shared between *Tarjan thread* and worker threads. There is no communication overhead. If to migrate this approach into distributed systems, we may consider to pass SCC only and let the worker threads to build the transitions locally to avoid the communication overhead. The is because the number of transitions of a SCC is often much larger than the number of vertices.

If the verification result is true, the number of states and transitions visited in the parallel and sequential version are same. If there is a counterexample, the parallel version may visit more states depending on when the counterexample is identified. If a counterexample is present in the first few SCCs encountered during the search, then the sequential version may find one quickly, while the parallel version may have forked multiple threads to search in more SCCs. Hence parallel version visits more states and transitions. On the other hand, if a counterexample is present only in the last few SCCs, the parallel version can be faster than the sequential version if the counterexample is identified quickly in one worker thread, which then terminates all other SCC checking. This is evidenced by the experiment results presented in Section 5. Notice that when there are more than one counterexamples in the system, it is possible that the parallel verification may produce different counterexample at different runs.

Regarding the soundness, the following theorem establishes correctness of the sequential algorithm. The proof for different fairness can be found in our technical report [30].

Theorem 1. *Let $\mathcal{L}$ be an LTS. Let ϕ be a property. Let F be a fairness type (i.e., EWF, PWF, ESF, PSF or SGF). $\mathcal{L} \vDash_F \phi$ if and only if the algorithm mc returns true.*

The following theorem states the correctness of the parallel algorithm *pmc*. We argue the total correctness of the parallel algorithm by showing it is terminating and equivalent to the sequential *mc* algorithm.

Theorem 2. *Let $\mathcal{L}$ be an LTS. Let ϕ be a property. Let F be a fairness type (i.e., EWF, PWF, ESF, PSF or SGF). $\mathcal{L} \vDash_F \phi$ if and only if the algorithm pmc returns true.*

Proof. Firstly, we show that the *pmc* algorithm is terminating. By the assumption, we know that the number of states is finite, so is the number of the SCCs. In *Tarjan thread*, the number of visited states and the pruned states are monotonically increasing, hence the Tarjan thread is terminating. Worker threads are terminating since they are working on the detected SCC and the number of pruned states are monotonically increasing. Since the number of SCC is finite, worker thread pool is terminating. Therefore *pmc* is terminating.

Secondly, we show that *pmc* returns the same result as *mc*. The key of this proof is to prove that each SCC analysis is independent of each other. If this true, then checking the SCCs in parallel is same as checking them sequentially. We have listed the four actions performed in the SCCs in Section 4.1, which can be applied independently.

Lastly, the correctness of data sharing and race condition prevention by using locks have been discussed in Section 4.2. We skip it here.   □

Following the above theorem, we conclude that the sequential algorithm and the parallel algorithm are equivalent in terms of correctness. Therefore as long as the reduction is compatible with sequential algorithm, then it is compatible with the parallel algorithm. For example, our previous work [32] shows that partial order reduction is possible by employing fairness annotations on individual events, which means this technique can also be used with our parallel algorithm. We remark that *pmc* is orthogonal to state reduction techniques like partial order reduction, symmetry reduction or data abstraction. Intuitively, the parallel algorithm would perform better since it may utilize more CPU power. Nonetheless, thread forking/terminating or communication between threads can be costly. We present detailed analysis using real-world examples as well as hand craft examples in the next section.

5   Experimental Results

Process Analysis Toolkit (hereafter PAT) is designed for systematic validation of distributed/concurrent systems using state-of-art model checking techniques. Its main functionalities include simulation, explicit on-the-fly model checking, and verification under fairness. The model checker combines complementary model checking techniques for system verification. In the following, we show its performance on both benchmark systems as well as recently developed population protocols, which require fairness for correctness. All the models (with configurable parameters) are embedded in the PAT package and available online at our web site http://pat.comp.nus.edu.sg.

Regarding the threads scheduling, there are two approaches. The first approach is to manually assign a newly created thread to a free CPU-core. If all CPU-cores are used, the new thread is pushed into the working queue and wait.The second approach is to make each thread as operating system thread[5], and let the OS CPU scheduler to do the scheduling. We compared the two approaches, it shows that when the size of the SCCs is big, the two approaches have same results. When the number of SCCs is big, the second approach is more efficient. We applied second approach in our experiments.

In our experiments below, *Size* denotes the number processes in the models. Besides the execution time of the sequential algorithm (*mc*) and parallel

---

[5] In our implementation, we use System.Threading.ThreadPool object in .NET framework 2.0 to create system threads in Microsoft Windows system.

Table 1. Experiment results on a PC running Windows XP with 2.83 GHz quad-core Intel Q9550 CPU and 2 GB memory

Model	Size	Avg SCC/ #SCC	SCC Ratio	EWF			ESF			SGF		
				Result	mc	pmc	Result	mc	pmc	Result	mc	pmc
DP	5	67/13	0.36	No	0.08	0.08	Yes	0.22	0.20	Yes	0.19	0.19
DP	6	178/21	0.38	No	0.13	0.13	Yes	0.97	0.84	Yes	0.86	0.78
DP	7	486/31	0.4	No	0.38	0.37	Yes	4.62	3.39	Yes	4.42	3.38
DP	8	1368/43	0.41	No	1.41	1.33	Yes	29.28	19.49	Yes	32.90	22.14
LE_C	3	22/3	0.33	Yes	0.11	0.11	Yes	0.11	0.11	Yes	0.10	0.10
LE_C	4	24/15	0.47	Yes	0.53	0.47	Yes	0.52	0.47	Yes	0.46	0.45
LE_C	5	34/43	0.58	Yes	4.04	3.66	Yes	4.03	3.65	Yes	3.66	3.49
LE_C	6	48/103	0.64	Yes	23.12	21.39	Yes	23.05	21.54	Yes	21.91	20.14
LE_C	7	66/227	0.68	Yes	128.8	124.4	Yes	129.5	124.3	Yes	133.9	127.2
LE_C	8	86/479	0.71	Yes	604.3	600.5	Yes	615.8	606.6	Yes	721.9	684.4
LE_R	3	9/268	0.36	No	0.11	0.11	No	0.12	0.12	Yes	1.40	1.27
LE_R	4	9/2652	0.4	No	0.11	0.28	No	0.59	0.60	Yes	21.65	15.73
LE_R	5	9/25274	0.42	No	0.71	0.72	No	2.22	2.19	Yes	587.0	456.4
TC_R	4	16/1	0.01	No	0.06	0.07	No	0.07	0.06	Yes	0.11	0.12
TC_R	5	60/1	0.01	No	0.08	0.08	No	0.08	0.08	Yes	0.45	0.48
TC_R	6	84/2	0.01	No	0.11	0.11	No	0.11	0.11	Yes	2.20	2.38
TC_R	7	210/2	0.01	No	0.14	0.14	No	0.15	0.16	Yes	11.28	12.31
TC_R	8	330/3	0.01	No	0.19	0.20	No	0.25	0.23	Yes	69.55	72.98
TC_R	9	756/3	0.01	No	0.27	0.31	No	0.36	0.37	Yes	494.4	572.7

algorithm (pmc), we present additional measurements which reflect the amount of workload pmc can put in parallel if the verification result is true[6]. One is the average size of nontrivial SCCs (denoted as *Avg SCC Size*) and the number of SCC (denoted as *#SCC*). A SCC is trivial if and only if it has only one state. Intuitively, the parallel algorithm gains more saving with larger and more SCCs. The other is the ratio of the number of states of all (non-trivial) SCCs and the whole state space (denoted as *SCC Ratio*). Intuitively, a higher *SCC Ratio* shall lead to more saving. The forking condition is that the SCC must have at least 100 states. '-' means out of memory. The unit of time measurement is second.

Table 1 summarizes the verification statistics on classic dinning philosophers problem (DP), and recently developed population protocols. The population protocols include leader election for complete networks (LE_C) [11], for network rings (LE_R) [11] and token circulation for network rings (TC_R) [1]. We modify the DP model so that it is deadlock-free (i.e., by letting one of the philosophers to pick up the forks in a different order). The property is that a philosopher never starves to death, i.e., $\Box\Diamond eat.0$, where $eat.0$ is the event of 0-th philosopher eating. The property for the leader election protocols is that eventually always there is one and only one leader in the network, i.e., $\Diamond\Box oneLeader$. Correctness of all these algorithms relies on different notions of fairness.

---

[6] When the property is false, *SCC Ratio* can be different for different runs.

Table 2. Experiment results on a PC running Windows XP with 2.83 GHz quad-core Intel Q9550 CPU and 2 GB memory

Model	Size	Avg SCC/ #SCC	SCC Ratio	EWF Result	mc	pmc	ESF Result	mc	pmc	SGF Result	mc	pmc
PAR1	5	10001/5	0.2	No	1.75	2.11	Yes	22.50	12.03	Yes	11.33	6.97
PAR1	6	10001/6	0.2	No	1.74	2.07	Yes	27.10	14.81	Yes	13.59	8.13
PAR1	7	10001/7	0.2	No	1.71	2.29	Yes	31.22	16.66	Yes	15.89	9.14
PAR1	8	10001/8	0.2	No	1.71	2.16	Yes	36.08	18.04	Yes	18.09	10.60
PAR1	9	10001/9	0.2	No	1.71	2.15	Yes	40.59	20.85	Yes	20.40	11.90
PAR1	10	10001/10	0.2	No	1.73	2.15	Yes	45.29	22.63	Yes	22.81	13.07
PAR2	4	20000/5	0.5	No	5.46	7.12	NA	-	-	Yes	8.87	5.52
PAR2	5	20000/6	0.5	No	6.05	9.53	NA	-	-	Yes	18.32	8.64
PAR2	6	20000/7	0.5	No	6.39	10.51	NA	-	-	Yes	21.37	9.32
PAR2	7	20000/8	0.5	No	6.90	11.41	NA	-	-	Yes	24.50	9.69
PAR2	8	20000/9	0.5	No	7.77	11.65	NA	-	-	Yes	27.86	11.82
PAR2	9	20000/10	0.5	No	8.06	12.76	NA	-	-	Yes	30.89	13.68
PAR3	7	2000/8	1	No	0.29	0.20	Yes	411.5	117.6	Yes	0.41	0.28
PAR3	8	2000/9	1	No	0.21	0.24	Yes	463.1	135.7	Yes	0.45	0.29
PAR3	9	2000/10	1	No	0.25	0.23	Yes	515.7	155.8	Yes	0.49	0.31

In Table 1, we can see that when the verification result is false, either *pmc* or *mc* can be faster, which is expected. When the verification result is true, *pmc* is faster in most of the cases, except in the case of model checking the TC_R example under strong global fairness. In this particular example, *SCC ratio* is very low (0.01), which means that there are many trivial SCCs. Furthermore, there are only few non-trivial SCCs. As a result, there is little work that can be separated out for the worker threads to speed up the model checking, and the communication overhead makes *pmc* slower. On the other hand, the *pmc* slowdown in this case is only several percents of *mc*, which shows that the communication overhead in *pmc* is low.

Table 2 summarizes the verification statistics on some hand craft examples to show the potential effectiveness of the parallel algorithm. We create three models (*PAR1*, *PAR2* and *PAR3*) such that the their state space contains several SCCs, each of which has big number of states. As a result, worker threads can be dispatched with substantial workload. Correctness of all these algorithms requires ESF and SGF.

In Table 2, we can see that *pmc* is working well in *PAR1* example, where the average SCC size is big and the SCC ratio is not very low. The performance is even better (60% speedup) when the SCC ratio increases to 0.5 in *PAR2* example. The *PAR3* example almost produces the ideal case (72% speedup) such that the four cores are fully loaded. Since there are more SCCs than cores, further speedup could be achieved if there were more cores. ESF case in *PAR2* gives a worst case mentioned in Section 4.3 for strong fairness checking, hence it ends up with out of memory exception.

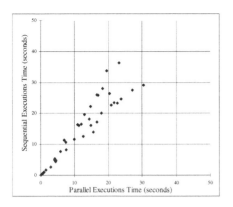

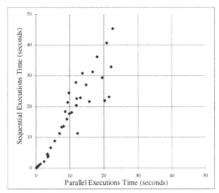

Fig. 6. Results on Intel Core2 6600 CPU   **Fig. 7.** Results on Intel Q9550 CPU

The experiment results in Table 1 and 2 confirm that the speedup of parallel verification relies on the size and the number of non-trivial SCCs. Each SCC has four analysis actions as described in Section 4.1. If the size of SCCs is big and/or the number of SCCs is more than the number of cores, each worker thread will make full use of the available CPU-cores. Overall, *pmc* performs better than *mc* for big average SCC size and high SCC ratio.

To study the scalability of our approach with different number of CPU cores, we conduct the same experiments (model checking examples in Table 1 and *PARA*1 example under strong global fairness)[7] on a dual-core CPU (Figure 6) and a quad-core CPU[8] (Figure 7). The coordinate of each point (x, y) in the graphs represents *mc* execution time and *pmc* execution time of a model correspondingly. From the figures we can see that, points in Figure 6 are scattered between line $y = x$ and $y = 2x$, while points in Figure 7 are scattered between line $y = 2x$ and $y = 3x$. The average speedup of the parallel algorithm is 22.9% for quad-core CPU and 11.2% for dual-core CPU. This suggests that our approach is scalable for more CPU cores in general.

Besides PAT, there are a number of model checkers which are designed for similar application domains. It is, however, not easy to compare PAT with them. For instance, the refinement checker FDR does not support shared variables/arrays, and therefore, FDR's model is significantly different from PAT's. Further, FDR has no support for multi-core. The model checker SPIN supports verification of LTL properties. The multi-core parallel algorithm in SPIN is designed for model checking based on nested depth-first search. Nested depth-first-search works well for verification under no fairness. It can be twisted to perform model checking under fairness in the price of significant computational overhead, which has been

---

[7] *PARA*2 and *PARA*3 have high average SCC size and SCC ratio which is rare in real systems, so we exclude them in the salability testing.

[8] Since we calculate the speedup of *pmc* compared to *mc*, the absolute speed of the two CPUs is not important.

shown in [31]. As a result, it makes little sense here to compare performance of our parallel algorithm with SPIN's.

6   Related Works

LTL parallel verification is an active research area due to the prevalence of the multi-core CPU and distributed systems. There are various approaches in the literature, as discussed below.

Holzmann proposed an extension of the SPIN model checker for dual-core machines in [17]. The algorithms keep their linear time complexity and the liveness checking algorithm supports full LTL. The algorithm for checking safety properties scales well to N-core systems. The algorithm for liveness checking, which is based on the original SPIN's nested DFS algorithm, can only be applied in dual-core systems. Furthermore, our approach handles different forms of fairness, while SPIN handles only process level weak fairness.

Lafuente [22] presented a cycle localization algorithm based on nested DFS, which is very similar to our ideas. In their approach, the main thread performs the first DFS to identify an accepting state, and the worker threads perform the second DFS to detect the fair cycle from the accepting state. Compared to this solution, our approach has the advantage that each SCC will be checked by one and only one worker thread.

A multi-core LTL model checking algorithm based on known distributed-memory algorithms is presented in [2]. This algorithm is linear for properties expressible as weak Büchi automata. However, the worst case complexity is quadratic. Our approach has no restriction on the types of LTL, and has linear time complexity in worst case.

A different approach to shared-memory model checking is presented in [19] based on CTL* translation to Hesitant Alternating Automata. The proposed algorithm uses non-emptiness game for deciding validity of the original formula and is therefore largely unrelated to the algorithms based on fair-cycle detection.

Barnat, Chaloupka and Pol gave a comprehensive survey in the distributed SCC decomposition algorithms [3]. We briefly list some of important ones in the following. These algorithms are designed for distributed systems and has quadratical or cubic order of complexity.

MAP. The idea of the Maximal Accepting Predecessor algorithm [6,8] relies on the fact that every accepting vertex inside an accepting cycle is its own predecessor. Direct implementation from this idea would give expensive computation and store all proper accepting predecessors of all (accepting) vertices. To solve this problem, the MAP algorithm stores only a single representative of all proper accepting predecessor. The time complexity of the algorithm is $O(a^2 \times m)$, where a is the number of accepting vertices and m is the number of edges.

OWCTY. The One Way Catch Them Young algorithm [12,9] is to try to repeatedly remove vertices from the graph that cannot lie on an accepting cycle. The two removal rules of this algorithm are explained as follows: (1) a vertex is removed from the graph if it has no successors in the graph (the vertex cannot lie on a cycle), and (2) a vertex is removed if it cannot reach an accepting vertex (a potential cycle the vertex lies on is non-accepting). The algorithm continues the removal steps until there are more vertices to be removed. In the end, either there are some vertices remaining in the graph meaning that the original graph contained an accepting cycle, or all vertices have been removed meaning that the original graph had no accepting cycles. The time complexity of the algorithm is $O(h \times m)$ where h is the height of the SCC quotient graph. Here the factor m comes from the computation of elimination rules while the factor h relates to the number of global iterations the removal rules must be applied.

NEGC. The idea behind the Negative Cycle Algorithm [7] is to transform the LTL model checking problem to the problem of negative cycle detection. Every edge of the graph outgoing from a non-accepting vertex is labeled with 0 while every edge outgoing from an accepting vertex is labeled with 1. Clearly, the graph contains a negative cycle if and only if it has an accepting cycle. The worst case time complexity of the algorithm is $O(n \times m)$, where n is the number of vertices and m is the number of edges.

OBF. This algorithm is based on a recent technique OWCTY-BWD-FWD (OBF) [4,5]. It identifies a number of independent subgraphs (called OBF slices) in $O(n + m)$ time, where n is the number of vertices and m is the number of edges. The slices are then decomposed using the FB algorithm. This algorithm assumes the input graph to be rooted, i.e., we have an initial vertex from which all other vertices are reachable. The time complexity of the algorithm is $O(n \times (n + m))$.

7   Conclusion

In this work, we proposed a parallel LTL-verification on fairness enhanced systems in multi-core shared-memory architecture. Based on the Tarjan's algorithm, our approach separated the SCC analysis into workers threads by careful algorithm design. Our approach is holistic, which does not only take care of LTL verification but also check the fairness constraints satisfaction in one goal. Fairness enhanced systems may contains big and complicated SCC structures in the state space. Our approach can split the workload to worker threads to achieve performance improvement. The solution is on-the-fly and the complexity is linear to the size of state space. We have implemented this technique in our home grown model checker PAT. The experimental results on real world systems suggested our solution is efficient and scalable to multi-cores.

It is a well known fact, that a distributed-memory, parallel algorithm is straightforwardly transformed into a shared-memory one. But not vise verse. One of the future work is to migrate our approach into distributed systems with the aim of minimizing the communication overhead. Furthermore, we will conduct more experiments in the future to see both the scalability and limitations with more CPU cores.

References

1. Angluin, D., Aspnes, J., Fischer, M.J., Jiang, H.: Self-stabilizing Population Protocols. In: Anderson, J.H., Prencipe, G., Wattenhofer, R. (eds.) OPODIS 2005. LNCS, vol. 3974, pp. 103–117. Springer, Heidelberg (2006)
2. Barnat, J., Brim, L., Ročkai, P.: Scalable Multi-core LTL Model-Checking. In: Bošnački, D., Edelkamp, S. (eds.) SPIN 2007. LNCS, vol. 4595, pp. 187–203. Springer, Heidelberg (2007)
3. Barnat, J., Chaloupka, J., Van De Pol, J.: Distributed Algorithms for SCC Decomposition. Journal of Logic and Computation (to appear, 2009)
4. Barnat, J., Chaloupka, J., van de Pol, J.: Improved Distributed Algorithms for SCC Decomposition. ENTCS 198(1), 63–77 (2008)
5. Barnat, J., Moravec, P.: Parallel Algorithms for Finding SCCs in Implicitly Given Graphs. In: Brim, L., Haverkort, B.R., Leucker, M., van de Pol, J. (eds.) FMICS 2006 and PDMC 2006. LNCS, vol. 4346, pp. 316–330. Springer, Heidelberg (2007)
6. Brim, L., Cerna, I., Moravec, P., Simsa, J.: Accepting Predecessors are Better than Back Edges in Distributed LTL Model-Checking. In: Hu, A.J., Martin, A.K. (eds.) FMCAD 2004. LNCS, vol. 3312, pp. 352–366. Springer, Heidelberg (2004)
7. Brim, L., Cerná, I., Krcál, P., Pelánek, R.: Distributed LTL Model Checking Based on Negative Cycle Detection. In: Hariharan, R., Mukund, M., Vinay, V. (eds.) FSTTCS 2001. LNCS, vol. 2245, p. 96. Springer, Heidelberg (2001)
8. Brim, L., Cerna, I., Moravec, P., Simsa, J.: How to Order Vertices for Distributed LTL Model-Checking Based on Accepting Predecessors. In: Proceedings of 4th International Workshop on Parallel and Distributed Methods in verification, pp. 1–12 (2005)
9. Cerna, I., Mu, F., Cerna, I., Cerna, I., Pelnek, R., Pelanek, R.: Distributed explicit fair cycle detection: Set based approach (2002)
10. Courcoubetis, C., Vardi, M.Y., Wolper, P., Yannakakis, M.: Memory-Efficient Algorithms for the Verification of Temporal Properties. Formal Methods in System Design 1(2/3), 275–288 (1992)
11. Fischer, M.J., Jiang, H.: Self-stabilizing Leader Election in Networks of Finite-state Anonymous Agents. In: Shvartsman, M.M.A.A. (ed.) OPODIS 2006. LNCS, vol. 4305, pp. 395–409. Springer, Heidelberg (2006)
12. Fisler, K., Fraer, R., Kamhi, G., Vardi, M.Y., Yang, Z.: Is There a Best Symbolic Cycle-Detection Algorithm? In: Margaria, T., Yi, W. (eds.) TACAS 2001. LNCS, vol. 2031, pp. 420–434. Springer, Heidelberg (2001)
13. Geldenhuys, J., Valmari, A.: More Efficient On-the-fly LTL Verification with Tarjan's Algorithm. Theoritical Computer Science 345(1), 60–82 (2005)
14. Giannakopoulou, D., Magee, J., Kramer, J.: Checking Progress with Action Priority: Is it Fair. In: Proceedings of the 7th ACM SIGSOFT Symposium on the Foundations of Software Engineering (FSE 1999), pp. 511–527 (1999)
15. Henzinger, M.R., Telle, J.A.: Faster Algorithms for the Nonemptiness of Streett Automata and for Communication Protocol Pruning. In: Karlsson, R., Lingas, A. (eds.) SWAT 1996. LNCS, vol. 1097, pp. 16–27. Springer, Heidelberg (1996)
16. Holzmann, G.J.: The SPIN Model Checker: Primer and Reference Manual. Addison Wesley, Reading (2003)
17. Holzmann, G.J., Bosnacki, D.: The Design of a Multicore Extension of the SPIN Model Checker. IEEE Trans. Softw. Eng. 33(10), 659–674 (2007)
18. Holzmann, G.J., Peled, D., Yannakakis, M.: On Nested Depth-first Search. In: The Spin Verification System, pp. 23–32 (1996)

19. Inggs, C.P., Barringer, H.: CTL* Model Checking on a Shared-memory Architecture. Form. Methods Syst. Des. 29(2), 135–155 (2006)
20. Kesten, Y., Pnueli, A., Raviv, L., Shahar, E.: Model Checking with Strong Fairness. Formal Methods and System Design 28(1), 57–84 (2006)
21. Kurshan, R.P.: Computer-Aided Verification of Coordinating Processes: The Automata-Theoretic Approach. Princeton university press, Princeton (1995)
22. Lafuente, A.L.: Simplified Distributed LTL Model Checking by Localizing Cycles. Technical report, Institute of Computer Science, Albert-Ludwings Universität Freiburg (2002)
23. Lamport, L.: Fairness and Hyperfairness. Distributed Computing 13(4), 239–245 (2000)
24. Lamport, L.: Proving the Correctness of Multiprocess Programs. IEEE Transactions on Software Engineering 3(2), 125–143 (1977)
25. Lehmann, D.J., Pnueli, A., Stavi, J.: Impartiality, Justice and Fairness: The Ethics of Concurrent Termination. In: Even, S., Kariv, O. (eds.) ICALP 1981. LNCS, vol. 115, pp. 264–277. Springer, Heidelberg (1981)
26. Musuvathi, M., Qadeer, S.: Fair Stateless Model Checking. In: ACM SIGPLAN 2008 Conference on Programming Language Design and Implementation (PLDI 2008), pp. 362–371. ACM, New York (2008)
27. Pnueli, A., Sa'ar, Y.: All You Need Is Compassion. In: Logozzo, F., Peled, D.A., Zuck, L.D. (eds.) VMCAI 2008. LNCS, vol. 4905, pp. 233–247. Springer, Heidelberg (2008)
28. Reif, J.H.: Depth-First Search is Inherently Sequential. Information Processing Letters 20(5), 229–234 (1985)
29. Sun, J., Liu, Y., Dong, J.S., Chen, C.Q.: Integrating Specification and Programs for System Modeling and Verification. In: Proceedings of the 3rd IEEE International Symposium on Theoretical Aspects of Software Engineering (TASE 2009), pp. 127–135 (2009)
30. Sun, J., Liu, Y., Dong, J.S., Pang, J.: Towards a Toolkit for Flexible and Efficient Verification under Fairness. Technical Report TRB2/09, National Univ. of Singapore (December 2008), http://www.comp.nus.edu.sg/~pat/report.ps
31. Sun, J., Liu, Y., Dong, J.S., Pang, J.: PAT: Towards Flexible Verification under Fairness. In: Proceedings of the 21th International Conference on Computer Aided Verification (CAV 2009), Grenoble, France, pp. 702–708 (2009)
32. Sun, J., Liu, Y., Dong, J.S., Wang, H.H.: Specifying and Verifying Event-based Fairness Enhanced Systems. In: Liu, S., Maibaum, T., Araki, K. (eds.) ICFEM 2008. LNCS, vol. 5256, pp. 318–337. Springer, Heidelberg (2008)
33. Tarjan, R.: Depth-first Search and Linear Graph Algorithms. SIAM Journal on Computing 2, 146–160 (1972)

Combining Static Model Checking with Dynamic Enforcement Using the Statecall Policy Language

Anil Madhavapeddy

Imperial College,
South Kensington, London SW1 2AZ, UK
a.madhavapeddy@imperial.ac.uk

Abstract. Internet protocols encapsulate a significant amount of state, making implementing the host software complex. In this paper, we define the Statecall Policy Language (SPL) which provides a usable middle ground between ad-hoc coding and formal reasoning. It enables programmers to embed automata in their code which can be statically model-checked using SPIN and dynamically enforced. The performance overheads are minimal, and the automata also provide higher-level debugging capabilities. We also describe some practical uses of SPL by describing the automata used in an SSH server written entirely in OCaml/SPL.

Constructing modern Internet servers is a difficult proposition, since the software must encapsulate a significant amount of state and deal with a variety of incoming packet types, complex configurations and versioning inconsistencies. Network applications are also expected to be liberal in interpreting received data packets and must reliably deal with timing and ordering issues arising from the "best-effort" nature of Internet data traffic.

Due to this complexity, mechanical verification techniques are very useful to guarantee safety, security and reliability properties. One mature formal method used to verify properties about systems is *model checking*. Software model-checking involves: (*i*) creating an abstract model of a complex application; (*ii*) validating this model against the application; and (*iii*) checking safety properties against the abstract model. To non-experts, steps (*i*) and (*ii*) are often the most daunting. How does one decide which aspects of the application to include in the abstract model? How does one determine whether the abstraction inadvertently "hides" critical bugs? If a counter-example is found, how does one determine whether this is a genuine bug or just a modeling artifact?

In this paper, we present the Statecall Policy Language (SPL) which simplifies the model specification and validation tasks with a view to making model checking more accessible to regular programmers. SPL is a high-level modelling language which enables developers to specify models in terms of allowable program events (e.g. valid sequences of received network packets). We have implemented a compiler that translates SPL into both PROMELA and a general-purpose programming language (e.g. OCaml). The generated PROMELA can be used with

K. Breitman and A. Cavalcanti (Eds.): ICFEM 2009, LNCS 5885, pp. 446–465, 2009.

SPIN [1] in order to check static properties of the model. The OCaml code provides an executable model in the form of a *safety monitor*. A developer can link this safety monitor against their application in order to *dynamically* ensure that the application's behaviour does not deviate from the model. If the safety monitor detects that the application has violated the model then it logs this event and terminates the application.

Although this technique simplifies model specification and validation it is, of course, not appropriate for all systems. For example, dynamically shutting down a fly-by-wire control system when a model violation is detected is not an option. However, we observe that there *is* a large class of applications where dynamic termination, while not desirable, is preferable to (say) a security breach. Melange [2] focusses on constructing correct, clean-room implementations of Internet applications using statically type-safe languages, and SPL delivers real benefits in this area. None of the major implementations of protocols such as HTTP (Apache), SMTP (Sendmail/Postfix), or DNS (BIND) are regularly model-checked by their development teams. All of them regularly suffer from serious security flaws ranging from low-level buffer overflows to subtle high-level protocol errors, some of which could have been caught by using model checking. In this paper, we use the Melange SSH [3] server as an example of how an application using SPL can be model-checked without sacrificing performance (§3.1) and enforcing critical security properties (§3.2) that are informally specified in the RFC documents.

There is no "perfect" way of specifying complex state machines, and the literature contains many different languages for this purpose (e.g. SDL [4], Estelle [5], Statemate [6], or Esterel [7]). In recognition of this, the SPL language is very specialised to expressing valid sequences of packets for Internet protocols and is translated into a more general intermediate "Control Flow Automaton" representation first proposed by Henzinger et al. [8]. The output code is generated from this graph, allowing for other state machine languages to be used in the future without requiring the backend code generators to be rewritten.

1   Statecall Policy Language

SPL is used to specify sequences of events which represent non-deterministic finite state automata. The automaton inputs are referred to as *statecalls*—these can represent any program events such as the transmission of receipt of network packets or the completion of some computation. The syntax of the language is written using a familiar 'C'-like syntax, with built-in support for non-deterministic choice operators in the style of Occam's ALT [9]. Statecalls are represented by capitalized identifiers, and SPL functions use lower-case identifiers. Semicolons are used to specify sequencing (e.g. S1; S2 specifies that the statecall S1 must occur before the statecall S2).

1.1   Case Study

Before specifying SPL more formally, we explain it via a simple case study—the UNIX `ping` utility which transmits and receives ICMP Echo requests and measures their latencies. A simple `ping` automaton with just 3 statecalls could be written as:

```
automaton ping() {
  Initialize;
  multiple (1..) {
   Transmit_Ping;
   Receive_Ping;
  }
}
```

This automaton guarantees that the statecalls must initially operate in the following order: `Initialize`, `Transmit_Ping`, and `Receive_Ping`. Since a realistic implementation of ping transmits and receives packets continuously, we also use the `multiple` keyword in our SPL specification. Using this automaton, the `ping` process can perform initialisation once, and then transmit and receive ping packets forever; an attempt to initialise more than once is not permitted. In a realistic network a ping response might never be received, and the non-deterministic `either`/`or` operator allows programmers to represent this scenario.

```
automaton ping() {
  Initialize;
  multiple (1..) {
    Transmit_Ping;
    either {
      Receive_Ping;
    } or {
      Timeout_Ping;
    };
  }
}
```

`ping` provides a number of command-line options that can modify the program behaviour. For example, `ping -c 10` requests that only 10 ICMP packets be sent in total, and `ping -w` specifies that we must never timeout, but wait forever for a ping reply. We represent these constraints by introducing *state variables* into SPL as follows:

```
automaton ping(int max_count, int count, bool can_timeout) {
  Initialize;
  during {
    count = 0;
    do {
      Transmit_Ping;
      either {
        Receive_Ping;
      } or (can_timeout) {
        Timeout_Ping;
      };
      count = count + 1;
    } until (count >= max_count);
```

```
  } handle {
    Sig_INFO;
    Print_Summary;
  };
}
```

Observe that the `either`/`or` constructs can be conditionally guarded in the style of Occam's ALT, and state variables can be assigned in an imperative style. A long-running `ping` process would need to receive UNIX signals at any point in its execution, take some action, and return to its original execution. Signal handlers are often a source of bugs due to their extremely asynchronous nature [10]—SPL provides a `during`/`handle` construct (used in the example above) which models them by permitting a state transition into alternative statement blocks during normal execution of an SPL specification.

Once we are satisfied that our SPL specification is of suitable granularity, the SPL compiler is run over it. The compiler outputs several targets: (*i*) a graphical visualisation using the Graphviz tool [11] as seen in Figure 1 for the example above; (*ii*) a non-deterministic model in the PROMELA language; and (*iii*) an executable model designed to be linked in with an application. The OCaml interface for the executable model is shown below:

```
exception Bad_statecall

type t = [ 'Initialize | 'Print_summary | 'Receive_ping
  | 'Sig_info | 'Timeout_ping | 'Transmit_ping ]

type s
val init : max_count:int -> count:int -> can_timeout:bool ->
  unit -> s
val tick : s -> t -> s
```

This code is linked in with the main `ping` application, and appropriate calls to initialize the automaton and invoke statecalls are inserted in the code. Crucially, we do not mandate a single style of invoking statecalls; instead the programmer can choose between automatic mechanisms (e.g. MPL [2] packet parsing code can automatically invoke statecalls when transmitting or receiving packets), language-assisted means (e.g. functional combinators, object inheritance, or pre-processors such as `cpp`), or even careful manual insertion in places where other methods are inconvenient.

1.2 Syntax and Typing Rules

SPL syntax is presented in Figure 2 with an extended Backus-Naur Form [12]. We represent terminals as *term*, tokens as `token`, alternation with {*one* | *two*}, optional elements as [*optional*], elements which must repeat once or more as (*term*)+ and elements which may appear never or many times as (*term*)*.

SPL is a first order imperative language, extended from Cardelli's simple imperative language [13]. We distinguish between *commands* (without a return value) and *expressions* which do have a return value. Function and automaton

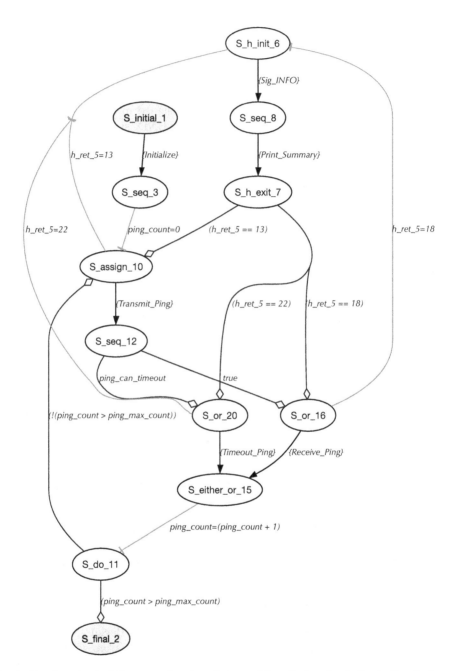

Fig. 1. Graph output of the example `ping` state machine. Red nodes indicate the start and final states, black edges are statecalls, blue edges are conditional, and green edges are state variable assignments.

$$main \rightarrow (fdecl)+ \ eof$$
$$fdecl \rightarrow \{\texttt{automaton} \mid \texttt{function}\} \ id \ [\ fargs \ ] \ fbody$$
$$fargs \rightarrow (\ \{\texttt{int} \ id \mid \texttt{bool} \ id\} \ [, \ fargs] \ )$$
$$fcall\text{-}args \rightarrow id \ [, \ fcall\text{-}args]$$
$$statecall\text{-}args \rightarrow statecall \ [, \ statecall\text{-}args]$$
$$fbody \rightarrow \{ \ (statement)^* \ \} \ [;]$$
$$int\text{-}range \rightarrow (\ [int] \ .. \ [int] \ ) \quad \mid \quad (\ int \ )$$
$$statement \rightarrow statecall \ ; \quad \mid \quad id \ (\ fcall\text{-}args \ ) \ ;$$
$$\mid \quad \texttt{always-allow} \ (\ statecall\text{-}args \ ) \ fbody$$
$$\mid \quad \texttt{multiple} \ int\text{-}range \ fbody \quad \mid \quad \texttt{optional} \ fbody$$
$$\mid \quad \texttt{either} \ [\ guard \ ] \ fbody \ (\texttt{or} \ [\ guard \ ] \ fbody)+$$
$$\mid \quad \texttt{do} \ fbody \ \texttt{until} \ guard \ ;$$
$$\mid \quad \texttt{while} \ guard \ fbody$$
$$\mid \quad id \ \texttt{=} \ expr \ ;$$
$$\mid \quad \texttt{during} \ fbody \ (\texttt{handle} \ fbody)+$$
$$\mid \quad \texttt{exit} \ ; \quad \mid \quad \texttt{abort} \ ;$$
$$guard \rightarrow (\ expr \ )$$
$$expr \rightarrow int \quad \mid \quad id \quad \mid \quad (\ expr \ )$$
$$\mid \quad expr \ \texttt{+} \ expr \quad \mid \quad expr \ \texttt{-} \ expr$$
$$\mid \quad expr \ \texttt{*} \ expr \quad \mid \quad expr \ \texttt{/} \ expr$$
$$\mid \quad \texttt{-} \ expr \quad \mid \quad \texttt{true} \quad \mid \quad \texttt{false}$$
$$\mid \quad expr \ \texttt{\&\&} \ expr \quad \mid \quad expr \ || \ expr \quad \mid \quad \texttt{not} \ expr$$
$$\mid \quad expr > expr \quad \mid \quad expr >= expr$$
$$\mid \quad expr < expr \quad \mid \quad expr <= expr$$
$$\mid \quad expr = expr$$

Fig. 2. EBNF grammar for SPL specifications

names are distinct, and are considered commands. Function types are written $\rho_1 \times \ldots \times \rho_i$, or abbreviated to ρ. Γ_α represents a global environment with type signatures for functions and Γ a per-function environment containing state variable bindings. SPL does not have any built-in functions, so all type signatures are obtained from the SPL specifications.

Table 1 lists the imperative type judgements and Table 2 establishes the basic typing rules. Note that procedure environments contain only the variables passed in as arguments to the function declaration, and no global variables are permitted. Table 3 and Table 4 list the type rules for expressions and statements.

Table 1. Type Judgments for SPL

$\Gamma \vdash \diamond$	Γ is a well-formed environment
$\Gamma \vdash A$	A is a well-formed type in Γ
$\Gamma \vdash C$	C is a well-formed command in Γ
$\Gamma \vdash E : A$	E is a well-formed expression of type A in Γ

Table 2. Basic environment and typing rules

(ENV ϕ)   (ENV x)   (TYPE INT)

$$\frac{}{\phi \vdash \diamond} \qquad \frac{\Gamma \vdash A \qquad I \notin dom(\Gamma)}{\Gamma, I : A \vdash \diamond} \qquad \frac{\Gamma \vdash \diamond}{\Gamma \vdash Int}$$

(TYPE BOOL)   (DECL PROC)

$$\frac{\Gamma \vdash \diamond}{\Gamma \vdash Bool} \qquad \frac{\phi, \boldsymbol{x} : \boldsymbol{\rho} \vdash C \qquad \Gamma_\alpha, I : \boldsymbol{\rho} \vdash \diamond}{\Gamma_\alpha \vdash (\mathbf{fun}\ I\ (\boldsymbol{x} \times \boldsymbol{\rho}) = C)}$$

Table 3. Expression typing rules

(EXPR BOOL)   (EXPR INT)   (EXPR VAL)

$$\frac{\Gamma \vdash \diamond \qquad x \in \{true, false\}}{\Gamma \vdash x : Bool} \qquad \frac{\Gamma \vdash \diamond}{\Gamma \vdash N : Int} \qquad \frac{\Gamma_1, I : A, \Gamma_2 \vdash \diamond}{\Gamma_1, I : A, \Gamma_2 \vdash I : A}$$

(EXPR NOT)   (EXPR BOOLOP)

$$\frac{\Gamma \vdash E_1 : Bool}{\Gamma \vdash \mathbf{not}\ E_1 : Bool} \qquad \frac{\Gamma \vdash E_1 : Bool \qquad \Gamma \vdash E_2 : Bool \qquad O_1 \in \{\mathbf{and, or}\}}{\Gamma \vdash O_1(E_1, E_2) : Bool}$$

(EXPR INTOP)

$$\frac{\Gamma \vdash E_1 : Int \qquad \Gamma \vdash E_2 : Int \qquad O_1 \in \{+, -, \times, \div\}}{\Gamma \vdash O_1(E_1, E_2) : Int}$$

(EXPR COMPOP)

$$\frac{\Gamma \vdash E_1 : Int \qquad \Gamma \vdash E_2 : Int \qquad O_1 \in \{=, >, \geq, <, \leq\}}{\Gamma \vdash O_1(E_1, E_2) : Bool}$$

Table 4. Command typing rules

(CMD ASSIGN)   (CMD SEQUENCE)   (CMD ALLOW)

$$\frac{\Gamma \vdash I : A \qquad \Gamma \vdash E : A}{\Gamma \vdash I \leftarrow E} \qquad \frac{\Gamma \vdash C_1 \qquad \Gamma \vdash C_2}{\Gamma \vdash C_1; C_2} \qquad \frac{\Gamma \vdash C}{\Gamma \vdash \mathbf{allow}\ C}$$

(CMD EITHER OR)   (CMD DO UNTIL)

$$\frac{\Gamma \vdash C_{1..n} \qquad \Gamma \vdash E_{1..n} : Bool}{\Gamma \vdash \mathbf{either}\ (C_1 \times E_1 \ldots C_n \times E_n)} \qquad \frac{\Gamma \vdash E : Bool \qquad \Gamma \vdash C}{\Gamma \vdash (\mathbf{until}\ E = C)}$$

(CMD MULTIPLE)   (CMD WHILE)

$$\frac{\Gamma \vdash E_1 : Int \qquad \Gamma \vdash E_2 : Int \qquad \Gamma \vdash C}{\Gamma \vdash (\mathbf{multiple}\ E_1\ E_2 = C)} \qquad \frac{\Gamma \vdash E : Bool \qquad \Gamma \vdash C}{\Gamma \vdash (\mathbf{while}\ E = C)}$$

(CMD FUNCTION CALL)

$$\frac{\Gamma_\alpha^1, I : \boldsymbol{\rho}, \Gamma_\alpha^2 \vdash \diamond \qquad \Gamma \vdash \boldsymbol{x} : \boldsymbol{\rho}}{\Gamma_\alpha^1, I : \boldsymbol{\rho}, \Gamma_\alpha^2 \vdash \mathbf{call}\ I\ \boldsymbol{x}}$$

(CMD EXIT)   (CMD ABORT)

$$\frac{}{\Gamma \vdash \mathbf{exit}} \qquad \frac{}{\Gamma \vdash \mathbf{abort}}$$

2   Intermediate Representation

This section defines the Control Flow Automaton graph used as an intermediate representation of SPL specifications (§2.1), the semantics of multiple automata in the same SPL specification (§2.2), and finally optimisations applied to the CFA to reduce the number of states (§2.3). The CFA is a good abstraction for a software-based non-deterministic model and it is often used by model extraction tools (e.g. BLAST [8]) as the representation into which C source code is converted. Since there are a myriad of state-machine languages similar to SPL which share the properties formalised by Schneider's software automata [14], our adoption of the CFA representation ensures that the back-ends of the SPL toolchain (e.g. the PROMELA output) remain useful even if the front-end language is changed into something specialised for another task.

2.1   Control Flow Automaton

The SPL compiler transforms specifications into an extended Control Flow Automaton (CFA) [8] graph. A CFA represents program states and a finite set of state variables in blocks, with the edges containing conditionals, assignments, statecalls or termination operations. The CFA is non-deterministic and multiple states can be active simultaneously. More formally, our *extended control flow automaton* C is a tuple $(Q, q_0, X, S, Op, \rightarrow)$ where Q is a finite set of control locations, q_0 is the initial control location, X a finite set of typed variables, S a finite set of statecalls, Op a set of operations, and $\rightarrow \subseteq (Q \times Op \times Q)$ a finite set of edges labeled with operations. An edge (q, op, q') can be denoted $q \xrightarrow{op} q'$. The set Op of operations contains: (*i*) *basic blocks* of instructions, which consist of finite sequences of assignments **svar** = **exp** where **svar** is a state variable from X and **exp** is an equivalently typed expression over X; (*ii*) *conditional predicates* **if(p)**, where **p** is a boolean expression over X that must be true for the edge to be taken; (*iii*) *statecall predicates* **msg(s)**, where **s** is a statecall (**s** $\in S$) received by the automaton; and (*iv*) *abort traps*, which immediately signal the termination of the automaton. From the perspective of a Mealy machine, the input alphabet Σ consists of statecall predicates and the output alphabet $\wedge$ is the remaining operations. Thus a CFA graph is driven purely by statecall inputs, and the other types of operations serve to hide the state space explosion of a typical software model.

The CFA graph is constructed from SPL statements by recursively applying transformation rules to an initial state I and a final state O. Figure 3 illustrates the transformations for the basic SPL statements diagrammatically with the circles and lines representing CFA nodes and edges. The diamonds indicate a recursive application of the transformation rules with the initial and final states mapped to the input and outputs of the diamond node. Nodes within the dashed ellipses (named α, β, γ and so on) are newly created by the transformation rule. The **abort** and **exit** keywords signal the end of the automaton and thus do not connect to their output states. Each transformation rule has an environment $(\Gamma \times \Delta)$ where Γ is the list of always allowed statecalls as seen in **allow** blocks and

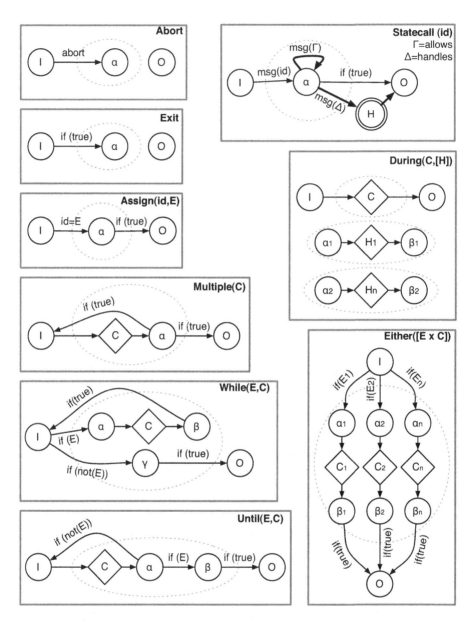

Fig. 3. Transformations of SPL statements into the corresponding CFA nodes

Δ represents statecalls which result in a transition to a handle clause (generated by the **during/handle** statement). A **during/handle** statement first creates all the handler nodes and transforms the main block with the handlers registered in the Δ environment. A **statecall** node creates a statecall edge and inserts appropriate edges to deal with **allow** and **during** handlers.

Some statements require the creation of new internal variables. The **multiple** call can optionally specify upper and lower bounds to the number of iterations; extra variables are automatically created to track these bounds in the CFA. **during/handle** statements create a new internal variable to track the state to which a handler must return. Function calls are either macro-expanded (if only called once) or temporary variables used to push and pop arguments in a single copy of the function graph (if called multiple times). An example of these internal variables can be seen in Figure 1 in our earlier `ping` sample.

2.2   Multiple Automata

It is often more convenient and readable to break down a complex protocol into smaller blocks which express the same protocol but with certain aspects factored out into simpler state machines. Accordingly, SPL specifications can define multiple automata, but the external interface hides this abstraction and only exposes a single, flat set of statecalls. The scope of automata names are global and flat; this is a deliberate design decision since the language is designed for light-weight abstractions that are embedded into portions of the main application code. Even a complex protocol such as SSH [3] can be broken down into smaller, more manageable automata—we have listed some of these in Appendix A. In this section, we explain how statecalls are routed to the individual automata contained in an SPL specification.

Each automaton executes in parallel and sees every statecall. If an automaton receives a statecall it was not expecting it reports an error. If *any* of the parallel automata report an error then the SPL model has been violated. When a statecall is received, it is dispatched *only* to automata which can potentially use that statecall at some stage in their execution.

More formally, let $\mathcal{A}$ represent an automaton or function definition in an SPL specification. Let $\mathcal{V}(\mathcal{A})$ represent the union of all the statecalls referenced in $\mathcal{A}$, and $\mathcal{F}(\mathcal{A})$ be the list of all functions called from $\mathcal{A}$. The *potentially visible statecalls* $\mathcal{P}(\mathcal{A})$ are the set of statecalls which the automaton $\mathcal{A}$ will use at some stage in its execution where $\mathcal{P}(\mathcal{A}) = \mathcal{V}(\mathcal{A}) \cup \{\mathcal{P}(\mathcal{F}_0) \dots \mathcal{P}(\mathcal{F}_n)\}$. A statecall is only dispatched to an automaton $\mathcal{A}$ if it is present in its potentially visible set $\mathcal{P}(\mathcal{A})$. Since the set of externally exposed statecalls $\mathcal{P}_{all} = \{\mathcal{P}(\mathcal{A}_0) \dots \mathcal{P}(\mathcal{A}_n)\}$ is calculated by the union of all the potentially visible sets of the automata contained in an SPL specification, it trivially follows that every statecall will be dispatched to at least one automaton.

This mechanism allows complex protocols such as SSH to be broken down into simpler automata which are still connected together by common messages. The SPL compiler can output the list of statecalls which are shared between automata as a development aid; in practise while specifying Internet protocols we have observed that most automata share only one or two statecalls between them (normally global messages to indicate protocol termination or auth status).

2.3   Optimisation

The transformation rules defined earlier (§2.1) result in a CFA which has a number of redundant edges (e.g. *if(true)* conditionals). The SPL compiler reduces the number of states in the CFA without modifying the graph semantics. We iterate over the graph and perform constant folding [15] to simplify conditional expressions. Since SPL only has expressions with booleans and integers, the folding is a simple recursive pattern match.

The CFA is then traversed to eliminate redundant nodes: (i) for a node Q_i, all edges from the node are of the form $Q_i \xrightarrow{if(true)} Q_o$ or (ii) for a node Q_o, all edges pointing to the node are of the form $Q_i \xrightarrow{if(true)} Q_o$. The initial state of the automaton is left unoptimised, so that automata can have a single entry point for simplicity.

3   Compiler Outputs

The SPL compiler outputs automata in: (i) OCaml to be embedded as a dynamic safety monitor; (ii) PROMELA to statically verify safety properties using a model checker such as SPIN; and (iii) HTML/AJAX to permit debugging of SPL models embedded in an executing application. Although we specifically describe an OCaml interface here, the compiler can also be easily extended to other type-safe languages (e.g. Java or C#), allowing application authors to write programs in their language of choice and still use the SPL tool-chain.

When describing each output, we will also analyze that output's use in the Melange SSH server. The Melange SSH server is written in pure OCaml, and uses the Meta Packet Language [2] to do the low-level packet parsing, and SPL to enforce the higher-level protocol constraints. The SSH protocol itself is defined in the form of Internet RFC documents [3].

3.1   OCaml

The OCaml output from the SPL compiler is designed to: (i) dynamically enforce the SPL model and raise an exception if it is violated; and (ii) provide real-time monitoring, debugging and logging of the SPL models. The SPL compiler generates OCaml code with a simple external interface which provides a: (i) variant type of statecalls for that model; (ii) constructor for a fresh automaton; and (iii) tick function which accepts a statecall and advances the automaton.

If a bad statecall is received, the automaton raises an exception. The interface is purely functional, thus allowing an automaton to be "rolled back" by keeping a list of previous automaton values.

The internal implementation takes several steps to make transitions as fast as possible. Since the only edges in the CFA which can "block" during execution are the statecall edges, all other edges are statically unrolled during compile-time code generation. When unrolling non-statecall edges during code generation, assignment operations are statically tracked by the SPL compiler in a symbol table. This permits the compiler to apply constant folding when the resultant expressions are used as part of conditional nodes (or when creating new state descriptors). Multiple conditional checks involving the same variable are grouped into a single pattern match (this is useful in SPL specs with **during/handle** clauses). These are necessary even when using the optimising OCaml compiler since they represent constraints present in the SPL specification which are difficult to spot in the more low-level OCaml code output.

The performance impact of several automata running in parallel in an application is minimal. In the Melange SSH server, written purely in OCaml and using SPL specifications to enforce constraints in the transport and connection layers of the protocol, it has around a 2-3% impact on the throughput of the server during bulk copy operations (see Figure 4). Some of the SPL specifications used in the SSH server are listed in Appendix A, with the full versions present in the Melange source code at `http://melange.recoil.org/`.

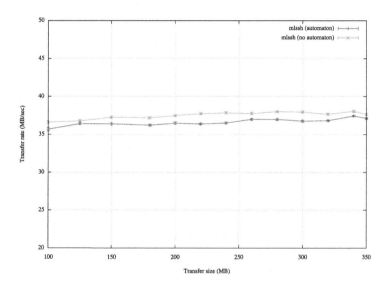

Fig. 4. Performance of the OCaml SSH server with and without the SPL automata

3.2   Model Checking

The SPL compiler also output PROMELA models from the SPL input, providing an easy way to statically reason about properties which are then dynamically enforced by the OCaml run-time automata. In the case of the SSH protocol, the SPL specification for the transport, authentication and global channel handling is a complex state machine, and an exhaustive safety verification in SPIN without any additional LTL constraints (i.e. testing assertions and invalid end-states) requires around 400MB of RAM and one minute to verify on a dual-G5 1.25GHz PowerMac. SPIN reports the following statistics:

```
State-vector 48 byte, depth reached 78709, errors: 0
1.41264e+07 states, stored (1.99736e+07 visited)
2.59918e+07 states, matched
4.59654e+07 transitions (= visited+matched)
7.85945e+07 atomic steps
```

The large number of atomic steps show the complexity reduction which results from the SPL compiler inserting `atomic` statements in the generated PROMELA to simulate the execution semantics of the OCaml safety monitors. Before this optimisation, messages would unnecessarily be interleaved and verification took orders of magnitude longer.

We now list some of the LTL formulae applied to the PROMELA output of the SSH global automaton and describe the security properties which they enforce. Unlike some other tools which translate state machine languages into PROMELA (e.g. Scott's SWIL language for interface descriptions [16]), we never require the manual modification of the PROMELA code (which would be dangerous since the equivalence between the model and the dynamically enforced SPL automaton would not be guaranteed any more). Instead, globally allocated state variables[1] are exposed within the model which can be referenced with LTL formulae, as shown below:

- $\Box(a \rightarrow \Box a)$ where (a $\leftarrow$ `transport_encrypted`) which informally reads "once the transport is encrypted, it will remain encrypted". This check ensures that the transport layer can never turn off encryption once a secure transport has been established for the lifetime of that connection.
- $\Box(a \rightarrow \Box(a \&\& b))$ where (a $\leftarrow$ `transport_serv_auth`) and (b $\leftarrow$ `transport_encrypted`) which informally reads "in the `transport` automaton, once `serv_auth` is `true`, both `serv_auth` and `encrypted` remain `true` forever". This guarantees that authentication can only happen over an encrypted connection.
- $\Box a$ where (a $\leftarrow$ `auth_success` + `auth_failed` < 2) informally reads "in the `auth` automaton, `success` and `failure` must never simultaneously be `true`". This restriction lets us use two boolean variables instead of a larger integer to store the 3 values for undecided, success or failure authentication states.
- $\Box(a \rightarrow X(b \parallel \Box\Diamond c))$ where (a $\leftarrow$ p == `Transmit_Auth_Success`) and (b $\leftarrow$ `auth_success`) and (c $\leftarrow$ `err`) informally reads "when an authentication success packet is transmitted, it must immediately be followed by the `success` variable being `true` or always eventually lead to an error."
- $\Box(a \rightarrow (b \parallel \Box\Diamond c))$ where (a $\leftarrow$ p == `Transmit_Transport_Accept_Auth`) and (b $\leftarrow$ `transport_encrypted`) and (c $\leftarrow$ `err`) which informally reads "if the authentication service is unlocked then the transport layer must be encrypted or an error always eventually occurs". This matches the security considerations section of the SSH authentication specification in RFC4252 [17] which states that "it assumed *(sic)* that this runs over a secure transport

---

[1] SPIN does not support partial order evaluation over local variables, so the SPL compiler safely promotes automaton-local variables to a global scope.

layer protocol, which has already authenticated the server machine, established an encrypted communications channel [...]".

– $\Box(a \rightarrow (b \ || \ \Box\Diamond c))$ where $(a \leftarrow p == \texttt{Receive\_Channel\_Open\_Session})$ and $(b \leftarrow \texttt{auth\_success})$ and $(c \leftarrow \texttt{err})$ which informally reads "requests to open a new channel are only allowed when authentication has been successful, or an error state is always eventually reached". This is in line with

Fig. 5. Screen capture of the AJAX debugger embedded into the SSH daemon, showing the global SPL automaton. The green states are valid statecalls, the pie chart shows the 5 most popular statecalls in real time, and the list on the left show recent statecalls.

the security considerations section of the SSH connection specification in RFC4254 [18] which states that "this protocol is assumed to run on top of a secure, authenticated transport".

These properties all reflect restrictions expressed informally in the SSH specifications [3,17,18], and can now be sure to either work correctly in the running SSH server, or terminate the connection to prevent a potential security breach.

3.3   AJAX Debugging

The SPL compiler can also include debugging stubs in the executable automata, most usefully in the form of HTML/AJAX code which can be accessed via a web browser. This page contains a real-time graphical view of all the automata embedded in the program, along with the set of valid states they can transition to next. Since the granularity of the SPL automata are chosen by the programmer, this is much more useful than the "raw" models obtained through static code analysis which often include a lot of superfluous information.

Figure 5 shows a screen capture of the SPL AJAX debugger single-stepping through the global SPL automaton for the Melange SSH server. The MLSSH server is blocked waiting for password authentication, having previously attempted to authenticate via null and public-key authentication. In our experience, the debugger was a valuable tool to debug complex protocol bugs in our implementation, as the single-stepping view via this debugger is significantly higher level than the alternative provided by either the native OCaml debugger or gdb.

4   Related Work

The Bandera tool-chain [19] is designed to ease the model-checking of Java source code. It includes components for program analysis and slicing, transformation, and visualisation. Bandera accepts Java source as input and requirements written in the Bandera Specification Language (BSL) [20]. A key design goal of BSL is to hide the intricacies of temporal logic by placing emphasis on common specification coding patterns (e.g. pre- and post-conditions to functions). BSL is also strongly tied to the source program code via references to variables and methods names. Much of Bandera's utility arises from its tools for model construction which eliminate redundant components [21], simplifying the eventual output.

The BLAST [8] project introduced the *lazy abstraction* paradigm for verifying safety properties about systems code. Lazy abstractions follows the following steps: (i) an abstraction is extracted from the source code; (ii) the abstraction is model-checked; and (iii) the model is then refined using counter-example analysis. The process is repeated until the model is sufficiently refined, and the resulting proof certificates are based on Proof Carrying Code [22]. This mechanism helps make the model extraction process more scalable by reducing the amount of time and effort required to create abstractions of systems code. In contrast to the conventional abtract-verify-refine loop, lazy abstraction builds abstract models on demand from the original source code. This results in a non-uniformedly detailed model which contains just enough detail to show a counter-example to the developer. SPL also provides an alternative way to provide non-uniform models by permitting the programmer to choose the level of granularity they want to write the models in.

Alur and Wang have tackled the problem of model checking real-world protocols by extracting a specification from RFCs and using symbolic refinement checking to verify the model against protocol implementations written in C [23]. They evaluate their technique by creating and verifying models of DHCP and PPP, and conclude that *"[manual model extraction] is unavoidable for extracting specification models since RFC documents typically describe the protocols in a tabular, but informal, format"*.

The Model-Carrying Code (MCC) project led by Sekar combines the model-extraction techniques described earlier with system call interception to provide a platform for the safe execution of untrusted binaries [24]. Untrusted code is bundled with a model of its security-relevant behaviour which can be formally verified against a local security policy by a model checker. The execution of the binary is dynamically verified by syscall interception to fit the model and the application terminated if a violation occurs. As Wagner and Soto point out [25], the low-level nature of syscall interception makes it easy for attackers to launch an observationally equivalent attack by crafting a valid sequence of syscalls, and so this technique is only useful as a last-resort if more formal and reliable verification techniques against the source code cannot be applied. We have drawn inspiration from the work described above, in particular the MCC approach of providing static models and dynamic enforcement, but our work operates at a higher level with explicit support from the application source code.

5   Conclusions

We have described the Statecall Policy language, which aims to provide a usable mechanism for programmers to integrate lightweight models into complex networked software. We solve the code/model equivalence problem by specifying models in our SPL language, and compiling them to multiple outputs for different purposes—model checking using SPIN by outputting PROMELA code, dynamical enforcement executables in OCaml, and even HTML/AJAX stubs for run-time debugging. It is currently targeted at applications written in OCaml and model checked using SPIN, but is simple to port to other languages and tools due to its use of the Control Flow Automaton intermediate graph.

We have also described practical uses of SPL in our complex Secure Shell server which uses several complex models to enforce critical security properties that are only informally specified in the official SSH RFCs.

We gratefully acknowledge funding from Intel Research and the UK Engineering and Physical Sciences Research Council grant EP/F024037/1.

References

1. Holzmann, G.J.: The SPIN Model Checker. Addison-Wesley, Reading (2003)
2. Madhavapeddy, A., Ho, A., Deegan, T., Scott, D., Sohan, R.: Melange: creating a functional internet. In: Ferreira, P., Gross, T.R., Veiga, L. (eds.) EuroSys, pp. 101–114. ACM, New York (2007)
3. Ylonen, T., Lonvick, C.: The Secure Shell (SSH) Protocol Architecture. RFC 4251 (Proposed Standard) (January 2006)
4. SDL: SDL forum society. Technical Report Recommendation Z.100, International Telecommunications Union, Geneva (1993)
5. ISO: Estelle—a formal description technique based on an extended state transition model. ISO 9074, International Organisation for Standardization, Geneva (1997)
6. Harel, D., Lachover, H., Naamad, A., Pnueli, A., Politi, M., Sherman, R., Shtul-Trauring, A.: Statemate: a working environment for the development of complex reactive systems. In: Proceedings of the 10th International Conference on Software Engineering (ICSE), pp. 396–406. IEEE Computer Society Press, Los Alamitos (1988)
7. Berry, G.: III. In: The Foundations of Esterel: Proof, Language, and Interaction (Essay in Honor of Robin Milner), pp. 425–454. MIT Press, Cambridge (2000)
8. Henzinger, T.A., Jhala, R., Majumdar, R., Necula, G.C., Sutre, G., Weimer, W.: Temporal-safety proofs for systems code. In: Brinksma, E., Larsen, K.G. (eds.) CAV 2002. LNCS, vol. 2404, pp. 526–538. Springer, Heidelberg (2002)
9. Jones, G.: Programming in Occam. Prentice-Hall, Hertfordshire (1986)
10. Chen, H., Wagner, D.: MOPS: an infrastructure for examining security properties of software. In: Proceedings of the 9th ACM Conference on Computer and Communications Security (CCS), pp. 235–244. ACM Press, New York (2002)
11. Gansner, E.R., North, S.C.: An open graph visualization system and its applications to software engineering. Software—Practice and Experience 30(11), 1203–1233 (2000)
12. Backus, J.W., Bauer, F.L., Green, J., Katz, C., McCarthy, J., Perlis, A.J., Rutishauser, H., Samelson, K., Vauquois, B., Wegstein, J.H., van Wijngaarden, A., Woodger, M.: Revised report on the algorithm language ALGOL 60. Communications of the ACM 6(1), 1–17 (1963)
13. Cardelli, L.: Type systems. In: Tucker, A.B. (ed.) The Computer Science and Engineering Handbook, pp. 2208–2236. CRC Press, Boca Raton (1997)
14. Schneider, F.B.: Enforceable security policies. ACM Transactions on Information Systems Security 3(1), 30–50 (2000)
15. Aho, A.V., Ullman, J.D.: Principles of Compiler Design. Computer Science and Information Processing. Addison-Wesley, Reading (1977)
16. Scott, D.J.: Abstracting Application-Level Security Policy for Ubiquitous Computing. PhD thesis, University of Cambridge (2005)
17. Ylonen, T., Lonvick, C.: The Secure Shell (SSH) Authentication Protocol. RFC 4252 (Proposed Standard) (January 2006)
18. Ylonen, T., Lonvick, C.: The Secure Shell (SSH) Connection Protocol. RFC 4254 (Proposed Standard) (January 2006)
19. Corbett, J.C., Dwyer, M.B., Hatcliff, J.: A language framework for expressing checkable properties of dynamic software. In: Havelund, K., Penix, J., Visser, W. (eds.) SPIN 2000. LNCS, vol. 1885, pp. 205–223. Springer, Heidelberg (2000)
20. Corbett, J.C., Dwyer, M.B., Hatcliff, J., Robby, Z.H.: Expressing checkable properties of dynamic systems: the Bandera Specification Language. International Journal on Software Tools for Technology Transfer 4(1), 34–56 (2002)

21. Corbett, J.C., Dwyer, M.B., Hatcliff, J., Laubach, S., Păsăreanu, C.S., Robby, Z.H.: Bandera: extracting finite-state models from Java source code. In: Proceedings of the 22nd International Conference on Software Engineering (ICSE), pp. 439–448. ACM Press, New York (2000)
22. Necula, G.C.: Proof-carrying code. In: Proceedings of the 24th ACM SIGPLAN-SIGACT Symposium on Principles of Programming Languages (POPL), Paris, France, pp. 106–119. ACM Press, New York (1997)
23. Alur, R., Wang, B.Y.: Verifying network protocol implementations by symbolic refinement checking. In: Berry, G., Comon, H., Finkel, A. (eds.) CAV 2001. LNCS, vol. 2102, pp. 169–181. Springer, Heidelberg (2001)
24. Sekar, R., Venkatakrishnan, V., Basu, S., Bhatkar, S., DuVarney, D.C.: Model-carrying code: a practical approach for safe execution of untrusted applications. In: Proceedings of the Nineteenth ACM symposium on Operating Systems Principles, pp. 15–28. ACM Press, New York (2003)
25. Wagner, D., Soto, P.: Mimicry attacks on host-based intrusion detection systems. In: Atluri, V. (ed.) Proceedings of the 9th ACM Conference on Computer and Communications Security (CCS), pp. 255–264. ACM, New York (2002)

A   SPL Policies for Secure Shell

In this appendix, we list an excerpt of the SPL policies for the Secure Shell (SSH) protocol. The full policies may be found in the Melange source code. There are two automata listed here which run in parallel (§2.2) and represent the transport and authentication layers respectively. The transport layer establishes an encrypted connection, and the authentication layer handles the negotiation of user credentials.

```
automaton transport (bool encrypted , bool serv_auth) {
  during {
    always_allow (Transmit_Transport_Debug ,
        Receive_Transport_Debug , Transmit_Transport_Ignore ,
        Receive_Transport_Ignore) {
      multiple {
      either {
        either {
          Transmit_Transport_KexInit;
          Receive_Transport_KexInit;
        } or (encrypted) {
          Receive_Transport_KexInit;
          Transmit_Transport_KexInit;
        }
        either {
          Expect_DHInit ;
          Receive_Dhgroupsha1_Init;
          Transmit_Dhgroupsha1_Reply;
        } or {
          Expect_GexInit ;
          Receive_Dhgexsha1_Request;
          Transmit_Dhgexsha1_Group;
```

```
            Receive_Dhgexsha1_Init;
            Transmit_Dhgexsha1_Reply;
          }
          Receive_Transport_NewKeys;
          Transmit_Transport_NewKeys;
          encrypted = true;
        } or (encrypted && !serv_auth) {
          Receive_Transport_ServiceReq_UserAuth;
          Transmit_Transport_ServiceAccept_UserAuth;
          serv_auth = true;
        }
      }
    }
  } handle {
    either { Signal_HUP; }
    or {
      either { Receive_Transport_Disconnect; }
      or {
        optional { Signal_QUIT; }
        Transmit_Transport_Disconnect;
        exit;
      }
    } or { Receive_Transport_Unimplemented; }
  }
}


automaton auth (bool success, bool failed) {
  Transmit_Transport_ServiceAccept_UserAuth;
  during {
    do {
      always_allow (Transmit_Auth_Banner) {
        either {
          Receive_Auth_Req_None;
          Transmit_Auth_Failure;
        } or {
          Receive_Auth_Req_Password_Request;
          either {
            Transmit_Auth_Success;
            success = true;
          } or {
            Transmit_Auth_Failure;
          }
        } or {
          Receive_Auth_Req_PublicKey_Request;
          either {
            Transmit_Auth_Success;
            success = true;
          } or {
            Transmit_Auth_Failure;
```

```
        }
      } or {
        Receive_Auth_Req_PublicKey_Check;
        either {
          Transmit_Auth_PublicKey_OK;
        } or {
          Transmit_Auth_Failure ;
        }
      } or {
        Notify_Auth_Permanent_Failure;
        failed = true;
      }
    }
  } until (success || failed);
} handle {
  Transmit_Transport_Disconnect;
  exit ;
}
}
```

Supporting Reuse of Event-B Developments through Generic Instantiation

Renato Silva and Michael Butler

School of Electronics and Computer Science
University of Southampton, UK
{ras07r,mjb}@ecs.soton.ac.uk

Abstract. It is believed that reusability in formal development should reduce the time and cost of formal modelling within a production environment. Along with the ability to reuse formal models, it is desirable to avoid unnecessary re-proof when reusing models. Event-B is a formal method that allows modelling and refinement of systems. Event-B supports generic developments through the context construct. Nevertheless Event-B lacks the ability to instantiate and reuse generic developments in other formal developments. We propose a way of instantiating generic models and extending the instantiation to a chain of refinements. We define sufficient proof obligations to ensure that the proofs associated to a generic development remain valid in an instantiated development thus avoiding re-proofs.

Keywords: formal methods, event-B, reusability, generic instantiation.

1 Introduction

Reusability has always been sought in several areas as a way to reduce time, cost and improve the productivity of developments [1]. Examples can be found in areas like software, mathematics and even formal methods. Generic Instantiation can be seen as a way of reusing components and solving difficulties raised by the construction of large and complex models [2,3]. The goal is to reuse generic developments (single model or a chain of refinements) and create components with similar properties instead of starting from scratch. Reusability is applied through the use of a *pattern* as the basic structure and afterwards each new component is generated through parameterisation.

We propose a generic instantiation approach for Event-B by instantiating machines. The instances inherit properties from the generic development (pattern) and afterwards are *parameterised* by renaming/replacing those properties to more specific names according to the instance. Proofs obligations are generated to ensure that assumptions used in the pattern are satisfied in the instantiation. In that sense our approach avoids re-proof pattern proof obligations in the instantiation. The models are developed in the Rodin platform [4], which is a toolset for Event-B [5]. A simple case study modelling a protocol communication is described to illustrate the use of instantiation.

K. Breitman and A. Cavalcanti (Eds.): ICFEM 2009, LNCS 5885, pp. 466–484, 2009.

A brief overview of the Event-B Language is given in Section 2. Section 3 defines how generic instantiation is interpreted by us. In section 4 instantiated machines are introduced. Section 5 gives an application of instantiation in combination with shared event composition. The application of instantiation to a chain of refinements is described in Section 6. Section 7 discusses an open question that arises when instantiating theorems and invariants in a pattern.

2   Event-B Language

Event-B is a formal methodology that uses mathematical techniques based on set theory and first order logic allowing the specification of systems. An abstract Event-B specification is divided into two parts: a static part called *context* and a dynamic part called *machine*. A machine *SEES* as many contexts as desired. The context consists of sets, constants and assumptions (axioms) of the system. Sets in the context can be seen as a collection of elements or a type definition. The machine contains the state variables whose values are assigned in *events*. Events can only occur when enable by their *guards* being true and as a result *actions* are executed. Events can have *parameters* that are local variables to the event and can be used by the guards or by the actions. The *INVARIANT* defines the dynamic properties of the specification. Proof obligations are generated to verify that the invariant is maintained before and after an event is enabled. Theorems are properties of the system that have proof obligations associated and usually are discharged based on other properties of the specified system.

An abstract Event-B specification can be refined by adding more details and becoming closer to the implementation (more concrete). A context *EXTENDS* an abstract context by adding sets, constants or axioms. Nonetheless the abstract context properties are still assumed. Refinement of a machine consists in refining existing events. The relation between variables in the concrete and abstract model is given by a *gluing invariant*. Proof obligations are generated to ensure that this invariant is preserved in the concrete model. Also it is possible to add new events that refine *skip* as long as the new events do not execute forever and the abstract events are not hampered.

3   Generic Instantiation

In order to explain our approach for Generic Instantiation we will use a simple case study. A protocol is modelled between two entities, Source and Destination, which communicate by sending messages through a channel. The content of the channel has a maximum dimension. To send a message it is necessary to add the content of the message to the channel. Based on the proposed requirements it is possible to create a context *ChannelParameters* to model the channel as seen in Fig. 1b.

The content of the message is of type *Message* and has a maximum dimension *max_size*. Figure 1a represents the machine side where a variable *channel* stores all the sent/received messages. The *channel* messages have type *Message* and

```
machine Channel sees ChannelParameters

variables channel

invariants
   @inv1 channel ⊆ Message
   @inv3 finite(channel)
   @inv2 card(channel) ≤ max_size

events
   event INITIALISATION
      then
         @act1 channel = ∅
   end

   event Send
      any m
      where
         @grd1 m ∈ Message
         @grd2 card(channel) < max_size
      then
         @act1 channel = channel ∪ {m}
   end

   event Receive
      any m
      where
         @grd1 m ∈ channel
      then
         @act1 channel = channel\{m}
   end
end
```

(a)

```
context ChannelParameters

constants max_size

sets Message

axioms
   @axm1 max_size ∈ N
end
```

(b)

Fig. 1. Machine *Channel* and respective context *ChannelParameters*

the number of messages in the channel is limited. Messages are introduced in the *channel* to be sent as seen in event *Send*. The event *Receive* models the reception of the message in the destination by extracting the messages from the *channel*. Elements in *ChannelParameters* context are the parameters (type and constant) for the *Channel* machine.

Now suppose we wish to model a bi-directional communication between two entities using two channels. Both channels are similar so an option is to *instantiate machine Channel* twice to create two instances: one channel called *Request* and the other *Response*. The protocol, represented in Fig. 2 starts by a message being sent from the Source. After arriving at the Destination, the reception of the message is acknowledged in the Source. Then a response is sent from the Destination and after arriving at the Source, it is also acknowledged in the Destination.

The instantiation of *Channel* is achieved by applying *machine instantiation*. An instance of the pattern *Channel* is created with more specific properties. A detailed description of the machine instantiation is described in Section 4. Moreover, a context containing the specific instances properties is required to model the protocol. In our case study we use the context *ProtocolTypes* in Fig. 3, where types *Request* and *Response* replace the more generic type *Message* and constants *qmax_size* and *pmax_size* replace *max_size*. This context must be provided by the modeller/developer.

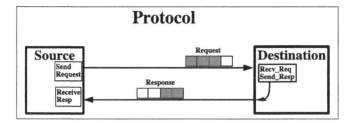

Fig. 2. Protocol diagram

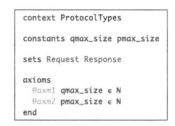

Fig. 3. ProtocolTypes Context

Abrial and Hallerstede [3] and Métayer et al [2] propose the use of generic instantiation for Event-B. It is suggested that the contexts of a development (equivalent to the pattern) can be merged and reused through instantiation in other developments. That proposal lacks a mechanism to apply the instantiation from the *pattern* to the instances. Therefore our work proposes a mechanism to instantiate machines and extend the instantiation to a refinement chain. The reusability of a development is expressed by instantiating a development (*pattern*) according to a more specific *problem*.

4 Generic Instantiation and Instantiated Machines

Inspired by the previous case study and having the ability to compose machines (Shared Event Composition plug-in [6]) and rename elements (Refactory plug-in[7]) in the Rodin platform, we propose an approach to instantiate machines. As mentioned the context plays an important role while instantiating since this is where the specific properties of the instance are defined (parameterisation). The use of context is briefly discussed before *instantiated machines* are introduced.

4.1 Contexts

As aforementioned, contexts in Event-B are the static part of a model containing properties of the modelled system through the use of axioms and theorems. Furthermore, having a closer look at the possible usage of contexts, there are two possible viewpoints:

Parameterisation: the context is seen only by one machine (or one chain of machine refinements) and defines specific properties for that machine (sets, constants, axioms, theorems). These properties are unique for that machine and any other machine would have different properties.

Sharing: a context is seen by several machines and there are some properties (sets, constants, axioms, theorems) that are shared by the machines. Therefore the context is used to share properties.

Several model developments mix both usages for the same context. For the ordinary modeller this distinction is not very clear and perhaps not so important. Our approach of generic instantiation reuses components and personalises each instance implying the use of **_Parameterisation_**.

4.2   Example of INSTANTIATED MACHINE

An INSTANTIATED MACHINE instantiates a generic machine (pattern). If the generic machine sees a context, then the context elements (sets and constants) have to be replaced by instance elements. The instance elements must exist already in a context seen by the instantiated machine (in our case study, this corresponds to ProtocolTypes - see Fig. 3).

Returning to the case study, the instantiated machine _QChannel_ that is an instance of the machine _Channel_ for requests looks like this:

```
INSTANTIATED MACHINE QChannel
INSTANTIATES Channel VIA ChannelParameters
SEES ProtocolTypes /* context containing the instance properties*/
REPLACE          /* replace parameters in ChannelParameters*/
    SETS Message := Request
    CONSTANTS max_size := qmax_size
RENAME          /* rename variables and events in machine Channel*/
    VARIABLES channel := qchannel
    EVENTS Send := QSend
           m := q   /*optional:rename parameter m in event Send*/
           Receive := Receive
           m := q /*optional:rename parameter m in event Receive*/
END
```

Fig. 4. Instantiated Machine: _QChannel_ instantiates _Channel_

Note that _ChannelParameters_ elements (sets and constants) are `replaced` because the replacement elements are already defined in _ProtocolTypes_. Machine elements (variables, parameters and events) are `renamed` since they did not exist before. The instantiated machine _PChannel_ that is an instance of _Channel_ for responses is similar.

Axioms in contexts are assumptions about the system and are used for discharging proofs obligations. When instantiating, we need to show that assumptions in the pattern are satisfied by the replacement sets and constants.

A possible solution is to convert the *pattern axioms* into *instantiated machine theorems* after the replacement is applied. A theorem has a proof obligation associated. By ensuring that a proof obligation related to each axiom is generated and discharged, we are confirming the correctness of the instantiation by satisfying the pattern assumptions (see theorem *thm1* in Fig. 5). "Expanding" machine *QChannel* can be seen in Fig. 5.

```
machine QChannel sees ProtocolTypes

variables qchannel

invariants
  @inv1 qchannel ⊆ Request
  @inv3 finite(qchannel)
  @inv2 card(qchannel) ≤ qmax_size
  theorem @thm1 qmax_size ∈ N

events
  event INITIALISATION
    then
      @act1 qchannel = ø
  end

  event QSend
    any q
    where
      @grd1 q ∈ Request
      @grd2 card(qchannel) < qmax_size
    then
      @act1 qchannel = qchannel ∪ {q}
  end

  event Receive
    any q
    where
      @grd1 q ∈ qchannel
    then
      @act1 qchannel = qchannel\{q}
  end
end
```

Fig. 5. Expanded version of instantiated machine QChannel

The instance *QChannel* sees the context *ProtocolTypes* (provided by the modeller/developer) that contains the context information for the instances. The type *Message* in context *ChannelParameters* is replaced by *Request* in *ProtocolTypes*, the constant *max_size* is replaced by *qmax_size*, the variable *channel* in *Channel* is renamed *qchannel* and event *Send* is renamed *QSend*. The axiom that exists in *ChannelParameters* is converted into a theorem in *QChannel* (but easily discharged by the axioms in *ProtocolTypes*). We convert the axiom *axm1* from the generic context *ChannelParameters*:

$$@axm1 \; max\_size \in \mathbb{N}$$

into the theorem *thm1* in the instance *QChannel*:

$$@thm1 \; qmax\_size \in \mathbb{N}$$

This results from the replacement of the constant *max_size* by *qmax_size*. A proof obligation is a sequent of the shape:

$$
\boxed{
\begin{array}{l}
Hypothesis \\
\vdash \\
Theorem
\end{array}
}
$$

For a machine theorem, the respective proof obligation is [8]:

$$
\boxed{
\begin{array}{l}
Axioms \\
Invariants \\
\vdash \\
Theorem
\end{array}
}
$$

For theorem *thm1*, the proof obligation to be generated is the following:

$$
\boxed{
\begin{array}{l}
qmax\_size \in \mathbb{N} \quad \text{/*axiom from } ProtocolTypes \text{*/} \\
pmax\_size \in \mathbb{N} \quad \text{/* axiom from } ProtocolTypes \text{*/} \\
qchannel \subseteq Request \text{ /*invariant from } QChannel \text{*/} \\
\ldots \\
\vdash \\
qmax\_size \in \mathbb{N}
\end{array}
}
$$

The first axiom of *ProtocolTypes* easily discharge this proof obligation. Note the expansion of *Qchannel* is not required in practice. We use it to show the meaning of an *instantiated machine*.

4.3   Definition of Generic Instantiation of Machines

Based on the instantiated machine *QChannel*, a general definition for generic instantiation of machines can be drawn. Considering Context *Ctx* and machine *M* in Fig. 6 together as a *pattern*, we can create a generic Instantiatiated Machine *IM* as seen in Fig. 7.

The context *D* contains the replacement properties (sets $DS_1, \ldots, DS_m$ and constants $DC_1, \ldots, DC_n$) for the elements in context *Ctx*. The variables, events and parameters are also renamed by new variables $nv_1, \ldots, nv_q$, new events $nev_1, \ldots, nev_r$ and new parameters $np_1, \ldots, np_s$. From the *pattern* we are able to create several instances that can be used in a more specific *problem*. During the creation of instances validity checks are required:

$$
\boxed{
\begin{array}{l}
\textbf{CONTEXT } Ctx \\
\textbf{SETS } S_1...S_m \\
\textbf{CONSTANTS } C_1...C_n \\
\textbf{AXIOMS } Ax_1...Ax_p
\end{array}
}
\qquad
\boxed{
\begin{array}{l}
\textbf{MACHINE } M \\
\textbf{SEES } Ctx \\
\textbf{VARIABLES } v_1...v_q \\
\textbf{EVENTS } ev_1...ev_r
\end{array}
}
$$

$$
\text{(a)} \qquad\qquad\qquad\qquad \text{(b)}
$$

Fig. 6. Generic view of a context and a machine

```
INSTANTIATED MACHINE IM
INSTANTIATES M VIA Ctx
SEES D                /* context containing the instance properties */
REPLACE               /* replace parameters defined in context C */
    SETS S₁ := DS₁,...,Sₘ := DSₘ /* Carrier Sets or Constants */
    CONSTANTS C₁ := DC₁,..., Cₙ := DCₙ
RENAME                /*rename elements in machine M*/
    VARIABLES v₁ := nv₁,..., v_q := nv_q      /* optional */
    EVENTS ev₁ := nev₁     /* optional */
           p₁ := np₁,..., p_s := np_s       /* parameters: optional */
           :
           ev_r := nev_r
END
```

Fig. 7. An Instantiated Machine

1. A static validation of replaced elements is required, e.g., a type must be replaced with a type, or a constant set and a constant with a constant.
2. All sets and constants should be replaced, i.e., no uninstantiated parameters.
3. A static check must be done to ensure that the instantiated machine specifies which generic context is being instantiated.

4.4 Avoiding Reproofs

As described above, a proof obligation (P.O.) is a sequent of the form $H \vdash G$ (short for *Hypothesis* $\vdash$ *Goal*). Renaming variable (or constant) v to w and type (carrier set) T to S results in instantiated P.O. as following:

$$[v := w] \; (H \vdash G) \; \text{(variable/constant instantiation)}$$
$$[T := S] \; (H \vdash G) \; \text{(type instantiation)}$$

$H \vdash G$ is valid means that the proof has been proved. We assume that if $H \vdash G$ is valid then any valid instantiation of $H \vdash G$ that avoids name clashes is also valid. Instantiation of variables and constants maintains validity since a sequent is implicitly universally quantified over its free variables. We are currently exploring a formal justification for why type instantiation maintains validity. Since instantiation maintains the validity of the sequent, the P.O. generated for the pattern can be reused in the instance and we avoid having to discharge the instantiated P.O..

5 Example of Instantiation and Composition

The creation of the instances is a intermediary step in the overall model development. In our case study, we model a protocol between entities that sends and receives messages. By using the created instances and the Shared Event Composition [9,10] plug-in for the Rodin platform we share events between Request

```
COMPOSED MACHINE Protocol
REFINES -
INCLUDES
     QChannel
     PChannel
EVENTS
     SendRequest
          Combines Events QChannel.QSend
     RecvReq_SendResp
          Combines Events QChannel.Receive || PChannel.Send
     RecvResp
          Combines Events combines PChannel.Receive
END
```

Fig. 8. Composed Machine Protocol

```
machine Protocol sees ProtocolTypes

variables qchannel pchannel

invariants
   @inv1 qchannel ⊆ Request
   @inv2 pchannel ⊆ Response
   @inv3 card(pchannel) ≤ pmax_size
   @inv4 card(qchannel) ≤ qmax_size
   theorem @QChannel/thm1 qmax_size ∈ N
   theorem @PChannel/thm2 pmax_size ∈ N

events
   event INITIALISATION
     then
        @act1 qchannel = ∅
        @act2 pchannel = ∅
   end
```
(a)

```
event SendRequest
   any q
   where
      @grd1 q ∈ Request
      @grd2 card(qchannel) < qmax_size
   then
      @act1 qchannel = qchannel ∪ {q}
end

event RecvReq_SendResp
   any q p
   where
      @grd1 q ∈ qchannel
      @grd2 p ∈ Response
      @grd3 card(pchannel) < pmax_size
   then
      @act1 pchannel = pchannel ∪ {p}
      @act2 qchannel = qchannel\{q}
end

event RecvResp
   any p
   where
      @grd1 p ∈ pchannel
   then
      @act1 pchannel = pchannel\{p}
   end
end
```
(b)

Fig. 9. *Machine Protocol*

and Response and model the protocol. A composed machine *Protocol* modelling this system can be seen in Fig. 8.

As seen in Fig. 2, while composing the instance machines *QChannel* and *PChannel* we add the events that are unique for each entity (*SendRequest* and *RecvResp*). *SendRequest* sends a message through the channel from Source to Destination. *RecvResp* models the reception of the response in the *Source* after being sent by Destination. Moreover the event that relates the communication between the two entities is also modelled (*RecvReq_SendResp*). The request is received and acknowledged and the response to that request is sent in parallel (from this combined event, a possible refinement is processing the request message before sending the response). We opt not to refine an abstract machine in Fig. 8 (*REFINES* clause is empty: "-") although it is possible. The composed machine *Protocol* corresponds to the expanded machine in Fig. 9.

The two instances of machine *Channel* model a bi-directional communication channel between two entities. This allows us to express the applicability of generic instantiation for modelling distributed systems without being restricted to this kind of system. When modelling a finite number of similar components with some specific individual properties, instantiated machines are a suitable option.

6   Generic Instantiation Applied to a Chain of Refinements

The above sections describe generic instantiation applied to individual machines. Although it is already an interesting way of reusing, in a large model it would be more interesting to instantiate a chain of machines, or in other words *instantiate a chain of refinements*. Suppose we have a development Dv containing several refinement levels $(Dv_1, Dv_2, \ldots, Dv_n)$. The most concrete model Dv_n matches a

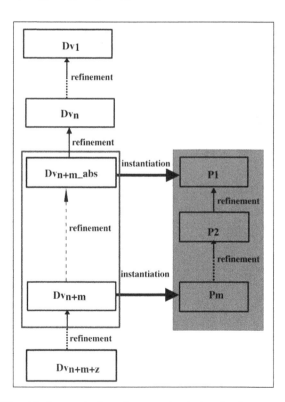

Fig. 10. Instantiation of a generic chain of refinements

generic model (pattern) P_1 that is part of a chain of refinements $P_1, P_2, \ldots, P_m$ as seen in Fig. 10. By applying generic instantiation we instantiate the pattern P_1 according to Dv_n. That instantiation is a refinement of Dv_n and it is called Dv_{n+m}_abs (the suffix *abs* stands for abstract). In addition we can extend the instantiation to one of the refinement layers of the pattern and apply it to the development Dv. As an outcome we get a further refinement layer for Dv_n for free (Dv_{n+m}_abs corresponds to the instantiation of P_1 and Dv_{n+m} corresponds to the instantiation of P_m). The refinement between Dv_{n+m}_abs and Dv_{n+m} does not introduce refinement proof obligations since the proof obligations were already discharged in the pattern chain. This follows from the instantiated machines where it is avoided the re-proof of pattern proof obligations. Afterwards Dv_{n+m} can be further refined to Dv_{n+m+z}. For a better understanding of this approach, we will refine our case study and apply an instantiation over the pattern chain.

6.1   Refinement of the Channel Case Study

We will refine the *Channel* machine. For the first refinement, the requirement is to include buffers before and after adding a message to the channel. A second refinement specifies the type *Message*. In particular, *Message* will be divided in two parts: *header* and *body*. The *header* of the *Message* contains the destination identification and the *body* represents the content of the message (data). *header* and *body* are based on the records proposal for Event-B suggested by Evans and Butler [11] and also in work developed by Rezazadeh et al [12].

The first refinement requires an introduction of two new variables *sending-Buffer* and *receivingBuffer* and a new event *addMessageBuffer* that loads the

```
machine Channel_M1 refines Channel
sees ChannelParameters

variables channel sendingBuffer
          receivingBuffer

invariants
    @inv1 sendingBuffer ⊆ Message
    @inv2 receivingBuffer ⊆ Message

events
    event INITIALISATION
      then
        @act1 channel = ∅
        @act2 sendingBuffer = ∅
        @act3 receivingBuffer = ∅
    end

    event addMessageBuffer
      any m
      where
        @grd1 m ∈ Message
        @grd2 m ∉ sendingBuffer
      then
        @act1 sendingBuffer=sendingBuffer∪{m}
    end
```
(a)

```
event Send refines Send
  any m
  where
    @grd1 sendingBuffer ≠ ∅
    @grd2 m ∈ sendingBuffer
    @grd3 card(channel) < max_size
  then
    @act1 channel = channel ∪ {m}
    @act2 sendingBuffer=sendingBuffer\{m}
end

event Receive refines Receive
  any m
  where
    @grd1 m ∈ channel
    @grd2 m ∉ receivingBuffer
  then
    @act1 channel = channel\{m}
    @act2 receivingBuffer=receivingBuffer∪{m}
end
```
(b)

Fig. 11. *Channel_M1*: refinement of *Channel*

```
context ChannelParameters_C2 extends ChannelParameters

constants header body

sets DATA DESTINATION

axioms
    @axm3 header ∈ Message → DESTINATION
    @axm4 body ∈ Message → DATA
end
```

Fig. 12. Context *ChannelParameters_C2*

```
machine Channel_M2 refines Channel_M1
sees ChannelParameters_C2

variables channel sendingBuffer
          receivingBuffer storeDATA

invariants
    @inv1 storeDATA ∈ DESTINATION ⇸ ℙ(DATA)

events
  event INITIALISATION
    then
        @act1 channel = ∅
        @act2 sendingBuffer = ∅
        @act3 receivingBuffer = ∅
        @act4 storeDATA = DESTINATION × {∅}
    end

  event addMessageBuffer
  refines addMessageBuffer
    any h b m
    where
        @grd1 header(m) = h
        @grd2 body(m) = b
        @grd3 m ∉ sendingBuffer
    then
        @act4 sendingBuffer=sendingBuffer∪{m}
    end
```
(a)

```
event send refines Send
    any m
    where
        @grd1 sendingBuffer ≠ ∅
        @grd2 m ∈ sendingBuffer
        @grd3 card(channel) < max_size
    then
        @act1 channel = channel ∪ {m}
        @act2 sendingBuffer=sendingBuffer\{m}
end

event receive refines Receive
    any m
    where
        @grd1 m ∈ channel
        @grd2 m ∉ receivingBuffer
    then
        @act1 channel = channel\{m}
        @act2 receivingBuffer=receivingBuffer∪{m}
end

event processMessage
    any m dest d
    where
        @grd1 m ∈ receivingBuffer
        @grd3 header(m) = dest
        @grd4 d = body(m)
        @grd5 dest ∈ dom(storeDATA)
    then
        @act1 storeDATA(dest)=storeDATA(dest)∪{d}
end
```
(b)

Fig. 13. *Channel_M2*: refinement of *Channel_M1*

message to *sendingBuffer* before being introduced in the channel in the *Send* event. The latter event reflects the introduction of the buffers. In the event *Receive*, messages in *channel* are extracted and loaded to *receivingBuffer* as seen in Fig. 11.

The second refinement is a data refinement over the type *Message* by dividing it in *header* and *body*. The *header* contains the destination identification and the *body* contains the data of the message. Constants *header* and *body* are defined in the context *ChannelParameters_C2* as in Fig. 12.

In Fig. 13 the machine *Channel_M2* data refines the variable *channel* and introduces a new event, *processMessage* that processes the received message after being retrieved from the receiving buffer. A variable *storeDATA* is also introduced to store the data that each destination receives.

6.2   Instantiation of a Chain of Refinements

We can consider the chain of refinements of *Channel* as a pattern. In that case, having all the proof obligations discharged we can reuse this pattern in a more specific development. The chain of refinements is seen as a single entity where it is possible to choose an *initial* and a *final* refinement level.

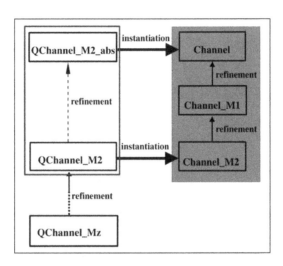

Fig. 14. Instantiation of a chain of refinements: *Channel* to *Channel_M2*

> **INSTANTIATED REFINEMENT** QChannel_M2
> **INSTANTIATES** Channel_M2 **VIA** ChannelParameters_C2
> **REFINES** -
> **SEES** ProtocolTypes_C2
> **REPLACE**
>   **SETS** *Message := Request*
>   **CONSTANTS** *max_size := qmax_size*
>   *header := qHeader*
>   *body := qBody*
> **RENAME**
>   **VARIABLES** *channel := qchannel*
>   *receivingBuffer := qReceivingBuffer*
>   *sendingBuffer := qSendingBuffer*
>   **EVENTS** *Send := QSend*
>   *m := q*
>   *receive := Receive*
>   *m := q*
> **END**

Fig. 15. Instantiation of a chain of refinements

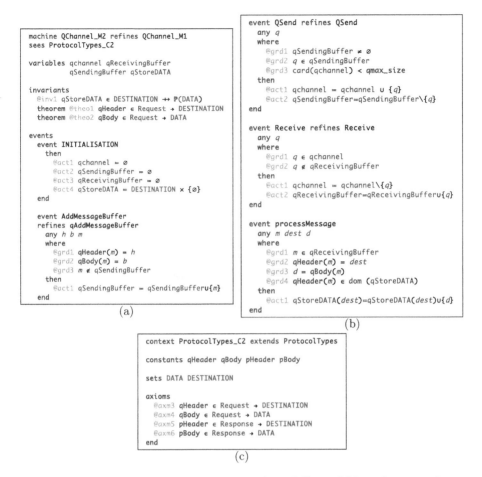

```
machine QChannel_M2 refines QChannel_M1
sees ProtocolTypes_C2

variables qchannel qReceivingBuffer
          qSendingBuffer qStoreDATA

invariants
   @inv1 qStoreDATA ∈ DESTINATION ⇸ ℙ(DATA)
   theorem @theo1 qHeader ∈ Request → DESTINATION
   theorem @theo2 qBody ∈ Request → DATA

events
  event INITIALISATION
    then
      @act1 qchannel = ∅
      @act2 qSendingBuffer = ∅
      @act3 qReceivingBuffer = ∅
      @act4 qStoreDATA = DESTINATION × {∅}
    end

  event AddMessageBuffer
  refines qAddMessageBuffer
    any h b m
    where
      @grd1 qHeader(m) = h
      @grd2 qBody(m) = b
      @grd3 m ∉ qSendingBuffer
    then
      @act1 qSendingBuffer = qSendingBuffer∪{m}
    end
```

(a)

```
event QSend refines QSend
  any q
  where
    @grd1 qSendingBuffer ≠ ∅
    @grd2 q ∈ qSendingBuffer
    @grd3 card(qchannel) < qmax_size
  then
    @act1 qchannel = qchannel ∪ {q}
    @act2 qSendingBuffer=qSendingBuffer\{q}
end

event Receive refines Receive
  any q
  where
    @grd1 q ∈ qchannel
    @grd2 q ∉ qReceivingBuffer
  then
    @act1 qchannel = qchannel\{q}
    @act2 qReceivingBuffer=qReceivingBuffer∪{q}
end

event processMessage
  any m dest d
  where
    @grd1 m ∈ qReceivingBuffer
    @grd2 qHeader(m) = dest
    @grd3 d = qBody(m)
    @grd4 qHeader(m) ∈ dom (qStoreDATA)
  then
    @act1 qStoreDATA(dest)=qStoreDATA(dest)∪{d}
end
```

(b)

```
context ProtocolTypes_C2 extends ProtocolTypes

constants qHeader qBody pHeader pBody

sets DATA DESTINATION

axioms
   @axm3 qHeader ∈ Request → DESTINATION
   @axm4 qBody ∈ Request → DATA
   @axm5 pHeader ∈ Response → DESTINATION
   @axm6 pBody ∈ Response → DATA
end
```

(c)

Fig. 16. Expanded version of instantiated machine *QChannel_M2* and context *ProtocolTypes_C2*

Using our case study, we intend to instantiate and refine *QChannel* with the chain of refinements of machine *Channel*, selecting *Channel* and *Channel_M2* as our initial and final refinement levels respectively. In Fig. 14 the shaded chain of refinement is seen as a single entity. After the selection of the two refinement levels to be instantiated, *QChannel_M2_abs* and *QChannel_M2* are created. *QChannel_M2* is treated as a refinement of *QChannel_M2_abs* as a consequence of the instantiation. Subsequently, *QChannel_M2* can be further refined to *QChannel_Mz*.

The refinement relationship between *Channel* and *Channel_M2* is ensured by discharging all the proof obligations in the chain of refinement (all the proofs are discharged automatically in the Rodin platform). By instantiating *Channel* and *Channel_M2* implicitly we are also referring to *Channel_M1*. Some of the properties of *Channel_M2* are inherited from *Channel_M1* (for instance the buffers) but for the instantiation purpose it is not necessary to incorporate *Channel_M1* explicitly. The instantiation of a chain of refinements follows the instantiation of a single machine as seen in Fig. 15.

The initial refinement level corresponds to the most abstract machine of the pattern. The final refinement level is any of the other refinement levels in the chain. The replacement and renaming is applied to the occurrences in both instances whenever applicable. Once again it is not necessary to "expand" *QChannel_M2* but that can be seen in Fig. 16.

In an instantiation of a chain of refinements, the pattern context is seen as a *flat context* comprising all the properties seen by the refinements until the selected final refinement level is reached. Therefore context *ProtocolTypes_C2* is the parameterisation context for *QChannel_M2* and extends *ProtocolTypes* similarly to the relation between contexts *ChannelParameters_C2* and *Channel-Parameters*. As before, axioms in *ProtocolTypes_C2* must be respected in the instance, so axioms are converted in theorems in *QChannel_M2*.

6.3   Definition of Generic Instantiation of Refinements

From the case study it is possible to draw a generic definition for the instantiation of a chain of refinements. If we consider a pattern that consists of a chain of refinements *M1*, *M2*, ... *Mt* , we can create a generic Instantiated Refinement *IR* as seen in Fig. 17.

The instantiated refinement *IR* instantiates one of the refinements of the pattern M_t via the parameterisation context Ctx_t. IR refines an abstract machine IR_0 and sees the context D_w containing the instance properties. The replacement and renaming are similar to the machine instantiation but apply to both M_1 and M_t. In addition to the validity checks for instantiated machines, instantiated refinements require:

INSTANTIATED REFINEMENT IR
INSTANTIATES M_t **VIA** Ctx_t
REFINES IR_0 /* abstract machine */
SEES D_w /* context containing the instance properties */
REPLACE   /* replace parameters defined in context C */
       SETS $S_1 := DS_1, \ldots, S_m := DS_m$ /* Carrier Sets or Constants */
       CONSTANTS $C_1 := DC_1, \ldots, C_n := DC_n$
RENAME   /*rename variables, events and params in M_1 to M_t*/
       VARIABLES $v_1 := nv_1, \ldots, v_q := nv_q$
       EVENTS $ev_1 := nev_1$ / * *optional* * /
              $p_1 := np_1, \ldots, p_s := np_s$ / * *parameters : optional* * /
              $\vdots$

              $ev_r := nev_r$
END

Fig. 17. An Instantiated Refinement

1. A static validation for the existence of a chain of refinements for M
   $(M_1, M_2, \ldots, M_t)$.
2. The types and constants in the contexts seen by the initial and final level of refinement should be instantiated.

The instantiation of refinements reuses the pattern proof obligations in the sense that the instantiation renames and replaces elements in the model but does not change the model itself (nor the respective properties). The correctness of the refinement instantiation relies in reusing the pattern proof obligations and ensuring the assumptions in the context parameterisation are satisfied in the instantiation.

7   Instantiating Theorems and Invariants

Theorems in contexts and machines are assertions about characteristics and properties of the system. Theorems have proof obligations associated that are discharged based on the model assumptions (axioms and invariants) . Once the theorems are discharged, they can be used as hypotheses for discharging other proof obligations in the model since they work as a consequence of the assumptions. On the other hand, invariants in machines are properties of the model that need to be maintained by all events.

An interesting question arises when a pattern is instantiated and contains theorems and invariants. If a proof obligation of a theorem is discharged by creating an instance we would not want to re-prove the theorem proof. Regarding the invariants and respective proof obligations we would have a similar situation where we would not want to discharge proof obligations in the instance if they were already discharged in the pattern. Ideally we would like to add to the instance the assumptions and assertions given by the theorems and invariants without re-proving them. Although addressed here as an open question, this situation suggests a different kind of theorem that does not exist in Event-B, a *pre-proved theorem* to be used in the instance. A *pre-proved theorem* would be similar to a theorem but it would not have associated a proof obligation. The invariants imported from the pattern fall under the same category where the respective proof obligations should not be re-generated. Informally the instances are just renaming and replacing elements without changing the semantics under the original pattern (if the validity checks are followed) so theorems and invariants would work as assumptions in the instantiated machine. The assumptions in the pattern (axioms) need to be satisfied by the instances through the generation of proof obligations but the same does not apply for invariants and theorems that are assertions in the pattern.

8   Conclusions

Reusability is of significant interest in the general software engineering research community. Advantages and disadvantages have been discussed in terms of how to reuse. Examples are given by Standish [1] and Cheng [13]. Reusing patterns in a style similar to design patterns is proposed in [14] using the KAOS specification language and temporal logic. The patterns are proved correct and complete and proofs can be reused. Sabatier [15] discusses the reuse of formal models as a detailed component specification or as a high level requirement and presents some real project examples. In classical B [16,17], reuse is expressed using the keywords *INCLUDES* and *USES* where an existing machine can be used in other developments. Instantiation is a way of reusing. Instantiation is well-established in areas such as mathematics and other formal methods like classical B or theorem provers like Isabelle [18]. [19] reuses Gang of Four (GoF) design pattern adapted to formal specifications (denominated specification patterns) for classical B. Several reuse mechanisms are suggested like instantiation, composition and extension. Proof obligations are also reused when the patterns are applied. Focusing on the instantiation, this is achieved by renaming sets (machine parameters), variables and operations. Unlike our work, this approach only defines patterns as single abstract machine whereas we define the parameterisation in contexts and extend the pattern to a chain of refinements. Abrial and Hallerstede [3] and Métayer et al [2] make use of generic instantiation for Event-B. It is proposed the flattening of the context in a way that the contexts of the pattern are merged and it is suggested the reuse by instantiating the flat context. Following that approach, we decide to propose an implementation of generic instantiation. The motivation for such implementation is concerned with reusability of components and existing developments. By creating an instance from a generic model, a new parameterised model is created based on the pattern with new specific properties.

Event-B supports generic developments but lacks capacity to instantiate and reuse those generic developments. As a solution, generic instantiation is applied to patterns and as an outcome instantiated machines are created and parameterised. An *instantiated machine* instantiates a generic machine, is parameterised by a context and the pattern elements are renamed/replaced according to the instance. In a similar style, an *instantiated refinement* instantiates a chain of refinements reusing the pattern proof obligations assuming that the instantiated proof obligations are as valid as the pattern ones. As future work we intend to prove this assumption. By quantifying the variables/constants and types we want to ensure that pattern proof obligations remain valid when instantiating. Event-B is not a high-order formalism: although it is possible to quantify variables and constants, it is not possible to quantify types. So we need to use a higher-order formalism to ensure that the instantiation of types maintains the validity of associated proof obligations. A practical case that models a communication protocol between two entities illustrates the advantages of using generic instantiation and in particular how to use our approach in the Rodin platform. Although a simple case study, we believe that it can be applied to more complex cases.

Further study is required to determine if context instantiation similar to instantiated machines is a worthwhile approach while modelling. Some methodological points will arise in a possible implementation of instantiated machines and refinements in the Rodin platform. As an example, Section 7 addresses the situation of instantiating theorems and invariants and is left as an open question. A future step for the instantiation of a chain of refinements is to study the possibility of selecting any of the refinement levels as the initial refinement level giving more freedom to the modeller. In a long term perspective, any refinement chain could be considered a pattern or a library of patterns should be provided when modelling: whenever a formal development fits in a pattern, instantiation could be applied taking advantage of the reusability of the model and respective proof obligations.

Acknowledgments. We would like to thank Jean-Raymond Abrial and Thai Son Hoang for valuable discussions about this paper. Also Hannah Warren for helping in the review of initial versions of the paper. We also thank the anonymous reviewers for their inputs and suggestions.

References

1. Standish, T.A.: An Essay on Software Reuse. IEEE Trans. Software Eng. 10(5), 494–497 (1984)
2. Métayer, C., Abrial, J.R., Voisin, L.: Event-B Language. Technical report, Deliverable 3.2, EU Project IST-511599 - RODIN (May 2005)
3. Abrial, J.R., Hallerstede, S.: Refinement, Decomposition, and Instantiation of Discrete Models: Application to Event-B. Fundam. Inf. 77(1-2), 1–28 (2007)
4. Rodin: RODIN project Homepage (September 2008), http://rodin.cs.ncl.ac.uk
5. Abrial, J.R., Butler, M.J., Hallerstede, S., Voisin, L.: An Open Extensible Tool Environment for Event-B. In: Liu, Z., He, J. (eds.) ICFEM 2006. LNCS, vol. 4260, pp. 588–605. Springer, Heidelberg (2006)
6. Silva, R., Butler, M.: Parallel Composition Using Event-B (July 2009), http://wiki.event-b.org/index.php/Parallel_Composition_using_Event-B
7. Silva, R.: Renaming Framework (July 2009), http://wiki.event-b.org/index.php/Refactoring_Framework
8. Abrial, J.R.: Summary of Event-B Proof Obligations (March 2008), http://www.docstoc.com/docs/7055755/Summary-of-Event-BProof-Obligations
9. Butler, M.: An Approach to the Design of Distributed Systems with B AMN. In: Till, D., Bowen, J., Hinchey, M.G. (eds.) ZUM 1997. LNCS, vol. 1212, pp. 221–241. Springer, Heidelberg (1997)
10. Butler, M.: Synchronisation-based Decomposition for Event-B. In: RODIN Deliverable D19 Intermediate report on methodology (2006)
11. Evans, N., Butler, M.: A Proposal for Records in Event-B. In: Misra, J., Nipkow, T., Sekerinski, E. (eds.) FM 2006. LNCS, vol. 4085, pp. 221–235. Springer, Heidelberg (2006)
12. Rezazadeh, A., Evans, N., Butler, M.: Redevelopment of an Industrial Case Study Using Event-B and Rodin. In: BCS-FACS Christmas 2007 Meeting - Formal Method In Industry (December 2007)
13. Cheng, J.: A Reusability-Based Software Development Environment. SIGSOFT Softw. Eng. Notes 19(2), 57–62 (1994)

14. Darimont, R., van Lamsweerde, A.: Formal Refinement Patterns for Goal-Driven Requirements Elaboration. In: SIGSOFT 1996: Proceedings of the 4th ACM SIGSOFT symposium on Foundations of software engineering, pp. 179–190. ACM, New York (1996)
15. Sabatier, D.: Reusing Formal Models. IFIP Congress Topical Sessions, 613–620 (2004)
16. Schneider, S.: The B method: an introduction. Palgrave (2001)
17. Abrial, J.R.: The B-Book: Assigning programs to meanings. Cambridge University Press, Cambridge (1996)
18. Paulson, L.C.: Isabelle. LNCS, vol. 828. Springer, Heidelberg (1994)
19. Blazy, S., Gervais, F., Laleau, R.: Reuse of Specification Patterns with the B Method. In: Bert, D., Bowen, J., King, S. (eds.) ZB 2003. LNCS, vol. 2651, pp. 40–57. Springer, Heidelberg (2003)

A Lazy Unbounded Model Checker for Event-B[*]

Paulo J. Matos[1], Bernd Fischer[1], and João Marques-Silva[2]

[1] Electronics and Computer Science, University of Southampton
{pocm,b.fischer}@ecs.soton.ac.uk
[2] School of Computer Science and Informatics, University College Dublin
jpms@ucd.ie

Abstract. Formal specification languages are traditionally supported by theorem provers, but recently model checkers have proven to be useful tools. In this paper we present Eboc, an explicit state model checker for Event-B. Eboc is based on lazy techniques that allow it to fairly perform an exhaustive state space search without bounding the size of the sets used in the specification. We describe the implementation of Eboc and provide a preliminary comparison with ProB, an existing bounded model checker for Classical B.

1 Introduction

Model checking has been the focus of many research papers in recent years, with successes in both hardware and software development. In formal methods, languages are usually supported by theorem provers but model checking has recently been investigated as well and model checkers have been developed for languages like Z [1,2,3], CSP [4], or Classical B [5]. This paper addresses the problem of model checking Event-B.

The B-method, originally devised by J.-R. Abrial [5], is a theory and methodology for the formal development of computer systems. It is used by industries in a range of critical domains, most notably railway control [6]. Event-B [7], an evolution of the Classical B, focuses on the formal development of discrete systems based on refinement. An Event-B specification consists of machines and contexts. A machine defines a state and several events which repeatedly update the state by means of update rules or *actions*, and so provide dynamics to the system. Contexts, which are seen by machines, provide static data to the model. Proof obligations ensure the correctness of the model and its dynamics [8], by for example assuring that invariants remain true after each event's actions.

In this paper, we describe Eboc, an explicit state model checker for Event-B. Like other model checkers, Eboc does not discharge proof obligations, but simulates the execution of the model, searching each state for an invariant violation. It thus complements theorem proving, which leaves users in the lurch if it fails to discharge a proof obligation, as the users cannot tell whether the proof obligation is provable in principle or not. In the latter case, Eboc will (eventually)

---

[*] This work is partially funded by EU project Coconut FP7-ICT-217069 and by EPSRC Grant EP/E012973/1.

K. Breitman and A. Cavalcanti (Eds.): ICFEM 2009, LNCS 5885, pp. 485–503, 2009.

MACHINE Simple
    VARIABLES x
    INVARIANTS
        $x \neq 5$
    INITIALISATION $\widehat{=}$
        $x := 0$
    EVENT Simple $\widehat{=}$
        ANY y WHERE $y \in \mathbb{Z}$ THEN $x := y$ END
END

Fig. 1. Simple machine causing a false claim in ProB's bounded model checking

find a counterexample, describing which state violates which invariant and how
it can be reached from the initial state. If the state space is finite, Eboc can
even search the complete state space and decisively show whether any invariant
is violated. Even if the state space is infinite and the proof obligation is provable
Eboc can search through enough of this space to give the user enough confidence
to proceed and try to discharge it manually.

Eboc's state space exploration is driven by a scheduler that expands all states
and searches for a violation of an invariant in the original (i.e., unbounded) state
space. Eboc traverses this potentially infinite state space by lazily enumerating
the values for any given variable such that no value is ever repeated and the space
is fairly covered. The way Eboc handles the problem of infinite search space is
fundamentally different than for example ProB [9], an existing model checker
for CLASSICAL B. ProB bounds the state space to be explored by bounding the
size of the deferred sets, the integers, the number of initial states computed,
and the number of enablings for each state. This up-front bounding however,
is of course problematic when the invariant is only violated for values outside
the bounds. Consider for example the (deliberately simple) machine shown in
Figure 1. Obviously, the invariant is violated if $y = 5$ is chosen. However, ProB's
default lower and upper bounds for the integers are -1 and 4, respectively, so
the guard will return no violation of the invariant. In this simple example it
is of course possible to inspect the model, see that a higher bound is required
and overwrite ProB's defaults, but with larger models this will generally become
harder, and eventually setting the right bound becomes a trial-and-error issue.
The problem is aggravated by the fact that if ProB returns no error, it is unclear
whether this is because the model is consistent with the invariants or because
the bounds are too restrictive. Moreover, more obscure problems might be due
to bounding the number of initial states computed by ProB or due to any other
bound imposed by ProB before the search starts. Our approach avoids these
bounds, thereby solving this problem. The solution involves the combination of
a lazy exploration of the values in the domain with a priority system that avoids
the search being deadlocked in a single infinite stream of values. This allows us
to fairly explore even infinite domains, or more precisely, given finite time, fairly
chosen finite subsets of unbounded size. In this context, laziness means that all
the nodes in the search space are considered however, they are only computed
when required for processing.

In Section 2 we present some background concepts important for the rest of the paper, in Section 3 we will present in detail the model checker for EVENT-B. Section 4 will focus on the architecture of the system and Section 5 will provide a preliminary comparison between our model checker and ProB with a discussion of the results. The paper finishes with an overview of related work in Section 6 and conclusions in Section 7.

2   Event-B Essentials

EVENT-B is a modelling notation and method for formal development of discrete systems based on refinement [10] which evolved from the B-Method [5]. Here, we give a brief overview of EVENT-B; for details see [7]. Since our model checker focuses on model checking the validity of invariants, we will ignore the concepts and constructs of EVENT-B that are irrelevant to this end. In particular, we will ignore the concept of refinement, which makes the specification of large and complex systems more tractable by gradually adding more details to an abstract base model. However, we are not constraining the amount of models that can be model checked: since model checking generally focuses on a specific refinement level, it is possible to *remove* the more abstract levels by flattening the model into the required level. Moreover, statuses and witnesses will not be discussed either since they are associated with the refinement of events. Similarly, we will not discuss theorems which are associated with contexts and machines, because they do not influence the execution of an EVENT-B machine.

An EVENT-B specification consists of machines which specify the behavioral properties of the model, and contexts which axiomatically provide static aspects of the model. EVENT-B's mathematical language is based on first-order logic and set theory (as in CLASSICAL B) and its syntax, type inference rules, and legibility rules are defined in [11].

Figure 2 presents a simple EVENT-B model which consists of a single machine and a single context. The context *Colors* consists of the deferred set Colors whose elements are left undefined, three constants and an axiom. The interpretation of the constants is given by the AXIOMS; in this case, the axioms specify that the deferred set consists of three different values represented by the identifiers red, green, and blue, respectively. The machine *Example* has two state variables x and y, which are initialized to 0 and red, respectively. It can see the *Colors* context, hence all the definitions of the context can be referred to in the machine. The machine defines an event e with two parameters xx and yy, a set of predicates referred to as *guards*, and a set of update rules referred to as *actions*. Events are guarded atomic actions that drive the execution of the model. Once all the variables are initialized, all events are checked for enabledness. An event is enabled if there is an assignment to its parameters that satisfies the guards in the current state. An enabled event is then chosen non-deterministically to be triggered and, once triggered, values are chosen non-deterministically for its parameters and the state is updated according to its actions. In the initial state $x = 0$, $y = $ red, e is enabled. Since this is the only event of the machine, it is

MACHINE Example   CONTEXT Colors
  SEES   SETS
    Colors   Colors
  VARIABLES
    x y CONSTANTS
  INVARIANTS   red green blue
    $x \in \mathbb{Z} \wedge y \in \text{Colors}$
    $x = 2 \Rightarrow y \neq \text{red}$ AXIOMS
  INITIALISATION $\;\widehat{=}\;$ $partition(\text{Colors}, \{\text{red}\}, \{\text{green}\}, \{\text{blue}\})$
    $x, y := 0, \text{red}$ END
  EVENT e $\;\widehat{=}\;$
    ANY
      xx yy
    WHERE
      $xx \in \mathbb{Z}$
      $yy \in \text{Colors}$
      $yy \neq y$
    THEN
      $x := x + xx$
      $y := yy$
    END
END

Fig. 2. Example EVENT-B specification

triggered and if for example $xx = 1$ and $yy = $ green are chosen as values for
the parameters, the new state becomes $x = 1$, $y = $ green. Note that $xx = 1$ and
$yy = $ red would not be a valid choice for the parameters as this would violate
the guard $yy \neq y$. Once a new state is generated, the process continues until no
event is enabled, in which case it is said the model reached a deadlock state.

The initialization of the state variables is given by a set of actions which can
take three forms:

$$\mathbf{v} := \mathbf{E}(\mathbf{c}) \tag{1}$$

$$v :\in S(\mathbf{c}) \tag{2}$$

$$\mathbf{v} :| \ P(\mathbf{v}', \mathbf{c}) \tag{3}$$

Here, $\mathbf{E}(\mathbf{c})$ represents a set of expressions over the seen constants, $S(\mathbf{c})$ is a single
set expression over the seen constants and $P(\mathbf{v}', \mathbf{c})$ is a before-after predicate,
where $\mathbf{v}'$ is the set of variables $\mathbf{v}$ in the after-state. The first form is a deterministic assignment form which assigns the value of each expression on the right-hand
side to the set of variables in the left-hand side in order. The second form is a
non-deterministic assignment form which assigns to the variable on the left-hand
side one of the elements of the set that result from the evaluation of $S(\mathbf{c})$. The
third form, which is the most general form, assigns a value non-deterministically
to the variables $\mathbf{v}$ that satisfy the predicate $P(\mathbf{v}', \mathbf{c})$. Event actions can, in general, also take different forms. However, we will assume without loss of generality

that all the non-determinism is represented in the guards and that event actions always take the deterministic form. The following is thus the canonical form used for events:

EVENT e $\hat{=}$ ANY **x** WHERE $P(\mathbf{v}, \mathbf{x}, \mathbf{c})$ THEN $\mathbf{v} := \mathbf{E}(\mathbf{v}, \mathbf{x}, \mathbf{c})$

Here, **x** represents the event's parameters whose scope are the the event's body and whose value are constrained by the guard $P(\mathbf{v}, \mathbf{x}, \mathbf{c})$. The guard enables the event and generates a new state through the application of the actions $\mathbf{v} := \mathbf{E}(\mathbf{v}, \mathbf{x}, \mathbf{c})$, which are analogous to the form shown in Equation (1).

Proof obligations play an important role in EVENT-B and their purpose is two-fold. On one hand, they show that a model is sound with respect to some behavioral semantics. On the other hand, they serve to verify properties of the model [8].

In this paper, we will focus on checking invariants. Invariants are the predicates that must be satisfied in all states of the model. EVENT-B ensures that a machine is consistent by constructing proof obligations that formalize the intuition that the machine preserves the invariant. Each event thus induces a proof obligation of the form:

$$\mathbf{I}(\mathbf{v}) \wedge \mathbf{P_e}(\mathbf{v}, \mathbf{x}, \mathbf{c}) \Rightarrow \mathbf{I}(\mathbf{v}') \tag{4}$$

Intuitively this means that if the invariants and the guard for event e hold in the current state, then the invariants also hold in the post-state. If this is proven for each event, then the machine is consistent. Eboc focuses on checking that these invariants are never violated. Eboc checks this by simulating the model, generating and exploring a state space by repeatedly applying all possible events that are enabled in the given state.

3   Explicit State Model Checking of EVENT-B

In contrast to ProB, Eboc performs a lazy, unbounded, explicit state search of an EVENT-B model. Before going into the details of how Eboc model checks an EVENT-B model, we present a brief discussion on what it means to do explicit state model checking of an EVENT-B model. Consider a slightly simplified version of event e of Figure 2:

EVENT e1 $\hat{=}$ WHEN $\top$ THEN $x := x + 1$

where x is always incremented. Consider also a second event:

EVENT e2 $\hat{=}$ ANY zz WHERE $zz \in \text{Colors} \wedge x \bmod 2 = 1$ THEN $x, y := x + 1, zz$

which increments x and non-deterministically chooses a new color for y if x is odd. Figure 3 shows the search tree for the machine of Figure 2 but with the events e and e1 above. The initial state is created and from it, all the enabled events are expanded: initially only event e because x is 0. In the resulting state both events are enabled however, four transitions occur to three different states.

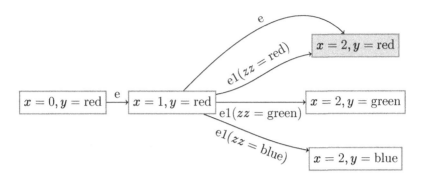

Fig. 3. Example of a search tree on an EVENT-B model

One transition is due to event e and the remaining three are due to the non-deterministic assignment of zz to one of the possible colors. Note what would have happened if there was a non-deterministic assignment to an integer variable, instead of a variable whose type is finite. The branching from this state would have been infinite. Current model checkers opt to bound these infinite sets so they can perform a search on the state space. However, our approach is to leave the infinite sets unbounded and lazily unroll them during search. Therefore, Eboc has the advantage of finding violations others may not find because their domains may be bounded to too restrictive values. This means that nothing is bound a priori and the search space (potentially infinite) is possibly exhaustively searched for a counterexample. However, this space is only unfolded when required. Therefore a counterexample, if it exists, is eventually found. The downside is that the model checker will not stop if the space is infinite and the model is correct. That is why we allow the user of Eboc to input a bound on the number nodes (which represent states in the system) to explore. In this case, Eboc assures the user that within that space no counterexample exists. The remainder of the section presents our approach in more detail.

3.1 Enumerations

In order to have an exhaustive search of an infinite state space, we need to have a methodology to list for every variable in the model all the values they can take, which are possibly infinite, so we need to lazily enumerate them. Whenever we need to choose non-deterministically a value for a given variable we take a value from a lazy stream of possible values (which depend on the type of the variable) and if the value does not fit the constraints the variable is subject to, we backtrack and try another. To this end, we discuss enumerations.

Consider again the simple example in Figure 1. Event Simple is always enabled, and can be triggered an infinite amount of times from a given state and for different values of y. From the initial state $x = 0$, each time we trigger event Simple we take a new y from the lazy stream of values $[0, -1, 1, -2, 2, \ldots]$, which generate the states $x = 0$, $x = -1$, $x = 1$, ... respectively. If instead the event was of the form:

EVENT Simple1 $\widehat{=}$ ANY y z WHERE $y \in \mathbb{Z} \wedge z \in$ Colors ...

where it can be assumed that Colors is the set defined in Figure 2, then we would need to lazily enumerate all values in $\mathbb{Z} \times Colors$, assign each of the values to y and z respectively and evaluate the state, thereby generating an infinite amount of states. The lazy stream this time would look like $[0 \mapsto$ red, $0 \mapsto$ green, $1 \mapsto$ red, $0 \mapsto$ blue, ...], where $x \mapsto y$ is EVENT-B's representation of the pair (x, y).

In general, an enumeration of a set S is a surjection f from $\mathbb{N}$ onto S. This definition allows that two different natural numbers have the same image under f, which is something we do not want for efficiency reasons, so f is, in our case, also injective.

EVENT-B has a flat type system that includes as basic types user defined sets, the booleans, the integers and cartesian product along with the powerset as type constructors. For each of these types we define enumerations that allow us to lazily step through each possible value induced by the type. However, we had to make sure these enumerations are not only injective but also fair. There are two dimensions to fairness:

1. it has to explore all the possible values the variable can have. For example, for an integer variable, it would not be fair to first explore all the positive number and then all the negative numbers because since the positive numbers are infinite the negative numbers would never be explored, even if given infinite time;

2. and, given a list of variables whose values we need to enumerate, we need to alternate the variable we change the value for next. For example, when enumerating all the values of a list of two integer variables, we cannot first enumerate all the values for the first and then, increase the second, enumerate all the values for the first and so on. If the first variable has an infinite domain, we end up never increasing the second variable. We need to alternate the variables to modify.

How each of the presented enumerations is fair will become clear during their presentation. To enumerate all possible values that a variable of given type can have, we will generate them recursively and them compose them. Assume a variable x has type $\mathbb{P}(\mathbb{Z} \times \text{BOOL})$ and the following enumerations:

– an enumeration h for powersets from $\mathbb{N}$ to $\mathbb{P}(\mathbb{N})$;
– an enumeration g for cartesian products from $\mathbb{N}$ to $\mathbb{N} \times \mathbb{N}$;
– an enumeration f_1 for integers from $\mathbb{N}$ to $\mathbb{Z}$, and;
– an enumeration f_2 for booleans from $\mathbb{N}$ to BOOL.

To obtain an enumeration for $\mathbb{P}(\mathbb{Z} \times \text{BOOL})$, we need to compose the above enumerations in the following way: given an n, we apply h to obtain a set of naturals $\{h_0, \ldots, h_s\}$. To every element of this set we apply g resulting in $\{g_{00} \mapsto g_{01}, \ldots, g_{s0} \mapsto g_{s1}\}$. Then we can apply f_1 to all the first elements of each pair and f_2 to all the second elements of each pair obtaining a set in $\mathbb{P}(\mathbb{Z} \times \text{BOOL})$: $\{f_{11} \mapsto f_{21}, \ldots, f_{1s} \mapsto f_{2s}\}$. This is a powerful method because it only requires us to define a few types of enumerations which by composition allows up to obtain enumerations for any possible EVENT-B type. The following enumerations will be defined:

- An enumeration for carrier sets S, mapping a subset of $\mathbb{N}$ to S;
- an enumeration for the integers, mapping $\mathbb{N}$ to $\mathbb{Z}$;
- an enumeration for the powerset, mapping $\mathbb{N}$ to $\mathbb{P}(\mathbb{N})$, and;
- an enumeration for fixed size lists, mapping $\mathbb{N}$ to $\mathbb{N} \times \ldots \times \mathbb{N}$. We require this enumeration to provide a lazy stream of values for a list of variables, for example, the list of local variables in an event. Furthermore, this enumeration for size 2 provides an enumeration of pairs.

The simplest enumeration is the one defined for user defined sets. Considering a set $S = \{s_0, s_1, \ldots, s_n\}$, the enumeration is a function that maps the first $n + 1$ natural numbers to each of the elements of the set S. An enumeration for the set Colors defined in the context shown in Figure 2 would be $\{0 \mapsto \text{red}, 1 \mapsto \text{green}, 2 \mapsto \text{blue}\}$.

The enumeration of the integers is given by a function f, where $f(x) = -(x + 1)/2$ if x is even and $f(x) = x/2$ otherwise. This generates an enumeration that jumps between the positive and negative numbers, without giving precedent to the positive or the negative numbers making it a fair enumeration for the whole set of integers.

Enumerating pairs is the same as enumerating lists of size 2. To enumerate lists, we enumerate first all of those whose elements sum 0, then all whose elements sum 1, and so on. This generates a diagonal perspective on the enumeration. Figure 4, on the left, represents diagrammatically how the enumeration proceeds for pairs of naturals. In the case of pairs, the only pair summing 0 is $0 \mapsto 0$, then all comes all of those summing 1: $0 \mapsto 1$ and $1 \mapsto 0$, and so on. Consider the enumeration of Colors $\times \mathbb{Z}$, where Colors is defined in Figure 2, in this case since Colors is finite, the enumeration will not generate pairs whose first element is bigger than 2, therefore having a diagrammatic representation as the one shown in the right of Figure 4.

Even though sometimes it is easy to find an explicit form as a function for an enumeration (as in the case of the integers), it is not so easy for more complex structures like lists or sets, so we will not pursue such representation and instead we will in these cases focus on how to go from one value to the next. The process of generating all lists *(enum sz s)* which have a specific sum can be thought of recursively as two cases:

1. $(enum\ 1\ s) \mathrel{\widehat{=}} (\mathbf{list}\ (\mathbf{list}\ s))$
2. $(enum\ sz\ s) \mathrel{\widehat{=}} ((\mathbf{cons}\ i\ (enum\ (-\ sz\ 1)\ (-\ s\ i)))\ \ldots)$

The first case is the base case that returns a list of all the lists of size 1 and a given sum. The second case builds all the lists of size *sz* and sum *s* by noting that the problem can be reduced by building on the lists one element smaller thus generating a recursive solution to the problem.

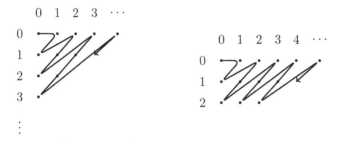

Fig. 4. Diagrammatic representation of enumeration of pairs in $\mathbb{N} \times \mathbb{N}$ (on the left) and $\{0, 1, 2\} \times \mathbb{N}$ (on the right)

Fig. 5. Diagrammatic representation of set enumeration with $step = 2$

The enumeration for sets is analogous to lists, with the constraint that two elements in a set cannot be the same and that we need to generate sets of different sizes in a fair order. We have a parameter which we called *step* that defines how many sets of size n we have to generate until we generate a set of size $n + 1$. As such, we can then lazily enumerate all the sets fairly by starting with the empty set and increasing their size. Figure 5 explains how the *step* parameter works, where $f(i) = s_i$, and f is a powerset enumeration.

3.2 Model Checking

In what follows we explain the search method used to find an invariant violation in Eboc through an example and discussing some important details in the end. Consider again the machine Example in Figure 2 and the part of the generated search tree in Figure 6.

In Figure 6, each of the shaded rectangles represent a state and the white rectangles with rounded corners represent choice points.

The simulation starts by setting up a choice point for the initial states. A choice point represents a suspension of an assignment, which might possibly have infinite results. This happens whenever a choice is required, as for example in the case of choosing a value for the parameters of an event or in the use of quantifiers.

In this case there is only one initial state since the initialization is deterministic, $x = 0$, $y = $ red, and therefore the choice point does not branch. Then, all events generate a suspension which represents a choice point for all the parameters. Event e generates a suspension for the choice of two parameters: $xx \in \mathbb{Z}$,

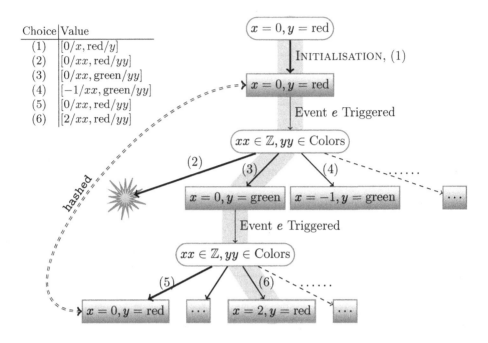

Fig. 6. Search space of the model shown in Figure 2

$yy \in$ Colors. As it can be seen in 6 we are representing states with rectangles with a gradient background and choice points with rectangles with rounded corners and white background. The choice points are where the lazy enumeration happens. In this case the scheduler will enumerate values of the for $\mathbb{Z} \times$ Colors. The first enumeration $xx = 0$, $yy =$ red generates no state since it violates one of the guards: $yy \neq y$. Note the thickness of the lines out of choice points, representing the priority with which a state is generated from a given choice. The next enumeration is: $xx = 0$, $yy =$ green generating the state $x = 0$, $y =$ green. This state generates again a suspension for the triggering of event e. At this point it is important to note the relevance of priorities in the search. The choice point has still infinitely many states to generate, but their priorities decrease as it generates more and more states from this. The second choice point has a infinitely more states to generate but the first state has again the highest possible priority and that will be the one that will be generated. The first enumeration is $xx \in \mathbb{Z}$, $yy \in$ red generating the state $x = 0$. $y =$ red but since states are hashed, the state is promptly discarded. From this point, both choice points will generate new states whose order will depend on their priorities. Once the second choice point tries the enumeration $x = 2$, $y =$ red, generating the state $x = 2$, $y =$ red the invariant evaluator, signals a violation and the process stops returning the trace: INITIALISATION, Event $e(xx = 0, yy =$ green$)$, $(x = 0$, $y =$ green$)$, Event $e(xx = 2, yy =$ red$)$, $(x = 2$, $y =$ red$)$. This is exactly the path shaded in Figure 6 and represents the path to the state violating the invariant.

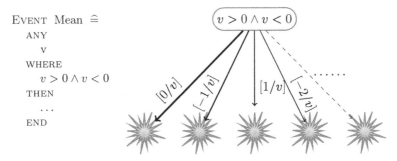

Fig. 7. Event and tree presenting an impossible guard to satisfy

This lazy method assures that all the space will be searched and if the model is finite the process will stop. If the model is infinite, the user either aborts the search after some time, or sets up the number of states that should be searched. This method generates a search tree that mixes depth with breadth first search and focusses the attention on the values which have the highest priority of generating a state which violates the invariant. For example, the enumeration of the integers starts at zero but it is possible to change the enumeration to allow it to start at any other point by adding to each of the values of the enumeration a specified offset. The priorities, which can be thought of as probabilities, are generated from a normal distribution. Note, that they are not exactly probabilities because their values range from 0 to 1, and the sum of all the priorities from a choice point does not sum 1.

Consider the event shown in Figure 7. This event has an impossible guard to satisfy which generates a choice point during the search that will never succeed in generating a state. The only reason why the search does not stop here in an infinite loop is because choice points generate branches with decreasing priority. After a while, depending on what the scheduler has on queue, the search will focus on some other part of the tree. This does not mean this choice point will be forgotten, but it will not be tried out as often as the rest. This is so that cases like $v > 1000000$ have a chance of ever generating a state.

EVENT-B supports definitions of constants whose value is constrained by a set of predicates, known as axioms. The model checking process handles them in the example same way as parameters. Constants are left undefined in the beginning and their value is only searched for once we notice an event needs their value. In this case, the choice point of the event will contain a choice for all the constants defined by the model constrained by all the axioms of the model and from that point onwards the scheduler will not worry about them anymore since below that branch their value is already assigned. This is highly inefficient: a value is assigned to all the constants once one of them is referenced, however, it should only be required to assign a value to the constants referenced in the event and those that require a value because they share the same constraint. For example, if an event uses a constant x constrained by the axioms $x < y$, then we need to assign a value to x and y but no other constant that might exist. We hope to

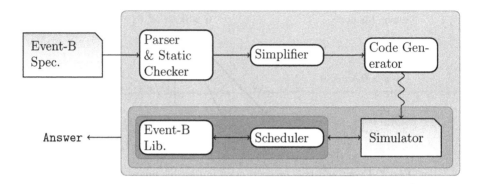

Fig. 8. Eboc system architecture

address this in the future to improve the efficiency of Eboc on models dealing with a lot of constants.

4 System Architecture

Eboc is fully implemented in PLT-Scheme [12] and was designed to be an easily extensible tool to work with EVENT-B models. Even though we implemented a model checker in the backend, it would be very easy to integrate other types of tools. We will focus this section on the system architecture and some implementation details which are important to understand how Eboc performs the lazy model checking.

Eboc is a command line tool that in its simplest form receives a file describing an EVENT-B specification and a natural number (the number of states to verify) and returns either that the verification was successful, or a trace to a state that violates one of the invariants. Figure 8 shows the system architecture. An EVENT-B specification is received as an argument and passed into the parser and static checker. The parser is responsible for generating an abstract syntax tree and the static checker besides assigning a type to each node through type inference, check that the tree is legible. The type inference and legibility rules for EVENT-B can be found in [11]. After the static check has been performed the simplifier does a series of simplifications to the model in order to simplify the simulation without affecting its performance. The code generator outputs the simulator code specific to the simulation of the input model which is linked to the scheduler and the EVENT-B library to produce the final answer.

4.1 Scheduling

The scheduling is performed by a function which given a search structure and the number of states to explore explores the state space of the model until either a violation is found or the number of states to explore has been reached.

```scheme
(define (begin-search! n s)
  (pq:enq! (search-igen s) ((search-igen s) 'prt))
  (let loop ((violations '()))
    (cond ((not (null? violations)) violations)
          ((> (search-ns s) n) '()) ; State bound achieved
          ((pq:empty?) '())         ; State space fully explored
          (else
            (let* ((element (pq:next-el!))) ;; Returns Removes high priority element
              (if (element 'empty?)
                  (loop '())
                  (let ((new-state (element 'stt)) (new-prt (element 'prt)))
                    (pq:enq! element new-prt)
                    (if (hashed? new-state)
                        (loop '())
                        (let ((vprops (foldl (λ (p acum)
                                               (if (p new-state)
                                                   acum
                                                   (cons p acum)))
                                             '()
                                             (search-props s))))
                          (incl! (set-search-ns! s))
                          (if (not (null? vprops))
                              (loop vprops)
                              (begin
                                (hash! new-state)
                                (for-each (λ (proc)
                                            (let* ((gen (proc new-state)))
                                              (when (not (gen 'empty?))
                                                (pq:enq! gen (gen 'prt)))))
                                          (search-evgen s))
                                (loop '()))))))))))))
```

Fig. 9. Simplified algorithm of the scheduler in pseudo-Scheme code

The search structure

```scheme
(define-struct search (ns igen evgen props))
```

has four elements, the number of states to explore, the initialization suspension, a list of suspension generators representing the events and a list of procedures that represent the properties that each state needs to verify.

Figure 9 shows a simplification of the scheduling algorithm. The functions *pq:enq!*, *pq:next-el*, and *pq:empty?* act on a global priority queue that contains suspensions and their respective priorities. These functions enqueue a suspension with a given priority, dequeue and remove the element with the highest priority from the queue and check if the queue is empty respectively. The scheduling function begins by enqueueing the initialization suspension which corresponds to the suspension that will generate all possible initialization states. Then it enters a loop that only stops on one of three conditions:

1. Either the number of violations found until now is not zero, in which case it returns the violations;
2. the number of states to explore as been reached, in which case it returns that no violations where found, or;
3. the queue is empty, which means that no states are left to explore and the whole state space has been explored.

Otherwise the procedures enters the *else* clause of the *cond* in the loop. Here we get the element with the highest priority in the queue. If this element is empty, meaning that no states are left to generate from this suspension, then we loop, otherwise we proceed by getting the new state the suspension has to generate (*new-state*) and the priority of the next state of the suspension (*new-prt*). Since the element was not empty, it is enqueued with the new priority and the code that follows handles the new state. If the new state has already been explored, then we loop and forget the new state, otherwise we increment the number of explored states and verify which properties have been violated in this state (*vprops*). If the number of violated properties is non-zero we loop with the violated properties to return to the user. If there are no violated properties in this state we hash the new state and enqueue all event suspensions that are not empty, meaning they generate some state and then we loop.

4.2   Code Generation and Simulation

Eboc makes use of units [13] in order to plugin automatically generated code. Code that simulates this model is generated, linked with the scheduler and the EVENT-B library, plugged into the main system and executed. Once the simulator terminates, its code is discarded and an answer is provided to the user.

The most important thing to consider is *what are suspensions?* Suspensions are closures over some variables that dictate how the next state is generated. Consider the following non-deterministic event NDet:

EVENT NDet $\widehat{=}$ ANY x WHEN $x > 0$ THEN $y := y + x$ END

The code generated for this particular event is shown in Figure 10. Each event generates a pair: guard/action procedures and it is the guard procedure that handles all the complexity related to non-determinism. The actions are always deterministic (which is not a restriction as described in section 2). The variable *enum* is a function that generates a lazy stream of values whose types are listed in the argument for *type-list-enumerator*, in this case *INT*. The closure receives a message which is then handled as appropriate. If a state is requested through the message *'stt*, then the local state is generated, the guard is evaluated and if the guard evaluates to true, the action is then invoked returning a new state. A pair of procedures, as shown in Figure 10, is generated per each event besides initialization code that sets up the search structure discussed in section 4.1 and the initial call to the *begin-search!* procedure. All this code is wrapped around a unit, which can be thought of as a pluggable module, compiled on the fly and linked to the main Eboc components.

4.3   Event-B Library

The EVENT-B deals with the evaluation of expressions and predicates. It mainly implements the operations of EVENT-B and provides two function: *eval-predicate* and *eval-expression* which evaluate a predicate or an expression respectively in a given state. Note that during the code generation each event guard and action

```
(define (NDet-guard state)
  (let* ((enum (type-list-enumerator '(INT)))
         (next-enum (enum))
         (next-prt (enum 'prt)))
    (λ (msg)
      (case msg
        ((empty?) (not next-enum))
        ((stt)
         (let ((local-state (map cons '(var:x) next-enum)))
           (begin0
             (if (eval-predicate '(> var:x 0) state local-state)
                 (NDet-action state local-state)
                 #f)
             (set! next-enum (enum))
             (set! next-prt (enum 'prt)))))
        ((prt) next-prt)))))

(define (NDet-action state local-state)
  (foldl (λ (assign-pair acum)
           (state-update acum
                         (car assign-pair)
                         (eval-expression (cdr assign-pair) state local-state)))
         state
         (list (cons 'var:y '(+ var:y var:x)))))
```

Fig. 10. Code generated for deterministic event NDet

contains symbolic expressions that represent EVENT-B predicates and expressions. All of this is done through code generation and the simulation is performed on a symbolic expression representation of EVENT-B.

5   Experiments

In this section we will report some preliminary experiments with Eboc. We will present four different models, show some results of their execution in ProB and Eboc and comment on the results.

All experiments were run on a Pentium-D 3.2GHz, with 2Gb of memory under a 64bit Gentoo Linux operating system with a timeout of 1200 seconds. Eboc was ran from the console and ProB was executed from its GUI. The measured time is shown always in seconds and in ProB reflects the time from the button to start the model checking is pushed until the experiment is completed (either because a violation is found or because the number of state to explore has been reached. For the remainder of this section, by *run* we mean a single execution of the model checkers with a given bound. Unless noted otherwise all the ProB runs were executed using the default settings of ProB-1.3.0-rc3 (compiled for 64bit). More over, ProB was set to only verify the invariants during model checking (which differs from the default option which includes also the check for deadlocks).

The first model is the Bakery1 model, which is distributed with ProB. It is a B model that we converted to EVENT-B syntax so that we could model check it with Eboc. This is a simple deterministic model where the invariants are not violated. The first row of Table 1 shows the timings for the execution of Eboc and ProB for different number of states to explore.

Table 1. Experimental results of running Eboc and ProB on four different models (runtime is shown in seconds)

	100 States		1000 States		10000 States		100000 States	
	Eboc	ProB	Eboc	ProB	Eboc	ProB	Eboc	ProB
Bakery1	3	1	4	2	13	11	141	317
Jukebox	3	1	4	59	10	217	108	>1200
Huffman	3	1	5	3	49	40	820	>1200
Consts	3	1	4	3	23	42	26	>1200

The Bakery1 model has four integer variables whose value is updated by six different events through simple arithmetic operations. One interesting point is that even though ProB is very fast for small number of states it gets slower as more and more states are explored until the point that it gets slower than Eboc. Given that this model has no invariant violation, none of the model checkers reported a violation.

The following model is the Jukebox and its experimentation table is shown in the second row of Table 1. The Jukebox is a model from a book about CLASSICAL B [14], which is also distributed by ProB as an example. Once again we converted the model from CLASSICAL B to EVENT-B so that we could use it with Eboc. The Jukebox machine sees a context that declares a deferred set and a constant, all of the machine events are non-deterministic and the update rules are set expressions.

In this example, after the first case ProB asked to increase the bound on the number of computed initializations because otherwise it would have no more states to explore. So, for all the bounds higher than 100, ProB default setting of computing 4 initializations was changed to 100. This is the reason why ProB got slower than Eboc for the remaining tests. Again, since there no violation of invariants in the model, none was reported.

Third row of Table 1 shows the experiments regarding the Huffman model by John Colley [15]. The model simulates the encoding and decoding of an infinite string of vowels from a fixed huffman tree. The model, which has 14 events, is non-deterministic and declares an enumerated set among several variables. The variables are sets or integers and most of the update rules deal with set expressions.

Eboc deals very well with these models and scaled very well. However ProB after a certain number of nodes have been explored the performance deteriorates very quickly. No invariant is violated and none of the model checker report a violation.

The Consts model is an artificial model created by us (ref. appendix A) to explore the handling of the constants when under a lot of non-determinism and which has a violation very far from the initial of the search. Last row of Table 1 shows the results for this experiment.

For the first 3 runs, neither of the model checkers found a violation and had similar performance (even though ProB already took three times more than Eboc on its third run). However, on the fourth run, Eboc found a violation after 26 seconds and ProB ran past the timeout without returning any violation. This is a case where ProB would not find the bug due to its default bounds and where Eboc had no problem finding the bound if given enough freedom to search the state space.

In conclusion, ProB is a very mature model checker with a wide range of options and model checking techniques. ProB seems to be extremelly fast for a small number of states (< 1000) but then its performance detiorates quickly. Unfortunately, at this point we did not any find real world examples that violate its invariant and where ProB is unable to detect it due to its restrictive bounds.

6 Related Work

Traditionally formal languages are supported by automated theorem provers with the notable exception of Alloy [16] which is supported by KodKod [17], a model finder.

However, other formal languages, more notably CLASSICAL B, Z and CSP, have already included a model checker to their available tools, but none has attempted to perform lazy unbounded model checking. Since the languages EVENT-B and CLASSICAL B are closely related we will concentrate our discussion in the B model checker, ProB.

ProB [9] is an animator, constraint-based checker and temporal bounded model checker for CLASSICAL B developed in SICStus Prolog. We will focus on its use as a bounded model checker. ProB requires the input of several types of bounds: bound on the size of the set of integers, bound on the number of computed initializations, and bound on the number of computed enablings (along with a timeout for computing them). Even though ProB provides default values for each of these, in practice there might be models whose faults lie outside the state space set by these bounds forcing the user to tweak them so that a faulty state can be reached. ProB as a model checker tries to find whether a machine violates its invariant by finding a sequence of operations that, starting from the initial state of the machine, navigates the machine into a state in which the invariant is violated. The exploration is done using an adaptation of the A* algorithm with cycle detection, and can be tuned to perform in the extreme cases as either a depth-first or breadth-first search. By default every node had 25% chance of being treated in a depth-first manner. ProB has been adapted over the years to check goals written in Linear Temporal Logic (LTL), and to model check Z, CSP and Promela [18]. ProB integrates symmetry reduction [19] and more recently, introduced support for EVENT-B.

On the subject of EVENT-B model checking, besides ProB we know about an attempt to use SAL, KodKod and BDDs to model check EVENT-B [20] however, at the time of writing there is no software available to experiment with.

7 Conclusions

In this paper we presented a new model checker for EVENT-B based on a lazy strategy to explore the state space of the models in an unbounded way. We focused our discussion around the problem we were trying to solve: *how to perform explicit state model checking and yet avoid bounding our domains?* We presented techniques to fairly enumerate the space of values of EVENT-B expressions, the model checking algorithm that makes use of these enumerations to lazily explore the state space and the Eboc system architecture details.

The work proposed in this paper is based on lazy streams coupled with a priority scheme and seems to work well in theory as well as in practice, even though there are still improvements to be made to the implementation in order to improve the efficiency of Eboc. Another important step is in finding complex case studies that demonstrate the importance of this approach and that Eboc is successful in finding invariants violations in these case studies, which would be otherwise impossible using bounded approaches.

References

1. Smith, G., Wildman, L.: Model checking Z specifications using SAL. In: Treharne, H., King, S., Henson, M., Schneider, S. (eds.) ZB 2005. LNCS, vol. 3455, pp. 85–103. Springer, Heidelberg (2005)
2. Derrick, J., North, S., Simons, T.: Issues in implementing a model checker for Z. In: Liu, Z., He, J. (eds.) ICFEM 2006. LNCS, vol. 4260, pp. 678–696. Springer, Heidelberg (2006)
3. Derrick, J., North, S., Simons, A.J.H.: Z2SAL - building a model checker for Z. In: Börger, E., Butler, M., Bowen, J.P., Boca, P. (eds.) ABZ 2008. LNCS, vol. 5238, pp. 280–293. Springer, Heidelberg (2008)
4. Hoare, C.A.: Communicating Sequential Processes. Prentice-Hall, Englewood Cliffs (1986)
5. Abrial, J.R.: The B-book: assigning programs to meanings. Cambridge University Press, Cambridge (1996)
6. Behm, P., Benoit, P., Faivre, A., Meynadier, J.M.: Météor: A successful application of B in a large project. In: Wing, J.M., Woodcock, J.C.P., Davies, J. (eds.) FM 1999. LNCS, vol. 1708, pp. 369–387. Springer, Heidelberg (1999)
7. Abrial, J.R.: Modeling in Event-B: Systems and Software Engineering. To be published by Cambridge University Press (2009)
8. Hallerstede, S.: On the purpose of Event-B proof obligations. In: Börger, E., Butler, M., Bowen, J.P., Boca, P. (eds.) ABZ 2008. LNCS, vol. 5238, pp. 125–138. Springer, Heidelberg (2008)
9. Leuschel, M., Butler, M.: ProB: A model checker for B. In: Araki, K., Gnesi, S., Mandrioli, D. (eds.) FME 2003. LNCS, vol. 2805, pp. 855–874. Springer, Heidelberg (2003)
10. Hallerstede, S.: Justifications for the Event-B modelling notation. In: Julliand, J., Kouchnarenko, O. (eds.) B 2007. LNCS, vol. 4355, pp. 49–63. Springer, Heidelberg (2006)
11. Métayer, C., Voisin, L.: The Event-B mathematical language (March 2009), http://wiki.event-b.org/index.php/Event-B_Mathematical_Language
12. Flatt, M., et al.: Reference: PLT Scheme. Reference Manual PLT-TR2009-reference-v4.2, PLT Scheme Inc. (June 2009)
13. Flatt, M., Felleisen, M.: Units: Cool modules for hot languages. In: Proc. Conf. on Programming Language Design and Implementation, SIGPLAN Notices, vol. 33(5), pp. 236–248. ACM, New York (1998)
14. Schneider, S.: The B-method — an introduction. Palgrave Macmillan, Basingstoke (2001)

15. Colley, J.: An Investigation into using Event-B for sub-system development in a SystemC TLM flow. Private Communication (July 2007)
16. Jackson, D.: Software Abstractions: Logic, Language, and Analysis. MIT Press, Cambridge (2006)
17. Torlak, E., Jackson, D.: Kodkod: A relational model finder. In: Grumberg, O., Huth, M. (eds.) TACAS 2007. LNCS, vol. 4424, pp. 632–647. Springer, Heidelberg (2007)
18. Leuschel, M., Plagge, D.: Seven at one stroke: LTL model checking for high-level specifications in B, Z, CSP, and more. Technical Report STUPS/2007/02, Institut für Informatik, Heinrich-Heine-Universität Düsseldorf (2007)
19. Spermann, C., Leuschel, M.: ProB gets nauty: Effective symmetry reduction for B and Z models. In: Proc. 2nd Intl. Symposium on Theoretical Aspects of Software Engineering, pp. 15–22. IEEE, Los Alamitos (2008)
20. Plagge, D., Leuschel, M., Lopatkin, I., Iliasov, A., Romanovsky, A.: SAL, Kodkod, and BDDs for validation of B models. lessons and outlook. In: Proc. 4th Workshop on Automated Formal Methods (June 2009)

A   Consts Model

MACHINE consts

SEES consts

VARIABLES x

EVENT e1 $\;\widehat{=}$
  ANY
    xx
  WHERE
    $\top$
  THEN
    $x := x + xx$
  END

EVENT e2 $\;\widehat{=}$
  ANY
    xx
  WHERE
    $xx > c2$
  THEN
    $x := xx + x + c1$
  END

EVENT e3 $\;\widehat{=}$
  WHEN
    $\top$
  THEN
    $x := c1 + c2 + x$
  END

INITIALISATION $\;\widehat{=}$
  $x := 0$

INVARIANTS
  $c1 = 2 \Rightarrow x \neq 150$
  $(x \geq -5000) \wedge (x \leq 5000)$
END

CONTEXT consts
  CONSTANTS $c1$ $c2$
  AXIOMS
    $c1 < c2$
END

Proof Assisted Model Checking for B⋆

Jens Bendisposto and Michael Leuschel

Institut für Informatik, Heinrich-Heine Universität Düsseldorf
Universitätsstr. 1, D-40225 Düsseldorf
{bendisposto,leuschel}@cs.uni-duesseldorf.de

Abstract. With the aid of the PROB Plugin, the Rodin Platform provides an integrated environment for editing, proving, animating and model checking Event-B models. This is of considerable benefit to the modeler, as it allows him to switch between the various tools to validate, debug and improve his or her models. The crucial idea of this paper is that the integrated platform also provides benefits to the tool developer, i.e., it allows easy access to information from other tools. Indeed, there has been considerable interest in combining model checking, proving and testing. In previous work we have already shown how a model checker can be used to complement the Event-B proving environment, by acting as a disprover. In this paper we show how the prover can help improve the efficiency of the animator and model checker.

Keywords: Model Checking, B-Method, Theorem Proving, Experiment, Tool Integration.

1 Introduction

There has been considerable interest in combining model checking, proving and testing (e.g., [22,23,25,11,28,4,12,15,13,14,32,29,24,5]). The Rodin platform for the formal Event-B notation provides an ideal framework for integrating these techniques. Indeed, Rodin is based on the extensible Eclipse platform and as such it is easy for provers, model checkers and other arbitrary tools to interact. In this paper we make use of this feature of Rodin to improve the PROB [18,19] model checking algorithm by using information provided by the various Rodin provers.

More concretely, in this paper we show how we can optimize the *consistency checking* of Event-B and B models, i.e., checking whether the invariants of the model hold in all reachable states. The key insight is that from the proof information we can deduce that certain events are guaranteed to preserve the correctness of specific parts of the invariant. By keeping track of which events lead to which states, we can avoid having to check a (sometimes considerable) amount of invariants.

⋆ This research is being carried out as part of the DFG funded research project GEPAVAS and the EU funded FP7 research project 214158: DEPLOY (Industrial deployment of advanced system engineering methods for high productivity and dependability).

The paper is structured as follows. In Section 2 we introduce the Event-B formal method and the Rodin platform, while in Section 3 we provide background about consistency checking and the PROB model checker, which itself already employs a combination of model checking and constraint solving techniques. In Section 4 we explain our approach to using proof information for optimizing the process of checking invariants in the PROB model checker, and present an improved model checking algorithm. Section 5 introduces a fully proven formal model of our approach. In Section 6 we evaluate our approach on a series of case studies, drawn from the Deploy project. The experiments show that there can be considerable benefit from exploiting proof information during model checking. In Section 7 we discuss how our method can be used in the context of classical B without easy access to proof information. We conclude with related work and discussions in Section 8.

2   Event-B and Rodin

Event-B is a formal method for state-based system modeling and analysis evolved from the B-method [1]. The B-method itself is derived from Z and based upon predicate logic combined with set theory and arithmetic, and provides several sophisticated data structures (sets, sequences, relations, higher-order functions) and operations on them (set union, intersection, relational composition, relational image, to name but a few).

An Event-B development consists of two types of artifacts: contexts and machines. The static properties are expressed in contexts, the dynamic properties of a system are specified in machines. A context contains definitions of carrier sets, constants as well as a set of axioms. A machine basically consists of finite sets of variables v and a finite set of events. The variables form the state of the machine, they are restricted and given a type by an invariant. The events describe transitions from one state into another state. An event has the form:

$$\text{event} \mathrel{\widehat{=}} \text{ANY } t \text{ WHERE } G(v,t) \text{ THEN } S(v,t) \text{ END}$$

It consists of a set of local variables t, a predicate $G(v,t)$, called the guard and a substitution $S(v,t)$. The guard restricts possible values for t and v. If the guard of an event is false, the event cannot occur and it is called disabled. The substitution S modifies some of the variables in v, it can use the old values of v and the local variables t. For instance, an event that chooses two natural numbers a, b and adds their product ab to the state variable $x \in v$ could be written as

$$\text{evt1} \mathrel{\widehat{=}} \text{ANY } a, b \text{ WHERE } a \in \mathbb{N} \wedge b \in \mathbb{N} \text{ THEN } x := x + ab \text{ END}$$

The Rodin tool [2] was developed within the EU funded project RODIN [26] and is an open platform for Event-B. The Rodin core puts emphasis on mathematical proof of models, while other plug-ins allow, for instance, UML-like editing, animation or model checking. The platform interactively checks a model, generates and discharges proof obligations for Event-B. These proof obligations deal with different aspects of the correctness of a model. In this paper we only deal with proofs that are related to invariant preservation, i.e., if the invariant holds in a state and we observe an event, the invariant still holds in the successor state:

$$I(v) \wedge G(v,t) \wedge S_{BA}(v,t,v') \Longrightarrow I(v')$$

By $S_{BA}(v,t,v')$ we mean the substitution S expressed as a Before-After predicate. The primed variables refer to the state after the event happened, the unprimed variables to the state before the event happened. In our small example, $S_{BA}(v,t,v')$ is the predicate $x' = x + ab$. If we want to express, that x is a positive integer, i.e. $x \in \mathbb{N}_1$, we need to prove:

$$x \in \mathbb{N}_1 \wedge a \in \mathbb{N} \wedge b \in \mathbb{N} \wedge x' = x + ab \Longrightarrow x' \in \mathbb{N}_1$$

This implication is obviously very easy to prove, in particular, it is possible to automatically discharge this obligation using the Rodin tool.

For each pair of invariant and event the Rodin Proof Obligation Generator, generates a proof obligation (PO) that needs to be discharged in order to prove correctness of a model as mentioned before. A reasonable number of these POs are discharged fully automatically by the tool. If an obligation is discharged, we know that if we observe an event and the invariant was valid before, then it will be valid afterwards. Before generating proof obligations, Rodin statically checks the model. Because this also includes type checking, the platform can eliminate a number of proof obligations that deal with typing only. For instance the invariant $x \in \mathbb{Z}$ does not give rise to any proof obligation, its correctness is guaranteed by the type checker.

The propagation and exploitation of this kind of proof information to help the model checker is the key concept of the combination of proving and model checking presented in this paper.

3   Consistency Checking and ProB

PROB [18,19] is an animator for B and Event-B built in Prolog using constraint-solving technology. It incorporates optimizations such as symmetry reduction (see, e.g., [30]) and has been successfully applied to several industrial case studies such as a cruise control system [18], parts of the Nokia Mobile Internet Technical Architecture (MITA) and the most recent one: the application of PROB to verify the properties of the San Juan Metro System deployment [20].

One core application of PROB is the *consistency checking* of a B model, i.e., checking whether the invariant of a B machine is satisfied in all initial states and whether the invariant is preserved by the operations of the machine. PROB achieves this by computing the *state space* of a B model, by

- computing all possible initializations of a model and
- by computing for every state all possible ways to enable events and computing the effects of these events (i.e., computing all possible successor states).

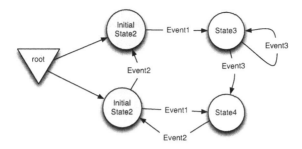

Fig. 1. A simple state space with four states

Graphically, the state space of a B model looks like in Figure 1. Note that the initial states are represented as successor states of a special root node.

PROB then checks the invariant for every state in the state space. (Note that PROB can also check assertions, deadlock absence and full LTL properties [21].)

Another interesting aspect is that PROB uses a mixture of depth-first and breadth-first evaluation of the state space, which can lead to considerable performance improvements in practice [17].

4   Proof-Supported Consistency Checking

The status of a proof obligation carries valuable information for other tools, such as a model checker. As described, PROB does an exhaustive search, i.e. it traverses the state space and verifies that the invariant is preserved in each state. This section describes how we incorporate proof information from Rodin into the PROB core.

Assuming we have a model, that contains the invariant $[I_1, I_2, I_3]^1$ and we follow an event *evt* to a new state. If we would, for instance, know that *evt* preserves I_1 and I_3, there would be no need to check these invariants. This kind of knowledge, which is precisely what we get from a prover, can potentially reduce the cost of invariant verification during the model checking.

The PROB plug-in translates a Rodin development, consisting of the model itself, its abstractions and all necessary contexts into a representation used by PROB. We evolved this translation process to also incorporate proof information, i.e., our representation contains a list of tuples (E_i, I_j) of all discharged POs, that is event E_i preserves invariant I_j.

Using all this information, we determine an individual invariant for each event that is defined in the machine. Because we only remove proven conjuncts, this specialized invariant is a subset of the model's invariant. When encountering a new state, we can evaluate the specialized invariant rather than the machine's full invariant.

---

[1] Sometimes it is handier to use a list of predicates rather than a single predicate, we use both notations equivalently. If we write $[P_1, P_2, \ldots, P_n]$, we mean the predicate $P_1 \wedge P2 \wedge \ldots \wedge P_n$.

As an example we can use the Event-B model shown in Figure 2. The full state space of this model and the proof status delivered by the automatic provers of the Rodin tool are shown in Figure 3.

VARIABLES
  f, x
INVARIANTS
  $inv1 :\ f \in \mathbb{N} \nrightarrow \mathbb{N}$
  $inv2 :\ x > 3$
EVENTS
Initialisation
$f := \{1 \mapsto 100\} || x := 10$
Event a $\widehat{=}$
$f := \{1 \mapsto 100\} || x := f(1)$
Event b $\widehat{=}$
$f := f \cup \{1 \mapsto 100\} || x := 100$

Fig. 2. Example for intersection of invariants

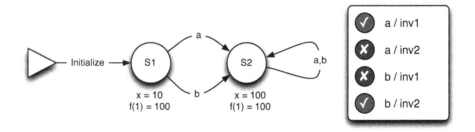

Fig. 3. State space of the model in figure 2

The proof status at the right shows, that Rodin is able to discharge the proof obligations $a/inv1$ and $b/inv2$ but not $a/inv2$ and $b/inv1$. This means, if a occurs, we can be sure that $f \in \mathbb{N} \nrightarrow \mathbb{N}$ holds in the successor state if it holds in the predecessor state. Analogously, we know, that if b occurs, we are sure, that $x > 3$ holds in the successor state if it holds in the predecessor state.

Consider a situation, where we already verified that all invariants hold for $S1$ and we are about to check $S2$ is consistent. We discovered two incoming transitions corresponding to the events a and b. From a, we can deduct that $f \in \mathbb{N} \nrightarrow \mathbb{N}$ holds. From b, we know that $x > 3$ holds. To verify $S2$, we need to check the intersection of unproven invariants, i.e., $\{f \in \mathbb{N} \nrightarrow \mathbb{N}\} \cap \{x > 3\} = \varnothing$, thus we already know that all invariants hold for $S2$.

This is of course only a tiny example but it demonstrates, that using proof information we are able to reduce the number of invariants for each event significantly, and sometimes by combining proof information from different events, we are able to get rid of the whole invariant. We actually have evidence that this is not only a theoretical possibility, but happens in real world specifications (see Section 6).

Algorithm 4.1 [*Proof-Supported Consistency Checking*]

> **Input:** An Event-B model with invariant $I = inv_1 \wedge \ldots \wedge inv_n$
> $Queue := \{root\}$; $Visited := \{\}$; $Graph := \{\}$
> **for all** events evt **do** $Unproven(evt) := \{inv_i \mid inv_i \text{ not proven for } evt\}$; **end do**
> **while** $Queue$ is not empty **do**
>   **if** random$(1) < \alpha$ **then**
> $state :=$ pop_from_front$(Queue)$; /* depth-first */
>   **else**
> $state :=$ pop_from_end$(Queue)$; /* breadth-first */
>   **end if**
>   **if** $\exists inv_i \in Inv(state)$ s.t. inv_i is false **then**
>   **return** counter-example trace in $Graph$
>   from $root$ to $state$
>   **else**
>   **for all** $succ, evt$ **such that** $state \rightarrow_{evt} succ$ **do**
> $Graph := Graph \cup \{state \rightarrow_{evt} succ\}$
>   **if** $succ \notin Visited$ **then**
>   push_to_front$(succ, Queue)$;
> $Visited := Visited \cup \{succ\}$
> $Inv(succ) := Unproven(evt)$
>   **else**
> $Inv(succ) := Inv(succ) \cap Unproven(evt)$
>   **end if**
>   **end if**
>   **end for**
>   **od**
>   **return** ok

Algorithm 4.1 describes PROB's consistency checking algorithm, we will justify it formally in section 5. The algorithm employs a standard queue data structure to store the unexplored nodes. The key operations are:

- Computing the successor states, i.e., "$state \rightarrow_{evt} succ$".
- Verification of the invariant "$\exists inv_i \in Inv(state)$ s.t. inv_i is false"
- Determining whether "$succ \notin Visited$"

The algorithm terminates when there are no further queued states to explore or when an error state is discovered. The underlined parts highlight the important differences with the algorithm in [19].

In contrast to the algorithm, the actual implementation does the calculation of the intersection ($Inv(succ) := Inv(succ) \cap Unproven(op)$) in a lazy manner, i.e., for each $state \notin Visited$, we store the event names as a list. As soon as we evaluate the invariant of a state, we calculate and evaluate the intersection on the fly. The reason is, that storing the invariant's predicate for each state is typically more expensive than storing the event names.

5   Verification

To show, that our approach is indeed correct, we developed a formal model of an abstraction of algorithm 4.1. We omitted few technical details, such as the way the state space is traversed by the actual implementation and also we omitted the fact, that our implementation always uses all available information. Instead, we have proven correctness for any traversal and any subset of the available information. Our model was developed using Event-B and fully proven in Rodin. The model is available as a Rodin 1.0 archive from http://deploy-eprints.ecs.soton.ac.uk/152/. In this paper we present only some parts of the model and some lemmas, without their proofs. All the proofs can be found in the file, we thus refer the reader to the Rodin model.

We used three carrier sets *STATES*, *INVARIANTS* and *EVENTS*. We assume, that these sets are finite. For invariants and events this is true by definition in Event-B, but the state space can in general be unbounded. However, the assumption of only dealing with finite state spaces is reasonable in the context of our particular model, because we can interpret the *STATES* set as the subset of all states that can be traversed by the model checker within some finite number of steps.[2] The following definitions are used to prove some properties of Event-B:

$$truth \subseteq STATES \times INVARIANTS$$
$$trans \subseteq STATES \times STATES$$
$$preserve = \{s \mid \{s\} \times INVARIANTS \subseteq truth\}$$
$$violate = STATES \setminus preserve$$
$$label \subseteq trans \times EVENTS$$
$$discharged \subseteq EVENTS \times INVARIANTS$$

The model also contains a set *truth*: pair of a state s and an invariant i is in *truth* if and only if i holds in s. The set *preserve* is defined as the set of states where each invariant holds, the relations *trans* and *label* describe, how two states are related, i.e. a triple $(s \mapsto t) \mapsto e$ is in *label* (and therefore $s \mapsto t \in trans$) if and only if t can be reached from s by executing e. The observation that is the foundation of all theorems we proved and is the following assumption:

$$\forall i, t \cdot (\exists s, e \cdot s \in preserve \land (s \mapsto t) \in trans \land$$

$$(s \mapsto t) \mapsto e \in label \land (e \mapsto i) \in discharged)$$

$$\Rightarrow (t \mapsto i) \in truth$$

The assumption is, that if we reach a state t from a state s where all invariants hold by executing an event e and we know, that the invariant i is preserved by e, we an be sure, that i holds in t. This statement is what we prove by discharging an invariant proof obligation in Event-B, thus it is reasonable to assume that it holds.

---

[2] Alternatively, we can remove this assumption from our Rodin models. This only means that we are not be able to prove termination of our algorithm; all other invariants and proofs remain unchanged.

We are now able to prove a lemma, that will capture the essence of our proposal; it is enough to find for each invariant i one event that preserves this invariant leading from a consistent state into a state t to prove, that all invariants hold in t.

Lemma 1. $\forall t \cdot t \in STATES \wedge (\forall i \cdot i \in INVARIANTS \wedge (\exists s, e \cdot s \in preserve \wedge e \in EVENTS \wedge (s \mapsto t) \in trans \wedge (s \mapsto t) \mapsto e \in label \wedge e \mapsto i \in discharged)) \Rightarrow t \in preserve$

Proof. All proofs have been done using Rodin and can be found in the model archive. □

We used five refinement steps to prove correctness of our algorithm. We will describe the first three steps, the last two steps are introduced to prove termination of new events. The first refinement step *mc0* contains two events **check_state_ok** and **check_state_broken**. The events take a yet unprocessed state and move it either into a set containing consistent or inconsistent states. Algorithm 5.1 shows the *check_state_ok* event, *check_state_broken* is defined analogously, except that it has the guard $s \notin preserve$ and it puts the state into the set *inv_broken*.

Algorithm 5.1 [Event *check_state_ok* from *mc0*]

```
event check_state_ok
  any s
  where
    s ∈ open
    s ∈ preserve
  then
    inv_ok := inv_ok ∪ {s}
    open := open \ {s}
end
```

At this very abstract level this machine specifies that our algorithm separates the states into two sets. If they belong to *preserve*, the states are moved into the set *inv_ok*. Otherwise, they are moved into *inv_broken*. Lemma 2 guarantees, that our model always generate correct results.

Lemma 2. *mc0 satisfies the invariants*

1. $inv\_ok \cup inv\_broken = STATES \setminus open$
2. $open = \varnothing \Rightarrow inv\_ok = preserve \wedge inv\_broken = violate$

The next refinement strengthens the guard and removes the explicit knowledge of the sets *preserve* and *violate*, the resulting proof obligation leads to lemma 3.

Lemma 3. *For all $s \in open$*

$$\{s\} \times INVARIANTS \setminus discharged[label[inv\_ok \lhd trans \rhd \{s\}]]) \subseteq truth$$

$$\Leftrightarrow s \in preserve$$

The third refinement introduces the algorithm. We introduce a new relation *invs_to_verify* in this refinement. The relation keeps track of those invariants, that need to be checked, in the initialization, we set *invs_to_verify* := *STATES*× *INVARIANTS*.

The algorithm has three different phases. It first selects a state that has not been processed yet then it checks if the invariant holds and moves the state into either *inv_ok* or *inv_broken*. Finally, it uses the information about discharged proofs to remove some elements from *invs_to_verify* as shown in algorithm 5.2.

Algorithm 5.2 [Event *mark_successor* from *mc2*]

```
event mark_successor
  any p s e
  where
    p ∈ inv_ok
    s ∈ trans[{p}]
    (p ↦ s) ↦ e ∈ label
    (p ↦ s) ↦ e ∉ marked
    ctrl = mark
  then
    invs_to_verify := invs_to_verify ◁ ({s} × (invs_to_verify[{s}] ∩ unproven[{e}]))
    marked := marked ∪ {(p ↦ s) ↦ e}
end
```

We take some state *s* and event *e*, where we know that *s* is reachable via *e* from a state *p*, where all invariants hold. Then we remove all invariants but those, that are not proven to be preserved by *e*. This corresponds to the calculation of the intersection in algorithm 4.1.

The main differences between the formal model and our implementation are, that the model does not explicitly describe how the states are chosen and the algorithm uses all available proof information while the formal model can use any subset. In addition, the model does not stop if it detects an invariant violation. We did not specify these details because it causes technical difficulties (e.g., we need the transitive closure of the *trans* relation) but does not seem to provide enough extra benefit.

Correctness of algorithm 4.1 is established by the fact that the outgoing edges of a *state* are added to the *Graph* only *after* the invariants have been checked for *state*. Hence, the removal of a preserved invariant only occurs *after* it has been established that the invariant is true before applying the event. This corresponds to the guard $p \in inv\_ok$. However, the proven proof obligations for an event only guarantee *preservation* of a particular invariant, not that this invariant is established by the event. Hence, if the invariant is false before applying the event, it could be false after the event, *even* if the corresponding proof obligation is proven and true. If one is not careful, one could easily set up cyclic dependencies and our algorithm would incorrectly infer that an incorrect model is correct.

6 Experimental Results

To verify that the combination of proving and model checking results in a considerable reduction of model checking effort, we prepared an experiment consisting of specifications we got from academia and industry. In addition we prepared a constructed example as one case, where the prover has a very high impact on the performance of the model checker. The rest of this section describes how we carried out the measurement. We will also briefly introduce the models and discuss the result for each of them. The experiment contains models where we expected to have a reasonable reduction and models where we expected to have only a minor or no impact.

6.1 Measurement

The latest development versions of PROB can do consistency checking of a refinement chain. Previous versions of PROB checked a specific refinement level only and removed all gluing invariants. We carried out both, single refinement level and multiple refinement level checks. The results have been gathered using a Mac Book Pro, 2.4 GHz Intel Core 2 Duo Computer with 4 GB RAM running Mac OS X 10.5. For the single level animation, we collected 40 samples for each model and calculated the average and standard deviation of the times measured in milliseconds. For the multi level animation, we collected 5 samples for each model. The result of the experiment is shown in tables 1, 2 and 3. The absolute values of tables 1 and 2 are very difficult to compare, because we used different versions of PROB.

Except for the case of the Siemens specification, we removed all interactive proofs from the models and used only those proof information, that Rodin was able to automatically generate using default settings. In the case of the Siemens model, we used both, a version with automatic proofs only and a development version with few additional interactive proofs; the development version was not fully proven.

6.2 Mondex

The mechanical verification of the Mondex Electronic Purse was proposed for the repository of the verification grand challenge in 2006. We use an Event-B model developed at the University of Southampton [8]. We have chosen two refinements from the model, m2 and m3. The refinement m2 is a rather big development step while the second refinement m3 was used to prove convergence of some events introduced in m2, in particular, m3 only contains gluing invariants.

In case of single refinement level checking, it is obvious that it is not possible to further simplify the invariant of m3 but we noticed, that we do not even lose performance caused by the additional specialization of the invariants. This is important because it is evidence, that our implementation's performance is in the order of the standard deviation in our measurement. For the case of m2, where we have machine invariants, we measured a reduction of about 12%.

In case of multiple refinement level checking, we have the only case, where we lost a bit of performance for m2. However, the absolute value is in the order of the standard deviation. For m3 we also did not get significant improvements of performance, most likely because the gluing invariant is very simple, actually it only contains simple equalities.

6.3   Siemens Deploy Mini Pilot

The Siemens Mini Pilot was developed within the Deploy Project. It is a specification of a fault-tolerant automatic train protection system, that ensures that only one train is allowed on a part of a track at a time. The Siemens model shows a very good reduction, as the invariants are rather complex. This model does contain a single machine, thus multi level refinement checking does not affect the speedup.

6.4   Scheduler

This model is an Event-B translation of the scheduler from [16]. The model describes a typical scheduler that allows a number of processes to enter a critical section. The experiment has shown, that the improvement using proof information is rather small, which was no surprise. The model has a state space that grows exponential when increasing the number of processes. It is rather cheap to check the invariant

$$ready \cap waiting = \varnothing \wedge active \cap (ready \cup waiting) = \varnothing \wedge active = \varnothing \Rightarrow ready = \varnothing$$

because the number of processes is small compared to the number of states. But nevertheless, we save a small amount of time in each state and these savings can sum up to a reasonable speedup. The scheduler also contains a single level of refinement.

6.5   Earley Parser

The model of the Earley parsing algorithm was developed and proven by Abrial. Like in the mondex example, we used two refinement steps that have different purposes. The second refinement step m2 contains a lot of invariants, while the m3 contains only very few of them. This is reflected in the savings we gained from using the proof information in the case of single refinement level checking. While m3 showed practically no improvement, in the m2 model the savings sum up to a reasonable amount of time. In the case of multiple refinement level checking the result are very different, while m2 is not affected, the m3 model benefits a lot. The reason is, that it contains several automatically proven gluing invariants.

6.6   SAP Deploy Mini Pilot

Like the Siemens model this is a Deploy pilot project. It is a model of system that coordinates transactions between seller and buyer agents. In the case of single refinement level case, we gain a very good speedup from using proof information, i.e., model checking takes less than half of the time. Like in the Siemens example, the model contains rather complicated invariants. In case of the multi refinement level checking the speedup is still good, but not as impressive as in single refinement level checking.

6.7   SSF Deploy Mini Pilot

The Space Systems Finland example is a model of a subsystem used for the ESA BepiColombo mission. The BepiColombo spacecraft will start in 2013 on its journey to Mercury. The model is a specification of parts of the BepiColombo On-Board software, that contains a core software and two subsystems used for tele command and telemetry of the scientific experiments, the Solar Intensity X-ray and particle Spectrometer (SIXS) and the Mercury Imaging X-ray Spectrometer (MIXS). The time for model checking could be reduced by 7% for a single refinement level and by 16% for multiple refinement checking.

6.8   Cooperative Crosslayer Congestion Control CXCC

CXCC [27] is a cross-layer approach to prevent congestion in wireless networks. The key concept is that, for each end-to-end connection, an intermediate node may only forward a packet towards the destination after its successor along the route has forwarded the previous one. The information that the successor node has successfully retrieved a package is gained by active listening. The model is described in [6]. The invariants used in the model are rather complex and thus we get a good improvement by using the proof information in both cases.

6.9   Constructed Example

The constructed example is mainly to show a case, where we get a huge saving from using the proofs. It basically contains an event, that increments a number x and an invariant $\forall a, b, c . a \in \mathbb{N} \wedge b \in \mathbb{N} \wedge c \in \mathbb{N} \Rightarrow (a = a \wedge b = b \wedge c = c \wedge x = x)$. Because the invariant contains the variable modified by the event, we cannot simply remove it. But Rodin can automatically prove that the event preserves the invariant, thus our tool is able to remove the whole invariant. Without proof information, PROB needs to enumerate all possible values for a,b and c which results in an expensive calculation.

7   Proof-Assisted Consistency Checking for Classical-B

In the setting of Event-B and the Rodin platform, PROB can rely on the other tools for providing type inference and as we have seen the proof information.

In the context of classical B, we are working on a tighter integration with Atelier B [31]. However, at the moment PROB does not have access to the proof information of classical B models.

PROB does perform some additional analyses of the model and annotates the AST (Abstract Syntax Tree) with additional information. For instance for each

Table 1. Experimental results (single refinement level check)

	w/o proof information [ms]	using proof information [ms]	Speedup-Factor
Mondex m3	1454 ± 5	1453 ± 5	1.00
Earley Parser m3	2803 ± 8	2776 ± 7	1.01
Earley Parser m2	140310 ± 93	131045 ± 86	1.07
SSF	31242 ± 64	29304 ± 44	1.07
Scheduler	9039 ± 15	8341 ± 14	1.08
Mondex m2	1863 ± 7	1665 ± 6	1.12
Siemens (auto proof)	54153 ± 50	25243 ± 22	2.15
Siemens	56541 ± 57	26230 ± 28	2.16
SAP	18126 ± 18	8280 ± 14	2.19
CXCC	18198 ± 21	6874 ± 12	2.65
Constructed Example	18396 ± 26	923 ± 8	19.93

Table 2. Experimental results (multiple refinement level check)

	w/o proof information [ms]	using proof information [ms]	Speedup-Factor
Mondex m2	1747 ± 21	1767 ± 38	0.99
Mondex m3	1910 ± 20	1893 ± 6	1.01
Earley Parser m2	309810 ± 938	292093 ± 1076	1.06
Scheduler	9387 ± 124	8167 ± 45	1.15
SSF	35447 ± 285	30590 ± 110	1.16
SAP	50783 ± 232	34927 ± 114	1.45
Earley Parser m3	7713 ± 40	5047 ± 15	1.53
Siemens (auto proof)	51560 ± 254	24127 ± 93	2.14
Siemens	51533 ± 297	23677 ± 117	2.18
CXCC	18470 ± 151	6700 ± 36	2.76
Constructed Example	18963 ± 31	967 ± 6	19.61

event we calculate a set of variables that are possibly modified. For instance if we analyze the operation[3]

$$Operation1 = BEGIN\ x := z \parallel y := y \wedge \{x \mapsto z\}\ END$$

the analysis will discover that the set of variables that could potentially influence the truth value of the invariant is $\{x, y\}$.

This analysis was originally used to verify the correct usage of SEES in the classical B-Method. The SEES construct was used in the predecessor of Event-B, so-called classical B, to structure different models. In classical B a machine can see another machine, i.e., it is allowed to call operations that do not modify the state of the other machine. To support this behavior, it was necessary to know if an operation has effect on state variables, that is the set of modified

---

[3] Operations are the equivalent of events in classical B.

Table 3. Number of invariants evaluated (single refinement level check)

	w/o Proof [#]	w Proof [#]	Savings [%]
Earley Parser m2	—	—	-
Mondex m3	440	440	0
Earley Parser m3	540	271	50
Constructed Example	42	22	50
SAP	48672	16392	66
Scheduler	20924	5231	75
Mondex m2	6600	1560	76
SSF	24985	5009	80
CXCC	88480	15368	83
Siemens	280000	10000	96
Siemens (auto proof)	280000	10000	96

variables is the empty set. It turned out, that the information is more valuable than originally thought, as it is equivalent to some proof obligation:

If u and v are disjoint sets of state variables, and the substitution of an operation is $S_{BA}(v, t, v')$ we know that $u = u'$ and thus a simplified proof obligation for the preservation of an invariant $I(u)$ over the variables u is

$$I(u) \wedge G(u \cup v, t) \wedge S_{BA}(v, t, v') \Rightarrow I(u)$$

which is obviously true. These kind of proof obligations are not generated by any of the proving environments for B we are aware of. In particular Rodin does not generate them. For a proving environment, this is a good idea as they do not contain valuable information for the user and they can be filtered out by simple syntax analysis. But for the model checker these proofs are very valuable; in most cases they allow us to reduce the number of invariants we need to check. As this type of proof information can be created from the syntax, we can use them even if we do not get proof information from Rodin, i.e., when working on classical B machines. As such, we were able to use Algorithm 4.1 also for classical B models and also obtain improvements of the model checking performance (although less impressive than for Event-B).

8   Conclusion and Future Work

First of all, we never found a model where using proof information significantly reduced the performance, i.e., the additional costs for calculating individual invariants for each state are rather low. Using proof information is the new default setting in PROB.

We got a number of models, in particular those coming from industry, where using the proof information has a high impact on the model checking time. In other cases, we gained only a bit or no improvement. This typically happens if the invariant is rather cheap to evaluate compared to the costs of calculating the guards of the events. We used an out-of-the-box version of Rodin[4] to produce our experimental results. Obviously, it is possible to further improve them by adding manual proof effort. In particular, it gives the user a chance to influence the speed of the model checker by proving invariant preservation for those parts that are difficult to evaluate, i.e., those predicates that need some kind of enumeration.

Related Work. A similar kind of integration of theorem proving into a model checker was previously described in [25]. In their work Pnueli and Shahar introduced a system to verfify CTL and LTL properties. This system works as a layer on top of CMU SMV and was sucessfully applied to fragments of the Futurebus+ system [10]. SAL is a framework and tool to combine different symbolic analysis [28], and can also be viewed as an integration of theorem proving and model checking. Mocha [3] is another work where a model checker is complemented by proof, mostly for assume-guarantee reasoning. Some more works using theorem proving and model checking together are [11,4,12,15].

In the context of B, the idea of using a model checker to assist a prover has already been exploited in practice. For example, in previous work [7] we have already shown how a model checker can be used to complement the proving environment, by acting as a disprover. In [7] it was also shown that sometimes the model checker can be used as a prover, namely when the underlying sets of the proof obligation are finite. This is for example the case for the vehicle function mentioned in [18]. Another example is the Hamming encoder in [9], where Dominique Cansell has used PROB to prove certain theorems which are difficult to prove with a classical prover (due to the large number of cases).

Future Work. We have done but a first step towards exploiting the full potential for integrating proving and model checking. For instance, we may feed the theorem prover with proof obligations generated by the model checker in order to speed up the model checking. A reasonable amount of time is spent evaluating the guards. If the model checker can use the theorem prover to prove that an event e is guaranteed to be disabled after an event f occurs, we can reduce the effort of checking guards. We may need to develop heuristics to find out when the model checker should try to get help from the provers.

Also we might feed information from the model checker back into the proving environment. If the state space is finite and we traverse all states, we can use this as a proof for invariant preservation. PROB restricts all sets to finite sets [19] to overcome the undecidability of B, so this needs to be handled with care. We need to ensure, that we do not miss states because PROB restricted some sets. Also we need to ensure that all states are reachable by the model checker, thus we may need some additional analysis of the model.

We also think of integrating a prover for classical B, to exploit proof information. The integration is most likely not as seamless as in Rodin and the costs of getting proof information is higher.

---

[4] For legal reasons, it is necessary to install the provers separately.

Although the cost of calculating the intersections of the invariants for each state is too low to measure it, the stored invariants take some memory. It might be possible to find a more efficient way to represent the intersections of invariants.

References

1. Abrial, J.-R.: The B-Book. Cambridge University Press, Cambridge (1996)
2. Abrial, J.-R., Butler, M., Hallerstede, S.: An open extensible tool environment for Event-B. In: Liu, Z., He, J. (eds.) ICFEM 2006. LNCS, vol. 4260, pp. 588–605. Springer, Heidelberg (2006)
3. Alur, R., Henzinger, T.A., Mang, F.Y.C., Qadeer, S., Rajamani, S.K., Tasiran, S.: Mocha: Modularity in model checking. In: Hu, A.J., Vardi, M.Y. (eds.) CAV 1998. LNCS, vol. 1427, pp. 521–525. Springer, Heidelberg (1998)
4. Arkoudas, K., Khurshid, S., Marinov, D., Rinard, M.C.: Integrating model checking and theorem proving for relational reasoning. In: Berghammer, R., Möller, B., Struth, G. (eds.) RelMiCS 2003. LNCS, vol. 3051, pp. 21–33. Springer, Heidelberg (2004)
5. Arons, T., Pnueli, A., Zuck, L.: Parameterized verification by probabilistic abstraction. In: Gordon, A.D. (ed.) FOSSACS 2003. LNCS, vol. 2620, pp. 87–102. Springer, Heidelberg (2003)
6. Bendisposto, J., Jastram, M., Leuschel, M., Lochert, C., Scheuermann, B., Weigelt, I.: Validating Wireless Congestion Control and Realiability Protocols using ProB and Rodin. FMWS 2008: Workshop on Formal Methods for Wireless Systems (August 2008)
7. Bendisposto, J., Leuschel, M., Ligot, O., Samia, M.: La validation de modèles event-b avec le plug-in prob pour rodin. Technique et Science Informatiques 27(8), 1065–1084 (2008)
8. Butler, M., Yadav, D.: An incremental development of the Mondex system in Event-B. Formal Aspects of Computing 20(1), 61–77 (2008)
9. Cansell, D., Hallerstede, S., Oliver, I.: UML-B specification and hardware implementation of a hamming coder/decoder. In: Mermet, J. (ed.) UML-B Specification for Proven Embedded Systems Design, ch. 16, November 2004. Kluwer Academic Publishers, Dordrecht (2004)
10. Clarke, E., Grumberg, O., Hiraishi, H., Jha, S.: Verification of the futurebus+ cache coherence protocol. Formal Methods in System Design (January 1995)
11. Dams, D., Hutter, D., Sidorova, N.: Using the inka prover to automate safety proofs in abstract interpretation - a case study. In: Bellegarde, F., Kouchnarenko, O. (eds.) Workshop on Modelling and Verification, C.I.S., Besançon, France (1999); Alternative title: Combining Theorem Proving and Model Checking - A Case Study
12. Dybjer, P., Haiyan, Q., Takeyama, M.: Verifying haskell programs by combining testing, model checking and interactive theorem proving. Information & Software Technology 46(15), 1011–1025 (2004)
13. Freitas, L.: Model Checking Circus. PhD thesis, University of York (2005)
14. Freitas, L., Woodcock, J., Cavalcanti, A.: State-rich model checking. Innovations Syst. Softw. Eng. 2(1), 49–64 (2006)
15. Gunter, E.L., Peled, D.: Model checking, testing and verification working together. Formal Asp. Comput. 17(2), 201–221 (2005)
16. Legeard, B., Peureux, F., Utting, M.: Automated boundary testing from Z and B. In: Eriksson, L.-H., Lindsay, P.A. (eds.) FME 2002. LNCS, vol. 2391, pp. 21–40. Springer, Heidelberg (2002)

17. Leuschel, M.: The high road to formal validation. In: Börger, E., Butler, M., Bowen, J.P., Boca, P. (eds.) ABZ 2008. LNCS, vol. 5238, pp. 4–23. Springer, Heidelberg (2008)

18. Leuschel, M., Butler, M.: ProB: A model checker for B. In: Araki, K., Gnesi, S., Mandrioli, D. (eds.) FME 2003. LNCS, vol. 2805, pp. 855–874. Springer, Heidelberg (2003)

19. Leuschel, M., Butler, M.J.: ProB: an automated analysis toolset for the B method. STTT 10(2), 185–203 (2008)

20. Leuschel, M., Falampin, J., Fritz, F., Plagge, D.: Automated property verification for large scale b models. In: Cavalcanti, A., Dams, D. (eds.) Proceedings FM 2009. LNCS, vol. 5850, pp. 708–723. Springer, Heidelberg (2009)

21. Leuschel, M., Plagge, D.: Seven at a stroke: LTL model checking for high-level specifications in B, Z, CSP, and more. In: Ameur, Y.A., Boniol, F., Wiels, V. (eds.) Proceedings Isola 2007, Cépaduès edn. Revue des Nouvelles Technologies de l'Information, vol. RNTI-SM-1, pp. 73–84 (2007)

22. Müller, O., Nipkow, T.: Combining model checking and deduction for i/o-automata. In: Brinksma, E., Steffen, B., Cleaveland, W.R., Larsen, K.G., Margaria, T. (eds.) TACAS 1995. LNCS, vol. 1019, pp. 1–16. Springer, Heidelberg (1995)

23. Owre, S., Rajan, S., Rushby, J., Shankar, N., Srivas, M.: PVS: Combining specification, proof checking, and model checking. In: Alur, R., Henzinger, T.A. (eds.) CAV 1996. LNCS, vol. 1102, pp. 411–414. Springer, Heidelberg (1996)

24. Pnueli, A., Ruah, S., Zuck, L.: Automatic deductive verification with invisible invariants. In: Margaria, T., Yi, W. (eds.) TACAS 2001. LNCS, vol. 2031, pp. 82–97. Springer, Heidelberg (2001)

25. Pnueli, A., Shahar, E.: A platform for combining deductive with algorithmic verification. In: Alur, R., Henzinger, T.A. (eds.) CAV 1996. LNCS, vol. 1102, pp. 184–195. Springer, Heidelberg (1996)

26. Romanovsky, A.: Rigorous Open Development Environment for Complex Systems - RODIN. ERCIM News 65, 40–41 (2006)

27. Scheuermann, B., Lochert, C., Mauve, M.: Implicit hop-by-hop congestion control in wireless multihop networks. In: Ad Hoc Networks (2007), doi:10.1016/j.adhoc.2007.01.001

28. Shankar, N.: Combining theorem proving and model checking through symbolic analysis. In: Palamidessi, C. (ed.) CONCUR 2000. LNCS, vol. 1877, pp. 1–16. Springer, Heidelberg (2000)

29. Sipma, H., Uribe, T., Manna, Z.: Deductive model checking. Formal Methods in System Design 15(1), 49–74 (1999)

30. Spermann, C., Leuschel, M.: ProB gets nauty: Effective symmetry reduction for B and Z models. In: Proceedings Symposium TASE 2008, Nanjing, China, pp. 15–22. IEEE, Los Alamitos (2008)

31. Steria, F.: Aix-en-Provence. In: Atelier B, User and Reference Manuals (1996), http://www.atelierb.societe.com

32. Uribe, T.: Combinations of model checking and theorem proving. In: Kirchner, H., Ringeissen, C. (eds.) Frocos 2000. LNCS (LNAI), vol. 1794, pp. 151–170. Springer, Heidelberg (2000)

Machine-Checked Sequencer for Critical Embedded Code Generator

Nassima Izerrouken[1,2], Marc Pantel[1], and Xavier Thirioux[1]

[1] University of Toulouse, IRIT-ENSEEIHT Laboratory
Toulouse, France
[2] Continental Automotive, Toulouse, France
{Nizerrou,Pantel,Thirioux}@enseeiht.fr

Abstract. This paper presents the development of a correct-by-construction block sequencer for GENEAUTO[1] a qualifiable (according to DO178B/ED12B recommendation) automatic code generator. It transforms SIMULINK models to MISRA C code for safety critical systems. Our approach which combines classical development process and formal specification and verification using proof-assistants, led to preliminary fruitful exchanges with certification authorities. We present parts of the classical user and tools requirements and derived formal specifications, implementation and verification for the correctness and termination of the block sequencer. This sequencer has been successfully applied to real-size industrial use cases from various transportation domain partners and led to requirement errors detection and a correct-by-construction implementation.

Keywords: automatic code generator, formal verification, software engineering, block sequencing, Coq proof assistant.

1 Introduction

Both the complexity of software in safety critical systems and the level of requirements from the certification authorities are rising regularly. Test-based verification of conformance between tool requirements (low level, conception related) and implementation (unit or integration related tests) are getting more and more expensive and less and less efficient w.r.t. the number of errors detected (according to several software departments in major industrial actors from the transportation domain). Test-based validation of user requirements and verification of conformance between user requirements (high level, specification related) and implementation (functional or deployment related tests) are mandatory and efficient but they occur very late in the development process.

Model driven engineering relies on the use of domain specific model verification in the development cycle and on automated code generation (ACG) from the verified models to software in order to avoid the costly and inefficient unit and integration tests. The use of model simulation and animation allows both early validation of user requirements and verification that tool requirements refine user requirements. The key point is not only to reduce the financial cost, but also to be able to do fast maintenance cycles.

---

[1] www.geneauto.org

K. Breitman and A. Cavalcanti (Eds.): ICFEM 2009, LNCS 5885, pp. 521–540, 2009.

In order to remove these tests on generated code, certification authorities require the ACG to be qualified, i.e. developed with the same kind of constraints as the safety critical system whose parts they will generate. ACG are handling modeling languages, it is thus quite difficult to define efficient test coverage criteria. This contribution presents the work done in the ITEA GENEAUTO project around the use of formal methods for the verification of some components of an ACG.

1.1 Motivation

The SIMULINK/STATEFLOW coupled tools from the MathWorks[2] are widely used in the domain of control and command systems for transportation. Several commercial code generators exist for SIMULINK (for example, Real-time workshop-embedded coder from the MathWorks and TargetLink from dSpace). However, to the authors knowledge, none of them have been qualified using formal technologies in the code generator. For instance, the code generator of SCADE/KCG accepts input models in SCADE[3] (model-based design toolset similar to SIMULINK) with LUSTRE-like synchronous semantics and generates C code. This code generator [1] is qualified using a classical development process: detailed specification and development cycle, test-based verification and analysis of potential sources of errors. Another example is the code generator presented in [2] where a formal verification is focused on the source code. However, code generator errors may invalidate correct source code. In addition, when classical tests are applied on the generated code, detected errors may include compiler errors as well as generated code errors. Hence the sequencer case study is particularly pertinent.

1.2 Previous Work

We presented in [3] a first block sequencer for GENEAUTO. In the beginning, it computes a total preorder of circuit blocks according to data-flow constraints, as illustrated in the figure 1(a). Then, it further distinguishes between equivalent blocks orders, thus providing a total order, using user provided block priorities and on the graphical position as done in SIMULINK. For example, let us consider the blocks with identical execution order such as *CompareToZero* and *Abs* illustrated in the figures 1(a) and 1(b), the block *Abs* cannot be evaluated before the block *CompareToZero* if the later has higher priority because its initial execution order is lower. Let us note that this algorithm also did not handle well the various kinds of control-flows. This previous work required a significant adaptation in order to handle both priorities and control-flows which are widely used in SIMULINK by industrial end users to manage side-effects (environment input/output and memory management).

1.3 Contribution

In this paper, we present the formal development of a correct-by-construction block sequencer for a qualifiable automatic code generator dedicated to safety critical real-time embedded systems. Our contribution is the integration of formal methods in a

[2] www.mathworks.com

[3] www.esterel-technologies.com

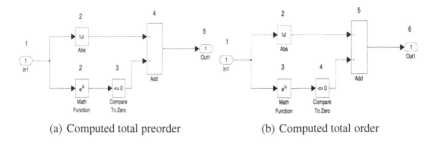

(a) Computed total preorder   (b) Computed total order

Fig. 1. SIMULINK data-flow model with conflict execution order

real qualifiable tool for the development of safety critical systems taking into account real industrial requirements and not only idealized academic ones. We rely on a formal specification of the input language derived from SIMULINK and of the user and tool requirements, to develop and to formally verify the sequencer. This approach allowed us to detect some requirement errors, remove unit tests and produce an error-free component (no bug reports related to the block sequencer so far after end users experiments, there are around 500 bug reports for the other components). First, we have transcribed the classical industrial requirements into a formal specification and developed the sequencing algorithm using the proof assistant COQ [4]. Extracted OCAML code from COQ preserves all properties proved in the specification. The extracted code is integrated in the classical development of the code generator tool chain as a qualified component.

1.4 Paper Outline

The remainder of this paper is organized as follows. Section 2 presents GENEAUTO, the code generator our work was integrated in, SIMULINK sequencing constraints and the derived requirements. Section 3 describes the specification of the input language of the code generator and dependency equations used in the sequencer. The sequencing algorithm is presented in Section 4. Section 5 outlines the main properties of the sequencer algorithm: its termination and correctness (related to execution order) properties. The code generator was applied to several real-size industrial applications from transportation domain. One case study among several industrial applications is illustrated in Section 6. Implementation and optimization aspects of the approach are discussed in Section 7. Some of earlier work on verification of code generators and compilers is sketched in Section 8. Concluding remarks and perspectives appear in Section 9.

2 Overview

2.1 Context

GENEAUTO's purpose is the development of a qualifiable automated code generator from a subset of SIMULINK and STATEFLOW to MISRA C (or any sequential

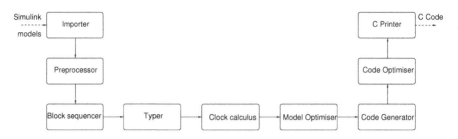

Fig. 2. GENEAUTO ACG architecture

programming language). The GENEAUTO toolset (cf. Figure 2) is composed of several elementary tools which exchange XML files representing either systems or code models:

- Model importer and exporter: converts model between GENEAUTO system model format and tool specific ones (currently SIMULINK/STATEFLOW and SCICOS);
- Preprocessor: expands virtual subsystems, check that elementary blocks are defined in the selected libraries, ...;
- Block sequencer: assigns a unique execution order fulfilling the data-flow, control-flow, user provided priority and assigned priority constraints (graphical position in SIMULINK);
- Block and signal type propagation and verification: forwards propagation of type information and verification that, for each block the computed and provided types are compatible with the block specific type as defined in the block library;
- Block and signal clock propagation and verification: System models are clock and event driven. GENEAUTO is restricted to events that are emitted on a clock basis (or buffered until the next cycle). Systems are thus synchronous. Clock information indicates if a value is available for a signal at a given clock cycle. This component does a forward propagation of clock information and verification that, for each block the computed and provided clocks are compatible with the block specific semantics as defined in the block library;
- System model optimizer: relies on clock information in order to apply transformation on the system model and reduce the memory or CPU time consumption;
- Code model generator: traverses the system model in the block execution order and produces for each block of the system model an appropriate code model according to the code pattern defined in the block library;
- Code model optimizer: applies local code restructuring rules in order to remove intermediate variables and factorize conditions. This reduces the overhead introduced by the code model generator technique;
- Target code generator: translates the generic code model to a specific target language (currently MISRA ANSI C, soon ADA).

This paper focuses on the development of the Block Sequencer, its verification using formal technologies and its integration into the tool chain development. Qualification of and compliance with SIMULINK execution model are the strongest constraints in the GENEAUTO project. GENEAUTO development process relies on the following classical steps: user and tool requirements specification, tool implementation, tool verification (the implementation fulfills the tool requirements), user verification and validation (the implementation fulfills the user requirements and intended uses).

Formal technologies have been applied in GENEAUTO in order to provide a formal specification of the requirements and implementation, and to prove that the implementation fulfills the requirements. Classical verification technologies such as proof reading or unit testing were applied where it was required or more efficient (for instance, to verify that the formal specification was correct w.r.t. the requirements written using natural language, to verify the input/output parts of the block sequencer, ...) Exchanges were conducted with certification authorities which concluded that the whole approach was sound w.r.t. the current rules of DO178B/ED12B and could be followed in order to produce a toolset that could be submitted to qualification in the appropriate domain.

2.2   Sequencing in SIMULINK

SIMULINK is a high-level graphical modeling language widely used in many application domains such as automotive and aerospace for the design of control and command systems. SIMULINK models are made of boxes linked by wires. Boxes are blocks and represent operators over the data carried by wires which stand for data signals (e.g., transporting values) or control signals (e.g., event signal for activating a sub-system).

Data-Flow Diagrams

In order to ease the development of the sequencer, we distinguish in our study between two kinds of SIMULINK blocks: combinatorial and sequential blocks without describing their operational semantics. Combinatorial blocks compute their outputs according to their inputs in the same clock instant. The sequencing of blocks linked only with data signals simply tracks data-flow propagation. An example of data-flow is illustrated in the figure 3. For instance, the *Divide* block must be executed after the *Sum* and *Gain1* blocks. A data-flow model expresses implicit concurrency between the blocks, however, we will focus on sequential execution of the blocks. A major requirement of the algorithm presented in this paper is that it must be deterministic and produces an unique execution order for each block in a SIMULINK model. This ordering must follow SIMULINK constraints which have been transcribed in GENEAUTO requirements.

Sequential blocks compute their outputs depending on the value of their inputs computed in previous cycles. For instance, the output of the block *UnitDelay*, in the figure 3,

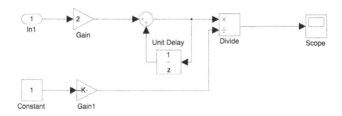

Fig. 3. SIMULINK data-flow circuit

is a copy of the value of its input from the previous clock cycle. Thus, the block *Sum* cannot be executed until the input value of *UnitDelay* computed in the previous cycle is read. Consequently, sequential blocks are split into *read* and *write* parts which are sequenced at two different steps. We only consider the read part and the other one is sequenced at the end of the cycle. Currently, we don't handle mixed blocks (combinatorial and sequential at the same time). However, any mixed block could be hierarchically decomposed to both pure combinatorial and sequential parts.

Control-Flow Diagrams

Control-flow is expressed using a mechanism similar to function call in programming languages (called "Function-call events and subsystems" in SIMULINK). A control signal links the controlling to the controlled blocks. The difficulty in models presenting imbricated control, as illustrated in the figure 4(a), is that we need to consider the transitive closure of the control relation, because the inputs of all controlled blocks must be available at the beginning of the execution of the root controlling blocks. The generated code related to *Function-Call* sub-systems is illustrated in Figure 4. For instance, to compute the sub-system g, it is required to compute the blocks controlled by g and their inputs. However, controlled sub-systems are often nested. Users can choose to inline the circuit by a pre-processing phase of the code generator. Non-inlined circuits are called atomic blocks and virtual otherwise. As a result, the execution of the sub-system f requires a prior evaluation of the input blocks $In1$, $In2$ and $In3$.

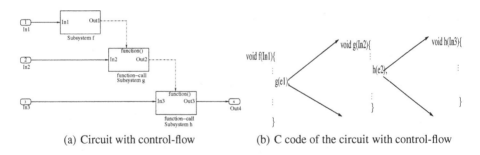

(a) Circuit with control-flow   (b) C code of the circuit with control-flow

Fig. 4. SIMULINK control-flow synthesis

Requirements for the Block Sequencing

The generated code must behave exactly as the model simulation provided by the SIMULINK tool. It is, thus, necessary that the sequencer algorithm meets requirements of SIMULINK, then sequencing constraints depend on:

– Data-flow: blocks computing values used by another block must be executed before;
– Control-flow: blocks linked by control-flows are considered as function calls in programs: caller blocks must be executed during callees blocks after their inputs;
– Sequential blocks: read part of *UnitDelay* blocks are executed before the write one;

- User priority: if two blocks cannot be sequenced with the above requirements, they must be sequenced using the user provided priority eventually defined in the model;
- Graphical position: if two blocks cannot be sequenced with the above requirements, they must be sequenced using the graphical position implicitly defined in the model.

Let us recall that the proposed sequencer is dedicated to mono-clock systems. Therefore, specification constraints of the input model include only data-flow and control-flow information and no clock data. However, these requirements did not provide an unique sequencing for all diagrams. This was exhibited during the translation to a formal specification. It was not possible to show that the result of the merging of these constraints produced a total ordering relation. This is related to the use of the graphical position by SIMULINK. It is used to order two blocks when all the other constraints are not concluding. Graphical positions are not required to be compatible with the other constraints, whereas SIMULINK requires the user priorities to be compatible with the data and control flows.

In order to overcome this default, we have introduced the notion of *inheritance* of user priority and position priority along the flows: a block inherits the priority and the position from the blocks that feeds it if these are stronger than its own. This allows us to derive a single block sequencing for any diagrams (Section 4.3).

3   Specification

We give a formal specification of the input language representing SIMULINK models inside the code generator, and then present a verified block sequencer.

3.1   GENEAUTO System Modeling Language

An input model called circuit is defined as a particular graph described by D. The input language of the code generator is described using the following simple grammar:

$$D ::= \langle G, E \rangle$$
$$G ::= \langle C_1, \ldots, C_n \rangle$$
$$E ::= \langle S_1, \ldots, S_m \rangle$$
$$C ::= B \mid D$$
$$B ::= op(\overrightarrow{i}, \overrightarrow{o}) \mid seq(\overrightarrow{i}, \overrightarrow{o})$$
$$S ::= data(s, t) \mid control(s, t) \quad (s, t \in \mathbb{N})$$

A SIMULINK block diagram D is described by G a sequence of nodes C_i and E a sequence of edges S_i. The *size* of a circuit represents the length of its node sequence. A node C can be a basic block B or a block sub-diagram D. Basic blocks can be: combinatorial blocks which compute outputs $\overrightarrow{o}$ according to all input parameters $\overrightarrow{i}$ of the block $op(\overrightarrow{i}, \overrightarrow{o})$, or sequential ones $seq(\overrightarrow{i}, \overrightarrow{o})$, characterized by the predicate $isSequential(\_)$, computing outputs according to input values from previous cycles. A sequential block cannot be involved in the control-flow. Blocks are linked by signals S that might be data signals $data(s, t)$ or control signals $control(s, t)$, where s and t are respectively positions of source and target nodes belonging to the node sequence of the concerned circuit, i.e. integers ranging from 0 to $(size - 1)$. For a given circuit A, we denote $A.In$ the set of its input blocks, $A.Out$ the set of its output blocks, $A.Callers$ the set of its controlling blocks, and finally $A.Callees$ the set of its controlled blocks.

This grammar is devoted to the sequencer component and must be extended to allow other analysis, such as type or clock verification. To simplify the presentation, we suppose that input models are flat. User can choose to inline the hierarchical circuits by a pre-processing phase in the code generator. This will not be detailed in this paper.

3.2 Dependency Equations

The adaptation of the rank calculus from our previous work to models with arbitrarily complex control-flow is not straightforward. Regarding requirements of Section 2, where data and control constraints are discussed, we propose, for a correct sequencing, to compute two sets of dependencies for each block, which must be propagated according to both data-flow and control-flow. In this section, the dependency equations are stated relatively to a circuit $d \in D$, which is left implicit when not needed. We use the terminology *event* to indicate start or end of the execution of a block.

- Input Dependencies (D_{in}): is the set of events that must have occurred in order to be able to start the execution of a block
- Output Dependencies (D_{out}): is the set of events that must have occurred in order to produce the output of a given block

Furthermore, a precise dependency specification must take into account the fact that a controlled block is executed inside its controller block. Thus we need to determine the start and end of blocks linked with control-flow. So, we tag blocks so that we distinguish between the start and end events of the execution for each block. Let *Call* and *Return* tags indicate respectively the beginning of reading inputs and writing outputs of a given block. We distinguish dependencies for combinatorial and sequential blocks. Thus, we define the domain of dependencies as $\Delta \triangleq \mathcal{P}(T)$ where $T \triangleq \{Call(i), Return(i) | i \in [0, size[\}$ is the type describing event constructors for each block.

Definition 1. *Input Dependencies D_{in}*

$$\forall A \ s.t. \ isSequential(A), \ D_{in}(A) \triangleq D_{out}(A.In) \ \cup \ Return(A) \qquad (1)$$

$$\forall A \ s.t. \ \neg isSequential(A), \ D_{in}(A) \triangleq D_{out}(A.In) \ \cup \ Return(A.In) \qquad (2)$$
$$\cup \ D_{in}(A.Callers) \ \cup \ Call(A.Callers)$$

The input values of a sequential block will be used in the next cycle, so they must be memorized. Thus, the start of sequential block execution (*cf.* equation 1) requires us to compute all blocks connected to its inputs blocks $(D_{out}(A.In))$ and write the output of the sequential block into memory $(Return(A))$. Before computing a combinatorial block (*cf.* equation 2), all the blocks connected to its inputs have to be finished $(D_{out}(A.In)$ and $Return(A.In))$ and all its controlling blocks must be ready to be called $(D_{in}(A.Callers)$ and $Call(A.Callers))$ before any other forthcoming event.

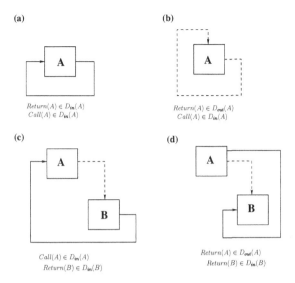

Fig. 5. SIMULINK Basic Loops

Definition 2. *Output Dependencies* D_{out}

$$\forall A \; s.t. \; isSequential(A), \; D_{out}(A) \triangleq Call(A) \tag{3}$$

$$\forall A \; s.t. \; \neg isSequential(A), \; D_{out}(A) \triangleq D_{out}(A.Callees) \cup Call(A) \tag{4}$$
$$\cup \; Return(A.Callees) \cup D_{in}(A)$$

The output of sequential blocks corresponds to read memory access $(Call(A))$. These accesses have to be executed first (*cf.* equation 3). The evaluation of the output of a given combinatorial block A (*cf.* equation 4) requires to compute its input blocks ($D_{in}(A)$ and $Call(A)$) and its controlled blocks must be ready to be finished ($D_{out}(A.Callees)$ and $Return(A.Callees)$) before any other forthcoming event.

3.3   Causality Issues

One main property related to design correctness for SIMULINK models is to verify the absence of causal loops. We differentiate two kinds of loops: data algebraic loop and control loop. Data algebraic loop, as illustrated by the most simple case of Figure 5(a), states that a given block inputs depend on the same block outputs at the same cycle. Control loop stands for a recursive call of the block (see Figure 5(b)). In such a case, the block may be executed, in the same cycle, an unbound number of times which is forbidden in finite time discrete SIMULINK control-flow. These two kinds of loops break the sequencing process. Consequently, models presenting such case must be rejected as model errors. Data and control loops can also be mixed as illustrated in the figures 5(c) and 5(d). These are considered as potential model errors in our analysis. Nevertheless SIMULINK accepts such models since it considers a default value (the one in the previous cycle) for data signals in case of non available values. All these errors are gathered under the following single property, inspired by the typical cases of Figure 5. Mimicking the SIMULINK distinction between potential and unquestionable errors would involve a more complex analysis, for instance detecting in advance pure data and control loops. Note that a pure control-flow or data-flow loop will be correctly spotted as a (potential) error, as $Return(b) \in D_{out}(b)$ holds in both cases.

Property 1. Absence of Loop related Potential Errors
$\forall\, b \in d,\ Return(b) \notin D_{out}(b)$

4 Sequencing Algorithm

4.1 Generic Framework

We define a generic framework, pertaining to the world of static analysis by least fixpoint computation, which computes for a given circuit the required information over blocks and signals. This information is defined by recursive equations according to the flow propagation. We apply the algorithm of Kleene to compute the least fixpoint of these equations. The generic framework will be instantiated to different analysis components of the code generator we are developing. It eases the development and allows the reuse of factorized proofs. The framework is parametrized by:

– Semantic domain: it represents the semantic information associated to circuit parts, such as block dependencies, types, clocks, etc.;
– Well-founded ordering: domain must be supplied with a well-founded ordering relation. This ordering is required to guide the undertaken analysis and ensures its termination;
– Lattice structure: the lattice operators will be used to express the abstract semantics of the blocks used in the flow equations based on the SIMULINK semantics and the user annotations;
– Transfer function: last, we need to propagate information between blocks and signals using a monotonic function with respect to the order relation.

4.2 Fixpoint Calculus

We define the domain of environments of size m as $\Gamma_m \triangleq \{i \in \mathbb{N} \mid i < m\} \to \Delta$. The main domain of input and output dependencies in our analysis is $\Theta \triangleq \Gamma_{size} \times \Gamma_{size}$. In order to propagate the dependencies through the circuit structure, we need a *transfer* function which spreads dependencies according to data-flow and control-flow.

Let $F : \Theta \to \Theta$ be the global transfer function where $\langle D_{in}, D_{out} \rangle = F(\langle D_{in}, D_{out} \rangle)$. F is composed of two transfer functions : E'_{in} the transfer function for input dependencies and E'_{out} the transfer function for output dependencies.

Definition 3. *Transfer function*

$$
\begin{aligned}
F &= \langle E_{in},\ E_{out} \rangle \mapsto \langle E'_{in},\ E'_{out} \rangle \\
E'_{in} &= A \mapsto
\begin{cases}
E_{out}(A.In) \cup Return(A.In) \\
\quad \cup E_{in}(A.Callees) & , when\ \neg isSequential(A) \\
E_{out}(A.In) \cup Return(A) & , when\ isSequential(A)
\end{cases} \\
E'_{out} &= A \mapsto \dots
\end{aligned}
$$

Initially, the calculus starts from an empty set of dependencies. The result $\langle D_{in}, D_{out} \rangle$ is computed as the least fixpoint of the transfer function F. Once the least fixpoint is reached, in our ordering analysis, we will be interested in output dependencies D_{out}, i.e. dependencies needed to finish execution of blocks. As for sequential blocks, following their usual decomposition into two *Read* and *Write* sub-blocks, comparing output dependencies amounts to considering only the *Read* part in our sequencing algorithm. For that purpose, relatively to a given element $\theta \in \Theta$ (in our case, the lfp of F), blocks are compared to each other via the following order relation defined on Δ. Notice that this relation is not to be confused with the global order relation on Θ needed to prove termination of the fixpoint calculus, as defined in Section 5.

Definition 4. *Order relation over block dependencies* ($\leq_\theta$) [4]
$$b \leq_\theta b' \triangleq snd(\theta)(b) \subseteq snd(\theta)(b')$$

However, all blocks are not necessarily comparable within $\leq_\theta$. Furthermore, additional requirements have to be considered.

4.3   Enforcing Additional Requirements

Aside from pure data and control flow dependencies, in SIMULINK we must take into account another sequencing constraints about blocks priorities. Priorities can be explicitly set by the user (user priority) or implicitly deduced from the circuit model which is based on the graphical position in SIMULINK (given priority). The last step of our sequencing algorithm consists in sorting, in decreasing order, output dependencies for each block using an order on priorities. Assume that $\alpha(b)$ (respectively $\beta(b)$) represents the user priority and the given priority for a block b.

Definition 5. *Lexicographical order over block priorities* $\leq_P$
$$b \leq_P b' \triangleq \alpha(b) < \alpha(b') \vee \alpha(b) = \alpha(b') \wedge \beta(b) < \beta(b'))$$

Let $\Sigma \triangleq \{b \mid Call(b) \in T\}^*$ be the set of *Call* events sequence. Assume a function $sort : \Delta \to \Sigma$ that sorts $Call(b)$ dependencies in decreasing order on b according to $\leq_P$, while removing $Return(b)$ dependencies. Therefore, the priority for a block is inherited from its dependencies. Moreover, we may immediately notice that two different blocks cannot have the same output dependencies, because the dependency of any block b contains at least the $Call(b)$ event. So considering them as sequences, lexicographically ordered, seems a natural way so to provide a total order between blocks. Also, first sorting the dependency sequence of a block b in decreasing priority order naturally allows us to emphasize greatest priorities.

Definition 6. *Lexicographical order over dependency sequences* $\leq_\Sigma$
$$\langle b_n, \ldots, b_1 \rangle \leq_\Sigma \langle b'_m, \ldots, b'_1 \rangle \triangleq$$
$$n = 0 \vee b_n <_P b'_m \vee (b_n =_P b'_m \wedge \langle b_{n-1}, \ldots b_1 \rangle \leq_\Sigma \langle b'_{m-1}, \ldots b'_1 \rangle)$$

Finally, blocks will be given an execution order, as their position in the following total order on blocks.

Definition 7. *Order relation over prioritized block dependencies* $\leq_{\theta^*}$
$$b \leq_{\theta^*} b' \triangleq sort(snd(\theta)(b)) \leq_\Sigma sort(snd(\theta)(b'))$$

---

[4] $snd(p)$ is the second projection of a pair p.

5   Formal Verification

One of the main purpose of GENEAUTO is to verify the code generator using formal methods and exchange with certification authorities about the acceptance of these technologies for qualification. The most important part of the development process is the verification phase. It consists in proving the conformance to requirements as well as auxiliary properties, such as termination of algorithms, correction of execution order with respect the circuit structure and loop detection.

5.1   Monotonicity of Transfer Function

This property states that each iterate of the transfer function F, starting from an initial empty set of dependencies, brings a new dependency set for a given block of the circuit, unless the fixpoint is reached. We define a relation order over pair of dependencies as:

Definition 8. *Well-founded order on main domain* $(\leq_\Theta)$

$$\langle \gamma_{in}, \gamma_{out} \rangle \leq_\Theta \langle \gamma'_{in}, \gamma'_{out} \rangle \triangleq \gamma_{in} \leq_{\Gamma_{size}} \gamma'_{in} \wedge \gamma_{out} \leq_{\Gamma_{size}} \gamma'_{out}$$
$$\gamma \leq_{\Gamma_{size}} \gamma' \triangleq \forall b \in d,\ \gamma(b) \subseteq \gamma'(b)$$

We need to prove that the transfer function is monotonic with respect to $\leq_\Theta$.

Theorem 1. *Monotonicity of* F

$$\forall \theta, \theta' \in \Theta,\ \theta \leq_\Theta \theta' \Rightarrow F(\theta) \leq_\Theta F(\theta')$$

Proof. We prove that both the input transfer function E'_{in} and the output transfer function E'_{out} are monotonic with respect to E_{in} and E_{out}. E'_{in} is monotonic as it is defined using the join operator which is monotonic. The proof can be conducted by structural decomposition. Symmetrically, E'_{out} is proved monotonic. Once the two auxiliary transfer functions are proved monotonic, the demonstration that F is monotonic is done structurally by applying the 2 above proofs.

5.2   Termination

One complex proof is to check whether the fixpoint calculus terminates. This property states that the computation of the successive iterates of F shall not loop.

Theorem 2. *The order relation* $\leq_\Theta$ *is well-founded.*

Proof. First, Δ, the set of subsets of T, is well-founded with respect to inclusion order as T is finite. Second, Γ_{size} well-foundedness is proved by induction on the circuit size. Finally, $\leq_\Theta$ is well-founded as a classical lattice product.

5.3   Order Correctness

The correctness order property ensures that the sequencing algorithm computes a correct order w.r.t. to the structure of input model. It must, first, implement the data-flow requirement.

Theorem 3. *Data-flow Order Correctness*

$$\forall b, b' \in d,\ \neg isSequential(b') \Rightarrow b \in b'.In \Rightarrow D_{out}(b) \subseteq D_{out}(b')$$

Proof. Let b and b' be blocks, block b' being combinatorial, such that $b \in b'.In$. By expanding the definition of $D_{in}(b')$ (resp. $D_{out}(b')$), we prove $D_{out}(b) \subseteq D_{in}(b')$ (resp. $D_{in}(b') \subseteq D_{out}(b')$). Then, the order correctness holds by transitivity.

Second, correctness order concerns also control-flows. Since a controlled block occurs inside a controlling one, this means that it is executed during the evaluation of its controlling block. We need to prove that a controlling block depends somehow on its controlled blocks.

Theorem 4. *Control-flow Order Correctness*
$\forall b, b' \in d, \ b \in b'.Callees \ \Rightarrow \ D_{out}(b) \subseteq D_{out}(b')$

Proof. Let b and b' be blocks, such that $b \in b'.Callees$. By expanding the definition of $D_{out}(b')$, we directly prove $D_{out}(b) \subseteq D_{out}(b')$.

Besides the principal theorems, some of which are sketched above, auxiliary theorems are proved in order to decompose complex demonstrations into simple lemmas. Notice that demonstrated theorems may be reused in other modules than the sequencer one (type, clocks, etc.).

6   Experimental Issues

The whole component implemented in COQ is correct-by-construction (around 500 reports were submitted for the other components, whereas, there was no bug reports related to the Block Sequencer). The extracted OCAML code is then integrated in the code generator as a qualified part. The specification and proofs are more that 4500 COQ code lines long, including input models data structure, sequencing and demonstrations of more than 130 theorems. Because of lack of space, the COQ development is not detailed in the paper. Nevertheless, it can be found at `http://izerrouken.perso. enseeiht.fr/`.

6.1   Integration of Elementary Tool

The source code of the elementary tool is extracted automatically in OCAML from the tool specification design and correctness proof using the program extractor from the COQ toolset. Currently, some parts (we have called *elementary tools*) in GENEAUTO are written with classical technologies using the JAVA programming language, and other parts are written with COQ and extracted to OCAML programming language. In order to interface the extracted code from COQ with the other parts of the GENEAUTO toolset, each elementary tool developed using formal technologies is composed of two software artifacts as illustrated in the figure 6.

The JAVA front-end model (reader and writer), on the one hand, relies on the common `Model Factory` to read and write the full XML model files representing the system and code models, and on the other hand executes the OCAML wrapper for the extracted implementation of the elementary tool from the COQ development. In order to exchange information with the concerned module, it writes simple text files which contain the minimal description of the model. This choice relies on simple verification

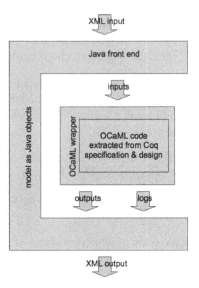

Fig. 6. Elementary tool architecture in GENEAUTO

of text files printers and parsers by cross-reading instead of the more complicated XML ones. Then, after executing OCAML wrapper, it reads a simple text file which contains minimal required information for building the outputs of the elementary tool. This artifact will also read the text log file produced by the OCAML model wrapper and output the messages through the standard GeneAuto logging facility. The OCAML wrapper which reads the simple text model file and computes the necessary information for the wrapper. For instance, the OCAML model sequencer computes the input and output dependencies, sorts the blocks according to the rules in the tool requirements, assigns an execution order to all blocks of the model and writes these to the execution order simple file. This artifact will also produce a log file.

6.2 Automotive Use Case

An industrial model is illustrated in figure 7. It exhibits the intricate mix of data and control flows. This use case is part of a larger Continental model describing functional behavior of the KNOCK reduction sub-system of a powertrain engine control function (gasoline for this model). We don't describe the operational part of the different blocks composing the studied system. Control signals are represented by dotted wires. The entire SIMULINK model has a hierarchical depth of 9 layers. It contains more than 5790 blocks (including subsystems, basic blocks as well as trigger/enabled ports). Sequencing the whole automotive system takes one second. The full code generator toolset including the formal Block Sequencer takes less than 18 seconds.

First, the OCAML wrapper indexes all blocks of the SIMULINK model. Then, the sequencing process starts computing input and output dependencies according to data and control flows. Due to lack of space, we will focus on sequencing some relevant blocks. For instance, the block READARRAY (which has the index 20) is connected through pure data-flow signals. The code generator tool shows the following fragments

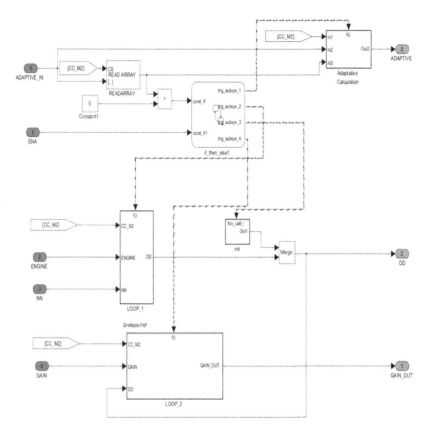

Fig. 7. Automotive powertrain engine control function

```
[INFO][TBlockSequencer_coq]09-07-15 21:38:56.667
[INFO] Input dependencies:
[INFO] block( 20 ) = {Call(Adaptive-In,CC-M2),
Return(Adaptive-In,CC-M2)}
[INFO][TBlockSequencer_coq]09-07-15 21:38:56.668
[INFO] Output dependencies:
[INFO] block( 20 ) = {Call(Adaptive-In,CC-M2,Readarray),
Return(Adaptive-In,CC-M2)}
```

Fig. 8. Evaluated dependencies for block READARRAY

of dependency calculus according respectively to READARRAY block and CC-M2 as shown in Figure 8 and Figure 9. To start evaluating the block READARRAY, the blocks ADAPTIVE-IN and CC-M2 have to be called (Call(ADAPTIVE-IN,CC-M2)) and finished (Return(ADAPTIVE-IN,CC-M2)). CC-M2 input dependencies is empty because there is no input to this block, while to produce its output, the block CC-M2 has to

```
[INFO][TBlockSequencer_coq]09-07-15 21:38:56.667
[INFO] Input dependencies:
[INFO] block( 1 ) = { }
[INFO][TBlockSequencer_coq]09-07-15 21:38:56.667
[INFO] Output dependencies:
[INFO] block( 1 ) = { Call(CC-M2) }
```

Fig. 9. Evaluated dependencies for block CC-M2

```
[INFO][TBlockSequencer_coq]09-07-15 21:38:56.667
[INFO]Input dependencies:
[INFO] block( 11 ) = { Call(ENA,Engine,NN,Adaptive-In,CC-M2,
Constant1,Relational,Readarray,IfThenElse1),
Return(ENA,Engine,NN,Adaptive-In,CC-M2,Constant1,
Relational,Readarray)}
[INFO][TBlockSequencer_coq]09-07-15 21:38:56.668
[INFO] Output dependencies:
[INFO] block( 11 ) = { Call(ENA,Engine,NN,Adaptive-In,CC-M2,
Constant1,Loop1,Relational,Readarray,IfThenElse1),
Return(ENA,Engine,NN,Adaptive-In,CC-M2,Constant1,
Relational,Readarray)}
```

Fig. 10. Evaluated dependencies for block LOOP-1

```
[INFO][TBlockSequencer_coq.]09-07-15 21:38:56.667
[INFO] Input dependencies:
[INFO] block( 16 ) = { Call(ENA,Adaptive-In,CC-M2,Constant1,
Math,Relational,Readarray,IfThenElse1),
Return(ENA,Adaptive-In,CC-M2,Constant1,Relational,
Readarray}
[INFO] Output dependencies:
[INFO][TBlockSequencer_coq]09-07-15 21:38:56.668
[INFO] block( 16 ) = { Call(ENA,Adaptive-In,CC-M2,Constant1,
Relational,Init,Readarray,IfThenElse1),
Return(ENA,Adaptive-In,CC-M2,Constant1,Relational,
Readarray}
```

Fig. 11. Evaluated dependencies for block INIT

execute its code (Call(CC-M2)). We remark that $D_{out}(\text{CC-M2}) \subset D_{out}(\text{READARRAY})$, consequently, the block CC-M2 is sequenced before READARRAY. All output dependencies are often not comparable. For instance, LOOP-1 and INIT are two incomparable blocks. They are indexed respectively 11 and 16 and their respective dependencies are shown in Figure 11 and Figure 10. In order to sequence the two incomparable blocks LOOP-1 and Init, only finished events are considered. So, the *Call* part of each output

Table 1. Industrial case studies size

Case Study	Satellite Orbit Control	"Knock" reduction Software	Airplane Flight Control System	Satellite Agile Control System	Sensor Networks
Model blocks	1085	5793	2800	1931	1108
Depth	8	9	7	6	7

dependency is sorted according to lexicographical order $\leq_P$ defined in Section 4.1. The resulting sorted sequence in decreasing order of output dependencies for LOOP-1 is:

⟨NN,ENGINE,ENA,RELATIONAL,CONSTANT1,READARRAY,ADAPTIVE-IN,CC-M2, LOOP1,IFTHENELSE1⟩

and the one for the block INIT is:

⟨ENA,RELATIONAL,CONSTANT1,READARRAY,ADAPTIVE-IN,CC-M2, INIT,IFTHENELSE1⟩

The two sequences are, then, element-wise compared using $\leq_\Sigma$ (cf. Section 4.1). In our case, the block ENA has higher priority than the block NN. Consequently, the block INIT is sequenced before the block LOOP-1.

6.3 Experimental Evaluation

Our scheduler was experimented on several industrial real-size applications. The code generator was successfully applied with the verified Block Sequencer to several industrial modules. Some case studies are illustrated in Table 1. Model blocks exhibits the blocks number of industrial case studies. The corresponding number of hierarchical nested levels is represented by depth. The cost of the sequencer is in line with the execution time of the others components. We have also applied the sequencer on "worst case" pipeline models of length 5000 with a memory cost of 2 Gb and runtime cost of 45 min on a 2.6 GHz core 2 duo.

7 Limitations and Optimization

In this section, we highlight some implementation issues about the sequencer module.

7.1 Efficient Handling of Integers

In COQ, data structures are defined using inductive types such as "nat" for the set of natural numbers. Then, the extracted OCAML code, reflecting the structure of COQ types, contains for instance the Peano integer coding for "nat". This coding allows to express any natural number as a unique sequence of S (successor) operators, followed by O (zero). For instance the number "3" is extracted as "S(S(S O))". Therefore, manipulating these Peano numbers is very costly in terms of memory and computing power. For instance, the addition $n + m$, instead of being executed in constant time as it is the case for primitive integers, is executed in time $O(n)$, as the result of a full recursive matching of its first parameter. The solution we have adopted so far consists in patching the extraction mechanism (as allowed by COQ), in order to map the original natural numbers to the primitive 32-bits integers of OCAML. As some arithmetical operations may now overflow, due to the fixed size of primitive integers, we make use of some *defensive programming* techniques, i.e. dynamically checked assertions about absence of overflows, in place of *offensive* techniques, i.e. proofs that manipulated integers always lie in a fixed range. Although this mapping is not formally proved harmless, it may still be fully qualified in our opinion, as the correction of our simple assertions surrounding our simple (primitive) arithmetical operations is easily done by careful code reading. Moreover, from a practical standpoint, GENEAUTO models are obviously unlikely to contain more elements than primitive integers would handle.

7.2 Efficient Handling of Function Applications

Still, the generated OCAML code without any further optimization can be very inefficient because of a rather undisciplined extraction mechanism. The extraction process tends first to replace some intermediate variables by their defining expressions (thus computing the value each time the variable is accessed) and second to perform some η-expansions, that adds extra parameters, turning straightaway evaluable expressions into functions (whose body is computed each time the function is applied). In our block sequencer, we chose to implement dependency environments ("D_{in}" and "D_{out}") as simple functions, which are plain first-class citizens in COQ, whereas specific data-structures, such as lists or hash-tables, would have deserved a special care and some related extra correction proofs. Concerning the fixpoint calculus of these functions, at each iteration the OCAML dependency evaluation ("E'_{in}" and "E'_{out}") of a given block computes over and over the dependencies of all related blocks, due to the extraction mechanism. The problem is solved by using a safe write once/read many caching mechanism, taking place during the extraction process, that puts once and for all evaluated values for an iteration in a local vector. The garbage collector allows the reuse of these vectors, so it doesn't affect the overall memory usage. Again, the management of these caches has been carefully designed in order to avoid any possible (unspecified) side-effect that would ruin the whole COQ development effort. Again, confidence in the correction of our caches seems easily obtainable by code proof reading.

8   Related Work

There exists a huge background of work related both to automatic code generation for model-based languages and to the verification of ACG. Large part of this work is dedicated to synchronous language-based models such as SCADE/KCG/LUSTRE, see [5,6,7,8]. Semantics of models supported by GENEAUTO, however, mix data-flow and control-flow. These can be expressed using synchronous languages (see [9,10]), but these do not allow us to easily respect the model/code structural traceability constraint expressed in GENEAUTO by several industrial partners. In addition to these works, semantics and features of code generation for synchronous languages are treated in [9,10,11,12], but besides the difficulty to handle traceability constraint, there is no formal verification applied to the code generator itself. The code generator of [2] focus on the verification of the source code. Important related works rely on compiler verification and validation, e.g., see [13,14], but the verification is focused on instances of compilation. A promising approach consists in the formal development of a correct-by-construction compiler, e.g. [15], our work is based on this later approach. However, there is a significant difference with our proposal. Formal technologies applied for proving compiler correctness usually rely on formal specification of the semantics of both input and output languages, the translation itself, and on the proof that the observed semantics of the source and target are always equivalent, similar or bi-similar. We have chosen in GENEAUTO not to depart too much from the usual industrial approach to qualification in order to ease its acceptance by certification authorities, thus we do not work at the semantic level directly. In fact, we developed a two-step approach: in a first step, tool components developers write a classical natural language specification of requirements that is translated in a formal specification used for a formal correct-by-construction development; then, in a second step, these requirements are proved correct w.r.t. the semantics of the languages. In this paper, we have focused on the first step.

9   Conclusion

We propose a formal framework for sequencing SIMULINK models as a first step for a qualified code generator for embedded critical systems. We have formally specified the input language of SIMULINK models, their requirements and formally implemented and verified the correctness properties of the sequencer. We think our work being challenging since the test phase is removed from the review process of the scheduler. The proposed tool not only produces a correct execution order with respect to requirements but also rejects models with loops. It appears that, once optimization problems were solved, we ended up with a prototype written in a pure functional style, that favorably compares in terms of memory and time consumption with the other GENEAUTO modules of similar complexity, that are still at this time hand-written in JAVA. The code source of the Block sequencer is now available at http://izerrouken.perso.enseeiht. fr/. Current and further work will include the development of other modules such as typing and clock calculus, on the one hand to improve the mixed classical/formal verification for qualification purpose and on the other hand to provide a complete ACG verified using formal technologies.

References

1. Pagano, B., Andrieu, O., Canou, B., Chailloux, E., Colaco, J.L., Moniot, T., Wang, P.: Certified development tools implementation in objective caml. In: Hudak, P., Warren, D.S. (eds.) PADL 2008. LNCS, vol. 4902, pp. 2–17. Springer, Heidelberg (2008)
2. Berry, G., Bouali, A., Fornari, X., Ledinot, E., Nassor, E., de Simone, R.: Esterel: a formal method applied to avionic software development. Sci. Comput. Program. 36(1), 5–25 (2000)
3. Izerrouken, N., Thirioux, X., Pantel, M., Strecker, M.: Certifying an Automated Code Generator Using Formal Tools: Preliminary Experiments in the GeneAuto Project. In: European Congress on Embedded Real-Time Software (ERTS), Toulouse, 29/01/2008-01/02/2008 (2008) (electronic medium), http://www.sia.fr

4. Bertot, Y., Castéran, P.: Interactive Theorem Proving and Program Development. Coq'Art: The Calculus of Inductive Constructions. Texts in Theoretical Computer Science. Springer, Heidelberg (2004)

5. Biernacki, D., Colaco, J.L., Hamon, G., Pouzet, M.: Clock-directed modular code generation of synchronous data-flow languages. In: ACM International Conference on Languages, Compilers, and Tools for Embedded Systems (LCTES), Tuscon, Arizona (June 2008)

6. Caspi, P., Hamon, G., Pouzet, M.: Synchronous Functional Programming with Lucid Synchrone. In: Real-Time Systems: Models and verification —Theory and tools. ISTE (2007)

7. Colaço, J.L., Hamon, G., Pouzet, M.: Mixing signals and modes in synchronous data-flow systems. In: ACM International Conference on Embedded Software (EMSOFT 2006), Seoul, South Korea (October 2006)

8. Colaço, J.L., Pouzet, M.: Type-based initialization analysis of a synchronous data-flow language. International Journal on Software Tools for Technology Transfer (STTT) 6(3), 245–255 (2004)

9. Caspi, P., Curic, A., Maignan, A., Sofronis, C., Tripakis, S.: Translating discrete-time simulink to lustre. In: Alur, R., Lee, I. (eds.) EMSOFT 2003. LNCS, vol. 2855, pp. 84–99. Springer, Heidelberg (2003)

10. Caspi, P., Curic, A., Maignan, A., Sofronis, C., Tripakis, S., Niebert, P.: From simulink to scade/lustre to tta: a layered approach for distributed embedded applications. In: ACM-SIGPLAN Languages, Compilers, and Tools for Embedded Systems, LCTES 2003 (2003)

11. Benveniste, A., Caillaud, B., Guernic, P.L.: Compositionality in dataflow synchronous languages: specification and distributed code generation 1, 2, 3. Information and Computation 163(1), 125–171 (2000)

12. Halbwachs, N., Raymond, P., Ratel, C.: Generating efficient code from data-flow programs. In: Third International Symposium on Programming Language Implementation and Logic Programming, Passau, Germany (August 1991)

13. Pnueli, A., Siegel, M., Singerman, E.: Translation validation. In: Steffen, B. (ed.) TACAS 1998. LNCS, vol. 1384, pp. 151–166. Springer, Heidelberg (1998)

14. Necula, G.C.: Translation validator for optimizing compilers. SIGPLAN Not. 35(5), 83–94 (2000)

15. Leroy, X.: Formal Certification of a Compiler Back-end or Programming a compiler with a Proof Assistant. In: POPL 2006, 33rd Symposium on Principles of Programming Languages (January 2006)

Implementing a Direct Method for Certificate Translation*

Gilles Barthe[1], Benjamin Grégoire[2], Sylvain Heraud[2],
César Kunz[1], and Anne Pacalet[2]

[1] IMDEA Software, Spain
[2] INRIA Sophia Antipolis - Méditerranée, France

Abstract. Certificate translation is a method that transforms certificates of source programs into certificates of their compilation. It provides strong guarantees on low-level code, and is useful for eliminating trust in the compiler (for high assurance code) and in the code producer for mobile code security. The theory of certificate translation has been developed in earlier work, but no implementation exists. As a result, it has been difficult to evaluate its practicality, and in particular the impact of certificate translation on the size of certificates.

In this paper, we report on the development of a certificate translator prototype. The tool takes as input a high-level program, defined in a small subset of the C programming language, and a logical specification *à la ACSL*, and computes a set of verification conditions for the Coq proof assistant. Once proof obligations are discharged, the tool compiles the source program into an intermediate RTL (i.e., three-address code) representation, and then performs a sequence of compiler optimizations. At each step, certificates are transformed automatically to produce a proof for the transformed programs. For optimizations that rely on arithmetic reasoning, such as constant propagation and common subexpression, the tool implements a new certificate translation strategy that minimizes certificate growth.

1 Introduction

Reasoning about source programs is important: it helps guarantee that programs have been correctly designed to meet some functionality, or some non-functional requirement. Reasoning about source programs is also successful: modern program verifiers for C, $C^\#$, Java, perform well, and their user base is growing across different areas of computer science.

Yet, reasoning about source programs does not provide guarantees about the behavior of executable code. The dissimilarity between a compliant source program and a misbehaved executable can arise on many accounts: the compiler may modify the functional semantics of the program, or it may preserve its functional semantics and yet alter its non-functional behavior (execution time, resource consumption), leading to security vulnerabilities or to ill-functioning

---

* Partially funded by the EU projects MOBIUS and HATS.

K. Breitman and A. Cavalcanti (Eds.): ICFEM 2009, LNCS 5885, pp. 541–560, 2009.

applications. Or, the executable code may be produced by a malicious third party that deliberately aims to provide users with code that does not respect the behavior of the source programs. Or, the compiled code might have been tampered prior to execution, for example for efficiency reasons. Thus, source code verification must be complemented with verification of executable code.

Program verification is costly, and there is little chance that programmers will agree to verify their source programs, and then to verify again the corresponding executable code. Verification across the compilation chain is even more problematic for source programs that are compiled to different targets, as the verification effort would need to be repeated for each potential target. Therefore, it is important to develop methods that allow transferring the results of source code verification to lower levels in the compilation chain.

Certificate translation is a method to transfer evidence from source programs to compiled programs. They manipulate so-called certificates, i.e. mathematical objects that capture program correctness proofs, and amenable to transformation by syntactic methods. In short, certificate translators are functions that map certificates of source programs, into certificates of their compilation.

The theory of certificate translation has been developed in previous work: in particular, Barthe *et al* [3] show in the setting of a RTL language that certificate translators exist for common program optimizations; later, Barthe and Kunz [2] show that certificate translators are guaranteed to exist under mild conditions. However, the theoretical development has not been matched by a practical implementation. As a result, it has not been possible to validate experimentally the theoretical developments, nor to assess the practicality of certificate translation.

In this paper, we report on a prototype implementation[1] of certificate translation for a subset of the C language. Although our verifier for C programs and our examples remain modest in comparison with the state-of-the-art (compared e.g. with Spec# [1] or Frama-C [5]), our work allows to draw for the first time some preliminary conclusions about the practicality of certificate translation. In particular, we are able to provide a preliminary analysis of the impact of certificate translation on the size of certificates, which is an essential metrics for Proof Carrying Code [7]—the initial motivation of our work. In addition to the tool, we report on a new method for transforming certificates for optimizations based on arithmetic reasoning, such as constant propagation, and common subexpression elimination. The method is simpler, in that it treats the certificate of the original program as a black-box, whereas the previous method in [3] involved weaving certificates, using a well-founded induction principle on the control flow graph of the program. In comparison, the new method also yields smaller certificates, and thus contributes to the practicality of certificate translation.

2   Overview

Figure 2 provides an overview of the tool. The tool operates on programs written in a subset of the C language. A program consists of a declaration of global

---

[1] The tool is available at http://mobius.inria.fr/CertificateTranslation

```
l₁  : i := 0;
l₂  : while (i < m){
l₃  :    j := 0;
l₄  :    while (j < p){
l₅  :       k := 0;
l₆  :       c[i * p + j] := 0;
l₇  :       while (k < n){
l₈  :          c[i * p + j] := c[i * p + j] + a[i * n + k] * b[k * p + j];
l₉  :          k := k + 1;
            }
l₁₀ :       j := j + 1;
         }
l₁₁ :    i := i + 1;
      }
l₁₂ : return 0
```

Fig. 1. Source code of matrix multiplication example

variables, followed by a sequence of function declarations. Each function defines the return type, the name and type of the formal parameters, a set of local variables, and the statement that defines its body. Variable types are restricted to integers and pointers to integer values. Statements include assignments to scalar and pointer variables, function invocation, conditional and loop statements. Program points can be labeled to be used as the target of a goto statement. Local declarations of pointer variables and expressions containing pointer arithmetic operations are not allowed.

Although minimalistic, the fragment considered is sufficiently expressive for writing many algorithms of interest. We have programmed (and verified) sorting algorithms, and algorithms that manipulate matrices. Our running example is a matrix multiplication algorithm.

Example 1 (Matrix Multiplication: source code). Consider as a running example the following algorithm, that computes the multiplication of two matrices a and b, and stores it in c. Matrices are encoded as uni-dimensional arrays; for example,

$$\begin{pmatrix} a & b \\ c & d \end{pmatrix}$$

is encoded as $\begin{pmatrix} a & b & c & d \end{pmatrix}$. More generally, if a $m \times n$ matrix A is represented by the uni-dimensional array a of size mn, we encode the array element $A_{i,j}$ as $a[i*n+j]$. The code is given in Figure 1. In the algorithm, the array variables a, b, and c represent a $m \times n$ matrix, a $n \times p$ matrix, and a $m \times p$ matrix, respectively. The l_is are program labels, and are used to add annotations in the program text.

The program verifier operates on annotated source programs. In order to support effective and modular verification, the program verifier requires that procedures are annotated with their preconditions and postconditions, and that loops are annotated with their invariants. However, the verifier allows assertions to be inserted at arbitrary points in the program, which is particularly useful to verify some non-functional properties. Procedure specifications are triples of the form $\langle$Pre, annot, Post$\rangle$, where Pre and Post are assertions and annot is a partial function from program labels to assertions. Assertions are written in a language similar to (but smaller than) the ACSL language used in the Frama-C project [5]; they are also allowed to refer to functions and predicates defined in an external Coq module. One minor difference with ACSL is that the specification language does not provide any syntactic sugar for modifiable clauses.

Example 2 (Matrix Multiplication: specification). The specification for matrix multiplication is given by the triple $\langle$Pre, annot, Post$\rangle$ where:

Pre $\doteq 0 < \mathsf{m} \wedge 0 < \mathsf{n} \wedge 0 < \mathsf{p}$
annot$(l_2) \doteq \forall i, j. \, ((0 \leq i < \mathsf{i}) \Rightarrow (0 \leq j < \mathsf{p}) \Rightarrow \mathsf{c}[i, j] = (\mathsf{a} \times \mathsf{b})[i, j]) \wedge \mathsf{i} \leq \mathsf{m}$
annot$(l_4) \doteq \forall j. ((0 \leq j < \mathsf{j}) \Rightarrow \mathsf{c}[\mathsf{i}, j] = (\mathsf{a} \times \mathsf{b})[\mathsf{i}, j]) \wedge (0 \leq \mathsf{j} \leq \mathsf{p}) \wedge$
$\qquad \forall i, j. \, ((0 \leq i < \mathsf{i}) \Rightarrow (0 \leq j < \mathsf{p}) \Rightarrow \mathsf{c}[i, j] = \mathsf{c}^{l_2}[i, j])$
annot$(l_7) \doteq \mathsf{c}[\mathsf{i}, \mathsf{j}] = \sum_{r=0}^{k-1}(\mathsf{a}[\mathsf{i}, r] * \mathsf{b}[r, \mathsf{j}]) \wedge (0 \leq \mathsf{j} \leq \mathsf{p}) \wedge$
$\qquad \forall j. \, ((0 \leq j < \mathsf{j}) \Rightarrow \mathsf{c}[\mathsf{i}, j] = \mathsf{c}^{l_4}[\mathsf{i}, j])$
Post $\doteq \forall i, j. \, ((0 \leq i < \mathsf{m}) \Rightarrow (0 \leq j < \mathsf{p}) \Rightarrow \mathsf{c}[i, j] = (\mathsf{a} \times \mathsf{b})[i, j])\}$

For notational convenience, we write $x[i, j]$ instead of $x[i * n + j]$ if the array x represents an $m \times n$ matrix. The postcondition ensures that the array c is the result of matrix multiplication between a and b, i.e. for every i and j, $\mathsf{c}[i, j]$ is equal to $\sum_{k=0}^{n-1} \mathsf{a}[i, k] * \mathsf{b}[k, j]$, denoted $(\mathsf{a} \times \mathsf{b})[i, j]$.

The innermost loop, defined in terms of the induction variable k, computes the sum $\sum_{k=0}^{n-1} \mathsf{a}[i, k] * \mathsf{b}[k, j]$, for the current value of the variables i and j. The first term in the conjunction that defines the loop invariant annot(l_7) expresses exactly this condition. In addition, annot(l_7) states that for any other pair (i', j') different from (i, j), the array value $\mathsf{c}[i', j']$ remains unmodified (c^{l_4} stands for the value of c before the assignment $k = 0$). The loop statements at labels l_2 and l_4 traverses the rows and columns of the matrix represented by c, respectively. The invariants annot(l_4) and annot(l_2) extend the condition $\mathsf{c}[\mathsf{i}, \mathsf{j}] = (\mathsf{a} \times \mathsf{b})[\mathsf{i}, \mathsf{j}]$ for the previous values of the variables j and i, respectively.

The program verifier generates for each annotated program a set of proof obligations. The generation of proof obligations proceeds in two phases: first, a symbolic execution algorithm is used to strengthen program annotations. Then, a weakest precondition calculus generates proof obligations using the strengthened annotations. In order to avoid bloated proof obligations, the weakest precondition calculus does not strengthen annotations with all the results of symbolic execution, but only with those that refer to variables that would appear in the proof obligation.

The use of symbolic execution to strengthen invariants allows users provide weaker specifications[2].

Example 3 (Matrix Multiplication: symbolic execution). At program point l_4, a standard VCgen would generate, for the execution that does not enter the loop,

---
[2] A similar technique is implemented in the Caveat tool, the predecessor of Frama-C.

User Input

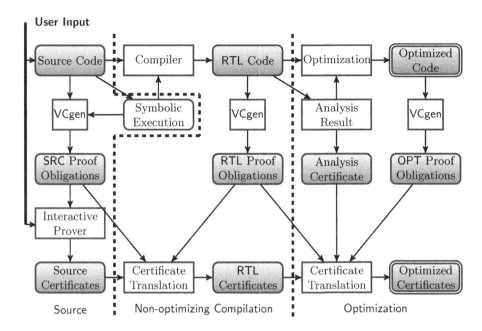

Fig. 2. Overall Tool Scheme

the proof obligation: $\mathsf{annot}(l_4) \Rightarrow \neg\mathsf{j} < \mathsf{p} \Rightarrow \mathsf{annot}(l_2)[^{\mathsf{i}+1}\!/_\mathsf{i}]$. Unfortunately, in this example the loop invariant $\mathsf{annot}(l_4)$ is not strong enough to discharge the proof obligation. In contrast, symbolic execution propagates automatically the condition provided by the outer invariants to strengthen the inner invariants, and generates provable proof obligations.

The obligations are collected in a Coq file, and must be discharged to guarantee that the program is correct w.r.t. its specification. This process is done interactively by the user, using the Coq proof assistant. The certificate of the program is the set of proof terms that are built automatically by Coq upon successful verification of the proof obligations.

Certificate translation starts after the user has completed the verification of the source program. The program is first compiled to an intermediate representation, written in a RTL language with arrays and procedure calls. The compiler from the source language to the target language does not perform any optimization, but replaces booleans, which do not exist in the RTL language, by integers—we do not discuss this transformation further.

Example 4 (Matrix multiplication: RTL code). The result of compiling the running example can be found in Figure 3. The boxes in gray show the optimized version of the RTL code, as explained in Section 5.2.

The checker of RTL programs is based on the same principles as the verifier for source programs: annotated RTL programs are sent to a weakest precondition calculus that generates a set of proof obligations; then the programs certificates

$$
\begin{array}{lll}
i := 0 & r_1 := i * p & r_{10} := r_9 + j \\
l_2 : \text{set } i^{l_2} := i & r_2 := r_1 + j & r_{11} := b[r_{10}] \\
\quad \text{set } j^{l_2} := j & c[r_2] := 0 & r_{12} := r_8 * r_{11} \\
\quad \text{set } k^{l_2} := k & l_7 : \text{set } k^{l_7} := k & r_{13} := r_5 + r_{12} \\
\quad \text{set } c^{l_2} := c & \quad \text{set } c^{l_7} := c & \boxed{r_{14} := i * p} \;\; \boxed{r_{14} := r_1} \\
l_2^b : \text{cjmp } i < m \; l_2^o & l_7^b : \text{cjmp } k < n \; l_7^o & \boxed{r_{15} := r_{14} + j} \;\; \boxed{r_{15} := r_2} \\
\quad \text{jmp } l_2' & \quad \text{jmp } l_7' & c[r_{16}] := r_{15} \\
l_2^o : j := 0 & l_7^o : \boxed{r_3 := i * p} \;\; \boxed{r_3 := r_1} & k := k + 1 \\
l_4 : \text{set } j^{l_4} := j & \quad\;\; \boxed{r_4 := r_3 + j} \;\; \boxed{r_4 := r_2} & \text{jmp } l_7 \\
\quad \text{set } k^{l_4} := k & r_5 := c[r_4] & l_7' : j := j + 1 \\
\quad \text{set } c^{l_4} := c & r_6 := i * n & \quad \text{jmp } l_4 \\
l_4^b : \text{cjmp } j < p \; l_4^o & r_7 := r_6 + k & l_4' : i := i + 1 \\
\quad \text{jmp } l_4' & r_8 := a[r_7] & \quad \text{jmp } l_2 \\
l_4^o : k := 0 & r_9 := k * p & \quad \text{return } 0
\end{array}
$$

Fig. 3. RTL representation of the matrix multiplication example

$$
\begin{array}{rl}
\textbf{integer expressions} & e ::= n \mid x \mid a[e] \mid e + e \mid e * e \mid \dots \\
\textbf{boolean expressions} & b ::= \text{true} \mid \text{false} \mid \neg b \mid b \wedge b \mid e \leq e \mid e = e \mid \dots \\
\textbf{statements} & c ::= \text{skip} \mid x := e \mid a[e] := e \mid c; c \\
& \quad\;\; \mid x := \text{invoke } f(e) \mid \text{return } e \\
& \quad\;\; \mid \text{if } b \text{ then } c \text{ else } c \mid \text{while } b \text{ do } c
\end{array}
$$

Fig. 4. Source Programs

are checked against the proof obligations. Unlike the verifier for source programs, the checker for RTL programs does not rely on symbolic execution—one reason for this discrepancy is that the RTL checker is trusted, and hence should be as simple as possible. To bridge the gap between the source code verifier and the RTL checker, the tool relies on a specification compiler that strengthens the original specification with the result of the symbolic execution. Although the proof obligations between source code and RTL programs are very similar, there are some minor differences that prevent directly reusing certificates—for many examples, including the running example, the proof obligations coincide syntactically. The tool implements a Coq tactic to transform the original certificates into certificates for their RTL compilation.

The tool then performs a series of optimizations: constant propagation, common subexpression elimination, partial redundancy elimination, and unreachable code elimination. For each optimization, the tool transforms the program, its specification and the certificates. This is done by comparing the original and final proof obligations as a black-box, instead of considering the definition of the compiler. Therefore, although we consider a particular compiler, the certificate transformation technique presented here can be applied to any optimization based on arithmetic simplification. However, it is not completely independent on the compiler, in that sense that the certificate transformation may fail if the transformation is not semantically correct.

As noted in [3], certificate translation require program analyzers to generate a certificate for the result of the analysis. The certificates of the analyses are then merged with the original certificates. In Section 5, we present a new method to perform the merging of certificates. Section 6 provide experimental results.

3 Source Program Verification

For the clarity of exposition, we base the presentation on a simpler language, restricting the heap model to array operations. The set of statements is given in Figure 4. $\mathcal{V}$ and $\mathcal{A}$ represent the set of scalar and array variables, respectively.

Scalar variables are local to the execution of a procedure body, and array variables are global to the execution of the whole program. Array variables represent pointers from a common and global heap. In order to avoid pointer aliasing, array variables hold distinct memory pointers, that are statically defined and cannot be modified along the execution of the program. To enforce this, assignments of the form $a := a'$, where a and a' are array variables, are not allowed in this paper. The program semantics is standard.

3.1 Specification

A procedure specification is provided by a set of logical formulae. The specification may refer to any program variable, and to the special purpose variable res that refers to the value returned by a procedure, and to ghost variables, which are used only for specification purposes. A particular subset of ghost variables are the *starred* variables $x^\star$, referring to the initial value of the variable x. In addition to starred variables, we consider also *labeled* variables. One can interpret the ghost variable x^l as standing for the value held by the program variable x at the program point l.

Preconditions are logical formulae that only refers to any array variable and any scalar arguments of the procedure. Postconditions can refer to the variable res, any array variables, and any ghost variable.

To compute verification conditions from a procedure and a specification $\langle \mathsf{Pre}, \mathsf{annot}, \mathsf{Post} \rangle$, the verification framework requires that every loop statement $l : \mathbf{while}\ b\ \mathbf{do}\ c$ is annotated, that is, that l is in $\mathsf{dom}(\mathsf{annot})$.

3.2 Symbolic Execution

In this section, we describe the invariant strengthening technique based on the symbolic propagation of invariants and path conditions.

A symbolic state is defined by a pair (S, C), where S is an execution store that maps variables to integer expressions composed of only ghost variables. Similarly, C is a formula whose every free variable is a ghost variable. We denote $[\![e]\!]S$ and $[\![\phi]\!]S$ the syntactic substitution in e and ϕ, respectively, of every variable v by Sv.

The symbolic execution of a statement c from a symbolic state (S, C) and returning the symbolic state (S', C'), is denoted $(S, C, c) \to (S', C')$. The rules that define the symbolic execution can be found in Figure 5. In the figure, a

$$\overline{\langle S, C, \textbf{skip}\rangle \to \langle S, C\rangle}$$

$$\overline{\langle S, C, a[e] := e'\rangle \to \langle [S : a \mapsto [\![a : e \mapsto e']\!]S], C\rangle}$$

$$\overline{\langle S, C, x := e\rangle \to \langle [S : x \mapsto [\![e]\!]S], C\rangle}$$

$$\overline{\langle S, C, l : x := \textbf{invoke } f(e)\rangle \to \langle [S : (x, a) \mapsto (x^l, a^l)], C\rangle}$$

$$\frac{\langle S, C, c_1\rangle \to \langle S_1, C_1\rangle \qquad \langle S_1, C_1\rangle \sqsubseteq_{l_2} \langle S_2, C_2\rangle \qquad \langle S_2, C_2, c_2\rangle \to \langle S', C'\rangle}{\langle S, C, l_1 : c_1; l_2 : c_2\rangle \to \langle S', C'\rangle}$$

$$\frac{\langle S, C \wedge [\![b]\!]S, c_1\rangle \to \langle S_t, C_t\rangle \qquad \langle S, C \wedge [\![\neg b]\!]S, c_2\rangle \to \langle S_f, C_f\rangle}{\langle S, C, l : \textbf{if } b \textbf{ then } c_1 \textbf{ else } c_2\rangle \to \langle S_t \oplus_l S_f, ([\![b]\!]S \Rightarrow C_t) \wedge ([\![\neg b]\!]S \Rightarrow C_f))}$$

$$\frac{\text{for all } x \text{ modifiable by } c, \; Sx = x^l \qquad \langle S, C \wedge [\![\textsf{annot}(l)]\!]S \wedge [\![b]\!]S, c\rangle \to \langle S', C'\rangle}{\langle S, C, l : \textbf{while } b \textbf{ do } c\rangle \to \langle S, C \wedge [\![\neg b]\!]S\rangle}$$

Fig. 5. Symbolic Execution Rules

stands for the array variables modified by the procedure f. The expression $[f : x \mapsto n]$ stands for the function f' such that $f'x = n$ and $f'y = fy$ for all $y \neq x$.

The symbolic execution is assumed to start in an initial state (S_0, C_0) such that S_0 maps every variable x to $x^\star$, that is, to its initial value. The execution proceeds by case analysis on the statement. In the following paragraphs we explain some of the execution rules:

Assignment: In the case of an assignment $x := e$, the symbolic store S is updated so that after the assignment is executed, the variable x holds the corresponding symbolic value $[\![e]\!]S$. A similar substitution is applied in the case of assignments to array variables.

Conditional statement: In the case of the conditional statement of the form **if** b **then** c_1 **else** c_2, each branch c_1 and c_2 is evaluated under the conditions b and $\neg b$, respectively. To this end, the symbolic conditional C is strengthened with the interpretation of the boolean expressions b and $\neg b$, denoted $[\![b]\!]S$ and $[\![\neg b]\!]S$, respectively. Finally, the symbolic states S_t and S_f, resulting from the execution of each branch are merged into a symbolic state $S_t \oplus_l S_f$. The definition of the merging operation preserves the assignments of variables in which S_t and S_f coincide. If S_t and S_f differ on a variable x, this variable is mapped to a fresh labeled variable x^l. That is

$$(S_1 \oplus_l S_2)x = \begin{cases} S_1 x & \text{if } S_1 x = S_2 x \\ x^l & \text{otherwise} \end{cases}$$

Loop statements: The execution of a loop statement may invalidate symbolic conditions if they refer to a variable that may be modified by the loop body. We follow thus a safe approach and require the symbolic execution to start in an initial state that sets every modifiable variable to a fresh ghost variable x^l, from which nothing is known. The loop body, is then executed in a state in which the interpretation of the guard $[\![b]\!]S$ is incorporated to the conditional C. As the final state, the conditional expression C is strengthened with the negation of the loop guard $[\![\neg b]\!][S : x \mapsto x^l]$.

The tool expects a procedure specification to provide the set of variables that each loop may modify. In return, the tool outputs a set of proof obligations that ensures the correctness of this part of the specification. To simplify the presentation, we assume here that the set of modifiable variables are automatically overapproximated by a static analysis.

Sequential composition: Loops statements require initial symbolic stores S to map modifiable variables to fresh ghost variables from which nothing is known in C. To satisfy this requirement, the composition rule allows one to weaken symbolic states. In the figure, $\langle S, C \rangle \sqsubseteq_l \langle S', C' \rangle$ is defined as $C = C'$, $\mathsf{dom}(S) = \mathsf{dom}(S')$ and for all $x \in \mathsf{dom}(S)$ we have $S(x) = S'(x)$ or $S'x = x^l$.

Note that the symbolic result can be arbitrarily weak by application of the rule for sequential composition, from the requirement $\langle S, C \rangle \sqsubseteq_l \langle S', C' \rangle$. However, since the only statement that put restrictions on the symbolic pre-state is the **while** statement, one can make it as strong as possible by choosing $S' = [S : x \mapsto x^l]$, where x represents every variable modifiable by the loop body, and l is the label of the loop statement. For any other case, one can simply choose $\langle S, C \rangle = \langle S', C' \rangle$. As a result, the symbolic execution becomes deterministic. Therefore, in the rest of the paper we associate every program label l to exactly one symbolic state, represented by the pair (S_l, C_l).

3.3   Verification Condition Generator

In this section we define a verification framework for source-level programs. A verification condition generator (VCgen) takes as input a source program and its specification, and returns a set of proof obligations. The validity of the generated proof obligations ensure that the program satisfies its specification.

The verification framework defined in this section relies on the symbolic execution presented in the paragraphs above. When computing the set of proof obligations, the VCgen strengthens invariants by incorporating the information that is computed by the symbolic analyzer.

The extraction of verification conditions are defined by the function VCG, formalized by the rules in Figure 6. During the computation, every reference to the intermediate specification annot is strengthened with the result of the symbolic execution, and denoted $\overline{\mathsf{annot}}$:

$$\overline{\mathsf{annot}}(l) \doteq \mathsf{annot}(l) \wedge C_l \wedge \bigwedge_{v \in \mathsf{dom}(S_l)} v = S_l(v)$$

Since the VCgen process incorporates the result of the symbolic analysis, the definition of VCG is tightly coupled with the symbolic execution rules. Indeed, the standard weakest precondition must be modified to deal with the fresh ghost

$$\overline{\mathsf{VCG}(\mathbf{skip}, \phi) = \langle \phi, \emptyset \rangle} \qquad \overline{\mathsf{VCG}(\mathbf{return}\ e, \phi) = \langle \mathsf{Post}[^e/_{\mathsf{res}}], \emptyset \rangle}$$

$$\overline{\mathsf{VCG}(l : x := e, \phi) = \langle \phi[^x/_{x^l}][^e/_x], \emptyset \rangle}$$

$$\overline{\mathsf{VCG}(l : a[e_1] := e_2, \phi) = \langle \phi[^a/_{a^l}][^{[a:e_1 \mapsto e_2]}/_a], \emptyset \rangle}$$

$$\frac{\Phi = \mathsf{Pre}_f[^e/_{x_f}] \wedge \forall \mathbf{res}, V'.\ \mathsf{Post}_f[^{V', V}/_{V, V\star}][^v/_{x_{f\star}}] \Rightarrow \phi[^a/_{a^l}][^v/_{v^l}][^{V'}/_V][^{\mathsf{res}}/_v]}{V \text{ array variables modified by } f}$$
$$\overline{\mathsf{VCG}(l : v := \mathbf{invoke}\ f(e), \phi) = \langle \Phi, \emptyset \rangle}$$

$$\frac{\mathsf{VCG}(c_1, \phi) = \langle \phi_1, \theta_1 \rangle \qquad \mathsf{VCG}(c_2, \phi) = \langle \phi_2, \theta_2 \rangle}{\mathsf{VCG}(\mathbf{if}\ b\ \mathbf{then}\ c_1\ \mathbf{else}\ c_2, \phi) = \langle b \Rightarrow \phi_1 \wedge \neg b \Rightarrow \phi_2, \theta_1 \cup \theta_2 \rangle}$$

$$\frac{\mathsf{VCG}(c, \overline{\mathsf{annot}}(l)[^x/_{x^l}]) = \langle \phi_1, \theta \rangle \qquad \Psi \doteq \overline{\mathsf{annot}}(l) \Rightarrow (b \Rightarrow \phi_1) \wedge (\neg b \Rightarrow \phi)}{\mathsf{VCG}(l : \mathbf{while}\ b\ \mathbf{do}\ c, \phi) = \langle \overline{\mathsf{annot}}(l)[^x/_{x^l}], \{\Psi\} \cup \theta \rangle}$$

$$\frac{\mathsf{VCG}(c_1, \phi_2) = \langle \phi_1, \theta_1 \rangle \qquad \mathsf{VCG}(c_2, \phi) = \langle \phi_2, \theta_2 \rangle}{\mathsf{VCG}(c_1 ; c_2, \phi) = \langle \phi_1, \theta_1 \cup \theta_2 \rangle}$$

$$\frac{\langle \phi, \theta \rangle = \mathsf{VCG}(c, \mathsf{Post}) \qquad c \text{ the body of } p}{\mathsf{PO}(p) \doteq \{\mathsf{Pre} \Rightarrow \phi[^{\vec{V}}/_{\vec{V}\star}]\} \cup \theta}$$

Fig. 6. Source Code VCgen Rules

variables that are introduced by the symbolic execution. Consider for instance the case of the function invocation $v := \mathbf{invoke}\ f(e)$. Recall that, from the definition of symbolic execution, the final state S' maps v to the fresh ghost variable v^l, and similarly with the arrays that may be modified by f. Then, one must substitute the ghost variable v^l by v, as well as a^l by a, for all array variable a that may be modified by f. A similar situation occurs with loop and conditional statements.

The set of verification conditions is defined as $\mathsf{PO}(p)$ in Figure 6. We say that a procedure p is correct with respect to its specification if $\mathsf{PO}(p)$ is a set of valid formulae. Let the judgment $\langle c, \sigma \rangle \rightsquigarrow \langle n, \sigma' \rangle$ represent the determinist execution of the statement c, starting in a state σ and returning a value n and a final state σ'. The VCgen defined above is sound, that is, the execution of a valid procedure p satisfies its specification. Formally, if c is the statement of a procedure that is valid w.r.t. $\langle \mathsf{Pre}, \mathsf{annot}, \mathsf{Post} \rangle$, and the σ satisfies the precondition Pre, the execution $\langle c, \sigma \rangle \rightsquigarrow \langle n, \sigma' \rangle$ implies that σ' satisfies the postcondition $\mathsf{Post}[^n/_{\mathsf{res}}]$.

Example 5. Consider again the source code specification provided in Example 2 for the matrix multiplication example. The program code between labels l_2 and l_4 does not modify the array c in the range $0 \leq i < \mathtt{i}$ and $0 \leq j < \mathtt{p}$. Therefore, the symbolic execution can propagate the information provided by the invariant $\mathsf{annot}(l_2)$:

$$\varphi \doteq \mathtt{i} = \mathtt{i}^{l_2} \wedge \forall i, j.\ ((0 \leq i < \mathtt{i}^{l_2}) \Rightarrow (0 \leq j < \mathtt{p}) \Rightarrow \mathtt{c}^{l_2}[i, j] = (\mathtt{a} \times \mathtt{b})[i, j])$$

to strengthen the invariant $\mathsf{annot}(l_4)$, making thus the specification valid. In this particular case, one can see that the new proof obligation is

$$\mathsf{annot}(l_4) \wedge \varphi \Rightarrow \left| \begin{array}{l} (\forall i, j. \, ((0 \leq i < \mathtt{i}) \Rightarrow (0 \leq j < \mathtt{p}) \Rightarrow \mathtt{c}[i,j] = (\mathtt{a} \times \mathtt{b})[i,j]) \\ \wedge \\ \forall j. \, ((0 \leq j < \mathtt{p}) \Rightarrow \mathtt{c}[\mathtt{i},j] = (\mathtt{a} \times \mathtt{b})[\mathtt{i},j])) \end{array} \right.$$

which is a valid logical formula.

4   RTL Program Checking

As a compiler intermediate program representation we assume a Register Transfer Language (RTL), that is, three-address based code. It is an unstructured low-level language with conditional jumps, assignments of atomic expressions and function invocations.

A RTL program is defined as a collection of RTL procedures. Each RTL procedure is defined by its formal parameters and a sequence of labeled low-level instructions. RTL instructions and expressions are defined in Figure 7.

In Figure 7, x stands for a scalar program variable or an integer constant and a stands for an array variable. Assignments involve at most one array access or two scalar variables. In the figure, $\bar{e}$ represents an atomic integer expression (one array access or an arithmetic operation between at most two scalar variables), e an integer expression as defined in the source program syntax, and $\hat{v}$ stands for a ghost variable. The symbol $\bowtie$ stands for any integer comparison. Since ghost variables cannot interfere with the program semantics, they can only appear on **set** instructions. RTL instructions include also a **return** instruction, procedure invocation and conditional and unconditional jumps.

For a RTL procedure p and a label l, we denote $p[l]$ the instruction located at the position with label l. For a label of a RTL procedure p, we define the successors labels, denoted $\mathsf{succ}(l)$, by case analysis on the instruction $p[l]$. For $p[l]$ equal to **return** x we have $\mathsf{succ}(l) = \emptyset$, for **jmp** l' we have $\mathsf{succ}(l) = \{l'\}$, and for **cjmp** l', $\mathsf{succ}(l) = \{l', l+1\}$, where $l+1$ is the label of the next instruction in the sequence p. In any other case, $\mathsf{succ}(l) = \{l+1\}$.

Program Verification. Procedure specifications are provided by triples of the form $\langle \mathsf{Pre}, \mathsf{annot}, \mathsf{Post} \rangle$, where Pre and Post are assertions representing the pre and postconditions and annot is a partial function that maps labels to assertions specifying the loop invariants. Pre, Post and annot are written in the same language and follow the same restrictions as source program specifications.

$$
\begin{array}{rl}
\textbf{(atomic expressions)} & \bar{e} ::= x \mid x + x \mid x * x \mid \ldots \mid a[x] \\
\textbf{(instructions)} & ins ::= \textbf{nop} \mid v := \bar{e} \mid a[x] := \bar{e} \\
& \quad \mid \textbf{invoke } f \, (\vec{x}) \mid \textbf{return } x \mid \textbf{set } \hat{v} := e \\
& \quad \mid \textbf{cjmp } x \bowtie x \, l \mid \textbf{jmp } l
\end{array}
$$

Fig. 7. RTL Instructions

$\mathsf{wpi}(l : \mathbf{nop}) = \mathsf{wp}(l + 1)$
$\mathsf{wpi}(l : v := e) = \mathsf{wp}(l + 1)[^e/_v]$
$\mathsf{wpi}(l : \mathbf{set}\ \hat{v} := e) = \mathsf{wp}(l + 1)[^e/_{\hat{v}}]$
$\mathsf{wpi}(l : a[v_1] := v_2) = \mathsf{wp}(l + 1)[^{[a:v_1 \mapsto v_2]}/_a]$
$\mathsf{wpi}(l : \mathbf{cjmp}\ v_1 \bowtie v_2\ l') = ((v_1 \bowtie v_2) \Rightarrow \mathsf{wp}(l')) \wedge (\neg(v_1 \bowtie v_2) \Rightarrow \mathsf{wp}(l + 1))$
$\mathsf{wpi}(l : \mathbf{invoke}\ f\ x) = \mathsf{Pre}_f[^x/_{x_f}] \wedge \forall_{\mathsf{res},a'} \mathsf{Post}_f[^{a',a}/_{a,a^\star}][^{x_f^\star}/_x] \Rightarrow \mathsf{wp}(l + 1)[^{a'}/_a]$
$\mathsf{wpi}(\mathbf{return}\ v) = \mathsf{Post}[^v/_{\mathsf{res}}]$

$$\mathsf{wp}(l) = \begin{cases} \mathsf{annot}(l) & \text{if } l \in \mathsf{dom}(\mathsf{annot}) \\ \mathsf{wpi}(l : p[l]) & \text{otherwise} \end{cases}$$

Fig. 8. RTL VCgen rules

To compute a set of proof obligations from a procedure p and its specification, the RTL checker requires that p is well-annotated. A procedure p with specification (Pre, annot, Post) is well-annotated if every cyclic path in its control flow graph contains at least one annotated label in dom(annot). The result of compiling a well-annotated source procedure is a well-annotated RTL procedure: without further ado, we thus consider only well-annotated programs.

For a RTL procedure p with specification $\langle \mathsf{Pre}, \mathsf{annot}, \mathsf{Post} \rangle$, the proof obligations are defined by the set:

$$\mathsf{po}(p) = \{\mathsf{Pre} \Rightarrow \mathsf{wp}(l_{\mathsf{in}})[^V/_{V^\star}]\} \cup \{\mathsf{annot}(l) \Rightarrow \mathsf{wpi}(l : p[l]) \mid l \in \mathsf{dom}(\mathsf{annot})\}$$

where the predicate transformers wpi and wp are defined in Figure 8. In the figure, a represents every array variable that may get modified by f. The assertion $\varphi[^V/_{V^\star}]$ stands for the substitution in φ of every array variable $a^\star \in V^\star$ by a.

Consider a RTL program such that every procedure is verified correct with respect to its specification. Then, as with source programs, every terminating execution of a procedure with specification $\langle \mathsf{Pre}, \mathsf{annot}, \mathsf{Post} \rangle$, from an initial state that satisfies the precondition Pre, will reach a final state satisfying the postcondition Post.

5   Certificate Translation

In this section, we deal with certificate transformation along a common compilation process. We show that the first compiler step, that is, non-optimizing compilation, preserves verification conditions up to minor differences. Then we explain how we deal with the transformation of certificates in the presence of compiler optimizations. We first provide an introduction to certificate translation in the most general case. Then, we provide a more ad-hoc technique, implemented in the tool, that considers a particular class of optimizations, for which the growth of the original certificate size is reduced.

5.1   Non-optimizing Compilation

The non-optimizing compiler transforms every source code statement into an intermediate RTL representation. The transformation is defined as a function

$$\mathcal{C}_{(l')}(v := e) = \mathcal{C}^{\text{e}}(v, e) :: \textbf{jmp } l'$$

$$\mathcal{C}_{(l')}(l : \textbf{if } b \textbf{ then } c_1 \textbf{ else } c_2) = \mathcal{C}^{\text{b}}_{(l_t, l_f)}(b) :: l_f : \mathcal{C}_{(l'')}(c_2) :: l_t : \mathcal{C}_{(l'')}(c_1) ::$$
$$l'' : \textbf{set } x^l := x :: \textbf{jmp } l'$$

$$\mathcal{C}_{(l')}(l : \textbf{while } b \textbf{ do } c) = l : \textbf{set } x^l := x :: l^b : \mathcal{C}^{\text{b}}_{(l_o, l')}(b) :: l_o : \mathcal{C}_{(l)}(c)$$

$$\mathcal{C}_{(l')}(v := \textbf{invoke } p(e_1, .., e_k)) = \mathcal{C}^{\text{e}}(v_1, e_1) :: .. :: \mathcal{C}^{\text{e}}(v_k, e_k) ::$$
$$v := \textbf{invoke } f(v_1, .., v_k) :: \textbf{set } v^l := v :: \textbf{set } a^l := a :: \textbf{jmp } l'$$

$$\mathcal{C}_{(l')}(c_1; c_2) = \mathcal{C}_{(l'')}(c_1) :: l'' : \mathcal{C}_{(l')}(c_2) :: \textbf{jmp } l'$$

$$\mathcal{C}_{(l')}(\textbf{return } e) = \mathcal{C}^{\text{e}}(v, e) :: \textbf{return } v$$

Fig. 9. Non-optimizing Compiler (Excerpt)

$\mathcal{C}$, shown in Figure 9, that takes a source code statement and a label l' where execution must continue after the execution of the compiled statement. In addition, auxiliary functions are defined, in order to compile boolean and integer expressions. $\mathcal{C}^{\text{b}}$ takes a boolean expression, and two output labels, to which execution must flow depending on the evaluation of the boolean expression. This function decomposes the evaluation of the boolean condition into two sequences of RTL instructions. Each of them evaluates an atomic conditional expression. Similarly, the function $\mathcal{C}^{\text{e}}$ takes a variable v and an expression e and returns RTL code that stores the evaluation of e in the variable v. It does so by decomposing the evaluation of the expression e into the evaluation of its atomic subexpressions.

Since we adopt a standard VCgen for RTL procedures, the compiler must incorporate the result of the symbolic execution, used to assist source code verification, to the specification of the resulting RTL procedure.

Consider a source code procedure p, with specification $\langle \text{Pre}, \text{annot}, \text{Post} \rangle$. Let $p' = l_{\text{in}} : \mathcal{C}_{(l_{\text{out}})}(c)$, where c is the body of p. We define the specification for p' as $\langle \text{Pre}, \text{annot}', \text{Post} \rangle$, where $\text{dom}(\text{annot}') = \{l^b \mid l \in \text{dom}(\text{annot})\}$ and

$$\text{annot}'(l^b) = \text{annot}(l) \wedge C_l \bigwedge_{v \in \text{dom}(S_l)} v = S_l(v)$$

and (S_l, C_l) is the result of the symbolic execution at the source program point labeled as l.

In order to deal with the ghost variables that appear in the final specification, the compilation of every statement that may introduce a ghost variable in the symbolic state must be followed by a **set** statement on that ghost variable.

Consider for instance the case of loop statements. Recall that for every variable x that may be modified by the loop, a **while** statement introduces a fresh ghost variable x^l in the symbolic state. Then, the VCG function is defined accordingly to deal with the introduction of these variables. In the case of a standard RTL verification, the compiler must introduce **set** statements in order to make the augmented specification valid. Similar criteria are used to define the compilation of conditional statements and function invocation. In Figure 9, x stands for every variable that may get modified by any of the two statements. In the case of function invocation, a stands for every array variable that the function may modify.

Consider a source procedure p with body c and specification $\langle \mathsf{Pre}, \mathsf{annot}, \mathsf{Post} \rangle$, and the RTL procedure $p' = l_{\mathsf{in}} : \mathcal{C}(c)$. From the definition of the non-optimizing compiler, one can show that the proof obligations in $\mathsf{PO}(p)$ are equivalent to the proof obligations in $\mathsf{po}(p')$. The only source of syntactic differences is due to the compilation of boolean expressions. For instance, for the statement c defined as **if** $b_1 \wedge b_2$ **then** c_1 **else** c_2, the function $\mathsf{VCG}(c, \varphi)$ returns a precondition of the form $(b_1 \wedge b_2 \Rightarrow \varphi_t) \wedge (\neg(b_1 \wedge b_2) \Rightarrow \varphi_f)$. If we compute the $\mathsf{wp}(l)$ for the subgraph that results from the compilation $l : \mathcal{C}_{(l')}(c)$ we get a precondition of the form $(b_1 \Rightarrow ((b_2 \Rightarrow \varphi_t) \wedge (\neg b_2 \Rightarrow \varphi_f))) \wedge (\neg b_1 \Rightarrow \varphi_f)$. Both assertions are trivially equivalent, but since proof obligations do not coincide syntactically, the tool implements a Coq tactic to transform the original certificates.

Example 6. The result of compiling the running example can be found in Figure 3. In this case, proof obligations coincide syntactically since every boolean condition of the source program is atomic.

Consider for instance one of the proof obligations for the code in Figure 3:

$$\mathsf{annot}'(l_4^b) \Rightarrow \left| \begin{array}{l} (j < p \Rightarrow \mathsf{annot}'(l_7^b)[^{\mathsf{k},\mathsf{c}}\!/_{\mathsf{k}^{l_4},\mathsf{c}^{l_4}}][^{[c:r_2 \mapsto 0]}\!/_c][^{r_1 + j}\!/_{r_2}][^{i * p}\!/_{r_1}][^{0}\!/_{\mathsf{k}}]) \wedge \\ (\neg j < p \Rightarrow \mathsf{Post}) \end{array} \right.$$

By definition of annot', and since r_1 and r_2 are fresh variables that do not appear in $\mathsf{annot}(l_7)$, this is equal to:

$$\overline{\mathsf{annot}}(l_4) \Rightarrow (j < p \Rightarrow \overline{\mathsf{annot}}(l_7)[^{\mathsf{k},\mathsf{c}}\!/_{\mathsf{k}^{l_4},\mathsf{c}^{l_4}}][^{[c:i*p+j \mapsto 0]}\!/_c][^{0}\!/_{\mathsf{k}}]) \wedge (\neg j < p \Rightarrow \mathsf{Post})$$

which coincides with the proof obligation computed for the source program at label l_4.

5.2   Optimizing Compilation

In this section, we describe how the tool implements a certificate translator in the context of a basic but common class of program transformations. Standard compiler optimizations operates in a two-step basis. First, an automatic analysis gathers static information from the procedure. Then, based on this information, a second compiler step transforms the code preserving the original semantics.

We provide first a representation of an analysis framework and a characterization of the result of an analysis. Then, we explain how the tool returns, in addition to the analysis results, a certificate of its representation in the verification setting. We then show that for these optimizations one can define a certificate translator that avoids the growth of certificate size caused by the more general technique developed in previous work [3].

Certifying Analyzers. In general, program transformations not only modify proof obligations, but may render the original specification invalid. For the class of optimizations considered in this paper, the certificate translator must strengthen the specification with the result of the analysis that motivates the program transformation. Therefore, a certificate translation procedure automatically generates a certificate for the analysis result, and then merges it with the original certificate.

An analysis module is implemented in the tool as a data type A that represents properties on states, and a transfer function T. The transfer function T takes an instruction ins and an element of type A and returns a new element in A. To give an intuition, if a state satisfies a property a, then the state after the execution of a satisfies the property $T(\text{ins}, a)$.

The result of the analysis, represented by a mapping S from program labels to elements in A, is computed by the tool by fixpoint approximation. For every label l, the property $S(l)$ characterizes the execution states that may reach that program point.

In order to certify the result of the analysis, the tool must define, for each analysis module, a function that maps every element a in A to its representation as a logical assertion. We omit, however, the application of this function and do not make the distinction between an element a in A and its logical representation.

From an analysis result S, the tool generates automatically a certificate for the procedure specification $\langle \text{true}, S, \text{true} \rangle$. First, the tool computes a set of verification conditions. Then, proof obligations are automatically discharged in Coq by application of the ring tactic, that solves equations on ring structures by associative and commutative rewriting.

Example 7. Consider for instance the analysis in which common-subexpression elimination is based. For the program in Figure 3, consider a labeling S, representing a result of the analysis such that $S(l_7^b) \doteq r_1 = \text{i} * \text{p} \wedge r_2 = \text{i} * \text{p} + \text{j}$ and $S(l) = \text{true}$ for $l \in \{l_2^b, l_4^b\}$. Ignoring for simplicity the symbolic execution process that strengthens invariants, the verification condition computed with specification $\langle \text{true}, S, \text{true} \rangle$ at label l_4^b has the form

$$\text{true} \Rightarrow (\text{j} < \text{p} \Rightarrow \text{true}) \wedge (\neg \text{j} < \text{p} \Rightarrow \text{i} * \text{p} = \text{i} * \text{p} \wedge \text{i} * \text{p} + \text{j} = \text{i} * \text{p} + \text{j})$$

At label l_7^b, the proof obligation is

$$r_1 = \text{i} * \text{p} \wedge r_2 = \text{i} * \text{p} + \text{j} \Rightarrow (\text{k} < \text{n} \Rightarrow r_1 = \text{i} * \text{p} \wedge r_2 = \text{i} * \text{p} + \text{j}) \wedge (\neg \text{k} < \text{n} \Rightarrow \text{true})$$

The implemented Coq tactic can clearly discharge these verification conditions.

Optimization Based on Arithmetic Simplification. The class of optimizations considered in this section consists in the replacement of expressions in the instructions of a RTL procedure, without modifying its control-flow graph.

We can formalize the result of applying these class of optimizations to a procedure p, as a procedure p' such that for every label l, $p'[l] = p[l]$ or one of the following conditions holds:

- $p[l] = \textbf{cjmp } x_1 \bowtie x_2 \ l'$ and $p'[l] = \textbf{cjmp } x_1' \bowtie x_2' \ l'$ for some variables or constants x_1, x_2, x_1' and x_2', or
- $p[l] = v := e$ and $p'[l] = v := e'$, or
- $p[l] = a[x] := e$ and $p'[l] = a[x'] := e'$, or
- $p[l] = \textbf{invoke } f(\vec{x})$ and $p'[l] = \textbf{invoke } f(\vec{x'})$, or
- $p[l] = \textbf{return } x$ and $p'[l] = \textbf{return } x'$.

for some atomic expressions x, x', e, e'.

$$\frac{}{\vdash e_1 \bowtie e_2 \sim e_1 \bowtie e_2} \qquad \frac{e_1 = e_1', e_2 = e_2' \vdash e_1 \bowtie e_2 \sim e_1' \bowtie e_2'}{}$$

$$\frac{e_1 = e_1' \vdash e_1 \bowtie e_2 \sim e_1' \bowtie e_2}{} \qquad \frac{e_2 = e_2' \vdash e_1 \bowtie e_2 \sim e_1 \bowtie e_2'}{}$$

$$\frac{\Gamma \vdash \phi \sim \phi'}{\Gamma \vdash \neg \phi \sim \neg \phi'} \qquad \frac{\Gamma \vdash \phi \sim \phi'}{\Gamma \vdash \forall v.\ \phi \sim \forall v.\ \phi'} \qquad \frac{\Gamma \vdash \phi \sim \phi' \qquad \Gamma' \vdash \psi \sim \psi'}{\Gamma, \Gamma' \vdash \phi \diamond \psi \sim \phi' \diamond \psi'} \diamond \in \{\wedge, \vee, \Rightarrow\}$$

Fig. 10. Definition of Structural Congruence

The main result of this characterization, is that the computation of verification conditions along the graph of the optimized program coincides in their logical structure with the original ones. That is, there is a syntactical correspondence between the logical formulae, up to substitution of equal expressions. This condition on a pair of assertions ϕ and ϕ' are formalized, for a set of equalities Γ, by the relation $\Gamma \vdash \phi \sim \phi'$ defined by the rules in Figure 10.

The tool relies on the fact that if p' is the result of applying arithmetic simplification to p, then, for every label l, there is a set of equations Γ' such that the relation $\Gamma' \vdash \mathsf{wpi}(p[l]) \sim \mathsf{wpi}(p'[l])$ holds.

Consider two logical formulae φ and φ', and assume they coincide modulo substitution of equalities in the set Γ, that is, $\Gamma \vdash \varphi \sim \varphi'$. It should be clear that from a set of certificates for the equalities in Γ, one can produce a certificate for the goal $\varphi \Rightarrow \varphi'$. The tool implements a tactic that produces this certificate, by traversing the logical structure of φ, and applying the Coq rewrite rule when needed, taking as input the certificate of the equations in Γ. In the following paragraphs, we explain how the tool obtains the certificates for the set of equations in Γ.

Consider the procedure p with specification $\langle \mathsf{Pre}, \mathsf{annot}, \mathsf{Post} \rangle$, and S a result of the analysis. Let p' be the result of transforming p by arithmetic simplification. Then, if the transformation is correct, for every label l there is a set Γ such that $\Gamma \vdash \mathsf{wp}_p(l) \sim \mathsf{wp}_{p'}(l)$, and such that $S(l)$ implies $e = e'$, for every $e = e'$ in Γ. Based on this result, the tool constructs a certificate of $S(l) \Rightarrow e = e'$, for every label l, and equality $e = e'$ in Γ, where Γ is such that $\Gamma \vdash \mathsf{wp}_p(l) \sim \mathsf{wp}_{p'}(l)$. It does so by relying on the Coq tactic ring. By composing these results the tool generates a certificate for the goal $S(l) \Rightarrow \mathsf{wp}_p(l) \Rightarrow \mathsf{wp}_{p'}(l)$ for every label l.

Then, the tool strengthens the original specification with the result of the analysis. The resulting specification $\langle \mathsf{Pre}, \mathsf{annot} \wedge S, \mathsf{Post} \rangle$ will be used also as the specification of the transformed program. To transform the certificates according to the new specification, the analysis is required to produce a certificate for its results, as explained before. Then, a Coq tactic implements a transformation that merges the certificate for the analysis with the original certificate. As a result, we have, for every $l \in \mathsf{annot}$, a proof for $\mathsf{annot}(l) \wedge S(l) \Rightarrow \mathsf{wpi}_p(l{:}p[l])$.

The tool then generates a certificate for the proof obligation corresponding to the transformed program $\mathsf{annot}(l) \wedge S(l) \Rightarrow \mathsf{wpi}_{p'}(l{:}p'[l])$. As mentioned above, the tool implements a Coq tactic, combining the ring tactic with rewriting of expressions, to discharge the goal $\mathsf{annot}(l) \Rightarrow \mathsf{wpi}_p(l : p[l]l) \Rightarrow \mathsf{wpi}_{p'}(l : p'[l])$. The final certificate is then created by composition of the latter certificate and the original certificate $\mathsf{annot}(l) \Rightarrow \mathsf{wpi}_p(l : p[l])$.

Example 8 (Matrix Multiplication: Common-subexpression elimination). From the analysis result computed in Example 7, one can apply common-subexpression elimination on the RTL code shown in Figure 3. In the figure, the optimization replaces the original instructions, in the white boxes, by the optimized instructions inside the gray boxes. The assignments are simplified taking advantage of the conditions $r_1 = \mathtt{i} * \mathtt{p}$ and $r_2 = \mathtt{i} * \mathtt{p} + \mathtt{j}$.

If we compute the proof obligation at label l_7^b in the RTL program of Figure 3 we get something of the form:

$$\mathsf{annot}'(l_7^b) \Rightarrow (\mathtt{k} < \mathtt{n} \Rightarrow \mathsf{annot}'(l_7^b)[^{[c:e_1 \mapsto e_2]}\!/_c][^{\mathtt{k}+1}\!/_{\mathtt{k}}]) \wedge \varphi$$

for some φ, where e_1 stands for $\mathtt{i} * \mathtt{p} + \mathtt{j}$ and e_2 stands for the expression $\mathtt{c}[\mathtt{i} * \mathtt{p} + \mathtt{j}] + \mathtt{a}[\mathtt{i} * \mathtt{n} + \mathtt{k}] * \mathtt{b}[\mathtt{k} * \mathtt{p} + \mathtt{j}]$. The corresponding proof obligation at label l_7^b in the optimized program of Figure 3 has the form:

$$\mathsf{annot}'(l_7^b) \Rightarrow (\mathtt{k} < \mathtt{n} \Rightarrow \mathsf{annot}'(l_7^b)[^{[c:e_1' \mapsto e_2']}\!/_c][^{\mathtt{k}+1}\!/_{\mathtt{k}}]) \wedge \varphi$$

where e_1' stands for r_2 and e_2 stands for $\mathtt{c}[r_2] + \mathtt{a}[\mathtt{i} * \mathtt{n} + \mathtt{k}] * \mathtt{b}[\mathtt{k} * \mathtt{p} + \mathtt{j}]$. Clearly, the two formulae differ only on the substitution of the terms e_1 by e_1', and e_2 by e_2'. The result of the analysis $r_2 = \mathtt{i} * \mathtt{p} + \mathtt{j}$ can prove the equations $e_1 = e_1'$ and $e_2 = e_2'$. Therefore, by strengthening the original annotation with the result of the analysis, the tool can generate a certificate for:

$$S(l_7^b) \wedge \mathsf{annot}'(l_7^b) \Rightarrow (\mathtt{k} < \mathtt{n} \Rightarrow \mathsf{annot}'(l_7^b)[^{[c:e_1' \mapsto e_2']}\!/_c][^{\mathtt{k}+1}\!/_{\mathtt{k}}] \wedge \varphi$$

Redundant Conditional Elimination. The tool also implements redundant conditional elimination, that replaces conditional instruction **cjmp** l' by a non-conditional jump **jmp** l' (or **jmp** $l+1$) if we can statically infer that a condition (or its negation) is always valid.

After the application of this transformation, for an annotated label l such that $p[l] = \mathbf{cjmp}\ v_1 \bowtie v_2\ l'$, the tool must provide, from a certificate of the form

$$\mathsf{annot}(l) \Rightarrow ((v_1 \bowtie v_2) \Rightarrow \mathsf{wp}(l')) \wedge (\neg(v_1 \bowtie v_2) \Rightarrow \mathsf{wp}(l+1))$$

a certificate for the transformed proof obligation: $\mathsf{annot}(l) \Rightarrow \varphi$ where φ is equal to $\mathsf{wp}(l')$ or $\mathsf{wp}(l+1)$ depending on which of the conditions $v_1 \bowtie v_2$ or $\neg(v_1 \bowtie v_2)$ is always valid. The transformation is restricted to the case in which the tool can automatically prove the condition $v_1 \bowtie v_2$ true or false. Therefore, it can straightforwardly generate a certificate for $\mathsf{wp}(l')$ or $\mathsf{wp}(l+1)$ from the certificate of the original proof obligation.

Dead Code Elimination. Another optimization implemented by the tool consists in removing unreachable program points from a sequence of labeled RTL instructions. This optimization is useful for the elimination of redundant conditional jumps. As a side effect, proof obligations are not modified. Instead, some of them may disappear if the optimization removes an unreachable annotated program label. Therefore, the new set of proof obligations is a subset of the original one, and no certificate transformation is needed.

6   Experimental Results

We have experimented with several examples to estimate the impact of certificate transformation in the size of the final certificates. Most of the examples are relatively small, but specifically suited to test the optimizations covered by the tool. To describe the size of certificates, we have considered the number of nodes of the tree structure that represents each Coq λ-term. In average, from the original certificate we have obtained a slight reduction on the certificate for the non-optimized RTL code. The size of the certificate of the result of the analysis is on average 0.43 times the size of the original certificate. Merging the RTL certificates with the certificates of the analysis yields certificates that are almost three times the size of the original certificate. Certificate translation for common-subexpression elimination increases the previous certificate by a factor of 1.46 on average. In total, the final certificates are on average approximately 4 times the size of the original certificates.

We show in the following table a more detailed analysis of the certificate size for the multiplication matrix example.

PO	Source	RTL	Analysis	Merge	CSE
Pre	2922	2960	109	7615	7615
annot(l_2)	8746	8272	138	23276	23276
annot(l_4)	33232	32418	261	86962	86962
annot(l_7)	95195	93907	229	178012	253575

The table shows each certificate size for each step of the compilation. The second column represents the original certificate discharged interactively by the tool user. The third column represents the certificate size after non-optimizing compilation. The fourth column represents the size of the certificate of the analysis result, automatically generated by the tool. The fifth column represents the certificate size after merging the certificate for the RTL program and the certificate for the result of the analysis. Finally, the last column show the certificate size for the optimized program.

Other optimizations, such as redundant conditional elimination and dead code elimination, reduce the size of certificates, since verification conditions are always simplified.

7   Concluding Remarks

This paper reports on a prototype implementation of certificate translation for a fragment of the C language to a RTL language. Although the prototype is modest with respect to state-of-the-art verification tools, it brings a practical perspective on certificate translation and complements the theoretical developments.

Related work. We refer to [3] for a more comprehensive account of related work, and only focus on closely related work. Most of the practical attempts to transfer evidence from source code to lower levels are based on type systems: type-preserving compilers [6,4] aim at translating typable source programs into typable lower level programs; sometimes, they also generate typing information that can be used to make type checking of compiled code more efficient. Certifying compilers [7] aim at translating typable source programs into provably correct lower level programs: they generate logical annotations from the typing derivations, and a certificate for the annotated programs. However, there are only few practical efforts to transform provable source code programs into provable lower level programs, and to generate certificates of the latter. Pavlova [9] implements a certificate translator for a non-optimizing compiler from Java to the JVM. Nordio *et al* [8] formalize non-optimizing proof-transforming compilers from Eiffel to MSIL.

Future work. Our prototype is still in a preliminary stage, and there are many opportunities for improvements and extensions. A first improvement would be to reduce certificate size. We envision two complementary efforts: firstly, one can reduce the size of certificates for source programs using hybrid methods, combining program analysis and program verification. Secondly, one can reduce the growth of certificates during strengthening by symbolic execution and by certificate translation using methods to slice unused parts of the specification; some work in this direction is reported in [10].

Extensions may also be pursued in two complementary efforts. Firstly, one may extend the compilation scheme from RTL to assembly, and provide a corresponding certificate translator. Compiling RTL to assembly involves defining calling conventions, linearizing code, and spilling. We believe that writing certificate translators for these transformations is feasible, and no more difficult than dealing with the optimizations studied here. Secondly, one may extend language coverage, and aim to cover increasingly large fragments of C.

An ambitious goal, that encompasses many of these directions, would be to build a certificate translator that uses Frama-C [5] as a front end.

References

1. Barnett, M., Leino, K.R.M., Schulte, W.: The Spec# programming system: An overview. In: Barthe, G., Burdy, L., Huisman, M., Lanet, J.-L., Muntean, T. (eds.) CASSIS 2004. LNCS, vol. 3362, pp. 49–69. Springer, Heidelberg (2005)
2. Barthe, G., Kunz, C.: Certificate translation in abstract interpretation. In: Drossopoulou, S. (ed.) ESOP 2008. LNCS, vol. 4960, pp. 368–382. Springer, Heidelberg (2008)
3. Barthe, G., Grégoire, B., Kunz, C., Rezk, T.: Certificate translation for optimizing compilers. ACM Transactions on Programming Languages and Systems 31(5), 18:1–18:45 (2009)

4. Chen, J., Hawblitzel, C., Perry, F., Emmi, M., Condit, J., Coetzee, D., Pratikakis, P.: Type-preserving compilation for large-scale optimizing object-oriented compilers. In: Proceedings of the ACM SIGPLAN 2008 Conference on Programming Language Design and Implementation, pp. 183–192. ACM, New York (2008)
5. Monate, B., Correnson, L.: Frama-C, `http://frama-c.cea.fr`
6. Morrisett, G., Walker, D., Crary, K., Glew, N.: From system F to typed assembly language. ACM Transactions on Programming Languages and Systems 21(3), 527–568 (1999); Expanded version of a paper presented at POPL 1998 (1998)
7. Necula, G.C.: Compiling with Proofs. PhD thesis, Carnegie Mellon University, Available as Technical Report CMU-CS-98-154 (October 1998)
8. Nordio, M., Müller, P., Meyer, B.: Proof-transforming compilation of eiffel programs. In: Paige, R. (ed.) TOOLS-EUROPE. LNBIP. Springer, Heidelberg (2008)
9. Pavlova, M.: Java bytecode verification and its applications. Thèse de doctorat, spécialité informatique, Université Nice Sophia Antipolis, France (January 2007)
10. Seo, S., Yang, H., Yi, K., Han, T.: Goal-directed weakening of abstract interpretation results. ACM Transactions on Programming Languages and Systems 29(6), 39:1–39:39 (2007)

Algorithmic Verification with Multiple and Nested Parameters

Antti Siirtola and Juha Kortelainen

University of Oulu, Department of Information Processing Science, P.O. Box 3000,
90014 University of Oulu, Finland
antti.siirtola@oulu.fi, juha.kortelainen@oulu.fi

Abstract. We consider parameterised verification problem, where parameters are sets and relations over these sets, typically used to denote sets of identities of replicated components and connections between the components. A specification and a system are given as (multiply) parameterised labelled transition systems, parameter values are encoded using first-order logic and correctness is understood as the traces refinement. We provide an algorithm that reduces the (infinite) set of parameter values to a finite one without changing the answer to the verification task, which can be then solved with the aid of existing tools. To the best of our knowledge, the algorithm is the most general one that is both complete and applicable to systems with multiple and nested parameters.

Keywords: parameterised verification, refinement checking, process algebra.

1 Introduction

Probably all real-life systems can be naturally modelled as parameterised finite-state machines. Unfortunately, the related verification task is undecidable in general [1], which means that all algorithmic solutions to the problem are somehow restricted. Typically, the number of parameters is limited (to one) and the state-space of the components of the system is not allowed to be parameter-dependent, which raises problems especially when modelling software applications. Moreover, many algorithms are not complete, i.e. guaranteed to provide an answer for all inputs, which means it is difficult know in advance when they are applicable. In practice, also the lack of tool support is a problem.

We address all these issues by improving the theory of labelled transition systems (LTSs) [2,3]. To enable parameterisation, LTS operators are replaced by symbolic equivalents and some actions and sets of actions are represented by variables leading to a structure we call an LTS schema. Hence, in our approach, parameters are sets and relations over these sets, typically used to denote sets of identities of replicated components and connections between the components. As the values of variables are fixed using a valuation, an instance of the LTS schema, an LTS, is obtained. Sets of valuations are expressed as a valuation formula, an expression of first-order logic. The parameterised verification problem can now be

K. Breitman and A. Cavalcanti (Eds.): ICFEM 2009, LNCS 5885, pp. 561–580, 2009.

stated as follows: given a specification and a system LTS schema and a valuation formula, determine whether the instance of the system LTS schema is correct with respect to the corresponding instance of the specification LTS schema for all valuations.

We present a complete algorithm that reduces the (infinite) set of valuations expressed as a valuation formula to a finite one without changing the answer to the verification task. Hence, after the application of the reduction algorithm, the problem can be solved using existing tools. The algorithm assumes that the traces refinement is used to establish correctness, the specification does not involve hiding, and existential quantification is not used to specify parameter values. The reduction exploits algebraic properties, mainly the precongruence, of the traces refinement, which allow the correctness of large system instances to be derived from that of small ones. The idea is introduced in [4] and it is called the precongruence reduction. The same paper also provides a simple algorithm that does the reduction automatically.

In this paper, we develop the concept of an LTS schema introduced in [4] further by allowing relation variables that can be used to represent system topology more precisely. We also propose a finite representation for (infinite) sets of valuations. This enables an enhanced reduction algorithm with a strictly wider application domain than the one in [4], which necessitates a full or empty relation between system components of the same type. Hence, the algorithm in [4] is not applicable to the shared resource system considered here, because a maximal irreflexive relation is needed to distinct between different users.

However, also the algorithm presented here has its restrictions. The sets of valuations arising from existential-free valuation formulae are downward closed, which informally means that we can study only specification-system that are closed under the removal of a replicated component. For example, systems with a star, bipartite and totally (un)connected topology are such, but those with a ring, linear or tree topology are not. However, if it is possible to capture the behaviour of the system from the viewpoint of any two components connected to each other using only finitely many LTS schemata, then one can study transitive closures of rings, arrays and forests instead, which are closed under the removal of a replicated component.

An other restriction is that in our formalism parameterisation is achieved through the use of replicated parallel composition, which roughly corresponds to replicated conjunction or universal quantification in logics. From the specification point of view it means that one can study for-all-type safety properties. For example, specifications of the form $\bigwedge_{x_1,\dots,x_k} f(x_1,\dots,x_k)$, where $x_1,\dots,x_k$ range over identities of different replicated components and $f(x_1,\dots,x_k)$ is a safety property related to $x_1,\dots,x_k$, can be represented in our formalism.

Systems expressible in our formalism are those that can be composed from finitely many parts each of which represents the system from the viewpoint of a fixed number of processes. In this sense, the most related works are the complete methods by Bouajjani et al. [5] and Emerson and Kahlon [6] that enable parameterised verification by providing bounds (cut-offs) for the values of parameters.

Request-take-release (RTR) systems considered by Bouajjani et al. [5] can be faithfully modelled from the view of two processes, because every illegal behaviour can be traced back to two processes served in a wrong order. Hence, RTR systems can be modelled as LTS schemata, which implies that the results in [5] concerning for-all-type safety properties can be obtained as an application of our theory.

Also systems with conjunctive guards considered by Emerson and Kahlon [6] can be expressed in our formalism, but those with disjunctive guards not. That is because every process must agree on the execution of a transition with a conjunctive guard, whereas a disjunctive guard can be enabled by a single process. Hence, systems with conjunctive guards can be modelled from the view of two processes, but by looking at the fixed number of processes it is impossible to say whether a disjunctive guard is disabled. Therefore, systems with disjunctive guards cannot be modelled in our formalism, but the results concerning conjunctive guards and for-all-type safety properties can be obtained as an application of our theory.

Other complete cut-off results are more or less incomparable to ours. In their other paper, Emerson and Kahlon consider systems with arbitrary many processes generated from the same template and properties related to one or two processes [7]. However, because transition guards can be disjunctive, the results are incomparable to ours.

The same applies to data-independence results of Wolper [8], and Lazić and Nowak [9,10]. These methods treat systems that can send and receive data values of an arbitrary large or infinite type, but the structure of a system is not allowed to be parameterised. On the other hand, as receiving of data cannot be naturally expressed using the replicated parallel composition, also data-independence results are incomparable to ours.

The results of Emerson and Namjoshi [11], Emerson and Kahlon [12,13] and Nazari and Thistle [14] are related to rings of processes communicating through token passing. The models of computation are (close to) LTSs, but the results are still incomparable to ours, because applying them outside rings is obviously difficult and applying our method to rings requires additional modelling work.

Clarke et al. [15] consider networks of homogeneous fixed-size processes communicating through token passing. Their results provide only an upper bound for the size of network graphs, but no method to determine the networks below the bound. Moreover, as only one process type is allowed and a family of networks does not have to be closed under the removal of a process, the method is incomparable to ours.

There are also methods that establish a cut-off by inductive reasoning [16,17,18,19], but they apply to rings of similar fixed-sized processes only and are not complete. An exception is the approach of Valmari and Tienari [19] which is shown to terminate if certain structural conditions are met [14]. An other exception is the method of Pyssysalo [18] that allows the state-space of the processes to be parameter-dependent. Nevertheless, all the methods are incomparable to ours.

Other parameterised verification methods are based on abstract interpretation or inductive reasoning, but despite few exceptions they are not fully algorithmic or guaranteed to terminate. The exceptions are based on either counter abstraction [20] or infinite-state verification algorithms [21] naturally applicable to systems with non-parameterised components only.

In the next section, the relevant parts of the theory of LTSs are reviewed. The formalism, LTS schemata, valuations and valuation formulae, is introduced in Sect. 3. Also the research problem and the precongruence reduction method for parameterised verification are presented in this section. The following section discusses modelling issues and presents a shared resource system used as a running example. In Sect. 5, the verification method is lifted in the level of valuations, and in the following section, an enhanced reduction algorithm is given. The paper concludes with discussion on future work.

2   Labelled Transition Systems

A labelled transition system, an LTS, is our fundamental model of computation [3]. Intuitively, an LTS is a graph the nodes of which are called states, the edges are labelled by actions and they are called transitions, and one of the states is marked as the initial one. To introduce LTSs formally, we assume a countably infinite set $\mathbb{A}$ of *atoms*. Tuples of atoms are called *actions*. The empty tuple $()$, also denoted by τ, is called the *invisible* action and the rest of the actions are *visible*. The set of all the visible actions is referred to by $\mathbb{V}$.

Definition 1 (LTS). *A labelled transition system is a four-tuple* $(S, \Sigma, R, \hat{s})$, *where* S *is a non-empty set of* states, $\Sigma \subseteq \mathbb{V}$ *is a set of visible actions,* $R \subseteq S \times (\Sigma \cup \{\tau\}) \times S$ *is a set of* transitions *and* $\hat{s} \in S$ *is the initial state.*

If $\mathcal{L} = (S, \Sigma, R, \hat{s})$ is an LTS, the set S is called the *state-space* of $\mathcal{L}$ and the set Σ, also denoted by $\mathrm{alph}(\mathcal{L})$, is said to be the *alphabet* of $\mathcal{L}$. The *size* of an LTS is the sum of the sizes of its state-space and alphabet. An LTS of finite size is simply called *finite*.

A system modelled as an LTS is typically built of smaller LTSs representing its parts. Let I be a finite index set and $\mathcal{L}_i = (S_i, \Sigma_i, R_i, \hat{s}_i)$ an LTS for every $i \in I$. The *parallel composition* of LTSs in the set $\{\mathcal{L}_i\}_{i \in I}$, denoted by $(\|_{i \in I} \mathcal{L}_i)$, is a four-tuple $(\prod_{i \in I} S_i, \bigcup_{i \in I} \Sigma_i, R_I, \hat{s}_I)$, where $\prod_{i \in I} S_i$ denotes the set of all functions $s : I \mapsto \bigcup_{i \in I} S_i$ is such that $s(i) \in S_i$ for all $i \in I$, $\hat{s}_I \in \prod_{i \in I} S_i$ such that $\hat{s}_I(i) = \hat{s}_i$ for all $i \in I$, and R_I consists of all tuples (s, α, s') such that either

- $\alpha \neq \tau$, $(s(i), \alpha, s'(i)) \in R_i$ whenever $\alpha \in \Sigma_i$ and $i \in I$, and $s(i) = s'(i)$ whenever $\alpha \notin \Sigma_i$ and $i \in I$; or
- $\alpha = \tau$ and there is $i \in I$ for which $(s(i), \tau, s'(i)) \in R_i$ and $s(j) = s'(j)$ for every $j \in I \setminus \{i\}$.

Hence, an LTS can execute a visible action α in the parallel composition, if and only if all the other LTSs having α in their alphabet can execute the action as well, but the invisible actions each LTS executes individually. If $I = \{1, \ldots, n\}$ or other totally ordered set, we can write $(\mathcal{L}_1 \parallel \ldots \parallel \mathcal{L}_n)$ or $\parallel_{i=1}^{n} \mathcal{L}_i$ alternatively for $\parallel_{i \in I} \mathcal{L}_i$. In this case, the states s of $\parallel_{i \in I} \mathcal{L}_i$ can be identified with tuples $(s(1), \ldots, s(n))$, which corresponds to the standard definition of the parallel composition.

Renaming and hiding are defined in the usual manner. Let $\mathcal{L} = (S, \Sigma, R, \hat{s})$ be an LTS, $\zeta : \mathbb{V} \mapsto \mathbb{V}$ a function and $\Lambda \subseteq \mathbb{V}$ a set of visible actions. The LTS $\mathcal{L}$ *renamed by* ζ is a four-tuple $(S, \{\zeta(\alpha) \mid \alpha \in \Sigma\}, R_\zeta, \hat{s})$, denoted by $\zeta(\mathcal{L})$, where R_ζ consists of all tuples $(s, \tau, s') \in R$ and all tuples $(s, \zeta(\alpha), s')$ such that $(s, \alpha, s') \in R$ and $\alpha \in \Sigma$. Hence, $\zeta(\mathcal{L})$ is obtained from $\mathcal{L}$ by mapping all the visible actions using ζ. The LTS $\mathcal{L}$ *hiding* Λ, is a four-tuple $(S, \Sigma \setminus \Lambda, R_\Lambda, \hat{s})$, denoted by $(\mathcal{L} \setminus \Lambda)$, where R_Λ consists of all tuples (s, α, s') such that either $\alpha \notin \Lambda$ and $(s, \alpha, s') \in R$, or $\alpha = \tau$ and there is $\beta \in \Lambda$ such that $(s, \beta, s') \in R$. Hence, $(\mathcal{L} \setminus \Lambda)$ is obtained from $\mathcal{L}$ by changing the transition labels in Λ to the invisible action and removing the actions in Λ from the alphabet. It is easy to see that the structures obtained from LTSs by parallel composition, hiding and renaming are LTSs, and that the operators preserve finiteness.

In the analysis of LTSs, we are usually interested in the sequences of visible actions reachable from the initial state. A finite alternating sequence of states and actions, $s_1 \alpha_1 s_2 \ldots \alpha_{n-1} s_n$, of an LTS $\mathcal{L}$, is a *path in $\mathcal{L}$ from* s_1, if (s_i, α_i, s_{i+1}) is a transition of $\mathcal{L}$ for every $i \in \{1, \ldots, n-1\}$. A finite sequence t of visible actions is a *trace (of $\mathcal{L}$)*, if there is path in $\mathcal{L}$ from the initial state such that t can be obtained from the path by removing all the states and the invisible actions. The set of all the traces of $\mathcal{L}$, the *traces of $\mathcal{L}$* for short, is referred to by $\mathrm{tr}(\mathcal{L})$.

An LTS $\mathcal{L}_2$ is a *traces refinement* of an LTS $\mathcal{L}_1$, denoted by $\mathcal{L}_1 \succeq_{\mathrm{tr}} \mathcal{L}_2$, if $\mathcal{L}_1$ and $\mathcal{L}_2$ have the same alphabet and $\mathrm{tr}(\mathcal{L}_2) \subseteq \mathrm{tr}(\mathcal{L}_1)$. If $\mathcal{L}_1 \succeq_{\mathrm{tr}} \mathcal{L}_2$ and $\mathcal{L}_2 \succeq_{\mathrm{tr}} \mathcal{L}_1$, denoted by $\mathcal{L}_1 =_{\mathrm{tr}} \mathcal{L}_2$, then $\mathcal{L}_1$ and $\mathcal{L}_2$ are called *traces equivalent* or one says that $\mathcal{L}_1$ is *traces equivalent to* $\mathcal{L}_2$. Clearly, $\succeq_{\mathrm{tr}}$ is a preorder, i.e. a reflexive and transitive relation, and $=_{\mathrm{tr}}$ is an equivalence in the set of LTSs. However, unlike in [3], we require the alphabets to match in the definition of the traces refinement. This is necessary to make the traces refinement a precongruence, because in our definition of the parallel composition the actions to be synchronised are not explicitly given but implicitly determined by the alphabets.

Proposition 2. *Let I and K be finite index sets, $\mathcal{L}_i$ and $\mathcal{L}_i'$ LTSs for all $i \in I$, $\mathcal{L}_{i,k}$ an LTS for all $(i, k) \in I \times K$, $\mathcal{L}, \mathcal{L}_1, \mathcal{L}_2$ LTSs, ζ a function: $\mathbb{V} \mapsto \mathbb{V}$ and Λ, Λ' sets of visible actions.*

1. $\parallel_{i \in I} \parallel_{k \in K} \mathcal{L}_{i,k} =_{\mathrm{tr}} \parallel_{k \in K} \parallel_{i \in I} \mathcal{L}_{i,k}$.
2. $\parallel_{i \in I} \mathcal{L}_i =_{\mathrm{tr}} \parallel_{j \in J} \parallel_{i \in I_j} \mathcal{L}_i$, *if J is an index set s.t. $\{I_j\}_{j \in J}$ is a partition of I.*
3. $\parallel_{i \in I} \mathcal{L}_i =_{\mathrm{tr}} \parallel_{i \in I, \Sigma(\mathcal{L}_i) \neq \emptyset} \mathcal{L}_i$.
4. $\parallel_{i \in I} \mathcal{L}_i =_{\mathrm{tr}} \mathcal{L}$, *if I is non-empty and $\mathcal{L}_i = \mathcal{L}$ for every $i \in I$.*
5. $\zeta(\parallel_{i \in I} \mathcal{L}_i) =_{\mathrm{tr}} \parallel_{i \in I} \zeta(\mathcal{L}_i)$, *if ζ is a bijection.*
6. $\zeta(\mathcal{L} \setminus \Lambda) =_{\mathrm{tr}} \zeta(\mathcal{L}) \setminus \{\zeta(\alpha) \mid \alpha \in \Lambda\}$, *if ζ is a bijection.*

7. $\|_{i \in I} (\mathcal{L}_i \setminus \Lambda) \succeq_{\mathrm{tr}} (\|_{i \in I} \mathcal{L}_i) \setminus \Lambda$.
8. $\mathcal{L} \setminus \Lambda =_{\mathrm{tr}} \mathcal{L}$, if Λ and $\mathrm{alph}(\mathcal{L})$ are disjoint.
9. $(\mathcal{L} \setminus \Lambda) \setminus \Lambda' =_{\mathrm{tr}} \mathcal{L} \setminus (\Lambda \cup \Lambda')$.
10. $\|_{i \in I} \mathcal{L}_i \succeq_{\mathrm{tr}} \|_{i \in I} \mathcal{L}_i'$, if $\mathcal{L}_i \succeq_{\mathrm{tr}} \mathcal{L}_i'$ for every $i \in I$.
11. $\zeta(\mathcal{L}_1) \succeq_{\mathrm{tr}} \zeta(\mathcal{L}_2)$, if $\mathcal{L}_1 \succeq_{\mathrm{tr}} \mathcal{L}_2$.
12. $\mathcal{L}_1 \setminus \Lambda \succeq_{\mathrm{tr}} \mathcal{L}_2 \setminus \Lambda$, if $\mathcal{L}_1 \succeq_{\mathrm{tr}} \mathcal{L}_2$.

Informally, the proposition states that (1) the order of successive parallel compositions can be changed, if the index sets are mutually independent, (2) the index set of a parallel composition can be partitioned, (3) LTSs with the empty alphabet and (4) redundant LTSs can be removed from the parallel composition, (5,6) bijective renaming can be pushed inside other operators, (7) pushing hiding inside the parallel composition results to an LTS greater in the preorder, (8) any LTS is an idempotent element with respect to hiding a set of actions disjoint from its alphabet, (9) successive hiding operators can be combined and vice versa, and (10–12) the operators preserve the traces refinement, which implies that the traces refinement is a precongruence. The proposition is based on the results in [2,3].

3   Formalism

A parameterised system and a related parameterised specification can be modelled as a family $\{(Spec_i, Sys_i)\}_{i \in I}$ of pairs of finite LTSs, where I denotes a (typically infinite) set of parameter values, and $Spec_i$ and Sys_i represent respectively the specification and the system with the parameter value $i \in I$. The system is considered to be correct with respect to a specification if and only if $Spec_i \succeq_{\mathrm{tr}} Sys_i$ for every $i \in I$. This way, it is possible to prove absence of illegal behaviour, i.e. to check safety or reachability properties [3].

Checking the correctness of a parameterised system modelled as a family of pairs of finite LTSs is obviously impossible in general. However, finite subsets of the family can be automatically checked, and in practical situations, the LTSs share a common structure, which could be exploited to reduce the number of refinement checks needed.

To formalise the structure of a specification and system LTS, three kinds of parameters, or variables, are introduced. *Atom variables* represents atoms and they are typically used to denote identities of system components. A non-empty tuple $(x_1, \ldots, x_k, a_1, \ldots, a_l)$, where $x_1, \ldots, x_k$ are atom variables, $a_1, \ldots, a_l$ are atoms and $k + l \in \mathbb{Z}_+$, is called an *action schema*. *Type variables* denote sets of atoms and they represent sets of identities of system components of the same kind. Finally, *relation variables* denote sets of tuples of atoms (i.e. sets of visible actions), and they are used to describe the topology of a system and relationships between its components. The sets of all the type, relation and atom variables are denoted by respectively $\mathbb{T}$, $\mathbb{G}$ and $\mathbb{X}$, and they are assumed to be countably infinite, disjoint and also disjoint from the set of atoms.

The structure of a parameterised LTS is represented as an LTS schema defined as follows.

Definition 3 (LTS schema). *An LTS schema is an expression obtained by finite application of the steps below. There are no other LTS schemata.*

1. *If S is a non-empty set of* states, Γ *is a set of action schemata,* $\Delta \subseteq S \times (\Gamma \cup \{\tau\}) \times S$ *is a set of* transition schemata *and* $\hat{s} \in S$ *is the* initial state, *then* $(S, \Gamma, \Delta, \hat{s})$ *is an (elementary) LTS schema.*
2. *If $\mathcal{P}_1$ and $\mathcal{P}_2$ are LTS schemata, then $(\mathcal{P}_1 \,\|\, \mathcal{P}_2)$ is a (parallel) LTS schema.*
3. *If $\mathcal{P}$ is an LTS schema, k is a positive integer, $T_1, \ldots, T_k$ are type variables, Π is a relation variable and $x_1, \ldots, x_k$ are distinct atom variables, then $(\|_{(x_1,\ldots,x_k) \in \Pi : T_1 \times \ldots \times T_k} \mathcal{P})$ is a $((\Pi\text{-})\text{replicated parallel})$ LTS schema.*
4. *If $\mathcal{P}$ is an LTS schema, Γ is a set of action schemata, k is a non-negative integer, $T_1, \ldots, T_k$ are type variables and $x_1, \ldots, x_k$ are distinct atom variables, then $(\mathcal{P} \setminus \bigcup_{(x_1,\ldots,x_k) \in T_1 \times \ldots \times T_k} \Gamma)$ is a (hiding) LTS schema.*

An LTS schema $\mathcal{P}$ is *finite*, if every set of states and every set of action schemata occurring in $\mathcal{P}$ is finite. An LTS schema $\mathcal{P}'$ is said to be an *LTS subschema* (of $\mathcal{P}$), if $\mathcal{P}'$ is a subexpression of $\mathcal{P}$. A structure $\bigcup_{(x_1,\ldots,x_k) \in T_1 \times \ldots \times T_k} \Gamma$ that is the part of a hiding LTS schema is called a *set schema*. An atom variable x is *free* in $\mathcal{P}$, if there is an occurrence of x in $\mathcal{P}$ that is not within an LTS subschema $\|_{(x_1,\ldots,x_k) \in \Pi : T_1 \times \ldots \times T_k} \mathcal{P}'$ nor within a set schema $\bigcup_{(x_1,\ldots,x_k) \in T_1 \times \ldots \times T_k} \Gamma$ such that $x = x_i$ for some $i \in \{1, \ldots, k\}$. An LTS schema with no free atom variable is said to be *closed*.

The parameters of an LTS schema are the type, relation and free atom variables occurring in it. The set of all the parameters of $\mathcal{P}$ is called the *signature* of $\mathcal{P}$ and it is denoted by $\mathrm{sig}(\mathcal{P})$. The set of all the atoms occurring in $\mathcal{P}$ is referred by $\mathrm{at}(\mathcal{P})$. If $\|_{(x_1,\ldots,x_k) \in \Pi : T_1 \times \ldots \times T_k} \mathcal{P}'$ is a replicated parallel LTS subschema of $\mathcal{P}$, then $T_1 \times \ldots \times T_k$ is a *type of* Π *(in $\mathcal{P}$)*. In practical situations, there is precisely one type for each relation variable in $\mathrm{sig}(\mathcal{P})$.

The parameter values are formally represented as a valuation, a partial function mapping atom, type and relation variables to respectively atoms, sets of atoms and sets of visible actions (sets of non-empty tuples of atoms), where the atoms occurring in the values of atom and relation variables are restricted to those occurring in the images of type variables.

Definition 4 (Valuation). *A valuation is a partial function*

$$\phi : \mathbb{X} \cup \mathbb{T} \cup \mathbb{G} \mapsto \mathbb{A} \cup \mathbb{P}(\mathbb{A}) \cup \mathbb{P}(\mathbb{V})$$

such that

- $\phi|_{\mathbb{T}}$ *maps type variables to finite, non-empty, disjoint sets of atoms,*
- $\phi|_{\mathbb{G}}$ *maps relation variables to $\bigcup_{k \in \mathbb{Z}_+} \bigcup_{A_1,\ldots,A_k \in \mathrm{im}(\phi|_{\mathbb{T}})} \mathbb{P}(A_1 \times \ldots \times A_k)$, and*
- $\phi|_{\mathbb{X}}$ *maps atom variables to $\bigcup_{A \in \mathrm{im}(\phi|_{\mathbb{T}})} A$.*

A valuation ϕ is said to be *compatible with* an LTS schema $\mathcal{P}$, if ϕ defines values for all the parameters of $\mathcal{P}$, the atoms occurring in $\mathcal{P}$ are not used in the values of variables (i.e. $\mathrm{at}(\mathcal{P}) \cap (\bigcup_{A \in \mathrm{im}(\phi|_{\mathbb{T}})} A) = \emptyset$) and whenever $T_1 \times \ldots \times T_k$ is a type of a relation variable Π in $\mathcal{P}$, then $\phi(\Pi)$ is a subset of $\phi(T_1) \times \ldots \times \phi(T_k)$.

If ϕ is compatible with $\mathcal{P}$, then the *instance* of $\mathcal{P}$ *(generated by ϕ)*, denoted by $[\![\mathcal{P}]\!]_\phi$, is obtained from $\mathcal{P}$ by first substituting the parameters according to ϕ, then converting symbolic operators to standard ones, and finally applying them as usual.

To define $[\![\mathcal{P}]\!]_\phi$ formally, let $x_1, \ldots, x_k$ be distinct atom variables and Π a relation variable in $\mathrm{sig}(\mathcal{P})$. We write $\phi[(x_1 \ldots, x_k) \mapsto \Pi]$ for the set of all valuations ϕ' such that

1. the domain of ϕ' is $\mathrm{dom}(\phi) \cup \{x_1, \ldots, x_k\}$,
2. $(\phi'(x_1), \ldots, \phi'(x_k)) \in \phi(\Pi)$ and
3. ϕ' maps the elements in $\mathrm{dom}(\phi') \setminus \{x_1, \ldots, x_k\}$ like ϕ does.

In other words, $\phi[(x_1, \ldots, x_k) \mapsto \Pi]$ denotes the set of all the valuations obtained by (re)defining ϕ for $x_1, \ldots, x_k$ such that the value of $(x_1, \ldots, x_k)$ is in $\phi(\Pi)$. A set $\phi[x_1 \mapsto T_1, \ldots, x_k \mapsto T_k]$, where $T_1, \ldots, T_k$ are type variables, of all valuations ϕ' obtained by (re)defining ϕ for $x_1, \ldots, x_k$ such that $\phi'(x_i) \in \phi(T_i)$ for all $i \in I$ is defined analogously.

Now, the instance of $\mathcal{P}$ generated by ϕ can be defined inductively as follows.

1. $[\![(S, \Gamma, \Delta, \hat{s})]\!]_\phi = (S, [\![\Gamma]\!]_\phi, [\![\Delta]\!]_\phi, \hat{s})$,

   where $[\![\Gamma]\!]_\phi$ and $[\![\Delta]\!]_\phi$ are obtained from respectively Γ and Δ by substituting $\phi(x)$ for every occurrence of an atom variable x.

2. $[\![(\mathcal{P}_1 \parallel \mathcal{P}_2)]\!]_\phi = [\![\mathcal{P}_1]\!]_\phi \parallel [\![\mathcal{P}_2]\!]_\phi$.

3. $[\![(\underset{(x_1,\ldots,x_k)\in\Pi:T_1\times\ldots\times T_k}{\parallel} \mathcal{P}')]\!]_\phi = \underset{\phi'\in\phi[(x_1,\ldots,x_k)\mapsto\Pi]}{\parallel} [\![\mathcal{P}']\!]_{\phi'}$.

4. $[\![(\mathcal{P}' \setminus \underset{(x_1,\ldots,x_k)\in T_1\times\ldots\times T_k}{\bigcup} \Gamma)]\!]_\phi = [\![\mathcal{P}']\!]_\phi \setminus \underset{\phi'\in\phi[x_1\mapsto T_1,\ldots,x_k\mapsto T_k]}{\bigcup} [\![\Gamma]\!]_{\phi'}$.

It is easy to see that the instance of an LTS schema is an LTS, and if the LTS schema is finite then all its instances are finite too.

We may now assume that a specification and a system are given as respectively LTS schemata $\mathcal{Q}$ and $\mathcal{P}$, and the allowed parameter values are encoded as a set Φ of valuations. The problem whether $[\![\mathcal{Q}]\!]_\phi \succeq_{\mathrm{tr}} [\![\mathcal{P}]\!]_\phi$ for all valuations $\phi \in \Phi$ compatible with $\mathcal{Q}$ and $\mathcal{P}$ is called *Parameterised Traces Refinement*. Our goal is to determine a finite subset Ψ of Φ such that the instances $\mathcal{Q}, \mathcal{P}, \Psi$ and $\mathcal{Q}, \mathcal{P}, \Phi$ of Parameterised Traces Refinement have the same answer.

Without loss of generality, we may assume that the valuations in Φ have the domain $\mathrm{sig}(\mathcal{Q}) \cup \mathrm{sig}(\mathcal{P})$, i.e. the valuations specify values precisely to the parameters of $\mathcal{Q}$ and $\mathcal{P}$. We also assume that the LTS schemata are finite, because we are interested in the verification of real systems. Without the loss of generality, we may then assume that the LTS schemata are closed as well, because finitely many atom variables can be eliminated by introducing new relation variables.

Now, suppose that we have proven the system correct with respect to the specification for finitely many parameter values. By exploiting the precongruence property, it is possible to generalise the result to specification-system instances that can be obtained from the examined ones by the application of LTS operators. In the best case, the whole system can be proven correct this way. The method is called *the precongruence reduction*. It is first introduced in [4] and captured in the following proposition.

Theorem 5. *Let $\mathcal{Q}$, $\mathcal{P}$, Φ be an instance of Parameterised Traces Refinement. If Ψ is a subset of Φ such that for every $\phi \in \Phi \setminus \Psi$ compatible with $\mathcal{Q}$ and $\mathcal{P}$ there are a positive integer n, an n-place function f that is a composition of parallel composition, renaming and hiding operators, and $\psi_1, \ldots, \psi_n \in \Psi$ compatible with $\mathcal{Q}$ and $\mathcal{P}$ such that*

$$[\![\mathcal{Q}]\!]_\phi \succeq_{\text{tr}} f([\![\mathcal{Q}]\!]_{\psi_1}, \ldots, [\![\mathcal{Q}]\!]_{\psi_n}) \text{ and } f([\![\mathcal{P}]\!]_{\psi_1}, \ldots, [\![\mathcal{P}]\!]_{\psi_n}) \succeq_{\text{tr}} [\![\mathcal{P}]\!]_\phi \,,$$

then the answer to $\mathcal{Q}$, $\mathcal{P}$, Ψ is the same as the answer to $\mathcal{Q}$, $\mathcal{P}$, Φ.

The theorem follows straightforwardly from the precongruence of traces refinement, see [4] for details.

Because checking traces refinement is a computationally expensive task, we want to pick Ψ in such a way that the valuations in Ψ generate small specification-system instances. Hence, it is sufficient to consider only functions f that are compositions of parallel composition and bijective renaming, because other operators do not help in constructing large instances. Such functions can be always represented in the form $\|_{i=1}^{n} \zeta_i(\cdot_i)$, where ζ_i is a bijection: $\mathbb{V} \mapsto \mathbb{V}$ for every $i \in \{1, \ldots, n\}$. So, assuming the family $\{[\![\mathcal{Q}]\!]_\phi, [\![\mathcal{P}]\!]_\phi\}_{\phi \in \Phi'}$, where Φ' is the set of all the valuations in Φ compatible with $\mathcal{Q}$ and $\mathcal{P}$, to be sufficiently closed under bijective renaming, one can do the generalisation from Ψ to Φ in two steps. First, one generalises the result to all the instances that can be obtained by bijective renaming, and after that to all the instances that can be represented as the parallel composition of those obtained in the first step.

To automate the reduction method, we still need a finite representation for sets of valuations. Because the main purpose of such a formalism is to encode the values of relation variables, using logics of some sort is a natural choice. For that purpose, we need to be able to pick atoms from the sets represented by type variables, compare them and test whether a tuple of them is in the set represented by a relation variable. These constructs are formalised as a valuation formula.

Definition 6 (Valuation formula). *A valuation formula is an expression generated by the Backus-Naur form grammar*

$$c ::= (x_1, x_2, \ldots, x_n) \in \Pi \mid x_0 = x_1 \mid (\neg c) \mid (c \wedge c) \mid (c \vee c) \mid (\forall x_0 \in T.c) \,,$$

where $x_0, x_1, x_2, \ldots, x_n$ denote any atom variables ($n \in \mathbb{Z}_+$), Π any relation variable and T any type variable.

The notation and concepts of a *valuation subformula*, a *free* atom variable, a *closed* valuation formula and the *signature* of a valuation formula are defined analogously to LTS schemata. A valuation formula is called *existential-free*, if no universal valuation subformula $\forall x \in T.c'$ occurs within a negated valuation subformula $\neg c''$.

We say that a valuation ϕ is *compatible* with a valuation formula c, if the signature of c is a subset of the domain of ϕ. If ϕ is compatible with c, then $[\![c]\!]_\phi$ denotes a formula obtained from c by substituting the variables in $\mathrm{sig}(c)$ according to ϕ. The formula $[\![c]\!]_\phi$ is called the *instance (of c) (generated by ϕ)* and it is evaluated in the usual way. Now, the set of valuations represented by a valuation formula c is naturally defined as the one the members of which satisfy c and have the domain $\mathrm{sig}(c)$. We write $\mathrm{va}(c)$ for the set of all valuations ϕ with the domain $\mathrm{sig}(c)$ such that $[\![c]\!]_\phi$ is true.

We may now concentrate on instances $\mathcal{Q}, \mathcal{P}, \mathrm{va}(c)$ of Parameterised Traces Refinement such that $\mathcal{Q}$ and $\mathcal{P}$ are closed, and c is a valuation formula for which $\mathrm{sig}(c) = \mathrm{sig}(\mathcal{Q}) \cup \mathrm{sig}(\mathcal{P})$.

4   Modelling Using LTS Schemata

Using LTS schemata to represent parameterised systems and specifications necessitates a compositional modelling technique; the system and the specification have to be constructed from smaller parts using a parallel composition such that each part represents the behaviour of the system or the specification from the viewpoint certain components. However, to successfully use the technique, i.e. to avoid introducing false positive verification results, one should recall that it is safe to replace the system with a bigger one and the specification with a smaller one in the preorder, but not otherwise.

Proposition 7. *Let Spec and Sys be LTSs, I a finite index set and $Spec_i$ and Sys_i LTSs for all $i \in I$ such that* $\mathrm{alph}(Spec) = \bigcup_{i \in I} \mathrm{alph}(Spec_i)$ *and* $\mathrm{alph}(Sys) = \bigcup_{i \in I} \mathrm{alph}(Sys_i)$.

1. *$Spec \succeq_{\mathrm{tr}} \|_{i \in I} Spec_i$ if and only if whenever t is a (minimal) sequence over $\mathrm{alph}(Spec)$ such that $t \notin \mathrm{tr}(Spec)$, there exists $i \in I$ such that the projection of t on $\mathrm{alph}(Spec_i)$ is not a trace of $Spec_i$.*
2. *$\|_{i \in I} Sys_i \succeq_{\mathrm{tr}} Sys$ if and only if $Sys_i \succeq_{\mathrm{tr}} Sys \setminus (\mathrm{alph}(Sys) \setminus \mathrm{alph}(Sys_i))$ for all $i \in I$.*

The proposition follows easily from the definitions.

Informally, the proposition states that when creating the specification from smaller parts, every illegal behaviour must be forbidden by some of the parts. Similarly, every part of the system model must cover all the behaviours of the system from its own point of view. In the context of LTS schemata, it means that we have to restrict our attention to systems and specifications the behaviour of which can be faithfully modelled from the viewpoint of a bounded number of components, because each elementary LTS schema can refer to finitely many components only.

The restriction could be overcome by introducing a replicated choice or equivalent construct. The replicated choice can be though as a dual of the replicated parallel composition. Whereas the instances composed in parallel can all make progress, the replicated choice picks only one the instances for execution. The construct is useful for modelling purposes, but it seems to be very difficult to include it in our formalism without making the problem undecidable.

As an example, consider a shared resource system with an arbitrary number of users and shared resources, where a user may get a read or write access to any resource after obtaining the corresponding lock. A resource itself has no mechanism for concurrency control and several users can hold a lock for a resource simultaneously only if all of them have only the read lock. Our goal is to formally prove it is not possible for a user to access a resource if an other one is writing to it.

The behaviour of a user u from the viewpoint of a single resource r is captured in an LTS schema $User$ in Fig. 1. Obtaining the read (write) lock for the resource is modelled by an action schema $(u, r, rdlock)$ (respectively $(u, r, wrlock)$) and releasing the lock by $(u, r, unlock)$, where u and r are atom variables. Reading (writing to) the resource is modelled using two action schemata, namely $(u, r, rdbeg)$ and $(u, r, rdend)$ (respectively $(u, r, wrbeg)$ and $(u, r, wrend)$) denoting respectively the beginning and the end of the event. The invisible actions represent user's other activities which may take place at any time.

Similarly, the behaviour of a lock from the viewpoint of a user and a resource is first captured in an LTS schema $Lock_1$. However, as the locking sequences of users are mutually dependent, the lock has to be modelled from the viewpoint of two users and a resource, too. This behaviour is captured in an LTS schema $Lock_2$ in Fig. 1, and $Lock_1$ can be now obtained from $Lock_2$ by removing transition schemata involving u_2. The resources are modelled in the level of action schemata only.

Clearly, the LTS schemata $User$, $Lock_1$ and $Lock_2$ capture all the behaviours of the system from their own point of view. By Proposition 7, the system model can be build by composing all the users and locks in parallel, which results to the LTS schema

$$SRS := (\underset{u\in *_U:U}{\|} \underset{r\in *_R:R}{\|} User) \| (\underset{r\in *_R:R}{\|} (\underset{(u_1,u_2)\in \neq_U:U\times U}{\|} Lock_2) \| (\underset{u_1\in *_U:U}{\|} Lock_1)) ,$$

where U and R are type variables denoting sets of respectively user and resource identifiers, $*_U$ and $*_R$ are relation variables representing the same sets as respectively U and R, and $\neq_U$ denotes the set of all pairs of distinct user identifiers.

The specification is formalised in a similar way as a lock; it is first modelled from the viewpoints of a resource and one and two users, and then all such parts are put together using the parallel composition. This gives the LTS schema

$$Mtx := \underset{r\in *_R:R}{\|} ((\underset{(u_1,u_2)\in \neq_U:U\times U}{\|} Prop_2) \| (\underset{u_1\in *_U:U}{\|} Prop_1)) ,$$

where $Prop_2$ is an LTS schema in Fig. 1 and $Prop_1$ is obtained from $Prop_2$ by removing transition schemata involving u_2. Note that Mtx is a correct model of the specification, because every illegal behaviour (two users access a resource simultaneously) is forbidden by some instance of $Prop_2$.

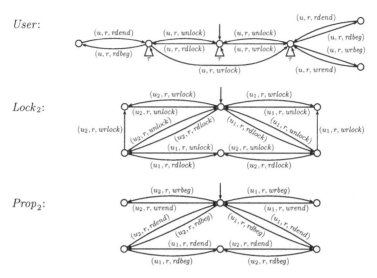

Fig. 1. Parts of the shared resource system

As the locking actions are irrelevant to the specification, the actions represented by $La := \bigcup_{(u,r) \in U \times R}\{(u, r, rdlock), (u, r, wrlock), (u, r, unlock)\}$ are hidden in the system model. The problem whether the system works correctly can be now formalised as an instance Mtx, $SRS \setminus La$, va(c_{SRS}) of Parameterised Traces Refinement, where c_{SRS} is a valuation formula

$$(\forall x \in U.x \in *_U) \wedge (\forall x \in R.x \in *_R) \wedge$$
$$\forall x_1 \in U.\forall x_2 \in U.(x_1 = x_2 \wedge \neg(x_1, x_2) \in \neq_U) \vee ((x_1, x_2) \in \neq_U \wedge \neg x_1 = x_2) .$$

It represents the set of valuations ϕ with the domain $\{U, R, *_R, *_U, \neq_U\}$ such that $\phi(T) = \phi(*_T)$ for $T \in \{U, R\}$ and $\phi(\neq_U) = \{(a_1, a_2) \mid a_1, a_2 \in \phi(U), a_1 \neq a_2\}$.

The algorithm in [4] applies to LTS schemata without relational parameters, so it is of no use here. Nevertheless, our intuition says that in order to prove the system correct one should check at least an instance with two users and a resource and another one with one user and one resource. Next, we show that it is actually sufficient and develop an enhanced algorithm for the task.

5 Precongruence Reduction for Valuations

Let $\phi_1, \phi_2 \in$ va(c_{SRS}) compatible with Mtx and $SRS \setminus La$ such that $\phi_i(R)$ is a singleton and $\phi_i(U)$ is a set of size i for both $i \in \{1, 2\}$. Using a finite-state refinement checker, like FDR2 [3], one can show that $[\![Mtx]\!]_{\phi_i} \succeq_{\text{tr}} [\![SRS \setminus La]\!]_{\phi_i}$ for both $i \in \{1, 2\}$. Hence, at least two instances of the shared resource system, one with two users and a resource and another one with a single user and a resource, work as specified.

By above, it is actually quite easy to believe that the system works correctly in the presence of any two users and any resource. In other words, $[\![Mtx]\!]_{\phi} \succeq_{\text{tr}}$

$[SRS \setminus La]_\phi$ for all $\phi \in \Phi'_{SRS}$, where Φ'_{SRS} denotes the set of all valuations $\phi \in \text{va}(c_{SRS})$ compatible with Mtx and $SRS \setminus La$ that map R to a singleton and U to a set of size two.

The result holds also more generally. One can generalise the verification results made using some valuations to all valuations that can be obtained from them using bijective mapping. We say that a valuation ϕ is *isomorphic* to a valuation ψ or that ϕ and ψ are *isomorphic*, denoted by $\phi \simeq \psi$, if they have the same domain and there is a bijection $g : \mathbb{A} \mapsto \mathbb{A}$ such that

1. $\psi(T) = \{g(a) \mid a \in \phi(T)\}$ for all type variables $T \in \text{dom}(\psi)$,
2. $\psi(x) = g(\phi(x))$ for all atom variables $x \in \text{dom}(\psi)$, and
3. $\psi(\Pi) = \{g^*(\alpha) \mid \alpha \in \phi(\Pi)\}$ for all relation variables $\Pi \in \text{dom}(\psi)$,

where g^* is a function: $\mathbb{V} \mapsto \mathbb{V}$ such that $g^*((a_1, \ldots, a_k)) = (g(a_1), \ldots, g(a_k))$ for all visible actions $(a_1, \ldots, a_k)$. Valuations ϕ and ψ that are not isomorphic are *non-isomorphic*, denoted by $\phi \not\simeq \psi$. Clearly, $\simeq$ is an equivalence in the set of valuations.

Lemma 8. *If ϕ and ψ are isomorphic valuations, then there is a bijection $g : \mathbb{A} \mapsto \mathbb{A}$ such that $g^*([\![\mathcal{P}]\!]_\phi) =_{\text{tr}} [\![\mathcal{P}]\!]_\psi$ whenever $\mathcal{P}$ is an LTS schema with which ϕ and ψ are compatible.*

The claim is evident and a generalisation of Lemma 3 in [4]. To formally prove it, take g to be a bijection: $\mathbb{A} \mapsto \mathbb{A}$ that maps ϕ to ψ and preserves the atoms not in $\bigcup_{A \in \text{im}(\phi|_T) \cup \text{im}(\psi|_T)} A$, take $\mathcal{P}$ to be any LTS schema with which ϕ and ψ are compatible, and proceed by induction on the structure of $\mathcal{P}$.

The lemma implies that adding or removing isomorphic valuations compatible with the system and specification LTS schema has no effect on the answer to the parameterised verification task. This is formally captured in the following proposition that follows straightforwardly from Lemma 8 and Theorem 5.

Proposition 9. *Let $\mathcal{Q}, \mathcal{P}, \Phi$ be an instance of Parameterised Traces Refinement such that the valuations in Φ are compatible with $\mathcal{Q}$ and $\mathcal{P}$. If Ψ is a subset of Φ containing a maximal set of representatives of $\simeq$ in Φ, then deciding $\mathcal{Q}, \mathcal{P}, \Phi$ gives the same answer as deciding $\mathcal{Q}, \mathcal{P}, \Psi$.*

To show that the correctness of any shared resource system instance can be derived from the correctness of instances with at most two users and a resource, by Theorem 5, it is sufficient to prove that for every $\phi \in \text{va}(c_{SRS})$ compatible with Mtx and $SRS \setminus La$ there is a finite non-empty set $\Theta \subseteq \Phi'_{SRS}$ of valuations such that $[\![Mtx]\!]_\phi \succeq_{\text{tr}} \|_{\theta \in \Theta} [\![Mtx]\!]_\theta$ and $\|_{\theta \in \Theta} [\![SRS \setminus La]\!]_\theta \succeq_{\text{tr}} [\![SRS \setminus La]\!]_\phi$.

Intuitively, the instances of Mtx generated by valuations in Θ should not be greater than $[\![Mtx]\!]_\phi$, which implies that also the valuations in Θ should be equal to or smaller than ϕ in some sense. Formally, a valuation θ is said to be *equal to or smaller than* ϕ, denoted by $\theta \leq \phi$, if the valuations have the same domain and

- $\theta(T) \subseteq \phi(T)$ for all type variables $T \in \text{dom}(\phi)$,
- $\theta(x) = \phi(x)$ for all atom variables $x \in \text{dom}(\phi)$ and

- $\theta(\Pi) = \phi(\Pi) \cap (\bigcup_{k \in \mathbb{Z}_+} \bigcup_{A_1, \dots, A_k \in \mathrm{im}(\theta|_\mathrm{T})} A_1 \times \dots \times A_k)$ for all relation variables $\Pi \in \mathrm{dom}(\phi)$.

Hence, we assume that $\theta \leq \phi$ for all $\theta \in \Theta$.

On the other hand, the valuations in Θ should contain enough information to construct $[\![Mtx]\!]_\phi$. Note that both $[\![Mtx]\!]_\phi$ and $\|_{\theta \in \Theta} [\![Mtx]\!]_\theta$ are created from instances of $Prop_2$ and $Prop_1$ using the parallel composition. Because the order in which LTSs are put in parallel and the number of times an LTS occurs in a parallel composition are insignificant from the viewpoint of the traces equivalence, and LTSs with the empty alphabet can be removed from a parallel composition, to prove that $[\![Mtx]\!]_\phi \succeq_\mathrm{tr} \|_{\theta \in \Theta} [\![Mtx]\!]_\theta$, it is sufficient to show that whenever an instance of $Prop_i$, where $i \in \{1, 2\}$, occurs in $[\![Mtx]\!]_\phi$, then it occurs also in $\|_{\theta \in \Theta} [\![Mtx]\!]_\theta$, and vice versa.

The precise form of an instance of $Prop_2$ depends on the values assigned to atom variables r, u_1, u_2. The values of these atom variables are picked from the values of relation variables $*_R$ and $\neq_U$ that occur in nested replicated parallel LTS schemata. We need to make sure that no matter how we pick the values of r and u_1, u_2 from $\phi(*_R)$ and $\phi(\neq_U)$, then there is some $\theta \in \Theta$ such that the values r and u_1, u_2 can be picked in the same way from $\theta(*_R)$ and $\theta(\neq_U)$. Similarly, an instance of $Prop_1$ is created by picking the values of r, u_1 from the values of relation variables $*_R$ and $*_U$ occurring in nested replicated parallel LTS schemata. Therefore, one must also guarantee that whenever $a_1 \in \phi(*_R)$ and $a_2 \in \phi(*_U)$ then there is $\theta \in \Theta$ such that $a_1 \in \theta(*_R)$ and $a_2 \in \theta(*_U)$.

The conditions above are satisfied if Θ consists of all valuations θ such that $\theta \leq \phi$, $|\theta(R)| = 1$ and $|\theta(U)| \leq 2$. It implies that every instance of $Prop_i$ that occurs in $[\![Mtx]\!]_\phi$ occurs in $\|_{\theta \in \Theta} [\![Mtx]\!]_\theta$, too, whenever $i \in \{1, 2\}$. On the other hand, because all the valuations in Θ are smaller than or equal to ϕ, it is easy to see that also the opposite holds. Hence, both the LTSs are created from the same instances of $Prop_2$ and $Prop_1$ using the parallel composition only, which actually implies that $[\![Mtx]\!]_\phi =_\mathrm{tr} \|_{\theta \in \Theta} [\![Mtx]\!]_\theta$.

The result can be generalised to any LTS schema $\mathcal{Q}$ that has no hiding LTS subschema. However, to generalise the restrictions concerning ϕ and Θ, the concept of nested relation variables has to be clarified. We say that LTS schemata $\mathcal{P}_0, \dots, \mathcal{P}_n$ are *nested* if $\mathcal{P}_i$ is an LTS subschema of $\mathcal{P}_{i-1}$ for all $i \in \{1, \dots, n\}$. A sequence $\Pi_1 \cdots \Pi_k$ of relation variables is called a *branch* of $\mathcal{Q}$, if there are nested LTS subschemata $\mathcal{Q}_1, \dots, \mathcal{Q}_k$ of $\mathcal{Q}$ such that $\mathcal{Q}_i$ is a Π_i-replicated LTS schema for all $i \in \{1, \dots, k\}$. Now, the to guarantee that $[\![\mathcal{Q}]\!]_\phi =_\mathrm{tr} \|_{\theta \in \Theta} [\![\mathcal{Q}]\!]_\theta$, we require that

P1 (ϕ, Θ) : $\theta \leq \phi$ for all $\theta \in \Theta$, and

P2 $(\mathcal{Q}, \phi, \Theta)$: whenever $\Pi_1 \cdots \Pi_k$ is a branch of $\mathcal{Q}$ and $\alpha_1, \dots, \alpha_k$ are actions in respectively $\phi(\Pi_1), \dots, \phi(\Pi_k)$, then there is $\theta \in \Theta$ such that $\alpha_i \in \theta(\Pi_i)$ for all $i \in \{1, \dots, k\}$.

Lemma 10. *If $\mathcal{Q}$ is an LTS schema which has no hiding LTS schema, ϕ a valuation compatible with $\mathcal{Q}$ and Θ a finite non-empty set of valuations such that $\mathbf{P1}(\phi, \Theta)$ and $\mathbf{P2}(\mathcal{Q}, \phi, \Theta)$, then $[\![\mathcal{Q}]\!]_\phi =_\mathrm{tr} \|_{\theta \in \Theta} [\![\mathcal{Q}]\!]_\theta$.*

The formal proof exploits Proposition 2 and proceeds by induction on the structure of $\mathcal{Q}$ using the lemma as an induction hypothesis. The lemma is a generalisation of Lemma 2 in [4].

To generalise the verification results made using two users and a resource to the whole system, we still have to show that $\|_{\theta \in \Theta} [\![SRS \setminus La]\!]_\theta \succeq_{\mathrm{tr}} [\![SRS \setminus La]\!]_\phi$. Using similar reasoning as earlier, one can see that the LTSs $\|_{\theta \in \Theta} [\![SRS \setminus La]\!]_\theta$ and $[\![SRS \setminus La]\!]_\phi$ are constructed from the same instances of *User*, *Lock*$_1$ and *Lock*$_2$ using the parallel composition and hiding. Moreover, it is quite easy to see that the same actions are hidden in the both the LTSs, which implies that the alphabets of the LTSs must match. However, because hiding takes place earlier in the former LTS, it may have more traces than the latter one. Therefore, $\|_{\theta \in \Theta} [\![SRS \setminus La]\!]_\theta \succeq_{\mathrm{tr}} [\![SRS \setminus La]\!]_\phi$. Also this result can be generalised to any LTS schema $\mathcal{P}$.

Lemma 11. *If $\mathcal{P}$ is an LTS schema, ϕ a valuation compatible with $\mathcal{P}$ and Θ a finite non-empty set of valuations such that $\mathbf{P1}(\phi, \Theta)$ and $\mathbf{P2}(\mathcal{P}, \phi, \Theta)$, then $\|_{\theta \in \Theta} [\![\mathcal{P}]\!]_\theta \succeq_{\mathrm{tr}} [\![\mathcal{P}]\!]_\phi$.*

The formal proof exploits Proposition 2 and proceeds by induction on the structure of $\mathcal{P}$ using the lemma as an induction hypothesis. The lemma is a generalisation of Lemma 1 in [4].

Hence, we have shown that every instance of the shared resource system and its specification can be represented as the parallel composition of smaller ones involving at most two users and a resource. Furthermore, all such small instances are shown to be correct, which by Theorem 5 implies the correctness of the whole shared resource system independent of the parameter values.

Generalisation of this result follows straightforwardly from Lemmas 10 and 11, and Theorem 5.

Proposition 12. *Let $\mathcal{Q}$, $\mathcal{P}$, Φ be an instance of Parameterised Traces Refinement such that $\mathcal{Q}$ has no hiding LTS subschema, and let Φ' be a subset of Φ. If for every $\phi \in \Phi \setminus \Phi'$ there is a finite non-empty subset Θ of Φ' such that $\mathbf{P1}(\phi, \Theta)$, $\mathbf{P2}(\mathcal{Q}, \phi, \Theta)$ and $\mathbf{P2}(\mathcal{P}, \phi, \Theta)$, then deciding $\mathcal{Q}$, $\mathcal{P}$, Φ gives the same answer as deciding $\mathcal{Q}$, $\mathcal{P}$, Φ'.*

6   Reduction Algorithm

Recall that our goal is to algorithmically reduce an instance $\mathcal{Q}$, $\mathcal{P}$, va(c) of Parameterised Traces Refinement to an instance $\mathcal{Q}$, $\mathcal{P}$, Ψ having the same answer, where the LTS schemata $\mathcal{Q}$ and $\mathcal{P}$ are closed, c is a valuation formula such that $\mathrm{sig}(c) = \mathrm{sig}(\mathcal{Q}) \cup \mathrm{sig}(\mathcal{P})$, and Ψ is a finite subset of va(c).

Unfortunately, there is no generic algorithmic solution to the problem. The reason is that one can simulate a Turing machine with an LTS schema. The full construction is far too complicated to be presented here, but the idea is that the behaviour of a cell of the tape of a Turing machine can be expressed as an elementary LTS schema that communicates with the neighbouring cells using token passing. The token carries state information and indicates the location of the read-write head. The model of the Turing machine is then obtained by enclosing the model of a cell in a Π-replicated parallel LTS schema such that a relation variable Π encodes a ring. For example, a question on Turing machine halting with the empty input, a famous undecidable problem, can be encoded this way.

Actually, using the precongruence reduction, it is not possible to reduce any instance of Parameterised Traces Refinement that represents a verification task of a family of systems with a ring topology. Intuitively, the reason is that large rings cannot be constructed from small ones without breaking the structure.

The reason why the method works in the case of the shared resource system is that the specification does not involve hiding and the set $\mathrm{va}(c_{SRS})$ of valuations is *downward closed*, which means that whenever a valuation ϕ is in the set and ψ is a valuation smaller than or equal to ϕ, then ψ is in the set, too. This property enables us to represent large specification-system instances as the parallel composition of smaller ones.

Now, an obvious question is that which valuation formulae represent downward closed sets of valuations. The answer is that those that are existential-free. Actually, allowing the use of existential quantification makes it possible to express rings and hence renders the problem undecidable, so the restriction to existential-free valuation formulae is very natural.

Lemma 13. *Let c be an existential-free valuation formula. If ϕ and ψ are valuations compatible with c such that $\psi \leq \phi$ and $[\![c]\!]_\phi$ is true, then $[\![c]\!]_\psi$ is true.*

Intuition behind the result is that if c is existential-free and $[\![c]\!]_\phi$ is true, and one removes some atoms from the values of type variables, the formula must be still satisfied, because type variables are used in quantification only, and if quantification over some set gives a positive result, then quantification over its subset must give a positive result, too. Moreover, as one cannot refer to atoms that do not occur in the values of type or free atom variables, it is also possible to take away actions involving removed atoms from the values of relation variables without making the formula false, which means that $[\![c]\!]_\psi$ must be true for all valuations $\psi \leq \phi$.

The formal proof proceeds by induction on the structure of the valuation formula using the lemma as an induction hypothesis strengthened by the claim that if c has no universal valuation subformula, then $[\![c]\!]_\phi$ is true if and only if $[\![c]\!]_\psi$ is true.

Now, we have limited our attention instances $\mathcal{Q}$, $\mathcal{P}$, $\mathrm{va}(c)$ of Parameterised Traces Refinement such that $\mathcal{Q}$ and $\mathcal{P}$ are closed, $\mathcal{Q}$ has no hiding LTS subschema and c is an existential-free valuation formula with the signature $\mathrm{sig}(\mathcal{Q}) \cup \mathrm{sig}(\mathcal{P})$. We show that for such instances one can always compute a finite subset Ψ of $\mathrm{va}(c)$ such that deciding $\mathcal{Q}, \mathcal{P}, \Psi$ gives the same answer as deciding $\mathcal{Q}, \mathcal{P}, \mathrm{va}(c)$.

Let Ψ be a subset of $\mathrm{va}(c)$ such that the valuations in Ψ are compatible with $\mathcal{Q}$ and $\mathcal{P}$. Then there is a subset of Φ' of $\mathrm{va}(c)$ such that Φ' contains all valuations in $\mathrm{va}(c)$ isomorphic to some valuations in Ψ. By Proposition 9, deciding $\mathcal{Q}, \mathcal{P}, \Psi$ gives the same answer as deciding $\mathcal{Q}, \mathcal{P}, \Phi'$. To guarantee that deciding $\mathcal{Q}, \mathcal{P}, \Phi'$ gives the same answer as deciding $\mathcal{Q}, \mathcal{P}, \mathrm{va}(c)$, it is sufficient to make sure that

Φ' is large enough to satisfy the assumptions of Proposition 12. In other words, for every $\phi \in \text{va}(c) \setminus \Phi'$ there has to be a finite non-empty subset Θ of Φ' such that $\mathbf{P1}(\phi, \Theta)$, $\mathbf{P2}(\mathcal{Q}, \phi, \Theta)$ and $\mathbf{P2}(\mathcal{P}, \phi, \Theta)$.

To see how large Φ' should be some new concepts are needed. Let T be a type variable, Π a relation variable and $\mathcal{R}$ an LTS schema. The T-*degree of* Π *(in* $\mathcal{R}$), denoted by $\deg_T(\Pi, \mathcal{P})$, is the maximum number of occurrences of T in a type of Π in $\mathcal{P}$. For example, $\deg_U(\neq_U, SRS)$ is two, $\deg_R(*_R, SRS)$ and $\deg_U(*_U, SRS)$ are one, and $\deg_U(*_R, SRS)$ is zero. Moreover, *the* T-*degree of* $\mathcal{R}$, denoted by $\deg_T(\mathcal{R})$, is the maximum number of occurrences of T in the types of relation variables in a branch of $\mathcal{R}$. In other words,

$$\deg_T(\mathcal{R}) = \max\{\deg_T(\Pi_1, \mathcal{R}) + \ldots + \deg_T(\Pi_n, \mathcal{R}) \mid \Pi_1 \cdots \Pi_n \text{ is a branch of } \mathcal{R}\} \ .$$

For example, the branches of Mtx are the empty sequence, $*_R$, $*_U$, $\neq_U$, $*_R*_U$ and $*_R \neq_U$. The LTS schema $SRS \setminus La$ has additionally the branch $*_U*_R$. Consequently, for both the LTS schemata, the U-degree is two and the R-degree is one.

Now, let ϕ be a valuation in $\text{va}(c) \setminus \Phi'$, $\Pi_1 \Pi_2 \cdots \Pi_n$ a branch of $\mathcal{R}$, where $\mathcal{R}$ is either $\mathcal{P}$ or $\mathcal{Q}$, and α_i an action in $\phi(\Pi_i)$ for all $i \in \{1, \ldots, n\}$. At worst, the atoms occurring in the actions $\alpha_1, \ldots, \alpha_n$ are all different. It means that for each type variable T in $\text{sig}(\mathcal{Q}) \cup \text{sig}(\mathcal{P})$, there are at most $\max\{\deg_T(\mathcal{Q}), \deg_T(\mathcal{P})\}$ atoms that occur both in the actions $\alpha_1, \ldots, \alpha_n$ and in $\phi(T)$. Because $\text{va}(c)$ is downward closed, it is sufficient that Φ' includes all valuations $\phi \in \text{va}(c)$ such that $|\phi(T)| \leq \max\{1, \deg_T(\mathcal{Q}), \deg_T(\mathcal{P})\}$ for all type variables $T \in \text{dom}(\phi)$.

In other words, if one first takes all valuations $\phi \in \text{va}(c)$ compatible with $\mathcal{Q}$ and $\mathcal{P}$ such that $|\phi(T)| \leq \max\{1, \deg_T(\mathcal{Q}), \deg_T(\mathcal{P})\}$ for all type variables $T \in \text{dom}(\phi)$, and then picks a maximal set of representatives of $\simeq$ among those, one obtains a subset Ψ of $\text{va}(c)$ such that $\mathcal{Q}, \mathcal{P}, \Psi$ gives the same answer as deciding $\mathcal{Q}, \mathcal{P}, \text{va}(c)$.

It is also quite easy to see that the set Ψ determined in such a way is finite, too. Consider the valuations in Ψ. The size of the values of type variables is bounded, so each type variable can have only finitely many essentially different (non-isomorphic) values. Moreover, because all the valuations $\psi \in \Psi$ are compatible with the LTS schemata and every relation variable $\Pi \in \text{dom}(\psi)$ occurs in $\mathcal{Q}$ or $\mathcal{P}$, the values of Π are limited to subsets of the values of its types. Hence, also every relation variable can have only finitely many non-isomorphic values. Finally, as all the valuations in Ψ are non-isomorphic and have the same finite domain which contains no atom variable, it is clear Ψ cannot be infinite. Hence, we have proved the following theorem.

Theorem 14. *Let $\mathcal{Q}$ and $\mathcal{P}$ be finite and closed LTS schemata and c a valuation formula such that $\text{sig}(c) = \text{sig}(\mathcal{P}) \cup \text{sig}(\mathcal{Q})$. If $\mathcal{Q}$ has no hiding LTS subschema and c is existential-free, then any maximal set Ψ of representatives of $\simeq$ in*

$$\{\phi \in \text{va}(c) \mid \phi \text{ is compatible with } \mathcal{Q} \text{ and } \mathcal{P}, \text{ and}$$
$$\forall T \in \text{dom}(\phi) \cap \mathbb{T}.|\phi(T)| \leq \max\{1, \deg_T(\mathcal{P}), \deg_T(\mathcal{Q})\}\}$$

is finite and deciding $\mathcal{Q}$, $\mathcal{P}$, $\text{va}(c)$ gives the same answer as deciding $\mathcal{Q}$, $\mathcal{P}$, Ψ.

---

input: closed finite LTS schemata $\mathcal{Q}$, $\mathcal{P}$ and an existential-free valuation formula c
    such that $\mathcal{Q}$ has no hiding LTS subschema and $\text{sig}(c) = \text{sig}(\mathcal{Q}) \cup \text{sig}(\mathcal{P})$
output: a finite subset Ψ of $\text{va}(c)$ such that deciding $\mathcal{Q}$, $\mathcal{P}$, Ψ
    gives the same answer as deciding $\mathcal{Q}$, $\mathcal{P}$, $\text{va}(c)$
let $T_1, \ldots, T_k$ be the type variables in $\text{sig}(c)$
let $\Psi := \emptyset$
for each $i \in \{1, \ldots, k\}$ let $l_i := \max\{1, \deg_T(\mathcal{Q}), \deg_T(\mathcal{P})\}$
let $a_{1,1}, \ldots, a_{1,l_1}, a_{2,1}, \ldots, a_{2,l_2}, \ldots, a_{k,1}, \ldots, a_{k,l_k}$ be distinct atoms
    different from those in $\text{at}(\mathcal{Q}) \cup \text{at}(\mathcal{P})$
for all $v \in \{1, \ldots, l_1\} \times \{1, \ldots, l_2\} \times \ldots \times \{1, \ldots, l_k\}$ do
    for all valuations ϕ compatible with $\mathcal{Q}$ and $\mathcal{P}$ such that
        $\text{dom}(\psi) = \text{sig}(c)$ and $\forall i \in \{1, \ldots, k\}.\psi(T_i) = \{a_{i,1}, \ldots, a_{i,v(i)}\}$ do
        if $[\![c]\!]_\phi$ is true and $\forall \psi \in \Psi.\phi \not\cong \psi$ then let $\Psi := \Psi \cup \{\phi\}$
    end do
end do
return Ψ

Fig. 2. Reduction algorithm

To automate the application of the theorem, one should be able to pick valuations from the set and perform isomorphism test between them. The latter task is actually not a problem, because it is clearly decidable for valuations with a finite domain. To perform the former task, one needs to know which atoms can be used for the values of type variables. Fortunately, any atoms not occurring in $\mathcal{Q}$ or $\mathcal{P}$ will do, because the set $\text{va}(c)$ is *isomorphism closed*, meaning that whenever a valuation ϕ in the set and ψ is a valuation isomorphic to ϕ, then ψ is in the set, too.

Lemma 15. *Let c be a valuation formula. If ϕ and ψ are isomorphic valuations compatible with c, then $[\![c]\!]_\phi$ is true if and only if $[\![c]\!]_\psi$ is true.*

The proof is straightforward and proceeds by induction on the structure of the valuation formula using the lemma as an induction hypothesis.

With this information, Theorem 14 converts straightforwardly to an algorithm in Fig. 2. It is obviously computationally quite complex, because it generates a great amount of valuations and performs isomorphism tests between them. On the other hand, the algorithm reduces a parameterised verification task to a finite one, so in this sense generating only finitely many valuations should be acceptable. Moreover, if one wants to avoid isomorphism testing, then one has to perform extra refinement checks. It does not make much sense, because testing isomorphism between valuations is generally simpler than checking traces refinement of instances generated by those valuations.

The algorithm is clearly applicable to Mtx, $SRS \setminus La$, c_{SRS}. Because the maximum of $\{1, \deg_T(Mtx), \deg_T(SRS \setminus La)\}$ is two for $T = U$ and one for $T = R$, and there are only two non-isomorphic valuations $\phi \in \text{va}(c_{SRS})$ such that $|\phi(U)| \leq 2$ and $|\phi(R)| \leq 1$, the algorithm produces the same result as we obtained earlier by manual reasoning.

7 Conclusions and Discussion

We have presented an algorithm that enables the infinite family of verification tasks arising from parameterised specification and system descriptions to be solved just by examining its finite subset. After that, the subset can be checked using existing refinement checkers. The algorithm allows the use of multiple and nested parameters, which makes it possible to express systems with components of a parameterised state-space. To the best of our knowledge, it is the most generic such an algorithm.

The most serious limitations of the algorithm are the lack of a replicated choice construct and restriction to existential-free valuation formulae. The former deficiency means that we have to restrict our attention to systems and specifications the behaviour of which can be faithfully captured in parts each of which represents the system or the specification from the viewpoint of a bounded number of components only. The latter restriction implies that we can study only specification-system families closed under the removal of a replicated component. For example, systems with a star, bipartite and totally (un)connected topology are such, but those with a ring, linear or tree topology are not.

Despite that, we have applied the results to verify taDOM+ tree-locking protocols [22] used in XML databases. The protocols were modelled as LTS schemata parameterised by the number of concurrent transactions and the size and the shape of a tree. In the case of these protocols, it is possible to describe the behaviour of a transaction from the viewpoint of a node and its arbitrary ancestor using finitely many LTS schemata, so we could study transitive closures of forests instead of trees. As the family of transitive closures of forests is closed under the removal of a node, it was possible to prove a mutual exclusion property for these protocols. The same property is earlier proved in [23] but using a theory tailored for the protocols.

Future work covers implementing and extending the algorithm. It looks like that with the cost of worse reduction, one can allow hiding in a specification LTS schema and richer semantic models that enable verification of deadlock and liveness properties. Generalising the approach that enables the analysis of systems with a linear, ring or tree topology is also a topic of future research.

Acknowledgements. The research is mainly funded by the Ministry of Education of Finland through Infotech Oulu Graduate School, and supported by Oulu University Scholarship Foundation and the Foundation of Tauno Tönning. The authors thank Antti Valmari for his comments and pointing out undecidability in the case of valuation formulae that are not existential-free.

References

1. Apt, K.R., Kozen, D.C.: Limits for automatic verification of finite-state concurrent systems. Inf. Process. Lett. 22(6), 307–309 (1986)
2. Hoare, C.A.R.: Communicating Sequential Processes. Prentice Hall, Englewood Cliffs (1985)
3. Roscoe, A.W.: The Theory and Practice of Concurrency. Prentice Hall, Englewood Cliffs (1997)

4. Siirtola, A., Kortelainen, J.: Parameterised process algebraic verification by pre-congruence reduction. In: ACSD 2009, pp. 158–167. IEEE, Los Alamitos (2009)
5. Bouajjani, A., Habermehl, P., Vojnar, T.: Verification of parametric concurrent systems with prioritised FIFO resource management. Form. Method. Syst. Des. 32(2), 129–172 (2008)
6. Emerson, E.A., Kahlon, V.: Reducing model checking of the many to the few. In: McAllester, D. (ed.) CADE 2000. LNCS, vol. 1831, pp. 236–254. Springer, Heidelberg (2000)
7. Emerson, E.A., Kahlon, V.: Exact and efficient verification of parameterized cache coherence protocols. In: Geist, D., Tronci, E. (eds.) CHARME 2003. LNCS, vol. 2860, pp. 247–262. Springer, Heidelberg (2003)
8. Wolper, P.: Expressing interesting properties of programs in propositional temporal logic. In: POPL 1986, pp. 184–193. ACM, New York (1986)
9. Lazić, R.S.: A Semantic Study of Data Independence with Applications to Model Checking. PhD thesis, Oxford University (2001)
10. Lazić, R.S., Nowak, D.: A unifying approach to data-independence. In: Palamidessi, C. (ed.) CONCUR 2000. LNCS, vol. 1877, pp. 581–595. Springer, Heidelberg (2000)
11. Emerson, E.A., Namjoshi, K.S.: On reasoning about rings. Int. J. Found. Comput. Sci. 14(4), 527–550 (2003)
12. Emerson, E.A., Kahlon, V.: Model checking large-scale and parameterized resource allocation systems. In: Katoen, J.-P., Stevens, P. (eds.) TACAS 2002. LNCS, vol. 2280, pp. 251–265. Springer, Heidelberg (2002)
13. Emerson, E.A., Kahlon, V.: Parameterized model checking of ring-based message passing systems. In: Marcinkowski, J., Tarlecki, A. (eds.) CSL 2004. LNCS, vol. 3210, pp. 325–339. Springer, Heidelberg (2004)
14. Nazari, S., Thistle, J.: Structural conditions for model-checking of parameterized networks. In: ACSD 2007, pp. 187–196. IEEE, Los Alamitos (2007)
15. Clarke, E., Talupur, M., Touili, T., Veith, H.: Verification by network decomposition. In: Gardner, P., Yoshida, N. (eds.) CONCUR 2004. LNCS, vol. 3170, pp. 276–291. Springer, Heidelberg (2004)
16. Konnov, I.V., Zakharov, V.A.: An approach to the verification of symmetric parameterized distributed systems. Program. Comput. Soft. 31(5), 225–236 (2005)
17. Li, J., Suzuki, I., Yamashita, M.: A new structural induction theorem for rings of temporal Petri nets. IEEE Trans. Softw. Eng. 20(2), 115–126 (1994)
18. Pyssysalo, T.: An induction theorem for ring protocols of processes described with predicate/transition nets. Research Report A37, Helsinki University of Technology (1996)
19. Valmari, A., Tienari, M.: An improved failures equivalence for finite-state systems with a reduction algorithm. In: PSTV 1991, pp. 3–18. North-Holland, Amsterdam (1991)
20. Delzanno, G., Raskin, J.F., Begin, L.V.: Towards the automated verification of multithreaded Java programs. In: Katoen, J.-P., Stevens, P. (eds.) TACAS 2002. LNCS, vol. 2280, pp. 173–187. Springer, Heidelberg (2002)
21. Bingham, J.D., Hu, A.J.: Empirically efficient verification for a class of infinite-state systems. In: Halbwachs, N., Zuck, L.D. (eds.) TACAS 2005. LNCS, vol. 3440, pp. 77–92. Springer, Heidelberg (2005)
22. Haustein, M., Härder, T.: Optimizing lock protocols for native XML processing. Data Knowl. Eng. 65(1), 147–173 (2008)
23. Siirtola, A., Valenta, M.: Verifying parameterized taDOM+ lock managers. In: Geffert, V., Karhumäki, J., Bertoni, A., Preneel, B., Návrat, P., Bieliková, M. (eds.) SOFSEM 2008. LNCS, vol. 4910, pp. 460–472. Springer, Heidelberg (2008)

Verifying Stateful Timed CSP Using Implicit Clocks and Zone Abstraction

Jun Sun, Yang Liu, Jin Song Dong, and Xian Zhang

School of Computing,
National University of Singapore
{sunj,liuyang,dongjs,zhangxi5}@comp.nus.edu.sg

Abstract. In this work, we study model checking of compositional real-time systems. A system is modeled using mutable data variables as well as a compositional timed process. Instead of explicitly manipulating clock variables, a number of compositional timed behavioral patterns are used to capture quantitative timing requirements, e.g. delay, timeout, deadline, timed interrupt, etc. A fully automated abstraction technique is developed to build an abstract finite state machine from the model. The idea is to dynamically create/delete clocks, and maintain/solve a constraint on the clocks. The abstract machine weakly bi-simulates the model and, therefore, LTL model checking or trace-refinement checking are sound and complete. We enhance our home-grown PAT model checker with the technique and show its usability via the verification of benchmark systems.

1 Introduction

Specification and verification of real-time systems are important research topics which have practical implications. During the last decade or so, a popular approach for specifying real-time systems is based on the notation Timed Automata [1,23]. Timed Automata are powerful in designing real-time models with explicit clock variables. Real-time constraints are captured by explicitly setting/resetting clock variables. A number of automatic verification support for Timed Automata have proven to be successful (e.g. UPPAAL [20], KRONOS [4] and RED [36]).

Models based on Timed Automata often adapt a simple structure, e.g. a network of Timed Automata with no hierarchy [20]. The benefit is that efficient model checking is made feasible. Nonetheless, designing and verifying compositional real-time systems is becoming an increasingly difficult task due to the widespread applications and increasing complexity of such systems. High-level requirements for real-time systems are often stated in terms of *deadline*, *time out*, and *timed interrupt* [18,11,22]. In industrial case studies of real-time system verification, system requirements are often structured into phases, which are then composed sequentially, in parallel and alternatively [14,19]. Unlike statecharts (with clocks) or timed process algebras, Timed Automata lack high-level compositional patterns for hierarchical design. As a result, users often need to manually cast those terms into a set of clock variables with carefully calculated clock constraints. The process is tedious and error-prone.

K. Breitman and A. Cavalcanti (Eds.): ICFEM 2009, LNCS 5885, pp. 581–600, 2009.

Contributions. We investigate an alternative approach for modeling and verifying compositional real-time systems. In this work, a system is modeled using a compositional timed process as well as mutable data variables and data operations. A rich set of process constructs are supported, a number of which are adapted from Timed CSP [30]. Additional behavioral patterns which are useful in modeling and analyzing real-time systems are introduced. Examples are *deadline* (which constrains a process to terminate within some time units), *timed interrupt*, etc. Instead of explicitly manipulating clock variables (as in Timed Automata), the time related process constructs are designed to build on implicit clocks. Further, we augment a system model with mutable variables and data structures (e.g. arrays, stacks, queues, or any user created data types), synchronous/asynchronous channels, etc.

In order to offer efficient mechanical verification support, a fully automated abstraction technique is developed to build an abstract finite state machine from the model. The idea is to dynamically create clocks (only if necessary) to capture constraints introduced by the timed process constructs. A clock may be shared for many constructs in order to reduce the number of clocks. Further, the clocks are deleted as early as possible. During system exploration, a constraint on the active clocks is maintained and solved using techniques based on Difference Bound Matrix (DBM [7]). We show that the abstraction is finite state and is subject to model checking. Further, it weakly bi-simulates the concrete model and, therefore, we may perform sound and complete LTL-X (i.e. LTL without the next operator) model checking or refinement checking upon the abstraction. We enhance our home-grown PAT model checker [33] (available at http://pat.comp.nus.edu.sg) with the technique and show its usability via automated verification of benchmark systems. We compare PAT with UPPAAL to show that our technique offers complementary support for analysis of real-time systems.

Section Organization. The remainder of the paper is organized as follows. Section 2 presents the syntax and operational semantics of a subset of our modeling language. Section 3 presents the zone abstraction using dynamical clocks. Section 4 discusses the soundness of the abstraction and its implication on model checking. Section 5 discusses automation of the technique in the PAT model checker. Section 6 reviews related work and discusses future research direction.

2   Language Syntax and Operational Semantics

In this section, we introduce the compositional language to model real-time systems and then define its operational semantics. Let Σ be the set of event names.

Definition 1 (LTS). *A labeled transition system is 3-tuple* $\mathcal{L} = (S, init, \rightarrow)$ *where* S *is a set of system configurations,* $init : S$ *is an initial system configuration and* $\rightarrow: S \times \Sigma \times S$ *is a labeled transition relation.*

A run of a LTS is a finite or infinite sequence of alternating configurations/events, i.e. $\langle s_0, e_0, s_1, e_1, \cdots \rangle$ such that $s_0 = init$ and $s_i \xrightarrow{e_i} s_{i+1}$ for all i. An execution is a sequence of events $\langle e_0, e_1, \cdots \rangle$ such that there exists a run $\langle s_0, e_0, s_1, e_1, \cdots \rangle$. For simplicity, we write $c \xrightarrow{x}$ to mean that there exists c' such that $c \xrightarrow{x} c'$.

2.1   Syntax

Definition 2 (Timed process). *A timed process (hereafter process) is defined by the following grammar*[1].

$$
\begin{array}{ll}
P = Stop \mid Skip & - primitives \\
\mid\ e \to P & - event\ prefixing \\
\mid\ [b]P & - state\ guard \\
\mid\ P \mid Q & - general\ choice \\
\mid\ P \parallel Q & - parallel\ composition \\
\mid\ P;\ Q & - sequential\ composition \\
\mid\ Wait[d] & - delay \\
\mid\ P\ timeout[d]\ Q & - timeout \\
\mid\ P\ interrupt[d]\ Q & - timed\ interrupt \\
\mid\ P\ deadline[d] & - deadline \\
\mid\ P \mathrel{\hat{=}} Q & - process\ definition
\end{array}
$$

where P and Q range over processes, $e \in \Sigma$ is an observable event, b is a Boolean expression on global variables or process parameters and d is an integer constant.

Process $Stop$ does nothing but idling. Process $Skip$ terminates (possibly after some idling). Process $e \to P$ engages in event e first and then behaves as P. Notice that e may be an abstract event or a data operation, e.g. written in the form of $e\{x = 5; y = 3; \}$ or an external C# program. The data operation may update data variables (and is assumed to be executed atomically). For simplicity, the resultant data valuation is written as $e(V)$. A guarded process is written as $[b]P$. If b is true, then it behaves as P, else it idles until b becomes true. Process $P \mid Q$ offers a choice between P and Q. Parallel composition of two processes is written as $P \parallel Q$, where P and Q may communicate via multi-party event synchronization or shared variables. Process $P;\ Q$ behaves as P until P terminates and then behaves as Q immediately.

A number of timed process constructs can be used to capture common real-time system behavior patterns. Without loss of generality, we assume d is an integer constant. Process $Wait[d]$ idles for exactly d time units. In process $P\ timeout[d]\ Q$, the first observable event of P shall occur before d time units elapse (since the process starts). Otherwise, Q takes over control after exactly d time units elapse. Process $P\ interrupt[d]\ Q$ behaves exactly as P (which may engage in multiple observable events) until d time units elapse, and then Q takes over control. Process $P\ deadline[d]$ constrains P to terminate before d time units. We remark additional process constructs (e.g. if-then-else, while, etc.) can be defined using the above. In this setting, clock variables are made implicit and hence they cannot be compared with each other directly, which potentially allows efficient clock manipulation and hence system verification.

Definition 3 (System model). *A system model is a 3-tuple $\mathcal{S} = (Var, init, P)$ where Var is a set of global variables, init is the initial valuation of the variables and P is a process.*

---

[1] Hiding, external/internal choice, waituntil and more are skipped for simplicity. It should be clear that the discussion applies to those operators.

Example 1 (Fischer's Algorithm). The following models Fischer's mutual exclusion algorithm.

var x $= -1$;
var ct $= 0$;
$Proc(i)$ $= [x = -1]Active(i)$
$Active(i) = (update.i\{x = i\} \rightarrow Skip)deadline[\delta]$;
         $Wait[\epsilon]$;
         if $(x = i)$ {
                $cs.i\{ct = ct + 1\} \rightarrow$
                $exit.i\{ct = ct - 1; \ x = -1\} \rightarrow Proc(i)$
         } *else* {
                $Proc(i)$
         }
$Protocol$ $= Proc(0) \parallel Proc(1) \parallel Proc(2)$;

where δ and ϵ are two integer constants with $\delta < \epsilon$; x and ct are global variables. The protocol is modeled as process *Protocol*, which is the parallel composition of three processes. Each of the three processes attempts to enter the critical section when x is -1, i.e. no other process is currently attempting. Once the process is active, it sets x to its identity i within δ time units (captured by $deadline[\delta]$). Then it idles for ϵ time units (captured by $Wait[\epsilon]$) and then checks whether x is still i. If so, it enters the critical section and leaves later. Otherwise, it restarts from the beginning.   □

2.2 Semantics

In order to define the operational semantics of a system model, we define the notion of a configuration to capture the global system state during system execution.

Definition 4 (System configuration). *A system configuration is a pair* $c = (V, P)$ *where* V *is a variable valuation function and* P *is a process.*

A transition of the system is of the form $c \xrightarrow{x} c'$ where c and c' are the system configurations before and after the transition respectively. We adopt the following naming convention for transition labels: t denotes a non-negative real number; τ denotes an invisible event; $\checkmark$ is the event of process termination; $e \in \Sigma \cup \{\checkmark\}$ is an observable event; $x \in \Sigma \cup \{\tau, \checkmark\}$. For instance, $c \xrightarrow{t} c'$ denotes a transition of t time units elapsing. In the following, we present the firing rules which are associated with the timed process constructs, adopting the approach in [29].

$$\frac{t \leq d}{(V, Wait[d]) \xrightarrow{t} (V, Wait[d - t])} \ [\ de1\ ] \qquad \frac{}{(V, Wait[0]) \xrightarrow{\tau} (V, Skip)} \ [\ de2\ ]$$

The above captures behaviors of process $Wait[d]$. Rule $de1$ states that the process may idle for any amount of time as long as it is less than or equal to d time units; Rule $de2$ states that the process terminates immediately after d becomes 0.

$$\frac{(V, P) \xrightarrow{e} (V', P')}{(V, P \ timeout[d] \ Q) \xrightarrow{e} (V', P')} \ [\ to1\ ]$$

$$\frac{(V,P) \xrightarrow{\tau} (V',P')}{(V,P\ timeout[d]\ Q) \xrightarrow{\tau} (V',P'\ timeout[d]\ Q)}\ [\ to2\ ]$$

$$\frac{(V,P) \xrightarrow{t} (V,P'), t \leq d}{(V,P\ timeout[d]\ Q) \xrightarrow{t} (V,P'\ timeout[d-t]\ Q)}\ [\ to3\ ]$$

$$\frac{}{(V,P\ timeout[0]\ Q) \xrightarrow{\tau} (V,Q)}\ [\ to4\ ]$$

If an observable event x can be engaged by P, then $P\ timeout[d]\ Q$ becomes P' (rule $to1$). An invisible transition does not solve the *choice* (rule $to2$). If P may idle for less than or equal to d time units, so is the composition (rule $to3$). When d becomes 0, Q takes over control by a silent transition (rule $to4$).

$$\frac{(V,P) \xrightarrow{x} (V',P')}{(V,P\ interrupt[d]\ Q) \xrightarrow{x} (V',P'\ interrupt[d]\ Q)}\ [\ it1\ ]$$

$$\frac{(V,P) \xrightarrow{t} (V,P'), t \leq d}{(V,P\ interrupt[d]\ Q) \xrightarrow{t} (V,P'\ interrupt[d-t]\ Q)}\ [\ it2\ ]$$

$$\frac{}{(V,P\ interrupt[0]\ Q) \xrightarrow{\tau} (V',Q)}\ [\ it3\ ]$$

Rule $it1$ states if P engages in event x, $P\ interrupt[d]\ Q$ becomes $P'\ interrupt[d]\ Q$. Rule $it2$ states that if P may idle for less than or equal to d time units, so is the composition. When d time units elapse, Q takes over by a τ-transition.

$$\frac{(V,P) \xrightarrow{x} (V',P')}{(V,P\ deadline[d]) \xrightarrow{x} (V',P'\ deadline[d])}\ [\ dl1\ ]$$

$$\frac{(V,P) \xrightarrow{t} (V,P'), t \leq d}{(V,P\ deadline[d]) \xrightarrow{t} (V,P'\ deadline[d-t])}\ [\ dl2\ ]$$

Intuitively, $P\ deadline[d]$ behaves exactly as P except that it must terminate before d time units. The rest of the rules are straightforward extensions of those introduced in [29], which are presented in Appendix A.

Definition 5 (Concrete transition system). *Let $S = (Var, init, P)$ be a system model. The concrete transition system corresponding to S is a LTS $\mathcal{L}_c^S = (C_c, init_c, \rightarrow)$ where C_c is the set of reachable concrete system configurations, $init_c$ is the initial configuration $(init, P)$ and $\rightarrow$ is the smallest transition relation closed under the firing rules.*

3   Zone Abstraction

For the sake of model checking, we assume that all variables have finite domains and the process forbids unbounded non-tail recursion. Nonetheless, the number of concrete configurations (and hence the concrete transition system) is infinite because of the time transitions. In the following, we apply zone abstraction to build an abstract configuration system. Different from zone abstraction applied to Timed Automata [7,38], we dynamically create/delete a set of clocks to precisely encode the timing requirements. We show that the abstract transition system is finite state and subject to model checking.

3.1   Clock Activation and De-activation

A clock is a variable ranging from 0 to some bounded natural number. Given a configuration (V, P), a clock is necessary to measure time elapsing if, and only if, a timed process is (e.g. $Wait[d]$, P $timeout[d]$ Q, P $interrupt[d]$ Q, or P $deadline[d]$) has been enabled. If a timed process (say $Wait[d]$) is enabled, we associate a clock (say tm) with the process to record time elapsing (written as $Wait[d]_{tm}$). The timing requirements can be captured using a constraint on the valuation of the clock. During system execution, multiple clocks may be used to capture quantitative timing constraints. A clock may become irrelevant as soon as the related process takes a transition. For instance, if P in P $timeout[d]_{tm}$ Q engages in an observable event, then the process transforms to P' and clock tm becomes irrelevant. It is known that model checking of real-time systems is exponential in the number of clocks. Therefore, it is desirable to use clocks only necessary and discharge them as early as possible.

Definition 6 (Abstract system configuration). *An abstract system configuration is a triple (V, P, D), where V is a variable valuation, P is a process and D is a zone.*

A *zone* is the maximal set of clock valuations satisfying a set of primitive clock constraints. A primitive constraint on a clock is of the form $tm \sim d$ where tm is a timer, d is a constant and $\sim$ is $\geq$, $=$, or $\leq$. Because clocks are implicit, clock readings cannot be compared directly. A zone is not empty if, and only if, the constraint is not false.

Next, we show how to systematically activate and de-activate clocks using process $Wait[d]$ and P $timeout[d]$ Q as examples. Let t be a fresh clock. Given an abstract configuration, we define function $\mathcal{A}(P, t)$ to recursively determine whether a clock is necessary and associate the clock with the relevant process constructs. A clock is necessary if and only if one (or more) timed pattern has just been enabled. For instance,

$$\mathcal{A}(Wait[d]_{t'}, t) = Wait[d]_{t'}$$
$$\mathcal{A}(Wait[d], t) \ \ = Wait[d]_t$$

where $Wait[d]_{t'}$ denotes that the timed pattern is associated with a clock t', whereas $Wait[d]$ denotes that it has not been associated with a clock. The intuition is for the former case, $\mathcal{A}$ does nothing and t is not used (since it is not necessary to introduce another clock); for the latter case, $\mathcal{A}$ associates t the the timer pattern. The following shows how to apply $\mathcal{A}$ to process P $timeout[d]$ Q.

$$\mathcal{A}(P \ timeout[d]_{t'}, t) \ = P \ timeout[d]_{t'} \ Q$$
$$\mathcal{A}(P \ timeout[d] \ Q, t) = \mathcal{A}(P) \ timeout[d]_t \ \mathcal{A}(Q)$$

$$
\begin{aligned}
\mathcal{A}(P \mid Q, t) &= \mathcal{A}(P, t) \mid \mathcal{A}(Q, t) \\
\mathcal{A}(P \parallel Q, t) &= \mathcal{A}(P, t) \parallel \mathcal{A}(Q, t) \\
\mathcal{A}(P;\ Q, t) &= \mathcal{A}(P, t);\ Q \\
\mathcal{A}(P, t) &= \mathcal{A}(Q, t) && -\text{if } P \cong Q \\
\mathcal{A}(Wait[d], t) &= \mathcal{A}(Wait[d]_t) \\
\mathcal{A}(P\ timeout[d]\ Q, t) &= \mathcal{A}(P, t)\ timeout[d]_t\ \mathcal{A}(Q, t) \\
\mathcal{A}(P\ interrupt[d]\ Q, t) &= \mathcal{A}(P, t)\ interrupt[d]_t\ \mathcal{A}(Q, t) \\
\mathcal{A}(P\ deadline[d], t) &= \mathcal{A}(P, t)\ deadline[d]_t
\end{aligned}
$$

Fig. 1. Clock activation: $\mathcal{A}(P, t)$ is P except the above cases

If a clock t' has already been associated with $P\ timeout[d]\ Q$, then function $\mathcal{A}$ simply returns the abstract configuration. Otherwise, it is associated with t and further $\mathcal{A}$ is applied to the sub-processes P and Q recursively. The complete definition of function $\mathcal{A}$ is presented in Figure 1. In an abuse of notation, given an abstract configuration $c = [V, P]_D$, we write $\mathcal{A}(c)$ to be $[V, \mathcal{A}(P)]_{D \wedge t=0}$ if t is used; otherwise $\mathcal{A}(c)$ is simply c.

A runtime clock may later be discarded when the time-related process has evolved such that the reading of the clock is no longer relevant. For instance, the clock associated with $P\ timeout[d]\ Q$ can be discarded when P engages in an observable event. It should be clear that we can identify the set of active runtime clocks by a similar procedure. To minimize clocks, all in-active runtime clocks, and the associated timing constraints, shall be pruned from D. Notice that t_G is never pruned. We assume a function $\mathcal{D}$ which performs clock de-activation in a sound and complete way.

3.2   Zone Abstraction

We define $D^\uparrow = \{t + d \mid t \in D \wedge d \in \mathbb{R}_+\}$, i.e. the zone obtained by delaying arbitrary amount of time. Notice that all clocks take the same pace. Next, we define function ι to compute the zone which can be reached by idling from a given abstract system configuration [38], presented in Figure 2. Given the current zone D, process $P\ timeout[d]_{tm}\ Q$ may keep idling as long as P may keep idling and the reading of clock tm is less or equal to d (so that $timeout$ has not occur). The rest are similarly defined.

In the following, we define the firing rules based on the abstract system configurations. The idea is to eliminate time transitions altogether and use the timing constraint to ensure that the time-related process constructs behave correctly. An abstract transition is of the form $(V, P, D) \xrightarrow{x} (V', P', D')$, where $x \in \Sigma \cup \{\checkmark, \tau\}$.

$$
\frac{}{(V, Wait[d]_{tm}, D) \xrightarrow{\tau} (V, Skip, D^\uparrow \wedge tm = d)} \quad [\ ade\ ]
$$

Process $Wait(d)$ idles for exactly d time units and then engages in event τ and the process transforms to $Skip$. Intuitively, it should be clear that this is 'equivalent' to the concrete firing rules. We will define what equivalence means later in this section.

$$\begin{aligned}
\iota(V, Stop, D) &= D^\uparrow \\
\iota(V, Skip, D) &= D^\uparrow \\
\iota(V, e \rightarrow P, D) &= D^\uparrow \\
\iota(V, [b]P, D) &= D^\uparrow \\
\iota(V, P \mid Q, D) &= \iota(V, P, D) \wedge \iota(V, Q, D) \\
\iota(V, P \parallel Q, D) &= \iota(V, P, D) \wedge \iota(V, Q, D) \\
\iota(V, P;\ Q, D) &= \iota(V, P, D) \\
\iota(V, Wait[d]_{tm}, D) &= D^\uparrow \wedge tm \leq d \\
\iota(V, P\ timeout[d]_{tm}\ Q, D) &= \iota(V, P, D) \wedge tm \leq d \\
\iota(V, P\ interrupt[d]_{tm}\ Q, D) &= \iota(V, P, D) \wedge tm \leq d \\
\iota(V, P\ deadline[d]_{tm}, D) &= \iota(V, P, D) \wedge tm \leq d \\
\iota(V, P, D) &= \iota(V, Q, D) \qquad\qquad -\text{if } P \mathrel{\hat{=}} Q
\end{aligned}$$

Fig. 2. Idling calculation

$$\frac{(V, P, D) \xrightarrow{\tau} (V', P', D')}{(V, P\ timeout[d]_{tm}\ Q, D) \xrightarrow{\tau} (V', P'\ timeout[d]_{tm}\ Q, D' \wedge tm \leq d)} \quad [\ ato1\ ]$$

$$\frac{(V, P, D) \xrightarrow{x} (V', P', D')}{(V, P\ timeout[d]_{tm}\ Q, D) \xrightarrow{x} (V', P', D' \wedge tm \leq d)} \quad [\ ato2\ ]$$

$$\frac{}{(V, P\ timeout[d]_{tm}\ Q, D) \xrightarrow{\tau} (V, Q, tm = d \wedge \iota(V, P, D))} \quad [\ ato3\ ]$$

Depending on when the first event of P takes place and whether it is observable, process $P\ timeout[d]\ Q$ behaves differently in three ways. An observable transition of P must occur no later than d time units since the process is enabled (rule $ato1$ and $ato2$). If the first transition is observable, then the *choice* is resolved (rule $ato2$). If it is silent, then the it transforms to $P'\ timeout[d]\ Q$. If P may delay more than d time units (captured by the constraint $\iota(V, P, D)$), then it times out after exactly d time units (rule $ato3$). The constraint $tm = d \wedge \iota(V, P, D)$ means that the delay is exactly d time units and P must be idling during the period.

$$\frac{(V, P, D) \xrightarrow{x} (V', P', D')}{(V, P\ interrupt[d]_{tm}\ Q, D) \xrightarrow{x} (V', P'\ interrupt[d]_{tm}\ Q, D' \wedge tm \leq d)} \quad [\ ait1\ ]$$

$$\frac{}{(V, P\ interrupt[d]_{tm}\ Q, D) \xrightarrow{\tau} (V, Q, tm = d \wedge \iota(V, P, D))} \quad [\ ait2\ ]$$

Process $P\ interrupt[d]\ Q$ behaves differently in two ways. Transitions of P must take place no later than d time units since the process is enabled (rule $ait1$). If P may delay more than d time units (captured by the constraint $\iota(V, P, D)$), then it is interrupted after exactly d time units (rule $ait2$).

Fig. 3. A simple example

$$\frac{(V, P, D) \xrightarrow{x} (V', P', D'), x \neq \checkmark}{(V, P \ deadline[d]_{tm}, D) \xrightarrow{x} (V', P' \ deadline[d]_{tm}, D' \wedge tm \leq d)} \ [\ adl\ ]$$

Process $P \ deadline[d]$ behaves exactly as P except that any transition must occur before d time units.

The rest of the firing rules is present in Appendix B. A transition is valid if, and only if, it conforms to the firing rules and the resultant zone is not empty. Intuitively, this means that a transition must be allowed by the untimed system and at the same time satisfy the additional timing requirement.

Definition 7 (Abstract transition system). *Let $S = (Var, init, P)$ be a system model. The abstract transition system corresponding to S is a LTS $\mathcal{L}_a^S = (C_a, init_a, \hookrightarrow)$ where C_a is the set of reachable valid abstract system configurations, $init_a$ is the initial configuration $(init, P, true)$ and $\hookrightarrow$ is the smallest transition relation satisfying $\forall c, c' : C_a. c \xrightarrow{e} c' \Leftrightarrow \mathcal{A}(c) \xrightarrow{e} \mathcal{D}(c')$.*

Example 2 (A simple example). Assume a model $(\varnothing, \varnothing, P)$ with no variable and P is $(a \rightarrow Wait[5]; \ b \rightarrow Stop) \ interrupt[3] \ c \rightarrow Stop$. The abstract transition system is shown in Figure 3, where transition label τ is skipped for simplicity. Let $\langle t_1, t_2 \rangle$ be a sequence of clocks. The following illustrates how to construct the abstract transition system. Let s_0 be $(\varnothing, P, true)$.

- Step 1: apply $\mathcal{A}$ to s_0 to get

  $$s_1 = (\varnothing, (a \rightarrow Wait[5]; \ b \rightarrow Stop) \ interrupt[3]_{t_1} \ c \rightarrow Stop, t_1 = 0)$$

- Step 2: apply rule $ait1$ to s_1 to get

  $$s_2 = (\varnothing, (Wait[5]; \ b \rightarrow Stop) \ interrupt[3]_{t_1} \ c \rightarrow Stop, 0 \leq t_1 \leq 3)$$

  Notice that $(t_1 = 0)^{\uparrow}$ equals to $t_1 \geq 0$.
- Step 3: apply $\mathcal{D}$ to s_2. The result is exactly s_2. We obtain the transition from state 1 to state 2.
- Step 4: apply rule $ait2$ to s_1 to get

  $$s_3 = (\varnothing, (c \rightarrow Stop), t_1 \geq 0 \wedge t_1 = 3)$$

  Notice that $\iota(\varnothing, a \rightarrow Wait[5]; \ b \rightarrow Stop, t_1 = 0)$ is $t_1 \geq 0$.
- Step 5: apply $\mathcal{D}$ to s_3 to get $s_4 = (\varnothing, (c \rightarrow Stop), true)$. We remark that because t_1 becomes inactive, it is pruned from the constraint. This generates the transition from state 1 to state 3.

– Step 6: apply $\mathcal{A}$ to s_2 to get

$$s_5 = (\varnothing, (\mathit{Wait}[5]_{t_2};\ b \to \mathit{Stop})\ \mathit{interrupt}[3]_{t_1}\ c \to \mathit{Stop},$$
$$0 \leq t_1 \leq 3 \wedge t_2 = 0)$$

– Step 7: apply rule $\mathit{ait}1$ to s_5, we get

$$s_6 = (\varnothing, (\mathit{Skip};\ b \to \mathit{Stop})\ \mathit{interrupt}[3]_{t_1}\ c \to \mathit{Stop}, 0 \leq t_1 \leq 3 \wedge t_2 = 5)$$

Notice that the timing constraint is false given that all timers take the same pace. Refer to next section on how this is discovered systematically.

– Step 8: apply rule $\mathit{ait}2$ to s_5 to get

$$s_7 = (\varnothing, c \to \mathit{Stop}, t_1 \geq 0 \wedge t_2 \geq 0 \wedge t_2 \leq 5 \wedge t_1 = 3)$$

– Step 9: apply $\mathcal{D}$ to s_7 to get s_4. Notice that both clocks are inactive and therefore pruned. This generates the transition from state 2 to state 3.
– Lastly, we generate the transition from state 3 to state 4. Notice that this transition involves no quantitative timing.

3.3 Zone Operations

In order to construct and verify the abstract transition system, we need efficient and sound procedures to manipulate zones. For instance, we need to determine whether a zone is empty or not. The procedure must be sound (so that a valid configuration is not missed) and complete (so that invalid configurations are ruled out).

A zone D can be equivalently represented as a difference bound matrices (DBM). Let $\{t_1, t_2, \cdots, t_n\}$ be a set of n clocks. Let t_0 be a dummy clock whose value is always 0. A DBM representing a constraint on the clocks contains $n + 1$ rows, each of which contains $n + 1$ elements. Let D_j^i represent entry (i, j) in the matrix. A DBM represents the constraint: $\forall i : 0 \mathrel{..} n.\ \forall j : 0 \mathrel{..} n.\ t_i - t_j \leq D_j^i$. The most important property of DBM is that there is a relatively efficient procedure to compute a unique canonical form. Given a DBM in canonical form, checking whether the zone is empty or not is as easy as looking up an entry in the matrix. DBM has been well studied [7,2,3]. In the following, we briefly introduce the relevant DBM operations/properties. We skip the discussion on rest of the zone operations (e.g. $D^\uparrow$, adding a constraint, etc.) as they resemble the discussion in [3].

Calculate canonical form. In theory, there are infinite different timing constraints which represent the zone. For instance, $0 \leq t_1 \leq 3 \wedge 0 \leq t_1 - t_2 \leq 3$ is equivalent to $0 \leq t_1 \leq 3 \wedge 0 \leq t_1 - t_2 \leq 3 \wedge t_2 \leq 1000$. In order to systematically compare two zones, we compute their unique canonical forms. In other words, we compute the tightest bound on each clock difference. If the clocks are viewed as vertices in a weighted graph and the clock difference as the label on the edge connecting two clocks, the tightest clock difference is the shortest path between the respective vertices. The Floyd-Warshall algorithm [12] thus can be used to compute the canonical from. Given that this algorithm is cubic in the number of clocks, it is desirable to reduce the number of clocks. Besides, the algorithm must be invoked if necessary and ideally (if possible) the result of performing an operation on a canonical DBM should be canonical.

Check satisfiability. In order to construct the abstract transition system, it is essential to check whether a zone is empty. Given the DBM representing a zone, it is unsatisfiable if, and only if, there is a clock which has a negative difference from itself, i.e. $t_k - t_k < 0$ for some k so that the constraint is false. If the DBM is in canonical form, then there exists at least one D_i^i which is negative. Further, it can be shown that the DBM is false if, and only if, D_0^0 is negative. Therefore, we compute the canonical form whenever it is necessary to check for satisfiability.

Add clocks. In our setting, clocks may be introduced during system exploration. We remark that clocks are a constant set in Timed Automata. Assume the new clock is t_k and the given DBM is canonical. The following shows how the DBM is updated with entries for t_k. For all i, $D_k^i = D_0^i$ and $D_i^k = D_i^0$ as the new clock always starts with value 0. By a simple argument, it can be shown the resultant DBM is canonical.

	t_0	t_1	$\cdots$	t_i	$\cdots$	t_{k-1}	$\mathbf{t_k}$
t_0	0	d_1^0	$\cdots$	d_i^0	$\cdots$	d_{k-1}^0	**0**
t_1	d_0^1	*	$\cdots$	*	$\cdots$	*	$\mathbf{d_0^1}$
$\cdots$	$\cdots$					$\cdots$	$\cdots$
t_i	d_0^i	*	$\cdots$	*	$\cdots$	*	$\mathbf{d_0^i}$
$\cdots$	$\cdots$					$\cdots$	$\cdots$
t_{k-1}	d_0^{k-1}	*	$\cdots$	*	$\cdots$	*	$\mathbf{d_0^{k-1}}$
$\mathbf{t_k}$	**0**	$\mathbf{d_1^0}$	$\cdots$	$\mathbf{d_i^0}$	$\cdots$	$\mathbf{d_{k-1}^0}$	**0**

Prune clocks. Because entries in a canonical DBM represent the tightest bound on clock differences, pruning clocks is simply to remove the relevant row and column in the table. It should be clear that the remaining DBM is canonical, i.e. the bounds can not be possibly tightened with less constraints.

Notice that the number of reachable timing constraints in canonical form are finite as proved in [7]. As a result, the abstraction system is finite state and therefore subject to model checking[2].

Example 3 (DBM manipulation example). The following illustrates how the DBM is transformed through system exploration in Example 2.

$\dfrac{\quad|\ t_0}{t_0\ |\ 0}$ $\xrightarrow{Step1}$

	t_0	t_1
t_0	0	0
t_1	0	0

$\xrightarrow{Step2}$

	t_0	t_1
t_0	0	0
t_1	3	0

$\xrightarrow{Step6}$

	t_0	t_1	t_2
t_0	0	0	0
t_1	3	0	3
t_2	0	0	0

$\xrightarrow{Step7}$

	t_0	t_1	t_2
t_0	0	0	-5
t_1	3	0	3
t_2	5	0	0

$\equiv$

	t_0	t_1	t_2
t_0	-2	-5	-7
t_1	1	-2	-4
t_2	1	-2	-4

$Step4 \downarrow$

	t_0	t_1
t_0	0	-3
t_1	3	0

$\xrightarrow{Step5}$ $\dfrac{\quad|\ t_0}{t_0\ |\ 0}$

$Step8 \downarrow$

	t_0	t_1	t_2
t_0	0	-3	0
t_1	3	0	3
t_2	∞	0	0

$\xrightarrow{Step9}$ $\dfrac{\quad|\ t_0}{t_0\ |\ 0}$

The DBM obtained after Step 7 is indeed false, i.e. after applying the Floyd-Warshall algorithm, D_0^0 is -2. $\qquad\square$

---

[2] Assume that the variable domains are finite and the reachable process expressions are finite.

4 System Verification

In this section, we prove that our abstraction is sound and complete with respect to a number of properties. The abstract transition system is shown to be equivalent to the concrete transition system using a specialized bi-simulation relationship [21]. We then show that two different system verification methods are sound.

In the concrete transition system, if a configuration (V', P') can be reached from (V, P) by idling only, we write $(V, P) \rightsquigarrow (V', P')$. By a simple argument, it can be shown that if $(V, P) \rightsquigarrow (V', P')$, then $V = V'$. We write $(V, P) \stackrel{x}{\rightsquigarrow} (V', P')$ if, and only if, there exists (V, P_1), (V', P_2) such that $(V, P) \rightsquigarrow (V, P_1)$ and $(V, P_1) \stackrel{x}{\rightarrow} (V', P_2)$ and $(V', P_2) \rightsquigarrow (V', P')$.

Definition 8 (Time abstract bi-simulation). *Let* $\mathcal{S} = (Var, init, P)$ *be a model. Let* $\mathcal{L}_c^{\mathcal{S}} = (C_c, init_c, \rightarrow)$ *and* $\mathcal{L}_a^{\mathcal{S}} = (C_a, init_a, \hookrightarrow)$ *be the concrete and abstract transition systems.* $\mathcal{L}_c$ *and* $\mathcal{L}_a$ *are time abstract bi-similar (hereafter bi-similar) if, and only if, there exists a binary relation* $\mathcal{R} : C_c \rightarrow C_a$ *such that* $(init_c, init_a) \in \mathcal{R}$ *and* $\forall x :$ $\Sigma \cup \{\checkmark, \tau\}$; $c = (V_c, P_c)$; $a = (V_a, P_a, D_a)$ *such that* $(c, a) \in \mathcal{R}$ *implies,*

– $V_c = V_a$,
– *if* $c \stackrel{x}{\rightsquigarrow} c'$, *then for some* a', $a \stackrel{x}{\hookrightarrow} a'$ *and* $(c', a') \in \mathcal{R}$.
– *if* $a \stackrel{x}{\hookrightarrow} a'$, *then for some* c', $c \stackrel{x}{\rightsquigarrow} c'$ *and* $(c', a') \in \mathcal{R}$.

We say that c and a are bi-similar, written as $c \sim a$, if, and only if, there exists $\mathcal{R}$ such that the transition systems are bi-similar. Notice that $\mathcal{L}_c$ and $\mathcal{L}_a$ are bi-similar if, and only if, $init_c \sim init_a$.

Theorem 1. *Let* $\mathcal{S} = (Var, init, P)$ *be a system model.* $\mathcal{L}_c^{\mathcal{S}}$ *and* $\mathcal{L}_a^{\mathcal{S}}$ *are time abstract bi-similar.*   □

By definition, it suffices to construct a binary relation which satisfies the condition. We present the proof based on structural induction in Appendix C. Time abstract bi-simulation is strong enough to guarantee soundness on verification of a number of useful properties.

LTL-X Model Checking. In this setting, the properties are linear temporal logic formulae without the next operator (i.e. LTL-X), constituted by propositions on global variables. Notice that no clocks are allowed in the property. The philosophy is that a critical property may often be independent of the speed of the hardware on which the system is deployed, whereas the model of the implementation shall incorporate known hardware limitations.

Example 4. Given Example 1, the following are some critical properties.

$$\Box ct \leq 1 \qquad \qquad \text{– safety property}$$
$$\Box (x = i \Rightarrow \Diamond cs.i) \qquad \text{– liveness property}$$

where $\Box$ and $\Diamond$ read as 'always' and 'eventually'. The first property precisely states mutual exclusion, i.e. at all time, there must not be 2 or more processes in the critical section. The second states that if process i is attempting to access the shared resource, it must eventually do so.

In order to reflect model checking results on the abstract transition system to the original system, we need to establish that the abstract transition system is equivalent to the concrete one with respect to LTL-X formulae. The idea is to show stutter equivalence between traces of the abstract system and the concrete system. Given two traces $tr_1 = \langle V_0, V_1, \cdots \rangle$ and $tr_2 = \langle V_0', V_1', \cdots \rangle$, tr_1 and tr_2 are stutter equivalent if, and only if, tr_1 and tr_2 can be partitioned into blocks, so that the variable valuation in the k-th block in tr_1 is the same as those in the k-th block of tr_2. Formally, tr_1 is stutter equivalent to tr_2 if, and only if, there are two infinite sequences of integers $0 < i_0 < i_1 < \cdots$ and $0 < j_0 < j_1 < \cdots$ such that for every block $k \geq 0$ holds $V_{s_{i_k}} = V_{s_{i_k+1}} = \cdots = V_{s_{i_{k+1}-1}} = V'_{s_{j_k}} = V'_{s_{j_k+1}} = \cdots = V'_{s_{j_{k+1}-1}}$. It is known that tr_1 satisfies a LTL-X property if, and only if, tr_2 does.

Let ϕ be such a property, we write $\mathcal{L} \vdash \phi$ to denote that the labeled transition system $\mathcal{L}$ satisfies ϕ, i.e. every trace of $\mathcal{L}$ satisfies ϕ.

Lemma 1. *Let $\mathcal{S} = (Var, init, P)$ be a system model. For every trace of the concrete transition system $\mathcal{L}_c$, there is a stutter equivalent trace of the abstract transition system $\mathcal{L}_a$ and vice versa.*

The above lemma can be proved by structural induction or implied from Theorem 1. Consequently, the following theorem can be proved straightforwardly.

Theorem 2. *Let $\mathcal{S} = (Var, init, P)$ be a system model. Let ϕ be a LTL-X formula constituted by propositions on Var. $\mathcal{L}_c^{\mathcal{S}} \vDash \phi$ if, and only if, $\mathcal{L}_a^{\mathcal{S}} \vDash \phi$.* □

Refinement Checking. In this setting, we investigate an alternative verification schema for finite system executions. That is, to verify whether the system satisfies the property by showing a refinement relationship between the system and a model which models the property. A variety of refinement relationships have been studied, e.g. trace-refinement, stable failures refinement and failures/divergence refinement [16]. In order to check refinement between two (timed) models, time abstraction must be applied to both models.

Example 5. Given the model presented in Example 1, a natural question is whether ϵ and δ are necessary or their values would make a difference. Equivalently, the former is to ask whether $(init, uProcotol)$ where $init = \{x \mapsto -1, ct \mapsto 0\}$ and $uProcotol$ defined as follows, trace-refines the original one $(init, Procotol)$.

$$
\begin{aligned}
uProc(i) &= [x = -1]uActive(i) \\
uActive(i) &= update.i\{x = i\} \rightarrow \\
&\qquad if\ (x = i)\ \{ \\
&\qquad\qquad cs.i\{ct = ct + 1\} \rightarrow \\
&\qquad\qquad exit.i\{ct = ct - 1;\ x = -1\} \rightarrow uProc(i) \\
&\qquad \}\ else\ \{ \\
&\qquad\qquad uProc(i) \\
&\qquad \} \\
uProtocol &= uProc(0)\ \|\ uProc(1)\ \|\ uProc(2);
\end{aligned}
$$

By showing trace refinement in both directions, we may establish trace equivalence. Or, the users may change the value of ϵ and δ check for equivalence. □

Let $\mathcal{L}$ be a LTS. A finite sequence of observable events, e.g. $\langle x_0, x_1, \cdots, x_m \rangle$, is a trace of $\mathcal{L}$ if, and only if, there exists a finite execution $\langle c_0, e_0, c_1, e_1, \cdots, e_n, c_{n+1} \rangle$ such that $\langle e_0, e_1, \cdots, e_n \rangle \upharpoonright \{\tau\} = \langle x_0, x_1, \cdots, x_m \rangle$ where $tr \upharpoonright X$ removes the events in X from the sequence tr. The set of all traces of $\mathcal{L}$ is written as $traces(\mathcal{L})$.

Given a finite trace tr and a configuration c in $\mathcal{L}$, we write c/tr to denote the set of system configurations that can be reached from c via trace tr or idling. Because of nondeterminism, multiple configurations can be reached via the same trace. The refusals are the sets of observable event sets which may be *refused*.

$$refusals(c) = \{X : \mathbb{P}\,\Sigma \mid \forall e : X \; \nexists c' \; c \overset{e}{\rightsquigarrow} c'\}$$

where $\mathbb{P}\,\Sigma$ is the power sets of Σ. The failures of $\mathcal{L}$ is defined as follows.

$$failures(\mathcal{S}) = \{(tr, X) \mid tr \in traces(\mathcal{L}) \wedge X \in refusals(init/tr)\}$$

If (tr, X) is a failure of the model, this means that the model can engage in the sequence of events recorded by tr, and then refuse to perform any event in X.

Definition 9. *Let $\mathcal{S}_i = (Var_i, init_i, P_i)$ where $i \in \{1, 2\}$ be two system models. $\mathcal{S}_1$ trace-refines $\mathcal{S}_2$ if, and only if, $traces(\mathcal{L}_c^{\mathcal{S}_1}) \subseteq traces(\mathcal{L}_c^{\mathcal{S}_2})$. $\mathcal{S}_1$ refines $\mathcal{S}_2$ in the failures semantics if, and only if, $traces(\mathcal{L}_c^{\mathcal{S}_1}) \subseteq traces(\mathcal{L}_c^{\mathcal{S}_2})$ and $failures(\mathcal{L}_c^{\mathcal{S}_1}) \subseteq failures(\mathcal{L}_c^{\mathcal{S}_2})$.*

In the following, we argue that it is sound and complete to show stable failures refinement (i.e. assuming both models are divergence-free) between the abstraction transition systems in order to show failures refinement between the concrete models.

Theorem 3. *Let $\mathcal{S}_i$ where $i \in \{1, 2\}$ be two models. $\mathcal{S}_1$ refines $\mathcal{S}_2$ in stable failures semantics iff $traces(\mathcal{L}_a^{\mathcal{S}_1}) \subseteq traces(\mathcal{L}_a^{\mathcal{S}_2})$ and $failures(\mathcal{L}_a^{\mathcal{S}_1}) \subseteq failures(\mathcal{L}_a^{\mathcal{S}_2})$.*   □

By Theorem 1, it should be clear that our abstraction preserves failures. Intuitively, this is because not only observable transitions but also τ-transitions are preserved by the abstraction. The theorem can then be proved straightforwardly. We remark that it is clear the failures refinement subsumes trace-refinement and, therefore, it too can be supported by only checking the abstract transition systems.

5   Implementation and Evaluation

PAT is a self-contained environment for system specification, simulation and verification. It supports multi-languages targeting concurrent/distributed systems. The techniques presented in this paper have been implemented in PAT. PAT verifies LTL properties using an on-the-fly automata-based approach [35]. PAT verifies refinement relationship using an on-the-fly simulation checking approach [32]. In the following, we present the experiments results on two bench models. The models and PAT are available at http://pat.comp.nus.edu.sg.

Table 1 shows the experiment results on the Fischer's mutual exclusion algorithm and a railway control system [38]. The data is obtained with Intel Core 2 Quad 9550 CPU at 2.83GHz and 2GB memory. In both examples, PAT performs reasonably well.

Table 1. Experiment results

Model	Size	Property	States/Transitions	PAT (s)
Fischer	4	$\Box\, ct \leq 1$	3452/8305	0.22
Fischer	5	$\Box\, ct \leq 1$	26496/73628	2.49
Fischer	6	$\Box\, ct \leq 1$	207856/654776	27.7
Fischer	7	$\Box\, ct \leq 1$	1620194/5725100	303
Fischer	4	$\Box\,(x = i \Rightarrow \Diamond cs.i)$	5835/16776	0.53
Fischer	5	$\Box\,(x = i \Rightarrow \Diamond cs.i)$	49907/169081	5.83
Fischer	6	$\Box\,(x = i \Rightarrow \Diamond cs.i)$	384763/1502480	70.5
Fischer	4	*Protocol refines uProtocol*	7741/18616	5.22
Fischer	5	*Protocol refines uProtocol*	72140/201292	126.3
Fischer	6	*Protocol refines uProtocol*	705171/2237880	3146
Railway Control	4	deadlock-free	853/1132	0.11
Railway Control	5	deadlock-free	4551/6115	0.42
Railway Control	6	deadlock-free	27787/37482	3.07
Railway Control	7	deadlock-free	195259/263641	24.2
Railway Control	8	deadlock-free	1563177/2111032	223.1
Railway Control	4	$\Box\,(appr.1 \rightarrow \Diamond leave.1)$	1504/1985	0.16
Railway Control	5	$\Box\,(appr.1 \rightarrow \Diamond leave.1)$	8137/10862	0.95
Railway Control	6	$\Box\,(appr.1 \rightarrow \Diamond leave.1)$	50458/67639	6.58
Railway Control	7	$\Box\,(appr.1 \rightarrow \Diamond leave.1)$	359335/482498	58.63

It handles 10^7 states/transition in a few hours, which is comparable to existing model checkers [17,28]. Further, a simple experiment shows that the computational overhead of calculating clocks/DBMs is around one third of the overall time.

The data on UPPAAL [20] or RED [36] verifying the same models has been omitted from the table. Because UPPAAL and PAT are based on a different modeling language, the results must be taken with a grain of salt. The state graph generated from a PAT model may contain unnecessary τ-transitions introduced by the compositional process constructs, e.g. the τ in rule $ato3$. In hand-crafted UPPAAL models, however, the τ-transitions may be removed by carefully manipulating the clock guards and grouping clock guards and events on the same transition. In such a setting, verification of the UPPAAL is faster (by a factor related to the number of such τ-transitions). However, our experiment show that if we manually construct a PAT model and a UPPAAL model with the same state graph, then PAT and UPPAAL have a similar performance.

6 Conclusion

This work is related to specification and verification of real-time systems. Compositional specification based on process algebras for real-time systems has been studied extensively, e.g. the algebra of timed processes ATP [31,24], CCS + real time [37] and timed CSP [26,30]. Verification support has been developed for these specification language. For instance, a preliminary PVS encoding of Timed CSP was presented in [5], which rely heavily on user interaction for formal proving of real-time systems.

In [38], a constraint solving method was proposed to verify CCS + real time. A number of verification support for ATP were evidenced in [25,6]. The modeling language Timed Automata [1] gathered more attention later on, especially in terms of mechanical verification. Several model checkers have been developed with Timed Automata (or a simplified version named timed safety automata [15]) being the core of their input languages [20,4,34]. The zone abstraction is closely related to works presented in [38], where a similar compositional abstraction method is discussed for CCS + real time. The difference is that we use implicit clocks and make the specification fully compositional. The soundness discussion of our abstraction is inspired by [21]. A remotely related modeling language is statecharts [13] with clocks, which too is compositional. This work follows the approach of Timed CSP and significantly extends the notion to cover a wide range of application domains. We developed a self-contained toolkit PAT to verify our models. To the best of our knowledge, there are few verification support for Timed CSP, e.g. the theorem proving approach documented in [5], the translation to UPPAAL models [8,9] and the approach based on constraint solving [10]. The PAT model checker is the first dedicated verification tool support for Timed CSP models adapting advanced verification techniques for real-time systems. In addition, PAT complements UPPAAL with the ability to check full LTL-X property and check refinement relationship. PAT is remotely related to the Spin model checker (on automata-based LTL model checking) [17] and the FDR refinement checker (on refinement checking) [28].

We remark that verification on CSP-based models has been traditional based on refinement checking [27], e.g. using the FDR checker [28]. One research direction we are currently investigating is to check timed refinement relationship between two timed models. The main challenge is that abstraction must be applied separately to two timed models and yet preserve timed trace/failures equivalence.

References

1. Alur, R., Dill, D.L.: A Theory of Timed Automata. Theoretical Computer Science 126, 183–235 (1994)
2. Behrmann, G., Larsen, K.G., Pearson, J., Weise, C., Yi, W.: Efficient Timed Reachability Analysis Using Clock Difference Diagrams. In: Halbwachs, N., Peled, D.A. (eds.) CAV 1999. LNCS, vol. 1633, pp. 341–353. Springer, Heidelberg (1999)
3. Bengtsson, J., Yi, W.: Timed Automata: Semantics, Algorithms and Tools. In: Desel, J., Reisig, W., Rozenberg, G. (eds.) Lectures on Concurrency and Petri Nets. LNCS, vol. 3098, pp. 87–124. Springer, Heidelberg (2004)
4. Bozga, M., Daws, C., Maler, O., Olivero, A., Tripakis, S., Yovine, S.: Kronos: A Model-Checking Tool for Real-Time Systems. In: Y. Vardi, M. (ed.) CAV 1998. LNCS, vol. 1427, pp. 546–550. Springer, Heidelberg (1998)
5. Brooke, P.: A Timed Semantics for a Hierarchical Design Notation. PhD thesis, University of York (1999)
6. Closse, E., Poize, M., Pulou, J., Sifakis, J., Venter, P., Weil, D., Yovine, S.: TAXYS: A Tool for the Development and Verification of Real-Time Embedded Systems. In: Berry, G., Comon, H., Finkel, A. (eds.) CAV 2001. LNCS, vol. 2102, pp. 391–395. Springer, Heidelberg (2001)
7. Dill, D.L.: Timing Assumptions and Verification of Finite-State Concurrent Systems. In: Sifakis, J. (ed.) CAV 1989. LNCS, vol. 407, pp. 197–212. Springer, Heidelberg (1990)

8. Dong, J.S., Hao, P., Qin, S.C., Sun, J., Yi, W.: Timed Patterns: TCOZ to Timed Automata. In: Davies, J., Schulte, W., Barnett, M. (eds.) ICFEM 2004. LNCS, vol. 3308, pp. 483–498. Springer, Heidelberg (2004)
9. Dong, J.S., Hao, P., Qin, S.C., Sun, J., Yi, W.: Timed Automata Patterns. IEEE Trans. Software Eng. 34(6), 844–859 (2008)
10. Dong, J.S., Hao, P., Sun, J., Zhang, X.: A Reasoning Method for Timed CSP Based on Constraint Solving. In: Liu, Z., He, J. (eds.) ICFEM 2006. LNCS, vol. 4260, pp. 342–359. Springer, Heidelberg (2006)
11. Dong, J.S., Mahony, B.P., Fulton, N.: Modeling Aircraft Mission Computer Task Rates. In: Woodcock, J.C.P., Davies, J., Wing, J.M. (eds.) FM 1999. LNCS, vol. 1709, p. 1855. Springer, Heidelberg (1999)
12. Floyd, R.W.: Algorithm 97: Shortest Path. Commun. ACM 5(6), 345 (1962)
13. Harel, D.: Some Thoughts on Statecharts, 13 Years Later. In: Grumberg, O. (ed.) CAV 1997. LNCS, vol. 1254, pp. 226–231. Springer, Heidelberg (1997)
14. Havelund, K., Skou, A., Larsen, K.G., Lund, K.: Formal Modeling and Analysis of an Audio/video Protocol: an Industrial Case Study using UPPAAL. In: RTSS 1997, pp. 2–13 (1997)
15. Henzinger, T.A., Nicollin, X., Sifakis, J., Yovine, S.: Symbolic Model Checking for Real-Time Systems. Information and Computation 111(2), 193–244 (1994)
16. Hoare, C.A.R.: Communicating Sequential Processes. International Series in Computer Science. Prentice-Hall, Englewood Cliffs (1985)
17. Holzmann, G.J.: The SPIN Model Checker: Primer and Reference Manual. Addison Wesley, Reading (2003)
18. Lai, L.M., Watson, P.: A Case Study in Timed CSP: The Railroad Crossing Problem. In: Maler, O. (ed.) HART 1997. LNCS, vol. 1201, pp. 69–74. Springer, Heidelberg (1997)
19. Larsen, K.G., Mikucionis, M., Nielsen, B., Skou, A.: Testing Real-time Embedded Software using UPPAAL-TRON: an Industrial Case Study. In: EMSOFT 2005, pp. 299–306 (2005)
20. Larsen, K.G., Pettersson, P., Wang, Y.: Uppaal in a Nutshell. International Journal on Software Tools for Technology Transfer 1(1-2), 134–152 (1997)
21. Larsen, K.G., Yi, W.: Time-abstracted Bisimulation: Implicit Specifications and Decidability. Information and Computation 134(2), 75–101 (1997)
22. Lindahl, M., Pettersson, P., Wang, Y.: Formal Design and Analysis of a Gearbox Controller. STTT 2001 3(3), 353–368 (2001)
23. Lynch, N.A., Vaandrager, F.W.: Action Transducers and Timed Automata. Formal Aspects of Computing 8(5), 499–538 (1996)
24. Nicollin, X., Sifakis, J.: The Algebra of Timed Processes, ATP: Theory and Application. Information and Computation 114(1), 131–178 (1994)
25. Nicollin, X., Sifakis, J., Yovine, S.: Compiling Real-Time Specifications into Extended Automata. IEEE Trans. Software Eng. 18(9), 794–804 (1992)
26. Reed, G.M., Roscoe, A.W.: A Timed Model for Communicating Sequential Processes. In: Kott, L. (ed.) ICALP 1986. LNCS, vol. 226, pp. 314–323. Springer, Heidelberg (1986)
27. Roscoe, A.W.: On the expressive power of csp refinement. Formal Asp. Comput. 17(2), 93–112 (2005)
28. Roscoe, A.W., Gardiner, P.H.B., Goldsmith, M., Hulance, J.R., Jackson, D.M., Scattergood, J.B.: Hierarchical compression for model-checking csp or how to check 10^{20} dining philosophers for deadlock. In: TACAS 1995. LNCS, vol. 1019, pp. 133–152. Springer, Heidelberg (1995)
29. Schneider, S.: An Operational Semantics for Timed CSP. Information and Computation 116(2), 193–213 (1995)
30. Schneider, S.: Concurrent and Real-time Systems. John Wiley and Sons, Chichester (2000)
31. Sifakis, J.: The Compositional Specification of Timed Systems - A Tutorial. In: Halbwachs, N., Peled, D.A. (eds.) CAV 1999. LNCS, vol. 1633, pp. 487–490. Springer, Heidelberg (1999)

32. Sun, J., Liu, Y., Dong, J.S.: Model Checking CSP Revisited: Introducing a Process Analysis Toolkit. In: Margaria, T., Steffen, B. (eds.) ISOLA 2008. CCIS, vol. 17, pp. 307–322. Springer, Heidelberg (2008)
33. Sun, J., Liu, Y., Dong, J.S., Pang, J.: PAT: Towards Flexible Verification under Fairness. In: CAV 2009. LNCS, vol. 5643, Springer, Heidelberg (2009)
34. Tasiran, S., Alur, R., Kurshan, R.P., Brayton, R.K.: Verifying Abstractions of Timed Systems. In: Sassone, V., Montanari, U. (eds.) CONCUR 1996. LNCS, vol. 1119, pp. 546–562. Springer, Heidelberg (1996)
35. Vardi, M.Y., Wolper, P.: An Automata-Theoretic Approach to Automatic Program Verification (Preliminary Report). In: Proc. of the Symposium on Logic in Computer Science (LICS 1986), pp. 332–344. IEEE Computer Society, Los Alamitos (1986)
36. Wang, F., Wu, R., Huang, G.: Verifying Timed and Linear Hybrid Rule-Systems with RED. In: SEKE 2005, pp. 448–454 (2005)
37. Yi, W.: CCS + Time = An Interleaving Model for Real Time Systems. In: Leach Albert, J., Monien, B., Rodríguez-Artalejo, M. (eds.) ICALP 1991. LNCS, vol. 510, pp. 217–228. Springer, Heidelberg (1991)
38. Yi, W., Pettersson, P., Daniels, M.: Automatic Verification of Real-time Communicating Systems by Constraint-Solving. In: FORTE 1994, pp. 243–258. Chapman & Hall, Boca Raton (1994)

Appendix A: Concrete Operational Semantics

The following are firing rules associated with process constructs other than those discussed in Section 2. They are extension of those presented previously by Schneider in [29]. $\alpha P \subseteq \Sigma \cup \{\checkmark\}$ is the alphabet of process P; $init(V, P)$ is the set of enabled events, as defined in [29]. In an abuse of notations, we use $\star$ to denote any event in $\Sigma \cup \{\tau, \checkmark\}$ or a real number.

$$\frac{}{(V, Stop) \xrightarrow{t} (V, Stop)} \; [\, st \,] \qquad\qquad \frac{}{(V, Skip) \xrightarrow{\checkmark} (V, Skip)} \; [\, sk1 \,]$$

$$\frac{}{(V, Skip) \xrightarrow{t} (V, Skip)} \; [\, sk2 \,] \qquad\qquad \frac{}{(V, e \to P) \xrightarrow{t} (V, e \to P)} \; [\, as1 \,]$$

$$\frac{}{(V, e \to P) \xrightarrow{e} (e(V), P)} \; [\, as2 \,] \qquad\qquad \frac{}{(V, [b]P) \xrightarrow{t} (V, [b]P)} \; [\, gu1 \,]$$

$$\frac{V \vDash b}{(V, [b]P) \xrightarrow{\tau} (V, P)} \; [\, gu2 \,] \qquad\qquad \frac{(V, P) \xrightarrow{x} (V', P')}{(V, P \mid Q) \xrightarrow{x} (V', P')} \; [\, ex1 \,]$$

$$\frac{(V, Q) \xrightarrow{x} (V', Q')}{(V, P \mid Q) \xrightarrow{x} (V', Q')} \; [\, ex2 \,] \qquad\qquad \frac{\begin{array}{c}(V, P) \xrightarrow{t} (V, P'), \\ (V, Q) \xrightarrow{t} (V, Q')\end{array}}{(V, P \mid Q) \xrightarrow{t} (V, P' \mid Q')} \; [\, ex3 \,]$$

$$\frac{(V, P) \xrightarrow{x} (V', P'), x \notin \alpha Q}{(V, P \parallel Q) \xrightarrow{x} (V', P' \parallel Q)} \; [\, pa1 \,] \qquad\qquad \frac{(V, Q) \xrightarrow{x} (V', Q'), x \notin \alpha P}{(V, P \parallel Q) \xrightarrow{x} (V', P \parallel Q')} \; [\, pa2 \,]$$

$$\frac{(V,P) \xrightarrow{x} (V,P'), (V,Q) \xrightarrow{x} (V,Q'), x \in (\alpha P \cap \alpha Q) \cup \mathbb{R}_+}{(V,P \parallel Q) \xrightarrow{x} (V,P' \parallel Q')} \ [\ pa3\ ]$$

$$\frac{(V,P) \xrightarrow{\checkmark} (V,P')}{(V,P;\ Q) \xrightarrow{\tau} (V,Q)} \ [\ pa4\ ] \qquad \frac{(V,P) \xrightarrow{t} (V',P'), \checkmark \notin init(V,P)}{(V,P;\ Q) \xrightarrow{t} (V',P';\ Q)} \ [\ se1\ ]$$

$$\frac{(V,P) \xrightarrow{x} (V',P'), \checkmark \notin init(V,P)}{(V,P;\ Q) \xrightarrow{x} (V',P';\ Q)} \ [\ se2\ ] \qquad \frac{(V,Q) \xrightarrow{\star} (V',Q'), P \mathrel{\widehat{=}} Q}{(V,P) \xrightarrow{\star} (V',Q')} \ [\ def\ ]$$

Appendix B: Abstract Operational Semantics

The following are abstract firing rules associated with process constructs other than those discussed in Section 2.

$$\frac{}{(V, Skip, D) \xrightarrow{\checkmark} (V, Stop, D^\uparrow)} \ [\ aki\ ] \qquad \frac{V \vDash b}{(V, [b]P, D) \xrightarrow{\tau} (V, P, D^\uparrow)} \ [\ agu\ ]$$

$$\frac{}{(V, e\{prg\} \to P, D) \xrightarrow{e} (prg(V), P, D^\uparrow)} \ [\ aev\ ]$$

$$\frac{(V, P, D) \xrightarrow{x} (V', P', D')}{(V, P \mid Q, D) \xrightarrow{x} (V', P', D' \wedge \iota(V, Q, D))} \ [\ aex1\ ]$$

$$\frac{(V, Q, D) \xrightarrow{x} (V', Q', D)}{(V, P \mid Q, D) \xrightarrow{x} (V', Q', D' \wedge \iota(V, P, D))} \ [\ aex2\ ]$$

$$\frac{(V, P, D) \xrightarrow{e} (V', P', D'), e \notin \alpha Q}{(V, P \parallel Q, D) \xrightarrow{e} (V', P' \parallel Q, D' \wedge \iota(V, Q, D))} \ [\ apa1\ ]$$

$$\frac{(V, Q, D) \xrightarrow{e} (V', Q', D'), e \notin \alpha P}{(V, P \parallel Q, D) \xrightarrow{e} (V', P \parallel Q', D' \wedge \iota(V, P, D))} \ [\ apa2\ ]$$

$$\frac{(V, P, D) \xrightarrow{e} (V, P', D'), (V, Q, D) \xrightarrow{e} (V, Q', D''), e \in \alpha P \cap \alpha Q}{(V, P \parallel Q, D) \xrightarrow{e} (V, P' \parallel Q', D' \wedge D'')} \ [\ apa3\ ]$$

$$\frac{(V, P, D) \xrightarrow{x} (V', P', D'), x \neq \checkmark}{(V, P;\ Q, D) \xrightarrow{x} (V', P';\ Q, D' \wedge (\checkmark \notin init(V, P) \vee D))} \ [\ ase1\ ]$$

$$\frac{(V, P, D) \xrightarrow{\checkmark} (V', P', D')}{(V, P;\ Q, D) \xrightarrow{\tau} (V, Q, D \wedge D')} \qquad \frac{(V, P, D) \xrightarrow{x} (V', P', D'), Q \mathrel{\widehat{=}} P}{(V, Q, D) \xrightarrow{x} (V', P', D')}$$

Appendix C: Proof of Theorem 1

Let $\mathcal{S} = (Var, i, P)$ be the model; $\mathcal{L}_c$ and $\mathcal{L}_a$ be the concrete and abstract transition system respectively. By definition, it suffices to construct a binary relation which satisfies the condition. The theorem is proved by structural induction on the all types of process expressions. The following are the base cases.

- $Stop$: $\mathcal{R} = \{(i, Stop) \mapsto (i, Stop, true)\}$. Trivially true.
- $Skip$: $\mathcal{R} = \{(i, Skip) \mapsto (i, Skip, true), (i, Stop) \mapsto (init, Stop, true)\}$. Trivially true.
- $Wait[d]$: $\mathcal{R} = \{(i, Wait[d]) \mapsto (i, Wait[d], true), (i, Skip) \mapsto (i, Skip, true), (i, Stop) \mapsto (i, Stop, true)\}$. The transition $(i, Wait[d]) \overset{\tau}{\rightsquigarrow} (i, Skip)$ of $\mathcal{L}_c$ corresponds to the transition $(i, Waid[d], true) \overset{\tau}{\hookrightarrow} (i, Skip, true)$. Notice that the clock introduced by function $\mathcal{A}$ would be pruned by $\mathcal{D}$. The rest is trivial.

Next, we prove the induction step.

- $e \rightarrow P$: $(i, e \rightarrow P)$ and $(i, e \rightarrow P, true)$ are bi-similar since $(i, e \rightarrow P) \overset{e}{\rightsquigarrow} (prg(i), P)$ (by rule $as1$ and $as2$) and $(i, e \rightarrow P, true) \overset{e}{\hookrightarrow} (e(i), P, true)$ (by rule aev), and $(e(i), P) \sim (e(i), P, true)$ (by hypothesis).
- $[b]P$: if $i \vDash b$, then $[b]P$ behaves exactly as P (rule $gu2$ and rule agu), hence by hypothesis, $(i, [b]P) \sim (i, [b]P, true)$. If $i \nvDash b$, then $[b]P$ behaves exactly as $Stop$ (rule $gu1$ and no abstract firing rule), hence $(i, [b]P) \sim (i, [b]P, true)$.
- $P \mid Q$: $P \mid Q$ behaves either as P or Q, in both cases, by hypothesis $(i, P \mid Q) \sim (i, P \mid Q, true)$.
- $P \parallel Q$: there is one-to-one correspondence on the concrete firing rules (rule $pa1$, $pa2$ and $pa3$) and the abstract firing rules ((rule $apa1$, $apa2$ and $apa3$)). It is clear that by hypothesis $(i, P \parallel Q) \sim (i, P \parallel Q, true)$.
- $P; Q$. Similarly as above.
- $P\ timeout[d]\ Q$: let the associated clock be tm. We show that each abstract transition is possible if, and only if, there is a corresponding concrete transition $(i, P) \rightsquigarrow (i', P')$. Rule $ato1$ is applicable if, and only if, $tm \leq d$ and (i, P, D) may perform a τ-transition. By hypothesis, (i, P, D) may perform a τ-transition if, and only if, (i, P) does. By rule $to2$, $to3$ and $to4$, a τ of P may happen if, and only if, $tm \leq d$. Therefore, we conclude rule $ato1$ is applicable if, and only if, there is a corresponding concrete transition. Similarly, we argue that rule $ato2$ and $ato3$ are applicable if, and only if, there is a corresponding concrete transition. This concludes that $(i, P\ timeout[d]\ Q) \sim (i, P\ timeout\ Q, true)$.
- $P\ interrupt[d]\ Q$: Similarly as above.
- $P\ deadline[d]$: Similarly as above.
- $P \cong Q$: By induction.

Modal Systems:
Specification, Refinement and Realisation[*]

Fernando L. Dotti[1,2], Alexei Iliasov[1],
Leila Ribeiro[3], and Alexander Romanovsky[1]

[1] Centre for Software Reliability, Newcastle University, UK
{alexei.iliasov,alexander.romanovsky}@newcastle.ac.uk
[2] Faculdade de Informática, PUCRS, Brazil
fernando.dotti@pucrs.br
[3] Instituto de Informática, UFRGS, Brazil
leila@inf.ufrgs.br

Abstract. Operation modes are useful structuring units that facilitate design of several safety-critical systems such as such as avionic, transportation and space systems. Although some support to the construction of modal systems can be found in the literature, modelling abstractions for the formal specification, analysis and correct construction of modal systems are still lacking.

This paper discusses existing support for the construction of modal systems and proposes both a formalisation and a refinement notion for modal systems. A modal system, specified using the proposed abstractions, can be realised using different specification languages. Complementing the contribution, we define the requirements for an Event-B model to realise a modal system specification. A case study illustrates the proposed approach.

1 Introduction

Several systems, many of them safety-critical ones, are modal, i.e., they are described using the notion of 'operation modes'. While there is no widely accepted definition of operation mode and modal system, several authors use operation modes to denote the expected system functionality under distinguished working conditions of the system. A modal system denotes the assembly of a set of such modes[1], related by mode transitions that represent the possible changes in the working conditions of a system, originated either by environmental changes or by system evolution.

Given the importance of modal systems, several abstractions for their modelling are provided. Examples of modal systems and a brief survey of modelling approaches are discussed in Section 2. That efforts not withstanding, there is

---

[*] This work is partially supported by the ICT DEPLOY IP and the EPSRC/UK TrAmS platform grant. Fernando L. Dotti is supported by CNPq/Brazil grant 200806/2008-4. Leila Ribeiro is supported by CNPq/Brazil grant 200779/2008-7.
[1] 'Mode' and 'operation mode' are used as synonyms.

K. Breitman and A. Cavalcanti (Eds.): ICFEM 2009, LNCS 5885, pp. 601–619, 2009.
© Springer-Verlag Berlin Heidelberg 2009

a lack of abstraction to allow the formal specification of modal systems as well as approaches to analysing and rigorously deriving implementations from these systems.

In our previous work [1], we introduced modal systems and discussed their use for structuring dependable systems (focusing specifically on the recovery and degradation modes).

As one contribution, this paper presents the formal definitions of the abstractions used to specify modal systems. According to our approach, a modal system is an abstract specification of the modes as well as mode transitions that may occur in a system. It does not specify concretely how the system operates while it is in some specific mode nor how mode transitions occur. It rather imposes requirements on concrete implementations, complementing traditional modelling but not replacing it. The construction of a concrete model that realizes a modal system specification can be done using any existing formalism. Therefore it is important to define when a concrete model realizes a modal system.

Event-B [2] is a state-based formal method closely related to Classical B [3]. It has been successfully used in several applications, having available tool support for both model specification and analysis. Another contribution of the paper are the satisfaction conditions stating when an Event-B model realises a modal system. A series of proof obligations on the Event-B model are derived from the modal system to show its satisfaction. The realisation of a modal system using state-based formal methods is especially interesting since the modal system helps to structure state-based systems.

A final contribution of this paper is the formalization of the notion of modal system refinement. A modal system can be step-wise detailed to model system requirements, allowing an organized way to construct the system and reason about its properties.

The rest of the paper is structured in 4 major parts: first, related work is surveyed in Section 2; second, modal systems and modal system refinement are formally defined in Sections 3 and 4; then Event-B is briefly introduced and its relation to modal systems defined in Sections 5 and 6; finally, Section 7 presents a case study to illustrate and evaluate the ideas introduced in the paper. Section 8 concludes the paper with a summary and an outline of future extensions of the approach.

2   Related Work

A considerable number of systems are described using the notion of 'operation modes', which serves to structure their operation. These are called 'modal systems'. For example, in [4,5] the authors specify and analyse the operation mode logics of space and avionic systems. In both avionics and space systems, modes denote phases of a flight and operational status of on-board instruments, among others. An extension of an Automated Highway System with degraded operation modes that tolerates several kinds of faults is discussed in [6]. The Steam Boiler Control [7], a classic case study showing the use of formal methods, is based on the notion of operation modes. More recent examples of the extensive use of modes for the specification of transportation and space systems can be found in [8].

The use of operation modes is very common in real-time systems. Timing properties are analysed considering operation modes of the system: deadlines to enter or leave modes, or to perform mode changes are investigated. Modecharts [9] focus on the specification of real-time properties of mode and mode switching. The authors propose modes both as partitions of the state space, representing different working conditions of the system, as well as a way to define control information in large state machines, imposing structure on the operation of the system. However, Modecharts lacks adequate support to specifying and reason about functional properties.

According to [10], also focused on real-time systems, a mode is characterized by a group of tasks. The system initiates in a given mode, with a specific set of active tasks. During system evolution or to react to external stimuli, the system may change modes. This involves stopping and starting tasks, keeping or changing parameters of tasks. The approach discusses real-time systems and how to meet deadlines. In such systems, a mode change may result in transient stages where tasks are deleted/created. Mode changes take time but are atomic - not iterrupted by other mode changes. The problem of meeting deadlines during mode changes in real-time systems is also addressed in [11].

Since the notion of operation modes is rather generic and many modal systems are critical, modelling abstractions to support modal system definitions appeared recently, which are not focused on real-time aspects. In the Architecture Analysis & Design Language (AADL) [12] a system is built out of communicating components and each component may have modes, representing alternative operational states. Modes serve to identify configurations of components. A state machine abstraction is used, such that a distinct configuration is a modal state and specific events cause transition among them. A component may have distinct behaviour according to the current mode.

The Dependability Requirement Engineering Process (DREP) [13] provides a methodology for developing modal systems using UML diagrams. A system is considered to offer a set of services and, depending on the mode, different subsets of services may be available. Switching modes means to change the configuration of the system such that the profile of offered services changes. Since DREP is specially focused on the representation of degraded service outcomes, some modes are specially discussed: normal, degraded, emergency and restricted. The use of modes to represent degraded system operation is commonly found in the literature [14].

According to our literature survey, none of the existing approaches discusses refinement of modal systems. Moreover, most of them are not formal, and thus can neither be used as a basis for formal development nor to check whether possible realisations are correct.

3   Modal Systems

As mentioned in the Introduction and observed in Section 2, operation modes are generally used to denote expected system functionality under distinguished working conditions of the system. A modal system consists of the assembly of a set of such modes related by mode transitions. As a brief example, the Steam Boiler Control [7] states that the *normal mode* is characterized by a working water level sensor and the water level in normal range - in such conditions the system works to keep the water level (read from sensor) in normal range. In the event of a detected failure of a water level sensor, the system switches to *rescue mode* where the sensor is not trusted - in such conditions the system operates differently, based on the amount of water pumped into the boiler and amount of steam generated. The case study in Section 7 discusses a cruise control system with several modes, each organized in similar way and related by transitions.

We are interested in how to specify, analyse and build correct modal systems. Instead of proposing a specification method, our approach is to provide abstractions that allow to formally specify the requirements of modal systems towards concrete models that realize them. A modal system specification is a complementary view on the system that does not replace traditional formal modelling. The construction of a concrete model that realises a modal system specification can be done using any existing formalism, provided it is possible to demonstrate that the model satisfies the modal system specification. This is further discussed in Section 6.

Due to the nature of modal systems, we follow a state-based approach to propose suitable abstractions. We consider that the state of a model is detailed enough to allow one to distinguish its different operating conditions and also to characterize required mode functionality and possible mode switching in terms of state transitions.

Below we introduce the necessary elements (in definitions 1 and 2) to formally define modal systems (definition 3).

Definition 1 (State, Invariant, Assumption, Guarantee). *Given a set of variables Var and a set of values Val, the state of a system is a (total) function $v : Var \to Val$. We denote as $State$ the set of all states. Invariant and assumption are predicates over state variables. A guarantee is a predicate over $Var \times Var'$, where $Var' = \{x'|x \in Var\}$. It is interpreted over $State \times State$. We assume that there is a special value called $Undef$ in Val, and the undefined state (a state in which all values are mapped to $Undef$) is called $Undef$.*

Invariant is a property preserved at each point in a systems life time. Often it is interpreted as a characterisation of safe states of a system. A guarantee is used to express the requirements towards the functionality of a mode, while an assumption expresses the requirements of a mode, to the rest of the system, to assure the functionality required by the guarantee. A pair assume/guarantee can be seen as a contract between the mode and the rest of the system, and is what defines a mode, as follows.

Definition 2 (Mode). *Given an invariant I, a Mode is a pair A/G where A is an assumption, G is a guarantee and:*

- *the assumption characterises a non-empty set of states: $\exists v \cdot A(v)$, assuring that a mode contributes to system functionality;*

- *G is feasible:* $\exists v, v' \cdot I(v) \wedge A(v) \Rightarrow G(v, v')$. *I.e. a mode should permit a concrete implementation of the required functionality;*
- *G preserves the invariant* I *and the mode's assumption* A:
  $I(v) \wedge A(v) \wedge G(v, v') \Rightarrow I(v') \wedge A(v')$.

Given a mode M_i *we denote its assumption by* A_i *and its guarantee by* G_i.

Concerning the last condition, it would not make sense if a guarantee would require the mode to violate the invariant. Also, we postulate that a mode guarantee should neither violate its assumption: this helps to clearly separate the specification of actions that may cause mode switching from those that preserve current mode, an important feature in modal systems.

Definition 3 (Mode Transition, Modal System). *Given a set of modes* M, *a transition* t *is a pair* (i, j), *with* $i, j \in M$. *A transition is denoted by* $i \rightsquigarrow j$, *and the source* i *and target* j *modes of a transition* t *are denoted by* $src(t)$ *and* $target(t)$, *respectively.*

A Modal System is a tuple $MSys = (Var, Val, I, M, T)$ *where:*

1. Var *is a set of variables of the system;*
2. Val *is the set of possible values for variables;*
3. I *is an invariant;*
4. M *is a finite set of modes* $(M_i = A_i/G_i)_{i \le n, n \in \mathbb{N}} \cup \{\top_M, \bot_M\}$ *such that*
   (a) $I(v) \Rightarrow A_1(v) \oplus \cdots \oplus A_n(v)$, *where* $\oplus$ *is the exclusive or operator. This implies that for each mode a different assumption is declared, that mode assumptions are exclusive, and that assumptions are valid with respect to the invariant.*
5. $T \subseteq M \times M$ *is a set of mode transitions, with the following restrictions:*
   (a) $i \rightsquigarrow \top_M \notin T \wedge \bot_M \rightsquigarrow j \notin T \wedge \top_M \rightsquigarrow \bot_M \notin T$
   (b) $\forall m \in M - \{\bot_M\} \cdot (\top_M, m) \in T^*$, *where* T^* *is the transitive closure of* T.

A modal system is an assembly of several modes (M) related by mode transitions (T). Modes $\top_M$ and $\bot_M$ are called start and terminal modes, respectively. It is assumed that a system is only in one mode at a time, represented by condition 4a. The meaning and implications of a system being simultaneously in more than one mode are not trivial and subject of further study. A mode transition is an atomic step switching from one source mode i to one destination mode j. The possible mode transitions of a modal system are defined by T. According to condition 5b, the start mode $\top_M$ is present in any modal system specification. A transition $\top_M \rightsquigarrow M_i$ defines that M_i is a possible initial mode of the modal system. Other such transitions may exist defining more than one initial mode. Some systems may be non-terminating, in which case there will be no mode transition to the terminal mode $\bot_M$. Condition 5a states that it is not possible to switch to a state before initialization or from the terminal mode to another mode; and during its lifetime a system enters at least one operation mode. Now we define the behavior of a modal system.

Definition 4 (Modal System Behaviour). *The behaviour of a modal system* $MSys = (Var, Val, I, M, T)$, *given by a transition system* $MST = (MState, S_0, \rightarrow)$ *where* $MState = \{\langle m, v \rangle \mid m \in \{1..n, \top_M, \bot_M\}$ *is a mode index and* v *is a state}; the initial state* S_0 *is* $\langle \top_M, Undef \rangle$ *and the transition relation* $\rightarrow$: $MState \rightarrow MState$ *is given by the rules:*

$$\boxed{start} \frac{\top_M \rightsquigarrow k \wedge A_k(v)}{\langle \top_M, Undef \rangle \rightarrow \langle k, v \rangle}$$

$$\boxed{internal} \frac{A_m(v) \wedge G_m(v, v') \wedge A_m(v')}{\langle m, v \rangle \rightarrow \langle m, v' \rangle}$$

$$\boxed{switching} \frac{m \rightsquigarrow n \wedge A_m(v) \wedge A_n(v')}{\langle m, v \rangle \rightarrow \langle n, v' \rangle}$$

The state of a system described using operation modes is a tuple $\langle m, v \rangle$ where m is the index of a current operation mode and v is the current system state. In the following, each of the transition rules is explained.

Initialisation. A system starts executing one of its initialization mode transitions $\langle \top_M, Undef \rangle \rightarrow \langle k, v \rangle$. The transition switches the system on, by establishing a possible state defined by $A_k(v)$, and places it into some system mode $M_k = A_k/G_k$. This behaviour is described by rule *start*.

Evolution. A modal system may evolve either performing internal or mode switching transitions. Rule *internal* states that while the system is in some mode m the state may evolve to a state v' satisfying both the corresponding guarantee $G_m(v, v')$ and the modes assumption $A_m(v')$. Rule *switching* states that the system may switch modes if there is a defined mode transition originating from the current mode. *Internal* and *switching* transitions compete with each other: at each step a non-deterministic choice is made among the enabled transitions.

Termination. A system terminates by executing one of terminating mode transition $t \rightsquigarrow \bot_M$. Not every system has to have this transition: a control system would be typically designed as never aborting. There can be any number of terminating mode transitions. Due to condition 5a, no mode transitions are possible after $\bot_M$ is reached

4   Refinement of Modal Systems

Modal System behavioural refinement details modes assumption or guarantee or both. A mode can also be detailed in more than one corresponding modes at the concrete level. Mode assumption cannot be strengthened during refinement. This is based on the understanding that an assumption is a requirement of a mode to its environment. As a system developer cannot assume control over the environment of a modelled system, a stronger requirement to an environment may not be realisable. On the other hand, a weaker requirement to an environment means that a system is more robust as it would remain operational in a wider range of environments. Therefore, weakening assumptions during refinement is desired. Symmetrically, a mode guarantee cannot be weakened as a mode guarantee is understood as a contract of a mode with the rest of a system and the system environment. In other words, weakening a mode guarantee could violate expectations of another system part.

Mode transitions must be consistently refined along with refinement of modes. The general rules for refining mode transitions are: (i) a mode transition present at an abstract model must have at least one corresponding transition at a concrete model. If a source mode of a transition is split into two new modes, the transition can be associated with any one of the new modes or both; (ii) no new transitions may appear relating an abstract mode to another mode; (iii) new transitions may be defined on concrete modes. Now we formalize the above discussed notion of behavioural mode refinement.

Definition 5 (Modal System Behavioural Refinement). *Given:*

- *a modal system $MSys_{abs} = (Var_{abs}, Val_{abs}, I_{abs}, M_{abs}, T_{abs})$; and*
- *a modal system $MSys_{cnc} = (Var_{cnc}, Val_{cnc}, I_{cnc}, M_{cnc}, T_{cnc})$*

a refinement of $MSys_{abs}$ into $MSys_{cnc}$ is defined by a pair $ref = (ref^M, ref^T)$ of functions $ref^M : M_{cnc} \to M_{abs}$ and $ref^T : T_{cnc} \to T_{abs}$ such that:

1. *ref^M is total, surjective and preserves the start and terminal modes; and ref^T is partial and surjective;*
2. *an abstract mode assumption is stronger than the disjunction of assumptions of its concrete modes: $\forall m \in M_{abs} \cdot \bigvee_{\forall j \cdot j \in M_{cnc} \wedge ref^M(j)=m} A_j \Leftarrow A_m$*
3. *an abstract mode guarantee is weaker than the disjunction of guarantees of its concrete modes: $\forall m \in M_{abs} \cdot \bigvee_{\forall j \cdot j \in M_{cnc} \wedge ref^M(j)=m} G_j \Rightarrow G_m$*
4. *concrete transitions not mapped to abstract ones have the same abstract mode as source and target (i.e. it was an internal, or non-observable, transition of an abstract mode): $\forall t \notin dom(ref^T) \cdot ref^M(src_{ref}(t)) = ref^M(target_{ref}(t))$*
5. *for all transition $t \in dom(ref^T)$, the squares bellow commute:*

$$
\begin{array}{ccc}
T_{abs} & \xrightarrow{\ src_{abs}\ } & M_{abs} \\
{\scriptstyle ref^T}\Big\uparrow & = & \Big\uparrow{\scriptstyle ref^M} \\
dom(T_{cnc}) & \xrightarrow[src_{cnc}]{} & M_{cnc}
\end{array}
\qquad
\begin{array}{ccc}
T_{abs} & \xrightarrow{\ target_{abs}\ } & M_{abs} \\
{\scriptstyle ref^T}\Big\uparrow & = & \Big\uparrow{\scriptstyle ref^M} \\
dom(T_{cnc}) & \xrightarrow[target_{cnc}]{} & M_{cnc}
\end{array}
$$

These conditions mean that: (1) all concrete modes have an abstract mode that they refine, and all abstract modes are refined by at least one concrete mode; and all abstract mode transitions are refined into one or more concrete mode transitions; (2) considering variables in the abstract system, concrete modes cover the same state space as the abstract one – it is not possible to restrict assumptions by refinement; (3) guarantees of the concrete system may be stronger (more deterministic) than the corresponding abstract ones; (4) if a transitions is added in a refinement step, it must have a non-observable effect on the abstract level (same source and target modes); (5) the transitions that are mapped to the abstract level (those in $dom(T_{cnc})$) must be consistent with the mapping of source and target modes.

Via data refinement, the set v of model variables may change to a new set u and model invariant $I(v)$ is replaced with a new invariant $J(v,u)$, often called a *gluing invariant*. The presence of old variables v in new invariant J allows a modeller to express a linking relation between the states of concrete and abstract models. Given a gluing invariant $J(v,u)$, data refinement can be added to definition 5 by extending conditions 2 and 3 respectively as:

$$\forall m \in M_{abs} \cdot \bigvee_{\forall j \cdot j \in M_{ref} \wedge ref^M(j)=m} J(v,u) \wedge A_j(u) \Leftarrow A_m(v)$$
$$\forall m \in M_{abs} \cdot \bigvee_{\forall j \cdot j \in M_{ref} \wedge ref^M(j)=m} J(v,u) \wedge J(v',u') \wedge G_j(u,u') \Rightarrow G_m(v,v')$$

Proposition 1. *Given:*

- *an abstract modal system $MSys_{abs} = (Var_{abs}, Val_{abs}, I_{abs}, M_{abs}, T_{abs})$;*
- *a concrete modal system $MSys_{cnc} = (Var_{cnc}, Val_{cnc}, I_{cnc}, M_{cnc}, T_{cnc})$;*
- *a refinement $ref = (ref^M, ref^T)$ where $ref^T : T_{cnc} \rightarrow T_{abs}$;*

any possible sequence of modes described by the transition system of $MSys_{cnc}$ can be translated into a possible sequence of modes described by the transition system of $MSys_{abs}$.

Proof. By definitions 3 and 4 the initial mode of a modal system is $\top_M$, and by definition 5 $ref^M(\top_M) = \top_M$. So $\top_M$ is initial in any sequence of modes described by both $MSys_{abs}$ and $MSys_{cnc}$. Now consider the concrete modal system in any mode m_{c1}, corresponding through ref^M to an abstract mode m_a. By definition 5, conditions 1 and 4, a mode transition in the concrete level is either a new transition or refinement of a transition in the abstract level.

Consider the first case: by condition 4 a new transition can be added only among modes that refine a same abstract mode. In this case, switching from m_{c1} to m_{c2}, both corresponding through ref^M to m_a, has no effect at the abstract level - m_a is kept.

Consider the second case: in definition 5, by conditions 1, 4 and 5, any mode transition, which is not new (case above), starting from m_{c1} refines a transition starting from m_a and any mode transition arriving in m_{c1} also refines a transition arriving in m_a. This means that m_{c1} may offer a subset of possibilities of transitions, compared to m_a. However, since ref^T is surjective (condition 1), all transitions where m_a is involved have to be mapped to the concrete level. Thus another mode m_{c2}, that have to be refined from m_a (due to condition 5), will be associated to transitions that, together with the transitions where m_{c1} is involved, are equivalent to the transitions of m_a. The switching from m_{c1} to m_{c2}, according to the case above, does not correspond to a mode change at the abstract level because m_{c1} and m_{c2} refine the same m_a. Thus, the transitions of m_{c1} and m_{c2} correspond the transitions where m_a is involved.

Since each refinement does not add new mode switching possibilities, except those that have no observable effect at the abstract level, and since the transitions involving concrete modes of a same abstract mode exactly cover the transitions involving the abstract mode, the observable sequence of modes of a concrete modal system can be translated to an observable sequence of modes of the respective abstract modal system by taking each concrete mode m_{ci} of the sequence and substituting by the corresponding abstract one $(ref^M(m_{ri}))$ while eliminating consecutive switchings to the same resulting abstract mode.   □

5   Event-B

Event-B [2] is a state-based formalism closely related to Classical B [3] and Action Systems [15].

Definition 6 (Event-B Model, Event). *An Event-B Model is defined by a tuple $EBModel = (c, s, P, v, I, R_I, E)$ where c are constants and s are sets known in the model; v are the model variables[2]; $P(c, s)$ is a collection of axioms constraining c and s; $I(c, s, v)$ is a model invariant limiting the possible states of v s.t. $\exists c, s, v \cdot P(c, s) \wedge I(c, s, v)$ - i.e. P and I characterise a non-empty set of model states; $R_I(c, s, v')$ is an initialisation action computing initial values for the model variables; and E is a set of model events.*

Given states v, v' an event is a tuple $e = (H, S)$ where $H(c, s, v)$ is the guard and $S(c, s, v, v')$ is the before-after predicate that defines a relation between current and next states. We also denote an event guard by $H(v)$, the before-after predicate by $S(v, v')$ and the initialization action by $R_I(v')$.

Model correctness is demonstrated by generating and discharging a collection of proof obligations. The model *consistency* condition states that whenever an event on an initialisation action is attempted, there exists a suitable new state v' such that the model invariant is maintained - $I(v')$. This is usually stated as two separate proof obligations: a feasibility $(I(v) \wedge H(v) \Rightarrow \exists v' \cdot S(v, v'))$ and an invariant satisfaction obligation $(I(v) \wedge H(v) \wedge S(v, v') \Rightarrow I(v'))$. The behaviour of an Event-B model is the transition system defined as follows.

Definition 7 (Event-B Model Behaviour). *Given $EBModel = (c, s, P, v, I, R_I, E)$, its behaviour is given by a transition system $BST = (BState, BS_0, \rightarrow)$ where: $BState = \{\langle v \rangle | v \text{ is a state}\} \cup Undef$, $BS_0 = Undef$, and $\rightarrow \subseteq BState \times BState$ is the transition relation given by the rules:*

$$\boxed{start}\frac{R_I(v') \wedge I(v')}{Undef \rightarrow \langle v' \rangle}$$

$$\boxed{transition}\frac{\exists (H, S) \in E \cdot I(v) \wedge H(v) \wedge S(v, v') \wedge I(v')}{\langle v \rangle \rightarrow \langle v' \rangle}$$

According to rule **start** the model is initialized to a state satisfying $R_I \wedge I$ and then, as long as there is an enabled event (rule **transition**), the model may evolve by firing an enabled event and computing the next state according to the event's before-after predicate. Events are atomic. In case there is more than one enabled event at a certain state, the demonic choice semantics applies. The semantics of an Event-B model is given in the form of proof semantics, based on Dijkstra's work on weakest preconditions [16].

---

[2] For convenience, as in [3], no distinction is made between a set of variables and a state of a system.

To refine model M one constructs a new model M' that is behaviourally equivalent to the old one. In Event-B, this is achieved by constructing a refinement mapping between M' and M and by discharging a number of refinement proof obligations.

An extensive tool support through the Rodin Platform makes Event-B especially attractiveA development environment for Event-B is supported. An integrated Eclipse-based development environment is actively developed, and open to third-party extensions in the form of Eclipse plug-ins. The main verification technique is theorem proving supported by a collection of theorem provers, but there is also some support for model checking[3].

6   Modal Systems and Event-B

As already discussed, a modal system defines a class of possible models which may be specified using established formal methods. Therefore, a consistency condition is needed such that we can evaluate if a given model satisfies a modal system. In this section we discuss first such condition and then how to enrich the set of proof obligations on an Event-B model to show that it satisfies a modal system specification.

Definition 8 (Modal System Consistency Conditions for an Event-B Model). *Given:*

- *an Event-B model* $EBModel = (c_E, s_E, P_E, v_E, I_E, R_{I_E}, E_E)$ *and*
- *a Modal System* $MSys = (Var_M, Val_M, I_M, M_M, T_M)$
  where $Var_M \subseteq v_E$;
- *a state projection function* $fs_{EtoM}(s_E) = s_M$ *that, given a state* s_E *of the Event-B Model, constructs the corresponding state* s_M *of the modal system by projecting the modal system state;*
- *a predicate projection function* $fp_{EtoM}(P_E) = P_M$ *that, given a predicate over* v_E *constructs the corresponding predicate over* Var_M;

EBModel satisfies MSys iff:

1. *both specify the same invariant on* Var_M: $fp_{EtoM}(I_E) = I_M$
2. *the initialisation is compatible, i.e. the initial state* $EBModel$ *is compatible with the assumption of any initial mode of* $MSys$:
   $$fp_{EtoM}(R_{I_E}) \Rightarrow \bigvee_{\forall t \in T_M \cdot src(t) = \top_M} A_{target(t)}$$
3. (a) *every transition* $t_E : s1_E \to s2_E$ *of the behaviour of* $EBModel$ *has a corresponding transition* $t_M : \langle m1, s1_M \rangle \to \langle m2, s2_M \rangle$ *in the behaviour of* $MSys$, *where* $fs_{EtoM}(s1_E) = s1_M \wedge fs_{EtoM}(s2_E) = s2_M$ *and* t_M *is either:*

---

[3] See Rodin Platform http://www.event-b.org/ (last accessed September 21st 2009). Rodin Development is supported by European Union ICT Projects DEPLOY (2008 to 2012) and RODIN (2004 to 2007).

    i. an internal transition of MSys, when $m1 = m2$ or
    ii. a switching transition of MSys, when $m1 \neq m2$;
(b) every transition $t_M : \langle m1, s1_M \rangle \rightarrow \langle m2, s2_M \rangle$ in the behaviour of MSys has a corresponding transition $t_E : s1_E \rightarrow s2_E$ of the behaviour of EBModel with $fs_{EtoM}(s1_E) = s1_M \wedge fs_{EtoM}(s2_E) = s2_M$.

The following proposition states the compatibility between the computations of the mode system and an Event-B model that realises it, according to Def. 8. Note that this realisation if not just a refinement relation because, besides requiring that the event-B model does not introduce new behavior, it requires also that the event-B model exhibits all possible behaviors defined in the mode system being realised.

Proposition 2. *Given:*

- *a Modal System $MSys = (Var_M, Val_M, I_M, M_M, T_M)$ where $Var_M \subseteq v_E$;*
- *an Event-B model $EBModel = (c_E, s_E, P_E, v_E, I_E, R_{I_E}, E_E)$ and*
- *function fs_{EtoM} and fp_{EtoM} as in Def. 8 ;*

any possible sequence in the transition system of MSys can be translated into a sequence described by the transition system of EBModel and vice versa.

Proof. Condition 1 of Def. 8 assures that the state space is the same (restricted to the variables of *MSys*).

First, we prove that given a transition sequence of *MSys*, we can generate a corresponding one for **EBModel**. Any sequence of *MSys* must start with a transition generated by rule **start**, that generates a state in which the assumption of some initial mode A_k is true. Since this state is also possible in the *EBModel* (because the state spaces are the same) and assumptions of a mode system are disjoint, condition 2 of Def. 8 ensures that there must be a transition generated by rule **startEvent** that leads to this state. From there on, 3b of Def. 8 guarantees that there is a corresponding transition in the transition system of *EBModel* for each transition of *MSys*.

The proof of the other direction (given a transition sequence of *EBModel*, a corresponding one for *MSsys* can be found) is analogous, using 3a of Def. 8. $\square$

Based on these consistency conditions, we now define the proof obligations that are necessary to discharge to show that an Event-B model satisfies a mode system. The first two proof obligations correspond to the first two consistency conditions. The other 3 are necessary to ensure condition 3.

Definition 9 (Proof Obligations).

PO1 (Invariant compatibility):

$$fp_{EtoM}(I_E) = I_M$$

PO2 (Initial state compatibility):

$$fp_{EtoM}(R_{I_E}) \Rightarrow \bigvee_{\forall t \in T_M \cdot src(t) = \top_M} A_{target(t)}$$

PO3 (Events/Modes compatibility):

$$\forall \; E_i = (H_i, S_i) \in E_{EBModel} \cdot \forall \; M_j = A_j/G_j \in M_{MSys}.$$
$$(H_i(v) \wedge A_j(v) \wedge S(v,v')) \Rightarrow \tag{1}$$
$$(\; (A_j(v') \wedge G_j(v,v')) \vee \tag{2}$$
$$((\exists M_k = A_k/G_k \in M_{MSys} \cdot A_k(v')) \wedge (j \rightsquigarrow k) \in T_{MSys}) \;) \tag{3}$$

PO4 (Event guard/Mode assumption compatibility):

$$\forall \; E_i = (H_i, S_i) \in E_{EBModel}, H_i(v) \Rightarrow \bigvee_{\forall M_j = A_j/G_j \in M_{MSys}} A_j(v)$$

PO5 (Events/Transitions compatibility):

$$\forall \; (i \rightsquigarrow j) \in T_{MSys}, M_i = (A_i/G_i), M_j = (A_j/G_j) \in M_{MSys}.$$
$$\exists E_k = (H_k, S_k) \in E_{EBModel} \wedge (H_k(v) \wedge A_i(v) \wedge S_k(v,v') \wedge A_j(v'))$$

Condition 3 of Def. 8 relates the transitions of Event-B Model and Modal System. Condition 3a states that any transition in the Event-B Model is a possible transition of the Modal System (3(a)i or 3(a)ii). This can be shown on the structure of events. Each event of the model, whenever enabled in a mode, will either: preserve the modes assumption and guarantee in case of 3(a)i or switch mode according to existing mode switching transition in case of 3(a)ii. Proof obligation **PO3** has to be discharged to cover this condition. If an event guard and a mode assumption are true (line 1), the event is possible in that mode. In this case the event either describes an internal transition (line 2) or a mode transition (line 3). In the first case, both assumption and guarantee of the current mode have to be preserved by the event. In the second case, the modal system specifies the possibility of such transition and the event establishes the new assumption.

Since our mode definition allows the invariant to be weaker than the conjunction of assumptions, it is needed to show that any event is enabled only when an assumption is, otherwise the event is specifying some behaviour that does nor match any mode definition. This is assured by discharging proof obligation **PO4**.

Condition 3b of Def. 8 states that all defined mode switching transitions have a corresponding event in the Event-B model. The corresponding proof obligation is **PO5**.

Reachability Properties. To completely assure condition 3b, it has to be shown, additionally to the given proof obligations, that each mode transition in the Modal System behaviour is possible in the Event-B model behaviour. Proof obligations to discharge such properties can not be generated in general, they are specific for each model. They can be assured either by structuring a model such that these properties can be proven or by using additional analysis techniques such as model checking.

7   Cruise Control Case Study

The Case Study is presented in the following parts: first we exemplify modelling with modes; then we discuss aspects of building an Event-B model to realise a modes specification; thirdly we exemplify proof obligations on the case study, and then general comments are made.

7.1   Modelling with Modes

The Cruise Control case study illustrates the proposed technique to the development of a simplified version of one of the DEPLOY case studies [8]. The system assists a driver in reaching and maintaining some predefined speed. In the current modelling we assume an idealised car and idealised driving conditions such that the car always responds to the commands and the actual speed is updated according to the control system commands.

Figure 1 presents the diagrams of the most abstract modal system for the cruise control (A) and the resulting models of three successive refinement steps (B to D). The assumption and guarantee for each mode is given in Figure 2. The diagrams use a visual notation loosely based on Modecharts [9]. A mode is represented by a box with mode name; a mode transition is an arrow connecting two modes. The direction of an arrow indicates the previous and next modes in a transition. Special modes $\top_M$ and $\bot_M$ are omitted so that initiating and terminating transitions appear connected with a single mode. Refinement is expressed by nesting boxes. A refined diagram with an outgoing arrow from an abstract mode is equivalent to outgoing arrows from each of the concrete modes.

At the most abstract level (Figure 1(A)) we introduce mode *IGNITION_CYCLE* to represent the activity from the instant the ignition is turned on to the instant it is turned off, represented by transitions *ignitionOn* and *ignitionOff*. During an ignition cycle, its guarantee must be respected independently of operation by the driver or by the cruise control. The model includes: the state of ignition (on/off) modelled by a boolean flag *ig*; the current speed of the car (a modelling approximation of an actual car speed), stored in variable *sa*; a safe speed limit *speedLimit* above which the car should not be; and a safe speed variation *maxSpeedV*. No memory is retained about states in the previous ignition cycle.

In the first refinement step *IGNITION_CYCLE* is refined by *DRIVER*, corresponding to the activity when cruise control is off, and *CRUISE_CONTROL*, when cruise control is active (Figure 1(B)). *on/off* interface buttons to activate/deactivate the cruise control are mapped to transition events *ccOn* and *ccOff*. This refinement introduces: the state of cruise control (on/off), modelled by boolean flag *cc*; the target speed that a cruise control is to achieve and maintain, represented by variable *st*; an allowance interval *isp* that determines how much actual speed could deviate from a target speed. The next refinement step (Figure 1(C)) introduces different operating strategies: if the difference between current (*sa*) and target (*st*) speeds is within an acceptable error interval (*isp*), the cruise control works to *MAINTAIN* the current speed. Otherwise, it employs different procedures to *APPROACH* the target speed. Switching from *DRIVER* to *CRUISE_CONTROL* may

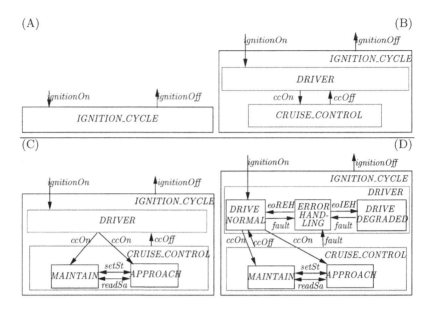

Fig. 1. Cruise control refinement steps (A) to (D)

either establish the assumptions of *APPROACH* or *MAINTAIN*, depending on the difference between *st* and *sa*. In either of these two modes the cruise control can be switched off and the control returned to the driver.

At any time failures of the surrounding components (e.g. airbag activated, low energy in battery, etc.) may happen and are signalled to the cruise control system. In the presence of an error, the control is returned to the driver and handling measures are activated. Errors can be reversible or irreversible. After being handled, the first ones allow the cruise control to become available again; the irreversible ones cause the cruise control to become unavailable during the ignition cycle. According to the last refinement step (Figure 1(D)), when an error is detected it is registered in an *error* variable. If an error is signalled in any of the system modes, the system switches to *ERROR_HANDLING*, where control is with the driver. Eventually error handling reestablishes *DRIVE_NORMAL*, with full functionality available, or switches to *DRIVE_DEGRADED* mode where the cruise control is not available. Note that although the guarantees of these three concrete modes from *DRIVER* are the same, they have distinct mode transition possibilities: in modes *DRIVE_DEGRADED* and *ERROR_HANDLING* the cruise control cannot be turned on. After finishing error handling the system continues in either normal or degraded mode.

7.2   Building an Event-B Model to Realise the Modal System

Once a modal system is sufficiently developed (but not necessarily finalised) one can start building an Event-B model implementing it. The static part of a model, such as variables and invariant is already elaborated to some degree in a modal

mode	assumption	guarantee
IGNITION_ CYCLE	ignition is on	keep speed under limit and (ac/de)celarate safely
	$ig = true$	$(sa < speedLimit) \land (|sa' - sa| < maxSpeedV)$
DRIVER	ignition cycle assumption and cruise control off	ignition cycle guarantee
	$ig = true \land cc = false$	$(sa < speedLimit) \land (|sa' - sa| < maxSpeedV)$
CRUISE_ CONTROL	ignition cycle assumption and cruise control on	ignition cycle guarantee and maintain or approach target speed or
	$ig = true \land cc = true$	$(sa < speedLimit) \land (|sa' - sa| < maxSpeedV) \land$ $(|sa' - st'| \leq isp \lor |sa' - st'| < |sa - st|)$
APPROACH	cruise control assumption and speed not close to target	cruise control guarantee and approach target speed
	$ig = true \land cc = true \land$ $|sa' - st'| > isp$	$(sa < speedLimit) \land (|sa' - sa| < maxSpeedV) \land$ $(|sa' - st'| < |sa - st|)$
MAINTAIN	cruise control assumption and speed close to target	cruise control guarantee and maintain target speed
	$ig = true \land cc = true \land$ $|sa' - st'| \leq isp$	$(sa < speedLimit) \land (|sa' - sa| < maxSpeedV) \land$ $(|sa' - st'| \leq isp)$
DRIVE_ NORMAL	driver assumption and and no error	driver guarantee (and cruise control available)
	$ig = true \land cc = false \land$ $error = false$	$(sa < speedLimit) \land$ $(|sa' - sa| < maxSpeedV)$
ERROR_ HAND-	driver assumption and error and handling not finished	driver guarantee and recovery measures (and cruise control not available)
	$ig = true \land cc = false \land$ $error = true \land eHand = true$	$(sa < speedLimit) \land$ $(|sa' - sa| < maxSpeedV)$
DRIVE_ DEGRADED	driver assumption and error and handling finished	driver guarantee (and cruise control not available)
	$ig = true \land cc = false \land$ $error = true \land eHand = false$	$(sa < speedLimit) \land$ $(|sa' - sa| < maxSpeedV)$

Fig. 2. Modes assumptions and guarantees

system specification. These are simply copied into an initial Event-B machine. Next, one has to study a mode diagram to grasp the general architecture of a system: the modes and the mode transitions. It helps to begin such a study with the most abstract diagram as it gives the understanding of the relation between the system modes.

We present excerpts from an Event-B model realising the modal system developed for the case study. For the most detailed modal specification, we have the Event-B declaration of variables and invariant on the right. It is merely a result of mechanically translating definitions from the modal specification into the Event-B syntax. The referenced context *cc_ctx* contains declarations of sets and constants such *SPEED* and *speedLimit*.

> **machine** *cruisecontrol*
> **sees** *cc_ctx*
> **variables** $ig, cc, sa, st, error$
> **invariant**
> $ig \in BOOL$
> $cc \in BOOL$
> $sa \in SPEED$
> $st \in SPEED$
> $st > 0$
> $error \in BOOL$
> $eHand \in BOOL$

Initially, the invariant has no interesting statements relating to the safety properties of the system. This is because in a modal system safety properties are put into the guarantees of individual modes. However, once it comes to the verification of an Event-B model against a modal specification the proof obligations (see Def. 9), derived from the condition that an event must satisfy a mode guarantee, would suggest additional invariants. Hence, the process of showing modes/Event-B consistency gradually adds more details into an Event-B model with each additional discharged proof obligation.

In Event-B an initialisation is a special event assigning initial values to all the model variables. While in a modal specification there is no explicit discussion of initialisation in terms of state computations, the conditions on all mode transitions originating at $\top_M$ result in a rather detailed characterisation of possible variable initialisations.

For the cruise control case study the initial state should satisfy the invariant and the assumption of the initiating mode 'Drive Normal' and thus the least constrained initialisation event has the form shown on the right.

```
initialisation
ig := TRUE ∥ cc := FALSE ∥
sa :∈ SPEED ∥ st :∈ ℕ₁ ∥
error := FALSE ∥ eHand :: BOOL
```

The non-deterministic initialisation of *sa* (car speed) should raise concerns as it contradicts our understanding that a car is initially stationary. There is, however, nothing the mode specification that tells this and it is one of those many details we have abstracted away in a mode specification. In this case we choose to strengthen the initialisation event and state that initially *sa* is zero. Obviously, such initialisation also satisfies the requirements to an event implementing initiating mode transitions. The counterpart of the initialisation event is an event halting the current ignition cycle. This is implemented with an event setting *ig* to $FALSE$:

$$ignition\_off = \textbf{when } ig = TRUE \textbf{ then } ig := FALSE \textbf{ end}$$

Let us now take a look at how a mode is implemented. There is no ready rule for generating events from a mode description. This is the part where a designer has the most freedom within the limits set by the assumption and guarantee of a mode. There is no limitation on the number of events realising a mode. As example, we have found it convenient to have two events for mode *Drive Normal Mode*, each responsible for either decrease or increase in vehicle speed.

$speed\_up = \textbf{any } si \textbf{ where}$	$speed\_down = \textbf{any } sd \textbf{ where}$
$si \in SPEED$	$sd \in SPEED$
$si < maxSpeedV$	$sd < maxSpeedV$
$sa + si < speedLimit$	$sa - sd \in SPEED$
$ig = TRUE$	$ig = TRUE$
$cc = FALSE$	$cc = FALSE$
$\textbf{then}$	$\textbf{then}$
$sa := sa + si$	$sa := sa - sd$
$\textbf{end}$	$\textbf{end}$

7.3   Examples of Proof Obligations Generated from the Modal System

Now we exemplify the application of the proof obligations in Def. 9 to the case study.

PO1 is discharged trivially because the Event-B model has the same variable definitions of the modal system and the same invariant.

PO2 reduces to prove that the initialization implies the assumption of the initial mode which is *Drive Normal Mode*.

According to **PO4**, for each of the events we have to demonstrate that it is enabled only when the mode assumption holds. For instance, for event *speed_up* we have:

$$\forall si \cdot si \in SPEED \wedge si < maxSpeedV \wedge$$
$$sa + si < speedLimit \wedge ig = TRUE \wedge cc = FALSE \implies$$
$$ig = TRUE \wedge cc = FALSE$$

According to **PO3**, it is required to show for each event that it either respects the mode guarantee (Def. 9, **PO3**, line 2) or that it switches to another mode according to a possible mode transition (line 3). Below we show the proof to event *speed_up* in respecting guarantee of *Drive Normal Mode*.

$$\forall si \cdot si \in SPEED \wedge si < maxSpeedV \wedge$$
$$sa + si < speedLimit \wedge ig = TRUE \wedge cc = FALSE \wedge$$
$$sa' = sa + si \wedge ig' = ig \wedge cc' = cc \wedge$$
$$st' = st \wedge error' = error \wedge eHand' = eHand \implies$$
$$ig' = TRUE \wedge cc' = FALSE \wedge$$
$$(sa' < speedLimit) \wedge |sa' - sa| < maxSpeedV$$

According to **PO5**, for each transition there must be at least one event implementing it. Event *ignition_off*, for instance, is shown to implement transitions from any mode to $\perp_M$.

The proof obligations, being formulated as Event-B theorem (extra conditions on Event-B models), are automatically discharged by the Rodin platform theorem prover. This is also true the rest of proof obligations, coming from modes and native to Event-B.

7.4   General Comments on the Case Study

From our experience, the construction of an Event-B from a modal specification is a fairly straightforward process. However, we have also found that, for the few initial development steps, constructing an Event-B model for each step of a modal system refinement makes little impact on understanding the system. This because a mode specification embodies basically the same information (albeit in a structured manner) as an abstract Event-B model.

On the other hand, in absence of a dedicated tool support for checking modal specifications, an Event-B implementation provides a verification platform in the form of the Rodin toolkit. This also defines how we see the application of the approach. A developer would start with translating requirements into a high-level modal specification. More requirements are captured by refining modes and, at some point, an Event-B model is constructed. For several further steps, modal and Event-B developments go hand-in-hand until no further detalisation can be done at the level of a modal specification. This would mark the final transition into an Event-B model. However, even at that point a modal specification is not forgotten. The consistency conditions proved at an earlier refinement are preserved through a refinement chain and thus, even after several refinement steps, an Event-B model still respects all the properties of a modal specification from which it was initially derived.

8 Conclusions

A representative class of critical systems employs the notion of operation modes. While this notion is supported in some languages [9,12], a formal definition for modal systems as well as approaches for their rigorous construction could not be found. Following previous work [1], in this paper we formalize modal systems and modal systems refinement. The use of modes and modal system refinement helps to organize system properties, to trace requirements into model definition and helps to impose control structure in the system. Such advantages are specially welcomed together with a state-based formal method. As a further contribution of this paper we take Event-B and show how to demonstrate that a model in Event-B is according to a modal system, i.e. respecting assumptions, guarantees and mode switchings. Although the satisfaction conditions were shown for Event-B, the same ideas can be generalised to other formal methods.

Using modal systems refinement and the notion of modal system consistency for an Event-B model, both defined in this paper, together with the common Event-B refinement notion, it is possible to build a concrete Event-B model $EBModel_C$ refining an $EBModel_A$ and show that it satisfies an $MSys_C$ which refines $MSys_A$. A natural extension of this work is to formally define restrictions on the refinement starting from $EBModel_A$ leading to $EBModel_C$ which by construction satisfies $MSys_C$. Such restrictions would be based on the refinement from $MSys_A$ to $MSys_C$. Additionally, in future work we intend to investigate the implications of mode concurrency.

Acknowledgements

We would like to thank John Fitzgerald for the valuable comments made on earlier versions of this work.

References

1. Iliasov, A., Dotti, F.L., Romanovsky, A.: Structuring specifications with modes. In: Proceedings of the fourth Latin-American Symposium on Dependable Computing, pp. 81–88. IEEE Computer Society, Los Alamitos (2009)

2. Abrial, J.R., Métayer, C.: Rodin deliverable 3.2 - event-b language. Technical report, Newcastle University, England (2005), http://rodin.cs.ncl.ac.uk
3. Abrial, J.R.: The B-Book: Assigning Programs to Meanings. Cambridge University Press, Cambridge (2005)
4. Butler, R.W.: Nasa technical memorandum 110255 an introduction to requirements capture using pvs: Specification of a simple autopilot (1996)
5. Miller, S.P.: Specifying the mode logic of a flight guidance system in core and scr. In: FMSP 1998: Proceedings of the second workshop on Formal methods in software practice, pp. 44–53. ACM, New York (1998)
6. Lygeros, J., Godbole, D.N., Broucke, M.E.: Design of an extended architecture for degraded modes of operation of ivhs. In: American Control Conference, pp. 3592–3596 (1995)
7. Abrial, J.R., Börger, E., Langmaack, H. (eds): Formal Methods for Industrial Applications, Specifying and Programming the Steam Boiler Control, the book grow out of a Dagstuhl Seminar (June 1995); Abrial, J.R., Börger, E., Langmaack, H. (eds.): Dagstuhl Seminar 1995. LNCS, vol. 1165. Springer, Heidelberg (1996)
8. Abrial, J.R., Bryans, J., Butler, M., Falampin, J., Hoang, T.S., Ilic, D., Latvala, T., Rossa, C., Roth, A., Varpaaniemi, K.: Report on knowledge transfer - deploy deliverable d5 (February 2009)
9. Jahanian, F., Mok, A.: Modechart: A specification language for real-time systems. IEEE Transactions on Software Engineering 20(12), 933–947 (1994)
10. Real, J., Crespo, A.: Mode change protocols for real-time systems: A survey and a new proposal. Real-Time Syst. 26(2), 161–197 (2004)
11. Fohler, G.: Realizing changes of operational modes with a pre run-time scheduled hard real-time system. In: Proceedings of the Second International Workshop on Responsive Computer Systems, pp. 287–300. Springer, Heidelberg (1992)
12. Peter, H., Feiler, D.P., Gluch, J.J.H.: The architecture analysis & design language (aadl): An introduction. Technical Note CMU/SEI-2006-TN-011, Software Engineering Institute - Carnegie Mellon University (2006)
13. Mustafiz, S., Kienzle, J., Berlizev, A.: Addressing degraded service outcomes and exceptional modes of operation in behavioural models. In: SERENE 2008: Proceedings of the 2008 RISE/EFTS Joint International Workshop on Software Engineering for Resilient Systems, pp. 19–28. ACM, New York (2008)
14. Robert, T., Fabre, J.C., Roy, M.: Application of Early Error Detection for Handling Degraded Modes of Operation. In: Waeselynck, H. (ed.) Proceedings of the 12th European Workshop on Dependable Computing, EWDC 2009 12th European Workshop on Dependable Computing, EWDC 2009, Toulouse, France, p. 3 (May 2009); Rapport LAAS 09171
15. Back, R.J., Sere, K.: Stepwise Refinement of Action Systems. In: van de Snepscheut, J.L.A. (ed.) Proceedings of the International Conference on Mathematics of Program Construction, 375th Anniversary of the Groningen University, London, UK, pp. 115–138. Springer, Heidelberg (1989)
16. Dijkstra, E.: A Discipline of Programming. Prentice-Hall International, Englewood Cliffs (1976)

Refinement-Preserving Co-evolution

Thomas Ruhroth and Heike Wehrheim

Universität Paderborn
Institut für Informatik
33098 Paderborn, Germany
{thomas.ruhroth,wehrheim}@uni-paderborn.de

Abstract. Software changes during its lifetime. Likewise, specifications change during their design time, e.g. by removing, adding or changing operations. In a refinement-based approach to software design, we moreover do not deal with a single but with a *chain* of specifications, related via refinement. Changes thus need to be consistently made to all specifications in the chain so as to keep the refinement structure.

In this paper, we describe such *co-evolutions* of specifications in the context of the formal method Object-Z. More specifically, given a particular evolution of a specification we show how to construct a corresponding evolution for its refinements. We furthermore formally prove our co-evolutions to maintain refinement, thus giving rise to a notion of *refinement-preserving co-evolution*.

1 Introduction

Today, Model Driven Development (MDD) is advocated as a means for designing high-quality software. The MDD approach puts models into the center of software design and proposes a stepwise development, from a platform-independent through a platform-specific model to the final implementation. In a formal approach to MDD, such models are written in a formal specification language, and the incrementally designed models are related by *refinement* [5, 3] to guarantee consistency of lower level with higher level specifications. This approach gives rise to a *chain* of specifications with a refinement ordering.

While in use, software changes along with its specifications. Every time a fault is detected or the requirements of a system change, models as well as software have to be modified. The ongoing continuous modification of software or specifications is referred to as *evolution*. This includes the correction of faults, the addition of new features, or the change of the architectural structure.

The main challenge evolution imposes on a formal MDD approach lies in the maintenance of the refinement structure: how can we guarantee that an evolution of the platform-independent model is consistently reflected in lower level models, i.e. how can we co-evolve all specifications in the chain while keeping their refinement relationship? Figure 1 graphically depicts this question for a chain of just two models: given a specification $Spec^A$, its refinement $Spec^C$ (these two forming our chain) and A's evolution into $\widehat{Spec^A}$, can we construct (from the

K. Breitman and A. Cavalcanti (Eds.): ICFEM 2009, LNCS 5885, pp. 620–638, 2009.

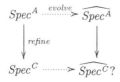

Fig. 1. Challenge: Constructing co-evolutions

known refinement between $Spec^A$ and $Spec^C$ and the known way of evolution) a specification $\widehat{Spec^C}$ out of $Spec^C$, such that $\widehat{Spec^C}$ is a refinement of $\widehat{Spec^A}$?

Co-evolution maintaining some sort of consistency between models has so far mainly been looked at in the area of UML models. Here, usually two sorts of consistency are distinguished: *vertical* consistency relates models at different levels of abstraction whereas *horizontal* consistency treats different views (or diagrams) within one model. The preservation of vertical consistency is for instance tackled in [25] and [1], horizontal consistency (there, deadlock-freedom) is treated in [6]. Consistency between models and corresponding implementations has been investigated in for instance [2, 10]. According to this classification into vertical and horizontal consistency, our interest is in finding co-evolutions which preserve vertical consistency, i.e. refinement. We moreover aim at employing our approach in a *formal* design with models written in a formal specification language, thus necessitating a precise definition of consistency (which is given when fixing a notion of refinement) and a formal proof of preservation for co-evolutions.

In the area of formal methods, an approach aiming at a similar task, however, with a different technique, has been proposed in [26]. The assumption there is that the chain of refinements has been constructed using some rules of a refinement calculus. Once the top level specification changes, the chain is tried to be rebuild by applying the same rules in the same order on the changed specification. In some cases, this necessitates manual adaptations of the constructed specifications. Similar in spirit is the technique proposed in [19] which assumes evolutions to be retrenchments and then calculates lower level models, much in the sense of [4] which calculates refinements. Contrary to these two approaches, we aim at constructing appropriate corresponding *evolutions* for the lower level models which, when applied, then - by construction - guarantee preservation of refinement.

In this paper, we thus present a *constructive* solution to the evolution of refinement chains that allows for a co-evolution of a specification and its refinements. As specification language we use the object-oriented state-based method Object-Z [23]. This gives us the necessary formal background and immediately supplies us with a definition of refinement, i.e. *data refinement*. The refinement chains will thus consist of Object-Z models related via data refinement. Given this setting, we then systematically investigate different forms of evolution (e.g. new variables, new operations, changes and removal of operations). For every such evolution we give rules for constructing the corresponding co-evolution on a refinement. We prove soundness of our construction, i.e. show that every such co-evolution preserves refinement.

2   Evolution: An Example

In this section we will provide an example of the evolution of a simple prepaid cash system, pas can sometimes be found in theme parks. A customer loads money to a card and can then pay with it. For simplicity, we concentrate on the payment only in the specification, loading is elided.

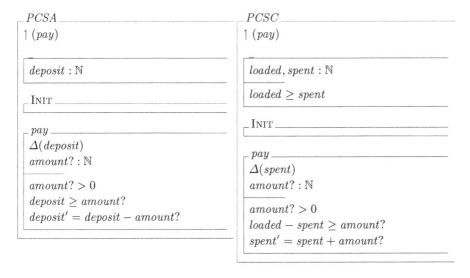

Fig. 2. Initial specification PCSA and its refinement PCSC

In the left part of Fig. 2, we see the Object-Z class *PCSA* (Prepaid Cash System A) which gives us the high level specification. The class description consists of a visibility list, a state and an init schema and, here one operation schema. In the example, the variable *deposit* defined in the state schema holds the amount of money which can be spent. The init schema is empty and thus allows for arbitrary values of *deposit*. The class furthermore defines one operation *pay* modelling the payment. The delta list ($\Delta(deposit)$) enumerates all state variables that can be changed by the operation. The input variable *amount?* of type natural number is the amount to be paid. In the lower part of the schema there are some constraints describing the operation, where primed variables always refer to the after state of the operation.

Next to the high level specification *PCSA*, we see one possible refinement called *PCSC*. In the following we will also refer to *PCSA* as the abstract or high level and to *PCSC* as the concrete or low level specification. The main difference between *PCSA* and *PCSC* is that for statistical reasons not the deposit but the money loaded on the system and that spent are being held in different variables. Operation *pay* consequently has to be adjusted to this idea. Specifications *PCSA* and *PCSC* are in a refinement relation. To see this, we have to give a formal definition of refinement.

As we are dealing with Object-Z specification here, we use data refinement [5], which is usually proven by downward and upward simulations. Here we concentrate on downward simulation[1]. It assumes that two Object-Z classes A and C are given, which both consist of a state schema, an initialization schema, and some operation schemas: $A = (State^A, Init^A, \{Op_i^A\}_{i \in I})$ and $C = (State^C, Init^C, \{Op_i^C\}_{i \in I})$, where I is some index set for operations. Note that I is the same for A and C and serves as an enumeration of the operations which constitute the interface of the class, i.e. its externally visible operations.

Definition 1. *C is a* downward simulation *of A, $A \sqsubseteq_{DS} C$, if there is a retrieve relation R between $State^A$ and $State^C$ such that the following holds:*

1. *Initialization:* $\forall\, State^C \bullet Init^C \Rightarrow (\exists\, State^A \bullet Init^A \wedge R)$,
2. *Applicability:* $\forall\, i \in I, \forall\, State^A, State^C \bullet R \Rightarrow (pre\, Op_i^A \Leftrightarrow pre\, Op_i^C)$,
3. *Correctness:* $\forall\, i \in I, \forall\, State^A, State^C, State^{C'} \bullet$
$$R \wedge Op_i^C \Rightarrow \exists\, State^{A'} \bullet R' \wedge Op_i^A.$$

A downward simulation ensures that every refinement of an abstract specification can be used as a substitute for the abstract specification. To this end, we need to show that the concrete specification can simulate the abstract one. Given a relation R between states of concrete and abstract, the first condition guarantees that every initial state of the concrete has a corresponding initial abstract state. The second condition guarantees that concrete and abstract operations are either both applicable in related states or both not, and condition 3 ensures compatible results of operation execution. In the definition we use $pre\, Op$, which denotes the precondition of the operation Op.

Definition 2 (Precondition [5]). *For an operation Op on state $State$, with inputs $Inps$ and outputs $Outs$, its precondition is defined by*

$$pre\, Op = \exists\, State';\; Outs \bullet Op.$$

Thus, $pre\, Op$ will be a schema on $State$ and $Inps$ indication for which before-state and inputs Op provides a possible after-state and output.

In the correctness condition, we use $State'$ to describe the after state of an operation, and use the retrieve relation R on the primed states (R'). Sometimes we also use the term downward simulation and refinement in the context of operations. In this case, this term refers to the applicability and correctness of a single operation.

In the remainder of this paper the class names of the abstract specification will always end with the letter A (abstract) and the refinements will end with the letter C (concrete). We will say that a class C *refines* a class A or is a *refinement* of A if there is a downward simulation from A to C. For $PCSA$ and $PCSC$ we can give a retrieve relation R such that $PCSC$ is a refinement of $PSCA$:

---

[1] All of our results given later hold in a similar way for upward simulations.

```
__R_____
  PCSA
  PCSC
  _____
  PCSA.deposit = PCSC.loaded - PCSC.spent
```

This relation relates the value of variable *deposit* to the values of *loaded* and *spent*.

Evolution of the initial specification. The two specifications give us our (two-elements only) refinement chain. Next, we carry out several evolutions on our top level specification *PCSA* as our cash system shall get more features. First (1) we want to add a bonus system so that the customer can gain bonuses, which can be used to gain benefits. Thus, in our first evolution we add a variable *bonus* and an operation *gainbonus* to *PCSA* resulting in the class in Fig. 3.

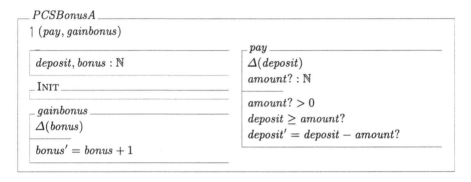

Fig. 3. Abstract class after first evolution

Specification *PCSBonusA* is next further evolved in several steps. Figure 4 shows the final abstract specification, the intermediate steps are elided. Using the bonus extension, it should be possible to pay and gain a bonus simultaneously, thus we add a further operation in the next evolution (evolution 2), which is simply the combination of the operations *pay* and *gainbonus* (defined as $payWithBonus \hat{=} pay \wedge gainbonus$). The third change (evolution 3) concerns the conversion of bonuses into money when a customer has collected at least 10 bonuses. This lets us add an operation *convertbonus*. Up to here, we have enhanced the specification with a bonus system, next we want the bonus pay to be the only pay function. Therefore, we hide the operation *pay* (evolution 4) and (evolution 5) expand the definition of *payWithBonus* so as to have a direct definition in a schema (not by a conjunction of schemas) and finally remove the now unused operation *pay* (evolution 6). The question is now whether and if yes, how, we can carry out corresponding evolutions on *PCSC* so as to keep the initially existing refinement relation between high and lower level specification.

___ *PCSBonus2A* _____

1 (*payWithBonus*, *gainbonus*, *convertbonus*)

_____	_ *gainbonus* _____
deposit, *bonus* : $\mathbb{N}$	$\Delta(bonus)$
_ INIT _____	$bonus' = bonus + 1$
_ *convertbonus* _____	_ *payWithBonus* _____
$\Delta(bonus, deposit)$	$\Delta(deposit, bonus)$
_____	$amount? : \mathbb{N}$
$bonus > 10$	_____
$bonus' = bonus - 10$	$amount? > 0$
$deposit' = deposit + 10$	$deposit \geq amount?$
	$deposit' = deposit - amount?$
	$bonus' = bonus + 1$

Fig. 4. Final abstract specification

3 Evolutions for Object-Z

Before answering the question raised in the last section, we will present a systematic view on evolutions and introduce a notation for evolutions in an object-oriented context.

Groves [9] has shown that for the Z notation it is sufficient for the description of evolutions to use schema operators together with the introduction of new schemas. In contrast to Z, where the basic unit is a schema which has a simple structure, in Object-Z the basic structure class has a complex interior. Therefore we have to consider more complex evolutions that consider the different parts such as state schema, init schema and different operation schemas. Table 1 gives a summary of evolutions for Object-Z as covered by our approach. These evolutions can be divided into groups that are distinguished by the sort (e.g. replacement or modification) and the location of the evolution (e.g. operation or state schema). The table gives - beside the name and the notation for an evolution - also the definition in terms of a class tuple and a condition. In the conditions we use some special helper functions which have been defined by Smith [23] for the Object-Z semantics: the function **vars** gives all variables of an operation or state, functions **input** and **output** return a set with the input resp. output variables of an operation.

To explain just one notation in more depth, consider evolution "Init Conjunction" on init schemas:

$$A[Init \wedge NInit/Init] \;\widehat{=}\; (State, Init \wedge NInit, \{Op_i\}_{i\in I})$$
$$\text{if } \mathbf{vars}(State) \supseteq \mathbf{vars}(NInit)$$

which defines the evolution to replace (/) schema *Init* with *Init* $\wedge$ *NInit* in an existing class $A = (State, Init, \{Op_i\}_{i\in I})$, i.e. to add a new conjunct to the init

schema assuming that the variables in the additional conjunct have all been defined in the state schema. In a similar way, modifications to operation schemas
are defined, also allowing for composing an existing operation with a new part
using the Object-Z operators of parallel composition, choice or sequential composition. A special type of evolutions are all sorts of *refactorings* (last line in the
table). Refactorings for instance remove unused parts or change the structure
of specifications while maintaining their behaviour. Often they also take additional parameters, hence we have added some optional argument $\langle para \rangle$ to their
definition. For a more detailed discussion see for instance [22].

Next, we define all of our evolutions of the previous section in terms of this
notation. The first evolution has added a variable and a new operation to *PCSA*.
This can be seen as conjoining the existing class with a new one containing just
this variable and schema, thus is an application of class evolution "Disjoint
Conjunction" (with class *Bonus*):

The second evolution has introduced an operation *payWithBonus* defined as a
conjunction of two existing operations. In Table 1 we find this evolution in the
part *New operation as combination of existing operations* labelled as *Conjunction*. In a similar way, we can describe all evolutions of the example, in summary
we thus carry out the following five evolutions:

$$PCSBonusA \cong PCSA \oslash BonusA \qquad (1)$$

$$PCSBonus0A \cong PCSBonusA \oplus \{payWithBonus \cong pay \wedge gainbonus\} \qquad (2)$$

$$PCSBonus1A \cong PCSBonus0A \oplus \{convertBonus\} \qquad (3)$$

$$PCSBonus2A \cong PCSBonus1A \backslash \{pay\} \qquad (4)$$

$$PCSBonus3A \cong ExpandOperation(PCSBonus2A, payWithBonus) \qquad (5)$$

$$PCSBonus4A \cong Remove(PCSBonus3A, pay) \qquad (6)$$

The last two evolutions are applications of refactorings: first with "Expand Operation" we expand the definition of *payWithBonus* (hence *payWithBonus* is the
parameter for this refactoring) to give a direct operation definition and then we
remove the unused operation *pay* (thus *pay* is the parameter here).

Having obtained a clear description of the evolutions, we now need to find
out how to carry out the corresponding co-evolution on *A*'s refinement *PCSC*.
Figure 5 illustrates the problem: we need to find six concrete specifications which
are refinements of the six abstract specifications constructed by our evolutions.

Table 1. Some Evolutions for Object-Z of a Class A. ($State$, $NInv$: state schema; A,B : classes; $Init$, $NInit$: init schemas; Op, $NSch$: operation schema; I : operation index set; $para$: some parameter for the refactoring).

Name	Symbol	Definition	Conditions
Evolutions of type class/class			
Conjunction	$A \wedge B$	$(State^A \wedge State^B, Init^A \wedge Init^B, \{Op_i\}_{i\in I})$	$\{Op_i\}_{i\in I} = \{Op_i^A\}_{i\in I\backslash B} \cup \{Op_i^B\}_{i\in I\backslash A} \cup \{Op_i^A \wedge Op_i^B\}_{i\in I_A\cap I_B}$
Disjunction	$A \vee B$	$(State^A \vee State^B, Init^A \vee Init^B, \{Op_i\}_{i\in I})$	$\{Op_i\}_{i\in I} = \{Op_i^A\}_{i\in I\backslash B} \cup \{Op_i^B\}_{i\in I\backslash A} \cup \{Op_i^A [] Op_i^B\}_{i\in I_A\cap I_B}$
Disjoint Conj.	$A \oslash B$	$(State^A \wedge State^B, Init^A \wedge Init^B, \{Op_i^A\}_{i\in I_A} \cup \{Op_i^B\}_{i\in I_B})$	$I_A \cap I_B = \varnothing \wedge \mathbf{vars}(State^A) \cap \mathbf{vars}(State^B) = \varnothing$
Disjoint Dis.	$A \oslash B$	$(State^A \vee State^B, Init^A \wedge Init^A, \{Op_i^B\}_{i\in I_B})$	$I_A \cap I_B = \varnothing \wedge \mathbf{vars}(State^A) \cap \mathbf{vars}(State^B) = \varnothing$
Evolutions of type Inv/Inv-schema			
Invar. Conjunction	$A[State \wedge NInv/State]$	$(State \wedge NInv, Init, \{Op_i\}_{i\in I})$	$\mathbf{vars}(State) \supseteq \mathbf{vars}(NInv)$
Invar. Disjunction	$A[State \vee NInv/State]$	$(State \vee NInv, Init, \{Op_i\}_{i\in I})$	$\mathbf{vars}(State) \supseteq \mathbf{vars}(NInv)$
Evolutions of type Init/Init-schema			
Init Conjunction	$A[Init \wedge NInit/Init]$	$(State, Init \wedge NInit, \{Op_i\}_{i\in I})$	$\mathbf{vars}(State) \supseteq \mathbf{vars}(NInit)$
Init Disjunction	$A[Init \vee NInit/Init]$	$(State, Init \vee NInit, \{Op_i\}_{i\in I})$	$\mathbf{vars}(State) \supseteq \mathbf{vars}(NInit)$
Modification of existing operations			
Conjunction	$A[Op_j \wedge NSch/Op_j]$	$(State, Init, \{Op_i\}_{i\in I\wedge\neq j} \cup \{Op_j \mathrel{\hat=} Op_j \wedge NSch\})$	$\mathbf{vars}(State) \cup \mathbf{input}(NSch) \cup \mathbf{output}(NSch) \supseteq \mathbf{vars}(NSch) \wedge j\in I$
Parallel	$A[Op_j \parallel NSch/Op_j]$	$(State, Init, \{Op_i\}_{i\in I\wedge\neq j} \cup \{Op_j \mathrel{\hat=} Op_j \parallel NSch\})$	$\mathbf{vars}(State) \cup \mathbf{input}(NSch) \cup \mathbf{output}(NSch) \supseteq \mathbf{vars}(NSch) \wedge j\in I$
Ass Parallel	$A[Op_j \parallel_! NSch/Op_j]$	$(State, Init, \{Op_i\}_{i\in I\wedge\neq j} \cup \{Op_j \mathrel{\hat=} Op_j \parallel_! NSch\})$	$\mathbf{vars}(State) \cup \mathbf{input}(NSch) \cup \mathbf{output}(NSch) \supseteq \mathbf{vars}(NSch) \wedge j\in I$
Choice	$A[Op_j [] NSch/Op_j]$	$(State, Init, \{Op_i\}_{i\in I\wedge\neq j} \cup \{Op_j \mathrel{\hat=} Op_j [] NSch\})$	$\mathbf{vars}(State) \cup \mathbf{input}(NSch) \cup \mathbf{output}(NSch) \supseteq \mathbf{vars}(NSch) \wedge j\in I$
Composition	$A[Op_j \,\text{\textcircled{9}}\, NSch/Op_j]$	$(State, Init, \{Op_i\}_{i\in I\wedge\neq j} \cup \{Op_j \mathrel{\hat=} Op_j \,\text{\textcircled{9}}\, NSch\})$	$\mathbf{vars}(State) \cup \mathbf{input}(NSch) \cup \mathbf{output}(NSch) \supseteq \mathbf{vars}(NSch) \wedge j\in I$
Class modification			
Hide Operation	$A\backslash\{Op_k\}$	$(State, Init, \{Op_i\}_{i\in I\backslash\{j\}})$	$j \in I$
Rename Operation	$A[Op_j/Op_k]$	$(State, Init, \{Op_i\}_{i\in I\backslash\{k\}} \cup \{Op_j\})$	$Op_j \mathrel{\hat=} Op_k$
New operations			
New Operation	$A \oplus Op_j$	$(State, Init, \{Op_i\}_{i\in I} \cup \{Op_j\})$	$j \notin I$
Copy Operation	$A \oplus_c Op_j$	$(State, Init, \{Op_i\}_{i\in I} \cup \{Op_j\})$	$j \notin I \wedge i \in I \wedge Op_j \mathrel{\hat=} Op_i$
New operation as combination of existing operations			
Conjunction	$A \oplus \{Op_j \wedge Op_k\}$	$(State, Init, \{Op_i\}_{i\in I} \cup \{Op_l \mathrel{\hat=} Op_j \wedge Op_k\})$	$j, k \in I \wedge l \notin I$
Parallel	$A \oplus \{Op_j \parallel Op_k\}$	$(State, Init, \{Op_i\}_{i\in I} \cup \{Op_l \mathrel{\hat=} Op_j \parallel Op_k\})$	$j, k \in I \wedge l \notin I$
Ass Parallel	$A \oplus \{Op_j \parallel_! Op_k\}$	$(State, Init, \{Op_i\}_{i\in I} \cup \{Op_l \mathrel{\hat=} Op_j \parallel_! Op_k\})$	$j, k \in I \wedge l \notin I$
Choice	$A \oplus \{Op_j [] Op_k\}$	$(State, Init, \{Op_i\}_{i\in I} \cup \{Op_l \mathrel{\hat=} Op_j [] Op_k\})$	$j, k \in I \wedge l \notin I$
Composition	$A \oplus \{Op_j \,\text{\textcircled{9}}\, Op_k\}$	$(State, Init, \{Op_i\}_{i\in I} \cup \{Op_l \mathrel{\hat=} Op_j \,\text{\textcircled{9}}\, Op_k\})$	$j, k \in I \wedge l \notin I$
Refactorings			
Refactoring	$refName(A, \langle para \rangle)$	depending on the type of refactoring	

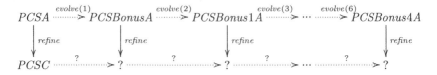

Fig. 5. Overview: Evolutions and missing refinements

4 Constructing Sound Co-evolutions

We have evolved the specification of *PCSA* several times using the evolutions described in the last section. In this section we answer the question, how to construct corresponding evolutions for the concrete level. The thus *co-evolutions* obtained should then preserve the refinement relationship between abstract and concrete specification. To this end, we will in the following provide rules for co-evolution steps, apply them to the example, and prove that they are refinement-preserving. The idea is to compute - using a given specification A, its evolution into $\widehat{A}$ and its refinement C - a new refinement $\widehat{C}$ of $\widehat{A}$ by applying a similar evolution to C.

Disjoint Class Conjunction. The first evolution step on the abstract specification in the example was a disjoint class conjunction. The idea now is to simply apply the same class conjunction on the more concrete specification. This is indeed a valid co-evolution as can be seen from the following theorem:

Theorem 1. (Class Conjunction) *Let A, B and C be Object-Z classes, C a refinement of A. Then $A \otimes B$ is refined by $C \otimes B$.*

Proof. Because the proof of the upward simulation is similar, we show only the proof for downward simulations. Let R_{AC} be the retrieve relation for the downward simulation between A and B and id_{State^B} the identity function on the state of B. Because of the condition for '"Disjoint Class Conjunction"' ($I_A \cap I_B = \varnothing \wedge I_C \cap I_B = \varnothing$) we can choose the retrieve relation between $A \otimes B$ and $C \otimes B$ as $R_{(A \otimes B)(C \otimes B)} = R_{AC} \wedge id_{State^B}$ and prove that this is a downward simulation:
Initialization:

$$\forall State^{C \otimes B} \bullet Init^{C \otimes B}$$
$$= \forall State^{C \otimes B} \bullet Init^C \wedge Init^B$$
$$\Rightarrow (\exists State^A \bullet Init^A \wedge R_{AC}) \wedge (\exists State^B \bullet Init^B \wedge id_{State^B})$$
$$= \exists State^A, State^B \bullet Init^A \wedge Init^B \wedge R_{AC} \wedge id_{State^B}$$
$$= \exists State^{A \otimes B} \bullet Init^{A \otimes B} \wedge R_{(A \otimes B)(C \otimes B)}$$

Applicability and Correctness: The idea of the proof is that for each operation we only have to consider the part of the state the operation works on. Because of the conditions for "Disjoint Class Conjunction" these states are disjoint and we can reduce each operation to its scope. We present as instance of these proofs the applicability proof of an operation introduced through the class A, the others are similar:

$$\forall i \in I_A \bullet \forall State^{A \otimes B}, State^{C \otimes B} \bullet R_{(A \otimes B)(C \otimes B)} \Rightarrow (\text{pre } Op_i^{AB} \Leftrightarrow \text{pre } Op_i^{CB})$$
$$\equiv \{ I_A \cap I_B = \varnothing \wedge I_C \cap I_B = \varnothing \text{ and Definition of } R_{(A \otimes B)(C \otimes B)} \}$$
$$\forall i \in I_A \bullet \forall State^A, State^C \bullet R_{AC} \Rightarrow (\text{pre } Op_i^A \Leftrightarrow \text{pre } Op_i^C) \qquad \square$$

Thus to obtain a valid refinement of $PCSBonusA$ (the abstract specification after the first evolution), we apply exactly the same evolution to class $PCSC$ resulting in the new class $PCSBonusC$:

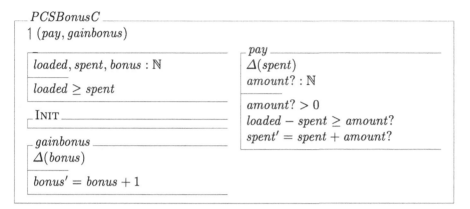

New operation as conjunction of existing operations. The second evolution concerned the addition of operation *payWithBonus* described by building a new operation as the combination of existing ones. In this case we combine the operations using the Object-Z conjunction operator. Thus, we can write this as (see (2) in Sec. 3):

$$A \oplus \{ Op_{new}^A \mathrel{\hat{=}} Op_1^A \wedge Op_2^A \}.$$

Unfortunately, we cannot just simply do the same kind of construction on the concrete specification using the corresponding concrete operations since this does not preserve refinement in every case. The issue of conjunction in Object-Z not being compositional has already been treated in [15]. In that work, compositionality is achieved by modifying the operations in such a way that a refinement relationship between operations only holds for the cases where conjunction is indeed compositional. Here, we take a different approach and will instead explicitly state preconditions on the application of operation conjunction in evolutions. Our setting here is the following: given classes A and C with operations Op_1^A, Op_2^A and Op_1^C, Op_2^C such that

$$Op_1^A \sqsubseteq Op_1^C$$
$$Op_2^A \sqsubseteq Op_2^C$$

we try to achieve $Op_1^A \wedge Op_2^A \sqsubseteq Op_1^C \wedge Op_2^C$. The correctness of this construction can depend on the existence of an after state in the conjoined operation. The set of possible after states can change through refinement (reduction of nondeterminism). Therefore, it is possible that there is no after state in the conjunction of the refined operations, while there is an after state in the conjunction of abstract operations, or - if both exist - they might not be related by the retrieve relation. In such cases refinement fails.

One possibility for ruling out these cases is to require that the operations to be conjoined operate on distinct parts of the state, and this separation is also reflected by the retrieve relation.

Definition 3. *Let A and C be Object-Z classes such that C refines A via the retrieve relation R. Classes A and C and the refinement are said to be* separable *with respect to variable sets V_1^A, V_2^A and V_1^C, V_2^C, $V_1^A \cap V_2^A = \varnothing$, $V_1^C \cap V_2^C = \varnothing$, if*

- *$State^A$ can be split into $State_1^A$, $State_2^A$, i.e. $State^A = State_1^A \wedge State_2^A$, such that $State_i^A$ contains variables from V_i^A only (and similarly for C), $i = 1, 2$, and*
- *R can be split into R_1, R_2, i.e. $R = R_1 \wedge R_2$, such that R_i contains variables from V_i^A and V_i^C only, $i = 1, 2$.*

A separable refinement effectively consists of two completely disjoint parts, which are moreover also completely unrelated in the state schemas, i.e. the state invariants never relate variables of these sets. Though this seems to be overly restrictive, it is in fact occuring quite often in evolutions, namely for instance always after having executed the evolution step disjoint class conjunction (which is the case in our example). For separable refinements we can allow for operation conjunction if the operations operate on these distinct parts of the classes.

Theorem 2. (New operation as conjunction of existing operations) *Let A and C be Object-Z classes such that C refines A under R, and let A, C and R be separable with respect to variable sets V_1^A, V_2^A and V_1^C, V_2^C.*
  Then the class $C \oplus \{ Op_{new}^C \mathrel{\widehat{=}} Op_1^C \wedge Op_2^C \}$ is a refinement of $A \oplus \{ Op_{new}^A \mathrel{\widehat{=}} Op_1^A \wedge Op_2^A \}$ if

$$\mathbf{vars}(Op_1^A) \subseteq V_1^A \wedge \mathbf{vars}(Op_2^A) \subseteq V_2^A \tag{i}$$

$$\mathbf{vars}(Op_1^C) \subseteq V_1^C \wedge \mathbf{vars}(Op_2^C) \subseteq V_2^C \tag{ii}$$

Proof. Again we only provide the proof for downward simulation. Let R be the retrieve relation showing downward simulation. The initialization condition as well as applicability and correctness for existing operations are straightforward. Only the new operation needs to be considered. We use Out_1, Out_2 to denote the output variables of Op_1^A, Op_1^C and Op_2^A, Op_2^C, respectively.

Applicability:

$$\forall State^A, State^C \bullet R \Rightarrow (\text{pre } Op_1^A \Leftrightarrow \text{pre } Op_1^C) \wedge$$
$$(\text{pre } Op_2^A \Leftrightarrow \text{pre } Op_2^C)$$
$$\Rightarrow \{ \text{ Definition of } pre \}$$
$$\forall State^A, State^C \bullet R \Rightarrow ((\exists State^{A'}, Out_1 \bullet Op_1^A) \Leftrightarrow \exists State^{C'}, Out_1 \bullet Op_1^C) \wedge$$
$$(\exists State^{A'}, Out_2 \bullet Op_2^A) \Leftrightarrow \exists State^{C'}, Out_2 \bullet Op_2^C)$$

$\Rightarrow \{$ Separability and i, ii $\}$

$\forall State^A, State^C \bullet R \Rightarrow ((\exists State_1^{A'}, Out_1 \bullet Op_1^A) \Leftrightarrow \exists State_1^{C'}, Out_1 \bullet Op_1^C) \wedge$
$\qquad\qquad\qquad\qquad (\exists State_2^{A'}, Out_2 \bullet Op_2^A) \Leftrightarrow \exists State_2^{C'}, Out_2 \bullet Op_2^C)$

$\Rightarrow \{$ take $State^{A'} := State_1^{A'} \wedge State_2^{A'}, State^{C'} := State_1^{C'} \wedge State_2^{C'},$
$\qquad Out := Out_1 \wedge Out_2\}$

$\forall State^A, State^C \bullet R \Rightarrow ((\exists State^{A'}, Out \bullet Op_1^A \wedge Op_2^A) \Leftrightarrow$
$\qquad\qquad\qquad\qquad \exists State^{C'}, Out \bullet Op_1^C \wedge Op_2^C)$

$\Rightarrow \{$ Definition of $pre\}$

$\forall State^A, State^C \bullet R \Rightarrow (\mathrm{pre}(Op_1^A \wedge Op_2^A) \Leftrightarrow \mathrm{pre}(Op_1^C \wedge Op_2^C))$

Correctness:

$\forall State^A, State^C, State^{C'} \bullet R \wedge Op_1^C \Rightarrow \exists State^{A'} \bullet Op_1^A \wedge R' \wedge$
$\qquad\qquad\qquad\qquad R \wedge Op_2^C \Rightarrow \exists State^{A'} \bullet Op_2^A \wedge R'$

$\Rightarrow \{$ Separability and i, ii$\}$

$\forall State^A, State^C, State^{C'}, State_1^A, State_2^A \mid State^A = State_1^A \wedge State_2^A \bullet$
$\quad (R \wedge Op_1^C \Rightarrow \exists State_1^{A'}, State_2^{A'} \bullet \Xi State_2^A \wedge Op_1^A \wedge R_1') \wedge$
$\quad (R \wedge Op_2^C \Rightarrow \exists State_1^{A'}, State_2^{A'} \bullet \Xi State_1^A \wedge Op_2^A \wedge R_2')$

$\Rightarrow \{\Delta(Op_1^A) \cap \mathbf{vars}(State_2^A) = \varnothing, \Delta(Op_2^A) \cap \mathbf{vars}(State_1^A) = \varnothing,$
$\qquad$ definition of schema conjunction in Object-Z $\}$

$\forall State^A, State^C, State^{C'}, State_1^A, State_2^A \mid State^A = State_1^A \wedge State_2^A \bullet$
$\quad R \wedge (Op_1^C \wedge Op_2^C) \Rightarrow \exists State_1^{A'}, State_2^{A'} \bullet (Op_1^A \wedge Op_2^A) \wedge R_1' \wedge R_2'$

$\Rightarrow \{$ take $State^{A'} := State_1^{A'} \wedge State_2^{A'}\}$

$\forall State^A, State^C, State^{C'} \bullet R \wedge (Op_1^C \wedge Op_2^C) \Rightarrow \exists State^{A'} \bullet (Op_1^A \wedge Op_2^A) \wedge R'$

$\qquad\qquad\qquad\qquad\qquad\qquad\qquad\qquad\qquad\qquad\qquad\qquad\qquad \square$

Thus, for the second evolution in our example we have to prove the side-conditions of Thm. 2, which are separability with the constraints (i) and (ii) on the conjoined operations. These are fulfilled which can be seen by

$\mathbf{vars}(pay^A) = \{deposit, amount?\} \subseteq \{deposit, amount?\} = V_1^A$
$\mathbf{vars}(gainBonus^A) = \{bonus\} \subseteq \{bonus\} = V_2^A$
$\mathbf{vars}(pay^C) = \{spent, loaded, amount?\} \subseteq \{spent, loaded, amount?\} = V_1^C$ and
$\mathbf{vars}(gainBonus^C) = \{bonus\} \subseteq V_2^C = \{bonus\}.$

As a consequence, we can apply the same evolution on the concrete specification as given in the class $PCSBonus0C$ (Fig. 6).

New operation. Evolution step (3) of the example is the addition of an operation with a completely new body. This is an interesting kind of evolution, because in contrast to the other evolutions in this paper, it requires to fully build a new operation in the concrete class. For defining the corresponding co-evolution we follow the approach for calculating refinements of [5], adapting them to our setting and thus specifically to Object-Z. [5] gives conditions for calculating operations in a refinement of a Z specification given a concrete state schema and retrieve relation R. The basic idea is to use the definition of refinement to

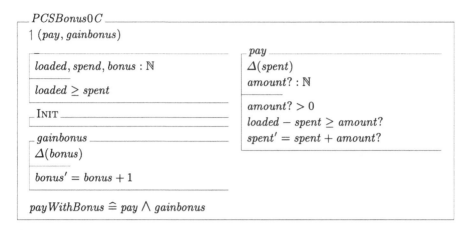

Fig. 6. Class $PCSBonus0C$

construct suitable concrete operations which are the weakest ones with respect to the relation R. We have to slightly adapt this result so as to cope with difference in Z and Object-Z data refinement (non-blocking vs. blocking semantics).

Theorem 3. *Let A and C be Object-Z classes such that C is a downward simulation of A under a retrieve relation R, and let Op^A_{new} be an additional operation for A.*

1. *For Op^C_{new} defined as*

$$Op^C_{new} \ \widehat{=}\ (\exists\, State^A \bullet R \land pre\ Op^A_{new}) \land (\forall\, State^A \bullet R \Rightarrow \exists\, State^{A'} \bullet R' \land Op^A_{new})$$

   we have

$$A \oplus Op^A_{new} \sqsubseteq_{ds} C \oplus Op^C_{new} \quad iff \quad pre\ Op^A_{new} \land R \Rightarrow pre\ Op^C_{new}$$

2. *If the retrieve relation R is furthermore functional from concrete to abstract, then for*

$$Op^C_{new} \ \widehat{=}\ \exists\, State^A;\ State^{A'} \bullet (R \land Op^A_{new} \land R')$$

   we get $A \oplus Op^A_{new} \sqsubseteq_{ds} C \oplus Op^C_{new}$.

This theorem is a direct corollary of Chapter 5 in [5]. To calculate the refinement we need the retrieve relation of the refinement of the classes before the evolution:

R_1
$PCSBonus0A$
$PCSBonus0C$

$PCSBonus0A.bonus = PCSBonus0C.bonus$
$PCSBonus0A.deposit = PCSBonus0C.loaded - PCSBonus0C.spent$

The retrieve relation R_1 of our example is functional from concrete to abstract, so we can use the second part of Thm. 3.

$$convertbonus^C \mathrel{\widehat{=}} \exists\, State^{PCSBonus1A};\ State^{PCSBonus1A'} \bullet (R \wedge$$
$$[\Delta(bonus, deposit) \mid bonus > 10 \wedge$$
$$bonus' = bonus - 10 \wedge$$
$$deposit' = deposit + 10]$$
$$\wedge R')$$
$$\equiv [\Delta(bonus, loaded, spent)$$
$$\mid bonus > 10$$
$$bonus' = bonus - 10$$
$$loaded' - spent' = loaded - spent + 10]$$

We have thus gained a valid refinement for $PCSBonus1A$. However, this refinement somehow does not match the intention of the concrete level in which the value of *loaded* should always be the total amount of money loaded to the system. The new operation *convertbonus* can nondeterministically change the values of *loaded* and *spent* as long as the condition holds, i.e. it could also increase both *loaded* and *spent*. This problem can be solved using an additional refinement step, which specializes the operation in the intended way. The result is given in Fig. 7. This additional refinement is possible since we have only calculated the weakest refinement.

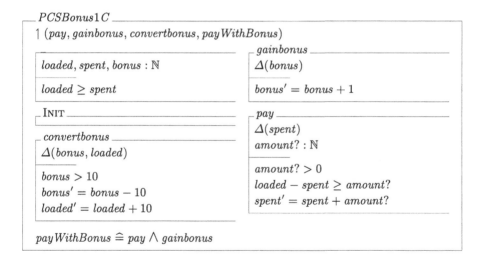

Fig. 7. Class $PCSBonus1C$

Hide operation. The next evolution is the hiding of an operation, *Hide operation* (evolution 4). Hiding removes an operation from the class' interface. In the refined specification we simply hide the same operation, resulting in a valid refinement chain.

Theorem 4. (Hide Operation) *Let A and C be two Object-Z classes such that C refines A. Then $A \backslash \{Op_d^A\}$ is refined by $C \backslash \{Op_d^C\}$ for $d \in I_A$.*

Proof. The proof is straightforward as initialisation condition as well as applicability and correctness of the remaining operations are kept.   □

Refactoring: Expanding an operation and removing unused operation. The last evolutions of the cash system were two refactorings: *PSCBonus2A* is simplified by expanding schema *payWithBonus* and finally removing the unused operation *pay*. Because refactorings are a well known topic for programming languages [18, 21, 7] as well as in formal methods [15, 22, 24, 14], we do not discuss the topic in detail here. For the description of refactorings special notations are used. For simplicity, we omit these notations and treat refactoring as functions, which takes some parameters describing the details of the refactoring. The assumption that we make about refactorings is that they are transformations which keep the *semantics* of specifications, i.e. unlike the other evolutions, applying refactorings only change the internal structure of specifications and never their meaning. Hence, whenever we apply a refactoring *refName* on a specification A using some parameter value *para*, we get $A \equiv refName(A, para)$ (where $A \equiv A'$ iff A refines A' and A' refines A).

Due to this propery of refactorings, they can trivially be shown to be refinement-preserving co-evolutions:

Theorem 5. *Let A and C be Object-Z classes such that C refines A, and let refName be the name of a refactoring and para some value for parameters. Then refName(A, para) is refined by refName(C, para).*

Proof
Follows from the fact that $A \equiv refName(A, para)$ and $C \equiv refName(C, para)$. □

In practice, refactorings are often used to prepare a change or enhancement of software, that is why we have presented them here in the context of evolutions. As co-evolutions for our example we simply apply the same refactoring with the same parameter to our concrete specification. This completes the evolutions of the example section. We have seen how to find a corresponding co-evolution for the concrete level for every evolution carried out on the abstract specification.

Replacement of operations and composition. Finally we address a common problem of evolutions which replace existing operations in classes where the operation is used for the definition of other operations. Since the operation *pay* in *PSCBonus0A* is used by the operation *payWithBonus*, we would change *payWithBonus* if we change *pay*. Thus, we might implicitly also evolve operations which use evolved operations. A similar problem occurs when we are dealing with a specification with several classes, potentially with one class having variables which reference objects of other classes. An evolution carried out in one class might thus affect several classes. Consequently the co-evolution has to be carried out on several classes in the refinement as well.

Table 2. Co-Evolutions (A,B,C: classes; Op, $NSch$: operation schema). The superscripts (e.g. Op^A) indicate the class the part belongs to. The tick-symbol (✓) indicates, that no conditions need to be fulfilled.

Evolution	Condition
Evolutions of type class/class	
$A \wedge B$ $\ldots C \wedge B$	Can be described by class conjunction (⊘) plus replace operation ($[Op_j \wedge NSch/Op_j]$)
$A \vee B$ $\ldots C \vee B$	Can be described by class disjunction (⊘) plus replace operation ($[Op_j \vee NSch/Op_j]$)
$A \oslash B$ $\ldots C \oslash B$	✓
$A \oslash B$ $\ldots C \oslash B$	
Modification of existing operations	
$A[Op_j^A \wedge NSch/Op_j^A]\ldots C[Op_j^C \wedge NSch/Op_j^C]$	See Theorem 2 and Paragraph "Replacement of operations and composition"
$A[Op_j^A \parallel NSch/Op_j^A]\ldots C[Op_j^C \parallel NSch/Op_j^C]$	Can be expressed in Terms of Conjunction
$A[Op_j^A \parallel_1 NSch/Op_j^A]\ldots C[Op_j^C \parallel_1 NSch/Op_j^C]$	Can be expressed in Terms of Conjunction
$A[Op_j^A \, \overset{\circ}{\circ}\, NSch/Op_j^A]\ldots C[Op_j^C \, \overset{\circ}{\circ}\, NSch/Op_j^C]$	Can be expressed in Terms of Conjunction
$A[Op_j^A \| NSch/Op_j^A]\ldots C[Op_j^C \| NSch/Op_j^C]$	✓
Class modification	
$A \backslash \{Op_j^A\}$ $\ldots C \backslash \{Op_j^C\}$	✓
$A[Op_j^A/Op_k^A]$ $\ldots C[Op_j^C/Op_k^C]$	✓
New operations	
$A \oplus Op_j^A$ $\ldots C \oplus Op_j^C$	See Theorem 3
$A \oplus_c Op_j^A$ $\ldots C \oplus_c Op_j^C$	✓
New operation as combination of existing operations	
$A \oplus \{Op_j^A \wedge NSch\}$ $\ldots C \oplus \{Op_j^C \wedge NSch\}$	See Theorem 2
$A \oplus \{Op_j^A \parallel NSch\}$ $\ldots C \oplus \{Op_j^C \parallel NSch\}$	Can be expressed in Terms of Conjunction
$A \oplus \{Op_j^A \parallel_1 NSch\}$ $\ldots C \oplus \{Op_j^C \parallel_1 NSch\}$	Can be expressed in Terms of Conjunction
$A \oplus \{Op_j^A \, \overset{\circ}{\circ}\, NSch\}$ $\ldots C \oplus \{Op_j^C \, \overset{\circ}{\circ}\, NSch\}$	Can be expressed in Terms of Conjunction
$A \oplus \{Op_j^A \| NSch\}$ $\ldots C \oplus \{Op_j^C \| NSch\}$	✓

Overview over refinement-preserving evolutions. The co-evolutions of the example and the corresponding theorems about preservation of refinement cover only some of the evolutions in Table 1. However, the other co-evolutions can be defined and proven correct in a similar way, often using corresponding side-conditions (if necessary at all). Table 2 gives some co-evolutions together with the side-conditions for refinement preservation. Some co-evolutions have no side condition (like Disjoint Conjunction), others can be composed out of other co-evolutions, e.g. $A \wedge B$ in Table 2. $A \wedge B$ can be done by first combining the disjoint parts: $A \oslash \hat{B}$ where $\hat{B}$ is the class B without the operations existing in class A. In the second step, all remaining operations of B are combined with the operations of $A \oslash \hat{B}$ using the evolution *modification of existing operations - conjunction*. Thus, the matching co-evolution is also the combination of these steps.

5   Conclusion and Related Work

In this paper we have presented behavior-preserving co-evolutions. In the design process, the evolution of a specification is used to adapt the model to changing requirements. Co-evolution is then the joint evolution of two or more specifications, often related to each other by some notion of consistency. In this paper we have analyzed the co-evolution of chains of specifications related by refinement. To this end, we first of all formally defined a number of evolutions of Object-Z specifications. Using these evolutions we have presented rules for co-evolution which ensure that refinement relationships are kept.

The evolutions in this paper are not dealing with inheritance. The extension to evolutions of classes in an inheritance structure is straightforward: leaf classes (classes which have no subclasses themselves), can be evolved in the described way, because the definition of semantic functions like **vars** already cope with the inheritance and the conditions thus do not change. Other classes, i.e. classes which have subclasses, can be evolved, if all their subclasses are also evolved in the same way. The co-evolution needs to be performed for the whole inheritance subtree simultaneously.

Related Work. We divide this section into two parts: evolutions for formal methods and, more importantly, co-evolution.

The notion of behavioral subtyping [13, 27] can be seen as a specific kind of evolution. Behavioural subtyping requires the evolved specification to retain a certain kind of consistency with the original specification, so as to allow for substitutability of new for old specification. Hence not all evolutions can be classified as being behavioural subtypes.

A notion of evolution derived from refinement is retrenchment [20]. Retrenchment weakens refinement in a controlled way. Retrenchment does not automatically guarantee preservation of refinement but - as already discussed in the introduction - can be used to construct co-evolutions for Z.

Co-evolution can address different layers of models or specifications, e.g in UML, different diagrams can be evolved together, such that they are still consistent after the co-evolution of these diagrams. Engels et al. [6] analyze co-evolutions on UML class and state diagrams. Kosiucznko [11] evolves UML class diagrams together with contracts given in OCL and lays a special focus on refactorings. Other works on UML ([25, 1]) focus mainly on consistency after a change and do not give a set of rules which can be used to express consistency preserving transformations.

Giese and Wagner [8] reinstall consistency between diagrams after the diagrams have been evolved separately. They use triple graph grammars to find the inconsistencies and a rule based approach to correct the found inconsistencies using an incremental procedure. Other approaches to reinstall the consistency are described amongst others in [16, 17].

The co-evolution of an agent-oriented conceptual model (i^*) and its representation in Z is described in [12]. In this work, they establish a mapping between i^* and Z which is then used to analyze the impact of a change in the i^* model. With this information the modeler can then change the Z specification.

A special case of evolution is refactoring which is required to not even change the behaviour of the specification to which it is applied. Refactorings are also sometimes considered in a co-evolution context [25]. Since they keep the behaviour of specification, refinement preservation is directly achieved.

References

[1] Briand, L.C., Labiche, Y., Yue, T.: Automated traceability analysis for UML model refinements. Inf. Softw. Technol. 51(2), 512–527 (2009)

[2] Cazzola, W., Pini, S., Ghoneim, A., Saake, G.: Co-evolving application code and design models by exploiting meta-data. In: SAC, pp. 1275–1279. ACM, New York (2007)

[3] de Roever, W.-P., Engelhardt, K.: Data Refinement: Model-Oriented Proof Methods and their Comparison. In: CUP (1998)

[4] Derrick, J., Boiten, E.A.: Calculating upward and downward simulations of state-based specifications. Information & Software Technology 41(13), 917–923 (1999)

[5] Derrick, J., Boiten, E.A.: Refinement in Z and Object-Z. Springer, Heidelberg (2001)

[6] Engels, G., Heckel, R., Malte Küster, J., Groenewegen, L.: Consistency-preserving model evolution through transformations. In: Jézéquel, J.-M., Hussmann, H., Cook, S. (eds.) UML 2002. LNCS, vol. 2460, pp. 212–226. Springer, Heidelberg (2002)

[7] Fowler, M.: Refactoring: Improving the Design of Existing Code. Addison Wesley, Reading (2004)

[8] Giese, H., Wagner, R.: From model transformation to incremental bidirectional model synchronization. Software and Systems Modeling 8(1) (2009)

[9] Groves, L.: A formal approach to program evolution. In: Proc. Workshop on Evolutionary Formal Software Development EFSD 2002 (July 2002)

[10] Henkel, J., Diwan, A.: Catchup!: capturing and replaying refactorings to support API evolution. In: ICSE 2005: Proceedings of the 27th international conference on Software engineering, pp. 274–283. ACM, New York (2005)

[11] Kosiuczenko, P.: Redesign of UML class diagrams: a formal approach. Software and Systems Modeling 8(2) (April 2009)

[12] Krishna, A., Ghose, A.K., Vilkomir, S.A.: Co-evolution of complementary formal and informal requirements. In: IWPSE 2004, pp. 159–164 (2004)

[13] Liskov, B., Wing, J.: A behavioural notion of subtyping. ACM Transactions on Programming Languages and Systems 16(6), 1811–1841 (1994)

[14] McComb, T.: Refactoring Object-Z Specifications. In: Wermelinger, M., Margaria-Steffen, T. (eds.) FASE 2004. LNCS, vol. 2984, pp. 69–83. Springer, Heidelberg (2004)

[15] McComb, T., Smith, G.: Compositional class refinement in Object-Z. In: Misra, J., Nipkow, T., Sekerinski, E. (eds.) FM 2006. LNCS, vol. 4085, pp. 205–220. Springer, Heidelberg (2006)

[16] Mens, T., Van Der Straeten, R., DHondt, M.: Detecting and resolving model inconsistencies using transformation dependency analysis. In: Model Driven Engineering Languages and Systems (2006)

[17] Olsen, T., Grundy, J.: Supporting traceability and inconsistency management between software artefacts. In: International Conference on Software Engineering and Applications, IASTED Press (2002)

[18] Opdyke, W.F.: Refactoring Object-Oriented Frameworks. PhD thesis, University of Illinois at Urbana-Champaign (1992)

[19] Poppleton, M., Groves, L.: Software evolution with refinement and retrenchment. In: RCS 2003: 2nd Annual Workshop on Refinement of Critical Systems (June 2003)

[20] Poppleton, M., Groves, L.: Formal perspectives on software evolution: from refinement to retrenchment. In: Software Evolution and Feedback: Theory and Practice, pp. 313–338 (2006)

[21] Roberts, D.B.: Practical Analysis For Refactoring. PhD thesis, University of Illinois at Urbana-Champaign (1999)

[22] Ruhroth, T., Wehrheim, H.: Refactoring object-oriented specifications with data and processes. In: Bonsangue, M.M., Johnsen, E.B. (eds.) FMOODS 2007. LNCS, vol. 4468, pp. 236–251. Springer, Heidelberg (2007)

[23] Smith, G.: The Object-Z Specification Language. Kluwer Academic Publishers, Dordrecht (2000)

[24] Stepney, S., Polack, F., Toyn, I.: A Z Patterns Catalogue I: Specification and refactorings, v0.1. Technical Report YCS-2003-349, University of York (2003)

[25] Van Der Straeten, R., Jonckers, V., Mens, T.: A formal approach to model refactoring and model refinement. Software and Systems Modeling 6(2), 139–162 (2007)

[26] Vadera, S.: Proof by analogy in mural. Formal Aspects of Computing 7 (1995)

[27] Wehrheim, H.: Behavioral subtyping relations for active objects. Formal Methods in System Design 23(2), 143–170 (2003)

Circular Coinduction with Special Contexts

Dorel Lucanu[1] and Grigore Roşu[2]

[1] Faculty of Computer Science
Alexandru Ioan Cuza University, Iaşi, Romania
dlucanu@info.uaic.ro
[2] Department of Computer Science
University of Illinois at Urbana-Champaign, USA
grosu@illinois.edu

Abstract. Coinductive proofs of behavioral equivalence often require human ingenuity, in that one is expected to provide a "good" relation extending one's goal with additional lemmas, making automation of coinduction a challenging problem. Since behavioral satisfaction is a Π_2^0-hard problem, one can only expect techniques and methods that approximate the behavioral equivalence. Circular coinduction is an automated technique to prove behavioral equivalence by systematically exploring the behaviors of the property to prove: if all behaviors are circular then the property holds. Empirical evidence shows that one of the major reasons for which circular coinduction does not terminate in practice is that the circular behaviors may be guarded by a context. However, not all contexts are safe. This paper proposes a large class of contexts which are safe guards for circular behaviors, called special contexts, and extends circular coinduction appropriately. The resulting technique has been implemented in the CIRC prover and experiments show that the new technique can prove many interesting behavioral properties fully automatically.

1 Introduction

Coinduction allows us to prove properties about infinite objects, such as, for example, streams of numbers or infinite behaviors of systems. Since many system specifications manifest infinite behaviors, coinduction is increasingly gaining interest among computer scientists. There are many efforts to mechanize proofs by coinduction, e.g., [8,18,6,19,13,17] among many others. Circular coinduction [19] is an automated technique to prove behavioral equivalence by systematically exploring the behaviors of the property to prove. More specifically, it derives the behavioral task until one obtains, on every derived path, either a truth or a cycle. Variants of circular coinduction have been implemented in at least three systems so far: in a behavioral extension of OBJ called BOBJ [19] (not maintained anymore), in Isabelle/HOL for CoCasl [13], and in CIRC [15].

Circular coinduction can be formalized as a three-rule proof system deriving pairs of the form $\mathcal{B} \cup \mathcal{F} \Vdash^{\circ} \mathcal{G}$, where $\mathcal{B}$ is the *(initial) specification* (or *initial hypotheses*), $\mathcal{F}$ is the set of *frozen hypotheses*, and $\mathcal{G}$ is the set of *goals* [22]

K. Breitman and A. Cavalcanti (Eds.): ICFEM 2009, LNCS 5885, pp. 639–659, 2009.

(see also Figure 2). Both the hypotheses and goals are sets of equations. The frozen hypotheses are written in a box (e.g., $\boxed{e}$), with the intuition that those cannot be used in contextual reasoning. The freezing operation is essential in proving the soundness of the circular coinduction. We illustrate the circular coinduction proof system using an intuitive behavioral specification of infinite streams. We do not assume the reader is familiar with behavioral specifications and/or coinduction, so our notions are explained in detail. We make use of conventional algebraic specification notation, briefly explained in Appendix A. Intuitively, a stream is an infinite sequence $x_1 : x_2 : x_3 : \ldots$. The derivatives Δ for streams are given by the operations head, hd, and tail, tl, defined by $hd(x : S) = x$ and $tl(x : S) = S$. The intuition for the derivatives is that they can be used to completely "derive" any stream, in that they can eventually reach, or observe, any of the stream's elements; derivatives are dual to constructors in inductive data types. Let STREAM be the specification of streams including besides data axioms the following operations defined in terms of head and tail:

$$odd, \ even : Stream \to Stream \qquad\qquad zip : Stream \times Stream \to Stream$$
$$hd(odd(S)) = hd(S) \qquad\qquad\qquad\quad hd(zip(S, S')) = hd(S)$$
$$tl(odd(S)) = even(tl(S)) \qquad\qquad\quad tl(zip(S, S')) = zip(S', tl(S))$$
$$even(S) = odd(tl(S))$$

Here are the intuitive definitions for the three stream operations above:

$$zip(x_1 : x_2 : \ldots, \ y_1 : y_2 : \ldots) = x_1 : y_1 : x_2 : y_2 : \ldots,$$
$$odd(x_1 : x_2 : x_3 : x_4 \ldots) = x_1 : x_3 : \ldots, \ \text{and} \ even(x_1 : x_2 : x_3 : x_4 : \ldots) = x_2 : x_4 : \ldots.$$

Streams S, S' are *behaviorally equivalent* in STREAM, written STREAM $\Vdash S = S'$, iff STREAM $\vdash hd(tl^i(S)) = hd(tl^i(S'))$ for $i = 0, 1, 2, \ldots$; this corresponds to the intuition that S and S' are indistinguishable under experiments using the derivatives. The behavioral equivalence $\Vdash$ over streams is a Π_2^0-hard problem [20], i.e., it is strictly harder than equational satisfaction; thus, there is no complete procedure to enumerate all the behavioral truths. Thus, the best we can do is to approximate behavioral equivalence, which is what circular coinduction does.

Since the circular coinductive deduction $\Vdash^{\circlearrowleft}$ is sound for the behavioral equivalence $\Vdash$ (see, e.g., Theorem 2), it follows that the following proof tree shows that STREAM $\Vdash e$, where e is the property $zip(odd(S), even(S)) = S$:

$$\text{STREAM} \cup \left\{ \boxed{zip(odd(S), even(S))} = \boxed{S} \right\} \Vdash^{\circlearrowleft} \emptyset$$

$$\text{STREAM} \cup \left\{ \boxed{zip(odd(S), even(S))} = \boxed{S} \right\} \vdash \boxed{hd(zip(odd(S), even(S)))} = \boxed{hd(S)}$$

$$\text{STREAM} \cup \left\{ \boxed{zip(odd(S), even(S))} = \boxed{S} \right\} \Vdash^{\circlearrowleft} \left\{ \boxed{hd(zip(odd(S), even(S)))} = \boxed{hd(S)} \right\}$$

$$\text{STREAM} \cup \left\{ \boxed{zip(odd(S), even(S))} = \boxed{S} \right\} \vdash \boxed{tl(zip(odd(S), even(S)))} = \boxed{tl(S)}$$

$$\text{STREAM} \cup \left\{ \boxed{zip(odd(S), even(S))} = \boxed{S} \right\} \Vdash^{\circlearrowleft} \left\{ \begin{array}{l} \boxed{hd(zip(odd(S), even(S)))} = \boxed{hd(S)}, \\ \boxed{tl(zip(odd(S), even(S)))} = \boxed{tl(S)} \end{array} \right\}$$

$$\text{STREAM} \qquad\qquad\qquad\qquad\qquad \Vdash^{\circlearrowleft} \left\{ \boxed{zip(odd(S), even(S))} = \boxed{S} \right\}$$

We give a "bottom-up" description of the above proof tree, as it is built by CIRC prover [15,14]. In the first step, STREAM $\Vdash e$ is reduced to showing that STREAM $\cup\,\{\boxed{e}\}\ \Vdash^{\circlearrowleft}\boxed{\Delta[e]}$, where (when e is an equation $t = t'$, $\boxed{e}$ is $\boxed{t}=\boxed{t'}$)

$$\Delta[e] = \{hd(zip(odd(S), even(S))) = hd(S), tl(zip(odd(S), even(S))) = tl(S)\}$$
$$= \{hd(zip(odd(S),odd(tl(S)))) = hd(S), tl(zip(odd(S),odd(tl(S)))) = tl(S)\},$$

where the definition of *even* was applied. The first equation in $\Delta[e]$ is discarded because it is a consequence of the STREAM axioms, $hd(zip(odd(S), odd(tl(S)))) = hd(odd(S)) = hd(S)$. The derivation of the second equation in $\Delta[e]$ is trickier: first, STREAM $\vdash \boxed{tl(zip(odd(S),odd(tl(S))))}=\boxed{zip(odd(tl(S)),odd(tl(tl(S))))}$ by the STREAM axioms, then STREAM $\cup\,\{\boxed{e}\}\vdash\boxed{zip(odd(tl(S)),odd(tl(tl(S))))}=\boxed{tl(S)}$ using the frozen hypothesis $\boxed{e}$ with the substitution $\theta(S) = tl(S)$, and finally by equational transitivity it follows that STREAM $\cup\,\{\boxed{e}\}\vdash\boxed{tl(zip(odd(S), odd(tl(S))))}=\boxed{tl(S)}$, so the second equation in $\Delta[e]$ is also discarded. Note that freezing is necessary, otherwise the derivatives in $\Delta[e]$ would follow by the congruence rule from e, no matter whether the property holds or not.

Many interesting properties like the above can be proved by simple circular coinduction. However, its success strictly depends upon the existence of a finite set of frozen equations $\mathcal{F}$ extending the original set of proof goals that would allow for the derivation of a circular coinductive proof (in the above example $\mathcal{F}$ is $\{\boxed{zip(odd(S), even(S))} = \boxed{S}\}$). Unfortunately, the Π_0^2-hardness result in [20] tells us that for some goals there is no such finite set of frozen equations.

Let us next discuss an example where the simple circular coinduction system fails to build a finite proof tree. A technique based on behavioral equivalence for checking well-definedness of stream operations is proposed in [27]. For instance, the well-definedness of *zip* follows by defining streams g and h by $hd(g) = hd(h) = 1$ (or any other constant), $tl(g) = zip(g, g)$, $tl(h) = zip(h, h)$, and then showing that STREAM $\Vdash g = h$.[1] Circular coinduction fails to find a proof for this property because the building process of the proof tree does not terminate. We show that a finite proof tree be quickly obtained if the additional hypotheses defined by the special contexts are used (a context is a term with a hole, written "$*$" in this paper; special contexts are defined in Section 4). Two special contexts are needed, namely $\Gamma = \{zip(*{:}Stream,S{:}Stream),zip(S{:}Stream,*{:}Stream)\}$. These contexts together with the frozen hypothesis (corresponding to the initial goal) yield the following two special hypotheses:

$$\Gamma[g=h] = \{zip(g,S{:}Stream) = zip(h,S{:}Stream), zip(S{:}Stream,g) = zip(S{:}Stream,h)\}.$$

Here is the proof tree generated by the extended proof system:

---

[1] The authors warmly thank Hans Zantema for supplying this example.

$\text{STREAM} \cup \{\boxed{g} = \boxed{h}\} \cup \boxed{\Gamma[g = h]} \; \Vdash^{\circlearrowleft} \; \emptyset$

$\text{STREAM} \cup \{\boxed{g} = \boxed{h}\} \cup \boxed{\Gamma[g = h]} \vdash \boxed{hd(g)} = \boxed{hd(h)}$

$\text{STREAM} \cup \{\boxed{g} = \boxed{h}\} \cup \boxed{\Gamma[g = h]} \; \Vdash^{\circlearrowleft} \; \left\{ \boxed{hd(g)} = \boxed{hd(h)} \right\}$

$\text{STREAM} \cup \{\boxed{g} = \boxed{h}\} \cup \boxed{\Gamma[g = h]} \vdash \boxed{tl(g)} = \boxed{tl(h)}$

$\text{STREAM} \cup \{\boxed{g} = \boxed{h}\} \cup \boxed{\Gamma[g = h]} \; \Vdash^{\circlearrowleft} \; \left\{ \begin{array}{c} \boxed{hd(g)} = \boxed{hd(h)}, \\ \boxed{tl(g)} = \boxed{tl(h)} \end{array} \right\}$

$\text{STREAM} \qquad\qquad\qquad\qquad \Vdash^{\circlearrowleft} \; \boxed{g} = \boxed{h}$

The special hypotheses are used in the deduction of $\boxed{tl(g)} = \boxed{tl(h)}$ (fourth line of the proof tree above) as follows: we have $tl(g) = zip(g, g)$ and $tl(h) = zip(h, h)$ as defining axioms, and $\boxed{zip(g, g)} = \boxed{zip(h, g)} = \boxed{zip(h, h)}$ follow from $\boxed{\Gamma[g = h]}$.

Special contexts must satisfy a certain well-foundedness condition w.r.t. derivatives (see Definition 5). Not all contexts are special. For example, if odd ($*$:$Stream$) were special then our proof system with special contexts would be unsound, as shown by the following scenario inspired from [10]. Let a and b be specified by $hd(a) = hd(b)$, $tl(a) = odd(a)$ and $tl^2(b) = odd(b)$, and let $odd(b) = a$ be the goal we want to prove. Applying the third rule, this goal is added as frozen hypothesis $\boxed{odd(b)} = \boxed{a}$ and the following two new goals are generated: $hd(odd(b)) = hd(a)$ and $tl(odd(b)) = tl(a)$. The former is eliminated by the second rule, and the latter is reduced to $odd(odd(b)) = odd(a)$. If we assume that $odd(*$:$Stream)$ is special, and hence the hypothesis $\boxed{odd(odd(b))} = \boxed{odd(a)}$ is automatically added, then we would wrongly deduce that $odd(b) = a$. A counter-example is given by $a = 0 : 0 : 1 : 2^\infty$ and $b = 0 : 1 : 0^\infty$.

In this paper we extend the basic circular coinduction proof system with the ability to use hypotheses defined by *special contexts*. The result is a more powerful proof system able to automatically prove a larger class of behavioral properties than that of [22]. The soundness of the new proof system is proved. The new system is effective for a given behavioral specification only if the special contexts are known. An algorithm that computes the special contexts is presented. Since the correctness proof and complexity of the algorithm needs more space, it will be presented in an extended version of this paper.

The techniques presented in this paper have been implemented and extensively evaluated in CIRC [15,14], a behavioral extension of Full Maude [5] tuned and optimized for automated and combined inductive and coinductive proving. CIRC implements the proof rules as reduction rules such that for an input $(\mathcal{B}, \mathcal{G})$, it incrementally computes $\mathcal{F}$ such that $\mathcal{B} \cup \mathcal{F} \Vdash^{\circlearrowleft} \mathcal{G}$. CIRC implements a criterion for automatic detection of special contexts and it can automatically prove both properties discussed above among many others *requiring special contexts*; for example, if the stream elements come from a commutative ring, CIRC can automatically prove that $zeros = 0{:}0{:}0{:}...$ and $[1] = 1{:}zeros$ are zero and unit elements for $\times$ (the convolution product), the distributivity of $\times$ over $+$ of streams, the equivalence of the two definitions for the Thue-Morse stream (see Example 9), the well-definedness of stream operations, etc. Similar properties are proved for the shuffle product of streams [24] and for infinite binary trees [25]. The special contexts are also useful for proving equivalences of basic process algebra (BPA) processes (see Example 8). All these and many other examples can be found on and executed using the online version of CIRC (`http://fsl.cs.uiuc.edu/CIRC`).

The rest of the paper is structured as follows. Sections 2 and 3 recall from [22] our proof theoretical approach for behavioral satisfaction and circular coinduction, focusing on the role of the freezing operator. Section 4 introduces the concept of special hypotheses as a closure operator and extends the coinductive circularity principle to the case when the special hypotheses are used. Then the concept of special context is introduced and it is shown how it yields a particular class of special hypotheses. Section 5 presents how the CIRC theorem prover implements both the circular coinduction and the special contexts. An algorithm for automatically computing special contexts is briefly presented.

2   Behavioral Specifications and Coinduction

We assume the reader familiar with the basics of many sorted algebraic specifications. A list of terms and notations used in this paper is given in Appendix A.

A *behavioral specification* is a pair $(\mathcal{B}, \Delta)$, where $\mathcal{B} = (S, \Sigma, E)$ is a many sorted algebraic specification and Δ is a set of Σ-contexts, called *derivatives*. If $\delta[*{:}h] \in \Delta$ then the sort h is called a *hidden sort*. Let $H \subseteq S$ be the set of all hidden sorts of $\mathcal{B}$. Remaining sorts are called *data, or visible, sorts*; let $V = S - H$ be their set. A *data operator* is an operator in Σ taking and returning only visible sorts; a *data term* is a term built with only data operators and variables of data sorts; a *data or visible, equation* is an equation built with only data terms. Equation "$(\forall X)\, t = t'$ if *cond*" is called a *hidden equation* iff the common sort of t and t' is hidden. We consider only equations whose conditions are conjunctions of visible equalities. If $\mathcal{G}$ is a set of Σ-equations, let *visible*$(\mathcal{G})$ and *hidden*$(\mathcal{G})$ be the sets of $\mathcal{G}$'s visible and hidden equations, respectively.

Sorts are thus split into hidden and visible, so that one can derive terms of hidden sort until they possibly become visible. Formally, a Δ-*experiment* is a Δ-context of visible sort, that is: (1) each $\delta[*{:}h] \in \Delta_v$ with $v \in V$ is an experiment, and (2) if $\delta[*{:}h] \in \Delta_{h'}$ and $C[*{:}h']$ is an experiment, then so is $C[\delta[*{:}h]]$. Note that we only consider unary contexts, that is, contexts with only one hole "$*$". If Δ is clear, we may write experiment for Δ-experiment and context for Δ-context.

Example 1. (*Streams*) A stream over D is an infinite sequence $a_1 : a_2 : a_3 : \dots$ whose elements a_i belong to D. In this paper we assume that $(D, +, \cdot, not)$ is a boolean ring (with 0 the unit for $+$, 1 the unit for $\cdot$, $not(0) = 1$, $not(1) = 0$, etc.). The operations over D can be extended to streams using corecursive equations:

$$a : s + a' : s' = (a + a') : (s + s')$$
$$a : s \times a' : s' = (a \cdot a') : (s \times a' : s' + [a] \times s'), \text{ where } [a] = a : 0^\infty$$
$$not(a : s) = not(a) : not(s)$$

If $s = a_1{:}a_2{:}a_3{:}\dots$ and $s' = a_1'{:}a_2'{:}a_3'{:}\dots$ are streams, then $s \times s'$ is the stream $(a_1 \cdot a_1') : (a_1 \cdot a_2' + a_2 \cdot a_1') : (a_1 \cdot a_3' + a_2 \cdot a_2' + a_3 \cdot a_1') : \dots$ and is called the *convolution product* of s and s'. Other stream operations, e.g., *zeros, ones, odd, even*, and *zip* can be defined like in Section 1. For more details on streams and their properties see, e.g., [23,24,27].

The equational part $\mathcal{B}$ of the behavioral specification of streams includes a hidden sort *Stream*, for streams, a visible sort *Data*, for elements of the streams, the operations over data and streams, and the equations over data (e.g., the axioms of the boolean ring) and streams. The set of the derivatives Δ includes two derivatives: $hd(*:Stream)$ and $tl(*:Stream)$. The experiments are of the form $hd(tl^i(*:Stream))$, where $i \geq 0$. Any specification of streams can be expressed in terms of the derivatives. For instance, the constant stream *zeros* and the convolution product are specified as follows:

$$hd(zeros) = 0 \qquad\qquad hd(S \times S') = hd(S) \cdot hd(S')$$
$$tl(zeros) = zeros \qquad\qquad tl(S \times S') = tl(S) \times S' + [hd(S)] \times tl(S')$$

The other operations are specified in a similar way. Let STREAM denote the behavioral specification of streams expressed in terms of the derivatives hd and tl.

Example 2. (*Processes*) We next consider the particular class of processes defined by basic process algebra (BPA) terms and guarded recursive specifications [9].

The equational specification of the processes is defined by the following items:

- a sort *Alph* for the atomic actions (the alphabet),
- a sort *Pid* for the process variables,
- a sort *Pexp* for the process terms (expressions),
- the constructors for the process terms (we regard subsorting as constructor):

$$Alph < Pexp \qquad\qquad Pid < Pexp$$
$$\_+\_ : Pexp\ Pexp \to Pexp \qquad \_;\_ : Pexp\ Pexp \to Pexp$$

which describe the grammar $p ::= a \mid X \mid p + p \mid p\,;p$, where p ranges over *Pexp*, a over *Alph*, and X over *Pid*,
- a sort *Peq* together with the constructor $\_=_{def}\_ : Pid\ Pexp \to Peq$ for the possibly recursive process equations,
- a sort *Set{Peq}* together with the constructors

$$Peq < Set\{Peq\} \qquad\qquad \_,\_ : Set\{Peq\}\ Set\{Peq\} \to Set\{Peq\}$$

and associativity/commutativity/idempotence axioms for sets of process equations, plus axioms ensuring that each *Pid* is defined at most once.

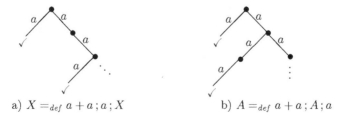

a) $X =_{def} a + a\,;a\,;X$ \qquad\qquad b) $A =_{def} a + a\,;A\,;a$

Fig. 1. Two infinitary completed trace equivalent processes

Fig. 1 shows two processes specified by guarded recursive equations. Recall that guarded recursive specifications allow a unique solution modulo bisimulation equivalence [9]. A specification like $X =_{def} a + X$ is not guarded.

The behavioral aspect we consider here is intended to capture the *infinitary completed trace equivalence* (see, e.g., [26]) and therefore it is given by two derivatives: $\_\{\_\} : Pexp \to Pexp$, with the intuitive meaning that $p\{a\}$ is the process $+\{q \mid p \xrightarrow{a} q\}$, and $\checkmark? : Pexp \to Bool$, with the intuitive meaning that an experiment $\checkmark?(p\{a_1\} \ldots \{a_n\})$ returns true if and only if $a_1 \ldots a_n$ is a completed trace for p, i.e., $p \xrightarrow{a_1} p_1 \ldots \xrightarrow{a_n} \checkmark$.

The problem is that the transition relation is partial and we work with derivatives which are totally defined. For instance, only an a-transition is defined for $a;p$. Since the derivatives are applied on all processes, we have to evaluate expressions like $a;p\{b\}$ with $b \neq a$. Therefore we consider two new process constants: $\perp$ with the meaning $p \xrightarrow{a} \perp$ iff there is no $q \neq \perp$ such that $p \xrightarrow{a} q$, and $\checkmark$ to denote the result obtained when we evaluate $a\{a\}$ (this corresponds to a successful termination).

We therefore consider only one hidden sort $Pexp$ and the derivatives $\Delta = \{*:Pexp\{A:Alph\}, \checkmark?(*:Pexp)\}$. The definitions of the process operations in terms of the derivatives are given by the following equations:

$$(p + q)\{a\} = p\{a\} + q\{a\} \qquad\qquad a\{a\} = \checkmark$$
$$\checkmark?(p + q) = \checkmark?(p) \vee \checkmark?(q) \qquad\qquad b\{a\} = \perp \text{ if } b \neq a$$
$$(p;q)\{a\} = p\{a\};q \text{ if } p \neq \checkmark \wedge p \neq \perp \qquad \checkmark?(a) = false \qquad \checkmark?(\checkmark) = true$$
$$\checkmark?(p;q) = \checkmark?(p) \wedge \checkmark?(q) \qquad\qquad \checkmark;p = p$$
$$X\{a\} = p\{a\} \text{ for each equation } X =_{def} p \qquad \checkmark\{a\} = \perp$$
$$\checkmark?(X) = false \qquad\qquad \perp;p = \perp \qquad \perp + p = p$$

Let BPA denote the above behavioral specification of the basic process algebra.

The theoretical results in this paper will be parametric in a given entailment relation $\vdash$ on many sorted equational specifications, which may, but is not enforced to, be the usual equational deduction relation [12]. For instance, it can also be the "rewriting" entailment relation ($E \vdash t = t'$ iff t and t' rewrite to the same term using E as a rewrite system), etc. We need though some properties of $\vdash$, which we axiomatize here by adapting to our context the general definition of entailment system as given in [16]. Fix a signature Σ.

Definition 1. *If Δ is a set of Σ-contexts, then a Δ-contextual entailment system is an (infix) relation $\vdash$ between sets of equations and equations, with: (reflexivity) $\{e\} \vdash e$; (monotonicity) If $E_1 \supseteq E_2$ and $E_2 \vdash e$ then $E_1 \vdash e$; (transitivity) If $E_1 \vdash E_2$ and $E_2 \vdash e$ then $E_1 \vdash e$; (Δ-congruence) If $E \vdash e$ then $E \vdash \Delta[e]$. In the above, E, E_1, E_2 range over sets of equations and e over equations; also, we tacitly extend $\vdash$ to relate two sets of equations: $E_1 \vdash E_2$ iff $E_1 \vdash e$ for any $e \in E_2$. We let $E^\bullet$ denote the set of equations $\{e \mid E \vdash e\}$.*

One can use the above to prove many properties of $\vdash$ on sets of equations. Here are some of them used later in the paper (their proofs are simple exercises):

$E \vdash \emptyset$, $E \vdash E$, if $E_1 \vdash E_2$ and $E_2 \vdash E_3$ then $E_1 \vdash E_3$, if $E_1 \vdash E_2$ then $E \cup E_1 \vdash E \cup E_2$, if $E_1 \vdash E_2$ then $E_1 \vdash \Delta[E_2]$, if $E_1 \vdash E_2$ then $E_1 \vdash E_1 \cup E_2$, if $E_1 \supseteq E_2$ then $E_1 \vdash E_2$, if $E \vdash E_1$ and $E \vdash E_2$ then $E \vdash E_1 \cup E_2$.

We take the liberty to slightly abuse the syntax of entailment and allow one to write a specification instead of a set of equations, with the obvious meaning: if $\mathcal{B} = (S, \Sigma, E)$ is a specification and e is a Σ-equation, then $\mathcal{B} \vdash e$ iff $E \vdash e$. Also, if $\mathcal{B} = (S, \Sigma, E)$ then we may write $\mathcal{B}^\bullet$ instead of $E^\bullet$.

Definition 2. $\mathcal{B}$ **behaviorally satisfies** equation e, written $\mathcal{B} \Vdash e$, iff: $\mathcal{B} \vdash e$ if e is visible, and $\mathcal{B} \vdash C[e]$ for each appropriate experiment C if e is hidden. Let $\equiv$ be the set of equations $\{e \mid \mathcal{B} \Vdash e\}$, called the **behavioral equivalence** of $\mathcal{B}$. A set of equations $\mathcal{G}$ is **behaviorally closed** iff $\mathcal{B} \vdash visible(\mathcal{G})$ and $\Delta[\mathcal{G} - \mathcal{B}^\bullet] \subseteq \mathcal{G}$.

For instance, if $(\forall X) t = t'$ is a stream equation, then STREAM $\Vdash (\forall X) t = t'$ if and only if $(\forall n \geq 0)$ STREAM $\vdash (\forall X) hd(tl^n(t)) = hd(tl^n(t'))$. Similarly, if $(\forall X) t = t'$ expresses a property over processes, then BPA $\Vdash (\forall X) t = t'$ if and only if $(\forall a_1 \ldots a_n)$ BPA $\vdash (\forall X) \checkmark?((t\{a_1\} \ldots \{a_n\})) = \checkmark?((t'\{a_1\} \ldots \{a_n\}))$. In both cases we assume that $\vdash$ is the equational deduction relation.

It can be shown that $\Vdash$ extends $\vdash$, i.e., if $\mathcal{B} \vdash e$ then $\mathcal{B} \Vdash e$ (see [22]). Our approach in this paper is proof-theoretical rather than model-theoretical, so our notion of behavioral equivalence is defined proof-theoretically rather than using models like in [11,3,1]; also, our $\equiv$ may contain conditional equations (of visible conditions). A behaviorally closed set $\mathcal{G}$ of equations is one whose visible equations are provable from $\mathcal{B}$ using the base entailment system and whose equations not provable from $\mathcal{B}$ using the base system remain in $\mathcal{G}$ when derived. Hence, the only way an equation can "escape" the derivation process in a behaviorally closed set is to be proved using the base entailment system $\vdash$.

Theorem 1. *(Coinduction)[22] For any behavioral specification, the behavioral equivalence $\equiv$ is the largest behaviorally closed set of equations.*

Theorem 1 is the foundation for the coinduction proving technique. An entailment-based coinductive proving technique is presented in [22]. The main idea is to find a set of equations G such that $\Delta(G) \subseteq \overline{G \cup \mathcal{B}^\bullet}$, where $\overline{\mathcal{E}}$ denotes the closure of $\mathcal{E}$ under substitution, symmetry, and transitivity.

Example 3. A proof by coinduction of the stream property $S \times zeros = zeros$ is given by $G = \{S \times zeros = zeros, S \times zeros + S' = S'\}$ and the following equations showing that $\Delta(G) \subseteq \mathcal{G} = \overline{G \cup \text{STREAM}^\bullet}$:

$$hd(S \times zeros) = hd(zeros) \qquad \text{(in STREAM}^\bullet)$$
$$hd(S \times zeros + S') = hd(S') \qquad \text{(in STREAM}^\bullet)$$
$$tl(S \times zeros) = tl(S) \times zeros + [hd(S)] \times zeros \quad \text{(in STREAM}^\bullet)$$
$$tl(S) \times zeros + [hd(S)] \times zeros = [hd(S)] \times zeros \ \text{(substitution)}$$

$$[hd(S)] \times zeros = zeros \qquad \text{(substitution)}$$
$$tl(S) \times zeros + [hd(S)] \times zeros = zeros \qquad \text{(transitivity)}$$
$$tl(S \times zeros) = zeros \qquad \text{(transitivity)}$$
$$tl(S \times zeros + S') = tl(S) \times zeros + [hd(S)] \times zeros + tl(S') \qquad \text{(in STREAM}^{\bullet}\text{)}$$
$$tl(S) \times zeros + [hd(S)] \times zeros + tl(S') = [hd(S)] \times zeros + tl(S') \quad \text{(substitution)}$$
$$[hd(S)] \times zeros + tl(S') = tl(S') \qquad \text{(substitution)}$$
$$tl(S \times zeros + S') = tl(S') \qquad \text{(transitivity)}$$

Example 4. Here we consider a proof by coinduction of a property over processes. Having the guarded recursive specification $U =_{def} a\,;V$, $V =_{def} b\,;U$, $Y =_{def} a\,;b\,;Y$, then $\{V = b\,;Y,\ U = Y\}$ together with the equations given below is a proof by coinduction of $U = Y$:

$$\checkmark?(U) = \checkmark?(Y) \quad \text{(in BPA}^{\bullet}\text{)} \qquad U\{b\} = Y\{b\} \qquad \text{(in BPA}^{\bullet}\text{)}$$
$$V\{a\} = b\,;Y\{a\} \quad \text{(in BPA}^{\bullet}\text{)} \qquad \checkmark?(V) = \checkmark?(b\,;Y) \quad \text{(in BPA}^{\bullet}\text{)}$$
$$V\{b\} = U \qquad \text{(in BPA}^{\bullet}\text{)} \qquad b\,;Y\{b\} = Y \qquad \text{(in BPA}^{\bullet}\text{)}$$
$$V\{b\} = b\,;Y\{b\} \quad \text{(transitivity)}$$

As seen in the examples above, coinductive proofs of behavioral equivalence require human intervention, to provide an appropriate behaviorally closed set of equations $\mathcal{G}$, which can be thought of as an "approximation" of $\equiv$. It is worth noting that it is virtually impossible to compute $\equiv$ precisely, because, as shown in [20], the problem of behavioral satisfaction is a Π_2^0 hard problem even for the particular specification of streams discussed in this paper. Circular coinduction [21,19,22] automates coinductive proving by dynamically inferring a suitable behaviorally closed set $\mathcal{G}$ including the property(ies) to prove.

3   Circular Coinduction

A key notion in our formalization and even implementation of circular coinduction is that of a "frozen" equation. The motivation underlying frozen equations is that they structurally inhibit their use underneath proper contexts; because of that, they will allow us to capture the above-mentioned informal notion of "circular behavior" elegantly, rigorously, and generally (modulo a restricted form of equational reasoning). Formally, let $(\mathcal{B}, \Delta)$ be a behavioral specification and let us extend its signature Σ with a new sort *Frozen* and a new operation $\boxed{-} : s \to$ *Frozen* for each sort s. If t is a term, then we call $\boxed{t}$ the *frozen (form of) t*. Note that freezing only acts on the original sorts in Σ, so double freezing, e.g., $\boxed{\boxed{t}}$, is not allowed. If e is an equation $(\forall X)\, t = t'$ if c, then we let $\boxed{e}$ be the *frozen equation* $(\forall X)\boxed{t} = \boxed{t'}$ if c; note that the condition c stays unfrozen, but recall that we only assume visible conditions. By analogy, we may call the equations over the original signature Σ *unfrozen equations*. If e is an (unfrozen) visible equation then $\boxed{e}$ is called a *frozen visible equation*; similarly when e is hidden. It is important to note here that if $E \cup \mathcal{F} \vdash \mathcal{G}$ for some unfrozen equation set E and frozen equation sets $\mathcal{F}$ and $\mathcal{G}$, it is not necessarily the case that $E \cup \mathcal{F} \vdash C[\mathcal{G}]$ for a context C. Freezing therefore inhibits the free application of the congruence deduction rule of equational reasoning.

Recall that, for generality, we work with an axiomatically defined entailment system in this paper. We next add two more axioms:

Definition 3. *A **Δ-contextual entailment system with freezing** is a Δ-contextual entailment system extended as above such that:*

(A1) If e is a visible unfrozen equation then $E \cup \mathcal{F} \vdash \boxed{e}$ iff $E \vdash e$;
(A2) $E \cup \mathcal{F} \vdash \mathcal{G}$ implies $E \cup \delta[\mathcal{F}] \vdash \delta[\mathcal{G}]$ for each $\delta \in \Delta$, equivalent to saying that for any Δ-context C, $E \cup \mathcal{F} \vdash \mathcal{G}$ implies $E \cup C[\mathcal{F}] \vdash C[\mathcal{G}]$.

(E ranges over unfrozen equations, and $\mathcal{F}$ and $\mathcal{G}$ over frozen hidden equations.)

Our working entailment system $\vdash$ is now defined over both unfrozen and frozen equations. It is easy to check these additional axioms for concrete entailment relations and to see that they are conservative [22].

Figure 2 defines circular coinduction as a proof system for deriving pairs of the form $\mathcal{B} \cup \mathcal{F} \Vdash^{\circlearrowleft} \mathcal{G}$, where $\mathcal{B}$ is the original behavioral specification, $\mathcal{F}$ is a set of *frozen hypotheses*, and $\mathcal{G}$ is a set of (frozen) *goals*. Initially, $\mathcal{F}$ is empty and $\mathcal{G}$ is the frozen version $\boxed{G}$ of the original goals G to prove. Circular coinduction iteratively attempts to complete $\boxed{G}$ to a behaviorally closed set of equations; freezing is necessary to inhibit the application of the congruence rule of equational deduction because, otherwise, the hypothesis of [Derive] would

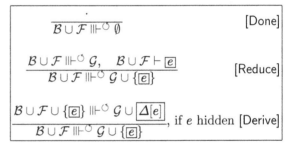

Fig. 2. *Circular coinduction as a proof system: If $\mathcal{B} \Vdash^{\circlearrowleft} \boxed{G}$ is derivable then $\mathcal{B} \Vdash G$*

hold superfluously whenever $\mathcal{B} \cup \mathcal{F} \Vdash^{\circlearrowleft} \mathcal{G}$ is derivable, so the proof system would be unsound. An example circular coinduction proof tree is presented in Section 1.

Theorem 2. *(soundness of circular coinduction)[22] If $\mathcal{B}$ is a behavioral specification and G is a set of equations such that $\mathcal{B} \Vdash^{\circlearrowleft} \boxed{G}$ is derivable using the proof system in Figure 2, then $\mathcal{B} \Vdash G$.*

4   Special Hypotheses and Special Contexts

We now show that circular coinduction can be extended by adding "on the fly" new hypothesis which are sound provided that the derivation process successfully terminates. The result is a better approximation of the behavioral equivalence.

Definition 4. *(special hypotheses) Let $(\mathcal{B}, \Delta)$ be a behavioral specification and F a set of hidden equations. Hidden equation e is a **special hypothesis** for F iff $(\forall C) \mathcal{B} \vdash C[e]$ whenever $\mathcal{B} \vdash C^{\leq}[F]$, where $C^{\leq}$ is the set of Δ-experiments D with $|D| \leq |C|$ ($|C|$ is the depth of C; see Appendix A). The set of special hypotheses for F, written $F^{\leq}$, is called the **special-hypothesis closure** of F.*

Therefore, a special hypothesis for a set of hidden equations F is a hidden equation e which holds under experiment C whenever the equations in F hold under all the experiments smaller than or equal to C (in depth, not in size). The intuition for special hypotheses, formalized in Theorem 3, is that they can be soundly used in reasoning when checking the closure of F under derivatives.

It is easy to check that $\cdot^{\leq}$ is a closure operator on sets of equations, that is, it is extensive ($F \subseteq F^{\leq}$), increasing ($F_1 \subseteq F_2$ implies $F_1^{\leq} \subseteq F_2^{\leq}$), and idempotent ($(F^{\leq})^{\leq} = F^{\leq}$). Also, $(\equiv\lceil_H)^{\leq} = \equiv\lceil_H$ and $\equiv\lceil_H \subseteq F^{\leq}$ for any hidden equation set F, where recall from Section 2 that H is the set of hidden sorts, so $\equiv\lceil_H$ is the set of hidden equations e such that $\mathcal{B} \Vdash e$; in particular, if $F \subseteq \equiv\lceil_H$ then $F^{\leq} = \equiv\lceil_H$. We next discuss some examples.

Example 5. If F consists of an equality of two streams $a = b$, then the following equations are in $F^{\leq}$: $S + a = S + b$, $a + S = b + S$, $S \times a = S \times b$, $a \times S = b \times S$, $not(a) = not(b)$, $zip(S, a) = zip(S, b)$, $zip(a, S) = zip(b, S)$, where S is a variable over streams. The equations $odd(a) = odd(b)$ and $even(a) = even(b)$ are not in $F^{\leq}$. For instance, we cannot deduce $hd(tl(odd(a))) = hd(tl(odd(b)))$ knowing only $hd(a) = hd(b)$ and $hd(tl(a)) = hd(tl(b))$ since $hd(tl(odd(a))) = hd(tl(tl(a)))$ and $hd(tl(odd(b))) = hd(tl(tl(b)))$.

The coinductive circularity principle (Theorem 2 in [22]) states that if F is a set of hidden equations such that $\mathcal{B} \cup \boxed{F} \vdash \boxed{\Delta(F)}$ then $\mathcal{B} \Vdash F$. This coinductive principle is the fundamental result underlying the soundness of circular coinduction. We next extend it by allowing $F^{\leq}$ instead of F as hypotheses:

Theorem 3. *(extended coinductive circularity principle)* *If F is a set of hidden equations such that $\mathcal{B} \cup \boxed{F^{\leq}} \vdash \boxed{\Delta[F]}$, then $\mathcal{B} \Vdash F^{\leq}$ (in fact, $F^{\leq} = \equiv\lceil_H$).*

Example 6. The additional equation $S \times zeros + S' = S'$ in Example 3 is special for $F = \{S \times zeros = zeros\}$, so, by Theorem 3, its frozen form can be used as hypothesis without including it into the initial set of goals.

In practice, one needs not add all the special hypotheses in $F^{\leq}$, but only those that help to derive $\boxed{\Delta[F]}$. Indeed, if SH is a subset of special hypotheses such that one can derive $\mathcal{B} \cup \boxed{SH} \cup \boxed{F} \vdash \boxed{\Delta[F]}$, then Theorem 3 implies $\mathcal{B} \Vdash SH \cup F$. In particular, if $SH = \emptyset$ then we obtain the coinductive circularity principle (Theorem 2 in [22]) as a special case. It is worthwhile noticing that no proof obligation is generated for the added special hypotheses; however, checking the condition in Definition 4 may not be trivial. In what follows we give a more effective approach to define useful special hypotheses, based on *special contexts*.

A first variant of special context was introduced in [10]: a context $\gamma[*:h]$ was called "special" in [10] iff for any experiment C for γ there is some experiment D with $|D| \leq |C|$ and $\mathcal{B} \vdash C[\gamma[*:h]] = D[*:h]$. The intuition for special contexts is therefore that whenever they appear at the bottom of an experiment they can be eliminated yielding a strictly smaller experiment. This way, again intuitively, their application on top of goals to prove does not change the behavioral validity status of those goals, so with our terminology above, their application on goals to prove can be added as special hypotheses. In what follows we formalize and prove this claim. Before we do so, motivated by practical needs, we first extend the definition of a special context by allowing the right hand side of the equation above, $D[*{:}h]$, to be replaced by any Σ-term whose occurrences of $*{:}h$ appear only in subterms of the form $D[*{:}h]$, where D is an experiment with $|D| \leq |C|$.

Definition 5. *(special contexts) Context $\gamma[*{:}h]$ is **special** iff for any experiment C for γ there is some term t such that $\mathcal{B} \vdash C[\gamma[*{:}h]] = t$ and each occurrence of $*{:}h$ in t appears only in a subterm in $C^{\leq}$ (see Definition 4).*

Example 7. For the streams specified in Example 1, the following are special contexts: $*{:}Stream + S{:}Stream, S{:}Stream + *{:}Stream, *{:}Stream \times S{:}Stream, S{:}Stream \times *{:}Stream, not(*{:}Stream), zip(*{:}Stream, S{:}Stream)$, and $zip(S{:}Stream, *{:}Stream)$. Moreover, any combination of these contexts (e.g., $(*{:}Stream \times S{:}Stream) + S'{:}Stream$) is special, as well. In contrast, $odd(*{:}Stream)$ and $even(*{:}Stream)$ are not special contexts: e.g., $\mathtt{STREAM} \vdash hd(tl(odd(*{:}Stream))) = hd(tl(tl(*{:}Stream)))$ and $|hd(tl(tl(*{:}Stream)))| > |hd(tl(*{:}Stream))|$.

The problem of detecting special contexts appears to be very hard in its full generality. However, in practice it turns out that a small number of special contexts and compositions of them, like described in Section 5, are sufficient. More precisely, it tends to suffice to search for special contexts among the operations already defined by the specification, focusing on particular arguments of them. For example, one may ask oneself if the operation zip on streams, with focus on its first argument, is a special context. To check that, all one needs to do is to show that for any experiment applied to the focused operation, in our case to $zip(*{:}Stream, S{:}Stream)$, one can, via equational deduction, reduce the overall depth to the $*$ variable. In our case, it is easy to see that a generic stream experiment $hd(tl^{n}(*{:}Stream))$ applied to $zip(*{:}Stream, S{:}Stream)$ will eventually reduce the depth to $*$: if $n = 0$ one gets $hd(*{:}Stream)$ of depth 1, so the depth is reduced by 1; if $n = 1$ one gets $hd(S{:}Steam)$ so there is no $*$ anymore; if $n \geq 2$ then one can apply the two depth-most tl operations on the $zip(*{:}Stream, S{:}Stream)$ context and obtain, via equational deduction, a new context $zip(tl(*{:}Stream), tl(S{:}Stream))$, so two tl operations have been removed and only one has been inserted above $*$. One can do the same for the other argument of zip. The above certify that zip is indeed special. While the above is not a fully general technique to find all the special contexts, it works so well in practice that we implemented it as integral part of the CIRC prover (Section 5).

From now on, we assume that $\vdash$ is also closed under substitution, that is, if $E \vdash e$ and θ is a substitution, then $E \vdash \theta(e)$. This requirement is reasonable and satisfied by any entailment system that we are aware of.

Theorem 4. *If F is a hidden equation set and γ a special context, $\gamma[F] \subseteq F^{\leq}$.*

Therefore, special contexts automatically yield a distinguished set of special hypotheses for any set of hidden equations. We empirically found that these distinguished special hypotheses are sufficient to prove all the behavioral properties that we and other colleagues considered so far, so we next extend our circular coinductive proof system with special contexts and then prove its soundness.

Let us replace the rule [Derive] in Figure 2 with the more general one below:

$$\frac{\mathcal{B} \cup \mathcal{F} \cup \{\boxed{e}\} \cup \boxed{\Gamma[e]} \Vvdash^{\circlearrowleft} \mathcal{G} \cup \boxed{\Delta[e]}}{\mathcal{B} \cup \mathcal{F} \Vvdash^{\circlearrowleft} \mathcal{G} \cup \{\boxed{e}\}}, \quad \begin{array}{l}\text{when } e \text{ is hidden and} \\ \Gamma \text{ is a set of special contexts}\end{array} \qquad [\mathsf{Derive}^{\mathsf{scx}}]$$

Theorem 5. ***(soundness of circular coinduction with special contexts)*** *If $\mathcal{B}$ is a behavioral specification and G is a set of equations such that $\mathcal{B} \Vvdash^{\circlearrowleft} \boxed{G}$ is derivable using the proof system extended with rule* [Derive^{scx}]*, then $\mathcal{B} \Vvdash G$.*

$$\begin{array}{l}
\hline
\mathsf{BPA} \cup \boxed{F_3} \cup \boxed{\Gamma_3} \Vvdash^{\circlearrowleft} \emptyset \\
\mathsf{BPA} \cup \boxed{F_3} \cup \boxed{\Gamma_3} \vdash \boxed{A\{a\}\{a\}\{a\}} = \boxed{X\{a\}\{a\}\{a\}} \\
\hline
\mathsf{BPA} \cup \boxed{F_3} \cup \boxed{\Gamma_3} \Vvdash^{\circlearrowleft} \boxed{A\{a\}\{a\}\{a\}} = \boxed{X\{a\}\{a\}\{a\}} \\
\mathsf{BPA} \cup \boxed{F_3} \cup \boxed{\Gamma_3} \vdash \boxed{\surd?(A\{a\}\{a\})} = \boxed{\surd?(X\{a\}\{a\})} \\
\hline
\mathsf{BPA} \cup \boxed{F_3} \cup \boxed{\Gamma_3} \Vvdash^{\circlearrowleft} \left\{\begin{array}{l} \boxed{A\{a\}\{a\}\{a\}} = \boxed{X\{a\}\{a\}\{a\}} \\ \boxed{\surd?(A\{a\}\{a\})} = \boxed{\surd?(X\{a\}\{a\})} \end{array}\right\} \\
\hline
\mathsf{BPA} \cup \boxed{F_2} \cup \boxed{\Gamma_2} \Vvdash^{\circlearrowleft} \boxed{A\{a\}\{a\}} = \boxed{X\{a\}\{a\}} \\
\mathsf{BPA} \cup \boxed{F_3} \cup \boxed{\Gamma_3} \vdash \boxed{\surd?(A\{a\})} = \boxed{\surd?(X\{a\})} \\
\hline
\mathsf{BPA} \cup \boxed{F_2} \cup \boxed{\Gamma_2} \Vvdash^{\circlearrowleft} \left\{\begin{array}{l} \boxed{A\{a\}\{a\}} = \boxed{X\{a\}\{a\}} \\ \boxed{\surd?(A\{a\})} = \boxed{\surd?(X\{a\})} \end{array}\right\} \\
\hline
\mathsf{BPA} \cup \boxed{F_1} \cup \boxed{\Gamma_1} \Vvdash^{\circlearrowleft} \boxed{A\{a\}} = \boxed{X\{a\}} \\
\mathsf{BPA} \cup \boxed{F_3} \cup \boxed{\Gamma_3} \vdash \boxed{\surd?(A)} = \boxed{\surd?(X)} \\
\hline
\mathsf{BPA} \cup \boxed{F_1} \cup \boxed{\Gamma_1} \Vvdash^{\circlearrowleft} \left\{\begin{array}{l} \boxed{A\{a\}} = \boxed{X\{a\}} \\ \boxed{\surd?(A)} = \boxed{\surd?(X)} \end{array}\right\} \\
\hline
\mathsf{BPA} \qquad\qquad\quad \Vvdash^{\circlearrowleft} \boxed{A} = \boxed{X}
\end{array}$$

Fig. 3. The proof tree for $\mathsf{BPA} \Vvdash^{\circlearrowleft} A = X$

Example 8. Figure 3 shows the proof tree for $\mathsf{BPA} \Vvdash^{\circlearrowleft} A = X$, where A and X are defined in Fig. 1. The following notations are used:

$$\begin{array}{lll}
F_1 = \{A = X\} & F_2 = F_1 \cup \{A\{a\} = X\{a\}\} & F_3 = F_2 \cup \{A\{a\}\{a\} = X\{a\}\{a\}\} \\
\Gamma_i = \Gamma(F_i) & \text{for } i = 1, 2, 3 &
\end{array}$$

where Γ is the closure under context composition of

$$\{p + {*}{:}Pexp,\ {*}{:}Pexp + p,\ p\,;{*}{:}Pexp,\ {*}{:}Pexp\,;p\}.$$

The role of the special hypotheses is explained by showing how $A\{a\}\{a\}\{a\} = X\{a\}\{a\}\{a\}$ is deduced:

$$
\begin{array}{ll}
A\{a\} = \checkmark + A\,;a & \text{(by the axioms in BPA)} \\
\checkmark + A\,;a = \checkmark + X\,;a & \text{(a special hypothesis in } \Gamma_1 \subset \Gamma_3\text{)} \\
(\checkmark + X\,;a)\{a\}\{a\} = \checkmark + X\,;a & \text{(by the axioms in BPA)} \\
A\{a\}\{a\}\{a\} = \checkmark + X\,;a & \text{(congruence \& transitivity)} \\
X\{a\} = \checkmark + a\,;X & \text{(by the axioms in BPA)} \\
X\{a\}\{a\}\{a\} = \checkmark + a\,;X & \text{(by the axioms in BPA)} \\
A\{a\}\{a\}\{a\} = X\{a\}\{a\}\{a\} & \text{(by the axioms in } F_2 \cup \Gamma_1 \subset F_3 \cup \Gamma_3\text{)}
\end{array}
$$

The special hypothesis used above is obtained as follows: we have $A = X$ in F_1, $A;a = X\,;a$ is in Γ_1 by using the special context $*{:}Pexp\,;p$, and $\checkmark + A\,;a = \checkmark + X\,;a$ is in Γ_1 by using the special context $p + *{:}Pexp$. The behavioral closure of $F_3 \cup \Gamma_3$ is an infinite set, hence this example exhibits the ability of the proof system with special contexts to handle infinite coinductive proofs.

Example 9. In this example we show that two (known) definitions for the famous Thue-Morse sequence (see, e.g., [2]) are equivalent. The Thue-Morse sequence is the stream of bits whose n-th bit is computed as follows: 1) write the number n

$$
\dfrac{\texttt{STREAM} \cup \boxed{F_4} \cup \boxed{\Gamma_4} \Vvdash^{\circlearrowleft} \emptyset}{\texttt{STREAM} \cup \boxed{F_4} \cup \boxed{\Gamma_4} \vdash \boxed{tl^2(f(S))} = \boxed{tl^2(zip(S, not(S)))}}
$$

$$
\dfrac{\texttt{STREAM} \cup \boxed{F_4} \cup \boxed{\Gamma_4} \Vvdash^{\circlearrowleft} \left\{\boxed{tl^2(f(S))} = \boxed{tl^2(zip(S, not(S)))}\right\}}{\texttt{STREAM} \cup \boxed{F_4} \cup \boxed{\Gamma_4} \vdash \boxed{hd(tl(f(S)))} = \boxed{hd(tl(zip(S, not(S))))}}
$$

$$
\dfrac{\texttt{STREAM} \cup \boxed{F_4} \cup \boxed{\Gamma_4} \Vvdash^{\circlearrowleft} \left\{\begin{array}{l}\boxed{tl^2(f(S))} = \boxed{tl^2(zip(S, not(S)))} \\ \boxed{hd(tl(f(S)))} = \boxed{hd(tl(zip(S, not(S))))}\end{array}\right\}}{\texttt{STREAM} \cup \boxed{F_4} \cup \boxed{\Gamma_4} \vdash \boxed{tl^2(morse)} = \boxed{tl^2(altMorse)}}
$$

$$
\dfrac{\texttt{STREAM} \cup \boxed{F_4} \cup \boxed{\Gamma_4} \Vvdash^{\circlearrowleft} \left\{\begin{array}{l}\boxed{tl^2(f(S))} = \boxed{tl^2(zip(S, not(S)))} \\ \boxed{hd(tl(f(S)))} = \boxed{hd(tl(zip(S, not(S))))} \\ \boxed{tl^2(morse)} = \boxed{tl^2(altMorse)}\end{array}\right\}}{\cdots}
$$

$$
\dfrac{\texttt{STREAM} \cup \boxed{F_1} \cup \boxed{\Gamma_1} \Vvdash^{\circlearrowleft} \left\{\boxed{f(S)} = \boxed{zip(S, not(S))},\ \boxed{tl(morse)} = \boxed{tl(altMorse)}\right\}}{\texttt{STREAM} \cup \boxed{F_1} \cup \boxed{\Gamma_1} \vdash \boxed{hd(morse)} = \boxed{hd(altMorse)}}
$$

$$
\dfrac{\texttt{STREAM} \cup \boxed{F_1} \cup \boxed{\Gamma_1} \Vvdash^{\circlearrowleft} \left\{\begin{array}{l}\boxed{f(S)} = \boxed{zip(S, not(S))} \\ \boxed{tl(morse)} = \boxed{tl(altMorse)},\ \boxed{hd(morse)} = \boxed{hd(altMorse)}\end{array}\right\}}{\texttt{STREAM} \Vvdash^{\circlearrowleft} \left\{\begin{array}{l}\boxed{f(S)} = \boxed{zip(S, not(S))} \\ \boxed{morse} = \boxed{altMorse}\end{array}\right\}}
$$

Fig. 4. The proof tree for $\texttt{STREAM} \Vvdash^{\circlearrowleft} \{morse = altMorse, f(S) = zip(S, not(S))\}$

in binary; if the number of ones in this binary expansion is odd then the n-th bit is 1; if even then the n-th bit is 0. The first definition we consider is given by

$$morse = 0 : zip(not(morse), tl(morse)).$$

The second definition uses an auxiliary function:

$$altMorse = f(0 : tl(altMorse)) \text{ where } f(a : s) = a : not(a) : f(s)$$

Figure 4 shows the (partial) proof tree for $\texttt{STREAM} \Vdash^{\circlearrowleft} morse = altMorse$, using the behavioral definitions expressed in terms of the derivatives head and tail. The proof of this property requires the following lemma: $f(S) = zip(S, not(S))$. Since the proof system is able to handle sets of goals, we prove the two properties simultaneously. Only the special hypotheses generated by the special context $f(*{:}Stream)$ are required. The following notations are used:

$$F_1 = \{morse = altMorse\} \qquad F_2 = F_1 \cup \{f(S) = zip(S, not(S))\}$$
$$F_3 = F_2 \cup \{tl(morse)=tl(altMorse)\} \quad F_4 = F_3 \cup \{tl(f(S))=tl(zip(S, not(S)))\}$$
$$\Gamma_i = \{f(t) = f(t') \mid t = t' \in F_i\}, \, i = 1, \dots, 4$$

In order to see the role of special hypotheses, we explain how $\boxed{tl^2(morse)} = \boxed{tl^2(altMorse)}$ is deduced. We get $tl^2(morse) = zip(tl(morse), not(tl(morse))) = f(tl(morse))$ and, similarly, $tl^2(altMorse) = f(tl(altMorse))$ by the definition of the operations. The conclusion follows now by applying the special hypothesis $f(tl(morse)) = f(tl(altMorse))$ from Γ_3. Again, the behavioral closure of $F_4 \cup \Gamma_4$ is an infinite set, hence this example exhibits the ability of the proof system with special contexts to handle infinite coinductive proofs.

It is worth noting that the above property can also be proved using the hypotheses generated by the special contexts in Example 7.

5   Implementation in CIRC

CIRC implements the circular coinduction proof system by the reduction rules in Fig. 5. The entailment relation used in CIRC is $\mathcal{E} \vdash_{\leftarrow} (\forall X)t = t'$ if $\wedge_i u_i = v_i$ iff $\mathrm{nf}(t) = \mathrm{nf}(t')$, where $\mathrm{nf}(t)$, the *normal form* of t, is computed as follows:

- the variables of the equations are turned into fresh constants;
- the condition equalities are added as equations to the specification;
- the equations in the specification are oriented and used as rewrite rules.

It is easy to see that the reduction rules [Done], [Reduce], and [Derive] implement the proof rules with the same names given in Fig. 2. The reduction rules [Normalize] and [Fail] have no correspondent in the proof system and are used to ease the user interaction with the prover. A failure does not necessarily mean that the answer is false. The failure relation $\mathcal{E} \nvdash_{\leftarrow} \boxed{e}$ says that the corresponding normal forms are different. Since we do not impose any confluence conditions on the specification, it is possible that the normal forms are different even if the equation is a $\vdash$-consequence of the current specification. So, a failing ending of the algorithm needs (human) analysis in order to know the source of the failure.

$$
\begin{array}{lll}
\text{[Done]} & : (\mathcal{B}, \mathcal{F}, \emptyset) \Rightarrow \cdot \\
\text{[Reduce]} & : (\mathcal{B}, \mathcal{F}, \mathcal{G} \cup \{\boxed{e}\}) \Rightarrow (\mathcal{B}, \mathcal{F}, \mathcal{G}) & \text{if } \mathcal{B} \cup \mathcal{F} \vdash_{\leftarrow} e \\
\text{[Derive]} & : (\mathcal{B}, \mathcal{F}, \mathcal{G} \cup \{\boxed{e}\}) \Rightarrow (\mathcal{B}, \mathcal{F} \cup \{\boxed{e}\}, \mathcal{G} \cup \{\boxed{\Delta(e)}\}) & \begin{array}{l}\text{if } \mathcal{B} \cup \mathcal{F} \nvdash_{\leftarrow} e \\ \text{and } e \text{ is hidden}\end{array} \\
\text{[Normalize]} & : (\mathcal{B}, \mathcal{F}, \mathcal{G} \cup \{\boxed{e}\}) \Rightarrow (\mathcal{B}, \mathcal{F}, \mathcal{G} \cup \{\boxed{\text{nf}(e)}\}) \\
\text{[Fail]} & : (\mathcal{B}, \mathcal{F}, \mathcal{G} \cup \{\boxed{e}\}) \Rightarrow \textit{fail} & \begin{array}{l}\text{if } \mathcal{B} \cup \mathcal{F} \nvdash_{\leftarrow} e \\ \text{and } e \text{ is visible}\end{array}
\end{array}
$$

Fig. 5. CIRC's reduction rules implementing the circular coinduction

However, since CIRC includes an implementation of the circular induction (it will be presented in a different paper), a technique similar to that in [4] can be used to check if the failed visible equation or the inequality of the two normal forms is an inductive theorem. More details about CIRC tool can be found in [14].

The implementation of the system extended with the special contexts is obtained by replacing the implementation of [Derive] with that of [Derive^{scx}]. In order to make the rule [Derive^{scx}] effective, we have to know which contexts are special. A less efficient way is to manually prove that some contexts are special and then include them in the behavioral specification. Though CIRC includes such a facility, it is more challenging and elegant to automatically detect the special contexts. If the composition $\gamma_1[\gamma_2]$ of two special contexts γ_1 and γ_2 is a special context as well, then it is enough to find a maximal subset Γ of contexts γ of minimal depth. An example of such Γ is given in Example 7. Knowing Γ, there is a very simple and efficient way to implement [Derive^{scx}]: for each special context $\gamma[*{:}h]$ in Γ, the following equation is added to the specification:

$$
\boxed{\gamma[x]} = \boxed{\gamma[y]} \quad \text{if} \quad \boxed{y} := \boxed{x}
$$

where the execution of the matching equation $\boxed{y} := \boxed{x}$ instantiates y by matching $\boxed{y}$ against the normal form of $\boxed{x}$. However, note that this elegant implementation works in our case thanks to the matching-in-condition mechanism specific to Maude. Let us explain how this mechanism works for $\gamma = *{:}Stream + S'$ and $\boxed{S \times zeros} = \boxed{zeros}$. If $x \mapsto S \times zeros$, then $\boxed{y} := \boxed{x}$ returns $y \mapsto zeros$. Replacing γ, x and y in $\boxed{\gamma[x]} = \boxed{\gamma[y]}$ we obtain the desired result: $S \times zeros + S' = zeros + S'$.

The algorithm used by CIRC for computing a set Γ of special contexts of minimal depth is quite complex and it will be presented in detail, together with its correctness and complexity, in an extended version. Here we briefly describe the intuition behind this algorithm.

We first introduce some notation. Let Ctx° be the set of contexts $f(x_1, \ldots, x_n)$ with $f \in \Sigma^{hidden}$, $x_i = *$ for exactly one hidden argument, say the ith, and in the rest x_j is a variable, where Σ^{hidden} is the set of operations with hidden result and at least one hidden argument. If C is a Δ-context, then the *hidden depth* $|C|^{\cdot}$ of C is defined by $|C|^{\cdot} = |C|$ if C is hidden, and $|C|^{\cdot} = |C| - 1$ if C is visible.

Thus, the hidden depth of a context is the number of operations in Σ^{hidden} on the path to $*$. If $k \geq -1$ and $\Gamma \subseteq Ctx^\circ$, then a (k, Γ)-*composite* is defined as:

1. any non-star variable and any constant is a $(-1, \Gamma)$-composite;
2. any Δ-context C is a $(|C|^\cdot, \Gamma)$-composite;
3. if $f : v_1 \ldots v_n \to v$ is a data operator or a generalized constant and t_i is a (k_i, Γ)-composite for $i = 1, \ldots, n$, then $f(t_1, \ldots, t_n)$ is a (k, Γ)-composite, where $k = \max\{k_1, \ldots, k_n\}$;
4. if $\gamma \in \Gamma$ and t is a (k, Γ)-composite, then $\gamma[t]$ is a (k, Γ)-composite;
5. if C is a Δ-context, t a (k, Γ)-composite with $k = -1$ or t of the form $g(t_1, \ldots, t_n)$ with g a generalized constant, then $C[t]$ is a (k, Γ)-composite.

The goal is to find a predicate $Comp(C, t)$ and a set $\Gamma \subseteq Ctx^\circ$ such that the predicate $Special(\Gamma)$, given by

$$Special(\Gamma) \stackrel{\text{def}}{=} (\forall \gamma \in \Gamma)(\forall \delta \in \Delta) \; Comp(\delta, \gamma),$$

implies that each Γ-context is special. If we have an algorithm for computing such a predicate $Comp(C, t)$, then the searching for a suitable Γ requires the evaluation of the predicate for a small set of pairs (C, t). The algorithm implemented in CIRC uses the following definition for $Comp(C, t)$: if C is a Δ-context and t is a (k, Γ)-composite term, then

$$Comp(C, t) \stackrel{\text{def}}{=} \mathcal{B} \vdash C[t] = t' \wedge t' \text{ is } (k', \Gamma)\text{-composite} \wedge k' \leq k + |C|^\cdot$$

If the property $Comp(\delta, \gamma)$ can be algorithmically checked for $\delta \in \Delta$ and $\gamma \in \Gamma$, then the property $Special(\Gamma)$ can be checked as well. So, the only thing we have to do is to find a suitable set Γ. Our algorithm starts with $\Gamma = Ctx^\circ$. For each $\delta \in \Delta$ and $\gamma \in \Gamma$, it computes the normal form of $\delta[\gamma]$ and it checks if this normal form is $(|\delta|^\cdot, \Gamma)$-composite (this can be algorithmically checked). If the answer is yes in all the cases, then $Special(\Gamma)$ holds and the algorithm returns Γ. If the answer is no for some δ and γ, then γ is removed from Γ and the algorithm is applied again over the new set Γ. The algorithm stops when the current set of contexts becomes empty (no special contexts found) or, as we have seen above, we have $Special(\Gamma)$. The following algorithmic description summarizes the procedure described above:

```
check (Γ)
   if Γ ≠ ∅
   then for each γ ∈ Γ
               for each δ ∈ Δ
                  if not Comp(δ, γ)
                     then return check(Γ \ {γ})
   return Γ
```

The special contexts basis Γ for a $\mathcal{B}$ is computed by the call check(Ctx°).

Here is an excerpt of the dialog with CIRC exhibiting how the special contexts in Example 9 are automatically computed:

```
Maude> (set auto contexts on .)
Maude> in stream
-------------------------------------------

The special contexts are:
*:Stream + V#2:Stream          not(*:Stream)
V#1:Stream + *:Stream          zip(*:Stream,V#2:Stream)
*:Stream x V#2:Stream          zip(V#1:Stream,*:Stream)
V#1:Stream x *:Stream
```

Setting on the switch `auto contexts`, CIRC automatically execute the algorithm computing the special contexts for each behavioral theory loaded after that. Recall that a behavioral theory includes, among other things, the declaration of the derivatives. We see that $f(*{:}Stream)$ is not found as a special context. This is because the definition of f is in terms of $hd(*{:}Stream)$, $hd(tl(*{:}Stream))$, and $tl(tl(*{:}Stream))$. The algorithm can be specialized for such cases and this specialization can be executed by introducing `check scx` command:

```
Maude> (check scx f(*:Stream) using hd(*:Stream) hd(tl(*:Stream))
                                     tl(tl(*:Stream)) .)
f(*:Stream) is a special context
```

We can use CIRC to see that the special contexts are essential in proving the properties described in Example 9. We first execute the circular coinduction without special contexts by setting the switch `auto contexts` off:

```
Maude> (set auto contexts off .)
Contexts will not be automatically computed.
Maude> in stream
Maude> (add goal f(S:Stream) = zip(S:Stream, not(S:Stream))
Maude> (add goal morse = altMorse .)
Maude> (coinduction .)
Stopped: the number of prover steps was exceeded.
```

The output message saying that the number of prover steps was exceeded is a clue that the algorithm does not terminate (we may check that by increasing the number of steps). Then we execute the algorithm with the special contexts:

```
Maude> (set auto contexts on .)
Maude> in stream
Maude> (add goal f(S:Stream) = zip(S:Stream, not(S:Stream)) .)
Maude> (add goal morse = altMorse .)
Maude> (coinduction .)
Proof succeeded.

  Number of derived goals: 8
  Number of proving steps performed: 41
  Maximum number of proving steps is set to: 256

Proved properties:

  tl(f(S:Stream)) = zip(not(S:Stream),tl(S:Stream))
  tl(morse) = tl(altMorse)
  f(S:Stream) = zip(S:Stream,not(S:Stream))
  morse = altMorse
```

We see that the algorithm successfully terminated this time. Moreover, it displays the set $\mathcal{F}$ of frozen hypotheses it discovered during the proving process. At this point, the user can display the proof tree like the one in Example 9 by introducing the command (`show proof .`). We encourage the interested reader to try the examples in this paper, as well as many others, in CIRC using its online web interface at `http://fsl.cs.uiuc.edu/CIRC` (all the examples discussed in this paper are already provided there).

6 Conclusion, More Related Work, and Future Work

The main contributions of this paper are: we introduced *special hypotheses* as a closure operator and use it to extend the coinductive circularity principle; we used *special contexts* to obtain a distinguished class of special hypotheses, and extended the circular coinductive proof system with special contexts; we explained how the circular coinductive proof system and its extension with special contexts are implemented in CIRC; we described an algorithm which automatically finds special contexts in a given specification (the algorithm is already implemented in CIRC); we showed on non-trivial examples that the special contexts are useful.

The proof system presented in this paper and its implementation in CIRC has its roots in the circular coinductive rewriting algorithm given in [10] and early implemented in the BOBJ system [19]. An advantage of our proof theoretical approach discussed in this paper, which extends with special contexts the one we previously proposed in [22], is that it can be relatively easily combined with proof plans and proof critics similar to those defined in [7]. A part of them are already supported in the current version of CIRC [14].

An important aspect of behavioral specifications, that we did not discuss in this paper, is that of well-definedness. An ingenious method for checking well-definedness of behavioral specifications over streams that follow a common corecursive specification style is given in [27], using a reduction to ordinary termination, which can further be checked using off-the-shelf termination tools. It would be interesting to explore the relationship between behavioral well-definedness and behavioral equivalence, and to understand under what conditions one could reduce behavioral equivalence to termination; an incipient discussion on this topic can be found in [27].

A closely related topic is observational logic; see [3] for a recent reference. In particular, our proof theoretic definition of the behavioral entailment relation $\Vdash$ is reminiscent of the infinitary proof system defined in [3]. We believe that our circular coinductive proof system can be seamlessly adapted to observational logic and also that CIRC can be used as is to do sound observational logic proofs.

Our next goal is to incorporate case analysis into our automated behavioral prover, CIRC, both at the level of its underlying proof system and within its algorithm that computes special contexts. Finally, even though CIRC provides support for combined inductive and coinductive proving, the proof theoretical foundations for circular induction still need to be elaborated in detail.

Acknowledgments. We are grateful to Hans Zantema for the fruitful discussion regarding the special contexts and to Georgiana Caltais and Eugen Goriac for implementing in a short time the algorithm computing the special contexts.

References

1. Adámek, J.: Introduction to coalgebra. Theory and Applications of Categories 14(8), 157–199 (2005)
2. Allouche, J.-P., Shallit, J.: The ubiquitous Prouhet-Thue-Morse sequence. In: SETA 1998, pp. 1–16. Springer, Heidelberg (1999)
3. Bidoit, M., Hennicker, R., Kurz, A.: Observational logic, constructor-based logic, and their duality. Theoretical Computer Science 3(298), 471–510 (2003)
4. Bouhoula, A., Rusinowitch, M.: Observational proofs by rewriting. Theoretical Computer Science 275(1-2), 675–698 (2002)
5. Clavel, M., Durán, F., Eker, S., Lincoln, P., Martí-Oliet, N., Meseguer, J., Talcott, C.L.: All about Maude - a high-performance logical framework, how to specify, program and verify systems in rewriting logic. In: All About Maude - A High-Performance Logical Framework. LNCS, vol. 4350. Springer, Heidelberg (2007)
6. Coquand, T.: Infinite objects in type theory. In: Barendregt, H., Nipkow, T. (eds.) TYPES 1993. LNCS, vol. 806, pp. 62–78. Springer, Heidelberg (1994)
7. Dennis, L.: Proof Planning Coinduction. PhD thesis, Edinburgh University (1998)
8. Dennis, L., Bundy, A., Green, I.: Using a generalisation critic to find bisimulations for coinductive proofs. In: McCune, W. (ed.) CADE 1997. LNCS (LNAI), vol. 1249, pp. 276–290. Springer, Heidelberg (1997)
9. Fokkink, W.: Introduction to Process Algebra. Springer, Berlin (2000)
10. Goguen, J., Lin, K., Roşu, G.: Conditional circular coinductive rewriting with case analysis. In: Wirsing, M., Pattinson, D., Hennicker, R. (eds.) WADT 2003. LNCS, vol. 2755, pp. 216–232. Springer, Heidelberg (2003)
11. Goguen, J., Malcolm, G.: A hidden agenda. Theoretical Computer Science 245(1), 55–101 (2000)
12. Goguen, J., Meseguer, J.: Completeness of Many-Sorted Equational Logic. Houston Journal of Mathematics 11(3), 307–334 (1985)
13. Hausmann, D., Mossakowski, T., Schröder, L.: Iterative circular coinduction for CoCasl in Isabelle/HOL. In: Cerioli, M. (ed.) FASE 2005. LNCS, vol. 3442, pp. 341–356. Springer, Heidelberg (2005)
14. Lucanu, D., Goriac, E.-I., Caltais, G., Roşu, G.: CIRC: A behavioral verification tool based on circular coinduction. In: Lenisa, M., Kurz, A., Tarlecki, A. (eds.) CALCO 2009. LNCS, vol. 5728, pp. 433–442. Springer, Heidelberg (2009)
15. Lucanu, D., Roşu, G.: Circ: A circular coinductive prover. In: Mossakowski, T., Montanari, U., Haveraaen, M. (eds.) CALCO 2007. LNCS, vol. 4624, pp. 372–378. Springer, Heidelberg (2007)
16. Meseguer, J.: General logics. In: Ebbinghaus, H.D., et al. (eds.) Logic Colloquium 1987, pp. 275–329. North Holland, Amsterdam (1989)
17. Niqui, M.: Coinductive formal reasoning in exact real arithmetic. Logical Methods in Computer Science 4(3:6), 1–40 (2008)
18. Paulson, L.C.: Mechanizing coinduction and corecursion in higher-order logic. Logic and Computation 7, 175–204 (1997)
19. Roşu, G.: Hidden Logic. PhD thesis, University of California at San Diego (2000)
20. Roşu, G.: Equality of streams is a Π_2^0-complete problem. In: ICFP 2006, pp. 184–191. ACM, New York (2006)
21. Roşu, G., Goguen, J.: Circular coinduction, Short paper. In: IJCAR 2001 (2001)

22. Roşu, G., Lucanu, D.: Circular Coinduction – A Proof Theoretical Foundation. In: Lenisa, M., Kurz, A., Tarlecki, A. (eds.) CALCO 2009. LNCS, vol. 5728, pp. 127–144. Springer, Heidelberg (2009)

23. Rutten, J.: Behavioural Differential Equations: A Coinductive Calculus of Streams, Automata, and Power Series. Theoretical Computer Science 308(1-3), 1–53 (2003)

24. Rutten, J.: A coinductive calculus of streams. Mathematical Structures in Computer Science 15(1), 93–147 (2005)

25. Silva, A., Rutten, J.: Behavioural differential equations and coinduction for binary trees. In: Leivant, D., de Queiroz, R. (eds.) WoLLIC 2007. LNCS, vol. 4576, pp. 322–336. Springer, Heidelberg (2007)

26. van Glabbeek, R.J.: The linear time - branching time spectrum II. In: Best, E. (ed.) CONCUR 1993. LNCS, vol. 715, pp. 66–81. Springer, Heidelberg (1993)

27. Zantema, H.: Well-definedness of streams by termination. In: Treinen, R. (ed.) RTA 2009. LNCS, vol. 5595, pp. 164–178. Springer, Heidelberg (2009)

A   Glossary

Signature. A signature Σ over the set of *sorts* S is a $(S^* \times S)$-indexed set of operation names. If $\sigma \in \Sigma_{w,s}$ then $w \in S^*$ is the *arity* of σ and s is the *sort* of σ; we typically write $\sigma : w \to s$ instead of $\sigma \in \Sigma_{w,s}$ when Σ is understood;

Constant = an operation whose arity is empty and written as $\sigma : \ \to s$.

Variable = a symbol x having associated a sort s and often written as $x{:}s$.

Σ-term. A Σ-term with variables in X is inductively defined as follows: any variable $x{:}s$ of sort s is a term of sorts s; any constant $\sigma : \ \to s$ in Σ is a term of sorts s; if $\sigma : s_1 \dots s_n \to s$ is an operation name in Σ, t_i is a term of sort s_i for each $i \in \{1, \dots, n\}$, then $\sigma(t_1, \dots, t_n)$ is a term of sort s.

Ground term = a term without variables.

Σ-equation = an expression e of the form $(\forall X)\, t = t'$ if $\bigwedge_{i \in \{1,\dots,n\}} u_i = v_i$ with t, t', u_i, and v_i Σ-terms with variables in X for all $i \in \{1, \dots, n\}$; the two terms appearing in any equality in an equation, that is the terms t, t' and each pair u_i, v_i for each $i \in \{1, \dots, n\}$, have, respectively, the same sort. When $n = 0$ we call the equation unconditional and omit the condition (i.e., we write it $(\forall X)\, t = t'$). The *sort of* e is the common sort of t and t'.

Σ-context (for sort s) = a Σ-term C which has one occurrence of a distinguished variable $*{:}s$ of sort s; we may write $C[*{:}s]$ instead of just C.

$|C|$ = the *depth* of the context C: $|*{:}s| = 0$ and $|C[\sigma[*{:}s]]| = |C| + 1$, $\sigma \in \Sigma$.

$C[e]$. If $C[*{:}s]$ is a context and e is an equation $(\forall X)\, t = t'$ if c of sort s, then $C[e]$ is the equation $(\forall X \cup Y)\, C[t] = C[t']$ if c, where Y is the set of non-star variables occurring in $C[*{:}s]$. When C is not a context (it does not include the star variable $*$), $C[e]$ is the identity equation $(\forall X)C = C$. So, a Σ-context C induces a partially defined *equation transformer* $e \mapsto C[e]$.

$C[E]$. If C a context and e an equation, then $C[E] = \{C[e] \mid e \in E\}$.

$\mathbf{C}_s$. If $\mathbf{C}$ is a set of contexts, $\mathbf{C}_s$ denotes all the contexts of sort s in $\mathbf{C}$.

$\mathbf{C}[e]$. If $\mathbf{C}$ is a set of contexts and e an equation, then $\mathbf{C}[e] = \{C[e] \mid C \in \mathbf{C}\}$.

$\mathbf{C}[E]$. If $\mathbf{C}$ is a set of contexts and E a set of equations, then $\mathbf{C}[E] = \bigcup_{e \in E} \mathbf{C}[e]$.

Algebraic specification or simply a *specification*, is a triple (S, Σ, E), where S is a set of sorts, Σ is a signature over S, and E is a set of Σ-equations.

The VSE Refinement Method in HETS

Mihai Codescu[1], Bruno Langenstein[2], Christian Maeder[1], and Till Mossakowski[1,3]

[1] German Research Center for Artificial Intelligence (DFKI GmbH), Bremen, Germany
[2] DFKI GmbH, Saarbrücken, Germany
[3] SFB/TR 8 Spatial Cognition, Bremen, Germany

Abstract. We present the integration of refinement method of VSE verification tool, successfully used in industrial applications, in the Heterogeneous Tool Set HETS. The connection is done via introducing the dynamic logic underlying VSE and two logic translations in the logic graph of HETS. Thus the logic-independent layers of HETS are not modified and its proof management formalism can be applied to VSE specifications.

1 Introduction

Heterogeneous specification becomes more and more important because complex systems are often specified using multiple viewpoints, involving various formalisms. Moreover, a formal software development process may lead to a change of formalism during the development. However, current research in integrated formal methods only deals with ad-hoc integrations of different formalisms.

The Heterogeneous Tool Set HETS [21,19], developed at DFKI Bremen, is a tool for heterogeneous multi-logic specification, interfacing various theorem provers, model checkers and model finders. The specification environment Verification Support Environment (VSE) [3], developed at DFKI Saarbrücken, provides an industrial-strength methodology for specification and verification of imperative programs.

We want to combine the best of both worlds by establishing a connection between the VSE prover and the HETS proof management. For VSE, this brings additionally flexibility: VSE specifications can now be verified not only with the VSE prover, but also with provers like SPASS [25] and Isabelle [23] which are interfaced with HETS. On the other hand, HETS benefits from VSE's industrial experience, including a practical relation between specification and programming languages together with the necessary poof support. Being interactive the VSE prover offers enough flexibility to tackle even challenging proof obligations, while a set of strong heuristics based on symbolic execution provide automation to keep the proof effort still small.

In order to understand the specific way of integrating HETS and VSE, one needs to understand the philosophy behind HETS. The central idea of HETS is to provide a general integration and proof management framework. One can think of HETS acting like a motherboard where different expansion cards can be plugged in, the expansion cards here being individual logics (with their analysis and proof tools) as well as logic translations. Of course, a tool like VSE provides analysis and proof tools for a specific logic, but not yet in a form that can directly be plugged into the HETS motherboard. The challenge hence is to encapsulate VSE in an expansion card that is

K. Breitman and A. Cavalcanti (Eds.): ICFEM 2009, LNCS 5885, pp. 660–678, 2009.

compatible to the HETS motherboard. The benefit of doing this is that for both verification and refinement, we can use the general proof management mechanisms of the HETS motherboard, instead of the specialised refinement tools hard-wired into VSE.

Moreover, the HETS motherboard already has plugged in a number of expansion cards (e.g., the theorem provers Isabelle, SPASS and more, as well as model finders) that can be used for VSE as well. The challenge is that typically, tools that shall be plugged into the HETS motherboard are not compatible with HETS expansion slots. Often, this is a matter of writing a suitable wrapper, but sometimes, also the specification of the expansion slot has to be enhanced. Of course, such enhancements should only be done for

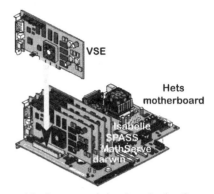

very good reasons — otherwise, one will end up with slots containing hundreds of special pins. Since VSE provides a special notion of refinement, one is tempted to enhance the specification of the expansion slot in this case. However, we will see that we can do without such an enhancement.

Related work includes ad-hoc integration of (tools for) formal methods, see e.g. the integrated formal methods conference series [17], and integrations of decision procedures, model checkers and automated theorem provers into interactive theorem provers [10,18]. However, these approaches are not as flexible as the HETSmotherboard/expansion card mechanism. In many approaches, the interfaces for these integrations are ad-hoc and not re-used in many different contexts. Moreover, we will see in Sect. 6 below that the use of *logic translations as first class citizens* in the expansion card mechanism is crucial for integrating VSE and HETS in a modular way. This clearly is a novel feature of our approach.

The paper is organised as follows: Section 2 contains an informal description of HETS and its foundations. In particular, the notions of *institution* and *institution comorphism* can be imagined as the specification of two different types of expansion slot on the HETS motherboard. Section 3 presents the VSE methodology, and in Section 4, its underlying dynamic logic is (for the first time) organised as an institution, aka as an expansion card that can easily be plugged into the HETS motherboard. Section 5 recalls the algebraic specification notion of refinement and compares the the way this concept is handled by HETS and VSE. In Section 6, we define two institution comorphisms, which can be thought of as further expansion cards that provide the VSE notion of refinement in HETS. In Section 7 we briefly present a standard example, illustrating the implementation of natural numbers as lists of binary digits, while Section 8 concludes the paper.

2   Presentation of HETS

HETS is a multi-logic proof management tool that heterogeneously integrates many languages, logics and tools on a strong semantic basis. The core of HETS is a heterogeneous extension of the specification language CASL, designed by the "Common Framework Initiative for Algebraic Specification and Development".

2.1   CASL

CASL has been designed from the outset as the central language in a family of languages. Soon sublanguages and extension of CASL, like the higher-order extension HASCASL, the coalgebraic extension COCASL, the modal logic extension MODAL-CASL the reactive extensions CASL-LTL and CSP-CASL and others emerged. Luckily, the CASL follows a separation of concerns — it has been designed in four different layers [2,4,9]:

basic specifications are unstructured collections of symbols, axioms and theorems, serving the specification of individual software modules. The specific logic chosen for CASL here is first-order logic with partial functions, subsorting and induction principles for datatypes;

structured specifications organise large specifications in a structured way, by allowing their translation, union, parameterisation. restriction to an export interface and more. Still, structured specifications only cover the specification of individual software modules;

architectural specifications allow for prescribing the structure of implementations, thereby also determining the degree of parallelism that is possible in letting different programmers independently develop implementations of different subparts;

specification libraries allow the storage and retrieval of collections of specifications, distributed over the Internet.

2.2   Institutions

A crucial point in the design of these layers is that the syntax and semantics of each layer is orthogonal to that of the other layers. In particular, the layer of basic specifications can be changed to a different language and logic (e.g. an extension of CASL, or even a logic completely unrelated to CASL), while retaining the other layers. The central abstraction principle to achieve this separation of layers is the formalisation of the notion of logical system as *institutions* [12], a notion that arose in the late 1970ies when Goguen and Burstall developed a semantics for the modular specification language Clear [7].

We recall informally this central notion here. An institution provides

- a notion of signature, carrying the context of user-defined (i.e. non-logical) symbols, and a notion of signature morphisms (translations between signatures);
- for each signature, notions of sentence and model, and a satisfaction relation between these;
- for each signature morphism, a sentence translation and a model reduction (the direction of the latter being opposite to the signature morphism), such that satisfaction is invariant under translation resp. reduction along signature morphisms.

A very prominent example is the institution $FOL^=$ of many-sorted first-order logic with equality. Signatures are many-sorted first-order signatures, i.e. many-sorted algebraic signatures enriched with predicate symbols. Models are many-sorted first-order structures, and model reduction is done by translating a symbol that needs to be interpreted along the signature morphism before looking up its interpretation in the model that is being reduced. Sentences are first-order formulas, and sentence translation means replacement of the translated symbols. Satisfaction is the usual satisfaction of a first-order sentence in a first-order structure.

The institution $CFOL^=$ adds sort generation constraints to $FOL^=$. These express that some of the carriers sets are generated by some of the operations (and possibly the other carrier sets). $SubPCFOL^=$, the CASL institution, further equips $CFOL^=$ with subsorting and partial functions (which, however, will not play a role in this paper).

With the notion of institution providing the abstraction barrier between the layer of basic specifications on the one hand and the other layers on the other hand, it was quite natural (though also a great challenge) to realise this abstraction barrier *also at the level of tools*. HETS provides an object-oriented interface for

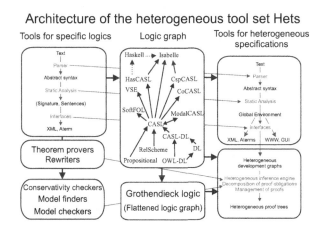

Architecture of the heterogeneous tool set Hets

logics and their proof tools, realised through a Haskell type class. This is exactly the specification of expansion slots mentioned in the introduction. This specification is heavily based on institutions, that is, the individual components of an institution are reflected in the interface. Of course, to be practically useful, the expansion slot specification contains additional components like concrete syntax, parsers, static analysis tools, and, last but not least, proof tools. The interface captures both interactive and automatic proof tools.

HETS allows for relating specifications written in different logics, e.g. CASL specifications can be imported for CASL extensions, or refinements can occur across different logics. In order to support this, HETS treats logic translations, formalised as *institution comorphisms (and morphisms)* [13], as first-class citizens (i.e., they are a different type of expansion card). An institution comorphism captures the idea of encoding or embedding between two institutions. It provides

- a translation of signatures (and signature morphisms),
- a translation of sentences,
- a translation of models (going backwards to the direction of the comorphism),

such that satisfaction is invariant under translation of sentences resp. models.

HETS is based on a *logic graph* of institutions and comorphisms, which is a parameter to the tools acting at the structured, architectural and library layers. The logic graph can be changed and extended without the need even to recompile those logic independent analysis tools. The architecture of HETS is shown in figure below. HETS' development graph component [20], inspired by the tool MAYA (a cousin of VSE, also developed in Saarbrücken) provides a proof management for heterogeneous specifications, relying on proof tools for the individual logics involved.

3   Presentation of VSE

The *Verification Support Environment* (VSE) is a tool that supports the formal development of complex large scale software systems from abstract high level specifications down to the code level. It provides both an administration system to manage structured formal specifications and a deductive component to maintain correctness on the various abstraction levels (see figure below). Taken together these components guarantee the overall correctness of the complete development. The structured approach allows the developer to combine specifications in an algebraic functional style with state based formal descriptions of concurrent systems.

VSE has been developed in two phases on behalf the German Bundesamt für Sicherheit in der Informationstechnik (BSI) to satisfy the needs in software developments according to the upcoming standards ITSEC and Common Criteria. Since then VSE has been successfully applied in several industrial and research projects, many of them being related to software evaluation [15,3,16,8]. The models developed with VSE comprise among others the control system of a heavy robot facility, the control system of a storm surge barrier, a formal security policy model conforming to the German signature law and protocols for chip card based biometric identification.

3.1   The VSE Methodology

VSE supports a development process that starts with a modular formal description of the *system model* and possibly together with separate *requirements* or *security objectives*. Logically the requirements have to be derivable from the system model. Therefore, the requirements lead to proof obligations that must be discharged by using the integrated deductive component of VSE.

In a *refinement process* the abstract system model can be related to more concrete models. This is in correspondence

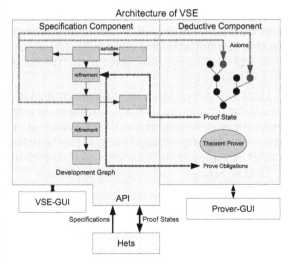

with a software development that starts from a high level design and then descends to the lower software layers such that in a sense higher layers are implemented based on lower layers. Each such step can be reflected by a *refinement step* in VSE. These steps involve programming notions in the form of abstract implementations, that can later be exploited to generate executable code. Each refinement step gives rise to proof obligations showing the correctness of the implementations. Refinements also can be used to prove consistency of specifications, because they describe a way how to construct a model. This plays a major role for the formal specifications required for Common Criteria, which only need to cover higher abstraction levels.

In addition to the *vertical* structure given by refinement steps, VSE also allows the specification to be structured *horizontally* to organise the specifications on one abstraction level. Each single (sub)specification can be refined vertically or further decomposed horizontally, such that the complete development is represented by a *development graph*. The deductive component is aware of this structure. And this is an important aspect for the interactive proof approach, as the structure helps the user to prove lemmas or proof obligations that require properties from various parts of the specification.

4 Institution of Dynamic Logic

VSE provides an interactive prover, which supports a Gentzen style natural deduction calculus for dynamic logic. This logic is an extension of first-order logic with two additional kinds of formulas that allow for reasoning about programs. One of them is the box formula $[\alpha]\varphi$, where α is a program written in an imperative language, and φ is a dynamic logic formula. The meaning of $[\alpha]\varphi$ can be roughly put as "After every terminating execution of α, φ holds.". The other new kind of formulas is the diamond formula $\langle\alpha\rangle\varphi$, which is the dual counter part of a box formula. The meaning of $\langle\alpha\rangle\varphi$ can be described as "After some terminating execution of α, φ holds".

We will now describe the formalisation of this dynamic logics as an institution, denoted $CDyn^=$, in some detail, because this has not been done in the literature so far. Moreover, as stated in the introduction, this step is crucial for turning VSE into an expansion card that can be plugged into the HETS motherboard.

4.1 Signatures

The starting point for dynamic logic signatures are the signatures of first-order logic with equality (FOL$^=$) that have the form $\Sigma_{\text{FOL}^=} = (S, F, P)$ consisting of a set S of sorts, a family F of function symbols and a family P of predicate symbols. Because we need to name procedures, we add a $S^* \times S^*$-sorted family $PR = (PR_{v,w})_{v,w \in S^*}$ of procedure symbols, leading to signatures of the form $\Sigma = (S, F, P, PR)$. We have two separate lists v and w of the argument sorts of the procedure symbols in $PR_{v,w}$, in order to distinguish the sorts of the input parameters (v) from those of the output parameters (w).

A signature morphism between two signatures maps sorts, operation symbols, predicate symbols and procedure symbols in a way such that argument and result sorts are preserved.

Moreover, it is assumed that all signatures have a sort *bool* together with two constants *true* and *false* on it and this subsignature is preserved by signature morphisms.

4.2 Sentences

Let $\Sigma = (S, F, P, PR)$ be a dynamic logic signature with $PR = (PR_{v,w})_{v,w \in S^*}$. For each sort s we assume a fixed countably infinite set $\mathbb{X}_s$ of variables of sort s such that the sets $\mathbb{X}_s$ are pairwise disjoint. We set $\mathbb{X} := \bigcup_{s \in S} \mathbb{X}_s$.

First we define the syntax of the programs that may appear in dynamic logic formulas. The programs contain Σ-terms, which are predicate logical terms of the signature $(S, (F_{v,s} \cup PR_{v,s})_{v \in S^*, s \in S}, P)$, i.e. in addition to variables and function symbols we allow symbols of predicates with a single result parameter to occur in these terms. The set $\mathbb{P}_\Sigma$ of Σ-programs is the smallest set containing:

- **abort**, **skip**
- $x := \tau$
- $\alpha; \beta$
- **var** $x : s = \tau$ **in** α
- **var** $x : s =$? **in** α
- **if** ε **then** α **else** β **fi**
- **while** ε **do** α **od**
- $p(x_1, x_2, ..., x_n; y_1, y_2, \ldots, y_m)$,

where $x, x_1, x_2, \ldots, x_n \in \mathbb{X}$ are variables, $y_1, y_2, \ldots, y_m \in \mathbb{X}$ are pairwise different variables, τ a Σ-term of the same sort s as $x \in \mathbb{X}$, ε a boolean Σ-formula (i.e. a Σ-formula without quantifiers, boxes and diamonds), $\alpha, \beta \in \mathbb{P}_\Sigma$, p a procedure symbol, such that the sorts of $x_1, \ldots, x_n, y_1, \ldots, y_m$ match the argument and result sorts of p.

These kinds of program statements can be explained informally as follows: **abort** is a program that never terminates. **skip** is a program that does nothing. $x := \tau$ is the assignment. **var** $x : s = \sigma$ **in** α is the deterministic form of a variable declaration which sets x to the value of σ. Its nondeterministic form **var** $x : s =$? **in** α sets x to an arbitrary value before executing α. $\alpha; \beta$ is the composition of the programs α and β, such that α is executed before β. The *conditional* **if** ε **then** α **else** β **fi** means that α is executed if ε holds, otherwise β is computed. Finally, the *loop* **while** ε **do** α **od** checks the condition ε, in case of validity executes α and repeats the loop.

There are three kinds of sentences that may occur in a Σ-dynamic logic specification.

1. The set of Dynamic Logic Σ-formulas is the smallest set containing
   - the (S, F, P)-first-order formulas φ
   - for any dynamic logic Σ-formulas φ, ψ, any variable x, and any Σ-program α the formulas $[\alpha]\varphi$, $\langle\alpha\rangle\varphi$ and $\neg\varphi$, $\varphi \wedge \psi$ and $\forall x.\varphi$;
2. Procedure definitions are expressions of the form:

$$\textbf{defprocs}$$
$$\textbf{procedure } p(x_1, \ldots, x_n, y_1, \ldots, y_m)\alpha$$
$$\cdots$$
$$\textbf{defprocsend}$$

where $p \in PR_{v,w}$ for some $v, w \in S^*$, $x_1, \ldots, x_n, y_1, \ldots, y_m$ are variables of the corresponding sorts in v, w, and $\alpha \in \mathbb{P}_\Sigma$ is a Σ-program with free variables from the set $\{x_1, \ldots, x_n, y_1, \ldots, y_m\}$.

3. *Restricted sort generation constraints* express that a set of values defined by restriction procedure can be generated by the given set of procedures, the *constructors*. Sort generation constraints in the export specification will give rise to proof obligations stated as a sentence of this kind. Syntactically a restricted sort generation constraints takes the form

$$\textbf{generated type } s ::= p_1(\dots)|p_2(\dots)|\dots|p_n(\dots) \textbf{ restricted by } r \ , \qquad (1)$$

where s is a sort symbol, $p_1,\dots,p_n$ are functional procedure symbols, the dots in $p_1(\dots)$ etc. have to be replaced by a list of the argument sorts, and r is a procedure symbol taking one argument of sort s. The meaning is, that all elements of sort s that fulfil the restriction r, i.e. for which r terminates, can be generated by the constructors $p_1, p_2, \dots, p_n$.

For any signature morphism $\varphi : \Sigma \rightarrow \Sigma'$, the translation of Σ-sentences along ϕ is done by translating each symbol according to the sort, operation symbol, predicate symbol and procedure symbol mappings respectively and by changing the sort of a variable $x : s$ to $\varphi(s)$. Notice that in the case of non-injective signature morphisms the disjointness condition on the sets of variables ensures us that no identifications between variables are made.

4.3   Models

Let $\Sigma = (S, F, P, PR)$ be a dynamic logic signature with $F = (F_{w,s})_{w \in S^*, s \in S}, P = (P_w)_{w \in S^*}, PR = (PR_{v,w})_{v,w \in S^*}$. A (dynamic logic) Σ-model M maps each sort symbol $s \in S$ to a carrier set M_s, each function symbol $f \in F_{w,s}$ to a total function $f : M_w \rightarrow M_s$, each predicate symbol $p \in P_w$ to a relation $p \subseteq M_w$ and each procedure symbol $pr \in PR_{v,w}$ to a relation $M_{pr} \subseteq M_v \times M_w$, where $M_{(s_1,\dots,s_n)}$ denotes $M_{s_1} \times M_{s_2} \times \cdots \times M_{s_n}$ for $(s_1, s_2, \dots, s_n) \in S^*$. Thus, such a model can be viewed as a $CFOL^=$ structure extended with the interpretation of procedure symbols.

For any signature morphism $\varphi : \Sigma \rightarrow \Sigma'$, the reduct of a Σ'-model inteprets x as the interpretation of $\varphi(x)$ in the original model, where x can be either a sort, a function symbol, a predicate symbol or a procedure symbol.

4.4   Satisfaction of Dynamic Logic Formulas

Semantics is defined in a Kripke-like manner. For a given signature Σ and a Σ-model M the (program) states are variable valuations, i.e. functions from the fixed infinite set $\mathbb{X}$ of variables to M, such that for each sort s variables $x \in \mathbb{X}_s$ are mapped to values of M_s. The semantics of a program α with respect to a model M is a predicate $.\llbracket \alpha \rrbracket^M .$ on two program states. $q\llbracket \alpha \rrbracket^M r$ can be read as: If α is started in state q it may terminate after having changed the state to r.

- $q\llbracket\textbf{skip}\rrbracket^M q$
- not $q\llbracket\textbf{abort}\rrbracket^M r$
- $q\llbracket x := \sigma \rrbracket^M r \Leftrightarrow r = q[x \leftarrow \sigma^{M,q}]$
- $q\llbracket x := p(\tau_1, \tau_2, \dots, \tau_n) \rrbracket r$
  $\Leftrightarrow q\llbracket\textbf{var } z_1 : s_1 = \tau_1, \dots, z_n : s_n = \tau_n \textbf{ in } x := p(z_1, z_2, \dots, z_n)\rrbracket r$

- $q[\![\alpha; \beta]\!]^M r \Leftrightarrow$ for some state $s : q[\![\alpha]\!]^M s$ and $s[\![\beta]\!]^M r$
- $q[\![\mathbf{var}\, x : s = \sigma; \alpha]\!]^M r \Leftrightarrow q[x := \sigma; \alpha]\!]^M r$
- $q[\![\mathbf{var}\, x : s =?; \alpha]\!]^M r \Leftrightarrow$ for some $a \in s^M : q[x \leftarrow a][\![\alpha]\!]^M r$
- $q[\![\mathbf{if}\,\varepsilon\,\mathbf{then}\,\alpha\,\mathbf{else}\,\beta\,\mathbf{fi}]\!]^M r \Leftrightarrow (q \models \varepsilon$ and $q[\![\alpha]\!]^M r)$ or $(q \models \neg\varepsilon$ and $q[\![\beta]\!]^M r)$
- $q[\![\mathbf{while}\,\varepsilon\,\mathbf{do}\,\alpha\,\mathbf{od}]\!]^M r \Leftrightarrow q([\![\mathbf{if}\,\varepsilon\,\mathbf{then}\,\alpha\,\mathbf{else}\,\mathbf{skip}\,\mathbf{fi}]\!]^M)^* r$ and $r \models \neg\varepsilon$
- $q[\![pr(x_1, \ldots, x_n; y_1, \ldots, y_m)]\!]^M r \Leftrightarrow pr_M(q(x_1), \ldots, q(x_n); r(y_1), \ldots, r(y_m))$

where for any program α, $([\![\alpha]\!]^M)^*$ is the reflexive transitive closure of the relation $[\![\alpha]\!]^M$, and the state $q[x \leftarrow a]$ is defined as $q[x \leftarrow a](y) = \begin{cases} q(y) & \text{if } y \neq x \\ a & \text{if } y = x \end{cases}$, σ is a Σ-term without predicate symbols and $\sigma^{M,q}$ is the evaluation of the term σ with respect to the model M and state q, $z_1 \in \mathbb{X}_{s_1}, z_2 \in \mathbb{X}_{s_2}, \ldots, z_n \in \mathbb{X}_{s_n}$ are variables not occurring in the terms $\tau_1, \tau_2, \ldots \tau_n$.

We define satisfaction on a model M and a program state r as follows:

- $M, r \models p(\sigma_1, \ldots \sigma_n) \Leftrightarrow p_M(\sigma_1^{M,r}, \sigma_2^{M,r}, \ldots, \sigma_n^{M,r})$
- $M, r \models \sigma = \tau \Leftrightarrow \sigma^{M,r} = \tau^{M,r}$
- $M, r \models \neg\varphi \Leftrightarrow M, r \not\models \varphi$
- $M, r \models \varphi \wedge \psi \Leftrightarrow M, r \models \varphi$ and $M, r \models \psi$
- $M, r \models \varphi \vee \psi \Leftrightarrow M, r \models \varphi$ or $M, r \models \psi$
- $M, r \models \forall x.\varphi \Leftrightarrow$ for all $a \in M_s: M, r[x \leftarrow a] \models \varphi$
- $M, r \models [\alpha]\varphi \Leftrightarrow$ for all program states q with $r[\![\alpha]\!]^M q: M, q \models \varphi$

The formula $\langle\alpha\rangle\varphi$ is to be read as an abbreviation for $\neg[\alpha]\neg\varphi$. Finally a formula φ holds on a model M ($M \models \varphi$), if for all program states r it holds on M and r ($M, r \models \varphi$).

4.5 Satisfaction of Procedure Definitions

The procedures in our model will not have any side effects (except for modifying the output parameters).

Unwinding a procedure call by replacing it by the body of the procedure and substituting the formal parameter variables by the actual parameters should not change the result of a program. Therefore, for a signature Σ a Σ-model M is a model of a procedure declaration

$$\mathbf{defprocs\ procedure}\, pr(x_1, \ldots, x_n, y_1, \ldots, y_m)\alpha\ \mathbf{defprocsend}$$

without recursion if

$$M \models \forall x_1, \ldots, x_n, r_1, \ldots, r_m :$$
$$(\langle pr(x_1, \ldots, x_n; y_1, \ldots, y_m)\rangle y_1 = r_1 \wedge \cdots \wedge y_m = r_m)$$
$$\Leftrightarrow \langle\alpha\rangle y_1 = r_1 \wedge \cdots \wedge y_m = r_m$$

holds. Abbreviating the procedure declaration as π, we then write $M \models \pi$. It is obvious how this can be extended to declarations of more than one procedure.

In the presence of recursion this is not sufficient to make the procedure definitions non-ambiguous and adequate to conventional semantics of programming languages.

Therefore, from several models complying with the definitions the minimal model with respect to some order will be chosen. The order compares the interpretations of the procedures symbols, such that the order relation $M_1 \leq M_2$ holds for two models M_1 and M_2 for the same signature $\Sigma = (S, F, P, PR)$, iff $pr_{M_1} \subseteq pr_{M_2}$ for all $pr \in PR$ and the interpretations of sort, function and predicate symbols are identical. Then we define that M satisfies a procedure declaration π ($M \models \pi$), iff $M \Vert\models \pi$, and for all other models M' only differing in the interpretations of the procedure symbols $pr_1, \ldots, pr_k$, $M' \Vert\models \pi$ implies $M \leq M'$.

4.6   Satisfaction of Restricted Sort Generation Constraints

A restricted sort generation constraint as in (1) is said to hold, iff the subset of the carrier on which the restriction procedure r terminates is generated by the constructor procedures $p_1, p_2, \ldots p_n$. In more detail: for each state s with $s \models \langle r(a) \rangle$ there must by a program α being the composition of calls of constructor procedures only such that for all states t, u with $t[\![\alpha]\!]u$ the equation $u(a) = s(a)$ holds.

Proposition 1. *The satisfaction condition for $CDyn^=$ holds and thus $CDyn^=$ is an institution.*

5   Refinement

The methodology of formal software development by stepwise refinement describes the ideal process (which in practice is more a loop with continuous feedback) as follows: starting from initial informal requirements, these are translated to a formal requirement specification, which is then further refined to a formal design specification and then to an executable program.

Simple refinements between specifications can be expressed as so-called views in CASL, which are just theory morphisms. The degree of looseness diminishes along a refinement (technically, the model class shrinks). For more complex refinements involving architectural decompositions (i.e. branching points in the emerging refinement tree), a refinement language has been designed [22]. Sometimes (e.g. when refining arrays to stacks with pointers), an observational interpretation of specification is needed. This means that values exhibiting the same observable behaviour are identified (that is, observational congruence is generated implicitly). This has been developed in theory to some degree [5], but not implemented in HETS yet. By contrast, the VSE specification language supports a refinement approach based on explicit submodels and congruences [24], an idea that dates back to Hoare [14]. This somewhat simpler approach has been successfully applied in practice, and moreover, it is linked with a code generation mechanism. Hence, integrating this approach into HETS brings considerable advantages.

VSE's refinements associate an abstract data type specification, called the *export specification* of the refinement, with an implementation. The implementation is based on another theory, called the *import specification* and contains several functional procedures written in an imperative language. These procedures use the functions and predicates of the import specifications. A so called *mapping* relates each sort of the export specification to a sort of the import specification, while the functions and procedures are mapped to procedures in the import specification.

A refinement describes the construction of a model for the signature of the export specification (export model) from a model of the import specification (import model). The functions and predicates are interpreted by the computations of the procedures. The elements of the carrier sets of the export model are constructed from the carrier sets of the import model. The implementations are allowed to represent a single value in the export specification by several values of the import specifications. For example, when implementing sets by lists, a set might be represented by any list containing all elements of the set in any order. Furthermore, VSE do not require that all values of a sort in the import specification really represent a value of the export specification. In the example below where we will implement natural numbers by binary words, we will exclude words with leading zeroes. In order to describe the construction of the carrier sets, the refinement contains two additional procedures for each sort: procedure defining a *congruence* relation and a procedure defining a *restriction*. The restriction terminates on all elements, that represent export specification values. The congruence relation determines the equivalence classes that represent the elements of the export model.

A refinement is *correct*, if for every import model the export model constructed according to the refinement is actually a model of the export theory. The VSE system generates proof obligations that are sufficient for the correctness.

6   VSE Refinement as an Institution Comorphism

When integrating VSE and its notion of refinement into HETS, a naive approach would extend HETS with a new notion of *restriction-quotient refinement link* in HETS, and would extend both the HETS motherboard and the expansion slot specification in way that makes it possible to deal with such refinement link. VSE easily could be turned into an expansion card that is able to prove these refinement links.

However, this approach has a severe disadvantage: the specification of expansion slots needs to be extended! If we did this for every tool that is newly integrated into HETS (and every tool comes with its own special features), we would quickly arrive at a very large and unmanageable expansion slot specification.

Fortunately, the heterogeneity of HETS offers a better solution: we can encode VSE refinement as ordinary refinement in HETS, with the help of an institution comorphism that does the actually restriction-quotient construction. With this approach, only the HETS logic graph needs to be extended by a logic and a comorphism; actually, we will see that two comorphisms are necessary. That is, we add two further expansion cards doing the work, while the logic-independent part of HETS, i.e. the motherboard and the expansion slot specification, can be left untouched!

6.1   The Refinement Comorphism

We model the refinement notion of VSE by a comorphism from the CASL institution $CFOL^=$ to the VSE institution $CDyn^=$. The intuition behind it can be summarised as follows. At the level of signatures, for each sort we need to introduce procedure symbols for the equality relation and for the restriction formula together with axioms specifying their expected behaviour, while for function and predicate symbols, we need to introduce procedure symbols for their implementations. For all these symbols, we assign no procedure definition but rather leave them loosely specified; in this way, the choice of a possible implementation is not restricted. The sentence translation is based on translation of terms into programs implementing the representation of the term. The model reduct performs the submodel/quotient construction, leaving out the values that do not satisfy the restriction formula and quotienting by the congruence generated by the equality procedure.

Each CASL signature (S, F, P) is mapped to the $CDyn^=$ theory, denoted $((S, \emptyset, \emptyset, PR), E)$. PR contains (1) for each sort s, a symbol $restr\_s \in PR_{[s],[]}$ for the *restriction formula* on the sort (the restriction predicate is then obtained as the set of values for which $restr\_s$ terminates) and a symbol $eq_s \in PR_{[s,s],[bool]}$ for the *equality* on the sort and (2) for each function symbol $f : w \rightarrow s \in F_{w,s}$, a symbol $f : w \rightarrow s \in PR_{w,[s]}$ and for each predicate symbol $p : w \in P_w$, a symbol $p : w \rightarrow [bool] \in PR_{w,[bool]}$.

The set of axioms E contains sentences saying that for each sort s, (1) eq_s is a congruence and it terminates for inputs satisfying the restriction and (2) the procedures that implement functions/predicates terminate for inputs satisfying the restriction and their results also satisfy the restriction. These properties are to be proven when providing an actual implementation. For space limitations reasons, we don't present these sentences in full detail but rather refer the reader to the general pattern of Fig. 1, which presents the symbols and the sentences introduced in the resulting VSE theory for each symbol of the CASL theory that is translated.

Given a CASL signature (S, F, P) and a model M' of its translation $((S, \emptyset, \emptyset, PR), E)$, we define the translation of M' to an (S, F, P)-model, denoted M. The interpretation of a sort s in M is constructed in two steps. First we take the subset $M_{restr\_s} \subseteq M'_s$ of elements, for which the restriction terminates. Then we take the quotient $M_{restr\_s}/_\equiv$ according to the congruence relation $\equiv$ defined by eq_s, such that for all $x_1, x_2 \in M'_s$,

CASL	VSE	VSE sentences
sort s	sort s $eq\_s \in PR_{[s,s],[bool]}$ $restr\_s \in PR_{[s],[]}$	$\langle restr\_s(x)\rangle true \quad\wedge\quad \langle restr\_s(y)\rangle true \quad\Rightarrow$ $\langle eq\_s(x,y;e)\rangle true$
		$\langle restr\_s(x)true\rangle \Rightarrow \langle eq\_s(x,x;e)\rangle e = true$ $\langle restr\_s(x)\rangle true \wedge \langle restr\_s(y)\rangle true \wedge \langle eq\_s(x,y;e)\rangle e = true \Rightarrow \langle eq\_s(y,x;e)\rangle e = true$
		$\langle restr\_s(x)\rangle true \quad\wedge\quad \langle restr\_s(y)\rangle true \quad\wedge$ $\langle restr\_s(z)\rangle true \quad\wedge\quad \langle eq\_s(x,y;e)\rangle e \;=\; true \quad\wedge$ $\langle eq\_s(y,z;e)\rangle e = true \Rightarrow \langle eq\_s(x,z;e)\rangle e = true$
$f \in F_{s \rightarrow t}$	$f \in PR_{[s],[t]}$	$\langle restr\_s(x)\rangle R \wedge \langle restr\_s(y)\rangle R \wedge \langle eq\_s(x,y;e)\rangle e = true \Rightarrow$ $\langle y1 := f(x;r1)\rangle\langle y2 := f(y;r2)\rangle\langle eq\_t(y1,y2,e)\rangle e = true$
		$\langle restr\_s(x)\rangle true \implies \langle f(x;y)\rangle\langle restr\_t(y)\rangle true$
$p \in P_s$	$p \in PR_{[s],[bool]}$	$\langle restr\_s(x)\rangle true \wedge \langle restr\_s(y)\rangle true \wedge \langle eq\_s(x,y;e)\rangle e = true \Rightarrow \langle p(x;r1)\rangle\langle p(y;r2)\rangle r1 = r2$
		$\langle restr\_s(x)\rangle true \Rightarrow \langle p(x;e)\rangle true$

Fig. 1. Summary of the signature translation part of the comorphism $CASL2VSERefine$ (for simplicity, only unary symbols are shown)

$x_1 \equiv x_2$ is equivalent to $M' \models \langle eq_s(x_1, x_2; y)\rangle y = true$. For each function symbol f, we define the value of M_f in the arguments $x_1, ..., x_n$ to be the value returned by the call of procedure M'_f on inputs $x_1, .., x_n$, that is $M_f(x_1, ..., x_n) = b$ if and only if $\langle M'_f(x_1, ..., x_n; y)\rangle y = b$. The axioms (1) and (2) in E ensure that M_f is total and well-defined. Similarly, for each predicate symbol p, $M_p(x_1, ..., x_n)$ holds iff $\langle M'_p(x_1, .., x_n; y)\rangle y = true$.

Sentence translation is based on translation of terms into programs that compute the representation of the term. Basically, each function application is translated to a procedure call of the implementing procedure, and new output variables are introduced:

- a variable x is mapped to $x := x$, where the left-hand side x is the output variable and the right-hand side x is the logical variable;
- an constant c is mapped to $c(; y)$, where c is now the procedure implementing the constant and y is a new output variable;
- a term $f(t_1, .., t_n)$ is mapped to $\alpha_1; ..\alpha_n; a := f(y_1, .., y_n)$, where α_i is the translation of t_i with the output variable y_i and a is a new output variable

Then the sentence translation is defined inductively:

- a equation $t_1 = t_2$ is translated to

$$\langle \alpha_1 \rangle; \langle \alpha_2 \rangle; \langle eq_s(y_1, y_2; y)\rangle y = true$$

where α_i is the translation of the term t_i, with the output variable y_i
- a predicate $p(t_1, .., t_n)$ is translated to

$$\langle \alpha_1 \rangle..\langle \alpha_n \rangle \langle p(y_1, .., y_n; y)\rangle y = true$$

where α_i is the translation of the term t_i, with the output variable y_i
- Boolean connectives of formulas are translated into the same connections of their translated formulas;
- for universally and existentially qualified formulas one also has to make sure that the bound variables are assigned a value that satisfies the restriction.

The complete translation is obtained by adding as hypotheses to the translation of the formula a list of formulas of type $\langle restr\_s(y)\rangle true$, where y is a free variable of the formula, of sort s. An example of how a CASL sentence is translated along $CASL2VSERefine$ comorphism will be introduced in the next section.

Sort generation constraints are translated to restricted sort generation constraints over implementing procedures. For example, assume we have in the abstract specification of natural numbers a sort generation constraint:

$$generated\ type\ nat\ ::=\ 0\mid suc\ (nat)$$

Then in the VSE theory resulting from translation along comorphism, the restricted sort generation constraint

$$\textbf{generated type } nat\ ::=\ 0\mid suc(nat)\ \textbf{restricted by } restr\_nat\ .$$

is introduced, where 0 and suc are now the procedures implementing the constructors (and have same name) and $restr\_nat$ is the restriction procedure symbol on sort nat.

The functoriality of the signature translation and the naturality of sentences and models translations follow in a quite standard way, therefore we ommit them in this presentation.

Theorem 1. *The satisfaction condition for the comorphism* $CASL2VSERefine$ *holds.*

Proof idea: As mentioned in section 2, the satisfaction conditions for comorphisms means that truth remains invariant to translations of sentences/model. In our particular case, the proof follows from noticing that given any term t in a arbitrary CASL signature and any VSE model M' of the translated signature, the interpretation of t in the reduct of the model M' coincides with the interpretation of the translation of the term t in M'.   ∎

Notice that this construction follows very faithfully the steps of the refinement method of VSE, as described in section 5. The export specification of VSE is a first-order specification that we can translate along the comorphism $CASL2VSERefine$ to generate the same kind of proof obligations that VSE would generate to prove correctness of a refinement. The difference is now they are built using abstract (i.e. loose) procedure names and actual implementations are to be later plugged in by means of a view which corresponds to the VSE mapping, with the exception that instead of pairing export specification symbols with implementations, the view rather pairs abstract procedures with implementations. Moreover, the correctness of the view ensures us that a model of the implementation reduces along the signature morphism induced by the view to a model of the translation of the original export specification, that can we further translate along the comorphism to obtain a model of the export specification. Thus we achieve that the model semantics of the refinement in VSE [1] and of the refinement expressed using the comorphism $CASL2VSERefine$ coincide.

Theorem 2. *The proof calculus for heterogeneous development graphs, combined with the VSE prover, can be used for discharging refinement proof obligations in a sound way.*

Proof idea: This follows from the soundness of the development graph calculus [20], the soundness of the VSE prover, and Thm. 1.   □

Unfortunately, we cannot expect completeness here, because first-order dynamic logic is not finitely axiomatisable [6].

6.2   Structuring in Context of Refinement

Consider the situation where a theory of a library (e.g. the natural numbers) or a parameter theory that will be instantiated later occurs both in the abstract and the refined specification. Such common import specifications should not be refined, but rather kept identically — and this is indeed the case in VSE.[1]

---

[1] This resembles a bit the notion of imports of parameterised specifications in CASL, where the import is shared between formal and actual parameter and is kept identically.

To handle this situation in the present context, the import of a first-order specification into a dynamic logic one is not done along the trivial inclusion comorphism from $CFOL^=$ to $CDyn^=$ — this would mean that the operations of the import need to be implemented as procedures. Instead, we define a comorphism, $CASL2VSEImport$, which, besides keeping the first-order part, will introduce for the symbols of import specification new procedure symbols, similarly to $CASL2VSERefine$. The difference is that this time the interpretation of procedure symbols is not loosely specified, but definitions are introduced in such a way that semantics is not affected. In the case of sorts, this requires that no element is restricted and equality procedure on the sort is the set-theoretic equality. In the case of functions, the procedure simply returns the value of the function in the given arguments, while in the case of predicates, the procedure returns true if the corresponding predicate holds. Sentences are translated identically, and the model reduct keeps interpretation of symbols.

For example, let us consider the situation in the diagram below, where the natural numbers are imported both in the abstract and the concrete specification (and the (heterogeneous) refinement link is represented by the double arrow):

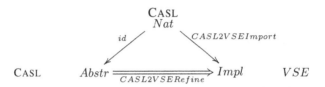

Fig. 2. The naturals occur both in the abstract requirement and in the implementation. The quotient represented by the double arrow is trivial for the naturals.

Assume there is a sort nat in Nat. When translating $Abstr$ to $CDyn^=$ along the refinement comorphism, we make no distinction between the sorts defined in $Abstr$ and the imported ones, so in the resulting translated theory we will have symbols for the restriction on sort nat and for equality. The second comorphism, used for imports, introduces the same symbols in $Impl$ and imposes that they are implemented as themselves: no element of nat is restricted and the identification is implemented as the strong equality. Thus, the expected behaviour is obtained: $Impl$ provides default implementations, introduced by the importing comorphism, such that the sort nat can be regarded as kept, modulo wrapping into procedures.

7   Example: Implementing Natural Numbers by Binary Words

As an example, we present the implementation of natural numbers as lists of binary digits, slightly abridged from [24].[2] The abstract CASL specification, NATS (introduced in Fig. 3), is the usual specification of natural numbers with 0, successor and addition with

---

[2] The complete example can be found at https://svn-agbkb.informatik.uni-bremen.de/Hets-lib/trunk/Refinement/natbin_refine.het.

spec NATS =
free type
$nats ::= zero\_n \mid succ\_n(nats)$
op $zero\_n : nats$
op $succ\_n : nats \rightarrow nats$
op $prdc\_n : nats \rightarrow nats$
op $add\_n : nats \times nats \rightarrow nats$
vars $m, n : nats$
• $prdc\_n(zero\_n) = zero\_n$
• $prdc\_n(succ\_n(m)) = m$
• $add\_n(m, zero\_n) = m$
• $add\_n(m, succ\_n(n))$
$= succ\_n(add\_n(m, n))$
end

Fig. 3. CASL specification of natural numbers

sort *nats*
PROCEDURES
$gn\_add\_n : IN\ nats,\ IN\ nats \rightarrow nats;$
$gn\_eq\_nats : IN\ nats,\ IN\ nats \rightarrow Boolean;$
$gn\_prdc\_n : IN\ nats \rightarrow nats;$
$gn\_restr\_nats : IN\ nats;$
$gn\_succ\_n : IN\ nats \rightarrow nats;$
$gn\_zero\_n : \rightarrow nats$
$\forall\ gn\_x0 : nats;\ gn\_x1 : nats;\ gn\_x2 : nats;$
$\qquad\qquad gn\_x3 : Boolean$
• $<:gn\_x1 := gn\_zero\_n;$
$\quad gn\_x0 := gn\_prdc\_n(gn\_x1);$
$\quad gn\_x2 := gn\_zero\_n;$
$\quad gn\_x3 := gn\_eq\_nats(gn\_x0, gn\_x2):>$
$\quad gn\_x3 = (op\ True : Boolean)$
...

Fig. 4. Natural numbers translated along CASL2VSERefine comorphism

the Peano axioms. In Fig. 4[3], we present a fragment of the theory obtained by translating NATS along the comorphism $CASL2VSERefine$: the resulting signature and the translation of the first axiom - the other three translated axioms and the sentences introduced by the comorphism are similar.

The VSE implementation, NATS-IMPL (Fig. 5), provides procedures for implementation of natural numbers as binary words, which are imported as data part along $CASL2VSEImport$[4] from the CASL specification BIN (here omitted). We illustrate the way the procedures are written with the example of the restriction procedure, nlz, which terminates whenever the given argument has no leading zeros. The implementation of the other procedures is similar and therefore omitted. Notice that the equality is in this case simply the equality on binary words.

Fig. 6 presents the view BINARY_ARITH expressing the fact that binary words, restricted to those with non-leading zeros, represent a refinement of natural numbers, where each symbol of NATS is implemented by the corresponding procedure in the symbol mapping of the view.

In figure 7, we present some of the proof obligations introduced by the view. Notice that they are translations of the sentences of the theory presented in Fig. 4 along the signature morphism induced by the view. The first two sentences that we included here are introduced by the signature translation of the comorphism and state that (1) equality terminates on inputs for which the restriction formula nlz holds and (2) the procedure implementing addition, i_add, terminates for valid inputs and the result is again valid. Also the translation of an axiom of NATS along the comorphism $CASL2VSERefine$ is presented.

---

[3] HETS uses $<: \alpha :> \phi$ as input syntax for $\langle \alpha \rangle \phi$.
[4] The Hets construction $SP\ with\ logic\ C$ translates a specification SP along the comorphism C.

spec NATS_IMPL =
  BIN **with logic** *CASL2VSEImport*
then *PROCEDURES*
  hnlz : IN bin; nlz : IN bin; i_badd : IN bin, IN bin, OUT bin, OUT bin;
  i_add : IN bin, IN bin → bin; i_prdc : IN bin → bin;
  i_succ : IN bin → bin; i_zero : → bin; eq : IN bin, IN bin → Boolean
  • *DEFPROCS*
  • *DEFPROCS*
      PROCEDURE hnlz(x)
        BEGIN
          IF x = b_zero THEN ABORT
          ELSE IF x = b_one THEN SKIP ELSE hnlz(pop(x)) FI
          FI
        END;
      PROCEDURE nlz(x)
        BEGIN IF x = b_zero THEN SKIP ELSE hnlz(x) FI END
    DEFPROCSEND
%% PROCEDURE i_zero(x) ...

Fig. 5. Implementation using lists of binary digits

view BINARY_ARITH : { NATS **with logic** *CASL2VSERefine* } **to** NATS_IMPL =
  nats ↦ bin, gn_restr_nats ↦ nlz, gn_eq_nats ↦ eq,
  gn_zero_n ↦ i_zero, gn_succ_n ↦ i_succ, gn_add_n ↦ i_add

Fig. 6. Natural numbers as binary words

%% Proof obligations introduced by the view
%% equality procedure terminates on valid inputs
$\forall$ *gn_x, gn_y : bin*• <:*nlz(gn_x)*:> *true* $\wedge$ <:*nlz(gn_y)*:> *true*
  $\Rightarrow$ <:*gn_b := eq(gn_x, gn_y)*:> *true*
%% procedure implementing addition terminates and gives valid results on valid inputs
$\forall$ *gn_x1, gn_x2 : bin* • <:*nlz(gn_x1)*:> *true* $\wedge$ <:*nlz(gn_x2)*:> *true*
  $\Rightarrow$ <:*gn_x := i_add(gn_x1, gn_x2)*:> <:*nlz(gn_x)*:> *true*
%% translation of : forall m : nats . add_n(m, zero_n) = m
  $\forall$ *gn_x0, gn_x1, gn_x2, gn_x3 : bin; gn_x4 : Boolean;*
  m : bin
  • <:*nlz(m)*:> *true*
  $\Rightarrow$ <:*gn_x1 := m ;*
      gn_x2 := i_zero;
      gn_x0 := i_add(gn_x1, gn_x2);
      gn_x3 := m;
      gn_x4 := eq(gn_x0, gn_x3):>
    gn_x4 = (op True : Boolean)

Fig. 7. Generated proof obligations

The two comorphisms have been implemented and are part of the latest HETS release; the VSE tool is also going to become available under public licence. Provided VSE is installed, the example can be fully checked in HETS.

8 Conclusions and Future Work

We have integrated VSE's mechanism of refining abstract specifications into procedural implementations into HETS. Via a new logic and two comorphisms, one of them doing the usual restriction-quotient construction, we could avoid entirely the introduction of new types of "refinement links" into HETS, but rather could re-use the present machinery of heterogeneous development graphs and thus demonstrate its flexibility. Visually spoken, we could avoid extending the HETS motherboard and expansion slot specification, but rather just construct several expansion cards related to VSE and plug them into the HETS motherboard.

However, there is a point when it actually makes sense to enhance the expansion slot specification. Currently, it is based on the assumption that expansion cards (aka theorem provers) can only handle flat unstructured theories. However, VSE can also handle structured theories, and takes advantage of the structuring during proof construction. Hence, we plan to extend the expansion slot specification in a way that allows the transmission (between HETS and VSE) of whole acyclic directed development graphs of theories with connecting definition links, reflecting the import hierarchy. We expect to use this enhancement of the expansion slot specification also for other theorem provers supporting structured theories, like Isabelle.

Another direction of future work will try to exploit synergy effects between VSE and HETS e.g. by using automatic provers like SPASS (which are now available through the integration) during some sample VSE refinement proofs. The refinement method could also be extended from first-order logic to the richer language CASL, which also features subsorting and partial functions.

Acknowledgements

Work on this paper has been supported by the German Federal Ministry of Education and Research (Project 01 IW 07002 FormalSafe). We thank Werner Stephan for conceptual discussions and Erwin R. Catesbeiana for pointing out a class of specifications particularly easily usable as targets of refinements.

References

1. Spezifikationssprache VSE-SL, part of the VSE documentation (1997)
2. Astesiano, E., Bidoit, M., Krieg-Brückner, B., Kirchner, H., Mosses, P.D., Sannella, D., Tarlecki, A.: CASL - the common algebraic specification language. Theoretical Computer Science 286, 153–196 (2002)
3. Autexier, S., Hutter, D., Langenstein, B., Mantel, H., Rock, G., Schairer, A., Stephan, W., Vogt, R., Wolpers, A.: VSE: Formal methods meet industrial needs. International Journal on Software Tools for Technology Transfer, Special issue on Mechanized Theorem Proving for Technology 3(1) (September 2000)

4. Bidoit, M., Mosses, P.D. (eds.): CASL User Manual. LNCS (IFIP Series), vol. 2900. Springer, Heidelberg (2004)
5. Bidoit, M., Sannella, D., Tarlecki, A.: Observational interpretation of CASL specifications. Math. Struct. in Comp. Sci. 18(2), 325–371 (2008)
6. Blackburn, P., van Benthem, J.F.A.K., Wolter, F.: Handbook of Modal Logic. Studies in Logic and Practical Reasoning, vol. 3. Elsevier Science Inc., New York (2006)
7. Burstall, R.M., Goguen, J.A.: The semantics of CLEAR, a specification language. In: Bjorner, D. (ed.) Abstract Software Specifications. LNCS, vol. 86, pp. 292–332. Springer, Heidelberg (1980)
8. Cheikhrouhou, L., Rock, G., Stephan, W., Schwan, M., Lassmann, G.: Verifying a chipcard-based biometric identification protocol in VSE. In: Górski, J. (ed.) SAFECOMP 2006. LNCS, vol. 4166, pp. 42–56. Springer, Heidelberg (2006)
9. Mosses, P.D. (ed.): CoFI (The Common Framework Initiative). Casl Reference Manual. LNCS, vol. 2960. Springer, Heidelberg (2004)
10. Dennis, L.A., Collins, G., Norrish, M., Boulton, R.J., Slind, K., Melham, T.F.: The prosper toolkit. STTT 4(2), 189–210 (2003)
11. Gentzen, G.: Untersuchungen über das logische Schließen I & II. Mathematische Zeitschrift 39, 176–210, 572–595 (1935)
12. Goguen, J.A., Burstall, R.M.: Institutions: Abstract model theory for specification and programming. Journal of the ACM 39(1), 95–146 (1992)
13. Goguen, J., Roşu, G.: Institution morphisms. Formal Aspects of Computing 13, 274–307 (2002)
14. Hoare, C.A.R.: Proof of correctness of data representations. Acta Inf. 1, 271–281 (1972)
15. Hutter, D., Langenstein, B., Rock, G., Siekmann, J., Stephan, W., Vogt, R.: Formal software development in the verification support environment. Journal of Experimental and Theoretical Artificial Intelligence 12(4), 383–406 (2000)
16. Langenstein, B., Vogt, R., Ullmann, M.: The use of formal methods for trusted digital signature devices. In: Etheredge, J.N., Manaris, B.Z. (eds.) FLAIRS Conference, pp. 336–340. AAAI Press, Menlo Park (2000)
17. Leuschel, M., Wehrheim, H. (eds.): IFM 2009. LNCS, vol. 5423. Springer, Heidelberg (2009)
18. Meng, J., Quigley, C., Paulson, L.C.: Automation for interactive proof: First prototype. Inf. Comput. 204(10), 1575–1596 (2006)
19. Mossakowski, T.: Heterogeneous Specification and the Heterogeneous Tool Set. Habilitation thesis, Universität Bremen (2005)
20. Mossakowski, T., Autexier, S., Hutter, D.: Development graphs – proof management for structured specifications. Journal of Logic and Algebraic Programming 67(1-2), 114–145 (2006)
21. Mossakowski, T., Maeder, C., Lüttich, K.: The Heterogeneous Tool Set. In: Grumberg, O., Huth, M. (eds.) TACAS 2007. LNCS, vol. 4424, pp. 519–522. Springer, Heidelberg (2007)
22. Mossakowski, T., Sannella, D., Tarlecki, A.: A simple refinement language for CASL. In: Fiadeiro, J.L., Mosses, P.D., Orejas, F. (eds.) WADT 2004. LNCS, vol. 3423, pp. 162–185. Springer, Heidelberg (2005)
23. Nipkow, T., Paulson, L.C., Wenzel, M.: Isabelle/HOL — A Proof Assistant for Higher-Order Logic. Springer, Heidelberg (2002)
24. Reif, W.: Verification of large software systems. In: Shyamasundar, R.K. (ed.) FSTTCS 1992. LNCS, vol. 652, pp. 241–252. Springer, Heidelberg (1992)
25. Weidenbach, C., Brahm, U., Hillenbrand, T., Keen, E., Theobalt, C., Topic, D.: SPASS version 2.0. In: Voronkov, A. (ed.) CADE 2002. LNCS (LNAI), vol. 2392, pp. 275–279. Springer, Heidelberg (2002)

A Compositional Approach on Modal Specifications for Timed Systems[*]

Nathalie Bertrand[1], Axel Legay[1],
Sophie Pinchinat[2], and Jean-Baptiste Raclet[3]

[1] INRIA Rennes, France
[2] IRISA & Université Rennes 1, France
[3] INRIA Rhône-Alpes, France

Abstract. On the one hand, modal specifications are classic, convenient, and expressive mathematical objects to represent interfaces of component-based systems. On the other hand, time is a crucial aspect of systems for practical applications, e.g. in the area of embedded systems. And yet, only few results exist on the design of timed component-based systems. In this paper, we propose a timed extension of modal specifications, together with fundamental operations (conjunction, product, and quotient) that enable to reason in a compositional way about timed system. The specifications are given as modal event-clock automata, where clock resets are easy to handle. We develop an entire theory that promotes efficient incremental design techniques.

1 Introduction

Nowadays, systems are tremendously big and complex, resulting from the assembling of several components. These many components are in general designed by teams, working independently but with a common agreement on what the interface of each component should be. As a consequence, mathematical foundations that allow to reason at the abstract level of interfaces, in order to infer properties of the global implementation, and to design or to advisedly (re)use components is a very active research area, known as *compositional reasoning* [16]. In a logical interpretation, interfaces are specifications and components that implement an interface are understood as models. Aiming at practical applications as the final goal, the software engineering point of view naturally leads to the following requirements for a good theory of interfaces.

1. *Satisfiability/Consistency and Satisfaction.* It should be decidable whether a specification admits a model, and whether a given component implements a given interface. Moreover, for the synthesis of components to be effective, satisfiable interfaces should always have finitely presentable models.
2. *Refinement and shared refinement. Refinement* of specifications [20,23] expresses inclusion of sets of models, and therefore allows to compare interfaces.

---

[*] This work was funded by the European project COMBEST, IST-STREP 215543.

K. Breitman and A. Cavalcanti (Eds.): ICFEM 2009, LNCS 5885, pp. 679–697, 2009.

Related to this implication-like concept, the intersection, or *greatest lower bound*, is an optimal interface refining two given interfaces.

3. *Compositionality of the abstraction.* The interface theory should also provide a combination operator on interfaces, reflecting the standard composition of models by, *e.g.* parallel product.

4. *Quotient.* Last but not least, a quotienting operation, dual to composition is crucial to perform incremental design. Intuitively, the quotient enables to describe a part of a global specification assuming another part is already realized by some component. Together with the composition $\otimes$ the quotient operator $\oslash$ enjoys the following fundamental property at the component level:

$$\mathcal{C}_2 \models \mathcal{S} \oslash \mathcal{S}_1 \Leftrightarrow \forall \mathcal{C}_1 \ [\mathcal{C}_1 \models \mathcal{S}_1 \Rightarrow \mathcal{C}_1 \otimes \mathcal{C}_2 \models \mathcal{S}] \qquad (\star)$$

where $\mathcal{S}, \mathcal{S}_i$ are interfaces, $\mathcal{C}, \mathcal{C}_i$ components, and $\models$ is the satisfaction relation.

Building good interface theories is the subject of intensive studies which have led to theories based on models such as interface automata [12,14], modal automata or specifications [5,19,22,23,24], and their respective timed extension [9,13]. Modal specifications are deterministic automata equipped with transitions of the following two types: *may* and *must*. The components that implement such interfaces are deterministic labeled transition systems; an alternative language-based semantics can therefore be considered, as presented in [22,23]. Informally, a must transition is available in every component that implements the modal specification, while a may transition needs not to be. Modal specifications are interpreted as logical specifications matching the conjunctive nu-calculus fragment of the mu-calculus [15]. As a corollary, but also proved directly in [22], satisfaction and consistency of modal specifications are decidable, and the finite model property holds. Refinement between modal specifications coincides with a standard notion of alternating simulation. Since components can be seen as specifications where all transitions are typed must (all possible implementation choices have been made), satisfaction is also expressed via alternating simulation. Shared refinement is effectively computed via a product-like construction. Combination of modal specifications, handling synchronization products *à la* Arnold and Nivat [6], and the dual quotient combinators can be efficiently handled in this setting [23].

Recently, a timed extension of the theory of modal specifications has been introduced [9], motivated by the fact that time can be a crucial parameter in practice, *e.g.* in embedded–system applications. In this piece of work, components are timed automata as defined in [1], and naturally, an effective and expressive region-based semantics allows to combine modalities and timing constraints.

In this paper, we build on this preliminary paper and develop a complete compositional approach for modal specifications of timed systems. This framework favors methodologies for an incremental design process: Assume a global system implementing specification $\mathcal{S}$ has to be synthesized, and assume a component implements interface $\mathcal{S}_1$. Computing $\mathcal{S} \oslash \mathcal{S}_1$ and synthesizing a model of $\mathcal{S} \oslash \mathcal{S}_1$ yields a component that, in $\otimes$-combination with the component for $\mathcal{S}_1$, will yield a model for the global interface $\mathcal{S}$, thanks to property $(\star)$. As a consequence, low complexity algorithms are needed for computing product and quotient, as well as for the satisfiability decision procedure.

The synchronous product of timed objects requires a tight control on clocks [1], and so should its dual quotient. Actually, developing the theory in the general framework where components can reset their clocks in an arbitrary manner is a difficult question. Indeed, computing the resets of clocks of a product or of a quotient depends on how the control of clocks is distributed among the components. This information has to be provided *a priori*, which requires an extra formalism. We therefore restrict the presentation to the class of components definable by event-clock automata [2]: in these timed automata, resets are fully determined by the actions. Interfaces whose models are event-clock automata are called *modal event-clock specifications* (MECS).

Inheriting from the region-based semantics of timed modal specifications [9], we study the satisfiability as well as the consistency problems for MECS. Satisfiability is PSPACE-complete, hence no harder than traditional decision problems in the class of timed automata. Refinement serves as a theoretical basis to develop the product and the quotient of MECS. We propose two equivalent characterizations of these operations. Not surprisingly according to the semantics, inefficient EXPTIME constructions via the region graphs of the MECS (seen as untimed specifications) are provided. More interestingly, we present alternative direct and efficient PTIME constructions.

The rest of the paper is organized as follows. In Section 2, we introduce the timed modal specification setting, with preliminaries on untimed modal specifications and the definition of modal event-clock specifications. Section 3 focuses on MECS and exposes effective techniques to compute the binary operations of greatest lower bound, product, and quotient. In Section 4, we compare our framework with the existing literature. Section 5 concludes the paper. A long version of the current paper, including proofs is available as a research report [8].

2   Timed Modal Specifications

In this section we recall the framework of *modal specifications* originaly defined in [18] twenty years ago (see [5] for a survey), and its timed extension, recently proposed in [9]: We discuss the semantic, the preorder refinement and the satisfiability problem for untimed and timed modal specifications.

2.1   Preliminaries on Untimed Specifications

A modal specification is an automaton equipped with two types of transitions: *must*-transitions, that are required and *may*-transitions, that are allowed. We fix Σ a finite set of actions.

Definition 2.1 (Modal specification). *A modal specification (MS) is a tuple* $\mathcal{R} = (P^{\perp}, \lambda^0, \Delta^m, \Delta^M)$ *where* $P^{\perp} = P \cup \perp$ *is a finite set of states with* $\perp \cap P = \emptyset$, $\lambda^0 \in P^{\perp}$ *is the unique initial state, and* $\Delta^M \subseteq \Delta^m \subseteq P \times \Sigma \times P^{\perp}$. Δ^M

and Δ^m *correspond respectively to* must-transitions *and* may-transitions. *We additionally assume that* Δ^m *is* deterministic *(hence so is* Δ^M*) and* complete, *that is, for every state* $p \in P$ *and every action* $a \in \Sigma$, *there is exactly one state* $\lambda \in P^\perp$ *such that* $(p, a, \lambda) \in \Delta^m$.

We use p (resp. λ) as typical element of P (resp. $P^\perp$). Note that completeness is not a restriction since from any incomplete specification, one can derive a complete one by adding may-transitions to a possibly new state $\perp \in \perp\!\!\!\perp$. Intuitively, in state $p \in P$ a-may transition to some state $\lambda \in \perp\!\!\!\perp$ labelled by action a means that action a is forbidden in p. This interpretation will become clearer when we define the set of models of a modal specification.

The condition $\Delta^M \subseteq \Delta^m$ naturally imposes that every required transition is also allowed; it guarantees the *local consistency* of the modal constraints. The set of states $\perp\!\!\!\perp$ denotes the "bad states" which carry local inconsistency. Elements of $\perp\!\!\!\perp$ are *sink states* with no outgoing transition since both Δ^M and Δ^m are subsets of $P \times \Sigma \times P^\perp$. *Global inconsistency* can be derived as follows: we let $\mathcal{I}$ be the set of *inconsistent* states that must lead (that is via a sequence of *must*-transitions) to a local inconsistency; states in $P^\perp \setminus \mathcal{I}$ are *consistent*. Formally $\mathcal{I} = \{\lambda_0 \mid \exists n \geq 0,\ \exists \lambda_1 \cdots \lambda_n \in P^\perp\ \exists a_1 \cdots a_n \in \Sigma \text{ s.t. } \lambda_n \in \perp\!\!\!\perp \text{ and } (\lambda_i, a_{i+1}, \lambda_{i+1}) \in \Delta^M\}$. Notice that in particular $\perp\!\!\!\perp \subseteq \mathcal{I}$. We say that the modal specification $\mathcal{R}$ is *consistent* whenever its initial state is consistent, i.e. $\lambda^0 \notin \mathcal{I}$; otherwise $\mathcal{R}$ is *inconsistent*.

In the following, we write or draw $p \xrightarrow{a} \lambda$ (resp. $p \dashrightarrow{a} \lambda$) to mean $(p, a, \lambda) \in \Delta^M$ (resp. $(p, a, \lambda) \in \Delta^m \setminus \Delta^M$); in other words, solid arrows denote *required* transition, whereas dashed arrow represent *allowed* but not required transitions.

Example 2.2. Consider a client for a given resource available in a system. The alphabet of actions includes: ***get*** when the resource is requested; ***grant*** in case of access to the resource; and, ***extra*** which occurs when a privileged access with extended time is requested.

In order to simplify the figures, states in $\perp\!\!\!\perp$ are not represented (except if they are necessary) and transitions of the form $q \dashrightarrow{a} \perp$ are not depicted. Action names may be preceded by some "!" or "?" when the occurrence of the actions respectively stems from the designed component or by its environment.

The modal specification Cl for the client in Fig. 1(a) specifies that a ***get*** request may be sent again. Moreover every ***get*** request *must* be granted. Additionally the client may request extended time at any moment.

Models of MS are *deterministic automata*[1], with possibly infinitely many states, which we shortly call *automata* in the sequel. An automaton is a structure of the form $\mathcal{M} = (M, m^0, \Delta)$ where M is a (possibly infinite) set of states, $m^0 \in M$ is a unique initial state, and $\Delta \subseteq M \times \Sigma \to M$ is a *partial* transition function. The model relation $\models$ defined below is a particular case of alternating simulation [4] between the model and the consistent part, if any, of the specification.

---

[1] Also called *deterministic labeled transition systems.*

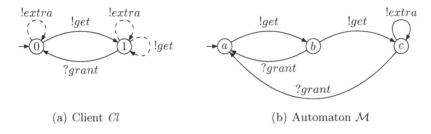

(a) Client Cl (b) Automaton $\mathcal{M}$

Fig. 1. The modal specification Cl accepts the automaton $\mathcal{M}$

Definition 2.3 (Model Relation). *Let* $\mathcal{R} = (P^{\perp}, \lambda^0, \Delta^m, \Delta^M)$ *be a* MS. *An automaton* $\mathcal{M} = (M, m^0, \Delta)$ *is a model of* $\mathcal{R}$, *written* $\mathcal{M} \models \mathcal{R}$, *if there exists a binary relation* $\rho \subseteq M \times (P \setminus \mathcal{I})$ *such that* $(m^0, \lambda^0) \in \rho$, *and for all* $(m, p) \in \rho$, *the following hold:* (1) *for every* $(p, a, \lambda) \in \Delta^M$ *there is a transition* $(m, a, m') \in \Delta$ *with* $(m', \lambda) \in \rho$, *and* (2) *for every* $(m, a, m') \in \Delta$ *there is a transition* $(p, a, \lambda) \in \Delta^m$ *with* $(m', \lambda) \in \rho$.

We denote by $\mathsf{Mod}(\mathcal{R})$, the set of models of an MS $\mathcal{R} = (P^{\perp}, \lambda^0, \Delta^m, \Delta^M)$.

Remark in Definition 2.3 that inconsistent states of the specification cannot appear in the relation ρ. Consequently, a transition of the form $(p, a, \lambda) \in \Delta^m$ where $\lambda \in \mathcal{I}$ is inconsistent interprets as: in any model, no a-transition from a state in relation with p is allowed. Moreover, for $\lambda^0 \in \mathcal{I}$ no ρ can exist and actually we have:

Lemma 2.4. *Let* $\mathcal{R}$ *be a* MS. $\mathsf{Mod}(\mathcal{R}) \neq \emptyset$ *if, and only if,* $\mathcal{R}$ *is consistent.*

Example 2.5. The automaton $\mathcal{M}$ in Fig. 1(b) is a model of the MS Cl in Fig. 1(a) as the binary relation $\rho = \{(a, 0), (b, 1), (c, 1)\}$ witnesses.

The semantic preorder between MS relies on an extension of Definition 2.3.

Definition 2.6 (Modal Refinement Preorder). *Given two* MS, $\mathcal{R}_1 = (P_1^{\perp}, \lambda_1^0, \Delta_1^m, \Delta_1^M)$ *and* $\mathcal{R}_2 = (P_2^{\perp}, \lambda_2^0, \Delta_2^m, \Delta_2^M)$, $\mathcal{R}_1$ *is a refinement of* $\mathcal{R}_2$, *written* $\mathcal{R}_1 \preceq \mathcal{R}_2$, *whenever there exists a binary relation* $\rho \subseteq (\mathcal{I}_1 \times \mathcal{I}_2) \cup (P_1^{\perp} \times (P_2 \setminus \mathcal{I}_2))$ *such that* $(\lambda_1^0, \lambda_2^0) \in \rho$, *and for all* $(\lambda_1, \lambda_2) \in \rho \cap ((P_1 \setminus \mathcal{I}_1) \times (P_2 \setminus \mathcal{I}_2))$:

(1) for every $(\lambda_2, a, \lambda_2') \in \Delta_2^M$ *there exists* $(\lambda_1, a, \lambda_1') \in \Delta_1^M$ *with* $(\lambda_1', \lambda_2') \in \rho$
(2) for every $(\lambda_1, a, \lambda_1') \in \Delta_1^m$ *there exists* $(\lambda_2, a, \lambda_2') \in \Delta_2^m$ *with* $(\lambda_1', \lambda_2') \in \rho$.

Definition 2.6 requires some explanations. First, by definition of the domain of ρ, an inconsistent state of $\mathcal{R}_2$ can only be refined as an inconsistent state in $\mathcal{R}_1$ whereas a consistent state in $\mathcal{R}_2$ can either be linked to a consistent or inconsistent state in $\mathcal{R}_1$. Moreover, for pairs of consistent states, Condition (1) ensures that all required transition in $\mathcal{R}_2$ are also required in $\mathcal{R}_1$, and Condition (2) guarantees that each possible transition in $\mathcal{R}_1$ is also allowed in $\mathcal{R}_2$.

Under our assumption that MS are deterministic, we can show that the pre-order $\preceq$ between MS matches the model inclusion preorder. We establish an intermediate result that exploits the embedding of automata into modal specifications.

Definition 2.7 (Embedding in MS). *An automaton* $\mathcal{M} = (M, m^0, \Delta)$ *can be interpreted as a modal specification* $\mathcal{M}^* = (M \cup \{\perp_*\}, m^0, \Delta_*^m, \Delta_*^M)$ *where* $\Delta = \Delta_*^M \subseteq \Delta_*^m$, *and* $(m, a, \perp_*) \in \Delta_*^m \setminus \Delta_*^M$ *when* $\Delta(m, a)$ *is undefined in* $\mathcal{M}$.

Lemma 2.8. *Given an automaton* $\mathcal{M}$ *and a* MS $\mathcal{R}$, $\mathcal{M} \models \mathcal{R}$ *iff* $\mathcal{M}^* \preceq \mathcal{R}$.

Proposition 2.9. *Let* $\mathcal{R}_1$ *and* $\mathcal{R}_2$ *be two* MS, *then:*

$$\mathcal{R}_1 \preceq \mathcal{R}_2 \text{ if, and only if, } \mathsf{Mod}(\mathcal{R}_1) \subseteq \mathsf{Mod}(\mathcal{R}_2).$$

Note that the determinism of modal specifications is crucial for the Proposition 2.9. In the nondeterministic case, modal refinement is not complete [20], that is $\mathsf{Mod}(\mathcal{R}_1) \subseteq \mathsf{Mod}(\mathcal{R}_2)$ does not imply $\mathcal{R}_1 \preceq \mathcal{R}_2$ in general.

As a consequence of Definition 2.6, inconsistent MS refine any MS, and consistent MS can only refine consistent MS. In the following, we write $\mathcal{R}_1 \equiv \mathcal{R}_2$, and say that $\mathcal{R}_1$ and $\mathcal{R}_2$ are *equivalent*, whenever $\mathcal{R}_1 \preceq \mathcal{R}_2$ and $\mathcal{R}_2 \preceq \mathcal{R}_1$. Remark that by merging all states of $\mathcal{I}$, every MS is equivalent to a MS where the set of inconsistent states is a singleton.

2.2   Modal Event-Clock Specifications

Let $\mathcal{X}$ be a finite set of *clocks* and let $\mathbb{R}_{\geq 0}$ denote the set of non-negative reals. A *clock valuation* over $\mathcal{X}$ is a mapping $\nu : \mathcal{X} \to \mathbb{R}_{\geq 0}$. The set of clock valuations over $\mathcal{X}$ is denoted $\mathcal{V}$; in particular, $\overline{0} \in \mathcal{V}$ is the clock valuation such that $\overline{0}(x) = 0$ for all $x \in \mathcal{X}$. Given $\nu \in \mathcal{V}$ and $t \in \mathbb{R}_{\geq 0}$, we let $(\nu + t) \in \mathcal{V}$ be the clock-valuation obtained by letting t time units elapse after ν, formally, $(\nu + t)(x) = \nu(x) + t$ for every $x \in \mathcal{X}$.

A *guard* over $\mathcal{X}$ is a finite conjunction of expressions of the form $x \sim c$ where $x \in \mathcal{X}$, $c \in \mathbb{N}$ is a *constant*, and $\sim \in \{<, \leq, =, \geq, >\}$. We then denote by $\xi[\mathcal{X}]$ the set of all guards over $\mathcal{X}$. For some fixed $N \in \mathbb{N}$, $\xi_N[\mathcal{X}]$ represents the set of guards involving only constants equal to or smaller than N. The *satisfaction relation* $\models \subseteq (\mathcal{V} \times \xi[\mathcal{X}])$ between clock valuations and guards is defined in a natural way and we write $\nu \models g$ whenever ν satisfies g. In the following, we will often abuse notation and write g to denote the guard g as well as the set of valuations which satisfy g.

Event-clock automata [2], form a subclass of timed automata where clock resets are not arbitrary: each action a comes with a clock x_a which is reset exactly when action a occurs. We consider event-clock automata with possibly infinitely many locations.

Definition 2.10 (Event-clock automata). *An* event-clock automaton (ECA) *over* Σ *is a tuple* $\mathcal{C} = (C, c^0, \delta)$ *where* C *is a set of states,* $c^0 \in C$ *is the initial state, and* $\delta \subseteq C \times \xi_N[\mathcal{X}_\Sigma] \times \Sigma \times C$ *is the transition relation (for some* $N \in \mathbb{N}$). *The pair* (Σ, N) *is the* signature *of* $\mathcal{C}$.

The semantics of an ECA is similar to the one of a timed automaton [1], except that the set of clocks that are reset by a transition is determined by the action of that transition: while firing a transition labeled by a, precisely clock x_a is reset. Event-clock automata do form a strict subclass of timed automata, but they enjoy nice properties: they are closed under union and intersection, and more interestingly they can be determinized (as opposed to the class of arbitrary timed automata). The determinizability of event-clock automata comes from the way clocks are reset and this property significantly eases the definition of binary operators (such as lower bound, product and quotient) on modal variants of event-clock automata.

For a fixed signature (Σ, N), a *region* is an equivalence class θ of clock-valuations that satisfy the same guards in $\xi_N[\mathcal{X}_\Sigma]$. We denote by Θ_N, or simply Θ, the set of all regions. Given a region $\theta \in \Theta$, we write $\mathsf{Succ}(\theta)$ for the union of all regions that can be obtained from θ by letting time elapse: $\mathsf{Succ}(\theta) = \{\theta'' \mid \exists \nu'' \in \theta'' \ \exists \nu \in \theta \ \exists t \in \mathbb{R}_{\geq 0} \text{ s.t. } \nu'' = \nu + t\}$.

Definition 2.11 (Region automaton [1]). *The* region automaton *associated to an ECA $\mathcal{C} = (C, c^0, \delta)$ is the automaton $R(\mathcal{C}) = (C \times \Theta, (c^0, \bar{0}), \Delta)$ over the alphabet $\Theta \times \Sigma$, where the set Δ of transitions is defined as follows: for each $c, c' \in C$, $\theta, \theta', \theta'' \in \Theta$, and $a \in \Sigma$, $((c, \theta), \theta'', a, (c', \theta')) \in \Delta$ whenever there exists $(c, g, a, c') \in \delta$ with $\theta'' \subseteq \mathsf{Succ}(\theta) \cap g$, and $\theta' = \theta''[x_a = 0]$ is the region obtained from θ'' by resetting clock x_a.*

Note that the region automata we consider extend the ones introduced in [1] since their transition labels keep track of the intermediate region where the action is fired. As a consequence, any automaton over the alphabet $\Theta \times \Sigma$ uniquely defines an ECA whose signature is of the form (Σ, N_Θ), with N_Θ determined by the set of regions Θ. We denote by T the natural injection of region automata into ECA; this mapping enables us to distinguish between the two interpretations of the same syntactic object: $R(\mathcal{C})$ is an automaton whereas $T(R(\mathcal{C}))$ is an ECA.

Definition 2.12 (Modal event-clock specification). *A modal event-clock specification (MECS) over the finite alphabet Σ is a tuple $\mathcal{S} = (Q^{\perp\!\!\!\perp}, \lambda^0, \delta^m, \delta^M)$ where*

- $Q^{\perp\!\!\!\perp} := Q \cup \perp\!\!\!\perp$ *is a finite set of* locations, *with $\perp\!\!\!\perp \cap Q = \emptyset$, and the initial state is $\lambda^0 \in Q^{\perp\!\!\!\perp}$.*
- $\delta^M \subseteq \delta^m \subseteq Q \times \xi[\mathcal{X}_\Sigma] \times \Sigma \times Q^{\perp\!\!\!\perp}$ *are finite sets of respectively* must- *and* may-transitions. *Given a may-transition $(q, g, a, \lambda) \in \delta^m$, q is the source state, λ is the destination state, $g \in \xi[\mathcal{X}_\Sigma]$ is the guard that specifies the valuations for which the transition can be taken, $a \in \Sigma$ is the action labeling the transition – recall that the only clock that is then reset is x_a.*

Moreover we require that δ^m is deterministic (hence, so is δ^M) and complete: for any state $q \in Q$, any action $a \in \Sigma$, and any clock valuation $\nu \in \mathcal{V}$, there is exactly one transition $(q, g, a, \lambda) \in \delta^m$ such that $\nu \models g$.

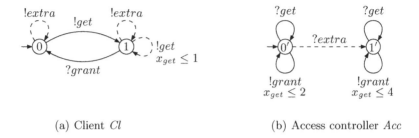

(a) Client Cl (b) Access controller Acc

Fig. 2. Client Cl and access controller Acc

Example 2.13. As an example of a MECS, we consider in Fig. 2(a) a timed variant of the client Cl introduced earlier. The clock corresponding to the action **get** is x_{get}.

In this example again, for simplification purposes, transitions of the form $q \xrightarrow{g,a} \bot$ are not depicted. As MECS are complete, these transitions can easily be recovered by taking $g = \neg(\bigvee_i g_i)$ where the g_i's are the guards appearing in the transitions of the form $q \xdashrightarrow{g_i,a} \lambda$ or $q \xrightarrow{g_i,a} \lambda$. When the guard of a transition is not indicated, it is implicitly true.

The MECS Cl for the client in Fig. 2(a) specifies that a **get** request may be sent again at most one time unit after the last request.

In the sequel, we generalize the graphical convention already used for untimed objects by writing $q \xdashrightarrow{g,a} \lambda'$ whenever $(q,g,a,\lambda') \in (\delta^m \setminus \delta^M)$ and $q \xrightarrow{g,a} \lambda'$ whenever $(q,g,a,\lambda') \in \delta^M$.

Remark that a natural untimed object associated to a MECS $\mathcal{S}$ is its region modal automaton, obtained by generalizing Definition 2.11 from event-clock automata to their modal extension. More precisely, $R(\mathcal{S})$ reflects the modalities of $\mathcal{S} = (Q^\bot, \lambda^0, \delta^m, \delta^M)$ as done in [9], the initial state is $(\lambda^0, \overline{0})$ and the set of locally inconsistent states in $R(\mathcal{S})$ is $\bot_{\mathcal{S}} \times \Theta$. A MECS $\mathcal{S}$ is said to be *inconsistent* if $R(\mathcal{S})$ is inconsistent; otherwise, it is *consistent*. Given a modal event-clock specification $\mathcal{S}$ over signature (Σ, N), $R(\mathcal{S})$ is a modal specification over the extended alphabet $\Sigma \times \Theta_N$; similarly, given an event-clock automaton $\mathcal{C}$, $R(\mathcal{C})$ is an automaton over alphabet $\Sigma \times \Theta_N$. Having this in mind, the model relation in the timed case is inherited from the one in the untimed case via the region construction:

Definition 2.14 (Model relation). *Let $\mathcal{S}$ be a* MECS. *An event-clock automaton $\mathcal{C}$ is a model of $\mathcal{S}$, written $\mathcal{C} \models \mathcal{S}$, if $R(\mathcal{C}) \models R(\mathcal{S})$.*

The set of models of a MECS $\mathcal{S}$, is defined by $\mathsf{Mod}(\mathcal{S}) := \{\mathcal{C} \mid \mathcal{C} \models \mathcal{S}\}$.

Observing that given a MECS $\mathcal{S}$, $R(T(R(\mathcal{S})))$ and $R(\mathcal{S})$ are isomorphic, we obtain the following:

Lemma 2.15. *Let $\mathcal{S}$ be a MECS. Then,* $\mathsf{Mod}(T(R(\mathcal{S}))) = \mathsf{Mod}(\mathcal{S})$.

In the spirit of Def.2.14 for the model relation, the *modal refinement preorder* between MECS also relies on a region-based construction:

Definition 2.16 (Modal refinement preorder). *Given two MECS $\mathcal{S}_1$ and $\mathcal{S}_2$, $\mathcal{S}_1$ refines $\mathcal{S}_2$, written $\mathcal{S}_1 \preceq \mathcal{S}_2$, whenever $R(\mathcal{S}_1) \preceq R(\mathcal{S}_2)$.*

As a corollary of the analogous results in the untimed setting on MS, it is decidable whether a MECS refines another one. Moreover, refinement and inclusion of models match:

Corollary 2.17. *Let $\mathcal{S}$, $\mathcal{S}_1$ and $\mathcal{S}_2$ be MECS. Then,*

- $\mathsf{Mod}(\mathcal{S}) \neq \emptyset$ *if, and only if $\mathcal{S}$ is consistent;*
- $\mathcal{S}_1 \preceq \mathcal{S}_2$ *if, and only if $\mathsf{Mod}(\mathcal{S}_1) \subseteq \mathsf{Mod}(\mathcal{S}_2)$.*

About consistency We recall that a specification is *consistent* if, and only if, it admits a model. According to Lemma 2.4, checking whether an untimed specification is consistent amounts to checking that the set of states $\perp\!\!\!\perp$ cannot be reached from its initial state by a sequence of must-transitions. The consistency problem is thus NLOGSPACE-complete for modal specifications and PSPACE-complete in the timed case.

3 Operations on Specifications

In this section, we introduce operations on modal event-clock specifications, which enable compositional reasoning. More precisely, we define the greatest lower bound, the product, and the quotient over MECS. For each of these operations, we establish important theoretical properties.

3.1 Greatest Lower Bound of MECS

We study the concept of *greatest lower bound*, which corresponds to the conjunction of two modal specifications and equivalently to their best shared refinement. We first recall the definition of the greatest lower bound in the untimed case. Let $\mathcal{R}_1 = (P_1^{\perp}, \lambda_1^0, \Delta_1^m, \Delta_1^M)$ and $\mathcal{R}_2 = (P_2^{\perp}, \lambda_2^0, \Delta_2^m, \Delta_2^M)$ be two MS. The *greatest lower bound* of $\mathcal{R}_1$ and $\mathcal{R}_2$ is $\mathcal{R}_1 \wedge \mathcal{R}_2 = (P^{\perp}, (\lambda_1^0, \lambda_2^0), \Delta_{\wedge}^m, \Delta_{\wedge}^M)$ with $P := P_1 \times P_2$, $\perp\!\!\!\perp := (\perp\!\!\!\perp_1 \times P_2^{\perp}) \cup (P_1^{\perp} \times \perp\!\!\!\perp_2)$, and whose transition relations are derived from the following rules:

$$\frac{\lambda_1 \overset{a}{\dashrightarrow} \lambda_1' \text{ and } \lambda_2 \overset{a}{\dashrightarrow} \lambda_2'}{(\lambda_1, \lambda_2) \overset{a}{\dashrightarrow} (\lambda_1', \lambda_2')} \ (Glb1) \qquad \frac{\lambda_1 \overset{a}{\longrightarrow} \lambda_1' \text{ and } \lambda_2 \overset{a}{\dashrightarrow} \lambda_2'}{(\lambda_1, \lambda_2) \overset{a}{\longrightarrow} (\lambda_1', \lambda_2')} \ (Glb2)$$

$$\frac{\lambda_1 \overset{a}{\dashrightarrow} \lambda_1' \text{ and } \lambda_2 \overset{a}{\longrightarrow} \lambda_2'}{(\lambda_1, \lambda_2) \overset{a}{\longrightarrow} (\lambda_1', \lambda_2')} \ (Glb3) \qquad \frac{\lambda_1 \overset{a}{\longrightarrow} \lambda_1' \text{ and } \lambda_2 \overset{a}{\longrightarrow} \lambda_2'}{(\lambda_1, \lambda_2) \overset{a}{\longrightarrow} (\lambda_1', \lambda_2')} \ (Glb4)$$

Remark in particular, that if in a state $\lambda = (\lambda_1, \lambda_2)$, we have the contradictory requirements that a is required ($\lambda_1 \overset{a}{\longrightarrow} \lambda_1' \in P_1$) and a should not happen ($\lambda_2 \overset{a}{\dashrightarrow} \lambda_2' \in \perp\!\!\!\perp_2$), then λ is inconsistent. This is indeed guaranteed by the definition of $\mathcal{R}_1 \wedge \mathcal{R}_2$ which imposes $P_1 \times \perp\!\!\!\perp_2 \subseteq \perp\!\!\!\perp$.

Greatest lower bound of MECS. The notion of greatest lower bound easily extends to MECS. Let $\mathcal{S}_1, \mathcal{S}_2$ be two MECS. The modalities for the transitions in $\mathcal{S}_1 \wedge \mathcal{S}_2$ are derived from those induced in the untimed case (Rules $(Glb1)$ to $(Glb4)$), and the labels of the transitions are obtained by intersecting the guards for common actions. As an example, Rule $(Glb1)$ becomes $(tGlb1)$ as follows.

$$\frac{\lambda_1 \xrightarrow{g_1,a} \lambda_1' \text{ and } \lambda_2 \xrightarrow{g_2,a} \lambda_2'}{(\lambda_1, \lambda_2) \xrightarrow{g_1 \wedge g_2, a} (\lambda_1', \lambda_2')} \ (tGlb1)$$

Thanks to Lemma 2.15, the set of models of a MECS $\mathcal{S}$ matches the set of models of its region version $T(R(\mathcal{S}))$. The following proposition characterizes the greatest lower bound of two MECS via the region graphs.

Proposition 3.1. *For any two* MECS $\mathcal{S}_1$ *and* $\mathcal{S}_2$, $R(\mathcal{S}_1 \wedge \mathcal{S}_2) \equiv R(\mathcal{S}_1) \wedge R(\mathcal{S}_2)$.

In Proposition 3.1, operator $\wedge$ is overloaded: on the right hand side, it corresponds to the greatest lower bound of MS whereas on the left hand side, it corresponds to the greatest lower bound of MECS.

Computing the conjunction of two MS via rules $(Gbl1)$ to $(Gbl4)$ is polynomial in the size of the arguments. Due to the construction of the region graphs, starting from two MECS $\mathcal{S}_1$ and $\mathcal{S}_2$ computing $R(\mathcal{S}_1) \wedge R(\mathcal{S}_2)$ is exponential. The direct construction of the greatest lower bound by using the timed variants of $(Gbl1)$ to $(Gbl4)$ is polynomial and therefore worth adopting for effective methods.

Finally, according to the above, one can establish that the greatest lower bound yields the intersection of the models.

Theorem 3.2. *For any two* MECS $\mathcal{S}_1$ *and* $\mathcal{S}_2$, $\mathrm{Mod}(\mathcal{S}_1 \wedge \mathcal{S}_2) = \mathrm{Mod}(\mathcal{S}_1) \cap \mathrm{Mod}(\mathcal{S}_2)$.

Application of the greatest lower bound is the following: in the design of a component one gives several specifications, each of them describing a particular requirement. The greatest lower bound of these specifications enables to check the compatibility of these requirements, by deciding consistency.

3.2   Product of MECS

The product of MECS relates to the synchronous parallel composition of models. For MS, it generalizes the synchronized product of automata $\mathcal{M}_1 \otimes \mathcal{M}_2$ that denotes the intersection of their behaviors (languages).

We first recall the product of MS: Let $\mathcal{R}_1 = (P_1^{\perp}, \lambda_1^0, \Delta_1^m, \Delta_1^M)$ and $\mathcal{R}_2 = (P_2^{\perp}, \lambda_2^0, \Delta_2^m, \Delta_2^M)$ be two MS over the same alphabet Σ. The product of $\mathcal{R}_1$ and $\mathcal{R}_2$, denoted by $\mathcal{R}_1 \otimes \mathcal{R}_2$, is the MS $(P^{\perp}, (\lambda_1^0, \lambda_2^0), \Delta_{\otimes}^m, \Delta_{\otimes}^M)$, with $P := P_1 \times P_2$, $\perp := (\perp_1 \times P_2^{\perp}) \cup (P_1^{\perp} \times \perp_2)$, and whose transitions are derived from the following rules:

$$\frac{\lambda_1 \dashrightarrow^{a} \lambda_1' \text{ and } \lambda_2 \dashrightarrow^{a} \lambda_2'}{(\lambda_1, \lambda_2) \dashrightarrow^{a} (\lambda_1', \lambda_2')} \ (Prod1) \qquad \frac{\lambda_1 \xrightarrow{a} \lambda_1' \text{ and } \lambda_2 \dashrightarrow^{a} \lambda_2'}{(\lambda_1, \lambda_2) \dashrightarrow^{a} (\lambda_1', \lambda_2')} \ (Prod2)$$

$$\frac{\lambda_1 \dashrightarrow^{a} \lambda_1' \text{ and } \lambda_2 \xrightarrow{a} \lambda_2'}{(\lambda_1, \lambda_2) \dashrightarrow^{a} (\lambda_1', \lambda_2')} \ (Prod3) \qquad \frac{\lambda_1 \xrightarrow{a} \lambda_1' \text{ and } \lambda_2 \xrightarrow{a} \lambda_2'}{(\lambda_1, \lambda_2) \xrightarrow{a} (\lambda_1', \lambda_2')} \ (Prod4)$$

Notice that Rules (*Prod*1) to (*Prod*4) uniformly consider consistent and inconsistent states.

Product of MECS. The product of MECS extends the synchronized product of ECA which consists in synchronizing transitions on action names and in taking the conjunction of the guards of the combined transitions.

Let $\mathcal{S}_1, \mathcal{S}_2$ be two MECS. The modalities for the transitions in $\mathcal{S}_1 \otimes \mathcal{S}_2$ are derived from those proposed in the untimed case, and the labels of the transitions are composed of the intersection of the guards together with the common action. For example, the timed version of (*Prod*1) becomes (*tProd*1) as follows.

$$\frac{\lambda_1 \xrightarrow{g_1, a} \lambda_1' \text{ and } \lambda_2 \xrightarrow{g_2, a} \lambda_2'}{(\lambda_1, \lambda_2) \xrightarrow{g_1 \wedge g_2, a} (\lambda_1', \lambda_2')} \quad (tProd1)$$

Similarly to Proposition 3.1 for the greatest lower bound, the product of MECS can be alternatively computed by building the product of the region graphs. This construction however causes an exponential blow-up whereas the direct construction is polynomial. Notice that operator $\otimes$ is overloaded to ease the presentation.

Proposition 3.3. $R(\mathcal{S}_1 \otimes \mathcal{S}_2) \equiv R(\mathcal{S}_1) \otimes R(\mathcal{S}_2)$.

In the untimed setting, it is known [23] that the product is monotonic with respect to the refinement, and that a product of models is a model of the product. Those properties extend to the timed case as stated in the following theorem.

Theorem 3.4 (Properties of the product). *For any* MECS $\mathcal{S}_1, \mathcal{S}_1', \mathcal{S}_2, \mathcal{S}_2'$, *and any* ECA $\mathcal{C}_1, \mathcal{C}_2$,

$$(\mathcal{S}_1 \preceq \mathcal{S}_2 \text{ and } \mathcal{S}_1' \preceq \mathcal{S}_2') \implies \mathcal{S}_1 \otimes \mathcal{S}_1' \preceq \mathcal{S}_2 \otimes \mathcal{S}_2'; \text{ and}$$
$$(\mathcal{C}_1 \models \mathcal{S}_1 \text{ and } \mathcal{C}_2 \models \mathcal{S}_2) \implies \mathcal{C}_1 \otimes \mathcal{C}_2 \models \mathcal{S}_1 \otimes \mathcal{S}_2.$$

As a consequence, the product operation satisfies the property of *independent implementability*, in the sense of [12]: an implementation of a specification of the form $\mathcal{S}_1 \otimes \mathcal{S}_2$ can be obtained by composing any two independent implementations of $\mathcal{S}_1$ and $\mathcal{S}_2$ respectively.

Example 3.5. The MECS *Acc* in Fig. 2(b) page 686 specifies the behavior of an access controller; the access to the resource will be granted for 2 time units after the reception of a **get** request. In case of a privileged access with an extra time, this duration will be extended to 4 time units.

The product $Cl \otimes Acc$ is depicted in Fig. 3(a). In the resulting specification, *extra* can now only occur *after* a **get** request. Timing constraints on the **grant** action issued from the access controller are also propagated.

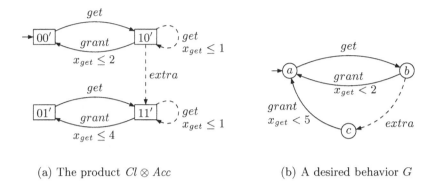

(a) The product $Cl \otimes Acc$ (b) A desired behavior G

Fig. 3. The global model $Cl \otimes Acc$ and its specified behavior G

3.3   Quotient of MECS

In this section, we define the *quotient operation*. Intuitively, the quotient describes a part of a global specification assuming another part will be realized by some component. We thus consider quotient of *specifications* which is different from the constructions studied in [17] where at least one of the operand is a system. We start by recalling the quotient operation on untimed modal specifications, then extend it to MECS.

In the untimed setting, we aim at defining an operation dual to the product of Section 3.2 in the following sense. Given two MS $\mathcal{R} = (P^{\perp}, \lambda^0, \Delta^m, \Delta^M)$ and $\mathcal{R}_1 = (P_1^{\perp}, \lambda_1^0, \Delta_1^m, \Delta_1^M)$, we want the *quotient* of $\mathcal{R}$ by $\mathcal{R}_1$ to be the MS written $\mathcal{R} \oslash \mathcal{R}_1$ which satisfies the following properties.

Proposition 3.6. *For every automaton $\mathcal{M}_2$,*

$$\mathcal{M}_2 \models \mathcal{R} \oslash \mathcal{R}_1 \Longleftrightarrow \forall \mathcal{M}_1. [\mathcal{M}_1 \models \mathcal{R}_1 \Rightarrow \mathcal{M}_1 \otimes \mathcal{M}_2 \models \mathcal{R}] \tag{1}$$

and $\mathcal{R} \oslash \mathcal{R}_1$ is the greatest such one, namely

$$\mathcal{R}_1 \otimes \mathcal{R}_2 \preceq \mathcal{R} \Longleftrightarrow \mathcal{R}_2 \preceq \mathcal{R} \oslash \mathcal{R}_1 \tag{2}$$

The definition of the quotient follows [23], but it is here revisited with a uniform way to handle both consistent and inconsistent states, as opposed to the original definition where so-called *pseudo-specifications* needed being considered.

Formally, the quotient of $\mathcal{R} = (P^{\perp}, \lambda^0, \Delta^m, \Delta^M)$ by $\mathcal{R}_1 = (P_1^{\perp}, \lambda_1^0, \Delta_1^m, \Delta_1^M)$ is the MS $\mathcal{R} \oslash \mathcal{R}_1 = (P'^{\perp}, (\lambda^0, \lambda_1^0), \Delta_{\oslash}^m, \Delta_{\oslash}^M)$, with $P' \subseteq (P \times P_1) \cup \{\top\}$, where $\top$ is fresh element, and the set $\perp'$ of locally inconsistent states of $\mathcal{R} \oslash \mathcal{R}_1$ contains at least an element $\perp'$ but also other elements: the rules below describe these elements as well as the set of transitions. Notation $\lambda \overset{a}{\dashrightarrow} \mathcal{I}$ means that the a-may-transition from λ leads to an inconsistent state in $\mathcal{I}$. We also use notations $\lambda \overset{a}{\dashrightarrow} P \setminus \mathcal{I}$, $\lambda \overset{a}{\longrightarrow} \mathcal{I}$, and $\lambda \overset{a}{\longrightarrow} P \setminus \mathcal{I}$ with the expected meaning, and $\lambda \overset{a}{\dashrightarrow}$ whenever there is no a-must-transition from state λ.

$$\frac{\lambda \in \mathcal{I} \text{ and } \lambda_1 \notin \mathcal{I}_1}{(\lambda, \lambda_1) \in \perp'} \; (I \wedge \neg I1) \qquad \frac{\lambda \in \mathcal{I} \text{ and } \lambda_1 \in \mathcal{I}_1}{(\lambda, \lambda_1) \xdashrightarrow{a} \top} \; (I \wedge I1)$$

$$\frac{\mathcal{I} \not\ni \lambda \xdashrightarrow{a} \text{ and } \lambda_1 \in \mathcal{I}_1}{(\lambda, \lambda_1) \in \perp'} \; (\neg Imust \wedge I1) \qquad \frac{\mathcal{I} \not\ni \lambda \xdashrightarrow{a} \text{ and } \lambda_1 \in \mathcal{I}_1}{(\lambda, \lambda_1) \xdashrightarrow{a} \top} \; (\neg Imay \wedge I1)$$

$$\frac{}{\top \xdashrightarrow{a} \top} \; (top)$$

Assume now that both λ and λ_1 are consistent, *i.e.*, $\lambda \notin \mathcal{I}$ and $\lambda_1 \notin \mathcal{I}_1$:

$$\frac{\lambda \xdashrightarrow{a} \mathcal{I} \text{ and } (\lambda_1 \xdashrightarrow{a} P_1 \setminus \mathcal{I}_1 \text{ or } \lambda_1 \xrightarrow{a} P_1 \setminus \mathcal{I}_1)}{(\lambda, \lambda_1) \xdashrightarrow{a} \perp'} \; (maynot)$$

$$\frac{\lambda \xdashrightarrow{a} \text{ and } \lambda_1 \xdashrightarrow{a} \mathcal{I}_1}{(\lambda, \lambda_1) \xdashrightarrow{a} \top} \; (may1)$$

$$\frac{\lambda \xdashrightarrow{a} \lambda' \notin \mathcal{I} \text{ and } (\lambda_1 \xdashrightarrow{a} \lambda_1' \notin \mathcal{I}_1 \text{ or } \lambda_1 \xrightarrow{a} \lambda_1' \notin \mathcal{I}_1)}{(\lambda, \lambda_1) \xdashrightarrow{a} (\lambda', \lambda_1')} \; (may2)$$

$$\frac{\lambda \xrightarrow{a} \lambda' \text{ and } \lambda_1 \xdashrightarrow{a} \lambda_1'}{(\lambda, \lambda_1) \in \perp'} \; (inconsistency)$$

$$\frac{\lambda \xrightarrow{a} \lambda' \text{ and } \lambda_1 \xrightarrow{a} \lambda_1'}{(\lambda, \lambda_1) \xrightarrow{a} (\lambda', \lambda_1')} \; (must)$$

We now give intuitive explanations for the rules above in particular with respect to the first requirement of Proposition 3.6. To do so, let $\mathcal{R}^\lambda$ be the MS informally defined as the sub-specification of $\mathcal{R}$ with initial state λ. When explaining a rule involving transitions outgoing λ in $\mathcal{R}$ and λ_1 in $\mathcal{R}_1$ we will thus speak about models in $\mathcal{R}^\lambda$, $\mathcal{R}_1^{\lambda_1}$ and $\mathcal{R}^\lambda \oslash \mathcal{R}_1^{\lambda_1}$. $\mathcal{R}^\lambda$ and $\mathcal{R}_1^{\lambda_1}$ are just introduced in order to be able to regard local models of $\mathcal{R}$ and $\mathcal{R}_1$ from states λ and λ_1. When, say $\lambda \in \mathcal{I}$, we have $\mathsf{Mod}(\mathcal{R}^\lambda) = \emptyset$.

Rule $(I \wedge \neg I_1)$ ensures that since there are no models for $\mathcal{R}^\lambda$ and there are models for $\mathcal{R}_1^{\lambda_1}$, there should not be models of $\mathcal{R}^\lambda \oslash \mathcal{R}_1^{\lambda_1}$, otherwise we would not have the right to left implication of Equation (1) in Proposition 3.6.

For Rules $(\neg Imust \wedge I1)$ and $(\neg Imay \wedge I1)$ (together with Rule (top)), since $\mathsf{Mod}(\mathcal{R}_1^{\lambda_1}) = \emptyset$, the right hand side of Equation (1) is trivially satisfied. Therefore in $(\neg Imust \wedge I1)$, the a-transition required from λ cannot be guaranteed; hence the quotient is not consistent. On the other hand for Rule $(\neg Imay \wedge I1)$, since nothing particular is required from λ for the a-transition, nothing either needs being required for models of the quotient; to guarantee Equation (2) of Proposition 3.6 (which states the maximality of the quotient) we set the quotient to be universal, *i.e.* it accepts every model.

Rule $(I \wedge I_1)$ together with Rule (top), is the case where both $\mathsf{Mod}(\mathcal{R}^\lambda) = \emptyset$ and $\mathsf{Mod}(\mathcal{R}_1^{\lambda_1}) = \emptyset$. In this case, the universal MS that accepts every model can be in the quotient, and this is what is chosen in order to get the greatest such MS, as required by Equation (2).

We now come to the set of rules where both λ and λ_1 are consistent ($\lambda \notin \mathcal{I}$ and $\lambda_1 \notin \mathcal{I}_1$), which by Lemma 2.4 amounts to say that $\mathsf{Mod}(\mathcal{R}^\lambda) \neq \emptyset$ and $\mathsf{Mod}(\mathcal{R}_1^{\lambda_1}) \neq \emptyset$.

In Rule $(may1)$, a is not possible from λ_1, and a is not mandatory from λ, it can therefore safely be authorized in the quotient. Rule $(maynot)$ deals with the case where a is forbidden in $\mathcal{R}^\lambda$, but is authorized or even mandatory in $\mathcal{R}_1^{\lambda_1}$: it should be forbidden in the quotient.

Rule $(may2)$ is very straightforward, as models of the quotient may have an a-transition irrespectively of what is required in $\mathcal{R}_1^{\lambda_1}$.

Finally, Rules $(inconsistency)$ and $(must)$ consider the case where we have must transitions in $\mathcal{R}^\lambda$. Rule $(inconsistency)$ corresponds to the inability of guaranteeing the a-transition required in $\mathcal{R}^\lambda$ since it may not exist in some models of $\mathcal{R}^{\lambda_1}$. Hence only an inconsistent MS can be considered so that Equation (1) holds. Rule $(must)$ is the simple case of must requirements; notice that we implicitly have $\lambda_1' \notin \mathcal{I}_1$, since by assumption $\lambda_1 \notin \mathcal{I}_1$.

One can easily verify that the conditions of the premises of Rules from $(I \wedge \neg I_1)$ to $(must)$ are exclusive, hence the quotient construction yields a deterministic object. Also, the quotient MS is complete.

Quotient of MECS. The quotient of a MECS $\mathcal{S} = (Q^{\perp\!\!\!\perp}, \lambda^0, \delta^m, \delta^M)$ by a MECS $\mathcal{S}_1 = (Q_1^{\perp\!\!\!\perp}, \lambda_1^0, \delta_1^m, \delta_1^M)$ is the MECS $\mathcal{S} \oslash \mathcal{S}_1 = (Q'^{\perp\!\!\!\perp}, (\lambda^0, \lambda_1^0), \delta_\oslash^m, \delta_\oslash^M)$, where $Q' \subseteq (Q \times Q_1) \cup \{\top\}$ and where the set of locally inconsistent states and the transition modalities follow the rules $(I \wedge \neg I_1)$ to $(must)$ of the untimed case; the guard of a transition is the conjunction of the local guards of $\mathcal{S}$ and $\mathcal{S}_1$. For example, the untimed rule $(must)$ becomes $(tmust)$ as follows.

$$\frac{\lambda \xrightarrow{g,a} \lambda' \text{ and } \lambda_1 \xrightarrow{g_1,a} \lambda_1'}{(\lambda, \lambda_1) \xrightarrow{g \wedge g_1, a} (\lambda', \lambda_1')} \ (tmust)$$

Besides, the rule $(ttop)$ is the following:

$$\frac{}{\top \xdashrightarrow{\text{true}, a} \top} \ (ttop)$$

This quotient operation for MECS can be used on ECA as the class of deterministic ECA can be embedded into the one of MECS; it suffices to type with must every existing transitions in the ECA, and to complete it by adding transitions typed by may to a state in $\perp\!\!\!\perp$. Assuming determinacy of event-clock automata is not restrictive, since they are known to be determinizable [2]. Observe that then the quotient of two event-clock automata is not an event-clock automaton since *e.g.* Rule $(\neg Imay \wedge I_1)$ introduces a may transition to the top state.

Finally, the quotienting operation yields a deterministic and complete specification. Hence:

Lemma 3.7. *Modal event-clock specifications are closed under quotient.*

As for the product operation, the quotient operation in the timed and untimed settings relate via the region construction (for the extended alphabet) as follows.

Proposition 3.8. $R(\mathcal{S} \oslash \mathcal{S}_1) \equiv R(\mathcal{S}) \oslash R(\mathcal{S}_1).$

The correctness of the quotient construction is stated by the following.

Theorem 3.9 (Properties of the quotient). *For any* MECS $\mathcal{S}, \mathcal{S}_1, \mathcal{S}_2$, *and any* ECA $\mathcal{C}_2$,

$$\mathcal{C}_2 \models \mathcal{S} \oslash \mathcal{S}_1 \iff \forall \mathcal{C}_1. \ [\mathcal{C}_1 \models \mathcal{S}_1 \Rightarrow \mathcal{C}_1 \otimes \mathcal{C}_2 \models \mathcal{S}]; \text{ and} \qquad (3)$$

$$\mathcal{S}_1 \otimes \mathcal{S}_2 \preceq \mathcal{S} \iff \mathcal{S}_2 \preceq \mathcal{S} \oslash \mathcal{S}_1. \qquad (4)$$

From a practical point of view, the quotient operation enables incremental design: consider a desired global specification $\mathcal{S}$, and the specification $\mathcal{S}_1$ of a preexisting component. By computing $\mathcal{S} \oslash \mathcal{S}_1$ and by checking its consistency, one can test whether a component implementing $\mathcal{S}_1$ can be reused in order to realize $\mathcal{S}$, or not. Note that by (4) the specification $\mathcal{S} \oslash \mathcal{S}_1$ is maximally permissive in the sense that it characterizes all components $\mathcal{C}_2$ such that for any $\mathcal{C}_1$ implementing $\mathcal{S}_1$, the composed system $\mathcal{C}_1 \otimes \mathcal{C}_2$ implements $\mathcal{S}$.

Example 3.10. A desired global behavior G is depicted in Fig. 3(b), page 690. It specifies that any **get** request must be fulfilled; the access to the resource is granted for 2 time units and 5 time units in the privileged mode.

A model of $G/(Cl \otimes Acc)$ will act as a protocol converter between Cl and the access controller Acc ; the overall obtained system will satisfy G. The MECS $G/(Cl \otimes Acc)$ is represented in Fig. 4. Not surprisingly, the state $c/11'$ is inconsistent. This is because, in the state $11'$ in Fig. 3(a), the resource is granted for 4 units of time whereas in the state c of the desired behavior G in Fig. 3(b), it must be granted for 5 units of time. To avoid this inconsistency, the transition *extra* from state $b/10'$ to $c/11'$ will not be implemented in any model of $G/(Cl \otimes Acc)$. Thus, the protocol converter will disallow the privileged mode.

The quotient operation we gave has nice properties: its construction is in essence a cartesian product, thus yielding a polynomial time complexity, as opposed to the exponential blow-up caused by the region graph construction of Proposition 3.8. Also the quotient, defined at the level of specifications and abstracting from a particular choice of implementations, amounts to quotienting logical statements denoted by specifications. In the untimed setting, the quotient operation is a particular case of the exponential construction introduced by [7] for arbitrary mu-calculus statements. However, we take here advantage of the restricted logical fragment covered by the modal specifications, namely the conjunction nu-calculus [15], to get an ad-hoc polynomial-time complexity of this quotient construction. The present contribution suggests a similar situation for a timed extension of the mu-calculus.

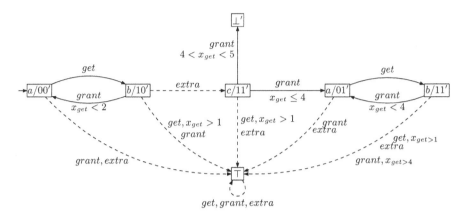

Fig. 4. The quotient $G/(Cl \otimes Acc)$

4   Related Work

Regarding a theory of interfaces, we compare our approach with the following settings: Interface automata of [12], timed interfaces of [13], and a timed extensions of modal specifications of [10].

Interface automata. In interface automata [13], an interface is represented by an input/output automaton [21], *i.e.*, an automaton whose transitions are typed with *input* and *output* rather than must and may modalities. The semantics of such an automaton is given by a two-player game: the *input* player represents the environment, and the *output* player represents the component itself. As explained [24], interfaces and modalities are in essence orthogonal to each other. Moreover, interface automata do not encompass any notion of model, and thus neither the model relation nor the consistency, because one cannot distinguish between interfaces and components. Alternatively, properties of interfaces are described in game-based logics, *e.g.*, ATL [3], with a high-cost complexity. Refinement between interface automata corresponds to the alternating refinement relation between games [4], *i.e.*, an interface refines another one if its environment is more permissive whereas its component is more restrictive. There is no notion of component reuse and shared refinement is defined in an ad-hoc manner [14]. Composition of interface automata differs from the one over modal specifications. Indeed, in interface automata, the game-based approach offers an optimistic treatment of composition: two interfaces can be composed if there exists at least one environment in which they can interact together in a safe way. In [19], Larsen et al. proposed *modal interfaces* that are modal specifications composed in a game-based manner. This work suggests that modal specifications subsume interface automata.

Timed interfaces. In [13], de Alfaro et al. proposed *timed interfaces* which extend timed automata just as interface automata extend automata. The composition of timed interfaces has only been partially studied, because of the underlying timed games semantics: in particular, an extra feature needs being incorporated to prevent players from winning by using Zeno strategies. Moreover, no refinement relation is defined. Recently, Chatain et al. [11] proposed a notion of alternating timed refinement between timed automata, implemented in the UPPAAL toolset [25]. In all cases, operations between specifications have not been investigated in a systematic way, and to our knowledge, no quotient construction has been addressed.

A timed extension of modal specifications. A timed extension of modal specifications appeared in [10] in a process algebra style. The formalism proposed is a variant of CCS whose semantics relies on the configuration graph rather than on the region graph, as done here. No logical characterization is developed, neither any notion of model relation (satisfaction) or consistency (satisfiability). Moreover, the quotient has not been considered at all.

5   Conclusion

Modal specifications offer a well-adapted algebraic framework for compositional reasoning on component-based systems, that enables incremental design as well as reuse of component. In this paper, we have presented a timed extension of modal specifications using event-clock timed automata. All essential features expected from a theory of interface (such as refinement, conjunction, satisfiability, product, and quotient) are fully addressed and efficiently treated in this framework.

Several research directions still need being investigated in the future. We aim at studying timed modal specifications in a broader framework than the one of MECS, since event-clock automata are strictly less expressive than timed automata. However, a generalization to arbitrary timed modal specifications raises complex issues on how different sets of clocks can be combined in the quotient. Another topic concerns a logical characterization of modal event-clock specifications (or even more general timed modal specifications), in the spirit of [15] who established the correspondence between simple modal specifications and conjunctive ν-calculus. Such characterization brings insight on the expressiveness of the specification formalism.

Acknowledgment. We are very thankful to the reviewers for relevant comments that helped us improving the paper.

References

1. Alur, R., Dill, D.L.: A theory of timed automata. Theoretical Computer Science 126(2), 183–235 (1994)
2. Alur, R., Fix, L., Henzinger, T.A.: Event-clock automata: A determinizable class of timed automata. Theoretical Computer Science 211, 1–13 (1999)
3. Alur, R., Henzinger, T.A., Kupferman, O.: Alternating-time temporal logic. Journal of the ACM 49(5), 672–713 (2002)

4. Alur, R., Henzinger, T.A., Kupferman, O., Vardi, M.Y.: Alternating refinement relations. In: Sangiorgi, D., de Simone, R. (eds.) CONCUR 1998. LNCS, vol. 1466, pp. 163–178. Springer, Heidelberg (1998)

5. Antonik, A., Huth, M., Larsen, K.G., Nyman, U., Wasowski, A.: 20 years of modal and mixed specifications. Bulletin of European Association of Theoretical Computer Science 1(94) (2008)

6. Arnold, A., Nivat, M.: Metric interpretations of infinite trees and semantics of non deterministic recursive programs. Theoretical Computer Science 11, 181–205 (1980)

7. Arnold, A., Vincent, A., Walukiewicz, I.: Games for synthesis of controllers with partial observation. Theoretical Computer Science 303(1), 7–34 (2003)

8. Bertrand, N., Legay, A., Pinchinat, S., Raclet, J.-B.: A compositional approach on modal specifications for timed systems. Technical report, INRIA 7039 (September 2009)

9. Bertrand, N., Pinchinat, S., Raclet, J.-B.: Refinement and consistency of timed modal specifications. In: Dediu, A.H., Ionescu, A.M., Martin-Vide, C. (eds.) LATA 2009. LNCS, vol. 5457, pp. 152–163. Springer, Heidelberg (2009)

10. Čerāns, K., Godskesen, J.C., Larsen, K.G.: Timed modal specification - theory and tools. In: Fermüller, C., Tammet, T., Leitsch, A., Zamov, N. (eds.) Resolution Methods for the Decision Problem. LNCS, vol. 679, pp. 253–267. Springer, Heidelberg (1993)

11. Chatain, T., David, A., Larsen, K.G.: Playing games with timed games. In: Proceedings of the 3rd IFAC Conference on Analysis and Design of Hybrid Systems, ADHS 2009 (to appear, 2009)

12. de Alfaro, L., Henzinger, T.A.: Interface automata. In: Proceedings of the 9th ACM SIGSOFT International Symposium on Foundations of Software Engineering (FSE 2001), pp. 109–120 (2001)

13. de Alfaro, L., Henzinger, T.A., Stoelinga, M.: Timed interfaces. In: Sangiovanni-Vincentelli, A.L., Sifakis, J. (eds.) EMSOFT 2002. LNCS, vol. 2491, pp. 108–122. Springer, Heidelberg (2002)

14. Doyen, L., Henzinger, T.A., Jobstmann, B., Petrov, T.: Interface theories with component reuse. In: Proceedings of the 8th International Conference on Embedded Software (EMSOFT 2008), pp. 79–88. ACM Press, New York (2008)

15. Feuillade, G., Pinchinat, S.: Modal specifications for the control theory of discrete-event systems. Discrete Event Dynamic Systems 17(2), 181–205 (2007)

16. Henzinger, T.A., Sifakis, J.: The embedded systems design challenge. In: Misra, J., Nipkow, T., Sekerinski, E. (eds.) FM 2006. LNCS, vol. 4085, pp. 1–15. Springer, Heidelberg (2006)

17. Jonsson, B., Larsen, K.G.: On the complexity of equation solving in process algebra. In: Proceedings of the International Joint Conference on Theory and Practice of Software Development (TAPSOFT 1991), pp. 381–396. Springer, Heidelberg (1991)

18. Larsen, K.G.: Modal specifications. In: Sifakis, J. (ed.) CAV 1989. LNCS, vol. 407, pp. 232–246. Springer, Heidelberg (1990)

19. Larsen, K.G., Nyman, U., Wasowski, A.: Modal i/o automata for interface and product line theories. In: De Nicola, R. (ed.) ESOP 2007. LNCS, vol. 4421, pp. 64–79. Springer, Heidelberg (2007)

20. Larsen, K.G., Nyman, U., Wasowski, A.: On modal refinement and consistency. In: Caires, L., Vasconcelos, V.T. (eds.) CONCUR 2007. LNCS, vol. 4703, pp. 105–119. Springer, Heidelberg (2007)

21. Lynch, N., Tuttle, M.R.: An introduction to Input/Output automata. CWI-quarterly 2(3) (1989)

22. Raclet, J.-B.: Quotient de spécifications pour la réutilisation de composants. PhD thesis, Université de Rennes I, december, In French (2007)
23. Raclet, J.-B.: Residual for component specifications. In: Proceedings of the 4th International Workshop on Formal Aspects of Component Software, FACS 2007 (2007)
24. Raclet, J.-B., Badouel, E., Benveniste, A., Caillaud, B., Passerone, R.: Why are modalities good for interface theories? In: Proceedings of the 9th International Conference on Application of Concurrency to System Design (ACSD 2009), pp. 127–199. IEEE Computer Society Press, Los Alamitos (2009)
25. The UPPAAL tool, http://www.uppaal.com/

An Efficient Translation of Timed-Arc Petri Nets to Networks of Timed Automata

Joakim Byg, Kenneth Yrke Jørgensen, and Jiří Srba*

Department of Computer Science
Aalborg University
Selma Lagerlöfs Vej 300
9220 Aalborg East, Denmark

Abstract. Bounded timed-arc Petri nets with read-arcs were recently proven equivalent to networks of timed automata, though the Petri net model cannot express urgent behaviour and the described mutual translations are rather inefficient. We propose an extension of timed-arc Petri nets with invariants to enforce urgency and with transport arcs to generalise the read-arcs. We also describe a novel translation from the extended timed-arc Petri net model to networks of timed automata. The translation is implemented in the tool TAPAAL and it uses UPPAAL as the verification engine. Our experiments confirm the efficiency of the translation and in some cases the translated models verify significantly faster than the native UPPAAL models do.

1 Introduction

Time dependent models have been intensively studied because of the current needs in software verification and development of embedded applications where several reliability and safety requirements depend, to a large extent, on the timing aspects. Among the most studied time dependent models are timed automata [3] and different time extensions of Petri nets (see e.g. [15]). A recent overview comparing these models has been given in [21].

We consider a particular extension of the Petri net model called *Timed-Arc Petri Nets* (TAPN) [7, 12] where an age (a real number) is assigned to each token in the net and time intervals on arcs restrict the ages of tokens that can be used to fire a transition. Recent studies show that bounded TAPN (where the maximum number of tokens in the net is a priori given) offer a similar expressive power as networks of timed automata, even though the models are conceptually different and suitable for modelling of different systems. Sifakis and Yovine [19] provided a translation of 1-safe timed-arc Petri nets into timed automata which preserves strong timed bisimilarity but their translation causes an exponential blow up in the size. Srba established in [20] a strong relationship (up to isomorphism of timed transition systems) between networks of timed automata and a

---

* The author is partially supported by Institute for Theoretical Computer Science (ITI), project No. 1M0545.

K. Breitman and A. Cavalcanti (Eds.): ICFEM 2009, LNCS 5885, pp. 698–716, 2009.

superclass of 1-safe TAPN extended with read-arcs. For reachability questions the reductions work in polynomial time. Recently Bouyer et al. [8] presented a reduction from bounded TAPN (with read-arcs) to 1-safe TAPN (with read-arcs), which preserves timed language equivalence (over finite words, infinite words and non-Zeno infinite words). Nevertheless the translations described in these papers are inefficient from a practical point of view as they either cause an exponential blow-up in the size or create a new parallel component with a fresh local clock (or more if the net is not 1-safe) for *each place* in the net, a situation where even most developed tools like UPPAAL [22] show often a poor performance. One limitation of the TAPN model is the impossibility to express urgent behaviour (a TAPN model can always in any marking delay for ever without taking any discrete transitions). While on one side this makes some problems like coverability and boundedness decidable even for unbounded nets [1, 2, 8, 16], it considerably limits the modelling power.

In this paper we extend the TAPN model with two new features: *invariants*[1] on places to enforce urgent behaviour and *transport arcs* that generalise the previously studied read-arcs [8, 20]. We then suggest a novel translation of TAPN to networks of timed automata where a fresh parallel component (with a local clock) is created for *every token* in the net. This is a conceptually orthogonal approach to the ones discussed in the previous works and it relies on different reduction techniques. The proposed translation also transforms safety and liveness logical formulae into equivalent formulae on networks of timed automata. One of the main advantages of this approach is the ability to use the *active clock reduction* and the *symmetry reduction* techniques available in the rich theory of timed automata.

The theory described in this paper translates TAPN models to UPPAAL-style of timed automata with handshake synchronization because UPPAAL is probably the most frequently used industrial-strength tool for verification of timed automata. For this reason, we chose at the moment not to use tools offering more general notions of synchronization like e.g. KRONOS [9] and our experiments confirm that the translation to timed automata with handshake synchronization was indeed a good choice as the verification using this approach is rather efficient. The suggested translations were implemented in a new tool TAPAAL [11], freely available at www.tapaal.net, which offers modelling, simulation and verification of timed-arc Petri nets with continuous time. We report here on two experiments: verification of the Fischer's mutual exclusion algorithm and the alternating bit protocol. The results are promising and the translated timed automata models verify in fact considerably faster than the native UPPAAL models do.

Related Tools. There is one related tool prototype for verification of timed-arc Petri nets mentioned in [2] where the authors discuss a coverability algorithm for general (unbounded) nets, though without any urgent behaviour. The tool does not seem to be maintained anymore. Time features (time stamps) connected to

---

[1] Invariants in our setting are time bounds restricting the ages of tokens in certain places. They should not be confused with transition/place invariant techniques studied in the theory of (untimed) Petri nets.

tokens can be modelled also in Coloured Petri Nets using CPN Tools [13], however, only discrete time semantics is implemented in CPN Tools with a limited
support for the automatic analysis.

A full version of this paper with complete proofs is available in [10].

2 Basic Definitions

A *timed labelled transition system* (TLTS) is a triple $T = (S, \mathcal{A}ct, \longrightarrow)$ where
S is a set of *states*, $\mathcal{A}ct$ is a set of *actions* where $\mathcal{A}ct \cap \mathbb{R}^{\geq 0} = \emptyset$ and $\mathbb{R}^{\geq 0}$ are
nonnegative real numbers, and $\longrightarrow \subseteq S \times (\mathcal{A}ct \cup \mathbb{R}^{\geq 0}) \times S$ is a *transition relation*.

We let $a, a_0, a_1, \ldots$ range over $\mathcal{A}ct$ and $d, d_0, d_1, \ldots$ over $\mathbb{R}^{\geq 0}$. We write $s \xrightarrow{a} s'$
if $(s, a, s') \in \longrightarrow$ for the *discrete transitions* and $s \xrightarrow{d} s'$ if $(s, d, s') \in \longrightarrow$ for the
delay transitions. We use the notations $s \xrightarrow{a}$ and $s \xrightarrow{d}$ if there exists some state
s' such that $s \xrightarrow{a} s'$ and $s \xrightarrow{d} s'$, respectively. By $s \longrightarrow s'$ we mean that either
$s \xrightarrow{a} s'$ for some $a \in \mathcal{A}ct$ or $s \xrightarrow{d} s'$ for some delay d. Let $s \in S$ and $d \in \mathbb{R}^{\geq 0}$.
By $s[d]$ we denote the unique (here we impose the standard *time-determinism*
assumption—see e.g. [5]) state s' such that $s \xrightarrow{d} s'$, provided that the delay d
is possible from s.

The set $\mathcal{I}$ of *time intervals* is defined by the following abstract syntax where
a and b range over $\mathbb{N}$ and $a < b$:

$$I ::= [a, b] \mid [a, a] \mid (a, b] \mid [a, b) \mid (a, b) \mid [a, \infty) \mid (a, \infty) .$$

The set $\mathcal{I}_{Inv}$ of *invariants* is a subset of intervals that include 0.

2.1 Logic for Safety and Liveness Properties

We shall now define a subset of Computation Tree Logic (CTL) used in the
tool TAPAAL [11] (essentially mimicking the logic used in UPPAAL, except for
the *leads-to* operator). Let $\mathcal{AP}$ be the set of atomic propositions. The logical
formulae are given by the following abstract syntax

$$\psi ::= \mathsf{EF}\, \varphi \mid \mathsf{EG}\, \varphi \mid \mathsf{AF}\, \varphi \mid \mathsf{AG}\, \varphi$$
$$\varphi ::= p \mid \neg \varphi \mid \varphi \wedge \varphi$$

where $p \in \mathcal{AP}$ and EF, EG, AF and AG are the standard CTL temporal operators.

The semantics of formulae is defined with respect to a given TLTS $T = (S, \mathcal{A}ct, \longrightarrow)$ together with a labelling function $\mu : S \to 2^{\mathcal{AP}}$ which assigns a set
of true atomic propositions to each state. The satisfaction relation $s \models \psi$ for a
state $s \in S$ and a formula ψ is defined inductively as follows:

- $s \models p$ iff $p \in \mu(s)$,
- $s \models \neg \varphi$ iff $s \not\models \varphi$,
- $s \models \varphi_1 \wedge \varphi_2$ iff $s \models \varphi_1$ and $s \models \varphi_2$,

- $s \models \mathsf{EF}\,\varphi$ iff $s \longrightarrow^* s'$ and $s' \models \varphi$
- $s \models \mathsf{EG}\,\varphi$ iff there is a (finite or infinite) alternating run ρ of the form

$$s = s_1 \xrightarrow{d_1} s_1' \xrightarrow{a_1} s_2 \xrightarrow{d_2} s_2' \xrightarrow{a_2} s_3 \xrightarrow{d_3} s_3' \xrightarrow{a_3} s_4 \xrightarrow{d_4} s_4' \xrightarrow{a_4} \ldots$$

such that for all i and for all d, $0 \le d \le d_i$, we have $s_i[d] \models \varphi$ and
(i) ρ is infinite, or
(ii) ρ is finite and ends in s_k where for all $d \in \mathbb{R}^{\ge 0}$ we have $s_k \xrightarrow{d}$ and $s_k[d] \models \varphi$, or
(iii) ρ is finite and ends in a state s' (where s' is either of the form s_k or s_k') such that whenever $s' \xrightarrow{d} s'[d]$ is possible for a $d \in \mathbb{R}^{\ge 0}$ then $s'[d] \models \varphi$ and there is no state s'' such that $s'[d] \xrightarrow{a} s''$ for any $a \in \mathcal{A}ct$,
- $s \models \mathsf{AF}\,\varphi$ iff $s \not\models \mathsf{EG}\,\neg\varphi$, and
- $s \models \mathsf{AG}\,\varphi$ iff $s \not\models \mathsf{EF}\,\neg\varphi$.

Remark 1. The formula $\mathsf{EG}\,\varphi$ means that there exists a *maximal* run such that at any point the formula φ is satisfied. The conditions (i), (ii) and (iii) list the three possibilities for a run to be maximal: (i) it consists of an infinite alternating sequence of actions and time delays, or (ii) it ends in a state where time can diverge, or (iii) it ends in a state from which no discrete transitions are possible after any time delay (this includes time-locks).

2.2   Timed-Arc Petri Nets

A *Timed-Arc Petri Net with transport arcs and place invariants* (TAPN) is a tuple $N = (P, T, F, c, F_{tarc}, c_{tarc}, \iota)$, where P is a finite set of *places*, T is a finite set of *transitions* such that $T \cap P = \emptyset$, $F \subseteq (P \times T) \cup (T \times P)$ is a *flow relation*, $c : F|_{P \times T} \to \mathcal{I}$ is a function assigning a time interval to every arc from a place to a transition, $F_{tarc} \subseteq (P \times T \times P)$ is the set of *transport arcs* that satisfy for all $(p, t, p') \in F_{tarc}$ and all $r \in P$:

$$\big((p, t, r) \in F_{tarc} \Rightarrow p' = r\big) \land \big((r, t, p') \in F_{tarc} \Rightarrow p = r\big) \land (p, t) \notin F \land (t, p') \notin F$$

$c_{tarc} : F_{tarc} \to \mathcal{I}$ is a function assigning a time interval to every transport arc, and $\iota : P \to \mathcal{I}_{Inv}$ is an *invariant assignment* of invariants to places.

Remark 2. The conditions imposed on the transport arcs guarantee for any given p and t that if there is a transport arc of the form (p, t, p') or (p'', t, p) then the places p' and p'' are unique. Whenever the places p' or p'' are not relevant for the context, we shall simply denote the transport arcs as $(p, t, \_)$ or $(\_, t, p)$.

The *preset* of a transition t in the net is defined as $\bullet t = \{p \in P \mid (p, t) \in F \lor (p, t, \_) \in F_{tarc}\}$, and the *postset* of a transition t is defined as $t^\bullet = \{p \in P \mid (t, p) \in F \lor (\_, t, p) \in F_{tarc}\}$. Without loss of generality assume that $|\bullet t \cup t^\bullet| > 0$ for any $t \in T$. By $\mathcal{B}(\mathbb{R}^{\ge 0})$ we denote the set of finite multisets on $\mathbb{R}^{\ge 0}$. For $B \in \mathcal{B}(\mathbb{R}^{\ge 0})$ and $d \in \mathbb{R}^{\ge 0}$ we let $B + d \stackrel{\text{def}}{=} \{b + d \mid b \in B\}$.

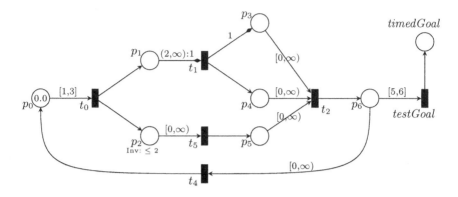

Fig. 1. Example of a marked TAPN

Let $N = (P, T, F, c, F_{tarc}, c_{tarc}, \iota)$ be a TAPN. A *marking* M on the net N is a function $M \colon P \to \mathcal{B}(\mathbb{R}^{\geq 0})$ such that every $p \in P$ and every $x \in M(p)$ satisfy $x \in \iota(p)$. Each place is thus assigned a certain number of tokens, and each token is annotated with a real number (*age*). We moreover consider only markings such that all their tokens satisfy the place invariants imposed by the invariant assignment ι. By $|M|$ we denote the total number of tokens in the marking M. The set of all markings on N is denoted by $\mathcal{M}(N)$. For a finite marking M (where $|M| < \infty$) we also use an alternative multiset notation $M = \{(p_1, r_1), (p_2, r_2), \ldots, (p_k, r_k)\}$ where $p_i \in P$ and $r_i \in \mathbb{R}^{\geq 0}$, which lists explicitly all tokens in the net by naming their positions and ages. A *marked TAPN* is a pair (N, M_0) where N is TAPN and M_0 is an initial marking. As *initial markings* we allow only markings with tokens of age 0.

Let us now outline the dynamics of TAPNs. We introduce two types of transition rules: *firing* of a transition and *time delay*.

For a TAPN N we say that a transition $t \in T$ is *enabled* in a marking M if

- in all places $p \in {}^\bullet t$ there is a token x such that its age belongs to the time interval on the arc from p to t, and
- if there is a transport arc of the form (p, t, p') then moreover the age of the token in p satisfies the invariant imposed by p'.

If a transition t is enabled then it can *fire*. It consumes one token (of an appropriate age) from each place in ${}^\bullet t$, and produces one new token to every place in $t^\bullet$. The age of the newly produced token is either 0 for the standard arcs, or it preserves the age of the consumed token for transport arcs.

Another behaviour of the net is a so-called *time delay* where all tokens in the net grow simultaneously older by a given time factor (a real number in general). A time delay is allowed only as long as invariants in all places are satisfied.

Example 1. Consider the marked TAPN from Fig. 1. There are 8 places (drawn as circles) and 6 transitions (drawn as rectangles) that are connected either by standard arcs (such that every arc from a place to a transition contains a time interval) or transport arcs like the one from p_1 to p_3 via t_1. Transport arcs via a given transition are numbered (the symbol :1 after the interval on the arc from p_1 to t_1 and the symbol 1 on the arc from t_1 to p_3) so that the routes for tokens that do not change their age after transition firing are clearly identified. The initial marking contains only one token in place p_0 of age 0 time units. Clearly, before t_0 can fire the net has to delay between 1 to 3 time units and after its firing two new tokens of age 0 are produced into p_1 and p_2. In fact, a longer delay of say 5 time units is also possible but then the transition t_0 will not be enabled again and the token in p_0 is sometimes referred to as a *dead token*. The place p_2 contains an invariant ensuring that tokens in that place cannot grow older than 2 time units. The other places do not show any invariant information, which implicitly means that their associated invariant is $[0, \infty)$. The transport arc between p_1 and p_3 ensures that when t_1 is fired the age of the token produced into p_3 is equal to the age of the token consumed in p_1 (the token produced to p_4 is of age 0).

Transition Firing. In a marking M, we can fire a transition t if it is enabled, i.e.

$$\forall p \in {}^\bullet t. \ \exists x \in M(p). \ [x \in c(p, t) \vee (x \in c_{tarc}(p, t, p') \wedge x \in \iota(p'))] \ .$$

Before firing t, we fix the sets $C_t^-(p)$ and $C_t^+(p)$ for all places $p \in P$ so that they satisfy the following equations (note that all operations are on multisets, and there may be several options for fixing these sets):

- for every $p \in P$ such that $(p, t) \in F$
  $C_t^-(p) = \{x\}$ where $x \in M(p)$ and $x \in c(p, t)$,
- for every $p \in P$ such that $(t, p) \in F$
  $C_t^+(p) = \{0\}$, and
- for every $p, p' \in P$ such that $(p, t, p') \in F_{tarc}$
  $C_t^-(p) = \{x\} = C_t^+(p')$ where $x \in M(p)$, $x \in c_{tarc}(p, t, p')$ and $x \in \iota(p')$;
- in all other cases (when the place in the argument is unrelated to the firing of the transition t) we set the above sets to $\emptyset$.

Firing a transition t in the marking M yields a new marking M' defined as

$$\forall p \in P. \ M'(p) \stackrel{\text{def}}{=} \left(M(p) \setminus C_t^-(p)\right) \cup C_t^+(p) \ .$$

Time Delays. In a marking M we can let time pass by $d \in \mathbb{R}^{\geq 0}$ time units if

$$\forall p \in P. \ \forall x \in M(p). \ (x + d) \in \iota(p)$$

and this time delay then yields a marking M' defined as

$$\forall p \in P. \ M'(p) \stackrel{\text{def}}{=} M(p) + d \ .$$

A given TAPN $N = (P, T, F, c, F_{tarc}, c_{tarc}, \iota)$ generates a TLTS $T(N) \stackrel{\text{def}}{=} (\mathcal{M}(N), T, \longrightarrow)$ where states are markings on N, the set of actions is T, and the transition relation $\longrightarrow$ is defined by $M \xrightarrow{t} M'$ whenever the firing of a transition t in a marking M yields a marking M', and $M \xrightarrow{d} M'$ whenever a time delay of d time units in a marking M yields a marking M'.

In a marked TAPN (N, M_0) we say that a marking M is reachable iff $M_0 \longrightarrow^* M$. The set of all reachable markings from marked TAPN (N, M_0) is denoted $\mathcal{M}(N, M_0)$. A marked net N is k-*bounded* if the total number of tokens in any of its reachable markings is less or equal to k. A marked net is called *bounded* if it is k-bounded for some k. A net N is of *degree* k if every transition $t \in T$ has exactly k incoming and exactly k outgoing arcs, formally $|{}^{\bullet}t| = |t^{\bullet}| = k$.

In order to argue about the validity of logical formulae on transition systems generated by timed-arc Petri nets, we also have to define the set of atomic propositions $\mathcal{AP}$ and the labelling function $\mu : \mathcal{M}(N) \to 2^{\mathcal{AP}}$. We let $\mathcal{AP} \overset{\text{def}}{=} \{p \bowtie n \mid p \in P, n \in \mathbb{N} \text{ and } \bowtie \in \{<, \leq, =, \geq, >\}\}$. The interpretation is that a proposition $(p \bowtie n)$ is true in marking M iff the number of tokens in the place p satisfies the proposition in question with respect to n, formally $\mu(M) \overset{\text{def}}{=} \{(p \bowtie n) \mid |M(p)| \bowtie n\}$, where $\bowtie$ is one of the (standard mathematical) operators in the above definition.

Given a marked TAPN (N, M_0) and a formula ψ, we shall write $M_0 \models_N \psi$ (or $M_0 \models \psi$ if N is clear from the context) whenever the marking M_0 satisfies the formula ψ in the TLTS $T(N)$.

Consider again the marked TAPN from Fig. 1. It is easy to verify that it satisfies e.g. the formula EF $(p_6 = 1)$ as the place p_6 can be easily marked. In our logic we do not consider queries that involve any timing information of tokens but such formulae can be still verified with the presented logic by adding new testing transitions like the one called *testGoal* moving tokens of the specified age from the place p_6 to *timedGoal*. Now the property whether p_6 can become marked with a token of age between 5 and 6 time units can be expressed as the formula EF $(timedGoal = 1)$. Similarly, by introducing a new place with a token and resetting its age when a certain transition is fired, one can measure the duration before some other transition is fired.

Remark 3. In standard P/T Petri nets there is a construction to ensure that a transition can be fired only if a token is present in a certain place, without removing the token. This is done by adding two arcs: one from the place to the transition and one in the opposite direction. A similar construction, however, does not work in TAPN with only standard arcs as consuming a (timed) token and returning it back resets its age. Hence an extension of the model with *read-arcs* was suggested in [20, 8]. A read-arc in TAPN setting is a special arc from a place to a transition which is labelled by a time interval. The semantics is that the transition can fire only if a token with its age in the given interval is present in the input place of the read-arc, however, the token is not consumed nor reset when the transition is fired. It is shown in [20, 8] that timed automata and bounded TAPN with read-arcs are equally expressive. Transport arcs, newly introduced in this paper, generalize the notion of read-arcs because a read-arc can be simulated by a pair of transport arcs which consume a token and return it back without resetting its age (the same trick as in P/T nets). On the other hand, transport arcs do not add any expressive power as we show in this paper that bounded TAPN with transport arcs can be also translated to timed automata. On the other hand, transport arcs are convenient for the modelling purposes because the encoding tricks used in simulating transport arcs by read-arcs are complex and they double the number of tokens in the net (as one token is used to simulate the token position and the other one to remember its age).

2.3   Networks of Timed Automata

Let C be a finite set of *clocks*. A *(time) valuation* of clocks from C is a function $v : C \to \mathbb{R}^{\geq 0}$. Let v be a valuation and $d \in \mathbb{R}^{\geq 0}$. We define a valuation $v + d : C \to \mathbb{R}^{\geq 0}$ by $(v + d)(x) \stackrel{\text{def}}{=} v(x) + d$ for every $x \in C$. For every set $R \subseteq C$ we define a valuation $v[R := 0] : C \to \mathbb{R}^{\geq 0}$ by $v[R := 0](x) \stackrel{\text{def}}{=} v(x)$ for $x \in C \setminus R$ and $v[R := 0](x) \stackrel{\text{def}}{=} 0$ for $x \in R$.

A *clock guard* is a partial function $g : C \hookrightarrow \mathcal{I}$ assigning a time interval to selected clocks. We denote the set of all clock guards as $\mathcal{G}(C)$. An *invariant* is a clock guard g where for every $x \in C$ holds $g(x) \in \mathcal{I}_{Inv}$ whenever $g(x)$ is defined. The set of all invariants is denoted by $\mathcal{G}_{Inv}(C)$. We say that a valuation v satisfies a guard $g \in \mathcal{G}(C)$ (written $v \models g$) iff $v(x) \in g(x)$ for all $x \in dom(g)$. To specify a guard g that only constrains the values of one clock x, we often use the notation $x \in I$ where $I = g(x)$.

A *timed automaton* (TA) is a tuple $A = (L, Act, C, \longrightarrow, \iota, \ell^0)$ where L is a finite set of *locations*, Act is a finite set *actions* such that $L \cap Act = \emptyset$, C is a finite set of *clocks*, $\longrightarrow \subseteq L \times \mathcal{G}(C) \times Act \times 2^C \times L$ is a finite *transition relation* written $\ell \xrightarrow{g,a,R} \ell'$ for $(\ell, g, a, R, \ell') \in \longrightarrow$, $\iota : L \to \mathcal{G}_{Inv}(C)$ is an *invariant assignment* of clock guards to the locations, and $\ell^0 \in L$ is an *initial* location.

A *configuration* of a timed automaton A is a pair (ℓ, v) where $\ell \in L$ is a location and $v : C \to \mathbb{R}^{\geq 0}$ is a clock valuation on C such that the location ℓ satisfies the respective invariant, i.e., $v \models \iota(\ell)$. We denote the set of all configurations of A by $Conf(A)$. An *initial configuration* of A is (ℓ^0, v^0) such that $v^0(x) \stackrel{\text{def}}{=} 0$ for all $x \in C$. We assume that the initial configuration always satisfies the invariant of the location ℓ^0, i.e., $(\ell^0, v^0) \in Conf(A)$.

A timed automaton $A = (L, Act, C, \longrightarrow, \iota, \ell^0)$ determines a TLTS $T(A) \stackrel{\text{def}}{=} (Conf(A), Act, \longrightarrow)$ where states are configuration of A and the transition relation $\longrightarrow$ is defined by

$(\ell, v) \xrightarrow{a} (\ell', v[R := 0])$ if $\ell \xrightarrow{g,a,R} \ell'$ in A s.t. $v \models g$ and $v[R := 0] \models \iota(\ell')$

$(\ell, v) \xrightarrow{d} (\ell, v + d)$ if $d \in \mathbb{R}^{\geq 0}$ and for all $d' \in [0, d]$ we have $v + d' \models \iota(\ell)$.

We shall adopt the handshake communication scheme as it is used in the tool UP-PAAL [22] for defining a parallel composition of automata. In the semantics, we consider only synchronization moves as independent moves of single components are not necessary for the reduction.

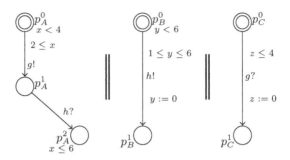

Fig. 2. Example of an NTA

Let $A_1, \ldots, A_n$ be timed automata where (for all i, $1 \le i \le n$) $A_i = (L_i, Act, C, \longrightarrow_i, \iota_i, \ell_i^0)$ and where Act and C are fixed sets of actions and clocks, respectively. We moreover require that Act is of the form $Act = Act_! \cup Act_?$ where $Act_! \stackrel{\text{def}}{=} \{a! \mid a \in Chan\}$ and $Act_? \stackrel{\text{def}}{=} \{a? \mid a \in Chan\}$ for a given nonempty set of *channel names Chan*. A *network of timed automata* (NTA) is a parallel composition of $A_1, \ldots, A_n$ denoted by $P = A_1 \| \cdots \| A_n$. Note that it is allowed to share the names of locations in different parallel components.

A *configuration* is a tuple $(\ell_1, \ldots, \ell_n, v)$ where $\ell_i \in L_i$ for all $1 \le i \le n$ and $v : C \to \mathbb{R}^{\ge 0}$ is a clock valuation on C such that for every i, $1 \le i \le n$, we have $v \models \iota_i(\ell_i)$. We denote the set of all configurations of P by $Conf(P)$. An *initial configuration* of P is $(\ell_1^0, \ldots, \ell_n^0, v^0)$ such that $v^0(x) \stackrel{\text{def}}{=} 0$ for all $x \in C$. As before we assume that $(\ell_1^0, \ldots, \ell_n^0, v^0) \in Conf(P)$.

An NTA P determines a TLTS $T(P) \stackrel{\text{def}}{=} (Conf(P), Chan, \longrightarrow)$ where states are the configurations of P, the discrete transitions are labelled by channel names, and the transition relation $\longrightarrow$ is defined by

- $(s_1, \ldots, s_j, \ldots, s_k, \ldots s_n, v) \stackrel{a}{\longrightarrow} (s_1, \ldots, s_j', \ldots, s_k', \ldots, s_n, v')$
  for $1 \le j \ne k \le n$ whenever
  - $s_j \xrightarrow{g_j, a!, R_j}_j s_j'$ and $v \models g_j$,
  - $s_k \xrightarrow{g_k, a?, R_k}_k s_k'$ and $v \models g_k$,
  - $v' = v[R_j \cup R_k := 0]$, and $(s_1, \ldots, s_j', \ldots, s_k', \ldots, s_n, v') \in Conf(P)$
- $(s_1, \ldots, s_n, v) \stackrel{d}{\longrightarrow} (s_1, \ldots, s_n, v + d)$
  if $d \in \mathbb{R}^{\ge 0}$ and $(s_i, v) \stackrel{d}{\longrightarrow}_i (s_i, v + d)$ for all i, $1 \le i \le n$.

Example 2. Consider the NTA in Fig. 2 with three parallel components A, B and C. We draw the parallel components as graphs where nodes represent locations together with their invariants and edges decorated by guards, synchronisation channels and clock updates represent the transition relation. The initial location of each component is marked with a double circle. In the following example of a computation in the network

$$(p_A^0, p_B^0, p_C^0, [x = 0, y = 0, z = 0]) \xrightarrow{3} (p_A^0, p_B^0, p_C^0, [x = 3, y = 3, z = 3]) \xrightarrow{g}$$

$$(p_A^1, p_B^0, p_C^1, [x = 3, y = 3, z = 0]) \xrightarrow{2.4} (p_A^1, p_B^0, p_C^1, [x = 5.4, y = 5.4, z = 2.4]) \xrightarrow{h}$$

$$(p_A^2, p_B^1, p_C^1, [x = 5.4, y = 0, z = 2.4]) \xrightarrow{0.6} (p_A^2, p_B^1, p_C^1, [x = 6, y = 0.6, z = 3])$$

we notice that in the last configuration the network is stuck as no further synchronization is possible and because of the invariant $x \le 6$ in place p_A^2 time cannot delay either.

In order to argue about validity of logical formulae on transition systems generated by networks of timed automata P, we have to define the set of atomic proposition $\mathcal{AP}$ and the labelling function $\mu : Conf(P) \rightarrow 2^{\mathcal{AP}}$. We let $\mathcal{AP} \stackrel{\text{def}}{=} \{(\#\ell \bowtie n) \mid \ell \in \cup_{i=1}^n L_i, \ n \in \mathbb{N} \text{ and } \bowtie \in \{<, \le, =, \ge, >\}\}$. The interpretation is that a proposition $(\#\ell \bowtie n)$ is true in a given configuration iff the number of parallel components that are currently in the location ℓ respects the given proposition with respect to n.

3   From Bounded TAPN to NTA

In this section we shall describe a reduction from bounded timed-arc Petri nets with invariants and transport arcs to networks of timed automata. We first describe a reduction from bounded nets to nets where each transition has exactly two input and two output places. In the second step this reduction is followed by a reduction to networks of timed automata.

3.1   From k-Bounded TAPN to TAPN of Degree 2

To translate a given k-bounded TAPN with transitions that have more than two input or output places into a TAPN of degree 2 we have to simulate a single transition firing in the original net by a series of transitions in the net of degree 2. The problem is that when firing a given transition in a number of steps, other transition firings may interleave—thus some extra behaviour can be introduced. To prevent this from happening, we introduce a new mutex-like place called p_{lock}, which contains a token that is consumed before the sequence of transition firings begins and the token is returned back after the simulation of the selected transition is ended.

  The translation is demonstrated in Fig. 3 where a simple 3-bounded TAPN is translated into a TAPN of degree 2. The idea is that the token in the place p_{lock} will travel through intermediate places $p(t_{in}^1)$, $p(t_{in}^2)$, $p(t_{out}^2)$, $p(t_{out}^1)$ and finally return to p_{lock}. When the first transition $p(t_{in}^1)$ is fired, a token of a suitable age from p_0 is consumed and placed in the holding place $p_h(t^1)$, then a token from p_1 is consumed and placed in $p_h(t^2)$. Because $|{}^\bullet t| < |t^\bullet|$ a special place called $p_{capacity}$ (used as a repository of the presently unused tokens) is created. By firing the transition t^3 a new token of age 0 is produced in p_3. And finally the tokens placed in $p_h(t^2)$ and $p_h(t^1)$ are moved to the appropriate output places

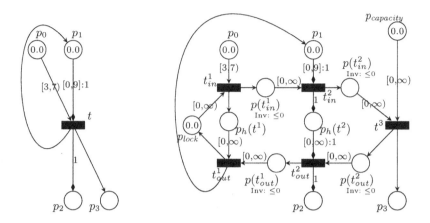

Fig. 3. An example of a 3-bounded net and the corresponding degree 2 net

by firing the transitions t_{out}^2 and t_{out}^1. Note that because of the invariants on the intermediate places, time cannot elapse during such a series of transition firing and so the age of the token in p_1 that is moved via the two transport arcs into p_2 is preserved. Notice that the use of holding places is essential as without them a token from p_0 can be consumed by t_{in}^1 while creating a new token in p_1. This may allow firing of t_{in}^2 even if there were no tokens in p_1 in the original net. Also notice that by this construction we may introduce extra deadlocks (e.g. if there is no token present in p_1 and the transition t_{in}^1 is fired). Nevertheless, for the verification of safety properties we can detect such situations as demonstrated in what follows.

Let us introduce some notation for a transition $t \in T$. We fix a set

$$
\begin{aligned}
Pairing(t) = &\{(p, I, p', tarc) \mid (p, t, p') \in F_{tarc}, I = c_{tarc}(p, t, p')\} \cup \\
&\{(p_1, I_1, p_1', normal), \ldots, (p_m, I_m, p_m', normal) \mid \\
&\{p_1, \ldots, p_\ell\} = \{p \mid (p, t) \in F\}, \ \{p_1', \ldots, p_{\ell'}'\} = \{p \mid (t, p) \in F\}, \\
&m = \max(\ell, \ell'), \ I_i = c(p_i, t) \text{ if } 1 \le i \le \ell \text{ else } I_i = [0, \infty), \\
&p_i = p_{capacity} \text{ if } \ell < i \le m, \ p_i' = p_{capacity} \text{ if } \ell' < i \le m\}
\end{aligned}
$$

and we define $\max(t) \stackrel{\text{def}}{=} \max(|{}^\bullet t|, |t^\bullet|)$. Note that the max operator with two arguments is the classical maximum of two numbers.

The intuition is that $Pairing(t)$ fixes the paths from input to output places on which the tokens travel when firing the transition t, and it also remembers the associated time intervals and the type of the path (*tarc* for transport arcs and *normal* for the standard arcs that reset the ages of produced tokens). Observe that for the example net in Fig. 3 where $\max(t) = 3$ a possible pairing operator (used in the reduction) looks like $Pairing(t) = \{(p_0, [3, 7), p_1, normal), (p_1, [0, 9], p_2, tarc), (p_{capacity}, [0, \infty), p_3, normal)\}$. Moreover, by $p \xrightarrow{I} t \longrightarrow p'$ we shall abbreviate the presence of an arc from p to

---

Algorithm 1. Translation from k-bounded TAPN to TAPN of degree 2

Input: A k-bounded TAPN $N = (P, T, F, c, F_{tarc}, c_{tarc}, \iota)$ with marking M_0.
Output: A TAPN $N' = (P', T', F', c', F_{tarc}{}', c_{tarc}{}', \iota')$ of degree 2 and M_0'.
begin

$\quad$ $P' := P \cup \{p_{lock}, p_{capacity}\} \cup \{p_h(t^i) \mid t \in T, \ 1 \leq i < \max(t)\}$
$\qquad\quad \cup \{p(t_{in}^i), p(t_{out}^i) \mid t \in T, \ 1 \leq i < \max(t)\}$

$\quad$ $T' := \{t_{in}^i, t_{out}^i \mid t \in T, \ 1 \leq i < \max(t)\} \cup \{t^{\max(t)}\}$

$\quad$ $\iota'(p) := \begin{cases} \iota(p) & \text{if } p \in P \\ [0,0] & \text{if } p \in \{p(t_{in}^i), p(t_{out}^i) \mid t \in T, \ 1 \leq i < \max(t)\} \\ [0,\infty) & \text{otherwise} \end{cases}$

$\quad$ **forall** $t \in T$ **do**

$\qquad$ $i := 1$

$\qquad$ **while** $|Pairing(t)| > 1$ **do**

$\qquad\quad$ Remove some $(p, I, p', type)$ from $Pairing(t)$ and add arcs

$\qquad\quad$ $p \xrightarrow{I} t_{in}^i \longrightarrow p_h(t^i)$ and $p_h(t^i) \xrightarrow{[0,\infty)} t_{out}^i \longrightarrow p'$ of type $type$.

$\qquad\quad$ $i := i + 1$

$\qquad$ Let $\{(p, I, p', type)\} := Pairing(t)$; add arcs $p \xrightarrow{I} t^i \longrightarrow p'$ of type $type$.

$\qquad$ Add normal arcs $p_{lock} \xrightarrow{[0,\infty)} t_{in}^1 \longrightarrow p(t_{in}^1)$ and $p(t_{out}^1) \xrightarrow{[0,\infty)} t_{out}^1 \longrightarrow p_{lock}$.

$\qquad$ Add normal arcs $p(t_{in}^i) \xrightarrow{[0,\infty)} t_{in}^{i+1} \longrightarrow p(t_{in}^{i+1})$ for $1 \leq i < \max(t) - 1$.

$\qquad$ Add normal arcs $p(t_{in}^{\max(t)-1}) \xrightarrow{[0,\infty)} t^{\max(t)} \longrightarrow p(t_{out}^{\max(t)-1})$.

$\qquad$ Add normal arcs $p(t_{out}^{i+1}) \xrightarrow{[0,\infty)} t_{out}^i \longrightarrow p(t_{out}^i)$ for $1 \leq i < \max(t) - 1$.

$\quad$ $M_0'(p) = \begin{cases} M_0(p) & \text{if } p \in P \\ \{0\} & \text{if } p = p_{lock} \\ \underbrace{\{0, \ldots, 0\}}_{k - |M_0|} & \text{if } p = p_{capacity} \\ \emptyset & \text{otherwise} \end{cases}$

end

---

t with the time interval I and an arc from t to p'; the type of the arcs (normal or transport) will be clear from the context. The translation is given in Alg. 1.

Notice that Alg. 1 for an input net $N = (P, T, F, c, F_{tarc}, c_{tarc}, \iota)$ creates an output net $N' = (P', T', F', c', F_{tarc}{}', c_{tarc}{}', \iota')$ such that

- $|P'| \leq |P| + 2 + 4(|F| + 2|F_{tarc}|)$,
- $|T'| \leq 2(|F| + 2|F_{tarc}|)$, and
- $|F'| + |F_{tarc}{}'| \leq 8(|F| + 2|F_{tarc}|)$.

Hence the translation causes only a linear growth in the size.

We shall now introduce a precise relationship between markings in a given marked k-bounded TAPN (N, M_0) and markings in the TAPN (N', M_0') constructed by Alg. 1. A marking $M' \in \mathcal{M}(N', M_0')$ is called *stable* iff $|M'(p_{lock})| = 1$. Let $M \in \mathcal{M}(N, M_0)$ and $M' \in \mathcal{M}(N', M_0')$. We say that M and M' correspond to each other, written $M \equiv M'$, if and only if

$$M'(p) = \begin{cases} M(p) & \text{if } p \in P \\ \{x\} & \text{if } p = p_{lock} \\ \{x_1, \ldots, x_{k-|M|}\} & \text{if } p = p_{capacity} \\ \emptyset & \text{otherwise} \end{cases} \quad \text{for some } x, x_1, \ldots, x_{k-|M|} \in \mathbb{R}^{\geq 0} .$$

Remark 4. Note that for a given marking M there may be many markings M' such that $M \equiv M'$, but whenever $M \equiv M'$ then M' is stable. Intuitively, the age of the token x in the place p_{lock} represents the time that has elapsed since the last transition firing.

Lemma 1. *Let (N, M_0) be a marked k-bounded TAPN and let (N', M'_0) be the marked TAPN of degree 2 constructed by Alg. 1. Let $M \in \mathcal{M}(N, M_0)$ and $M' \in \mathcal{M}(N', M'_0)$ such that $M \equiv M'$.*

1. *If $M \xrightarrow{t} M_1$ then $M' \longrightarrow^* M'_1$ such that $M_1 \equiv M'_1$ and the sequence by which M'_1 is reached from M' contains only discrete transitions.*
2. *If $M \xrightarrow{d} M_1$ then $M' \xrightarrow{d} M'_1$ such that $M_1 \equiv M'_1$.*
3. *If $M' \longrightarrow^* M'_1$, M'_1 is stable, none of the intermediate markings between M' and M'_1 are stable, and the first transition is not a time delay, then $M \xrightarrow{t} M_1$ for some $t \in T$ such that $M_1 \equiv M'_1$.*
4. *If $M' \xrightarrow{d} M'_1$ then $M \xrightarrow{d} M_1$ such that $M_1 \equiv M'_1$.*

We now describe how to translate queries. Formulae of the form $\psi = \mathsf{EF}\,\varphi$ are translated into $\psi' = \mathsf{EF}(\varphi \wedge p_{lock} = 1)$, and formulae of the form $\psi = \mathsf{AG}\,\varphi$ are translated into $\psi' = \mathsf{AG}(\varphi \vee p_{lock} = 0)$.

Theorem 1. *Let (N, M_0) be a marked k-bounded TAPN and let ψ be a formula of the form $\mathsf{EF}\,\varphi$ or $\mathsf{AG}\,\varphi$. Let (N', M'_0) be the marked TAPN of degree 2 constructed by Alg. 1 and let ψ' be the formula defined above. Then $M_0 \models_N \psi \Longleftrightarrow M'_0 \models_{N'} \psi'$.*

Proof. Notice that the translation returns M'_0 such that $M_0 \equiv M'_0$. We will use this fact implicitly in the arguments to follow. First, we prove the theorem for the EF operator.

"$\Rightarrow$" (EF): Let $M_0 \models \mathsf{EF}\,\varphi$, which means that $M_0 \longrightarrow^* M$ such that $M \models \varphi$. By repeatedly using Lemma 1 we get that $M'_0 \longrightarrow^* M'$ such that $M \equiv M'$, which gives that $M' \models \varphi$. Because M' is stable we get $M' \models \varphi \wedge p_{lock} = 1$ and this implies that $M'_0 \models \mathsf{EF}(\varphi \wedge p_{lock} = 1)$.

"$\Leftarrow$" (EF): Let $M'_0 \models \mathsf{EF}(\varphi \wedge p_{lock} = 1)$. This means that $M'_0 \longrightarrow^* M'$ such that M' is stable and $M' \models \varphi$. By repeatedly using Lemma 1 we get that $M_0 \longrightarrow^* M$ such that $M \equiv M'$, which means that $M \models \varphi$ and hence $M_0 \models \mathsf{EF}\,\varphi$.

The validity of the theorem for the AG operator follows for the definition and the above proved facts about EF as follows: $M_0 \models \mathsf{AG}\,\varphi \iff M_0 \not\models \mathsf{EF}\,\neg\varphi \iff M'_0 \not\models \mathsf{EF}(\neg\varphi \wedge p_{lock} = 1) \iff M'_0 \not\models \mathsf{EF}\neg(\varphi \vee p_{lock} \neq 1) \iff M'_0 \not\models \mathsf{EF}\neg(\varphi \vee p_{lock} = 0) \iff M'_0 \models \mathsf{AG}(\varphi \vee p_{lock} = 0)$. $\qquad\square$

3.2   From TAPN of Degree 2 to Networks of Timed Automata

We can now assume a given net of degree 2 produced by our previous translation and we will continue with a construction of a network of timed automata. The idea of the translation is to represent each token in the net by a single timed automaton with one local clock, and to simulate a transition firing by a handshake synchronisation on a channel named after the transition.

The intuition is described on an example in Fig. 4. We can see that every place in the net gives rise to an identically named location in the parallel component corresponding to a given token, while all invariants are carried over. Time intervals on arcs are naturally transformed into guards and the local clocks of each parallel component are reset if and only if the transitions correspond to normal arcs. In fact, the timed automata for all tokens in the net are identical, except for their initial locations that are determined by the placement of tokens in the initial marking and the names of local clocks. The full translation is given in Alg. 2. For a TAPN of degree 2 with k tokens we hence create k parallel components, each of them of a proportional size to the input net.

As for the first translation, we shall define a correspondence relation $\equiv$ between markings in the net and configurations of the constructed network of timed automata. Let $M = \{(p_1, r_1), (p_2, r_2), \cdots, (p_k, r_k)\}$ be a marking a TAPN of degree 2 and let $s = (l_1, \cdots, l_k, v)$ be a configuration of the constructed NTA. We write $M \equiv s$ if and only if for some permutation $\{j_1, j_2, \cdots, j_k\} = \{1, 2, \cdots, k\}$ we have $p_i = l_{j_i}$ and $v(x_{j_i}) = r_i$ for all i, $1 \leq i \leq k$.

Lemma 2. *Let (N, M_0) be a marked TAPN of degree 2. Let P_{TA} be the NTA constructed from (N, M_0). Let $M \in \mathcal{M}(N, M_0)$ and let s be a reachable configuration of P_{TA} such that $M \equiv s$.*

1. If $M \xrightarrow{t} M'$ then $s \xrightarrow{t} s'$ and $M' \equiv s'$.
2. If $M \xrightarrow{d} M'$ then $s \xrightarrow{d} s'$ and $M' \equiv s'$.
3. If $s \xrightarrow{t} s'$ then $M \xrightarrow{t} M'$ and $M' \equiv s'$.
4. If $s \xrightarrow{d} s'$ then $M \xrightarrow{d} M'$ and $M' \equiv s'$.

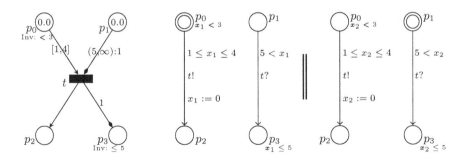

Fig. 4. An example of the translation from TAPN to NTA

Algorithm 2. Algorithm for translation of TAPN of degree 2 to NTA

Input: A TAPN $N = (P, T, F, c, F_{tarc}, c_{tarc}, \iota)$ of degree 2 and a marking M_0.
Output: An NTA $P_{TA} = A_1 \| A_2 \| \ldots \| A_{|M_0|}$ where $A_i = (L, \mathcal{A}ct, C, \longrightarrow_i, \iota_i, \ell_i^0)$.
begin

    $L := P; \ \mathcal{A}ct := \{t!, \ t? \mid t \in T\}; \ C := \{x_1, x_2, \ldots, x_{|M_0|}\}$
    forall $t \in T$ **do**

        Let $\{(p_1, I_1, p_1', type_1), (p_2, I_2, p_2', type_2)\} := Pairing(t)$.
        for $i := 1$ *to* $|M_0|$ **do**

            Add $p_1 \xrightarrow{\ x_i \in I_1, t!, R\ }_i p_1'$ s.t. $R = \{x_i\}$ if $type_1 = normal$ else $R = \emptyset$.
            Add $p_2 \xrightarrow{\ x_i \in I_2, t?, R\ }_i p_2'$ s.t. $R = \{x_i\}$ if $type_2 = normal$ else $R = \emptyset$.

    $i := 1; \ $ **forall** $p \in P,$ **forall** $Token \in M_0(p)$ **do** $\ \ell_i^0 := p; \ i := i + 1;$
    for $i := 1$ *to* $|M_0|$ **do forall** $p \in P$ **do** $\iota_i(p)(x_i) := \iota(p)$

end

Let ψ be a formula of our logic. By ψ' we denote a formula where atomic Petri net propositions of the form $(p \bowtie n)$ are replaced with propositions $(\#p \bowtie n)$ in the network of timed automata.

Theorem 2. *Let (N, M_0) be a marked TAPN of degree 2 and let ψ be a formula of the form* $\mathsf{EF}\,\varphi$, $\mathsf{AG}\,\varphi$, $\mathsf{EG}\,\varphi$ *or* $\mathsf{AF}\,\varphi$. *Let P_{TA} be an NTA constructed by Alg. 2 with the initial configuration $s_0 = (\ell_1^0, \ell_2^0, \ldots, \ell_{|M_0|}^0, v_0)$ and let ψ' be the formula defined above. Then $M_0 \models_N \psi \iff s_0 \models_{P_{TA}} \psi'$.*

Proof. Notice that the correspondence relation $\equiv$ is in fact a timed bisimulation and moreover $M \equiv s$ means that $M \models_N \varphi$ iff $s \models_{P_{TA}} \varphi'$ for every φ which is a Boolean combination of atomic propositions in the Petri net and φ' is the translated formula where every occurrence of $(p \bowtie n)$ is replaced with $(\#p \bowtie n)$. Because timed bisimilarity preserves TCTL model checking (and hence also our logic) and the atomic propositions do not distinguish between configurations related by the correspondence relation $\equiv$, we have established the validity of the theorem. $\qquad\square$

3.3 Final Remarks

In a summary, for safety properties (EF and AG) we provided a translation from bounded timed-arc Petri nets to networks of timed automata by combining Theorem 1 and Theorem 2. For liveness properties we achieved such a translation for nets of degree 2 by using Theorem 2. Even though many net models of real-systems are already of degree 2 or can be easily modified so that Theorem 2 becomes applicable, for the nets where it is necessary to have transitions with more than two input places other translations have to be designed. The main obstacle is that the translation presented in Alg. 1 introduces new time-locks which cannot be distinguished from the time-locks in the original net.

4   Experiments

We shall now report on two experiments testing the efficiency of the translations from Section 3. The translations were implemented in the tool TAPAAL [11] and the models used in the experiments can be downloaded at www.tapaal.net. The reported running times were measured on a Dell PowerEdge 2950, with a 2.5 GHz, Dual Core Intel Xeon 5420 processor and 32GB ram. Notice, however, that UPPAAL utilises only one core and addresses at most 4GB of RAM.

4.1   Fischer's Protocol for Mutual Exclusion

Fischer's protocol [14] for ensuring mutual exclusion for a number of timed processes is a well-known protocol used for testing performances of tools. It is an easily scalable algorithm and provides a suitable case study for our translation because it requires that every process has its own independent clock. In other tools for Petri nets, such as TINA [6] and ROMEO [18], it is inconvenient to model Fischer's protocol as here clocks are usually associated to transitions and hence the number of processes is a priory fixed. One has to necessarily modify the static structure of the net when more processes need to be considered. In our approach we only need to add extra tokens to the same underlying net in order to increase the number of processes. The timed-arc Petri net model of Fischer's protocol is taken from [2] and it is available as an example in the TAPAAL distribution.

We verified the correctness of the Fischer's protocol for a different number of processes. The results were compared with the verification times of the UPPAAL model of Fischer's protocol from the UPPAAL demo folder. The experiments were run with symmetry reduction turned on, both in TAPAAL and UPPAAL, and with the default search options. The verification results are presented in Fig. 5. Here TAPAAL standard reduction is the one from Section 3 and TAPAAL optimised reduction replaces the locking token in the net with a global Boolean

# Processes	Time in seconds			Speed-up
	UPPAAL	TAPAAL		
	Default	Standard	Optimised	
50	7.8	9.8	4.5	73 %
60	18.7	21.1	8.9	110 %
70	40.5	42.0	17.0	138 %
80	78.2	75.7	30.4	157 %
90	138.7	136.1	49.7	179 %
100	235.9	206.4	77.3	205 %
150	31m	22m	8m	293 %
200	2h 22m	1h 25m	29m	393 %
300	22h 7m	10h 6m	3h 24m	549 %
400	–	–	14h 9m	–

Fig. 5. Fischer's Protocol with Symmetry Reduction Turned On

variable in order to reduce the size of the produced UPPAAL templates. Details of the optimised translation are given in [10]. The speed-up column compares the running times between the UPPAAL model and the model produced by the TAPAAL optimised reduction. Even though the number of explored states in the network produced by TAPAAL is about two times as many as the ones in the native UPPAAL model, the verification times are significantly shorter. The reason for this seems to be the fact that the sizes of zones in the TAPAAL produced model are smaller and hence the expensive operation of zone inclusion checking is faster in our approach.

4.2   Alternating Bit Protocol

Alternating Bit Protocol (ABP) [4] is a simple instance of a sliding window protocol with windows of size one. ABP is an unbounded protocol, since in communication between a sender and a receiver, an arbitrary number of messages (each with an individual time-stamp) can be in transfer via a lossy communication media. Details of the model are given in the full version [10].

In Fig. 6 we present the verification results for a fixed number of messages in the system. The translation described in Section 3 allows us to verify the protocol for up to 50 messages in less than two hours. For comparison we created a UPPAAL model of ABP where all messages in the system are symmetric. Notice that the standard translation, contrary to the results from Fischer's protocol, is considerately faster than the optimised translation, which is comparable with the native UPPAAL model we created. The reason seems to be the same as in Fischer's protocol: even though the number of stored and explored states is about twice as large, the zones are less complex and hence the inclusion check is faster.

In the future work we plan to study in detail this phenomenon and optimise the reductions (perhaps depending on the analysis of the concrete net) in order to achieve a further improvement in verification of TAPN models.

# Messages	Time in seconds		
	UPPAAL	TAPAAL	
	Default	Standard	Optimised
12	7.7	2.4	8.9
13	17.6	3.6	21.8
14	19.4	5.1	62.6
15	136	7.3	192.2
16	10m	10.1	11m
17	32m	13.7	35m
20	18h 37m	32.5	19h 34m
30	–	5m	–
40	–	29m	–
50	–	1h 52m	–

Fig. 6. Alternating Bit Protocol with Symmetry Reduction Turned On

5   Conclusion

We studied timed-arc Petri nets extended with invariants on places and with transport arcs—new features that allow for a more convenient modelling of systems. The extended Petri net model with a bounded number of tokens was translated to networks of timed automata, preserving logical queries formulated in a subset of CTL. We employed a novel translation where a new component in the timed automata network was created for each token in the net.

The presented approach for verification of bounded timed-arc Petri nets is efficient as documented on two case studies modelled in the tool TAPAAL and in fact we outperform in the verification times of native UPPAAL models. We kept the considered logic simple and it is essentially identical with the presently implemented logical queries in UPPAAL. Nevertheless, we sketched that verification of TCTL queries and reasoning about the exact ages of tokens can be done by simple encoding tricks.

One cannot hope for a fully automatic verification of unbounded timed-arc Petri nets as, for example, the reachability problem becomes already undecidable [17]. On the other hand, the chosen reduction strategy enables one to further extend the bounded model with e.g. urgent transitions, priorities, cost, probability and game semantics, requiring only minor changes in the proposed reductions. In the future work we shall address these issues.

Acknowledgments. We would like to thank Alexandre David, Krishna Prasad Gundam and Ye Tian for their comments and suggestions. We also thank the anonymous reviewers for their feedback.

References

[1] Abdulla, P.A., Mahata, P., Mayr, R.: Dense-timed Petri nets: Checking zenoness, token liveness and boundedness. Logical Methods in Computer Science 3(1), 1–61 (2007)

[2] Abdulla, P.A., Nylén, A.: Timed Petri nets and BQOs. In: Colom, J.-M., Koutny, M. (eds.) ICATPN 2001. LNCS, vol. 2075, pp. 53–70. Springer, Heidelberg (2001)

[3] Alur, R., Dill, D.: A theory of timed automata. Theoretical Computer Science 126(2), 183–235 (1994)

[4] Bartlett, K.A., Scantlebury, R.A., Wilkinson, P.T.: A note on reliable full-duplex transmission over half-duplex links. Commun. ACM 12(5), 260–261 (1969)

[5] Berthomieu, B., Peres, F., Vernadat, F.: Bridging the gap between timed automata and bounded time Petri nets. In: Asarin, E., Bouyer, P. (eds.) FORMATS 2006. LNCS, vol. 4202, pp. 82–97. Springer, Heidelberg (2006)

[6] Berthomieu, B., Ribet, P.-O., Vernadat, F.: The tool TINA — construction of abstract state spaces for Petri nets and time Petri nets. International Journal of Production Research 42(14), 2741–2756 (2004)

[7] Bolognesi, T., Lucidi, F., Trigila, S.: From timed Petri nets to timed LOTOS. In: Proceedings of the IFIP WG 6.1 Tenth International Symposium on Protocol Specification, Testing and Verification (Ottawa 1990), pp. 1–14 (1990)

[8] Bouyer, P., Haddad, S., Reynier, P.-A.: Timed Petri nets and timed automata: On the discriminating power of Zeno sequences. Information and Computation 206(1), 73–107 (2008)

[9] Bozga, M., Daws, C., Maler, O., Olivero, A., Tripakis, S., Yovine, S.: Kronos: A model-checking tool for real-time systems. In: Y. Vardi, M. (ed.) CAV 1998. LNCS, vol. 1427, pp. 546–550. Springer, Heidelberg (1998)

[10] Byg, J., Joergensen, K.Y., Srba, J.: An efficient translation of timed-arc Petri nets to networks of timed-automata. Technical Report FIMU-RS-2009-06, Faculty of Infomatics, Masaryk University (2009)

[11] Byg, J., Joergensen, K.Y., Srba, J.: TAPAAL: Editor, simulator and verifier of timed-arc Petri nets. In: Liu, Z., Ravn, A.P. (eds.) ATVA 2009. LNCS, vol. 5799, pp. 84–89. Springer, Heidelberg (2009)

[12] Hanisch, H.M.: Analysis of place/transition nets with timed-arcs and its application to batch process control. In: Ajmone Marsan, M. (ed.) ICATPN 1993. LNCS, vol. 691, pp. 282–299. Springer, Heidelberg (1993)

[13] Jensen, K., Kristensen, L., Wells, L.: Coloured Petri nets and CPN tools for modelling and validation of concurrent systems. International Journal on Software Tools for Technology Transfer (STTT) 9(3), 213–254 (2007)

[14] Lamport, L.: A fast mutual exclusion algorithm. ACM Transactions on Computer Systems 5(1), 1–11 (1987)

[15] Penczek, W., Pólrola, A.: Advances in Verification of Time Petri Nets and Timed Automata: A Temporal Logic Approach. Springer, Heidelberg (2006)

[16] Valero Ruiz, V., de Frutos Escrig, D., Marroquin Alonso, O.: Decidability of Properties of Timed-Arc Petri Nets. In: Nielsen, M., Simpson, D. (eds.) ICATPN 2000. LNCS, vol. 1825, pp. 187–206. Springer, Heidelberg (2000)

[17] Valero Ruiz, V., Cuartero Gomez, F., de Frutos Escrig, D.: On non-decidability of reachability for timed-arc Petri nets. In: Proceedings of the 8th International Workshop on Petri Net and Performance Models (PNPM 1999), pp. 188–196 (1999)

[18] Seidner, Ch., Gardey, G., Lime, D., Magnin, M., Roux, O.: Romeo: A tool for time Petri net analysis., http://romeo.rts-software.org/

[19] Sifakis, J., Yovine, S.: Compositional specification of timed systems. In: Puech, C., Reischuk, R. (eds.) STACS 1996. LNCS, vol. 1046, pp. 347–359. Springer, Heidelberg (1996)

[20] Srba, J.: Timed-arc Petri nets vs. networks of timed automata. In: Ciardo, G., Darondeau, P. (eds.) ICATPN 2005. LNCS, vol. 3536, pp. 385–402. Springer, Heidelberg (2005)

[21] Srba, J.: Comparing the expressiveness of timed automata and timed extensions of Petri nets. In: Cassez, F., Jard, C. (eds.) FORMATS 2008. LNCS, vol. 5215, pp. 15–32. Springer, Heidelberg (2008)

[22] UPPAAL, http://www.uppaal.com

Verifying Ptolemy II Discrete-Event Models Using Real-Time Maude

Kyungmin Bae[1], Peter Csaba Ölveczky[2], Thomas Huining Feng[3],
and Stavros Tripakis[3]

[1] University of Illinois at Urbana-Champaign
[2] University of Oslo
[3] University of California, Berkeley

Abstract. This paper shows how Ptolemy II discrete-event (DE) models can be formally analyzed using Real-Time Maude. We formalize in Real-Time Maude the semantics of a subset of hierarchical Ptolemy II DE models, and explain how the code generation infrastructure of Ptolemy II has been used to automatically synthesize a Real-Time Maude verification model from a Ptolemy II design model. This enables a model-engineering process that combines the convenience of Ptolemy II DE modeling and simulation with formal verification in Real-Time Maude.

1 Introduction

Model-based design principles put the construction of models at the center of embedded system design processes [16,9]. Useful models are executable, providing simulations of system functionality, performance, power consumption, or other properties. Ideally, models are translated (code generated) automatically to produce deployable embedded software. Commercial examples of such modeling and code generation frameworks include Real-Time Workshop (from The MathWorks) and TargetLink (from dSpace), which generate code from Simulink models, and LabVIEW Embedded, from National Instruments. Models can also be used to guide formal verification, which can provide proofs of safety properties or identification of security vulnerabilities.

Ptolemy II is a well-established modeling and simulation tool, developed at UC Berkeley, that provides a powerful and intuitive graphical modeling language to allow a user to build hierarchical models that combine different models of computations [6]. In this paper, we focus on discrete-event (DE) models, which are explicit about timing behavior of systems. Discrete-event modeling is a time honored and widely used approach for system simulation [8]. More recently, it has been proposed as basis for synthesis of embedded real-time software [17]. The Ptolemy II realization of DE has a rigorous formal semantics rooted in the fixed-point semantics of synchronous languages [11].

This paper describes our work on enriching a significant subset of hierarchical Ptolemy II DE models with *formal verification* capabilities using Real-Time Maude [13] as back-end. Real-Time Maude is a high-performance tool that

K. Breitman and A. Cavalcanti (Eds.): ICFEM 2009, LNCS 5885, pp. 717–736, 2009.

extends the rewriting-logic-based Maude [3] system to support the formal specification and analysis of object-based real-time systems. Real-Time Maude provides a spectrum of formal analysis methods, including rewriting for simulation purposes, reachability analysis, and linear temporal logic (LTL) model checking.

In particular, we explain how we have enriched Ptolemy II DE models with formal verification capabilities by:

1. Formalizing the semantics of transparent hierarchical Ptolemy II DE models in Real-Time Maude.
2. Defining useful atomic state propositions, so that the Ptolemy user can specify temporal logic properties to be verified without understanding how Ptolemy models are represented in Real-Time Maude.
3. Using Ptolemy II's code generation infrastructure [18] to automatically synthesize a Real-Time Maude verification model from a Ptolemy design model, and by explaining how both code generation and verification have been integrated into Ptolemy, so that a Ptolemy model can be verified within Ptolemy.

This integration of Ptolemy II and Real-Time Maude enables a model-engineering process that combines the convenience of Ptolemy II modeling with formal verification in Real-Time Maude.

The main contributions of our work are:

- Enriching Ptolemy with formal verification capabilities to verify properties, such as the liveness property in Section 6, that cannot be checked using Ptolemy simulations. Furthermore, the synthesized verification model can be formally analyzed w.r.t. other properties (e.g., determinism, etc.).
- We show how Real-Time Maude can define the semantics of synchronous languages with fixed-point semantics. These techniques should be useful for defining the formal semantics of other synchronous languages. Our semantics also provides a basis for extensions to, e.g., *probabilistic* Ptolemy models, that can then be subjected to *statistical model checking* using tools like VeStA [15].

Our work is conducted in the context of the NAOMI project [4], where Lockheed Martin Advanced Technology Laboratories (LM ATL), UC Berkeley, UIUC, and Vanderbilt University work together to develop a multi-modeling design methodology. A key part of this project is the systematic use of model transformations and code generation to maintain consistency across models.

Section 2 briefly introduces Ptolemy II and Real-Time Maude. The Real-Time Maude semantics of Ptolemy II DE models is described in Section 3. Section 4 presents the atomic propositions that allow the user to specify his/her LTL properties without having the understand the Real-Time Maude translation of a Ptolemy model. Section 5 explains the Real-Time Maude code generation and integration into Ptolemy. Section 6 illustrates the use of our techniques to verify a Ptolemy model. Finally, Section 7 presents some related work and Section 8 gives some concluding remarks. More details about the Real-Time Maude semantics of Ptolemy DE, as well as three additional verification case studies, can be found in the longer technical report [1].

2   Preliminaries on Real-Time Maude and Ptolemy

2.1   Rewriting Logic and Real-Time Maude

Modeling. A Real-Time Maude *timed module* specifies a *real-time rewrite theory* of the form (Σ, E, IR, TR), where:

- (Σ, E) is a *membership equational logic* [3] theory with Σ a signature[1] and E a set of *confluent and terminating conditional equations*. (Σ, E) specifies the system's state space as an algebraic data type, and must contain a specification of a sort `Time` modeling the (discrete or dense) time domain.
- IR is a set of (possibly conditional) *labeled instantaneous rewrite rules* specifying the system's *instantaneous* (i.e., zero-time) local transitions, written `rl [`l`]` : t `=>` t', where l is a *label*. Such a rule specifies a *one-step transition* from an instance of t to the corresponding instance of t'. The rules are applied *modulo* the equations E.[2]
- TR is a set of *tick (rewrite) rules*, written with syntax

  `rl [`l`]` : `{`t`}` `=>` `{`t'`}` `in time` τ `.`

  that model time elapse. `{_}` is a built-in constructor of sort `GlobalSystem`, and τ is a term of sort `Time` that denotes the *duration* of the rewrite.

The initial state must be a ground term of sort `GlobalSystem` and must be reducible to a term of the form `{`t`}` using the equations in the specifications.

The Real-Time Maude syntax is fairly intuitive. For example, function symbols, or *operators*, are declared with the syntax `op` f : $s_1 \ldots s_n$ `->` s. f is the name of the operator; $s_1 \ldots s_n$ are the sorts of the arguments of f; and s is its (value) *sort*. Equations are written with syntax `eq` $t = t'$, and `ceq` $t = t'$ `if` *cond* for conditional equations. The mathematical variables in such statements are declared with the keywords `var` and `vars`. We refer to [3] for more details on the syntax of Real-Time Maude.

We make extensive use of the fact that an equation $f(t_1, \ldots, t_n) = t$ with the `owise` (for "otherwise") attribute can be applied to a subterm $f(\ldots)$ only if no other equation with left-hand side $f(u_1, \ldots, u_n)$ can be applied.[3]

In object-oriented Real-Time Maude modules, a *class* declaration

  `class` C `|` att_1 : s_1, $\ldots$, att_n : s_n `.`

declares a class C with attributes att_1 to att_n of sorts s_1 to s_n. An *object* of class C in a given state is represented as a term `<` O `:` C `|` att_1 `:` $val_1, ..., att_n$ `:` val_n `>` of sort `Object`, where O, of sort `Oid`, is the object's *identifier*, and where val_1 to val_n are the current values of the attributes att_1 to att_n. In a concurrent

---

[1] i.e., Σ is a set of declarations of *sorts*, *subsorts*, and *function symbols*.

[2] E is a union $E' \cup A$, where A is a set of equational axioms such as associativity, commutativity, and identity, so that deduction is performed *modulo* A. Operationally, a term is reduced to its E'-normal form modulo A before any rewrite rule is applied.

[3] A specification with `owise` equations can be transformed to an equivalent system without such equations [3].

object-oriented system, the state is a term of the sort `Configuration`. It has the structure of a *multiset* made up of objects and messages. Multiset union for configurations is denoted by a juxtaposition operator (empty syntax) that is declared associative and commutative, so that rewriting is *multiset rewriting* supported directly in Real-Time Maude.

The dynamic behavior of concurrent object systems is axiomatized by specifying each of its transition patterns by a rewrite rule. For example, the rule

```
rl [l] :  < O : C | a1 : 0, a2 : y, a3 : w, a4 : z >  =>
          < O : C | a1 : T, a2 : y, a3 : y + w, a4 : z >
```

defines a parameterized family of transitions (one for each substitution instance) which can be applied whenever the attribute `a1` of an object `O` of class `C` has the value `0`, with the effect of altering the attributes `a1` and `a3` of the object. "Irrelevant" attributes (such as `a4`, and the *right-hand side occurrence* of `a2`) need not be mentioned in a rule (or equation).

A *subclass* inherits all the attributes and rules of its superclasses.

Formal Analysis. A Real-Time Maude specification is *executable*, and the tool offers a variety of formal analysis methods. The *rewrite* command simulates *one* behavior of the system *up to a certain duration*. It is written with syntax (`trew` t `in time <=` τ `.`), where t is the initial state and τ is a term of sort `Time`. The *search* command uses a breadth-first strategy to analyze all possible behaviors of the system, by checking whether a state matching a *pattern* and satisfying a *condition* can be reached from the initial state.

Real-Time Maude also extends Maude's *linear temporal logic model checker* to check whether each behavior, possibly up to a certain time bound, satisfies a temporal logic formula. *State propositions* are terms of sort `Prop`, and their semantics should be given by (possibly conditional) equations of the form

$$\{statePattern\} \mathrel{|=} prop = b$$

for b a term of sort `Bool`, which defines the state proposition *prop* to hold in all states $\{t\}$ where $\{t\}$ `|=` *prop* evaluates to `true`. A temporal logic *formula* is constructed by state propositions and temporal logic operators such as `True`, `False`, `~` (negation), `/\`, `\/`, `->` (implication), `[]` ("always"), `<>` ("eventually"), and `U` ("until"). The time-bounded model checking command has syntax

(`mc` t `|=t` *formula* `in time <=` τ `.`)

for initial state t and temporal logic formula *formula* .

2.2   Ptolemy II and Its DE Model of Computation

The Ptolemy project[4] studies modeling, simulation, and design of concurrent, real-time, embedded systems. The key underlying principle in the project is the

---

[4] http://ptolemy.eecs.berkeley.edu/

use of well-defined *models of computation* (MoCs) that govern the interaction
between concurrent components. A major problem area being addressed is the
use of *heterogeneous* mixtures of MoCs [6]. A result of the project is a software
system called Ptolemy II, implemented in Java. Ptolemy II allows a user to build
hierarchical models that combine different MoCs, including state machines, data
flow, and discrete-event models. Models can be visually designed and simulated.
In addition, Ptolemy II's *code generation* capabilities allow models to be translated into models in other languages or into imperative code, e.g., in C and Java.

Discrete-Event Models in Ptolemy II. The focus of this paper is the formalization of a *subset* of Ptolemy II *discrete-event* (DE) models in Real-Time
Maude. A Ptolemy II model is a hierarchical composition of *actors* with *connections* between the actors' *input ports* and *output ports*. The actors represent
data manipulation units, whose execution is governed by a special attribute belonging to the model called *director*. Such a model can itself be treated as an
actor, that we call a *composite actor*. (Non-composite actors are called *atomic
actors*.) Ptolemy II also supports *modal models*, which are models with finite
state machine controllers. See Section 2.3 for an example of a Ptolemy II model.

   DE actors consume and produce *events* at their input and output ports, according to the *tagged signal model* [10]. A tagged event is a pair (v, t) where v is
a *value* in a complete partial order (CPO) and t is a *tag*, modeling the time at
which the event occurs. Ptolemy II DE models use *super-dense* time, in which
a tag t is a pair $(\tau, n) \in \mathbb{R}_{\geq 0} \times \mathbb{N}$, where τ is the *timestamp* that indicates the
model time when this event occurs, and n is the *microstep index*. Super-dense
time is useful for modeling multiple events that happen at the same time (i.e.,
have the same timestamp), but in sequence, where perhaps some events cause
other events. Super-dense tags are totally ordered using a *lexicographic* order:
$(\tau_1, n_1) \leq (\tau_2, n_2)$ iff $\tau_1 < \tau_2$, or $\tau_1 = \tau_2$ and $n_1 \leq n_2$.

   The semantics of Ptolemy II DE models [10] combines a synchronous-reactive
fixed-point iteration with advancement of time governed by an event queue [11].
Events in that queue are ordered by their tags. Operation proceeds by iterations,
each time removing one or more events with the smallest tag from the queue.
That tag is considered the current *model time*. The removed events are fed to
their designated actors. After that, actors with events available are executed,
which may generate new events into the queue. A difference between Ptolemy II
and standard DE simulators is that, at any model time (τ, n), the semantics is
defined as the *least fixed-point* of a set of equations, similarly to a synchronous
model [5]. This allows Ptolemy II models to have arbitrary *feedback loops*. Semantics of such models can always be given although they may result in *unknown*
(*bottom*) values, in case the model contains *causality cycles*. Conceptually, the
semantics can be captured as shown in Figure 1.

Code Generation Infrastructure. Ptolemy II offers a code generation framework using an *adapter-based mechanism*. A *codegen adapter* is a component that
generates code for a Ptolemy II actor. An adapter essentially consists of a Java
class file and a *code template* file that together specify the actor's behavior. The

```
Q := empty; // Initialize the event queue to be empty.
for each actor A do
  A.inititialize(); // Initialize A; may generate new events in Q

while Q is not empty do
  E := set of all events in Q with smallest tag;
  remove elements of E from Q;
  initialize ports with values in E or "unknown" (bottom of CPO);
  while port values changed do
    for each actor A receiving new values do
      if A.prefire() then  // Determine whether A needs to be fired
        A.fire(); // May increase port values according to CPO
  end while;        // Fixed-point reached for the current tag
  for each actor A that has been fired do
    A.postfire(); // Updates actor state; may generate new events in Q
end while;
```

Fig. 1. Pseudo-code of Ptolemy II DE semantics

code template file contains code blocks written in the target language. Supplied with a set of adapters and an initial model, the code generation framework examines the model structure and invokes the adapters to harvest code blocks from the code template files. The main advantage of this scheme is that it decouples the writing of Java code and target code (otherwise the target code would be wrapped in strings and interspersed with Java code).

2.3   Example: A Simple Traffic Light System

Figure 2 shows a Ptolemy DE model of a simple non-fault-tolerant traffic light system consisting of one car light and one pedestrian light at a pedestrian

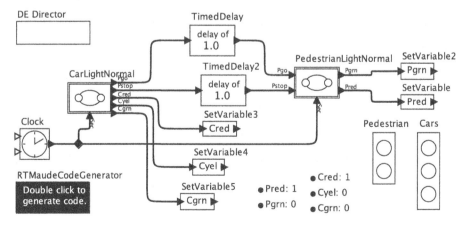

Fig. 2. Simple Traffic Light model in Ptolemy II

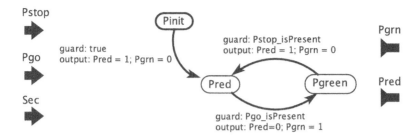

Fig. 3. The `PedestrianLightNormal` FSM actor

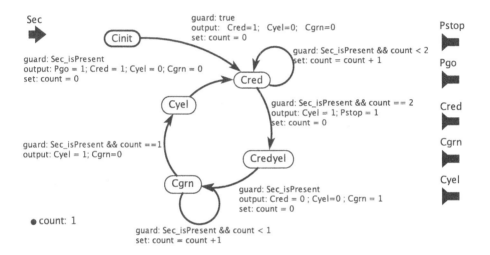

Fig. 4. The `CarLightNormal` FSM actor

crossing. Each traffic light is represented by a set of *set variable* actors (`Pred` and `Pgrn` represent the pedestrian light, and `Cred`, `Cyel`, and `Cgrn` represent the car light). A light is considered to be *on* iff the corresponding variable has the value 1. The lights are controlled by the two *finite state machine* (FSM) actors `CarLightNormal` and `PedestrianLightNormal` that send values to set the variables; in addition, `CarLightNormal` sends signals to the `PedestrianLight-Normal` actor through its `Pgo` and `Pstop` output ports. These signals are received by the `PedestrianLightNormal` actor after a *delay* of one time unit.

Figure 3 shows the FSM actor `PedestrianLightNormal`. This actor has three input ports (`Pstop`, `Pgo`, and `Sec`), two output ports (`Pgrn` and `Pred`), three internal states, and three transitions. This actor reacts to signals from the car light (by way of the delay actors) by turning the pedestrian lights on and off. For example, if the actor is in local state `Pred` and receives input through its `Pgo` input port, then it goes to state `Pgreen`, outputs the value 0 through its `Pred` output port, and outputs the value 1 through its `Pgrn` port.

Figure 4 shows the FSM actor `CarLightNormal`. Assuming that the *clock* actor sends a signal every time unit, we notice, e.g., that one time unit after both the red and yellow car lights are on, these are turned off and the green car light is turned on by sending the appropriate values to the variables (`output:` `Cred = 0; Cyel = 0; Cgrn = 1`). The car light then stays green for two time units before turning yellow.

3   Real-Time Maude Semantics of Ptolemy DE Models

This section gives a brief overview of the Real-Time Maude formalization of the Ptolemy DE semantics that is the basis for our work. Due to the lack of space, and in order to convey our ideas without introducing too much detail, we present a slightly simplified version of our semantics, in that we present a semantics for

1. *flat* Ptolemy models; that is, models without hierarchical actors, and
2. assume that all Ptolemy expressions are *constants*.

The report [1] explains the Real-Time Maude semantics that we actually use, and that covers the subset of Ptolemy listed in Section 3.1, including hierarchical actors and expressions with variables. The entire executable Real-Time Maude semantics is available at `http://www.ifi.uio.no/RealTimeMaude/Ptolemy`.

3.1   Supported Subset of Ptolemy

We currently support Real-Time Maude analysis of *transparent discrete event* (DE) Ptolemy models; that is, DE models where subdiagrams are also executed under the DE director. We support composite actors, modal models, and the following atomic actors: finite state machine (FSM), timed delay, variable delay, clock, current time, timer, noninterruptible timer, pulse, ramp, timed plotter, set variable, and single event actors. We also support connections with multiple destinations, split signals, and both single ports and multi-input ports.

3.2   Representing Flat Ptolemy DE Models in Real-Time Maude

This section explains how a Ptolemy model is represented as a Real-Time Maude term in (the slightly simplified version of) our semantics. We only show the representation for a small subset of the actors listed above, and refer to [1] for the definition of the other actors.

Our Real-Time Maude semantics is defined in an object-oriented style, where the global state has the form of a *multiset*

{*actors   connections*   < global : EventQueue | queue : *event queue* >}

where

- *actors* are objects corresponding to the actor instances in the Ptolemy model,
- *connections* are the connections between the ports of the different actors, and
- < global : EventQueue | queue : *event queue* > is an object whose queue attribute denotes the global event queue.

Actors. Each Ptolemy actor is modeled in Real-Time Maude as an object instance of a subclass of the following class `Actor`:

```
class Actor | ports : Configuration,  parameters : ValueMap .
```

The `ports` attribute denotes the set of *ports* of the actor. In our model, a port is modeled as an object, as shown below. The `parameters` attribute represents the *parameters* of the corresponding Ptolemy actor, together with their values, as a semicolon-separated set of terms of the form '*parameter-name* |-> *value*.

Current Time. Ptolemy's *current time* actor produces an output token on each firing with a value that is the current model time. In Real-Time Maude, such actors are represented as object instances of the following class that extends the class `Actor` with an attribute `current-time` denoting the current "model time":

```
class CurrentTime | current-time : Time .    subclass CurrentTime < Actor .
```

Timed Delay. A *timed delay* actor propagates an incoming event after a given time delay. If the *delay* parameter is 0.0, then there is a "microstep" delay on the generation of the output event. Since the *delay* parameter is represented in the `parameters` attribute of `Actor`, this subclass does not add any attributes:

```
class Delay .        subclass Delay < Actor .
```

Set Variable. This actor contains a variable that is set by a signal:

```
class SetVariable | variableName : VarId .    subclass SetVariable < Actor .
```

Finite State Machine (FSM) Actors. An FSM actor is a transition system containing finite sets of states (or "locations"), local variables, and transitions. A transition has a guard expression, and can contain a set of output actions and variable assignments. When an FSM actor is fired, there is never more than one enabled transition. If there is exactly one enabled transition then it is chosen and the actions contained by the transition are executed. Under the DE director, only one transition step is performed in each iteration.

An `FSM-Actor` is then characterized by its *current state*, its transitions, and the current values of its local variables:

```
class FSM-Actor | currState : Location,   initState : Location,
                  variables : ValueMap,   transitions : TransitionSet .
subclass FSM-Actor < Actor .
```

A location is the sort of the local "states" of the transition system. In particular, quoted identifiers (`Qids`) are state names. We model the transitions as a semicolon-separated set of transitions of the form

$$s_1 \dashrightarrow s_2 \ \{\texttt{guard:} \ g \ \texttt{output:} \ p_{i_1} \text{|->} e_{i'_1} ; \ldots ; \ p_{i_k} \text{|->} e_{i'_k} \ \texttt{set:} \ v_{j_1} \text{|->} e_{j'_1} ; \ldots ; \ v_{j_l} \text{|->} e_{j'_l}\}$$

for state/locations s_1 and s_2, port names p_i, variables v_i, and expressions e_i.

Ports. A *port* is represented as an object, with a name (the identifier of the port object), a status (unknown, present, or absent), and a value. We also have subclasses for input and output ports:

```
class Port | status : PortStatus, value : Value .
class InPort .     subclass InPort < Port .
class OutPort .    subclass OutPort < Port .

sort PortStatus .  ops unknown present absent : -> PortStatus [ctor] .
```

Connections. A connection is represented as a term p_o ==> $p_{i_1};\dots;p_{i_n}$ of sort Connection, where the p_js have the form $a!p$ for a a name of an actor and p a name of a port. Such a connection connects the output port p_o to all the input ports $p_{i_1},\dots,p_{i_n}$ Since connections appear in configurations, the sort Connection is defined to be a subsort of the sort Object.

The Global Event Queue. The global event queue is represented by an object

```
< global : EventQueue | eventQueue : event queue >
```

where *event queue* is an ::-separated list, ordered according to time until firing, of terms of the form

set of events ; *time to fire* ; *microstep*

where the *set of events* is a set of events, each event characterized by the "global port name" where the generated event should be output and the corresponding value, *time to fire* denotes the time *until* the events are supposed to fire, and *microstep* is the additional "microstep" until the event fires.

Example: Representing the Flat Traffic Light Model. Consider the flat non-fault-tolerant traffic light system given in Section 2.3. The Real-Time Maude representation of the TimedDelay2 delay actor is then

```
< 'TimedDelay2 : Delay |
      parameters : 'delay |-> # 1.0,
      ports : < 'input : InPort | value : # 0, status : absent >
              < 'output : OutPort | value : # 0, status : absent > >
```

Likewise, the FSM actor CarLightNormal is represented as the term[5]

```
< 'CarLightNormal : FSM-Actor |
    initState : 'Cinit, currState : 'Cinit, variables : 'count |-> # 1,
    ports : < 'Sec : InPort | value : # 0, status : absent >
            < 'Pgo : OutPort | value : # 0, status : absent >
            ... ,
    transitions :
      ('Cinit --> 'Cred
```

---

[5] To save space, some terms are replaced by '...'

```
{guard: (# true)
 output: ('Cred |-> # 1) ; ('Cyel |-> # 0) ; ('Cgrn |-> # 0)
 set: 'count |-> # 0}) ;
('Cred --> 'Cred
 {guard: (isPresent('Sec) && ('count lessThan # 2))
  output: emptyMap  set: 'count |-> ('count + # 1)}) ; ... > .
```

The connection from the output port output of the Clock actor to the input port Sec of CarLightNormal and the input port Sec of PedestrianLightNormal is represented by the term

```
('Clock ! 'output) ==> ('PedestrianLightNormal ! 'Sec) ; ('CarLightNormal ! 'Sec)
```

The entire state thus consists of two FSM actor objects, ten connections, two delay objects, five SetVariable objects, and the global event queue object.

3.3   Specifying the behavior of Flat DE Models

As explained in Section 2.2, the behavior of Ptolemy DE models can be summarized as repeatedly performing the following actions:

– Advance time until the time to fire the first events in the queue is $(0, 0)$.
– Then an iteration of the system is performed. That is:
  1. (Prefire) The events that are supposed to fire are added to the corresponding output ports; the status of all other ports is set to unknown.
  2. (Fire) Then the *fixed point* of all ports is computed by gradually increasing the knowledge about the presence/absence of inputs to and output from ports until a fixed-point is reached.
  3. (Postfire) Finally, states are updated for actors with inputs or scheduled events, and new events are generated and inserted into the event queue.

The following tick rule advances time until the time when the first events in the event queue are scheduled (we first declare all the variables used):

```
vars SYSTEM OBJECTS PORTS PORTS' REST : ObjectConfiguration . var N : Nat .
vars O O' : Oid . var EVTS : Events . var NZT : NzTime . var NZ : NzNat .
vars P P' : PortId . var QUEUE : EventQueue . vars T T' : Time .
var PS : PortStatus . var EPIS : EportIdSet . vars V TV : Value .
var VAL : ValueMap . vars STATE STATE' : Location .
var BODY : TransBody . var TG : TransGuard . var TRANSSET : TransitionSet .

rl [tick] :
   {SYSTEM  < global : EventQueue | queue : (EVTS ; NZT ; N) :: QUEUE >}
   =>
   {delta(SYSTEM, NZT)
     < global : EventQueue | queue : (EVTS ; 0 ; N) :: delta(QUEUE, NZT) >}
   in time NZT .
```

In this rule, the first element in the event queue has non-zero delay NZT. Time is advanced by this amount NZT, and, as a consequence, the (first component of the) event timer goes to zero. In addition, the function delta is applied to all the other objects (denoted by SYSTEM) in the system. The function delta defines effect of time elapse on the objects. This function is also applied to the other elements in the event queue, where it decreases the remaining time of each event set by the elapsed time NZT (where x monus y equals $\max(0, x - y)$):

```
op delta : EventQueue Time -> EventQueue .
eq delta((EVTS ; T ; N) :: QUEUE, T')
   = (EVTS ; T monus T' ; N) :: delta(QUEUE, T') .
eq delta(nil, T) = nil .
```

The function delta on configurations distributes over the elements in the configuration, and must be defined on single objects, as shown later.

The next rule is a "microstep tick rule" that advances "time" with some microsteps if needed to enable the first events in the event queue:

```
rl [shortTick] :
  {SYSTEM < global : EventQueue | queue : (EVTS ; 0 ; NZ) :: QUEUE >}
 =>
  {SYSTEM < global : EventQueue | queue : (EVTS ; 0 ; 0) :: QUEUE >} .
```

Finally, when the remaining time and microsteps of the first events in the event queue are both zero, an iteration of the system can be performed:

```
rl [executeStep] :
  {SYSTEM < global : EventQueue | queue : (EVTS ; 0 ; 0) :: QUEUE >}
 =>
  {< global : EventQueue | queue : QUEUE >
   postfireAll(portFixPoints(addEventsToPorts(EVTS, prefire(SYSTEM))))} .
```

The function prefire initializes each actor before firing. In particular, it sets the status of each port to unknown. The operator addEventsToPorts inserts the events scheduled to fire into the corresponding output ports. The portFixPoints function then finds the fixed points for all the ports (fire), and postfire "executes" the steps on the computed port fixed-points by changing the states of the objects and generating new events and inserting them into the global event queue. These functions have sort Configuration, whereas the equations defining them involve variables of the subsort ObjectConfiguration, ensuring that each function has finished computing before the "next" function is computed:

```
ops prefire portFixPoints postfire : Configuration -> Configuration .
```

To completely define the behavior of a system, we must define the functions prefire, portFixPoints, postfire, and delta on the different actors.

Initialize Actors. In our simplified setting, the `prefire` function just clears all the ports, that is, sets their `status` to `unknown`:

```
eq prefire(< O : Actor | ports : PORTS > REST)
    = < O : Actor | ports : clearPorts(PORTS) >   prefire(REST) .
eq prefire(SYSTEM) = SYSTEM [owise] .

op clearPorts : Configuration -> Configuration .
eq clearPorts(< P : Port | status : PS > PORTS)
    = < P : Port | status : unknown > clearPorts(PORTS) .
eq clearPorts(none) = none .
```

Computing the Fixed-Point for Ports. The idea behind the definition of the function `portFixPoints`, that computes the fixed-point for the values of all the ports, is simple. The state has the form `portFixPoints`(*actors and connections*), where initially, the only port information are the events scheduled for this iteration. For each possible case when the status of an `unknown` port can be determined to be either `present` or `absent`, there is an equation

```
eq portFixPoints(< O : ... | ports : < P : Port | status : unknown > PORTS,
                            ... >
                connections and other objects) =
   portFixPoints(< O : ... | ports : < P : Port | status : present,
                                                value : ... > PORTS, ... >
                connections and other objects) .
```

(and similarly for deciding that input/output is `absent`). The fixed-point is reached when no such equation can be applied. The `portFixPoints` operator is then removed by using the `owise` construct of Real-Time Maude:

```
eq portFixPoints(OBJECTS) = OBJECTS [owise] .
```

The following equation propagates port status from a "known" output port to a connecting `unknown` input port. The present/absent `status` (and possibly the `value`) of the output port P of actor O is propagated to the input port P' of the actor O' through the connection (O ! P) ==> ((O' ! P') ; EPIS):

```
ceq portFixPoints(
      < O : Actor |
              ports :  < P : OutPort | status : PS, value : V > PORTS >
      ((O ! P) ==> ((O' ! P') ; EPIS))
      < O' : Actor | ports : < P' : InPort | status : unknown > PORTS' >
      REST)
  = portFixPoints(< O : Actor | >  ((O ! P) ==> ((O' ! P') ; EPIS))
      < O' : Actor |
              ports : < P' : InPort | status : PS, value : V > PORTS' >
      REST)
   if PS =/= unknown .
```

The `portFixPoints` function must then be defined for each kind of actor to decide whether the actor produces any output in a given port. For example, the *timed delay* actor does not produce any output in this iteration as a result of any input. Therefore, if its `status` is `unknown` (that is, the delay actor did not schedule an event for this iteration), its output port should be set to `absent`:

```
eq portFixPoints(
    < O : Delay | ports : < P : OutPort | status : unknown > PORTS > REST)
 = portFixPoints(
    < O : Delay | ports : < P : OutPort | status : absent > PORTS > REST) .
```

Other actors generate immediate output when receiving input. For example, when a *current time* actor fires, it outputs the current model time:

```
ceq portFixPoints(
    < O : CurrentTime | current-time : T,
                        ports : < P : InPort | status : PS >
                                < P' : OutPort | status : unknown > >
    REST)
 = portFixPoints(
    < O : CurrentTime | ports : < P : InPort | >
                                < P' : OutPort | status : PS, value : # T >
    REST)
  if PS =/= unknown .
```

The definition of `portFixPoints` for FSM actors relies on the assumption that at most one transition is enabled at any time. In the following conditional equation, one transition from the current state `STATE` is enabled. In addition, there is *some* input to the actor (through input port P'), and some output ports have status `unknown`. The function `updateOutPorts` then updates the status and the values of the output ports according to the current state and input:

```
ceq portFixPoints(< O : FSM-Actor |
                        ports : < P' : InPort | status : present >
                                < P : OutPort | status : unknown > PORTS,
                        currState : STATE, variables : VAL,
                        transitions : (STATE --> STATE' {BODY}) ; TRANSSET >
                   REST)
  = portFixPoints(< O : FSM-Actor |
                        ports : updateOutPorts(VAL, BODY,
                                < P : OutPort | > < P' : InPort | > PORTS) >
                   REST)
 if transApplicable(< P : OutPort | > < P' : InPort | > PORTS, VAL, BODY) .
```

Another equation sets all output ports to `absent` if there is enough information to determine that no transition can become enabled in the current round.

Postfire. The `postfire` function updates internal states and generates new events that are inserted into the event queue. The `postfire` function distributes over the actor objects in the configuration. An *owise* equation defines `postfire` to be the identity function (that neither generates a future event nor changes its local state) on those actors that do not have other equations defining `postfire`.

If a time *delay* actor has input in its `'input` port, then it generates an event with a delay equal to the current value of the `'delay` parameter. If this delay is `0.0`, the microstep is `1`, otherwise the microstep is `0`. This event is added to the global event queue using the `addEvent` function that adds the new event into the correct place in the event queue:

```
eq postfire(
    < O : Delay | ports : < 'input : InPort | status : present, value : V >
                        < 'output : OutPort | >,
                parameters : 'delay |-> TV ; MEM >)
  < global : EventQueue | queue : EQ >
  =
  < O : Delay | >
  < global : EventQueue | queue : addEvent(event(O ! 'output, V), toTime(TV),
                                if toTime(TV) == 0 then 1 else 0 fi, EQ) > .
```

An FSM actor does not generate future events, but `postfire` updates the location and variables of the actor if it has input and has an enabled transition:

```
ceq postfire(< O : FSM-Actor |
                ports : < P : InPort | status : present > PORTS,
                variables : VAL,  currState : STATE,
                transitions : STATE --> STATE' {guard: TG output: OL set: AL}
                        ; TRANSSET) >)
  = < O : FSM-Actor | variables : updateValues(VAL, AL), currState : STATE' >
if transApplicable(< P : InPort | > PORTS, VAL, guard: TG output: OL set: AL) .
```

Defining Timed Behavior. Finally, we must define the function `delta`, that specifies the effect of time elapse, on single actors. Time elapse affects the internal state of `CurrentTime` actors by increasing the value of the `current-time` attribute according to the elapsed time. Time elapse does not affect the other actors we discuss here:

```
eq delta(< O : CurrentTime | current-time : T >, T') =
        < O : CurrentTime | current-time : T + T' > .

eq delta(O:Object, T) = O:Object [owise] .
```

Defining Initial Events. The initial state is defined as the term

```
{init(< global : EventQueue | queue : nil >  actors )  connections}
```

where `init` adds the initial events of the system to the global event queue.

4   Formal Analysis of Ptolemy II DE Models

As mentioned in Section 2.1, the Real-Time Maude verification model synthesized from a Ptolemy design model can be analyzed in different ways. In this
paper, we focus on linear temporal logic (LTL) model checking.

In Real-Time Maude, an LTL formula is constructed from a set of (possibly
parametric) *atomic state propositions* and the usual LTL operators, such as /\
(conjunction), ~ (negation), [] ("always"), <> ("eventually"), etc. Having to
define atomic state propositions makes the verification process nontrivial for
the Ptolemy user, since it requires some knowledge of the Real-Time Maude
representation of the Ptolemy model, as well as the ability to define functions
in Maude. To free the user from this burden, we have predefined some generic
atomic propositions. For example, the property

$$actorId \mid var_1 = value_1, \dots, var_n = value_n$$

holds in a state if the value of each "variable" var_i in the **parameters**s of an
actor equals $value_i$ for each $i \in \{1, \dots, n\}$. Here, $actorId$ is the *global actor name*
of a given actor (see below). For FSM actors (and modal models), the property

$$actorId \text{ @ } location$$

holds if and only if the FSM actor with global name $actorId$ is in location (or
"local state") $location$. Since we may analyze also hierarchical models, the global
actor name $actorId$ in the above formulas must be a list $m \cdot o_1 \cdot o_2 \cdot \dots \cdot o_n$, for
$n \geq 0$, where m is the name of the (top-level) model, o_1 is the object name of a
top-level actor in this model, and o_{i+1} is the name of an inner actor of the actor
o_i. Section 6 shows how these propositions can be used to verify Ptolemy models.

5   Code Generation and Integration with Ptolemy

This section shows how Ptolemy's adapter code generation infrastructure has
been used to automatically generate Real-Time Maude code from a Ptolemy DE
model, and to integrate Real-Time Maude analysis of DE models into Ptolemy.

5.1   Implementing the Real-Time Maude Code Generator

Ptolemy gives the user the possibility of adding a "code generation button" to a
(top-level) Ptolemy model. When this button is double-clicked, Ptolemy opens a
dialog window which allows the user to start code generation and give commands
to execute the generated code.

Ptolemy provides an *adapter* infrastructure to support the generation of code
into any target language. In particular, Ptolemy provides a Java class `Code-`
`GeneratorHelper` that contains utility methods such as `getComponent()`, which
returns a (Java) object containing all information about an actor, including
its name, parameters, ports, inner actors, etc. This class furthermore contains
"skeleton" functions like `String generateFireCode()`, which should generate
the code executed when the actor is "fired," `Set getSharedCode()`, which should
generate code shared by multiple instances of the same actor class, and so on.

An adapter class may have an associated *template file* containing code blocks of the form /***header(*parameters*)***/ *code pattern* /**/, where the *code pattern* is code written in the target language, but that can be parametrized with variables, and also have macro functions. Macros are prefixed with '$'.

The Real-Time Maude code generation is implemented by redefining the functions getSharedCode() and generateFireCode() in the adapter class for each type of actor. For each adapter class A, its associated template file includes a code block with header semantics_A that is just the Real-Time Maude module defining the formal semantics of the actor A! The template file also includes a code block with header attr_A that defines the attributes of the actor and their initial values. In Ptolemy, each actor class is a subclass of the class Entity. Therefore, we defined an adapter class for Entity that is a superclass of every actor adapter class. The template file for Entity hence contains

```
/***semantics_Entity***/
(tomod ACTOR is
...
  class Actor | ports : Configuration,  parameters : ValueMap .
...
endtom)
/**/

/***fireBlock($attr_terms)***/
< '$info(name) : $info(class) | $attr_terms >
/**/

/***attr_Entity***/
ports : ($info(ports)),
parameters : ($info(parameters))
/**/
```

The parameter attr_terms will be replaced by set of attr_*Actor* code blocks for each *Actor* a super class of the given actor. $info is a macro that uses Ptolemy's getComponent() to extract information, such as the name, the class, etc., about the actor instance. Likewise, the template file for CurrentTime contains

```
/***semantics_CurrentTime***/
(tomod CURRENT-TIME is inc ACTOR .
  ...
  class CurrentTime | current-time : Time .   subclass CurrentTime < Actor .
  ...
  eq portFixPoints(...) = ... .
endtom)
/**/

/***attr_CurrentTime***/
current-time : 0
/**/
```

The function `getSharedCode()` is used to generate the Real-Time Maude modules defining the semantics of those actors that appear in the Ptolemy model, and is defined as a Java function that returns the set of all code blocks (from the related template files) whose header starts with "`semantics`." Hence, for a `CurrentTime` actor, `getSharedCode()` returns the above two Real-Time Maude modules (and adds modules for LTL model checking in the same way).

The function `generateFireCode()` is used to generate the Real-Time Maude term representing the (initial state of the) given Ptolemy model. It generates the code from the code templates with header `fireBlock` and `$attr` in the appropriate adapter classes; that is, a Real-Time Maude object corresponding to the initial state of the actor.

5.2   Verifying Ptolemy DE Models from within Ptolemy

We have integrated *both* code generation and *verification* into Ptolemy, so that a Ptolemy DE model can be verified by pushing the *RTMaudeCodeGenerator* button in the Ptolemy model. The dialog window that then pops up allows the user to write his/her simulation and model checking commands. After clicking the `Generate` button of the dialog window, the generated Real-Time Maude code and the result of executing the analysis commands are shown in the dialog box.

6   Examples and Case Studies

This section shows how the LTL model checking infrastructure in Section 4 and the Real-Time Maude code generation can be used to verify Ptolemy DE models.

Verifying the Traffic Light Model. In the Ptolemy model in Section 2.3, each traffic light is represented by set of variables. The safety property we want to verify is that it is never the case that both the car light and the pedestrian light show green at the same time. If the name of the model is `'DE_SimpleTrafficLight`, then (`'DE_SimpleTrafficLight | ('Pgrn = # 1, 'Cgrn = # 1)`) holds in all states where the `Pgrn` and `Cgrn` variables both have the value 1. The safety property we are interested in, that such a state can *never* be reached, can be defined as the LTL formula

```
[] ~ ('DE_SimpleTrafficLight | ('Pgrn = # 1, 'Cgrn = # 1))
```

Alternatively, the LTL formula

```
[] ~ ('DE_SimpleTrafficLight . 'CarLightNormal @ 'Cgrn /\
      'DE_SimpleTrafficLight . 'PedestrianLightNormal @ 'Pgreen)
```

states that it is never the case that the `CarLightNormal` FSM actor is in local state `Cgrn` when the `PedestrianLightNormal` actor is in local state `Pgreen`.

We can also check the liveness property that both pedestrian and cars can cross infinitely often. That is, it is infinitely often the case the pedestrian light is green when the car light is *not* green, and it also infinitely often the case the car light is green when the pedestrian light is not green:

```
    []<> ('DE_SimpleTrafficLight | ('Pgrn = # 1, 'Cgrn = # 0))
 /\ []<> ('DE_SimpleTrafficLight | ('Pgrn = # 0, 'Cgrn = # 1))
```

As explained in Section 5.2, these formulas can be entered into the dialog box that pops up when the `RTMaudeCodeGenerator` button is clicked in the Ptolemy model; the dialog box will then display the results of the verification.

Other Examples and Case Studies. We have also verified the following three larger Ptolemy DE models in the same way (see [1] for details):

1. A *hierarchical* fault-tolerant extension of the traffic light system,
2. the railroad crossing benchmark, and
3. an assembly line system originally due to Misra.

7   Related Work

A preliminary exploration of translations of *synchronous reactive* (i.e., untimed) Ptolemy II models into Kripke structures, that can be analyzed by the NuSMV model checker, and of DE models into communicating timed automata is given in [2]. However, they require *data abstraction* to map models into finitary automata, and they do not use the code generation framework. On the other hand, Maude has been used to give semantics to a wide range of programming and modeling languages (see, e.g., [7,12]). Real-Time Maude is also used to analyze AADL [14] models of avionics embedded systems, but we are not aware of any translation of a synchronous real-time language into Maude or Real-Time Maude.

8   Concluding Remarks

We have formalized the semantics of a significant subset of transparent hierarchical Ptolemy II DE models in Real-Time Maude, and have shown how such Ptolemy design models can be verified by integrating Real-Time Maude code generation and model checking into Ptolemy, enabling a model-engineering process for embedded systems that leverages the convenience of Ptolemy II DE modeling and simulation with the formal verification of Real-Time Maude.

This work should continue in different directions. We should cover larger subsets of Ptolemy II and verify larger and more sophisticated applications. We should also add other relevant analysis methods, such as, e.g., statistical model checking to analyze probabilistic Ptolemy II models. Finally, counterexamples from Real-Time Maude verification should be visualized in Ptolemy II.

Acknowledgments. This work is part of the Lockheed Martin Advanced Technology Laboratories' NAOMI project. We thank the members of the NAOMI project for enabling and encouraging this research; Christopher Brooks, Chihhong Patrick Cheng, Edward A. Lee, and Man-Kit Leung for discussions on Ptolemy II; Edward A. Lee for suggestions to drafts of this paper; José Meseguer for encouraging us to study the formal semantics of Ptolemy in Real-Time Maude; and Lockheed Martin, through the NAOMI project, and The Research Council of Norway for financial support.

References

1. Bae, K., Ölveczky, P., Feng, T.H., Tripakis, S.: Verifying Ptolemy II discrete-event models using Real-Time Maude (2009),
   http://www.ifi.uio.no/RealTimeMaude/Ptolemy
2. Cheng, C.P., Fristoe, T., Lee, E.A.: Applied verification: The Ptolemy approach. Technical Report UCB/EECS-2008-41, EECS Department, University of California, Berkeley (April 2008)
3. Clavel, M., Durán, F., Eker, S., Lincoln, P., Mart-Oliet, N., Meseguer, J., Talcott, C.: All About Maude - A High-Performance Logical Framework. LNCS, vol. 4350. Springer, Heidelberg (2007)
4. Denton, T., Jones, E., Srinivasan, S., Owens, K., Buskens, R.W.: NAOMI – an experimental platform for multi-modeling. In: Czarnecki, K., Ober, I., Bruel, J.-M., Uhl, A., Völter, M. (eds.) MODELS 2008. LNCS, vol. 5301, pp. 143–157. Springer, Heidelberg (2008)
5. Edwards, S., Lee, E.: The semantics and execution of a synchronous block-diagram language. Science of Computer Programming 48(22), 21–42 (2003)
6. Eker, J., Janneck, J.W., Lee, E.A., Liu, J., Liu, X., Ludvig, J., Neuendorffer, S., Sachs, S., Xiong, Y.: Taming heterogeneity—the Ptolemy approach. Proceedings of the IEEE 91(2), 127–144 (2003)
7. Farzan, A., Chen, F., Meseguer, J., Rosu, G.: Formal analysis of Java programs in JavaFAN. In: Alur, R., Peled, D.A. (eds.) CAV 2004. LNCS, vol. 3114, pp. 501–505. Springer, Heidelberg (2004)
8. Fishman, G.S.: Discrete-Event Simulation: Modeling, Programming, and Analysis. Springer, Heidelberg (2001)
9. Giese, H., Karsai, G., Lee, E., Rumpe, B., Schätz, B. (eds.): Model-based Engineering of Embedded Real-time Systems. Dagstuhl Seminar Proc. 07451 (2007)
10. Lee, E.A.: Modeling concurrent real-time processes using discrete events. Annals of Software Engineering 7(1-4), 25–45 (1999)
11. Lee, E.A., Zheng, H.: Leveraging synchronous language principles for heterogeneous modeling and design of embedded systems. In: EMSOFT. ACM, New York (2007)
12. Meseguer, J., Rosu, G.: The rewriting logic semantics project. Theoretical Computer Science 373(3), 213–237 (2007)
13. Ölveczky, P.C., Meseguer, J.: Semantics and pragmatics of Real-Time Maude. Higher-Order and Symbolic Computation 20(1-2), 161–196 (2007)
14. SAE: AADL (2007), http://www.aadl.info/
15. Sen, K., Viswanathan, M., Agha, G.A.: VeStA: A statistical model-checker and analyzer for probabilistic systems. In: QEST 2005. IEEE, Los Alamitos (2005)
16. Sztipanovits, J., Karsai, G.: Model-integrated computing. IEEE Computer, 110–112 (1997)
17. Zhao, Y., Lee, E.A., Liu, J.: A programming model for time-synchronized distributed real-time systems. In: RTAS 2007. IEEE, Los Alamitos (2007)
18. Zhou, G., Leung, M.K., Lee, E.A.: A code generation framework for actor-oriented models with partial evaluation. In: Lee, Y.-H., Kim, H.-N., Kim, J., Park, Y.W., Yang, L.T., Kim, S.W. (eds.) ICESS 2007. LNCS, vol. 4523, pp. 193–206. Springer, Heidelberg (2007)

Specifying and Verifying Business Processes Using PPML

Germán Regis[1], Nazareno Aguirre[1], and Tom Maibaum[2]

[1] Departamento de Computación, FCEFQyN, Universidad Nacional de Río Cuarto and CONICET, Ruta 36 Km. 601, Río Cuarto (5800), Córdoba, Argentina
{gregis,naguirre}@dc.exa.unrc.edu.ar
[2] Department of Computing & Software, McMaster University, 1280 Main St. West, Hamilton, Ontario, Canada L8S 4K1
tom@maibaum.org

Abstract. The *Product Process Modeling Language* (PPML) is a formal language for the specification of business processes, which has a formal semantics based on timed transition systems. As opposed to other business process modeling languages, PPML puts an emphasis on *products* (not only processes), allowing the specifier to describe properties of these, and how processes affect them. This facilitates modeling of business processes, and combined with other characteristics of the language, most notably timing constraints in the form of time bounds associated with processes, makes it an expressive vehicle for modeling business processes.

PPML is more a formalism than an actual modeling language, since no syntax was ever defined for the formalism. In this paper, we define a suitable syntax for PPML models, and provide a formal semantics for the extended language in terms of timed automata. The formal semantics is given as a translation from PPML into UPPAAL. This formal semantics enables us to straightforwardly employ the UPPAAL model checker in order to verify real time properties of PPML specifications.

We show some of the benefits of a product-oriented language for business process modeling, the details of our translation and the results of the use of the UPPAAL model checker for PPML specifications via a simple case study, regarding a motherboard production line.

1 Introduction

The constant effort of different organizations for improving their business and manufacturing processes for efficiency and control has led to the development of languages and methods for business process modeling and analysis. Currently, there exist several business process modeling languages, such as BPEL, WS-CDL [14], etc. Most of these have been defined with a significant emphasis on modeling service oriented systems [1], and generally lack a formal semantics, which makes them less suitable for automated analysis.

PPML [19], on the other hand, is a *formal* business process modeling language based on timed state transition systems [18]. PPML models are composed of *processes*, and their effects on *products*. Also, processes may include temporal

---

K. Breitman and A. Cavalcanti (Eds.): ICFEM 2009, LNCS 5885, pp. 737–756, 2009.

bounds, which enable one to specify timing constraints. These features make the language appropriate for modeling concurrency related restrictions, process synchronizations, etc. The main difference with other languages is that, in PPML, *products* are explicit referents of the model. This provides us with greater flexibility, compared to other business process modeling formalisms, particularly when describing models in which products are complex, and their description is as important as that of processes. We believe that having the possibility of describing products and their structure is essential in cases in which the information flow of processes and how products evolve in these processes need to be explicitly specified, e.g., for stating invariants, properties describing relationships between different products (or different states of the same product), etc. Some situations in which this is clearly observed are the specification of certain industrial processes, protocol descriptions such as CORBA, etc. PPML also allows us to describe the structural state of products in particular moments in time; for instance, one can describe the state of a product before and after a process is executed on it. This facilitates the description of properties regarding product traceability, and other properties not directly associated with the processes, but with the products and their evolution in the system.

In the last two decades, the development of algorithmic methods for software/hardware verification has led to powerful analysis mechanisms, such as model checking [6]. These mechanisms have been enhanced by increasing computer power, and, in the last decade or so, various tools for automated analysis/verification have been developed, and are being used in practice. Many systems have requirements associated with real time (e.g., requirements associated with response within some preestablished bounds, etc.). For these kinds of systems and properties, there exist special model checking tools, most notably the tools Kronos [8] and UPPAAL [3]. Various kinds of timing constraints are often found in business process descriptions (cf. [15] page 3, [26] Section 1.7), and therefore, as it will be made clearer later on, we can benefit from the use of model checking tools for real-time for analyzing business process specifications.

We are interested in formally specifying business processes using a richer language for specifying products and their characteristics, as opposed to what is normally found in business process modeling notations. Moreover, we are also interested in verifying properties of these models, in particular real time properties.

The PPML formalism has been carefully defined, and various of its features have been thoroughly studied [19]. We refer both to the language and the logic as PPML, as opposed to [19], where PPML is the logic underlying the language, and the language is called *Mensurae*. Since no formal, precise syntax has been provided for PPML, we define a suitable syntax for it, extending the original language. Moreover, we also provide an encoding of the extended language into the language associated with the UPPAAL model checking tool. This translation provides the language with a formal semantics based on timed automata, the semantic formalism behind UPPAAL. We describe the above mentioned encoding, and develop a case study, based on a simplified version of a motherboard production line. This will enable us to justify the usefulness of the encoding, for verifying interesting real time properties associated with business process specification.

The paper proceeds as follows. First we describe the PPML language and provide an overview of the UPPAAL language and tool. We then present our extension of PPML, its formal syntax as well as the proposed semantics, as a translation from PPML into the language of the UPPAAL model checker. We use our case study as a reference for the presentation. We also use the translation in order to verify properties associated with the case study. Finally, we discuss related work in the area and draw some conclusions.

2 An Overview of PPML

PPML is a formal language which can be used to model business processes [19]. The basics of the method underlying the language are described in [17]. PPML has three basic constructs: *products*, *processes* and *gates*. *Products* are entities characterized by a set of measurable attributes. Products can be manipulated by processes. *Processes* are entities that represent behaviours, which are not necessarily instantaneous, i.e, they can take some time to be completed. They are modeled via "single input, single output" tasks. If multiple inputs are necessary, these have to be put together in a composite product. The main element employed for composing/decomposing products, to be processed by processes, is the *gate*. Basically, there exist three types of gate, namely, the *multiplexer*, the *demultiplexer* and the *semaphore*.

One can also associate timing constraints with processes. This is done in PPML via two bounds associated with processes: a lower bound (minimum time that the process needs to fulfill its task) and an upper bound (maximum time that the process can spend to complete its work).

2.1 Products

Products represent empirical referent objects (i.e., "things" in the world being modeled). Products are characterized by their measurable attributes, e.g., length, weight, color, etc. These characteristics may be directly observable or can be calculated by functions applied to values of other existing features. The characteristics associated with a product entity must be given in a suitable measurement scale [9].

In order to define products, we assume a first order theory presentation $\langle \Sigma, A \rangle$, called a proto-product, which defines the basic types (e.g., for attributes) necessary for products, including a sort of codes ($Code$), a sort of names ($Name$), and a sort for instants ($Time$, which corresponds to a discrete totally ordered set with a first element).

Products can then be either *atomic*, *composite* or *structured*. An *atomic product* P is a tuple $\langle code\_number_P, product\_name_P, time_P, attributes_P \rangle$, where $code\_number_P$ is a $Code$ constant, used to identify products; $product\_name_P$ is a constant of sort $Name$, which allows one to refer to particular products; $time_P$ is a constant of sort $Time$, and it is the *time stamp* of the product P, indicating the last time that the product's attributes have been updated; $attributes_P \subseteq \Sigma$ is a set of attributes, the measurable characteristics of the corresponding empirical referent (i.e., the entity in the real world being modeled by the product). Certain attributes, called *direct_attributes_P*, may be directly measured by means of appropriate measurement procedures, while others, *derived_attributes_P*, are calculated using rules and laws governed by the *axioms* A. As an example, suppose that we need to model a memory bank with some basic characteristics such as the memory's size and a flag indicating if the memory was tested or not:

$$\langle code\_memory, memory, 0, \{size : nat, tested : bool\}\rangle.$$

A *composite product* P is either:

- a pair $P = \langle code\_number_P, \otimes(P_{c1}, .., P_{cn})\rangle$ where $\otimes(P_{c1}, .., P_{cn})$ is an injection of the components P_{ci} into the cartesian product. This type of composite product is used to blend products emerging from several previous processes. This is useful, in particular, for synchronizing products in time, to be consumed as inputs by other processes,
- a pair $P = \langle code\_number_P, \iota(\mathcal{P})\rangle$ where $\mathcal{P}$ is a finite set of products and $\iota(\mathcal{P}) \in \mathcal{P}$. This type is the *choice* product and is used in situations where an input from any one of some previous processes is chosen based on some defined condition.

Products that need to be treated as atomic artifacts, but whose definitions are given in terms of constituent parts, are not the same as composite products. These are a particular kind of product, called a *structured* product.

A *structured product* P may be *refined* (or specialized), which corresponds in logic to extending the presentation $\langle \Sigma, A \rangle$ to some new proto-product $\langle \Sigma', A' \rangle$ by adding some new constants, functions and relations, or *aggregate*, which corresponds to a type of product that allows us to aggregate several constituent products into a new atomic product.

As it can be observed in the above specification, structured product descriptions are akin of classes in object orientation. The *instances* of these product descriptions will represent the individual referents in the real world. That is, the instances of product descriptions will be involved in the executions of processes.

2.2   Processes

A process models an empirical referent process (i.e., some real world process or procedure) that transforms an input product into an output one. As for products, the processes may be *atomic* (a process without internal constituent "subprocesses") or *structured*. They model input/output transformations. In order to carry out these transformations, each process has a *virtual machine* that interprets its basic commands. Intuitively, a virtual machine is an object system with routines, representing basic actions that it is capable of doing, such as assignments in a conventional programming language.

In order to specify a process, we define what input/output transformations are required using basic actions or some combinations of these, via some control structure of the virtual machine internal to the process. Not all actions of the virtual machine are under the control of the process. *Environmentally* controlled actions may appear. Another control structure that can be useful is parallel execution.

The formalization of the concept of the virtual machine is based on *object specifications* [10] and consists of a logical framework based on timed transition systems, called RETOOL [4]. The RETOOL semantics is based on the notion of computation over a timed object frame. The specification (theory presentation) describing the virtual machine is a pair consisting of a signature and a collection of sentences describing the behaviour of the system [19].

The definition of a process is given as a *transaction* defining a computation segment of the underlying virtual machine. It is specified by five elements, namely, the initial and final conditions (q, p), the invariant I, and the lower and upper bounds (l, u). The initial condition q specifies the states in which the transaction can be initiated; the final condition describes the states in which the transaction finishes (i.e., a kind of postcondition); the invariant I is a property that is supposed to hold throughout the execution of the transaction (e.g., requiring that the equipment being used for the process is not unplugged during the execution of the process!); finally, the lower and upper bounds l and u state the minimum and maximum time that the execution of the transaction can take, in order to be completed.

A process behaviour, i.e., its associated transfer function (how the input product is transformed into the output product), can then be formally characterized by a formula $(q, I)_l \Delta^u p$, which is interpreted with respect to a timed state sequence $\langle \sigma, T \rangle$ for a timed object frame, (where σ is an infinite sequence of states and T is an infinite sequence of corresponding times), and an instant i of time (the current time), in the following way: $\sigma, T, i \vDash (q, I)_l \Delta^u p$ iff, for some k such that $i + l < k \leq i + u$; $\sigma, T, i \vDash q$, $\sigma, T, k \vDash p$ and $\sigma, T, n \vDash I$ hold, for every $i \leq n \leq k$.

An *atomic process* p is a pair $\langle proc, VM \rangle$, where VM is the process' virtual machine (an object specification [4]) and $proc = \langle process\_code, process\_name, P_I, P_O, (q, I)_l \Delta^u p \rangle$; $process\_code, process\_name$ are state variables of the sorts used for process codes and names, respectively. These variables are rigid (i.e., their interpretations are immutable along computations), and their sorts are assumed to be defined and specified in the proto-product $\langle \Sigma, A \rangle$. P_I, P_O are the input and output products and $(q, I)_l \Delta^u p$ is the specification of the properties of the process (i.e., its associated *transfer function*). Consider, for instance, the following tuple describing an atomic tester process:

$$\langle code, tester, memory, memory, (\neg memory.tested, true)_5 \Delta^{10} memory.tested \rangle$$

This tester process takes as input a non tested memory bank, and after i units of time ($5 \leq i \leq 10$), the process returns a tested memory bank. For the sake of simplicity we skip the description of the virtual machine for this process.

2.3   Gates

In order to make processes interact, by interconnecting them via products, it is often necessary to combine products to build composite ones, or decompose products, for instance for feeding other processes with the parts. In order to do this, PPML provides the concept of gate. Besides gates for composing/decomposing products, there is a third kind of gate, the semaphore, which is useful for synchronization. Gates are useful for modeling transfer functions that can be regarded as instantaneous because the time taken is trivial and where the single input/single output constraint is not met by purely trivial marshalling activities. The types of gates are formally defined as follows:

- A multiplexer is a tuple $M = \langle multiplexer\_code, \mathcal{P}, P, F \rangle$, where $multiplexer\_code$ is a fixed value used to identify the gate, $\mathcal{P}$ is the set of input products, P is the output product of the multiplexer and F is the multiplexer action function defining P explicitly in terms of the set of input products $\mathcal{P}$.
- A demultiplexer is the dual of a multiplexer. In this case, the output products are defined as projections of the input product.
- A semaphore is a tuple $S = \langle semaphore\_code, P, S \rangle$, where $semaphore\_code$ is a fixed value used to identify the semaphore, P is the input/output product and S is the condition that must be satisfied to continue.

Graphically, gates are depicted as shown in Fig. 1 2 3, As an example, consider a multiplexer gate that receives a memory bank and a processor and returns a composite product putting together the input products. This is specified as follows:

$$\langle code_M, \{mem, proc\}, \langle code_P, \otimes(p_1, p_2) \rangle, \{(mem, p_1), (proc, p_2)\} \rangle$$

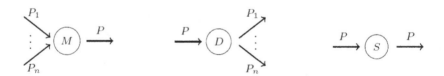

Fig. 1. Multiplexer   **Fig. 2.** Demultiplexer   **Fig. 3.** Semaphore

2.4   Framework Processes

When modeling complex empirical referents, it is often the case that one needs mechanisms providing us with *abstraction* and *encapsulation*, in order to deal with complexity. This is the usual situation when one decides to model processes in a bottom up way, i.e., modeling simpler processes first and composing these later on, as well as in top down approaches, i.e., modeling complex processes abstractly first and later on refining these into more detailed subprocesses [2]. PPML provides facilities for dealing with abstraction and encapsulation, particularly the notion of *framework process*. Framework processes are defined via process combinators. These are the following: Let $p1 = \langle p1_code, p1_name, p1_I, p1_O, $

$(q_{p1}, I_{p1})_{l_{p1}} \Delta^{u_{p1}} p_{p1}\rangle$ and $p2 = \langle p2\_code, p2\_name, p2_I, p2_O, (q_{p2}, I_{p2})_{l_{p2}} \Delta^{u_{p2}} p_{p2}\rangle$ be two processes,

- *Sequential combination*: Denoted as $p_1; p_2$, combines two processes into a new one $p = \langle p\_code, p\_name, p1_I, p2_O, (q_{p1}, I_p)_{l_{p1}+l_{p2}} \Delta^{u_{p1}+u_{p2}} p_{p2}\rangle$, in the expected way. The *p_code* and *p_name* "fields" have new unique *code* and *name*, respectively. The invariant I_p requires that the initial condition of the first of the processes holds, while the invariant I_{p1} holds for some time not exceeding u_{p1} units of time; after that, the final condition p_{p1} becomes true in at least l_{p1} units of time. Then, eventually the initial condition q_{p2} holds, while the invariant I_{p2} holds, from that point onwards, for at most u_{p2} units of time; after that, the final condition p_{p2} becomes true in at least l_{p2} units of time.
- *Semaphore (conditional) combination*: The semaphore composition of $p1$ and $p2$, denoted by $p1;_s p2$, is defined as for the sequential composition, but the invariant of the transfer function is strengthened in the sense that s (semaphore condition) must be true in order to start the second process.
- *Parallel combination*: Let $m_O = \langle multiplexer\_code, \mathcal{P}_O, P_O, F_O\rangle$ and $d_I = \langle demultiplexer\_code, P_I, \mathcal{P}_I, F_I\rangle$ be a multiplexer and a demultiplexer, respectively, each defined over the set of input and output products of $p1$ and $p2$. Then, the parallel composition p of $p1$ and $p2$ with respect to m_O and d_I, denoted by $[p1; p2](d_I, m_O)$ is defined as follows: The *process_code* and *process_name* "fields" of p have new unique *code* and *name* respectively. The input of p is the input of d_I and its output is the output of m_O. The transfer function τ of p is $(q_{p1} \wedge q_{p2}, I_p)_{max((l_{p1}, l_{p2}))} \Delta^{max((u_{p1}, u_{p2}))}(p_{p1} \wedge p_{p2})$, where the invariant I_p is defined as $(q_{p1} \wedge q_{p2}) \Rightarrow (\tau_1[(p_{p1}\mathcal{U}(p_{p1} \wedge p_{p2}))/p_{p1}] \wedge (\tau_2[(p_{p2}\mathcal{U}(p_{p1} \wedge p_{p2}))/p_{p2}]))$ (where $\tau[(p\mathcal{U}q)/r]$ denotes the replacement of the final condition r in τ by the condition $(p\mathcal{U}q)$). The symbol "$\mathcal{U}$" denotes the well known strong until temporal operator. This requires that, when the two processes are ready to start, they are executed in parallel. Further, when one of them finishes, it must wait for the other process to reach its final state.

A *framework process* p is an *atomic* process composed of a set of constituent processes $\{p_1, ..., p_n\}$ using the combinators defined above. We denote framework processes by pairs of the form $\langle p, fw.exp\rangle$, where p is the standard PPML definition of process and $fw.exp$ is the specification of the constituent processes in terms of the combinators.

3 UPPAAL

UPPAAL is a toolbox for the verification of real-time systems. It is based on the theory of timed automata, and provides a subset of CTL (computational tree logic) as a query language to specify properties to be checked. A model in UPPAAL is a set of instances of *templates* which can be communicated by means of various kinds of communication channels.

An UPPAAL specification consists of three parts: *global declarations*, *schemas* (automata templates) with their corresponding *local declarations*, and the *system specification*.

3.1   Declarations

The global declaration, or the local declaration of a template, may include the definition of variables, arrays, registers or types (as in the C programming language). There exist four predefined types: int (integers), bool (booleans), clock (clocks), and chan (communications channels). The communications channels can be *basic*, *urgent* or *broadcast*. Constants can also be defined, using the *const* keyword. UPPAAL provides a rich language for the declaration of functions that can be invoked in the templates. Parameters, conditional sentences and iterative sentences, such as 'while' or 'for' statements, can also be specified.

3.2   Templates

Templates are defined as *extended timed automata*. An automaton consists of *locations* and *edges*, and can also have local declarations and parameters (by value or by reference).

Locations can be labeled (reference names). We can specify *invariants* in the location, indicating that some condition must hold in the state. The invariant expressions can only be conjunctions of simple conditions over clocks, or boolean expressions without clock variables. Conditions involving lower bounds on clocks are not allowed. There are three modifiers for a template's locations: *initial* (each template must have exactly one initial state), *urgent* (time stops while a process is in one of these states), and *committed* (time stops while a process is in one of these states, as for urgent locations, but they also bind the system scheduler to choose one of the committed locations in the next transition).

Locations are connected by *edges*. The edges can be annotated with *selections*, *guards*, *synchronizations* or *updates*.

- *Selections*: Selections non-deterministically bind a given identifier to a value in a given range. The other three labels of an edge are within the scope of this binding.
- *Guards*: An edge is enabled in a state if and only if the guard in it evaluates to true.
- *Synchronization*:Processes can synchronize over channels. Edges labeled with complementary actions over a common channel synchronize.
- *Updates*: When an edge is "executed", the update expression of the edge is evaluated. The side effect of this expression changes the state of the system.

When two processes are synchronized, both synchronized edges are *fired* at the same time. Their corresponding updates are performed in an ordered manner: first the update of the *sending* process, and then the update of the *receiver*. Notice that the edges allow only for a single synchronizing channel. *Broadcast* channels represent one-to-many synchronizations, since the sender and all the receiver edges are fired at the same time.

3.3   System Specification

The specification of a system model consists of one or more concurrent processes (template instances), variables and communication channels. The variables, channels and functions defined at this level are not available in the templates.

3.4   Temporal Properties

UPPAAL provides a CTL temporal logic [20], with some restrictions (only one path quantifier), as a query language. Thus, the allowed query formulas are the following:

- $E \diamond q$: evaluates to true for a timed transition system if and only if there is a sequence of alternating delay transitions and action transitions $s_0 \to \cdots \to s_n$, where s_0 is the initial state and s_n satisfies q.
- $A \square q$: evaluates to true if and only if every reachable state satisfies q.
- $E \square q$: evaluates to true for a timed transition system if and only if there is a sequence of alternating delay or action transitions $s_0 \to s_1 \to \cdots \to s_i \to \cdots$ for which q holds in all states s_i.
- $A \diamond q$: evaluates to true if and only if all possible transition sequences eventually reach a state satisfying q.

In the above formulas, q is a well formed logical expression. The variables or states of a process in an expression can be referenced. For instance,

$$A \square Motherboard.End \to Motherboard.hasProcessor$$

expresses that, for all execution sequences, it is always the case that, if a motherboard is in its end state, then it must have a processor (its *hasProcessor* variable is set to true).

4   PPML Syntax and Extensions

In previous work on PPML, all the elements that are part of business process specifications are formally defined, but no actual syntax for the specifications is proposed. In order to provide a suitable high level syntax for specifying PPML models, we propose a syntax for products, processes and gates. This syntax has two objectives, namely, it allows us to provide a more flexible and user friendly way of writing PPML specifications (as in other business description languages), and to standardize the syntax so that tools for the language, such as parsers and analyzers, can be built.

For the sake of simplicity, we will mainly show the proposed syntax for PPML using a case study as a reference. The case study is the following. Suppose that we need to model a simplified version of part of a production line of a company that assembles motherboards. In this simplification, the assembly process receives as initial source products base motherboards, with two (empty) slots, one for a processor, and the other for a memory bank. Once assembled, each base motherboard is complemented with a processor and a memory bank, each seated in its corresponding slot. At the end of the manufacturing process, the assembled motherboard is tested, more precisely, the motherboard is tested in combination with the memory bank, and in combination with the processor. In order to reduce the manufacturing time, these tests can be done in parallel by two independent testing processes.

Motherboards are structured products. Consider the definition of the *Motherboard* product shown in Fig. 4, and illustrating the syntax of products.

```
Product MotherBoard {
    Proccessor MProccessor,
    Memory MMemory,
    int Proccessor_Socket,
    boolean hasProcessor,
    boolean hasMemory,
    boolean tested
}
```

Fig. 4. Structured Product *MotherBoard*

As it can be observed, structured product descriptions are akin to classes in object orientation (although is not shown in the example, the only kind of "method" allowed in product specifications are the definitions of derived attributes). The instances of products will be involved in the executions of processes.

When modeling business processes, one often finds situations in which certain products are built or transformed in several steps. In these cases, sometimes the state of some of the products' attributes being built or transformed are unknown, e.g., when these have not yet been assigned a particular value. In order to model these situations, it is necessary to introduce *null values*.

In order to illustrate a *process* definition, let us model part of the motherboard production line, namely the process that takes a motherboard without processor and a processor, and returns the partially assembled motherboard resulting from seating the processor in its corresponding slot in the motherboard. The input product is a composite product, consisting of a motherboard without processor, and a processor. The initial condition requires the compatibility of sockets and the processor slot in the motherboard being empty. The invariant for this process should specify that the processor cannot be assembled in parallel with the seating of the memory for this motherboard. The output product is simply the original motherboard with the processor put in its corresponding slot. We might associate time bounds with this process, for instance saying that the process cannot take less than 5 units of time to be performed, and it takes 10 units of time or less to be completed. This process is specified, in our proposed syntax, in Fig. 5.

Due to space restrictions, we include here only the formal syntax of atomic and structured products (see Fig. 6) and atomic processes (see Fig. 7). More complex processes, composed of simpler ones, are easier to express using a graphical notation, as we will see later on in the paper.

```
Process assem_1 {
  input: [Motherboard Mother_in; Proccessor Proc_in],
  output: MotherBoard Mother_out,
  invariant: Mother_in.HasMemory == false,
  requires: Mother_in.Proccessor_Socket == Proc_in.Proccessor_Socket
          && Mother_in.HasProccessor=false,
  ensure: Mother_out == Mother_in && Mother_in.MProcessor == Proc_in
          && Mother_in.hasProcessor == true,
  l_time: 5 ,
  u_time:10
}
```

Fig. 5. Process that assembles a motherboard and a processor

Product	→ 'Product' Product_name '{' Product_body '}'
Product_body	→ Product_refs ',' Product_atts | Product_atts
Product_refs	→ Product_ref ',' Product_refs | Product_ref
Product_atts	→ Product_att ',' Product_atts | Product_att
Product_ref	→ Product_ref_name Product_ref_ID
Product_att	→ Product_direct_att | Product_derived_att
Product_direct_att	→ Product_att_type Product_att_ID
Product_derived_att	→ Product_att_type Product_att_ID '=' Expression
Product_att_type	→ 'int' | 'boolean'
Expression	→ Expression Binary_op Expression | Unary_op Expression
	| Product_att_ID | Product_ref_name'.'Product_att_ID
	| '('Expression')' | NAT_const | BOOLEAN_const
Binary_op	→ '+' | '-' | '*' | '/' | '==' | 'and' | 'or' | '&&' | '||'
Unary_op	→ '-' | 'not' | '!'

Fig. 6. BNF for the syntax of atomic and structured products

Process	→ 'Process' Process_name '{' Process_body '}'
Process_body	→ 'input:' Input_def ',' 'output:' Output_def ','
	'invariant:' Invariant_def ',' 'requires:' Requires_def ','
	'ensures:' Ensure_def ',' Times_def
Input_def	→ Product_ref | Composite_product_ref
Output_def	→ Product_ref | Composite_product_ref
Invariant_def	→ Expression
Requires_def	→ Expression
Ensure_def	→ Expression
Times_def	→ 'l_time :' NAT ',' 'u_time :' NAT

Fig. 7. BNF for the syntax of atomic processes

5   From PPML to UPPAAL

With the aim of verifying temporal properties of PPML specifications, and providing a semantics for PPML in terms of timed automata, we propose a translation

from PPML into UPPAAL. This will enable us, in particular, to employ the UP-
PAAL model checker for verifying real time properties of PPML models.

Essentially, the encoding of PPML into UPPAAL is defined in the following
way. Each product class will correspond to a template, which will represent the
product states in the system (i.e., all states that the product can have in the
system) and a type that represents the product configuration, i.e., a structure
that describes the product's attributes.

Processes are encoded as templates that mimic the PPML processes' behaviours in the system.

Gates are encoded as arrays of integers, declared as global variables. The
values of an array representing a gate will correspond to the presence of the
expected product at a given instant in the system. More precisely, if the array
has in position i a value $n \neq 0$, then n is the code of a product available as input
for the gate at instant i. Code 0 represents the absence of products. Since codes
are unique for each product, they can be interpreted as references (with 0 being
the null reference).

The encoding of gates is merged with those of products and process templates,
in the following way:

– For a multiplexer gate M, the process that waits for the gate's output will
  have a conditional transition, checking whether $M[i] \neq 0$, for every i. All
  the products to be collected at the gate will also have in their corresponding
  templates a conditional transition checking whether the values in their corresponding positions in the gate are 0. If the condition holds and the transition
  is fired, the products update the array values with their corresponding codes.
– For a demultiplexer gate D, each process waiting for D's output checks if its
  input product is available.
– Semaphore gates are encoded as multiplexers, but with the process transition
  including an extra condition corresponding to the semaphore pass condition.

As is usual in model checking, we are forced to consider finite state systems, and
thus we have to consider a maximum number of instances for product classes.
For each product class (e.g., motherboard in our case study), we declare an array
whose length is the maximum number of instances of the class, and which will
hold the values of the attributes of these instances. For each process, we declare
a broadcast channel, which is shared between the process and its input products,
and is used to synchronize the start and finish tasks. The process manipulates
products by updating their attributes, stored in the corresponding data array.

The independence of templates for processes and products enables us to provide a flexible parametrization of the system domain. For example, we can change
the number of instances of products very easily, without altering the other con-
stituents of the system. In our case study, for instance, we exploit this flexibility
in order to "test" the system using different numbers of motherboards, processors
and memory banks.

In order to illustrate the encoding, let us consider the process depicted in
Fig. 8.

Fig. 8. Diagram for PPML process: $assem_1;assem_2;[test_1;test_2](D_1,M_3)$

The assembly process begins with the process $assem_1$ that takes a motherboard and a processor, and returns them assembled with a delay between 5 and 10 units of time. The next process is $assem_2$, which receives the output of the previous process and a memory bank, and assembles them with the same temporal bounds as the previous process. After that, the components are tested in parallel by the processes $test_1$ and $test_2$, whose lower and upper time bounds are 3 and 5 units of time.

5.1   Translation of Products

For each PPML product we generate:

- As global declarations, a range definition $0..n$ of integers, which specifies n instances of the product. These values will be used as codes for each of the system products, with 0 representing the *null* product. For each product class, a *struct type* declaration containing the data information of the product is also defined. In the case of a structured product, for each of its components, its type will have a variable of the corresponding product type. These variables will have the code of the composite product, or the value 0 (null, for incomplete products). Finally we declare an array of the product class type, whose length is the number of product instances. This array will contain the data values associated with these instances.
- A template with:
  - A clock variable declaration (time of the product in the system).
  - A function definition that updates its derived attributes.
  - A *constant*, used for representing the codes of the instances of products in the system.
  - *Locations*: an initial location, a location for each gate or process that manipulates it, and a final location.
  - *Edges*: without loss of generality, let us assume that we have a gate before every process. Thus we have two possible scenarios for edges: the edges go from a gate location to a process location, or from process locations to gate locations. Edges of the form (e_{gate}, e_{proc}), corresponding to the first of the scenarios described, are labeled with a conditional array gate update, where the update data is its code, and the condition expressing that the gate's product port is empty. Edges of the form (e_{proc}, e_{gate}), corresponding to the second kind of scenario described, are labeled with

a waiting message in the channel corresponding to the process whose code is in the gate. It also includes a call to the function that describes the updates of its calculated attributes.

When products are "copied" by a demultiplexer, all possible interleavings of processes modifying the product are taken into consideration.

– The instances of templates are declared in the system declarations.

As an example of product encoding, consider the specification given in Fig. 9, which is the result of encoding the memory product.

Global Declarations

```
//number of instances 2
 typedef int[1,2] n_memories;
//number of instances 2 + null
 typedef int[0,2] n_memories0;
//Prod. Structures declarations
 typedef struct {
   int size;
   bool assembled;
   bool tested ;
 } TMemory;
//Arrays for Prod. attr. values
 TMemory
     DataMemories[n_memories];
```

Template Declarations

```
clock x;
//Calculated Attr. Update
void UpdateAttr(){}
```

System Declarations

```
Memories (const n_memories id)
  := Memory(id);
```

Template states and edges

$e1$: Initial State (M_2)

$l1$: Guard: gMult2[1]== 0;
        Update: gMult2[1]:= id

$e2$: assem$_2$

$l2$: Guard: gMultiplexer2[1]== id
        Sync.: cassem2?
        Update: UpdateAttr()

$e3$: D_1

$l3$: Guard: gMultiplexer3[1]== 0;
        Update: gMult3[1]:=id

$e4$: test$_2$

$l4$: Guard: gMult3[1]== id
        Sync.: ctest2?
        Update: UpdateAttr()

$e5$: Final State (M_3)

Fig. 9. *Memory* Product translation

5.2   Translation of Processes

For each PPML process we generate:

– As global system declarations, channels to communicate the process with the products it is fed with, i.e., one channel and a variable of the corresponding code type are declared for each product involved in the process. The marshalled input products are simulated by the synchronizations of the above declared channels. We also generate a *broadcast* channel used by the process to "inform" the products that they are being processed.

- A template with:
  - A clock variable declaration (time within current process).
  - An initial location.
  - An update function, which expresses the action that the process performs on the products being processed. This is defined as an update of attributes of the products involved, defined as global shared variables.
  - The locations corresponding to: the idle process's location (a location for awaiting the arrival of products), a ready to process location (a location for the state in which all required products are queued for processing), and a final location (for the post-process state).
  - An edge connecting the idle location with the ready location, labeled with the condition that every array cell (codes of necessary products to start) be nonzero, and resetting its internal clock.

    The edge from the ready location to the post-processing location represents the activity of the process. So, it is labeled with the time constraints over the internal process clock, a broadcasting signal to the products involved and the update function call described above. Finally, an edge connecting the post-processing and idle locations is included, for resetting the process to receive a new job.
- In the system declarations, we create an instance for each process template.

As an example clarifying the process encoding, consider the specification shown in Fig. 10, which is the result of encoding the process of assembling a motherboard with a memory bank.

Global Declarations

```
//processing communication channel
broadcast chan cAssem2;
```

Template Declarations

```
clock x;
//Process Updates
void pAssem2(){
  //MotherBoard Update;
  DataMotherB[gMult2[0]].id_Memory:=
  gMult2[1];
}
```

System Declarations

```
Assem20 = Assem2();
```

States and Edges

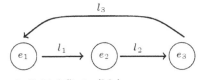

e1: Initial State (M_2)
l1: Guard: gMult2[0]!=0 and
    gMult2[1]!=0
    Update: x:=0;
e2: Pre-assem2
l2: Guard: x >=3 && x<=5
    Sync.: cassem2!
e3: Pos-assem2
l3: Update: x:=0;
    gMult2[0]:= 0;
    gMult2[1]:= 0;

Fig. 10. assem2 Process translation

5.3   System Specification and Verification of Real Time Properties

We finish the specification of the system by defining the product and process templates. Once this is done, we have a complete UPPAAL specification, and we can employ the UPPAAL model checker in order to verify real time properties of our PPML model.

For our case study, we considered the following properties for verification:
1) *Processors and memory chips cannot be shared by (different) motherboards.*

```
A[] forall (i:n_motherboards) forall (j:n_motherboards)
 i != j imply ((MotherBoards(i).End and MotherBoards(j).End)
 imply (DataMotherBoards[i].id_Memory != DataMotherBoards[j].id_Memory
 and DataMotherBoards[i].id_Processor!=DataMotherBoards[j].id_Processor))
```

2) *Every motherboard that reaches the final location has its processor and memory already tested.*

```
A[] forall (i:n_motherboards) (MotherBoards(i).End imply
 DataMotherBoards[i].tested)
```

3) *The processing of the motherboards can be completed in less than 14 units of time.*
Notice that this corresponds to the testing phases being performed in parallel.

```
E<> exists(i:n_motherboards)(MotherBoards(i).End and
 MotherBoards(i).x<=13)
```

4) *There exists the possibility that all motherboards can be assembled and tested successfully.*

```
E<> forall(i:n_motherboards)(DataMotherBoards[i].tested)
```

The above properties were verified in a PC with an 2.33GHz Intel Core2 Duo CPU processor, with 2GB of DDR2 memory, running GNU/Linux with kernel version 2.6.28-11. The UPPAAL version employed was 4.1.1. The details of the verifications are summarized in the following time table:

	Test 1	Test 2	Test 3	Test 4	Test 5
1)	0,231 s	4,651 s	22,093 m	2,694 m	-
2)	0,013 s	2,583 s	14,371 m	2,413 m	-
3)	0,001 s	0,792 s	1,642 s	1,931 s	20,053 s
4)	0,001 s	3,970 s	13,339 m	6,017 m	-

In the above table, (s) indicates seconds, (m) minutes and (-) indicates that the verification process was stopped after the system memory was exhausted, i.e., when the amount of virtual memory used doubled the size of real (hard) memory. At this point the trashing process made the verification infeasible. The experiments associated with the columns of the table, referred to as "tests", are the following:

- Test 1: 2 instances of each of the products, i.e., two motherboards, two processors and two memories.
- Test 2: 3 instances of each of the products.
- Test 3: 4 instances of each of the products.
- Test 4: three instances of motherboards and, five instances of processors and memories.
- Test 5: 6 instances of each of the products.

Notice that the experiments were carried out with quantities of processors and memories sufficient for assembling all the instances of Motherboard, i.e., *at least* one processor and one memory per motherboard. If we run the verification with fewer instances of memories or processors than instances of motherboards, some properties, such as, for instance, properties 2 and 4, may not be satisfied by the model.

These experiments are not only provided for illustration purposes, but also to show how limited the straightforward real time model checking is, for these kinds of specifications. Indeed, even though our case study is rather small, the number of instances of products that the model checker is able to deal with (in a standard desktop computer) is also quite small. The reader might argue that the inefficiency might be due to our translation; however, checking an ad hoc UPPAAL characterisation of the described case study yielded similar analysis results.

This fact shows that abstraction mechanisms, such as those supported by PPML via framework processes, are crucial for scaling up the analysis tasks. We plan, as future work, to take advantage of framework processes in order to improve the analyzability of PPML specifications (most likely, employing abstraction techniques).

6 Related Work and Conclusions

There are several approaches proposing formalizations for business process languages and their web services extensions, such as BPEL and WS-BPEL. A survey of formal verification for business process modelling approaches can be found in [22], where a classification of proposals for formally analyzing business processes is presented. Three kinds of formal semantics are the focus of the survey, namely automata, Petri nets and process algebra based semantics. Exhaustive reviews of approaches in the area of business process modeling and analysis are also presented in [11,12], where a translation from UML web services into FSP is proposed, so that web service specifications can be analyzed using LTSA.

Some approaches focus on providing formal semantics for the Business Process Modeling Notation (BPMN), such as for instance the works presented in [27,29]. Such semantics allows for the analysis of compatibility of business collaborations at design level. It also enables a pattern-based approach to the specification of behavioural properties (which can be verified), using Dwyer et al.'s approach. The same authors present a relative-timed semantic model for BPMN [28], and show how properties can be automatically verified using model checking via the

FDR tool. Another related approach is that presented in [16], where a semi automated translation from business process diagrams (BPD) into TLA+ is presented, using Petri nets as an intermediate formalism for the translation. This (conservative) translation allows one to model check properties of business processes, expressed as TLA formulas, using the TCL model checker.

A BPEL formalization, closely related to ours, is proposed in [23], mapping BPEL into timed automata. This formalization allows for checking deadlock freedom and reachability properties via the UPPAAL model checker, and is integrated into the ActiveBPEL tool. Other related approaches based on BPEL and BPEL4WS are the business process formalizations associated with the study of transactions and fault handling via compensations [24].

Other attempts at formalizing and analyzing workflow languages, such as UML activity diagrams, have been proposed; an example of this is that presented in [13], translating these kinds of diagrams into PROMELA (the language of the SPIN model checker). There exist various approaches providing formal semantics for workflow languages based on Petri nets or timed extensions of Petri nets [25].

A primary difference of our approach with respect to the ones described above is that PPML puts an emphasis on product description that, as far as we are aware of, is not available in any other business process modeling language. This capability enables the specifier to "balance" the description of business processes adequately, using a rich language for describing products in order to make process descriptions simpler. The language also offers timing constraints, given in the form of two bounds associated with processes, the lower and upper bounds. These are useful features with an intuitive meaning, that enable the specifier to annotate activities with timing restrictions, so that timing related properties, such as throughput or response time, can be analyzed. We took into consideration these characteristics of the language, and proposed a translation from PPML into UPPAAL, so that real time properties of PPML models can be verified using model checking. The query language (the language for expressing the properties to be checked) is a rather expressive language (computational tree logic with certain restrictions), enabling one to specify a wide range of properties, including safety and liveness properties. We have introduced a syntax for the language (the constituent elements of the formalisms have been formally defined in previous work, but no appropriate syntax for the language was provided), and an encoding of the language into UPPAAL, that provides, indirectly, a timed automata semantics of the language, and the direct possibility of model checking specifications. We have also illustrated the verification of some sample properties, using the proposed translation into UPPAAL.

Currently, we are developing a software tool to assist in the creation of PPML models, and the translation of PPML models into UPPAAL is being developed as a plug-in of this tool. We believe that PPML is a language that is useful for the formal specification (and now the analysis) of industrial processes. Directions for future work include developing abstract interpretation mechanisms associated with PPML models, so that the verification via model checking can be improved (by tackling the well known state explosion problem). More precisely, we plan to work on predicate abstraction [7] techniques for PPML analysis, exploiting the framework processes available in the language.

We also plan to prove that the new semantics, that is indirectly provided for the language via the encoding into UPPAAL, is in fact compatible with the original timed transition systems semantics of PPML given in [19].

Acknowledgements

The first two authors were partially supported by CONICET, the Argentinian Agency for Scientific and Technological Promotion (ANPCyT) and the Ministry of Science and Technology of the Province of Córdoba in Argentina. The third author was partially supported by McMaster University, the Canada Research Chair programme, and the Natural Sciences and Engineering Council of Canada.

References

1. Andrews, T., et al.: Business Process Execution Language for Web Services version 1.1, http://download.boulder.ibm.com/ibmdl/pub/software/dw/specs/ws-bpel/ws-bpel.pdf
2. Baum, G., Frias, M.F., Maibaum, T.S.E.: A Logic for Real-Time Systems Specification. In: Algebraic Semantics, and Equational Calculus, AMAST, pp. 91–105 (1998)
3. Bengtsson, J., et al.: UPPAAL- A Tool Suite for the Automatic Verification of Real-time Systems. In: Alur, R., Sontag, E.D., Henzinger, T.A. (eds.) HS 1995. LNCS, vol. 1066, pp. 232–243. Springer, Heidelberg (1996)
4. Carvalho, S., Fiadeiro, J., Haeusler, E.: A Formal Approach to Real-Time Object Oriented Software. In: Proceedings of the Workshop on Real-Time Programming IFAP/IFIP, Lyon, France, pp. 91–96 (1997)
5. Clarke, E.M., Emerson, E.A., Sistla, A.P.: Automatic verification of finite-state concurrent systems using temporal logic specifications. ACM Transactions on Programming Languages and Systems 8, 244–263 (1986)
6. Clarke, E., Grumberg, O., Peled, D.: Model Checking. MIT Press, Cambridge (2000)
7. Das, S., Dill, D., Park, S.: Experience with Predicate Abstraction. In: 11th International Conference on Computer-Aided Verification, pp. 160–172. Springer, Heidelberg (1999)
8. Daws, C., et al.: The Tool KRONOS. In: Alur, R., Sontag, E.D., Henzinger, T.A. (eds.) HS 1995. LNCS, vol. 1066, pp. 208–219. Springer, Heidelberg (1996)
9. Fenton, N., Pfleeger, S.L.L.: Software Metrics: A Rigorous and Practical Approach, Course Technology 2nd edn. (1998)
10. Fiadeiro, J., Maibaum, T.: Temporal Theories as Modularisation Units for Concurrent System Specification. In: Formal Aspects of Computing, pp. 239–272 (1992)
11. Foster, H., et al.: LTSA-WS: A Tool for Model-based Verification of Web Service Compositions and Choreography. In: 28th International Conference on Software Engineering (ICSE 2006), pp. 771–774 (2006)
12. Foster, H., et al.: WS-Engineer: A Model-Based Approach to Engineering Web Service Compositions and Choreography. In: Test and Analysis of W.S., pp. 87–119 (2007)

13. Guelfi, N., Mammar, A.: A Formal Semantics of Timed Activity Diagrams and its PROMELA Translation. In: APSEC, pp. 283–290 (2005)
14. Kavantzas, N., et al.: Web Services Choreography Description Language Version 1.0, http://www.w3.org/2002/ws/chor/edcopies/cdl/cdl.html
15. Koehler, J., Tirenni, G., Kumaran, S.: From Business Process Model to Consistent Implementation: A Case for Formal Verification Methods. In: 6th International Enterprise Distributed Object Computing Conference (EDOC 2002), pp. 96–106. IEEE Computer Society, Los Alamitos (2002)
16. Masalagiu, C., et al.: A Rigorous Methodology for Specification and Verification of Business Processes. In: Formal Aspects of Computing. Springer, London (2009)
17. Myers, M., Kaposi, A.: A First Systems Book: Technology and Management, 2nd edn. Imperial College Press, London (2004)
18. Henzinger, T.A., Manna, Z., Pnueli, A.: Timed Transition Systems (1996)
19. Maibaum, T.S.E.: An Overview of The Mensurae Language: Specifying Business Processes. In: Rigorous Object-Oriented Methods, BCS (2000)
20. Manna, Z., Pnueli, A.: The Temporal Logic of Reactive and Concurrent Systems - Specification. Springer, Heidelberg (1991)
21. Manna, Z., Pnueli, A.: Temporal Verification of Reactive Systems -Safety. Springer, Heidelberg (1995)
22. Morimoto, S.: A Survey of Formal Verification for Business Process Modeling. In: ICCS 2008, pp. 514–522 (2008)
23. Qian, Y., et al.: Tool Support for BPEL Verification in ActiveBPEL Engine. In: Australian Software Engineering Conference, pp. 90–100. IEEE Computer Society, Los Alamitos (2007)
24. Qiu, Z., et al.: Semantics of {BPEL4WS}-Like Fault and Compensation Handling. In: Proceedings of the International Symposium on Formal Methods 2005, pp. 350–365. Springer, Heidelberg (2005)
25. Van der Aalst, W., Ter Hofstede, A.: YAWL: Yet Another Workflow Language. Information Systems 30, 245–275 (2003)
26. W3C, Web Service Choreography Interface 1.0 (2002), http://www.w3.org/TR/wsci
27. Wong, P.Y.H., Gibbons, J.: A Process Semantics for BPMN. In: Liu, S., Maibaum, T., Araki, K. (eds.) ICFEM 2008. LNCS, vol. 5256, pp. 355–374. Springer, Heidelberg (2008)
28. Wong, P.Y.H., Gibbons, J.: A Relative Timed Semantics for BPMN. In: Proceedings of 7th International Workshop on the Foundations of Coordination Languages and Software Architectures. ENTCS (2008)
29. Wong, P.Y.H., Gibbons, J.: Property Specifications for Workflow Modelling. In: Leuschel, M., Wehrheim, H. (eds.) IFM 2009. LNCS, vol. 5423, pp. 56–71. Springer, Heidelberg (2009)

Author Index

Aguirre, Nazareno 737
Ahrendt, Wolfgang 387
Aichernig, Bernhard K. 206

Bae, Kyungmin 717
Barnat, Jiří 407
Barthe, Gilles 541
Basu, Samik 326
Bendisposto, Jens 504
Bertrand, Nathalie 679
Bokor, Péter 147
Brandl, Harald 206
Brim, Luboš 407
Broy, Manfred 1
Butler, Michael 466
Byg, Joakim 698

Cavalli, Ana 186
Chen, Xihui 107
Codescu, Mihai 660
Cristiá, Maximiliano 167

de Boer, Frank S. 367
de Halleux, Peli 49
Dong, Jin Song 426, 581
Dotti, Fernando L. 601
Dylla, Maximilian 387

Feng, Thomas Huining 717
Ferrante, Alessandro 306
Fischer, Bernd 485
Foo, Ernest 127

Ganov, Svetoslav 69
Ghosh, Arka P. 326
Grabe, Immo 367
Grégoire, Benjamin 541
Grigorenko, Pavel 49

Hardin, David 266
He, Ru 326
Heraud, Sylvain 541
Hiratzka, T. Douglas 266
Hwang, Iksoon 186

Iliasov, Alexei 601
Izerrouken, Nassima 521

Jaghoori, Mohammad Mahdi 367
Johnson, D. Randolph 266
Jørgensen, Kenneth Yrke 698

Ke, Wei 347
Khurshid, Sarfraz 69, 88
Killmar, Chip 69
Kortelainen, Juha 561
Krenn, Willibald 206
Kunz, César 541

Langenstein, Bruno 660
Legay, Axel 679
Leuschel, Michael 504
Liu, Yang 426, 581
Liu, Zhiming 347
Lucanu, Dorel 639

Madhavapeddy, Anil 446
Maeder, Christian 660
Maibaum, Tom 737
Marques-Silva, João 485
Matos, Paulo J. 485
Merayo, Mercedes G. 186
Monetti, Pablo Rodríguez 167
Mossakowski, Till 660
Mota, Alexandre 20

Napoli, Margherita 306
Nogueira, Sidney 20
Núñez, Manuel 186

Ölveczky, Peter Csaba 717
Ouyang, Chun 127

Pacalet, Anne 541
Pang, Jun 107
Pantel, Marc 521
Parente, Mimmo 306
Perry, Dewayne E. 69
Pinchinat, Sophie 679
Platzer, André 246
Pronk, C. (Kees) 226

Quesel, Jan-David   246

Raclet, Jean-Baptiste   679
Regis, Germán   737
Ribeiro, Leila   601
Ročkai, Petr   407
Romanovsky, Alexander   601
Roşu, Grigore   639
Ruhroth, Thomas   620

Sampaio, Augusto   20
Serafini, Marco   147
Siddiqui, Junaid Haroon   88
Siirtola, Antti   561
Silva, Renato   466
Smith, Jason   127
Srba, Jiří   698
Stam, Andries   367
Sun, Jun   426, 581
Suri, Neeraj   147
Suriadi, Suriadi   127

Taverne, Paul   226
Thirioux, Xavier   521
Tillmann, Nikolai   49
Tripakis, Stavros   717

van Deursen, Ton   107
Veanes, Margus   49
Veith, Helmut   147

Wagner, Lucas   266
Wang, Shuling   347
Wehrheim, Heike   620
Whalen, Michael   266

Yi, Wang   367

Zhang, Wenhui   286
Zhang, Xian   581
Zhao, Liang   347